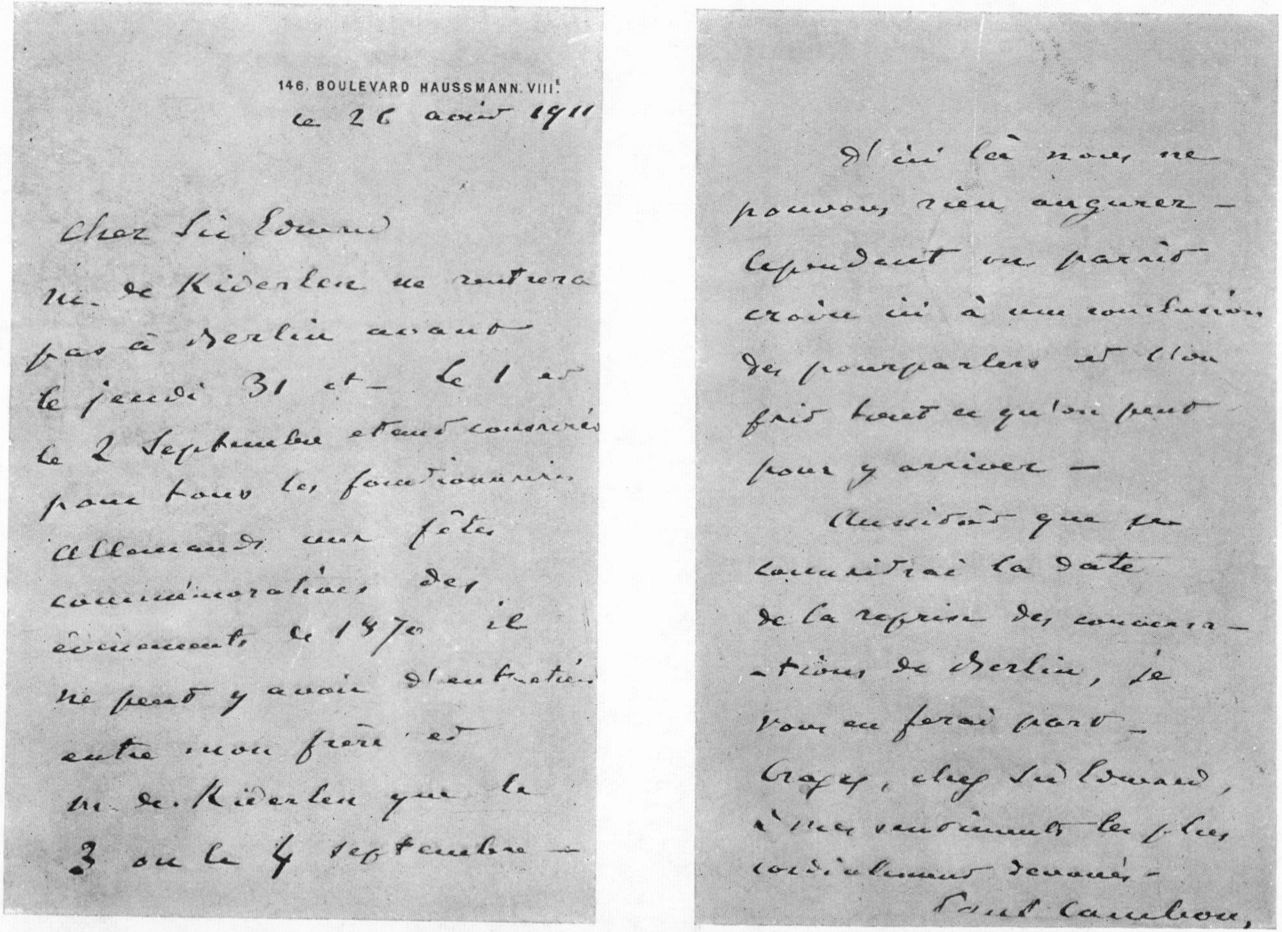
146, BOULEVARD HAUSSMANN. VIIIe

le 26 août 1911

Cher Sir Edward

M. de Kiderlen ne rentrera pas à Berlin avant le jeudi 31 et — le 1 et le 2 Septembre étant consacrés pour tous les fonctionnaires allemands aux fêtes commémoratives des événements de 1870 il ne peut y avoir d'entretien entre mon frère et M. de Kiderlen que le 3 ou le 4 septembre —

D'ici là nous ne pouvons rien augurer — cependant on paraît croire ici à une conclusion des pourparlers et l'on fait tout ce qu'on peut pour y arriver —

Aussitôt que je connaîtrai la date de la reprise des conversations de Berlin, je vous en ferai part —

Croyez, cher Sir Edward, à mes sentiments les plus cordialement dévoués —

Paul Cambon

Facsimile of Private Letter from M. Paul Cambon to Sir Edward [Lord] Grey, p. 489.

[Grey MSS., Vol. 13.]

British Documents on the Origins of the War

1898–1914

Edited by G. P. GOOCH, D.Litt., F.B.A., and
HAROLD TEMPERLEY, Litt.D., F.B.A.

Vol. VII

THE AGADIR CRISIS

LONDON:

1932

59—2—7

(*Crown Copyright Reserved*)

JOHNSON REPRINT CORPORATION
111 Fifth Avenue, New York, N.Y. 10003

JOHNSON REPRINT COMPANY LTD.
Berkeley Square House, London, W.1

Reprinted from a copy in the collections of
The New York Public Library
Astor, Lenox and Tilden Foundations

First reprinting, 1967, Johnson Reprint Corporation
Printed in the United States of America

VOLUME VII

THE AGADIR CRISIS

Edited by
G. P. GOOCH, D.Litt., and HAROLD TEMPERLEY, Litt.D.,
with the assistance of
LILLIAN M. PENSON, Ph.D.

Table of Contents.

Wt. 8085/615 2000 1/32 F.O.P. [19656] Gp. 37

Foreword to Volume VII.

THE decision to publish a selection from the British Documents dealing with the origins of the War was taken by Mr. Ramsay MacDonald, Prime Minister and Secretary of State for Foreign Affairs, in the summer of 1924. It was confirmed and announced by Mr. (now Sir) Austen Chamberlain in a letter of the 28th November, 1924 (published in "The Times" on the 3rd December), addressed to Dr. R. W. Seton-Watson. Some extracts from this letter were published by the Editors in the Foreword to Volume XI, and it need only be said here that the Secretary of State for Foreign Affairs referred to "impartiality and accuracy" as being the necessary qualifications for any work which the Editors were to publish.

The seventh Volume is devoted to the second Moroccan crisis, which was too large and important an item to fit into the chronological framework of Volume VI. The history of the Moroccan problem is resumed at the point where it was left in Volume III. Great Britain and France took advantage of the *détente* which followed the Conference of Algeciras to sign agreements with Spain in 1907 for the maintenance of the *status quo* in the Western Mediterranean and on the North Atlantic coast. The unavowed object of the two Governments was to avert unacceptable demands by Germany at Madrid, and their motive was fully understood at Berlin. It was, however, in Morocco itself that the Franco-German rivalry was mainly displayed. The arrest of the Casablanca deserters in 1908 provoked a sharp crisis, and though a *rapprochement* took place in 1909 the proposed economic condominium broke down within two years.

The expedition to Fez in April 1911 inaugurated the period of acute tension which lasted without interruption until the signature of the Moroccan and Congo agreements on November 4. The crisis fills three-quarters of the volume. The materials are so full and the subject is of such outstanding importance in the development of the European situation that it has been thought well to present the story in detail. The despatches of Sir Edward Goschen from Berlin, of Sir Francis Bertie from Paris, and of Sir Maurice de Bunsen from Madrid provide a vivid picture of every phase of the dispute, while the copious extracts from the Continental press illustrate public opinion in the European capitals. For the first time the policy of the British Foreign Office during the most dangerous moments of the last decade of peace is revealed almost from day to day. Among many points of interest may be noted the British effort to secure consideration for the interests of Spain in Morocco (pp. 603–4, 621); a conversation with General Joffre (pp. 632–4); the cancellation of a meeting between British and German squadrons at Molde at the height of the crisis in July (pp. 622–6); and the strange *rôle* of Isvolski, who had no wish to see Russian blood flow for a purely French interest (Chapter LVII). A final chapter illustrates French, British and German opinion after the signing of the treaties. *Appendix I* gives an interesting report of the way in which finance reacted on politics in Germany during the crisis. French opinion, as reflected from the debate in the French Chamber, is reproduced (*App. II*). A Memorandum by Sir Eyre Crowe written in January 1912 embodies his grave reflections on the recent crisis (*App. III*). Once again the private papers of Sir Edward Grey and Lord Carnock have proved of invaluable assistance, not only in interpreting the attitude of the Secretary of State and his principal adviser, but in revealing the inmost thoughts of the British representatives abroad, as expressed in their confidential correspondence. It is as well to mention again the statement of Lord Grey (already quoted in Volume VI, p. ix): "I did not, however, regard anything except my own letters and official papers as deciding policy."

In accordance with the practice of the Foreign Office, observed in the preceding volumes, the documents in the present volume containing information supplied or opinions expressed by certain Foreign Governments have been communicated to them for their agreement. The response has been less completely satisfactory than usual. At the wish of one Foreign Government a few passages considered likely to offend the susceptibilities of another Foreign Government have been omitted. These omissions, however, are in no single instance concerned with questions of policy. In this volume, as in all its predecessors, the Editors have omitted nothing which they consider essential to the understanding of the history of the period. In this connexion they beg to draw attention to their statement (made originally on p. viii of Volume III, and referred to on p. viii of Volume IV) " that they would feel compelled to resign if any attempt were made to insist on the omission of any document which is, in their view, vital or essential." In addition to despatches and telegrams, there are memoranda and minutes which are properly official documents. No objection has been raised by His Majesty's Secretary of State for Foreign Affairs to the publication in this volume of any documents of the above kind, nor to the publication of certain similar papers or of private letters, which are not properly official documents, but which are preserved in the Foreign Office.

From the point of view of historical criticism *Appendix VI* dealing with the movements of German warships to and from Agadir in 1911 deserves special mention. The question of the date of the arrival of S.M.S. Panther at Agadir caused the Editors great perplexity, as it could not be determined finally either from the statements in the *Grosse Politik* or the reports of the British consular officials or those received by the British Admiralty. It was possible to ascertain the facts only by an application to the German Government. They have courteously supplied information from their Naval Archives which seems to reconcile the conflicting views. The whole incident is considered by the Editors to be worth noting as an example of the difficulties of ascertaining historical truth even when evidence in abundant, and when there is no reason for anyone to conceal the truth. The Editors think that this example ought to be emphasized, as the discovery of the facts is by no means always possible or as easy as in the case indicated.

The Editors think they may here state their reasons for adopting the topical, instead of the chronological, method in the arrangement of their volumes. The topical method was used in the *Grosse Politik*. It grouped material into chapters and sections, dealing with particular issues and subjects. The chronological method, adopted in the French *Documents Diplomatiques*, displays the documents as they appear from day to day and week to week, without any attempt to sift them out under headings. It adds, however, a classified list by which the main subjects can be found. The Editors do not presume to decide on the advantages of either method as applied to other countries, where the practice may be different from their own. They believe, however, that the topical method is essential for displaying the workings of British policy. For when a crisis arises in England, or when a particular question comes up for decision before the Cabinet, the previous papers relating to the topic are printed and circulated to the Cabinet in special sections. Indeed, the normal arrangement of the Foreign Office *Confidential Print* is in printed sections devoted to topics of special interest as they arise, *e.g.*, Congo, China, Spanish-American War, Algeciras Conference, etc. The same treatment is shown when summaries of special questions are made to facilitate decision by the Foreign Secretary or the Cabinet. They are influenced in their decisions by following the development of the problem or of the crisis from documents or summaries extending backwards for six months or longer. Consequently the Editors feel that, in adopting the topical method, they are presenting the problems and decisions to their readers in much the same way as they appeared to the Cabinet and Foreign Secretary at the time. These reasons seemed to them to make the topical method of treatment the preferable one, so far as British policy is concerned.

His Majesty the King has graciously consented to the publication of his own minutes and those of King Edward. The Editors desire also to acknowledge the friendly assistance and advice of various officials at the Foreign Office, among whom they would like to mention the Librarian, Mr. Stephen Gaselee, C.B.E., and Mr. J. W. Field, O.B.E. They wish also to thank the officials of the Record Office in London, Mr. Wright, who is in charge of the Diplomatic and Embassy Archives formerly at Cambridge and now at Canterbury, and Miss E. M. Keate and Miss Priscilla BoysSmith, who assisted in the preparation of the volume for press.

G. P. GOOCH.

HAROLD TEMPERLEY.

Note on the Arrangement of Documents, &c.

THE technical arrangement and details of this volume are very similar in principle to those of Volumes III, IV and VI. The material deals mainly with one theme, the Agadir crisis. The amount of detail is more considerable than in most of the earlier volumes, the events of the period April to November 1911 being given with great fullness.

Within the chapters and their sub-sections the papers are placed in chronological order as in previous volumes; and, as before, chronological order means the date of despatch, whether to or from London, not the date of its receipt. The latter date is often added, and readers should be careful to note it.

In the earlier part of the volume most of the documents are taken from the official series of Foreign Office papers in the Public Record Office. The classification of these papers for the period 1898–1905 was thus described in the note prefaced to Volumes I and II (p. ix) :—

"They are classified mainly by country (F.O. France, etc.), and within countries by years. For each year the diplomatic documents are separated from the commercial and other classes. Within the diplomatic class there are volumes of outgoing and incoming despatches, outgoing and incoming telegrams, communications with the Foreign Ambassador ('Domestic') and with other Government Departments ('Various'). Papers relating to certain subjects have been specially treated. Some have been placed together in a miscellaneous series (F.O. General), as in the case of the Hague Peace Conference. In other instances all papers relating to a certain geographical area have been placed together, as with African affairs (after 1899) and the affairs of Morocco. Correspondence with the British representative at Paris or elsewhere appears in these cases under F.O. Africa and F.O. Morocco. A third method was to separate the correspondence relating to a special aspect of affairs from the other papers of the country concerned, thus removing them from chronological sequence. This was the case with despatches on African affairs down to 1899, which appear in special series of F.O. France (Africa), F.O. Germany (Africa), etc."

The note prefaced to Volume III (pp. ix–x) described further the arrangement inaugurated at the beginning of 1906 :—

"A new system was inaugurated at the beginning of the year 1906. From that date all papers, irrespective of country, are first divided into certain general categories, 'Political' (the former 'diplomatic'), Commercial, Consular, Treaty, etc. The papers are, however, not removed from their original files, the contents of each file being treated as one document. The files of papers are classified within the general categories according to the country to which their subject most properly belongs. The volumes containing papers relating to any country are therefore in a sub-section of the main series, and these sub-sections are arranged in alphabetical order (e.g., Political, Abyssinia, etc.). Previously the correspondence with, say, the British Ambassador at Paris was kept distinct from the communications of the French Ambassador in London, the latter being termed 'Domestic.' This distinction is now abolished and all papers relating to a subject are placed together in one file or in a series of files. The historian finds many difficulties in this arrangement, as the files are not arranged in the volumes in chronological or alphabetical sequence. The Foreign Office overcomes these difficulties by compiling a manuscript register of the contents, but this method cannot be used so satisfactorily by the historian. It is to be feared that the new arrangement makes it more difficult for the historian to be sure he has found all the papers relating to a given incident.''

The Editors are informed that the system of arrangement started in 1906 will be continued for the remainder of the period down to the outbreak of the War; but at present this process of arrangement in bound volumes has reached only to the year 1910, and the work for that year is not yet complete. Beyond this date the documents are still at the Foreign Office in the original loose files, and have not been sorted into any regular sequence. The task of surveying the available material is thus one of great difficulty. The Editors hope that it has been fulfilled adequately by the combination of three methods. A large proportion of the more important papers are printed in the bound volumes of the many series of the *Confidential Print*, and from the references given to these access to the originals in the Foreign Office files is easy. The printed texts can then be checked and the notes and minutes reproduced from the originals. Secondly, application has been made to the Foreign Office library staff for papers to which accidental reference has been found. Thirdly, the Foreign Office registers of despatches and telegrams sent to or received from every British Embassy or Legation have been at the disposal of the Editors for the purpose of searching for documents not otherwise to be found. It is hoped that by the use of these means the danger of material omissions has been overcome; but the position is not nearly so satisfactory as in the period for which a strict chronological series exists.

The Editors have already recorded in previous volumes their regret for the fact that the Embassy archives for the period after 1905 are not generally available. With the exception of Japan (to 1910) and Russia, the Embassies and Legations have not yet sent their later papers to England. In connection with the present volume, however, a search was made in the Embassy archives at Paris, though no additional material was found as a result. This helps to confirm the judgment previously expressed by the Editors that the records are more exact and complete after 1906. There are certainly very few cases in the present volume in which the original texts of documents occurring in the *Confidential Print* have proved impossible to trace.

The private collections available at the Foreign Office are more complete after the beginning of the year 1906. Many letters have been printed from the private correspondence of Sir Edward (Lord) Grey and from that of Sir Arthur Nicolson (Lord Carnock). The papers of Sir Charles (Lord) Hardinge and those of Lord Lansdowne are also now available for use, and a full selection from them will be published in a later volume.

The value of minutes increases as a later period is reached, and the present volume contains many of great interest by King Edward, Sir Edward Grey, Sir Charles (later Lord) Hardinge, Mr. (later Sir) Eyre Crowe, and others.

The text printed is in every case verbally identical with that given in the source whose reference appears at the head of the document. The text of the out-going despatches and telegrams is therefore that of the draft retained by the Foreign Office. In the case of in-coming telegrams, the text is that of the original decypher (except where otherwise indicated); in some cases this shows a *lacuna* between round brackets where the date of a previous telegram is omitted, and this, too, has been reproduced. Cross references have been given throughout, so that no difficulty of identification should arise.

As previously stated the spelling of proper names, capitalisation and punctuation have also been reproduced exactly, even where the spelling, as frequently happens, is inconsistent.

Plan of Volume VII.

Chapter L deals with the Mediterranean Naval Agreements between Great Britain, Spain and France concluded in May 1907, for the maintenance of the *status quo* in the Western Mediterranean and on the North Atlantic coast. It was desired to remove any danger to the security of Gibraltar, and to strengthen Spain in resisting demands for concessions from another Power.

Moroccan disputes and agreements from 1907 to the end of 1910 are the topic of *Chapter LI.* The first section is devoted to the French bombardment of Casablanca in 1907; the second to the recognition of Mulai Hafid by the Powers in 1908; the third to the brief crisis arising from the arrest of foreign deserters at Casablanca in September 1908; the fourth to the Franco-German Agreement of February 1909, which recognised the special political interest of France in Morocco and envisaged economic co-operation between the two Powers. The fifth and sixth sections relate to the Franco-Moroccan and Hispano-Moroccan Conventions of 1910.

Chapter LII describes the motives and progress of the expedition to Fez in April–May, 1911, and the excitement which it aroused in Germany and Spain. The numerous despatches of Sir Maurice de Bunsen from Madrid are of special value during this period of growing tension.

The first result of the expedition to Fez is shown in *Chapter LIII*, which deals with the arrival of Spanish troops at Laraiche and Alcazar in June, a measure described by the Spanish Government as precautionary and provisional.

Chapter LIV opens with the momentous announcement by the German Government on July 1 that the gunboat *Panther* was being despatched to the closed port of Agadir, and describes at length the dicussions that took place between Great Britain and France down to July 21.

The theme of *Chapter LV* is Mr. Lloyd George's historic declaration at the Mansion House on July 21, with its formidable reactions in Germany during the first week after its delivery.

Chapter LVI describes the development of the crisis and the attitude of the German press during the first three weeks of August. The views of the Emperor William II, as reported in a despatch from Sir Edward Goschen and a Memorandum by Sir John French on returning from the German manœuvres, will be found of special interest.

Chapter LVII deals with the Russian *démarche* of September 1, advising the French Government to avoid a war with Germany by timely concessions. This step, however, as is shown by a despatch from Sir George Buchanan, represented the attitude of M. Isvolski, the Russian Ambassador at Paris, rather than of the Emperor, who promised full support in case of necessity.

Chapter LVIII embraces the later phases of the long crisis, presents the successive drafts of the Moroccan and Congo treaties, and concludes with their signature on November 4. It also records the parallel endeavours of the French Government, in which the British Ambassador at Madrid played a useful part, to reach an agreement with Spain.

In *Chapter LIX* the diplomatic narrative is interrupted in order to present some documents of a naval and military character. The most interesting items concern the secret and succesful endeavour, initiated by Herr von Kiderlen-Waechter, to avoid a meeting of British and German squadrons at Molde during the most critical days of July on the ground that indiscreet utterances by the Emperor might complicate the situation, and the continuance of non-binding conversations between French and British military experts. In connection with the latter special importance attaches to the Memorandum by Brigadier-General Sir G. N. Nicolson of November 6, 1911, and the record of a meeting held in July 1911 between General Dubail and General Wilson (pp. 626–632).

The aftermath of the crisis is the theme of *Chapter LX*, which reprints the public statements of the German Chancellor, Herr von Kiderlen-Waechter and Sir Edward Grey; summarises the Parliamentary debates in Berlin and Paris, and analyses the publications of the Continental press down to the end of 1911.

The volume ends with some important appendices. *Appendix I* reprints a report on the German financial crisis by Sir Francis Oppenheimer, British Consul-General in Frankfurt, which is of interest as showing how far German diplomacy was susceptible to financial pressure. *Appendix II* gives the debate of December 15, 1911, in the French Chamber on the Moroccan treaties. *Appendix III* contains a Memorandum on the Franco-German negotiations by Sir Eyre Crowe, written in January 1912. *Appendix IV* reprints agreements concerning Morocco of 1904, 1909, and 1911. *Appendix V* throws light on the so-called "Cartwright Interview," of August 26, 1911. The last *Appendix* summarises information from the British Admiralty and from other sources as to the movements of the German warships S.M.S. *Berlin, Eber* and *Panther* in July 1911.

List of Principal Editorial Notes.

List of Abbreviations.

A. & P. ... ... British Parliamentary Papers, *Accounts and Papers.*

Caillaux ... ... J. Caillaux: *Agadir. Ma Politique Extérieure* (Paris, 1919).

Churchill ... ... Winston Churchill: *The World Crisis, 1911–14* (1923).

G.P. ... ... *Die Grosse Politik der Europäischen Kabinett.*

Jäckh ... ... E. Jäckh: *Kiderlen-Wächter : der Staatsmann und Mensch. Briefwechsel und Nachlass* (2 vols., Berlin, 1924).

Martens ... ... G. F. de Martens: *Nouveau Recueil Général de Traités, 1908–13, 3me Série* (Leipzig, 1913).

Mermeix ... ... Pseudonym for G. Terrail, *La chronique de l'an* 1911 *qui contient le récit des Négociations officielles et des Négociations secrètes à propos du Maroc et du Congo* (Paris, 1912).

Nicolson ... ... Harold Nicolson: *Sir Arthur Nicolson, Bart., First Lord Carnock: a study in the old diplomacy* (1849–1928) (1930).

Ö.-U.A. ... ... *Österreich-Ungarns Aussenpolitik, 1908–14.*

Parl. Deb. ... ... *Parliamentary Debates* (*House of Lords, or House of Commons*).

Siebert ... ... B. de Siebert: *Entente Diplomacy and the World*, edited, arranged and annotated by G. A. Schreiner (New York and London, 1921).
[This is an English translation, with the addition of a chronological list of documents by the American Editor, of *Diplomatische Aktenstücke zur Geschichte der Ententepolitik der Vorkriegsjahre* (Berlin and Leipzig, 1921).]

Siebert-Benckendorff .. This refers to a new German edition of the above by Herr von Siebert, containing a number of additions. It is entitled *Graf Benckendorffs Diplomatischer Schriftwechsel* (Berlin and Leipzig, 1928).

Tardieu... ... ... A. Tardieu: *Le Mystère d'Agadir* (Paris, 1912).

Twenty-Five Years ... Lord Grey: *Twenty-Five Years, 1892–1916* (2 vols., 1925).

Names of Writers of Minutes.

F. D. A. = Mr. F. D. Acland ... ... Parliamentary Under-Secretary of State for Foreign Affairs, 1911–5.

E. B. = Sir Eric Barrington ... ... Private Secretary to the Marquess of Landsdowne, 1900–5; Assistant Under-Secretary of State for Foreign Affairs, 1906–7.

H. C. B. = Sir Henry Campbell-Bannerman ... Prime Minister and First Lord of the Treasury, 1905–08.

E. A. C. = Mr. (later Sir E.) Crowe ... ... Senior Clerk, Foreign Office, 1906–12; Assistant Under-Secretary of State for Foreign Affairs, 1912–20; Permanent Under-Secretary of State for Foreign Affairs, 1920–5.

F. A. C. = Mr. (later Sir) F. A. Campbell ... Assistant Under-Secretary of State for Foreign Affairs, 1902–11.

E. D. = Hon. James (later Sir) Eric Drummond Assistant Clerk, Foreign Office, 1910–8.

W. E. D. = Sir W. E. Davidson, K.C. ... ... Appointed Legal Adviser to the Foreign Office, 1886; Acting Councillor of Embassy in the Diplomatic Service, 1910.

F. = Baron Fitzmaurice of Leigh ... Parliamentary Under-Secretary of State for Foreign Affairs, 1905–8.

E. G. = Sir Edward (later Viscount) Grey (of Fallodon) Secretary of State for Foreign Affairs, December 11, 1905–December 11, 1916.

C. H. = Sir Charles (later Baron) Hardinge (of Penshurst) Assistant Under-Secretary of State for Foreign Affairs, 1903–4; Ambassador at St. Petersburgh, 1904–6; Permanent Under-Secretary of State for Foreign Affairs, 1906–10; Viceroy and Governor-General of India, 1910–6.

G. E. P. H. = Mr. G. E. P. Hertslet ... ... Staff Officer, Librarian's Department, Foreign Office.

W. L. = Mr. (later Sir) W. Langley ... ... Senior Clerk, Foreign Office, 1902–7; Assistant Under-Secretary of State for Foreign Affairs, 1907–18.

C. H. M. ⎱ H.M. ⎰ = Mr. (later Sir) C. H. Montgomery ... Assistant Private Secretary to Sir Henry Campbell-Bannerman, Prime Minister, 1908; Précis Writer to Sir Edward Grey, 1908–10; Assistant Clerk, Foreign Office, 1910–6.

L. M. = Mr. (later Sir) Louis Mallet ... ... Private Secretary to Sir Edward Grey, 1905–6; Senior Clerk, 1906–7; Assistant Under-Secretary of State for Foreign Affairs, 1907–13.

M. = Mr. (later Viscount) Morley (of Blackburn) Secretary of State for India, 1905–10, and March–May, 1911; Lord President of the Council, 1910–4; in temporary charge of the Foreign Office, July, 1911.

A. N. = Sir Arthur Nicolson (later Baron Carnock) Ambassador at Madrid, 1905; British Representative at the Algeciras Conference on Affairs of Morocco, 1906; Ambassador at St. Petersburgh, 1906–10; Permanent Under-Secretary of State for Foreign Affairs, 1910–6.

H. N. = Mr. H. C. Norman ... ... 2nd Secretary at St. Petersburgh, 1903–6; employed in Foreign Office, 1906–14; Councillor at Buenos Aires, 1914.

A. P. = Mr. A. Parker ... ... Junior Clerk, Foreign Office, 1906–12; Assistant Clerk, 1912–7; Librarian, 1918–9.

G. S. S. = Mr. G. S. Spicer ... ... Private Secretary to Sir T. Sanderson, 1903–6; and to Sir C. Hardinge, 1906; Assistant Clerk, 1906–12; Senior Clerk, 1912–9.

G. H. V. = Mr. G. H. Villiers ... ... Clerk in Foreign Office, 1903–13.

Minutes by King Edward.

(These are attached to the following despatches.)

Minutes by King George.

(These are attached to the following despatches.)

LIST OF DOCUMENTS.

Chapter L.

The Mediterranean Naval Agreements between Great Britain, Spain and France of May 16, 1907.

Chapter LI.

Moroccan Disputes and Agreements, 1907–10.

I.—THE BOMBARDMENT OF CASABLANCA.

IV.—THE FRANCO-GERMAN AGREEMENT OF FEBRUARY 1909.

Chapter LII.

The Expedition to Fez.

XXXV

Chapter LIII.

The Spanish Landing at Larache and Alcazar and its Results.

Chapter LIV.

The Sending of the "Panther" and its effects.

Chapter LV.

Mr. Lloyd George's Speech of July 21, and its Results.

Chapter LVI.

The Approach to the Crisis, July 29–August 21, 1911.

d

Chapter LVII.

The Russian Démarche.

Chapter LVIII.

The Crisis and its Settlement, August 21–November 4, 1911.

Chapter LIX.

Naval and Military Negotiations.

I.—THE MOLDE INCIDENT, JULY 14–JULY 26, 1911.

II.—GENERAL.

Chapter LX.

The Aftermath, Press and Public Opinion.

Appendix I.

Appendix II.

Appendix III.

Appendix IV.

Appendix V.

Appendix VI.

CHAPTER L.

THE MEDITERRANEAN NAVAL AGREEMENTS BETWEEN GREAT BRITAIN, SPAIN AND FRANCE OF MAY 16, 1907.

[*ED. NOTE.*—For some years previous to 1898 a discussion had gone on between the Spanish and British Governments with reference to the position of Spanish guns near Gibraltar. During the year 1898 an interesting project for closer union between the two countries arose, which is thus described in the Annual Report on Spain for 1906.[1]

" 63. It remains, however, an interesting speculation to inquire whether no means exist of attaching Spain permanently to the side of England by a formal Treaty. Señor Moret's original suggestion, if indeed it emanated from him, was for a kind of offensive and defensive alliance. As approved by His Majesty's Government, and submitted confidentially on the 30th October, 1898, to the Queen Regent of Spain and to the Spanish Government by Sir Henry Drummond Wolff, it took the form of a draft Convention to the following effect :—

(1.) To secure the peace of the Mediterranean, &c., there shall be perpetual peace between England and Spain.
(2.) In case of war, Spain will not side with England's enemies, but give aid to England to the best of her ability and resources.
(3.) In pursuance of the Treaty of Utrecht (ceding Gibraltar without any exception or impediment whatever) Spain will defend Gibraltar from all land attack, undertaking not to construct any works of fortification or batteries, or mount any guns other than field guns within gunshot of Gibraltar—that is, for the present, 7 miles.
(4.) England may enlist Spanish soldiers in time of war.
(5.) If Spain becomes involved in war, England will assist her by preventing any hostile force from landing in the Bay of Algeciras or on the coast within gunshot of Gibraltar, and by undertaking the defence on the part of Spain of the Balearic and Canary Islands.

Proposed alternative Treaty.

64. Spain replied rejecting the above as involving obligations which in her then condition she would be incapable of fulfilling. She proposed the following alternative, which was, however, eventually rejected by His Majesty's Government as useless, and possibly restrictive of British freedom of action in the event of war :—

(1.) Spain will guarantee that Gibraltar shall not be attacked by Spanish forces, or by the forces of a Power at war with England operating from Spanish territory.
(2.) England to undertake that, in time of war, she will not conduct military operations on Spanish territory, continental or insular, and that on the demand of Spain, but not otherwise, she will navally assist to prevent violation of Spanish territory."

The subject however seems to have been then dropped, although, as the following extract shows, the particular question as to the Spanish guns was settled by a secret exchange of notes of an amicable kind.

" 61. . . . . Sir Henry Drummond Wolff's note in reply was dated the 17th March, 1899. In it he expressed the satisfaction of His Majesty's Government at the above friendly assurances, and added that, on their part, His Majesty's Government wished to assure the Spanish Government that they had at no time entertained the idea of making this question a ground for demanding further territorial acquisitions, and that they will be ready, if occasion should arise, to give their military and naval assistance for preventing any hostile landing on the coast of the Bay of Algeciras or any attack by sea on that coast."

Some further excitement arose in 1901 when Mr. Gibson Bowles drew attention in the House of Commons to the exposed nature of the harbour of Gibraltar and to the necessity which might arise of defending it by a hostile offensive in Spanish territory. The British Government

---

[1] [Enclosure in despatch No. 78, Sir M. de Bunsen to Sir E. Grey, D. April 27, R. May 4, 1907. F.O. 371/336.]

gave satisfactory assurances to Spain at this time, and though there was popular excitement in Spain it gradually subsided. The friendly relations instituted between France and England in 1904, and the latter's endeavour to improve Franco-Spanish relations, greatly improved the situation and tended to bring Spain and England more together. But no definite step forward was taken until the State visit of King Alfonso XIII to England was made in 1905.]

No. 1.

The Marquess of Lansdowne to Mr. Cartwright.

F.O. Spain 2208.
(No. 64.)   Confidential.
Sir,   *Foreign Office, June 8, 1905.*

The King of Spain was pleased to give me an audience this morning at Buckingham Palace.([1]) His Majesty expressed himself in the most cordial terms with regard to the relations between Spain and Great Britain, and dwelt with the utmost satisfaction upon the manner in which he had been received in this country.

I subsequently had an interview of some length with M. de Villa-Urrutia, who was also most friendly in his language. We discussed at some length the situation which had arisen with regard to Morocco. His Excellency had not yet seen the German Circular which Count Metternich communicated to me on the 6th instant.([2]) He told me however that the Spanish Government had discouraged the proposal made by the Moorish Government, and were prepared to act with this country and with France in dealing with any similar proposals. They would indeed be ready to join with us in an identical reply. We agreed however that having regard to the situation created by M. Delcassé's resignation, it might be better to defer a decision as to the manner in which the German Circular should be received until more was known of the attitude of the French Government. His Excellency suggested that if the French Government, in order to placate Germany, were to agree to a Conference, it would be difficult for the other Powers to object. In reference to the appeal made by the German Government to the Madrid Convention of 1880, His Excellency observed that he had always regarded that Convention as dealing entirely with the rights of protected persons and matters closely connected with them.

I told His Excellency, explaining that I did so unofficially and without authority from my colleagues, that it had occurred to me of late that a mutually advantageous arrangement might be made between Spain and Great Britain, under which Spain might undertake that she would not alienate to a third Power some of the important strategic points included in her possessions. I referred in particular to the places owned by Spain on the Moorish sea-board, the Balearic Islands, the Canaries, and Fernando Po. The kind of arrangement which I had in my mind was that Spain might agree not to alienate any of these, and that we should undertake to support her in denying them to any other Power which might attempt to wrest them from her. I thought however that if any such understanding were to be arrived at, it would be expected by His Majesty's Government that some arrangement should be made for the purpose of securing Gibraltar from exposure to attack from the Spanish mainland.

His Excellency received my suggestion in the most friendly manner. He observed that France had at one time certainly taken an interest in the future of the Balearic Islands, which might have been of great value to her in the event of a war with England. I said that whatever might be decided, our relations with

---

([1]) [His Majesty King Alfonso XIII arrived in England on June 5, and remained there until June 10.]

([2]) [*cp. Gooch & Temperley*, Vol. III, p. 92, No. 116.]

France were of such a kind that in my opinion nothing could be settled as to the disposal of these places except with the full knowledge of the French Government. His Excellency told me that he would have much pleasure in considering my suggestion, and discussing it further with me at a future time.(³)

[I am, etc.]
L[ANSDOWNE].

(³) [Owing to Ministerial changes in Spain these negotiations were not continued.]

[*ED. NOTE.*—On June 26, 1905, Sir A. Nicolson telegraphed to Lord Lansdowne from Madrid (No. 48, Confidential) : '' Would Y[our] L[ordship] like me to speak to new Gov[ernmen]t in regard to questions mentioned to M[inister for] F[oreign] A[ffairs] when in London as stated in your despatch No. 64 to Mr. Cartwright? I think that the moment is a favourable one.'' To this Lord Lansdowne replied in Tel. No. 44 of June 27, 1905 : '' It seems to us doubtful whether you should broach the subject so soon : but use your own discretion.'' Sir A. Nicolson took advantage of this permission to mention the matter to the Spanish Minister of State (Señor Sanchez Roman) and to the Prime Minister (Señor Montero Rios) saying that he '' did not ask for a reply at present but merely wished them to think over it.'' He also mentioned the matter to the King (*v.* Tel. No. 49 from Sir A. Nicolson of July 4, 1905). He asked for permission to inform M. Jules Cambon of what he had done. This permission was given by Lord Lansdowne in Tel. No. 46 of July 4, 1905. For these telegrams *v.* F.O. Spain 2211.]

No. 2.

Sir A. Nicolson to Lord Lansdowne.

F.O. Spain 2210.
(No. 189.) Confidential.
My Lord,   *Madrid, October* 25, 1905.

I had a conversation today with Señor Moret, and as it is thought probable that before long he will replace the present Prime Minister, his views on political questions may be of interest to Your Lordship.

Señor Moret, in speaking of the international position of Spain, was strongly of opinion that the present moment was most propitious for establishing on a solid basis the relations between his country and Great Britain. Speaking as a Spaniard he was desirous of obtaining from Great Britain an assurance that she would guarantee the insular possessions of Spain from hostile attack, while Spain on her side would give pledges so that no fears should in future exist as to the security of Gibraltar from land attack. This project was in fact the revival of one which had in a measure been treated with the Sagasta Cabinet, when he himself was Foreign Minister, but had not been pushed to a conclusion owing to the fear of Señor Sagasta of wounding the susceptibilities, if not of arousing the hostility of France. The political situation had since then undergone a great change by the existing close intimacy between Great Britain and France; and if the latter Power could be brought into an arrangement which would also set the mind of Spain at rest as regards her land frontier, so much the better.

The advantages which would accrue to Spain would be incalculable, as once exempt from all fear of a land or sea attack, she could lessen her military and naval burdens, and devote herself with a feeling of perfect safety to the much needed development of her internal resources. On the other hand both Great Britain and France would be free from any anxiety as to Spain being seduced or forced into engagements with other Powers of an embarrassing nature.

There was among thoughtful men of all parties in Spain a strong feeling that Great Britain was the natural friend and ally of their country, and that she was the only Power whose amity was of real practical value and on whom they could depend with absolute confidence. France by herself was regarded as a Power of doubtful strength and consistency : and recent incidents had much diminished her prestige in the eyes of the Spaniards. He knew France well, and he feared that the growth of luxury on the one hand, and the anti-religious and socialistic propagandas on the other, has [*sic*] sapped the foundations of political morality and also of the discipline and cohesion of the armed forces. He doubted if there were much virile patriotism in the country, or if the people of France would brace themselves up to any serious sacrifice. Peace at any price and the undisturbed enjoyment of their material comforts were, he was afraid, becoming the watchwords of the majority of the French nation.

Señor Moret said that he viewed with great anxiety the visit of King Alfonso to Berlin. His Majesty was young and inexperienced and, although he was aware that His Majesty was at present sincerely desirous of maintaining the friendliest and closest relations with the British Court and with His Majesty's Government, he feared that he might be impressed by the strong, and at the same time attractive personality of the German Emperor. The latter Sovereign, he was convinced, was desirous of winning King Alfonso over to his own views and aims, which could not be beneficial to Spain, and would in all probability exert himself towards inducing his youthful guest to enter into some engagements or undertakings.

It was, in these circumstances, essential that the King should have by his side some competent and experienced Minister, ready to guide and advise His Majesty on sudden occasions. The present Foreign Minister was ill qualified for such a duty ; but he had reason to believe that before the visit to Berlin commenced, the approaching reorganization of the Spanish Ministry would lead to the portfolio of Foreign Affairs being entrusted to other hands.

The above is a short summary of the views of Señor Moret in regard to the future policy of Spain, and which it is possible he may endeavour to realize if he assumes office. I was somewhat surprised at the marked distrust which he manifested in regard to Germany, as he has hitherto been regarded as being to a certain extent an advocate of German as opposed to French influence ; and he has always been in intimate intercourse with the German Embassy.

I have, &c.
A. NICOLSON.

No. 3.

Minute by Sir C. Hardinge.

F.O. 371/364.
285/285/07/41. *Foreign Office, December 8,* 1906.

Article VII of the Secret Convention concluded between the French and Spanish Gov[ernmen]ts on Oct[ober] 3 1904 relating to Morocco is in the following terms :—

"L'Espagne s'engage à n'aliéner ni à céder sous aucune forme, même à titre temporaire, tout ou partie des territoires désignés aux Articles II, IV et V de la présente Convention."(¹)

(These Articles contain the definition and demarcation of the French and Spanish spheres of influence in Morocco.)

From our point of view this Article contains a serious flaw, since there is nothing in this Article to prevent Spain from ceding such territories to France nor, in the event of war between France and Spain, of ceding them to any other Power. The fact that the Convention had been formally communicated to H[is] M[ajesty's] Gov[ernmen]t would not be sufficient to make the pledge under such circ[umstanc]es obligatory upon Spain. It is therefore very desirable that Spain should take the same engagement to us also.

(¹) [*v. infra,* pp. 827–8, *App.* IV; also printed in *Gooch & Temperley,* Vol. III, p. 51, No. 59.]

An opportunity for this would occur if the negotiations were commenced which Lord Lansdowne suggested to M. de Villa Urrutia when the latter was in London as Special Ambassador during the visit of the King of Spain to England in 1905, and which have had no sequel. I enclose Lord Lansdowne's record of his conversation.(²)

As M. de Villa Urrutia is now Spanish Ambassador here, and as the Spanish Government appear to be very favourably disposed towards us it might be worth while reminding the Spanish Ambassador of Lord Lansdowne's conversation and inquiring as to the views of the Spanish Gov[ernmen]t upon his suggestions.

C. H.
Dec. 8, 1906.

(²) [v. supra, pp. 2–3, No. 1.]

No. 4.

Sir Edward Grey to Sir H. Campbell-Bannerman.

F.O. 371/364.
285/285/07/41.
Private.

My dear Sir Henry,   *Foreign Office, December 12, 1906.*

Hardinge has been looking into this point connected with Spain and Morocco and Gibraltar. (It would be a distinct advantage to be assured that the part of the Morocco coast, which belongs to the Spanish sphere should not pass into hands likely or able to use it to our disadvantage.

On the other hand Lord Lansdowne's proposal would entail a new treaty obligation upon us and I do not desire to multiply treaty obligations, though this particular one would probably not entail action at any time.)(¹)

The balance of my mind would be decided by whether security for Gibraltar could be obtained and is an object of great importance to us, needing better security.

Shall the Admiralty be consulted upon this point first with a view to bringing it before the C[ommittee of] I[mperial] D[efence]?

Yours sincerely,
E. GREY.

MINUTE.

I think we should have the views of the Adm[iralt]y but I doubt if we are likely to obtain any guarantee for Gibraltar on the land side.

H. C.-B.
13/

(¹) [The section in brackets was printed for circulation to the Committee of Imperial Defence, with the following addition : " The question of the necessity for making further provision for the Security of Gibraltar and of the possibility of attaining this object by the means proposed would exercise a determining influence on my decision in the matter." The texts of Lord Lansdowne's despatch to Mr. Cartwright, No. 64 of June 8, 1905 (*supra*, pp. 2–3, No. 1), and of Sir C. Hardinge's minute (*supra*, pp. 4–5, No. 3) were circulated at the same time.]

No. 5.

Mr. Haldane to Sir Edward Grey.

F.O. 371/364.
285/285/07/41.

My dear Edward,   28, *Queen Anne's Gate, December* 15, 1906.

I do not think that any guarantee against threats from the Spanish side of Gibraltar would be worth much—excepting morally. From a military point of view I feel pretty sure my people would say that nothing was added.

But this might be discussed at the C[ommittee of] I[mperial] D[efence] Meeting on Thursday morning.

Yours ever,
R. B. HALDANE.

No. 6.

Sir F. Bertie to Sir Edward Grey.

F.O. 371/135.
43372/8457/06/41.
(No. 542.)   Secret.
Sir,

Paris, D. *December 24, 1906.*
R. *December 27, 1906.*

I have reason to believe that the French Government are much exercised as to the designs which the German Government may entertain in regard to the island possessions of Spain. The present moment might therefore be a favourable one for reviving with the Spanish Government the question of an undertaking by England to assist Spain in resisting aggression on Fernando Po, the Canaries and the Balearic Islands in return for an engagement by Spain that she will not in any way alienate by lease, concession or otherwise her rights in those Islands and will not erect works or place guns in the vicinity of Gibraltar which could threaten its safety or that of its anchorage.

The security of Gibraltar not being a permanent French interest such an arrangement as the one which I have referred to might not in ordinary circumstances have met with the approval of the French Government. It might indeed have been strongly but secretly opposed even quite lately; but if, as I understand, the French Government suspect the German Government of designs in the Balearic Islands, as well as in the Canaries, they might well be prepared to forego the possible advantage to France at some future date of Spain being able at French instigation to place guns in a position to threaten Gibraltar. France would feel assured that Germany would be precluded from using the Balearic Islands as a Naval Base in a war with France.

I have, &c.
FRANCIS BERTIE.

No. 7.

Sir F. Bertie to Sir Edward Grey.

Private.([1])
My dear Grey,

Paris, *December 25, 1906.*

In the time of Lord Salisbury's Government our relations with Spain were strained nearly to breaking point owing to the erection on the Spanish mainland of military works threatening the safety of Gibraltar.

In 1902 I suggested to Lansdowne an arrangement with Spain by which we should repudiate any designs on Spanish territory on the mainland and her Islands and undertake to assist her in defending the Islands in return for an engagement by Spain that she would not erect works or place guns in a position to threaten the safety of Gibraltar, and that she would not alienate in any way her Island property.

Not long after this something was said to the Spanish Government disclaiming any covetousness on our part. The pourparlers did not go far I think. The frequent changes of Government in Spain were an obstacle to negotiations.

([1]) [Grey MSS., Vol. 10.]

In July 1905 Nicolson spoke on the subject to the Spanish Prime Minister and to the King of Spain and he asked permission to inform the French Ambassador of what he had done. I was in England on leave when I saw Nicolson's telegram and I suggested that inasmuch as the safety of Gibraltar was not a permanent French interest it would be dangerous to communicate to the French Ambassador the subject of the negotiations. It was however too late to stop Nicolson doing so.([2])

I mention these details for the following reasons.

Cambon (Paul) when he came to see me on the 22nd instant said, when speaking of the Canaries Cables question and the designs of Germany, that it would perhaps be as well to make some arrangement between France England and Spain for the preservations of the *status quo* in the Mediterranean. The difficulty would be to devise a form which would secure that end without wounding Spanish susceptibilities. He thought that the three Powers might assure each other that they would not alienate, or grant concessions to Foreign Governments in, their Island Possessions. The British Government were not likely to wish to grant concessions in Malta and the French Government would have no desire to grant concessions in Corsica. With regard to the Spanish Islands it was of vital importance to France that no Foreign State should get a footing in the Balearic Islands. Germany had at one time made proposals to establish Ship Building works at Ferrol for the benefit of the Spanish Government. Germany might make similar proposals for an establishment or a concession of some sort in the Balearic Islands. Any understanding between the three Powers should include the Islands off the West Coast of Africa and in the Atlantic.

Yesterday evening in the course of my interview with Pichon on the subject of the Cable to the Canaries, he mentioned his fears in regard to German designs there and in the Balearic Islands. He said that in the Direction Politique of his Department there was a recollection of some pourparlers or communications of some kind about Spanish Islands, no dossier of the matter could however be found, but it was a question which required study. He did not ask me whether I knew anything about the matter and I did not say anything to encourage him to continue the subject.

My idea is that the French Ambassador at Madrid in talking over the Canaries Cable question with his brother, the Ambassador in London, has told him of the information given to him (Jules Cambon) by Nicolson. The two brothers had an interview with Pichon on the 22nd instant and probably told him of the communication made by Nicolson and suggested to him that the best way to block German designs would be an arrangement such as Cambon (Paul) had sketched out to me.

The safety of Gibraltar is a solid British interest and a sacrifice to secure it by such an arrangement as I suggested in 1902 would be justified in public opinion in England, and Foreign Powers would have no just cause for complaint. They cannot admit that they have designs on the Possessions of Spain. We have not only the right but the duty to obtain security for Gibraltar, and in return we only assure to Spain that to which she has a right and we at the same time, whilst keeping out ourselves from her Islands, keep out all the others.

In view of the nervousness of the French Government as to the ambitions of Germany I think that they might perhaps in present circumstances swallow the security of Gibraltar if they can feel that we shall prevent the Germans from getting a footing in the Canaries and the Balearic Islands. As matters stand, if we get on bad terms with the French they can instigate the Spaniards to put up works threatening Gibraltar. It would be no breach of any engagement on the part of Spain and we should have a renewal of strained relations with her and no remedy except an ultimatum.

Some naval experts may advise that the occupation by Germany of the Canaries

([2]) [*cp. supra*, p. 3, *Ed. note.*]

and other Islands would not harm us, that it would necessitate a distribution of her Naval Forces in time of War which would be of advantage to us and that we should be able to turn them out whenever we wished to do so. Other experts might think otherwise. Experts very often differ *e.g.* the varying opinions as to the value to us of Wei-hai-wei.

Yours sincerely,
FRANCIS BERTIE.

No. 8.

Sir F. Bertie to Sir Edward Grey.

Private & Confidential.([1])
My dear Grey,   *Paris, January* 3, 1907.

The French know quite well that it is as much a British as a French interest to keep the Germans out of the Spanish Islands. It will not be advisable to let the French Government think or to give the French Press ground for saying that in order to protect British interests we are using French interests in Morocco and our obligation to support them as a lever wherewith to oppose the laying of a German Cable in the Canaries.

The interests of the Eastern Telegraph Company and the investment of British as well as of French Capital in the proposed Spanish Cable is quite sufficient to justify our opposition to the German Cable. If the positions were reversed and the Germans stood in our shoes they would oppose tooth and nail a British application to the Spanish Government for a Concession to a British Cable Company of landing rights in the Canaries.

As Gibraltar appears to be at the mercy of mortars placed in Spanish ground invisible from Gibraltar is it not of vital importance to make sacrifices to retain the permanent friendship of Spain and therefore to guarantee to her her island property? Some people seem to think that we cannot prevent Germany from acquiring Coaling Stations and so becoming a Naval Power formidable to our commerce in time of war in other parts of the world than the North Sea, but where can she obtain coaling Stations not British or French? We are bound to defend Portuguese Possessions. There remains therefore only Spanish and Dutch property available : for the United States may be trusted to prevent the acquisition by Germany of anything in the West Indies. As matters stand if the Germans established interests in Spanish Possessions they might, as was proposed in the case of Fernando Po, get up a quarrel between a German individual and the Spanish local authorities and seize an Island. In such case it might perhaps be difficult for us to find good ground to interfere, whereas if we were bound by Convention with Spain to assist her in defending her islands the Germans would take good care not to push matters unless they desired war with us. The safety of Gibraltar might be used as the ostensible reason for an arrangement with Spain though the maintenance of the integrity of Spain in the interests of the balance of power is really quite sufficient justification for a guarantee by us.

We used to consider isolation as splendid but in view of the growing strength of Germany can we any longer afford to do so? Does it not become necessary to take every possible precaution for the maintenance of the *status quo* and the preservation of the balance of Power in the European System?

Yours sincerely,
FRANCIS BERTIE.

([1]) [Grey MSS., Vol. 11.]

No. 9.

Sir M. de Bunsen to Sir Edward Grey.

F.O. 371/364.
786/285/07/41.   *Madrid,* D. *January* 7, 1907, 8·30 P.M.
Tel. (No. 1.) Very Confidential.   R. *January* 8, 1907, 7·30 A.M.

French Ambassador(¹) has suddenly propounded the proposal that France and England should guarantee integrity of Spanish possessions in the Western Mediterranean and in the Atlantic Ocean, with special reference to the Balearic and Canary Islands and Spanish posts on Morocco coast. His Excellency has read to the King and Minister for Foreign Affairs a draft Convention to above effect. Idea is to attach Spain more firmly to England and France; to prevent her from seeking other alliances, and to strengthen her in refusing inconvenient foreign demands for concessions within Spanish territory.

This proposal bears some resemblance to one which was mooted by my predecessor, and which was founded on guarantee of Spanish possessions in exchange for certain assurances in respect to Gibraltar.

I have had this in mind, but no Spanish Government since my arrival at Madrid has seemed to me sufficiently secure to warrant renewal of proposal.

In its new form I doubt whether it would have much chance of success.

Spain would much prefer a Treaty with England alone, or at least that the initiative should be English and not French. I also think it would be exceedingly difficult to devise formula which Spain could accept binding her to raise no fortification within range of Gibraltar.

French proposal does not mention Gibraltar.

Spanish Government have been somewhat taken aback by the French Ambassador's action, and in matter of such importance they would not proceed without consulting Opposition leaders.

MINUTES.

The French proceeding is not only maladroit in itself, but also very inconsiderate as regards this country. It is quite improper that definite proposals should be made, committing H[is] M[ajesty's] G[overnment] in so momentous a matter, without their being even informed of the intention to do so. I think this requires a somewhat decided representation to the French Gov[ernmen]t.

Qu[ery] Repeat to Paris and instruct Sir F. Bertie to represent that action of French Gov[ernmen]t have placed H[is] M[ajesty's] G[overnment] in a most embarrassing position which would have been avoided if H[is] M[ajesty's] G[overnment] had been duly and in proper time consulted before Spain was approached with a formal proposal committing them to political action of the most serious character.

E. A. C.
Jan. 8.

The action of the French Gov[ernmen]t is certainly very extraordinary, but it w[oul]d probably be better to send for M. Cambon and speak to him in the sense suggested, than to instruct Sir F. Bertie. The above might however be conveyed to him as the first impression of H[is] M[ajesty's] G[overnment], without instructions to communicate it. (See his desp[atch] No. 542, Secret, of Dec. 23.) (²) It is difficult to see where the " entente " comes in if this sort of thing is done without consulting us.

E. B.

I will wait till I see M. Cambon to-morrow. The French have spoilt the pitch by running over it in advance.

E. G.

(¹) [It is stated in Annual Report on Spain (1906), § 66 (F.O. 371/334. 5354/1267/07/41), that M. Jules Cambon " was confidentially informed of the state of the question [Anglo-Spanish negotiation] in 1905." *cp.* also *supra,* p. 7, No. 7, and p. 3, *Ed.* note, where it is stated that Sir A. Nicolson made a communication to M. Jules Cambon on this subject.]

(²) [*v. supra,* p. 6, No. 6. It is of the 24th.]

No. 10.

Sir Edward Grey to Sir F. Bertie.

F.O. 371/364.
1606/285/07/41.
(No. 21.)
Sir,   *Foreign Office, January 9, 1907.*

M. Cambon told me to-day that his brother, M. Jules Cambon, who was to leave Madrid in a few weeks' time, had felt the importance of coming to some arrangement with Spain which would prevent Spain from yielding to German pressure, which was constantly being exercised with the object of securing some German footing in the Mediterranean. M. Jules Cambon said the present moment was favourable, because the King of Spain very much resented this pressure, and he had, therefore, drawn up a sort of draft Convention,(¹) which M. Paul Cambon showed to me, and which he explained was not a draft of the French Government, but emanated solely from his brother. All that had been done so far was that the idea had been mentioned to M. Pichon, and M. Pichon had expressed a desire that the idea should be put before me. The Convention was to the effect that England, Spain, and France should all guarantee one another's possessions in the region of the Mediterranean. It was put in this form because M. Jules Cambon felt it absolutely necessary that Spanish susceptibility should be soothed by a treaty on terms of perfect equality. M. Cambon said it would be very desirable that, if the matter was to be taken up, this should be done before his brother left Madrid in February.

I said this would be a difficult matter, because it was one on which I should have to consult my Colleagues, and they would not meet before February.(²)

I would, however, tell him I found that, a year and a-half ago, Lord Lansdowne had mentioned this subject to the Marquis de Villa Urrutia,(³) who was then accompanying the King of Spain on a visit to England. Lord Lansdowne had put forward as his own personal suggestion that a mutually advantageous arrangement might be made between Spain and Great Britain by which Spain should complete her arrangement with France on the subject of Morocco, by promising not to cede to any other Power any portion of the Morocco coast which was hers, and not to place guns or forts in such a position as to impair the security of Gibraltar. England in return would undertake to support Spain in resisting any attempt to deprive her of places which she owned on the Morocco seaboard or of her Islands.

I asked M. Cambon to observe that this would have been an arrangement of perfect equality. Spain would have given us a concession in the form of security for Gibraltar, and our guarantee of her would nave been in return for what she had given to us. Lord Lansdowne had told M. de Villa Urrutia at the time that, if anything was to be settled in this way, it must be with the full knowledge of the French Government.

Nothing had passed since then. But quite lately my attention had been drawn to what Lord Lansdowne had said, and I had spoken to the Prime Minister and to one or two of my Colleagues on the subject, with the view of discussing the matter with them. But I had not intended to say anything on the matter either to the French Government or to the Spanish Government until the question had been discussed.

I could not take the matter further without more consideration, and I should not have mentioned it yet had M. Cambon not raised it.

(¹) [*v. infra*, pp. 12–13, No. 13.]
(²) [The substance of the above part of this despatch was telegraphed to Sir M. de Bunsen in Tel. No. 4 of January 10. (F.O. 371/364. 786/285/07/41.)]
(³) [*v. supra*, pp. 2–3, No. 1.]

I observed that Spain never liked to be hurried, and at the present time I thought she was particularly little in a disposition to be hurried in the matter.

[I am, &c.]

E. G[REY].

No. 11.

Sir Edward Grey to Sir M. de Bunsen.

F.O. 371/364.
4655/285/07/41.
(No. 24.) Secret.
Sir,   *Foreign Office, February 7, 1907.*

I asked the Spanish Ambassador today whether he remembered a conversation which Lord Lansdowne had with him some time ago, when he accompanied the King of Spain on a visit to England.([1]) Lord Lansdowne had suggested as possible an agreement between Spain and England by which Spain would promise not to part with any portion of the Morocco coast which belonged to her, nor to allow operations which would imperil Gibraltar; England, in return, would promise to support Spain in defending her African possessions and her Islands if any other Power attempted to take them from her.

The Ambassador said he did remember the conversation, and then told me of the proposal made by M. Jules Cambon at Madrid with regard to a tripartite agreement between France, Spain, and England for the mutual protection of their possessions in that region.([2])

The views of the Spanish Government with regard to the question were that it was too soon for them to attempt so important a matter. It was one on which the Opposition would have to be consulted. The Opposition was very disunited in Spain, and had several leaders, all of whom would have to be taken into confidence; in these circumstances, the matter could hardly be negotiated without publicity. His Government further felt that, in engagements of this kind, it was always the weaker or smaller Power that fared worst. They desired to work with England and France, and to remain on the same cordial terms with them as at present, especially with England, whose influence they felt might be exercised very beneficially in the case of any difference arising between France and Spain in Morocco. But they felt that this good disposition, while it was as strong as it was now between all three Countries, might prove even better than any written engagement in practical results. They were, however, favourable in principle to such proposals as had been made.

I observed that Lord Lansdowne's proposal was not the same as that of M. Cambon. The part of it which related to Morocco and Gibraltar was more suitable for a dual treaty between Spain and England, for France had not the same local standing in regard to engagements concerning Gibraltar, and she already had her own Treaty with Spain respecting the coast of Morocco, whereas no arrangement of that kind existed between Spain and ourselves. This part of a Treaty, should one be made, would therefore be more appropriately a dual arrangement, though it would be communicated to the French.

The Ambassador said the Spanish Government were quite willing that Gibraltar should remain secured to us, but they might find difficulty in actually mentioning it in a Treaty.

I told him that the suggestions I was making were entirely personal. On so important a matter, I should have to consult my Colleagues before being able to speak on their behalf. But it was hardly worth while to ask them to consider the

([1]) [*v. supra*, pp. 2–3, No. 1.]
([2]) [*cp.* immediately preceding document; and *v. infra*, pp. 12–13, No. 13.]

matter with a view to authorising any proposal until I knew whether the Spanish Government were at all inclined to consider the question. If they were favourable to it in principle, it was for them to consider what form a proposal should take.

The Ambassador said he had no record of his conversation with Lord Lansdowne, and only remembered its general purport.

I promised to send him a short record of the conversation.

[I am, &c.]
E. G[REY].

No. 12.

Sir Edward Grey to Sir M. de Bunsen.

F.O. 371/364.
4996/285/07/41.
(No. 25.)   Secret.
Sir,   *Foreign Office, February* 13, 1907.

The Spanish Ambassador spoke to me to-day with reference to the summary which I had sent him of Lord Lansdowne's conversation with him.(¹)

He said it agreed entirely with his recollections, and it seemed to him also to agree very much in substance with the proposals which France had now made.¹ He thought, therefore, that as France was in any case to be informed from the beginning as to what was passing it would be more natural if France were to be associated with any arrangement that was come to.

I agreed with this view, and explained that the idea of a dual arrangement had no doubt originated at first from the fact that France already had an arrangement with Spain about the Morocco coast, and Lord Lansdowne had intended ours to be complementary to that. But the position had changed, since France had now made proposals of her own, and I quite agreed that she should be a party to anything that was done.

But the most important point was that we should know what form Spain would like any proposal to take. I should have to submit the matter to my Colleagues, and the first enquiry they would make of me would be whether Spain wished an arrangement to be made or not. If I had to reply that I did not know, they would feel unable to consider so important a matter without knowing what the wishes of Spain were. We had no intention whatever of urging anything that Spain did not desire, and I had only sent the Ambassador Lord Lansdowne's proposals in order that the Spanish Government might start the consideration of the subject with everything before them.

[I am, &c.]
E. G[REY].

(¹) [*v. supra.* pp. 2–3, No. 1.]

No. 13.

Communication from M. Paul Cambon, February 14, 1907.

Draft Note by M. Jules Cambon.

F.O. 371/364.
5103/285/07/41.

Les Gouvernements de la République Française de S[a] M[ajesté] le Roi d'Espagne, et de S[a] M[ajesté] le Roi d'Angleterre etc., également désireux de prévenir toute complication de nature à troubler l'équilibre européen et la paix générale, sont tombés d'accord qu'il est essentiel de maintenir le statu quo territorial en ce qui concerne leurs possessions maritimes respectives dans le bassin de la Méditerranée et dans la partie de l'Atlantique qui baigne les côtes de l'Europe et de l'Afrique.

En conséquence ils sont convenus de ne céder à aucune tierce Puissance, par voie de vente, de location, d'échange ou autrement, aucune île, aucun port, ni aucun point des côtes faisant partie des dites possessions. Ils ne céderont également aucun droit de pêche, aucun dépôt de charbon, non plus qu'aucun autre établissement quelconque pouvant entraîner une occupation permanente de la part d'une tierce Puissance ou de ses nationaux.

Dans le cas où l'un des trois Gouvernements serait saisi d'une proposition émanée d'une tierce Puissance ou de nationaux d'une tierce Puissance, tendant soit à la cession d'une portion de leurs territoires respectifs, soit à son occupation à titre permanent, il est convenu qu'il la communiquerait aux deux autres Gouvernements et que ceux-ci lui prêteraient leur appui diplomatique pour le maintien du statu quo territorial ci-dessus visé.

L'Ambassadeur soussigné, dûment autorisé à cet effet, donne acte à M. . . . . de l'assentiment de son Gouvernement à la présente Note.

MINUTE.

M. Cambon gave me this as an informal and personal draft, which M. Jules Cambon had drawn up on his own account, but which had been shown to Senor Maura, who was favourable to it.

E. G.
14 : 2 : 07.

No. 14.

Sir Edward Grey to Sir F. Bertie.

F.O. 371/364.
5552/285/07/41.
(No. 83.) Secret.

Sir, *Foreign Office, February* 14, 1907.

M. Cambon represented to me to-day that, in place of the dual arrangement which Lord Lansdowne had suggested to Spain, it would be much better to have a tripartite agreement, as all three Powers were interested.

It was to the interest of England to have Gibraltar guaranteed. It was very much to the interest of France that no hostile Power should be in possession of the Balearic Islands. England and France equally had an interest in seeing the Canaries remain Spanish. France also attached importance to Fernando Po. While to Spain it would be a great advantage to have a guarantee of her possessions from England and France.

I said I agreed that this was so and that if anything was done it should be between all three Powers. But my conversations with M. de Villa Urrutia had been directed to finding out what it was that Spain really wished. I should have to put this matter before my Colleagues, and I should certainly make no progress with them until I was in a position to say what Spain's wishes were. They would certainly not agree to urge Spain to do anything she did not really desire.

M. Cambon thought it might be very desirable that Italy should eventually be associated with such an arrangement for the maintenance of the *status quo* in the Mediterranean. But he doubted whether anything could be done with regard to Italy at present. It was essential that England, France, and Spain should be thoroughly agreed first.

[I am, &c.]
E. G[REY].

No. 15.

Sir M. de Bunsen to Sir Edward Grey.

F.O. 371/364.
6849/285/07/41.
(No. 43.)   Secret.   *Madrid,* D. *February* 22, 1907.
Sir,   R. *March* 2, 1907.

I have had the honour to receive your secret despatches Nos. 24 and 25 of the 7th and 13th instant,(¹) in which you have had the goodness to inform me of your conversations with the Spanish Ambassador in London on the subject of a possible agreement between Spain and England, on the basis suggested by Lord Lansdowne to His Excellency on the occasion of the King of Spain's visit to England in the summer of 1905.

I understand that it now rests with the Spanish Government to state their views in the matter, after full consideration of the summary of Lord Lansdowne's conversation with Señor de Villa Urrutia, which you placed in His Excellency's hands.

Meanwhile I may remark that the difficulty which Señor de Villa Urrutia said was felt by the Spanish Government owing to the condition of the Liberal Opposition, which was very disunited and had several leaders, all of whom would have to be taken into confidence in a matter of such importance, has now largely disappeared. As reported in a separate despatch, the Principal Liberal Statesmen, apart from the radical group led by Señor Canalejas, have held a formal meeting, at which Señor Moret was unanimously chosen as the leader of the Liberal Party. Señor Moret is therefore clearly indicated as the person who would have to be consulted on the opposition side, and I have good reason to believe that he would be likely to take a favourable view of the proposal in question. When Señor Moret was in Office on my arrival in Madrid in the Spring of last year he more than once expressed to me his opinion that Gibraltar ought to be regarded rather as a link between the two countries than as a bone of contention, and his language on this subject leads me to think that it is extremely probable that Señor Moret was the Spanish Statesman who made to Sir Henry Drummond Wolf on September 11th 1898 the first proposal for an understanding between Spain and England of the kind that is now contemplated.

One of the chief difficulties to be surmounted, in the event of the present Spanish Government taking up the idea, seems to me to be in the expectation, to which I presume we still hold, that, in Lord Lansdowne's language "some arrangement should be made for the purpose of securing Gibraltar from exposure to attack from the Spanish mainland."

This point was very fully gone into in the discussion to which the erection of certain works opposite Gibraltar gave rise in the year 1898. . . .(²)

I may mention however, in further illustration of Señor Moret's attitude on the question, that, in a conversation with Sir Arthur Nicolson in October 1905(³) His Excellency, who shortly afterwards became Prime Minister, expressed himself as very anxious to bring about a closer union between Spain and England, her natural ally, on the basis of a guarantee of the Spanish Islands in exchange for a pledge giving Gibraltar security from a land attack.

The present Spanish Government ought therefore to find no difficulty in securing the concurrence of their political opponents in a scheme designed to give effect to the policy outlined by the Liberal Leader.

(¹) [*v. supra,* pp. 11–12. Nos. 11 and 12.]
(²) [This part of the despatch is omitted because it merely contains a sketch of the history of the question between 1898–1904 already summarised at the beginning of the chapter. *v. supra,* pp. 1–2, *Ed. note.*]
(³) [*v. supra,* pp. 3–4, No. 2.]

It will be difficult, however, to convert the declarations concerning the works opposite Gibraltar, made in the exchange of Notes in 1899,([4]) into a formula of a more permanent and formal character, such as would both satisfy His Majesty's Government and prove acceptable to Spain.

> I have, &c.
> MAURICE DE BUNSEN.

([4]) [*v. supra*, p. 1, *Ed. note.*]

[*ED. NOTE.*—The minutes of the 96th Meeting of the Committee of Imperial Defence, February 28, 1907, show that the question of Gibraltar was discussed and a view expressed, among others, " that it would be an advantage from the naval and military point of view if Spain would undertake not . . . . to alienate any of her external possessions to any other Power, Great Britain on her side undertaking to guarantee those possessions against foreign occupation. It is desirable that France should be a party to this arrangement." An extract from these minutes was communicated to the Foreign Office on April 30, 1907. No action appears to have resulted. *v.* F.O. 371/364. 14116/285/07/41.]

No. 16.

Sir M. de Bunsen to Sir Edward Grey.

F.O. 371/364.   *Madrid, February* 28, 1907.
6675/285/07/41.   D. 4·30 P.M.
Tel. (No. 7.) Secret.   R. 8 P.M.

Your despatches Nos. 24 and 25, Secret, of 7th February and 13th February,([1]) and my despatch No. 43, Secret, of 22nd February,([2]) now on its way.

French Ambassador had an interview with the President of the Council yesterday on the subject of the proposed Convention. He found his Excellency well disposed, and he urged that instructions should be sent to Spanish Ambassador in London.

French Ambassador thinks that the negotiations should be pursued in London, and not at Madrid, where everything leaks out, or in Paris, where Spanish Ambassador is not to be trusted. He is left under the impression that an Agreement will not be difficult provided that (1) we do not insist on a guarantee of Gibraltar and Malta, and (2) that the Agreement takes the form of a single instrument signed on terms of equality between the three countries.

([1]) [*v. supra*, pp. 11–12, Nos. 11 and 12.]
([2]) [*v.* immediately preceding document.]

No. 17.

M. Jules Cambon's Draft Note of February 14, 1907, as amended by Señor de Villa Urrutia, and communicated by him to Sir Edward Grey on March 25, 1907.([1])

F.O. 371/364.
9873/285/07/41.

Les Gouvernements de la République Française, de Sa Majesté le Roi d'Espagne, et de Sa Majesté le Roi d'Angleterre, etc., également désireux de prévenir toute complication de nature à troubler l'équilibre Européen et la paix générale, sont tombés d'accord qu'il est essentiel de maintenir le *statu quo* territorial en ce qui

([1]) [For M. Jules Cambon's draft note of February 14 before amendment, *v. supra*, pp. 12–13, No. 13.]

concerne leurs possessions maritimes respectives dans le bassin de la Méditerranée et dans la partie de l'Atlantique qui baigne les côtes de l'Europe et de l'Afrique.

En conséquence ils sont convenus de ne céder à aucune tierce Puissance, par voie de vente, de location, d'échange, ou autrement, aucune île, aucun port, ni aucun point des côtes faisant partie des dites possessions. Ils ne céderont également aucun droit de pêche, aucun dépôt de charbon, non plus qu'aucun autre établissement quelconque pouvant entraîner une occupation permanente de la part d'une tierce Puissance ou de ses nationaux.

Dans le cas où l'un des trois Gouvernements serait saisi d'une proposition émanée d'une tierce Puissance ou de nationaux d'une tierce Puissance, tendant soit à la cession d'une portion de leurs territoires respectifs, soit à son occupation à titre permanent, il est convenu qu'il la communiquerait aux deux autres Gouvernements et que ceux-ci lui prêteraient leur appui diplomatique pour le maintien du *statu quo* territorial ci-dessus visé.

Pour le cas où l'action agressive de tierces Puissances mettrait en question le principe du statu quo dans les limites visées par le paragraphe premier, les trois Gouvernements se réservent d'aviser éventuellement aux moyens d'en assurer la sauvegarde.(²)

L'Ambassadeur soussigné, dûment autorisé à cet effet, donne acte à M. de l'assentiment de son Gouvernement à la présente note.

(²) [This paragraph is the amendment proposed by Señor de Villa Urrutia. The whole text was sent to Sir M. de Bunsen as an enclosure in Sir Edward Grey's despatch No. 48 of March 25. (*v.* immediately succeeding document.)]

No. 18.

Sir Edward Grey to Sir M. de Bunsen.

F.O. 371/364.
9873/285/07/41.
(No. 48.) Secret.
Sir,
                                                          Foreign Office, March 25, 1907.
   The Spanish Ambassador informed me to-day that he had heard from his Government with reference to the suggested tripartite Agreement between England, France, and Spain.

The Spanish Government were very favourably disposed to any thing which would strengthen the good relations between England and Spain, and they had no capital objection to the principle of M. Jules Cambon's draft.(¹) But it seemed to them more theoretical than practical.

With regard to the first clause, they felt that it was a little ambiguous, and scarcely recognised sufficiently that the maintenance of the *status quo* as regards the maritime possessions of England and France was just as important to Spain as the maintenance of the *status quo* of the Spanish maritime possessions was to England and France. But the Spanish Ambassador agreed that this criticism was one of form.

The Spanish Government thought that the second clause of M. Cambon's draft did not look well. It was out of the question that England or France should cede any of their possessions, and this paragraph therefore looked as if it were put in with reference solely to Spain. And, as a matter of fact, the object of it was covered by the third clause, to which the Spanish Government had no objection. In any case, they thought that in the second clause there should be no mention of fishing rights, because Spain might wish to give to a neighbour, such as Portugal, reciprocal rights of fishing which she would not extend to any more distant Power.

But, on the whole draft, the Spanish Ambassador observed that there was no indication of steps to be taken to maintain the *status quo*. And he handed me a

(¹) [*v. supra*, pp. 12–13, No. 13, and pp. 15–16, No. 17.]

draft of a clause based on the wording of the Agreement which Russia and France had made after the Anglo-Japanese Alliance.

He was very anxious that I should consider this, and let him know our views with regard to it before he left for Carthagena.

I said I must have time to consider it.

[I am, &c.]
E. G[REY].

No. 19.

Memorandum by Sir C. Hardinge.

F.O. 371/364.
10124/285/07/41.
Secret.

March 25, 1907.

The proposal made by Lord Lansdowne on the 8th of June, 1905([1]) for a mutual agreement between Spain and Great Britain not to alienate to a third Power the Spanish islands in the Mediterranean and Atlantic and the places owned on the Moorish sea-board has been replaced by a proposal made to the Spanish Government by the French Ambassador at Madrid for a tripartite agreement between England, France and Spain. The object of the proposed agreement is to strengthen Spain in refusing inconvenient demands for concessions within Spanish territory, to attach her more firmly to England and France, and to prevent her seeking other Alliances.

The Spanish Government and the Chief of the Opposition are said to be favourably disposed towards a tripartite agreement and the Spanish Ambassador has been told that he will receive instructions to make a communication to His Majesty's Government before he leaves London to take part in the ceremonies at Carthagena.

The chief objection on the part of His Majesty's Government to the proposed tripartite agreement is the necessity which it would entail of absolute secrecy. Otherwise it would be seriously resented by Germany who would regard it as aimed at her; it would appear as a tightening of the net spread around German political activity; and might act as a sufficient provocation to Germany to drive her into hostile action of some kind.

The idea does not however appear to have been favourably received by the King of Spain who made a counterproposal that there should be an arrangement with England alone, by which England should in time of war have free use of Spanish ports and arsenals in return for an undertaking to defend the Spanish coasts from attack by any other Power.

This suggestion is quite unacceptable, since it would, in the first instance impose a very serious obligation and duty upon British naval forces in time of war, and the use of Spanish ports and arsenals would necessarily be regarded by the enemy as a breach of neutrality and an act of belligerency by Spain.

Both the tripartite agreement and the King of Spain's proposal appear to be open to serious objection, and, as it would now be impossible to revert to Lord Lansdowne's original proposal, the question arises whether the matter should not be allowed to drop, or whether the agreement might not be reduced to an exchange of notes between the British and Spanish Governments by which they agree not to cede, lease, etc., ... ([2]) their islands, ports, etc. . . . . without consulting each other. This would probably be equally efficacious, it would entail no obligation upon us and Germany would have no cause for complaint.

March 25, 1907.

C. H.

([1]) [*v. supra*, pp. 2–3, No. 1.]
([2]) [The omission marks in this document appear in the original.]

[19656]

c

No. 20.

Minute by Sir C. Hardinge.

F.O. 371/364.
16168/285/07/41.
Sir E. Grey,   *Foreign Office, March* 28, 1907.

This is an amended text of the proposed notes([1]) to be exchanged between the British and Spanish Gov[ernmen]ts which should, I think, meet the objections raised yesterday verbally by the Spanish Amb[assado]r.

I should like, if you agree, to offer this text when at Carthagena as a purely *tentative* proposal.

C. H.

Yes. E. G.

([1]) [*v.* immediately succeeding document.]

No. 21.

Basis of Notes to be exchanged between the British and Spanish Governments.([1])

F.O. 371/364.
16168/285/07/41.   *March* 28, 1907.

Animated by the desire to contribute in every possible way to the maintenance of peace, and convinced that the preservation of the territorial *status quo* and of the national rights of $\frac{\text{Great Britain and Spain}}{\text{Spain and Great Britain}}$ in the Mediterranean and in that part of the Atlantic Ocean which washes the shores of Europe and Africa must materially serve this end, and is moreover to the mutual advantage of the two nations bound to each other by the closest ties of ancient friendship and of community of interests;

The Government of His $\frac{\text{Britannic}}{\text{Most Catholic}}$ Majesty desire to lay before that of His $\frac{\text{Most Catholic}}{\text{Britannic}}$ Majesty the following declaration of policy, in the confident hope that it will not only still further strengthen the good understanding so happily existing between them, but will also promote the cause of peace :—

The general policy of the government of His $\frac{\text{Britannic}}{\text{Most Catholic}}$ Majesty in the regions above defined is directed to the maintenance of the territorial *status quo*, and in pursuance of this policy, they are firmly resolved to preserve intact the national rights of the $\frac{\text{British}}{\text{Spanish}}$ Crown over its insular and maritime possessions in those regions.

In the event of any action being taken or threatened by a third Power which in the opinion of the government of His $\frac{\text{Britannic}}{\text{Most Catholic}}$ Majesty would alter or tend to alter the existing territorial *status quo* in the said regions they will communicate with the government of His $\frac{\text{Most Catholic}}{\text{Britannic}}$ Majesty in order to afford them the opportunity to concert, if desired, by mutual agreement, the course of action which the two Powers shall adopt in common.

([1]) [A French translation was appended.]

No. 22.

Sir F. Bertie to Sir Edward Grey.

F.O. 371/364.
10488/285/07/17.
(No. 169.)   Confidential.   *Paris*, D. *March* 31, 1907.
Sir,   R. *April* 2, 1907.

Yesterday was the day named by the French Minister for Foreign Affairs for the signature of the Additional Agreement to the Convention between Great Britain and France of December 1, 1897, respecting the exchange of Postal Parcels between India and France. Soon after the middle of the day I received a message from Monsieur Pichon that he was ill and was obliged to take to his bed and that he would send the Agreement to me for my signature. Two hours later he telephoned that he was better and would get up to receive me.

After we had signed the Agreement Monsieur Pichon said that he was glad of the opportunity to see me as he desired to acquaint me with certain matters indicative of the attitude of Germany towards France and England. The German Emperor in conversation with a person whom His Excellency did not name, but who I learnt to-day from the President of the Council was the French Chargé d'Affaires at Berlin, had been very violent in regard to the King of England and the King of Italy. His Imperial Majesty had attributed to the extraordinary and sinister influence of His Majesty King Edward all the grievances of which Germany had reason to complain, the understanding between England and France aimed against Germany, the approaching Agreements between Russia and Japan, between Russia and England and between France and Japan, the anti-German attitude of Spain, the perverse conduct of Italy in supporting England in advocating a discussion at the Hague Conference of a reduction or a limitation of expenditure in armaments.

Monsieur Pichon stated that he had absolutely trustworthy information that the German Ambassador at Paris was engaged in a campaign of intrigue with a portion of the French Press and certain Parliamentary Persons to get up a movement in favour of an understanding between France and Germany ; and £20,000 had been placed at the Ambassador's disposal for the purpose of founding a French newspaper to advocate such a policy.

The situation was at present not very serious, but what he had told me showed that there would be a renewal of the attempts by Germany to destroy the good under-standing between France and England, and the French and British Governments must be on their guard for with the German Emperor's temperament it was impossible to say from one day to another what His Majesty might do or say. The French Govern-ment were determined to remain loyal to the understanding with England and the newspaper Articles which no doubt I had noticed advocating an arrangement with Germany in neglect of British interests were entirely contrary to the views of the French Government. Dr. Schiemann had lately been in Paris ostensibly for the purpose of consulting some archives of the years 1831 and 1832. This was merely a pretext. He had come to intrigue against the Understanding between France and England. Monsieur Pichon had avoided receiving him and had managed to make Dr. Schiemann's stay in Paris so unpleasant owing to his being so much under the notice of newspaper correspondents and therefore so fruitless as regards secret inter-views with political persons of Germanophil tendencies that he had left the Capital.

I observed to Monsieur Pichon that Austria-Hungary appeared to be more than ever under the influence of Germany, and I asked him whether Germany could rely equally on Italy. His Excellency replied that though Italy was a Member of the Triplice no Italian Government could give active support to Austria and Germany against France ; that the interest of Italy was to rely on England and France rather than on Germany : that she was now on excellent terms with France and that her policy must always be largely dependent on that of England. He had no fear in present circumstances of Italy giving any trouble to France.

I saw Monsieur Clemenceau this afternoon. He asked me whether Monsieur Pichon had shown to me the report from the French Chargé d'Affaires at Berlin of a conversation with the Emperor William, and on my saying that His Excellency had told me of the conversation he said " well next time you see him make him show it to you." Monsieur Clemenceau then inquired how the negotiations between you and the Spanish Ambassador in London were getting on. He hoped that they would soon be concluded. I said that the Spanish Government found it difficult to mention our possession of Gibraltar, but that you hoped to come to some Agreement which though it might not be in the form at first suggested would secure the main objects which England, France and Spain had in view. Monsieur Clemenceau observed that owing to the internal questions in France it would be of the utmost importance that the negotiations with Spain and other outstanding questions in which France and England are both interested should be settled within the next month from now. I take this to mean that Monsieur Clemenceau foresees the possibility of his Government falling soon after the reassembling of the Chambers on the 7th of May and that he wishes France to be before then committed to an arrangement for securing the Spanish Island Possessions against German designs, and to an Agreement in regard to the Bagdad Railway.

I have, &c.

FRANCIS BERTIE.

MINUTES.

So long as the emperor believes that by intrigues and threats he can prevent other Powers from entering into mutually advantageous but entirely inoffensive agreements, so long will he and the German government continue to alarm the whole world by their proceedings. This will only cease when Germany has become convinced by experience that other Powers will not allow themselves to be dictated to or interfered with in questions of foreign policy, or cajoled or bullied into modelling their international relations in conformity with German designs. It is most necessary that the several Powers should stand firm in resisting the absurd proposition that unless they continue to quarrel among themselves, they commit an offence against Germany. The latter is fortunately quite powerless at present, and probably for some time to come, to prevent other Powers from serving their mutual interests by cooperation, and the more their friendly and non-aggressive association is strengthened, the sooner is it likely that Germany will renounce the useless policy of endeavouring to sow discord among them.

If the Spanish negotiation could be brought to a successful issue soon it would probably have a beneficial and tranquillizing effect on the general situation, if only because an accomplished fact is more readily accepted than an uncertainty which leaves the hope of a successful countermove open.

It is however for consideration whether France might not be asked to stand out of the Spanish negotiation altogether for the present, and to come in only if and when Germany did likewise. The object which M. Clemenceau's government has in view would be equally well served if England, simultaneously with her exchange of notes with Spain, were to give France an understanding to communicate with her in the case of a design against the Spanish possessions becoming apparent.

As regards the Bagdad railway I fear the prospects of arriving at a satisfactory arrangement before May 7 are very remote. Yet it is clear that a change of government in France might lead to an understanding being come to between the French and German bankers which would materially prejudice our position.

E. A. C.   Ap[ril] 2.

The language of the German Emperor need not necessarily represent the opinion of the German Gov[ernmen]t, but there is no doubt a belief in Germany that the main object of H[is] M[ajesty's] G[overnment] is to isolate her.

E. B.

We shall be able to put the French in possession of our views about the Bagdad R[ailwa]y this month, but an agreement with Germany may be a long way off.

E. G.

No. 23.

Sir Edward Grey to Sir F. Bertie.

F.O. 371/364.
11580/285/07/41.
Private.

My dear Bertie.   *Foreign Office, April 5, 1907.*

Cambon is away, and will not be back for some time. Meanwhile, Hardinge has gone to meet the King at Carthagena. Some conversation is sure to take place there on the subject of an agreement with Spain, and I should like M. Pichon to know the turn which it is likely to take. The thing is too vague to form the subject of a written communication, and as Cambon is away it would be desirable for you to tell M. Pichon verbally.

Before the Spanish Ambassador left London, he gave me the views of the Spanish Government on the French draft. They were, on the whole, favourable but he evidently wanted something in the form of a guarantee added to it.

I have two difficulties about this. In the first place, we cannot do such a thing secretly. What we do will have to be disclosed to Parliament. In the second place, if I have to lay before Parliament something which entails an obligation, I shall have the most searching questions addressed to me as to what I have got in return for it. I shall be asked point blank whether we have got any engagement about Gibraltar, and, if not, whether it is quite clear that Gibraltar is covered and intended by the Treaty.

When Lord Lansdowne first mentioned the matter to Villa Urrutia some time ago, he laid half the stress upon Gibraltar, and public opinion here would expect a very explicit statement about it.

Now, the Spanish Government will not like to mention Gibraltar in the Treaty, and it will be difficult for the French to do so. If no mention is made, it will not be agreeable if I have to explain later on that I regard the Spanish Government as having undertaken obligations with regard to Gibraltar.

I am, therefore, inclined to think that it might be better to have an exchange of Notes between ourselves and Spain which could be published without provoking any awkward questions. The Note would be to the effect that the general policy, both of Great Britain and Spain, in the Mediterranean, and in that part of the Atlantic which washes the shores of Europe and Africa, is directed to the maintenance of the territorial *status quo*; that, in pursuance of this policy, we are each of us resolved to preserve intact our respective national rights over our insular and maritime possessions in those regions; and that, in the event of any action being taken or threatened by a third Power, which in the opinion of either the British or the Spanish Government would alter, or tend to alter, the existing territorial *status quo* in those regions, the Government concerned will communicate with the other in order to afford the opportunity to concert, if desired, by mutual agreement the course of action which shall be adopted.

It would be possible for France to supplement the Agreement which she has already with Spain by a similar Note, or if that is thought unnecessary we should be prepared to give France an assurance that, in the event of either Spain consulting us or our consulting Spain as contemplated by the Note, we would inform the French Government.

Yours sincerely,
E. GREY.

No. 24.

Sir F. Bertie to Sir Edward Grey.

F.O. 371/364.
11580/285/07/41.

Private and Confidential.   Paris, D. *April* 7, 1907.

My dear Grey,   R. *April* 8, 1907.

I saw Pichon and afterwards Clemenceau yesterday on the subject of your letter of the 5th instant(¹) respecting the negotiations with Spain in regard to the maintenance of the *status quo* in the Mediterranean and that part of the Atlantic which washes the shores of Europe and Africa.

Pichon said that he considered that what you suggest would meet the requirements of the case, and it would avoid the appearance of a Triplice, but he evidently wished that Clemenceau (whom I told him I intended to see on the subject as he had spoken to me about it) should pronounce himself.

Clemenceau said that he would have preferred an agreement to an exchange of Notes; but he admitted the difficulty for Spain of endorsing by a written engagement our right to Gibraltar and your objection to secrecy and the force of what you say as to the Parliamentary objections to not mentioning Gibraltar in an Agreement entailing an obligation on the part of England.

Clemenceau therefore authorized me to say that in view of all the circumstances of the case he concurs in the proposal for an exchange of Notes, and he hopes that a satisfactory conclusion will be come to during the visit of the King to the King of Spain. He says that further delay might enable Germany to prevent an arrangement with Spain.

Yours sincerely,
FRANCIS BERTIE.

(¹) [*v.* immediately preceding document.]

No. 25.

Sir C. Hardinge to Sir Edward Grey.(¹)

F.O. 371/364.
11372/285/07/41.   *Carthagena*, D. *April* 9, 1907, 8 P.M.

Tel. (No. 3.)   Secret.   R. *April* 10, 1907, 7·30 A.M.

Agreement respecting Spanish Islands.

I had an interview yesterday with the M[inister for] F[oreign] A[ffairs] and Spanish Ambassador in London and, having explained at length your views, submitted text approved by you as the basis of notes to be exchanged. The result of interview was not hopeful as they insisted on text of agreement being of a tripartite form and said that they would submit a counter-project to-day.

Last night I spoke both to the King of Spain and the Prime Minister and urged upon them your views.

At an interview which I have just had with the Prime Minister and M[inister for] F[oreign] A[ffairs] I found a complete change in the situation. The Prime Minister told me that he fully appreciated force of Parliamentary and other political considerations which I had urged yesterday and which he regarded as unanswerable. He accepted the proposal of an exchange of notes provided the French Government would agree, and added that he could suggest no modifications of our text but that he wished for a short time for reflection upon its terms.

I was fortunately able to communicate to him the contents of your private telegram(²) which I received this morning at which he seemed greatly pleased and

(¹) [Repeated to Paris as No. 19 of April 10.]
(²) [In his private telegram of April 8, 1907, Sir Edward Grey informed Sir C. Hardinge that Sir F. Bertie had communicated to the French Prime Minister and Minister for Foreign Affairs the form of the proposed agreements between Great Britain and Spain and the purport of the notes to be exchanged. Both Ministers approved and hoped that satisfactory arrangements would be reached.]

said that all he would ask would be that the French Gov[ernmen]t should exchange with the Spanish Gov[ernmen]t notes in exactly same terms as ours and on same date.

The Spanish Ambassador in London and Sir M. de Bunsen were also present at the interview.

No. 26.

Sir C. Hardinge to Sir Edward Grey.

F.O. 371/364.
13877/285/07/41.
My dear Grey,

His Majesty's Yacht " Victoria and Albert,"([1])
D. *April 9, 1907.*
R. *April 12, 1907.*

I arranged a meeting yesterday afternoon with the Minister for F[oreign] A[ffairs] and Villa Urrutia on board the Spanish Royal Yacht to discuss the proposed exchange of notes. Bunsen came with me.

I explained to them at some length the historical side of the question, the advantages which the arrangement as first proposed presented from the point of view of public opinion in England, and the objections which any agreement which must be kept secret must necessarily have from the constitutional and parliamentary aspect. I then submitted to them the proposal that we and the French (if they desire it) should make an exchange of notes with the Spanish Gov[ernmen]t of which the purport should be based on the lines of the draft which you had approved and of which I gave them a copy in English and French.

I found at once that the question had been already discussed by the Spanish Gov[ernmen]t, evidently on the information given by Villa Urrutia, and the Minister for F[oreign] A[ffairs] made to me a formal statement that the policy of the Spanish Gov[ernmen]t is based on close co-operation with England and France, and that consequently no agreement would be possible that was not of a tripartite character. I pointed out that the threefold form of the agreement could be maintained by the French Gov[ernmen]t exchanging notes with them simultaneously of a similar character, but to this they objected that if we and the French exchanged notes with them there would be nothing to prevent any other Power doing the same thing, and this would entirely spoil in their opinion the moral effect of an agreement with England and France, while if the arrangement was of a tripartite character there would be no question of a fourth Power coming in. I drew their attention to the fact that a tripartite agreement might be regarded by other Powers as an unfriendly coalition to meet certain eventualities, and this they fully recognised, but stated that the solidarity of the interests of the three Powers in the Mediterranean and the Atlantic were so self-evident that they were convinced that a formula could be found to meet the circumstances of the case which would not wound the susceptibilities of any other Power. I reminded them that any formula that might be found would have to be of such a nature as could be laid before Parliament if desired, and they pointed out that equally they would have to publish their notes if we published ours and to them the result would be precisely the same as publishing a tripartite agreement.

I observed to them that we, the French and they are apparently of one mind as to what should be done, but seem to differ as to the mode of doing it and I asked if they would make a proposal to satisfy themselves and meet our objections. This they said they would do with the assistance of the Prime Minister, and when I saw the latter at a State banquet on board a Spanish ship last night I settled for a meeting to-day with him and the Minister for F[oreign] A[ffairs]. I availed myself

([1]) [On April 8, 1907, King Edward and Queen Alexandra visited King Alfonso off Carthagena. For various comments on the significance of this visit, *v.* Sir Sidney Lee : *King Edward VII* (1927), Vol. II, pp. 538–40.]

of that occasion to urge your views upon him and I spoke to the King of Spain in the same sense.

This afternoon Bunsen and I went again on board the Spanish yacht and had an interview with the Prime Minister, the Min[iste]r for F[oreign] A[ffairs] and Villa Urrutia. I found the situation had entirely changed. The Prime Minister, who is evidently a strong man and dominates the situation took the lead and told me that although he would have preferred a tripartite agreement as at first suggested by M. Jules Cambon he fully appreciated the force of the parliamentary objections to a secret agreement and the political objections to any arrangement which could possibly be regarded as an unfriendly coalition against any other Power. That Spain was more concerned than any other Power in avoiding giving offence to Germany, but that he would welcome any arrangement that would be likely to give his country greater security as regards her island possessions in the Mediterranean and Atlantic. He would therefore accept your proposal of an exchange of notes provided that the French Gov[ernmen]t would do the same, and he said that although he had carefully examined the text of the basis of the notes he thought it contained all that was desired and could suggest no alterations. He asked however for a little time for reflection upon its terms. I replied that having agreed in principle to our proposal we had no desire to rush him and that if he should wish to suggest any verbal change I was quite sure you would give it the most attentive consideration. At the same time I showed to him the text of your private tel[egram] which I received this morning and I asked Villa Urrutia to translate it to him in Spanish. He seemed greatly pleased at the French having concurred with our proposal and said that as soon as he had finally agreed upon the text of the notes to be exchanged, all he would ask would be that the same note should be exchanged by the Spanish and French Gov[ernmen]ts and on the same date as our's. This would make the connection between the two.

He asked me if we would publish our note and I replied that I thought it probable, but that he might rest assured that we would not do so without first consulting the Spanish Gov[ernmen]t. He agreed with me in thinking that the publication of a note in the terms we had suggested could offend nobody.

Altogether it was a satisfactory interview and I was greatly relieved that they have accepted your proposal to-day, of which I had not much hope yesterday.

I think we should give the text of our note to Geoffray or Bertie and try to get that definitely accepted by the French Gov[ernmen]t so that the French exchange of notes can be made at Madrid and our's in London. It must be remembered that it is undesirable to carry on the Franco-Spanish negotiations in Paris as the Spanish Amb[assado]r there would immediately inform Radolin.

Please excuse a long letter but I wished to give you the fullest possible details.

Yours very sincerely,

CHARLES HARDINGE.

No. 27.

Sir Edward Grey to Sir F. Bertie.

F.O. 371/364.
11372/285/07/41.
Tel. (No. 20.) Secret.   *Foreign Office, April 10, 1907.*

Please communicate to M. Pichon without delay copy of proposed text of notes which might be exchanged between British and Spanish governments, which I understand Sir C. Hardinge has sent to you. If the French agree to it, it would be desirable that they should intimate this to the Spanish Gov[ernmen]t, who evidently desire to be assured that such an exchange of notes would be acceptable to France.

No. 28.

Sir F. Bertie to Sir Edward Grey.

F.O. 371/364.
11580/285/07/41.
(No. 90.) Secret.   *Paris, D. April 11, 1907.*
Sir,   R. *April 12, 1907.*

I had the honour to receive yesterday evening your secret telegrams Nos. 19([1])
20([2]) and 21([3]) of yesterday, and the texts of the notes therein referred to reached
me this morning in your despatch No. 211 of yesterday.([4])

As the Minister for Foreign Affairs is absent from Paris I asked for an interview
with the President of the Council and he received me this morning. I gave to His
Excellency copies of the English and French texts of the notes which it is proposed
should be exchanged between His Majesty's Government and the Spanish Government
relative to the preservation of the territorial *status quo* and of the national rights of
Great Britain and Spain in the Mediterranean and in that part of the Atlantic which
washes the shores of Europe and Africa. I told M. Clemenceau that Sir Charles
Hardinge at an interview which he had had at Carthagena with the Spanish Minister
for Foreign Affairs and the Spanish Ambassador in London found that they insisted
very much on the Agreement being in a Tripartite form and proposed to produce a
counter-project; but that Sir Charles Hardinge having urged on His Majesty the King
of Spain and His Prime Minister your reasons for preferring an exchange of notes, the
Prime Minister had informed him on the following day at an interview at which the
Minister for Foreign Affairs, the Spanish Ambassador in London and His Majesty's
Ambassador at Madrid were present that he fully appreciated the force of the Parliamentary and political considerations which led you to object to a Tripartite Agreement
and that he regarded them as unanswerable. He therefore accepted the proposal for
an exchange of notes subject to the concurrence of the French Government and he
intimated the desire that there should be an exchange of notes between the French
and Spanish Governments in the same terms and on the same date as those to be
exchanged between the British and Spanish Governments.

I asked M. Clemenceau whether he concurred in the terms of the notes which
I had communicated to him and would authorise the French Ambassador at Madrid to
make an exchange of identic notes with the Spanish Minister for Foreign Affairs.

M. Clemenceau read the French text twice and then said that though he would
have preferred a Tripartite Agreement he realised the force of the Parliamentary and
political objections which you had to that form and he considered that the proposed
exchange of notes would answer the purpose in view. He therefore accepted the
proposal on behalf of the French Government and the requisite instructions would be
sent at once to the French Ambassador at Madrid to effect a like exchange of notes
with the Spanish Government. His Excellency pointed out that in the French text
which I had given to him in the third paragraph the wording ought to be "ce Gouvernement est fermement résolu à conserver" etc., instead of "ce gouvernement est
fermement résolu de conserver" etc.

I have, &c.
FRANCIS BERTIE.

([1]) [Repeating Sir C. Hardinge's telegram No. 3, Secret, of April 9, *v. supra*, pp. 22–3, No. 25.]
([2]) [*v.* immediately preceding document.]
([3]) [Sir Edward Grey's telegram No. 21 of April 10, D. 1·55 P.M., merely stated that a copy
of the text of the proposed note and a French translation were being sent by special bag.]
([4]) [Sir Edward Grey's despatch No. 211 of April 10, merely enclosed the texts of the
proposed notes.]

No. 29.

Sir F. Bertie to Sir Edward Grey.

F.O. 371/364.   *Paris, April* 16, 1907.
12262/285/07/41.   D. 8·12 A.M.
Tel. (No. 14.) Secret.   R. 11 A.M.

President of Council told me this evening that the Spanish Gov[ernmen]t are very insistent on the arrangement in regard to *status quo* in Mediterranean and Atlantic being a Tripartite Agreement. Spanish Ambassador has spoken to this effect at the Ministry of Foreign Affairs but has not yet seen M[inister for] F[oreign] A[ffairs] on the subject. I reminded President of the Council that the Spanish Prime Minister had accepted the proposal for an exchange of notes on your objections to Tripartite Agreement being explained to him by Sir C. Hardinge. President of Council said that nevertheless Spanish Gov[ernmen]t were very insistent for the tripartite form and that though notes might answer same purpose a Tripartite Agreement would be the preferable form.

French Ambassador in London will be in Paris to-morrow or next day and Spanish preference for tripartite form will be considered with him before French M[inister for] F[oreign] A[ffairs] discusses question with Spanish Ambassador.

President of Council did not ask me to communicate to you this information. Probably he will consider with M. Cambon whether you should be urged to reconsider your view as to form of the arrangement with Spain.

No. 30.

Sir F. Bertie to Sir Edward Grey.

F.O. 371/364.   *Paris, April* 17, 1907.
12433/285/07/41.   D. 8·25 P.M.
Tel. (No. 15.)   R. 10 P.M.

Minister for F[oreign] A[ffairs] told me this evening that there had been a consultation this morning between the President of the Council himself and the French Ambassador in London, that they were agreed on the great benefit of the proposed agreement in regard to *status quo* in the Mediterranean and Atlantic. Their only regret was that you objected to its being in a tripartite form. M. Cambon will return to London tomorrow and will make some suggestions to you in regard to wording of notes, which form of agreement French Gov[ernmen]t will accept if you still object to the tripartite form. He understood that what you propose is that notes shall be exchanged between British and Spanish Governments, between the French and Spanish Governments and British and French Governments.

Minister for F[oreign] A[ffairs] said that he supposed and hoped that exchange of notes would be kept secret.

I told him that something would be sure to leak out about the agreement and that if you were questioned in Parliament on the subject you could not deny fact of an arrangement having been made, and that as it will only provide for the three Powers keeping what belongs to them no other Power will have reasonable cause to object.

Minister for F[oreign] A[ffairs] told me that Spanish Ambassador at Paris had been made acquainted by his Gov[ernmen]t with the details of the proposed agreement and had been to see him on the subject today. He did not say whether the Ambassador had advocated a tripartite form.

MINUTES.

M. Cambon will no doubt fully explain the views of his government when he comes to see Sir Edward Grey.

There is, I think, much force in Sir F. Bertie's remark, with reference to the question of secrecy, that the fact of an arrangement having been come to is sure to leak out.

I pointed out in a memorandum([1]) some time ago that the probability of this happening, made it desirable seriously to consider the question of forestalling any misunderstanding, such as would be sure to arise out of incomplete and inaccurate reports getting about, by making at once a friendly and unofficial communication to the German ambassador. The reasons which in my memorandum I set out in favour of such a course still seem to me very strong ones.

E. A. C. Ap[ril] 18.

It w[oul]d be better to confide in Germany than to let her find out by accident, but we s[houl]d have to get the consent of France and Spain.

E. B.

It is too early to say anything to Germany yet : we must first know what form the thing is to take. I should like to see Mr. Crowe's Memorandum again.

E. G.

Sir C. Hardinge discussed this question with Sir E. Grey April 25.

C. H. M.
25.4.07.

([1]) [Dated January 1, 1907. *v. Gooch & Temperley*, Vol. III, pp. 397–420, *App.* A.]

No. 31.

Sir F. Bertie to Sir Edward Grey.

Private and Confidential.([1])

My dear Grey, 						*Paris, April* 18, 1907.
Your letter of the 13th instant reached me to-day.([2]) The French *do* consent to an exchange of notes *re* the Mediterranean &c. *status quo* if you maintain your affection for that form. They prefer the tripartite form and the insistence of the Spaniards on that form if it now exists is probably due to French prompting. Cambon will I suppose see you tomorrow. It seems to me important that the Agreement whatever form it may take should be concluded as soon as possible, for if the Germans get wind of the intention to make such an arrangement they may threaten and frighten the Spaniards, and the French would be more happy with a " fait accompli " than have to sign in face of German objections.

As to attempts to persuade the French to do a deal with Germany about the Bagdad Railway and Morocco to which you refer I do not think that anything will come of it with the present French Government so long as they feel confidence in our friendship and support, but if the Government fall which everybody says is certain the Germans will no doubt try to squeeze something out of the next Ministry.

Yours sincerely,
FRANCIS BERTIE.

([1]) [Grey MSS., Vol. 11.]
([2]) [In this letter Sir Edward Grey stated that " the consent of the French to an exchange of Notes is essential to enable Spain to make up her mind." Grey MSS., Vol. 11.]

No. 32.

Sir Edward Grey to Sir F. Bertie.

F.O. 371/364.
12927/285/07/41.
(No. 238.) Secret.
Sir, 						*Foreign Office, April* 19, 1907.
M. Cambon spoke to me to-day with regard to the proposed exchange of Notes with Spain.

He pressed me as to why we preferred an exchange of Notes to a tripartite arrangement, and asked me particularly whether it was the case that my Colleagues preferred that form.

I said it was the case that they preferred that form, and I thought there were very good reasons for this preference. We should have to publish whatever arrangement we made. And if it was in the form of the tripartite Treaty originally proposed by France, to which Spain had added an Article, I should be asked searching questions in the House of Commons with regard to Gibraltar. The proposed exchange of Notes would provoke fewer questions, and if pressed I should be able to speak more freely about Gibraltar, which every one knew was our chief interest in the matter, in regard to Notes exchanged with Spain than I should in regard to a tripartite arrangement. If I were to say, in connection with a tripartite arrangement, that it was of great benefit to us because Gibraltar had been guaranteed, this would surely provoke questions in the French Chamber as to whether the French Government had undertaken obligations to guarantee Gibraltar.

M. Cambon said that the French Government were prepared to accept an exchange of Notes. They would exchange a Note with Spain similar to the one we exchanged with Spain, and they would then propose that we and they should communicate to each other the Notes which we had respectively exchanged with Spain. He could not say whether the French Government would publish their Note, and if we published ours it would, therefore, be desirable that we should not mention the fact of the communication to France.

I told him I saw no difficulty in that. With regard to the wording of the Notes, our wording had been put forward as a "projet," and I would wait until I heard from the Spanish Government whether they had any alterations to suggest.

I also told M. Cambon that King Edward's visit to the King of Italy had no political significance, and was entirely a visit of courtesy which had not been in the original programme. But it was an added advantage to the exchange of Notes that, if later on Italy desired to exchange a similar Note with Spain, she would be able to do so much more easily than she could adhere to a tripartite arrangement.

M. Cambon was of opinion that it was premature to say anything to Italy, and with this I entirely agreed.

[I am, &c.]
E. G[REY].

No. 33.

Sir Edward Grey to Sir M. de Bunsen.

F.O. 371/364.
13878/285/07/41.
(No. 65.) Secret.
Sir, *Foreign Office, April 26, 1907.*

The Spanish Ambassador told me to-day that he had heard from M. Cambon the terms of the Note which the French Government proposed that we should exchange with them respecting the Spanish Agreement.

The Spanish Ambassador explained to me that his Government did not like the idea of this Note, as it implied a promise between England and France to talk apart regarding things which affected Spain.

I said that I had raised objection to the Note on the ground that, if we published the Spanish Note, we should have to publish the French Note also, and this France did not desire. And I had proposed that I should, in conversation, express satisfaction to the French at seeing them so entirely in agreement with us as to the policy which they desired in that part of the Mediterranean and its neighbourhood : an agreement which must be a guarantee that we should find ourselves in co-operation regarding any questions which might arise in connection with those regions.

The Spanish Ambassador said this was open to no objection, and told me that he had already informed M. Cambon of his views respecting the proposed Note.

[I am, &c.]
E. G[REY].

No. 34.

Memorandum for the Cabinet by Sir Edward Grey.

F.O. 371/364.
16168/285/07/41.
(Secret.)   *Foreign Office, April 26, 1907.*

I circulate to the Cabinet the text of the note to be exchanged between the British and the Spanish Governments.(¹)

Some time ago the matter was raised by Lord Lansdowne in a conversation, a record of which is annexed.(²) It was subsequently represented to me that, though France has a satisfactory understanding with Spain as regards the Morocco coast, we have no such understanding, and might one day find that Spain had ceded something on the Morocco coast to another Power that would impair or destroy the value of Gibraltar to us. The Committee of Defence expressed a strong opinion that this should be guarded against if possible.(³)

What has precipitated the matter, however, is that the French Government presented to the Spanish Government the draft Treaty annexed, to which the Spanish Government desired to add the paragraph in italics, and to which we were invited to adhere.(⁴)

For various reasons, which I will explain if necessary, it seemed to me preferable to have a simple exchange of notes between England and Spain in a form which was as little aggressive as possible, and which yet would make it clear that there was a community of interest between ourselves and Spain in maintaining our respective possessions intact, and would insure that no change took place behind our backs.

Spain is ready to agree to this, and, after a great deal of discussion, France has agreed, though reluctantly, to abandon the idea of a Tripartite Treaty, and to make her own arrangement with Spain separately.

The desire of France and Spain, and the opinion of our own Defence Committee, made it clear to me that it was impossible not to do something. And, in view of our Agreement with France about Morocco and that of France with Spain, it was desirable that we also should have some definite understanding with Spain. For us to have declined any proposals of the kind would have had a most prejudicial effect upon our relations with each of them, and probably also upon their relations with each other.

        E. G.

(¹) [*v. supra,* p. 18, No. 21.]
(²) [*v. supra,* pp. 2–3, No. 1.]
(³) [*cp. supra,* p. 5, No. 4, *note,* and p. 15, *Ed. note.*]
(⁴) [*v. supra,* pp. 15–16, No. 17.]

No. 35.

Sir F. Bertie to Sir Edward Grey.

F.O. 371/364.   *Paris, May 4, 1907.*
14543/285/07/41.   D. 1·22 P.M.
Tel. (No. 17.) Secret.   R. 3·15 P.M.

Min[iste]r for Foreign Affairs is very much perturbed at your intention (communicated to him by Spanish Ambassador) to publish notes to be exchanged with Spain. He says that such publication will inevitably lead to interpellations in French Parliament spontaneous or instigated by Germany. He will not be able to deny that there have been exchanges of ideas with Spanish Gov[ernmen]t and he may have to publish the notes exchanged between France and Spain, either to show that the French Gov[ernmen]t have not neglected French interests or under pressure from the Spanish Gov[ernmen]t who would object to appearance of Spain being under the protection of England and might publish notes in order to remove such appearance. The notes might, M[inister for] F[oreign] A[ffairs] says, be represented by German Gov[ernmen]t as being directed against Germany and as a provocation. He strongly urges that notes should be kept secret and that nothing should be said in Parliament except under pressure, and then only that there have been exchanges of views in regard to the respective interests of England and Spain in the Mediterranean. He would if interrogated in the French Parliament give a similar answer as regards France and Spain.

M. Pichon has instructed M. Cambon to make representations to you on this question.

The Spanish Ambassador has suggested the notes should be signed and exchanged at Madrid in order that the arrangement between Spain and England and between Spain and France may be simultaneous and in order that Spanish text may be correctly settled there. To this M. Pichon objects that the French Ambassador has not yet taken up his post at Madrid and that the note is too important to be signed by the Chargé d'Affaires who moreover has no full powers; and with regard to Spanish text, H[is] E[xcellency] suggests that it should be forwarded by the Spanish Gov[ernmen]t to their Ambassador at Paris, with authority to sign.

May 9 was mentioned by the Ambassador as a suitable date for the signature of notes.

MINUTES.

I always understood that as one of the main reasons against a tripartite formal " agreement " was the necessity to publish such an agreement, so the advantage of substituting an exchange of notes consisted partly in there being no necessity to publish.

Neither France nor Spain desires publication, nor does there seem any reason why we should hold to it. The question of communicating with Germany is a different matter. As regards the objections, on grounds of form chiefly, urged by M. Pichon against signature at Madrid, I confess they do not seem to me to be very weighty. But if France does attach value to these questions of form, it will not be easy to dissuade them [sic].

I still think there would be an advantage if the British and Spanish notes were exchanged at Madrid. We need not object to the Franco-Spanish exchange taking place simultaneously at Paris.(1)

Qu; suggest this course to the French and Spanish governments, telegraphing the necessary instructions to Paris and Madrid, adding assurance that H[is] M[ajesty's] G[overnment] do not wish to publish for the present.

E. A. C.
May 4.

Sir E. Grey will probably wish to wait until he has seen M. Cambon.

E. B.

This can wait till Monday.

C. H.

I do not want to hurry publication, but one of the reasons for an exchange of notes was to have one note in a form which could be published.

E. G.

(1) [Marginal comment by Sir E. Barrington : " This seems to be the most obvious solution. E. B."]

No. 36.

Sir Edward Grey to Sir F. Bertie.

F.O. 371/364.
14543/285/07/41.
Tel. (No. 29.) Secret. *Foreign Office, May 6, 1907.*

Y[ou]r tel[egram] No. 17.(1)

I told M. Cambon to-day that we had not decided upon the immediate publication of the Spanish note and did not desire it, but that publication might be forced by questions in Parliament.

M. Cambon then suggested the substitution of such a sentence as " if circ[umstanc]es arose " for the allusion to the third Power in the concluding paragraph of the note.

I said I would agree if France and Spain desired it.

(1) [v. immediately preceding document.]

31

No. 37.

Sir Edward Grey to Sir F. Bertie.

F.O. 371/364.
14543/285/07/41.
(No. 277.)
Sir,
                                        Foreign Office, May 6, 1907.
M. Cambon explained to me to-day the difficulty which the French Government felt about the publication of the Note exchanged with Spain.

It appeared that, if we published our Note, Spain would be obliged to publish the French Note also.

I said we had not decided upon immediate publication, and did not desire it. But publication might be forced by questions in Parliament; and later on, when it became known that the Germans had got a Cable concession to the Canaries under certain conditions, it might be desirable to publish our Note in order to correct erroneous impressions.

M. Cambon then asked me whether the words " a third Power " could not be modified. Some such words as " if circumstances arose " might be substituted for them.

I said I should not object to a modification of that kind if France and Spain desired it.

                                        I am, &c.
                                        E. GREY.

No. 38.

Sir Edward Grey to Sir F. Bertie.

F.O. 371/364.
15404/285/07/41.
(No. 286.) Secret.
Sir,
                                        Foreign Office, May 9, 1907.
M. Cambon told me today that M. Pichon had agreed to the modification in the Spanish Note, eliminating the phrase " a third Power," which M. Cambon had proposed to me the other day.

M. Pichon also hoped that we would not publish the Note before the month of August.

I said I would be quite willing not to publish the Note before that, and we might even not publish till later still, unless my hand was forced by questions in Parliament. In any case, I would let the French Government know before we decided to publish, whatever the time might be.

                                        [I am, &c.]
                                        E. G[REY].

[*ED. NOTE.*—On May 16. the following notes were exchanged by Sir Edward Grey and Señor de Villa Urrutia. On the same day M. Paul Cambon and Señor de Villa Urrutia communicated to Sir Edward Grey copies of the notes exchanged between France and Spain. *v. infra*, pp. 33–4, No. 41; and Sir Edward Grey and M. Paul Cambon presented to one another the *aide-mémoires* printed *infra*, pp. 34–5, Nos. 42 and 43.]

No. 39.

Sir Edward Grey to Señor de Villa Urrutia.

F.O. 371/364.
16168/285/07/41.
Your Excellency,   *Foreign Office, May 16, 1907.*

Animated by the desire to contribute in every possible way to the maintenance of peace, and convinced that the preservation of the territorial *status quo* and of the rights of Great Britain and Spain in the Mediterranean and in that part of the Atlantic Ocean which washes the shores of Europe and Africa must materially serve this end, and is, moreover, to the mutual advantage of the two nations bound to each other by the closest ties of ancient friendship and of community of interests :

The Government of His Britannic Majesty desire to lay before that of His Catholic Majesty the following declaration of policy, in the confident hope that it will not only still further strengthen the good understanding so happily existing between them, but will also promote the cause of peace :—

The general policy of the Government of His Britannic Majesty in the regions above defined is directed to the maintenance of the territorial *status quo*, and in pursuance of this policy they are firmly resolved to preserve intact the rights of the British Crown over its insular and maritime possessions in those regions.

Should circ[umstance]s arise which, in the opinion of the Government of His Britannic Majesty, would alter, or tend to alter, the existing territorial *status quo* in the said regions, they will communicate with the Government of His Catholic Majesty, in order to afford them the opportunity to concert, if desired, by mutual agreement the course of action which the two Powers shall adopt in common.

I have, &c.
(Signed)   E. GREY.

No. 40.

Señor de Villa Urrutia to Sir Edward Grey.([1])

F.O. 371/364.
16168/285/07/41.   *Embajada de España en Londres,*
Señor Ministro,   *16 de Mayo de* 1907.

Animado del deseo de contribuir por todos los medios posibles á la conservación de la paz y convencido de que el mantenimiento del "statu quo" territorial y de los derechos de España y de la Gran Bretaña en el Mediterráneo y en la parte del Atlantico que baña las costas de Europa y de Africa, debe servir eficazmente para alcanzar ese fin, siendo al mismo tiempo beneficioso para ambas Naciones, unidas además por los lazos de secular amistad y por la comunidad de intereses :

El Gobierno de Su Majestad Católica desea poner en conocimiento del Gobierno de Su Majestad Británica la declaración cuyo tenor sigue, con la firme esperanza de que contribuirá, no solamente á afianzar la buena inteligencia que tan felizmente existe entre ambos Gobiernos, sino también á servir la causa de la paz :

La política general del Gobierno de Su Majestad Católica en las regiones arriba indicadas tiene por objeto el mantenimiento del "statu quo" territorial y, conforme á tal política, dicho Gobierno está firmemente resuelto á conservar intactos los

([1]) [The original Note is in the Foreign Office. The English translation is omitted, as the Spanish note is, *mutatis mutandis*, the same as Sir Edward Grey's note, reproduced above, with one or two slight verbal differences.]

derechos de la Corona española sobre sus posesiones insulares y marítimas situadas en las referidas regiones.

En el caso de que nuevas circunstancias, según la opinión del Gobierno de Su Majestad Católica pudiesen modificar ó contribuir á modificar el "statu quo" territorial actual, dicho Gobierno entrará en comunicación con el Gobierno de Su Majestad Británica á fin de poner á ambos Gobiernos en condiciones de concertarse, si lo juzgan oportuno, respecto á las medidas que hubieran de tomarse en común.

Aprovecho esta ocasión, para reiterar á Vuestra Excelencia las seguridades de la alta consideración,

Con que soy,

Señor Ministro,

De Vuestra Excelencia,

Atento seguro servidor,

W. R. DE VILLA-URRUTIA.

Sr. Muy Hon. Sir Edward Grey, Bart., M.P.

[*ED. NOTE.*—The two notes above were presented to Parliament June 16, 1907. *v. A. & P.* (1907), C, (*Cd.* 3576), pp. 1–3.]

No. 41.

Notes exchanged between the French Minister for Foreign Affairs and the Spanish Ambassador at Paris, May 16, 1907.

I.—*M. Pichon to Señor Leon y Castillo.*

F.O. 371/364.
16168/285/07/41.

Animé du désir de contribuer par tous les moyens possibles à la conservation de la paix, et convaincu que le maintien du *statu quo* territorial et des droits de la France et de l'Espagne dans la Méditerranée et dans la partie de l'Atlantique qui baigne les côtes de l'Europe et de l'Afrique doit servir efficacement à atteindre ce but, tout en étant profitable aux deux nations qu'unissent d'ailleurs les liens d'une amitié séculaire et la communauté des intérêts :

Le Gouvernement de la République Française désire porter à la connaissance du Gouvernement de Sa Majesté Catholique la déclaration dont la teneur suit, avec le ferme espoir qu'elle contribuera non seulement à affermir la bonne entente qui existe si heureusement entre les deux Gouvernements, mais aussi à servir la cause de la paix :

La politique générale du Gouvernement de la République Française dans les régions susindiquées a pour objet le maintien du *statu quo* territorial, et, conformément à cette politique, ce Gouvernement est fermement résolu à conserver intacts les droits de la République Française sur ses possessions insulaires et maritimes situées dans les dites régions.

Dans le cas où se produiraient de nouvelles circonstances qui, selon l'opinion du Gouvernement de la République Française, seraient de nature ou à modifier ou à contribuer à modifier le *statu quo* territorial actuel, ce Gouvernement entrera en communication avec le Gouvernement de Sa Majesté Catholique, afin de mettre les deux Gouvernements en état de se concerter, s'il est jugé désirable, sur les mesures à prendre en commun.

(Signé)   S. PICHON.

Paris, le 16 Mai, 1907.

II.—*Señor Leon y Castillo to M. Pichon.*

Animado del deseo de contribuir por todos los medios posibles á la conservación de la paz y convencido de que el mantenimiento del *statu quo* territorial y de los derechos de España y de Francia en el Mediterráneo y en la parte del Atlántico que

[19656]

D

baña las costas de Europa y de Africa, debe servir eficazmente para alcanzar ese fin, siendo al mismo tiempo beneficioso para ambas Naciones, unidas además por los lazos de secular amistad y por la comunidad de intereses;

El Gobierno de Su Majestad Católica desea poner en conocimiento del Gobierno de la República Francesa la declaración cuyo tenor sigue, con la firme esperanza de que contribuirá, no solamente á afianzar la buena inteligencia que tan felizmente existe entre ambos Gobiernos, sino también á servir la causa de la paz:

La política general del Gobierno de Su Majestad Católica en las regiones arriba indicadas tiene por objeto el mantenimiento del *statu quo* territorial y, conforme á tal política, dicho Gobierno está firmemente resuelto á conservar intactos los derechos de la Corona Española sobre sus posesiones insulares y marítimas situadas en las referidas regiones.

En el caso de que nuevas circunstancias, según la opinión del Gobierno de Su Majestad Católica, pudiesen modificar ó contribuir á modificar el *statu quo* territorial actual, dicho Gobierno entrará en comunicación con el Gobierno de la República Francesa, á fin de poner á ambos Gobiernos en condiciones de concertarse, si lo juzgan oportuno, respecto á las medidas que hubieran de tomarse en común.

(Firmado)   F. DE LEON Y CASTILLO.

Paris, 16 de Mayo de 1907.

[*ED. NOTE.*—The French translation is omitted as the note is *mutatis mutandis* that signed by M. Pichon. For a similar reason the Spanish translation of the French note is omitted.]

No. 42.

Declaration made by Sir Edward Grey to M. Paul Cambon.

Aide-mémoire.

F.O. 371/364.
16168/285/07/41.   *Foreign Office, May 16, 1907.*

Sir Edward Grey took note with satisfaction of the identity of French policy with that of Great Britain and Spain in the regions defined in the notes which had been exchanged between these two Powers.

He observed that if, in the circumstances alluded to in those notes, it should become necessary for the British Government to communicate with that of Spain, or the Spanish Government to communicate with that of Great Britain, both would now be able to communicate with the French Government also, knowing that France takes the same view, and is as firmly resolved to preserve intact her rights over her insular and maritime possessions in the regions referred to, as are Great Britain and Spain to preserve those of their respective countries.

E. G.

No. 43.

Declaration made by M. Paul Cambon to Sir Edward Grey.

Aide-mémoire.

F.O. 371/364.
16168/285/07/41.   *Ambassade de France, Albert Gate, Londres.*

L'Ambassadeur de France exprime au nom de son Gouvernement à Sir Edward Grey toute sa satisfaction de l'accord intervenu simultanément aujourd'hui entre le Gouvernement de Sa Majesté Britannique et le Gouvernement de Sa Majesté Catholique d'une part, et entre le Gouvernement de la République Française et celui de Sa Majesté Catholique d'autre part.

Il est chargé de faire savoir au Gouvernement Britannique que, dans le cas où les éventualités prévues dans les notes en date de ce jour viendraient à se réaliser, le Gouvernement de la République Française serait prêt à se concerter avec le Gouvernement Britannique en même temps qu'avec le Gouvernement Espagnol.

Le 16 Mai, 1907.

No. 44.

Sir Edward Grey to Sir F. Bertie.(¹)

F.O. 371/364.
16168/285/07/41.
(No. 298.)   Secret.
Sir,   *Foreign Office, May* 17, 1907.

I transmit to your excellency herewith copies of the notes which I exchanged yesterday with the Spanish ambassador at this Court,(²) containing a declaration of policy, by which the British and Spanish governments agree to be guided in dealing with the insular and maritime possessions of their respective countries in the Mediterranean and that part of the Atlantic which washes its European and African shores.

The French ambassador was present at the signature of the notes, and, immediately afterwards, handed to me copies of the notes recording, *mutatis mutandis,* similar declarations of policy, which were exchanged yesterday at Paris between the French Minister for Foreign Affairs and the Spanish ambassador at that capital. I attach these papers, of which duplicates were also communicated to me by Señor de Villa Urrutia.*

I should explain that the text of the two notes addressed to me and to Monsieur Pichon respectively by the Spanish ambassadors here and at Paris, is in the Spanish language, and that the versions which accompany this despatch, are English and French literal translations.*

The formality of exchange and communication having been completed, I made a verbal declaration to the French ambassador in the terms recorded in the annexed *aide-mémoire* and His Excellency replied by a counter declaration of which I also inclose the text.(³)

[I have, &c.
E. GREY.]

(¹) [Also to Sir M. de Bunsen, No. 78, Secret.]
(²) [*v. supra,* pp. 32–3, Nos. 39 and 40.]
(³) [*v.* immediately preceding document.]
* Omitted in desp[atch] to Madrid, because the enclo[sure]s were sent in print.

No. 45.

Sir Edward Grey to Sir M. de Bunsen.

F.O. 371/364.
17395/285/07/41.   *Foreign Office, May* 28, 1907.
Tel.   (No. 16.)   D. 5·30 P.M.

There is reason to suppose that notes exchanged with Spain are already known. M. Cambon proposes that Spanish Ambassadors at Rome and Vienna should communicate copies to Italian and Austrian Governments as the two Powers interested in *status quo* in Mediterranean generally.   French and British Ambassadors could do the same at Rome and Vienna.   On the same day the respective Ambassadors at Berlin and St. Petersburgh would be instructed to inform German and Russian Governments verbally of the tenour of the communication made to the Austrian and Italian Governments and of the reason for it and to say that as a matter of courtesy a copy of the notes would be given to the German and Russian Governments when received.

You should consult your French colleague and when he has received similar instructions join with him in proposing this course to the Spanish Government and ask their assent to it.

No. 46.

Memorandum by Mr. W. Tyrrell.

F.O. 371/364.
18554/285/07/41.   *Foreign Office, June 3, 1907.*

M. Cambon called to-day to say that M. Pichon had discussed the question of the communication of the Spanish Notes with M. Barrère, the French Ambassador in Rome, M. Révoil, the French Ambassador in Madrid, and himself, as all three happened to be in Paris. And he was authorized by M. Pichon to say that the French Government have no objection to offer to the proposal of the Spanish Government that the communication should be made to all the Powers. But in view of the special position of Italy in the Mediterranean, and the particular engagements towards Italy which France and England had with regard to the Mediterranean, the French Government thought it desirable that the Representatives of England, France, and Spain at Rome should be instructed to concert among themselves as to the language in which they should communicate confidentially, say 48 hours before the general communication of the Notes, the substance of them, to the Italian Gov[ernmen]t, intimating at the same time that they do this in view of Italy's special interests in maintaining the "status quo" in the Mediterranean.

France proposes to make a communication simultaneously with the above one at St. Petersburg, Russia being her ally.

M. Cambon thought it also most desirable that the Representatives of England, France, and Spain should receive instructions to hold more or less the same language if asked for the reasons which led to the exchange of Notes. Thus, France would state that as a Power possessing Colonies in Africa both on the Mediterranean and the Atlantic shores she was keenly alive to no great military Power establishing herself in the Balearic Islands or the Canaries; while England was specially interested in safeguarding her present position at Gibraltar.

M. Cambon proposes to speak to you to-morrow at 4, unless he hears to the contrary.

Sir C. Hardinge thinks it desirable that you should press M. Cambon to explain what leakage has occurred which makes the communication of the notes necessary. As far as we know no leakage has occurred up till now, but merely an attempt on the part of a Paris journalist to "bluff" the Head of the French Press Bureau into committing an indiscretion.

From every point of view it would be preferable to defer communication until the close of the session.

W. T.

No. 47.

Sir Edward Grey to Mr. des Graz.([1])

F.O. 371/364.
18554/285/07/41.
(No. 79.) Secret.
Sir,   *Foreign Office, June 6, 1907.*

I enclose herewith copies of the notes exchanged on the 16th May by the Spanish Ambassador and myself defining the policy of the British and Spanish Gov[ernment]s

---

([1]) [Similar instructions were sent to the British representatives at St. Petersburgh, Berlin, Vienna and Lisbon.]

for the preservation of the *status quo* and of the rights of Great Britain and Spain in the Mediterranean and in that part of the Atlantic Ocean which washes the shores of Europe and Africa.(²)

I have to request you to concert with your French and Spanish Colleagues with a view to communicating verbally to the Italian Gov[ernmen]t on Wednesday the 12th instant the contents of the above mentioned notes. You should explain to Signor Tittoni that although it is the intention of H[is] M[ajesty's] G[overnment] to communicate copies of the notes to the Gov[ernment]s of Germany, Russia and Austria as well as Italy I have, in view of our previous agreements with Italy thought it courteous to inform the Italian Gov[ernmen]t of what had taken place before communicating with the other Powers, feeling confident that the aims of the British and Spanish Gov[ernment]s will be in entire accord with those of the Gov[ernmen]t of Italy. You should also communicate a copy of the notes to Signor Tittoni on Saturday the 15th inst[ant], that being the date agreed upon for its communication to the other Powers.

If inquiry is made of you as to there being any special object to be obtained by H[is] M[ajesty's] G[overnment] in the conclusion of such an agreement you are authorised to state that, in view of the progress made of late years in the construction of submarines and in the perfection of arms of offence it has been the desire of H[is] M[ajesty's] G[overnment] to assure the safety of the British possessions at Gibraltar by securing the protection of British and Spanish interests in the regions indicated in the notes exchanged and confirming friendly relations with Spain.

[I am, &c.
E. GREY.]

(²) [*v. supra*, pp. 32–3, Nos. 39 and 40.]

No. 48.

Sir Edward Grey to Sir F. Lascelles.(¹)

F.O. 371/364.
19203/285/07/41.
(No. 167.) Secret.
Sir,   *Foreign Office, June 6, 1907.*

I enclose herewith copies of notes exchanged on the 16th ultimo by the Spanish ambassador and myself, defining the policy of the Spanish and British governments for the preservation of the territorial *status quo* and of the rights of Spain and Great Britain in the Mediterranean and in that part of the Atlantic Ocean which washes the shores of Europe and Africa.(²)

I have to request Your Excellency to concert with your French and Spanish colleagues with the view of communicating to the German government on Saturday the 15th instant copies of these notes.

If enquiry is made of you as to there being any special object to be obtained by H[is] M[ajesty's] G[overnment] in the conclusion of such an agreement, you are authorised to state that, in view of the progress made of late years · in the construction of submarines and in the perfection of arms of offence, it has been the desire of H[is] M[ajesty's] G[overnment] to assure the safety of the British possessions at Gibraltar by securing the protection of British and Spanish interests in the regions indicated in the notes exchanged, and confirming our friendly relations with Spain.

I have communicated a copy of the present instructions confidentially to the French ambassador at this Court.

[I am, &c.
E. GREY.]

(¹) [Also to Sir E. Goschen, No. 47, Secret, *mutatis mutandis.*]
(²) [*v. supra*, pp. 32–3, Nos. 39 and 40.]

No. 49.

Sir Edward Grey to Sir F. Lascelles.(¹)

F.O. 371/364.
19203/285/07/41.
(No. 168.) Secret.
Sir,   *Foreign Office, June 6, 1907.*
    With reference to my immediately preceding despatch, I need hardly point out
to Your Excellency that the policy of H[is] M[ajesty's] G[overnment] is practically
the same as that embodied in the agreement concluded in 1887 between Great
Britain and Italy to which Austria-Hungary, with the concurrence and approval of
the German Government, immediately afterwards became a party.(²)

[I am, &c.
E. GREY.]

    (¹) [Also to Sir E. Goschen, No. 48, Secret.]
    (²) [Reference to the agreement of 1887 will be made in *Gooch & Temperley*, Vol. VIII. The
text is in A. F. Pribram : *The Secret Treaties of Austria-Hungary* (Harvard University Press,
1920), Vol. I, pp. 94–103.]

No. 50.

Sir Edward Grey to Sir F. Bertie.

F.O. 371/364.
19408/285/07/41.
(No. 340.) Secret.
Sir,   *Foreign Office, June 8, 1907.*
    M. Cambon showed me to-day the instructions which his Government proposed
to send respecting the communication of the French and Spanish Notes.
    He reminded me that, in the Agreement of 1904, England and France had
promised each other diplomatic support. The action of Germany changed this into
something like an alliance. He wished to know now whether, if Germany brought
pressure to bear on France or Spain in consequence of the Spanish Notes, English
support would be forthcoming.
    I replied that I could not see how Germany could attempt to disturb the
agreement which France had with Spain without also disturbing that which England
had made with Spain in the Note signed simultaneously.
    But, in any case, the regions affected by these Notes were very near to Morocco,
and I should regard the spirit of the Agreement of 1904 as applying to the provisions
of these Notes, and the same support would be forthcoming as we had given in
connection with the 1904 Agreement.

[I am, &c.]
E. G[REY].

No. 51.

Sir Edward Grey to Sir F. Villiers.

F.O. 371/364.
19203/285/07/41.   *Foreign Office, June 11, 1907.*
Tel. (No. 4.) Secret.   D. 4·25 P.M.
    Agreements have recently been signed in the shape of notes exchanged
between Great Britain, France and Spain for the preservation of the *status quo* in
the Mediterranean and that part of the Atlantic which touches the shores of Europe
and Africa.
    Copies of these agreements will be communicated on the 15th inst[ant] to the
Gov[ernmen]ts of Italy, Russia, Germany and Austria by the Ambassadors of the

3 Powers, at their respective Courts and you should concert with your French and Spanish Colleagues with a view to making a similar communication to the Portuguese Gov[ernmen]t on the same day.([1])

You should apply to the Spanish Representative at Lisbon for copies of the notes exchanged between Great Britain and Spain, of which, I understand, he has received an English version.

([1]) [Tel. No. 6 of June 15, received on the same day states that communication was made as directed on that day.]

No. 52.

Sir Edward Grey to Sir E. Egerton.([1])

F.O. 371/364.
19203/285/07/41.
Tel. (No. 10.) Secret.   Foreign Office, June 12, 1907.

It will be unnecessary to concert with Spanish Ambassador for comm[unicatio]n to Italian Gov[ernmen]t of Spanish note. You should act with your French Colleague alone.

MINUTE.

M. Cambon called this afternoon and explained that, the Spanish Govern[men]t having no agreement with Italy, there was no reason for the Spanish Amb[assado]r to act with the British and French Amb[assado]rs at Rome.

C. H.
11 June.

([1]) [Sir E. Egerton had returned to Rome on June 11.]

No. 53.

Sir E. Egerton to Sir Edward Grey.

F.O. 371/364.
19946/285/07/41.
(No. 103.) Secret.   Rome, D. June 12, 1907.
Sir,   R. June 17, 1907.

In accordance with the instructions contained in your despatch No. 79, Secret of the 6th instant([1]) I spoke to the French and Spanish Ambassadors yesterday as to the form of communicating verbally to the Minister for Foreign Affairs the notes exchanged defining the policy of the three Governments for the preservation of the Status Quo and of the rights of each in the Mediterranean and that part of the Atlantic Ocean which washes the shores of Europe and Africa.

The Spanish Ambassador, who to-day had to present his letters of recall, had no instructions to make this verbal communication; but informed me that on Saturday next the 15th June the Chargé d'Affaires of Spain would officially communicate copies of the notes to Signor Tittoni.

Consequently Monsieur Barrère and I alone read confidentially to-day to the Italian Minister in separate interviews the Exchanged notes. Signor Tittoni appeared pleased with the communication. Approving of the step taken as natural under the circumstances, he expressed himself as extremely sensible of the courtesy shewn by the previous communication of the agreement to the Italian Government.

([1]) [v. supra, pp. 36-7, No. 47.]

Monsieur Barrère told me that Signor Tittoni likewise received the verbal communication with evident satisfaction and promised to consider it as confidential.

On the 15th instant I shall make, as instructed, the official communication of the notes.

I have, &c.
EDWIN H. EGERTON.

MINUTE.

Nevertheless Signor Tittoni must have comm[unicate]d the contents both to Vienna and Berlin and also to the Press.

C. H.
E. G.

No. 54.

Sir A. Nicolson to Sir Edward Grey.

F.O. 371/364.
20717/285/07/41.
(No. 320.) Confidential.
Sir,

St. *Petersburgh*, D. *June* 15, 1907.
R. *June* 24, 1907.

By arrangement with my French and Spanish Colleagues we severally called on M. Isvolsky this morning, and I handed to him a copy of the note which you addressed to the Spanish Ambassador on May 16th 1907 defining the policy of the British and Spanish Governments for the preservation of the *Status quo*, and of the rights of Great Britain and Spain in the Mediterranean and in that part of the Atlantic Ocean which washes the shores of Europe and Africa.([1]) The Spanish Ambassador had handed to His Excellency previous to my visit, a copy of the note which Señor de Villa Urrutia had addressed to you on the 16th May last.([2])

M. Isvolsky, in thanking me for the communication, said that he would wish to remark, quite unofficially, that he feared that this new agreement would revive the " nervosité " at Berlin which had been manifested in connection with the Royal visits to Cartagena and Gaeta. It might be possible that Germany might consider that a fresh effort was being made to isolate her and that she might now seek for an opportunity of herself making some agreements in order to counterbalance those which of late had been concluded without her participation. He did not quite see, moreover, what was the precise object or necessity of the interchange of notes with the Spanish Government.

I told His Excellency that of late there had been considerable development in the weapons of maritime offence especially of those which could be employed in narrow waters, and that it was incumbent on us to take such precautions as were possible to safeguard the position of Gibraltar and its harbour and docks. It was self-evident that the principal factor with whom we had to deal in this direction was Spain, and an agreement with her was therefore natural. As to the possibility of the accord arousing displeasure at Berlin, I could not conceive why it should do so. All recent accords were fresh guarantees of peace, and if Germany followed our example I was sure that we should all welcome her adherence to the principle of friendly understandings. The notes would be communicated at Berlin to-day, and we should hear shortly how they had been received. M. Isvolsky said that no one would be better pleased than himself if his fears proved to be unfounded.

His Excellency said that there was another point which had struck him. He understood that copies of the notes were also to be communicated to the Japanese Government. This was quite a new departure, and he did not know if it were wise

([1]) [*v. supra*, p. 32, No. 39.]
([2]) [*v. supra*, pp. 32–3, No. 40.]

to bring Japan into a concert of European Powers in matters concerning the Mediterranean and the Atlantic. He observed that our alliance with Japan was in a measure enlarging its sphere. The second Treaty of Alliance had extended the sphere of the former, and now we were placing Japan on an equal footing with the other Great Powers in questions which were far removed from her waters. I told His Excellency that it seemed to me that we as the ally of Japan could hardly abstain from bringing to her knowledge, equally with others, the agreements which we made with another Power, and that Japan was entitled to be considered as a Great Power. A similar communication was also being made to the Government of the United States who were not a European Power. M. Isvolsky said that he did not dispute that Japan was a Great Power; and in respect to the United States they were parties to the Madrid Convention of 1880 and to the Algeciras Act and had, therefore, already participated in matters dealing with the regions indicated in the notes which had recently been exchanged. He did not wish to lay undue stress on his observations; he merely wished to remark that we were creating a new departure.

M. Isvolsky said that there was one other point to which he desired to allude, and that was that M. Bompard had intimated to him that the communication of the notes was confidential. He would of course treat the communication as being of a confidential nature, but he doubted if the secrecy could be long maintained when it had been confided to so many Governments, but if premature leakage did occur it would not be from the side of Russia. He repeated that the remarks which he had made were purely of a conversational character, and I said that I quite understood that he had not been speaking in an official capacity.

I have, &c.

A. NICOLSON.

MINUTES.

We have since heard that Russia and Germany are negotiating a similar agreement in regard to the *status quo* in the Baltic.([3])

G. S. S.
E. B.

As a matter of fact M. Isvolsky had already informed Berlin as Dr. Muhlberg stated to Sir F. Lascelles.

C. H.

I see no objection to an agreement on the part of Russia and Germany respecting the Baltic on similar lines.

E. G.

([3]) [The subject of these negotiations will be treated in *Gooch & Temperley*, Vol. VIII.]

No. 55.

Sir F. Villiers to Sir Edward Grey.

F.O. 371/364.
20810/285/07/36.
(No. 43.) Secret.   *Lisbon,* D. *June* 15, 1907.
Sir,   R. *June* 24, 1907.

I have the honour to report that I acted this afternoon upon the instructions contained in your telegram No. 4 Secret, of the 11th instant,([1]) and, in concert with the French and Spanish Ministers, communicated confidentially to the Minister for Foreign Affairs the Agreement recently concluded by an exchange of notes between Great Britain, France and Spain. The instructions given to the French Minister mentioned an arrangement that in all cases, at Berlin and elsewhere, the first communication

([1]) [*v. supra*, pp. 38–9, No. 51.]

should be made by the Spanish Representative who was to be supported by similar communications on the part of the French and then of the British Representative. The Spanish Minister also understood that this was the intention of our three Governments, and we accordingly adopted this mode of procedure.

My colleagues and I derived the impression from our interviews with Senhor Monteiro that he felt much satisfaction both at the contents of the notes and at the fact of their having been communicated to the Portuguese Government. He accepted the Agreement, when talking to me after I had presented the text of your note, as complementary to the *entente* with France and the Treaty with Portugal. A "bloc" had been created, to use his own expression, which would maintain the *Status Quo* in the regions defined and protect the interests of the Powers concerned. This was a most important contribution to the elements which make for peace.

I have, &c.
F. H. VILLIERS.

No. 56.

Sir F. Lascelles to Sir Edward Grey.

F.O. 371/364.
20454/285/07/41.
(No. 288.) Confidential.
Sir,

Berlin, D. *June* 16, 1907.
R. *June* 21, 1907.

In obedience to the instructions contained in your despatch No. 167 Secret of the 6th instant,(¹) I did not fail to concert with my French and Spanish Colleagues with the view of communicating to the German Government the copies of the Notes exchanged by you and the Spanish Ambassador in London on the 16th ultimo. It was arranged that Mr. Polo de Bernabé should apply for an interview with Herr von Mühlberg who is at present in charge of the Imperial Ministry for Foreign Affairs, at noon yesterday, that Mr. Cambon should then ask to be received and that I should apply for my interview after my two colleagues had made their communications.

Mr. Polo de Bernabé whose interview with Herr von Mühlberg took place at noon yesterday was good enough to call upon me on leaving the Ministry for Foreign Affairs. He said that Herr von Mühlberg had evidently not been pleased with the communication, he had read the Notes with great attention and had said with some irritation that he supposed it was an attempt to bring about universal Peace. He could understand that Spain and England might have an interest in coming to an agreement about their territorial possessions, but what interest could France have in such an arrangement? He asked whether it was intended to publish the Notes. Mr. Polo de Bernabé had replied that his instructions were to communicate the Notes confidentially to the German Government as a matter of courtesy, but that he did not think it was intended to publish them at present. Herr von Mühlberg thanked Mr. Polo de Bernabé for the communication which however he understood had already been made to the Russian Government.

On going to the Ministry for Foreign Affairs at 6·30 I met Mr. Cambon who had just left it. He said that Herr von Mühlberg had been most amiable, "all sugar and honey." He had said that he understood that England and Spain could have some interest in mutually guaranteeing their territorial possessions, but he failed to see what interest France had in the matter, and he asked whether the term "Mediterranean" included the Adriatic. Mr. Cambon had replied that France was in the first place a neighbour of Spain, and in the second place had possessions on the South Coast of the Mediterranean, viz., Algiers and Tunis which gave her an interest in all the waters which washed that coast. He rejoiced that his Government had come to an arrangement with Spain which showed the friendly feeling with which the two Governments were animated,(²) and nothing could give him greater

(¹) [*v. supra*, p. 37, No. 48.]
(²) [Marginal comment by Sir C. Hardinge : " rather well put. C. H."]

pleasure than to sign a similar agreement with Germany. Herr von Mühlberg having observed that there were no questions between France and Germany to which such an agreement would apply, Mr. Cambon replied that it might ·be possible to find some, as the object of his mission was to bring about a friendly understanding between the two countries. Herr von Mühlberg had suggested an early publication of the Notes, and Mr. Cambon was about to telegraph to his Government in this sense.

In my interview with Herr von Mühlberg, I began by stating that he must be aware of the object of my visit, and at once handed him the copies of the notes. He read them and said he had already studied them in the copies which had been given him by my Spanish and French Colleagues. He could understand that it would be an advantage to Spain to have her possessions guaranteed by England and France, but, he did not see what advantage these two Powers had obtained. There was moreover no guarantee, but merely a statement that each Power intended to keep what she had got. He was not aware that any one disputed their possession. Then assuming a joking expression, His Excellency said that the course of History would not be altered by a little paper "un petit papier" like this, and what, he asked, would happen if war again broke out between Spain and the United States and the latter fitted out a fleet to attack one of the Spanish possessions. I replied in the same tone that the course of history would certainly not be altered by any paper whether big or little, but that if the United States, or indeed any other Power were to seize a Spanish Port or island, the *status quo* referred to in the Notes would be changed and I had no doubt that the Signatory Powers would consult as to what measures should be taken. Herr von Mühlberg said that it seemed to him that the Japanese in their convention with the French had made a better bargain than Spain had done in her exchange of Notes with England and France. Japan had been guaranteed in the possession of Port Arthur.

Assuming a more serious tone, Herr von Mühlberg considered that it would be advisable to publish the Notes at once, so as to avoid the unfavourable criticisms in the Press of which he already saw symptoms. A statement had already appeared in a French paper, the "Messidor" that a new Triple Alliance had been formed which no doubt would create a painful impression in Germany and give rise to considerable criticism. His Excellency also asked me from whom the initiative of these notes proceeded. I replied that I had absolutely no knowledge on this point, but speaking entirely on my own responsibility, and without instructions, I could tell him that I knew that for many years past attempts had from time to time been made by the British Representatives at Madrid to conclude an arrangement with the Spanish Government, by which the security of Gibraltar as a British possession should be assured. Hitherto these attempts had failed and I had therefore no doubt that the exchange of Notes which had now taken place was agreeable to His Majesty's Government, but I was utterly unable to say whether they had taken the initiative in proposing them. Herr von Mühlberg again urged the advisability of the immediate publication of the Notes, and on leaving His Excellency, I had the honour of forwarding to you my telegram No. 15 of yesterday's date.([3])

I have, &c.

FRANK C. LASCELLES.

MINUTES.

Herr v[on] Muhlberg's enquiry as to whether the agreement extends to the Adriatic. It might perhaps be so interpreted, only neither G[rea]t Britain nor Spain have possessions there.

E. B.

Sir F. Lascelles brought out the point that these negotiations were not on our part of recent date.

C. H.

That was useful.

E. G.

([3]) [Not reproduced.]

No. 57.

Sir E. Goschen to Sir Edward Grey

F.O. 371/364.
20477/285/07/41.
(No. 78.) Secret.
Sir,

Vienna, D. June 16, 1907.
R. June 21, 1907.

I have the honour to report that, in accordance with the instructions contained in your despatch marked Secret No. 47 of the 6th instant,(¹) I yesterday communicated to the Minister for Foreign Affairs, after consultation with my French and Spanish colleagues, copies of the Notes exchanged between you and the Spanish Ambassador in London defining the policy of the Spanish and British Governments for the preservation of the territorial *status quo* and of the rights of Spain and Great Britain in the Mediterranean and in the part of the Atlantic Ocean which washes the shores of Europe and Africa.

Baron d'Aehrenthal had earlier in the afternoon received my Spanish and French colleagues, who had both received instructions laying down the order in which we were to be received, namely, the Marquis of Casa Calvo first, then Monsieur Crozier and then myself.

His Excellency, after stating that he had been for some time expecting some such communication, told me that for the moment he had not much to say on the subject, and that he would reserve any observations he might have to make until he had had time to study the question in all its bearings. He would, however, ask me, as he had asked my colleagues, to explain to him what part of the Mediterranean was referred to in the Notes. He asked this, he said, because the Mediterranean covered a large area and there were other Powers, including Austria-Hungary, who had rights within or near that area.

In reply I referred His Excellency to the third paragraph of the Notes exchanged, from which he would see that the general policy of the two Governments was directed to the maintenance of the territorial *status quo*, and that, in pursuance of that policy, they were resolved to preserve intact their rights over their insular and maritime possessions in the Mediterranean and the other regions indicated. His Excellency must know what these regions were. Baron d'Aehrenthal replied, "Yes! you have Gibraltar and Malta, but who is threatening those possessions? From all I have heard, there is no prospect of the peace of Europe being disturbed, and I can hardly see the necessity of these sudden precautions." To this I replied that I fully shared his opinion that the outlook was peaceful, and that I was sure he would agree with me that the time of peace was the time to make precautionary arrangements and not leave such matters to chance in times of difficulty and danger. As he pressed me further on the subject, I made use of the observations you had authorized me to make on the subject of Gibraltar and the changed conditions which the perfection of submarines and of arms of offence had introduced into modern warfare. His Excellency reiterated his observation that he was not aware of any danger which threatened Gibraltar, but admitted that we had every right to take whatever precautions we might deem necessary. As his Excellency returned to the question of the object of these Notes being interchanged, I reminded him that the policy of His Majesty's Government was practically the same as that embodied in the Agreement concluded in 1887 between Great Britain and Italy, to which Austria had subsequently become a party. His Excellency replied that, as I well knew, Austria-Hungary was a conservative Power and that the maintenance of the *status quo* everywhere and under all possible circumstances was one of the cardinal points of her policy. In reply I ventured to tell His Excellency that His Majesty's Government was well aware that such was the case, and was therefore confident that the present exchange of Notes which had the

(¹) [*v. supra,* p. 37, No. 48, and *note* (¹).]

maintenance of the *status quo* and the general preservation of peace as its chief object, would be in entire harmony with Austro-Hungarian policy, and thoroughly coincide with the views of the Austro-Hungarian Government.

His Excellency smiled, but said that he must reserve his opinion for the moment.

Baron d'Aehrenthal's tone was most friendly throughout our conversation, but I am bound to state that he looked rather worried and preoccupied.

The Spanish Ambassador came to see me in the evening, and told me that Baron d'Aehrenthal had pushed him very hard, and that the conversation had at times taken a very difficult and embarrassing turn. His Excellency had begun by stating that ever since the meeting at Cartagena he had expected that some arrangement would be made between Spain and Great Britain. The grounds for this expectation were obvious, and the result would come as a surprise to no one. It was quite different, however, with the arrangement with France; this was at all events a surprise. He was aware, and the Spanish Ambassador, who had only lately occupied a high position in the Spanish Foreign Office, must be aware that up to a comparatively recent period there had been no idea of such an arrangement. What was the reason for this sudden change of policy? Who had taken the initiative? Or perhaps was it pressure? and from whom had that pressure come? The Marquis de Casa Calvo told me that these questions followed each other so rapidly that he could scarcely find time to answer, as he had wished to do, that the arrangement with England had been prompted both by the wish of the Spanish Government to confirm the relations with Great Britain which circumstances had rendered so friendly and intimate, and also by the obvious necessity of coming to a decision some time or another, and better in time of peace, as to their future relations with the Power predominant at sea. That the extent of their coast and the number of their maritime and insular possessions, some of which were particularly open to attack, rendered such a decision absolutely necessary. That their policy towards France had been guided by similar considerations. That Spanish groups of islands lay between France and her African possessions, and circumstances might arise which would place the Spanish Government in a difficult, not to say dangerous, position. What more natural then than that they should insure themselves against every possible danger? He had added that both these understandings were of a purely defensive nature, and that he was sure that Baron d'Aehrenthal would understand that their policy was dictated by prudence and had not the slightest taint of aggression in any form whatever. Baron d'Aehrenthal, however, had persisted in his idea that there must have been pressure of some sort brought upon Spain, and his last words were "Cannot you tell me in the strictest confidence whether it is not a menace on the part of some Power which has driven your Government to adopt its present policy?"

The Marquis of Casa Calvo replied that he was certainly not cognizant of anything of the sort, and that he thought that the policy of the Spanish Government was fully to be accounted for by the motives he had given.

My French colleague informs me that his interview with Baron d'Aehrenthal passed off in the most friendly manner. His Excellency had, however, asked him many searching questions and had generally seemed rather perturbed by the communication. M. Crozier added that, in replying to Baron d'Aehrenthal's questions, he had based his arguments on the necessity for France to take necessary precautions to keep her communications with her African possessions free and open, as far as Spain was concerned, under all possible circumstances and upon the fact that such a precautionary arrangement did not, and could not, interfere in any way with the legitimate aims and policy of any other Power. Baron d'Aehrenthal had seemed fairly satisfied, but had said that for the present he would defer any definite expression of opinion.

Yesterday morning the "Neue Freie Press" reproduced an article from the French paper "Messidor" announcing that England, France and Spain had concluded an alliance. It also reprinted the *démenti* published by the agence Havas.

To-day it has a short article entitled "The new Triple Alliance," stating that, in spite of all *démentis*, this alliance had been made. Its concluding words are as follows :—

"The highly important news of the conclusion of an alliance between these three Mediterranean Powers will certainly make a deep impression in Germany; it touches moreover the interests of Austria-Hungary, and more especially those of Italy, who finds herself face to face with this alliance on her very shores."

I have. &c.
W. E. GOSCHEN.

No. 58.

Sir Edward Grey to Sir E. Goschen.

F.O. 371/364.
20330/285/07/41.
(No. 54.)

Sir,   *Foreign Office, June 17, 1907.*

Count Mensdorff came to see me to-day, as he was going away for a week, and asked me whether I had anything to say to him.

I told him of the communication which had been made at Vienna about the Spanish Note, and explained to him that, as far as we were concerned, the matter had originated more than two years ago in connection with Gibraltar.

He would no doubt have observed that, under modern conditions, the security of Gibraltar was more than ever important to us. It had been taken into consideration in the Agreement with France about Morocco in 1904, when it was stipulated that certain parts of the coast opposite should not be fortified. We desired to complete this security by recognition with Spain that we would both maintain our respective possessions in that region, and preserve the *status quo.*

[I am, &c.]
E. G[REY].

No. 59.

Mr. Lister to Sir Edward Grey.

F.O. 371/255.
21321/21321/07/17.
(No. 324.)

Sir,   *Paris, D. June 27, 1907.*
                                           R. June 29, 1907.

The "Echo de Paris" published in its issue of yesterday's date a telegram from its correspondent in Frankfort to the effect that Monsieur Pichon had granted an interview to the Paris representative of the Frankfort Gazette respecting the Franco-Spanish Agreement relative to the Mediterranean and Atlantic.

Monsieur Pichon was reported as having stated that it was a question of an *entente* not of an alliance and there was nothing behind it. He added that he did not see what questions could arise between France and Germany which could not be arranged by those peaceful methods to which his country was attached.

I have been able to obtain copies of the Frankfort Gazette in which His Excellency's declaration is published, and I have the honour to transmit them to you herewith.([1])

I have, &c.
REGINALD LISTER.

([1]) [Not reproduced.]

No. 60.

Sir Edward Grey to Count de Salis.

F.O. 371/364.
21844/285/07/41.
(No. 187.)   Secret.
Sir,   *Foreign Office, June* 27, 1907.

To-day, after some mutually agreeable observations on the subject of the German Emperor's Visit, and the amicable tendency of discussions at The Hague, with which we both expressed satisfaction, Count Metternich observed that the Spanish Note had been published.

I replied that Herr von Muhlberg had, when the Note was communicated to him, expressed the opinion that, on the whole, it might be well to publish it soon.

Count Metternich asked whether these negotiations with Spain had taken a long time, and how they had originated.

I said that, as far as we were concerned, they had originated under the late Government, with the object of securing Gibraltar. In our Agreement with France, we had an arrangement that certain parts of the coast of Morocco should not be fortified if they passed out of the Sultan's hands : but we had no similar arrangement with Spain. For a year or more the matter had remained in abeyance, but I had taken it up again a few months ago. About the same time I heard that France also desired something of the same kind with regard to her possessions ; but as far as we were concerned the matter had originated independently.

Count Metternich asked whether the matter had been discussed at Carthagena.([1])

I said certainly it had been discussed there by Sir Charles Hardinge. I had begun the negotiations here before the King's Visit to Carthagena, but it was found very convenient that Sir Charles Hardinge should take the opportunity of his being there to continue them at first hand with the Spanish Government.

Count Metternich asked how much was included by the expressions of the Agreement, the terms of which appeared to be very comprehensive.

I told him they referred to the Spanish and British possessions which were indicated, and the regions in which they were situated.

He asked whether, for instance, Malta would be included.

I thought that certainly, if we gave up Malta, we should inform the Spanish Government before doing so.

He then asked whether Cyprus would be included.

I thought that Cyprus was too remote, and would be more properly the subject of a communication to Italy, with whom, as he knew, we had once made an arrangement of a similar kind respecting the Mediterranean.

Count Metternich said of course he knew very well of that arrangement, which had practically been negotiated here (by which I understood him to mean the German Embassy in London).

I remarked that I thought that arrangement had been couched in stronger terms than our Note with Spain.

([1]) [*v. supra*, pp. 22–4, Nos. 25 and 26.]

Count Metternich said that his recollection of it was that it was an exchange of views, and I told him that the views exchanged were of the same kind, in principle, as those in the Spanish Note.

Count Metternich asked me whether the arrangement with Italy was still in force.

I said that I had done nothing with regard to it since I came into Office. I had not discussed it with the Italian Government, and it remained in exactly the same position as I had found it.

[I am, &c.]

E. G[REY]

No. 61.

Mr. Lister to Sir Edward Grey.

F.O. 371/255.
22532/22531/07/17.
(No. 338.)
Sir,

Paris, D. *July* 6, 1907.
R. *July* 8, 1907.

With reference to my immediately preceding despatch, I have the honour to report that the Minister for Foreign Affairs yesterday gave an explanation in the Chamber of Deputies, in answer to an interpellation of Baron Denys Cochin, of the reasons which had guided the French Government in coming to an Arrangement with Spain as to the *status quo* in the Mediterranean and Atlantic. I enclose herein the text of His Excellency's statement extracted from the "Journal Officiel" of to-day's date.([1])

M. Pichon declared that the Agreement with Spain had no direct connection with the Moroccan question but was the consummation of the policy followed by the Cabinets of Paris and Madrid for the last ten years. He described its eminently pacific and conservative character, and stated that no one could take umbrage at it, unless they harboured designs of territorial conquest at the expense of France and Spain. The Agreements with Spain on the part of France and Great Britain, which were drawn up in identical terms, were an additional guarantee of peace, and for his part he could not consider, as M. Denys Cochin had wished to show, that it was a misguided policy to give a concrete form to a mutual desire for the maintenance of peace, and to ensure thereby that the sentiments underlying such a desire should be safeguarded against any modifications which might result from a possible change of the persons in power. The intimate geographical connection of the two Countries had brought about a political connection. The two Governments had given full publicity to their Agreement and had notified all the Governments of its conclusion. It contained no secret clause, and was aimed against no one, neither was it a triple alliance as had been asserted. It merely afforded to the two Signatory Powers an additional security.

M. Pichon stated that no ill-humour had manifested itself in any quarter with regard to the Agreement, and he blamed the irresponsible way in which certain papers had treated this matter and which was capable of provoking unfriendly manifestations ("toutes les malveillances"). After this reproof of the attitude of certain Opposition organs, His Excellency went on to say that the remark recently made by Prince Bülow in the Reichstag that the greatness of Germany was not based on the disunion of other Powers was entirely true and most reassuring; no one in the Europe of the twentieth century would seek to fortify themselves at the expense of others by bringing about divisions and struggles which, at a time when the invincible tendency of nations was to draw closer to one another, would only end in internal conflicts.

The effect made on the Chamber by the explicit and straightforward declarations of M. Pichon, both as regards Morocco and more general international relations was

([1]) [Not reproduced.]

very marked.   M. Denys Cochin rose again, evidently with the desire to counteract
the general satisfaction thus shown in the foreign policy of the Government, and
carped at various points made by M. Pichon in his justification of the Government
policy.   A remark made by him, in a sarcastic tone, that, if it were the case that
the greatness of Germany was founded on the disunion of other Powers, the present
situation would be a disagreeable one for her, was received in a manner which
showed that the Chamber considered M. Denys Cochin's observation to be anything
but tactful after the recognition of the courteous and correct attitude of that Power
just made by the Minister for Foreign Affairs.

I think that it is not too much to say that on the eve of the departure of the
Legislature for a Recess of three months the general opinion both in Parliament
and in the country is that the present situation of France in international politics
is an eminently satisfactory one, and that the conduct of foreign affairs by the
present Cabinet gives no ground for reasonable criticism.

I have, &c.
REGINALD LISTER.

No. 62.

Extract from Annual Reports for Spain and Austria-Hungary for the Year 1907.

(a)

Extract from the Annual Report for Spain for the Year 1907.

(Enclosure in Sir M. de Bunsen's Despatch No. 25, D. February 14, 1908,
R. February 22, 1908.)

General Attitude of Germany.

F.O. 6189/6189/08/41.
129. During the year 1907 the German Embassy at Madrid exercised less pressure
than in previous years in endeavouring to loosen the ties by which Spain is bound, in
foreign politics, to France and England.   M. de Radowitz has repeatedly declared to
the Spanish Foreign Minister that Germany has no desire to interfere between France
and Spain on the one hand and Morocco on the other, so long as the provisions of the
Algeciras Act are kept in view.

130. His Excellency showed, however, great irritation over the exchange of notes
which took place in London and Paris on the 16th May in respect of the maintenance
of the *status quo* in the Mediterranean and Atlantic.([1])   He resented the ignorance in
which he had been kept of the negotiations by which that Agreement was preceded.
The Spanish Government, though understanding and even proclaiming the special
character of its relations with England and France, continues to show nervousness
whenever any course is proposed to which Germany might be expected to take exception.   Señor Maura lays stress on the international aspects of the Algeciras Act rather
than on those of its provisions which assign a prominent part to France and Spain, and
it is said by those who know him well that he is apt to lend a ready ear to German
advice in respect of the action of Spain in Morocco.

131. M. de Radowitz' approaching retirement into private life has been officially
announced.

([1]) [*v. supra*, pp. 32–4. Nos. 39–41.]

(b).

Extract from the Annual Report for Austria-Hungary for the Year 1907.

(Enclosure in Sir E. Goschen's Despatch No. 72, D. May 11, 1908, R. May 18, 1908.)

The Spanish Agreements.

F.O. 16971/16971/08/18.

32. On the 6th June copies of the notes exchanged between the Governments of Great Britain and Spain, and France and Spain, on the subject of the maintenance of the *status quo* in the Mediterranean and that part of the Atlantic which washes the shores of Europe and Africa were communicated to Baron d'Aehrenthal.([1]) As regards the Anglo-Spanish notes, he said that ever since the Royal meeting at Cartagena he had been expecting to receive a communication of this nature. He was therefore in no way surprised to receive my communication. He then asked to what parts of the Mediterranean the notes referred, observing at the same time that the Mediterranean covered a large area near to, or within, which other Powers, including Austria-Hungary, had interests. On being satisfied on this point, his Excellency expressed his surprise that His Majesty's Government should think it necessary in a time of profound peace to take such precautions for the safety of Gibraltar and Malta, as surely no one dreamt of attacking those possessions. Still, no doubt Great Britain knew her own business best, and he had no fault to find with her policy in this respect, especially as it aimed at the maintenance of the *status quo*, a policy to which a conservative country like Austria-Hungary could have no objection.

33. His language was quite friendly, but he let it be seen that in his inner mind he was thinking that the Agreements were in some way directed against Germany; as, while admitting finally that the Agreement between Great Britain and Spain in no way affected Austro-Hungarian, or even Italian, interests, he clung to the idea that it must be directed against some Power, and said: "If one closes one's door, it is in order to keep some one out." I ventured to point out to him that this was not necessarily always the case, and reminded him that the present policy of His Majesty's Government was practically the same as that embodied in the Agreement concluded between Great Britain and Italy in 1887, to which Austria-Hungary had subsequently become a party. His Excellency replied that any Agreement between any Powers which made for peace was agreeable to the Austro-Hungarian Government, but that he would reserve his definite opinion upon the present Agreement until he had studied it in all its bearings. So far as I am personally concerned, he has never to this day mentioned the subject again.

34. His Excellency's language to the French Ambassador, who had on the same day communicated the Franco-Spanish note, was similar to that which he had used to me, but with the Spanish Ambassador he went more into detail. He said that, for various reasons, such as the intimate relations between the two Courts, he had expected and could understand the Agreement between Spain and Great Britain. The Agreement between Spain and France was, however, a very different matter, and could not fail to cause general surprise. He was aware—and the Spanish Ambassador, who had only lately occupied a high position in the Spanish Foreign Office, must also be aware—that up to a comparatively recent period there had been no idea of such an Arrangement. What had been the cause for such a sudden change of policy? Who had taken the initiative? Or, perhaps, was it pressure of circumstances? And if so, in what quarter had these circumstances arisen? The Spanish Ambassador explained the motives of his Government in making these Agreements, adding that they were of a purely defensive character, and that he was sure that Baron d'Aehrenthal would understand that the policy of the Spanish Government was dictated solely by prudence and had not the slightest taint of

---

 ([1]) [Instructions for the communication of these notes were sent on June 6, *v. supra*, p. 37, No. 48, and *note* ([1]). The actual communication was made on the 15th, *v. supra*, pp. 44–6, No. 57.]

aggression in any form whatsoever. Baron d'Aehrenthal, however, persisted in the idea that pressure of some sort must have been brought to bear upon Spain, and finally asked the Marquis of Casa Calvo to tell him confidentially whether it was not a menace or some action on the part of some Great Power which had led the Spanish Government to throw in her lot with the two leading naval Powers. The Marquis of Casa Calvo replied that he was certainly not cognizant of anything of the sort, and that M. d'Aehrenthal might be assured that the motives he had given fully accounted for the policy of his Government.

35. The impression left on my mind by the foregoing conversations was that he did his best to speak pleasantly on a subject which was disagreeable to him, but let us clearly see that he regarded the Agreements with considerable suspicion. Nevertheless, in his speech before the Delegations his Excellency alluded to these Agreements as having, together with the meetings of Monarchs and statesmen, contributed in no small degree to the marked improvement of the general political situation and to the consolidation of the peace of Europe.

CHAPTER LI.

MOROCCAN DISPUTES AND AGREEMENTS, 1907-10.

I.—THE BOMBARDMENT OF CASABLANCA.

[ED. NOTE.—On July 30, 1907, a native mob killed nine Europeans engaged on harbour works at Casablanca, of whom three were French. When a French cruiser arrived on August 1, order had been restored; but the landing of a small detachment of troops on August 5 was followed by street fighting and a bombardment of the city. cp. G.P., XXIV, ch. 179, and Livre Jaune, Affaires du Maroc, III, (1906–1907), pp. 282–405, and IV, (1907–8).]

No. 63.

Sir G. Lowther to Sir Edward Grey.

F.O. 371/287.
25603/25603/07/28.　　　　　　　　　*Tangier,* D. *July* 31, 1907, 6·30 P.M.
Tel.　(No. 70.)　　　　　　　　　　　R. *August* 1, 1907, 8 A.M.

Serious disturbances yesterday at Dar-al-Baida.

Neighbouring tribes objecting to French port works and control of Customs. British Consul says he is of opinion that a ship of war or ships of war should be immediately sent. A French ship of war is leaving here to-day for Dar-al-Baida. British Colony consists of 140.

MINUTES.

Q[uestio]n Admiralty and say that S[ecretary] of S[tate] is of opinion that a ship of war should be despatched to Dar-al-Baida at once for the protection of B[ritish] s[ubject]s there. Request Sir F. Bertie to inform French Gov[ernmen]t that a ship will be sent.

W. L.
C. H.

The whole thing appears to be directed against the French works and the people employed on them. I am not clear that more than one ship of war is required and the French are sending one at least.

We had better telegraph to Sir F. Bertie to ask the French Gov[ernmen]t to let us know what steps they are taking and say that the British Consul has asked for a ship, but we wish to know their views as to the situation before sending one.

E. G.

[ED. NOTE.—On August 1, Sir E. Grey telegraphed to Sir F. Bertie (Tel No. 60, D. 4·15 P.M.) instructing him to ascertain what steps the French Government were taking. The following minute by Sir C. Hardinge of the same day shows that information had been received on this point from M. Cambon before Sir F. Bertie replied.

MINUTE.

F.O. 371/387.
25884/25603/07/28.

M. Cambon called this afternoon, by instruction from his Gov[ernmen]t, to state that the French Gov[ernmen]t were sending the cruiser Galilée from Tangier and the cruiser " Forbin " from the Azores to Casablanca, and that two more ships were being prepared at Toulon in case of a further emergency arising.

C. H.
Aug. 1, 1907.
E. G.

According to M. Cambon, Sir C. Hardinge declared that the British Government did not intend to intervene, but expressed the hope that the French Government would adopt energetic measures. *v. Livre Jaune, Affaires du Maroc,* III, (Paris, 1906-7), p. 285.

Sir E. Grey telegraphed on August 7 to Sir F. Bertie (No. 63) asking him to inform the French Government that we did not intend to send a ship, but relied on the force sent by France to protect British subjects if in danger.]

No. 64.

Sir Edward Grey to Sir G. Lowther.

F.O. 371/287.
25769/25603/07/28.
Tel.   (No. 47.)

Foreign Office, August 2, 1907.
D. 6 P.M.

Your tel[egram] No. 72.(¹)

We have informed French Gov[ernmen]t that Consul has asked for ship of war but that in view of measures taken by them we are not sending one. To do so might possibly entail the despatch of ships by other Powers, and if the French disembark troops it would be inconvenient that other Powers should do the same. The force they are sending should be sufficient to give protection.

(Repeat to Paris No. 61, Madrid No. 30.)

(¹) [Not reproduced. It stated that " information just received " indicated that the Dar-el-Baida rising was at present " purely anti-French."]

No. 65.

Sir F. Lascelles to Sir Edward Grey.

F.O. 371/287.
26861/25603/07/28 A.
(No. 347.)
Sir,

Berlin, D. August 4, 1907.
R. *August 12, 1907.*

The disturbances which have recently taken place in Casablanca have been given great prominence in the columns of the German newspapers. The efforts of the press are chiefly directed to proving that German interference in Morocco has not encouraged the Moors to combat the restoration of order. A semi-official article in the " Kölnische Zeitung " explains that the desire which is expressed in the " Temps " for the immediate establishment of an efficient police at Daralbaida is echoed in Germany. The " Frankfurter Zeitung," in a long article on the events at Daralbaida, combats the theory put forward in the French press that Germany, in order to carry out the spirit of the Algeciras Agreement, should not content herself alone with refraining from placing difficulties in the way of France and Spain, but that she should cause the Sultan to be informed that the efforts of France and Spain to pacify Morocco are cordially supported by Germany. The " Frankfurter " declares that it is no doubt true that France should have moral and diplomatic support from the other Signatory Powers of the Algeciras Agreement, but it enquires whether such support has ever been withheld. A message from Germany to the Sultan at this juncture to the effect that she would not help him against the French would be totally useless. The Sultan and his advisers are not more foolish than other men, and by this time they must have grasped the fact that nothing tangible has followed the " Tangier visit " and that they must deal with the French alone. If some fanatics do not yet understand this, they can very soon be taught that Frenchmen cannot be stoned to death with impunity. The articles are not very friendly to France, and the massacre of French citizens is treated with a levity which would certainly not have been the case, had any of the victims been of German origin. It is interesting in this connection to compare the anger which the press expresses at the supposed insults offered by Tyrolese Irredentists to a party of German tourists who have just paid a visit to the German speaking parts of the Tyrol. The Austrian Government are abused for not having prevented this "outrage," and apologies and satisfaction are demanded. The murder of a number of Frenchmen in Morocco is looked upon as a mere outburst of fanaticism for which the Makhzen can scarcely be blamed, and the French are told that it was more or less their own fault for not having established a proper police force at Daralbaida which in the interests of all the European Powers, they should have done long ago.

Some papers compare the recent massacre with the murder of Dr. Mauchamp at Marrakesh. The "Vossische Zeitung" points out that the latter crime led to the French occupation of Ujda, and it expresses its fears that France will now proceed to the occupation of further Moorish territory, and that the other Powers, supporting themselves on the Algeciras Agreement, may not be so ready to assume an attitude of unconcern as they did in the case of the seizure of Ujda.

There has been no expression of opinion on the matter by the Government, except the statement in the 'Kölnische Zeitung' that Germany desires to see proper police established at Daralbaida, but in view of the recent occurrences, it is interesting to bear in mind Prince Bülow's statement to Monsieur Huret that the French could be quite sure that Germany will not place difficulties in their way in Morocco.

I have, &c.

FRANK C. LASCELLES.

MINUTES.

There are several references in this Despatch to the desire to see proper police established at Dar-al-Baida. This can hardly mean the police contemplated in the Algeciras Act as no one would have confidence in a Moorish police at this moment.

One can therefore only imagine that the Germans will make no difficulty about a police force composed of French and Spaniards.

W. L.

It may mean that Germany intends to stipulate that the objective is to be the police contemplated by the Algeciras Act and that any other measures are to be regarded as temporary and provisional.

E. G.

No. 66.

Sir F. Bertie to Sir Edward Grey.

Paris, August 5, 1907.

F.O. 371/287.
26005/25603/07/28.   D. 2·30 P.M.
Tel. (No. 36.)   R. 5·10 P.M.

Political Director informs me that cruiser "Du Chayla" has been ordered to Mazagan in view of reports of agitation there. French force for Morocco will consist of not less than 3,000 men, with battery of artillery. French Government have every confidence in naval and military Commanders. Former is acquainted with Casa Blanca. They will soon have enough ships and men off Moorish coast to be able to deal rapidly with any emergency. Their action will be confined to re-establishing order at Casa Blanca and punishing offenders, and providing for safety of Europeans at other ports if threatened.

No advance into the interior is contemplated, but any disturbing elements round the towns may have to be dispersed. Measures will be taken in agreement with Spain to hasten organization of police; it is probable that forces will not be withdrawn till this has been accomplished, as risk cannot be run of repetition of similar incidents. Announcement of energetic action has been well received in France and abroad, and Political Director stated that Austrian Ambassador had informed Minister for Foreign Affairs that his Government hoped that France [would] "strike hard." Minister for Foreign Affairs inferred from this that German Government entirely concurred in necessity for strong measures.

No. 67.

M. Geoffray to Sir Charles Hardinge.

F.O. 371/287.
26265/25603/07/28.
Cher Sir Charles Hardinge,

Ambassade de France à Londres,
Le 5 Août, 1907.

Notre Chargé d'affaires à Tanger vient de faire savoir à M. Pichon que votre ministre en Maroc lui a signalé la situation menaçante qui regnerait à Magazan, en lui demandant une protection éventuelle pour les sujets britanniques.

Je m'empresse de vous informer, pour répondre aux directions de notre Ministre des Affaires Etrangères, que notre croiseur le "Du Chayla" mouillera aujourd'hui même devant Magazan.

Bien sincèrement à vous,
GEOFFRAY.

MINUTE.

I have written to M. Geoffray thanking him for his communication and for the steps taken.

I have also told him that inquiries are being made at the Admiralty as to the reasons for the departure of the Antrim from Gibraltar for Casablanca, contrary to Sir E. Grey's wishes, and asking for her recall so as to avoid the despatch of other vessels to that port, which are neither French nor Spanish.

C. H.
E. G.

No. 68.

Sir Edward Grey to Sir F. Bertie.

F.O. 371/287.
26584/25603/07/28.
(No. 435.)
Sir,

Foreign Office, August 7, 1907.

M. Cambon handed me to-day the statement of which a copy is sent herewith, as to the action taken at Casablanca.

I said the French Government evidently had no choice except to act as they had done, and it was probably better that they should have been forced to take strong measures than half-measures.([1])

[I am, &c.]
E. G[REY].

Enclosure in No. 68.

Note communicated by M. Paul Cambon, August 7, 1907.

Ambassade de France à Londres.

Les événements ont devancé les mesures arrêtées par le Gouvernement de la République à la suite des récents attentats commis à Casablanca, mesures qui allaient être portées à la connaissance des Gouvernements intéressés.

En présence de l'impuissance manifeste du Gouvernement Marocain à se faire obéir de ses sujets et à pourvoir à la sauvegarde des ressortissants étrangers, l'urgente nécessité s'affirme de plus en plus d'organiser la police dans les ports du Maroc. Le maintien et le respect de la haute autorité de S[a] M[ajesté] Chérifienne y sont intéressés au premier degré. C'est pénétré de ces sentiments que le Gouvernement de la République donnera suite aux mesures auxquelles il avait résolu de recourir en

([1]) [For M. Cambon's report *v. Livre Jaune, Affaires du Maroc,* III, (1906–7), p. 316.]

respectant scrupuleusement l'intégrité du Maroc et la souveraineté du Sultan. L'ordre et la sécurité, la liberté des transactions commerciales seront garanties à Casablanca par des forces suffisantes. Un châtiment exemplaire sera infligé aux indigènes responsables des massacres et des attentats d'hier.

Ces opérations seront accompagnées de l'organisation immédiate d'une police de la ville et de la banlieue de concert avec le Gouvernement Espagnol.

Londres, le 7 Août 1907.

No. 69.

Sir F. Bertie to Sir Edward Grey.

F.O. 371/287.
26603/25603/07/28 A.
(No. 394.)
Sir,

Paris, D. August 8, 1907.
R. *August* 9, 1907.

Mr. Lister saw the Political Director to-day and communicated to him the substance of your telegram to His Majesty's Ambassador at Madrid No. 37 of yesterday's date,([1]) relative to the importance of complete co-operation between the French and Spanish Governments at Casablanca. M. Louis said that the instruction to Sir M. de Bunsen was exactly what the French Government had wanted and that M. Pichon would be much gratified at the action of His Majesty's Government. The statement that the latter could not see any risk in the co-operation of the two Governments was, he considered, particularly valuable.

M. Louis then read Mr. Lister the note which had been presented to the various Powers, recounting what had occurred at Casablanca, and explaining the reasons for the French action. It should of course, he said, have been a joint communication by France and Spain, but the Spanish Government again were not ready, and the French Government were of opinion that the matter admitted of no delay. The Spanish Government had accepted the inevitable, and he believed that their representatives abroad had now made a statement to the various Governments concerned to the effect that they concurred absolutely in the communication made by the French Government.

M. Louis drew Mr. Lister's attention to the wording of the last sentence of the note in which the expression "organisation d'une police" not of "la police" is used. He said that in the present condition of affairs it was out of the question to think of a police constituted according to the provisions of the Algeciras Act, consisting that is to say, of a force of Moors with French and Spanish officers. A police of Frenchmen and Spaniards would be formed immediately, and as soon as circumstances permitted and the suitable Moors were available the force would be transformed to meet the stipulations of the Algeciras Act. He imagined that the men would be recruited from the troops now being landed; mainly no doubt from the Algerian regiments, as it was important that they should have a knowledge of Arabic. This, as far as the French were concerned, need not take more than a day or two. The recent experience had been unsolicited; it had been forced upon them and had been dearly bought; at the same time he could not help thinking that it might prove beneficial, as it had opened the eyes of Europe to the real state of affairs and might save France and Spain from even more disagreeable surprises in the future. Croakers expressed the opinion that things would go even worse, but he is of opinion that the recent outburst was the result of the impunity which for the last year has been enjoyed by the perpetrators on a smaller scale of outrages of a similar nature.

M. Louis said that at Berlin all was honey ("on est tout miel"); that when M. Jules Cambon communicated the French note to M. Tchirschky, the latter, after reading it said "C'est parfait, vous avez fait exactement ce qu'il fallait."

([1]) [Not reproduced.]

Mr. Lister informed M. Louis that there was absolutely no truth in the report that H.M.S. Antrim had left for Casablanca, and that she was still at Gibraltar, and he expressed himself very grateful for this precise information.

Mr. Lister also availed himself of the opportunity to congratulate M. Louis on his promotion to the rank of a "Grand Officier" of the Legion of Honour, a distinction which has rarely been conferred on the official occupying his post at the Quai d'Orsay.

I have, &c.

(For His Majesty's Ambassador),

REGINALD LISTER.

No. 70.

Sir F. Lascelles to Sir Edward Grey.

F.O. 371/287.
26865/25603/07/28 A.
(No. 353.)   Confidential.

Berlin, D. August 8, 1907.

Sir,   R. *August 12, 1907.*

Monsieur Jules Cambon, the French Ambassador, returned to Berlin yesterday morning in order to communicate to the German Government the note which the French Government have addressed to the Signatory Powers of the Act of Algeciras on recent events at Casablanca. Monsieur Cambon informs me that his interview with Herr von Tschirschky was entirely satisfactory. His Excellency had even gone so far as to assure Monsieur Cambon that the French Government could count upon the complete sympathy of the German Government in the action which they had been called upon to take at Casablanca.

I have, &c.

FRANK C. LASCELLES.

MINUTE.

The Germans seem now to display every desire to be as nice as possible towards the French in Morocco. They must have quite satisfied themselves that the baiting policy they were pursuing up till about a year ago would not pay them, (but they will expect to be paid for a change of policy).([1])

W. A. S.
G. S. S.
W. L.
E. G.

([1]) [The last clause, shown here in round brackets, was added by Sir E. Grey.]

No. 71

Sir Edward Grey to Sir M. de Bunsen.

F.O. 371/287.
26811/25603/07/28.
(No. 116.)
Sir,   *Foreign Office, August 15, 1907.*

The Spanish Minister called at this Office on the 9th instant and handed to Sir C. Hardinge the memorandum, of which a translation is enclosed, explanatory of the proposals of the French and Spanish Gov[ernmen]ts for the maintenance of order in Morocco.

Sir C. Hardinge took the opportunity of impressing upon the Marquis de Villalobar the importance which H[is] M[ajesty's] Gov[ernmen]t attach to harmonious co-operation between France and Spain which appears to them to offer the only means of confining the necessary operations within proper limits and of preventing international complications.

Sir C. Hardinge observed that, in spite of the requests received from H[is] M[ajesty's] Consul, H[is] M[ajesty's] Gov[ernmen]t had refrained from sending a warship to Casablanca, in order to avoid the despatch of other foreign vessels of war, and that they trusted to the French and Spanish military and naval authorities to take the proper measures for safeguarding the lives and property of British subjects in the seaport towns of Morocco.

The Marquis de Villalobar admitted that his Gov[ernmen]t had been slow to act and said that he would telegraph to them in the sense of Sir C. Hardinge's remarks.

[I am, &c.
E. GREY.]

Enclosure in No. 71.

Memorandum.

(Translation.)   *Spanish Embassy.*

The recent crimes committed at Casablanca having demonstrated the impotence of the Moorish Gov[ernmen]t to make itself obeyed by its subjects and to protect foreigners, render it more urgent than ever to organize the police in the ports of the Empire. It is a matter which concerns the maintenance and the prestige of the Sultan's high authority. With this object the Gov[ernmen]t of His Most Catholic Majesty have concerted measures with the Gov[ernmen]t of the French Republic respecting the organization of a police charged with the protection of the town and environs of Casablanca and by means thereof and of the measures which will have to be adopted as far as scrupulous respect for the integrity of Morocco and the sovereignty of the Sultan permit, for the assurance of order and liberty of mercantile transactions in those regions. These would be guaranteed and those responsible for the events above mentioned would not remain unpunished.

In order to carry out the principle which has been adopted and to pursue the course which they have set before themselves, the Gov[ernmen]t of His Most Catholic Majesty desire that the Powers should have cognizance of the foregoing.

London, Aug[ust] 8th, 1907.

No. 72.

Sir Edward Grey to Sir F. Bertie.

F.O. 371/287.
26603/25603/07/28 A.
(No. 449.)
Sir,   *Foreign Office, August* 15, 1907.

I transmit herewith to Y[our] E[xcellency] a copy of a despatch addressed to H[is] M[ajesty's] Ambassador at Madrid([1]) recording a conversation which Sir Charles Hardinge had on the 9th instant with the Spanish Minister on the subject of the action which is being taken by the French and Spanish Gov[ernmen]ts in consequence of the prevailing disturbances in Morocco.

On the 10th instant, the Marquis de Villalobar called again to see Sir C. Hardinge and stated that he had received a telegram from his Gov[ernmen]t saying that there was now complete co-operation with the French Gov[ernmen]t in Moroccan affairs within the limits of the Algeciras Act. M. de Villalobar explained that, the Spanish Gov[ernmen]t were very anxious to do nothing which could expose them to attack

([1]) [v. immediately preceding document.]

from other Powers for taking action outside the Algeciras Act and that they feared a forward policy on the part of France. He asked whether H[is] M[ajesty's] Gov[ernmen]t could not draw the attention of the French Gov[ernmen]t to the necessity for prudence.

It appears to me possible that, in speaking thus, M. de Villalobar had in view the intention of the French Gov[ernmen]t to organise a temporary police force for service in Morocco composed of Frenchmen and Spaniards, to which reference is made in Y[our] E[xcellency]'s despatch No. 394 of the 8th instant.(²) Such a step seems to me to offer at the present moment the only means of providing for the safety of the Europeans at the open ports when the time comes for the withdrawal of the military and naval forces, but it would presumably be adopted as a temporary measure pending the formation of the police force contemplated by the Algeciras Act.

[I am, &c.]
E. G[REY].

(²) [v. supra, pp. 56–7, No. 69.]

No. 73.

Sir Edward Grey to Sir F. Bertie.

F.O. 371/354.
28631/28631/07/44.
(No. 472. Confidential.)

Sir,　　　　　　　　　　　　　　*Foreign Office, August 22, 1907.*

I told M. Geoffray to-day that, though I had not yet seen Sir Charles Hardinge, he had sent me a written account of his interview with Prince Bülow.

It had been very favourable and friendly in tone. . . . .(¹)

With regard to Morocco, Prince Bülow had said that he was most anxious for an improvement in the relations between France and Germany. He thought this could be effected by a display of tact on both sides, especially on the part of the local representatives of the two Powers. He was convinced that France had no intention of attacking Germany. And he gave most formal assurances that Germany had no intention of attacking France, nor of creating difficulties for her in Morocco. He realised the difficulties which France already had in Morocco, and he did not desire to increase them. He had sent instructions that the Moorish authorities were to be made to understand that, as long as France and Spain acted in conformity with, and within the limits of, the Algeciras Act, the Moorish authorities would have no support from the German Government or German representatives in opposition to France and Spain. All Prince Bülow wanted was that German traders and merchants should not be unfairly treated by the French authorities, and should not be excluded from fair competition.

M. Geoffray said all that France desired was to act in conformity with the Algeciras Act—he further observed that during the last few weeks there had been a favourable change in the attitude of the German Legation in Morocco.

I said it was very likely that, when Prince Bülow spoke of the need for tact on the part of local representatives, he had Dr. Rosen in his mind. . . . .(¹)

[I am, &c.]
E. G[REY].

(¹) [The passages here omitted refer to the incursion of Morenga into German South-West Africa, the Hague Conference, the Anglo-Russian Agreement, and the questions of the Bagdad Railway and Macedonia. The despatch is printed in full in *Gooch & Temperley*, Vol. VI, pp. 47–48, No. 28.]

No. 74.

Sir M. de Bunsen to Sir Edward Grey.

F.O. 371/288.
28980/25603/07/28 A.   *Madrid,* D. *August* 28, 1907, 10 P.M.
Tel. (No. 44.)   R. *August* 29, 1907, 7 A.M.
  Confidential. Morocco.

President of the Council has given me in detail his views on the situation. They may be summed up as follows : France, without stopping to consult Spain, embarked on a course having no visible issue except that of rendering the execution of the Algeciras programme tenfold more difficult than before. Spain would have been justified in refusing to follow her in conducting military operations outside the Spanish sphere as defined by secret convention with France of October 1904. She preferred to give a public sign of her desire to proceed with France as far as possible by sending a police force of 400 to Casablanca. But she is not to be enticed into using it as an army or for other purpose than that of maintaining order and defending itself if actually attacked. Spain will continue her efforts to carry out engagements she made at Algeciras, but for anything beyond she must first secure the concurrence of the signatory Powers.

Spanish Ambassador at Paris reported yesterday by telegraph that the French Minister for Foreign Affairs suggested whether the object both sides had in view could not be better secured by abandoning the attempt to combine operations at any port and by assigning to each country the task of preserving order on the coast line within its own sphere. President of the Council is replying that he thinks proposal well worth consideration but only on the understanding, so far as Spanish sphere is concerned, that Spain shall be at liberty to consider at each point how her object can best be secured and that Spain shall give no undertaking to occupy any point by force, as he fears perhaps France intends shall be done. Tangier of course would have to be subject to special arrangements and consent of all the Powers would be necessary.

President of the Council was anxious to learn your views on the French proposal. I said that the great point was that the two Powers should agree.
  (Repeated to Tangier.)

MINUTES.

If we answer now all we can say, it seems to me, is that we should much deprecate any appearance of want of Agreement between the 2 Powers, and that the Spanish Gov[ernmen]t may be assured that any course on which they are agreed whether in the sense of the suggestion of the French Minister for F[oreign] A[ffairs], or otherwise will be supported by H[is] M[ajesty's] Gov[ernment], or something general of this sort.

I think, however, we might leave this tel[egram] unanswered until we hear from the French.
                                                                              F. A. C.
                                                                              29 Aug.

Sir F. Bertie should ascertain the view of the French Gov[ernmen]t first before we come to a decision to give advice.
                                                                              E. G.

No. 75.

Sir F. Bertie to Sir Edward Grey.

F.O. 371/288.
29164/25603/07/28 A.
(No. 422.) Confidential.   *Paris,* D. *August* 30, 1907.
Sir,   R. *August* 31, 1907.

I called on Monsieur Clemenceau yesterday as I had not seen him since his return to Paris from his cure at Carlsbad. His Excellency said that he had heard that I had made representations at the Ministry for Foreign Affairs on the subject of the fears of foreign residents at Tangier of a rising which the French forces would be unable to deal with. I explained to His Excellency the communication which I had made on behalf of His Majesty's Government and the assurances which had been given to me and which I had no doubt would be considered satisfactory by His Majesty's Government. Monsieur Clemenceau then told me that Prince Bülow had assured the French Ambassador that Germany had no intention or desire to impede any action that France might take so long as no attempt was made to upset the Algeciras Arrangements. As the French had no intention of doing anything beyond maintaining order and security for life at the ports and their immediate vicinities and to exact reparation for the outrages committed against Frenchmen there was nothing to which the German Government could reasonably object. No more troops than might be required for these objects would be sent to the Morocco Ports.

I have, &c.
FRANCIS BERTIE.

No. 76.

Sir F. Bertie to Sir Edward Grey.

F.O. 371/288.
29166/25603/07/28 A.
(No. 424.)   *Paris,* D. *August* 30, 1907.
Sir,   R. *August* 31, 1907.

I had the honour to receive last night your telegram No. 93(¹) of yesterday and the one from His Majesty's Minister [*sic*] at Madrid therein referred to (No. 44 Confidential August 29th).(²) This morning I asked Monsieur Pichon to receive me, and I saw him at 12 o'clock. I told His Excellency that the Spanish Government had sought your advice on a matter respecting which you would wish to learn the views of the French Government before making a reply.

Monsieur Pichon stated that the attitude of the Spanish Government regarding Morocco was anything but satisfactory and he could only hope that they would soon be brought to deal with the question in a reasonable manner.

I then informed His Excellency that, in the opinion of the Spanish Government the course adopted by the French Government, on which they had not been consulted will render the execution of the Algeciras Programme much more difficult than hitherto. They consider that Spain would have been justified in refusing to join in military operations outside the Spanish sphere defined by the Secret Convention of 1904. As however she wished to act with France as far as possible she sent a Police Force of 400 men to Casa Blanca. This force is intended solely for the purpose of maintaining order and for self-defence if attacked. Spain is ready to carry out her engagements undertaken at Algeciras, but for anything beyond them she must, the Spanish Government hold, seek the concurrence of the Signatory Powers. The Spanish Government are, they say, considering a proposal from the French Government viz. that France and Spain shall each undertake the preservation of order on the coast lying within its own sphere. They desire however to reserve for themselves liberty to consider at each point how their object can best be secured, and to give no undertaking to occupy any point by force. Any measures in regard to Tangier would, they consider, have to be the subject of special arrangements to which the consent of all the Powers would be necessary.

Monsieur Pichon said that he expected to see the Spanish Ambassador this afternoon and would after then be better able to state the views of the French Government.

(¹) [Not reproduced. In it, (F.O. 371/288. 28980/25603/07/28 A), Sir Edward Grey expressed the desire to learn the views of the French Government before replying to Sir M. de Bunsen's Tel. No. 44. *v. supra*, p. 60, No. 74.]

(²) [*v. supra*, p. 60, No. 74.]

Later in the day I received a message requesting me to call at the Quai d'Orsay at 6 o'clock. The Ambassador was with the Minister when I arrived and when he came away from his interview he told me that Monsieur Pichon had informed him that I had enquired of him whether the French Government felt able to maintain order and protect the lives of foreigners at Tangier as the British Residents there had expressed their apprehension as to what might take place and had asked that a British Ship of War should be sent thither, but that His Majesty's Government on receiving explanations from the French Government as to the means at their disposal for ensuring the security of foreigners had considered them satisfactory and had determined not to send a ship.

I told the Marquis del Muni what had passed on the subject between the Minister for Foreign Affairs and myself, and I suggested to him that if a British ship were sent the ships of other nationalities would probably appear also and the Morocco international complications would begin again. I then went in to see M. Pichon. His Excellency informed me that the Spanish Ambassador had by order of the Spanish Government expressed to him their surprise that the French Government should without consulting with them have sent another big ship of war to Tangier with troops and further reinforcements to Casa Blanca bringing the force there up to over 8,000 men. These measures looked like preparations for a military expedition which was not at all in the programme anticipated by the Spanish Government.

Monsieur Pichon had, he told me, replied that the additional ship for Tangier had already started, that it was a cruiser of some 7,000 tons, and that it had on board a landing contingent of 150 men. The other ship at Tangier having a light landing contingent there would be the possibility of landing in all 300 men, which would not be too much for the protection of Tangier with the support of the ships. It could not be regarded as a preparation for a military expedition nor could the additional troops sent to Casa Blanca be so regarded. The troops actually there were 4,444 and the reinforcement of 2,000 men would bring the total force up to 6,444, from which must be deducted the non-effectives, so that the fighting force could not be considered as more than adequate to prevent the tribes from successfully attacking Casa Blanca and its immediate vicinity. The French Government had no intention of embarking on an expedition into the interior. It must however be borne in mind by the Spanish Government that the Powers had delegated to France and Spain certain duties and responsibilities in regard to Morocco. The French Government were quite ready to discuss with the Spanish Government the measures to be taken but they could not incur the risk of leaving Tangier unprotected and wait till an agreement had been come to with the Spanish Government before making precautionary arrangements. What would the Powers, what would the French Parliament say if owing to the dilatoriness or inaction of France and Spain there were a massacre of foreigners at Tangier? M. Pichon could not take on himself such a responsibility, but now that preparations had been made he would be quite ready to discuss the question in detail with the Spanish Government. He could not admit that the concurrence of the Powers must be sought for what the French Government have done and intend to do for the protection of Tangier and the foreigners there. The question of the organisation of the Police was also a matter for discussion but for the time it was in abeyance owing to the state of affairs at the ports of Morocco.

M. Pichon informed me that it was possible that the Spanish Ambassador might go to San Sebastian to explain personally to the Spanish Prime Minister the intentions and views of the French Government and to assure him that there is no question of a military expedition into the interior of Morocco. M. Pichon trusts that His Majesty's Government will use their influence with the Spanish Government to bring them to adopt the policy of working in accord with France on the bases which he explained to the Spanish Ambassador.

I have, &c.
FRANCIS BERTIE.

MINUTE.

Morocco.

The Spanish Minister was much more satisfactory to-day. I read to him the telegram to Sir M. de Bunsen you drafted(³) expressing confidence that the French did not desire any expedition into the interior and your hopes for continued Spanish co-operation with France. He said he was reporting to Madrid in this sense, and I gathered that he thought that the Spanish Gov[ernmen]t *now* realised that there was no other policy open to them than loyal co-operation with France.

I said you would be very glad to hear it.

F. A. C.
    Sep. 2, '07.
E. G.

(³) [*v.* immediately succeeding document.]

No. 77.

Sir Edward Grey to Sir M. de Bunsen.

F.O. 371/288.
29166/25603/07/28 A.   *Foreign Office, September* 2, 1907.
Tel. (No. 61.)   D. 2·30 P.M.

Your telegram No. 44 (of Aug[ust] 28).(¹)

You can assure Spanish Gov[ernmen]t that we have every confidence that French Gov[ernmen]t desire to avoid an expedition into the interior and that but for the measures they have already taken we should have been obliged in answer to demands from British residents to send a ship to protect them at Tangier. In view of fact that policing of ports is entrusted to France and Spain this would have led to most undesirable complications. We sincerely hope therefore that Spain will continue to co-operate with France in giving protection at the ports on bases explained to Spanish Ambassador by M. Pichon.

(Sir F. Bertie should be informed.)(²)

(¹) [*v. supra*, p. 60, No. 74.]
(²) [This telegram was repeated to Paris as Tel. 95, in accordance with the note at the foot of the above draft. It was also repeated to Tangier as Tel. 89.]

No. 78.

Sir F. Lascelles to Sir Edward Grey.

F.O. 371/288.
30849/25603/07/28 A.
(No. 399.) Confidential.   *Berlin, D. September* 11, 1907.
Sir,   R. *September* 16, 1907.

The Spanish Ambassador was good enough to call upon me shortly after my return from Homburg and spoke at considerable length about the situation caused by recent events in Morocco, and the attitude which the German Government had assumed towards it. It was evident that the necessity under which France and Spain found themselves to send a military force for the purpose of maintaining order in the Moroccan ports was an infringement of the Act of Algeciras which contemplated the creation of a Police force composed of Moors. Both France and Spain had explained that they had been compelled by the force of circumstances to take this action and that their occupation of the Moorish Ports was only temporary and would cease as soon as it was possible to organize a Moorish Police Force in accordance with the Act of Algeciras. The German Government had accepted this explanation and Mr. Polo de Bernabé was convinced that they had no wish to raise difficulties. He believed that the German Government, or at all events Prince Bülow, had realised the fact that the former somewhat truculent methods of German diplomacy had not only not been of advantage to Germany but had even reduced her to a position of isolation among the Powers. It would seem therefore that he intended to alter his tactics and to assume a friendly aspect towards foreign countries. The improvement of the relations between England and Germany was a step in this direction and there could be little doubt of his desire to come to a good understanding with France. Mr. Polo de Bernabé did not anticipate that the German Government would object to the action of France and Spain in Morocco. He had however been struck by a remark which had fallen from Herr von Tschirschky in his conversations on the subject, to the effect that according to the information received by the German Government, the bombardment of Casablanca had been an unnecessary operation. Herr von Tschirschky must have known that it was a matter of regret to the Spanish Government to be obliged to take active measures in Morocco, and that it was only the conviction of the necessity of doing so and their determination to fulfil their obligation towards France that had induced them to join her in military operations. Mr. Polo de Bernabé wondered what Herr von Tschirschky's object was in making this observation. Was it for the purpose of sowing distrust between Spain and France, or was it for the purpose of being able to say later that the German Government, although they raised no objection to the action which France and Spain thought it necessary to take, did not see sufficient justification for such extreme measures the responsibility for which must fall upon them.

I replied that it was evident that the joint action of France and Spain could not be otherwise than distasteful to the German Government, and I could understand that Herr von Tschirschky should wish to make it clear that the German Government had not incurred any responsibility. I had however the impression that the German Government sincerely desired to avoid complications and really wished for the establishment of better relations between themselves and France, and I did not therefore think that they would raise objections to the course which France and Spain might think it necessary to pursue under the stress of circumstances and as a purely provisional measure.

Mr. Polo de Bernabé said that he was also under the impression that the German Government did not intend to raise difficulties, but he had been somewhat disturbed at Herr von Tschirschky's utterances, which, it was true, he had explained as being the expression of his personal opinion. In conclusion Mr. Polo de Bernabé begged me to consider what he had said as strictly confidential.

I have, &c.

F. C. LASCELLES.

No. 79.

Sir F. Lascelles to Sir Edward Grey.

F.O. 371/288.
30853/25603/07/28 A.
(No. 403.) Confidential.   *Berlin,* D. *September* 12, 1907.
Sir,   R. *September* 16, 1907.

I called the day before yesterday upon Herr von Tschirschky whom I had not an opportunity of seeing earlier since my return to Berlin. I said that I had read with great pleasure the account which Sir Charles Hardinge had given of the conversations which he had had with the Emperor and Prince Bülow at Wilhelmshöhe,(¹) and that I had heard from the Emperor himself that His Majesty had been greatly pleased by the visit which he had received from the King.

(¹) [*v. Gooch & Temperley*, Vol. VI, pp. 43–6.]

The conversation then turned upon the state of affairs in Morocco. Herr von Tschirschky referred to the reply of the German Government to the French Note(²) which I had no doubt seen in the North German Gazette, as a proof of the desire of the German Government not to raise difficulties. I said that I had understood the note in that sense, and I gathered that it was the wish of the German Government that the events in Morocco should not give rise to any complication with Foreign Powers. Herr on Tschirschky replied that this was certainly the case, and that the German Government had the sincere desire of living on good terms with all the Powers. The state of affairs in Morocco was no doubt very complicated but he did not anticipate that it would give rise to serious complications. He had received information that several of the Moroccan tribes had expressed the desire of entering into negotiations with the French, and this he hoped might bring about a satisfactory solution.

I have, &c.
FRANK C. LASCELLES.

(²) [v. supra, pp. 55–6, No. 68, encl.]

No. 80.

Sir Edward Grey to Sir F. Bertie.

F.O. 371/288.
31226/25603/07/28.
(No. 520.)
Sir,   *Foreign Office, September* 17, 1907.

I told M. Cambon to-day that the Spanish Minister had asked us to support at Paris the request that the Spaniards should have the superior command at Tangier : the French policing the outside zone and they the inside, but their commanding officer holding the superior rank. I had understood that M. Pichon had agreed to this, and if so I did not see where the difficulty lay.

M. Cambon said that M. Pichon had not agreed. He had thought it hopeless to reopen the discussion with Spain upon old arrangements, for it would be endless. What he had proposed was that, in the event of a disembarcation at Tangier becoming necessary, the French and Spanish Governments should come to an understanding as to the command. It was impossible to bring in the old arrangements for in the case of a crisis the Spaniards would not be ready. It was practically certain that the French would be there first, and would have to take what measures might be necessary.

He asked me to advise Spain to agree to the French proposal. He informed me that Spain, at the same time as she approached us, had approached the German Government on the same subject, which was an unfavourable sign.

I said I would give the Spanish Minister the answer which M. Cambon had given me.

M. Cambon said he expected the tribes round Casablanca would accept the French conditions. Great trouble had arisen because General Drude had not been able to take sufficient measures at first, but the strong measures taken since had had a calming effect.

I told M. Cambon that a point which persistently recurred in the conversation of the Spaniards was their anxiety about the secret agreement with France respecting Morocco,(¹) and I suggested that an assurance from France to Spain that measures

(¹) [v. infra, pp. 67–9, No. 82, encl. 2.]

[19656]   F

taken in Morocco to meet an emergency would not prejudice the secret agreement, if circumstances should in the future bring that agreement into operation, might have a calming effect.

[I am, &c.]
E. G[REY].

No. 81.

Sir F. Lascelles to Sir Edward Grey.

F.O. 371/262.
33223/29500/07/18.
(No. 436.)   Confidential.   *Berlin, D. October* 3, 1907.
Sir,   R. *October* 7, 1907.

Mr. Jules Cambon, who has recently returned to Berlin from leave of absence, has been good enough to give me an account of the visit which he paid to Prince Bülow at Norderney. He said that nothing could exceed the amiability of Prince Bülow's reception of him, and the conversations which they had had together were marked by great cordiality. It was evident to Mr. Cambon that Prince Bülow attached considerable importance to receiving him at Norderney and not at Berlin, as after Mr. Cambon had expressed his readiness to go to Norderney, Prince Bülow had spent some days in Berlin for the purpose of consulting his dentist. The interview might have taken place then, and Mr. Cambon gathered that Prince Bülow wished to give the impression that it was the French Ambassador rather than the German Chancellor who was the more anxious that the interview should take place. To this M. Cambon had no objection, and although Prince Bülow, as is his usual custom, indulged in vague generalities and did not say anything very definite, he gave Mr. Cambon to understand that the German Government had no wish or intention of raising difficulties for France in Morocco.

The recent action of the German Government had confirmed the impression which Mr. Cambon had received from his conversation with Prince Bülow. They had admitted the right of search of German vessels by France and Spain for the purpose of stopping the contraband traffic of arms and ammunition into Morocco. It is true that it would have been difficult for the German Government to have withheld their consent to this measure which had been accepted by His Majesty's Government, and it would have been more satisfactory if they had not limited its operation to six months, as it was scarcely to be hoped that order would be re-established within that period. He hoped however that there would not be much difficulty in inducing the German Government to agree to a prolongation of the term. He feared indeed that much greater difficulties might be anticipated from the Spanish Government, whose action throughout the crisis had been far from satisfactory, and who might object to take strong measures against their own subjects, who, he understood, were the principal offenders.

I have, &c.
FRANK C. LASCELLES.

No. 82.

Mr. Grant Duff to Sir Edward Grey.

F.O. 371/281.
34573/435/07/28.
(No. 156.)   Secret.   *Madrid, D. October* 12, 1907.
Sir,   R. *October* 19, 1907.

In recent despatches regarding the situation in Morocco His Majesty's Ambassador has alluded to a Secret Agreement signed in February last between

France and Spain regarding the organisation of the Sherifian Police under the terms of the Algeciras Act.

Before proceeding on leave Sir Maurice de Bunsen instructed me to endeavour to obtain a copy of this agreement from the Spanish Government and on Monday last I asked Señor Allendesalazar whether he would have any objection to complying with the Ambassador's wish.

His Excellency replied that he did not think there was any objection but promised to let me know in a few days.

I have now the honour to enclose a copy of Señor Allendesalazar's private letter confidentially communicating to me a copy in Spanish of the text of the Secret Agreement, of which I transmit a translation.

You will see from Señor Allendesalazar's letter that by the terms of the Agreement, at Casablanca, the senior Spanish instructor is to take command of the extra-urban zone and of reinforcements furnished if required by the urban force, and at Tangier the French senior instructor is to be in command. In practice, however, at Casablanca, owing to that town being situated in the French sphere of influence, the Spanish Government have acquiesced in the command being held by a French officer. Having made this concession the Spanish Government expect that should a similar situation arise at Tangier, which is within the Spanish sphere, the same consideration shall be shown them by the French Government and that the Chief Command shall be exercised by a Spanish officer. Señor Allendesalazar adds that the view of the Spanish Government is based not on Article 2 of the enclosed Agreement but on the spirit of that Agreement combined with the arrangement come to in 1904.

I have, &c.
EVELYN GRANT DUFF.

Enclosure 1 in No. 82.

Señor Allendesalazar to Mr. E. Grant Duff.

Monsieur le Chargé d'Affaires,   *Le 10 octobre,* 1907.

Conformément au désir que vous avez bien voulu m'exprimer à notre dernier entretien, j'ai l'avantage de vous faire parvenir, à titre strictement confidentiel, le texte de l'accord hispano-français du 23 février 1907 concernant la police au Maroc.

Vous ne manquerez pas d'observer que, pour les opérations de la zone extra-urbaine à Tanger et le recours qu'elles comporteraient à l'effectif urbain, les articles 1 et 2 stipulent que c'est l'officier français le plus élevé en grade qui prêtera son concours au commandement. Une situation équivalente était assurée à Casablanca à l'officier instructeur supérieur espagnol.

Les circonstances ont apporté toutefois ce changement : qu'en pratique la France a la suprématie à Casablanca. Le Gouvernement Royal s'y est prêté, tenant compte que cette ville est placée dans la sphère d'influence française. Mais il se croit à son tour en mesure d'invoquer une considération du même genre, dans le cas de Tanger, sphère d'influence espagnole.

Ce n'est pas donc, sur l'article 2 de l'accord du 23 février 1907 mais sur l'esprit de cette Convention, combiné avec les arrangements de 1904, que nous nous sommes basés lorsque nous avons demandé que le commandement des forces hispano-françaises, qui seraient éventuellement envoyées à Tanger pour y maintenir l'ordre, soit exercé par un officier espagnol.

Veuillez croire à mes sentiments distingués,
MANUEL ALLENDESALAZAR.

Enclosure 2 in No. 82.

Agreement between France and Spain, signed at Paris, February 23, 1907.

The Government of His Majesty the King of Spain and the Government of the French Republic deeming it convenient to define the limits in which each shall assist in the organisation of the Sherifian Police according to the terms laid down at the International Conference at Algeciras, have agreed on the following conditions :

At Tangier and Casablanca the police force shall be divided into two sections, one in charge of the urban and the other in charge of the extra-urban zone.

At Tangier the two zones shall be respectively delimited by the line of demarcation traced in the map annexed to the present act. The urban zone shall include :

1.—The walled city and the port as far as a line which proceeds from the sea, below the slope leading to the Dar Debagh Gate and enclosing the Romea theatre.

2.—The entire plateau of the Marchan from Bab-el-Fahz and the Camino del Monte (along which the urban police shall have the right to pass in order to communicate for purposes of duty with the Marchan) as far as the Rio de los Judios. The Spanish Hospital and the Convent of the Spanish Mission shall be considered to form part of this zone and in order to reach these buildings the urban police shall have the right to pass along the road leading from the Camino del Monte to the Barriada de San Francisco.

The Electric Light Factory shall also be considered part of this zone and the urban police in order to reach the said factory shall have the right to make use of the neighbouring roads.

The zone named extra-urban shall include, inclusive of the Camio del Monte, all the territory situated without the first zone. The French Hospital shall, in the same manner, be considered as forming part of this zone and the extra urban police shall have, in order to reach it, the right to make use of the roads leading to it.

At Casablanca the zone named urban shall include the gate and city as far as the intersection of the Marrakech Road and the Oued bou Zekour. The zone named extra-urban shall include the whole of the territory situated outside the first-named zone.

At Tangier the police shall be organised in the urban zone by Spanish instructors, and in the extra-urban zone by French instructors.

At Casablanca, the police shall be organised in the urban zone by French instructors and in the extra-urban zone by Spanish instructors.

Article 2.

At Tangier and Casablanca the officer instructor of the force charged with policing the extra-urban zone shall be superior in rank to the instructor of the force charged with policing the urban zone.

When the interests of public safety necessitate the co-operation of the two forces, the assistance which the instructors shall lend to the Morocco Authorities (Art[icle] 4 of the Algeciras Act) shall be regulated in the following manner :

In operations in the extra-urban zone and as regards the assistance required from the urban force, the instructor highest in rank of the extra-urban police shall be in command.

In the case of operations in the urban zone when it is necessary to have recourse to a portion of the extra-urban force, the instructor of the urban police shall be in command.

Except in these cases, the urban and extra-urban police, organised according to art[icle]s 1 and 4, shall carry out their duties separately. Measures shall be adopted with a view to securing the agreement of the regulations and ordinances to be applied to the urban and extra-urban zones of each of the towns for the organization and working of the police.

The senior officer at Tangier and Casablanca shall have the rank of commandant.

Article 3.

At Tangier and Casablanca the urban police will consist for the most part of infantry; the extra-urban police will be mostly composed of cavalry.

Article 4.

The total effective strength of the police force which is to be organised in the 8 Moorish ports, open to trade, will amount to 2,500 men. The number of officer-instructors belonging to the two countries will be 20; that of the non-commissioned officer-instructors 40.

In accordance with the prescriptions of the general act of the Algeciras Conference, the police will be distributed as follows :—

At Tangier. 200 men, 2 officers and 4 non-commissioned officers in the urban zone.

400 men with 3 officers and 6 non-commissioned officers in the extra-urban zone.

At Casablanca. 100 men, 1 officer and 2 non-commissioned officers in the urban zone.

300 men, 2 officers and 4 non-commissioned officers in the extra-urban zone.

At Tetuan and Larache. 500 men, 4 officers and 7 non-commissioned officers.

At Rabat, Saffi, Mazagan and Mogador. 1,000 men, 8 officers and 17 non-commissioned officers.

Article 5.

The Spanish and the French instructor of highest rank, designated by Article 4 of the Algeciras Act to determine, in conjunction with the Shereefian Minister of War or his delegate and the Inspector, the regulations and arrangements necessary to ensure the recruiting, discipline, instruction and administration of the police corps, will be in constant communication for this purpose as well as in regard to the conditions of the contract to be drawn up between the instructors and the Maghzen.

Article 6.

All differences between the instructors of the 2 countries in regard to their reciprocal powers, will be settled by the French and Spanish diplomatic representatives at Tangier in the spirit of cordial harmony which happily presides over the relations between France and Spain in respect to affairs in Morocco.

In faith of which the undersigned, duly authorized to that effect, &c.

Done, in duplicate, at Paris, February 23, 1907.

(sig) F. de Leon y Castillo.   (sig) S. Pichon.

Additional Article (Secret).

Should circumstances arise in the urban zone to necessitate the concentration of the larger portion of both forces, the French and Spanish Ministers will have to agree upon the share which each will have to take in the command (los Ministros de España y de Francia deberan ponerse de acuerdo acerca del concurso que haya de prestarse al mando).

No. 83.

Sir F. Bertie to Sir Edward Grey.

F.O. 371/291.
36844/32288/07/28 A.
(No. 533.)   Confidential.   *Paris, D. November* 6, 1907.
Sir,   R. *November* 8, 1907.

I had been invited to shoot at Marly to-day with the President of the Republic and I knew that I should meet the Minister for Foreign Affairs, but as I did not feel at all sure that he would be able to give me details of the negotiations at Rabat between the French Minister and the Sultan of Morocco I requested Mr. Lister to endeavour to ascertain them from the Political Director at the Ministry for Foreign Affairs. I have the honour to transmit to you herewith a copy of a Memorandum by Mr. Lister of his conversation with Monsieur Louis.

At Marly I inquired of Monsieur Pichon whether the negotiations at Rabat had been satisfactory to the French Government, and on his replying in the affirmative I asked him whether he could give me any details. His Excellency said that he would be happy to do so for your confidential information. On the way back to Paris he told me that he would desire Monsieur Louis to give me full particulars as he himself would be in the country to-morrow shooting.

Mr. Lister's Memorandum supplies that information.

[I have, &c.]
FRANCIS BERTIE.

Enclosure in No. 83.

Memorandum by Mr. Lister.

In the course of conversation with the Political Director of the Ministry for Foreign Affairs to-day I enquired whether the French Government were satisfied with the course of the negotiations on which Monsieur Regnault had been engaged with the Sultan of Morocco at Rabat. Monsieur Louis replied in the affirmative. The results he said would be published in the Yellow Book on Morocco, but the importance of the points gained would be minimized, in order not to create fresh difficulties for the Sultan with his subjects. He would however tell me in confidence that the Sultan had consented to recognize the Agreements of 1901 and 1902 with regard to the frontier, and had solemnly undertaken to enforce their provisions. This was really all that the French Government demanded and they were consequently very well satisfied. General Lyautey had taken part in the negotiations, and there was no doubt that his knowledge of Moorish mentality had contributed in no small measure to their success.

With regard to the punishment of the murderers of M. Charbonnier and Dr. Mauchamp, Monsieur Louis hoped that the Sultan would continue in his present frame of mind, and eventually give satisfaction to the French demands, but of course for the moment nothing could be done at Marrakesh.

The position in the South, he said, had improved, to judge by the various reports which reached the Ministry. Caid Anflous a "mauvais garnement" but none the less a dangerous enemy had deserted Mulay Hafid, and other desertions had followed. He attributed this more satisfactory state of affairs to the presence of Ben Ghazi, one of the few men of vigour round the Sultan, who had been sent to Mogador at the request of Monsieur Regnault.

There was no doubt that it was impossible to exaggerate the penury of the Sultan. A few millions of francs had been advanced to him indirectly by the French Government through the State Bank, the Société Algérienne etc., and precautions had been taken to insure it's [*sic*] being spent on the purposes for which it was intended, but this state of affairs could not go on indefinitely and a loan was absolutely necessary.

The pacification around Casablanca seemed to be progressing but slowly, the position being complicated by the fact that on the one hand the emissaries of Abd el Aziz were men of no vigour, and on the other many of the neighbouring tribes were in constant contact with Mulay Hafid.

Paris, November 6th, 1907.

No. 84.

Sir Edward Grey to Sir F. Bertie.

F.O. 371/289.
37053/27896/07/28.
(No. 624.)

Sir,   *Foreign Office, November 11, 1907.*

The French Ambassador called at this Office on the 8th instant and read to Sir Charles Hardinge the reply of the German Gov[ernmen]t to the Franco-Spanish proposal for the institution of an international commission to enquire into the claims arising out of the disturbances at Casablanca in August last.

The German note drew attention to the fact that a German Commission had already been appointed to enquire into the losses sustained by German subjects at Casablanca and that certain sums had already been advanced as first assistance to the most needy of the German claimants.

As regards the Franco-Spanish proposal, the German Gov[ernmen]t agreed to adhere to it on condition :—

1. That all claims accepted and fixed by the German Commission should be accepted without question and without revision by the International Commission, and
2. That any ulterior claims which might be presented by German subjects should be presented to and accepted by the International Commission on the same basis of evaluation.

M. Cambon said that the French Gov[ernmen]t considered these conditions quite inadmissible and that they intended to send him further instructions after consultation with the Spanish Gov[ernmen]t.

In reply to H[is] E[xcellency]'s invitation to express his opinion upon the attitude of the German Gov[ernmen]t, Sir C. Hardinge said that his own personal view was that German claims had no right to a privileged position and that he was unable to understand for what reason the British Delegate on the proposed International Commission should be compelled to accept a valuation of German claims made by a German Commission, whilst the German delegate was permitted to have a voice in the estimation of British claims. For this reason Sir C. Hardinge said that he regarded the German conditions as impossible of acceptance.

[I am, &c.
E. GREY.]

No. 85.

Sir Edward Grey to Count de Salis.

F.O. 371/289.
37768/27896/07/28.
(No. 329.)

Sir,   *Foreign Office, November 13, 1907.*

In the course of my conversation with Herr von Schoen at Windsor([1]) last night I spoke on the subject of the Casa Blanca claims, and explained that the German

([1]) [The subject of the visit of the Emperor William II to Windsor in November 1907 is treated in *Gooch & Temperley*, Vol. VI, pp. 78–107.]

condition would turn the International Commission into a mere clerk for registering claims.

We had been bound to accept the proposal of an International Commission, because of the precedent we ourselves had set with regard to the Alexandria claims.

But if German claims were to be admitted without discussion, and yet the German Representative was to have a voice in settling British claims, the position would be one which we could not accept.

Herr von Schoen said his difficulty was that the Germans had already established a Commission. He could not dissolve it, or stop its work : in fact, he would be thrown out if he attempted to do so.

I suggested that it might be possible to find some compromise by which the investigations of the German Commission on questions of fact would be accepted by the International Commission, and by which it would be left to the latter commission to decide on what principles compensation should be fixed and paid. This, however, was a matter to be discussed with the French and Spanish Governments.

[I am, &c.]
E. G[REY].

No. 86.

Sir Edward Grey to Count de Salis.

F.O: 371/292.
37769/37769/07/28.
(No. 330.)

Sir,   *Foreign Office, November* 13, 1907.

In the course of my conversation with Herr von Schoen at Windsor last night I told him, with regard to the general relations between the two countries, that since the Algeciras Conference those relations had been gradually improving.

But, as Herr von Schoen knew, we had an Agreement with France to give her diplomatic support in Morocco, and when difficulties arose there between France and Germany it made things difficult between Germany and us.

Herr von Schoen said, without hesitation, and very decidedly, that Germany did not intend to make difficulties in Morocco. He spoke of this in a friendly and decided tone, as if he wished to dissipate any anxiety on that point, and did not feel any himself.[1]

[I am, &c.]
E. G[REY].

[1] [For Herr von Schoen's report, *v. G.P.,* XXIV, pp. 17–21.]

No. 87.

Sir G. Lowther to Sir Edward Grey.

F.O. 371/292.
40914/40914/07/28.
(No. 469.)   *Tangier, D. December* 4, 1907.
Sir,   R. *December* 14, 1907.

French Troops have now been at Casablanca for four months and French men-of-war at all ports of Morocco, and it is not unreasonable to ask what has been the result of all this expenditure, and if a negative one, wherein lie the reasons and what is the remedy for the situation.

A study of the Yellow Book published last month will undoubtedly bring home to the reader the conviction that recent French policy in Morocco, with the exception perhaps of the precipitate landing of the insufficient force at Casablanca, has been marked by a certain timidity and prudence carried almost to excess. There has hardly been a corner of the Empire in which France has not had just grievances. The action of the tribes on the Algero-Moroccan frontier, the openly-declared anti-French attitude of Ma-el-Ainin in Mauritania with scarcely veiled threats of a holy war on the Senegal frontier. The murder here of Charbonnier and that of Doctor Mauchamp at Marakech; the attempted assassination of de Gironcourt at Fez, and finally the brutal murders of the French workmen at Casablanca. All these grievances have remained without any satisfaction being accorded. France has had to content herself with promises alone, and these given with a very bad grace. Indeed to these provocations might be added the suspicion that some of the crimes occurred with the support, or at least the silent acquiescence, of the Makhzen Authorities.

The apparent long-suffering attitude displayed by France, which by the people of this country is freely construed into one of timidity, has not failed to give the Arabs encouragement. It cannot truly be said that there is any strong fanatical feeling among the people of Morocco, but a fanatical cry has been raised to incite the lukewarm to join in resisting what all believe to be an intention on the part of the French to secure, slowly perhaps, but surely their country. To these must be added a large number whose only desire is to see disorder rife under a weak Makhzen, and consequently immunity from all taxation and a free hand to plunder. To nearly all it is immaterial who their Sultan may be. No feeling that can be construed into loyalty exists for the reigning Sultan or his brother on the part of their respective adherents.

Little support has been given by foreigners living in Morocco to French penetration. Firms long established here having time-worn relations with the native traders have adapted themselves to their special systems of doing business, and see with distrust and doubt the advent of a new organization which will inevitably be counter to that which commends itself to their conservative ideas. They fear and they judge by reports of experiences of others elsewhere that, with a French control of the Customs Houses, instead of having to deal with pliable Moorish Officials, they would come into contact with French controllers who might be apt to discriminate in favour of citizens of their own nationality to the disadvantage of other foreign merchants.

The result of all this is that anarchy, which has been for some years dormant with occasional explosions, is now general throughout the Empire and that the number of tribes over which the Sultan had still some semblance of authority has dwindled almost to vanishing point. Endless are the reasons which have produced this distressing state of affairs. Indecision and a marked antipathy for warfare on the part of the present Sultan; incapacity and dishonesty on the part of his Viziers and Governors have gradually encouraged the tribes to resist authority and to refuse to contribute to the Exchequer.

Whether the Sultan Abdul Aziz succeeds in maintaining himself on the throne or whether his brother Mulai Hafid[1] is successful in deposing him, there appears to be no remedy to the present disorder but intervention of some kind. The period of "pacific penetration," so glibly spoken of as a panacea seems to have passed and to have proved a failure. To continue providing the Sultan with doles of money which are wasted on armies whose men desert and sell their arms at the first sound of battle to the nearest tribesmen will not restore the country to order. To land a few men at different ports and endeavour to strike terror into the people by the presence of battleships will affect no one living outside the walls of the threatened towns. Of this we have had ample evidence at Casablanca where, after four months, it may be said that the effect produced on the tribes has been merely one of a necessity for caution in attack, and the conviction has been borne in upon them that the French are unable to leave their base. Casablanca has momentarily been ruined, the neighbouring tribes will lose this year's crops, but no fear or respect has been

(1) [Mulai Hafid proclaimed himself Sultan instead of his brother on August 17, 1907.]

instilled into them, and Casablanca threatens to drift into a position analogous to one of the Spanish Presidios on the Mediterranean Coast.

That there should be a marked hesitation on the part of France to embark on a policy which might entail a military expedition into the interior on a large scale is comprehensible, but I am inclined to the belief that this would not be necessary. France might adopt the system followed with success by previous Sultans, namely by severely punishing those tribes which, having acquired wealth, show signs of too great an independence; but the lesson should be a severe one, and the punishment once inflicted on the tribes in the immediate hinterland of the coast ports, should prove so salutary that a frequent repetition would hardly be required.

To this it may be objected that such action would hardly be in accordance with the provisions of the Act of Algeciras, but in face of the repeated grievances suffered by France, some efforts in obtaining redress could hardly meet with general objection, but it is outside my province to examine into the nature and strength of the opposition that might be raised.

Sultan Abdul Aziz has, it may be said, proved himself incapable of restoring order in his country in spite of the gold furnished to him with the assistance of France, and the fact that even His Majesty's jewels have been engaged would indicate that there are no other resources available. Consequently a more vigorous assistance is absolutely indispensable if Abdul Aziz is to be seriously supported, and it is questionable whether the apparent hesitation of France will eventually prove of advantage either to herself or to this country.

I have, &c.
GERARD LOWTHER.

II.—THE RECOGNITION OF MULAI HAFID.

[*ED. NOTE.*—For the subject of this section *cp. G.P.*, XXIV, ch. 181, and *Livre Jaune, Affaires du Maroc*, IV and V, (1907–8 and 1908–10).]

No. 88.

Sir Edward Grey to Sir M. de Bunsen.

F.O. 371/484.
2775/1581/08/28.
(No. 13.)
Sir,   *Foreign Office, January 22, 1908.*

The Spanish Ambassador spoke to me to-day at great length about Morocco. He said that France was supporting the present Sultan in various ways, and Spain did not wish to be brought into the quarrel between the Sultan and his rival; but she had no objection to France continuing to give support to the Sultan, as at present, by ways that did not appear.

I said I was sure France did not wish to be drawn into an expedition into the interior of Morocco; that would be entirely contrary to M. Clémenceau's policy; but she was taking steps to protect life and property in the sea ports.

The Ambassador then spoke of the Spanish apprehensions with regard to the action of Captain Fournier at Tangier. For a long time, he had done nothing there, but now he was drilling two or three thousand troops. The Spaniards considered that after their Secret Agreement with France, Captain Fournier ought not to have remained at Tangier. They considered it very undesirable that the interests of France should be strengthened in this way in parts of Morocco which would fall to Spain under the

Secret Agreement. They would have no objection if Captain Fournier drilled troops in other places. They considered that his doing so at Tangier would be contrary to the Algeciras Act, and his action would certainly throw into the shade the 250 police which were to be established there under Spanish auspices. Spain had consented to the joint policing force at Tangier in order not to reveal any thing about the Secret Agreement, and it would be unfair that alongside the 250 police there should be 2000 or 3000 troops under French Officers. His Government were very anxious to have my advice.

I said I understood that the French Government had given explanations to the Spanish Government about the matter. I could not see that the Secret Agreement would be impaired by any thing which might happen before it came into force. It would come into force only if Morocco was partitioned, and the fact that a French Officer who was in the employ of the Sultan was drilling troops in the Tangier district now could not prejudice the rights of Spain if the Sultan's authority disappeared and that part of Morocco was handed over to Spanish occupation. Under our Agreement with France about Morocco, nothing had been reserved to us similar to what had been reserved to Spain under her agreement with France, and yet France had never raised any objection to the position of Kaid Maclean, or claimed that it was inconsistent with the Agreement.

The Spanish Ambassador still maintained that a strong French party would be created in Tangier, and that would be injurious to Spain should that part of Morocco fall to her. He urged as an illustration that, even if the British occupation was withdrawn from Egypt to-morrow, the fact of our having been in occupation would give us great influence in Egypt.

I said I did not think there was an analogy between the two cases. As a matter of fact, if the British occupation were to be withdrawn to-morrow, and not only that but succeeded by the occupation of another Power in the same way as Spain would occupy the Tangier district, the British influence in Egypt would not be worth much. I further reminded the Ambassador that I heard it was an understanding that, as long as Morocco remained independent, the special diplomatic position of Tangier should continue to be recognised.

The Ambassador said this was the case, but Spain considered that France should not have a superior force in the district.

I told him I could only say, at present, that I understood what the Spanish susceptibilities in the matter were.

[I am, &c.]
E. G[REY].

No. 89.

Sir Edward Grey to Sir F. Bertie.

F.O. 371/484.
2656/2656/09/28.
(No. 40.)
Sir,   *Foreign Office, January* 27, 1908.

The French Ambassador called at this Office on the 22nd instant, and stated that the German Chargé d'Affaires at Paris had told Monsieur Pichon that the German Minister at Tangier had received a communication from Sultan Abdul Aziz asking for the intervention of Germany to prevent France from violating the Treaty of Algeciras. Baron Rosen had been instructed to reply that if there had been violations of the Treaty of Algeciras by France the proper course would be for the Sultan to warn all the Signatory Powers and not to address himself to Germany alone. If, however, the Sultan would specify in what the violation consists, the German Government would mention it to the French Government.

The German Chargé d'Affaires further informed Monsieur Pichon that Baron Rosen had received a message from Mulai Hafid asking that the German Government would prevent the French from supporting his brother in the struggle now going on between them.

Monsieur Pichon told the German Chargé d'Affaires, in reply, that the French Government had in no sense violated the Treaty of Algeciras and that it is their firm intention to act strictly within its limits. They had no idea of making a serious expedition into the interior or of occupying Fez or Marakesh. Their intention was to limit their action to the coast towns and to take steps for the protection of the lives and property of Europeans.

As regards Mulai Hafid, the French Government had, Monsieur Pichon observed, assumed an attitude of complete reserve towards the Sultan Abdul Aziz and would take no part in the struggle. The German Government should remember that the Sultan Abdul Aziz was still the recognised Sovereign, while Mulai Hafid represented revolutionary fanaticism, and that if in the end Mulai Hafid should succeed in overthrowing his brother, the result could only be complete chaos in Morocco.

The German Chargé d'Affaires was referred to a complete statement which Monsieur Pichon said he intended to make in the Chamber of Deputies on the 24th instant.

[I am, &c.
E. GREY.]

No. 90.

Sir Edward Grey to Sir M. de Bunsen.

F.O. 371/485.
4711/4711/08/28.
(No. 19.)
Sir,   *Foreign Office, February 7, 1908.*
I had some further conversation with the Spanish Ambassador to-day on the subject of Morocco.

He explained to me that some time ago the Germans had represented to him that, after the Anglo-French Agreement of 1904 was made, Spain would get on very well with France as long as she had German support, by which she could be backed in differences with France; and that, as England was coming to terms with France, England would naturally take the French side, and Spain would not get such effective support from her as she could get from Germany.

The Ambassador told me that he had considered that the relations of Spain with France could not be comfortable if Spain was backed by any one who was on bad terms with France, and he had therefore preferred the present situation.

I said I thought Spain was much safer under the present arrangement. The result of the Algeciras Conference had been that she and France were now two partners in a special position in Morocco. It was much better for her to be thus in Morocco with a partner with whom she had a satisfactory Secret Agreement than to have other Powers, with whom she had no arrangement, brought into Morocco.

As far as we were concerned, our only desire was to see things work smoothly between Spain and France. We had no other object in view, and there was no price to pay for our friendship.

[I am, &c.]
E. G[REY].

No. 91.

Mr. Herbert White to Mr. Crowe.

F.O. 371/485.
7417/7417/08/28.
Dear Mr. Crowe, *Tangier, February* **23,** 1908.

I enclose herewith extracts from a letter I have received from Dr. Verdon, to whom the Sultan sometimes talks very freely. The points mentioned by him are not new, but I was not aware that Mr. Regnault held any formal document in regard to them under the Sultan's seal.

1. We reported some time since that Commandant Fariau, Chief of the French Military Mission at the Court, is acting as Financial Adviser until the appointment of a Civilian.

2. This would appear to show that the Spaniards have some cause for their uneasiness at the training of Moorish troops here by Commandant Fournié.

The Germans will not be pleased if the services of these officers are dispensed with, but it will be difficult for them to insist on their retention.

Presumably the French would be glad to see Maclean leave also. He is quite ready to retire if a good pension is offered to him. I propose, at his suggestion, to mention the matter privately to Count St. Aulaire.

3. I do not understand how this can be in view of the formal arrangement with Spain, which has been accepted by the Powers.

4. M. Guiot informed me of this some time ago, the idea being that his department (representing the Bond Holders) who already have the control of the Custom Houses, should undertake that of the lighter service. He however went fully into the matter, having returned from Paris for the purpose, and came to the conclusion that it would be better to have nothing to do with it. The service can only be carried on at a loss to the Government, and is bristling with difficulties and troublesome questions, and he advised M. Regnault to let the matter drop.

The Marchica affair has caused some stir. I hear from Dr. Verdon that the French object to the action of Spain, and it is probably on their private representations that the Moorish Government have been so energetic in their protests. I cannot help thinking, however, that the denials of the Court both as to the appeal to Germany and as to the Marchica affair are no more true than their old denial of the request to Maclean to obtain protection for Menebhi. They are always ready to deny anything they have agreed to verbally, if subsequently found to be inconvenient.

It seems quite possible that M. Regnault will return to Rabat for a short time, as requested by the Sultan. M. Gaillard, French Consul at Rabat, told Dr. Verdon that he hoped he would come.

The French have had some more serious fighting lately. Madden thinks their forces will have to be considerably strengthened, though he believes they must now have about 14,000 men there—more than they give out.

I hear that our Casablanca merchants are much upset over the deduction of 5 per cent. from the amounts they may be awarded as compensation for their losses. They say that they will in any case be heavy losers and they consider the cost of the enquiry should be born[e] by the Moorish Government and not by them. None of the principal merchants have yet signed the undertaking, but doubtless wiser counsels will prevail and they will eventually sign. I have only received a private letter on the subject from Madden yet, but presume I shall shortly receive a despatch, copy of which I will forward.

Dr. Verdon has sent me, for delivery to Kaid Maclean to forward to Raisuli, the Sultan's reply to the latter's letter, copy of which went by last bag. The letter is closed, so I do not know its contents, but Verdon says it is "a nice letter."

Yours sincerely,
HERBERT WHITE.

Enclosure in No. 91.

Dr. Verdon to Mr. White.

Extracts. *Rabat, February* 11, 1908.

The Sultan cannot understand the lack of energy on the part of the French, and yesterday he got very excited and told me the following facts, which I believe were to be kept private until the loan was settled. I beg you will regard them as private, as I do not wish the Sultan to know that I have told anyone.

When M. Regnault was in Rabat he obtained a written promise or agreement from the Sultan, sealed with the Sultan's seal, stating that—

1. The French should administer the finances of the Moorish Government for a certain number of years.
2. The Sultan's army to be trained by Frenchmen only, the two German Officers in the Moorish service to leave; also a force of three to four thousand men to be formed at Tangier and to be trained by Frenchmen only, not by Spaniards.
3. The control of the contraband of arms to be entirely in the hands of the French.
4. The lighter service of the ports to be in the hands of the French.

There were other clauses in the agreement, but the Sultan led me to understand that the above were the more important.

The Sultan complains that the French did not keep the agreement private, and that one of M. Regnault's Secretaries told a Moor that the finances were to be under French control, and the Moor informed Kitani, and this was the cause of Kitani's action at Fez. . . . .

P.S.—I have just returned from the Palace. . . . . The Sultan told me not to mention to anyone our conversation of yesterday in regard to the secret agreement between M. Regnault and himself. He said he ought not to have told me, but he was excited at the time. I feel it my duty to tell you; I am sure you will be careful that no one else at Tangier gets the information.

MINUTES.

1. We know about.
2. It will be difficult for the French to justify their respect for the Algeciras Act if they wish to exercise exclusive control over the force to be raised at Tangier.
3. This may be a mistake. The Spaniards are quite unlikely to take any active part in controlling the contraband trade themselves; and great opposition would surely be aroused if the joint control were to be abandoned in favour of France alone.
4. Commercial Dep[artmen]t.
Our merchants apparently consider that there *is* something to be made out of the lighter service, and M. Guiot apparently that there is not.
As regards the deduction of 5% from the amount awarded to the claimants at Casablanca this sum has been fixed upon, by precedent, to pay the expenses of the British Rep[resentati]ve on the International Commission.

G. S. S.

The information is highly interesting. It tends to show that the French are not acting straightforwardly towards the Spaniards. But they will no doubt contend that the training of the Moorish *army* is a thing quite apart from the organisation of the *police*. And it must be admitted that there is nothing in the Algeciras Act to prevent the appointment by the Sultan of French officers to the command of his troops. Nor can it be strictly speaking claimed that such an arrangement would violate the spirit of the preamble of the Algeciras Act which lays down that the reforms in Morocco must be based " on the triple principle of the sovereignty and independence of H.M. the Sultan, the integrity of his dominions, and economic liberty without any inequality." No part of this triple principle is violated by the French having the most complete control of the army so long as this is freely accorded by the Sultan and subject to being revoked by him. There were until quite recently two Prussian officers in the Sultan's service, and, to quote a somewhat analogous case, there is a guard of Persian cossacks under Russian officers at Tehran.

On the other hand it is difficult to understand how, consistently with the Algeciras Act, the control of the contraband-of-arms supervision service can be placed in French hands. We cannot however criticise such an arrangement without being in possession of the full particulars of the scheme.

It is significant that the French have kept us in the dark as regards the existence of this agreement. This is quite in accord with their general attitude towards us. But perhaps it is as well that we should be, officially, and so far as France is concerned, in ignorance of arrangements which, if we were cognizant of them, might compel us to disapprove.

Qu[ery]. Copy Paris, Secret, and thank Mr. White for his communication assuring him that the information will be regarded as strictly confidential.

E. A. C.
March 3.

It is only natural that the French should wish to get rid of the German officers with the Moorish Army, and they can fairly argue that Commandant Fournié's force is quite distinct from the Police.

It has always been expected that they would do most of the work respecting contraband as the Spaniards entered unwillingly into the arrangement for joint control. As, however, the arrangement exists one can only believe that the Sultan has not correctly described this part of his new agreement with the French, or that it applies to arrangements which are to come into force after the joint control is at an end.

The action about Mar Chica is most unfriendly to the Spaniards, and seems unnecessary as Mar Chica is in the Spanish sphere.

W. L.

It is a pity that the troops organised by French officers are not kept at places within the French sphere. This sort of news if it reaches the Spaniards must excite distrust.

C. H.
E. G.

This also is the sort of thing which however technically justifiable—for the reasons given by Mr. Crowe in his minute—would be eagerly seized hold of by the Germans, if they wished to find a stick wherewith to beat the French and themselves get clear of the Algeciras Act.

F.

No. 92.

Sir F. Lascelles to Sir Edward Grey.

F.O. 371/484.
10718/2656/08/28A.
(No. 143.)   Confidential.   *Berlin, D. March 27, 1908.*
Sir,   R. *March 30, 1908.*

I had yesterday some conversation with my French colleague on the subject of the speeches on the Foreign Policy of Germany delivered by Prince Bülow and Herr von Schoen in the Reichstag on the 24th instant, a report of which I had the honour to forward to you in my despatch No. 132 of the 25th instant.(¹)

Mr. Cambon said he was completely satisfied with the language held by Prince Bülow and Herr von Schoen about Morocco. It was certainly intended to be conciliatory and he trusted it would be considered so in Paris. Herr von Schoen had previously informed him that a debate about Morocco was inevitable, and that it was probable that in the course of it, some of the speakers would severely criticize the action of France in that country. He himself would be called upon to reply and he would do his utmost to do so in a conciliatory manner, although he would be bound to assert that the German Government would take care to safeguard German interests in Morocco. Herr von Schoen having noticed that Count Berckheim, the Councillor of the French Embassy, was present in the Reichstag during a speech, sent a message to him to ask him to come to his room, and then prepared a résumé of his speech, which he requested him to hand to Mr. Cambon, a civility with which Mr. Cambon was much gratified.

(¹) [Not reproduced.]

Mr. Cambon said in conclusion that he had sent a report to his Government to the effect that the German Government desired to deal with the Moroccan question in a conciliatory sense, and that he hoped that this would be recognised in Paris.

I told Mr. Cambon that the impression I had received on reading the speeches was that the German Government wished to convey their desire for friendly relations with France, and indeed for all other countries, but that I thought that His Serene Highness' remarks about Macedonia might have been couched in more fortunate language. Mr. Cambon agreed that Prince Bülow's observations as to the danger of introducing innovations into Macedonia, might be held to apply to the question of the nomination of a Governor General, but they were of a vague and general character and did not constitute a reply to your proposal.

It has occurred to me that Prince Bülow, who according to a statement in the papers is about to pay a visit to Baron d'Aehrenthal at Vienna may have been guided by a wish to indicate to that statesman that he might count upon the support of the German Government in his Macedonian Policy.

I have, &c.
FRANK C. LASCELLES.

No. 93.

Sir F. Lascelles to Sir Edward Grey.

F.O. 371/482.
16014/1013/08/28.
(No. 210.) Confidential.   Berlin, D. *May* 6, 1908.
Sir,   R. *May* 11, 1908.

With reference to my Telegram No. 14 of this day's date,([1]) I have the honour to report that the French Ambassador called upon me this morning and spoke at considerable length of the conversations he had recently had with Herr von Schoen with regard to the reception to be accorded to the emissaries of Mulai Hafid who were now on their way to Berlin. He had pointed out that Mulai Hafid was a rebel against his brother and had no power of appointing representatives to foreign powers. Herr von Schoen had agreed to this and said there could be no question of recognizing the emissaries or of giving them an official reception. At the same time it would be interesting to hear what they had to say, and although he would not receive them himself, he thought it would be advisable that the Under Secretary of State should do so. M. Cambon strongly demurred to this and urged that they should not be received either officially or officiously.

At a subsequent interview during which Herr von Schoen had shown considerable annoyance at an article which had appeared in the "Temps," and which M. Cambon himself considered unnecessarily violent and singularly inopportune, Herr von Schoen dwelt upon the difficult position in which he found himself. He had no wish to do anything which would add to the difficulties which France was encountering in Morocco, but at the same time he had to protect German interests. He had received reports from the German residents in Morocco to the effect that the chances of Mulai Hafid were quite as good as those of Abdul Aziz and that it would be little short of a calamity if the port of Saffi were to be recaptured for Abdul Aziz either by the French or by Abdul Aziz himself with French assistance. M. Cambon was able to reply that it was perfectly natural that the German residents should have reported in this sense. They were all traders, including the German Consul at Saffi, and as long as that port was in possession of Mulai Hafid, no customs dues were levied and the merchants, the great majority of whom at Saffi were Germans, were able

([1]) [Not reproduced as its tenour is indicated.]

to import their goods free of duty. They had taken full advantage of this privilege, and there could be no doubt that they had furnished Mulai Hafid with supplies including arms and ammunition. It was evident that they should wish this state of things to continue, although it might cause some embarrassment to the German Government, who could not divest themselves of responsibility for the acts of their subjects. Herr von Schoen also alluded to the unfavourable criticisms which had been made on the White Book, which has recently been published, and he feared that he would be violently attacked in the German Press unless he could show that he had not neglected German interests. M. Cambon replied that he certainly would never be able to make any one in Paris believe that the German Government were afraid of the German Press, and Herr von Schoen subsequently admitted that if he could show that the German Government had given proper protection to German interests, the Press would probably follow the indications which might be given to them. M. Cambon took note of the admission that there were circumstances under which the German Government gave "indications" to the Press.

A third conversation took place in which Herr von Schoen informed M. Cambon that it had now been arranged that Mulai Hafid's emissaries should be received not by him or Herr Stemrich but by the Secretary of the German Legation at Tangier, who happened to be in Berlin, and who spoke Arabic. M. Cambon asked that the reception should not take place at the Foreign Office but in the Secretary's private apartments, but Herr von Schoen pointed out that this would be impossible, as the apartments consisted of one room on the fourth floor of an hotel.

This was how the matter stood when Herr von Schoen had to leave Berlin to be in attendance on the Emperor at Vienna. M. Cambon is convinced that Herr von Schoen sincerely desires to avoid any action which would increase the difficulties of France in Morocco; he believes, though with less conviction, that Prince Bülow has the same desire, but he fears that there may be others in the Ministry of Foreign Affairs who would not be sorry to see those difficulties increased rather than diminished. He hopes however that the news of the occupation of Saffi by the forces of Abdul Aziz, which reached Berlin after Herr von Schoen's departure, may induce Mulai Hafid's emissaries to give up their journey and to return to Morocco at once. If, however, they should come to Berlin, and call upon the Ambassadors, what attitude should I adopt? He himself would certainly refuse to receive them.

I replied that it was out of the question that they should be received in any official capacity, but that if they expressed a wish to call upon me, I should be disposed to treat the visit as a private one, but that I would apply to you for instructions as to how I should act.

I have, &c.
FRANK C. LASCELLES.

No. 94.

Sir F. Lascelles to Sir Edward Grey.

F.O. 371/486.
18740/18740/08/28.
(No. 247.) Confidential.   *Berlin, D. May* 27, 1908.
Sir,   R. *June* 1, 1908.

M. Cambon informed me yesterday that on the previous evening he had called upon Herr von Schoen to communicate to him, by order of his Government, the instructions recently given to General d'Amade to abstain from further military operations and to make preparations for the eventual withdrawal of the French troops from Morocco. It was intended to leave military posts composed of French and Moroccan troops at certain places in the Schauja territory which should by degrees be left entirely in the hands of Moroccan troops. M. Cambon had been careful to point out that the instructions to General d'Amade were a proof of the desire of the French Government to withdraw their troops from Morocco but that it was not to be expected that they would be able to do so at once; indeed he feared that some considerable time would elapse before they found themselves in a position to carry out their intentions.

A report having reached M. Cambon that a representation was likely to be made to the German Government to induce them to recognise Mulai Hafid as Sultan of Morocco, he thought it advisable to return to the Foreign Office yesterday, Herr von Schoen's reception day, for the purpose of drawing His Excellency's attention to this report. He argued that it would not be competent for one of the Signatory Powers of the Act of Algeciras to recognise a successor to Abdul Aziz with whom the Act had been concluded, without the consent of the other Signatories. It was of course possible that Abdul Aziz should cease to be Sultan of Morocco; he might die; he might abdicate after being defeated by Mulai Hafid, but even if he disappeared altogether it would be necessary for all the Signatories of the Algeciras Act to agree as to whom they would recognize as his successor. It was by no means certain that Mulai Hafid, even if he should be successful against Abdul Aziz, would be able to consolidate his power in Morocco to such an extent as to make it advisable to recognise him as Sultan. If therefore one of the Powers were to recognise him without consulting the others, it would be open to any of them to put forward a rival candidate. It was possible that the Spaniards might prefer El Roghi, who exercised considerable Authority in the neighbourhood of Melilla, and it was conceivable that the French might prefer the Shereef of Wazan who was a personage of great importance.

M. Cambon thoroughly believes that Herr von Schoen, and indeed the German Government as a whole, are sincere in their desire that the Moroccan questions should not give rise to further complications, and would be glad to see the difficulties with which France has to contend removed, so that she should be able to carry out her intention of withdrawing her troops, and he hopes that the warning he has given against the premature recognition of Mulai Hafid by the German Government alone, may not remain without effect.

I have, &c.
FRANK C. LASCELLES.

No. 95.

Mr. White to Sir Edward Grey.

F.O. 371/487.   *Tangier, August* 31, 1908.
30358/30358/08/28.   D. 6·45 P.M.
Tel. (No. 53.)   R. 9·30 P.M.

I am informed that Dr. Vassel has left for Fez to-day, to resume his duties as German Consul there. His departure was kept secret by the German Legation. Preparations for journey have been made very secretly.

MINUTES.

In June last Mulai Hafid asked the Powers to send back Cons[ula]r officers and lady doctors to Fez. It was decided here that it would be premature to do so, but we communicated with the French Gov[ernmen]t, who promised to let us know if and when they sent back their Consul to Fez.

M. Regnault is no doubt as well aware as Mr. White of this latest German move and will have reported it to his Gov[ernmen]t. Until Mulai Hafid has been recognized the French will not send their Consul to Fez, and we need not move till they do.

G. H. V.
1.9.08.

This is a piece of sharp practice on the part of Germany. She wishes to be first in with Mulai Hafid. The proceeding is all the more irregular because all the foreign representatives are still accredited to Abdul Aziz.

Dr. Vassel has been the German representative on the Casablanca claims commission, and Mr. Thorne, our commissioner, has told me he has no words for the unscrupulous and " dirty " manner in which Dr. Vassel has acted in regard to German and Austrian claims. He lived with an uncle, who is one of the principal German claimants at Casablanca. At any rate Dr. Vassel will not be missed there.

E. A. C.
Sept. 1.

No action is required.

F. A. C.
1.9.
E. G.

No. 96.

Sir F. Bertie to Sir Edward Grey.

F.O. 371/483.
30579/1013/08/28A.
(No. 328.)   *Paris,* D. *September* 2, 1908.
Sir,   R. *September* 3, 1908.

I have the honour to transmit to you herewith the text of a communiqué which has appeared in the " Temps " of this evening's issue relative to the question of recognising Mulai Hafid as Sultan of Morocco.

The communiqué states that in view of the attitude of Germany towards this question as set forth in the " North German Gazette," and in view of the insinuations as to France's attitude contained in the note published by that journal, it is necessary to affirm the principles which have decided the French Government's point of view. These principles, which are four in number, are stated categorically. The view on these four points adopted by France and Spain is known to all the Governments, and has hitherto met with no objection from the German Government.

I have, &c.
FRANCIS BERTIE.

Enclosure in No. 96.

Extract from " Le Temps " of September 3, 1908.

LA FRANCE, L'ALLEMAGNE ET LE MAROC.

La note de la *Gazette de l'Allemagne du Nord*, complétée par les commentaires des journaux allemands que nous avons donnés plus haut, semble indiquer que si l'Allemagne insiste pour la prompte reconnaissance (*rasche Anerkennung*) de Moulaï Hafid, c'est que la France se serait dérobée à cette reconnaissance, en manœuvrant avec une lenteur calculée pour maintenir une situation équivoque.

En présence de cette insinuation, nous avons cru devoir préciser nettement l'attitude de la France depuis que la question s'est posée. Voici, à ce sujet, les renseignements qui nous ont été fournis.

Dès le lendemain de la proclamation de Moulaï Hafid à Tanger, la France, qui, par l'organe de M. Regnault, avait répondu à Mnebhi et à El Guebbas qu'elle se désintéressait de la question dynastique et n'exigeait que le maintien de l'ordre, a précisé son point de vue dans les affirmations suivantes :

1. *Il est nécessaire que les puissances étudient d'abord les garanties à obtenir pour les intérêts européens.*
2. *L'entente des puissances sur ces garanties est aussi nécessaire que ces garanties elles-mêmes.*

[19656]   G 2

3. *Il y a encore trop d'inconnu dans la situation intérieure du Maroc pour qu'une décision puisse être prise avant complète information.*

4. *Sous ces réserves, la France n'a montré à aucun moment le parti pris de ne pas reconnaître Moulaï Hafid. Elle entend seulement que sa situation de fait soit précisée.*

La France et l'Espagne ont, dès le 26 août, envisagé ces quatre propositions pour soumettre aux puissances les conclusions qu'elles devaient leur suggérer.

Leur point de vue ainsi défini, est connu de toutes les chancelleries.

Il n'avait provoqué jusqu'ici aucune objection du gouvernement allemand.

MINUTES.

An important communiqué.

The views of the French Gov[ernmen]t were of course known to H[is] M[ajesty's] Gov[ernmen]t, but it is a good thing that they should be stated in the press.

It appears that the latest German move was instigated by the Spanish Gov[ernmen]t.

G. H. V.
3.9.08.

The action of the German gov[ernmen]t is likely to produce again a state of considerable tension.

It seems clear that that action is designed to serve the interests of the German parliamentary situation in the first instance. The recent articles in the Frankfort Gazette to which Sir F. Oppenheimer drew attention dwelt strongly on the necessity for Prince Bülow's "doing something" to show the people that Germany was successful in some one thing in the world of foreign politics. Any act of aggressiveness in Morocco or against France anywhere will always be popular in Germany and it seems not far fetched to read in the latest phase of German policy in Morocco the answer of Prince Bülow to the challenge of the Frankfurt Gazette— unless, which is not at all impossible, the whole scheme, including the articles in that paper, which nominally attacked him, emanated in its entirety from Prince Bülow himself.

In any case it seems to me that we are face to face with a situation resembling that which preceded the fall of M. Delcassé, and we may expect the beginning of another dose of bullying administered to the French gov[ernmen]t. It is all the more important in these circumstances that France and the Powers which support her should be most careful to make no mistake and to do strictly what is right internationally. So far it looks as if Germany would again place herself technically in the wrong.

E. A. C.
Sept. 3.

I should say Germany had already placed herself in the wrong. She ought not to have sent her Consul back to Fez without any consultation with the Powers interested, and she ought surely before launching and publishing her proposal to recognize the new Sultan to have sounded the French and Spanish Gov[ernmen]ts.

F. A. C.
3.9.
E. G.

No. 97.

Mr. Wyndham to Sir Edward Grey.

F.O. 371/483.
30694/1013/08/28A.
Tel. (No. 35.)

Rome, September 3, 1908.
D. 6 P.M.
R. 11·20 P.M.

Morocco.

French Chargé d'Affaires tells me that the German Chargé d'Affaires has suggested to the Italian Government desirability of recognition of Mulai Hafid.

No. 98.

Sir F. Bertie to Sir Edward Grey.

F.O. 371/483.
30703/1013/08/28A.
(No. 335.) Confidential.
Sir,

Paris, D. September 3, 1908.
R. September 4, 1908.

When I called on the Minister for Foreign Affairs yesterday afternoon by appointment to speak to him on matters concerning Turkey, I found him in a state of irritation at the statements made in the German inspired Press in regard to an immediate recognition of Mulai Hafid as Sultan of Morocco, and at an official communication made in his absence from Paris to the Political Director by the German Chargé d'Affaires expressing the opinion of the German Government that in the interest of the pacification of Morocco Mulai Hafid should be recognised at once. His Excellency had, he told me, hurried back to Paris in consequence of this communication and was to receive the German Chargé d'Affaires in half-an-hour's time. A like communication had, he informed me, been made by the German Government to the other Powers, and he intended, he said, to express to the German Representative his surprise that the German Government should separate themselves from the other Governments by sending Dr. Vassel, the German consul, to Fez which could not but cause a bad effect, and by proposing that Mulai Hafid should be recognised by the Powers without first obtaining from him guarantees as to his observance of the engagements taken by Abdul Aziz and his Government. He further intended to tell Baron Lancken that the conditions on which Mulai Hafid might be recognised had been considered by the French and Spanish Governments in consultation and that they would shortly communicate their views to the other Powers with whom it would rest to decide whether they would support the German proposal for an immediate and unconditional recognition of Mulai Hafid or the Franco-Spanish proposals.

Monsieur Pichon then told me that he was convinced that this last move of the German Government was a further attempt to alienate France from her friendship and intimacy with England. It was he did not doubt the result of Dr. Rosen's visit to Prince Bülow. The German Representative at Tangier had lately been saying that it was so regrettable that Morocco should be the stumbling block to good relations between France and Germany; that if the question were settled between them, the two countries could together arrange the affairs of the world, etc. The Germans hoped by constant opposition to the policy of France to convince her that the best thing for her to do would be to make terms with Germany and give up the understanding with England which could do France no real good as against Germany. On this I observed that supposing the German Government succeeded in persuading France to adopt such a policy she would then be in tow of Germany and whenever France did not act as the German Government might desire, they would give her to understand that they would come to an understanding with England to the detriment of France. It would be a repetition of the German policy anterior to the Anglo-French Agreements of 1904, namely, playing France against England and England against France. Monsieur Pichon concurred, and said that the French Government were not going to fall into German traps. Luckily their diplomacy was very awkward and transparent.

I have, &c.
FRANCIS BERTIE.

MINUTES.

Unless the Spanish Gov[ernmen]t are at the bottom of the latest German move it is very inexplicable. But it seems inconceivable that after the experience of the last few years, when each anti-French move on the part of the Germans has had the result of strengthening the *entente cordiale*, that [sic] the Germans should still be trying the same game.

G. H. V.
4.9.08.

The French gov[ernmen]t are apparently seeing in the present German attitude a return to the tactics which preceded the fall of Delcassé. They are probably right and it is well to remember that Herr von Holstein and Dr. Kriege who were the soul of Germany's anti-French policy then and hoped by following it to break up the Anglo-French " entente," are known to be again in high favour with Prince Bülow. I have been told on good authority that Herr von Holstein, in spite of his retirement from the public service, is daily at the Foreign Office in Berlin.

Dr. Kriege repeatedly told me at The Hague that the German authorities were beginning to see what a mistake they had made in being conciliatory at Algeciras. He himself had strongly urged the policy of Germany standing out and if necessary breaking up the conference, and he was convinced that to such a policy Germany ought to return. (It was Dr. Kriege who drafted most of the " intransigeant " despatches and notes to the French which were subsequently published in the Yellow Book). Kriege and Holstein are closely allied.

E. A. C.
Sept. 4.

But as M. Pichon observed, it is all very transparent.

F. A. C.
4.9.
E. G.

No. 99.

Sir F. Lascelles to Sir Edward Grey.

F.O. 371/483.
30936/1013/08/28A.
(No. 394.)   Confidential.   *Berlin,* D. *September* 3, 1908.
Sir,   R. *September* 7, 1908.

Having returned to Berlin from Homburg yesterday evening I called on Herr Stemrich by appointment at noon to-day. After an allusion to the recent meeting of the King and the Emperor at Friedrichshof([1]) which had highly gratified His Imperial Majesty who had telegraphed an account of the conversation he had had both with His Majesty and Sir Charles Hardinge, the conversation turned upon the situation in Morocco and the suggestion which had been made by the German Government that the Powers should consider the advisability of recognising Mulai Hafid as Sultan. For a considerable time past, the German Government had looked upon him as the *de facto* ruler of the country, and had been urged by the German residents in Morocco to acknowledge him as such. There had been some question in the newspapers as to the conditions which the Powers might attach to their recognition. These conditions were of two sorts, 1st General, such as would be covered by an assurance given by Mulai Hafid that he would acknowledge the binding force of the Algeciras Act and previous Treaties; 2nd Particular, as it was conceivable that some of the Powers might think it necessary to obtain more definite assurances from the new Sultan. Herr Stemrich believed that the majority of the Powers would be satisfied with the conditions of the first category and it was with the object of ascertaining their views on this subject that the German Representatives in foreign countries had been instructed to approach the Governments to which they were accredited. Herr Stemrich believed that the recognition of Mulai Hafid would be of great assistance to him in restoring order in Morocco.

Herr Stemrich said that the French press had been somewhat excited by the instructions which had been given to the German Consul at Fez to return to his post. He could not understand the objections which had been raised. Herr Vassel had no diplomatic character and his presence at or absence from Fez would have no political importance. He would merely look after German interests which had suffered in consequence of his absence from his post.

I have, &c.
FRANK C. LASCELLES.

([1]) [The subject of this meeting is treated in *Gooch & Temperley*, Vol. VI, pp. 173–200.]

No. 100.

Sir Edward Grey to Sir F. Lascelles.([1])

F.O. 371/483.
30694/1013/08/28A.
Tel. (No. 82.)

Foreign Office, September 5, 1908.
D. 6·45 P.M.

H[is] M[ajesty's] G[overnment] entirely agree with French and Spanish gov[ernmen]ts as to the inadvisability of recognizing Mulai Hafid without previously securing from him satisfactory guarantees that he will observe Algeciras Act and other obligations entered into by Morocco. Unless this point is settled, the subsequent confusion may be worse than ever. It seems to H[is] M[ajesty's] Gov[ernmen]t most important in the interests of all the Powers signatory of the Algeciras Act that they should show unanimity about it, and they await the Franco-Spanish proposals.

You should when the subject is referred to, explain that this is our view.

([1]) [This telegram was repeated to Berlin, St. Petersburgh, Washington, Lisbon, Brussels, The Hague, Stockholm, Rome, Paris and Madrid.]

No. 101.

Sir M. de Bunsen to Sir Edward Grey.

F.O. 371/483.
31558/1013/08/28A.
(No. 122.)
Sir,

San Sebastian, D. *September 7, 1908.*
R. *September 11, 1908.*

The terms on which Mulai Hafid shall be recognised as Sultan of Morocco have been during the last week the subject of continued discussion between the French and Spanish Governments. Spain has long been convinced that the star of Mulai Hafid was in the ascendant, and many weeks before the defeat of Abdul Aziz on August 19, she raised at Paris the question of Mulai Hafid's eventual recognition, and urged the expediency of an early agreement with France as to the conditions to be attached to it. Rightly or wrongly she suspected the French of supplying Abdul Aziz secretly with the means of prolonging a hopeless struggle. She determined to discourage this tendency and pressed for the abandonment of what she thought was already a lost cause. Her chief motive was perhaps her continued dislike of the existing situation at Casablanca, and her hope that the inauguration of a new reign might lead to arrangements being made which would enable France to withdraw from the occupation of that region. The French Government not unnaturally declined to follow a Spanish lead in the matter. So long as Abdul Aziz remained in the field they saw no necessity to prepare for a possible turning of the tables. But since the headlong flight of Abdul Aziz into the French camp they have admitted that the new order of things will have to be faced. The only question remaining was as to the conditions to be imposed upon the new Sultan.

A French draft, embodying the French proposals on these points in the form of a note for communication to the Powers, reached San Sebastian a few days ago. The French Chargé d'Affaires was good enough to allow me to glance at it. It was a rather lengthy document, including, among the conditions, not only full recognition by Mulai Hafid of the Algeciras Act and of subsequent agreements founded upon it, but also acceptance of liability for the Casablanca indemnities, for adequate provision in favour of Abdul Aziz, and for maintenance of safe communication between Fez, Tangier, Meknes and Marrakesh. It further reserved to the countries concerned the right to approach the new Sultan separately and independently with a view to repayment of the cost of military operations in Morocco. It required also that Mulai Hafid should afford proof of his being in a position to maintain order, and to restrain the hostile movement against the French on the eastern frontier. Subject to receiving satisfactory assurances on these points, France and Spain recommended, in the proposed note, that Mulai Hafid should be acknowledged as Sultan.

Señor Allendesalazar, Minister for Foreign Affairs, had been absent from San Sebastian for about a fortnight. I saw him immediately after his return and was glad to be enabled to report, in my telegram No. 28 of September 1st,(¹) that His Excellency had informed me that the conditions of recognition were practically settled between the French and Spanish Governments. His Excellency was, I think, a little premature in his statement, which agreed also with the French Chargé d'Affaires' first impressions. In point of fact, there were still differences of opinion requiring more than a mere revision of the text to bring the two Governments into agreement. Señor Allendesalazar had admitted to me that he did not like the paragraph relating to collection of a kind of war indemnity.

It has, I believe, since been agreed that the conditions as to a pension for Abdul Aziz, maintenance of communications in the interior, proof to be afforded by the Sultan of ability to fulfil his engagements, and as to restraint to be imposed on the more than semi-independent tribes along the eastern frontier, should be reserved for subsequent negotiation between the countries specially concerned and the new Sultan, and that they should not be submitted to the Powers as a necessary preliminary to recognition. In other words, the note to the Powers has been put by Spain into a form which would enable all the Powers to accept it without discussion. The object of a speedy recognition would thus be facilitated.

The new draft left San Sebastian for Paris, as I am informed, on the 5th instant. M. Daeschner, the French Chargé d'Affaires, considers that the modifications made in it are quite reasonable, and that his Government is likely to accept them. The note would, in any case, be issued to the Algeciras Powers within a few days.

The anxiety of Spain to hasten recognition led her to take an imprudent step. Hoping to obtain from all quarters an expression of opinion agreeing with their own, the Spanish Government instructed their representatives abroad to gather any information they could as to the views held on the question in the various capitals. The instruction seems to have been carried out by the Spanish Ambassador in Berlin in a manner which made it appear that Spain was taking the initiative in urging the Powers to recognise Mulai Hafid. My telegrams Nos. 31 and 32, both of the 4th instant,(²) have reported the Foreign Minister's explanations. His Excellency declared that he had only wished to elicit the opinions of other Governments to serve as a guide in concerting with France the terms of the note to the Powers. He disclaimed any idea of separating himself from the French or of encouraging Germany to take independent action. As, however, the impression was manifestly produced that Spain was taking an independent line of action, I have not failed, as stated in the last mentioned telegram, to represent to Señor Allendesalazar the great importance of avoiding, at this juncture, any semblance of divergent action as between the two countries mainly concerned.

His Excellency promised to clear up any misapprehension that might still exist on this point. The Prime Minister was giving assurances to newspaper correspondents which could not fail to destroy the illusion that Spain was taking an independent initiative.

Señor Allendesalazar went on to explain the importance he attached to cutting down considerably the original French text of the proposed note. He did not doubt that France would acquiesce in the eliminations which he was suggesting, and that the result would be a communication to the Powers in which the latter could acquiesce without wasting time over further discussions.

The action of Germany in proclaiming her attitude as regards the recognition of Mulai Hafid without waiting for the result of the conferences which she knew were

(¹) [Not reproduced as its tenour is indicated.]
(²) [Not reproduced as their tenour is indicated.]

proceeding between France and Spain has not caused in Spain the irritation which is so apparent in the press of all the principal countries outside Germany, and even in some of the German newspapers.

The reason, no doubt, is that the German view of the situation is more to the liking of Spain than the French view. Like Germany, Spain has chafed under the long hesitation of France to give up Abdul Aziz. Like Germany, she has from the first severely criticized the chain of events at Casablanca—the first landing of a small French detachment before the reinforcements had reached the port, the hasty bombardment on the initiative apparently, of a French naval officer of subordinate rank, the despatch of the French punitive force which has grown into the dimensions of a large army of occupation, holding the country far into the interior. The Spanish army has most unwillingly acquiesced in the position assigned to the small Spanish military detachment at Casablanca. In short, as I have often had occasion to point out, the policy of joint action with France is very reluctantly accepted only as a disagreeable political necessity. German condemnation of French proceedings in Morocco finds, therefore, a certain echo in Spain, and it explains, I think, the remark made to me yesterday by my German colleague, M. de Radowitz, that he has nothing but praise for the prudent handling by Spain of the Morocco question, and that, on his return to Spain a few days ago to deliver his letters of recall, he found Señor Allendesalazar in a very sensible frame of mind.

It is of course an object of German policy to detect and expose, if she can, any signs of weakening of the Spanish understanding with France and England. I do not believe, nor does my French colleague believe, that any such weakening is taking place. But it is no doubt a fact that there are many points on which Spain agrees with German criticism of French action in Morocco. This, however, does not prevent the Spanish Government, as I am repeatedly assured by the Foreign Minister, from pursuing their adopted policy of co-operation with France, on the lines of the General Act of Algeciras, while keeping their eyes constantly fixed on their secret convention with France by which their claims to preponderance along the northern coast of Morocco would seem to be recognised.

M. de Radowitz has returned to Spain in a highly irritable frame of mind. To my remark that it was not quite easy to understand the initiative sought to be taken by the German Government at a moment when no one disputed Mulai Hafid's claims to speedy recognition and when Spain and France were working together to that end, he said that Germany's stock of patience was at an end, that she could no longer tolerate the interruption of her trade with Morocco, and that the policy of France in that country was very offensive to Germany. His present language contrasts forcibly with that which he has been holding in Madrid till a few months ago, to the effect namely, that Germany was tired of the Morocco question, and that the French occupation of Ujda left her entirely cold. He is now in a very aggressive mood, reflecting possibly the state of feeling in Germany when he left that country only a few days ago.

I have, &c.
MAURICE DE BUNSEN.

MINUTES.

An excellent despatch giving a clear account of the feeling in Spain in regard to the Morocco question. The actual facts have been reported in Sir M. de Bunsen's various telegrams.
The attitude of the German Ambassador is significant.

G. H. V.
11.9.08.

It is important to note the confirmation we receive from many quarters that a complete change has suddenly been made in the general attitude of the German government. The present despatch illustrates this by the changed tone of M. de Radowitz. But more significant than anything else is the provocative language of the German inspired papers. It is only a short time ago that M. von Schoen informed Sir F. Lascelles that he was entirely satisfied with the loyal and straightforward attitude of France, that he had no fault whatever to find in their behaviour in the Morocco question, and that he was much put out and seriously inconvenienced by the way in which the German press continued to criticise and abuse the French government.

It is impossible to say that anything has since been done by France to warrant the complete turnabout executed by Germany and the biting anti-French articles launched in all the semi-official German papers.

Without wishing to be alarmist, I think this development is of a kind to cause legitimate anxiety. It does not seem altogether unlikely that Prince Bülow may resort to another bullying campaign intended to frighten and cow France into a yielding mood. It is at least possible that France will not this time be as conciliatory as was M. Rouvier's government when they dismissed M. Delcassé.

We know of the existence of a strong and pent-up feeling of rage in Germany at the want of success she has lately had in the domain of foreign policy, and of an inclination, to put it mildly, in high quarters, not to stem the flood of popular passions. Although this may be a game of parliamentary tactics on Prince Bülow's part, the dangers involved in that game are none the less real. If an " untoward event " were to occur anywhere, it should be remembered that the present is the very time when Germany is most ready for an armed adventure. Her army is at its fullest strength and at its highest degree of readiness. Her fleet is in the same condition. By October when the reservists and time-expired men leave the colours and the ships, the situation would be less favourable.

It cannot be said that we are entering a period of specially " strained relations " with Germany. But the latter's relations with France are in that condition in which a spark might explode the powder. And should, by any unfortunate coincidence, anything happen just now that looked like the beginning of a serious movement in India or Egypt or elsewhere against British power, any hesitation that Germany might feel as to embarking on a warlike policy, would probably disappear or be materially diminished.

I therefore think that special care and vigilance would be appropriate during the next four weeks.

E. A. C.
Sept. 11.

We can only hope that the present mood in Germany will pass; which it will if no " untoward incident " occurs.

F. A. C.
12.9.
C. H.

The situation is not comfortable.

E. G.

MINUTE BY KING EDWARD.

The action of the German Gov[ernmen]t is indeed greatly to be deplored!

E.R.

No. 102.

Sir Edward Grey to Sir F. Lascelles.

F.O. 371/483.
30762/1013/08/28.
(No. 243.)
Sir,

Foreign Office, September 7, 1908.

The German Chargé d'Affaires called at the Foreign Office on the 1st inst[ant](1) and informed Sir F. Campbell that he had been instructed to represent that in the opinion of the German Gov[ernmen]t the time had now come when the Powers Signatory of the Act of Algeciras should agree to recognise Mulai Hafid as Sultan in order to put an end to the state of anarchy and disorder which had so long prevailed in Morocco. He was also instructed to say that the return of the German Consul to Fez was connected with some long outstanding claims and had no political significance.

Sir F. Campbell enquired whether the German Gov[ernmen]t proposed to make any conditions with regard to Mulai Hafid's recognition. Herr von Stumm replied that his instructions were silent on the point, but he thought not

(1) [*cp. G.P.,* XXIV, p. 395.]

Sir F. Campbell observed that H[is] M[ajesty's] Gov[ernmen]t had some reason to believe that the French Gov[ernmen]t contemplated addressing the Powers on the subject of Mulai Hafid's recognition and if this were so H[is] M[ajesty's] Gov[ernmen]t would probably wish, before answering the German Gov[ernmen]t, to know whether the French Gov[ernmen]t suggested attaching any conditions to the recognition.

[I am, &c.

E. GREY.]

MINUTES.

We shall no doubt hear from the French their answer to this. There should certainly be conditions attached to the recognition of Mulai Hafid.

E. G.

No. 103.

Sir F. Lascelles to Sir Edward Grey.

F.O. 371/483.
31758/1013/08/28A.
(No. 408.) Confidential.
Sir,

Berlin, D. *September* 11, 1908.
R. *September* 14, 1908.

The French Chargé d'Affaires called upon me yesterday morning and expressed considerable annoyance at the article published in the Süddeutsche Reichskorrespondenz on the 9th instant, a translation of which I had the honour to inclose in my despatch No. 406 of yesterday's date.([1])

Baron Berckheim said that it was disappointing after the conciliatory language which Herr Stemrich had held to him, to find that a paper which is known to be Prince Bülow's organ has thought it necessary to publish a statement which could not fail to excite great irritation in France. He took especial exception to the concluding paragraph which was intended to convey the impression that an attempt had been made to oust Germany out of Morocco, and he considered the expression " fein leise ausgeschaltet " as especially offensive. He had confined himself to forwarding a translation of this article to his Government without comment, but it had been telegraphed to Paris by the correspondent of the Havas Agency and would no doubt lead to further recriminations in the French Press. He would be very grateful for any advice I could give him as to whether he should make a complaint to Herr Stemrich.

I replied that although it was well known that the newspaper in question was frequently used by Prince Bülow, it was not acknowledged as an official organ, and the article in question had not been reproduced by the North German Gazette although it had been copied by nearly all the other papers. It struck me as possible that Prince Bülow, who has of late been somewhat severely attacked in the German Press on account of his policy with regard to Morocco, may have chosen this method of attempting to justify himself in the eyes of his countrymen and had done so in a somewhat clumsy fashion. I doubted whether he intended to offend France, and as long as the official language of the German Government continued to be correct, I should be inclined not to attach too much importance to a newspaper article, even though there was reason to believe that it had been directly inspired. As a matter of fact the German Government were still waiting for the proposals which France and Spain were about to make with regard to the guarantees to be given by Mulai Hafid as a condition of his recognition. There were no doubt excellent reasons for the delay which had occurred in formulating these proposals, but I could understand that the German Government who had expressed the opinion that the early recognition of Mulai Hafid would contribute to the restoration of order in Morocco, might become impatient. I thought that Baron Berckheim might take an opportunity of pointing out to Herr Stemrich in the course

([1]) [Not reproduced.]

of conversation that the publication of the article would not facilitate the course of the negotiations, but I thought at the same time that it would be inadvisable for him to make a formal complaint. I believed that the German Government really desired to avoid any international complication and that it would be better to see what reception they gave to the Franco-Spanish proposals for the recognition of Mulai Hafid, before complaining of an unofficial statement in a newspaper, probably intended for home consumption, the clumsiness of which did not seem to me to redound to the credit of German diplomacy.

I have, &c.

FRANK C. LASCELLES.

MINUTES.

Sir F. Lascelles gave sound advice. The article was offensive but Baron Berckheim would have got no satisfaction by complaining—he probably would have been snubbed.

? Approve Sir F. Lascelles' language.

G. H. V.
14.9.08.

On the theory that Germany wants to " avoid complications," his (Prince Bulow's?)(²) actions are not intelligible.

E. A. C.
Sept. 14.

But the French w[oul]d have made matters worse by sending in a formal complaint.

F. A. C.
14.9.
C. H.
E. G.

(²) [Added in Sir C. Hardinge's hand-writing.]

No. 104.

Sir F. Bertie to Sir Edward Grey.

F.O. 371/483.
32052/1013/08/28A.
(No. 350.) Confidential.   *Paris,* D. *September* 13, 1908.
Sir,   R. *September* 15, 1908.

I have the honour to transmit to you herewith a Memorandum by Mr. Lister of a conversation which he had with M. Pichon on the 10th instant on the subject of the recent proceedings of the German Government in regard to Morocco, the interview of the German Chargé d'Affaires with His Excellency, the policy of the French Government and the relations between France and Germany and between Germany and England.

In view of the observations made to Mr. Lister by M. Pichon I asked M. Clemenceau on the 11th instant, when I paid him a visit, whether he was at all anxious in regard to the attitude of Germany. He replied that he did not think that the German Government meant to push matters to any serious extent, but the danger was that with a Ruler with the impetuous temperament of The Emperor it was impossible to feel sure to what lengths he might not unintentionally go, and the French Government would most assuredly not give way in the question of the unconditional recognition of Mulai Hafid so unexpectedly and so brusquely proposed by the German Government. Their policy was to endeavour to separate France and England and to take every opportunity of being disagreeable to both those countries and hampering their action so as to impress on each that nothing could be done without the consent of Germany and to prevail on one or the other to come to an understanding with her apart from the other.

I have, &c.
FRANCIS BERTIE.

Enclosure in No. 104.

Memorandum by Mr. Lister.

I saw Monsieur Pichon this afternoon and he gave me an account of his recent interview with Baron Lancken on the subject of Morocco. He had told the latter that he was at a loss to understand the action of Germany in proposing to recognize Mulay Hafid, when she knew that France and Spain were engaged in drawing up a Note on the subject to be submitted to the Powers, and now in sending Dr. Vassel up to Fez. Baron Lancken had appeared excessively embarrassed and seemed unable to give any direct reply : he said that the tension between the two Powers was most regrettable : that the Press embittered the situation, and finally asked Monsieur Pichon if he could not make him another declaration to the effect that France intended to evacuate Morocco. His demand, Monsieur Pichon said, astounded him : he answered that he had made a declaration to that effect at the Tribune of the Chamber, that French policy in Morocco had been absolutely loyal throughout, but that now, after Germany's recent action in Morocco, he declined to make any declaration : France would do as she thought fit.

The Franco-Spanish Note, he told me, was practically settled and would be submitted Saturday or Monday. France was quite determined not to give way before Germany. She had common sense, and the Powers with her—he did not see how even Austria could support German action. He would rather, he said, retire from public life altogether, than be the instrument of inflicting such a humiliation on his country. This was the feeling of all the Cabinet.

He said that he felt that the situation was becoming serious and although he did not anticipate an explosion in Morocco it was useless to shut one's eyes to the fact that relations between France and Germany and England and Germany were very much more strained than they had been for some time past.

British Embassy, Paris, September 10th, 1908.

MINUTES.

The action of the German Chargé d'Affaires in demanding a declaration to the effect that France would now evacuate Morocco is corroborative evidence that what Germany wants is to be able to come before the public at home with something in the nature of a national triumph and of French humiliation. It recalls the incident when after Mr. Chamberlain's famous " I have said what I have said " the German Chancellor tried his hardest to get out of Lord Lansdowne an apology or " explanation " which he wanted—avowedly—to use in the Reichstag for the purpose of soothing public opinion.

The French are clearly not in a temper to allow themselves to be bullied.

E. A. C.
Sept. 15.

That is so apparently, but probably the Germans are equally well aware of it, and will not therefore " push matters to any serious extent."

F. A. C.
15.9.

M. Clemenceau's language is open to the charge of exaggeration.

C. H.
E. G.

No. 105.

Mr. White to Sir Edward Grey.

F.O. 371/483.
32585/1013/08/28.
(No. 228.)
Sir,

Tangier, D. September 13, 1908.
R. September 21, 1908.

The Proclamation of Mulai Hafid at Saffi on the 5th and at Mogador on the 9th instant completes the recognition of the new Sultan throughout the whole country, except the Showia province, which is under French occupation, and the neighbourhood of M'Touga, where the Kaid is apparently still holding his own. The son and successor of the murdered Kaid Anfloos has caused Mulai Hafid to be proclaimed in Haha, and even Oujda, notwithstanding the presence of the French, who remained scrupulously neutral, has followed the example of the other towns and declared for the same Prince.

Everywhere the proclamation has passed off quietly and, though at Rabat the situaticn at one time caused anxiety, at no single place have there been any disturbances, but merely feasting and popular rejoicings, that have had the appearance of being genuine.

It was feared that trouble might be caused by the troops whose pay was stopped owing to the refusal of the State Bank to pay out any of the Makhzen funds until the position of the rival Sultans was definitely settled. The difficulty has however been got over by an order on the bank signed jointly by Cid El Mokri, as representing Mulai Abdelaziz, and by Cid Guebbas on behalf of Mulai Hafid.

Acting on the advice of the Tangier notables and possibly also of the German Legation Mulai Hafid has addressed a letter to the Doyen of the Diplomatic Body reaffirming his determination to observe the Algeciras Act and other Treaties entered into by his predecessors and requesting that, having been now proclaimed throughout these realms, he be recognized by the Powers also as Sultan. I have the honour to transmit herewith translation of this letter which was delivered yesterday;([1]) it has been well timed, arriving as it does just after the submission of Saffi and Mogador; it will also be in the hands of the Powers when they receive communication of the Franco-Spanish note.([2])

Hadj Dris Benjelun, whose departure for Fez was reported in my despatch No. 214 of the 26th ultimo,([3]) has left Fez on his return journey and is expected to arrive here to-day or to-morrow. In letters written before his departure he stated that Mulai Hafid had received him very well and he expressed his intention of following the advice tendered by Cid el Menebhi, Cid Torres, Cid Guebbas and other Tangier notables.

I have, &c.
HERBERT E. WHITE.

MINUTES.

The form in which the recognition of the new sultan by the treaty Powers should be made, will have before long to be considered. On the occasion of the notification to the sultan of the Algeciras Act, the dean of the diplomatic body went in special mission to Fez. This may perhaps serve as a precedent. But several of the Powers may prefer to send each their own Minister. The new British Minister will in any case, presumably, have to proceed to Fez.

The Librarian might say what was done when Abdul Aziz came to the throne.

E. A. C.
Sept. 21.

See Library memorandum annexed. Perhaps Sir F. Bertie could ascertain, when an opportunity offers for enquiring, what the French propose to do.

E. A. C.
Sept. 23.

No steps were taken for the recognition of Abdul Aziz until the official notification of the death of Mulai Hassan, and of the accession of Abdul Aziz, was received by the Foreign R[epresentatives] at Tangier on the 14th June, 1894.

A meeting of the Diplomatic Body was held at the British Legation at Tangier, on the 17th June, at which a draft reply to the Vizier for Foreign Affairs was considered and adopted by the British, French, Spanish and Portuguese Ministers and the Italian Chargé d'Affaires, and which formed the basis of the official action of the United States Consul-General. After expressions of condolence and felicitation, the Note went on to say that the signatories had received instructions to pay a visit to the Sultan, in order to convey to him the verbal expression of the friendly sentiments of their respective Gov[ernmen]ts, at whatever time and place it might be convenient to him. (Confl. 6518, page 204.)

([1]) [Not reproduced.]
([2]) [v. immediately succeeding document.]
([3]) [Not reproduced. It gives a detailed account of Moroccan internal affairs and the influence exercised by Cid el Menehbi.]

The instructions to the Austro-Hungarian, Belgian and German Ministers did not permit them to propose paying a visit to the new Sultan.

The Notes were conveyed to Rabat by the Spanish cruiser " Condé Venadito."

The Vizier, in his reply to the Foreign R[epresentatives], said that he regarded the proposed visit to the Sultan as a token of friendship, and that it would have given the Sultan great pleasure to receive them, but that as he was on the point of leaving for Mequinez and Fez, to arrange the affairs of the tribes, it must be unavoidably deferred until he was more consoled [sic] and affairs should have assumed a perfectly satisfactory condition. (Confl. 6561, page 6.)

Sir E. Satow proceeded to Fez, to present his credentials to Abdul Aziz, in October 1894.

G. E. P. HERTSLET,

F.O., 23 Sept., 1908.

This might be deferred. I spoke to M. de Fleuriau of the French Embassy on the point the other day, and I understood from him that when all the replies of the Powers had reached Paris, the French, or French and Spanish Gov[ernmen]ts would suggest what was to be done.(4)

F. A. C.

24/9.

C. H.

E. G.

(4) [For the note which was later drawn up v. infra, pp. 104–5, No. 114.]

No. 106.

Note communicated by M. Paul Cambon, September 14, 1908.(1)

F.O. 371/483.

32016/1013/08/28.

La résolution que le Sultan Adb-el-Aziz [sic : Abd-el-Aziz] vient de prendre, en renonçant à la lutte contre Moulay-Hafid, place les Puissances en présence d'une situation qui s'impose à leur examen. L'attitude même qu'elles ont gardée au cours de ce conflit, leur entente sur leurs intérêts communs au Maroc et les principes dont elles sont déjà convenues lorsqu'elles ont eu à examiner la question marocaine à Algésiras, rendent d'ailleurs très aisée la conformité des vues sur cette situation.

La France et l'Espagne, chargées d'assurer l'exécution des mesures les plus importantes prises par la Conférence d'Algésiras pour la sauvegarde des colonies étrangères dans l'Empire Chérifien, et spécialement intéressées dans les affaires marocaines par leur qualité de Puissances limitrophes, croient devoir soumettre aux Cabinets les observations que leur suggère la substitution d'un nouveau Gouvernement de fait au Makhsen d'Abd-el-Aziz.

Il apparaît tout d'abord, et ce sera sans doute le sentiment unanime des Puissances, qu'il est désirable d'affirmer dans cette occasion, au regard du Maroc, leur solidarité et leur complet accord, et il semble que le meilleur moyen d'établir l'entente nécessaire soit d'admettre la règle que les divers Gouvernements ne subordonneront la reconnaissance officielle du nouveau Makhzen qu'à l'obtention de garanties et de satisfactions communes à tous les intérêts étrangers.

Les Gouvernements Français et Espagnol estiment que les garanties à obtenir du nouveau mahksen devraient porter sur les points suivants :

Le nouveau Sultan déclarerait adhérer d'une façon générale à toutes les dispositions de l'Acte d'Algésiras ainsi qu'à tous les règlements d'application, prévus par cet acte, qui ont été déjà établis et approuvés par le Corps Diplomatique à Tanger, aux Commissions instituées en vertu de ces règlements, aux décisions chérifiennes et mesures quelconques prises à ce sujet.

On ne saurait oublier, en effet, que si cet acte constitue la consécration internationale de l'indépendance de l'Empire Chérifien, il assure en même temps la sauvegarde des intérêts étrangers au Maroc.

(1) [An identic communication was made on the same date by the Spanish Ambassador.]

Devraient être confirmés également les droits conférés à la France et à l'Espagne, avec l'agrément des Puissances, pour la surveillance sur mer de la contrebande des armes.

Le nouveau Gouvernement devrait accepter l'ensemble des autres traités et engagements conclus par les précédents Souverains du Maroc avec les Puissances, les arrangements passés avec le Corps Diplomatique et les contrats avec les particuliers : il assumerait aussi la responsabilité des dettes contractées par Abd-el-Aziz. Les dettes souscrites au bénéfice de particuliers seraient soumises à une vérification dont les conditions seront ultérieurement déterminées.

Le règlement des dommages causés par les troubles de Casablanca se poursuivra devant la Commission Internationale actuellement en fonctions. Le Sultan assumera la responsabilité effective et pécuniaire des décisions de cette commission dont il confirmera les attributions.

Les événements démontrent la nécessité absolue que le nouveau Sultan manifeste publiquement et officiellement, au regard de son peuple, sa ferme intention d'entretenir avec les Gouvernements étrangers et leurs nationaux des relations conformes au droit des gens.

Il devrait donc désavouer et arrêter les appels à la guerre sainte : il adresserait dans ce but aux Gouverneurs des tribus et des villes des lettres chérifiennes qui seraient destinées à prévenir ou calmer toute agitation et tout acte offensif, tant à l'intérieur que sur les frontières du Maroc. Le Sultan doit s'engager à adopter immédiatement toutes les mesures nécessaires pour assurer la sécurité et la liberté des communications autour des ports et sur les principales routes de l'intérieur.

Ces garanties étant obtenues, rien ne s'opposerait plus à ce qu'une demande officielle de reconnaissance faite par Moulay Hafid fût accueillie par les Puissances. Le Sultan déclarera que cela n'implique pour les Gouvernements étrangers aucune renonciation à poursuivre le règlement des questions qui touchent exclusivement à leurs intérêts respectifs, ni aucun préjudice à leur droit de poursuivre ce règlement. C'est ainsi que la France et l'Espagne se réservent de se faire rembourser leurs frais d'opérations militaires et de réclamer directement le paiement d'indemnités pour le meurtre de leurs nationaux.

D'autre part il conviendrait que le nouveau Sultan se prêtât à un règlement honorable de la situation personnelle d'Abd-el-Aziz et les Puissances lui recommanderont pour un traitement équitable les fonctionnaires de son prédécesseur.

Albert Gate House, le 14 *Septembre,* 1908.

MINUTE.

Recognition of Mulai Hafid.

The French and Spanish Ambassadors called and left the accompanying communications—which were said to be identical—detailing they [*sic*] conditions on which the two Governments were agreed that the recognition of Mulai Hafid by the Powers might be assented to.

The only observation I made, and that as a personal view, was that if Morocco was to be made responsible for repayment of all the military expenses of France and Spain, there might be some difficulty in finding the money.

M. Cambon said, "We shall see," and pointed out that Mulai Hafid was not asked to declare the Moorish Gov[ernmen]t responsible for such expenses but only to admit that his recognition did not imply any renunciation on the part of the Powers to claim a settlement of questions relating to their respective interests.

The Ambassadors hoped that they might be favoured with the reply of H[is] M[ajesty's] Gov[ernment] as soon as possible.[2]

F. A. C.
14 Sept., 1908.

(2) [*v. infra*, p. 99, No. 109.]

No. 107.

Sir F. Lascelles to Sir Edward Grey.

F.O. 371/487.
32322/32322/08/28A.
(No. 414.)   Berlin, D. September 14, 1908.
Sir,   R. September 17, 1908.

The temporary lull in the development of Moroccan affairs is being made use of by the German press for the purpose of indulging in violent diatribes against the French and other foreign presses for their hostile attitude towards Germany and German action in particular with regard to Morocco. During the last few days the Kölnische Zeitung, which always devotes its special attention to African and Colonial affairs, has been teeming with articles and telegrams of an argumentative or recriminating character, from its correspondent at Tangier, and its views have been extensively reproduced throughout the other German papers. . . . .([1])

I have, &c.
FRANK C. LASCELLES.

MINUTES.

The violent press campaign against France is another sign of the times.

G. H. V.
17.9.08

An article in the Cologne Gazette of the 16th breathes nothing but peace and painful surprise at having been misunderstood. France having in her note declared that she is determined to remain on the ground of common European interest in Morocco, Germany is entirely satisfied, because she desires nothing else. The attitude of France and Spain in expressing readiness to recognize Mulai Hafid on conditions, is described as following exactly the principles which had been laid down in the German communication to the Powers!

It is, in view of past experiences, perhaps too early to say : " All's well that ends well "; but clearly the Germans are once more executing a strategical movement to the rear.

E. A. C.
Sept. 17.

One is inclined to wish that the English and French press would combine never to mention Germany, though I suppose she would then take offence at that and complain of being boycotted.

F. A. C.
17.9.
C. H.
E. G.

([1]) [The rest of this despatch summarises in detail articles from various German papers.]

No. 108.

Mr. White to Sir Edward Grey.

F.O. 371/487.
33458/30358/08/28.
(No. 230.)   Tangier, D. September 16, 1908.
Sir,   R. September 28, 1908.

I enquired of Cid el Menebhi this morning whether he had any reliable information as to the language held by Dr. Vassel to Mulai Hafid since his arrival at Fez.

He replied that he had received letters on the subject and had also heard through Hadj Dris Benjelun, who had just returned from Fez. Up to the date of his latest information Dr. Vassel had had two interviews with Mulai Hafid. At the first he had conveyed complimentary messages from his Government, and, referring to the services

[19656]   H

they had already rendered to his cause, gave assurances of their desire to render him further assistance in every way. Mulai Hafid expressed his gratitude for the past services as well as for the assurances as to the future, and sent suitable complimentary messages in return. He was careful, however, not to commit himself in any way. At the second interview Dr. Vassel, it appears, was more explicit and requested Mulai Hafid to undertake to consult his Government in all matters, asking that he should take no decision in regard to any proposal or request put forward by the French or other Legation without first consulting them. He asked Mulai Hafid categorically whether he would engage to do this and to act upon the advice they might give, stating that he had to communicate his reply to his Government. Mulai Hafid replied that it was a serious matter and he must take time to consider it before coming to a decision. On the following day he sent a verbal reply to Dr. Vassel through the deputy of the Grand Vizier, to the effect that it was impossible for him to give the undertaking desired : he must reserve his liberty of action in all cases.

Dr. Vassel also spoke of the imprisonment of Kaid R'miki, and endeavoured to obtain orders for his immediate release, but here again Mulai Hafid put him off, saying he was certain Cid el Menebhi had not acted in the matter without good cause, and that he would take no decision without being in possession of his report.

Cid el Menebhi is convinced that the foregoing account of what passed between Dr. Vassel and Mulai Hafid is accurate. At the same time it must be borne in mind that implicit reliance cannot be placed on any information that has been derived from Moorish sources. That Dr. Vassel has not found Mulai Hafid as clay in his hand appears from a letter he has addressed to Mr. Consular Agent Carleton, of which I have the honour to transmit an extract herewith. The probability is that Mulai Hafid will consult Dr. Vassel in many matters, without however necessarily giving him full information even about the matter in question, and without following his advice unless it falls in with his own views.

Cid el Menebhi evidently anticipates that Mulai Hafid will endeavour to revert to old methods and will avoid putting himself in the hands of any Power—Germany, France or other—he will endeavour to govern without the help of Europeans, introducing however such reforms as may be possible with Moorish officials. He will maintain existing institutions, such as Custom control, police, &c. : and will do his best to increase his revenues by allowing the working of mines in certain districts and adopting such other methods as would be received by the people. I am inclined to think however that Cid el Menebhi will find he is mistaken and that Mulai Hafid will not be so averse to the employment of Europeans as he seems to anticipate.

I have, &c.

HERBERT E. WHITE.

Enclosure in No. 108.

Extract of letter from Dr. Vassel to Mr. Consular Agent Carleton.

The new Makhzen gives me a distinctly good impression of solidity and political insight. Surely they will be neither French nor German nor anything else but Moorish. No threatening and no sweetness will do with them. Instead of slimness and persuasion European diplomacy will have to use reasonable arguments with them. Mere instigation will not do, it will require a bothsided negotiation on terms.

This was clearly to be noticed in the Remiki case. In a day or two you will hear all about it. The final solution is an almost mathematical medium between the interests of the Remiki family and the necessity of avoiding unpleasantness to Menebhi.

TH. VASSEL.

MINUTES.

If true, this report of Dr. Vassel's proceedings is sensational news. It appears that Dr. Vassel explicitly asked, on behalf of his Gov[ernmen]t, that Mulai Hafid should do nothing without first consulting the German Gov[ernmen]t! German diplomacy has once more over-reached itself, and we are given another instance of the ultimate value of the underhand methods Germany employs.

It must be noted however that Mr. White is rather inclined to disbelieve the story.

G. H. V.
28.9.08.

That Dr. Vassel said something of the sort is only too probable. It is exactly what Count Tattenbach at one time suggested to Abdul Aziz.

E. A. C.
Sept. 28.
F. A. C.
28/9.
C. H.
E. G.

No. 109.

Sir Edward Grey to M. Paul Cambon and Señor de Villa Urrutia.

F.O. 371/483.
32016/1013/08/28A.
Y[our] E[xcellency],　　　　　　　　　*Foreign Office, September* 17, 1908.

H[is] M[ajesty's] Gov[ernmen]t have given careful consideration to the Note which Y[our] E[xcellency] was good enough to communicate to me on the 14th inst[ant] with regard to the recognition of Mulai Hafid as Sultan of Morocco.(¹)

I have the honour to inform Y[our] E[xcellency] that H[is] M[ajesty's] Gov[ernmen]t agree with the $\frac{\text{French}}{\text{Spanish}}$. Gov[ernmen]t that the recognition of Mulai Hafid by the Powers should be made dependent on his acceptance of the terms set forth in your Note.

A similar communication has been addressed to the $\frac{\text{Spanish}}{\text{French}}$ Ambassador.

[I have, &c.]
E. G[REY].

(¹) [*v. supra*, pp. 95–6, No. 106.]

No. 110.

Sir Edward Grey to Sir F. Lascelles.(¹)

F.O. 371/483.
32016/1013/08/28.　　　　　　　　　*Foreign Office, September* 17, 1908.
Tel. (No. 86.)　　　　　　　　　　　D. 5·30 P.M.

Morocco.

H[is] M[ajesty's] Gov[ernmen]t have informed French and Spanish Gov[ern-men]ts that they agree to recognition of Mulai Hafid subject to conditions set forth in Franco-Spanish notes.(²)

(¹) [Repeated to Sir E. Goschen, Tel. No. 75; Sir A. Hardinge, Tel. No. 6; Mr. Howard, Tel. No. 104; Mr. Wyndham, Tel. No. 84; Sir H. Howard, Tel. No. 4; Mr. Rennie. Tel. No. 15; Sir A. Nicolson, Tel. No. 368; Mr. Dering, Tel. No. 21; Mr. White, Tel. No. 32; Sir F. Bertie, Tel. No. 142; and to Sir M. de Bunsen, Tel. No. 15.]

(²) [*v. supra*, pp. 95–6, No. 106, and *note* (¹).]

No. 111.

Sir M. de Bunsen to Sir Edward Grey.

F.O. 371/483.
32921/1013/08/28A.
(No. 126.)   Confidential.   *San Sebastian,* D. *September* 17, 1908.
Sir,   R. *September* 23, 1908.
    I had some conversation last night with M. Révoil, French Ambassador, on his return to San Sebastian after an absence of some weeks in France. His Excellency having been lately summoned to Paris to confer with M. Pichon on the situation in Morocco, I asked him what impression had been produced on the French Government by recent events. He said that the extreme zeal of Germany to get Mulai Hafid recognized immediately and without guarantees has been regarded as another instance of the unintelligent and inconsistent manner in which Germany conducted her policy in Morocco. The avowed object of Mulai Hafid's recognition had not been advanced a single day, and the obvious German desire to curry favour with the new Sultan could only lead, if successful, to a further conflict of opposing interests at Fez, by which the pacification of the country might be indefinitely delayed. The French Government hoped, however, that the naturally strong position which they occupied as a neighbouring Power would lead Mulai Hafid to understand that he will be compelled in the long run to follow French advice. M. Révoil thought the terms of the Franco-Spanish notes which were communicated on the 14th instant to the Powers were such as to render the concurrence of the other Powers very easy to the latter. The conditions attached to recognition were only such as interested all the Algeciras Powers jointly. As to the rights which France and Spain reserved to themselves to recover separately indemnities for war expenses and other special claims, happily France was in a position to insist on what she might decide to exact, for she would certainly refuse to evacuate the country behind Casablanca till her just demands had been met. His Excellency did not think that anything like the entire expenses of her military operations would be demanded. These amounted to a great deal over 100 millions of francs, but probably not more than 50 millions would be asked, in the Ambassador's opinion, with easy terms for payments spread over a considerable period.

I have, &c.
MAURICE DE BUNSEN.

No. 112.

Sir F. Cartwright to Sir Edward Grey.

F.O. 371/483.
32706/1013/08/28A.
(No. 96.)   *Munich,* D. *September* 18, 1908.
Sir,   R. *September* 21, 1908.
    The mouthpiece of the German Government, the " Norddeutsche Allgemeine Zeitung," in commenting upon the steps taken by Germany to obtain the prompt recognition of Mulay Hafid as Sultan of Morocco, recently observed that " it is not without interest to note that the attacks made by the foreign press on the German communication to the Powers through a misunderstanding of the same have been much more virulent and unfriendly in the English than in the French newspapers." In referring to this remark of the Berlin official organ, some South German newspapers declare that this is nothing new to the German public, and that England in addition to working up the French newspapers against this country, does the same with the American press. Attention is widely called here to this first test of the little value

of the meeting at Cronberg between King Edward and the Kaiser. This meeting had been generally celebrated throughout the country as the first sign of a sincere desire on the part of Great Britain to draw closer to and to show friendship towards Germany, and it was thought to be the basis on which the Emperor had founded the peaceful declarations which formed the main point of his speech delivered at Strasburg.

What has become of all these hopes for a renewal of real friendship for Germany on the part of Great Britain? Germans say that at the first opportunity the British press violently attacks the German Government for doing what seemed most sensible, namely to recognize without loss of time as Sultan of Morocco the man who had succeeded in making himself master of the country. Here it is believed that what really irritates the British press on the present occasion is, that after a long period of reserve with regard to Morocco, Germany has again suddenly taken the initiative in the affairs of that country. The attacks of the British press are interpreted here in many quarters as a sign that British public opinion will not allow itself to be controlled even by King Edward, and that when His Majesty went to Cronberg in a friendly spirit towards Germany, he was not bringing there with him the real approval of the British nation. Many newspapers assert that it is no use indulging in the illusion that Great Britain harbours any genuine friendly disposition towards Germany, and that therefore sooner or later a point will be reached when an acute crisis will occur between the two countries: consequently Germany must prepare herself for all eventualities.

To quote the Stuttgart " Schwäbischer Merkur ": " The best explanation which may perhaps be given of the renewed British press attacks upon Germany is that the meeting at Cronberg and all that pertains to it has made absolutely no change in the regrettable state of things which previously existed between England and Germany. On the contrary England intends to pursue her restless European policy to the bitter end . . . . .([1]) We Germans, however, may be satisfied that according to all present appearances our Government do not intend to allow what took place at Cronberg to compel them to be submissive and yielding to certain European Powers on the present occasion."

Although the more chauvinistic press here welcomes Germany's action to obtain the recognition of Mulay Hafid as Sultan of Morocco, there are not a few people who hold a different opinion, and the Roman Catholic and the Social Democratic organs do not withhold their criticisms of the Imperial Government. According to them France blundered into an impossible position in Morocco, where she was spending her money in obtaining but futile results, and where her army was far from gathering any laurels. The wise policy for Germany to pursue would have been to push France still more deeply into the Moroccan adventure, as by doing so there. was a probability that the French army would gradually become disorganised and therefore rendered less efficient as against Germany. The Munich " Bayerischer Kurier " asserts that public opinion in France was becoming very dissatisfied with Monsieur Clemenceau's Government on account of the way in which they had conducted Moroccan affairs. Fortunately for Monsieur Clemenceau Germany has once more committed a mistake and by throwing down as it were the gauntlet to France she has again turned all parties in that country against herself.

It may interest you to know that in some quarters the Kaiser is being held personally responsible for the sudden recent action of Germany in Morocco. Prince Bülow remained at Norderney at the moment when the Imperial Government decided to take steps to obtain the recognition of Mulay Hafid as Sultan, while the Emperor left Strasburg on the 31st of August for Berlin, where he remained until September the 3rd, then returning to the former city. Was the visit to Berlin merely undertaken to attend the Sedan Parade or for other reasons? This is the question which many people are asking themselves here, and some newspapers observe that whoever may be responsible for inspiring the German communication with regard to Mulay Hafid's

([1]) [Thus in original.]

recognition as Sultan, it is again a case of hasty action based upon bad information, and they say that it is quite evident that Great Britain will be able to group together a considerable number of the Powers who will return a negative answer to Germany's proposals. Therefore by her precipitate action Germany has again exposed herself to a rebuff which will further damage her diplomatic prestige in the world and lend colour to the old accusation that she is always seeking to disturb the peace of Europe.

As regards the recent Franco-Spanish Note, it may be said that the German newspapers as a rule express the opinion that it cannot be accepted as it stands : for them the chief objection to the Note lies in the principle it sanctions, that each Power shall settle her financial claims against Morocco separately with the Sultan, and not in common. To admit this, according to German opinion, would be to hand over the resources of Morocco for many years to come to France alone, as her claims for military expenditure are already enormous.

The Munich "Neueste Nachrichten," which has always advocated a vigorous German policy in Morocco, expresses itself in bitter terms over the present situation. It does not believe that Prince Bülow will have the courage to carry through the recognition of Mulay Hafid "coûte que coûte." In referring to the possible acceptance of the Franco-Spanish Note—which would involve a breach of the Algeciras Act— it says : "Whether there is yet time to prevent this miserable result, which would mean the permanent occupation of Oudsha and Casa Blanca by France and the placing of Mulay Hafid under her tutelage, is doubtful : it is sad to think that the policy which was initiated with such brilliancy by the Kaiser's visit to Tangier, should have been so completely shipwrecked by the inconsequent and inefficient manner in which our Foreign Office have followed it up."

In conclusion I may say that the moderate "Frankfort Gazette" points out that mistakes have been made with regard to Morocco both by the French and by the German Governments, and that if the Moroccan question continues to be treated by these two Powers merely as one which involves the gain or loss of prestige, no satisfactory solution is likely to be found for it, and the German and French people will end by being thoroughly dissatisfied with the present management of their national interests.

I have, &c.
FAIRFAX L. CARTWRIGHT.

No. 113.

M. Paul Cambon to Foreign Office.([1])

F.O. 371/483.
33634/1013/08/28.
Privée.   *Ambassade de France à Londres,*
Cher Sir Francis,   *le 26 Septembre,* 1908.

Je vous envoie, à titre privé, la copie de la note allemande en réponse à la note Franco Espagnole relative à la reconnaissance de Moulay Hafid.

Votre sincèrement,
PAUL CAMBON.

Enclosure in No. 113.

Reply of German Government to Franco-Spanish Note.

Le Gouvernement Impérial a eu l'honneur de recevoir la note par laquelle les Gouvernements français et espagnol, animés, comme le Cabinet de Berlin, du désir d'aborder, sans retard, la solution des questions que soulève la nouvelle situation créée au Maroc par l'issue de la lutte entre les deux Sultans, ont bien voulu lui faire connaître leur manière de voir à ce sujet.

([1]) [The German reply was also communicated by Herr von Stumm on the same day.]

La chancellerie Impériale est heureuse de se trouver d'accord avec les cabinets de Paris et de Madrid dans la pensée qu'il est de l'intérêt de toutes les puissances signataires de l'Acte général d'Algésiras de se concerter en vue de l'attitude à prendre en présence de cette nouvelle situation. Estimant, comme eux, qu'il est désirable d'affirmer au regard du Maroc, la solidarité et l'accord des Puissances, le Gouvernement Impérial s'empresse de contribuer, dès à présent, pour sa part à l'établissement d'une entente de principe en se déclarant partisan de l'idée que la reconnaissance officielle du nouveau Maghzen, quelque désirable qu'il soit dans l'intérêt de l'apaisement du Maroc et de la reprise régulière des affaires d'en accélérer l'accomplissement, devrait être précédée de l'obtention de garanties et de satisfactions communes à tous les intérêts étrangers.

N'ayant point d'intérêts particuliers au Maroc, n'y aspirant ni à des avantages spéciaux ni à une position de faveur, ne s'inspirant que des principes consacrés par l'œuvre d'Algésiras, l'Allemagne éprouvera une véritable satisfaction à voir renaître dans l'Empire Chérifien le calme la paix et la sécurité et à y voir s'établir un ordre de choses représentant la mise en pratique complète et définitive des dispositions générales et particulières de l'Acte d'Algésiras.

Partant de ces points de vue généraux, le Gouvernement Allemand, après un examen attentif et approfondi des propositions que les Gouvernements français et espagnol ont bien voulu lui présenter croit pouvoir exposer sa manière de voir ainsi qu'il suit :

Le Gouvernement Impérial est tout prêt à s'associer à une démarche ayant pour but de faire donner par Moulay Hafid les garanties requises par la situation.

Ces garanties devant être inspirées par les intérêts communs de tous les étrangers, le Gouvernement Allemand est d'avis qu'afin d'accentuer la solidarité de l'entente des Puissances, la démarche dont il s'agit devra être faite par le Corps diplomatique résidant à Tanger par l'entremise de son doyen, procédé qui a été suivi lorsqu'il s'est agi d'obtenir l'adhésion à l'Acte général d'Algésiras du Sultan Abd ul Aziz.

Sous ce rapport, il paraît de bon augure que le Corps diplomatique de Tanger ait été récemment saisi d'une lettre de Moulay Hafid, contenant la notification formelle de son avènement au trône et demandant sa reconnaissance. Dans cette lettre, le Sultan donne des assurances formelles et précises sur la manière dont il entend gouverner et notamment sur sa ferme intention de se conformer en tous points à l'Acte d'Algésiras et aux autres obligations contiguës à cet acte.

Le Gouvernement Impérial estime que cette lettre constitue un fait nouveau dont la portée ne saurait échapper à l'attention des Puissances et il aime à espérer que les Gouvernements de France et d'Espagne, dans un esprit d'équité et de haute sagesse, seront prêts à examiner la question de savoir si les conditions formulées dans leur note ne pourraient pas, pour une certaine part, être considérées comme satisfaites par la lettre de Moulay Hafid.

Pour ce qui est du détail des garanties proposées, les observations suivantes se présentent, toujours sous les réserves qui découlent des remarques précédentes concernant la lettre de Moulay Hafid.

Il conviendrait que le Sultan déclarât adhérer d'une façon générale à toutes les dispositions de l'Acte d'Algésiras ainsi qu'à tous les règlements d'application prévus par cet Acte et établis ou approuvés par le Corps Diplomatique de Tanger, aux commissions instituées en vertu de ces règlements, aux décisions chérifiennes et mesures quelconques prises à ce sujet dans l'exercice du droit public marocain.

De même, le Gouvernement Impérial n'a pas d'objection à la confirmation des droits conférés à titre transitoire à la France et à l'Espagne, avec l'agrément des Puissances, pour la surveillance sur mer de la contrebande des armes. Il y a, d'ailleurs, lieu de faire remarquer que ces droits expirent à la fin de l'année courante.

D'autre part, le Gouvernement Impérial est tout disposé à reconnaître, en principe, que le nouveau gouvernement marocain devra accepter l'ensemble des autres traités et arrangements conclus par les précédents souverains du Maroc avec les Puissances, les arrangements passés avec le Corps Diplomatique et même les contrats avec les particuliers; qu'il devra en outre, assumer la responsabilité des dettes contractées par Abd ul Aziz pendant la période de sa souveraineté. Il est bien entendu que les contrats passés avec les particuliers et les dettes créées à une époque postérieure à la mise en vigueur de l'Acte d'Algésiras ne pourraient être reconnus qu'autant qu'ils se trouveraient être conformes aux prescriptions de cet Acte. Les contrats et dettes non conformes à ces prescriptions ne pourraient pas figurer, à l'avis du Gouvernement Allemand, parmi les obligations à présenter au Sultan au nom de la totalité des Puissances.

Le règlement des dommages causés par les troubles de Casablanca se poursuivra utilement devant la commission internationale actuellement en fonction dont le Sultan aurait à confirmer les attributions.

Le Gouvernement Impérial est prêt à proposer, avec les autres Gouvernements, au Sultan, qu'il manifeste publiquement et officiellement au regard de son peuple sa ferme intention d'entretenir avec les Gouvernements étrangers et leurs nationaux des relations conformes au droit des gens, et qu'il s'engage à préparer dès à présent toutes les mesures nécessaires pour établir la sécurité et la liberté des communications dans l'Empire Chérifien.

Ne mettant pas en doute les intentions pacifiques de Moulay Hafid, le Gouvernement Impérial estime toutefois qu'il conviendrait de lui laisser une certaine liberté d'action afin d'éviter une nouvelle effervescence parmi la population musulmane et le renouvellement d'évènements qui compromettraient sérieusement l'établissement d'un gouvernement stable, seule garantie d'un développement qui soit conforme aux intérêts communs des Puissances.

Le Gouvernement Allemand reconnaît qu'il appartient aux Gouvernements français et espagnol de régler avec le Maroc la question des frais de leurs opérations militaires et leurs réclamations motivées par le meurtre de leurs nationaux. Il a la confiance que les Gouvernements français et espagnol tiendront compte du fait que la situation financière du Maroc présente un intérêt général.

Enfin, le Gouvernement Impérial ne voit pas d'inconvénient à ce que le nouveau Sultan soit invité à régler d'une manière honorable et équitable la situation personnelle d'Abd ul Aziz et de ses fonctionnaires.

No. 114.

Communication from French and Spanish Embassies, October 19, 1908.

Note à faire parvenir à Moulay Hafid par l'entremise du Doyen du Corps Diplomatique à Tanger.

F.O. 371/483.
36447/1013/08/28.

Les Gouvernements signataires de l'Acte d'Algésiras ont reçu la lettre en date du 6 Septembre dernier que Moulay Hafid leur a fait parvenir par l'intermédiaire du Doyen du Corps Diplomatique à Tanger et par laquelle il annonçait qu'ayant été proclamé par tous les habitants de l'Empire du Mogreb il demandait à être reconnu par les Puissances comme Sultan du Maroc. Il offrait en même temps de reconnaître toutes les Conventions publiques passées avec les Puissances par ses prédécesseurs et en particulier la Convention d'Algésiras ainsi que tous les règlements et décisions dans lesquels est intervenu le Corps Diplomatique à Tanger pour assurer l'exécution de cet Acte. Les Gouvernements des pays représentés au Maroc ont accueilli avec satisfaction la déclaration spontanée de Moulay Hafid qui mérite leur approbation.

Mais, afin d'éviter à l'avenir toute interprétation erronée sur la portée de ses paroles, ils croient devoir en préciser la signification et en déduire expressément les conséquences dans l'intérêt même des rapports d'amitié et de confiance qu'ils veulent entretenir avec l'autorité souveraine de l'Empire Chérifien.

Ils considèrent qu'en acceptant les traités passés par ses prédécesseurs avec les différentes Puissances, Moulay Hafid adhère à toutes les disposit'ons de l'Acte d'Algésiras, ainsi qu'à tous les règlements d'application prévus par cet Acte et établis ou approuvés par le Corps Diplomatique à Tanger, aux Commissions institués [*sic*] en vertu de ces règlements, aux décisions chérifiennes et mesures quelconques prises à ce sujet, aux engagements et obligations de tout genre résultant d'arrangements avec le Corps Diplomatique à Tanger ou de contrats réguliers avec des particuliers.

Moulay Hafid assume par voie de conséquence la responsabilité des dettes contracteés par Abdul Aziz jusqu'au jour où ce dernier, en vue de sa renonciation au trône, a entamé des négociations par l'intermédiaire de Menebbi [*sic*]. Toutefois les dettes qui auraient été souscrites au bénéfice des particuliers seront soumises à une vérification dont les conditions seront ultérieurement déterminées sur la base de l'Acte d'Algésiras. Une des conditions principales du maintien de l'ordre est l'accord relatif à la police chérifienne dans les ports et le mandat qui, avec l'approbation des autres Puissances, a été donné temporairement à la France et à l'Espagne pour surveiller la contrebande maritime des armes. Il est entendu qu'aucune atteinte ne sera portée par l'autorité chérifienne à ces garanties.

D'autre part Abdul Aziz ayant provoqué la réunion à Casablanca d'une Commission Internationale chargée de régler les indemnités dues par le Gouvernement Marocain à raison des dommages causés par les troubles survenus dans cette région, et cette mesure ayant reçu l'assentiment des Puissances qui ont envoyé leurs délégués, il importe que la Commission reprenne dans le plus bref délai avec les mêmes attributions que précédemment ses travaux momentanément interrompus.

Une autre conséquence de l'acceptation des traités est l'obligation pour le Sultan de faire le nécessaire afin d'apporter la sécurité à ses sujets et aux colonies étrangères dans toutes les régions de l'Empire. Il convient par suite de procéder dans des conditions en harmonie avec l'Acte d'Algésiras à toutes les mesures indispensables pour garantir la sûreté et la liberté des communications, de manière à permettre l'établissement d'un gouvernement stable, qui soit conformes à l'intérêt de tous. Il convient aussi que Moulay Hafid le fasse savoir d'une manière officielle au peuple marocain en lui disant en même temps que sa volonté est de maintenir avec tous les pays et leurs nationaux des relations conformes au droit des gens, ainsi que cela doit être entre pays amis et qui se respectent réciproquement.

Ces questions sont celles qui intéressent toutes les Puissances. Il en est d'autres qui ne concernent que certaines d'entre elles. En reconnaissant un nouveau Sultan, aucune Puissance ne renonce à son droit de poursuivre avec lui le règlement des questions qui touchent exclusivement chacune d'elles en particulier.

C'est ainsi que la France et l'Espagne ont déclaré qu'elles se réservaient de poursuivre directement avec le Maghzen le remboursement des dépenses qu'elles ont faites pour assurer la tranquillité dans certaines régions du Maroc au moyen d'expéditions militaires indispensables. C'est également avec le Maghzen que la France et l'Espagne, comme aussi les autres Puissances qui se trouvent actuellement dans le même cas, traiteront la question des indemnités dues pour le meurtre de leurs nationaux.

Si, comme les Puissances l'ont toutes compris à la lecture de la lettre de Moulay Hafid, ces explications répondent exactement à sa pensée, elles lui demandent de vouloir bien les en informer en termes exprès afin qu'elles puissent le reconnaître comme Sultan légitime du Maroc. Elles le prient de leur transmettre cette réponse par l'intermédiaire du Doyen du Corps Diplomatique à Tanger.

Elles ne doutent pas qu'il ne comprenne qu'il doit à son frère Abdul Aziz les moyens de mener une existence digne d'un prince qui le touche de si près et qui a occupé le trône impérial de ses ancêtres. Elles espèrent aussi qu'il traitera équitablement les fonctionnaires qui ont fait partie du Maghzen d'Abdul Aziz.

MINUTE.

Sir E. Grey,

The French Councillor and Spanish Ch[argé] d'Affaires called to-day and communicated a copy of the note which it is proposed to address to Mulai Hafid through the Doyen of the

Diplomatic Corps at Tangier containing the conditions of his recognition as Sultan. They asked that instr[uctio]ns might be given to H[is] M[ajesty's] Representative to sign it.

I accepted the note and said that I would submit it to you for an early reply.([1])

C. H.

Oct. 19, 1908.

E. G.

([1]) [On October 22, 1908, in Despatch No. 170, (F.O. 371/483. 36447/1013/08/28), Sir Edward Grey forwarded a copy of the above note to Mr. White at Tangier authorizing him " when asked to do so, to sign the note as at present drafted."]

No. 115.

Count de Salis to Sir Edward Grey.

F.O. 371/483.

37911/1013/08/28A.

(No. 484.)   Confidential.

Berlin, D. *October* 30, 1908.

Sir,

R. *November* 2, 1908.

With reference to Sir F. Lascelles' despatch No. 461 of the 20th instant,([1]) the French Ambassador told me this morning that a few days ago Herr von Schoen in the course of conversation with reference to the draft of the note to be presented to Muley Hafid by the diplomatic body at Tangier with regard to his recognition as Sultan, remarked that in the opinion of the German Foreign Office Muley Hafid had been the rightful Sultan since the 5th of January, the date on which his accession had been proclaimed by the mullahs at Fez. Monsieur Jules Cambon replied that he could not accept this view; the German Government had evidently not held it last spring when they refused to receive officially Muley Hafid's envoys.([2]) No doubt there were Germans who had made contracts with Muley Hafid while he was fighting against his brother, and who were desirous of seeing any such date adopted. To a remark from Herr von Schoen that there were also perhaps Frenchmen who had continued to furnish supplies to Abdul Aziz after his cause was virtually lost, Monsieur Cambon rejoined that of course claims on any such account would have to be closely examined, but that the French Government could not admit that Abdul Aziz had ceased to be Sultan until he himself began talking of abdication, which would be about the 10th of September last, nor that Muley Hafid had become his legitimate successor until his formal recognition had taken place.

Herr von Schoen had presumably abandoned the contention, since yesterday he definitely informed Monsieur Cambon that his Government agreed to the note and had no observations to offer. The communication was made verbally but Monsieur Cambon added that he would place the matter on record by writing a formal note expressing thanks for the decision of the German Government.

I have, &c.

J. DE SALIS.

([1]) [*v. infra*, pp. 113–4, No. 125.]

([2]) [*v. supra*, pp. 80–1, No. 93.]

No. 116.

Sir F. Bertie to Sir Edward Grey.

F.O. 371/488.

41031/41031/08/28A.

(No. 477.)

Paris, D. *November* 23, 1908.

Sir,

R. *November* 24, 1908.

I have the honour to transmit to you herewith copies of the Yellow Book just published by the French Government respecting Moroccan affairs.([1]) It consists of

([1]) [Not reproduced. The volume concerned is *Livre Jaune, Affaires du Maroc,* IV, (1907–8).]

four hundred and sixty-nine documents covering the period from October 12, 1907, to October 14, 1908, and deals with the various questions with which French Diplomacy has been occupied during that period with the exception of the incident of the deserters at Casablanca,(²) as to which no papers are now published.

I would draw your attention to the account of an interview between the French Ambassador at Berlin and Prince Bülow on March 30 last (p. 188). Prince Bülow told M. Cambon that he could not repeat too often what he had already said to him at Norderney. The commercial question in Morocco was the only one which preoccupied the German Government, the only one which stirred public opinion and the only one which might raise difficulties between the two countries. Germany had had such an enormous economic expansion during the last thirty years that any impediment to commercial liberty seemed to her difficult to bear. He pointed out to M. Cambon that the tendency of French policy with regard to French colonial possessions was to shut out foreigners. England's tendency was, on the contrary, to show a liberal spirit in economic matters which had had a favourable result in her colonies, and he drew His Excellency's attention to the fact that practically all the speakers in the Reichstag had been the mouthpiece of German commercial grievances. It was his conviction that if German commerce had had during the past year or eighteen months no grievances to complain of, the French Government would have had no difficulties in Morocco. M. Jules Cambon observed in reply that German trade at Casablanca had been on the increase.

The "Temps" publishes a leading article on the Yellow Book approving M. Pichon's policy in his attitude towards European Powers in any negotiations respecting Moroccan affairs. On the other hand, the policy of the French Government in Morocco itself is sharply criticised as weak and incoherent, and is summed up as resulting in the abandonment of Abdul Aziz and capitulation before Mulai Hafid. The Government, the article states, refused to listen to the unanimous advice of their Agents in Morocco, and allowed Mulai Hafid to grow in power instead of crushing him in time.

This criticism is the usual one made by the "Temps" which has consistently advocated a more forward policy in Morocco than was favoured by the Government or approved by the Chamber.

The "Journal des Débats," on the other hand writes in an approving manner as to the restraint shown by the Government in resisting all temptation to take sides in the internal conflict between Mulai Hafid and Abdul Aziz.

I have, &c.
FRANCIS BERTIE.

(²) [v. infra, pp. 109–31.]

No. 117.

Mr. Lister to Sir Edward Grey.

F.O. 371/483.
41268/1013/08/28.
Tel. (No. 70.)   *Tangier, November* 25, 1908.

Mulai Hafid was proclaimed at Casablanca yesterday after departure of Abdelaziz, who landed privately at Harris Villa on French launch at 5·45 this morning.

No. 118.

Sir M. de Bunsen to Sir Edward Grey.

F.O. 371/483.
44496/1013/08/28A.
(No. 184.)   Confidential.   *Madrid,* D. *December* 17, 1908.
Sir,   R. *December* 21, 1908.

The French Ambassador informs me that the text of the note to the Maghzen expressing recognition by the Powers of Mulai Hafid as Sultan was concerted between himself and the Spanish Foreign Minister a few days ago, and will probably be submitted to-day by the French and Spanish Representatives at the various capitals for approval by the Governments concerned. M. Révoil states that in drafting the note he was careful to employ no expressions which did not conform closely to the language already accepted at Berlin and which was embodied in the note of November 18,(¹) since accepted by the new Sultan as defining with sufficient accuracy the attitude he is prepared to adopt towards the Powers.

His Excellency does not anticipate that any Government will raise objections to the proposed text, or that any considerable delay can now occur before Mulai Hafid is definitely recognised. He would feel better satisfied with this result if Mulai Hafid had not already gained a character which promises anything but well for the future. M. Révoil hears that imprisonment and torture are being unsparingly applied at Fez to adherents of the old régime. It would not greatly surprise him to learn that the death of the ex-Minister Ben Sliman was caused by foul play. All the reports he has received depict the new Sultan as harsh and cruel, contrasting very unpleasantly with his weak but well-meaning predecessor. M. Révoil has hopes that some man of strong character may emerge who will keep Mulai Hafid under proper restraint. El Menebhi, he thinks, might have played this part, with Ben Sliman to assist him. Whether single-handed he is equal to such a task, the Ambassador is inclined to doubt.

M. Révoil has had a conversation with Señor Allendesalazar on recent events in the Riff country. He is always very sensitive to Spanish movements in that region. The flight of the Roghi he feared might lead to an advance of Spanish troops from Melilla. The pretext would be the protection of Spanish property in the mining district. Once such a movement began it would be difficult to check it. M. Révoil was glad, therefore, to receive from the Minister for Foreign Affairs an assurance that nothing of the kind is in contemplation, at least for the present.

Señor Allendesalazar had derived some comfort from the visits paid a few days ago by several neighbouring tribal chiefs to General Marina at Melilla. This seemed to portend a friendly attitude on the part of the tribes. But no doubt the situation outside the walls of Melilla was greatly disturbed, and the Spanish Government intended, he said, to insist on the new Sultan fulfilling his Treaty obligation to keep order there, as soon as circumstances permit.

M. Révoil is satisfied with these declarations for the present. He thought it as well, however, to remind the Minister of the clause in the Secret Treaty of October, 1904, which requires Spain to secure the concurrence of France before taking any important step in the northern portion of Morocco. Señor Allendesalazar said the Spanish Government had no desire to conceal its intentions from the French Government, with which it claimed to be loyally co-operating in all matters relating to that country.

I have, &c.
MAURICE DE BUNSEN.

(¹) [Not reproduced. It consisted of the note of October 19 (*v. supra,* pp. 104–5, No. 114), enclosed in a letter for presentation to Mulai Hafid.]

III.—THE CASABLANCA DESERTERS' INCIDENT.

[*ED. NOTE.*—For the subject of this section *cp. G.P.*, XXIV, ch. 180, and Herr von Schoen : *The Memoirs of an Ambassador* (1922), pp. 90–4.]

No. 119.

Sir F. Bertie to Sir Edward Grey.

F.O. 371/488.
33655/33655/08/28A.
(No. 368.)   Confidential.   *Paris,* D. *September* 28, 1908.
Sir,   R. *September* 29, 1908.

I went to the Quai d'Orsay this afternoon to endeavour to obtain some information in regard to the incident at Casablanca.([1])   I saw Monsieur Pichon who was expecting a visit from the German Chargé d'Affaires, Baron von Lancken.   His Excellency told me that the French Government had not yet received a detailed account but they believed that the German Consulate at Casablanca had constituted itself a sort of Agency for desertion.   Of the six deserters who had been received at the Consulate and were when arrested by the French Authorities being conducted by the Consul's Secretary and a native employé to the Quai for embarkation on a German vessel, there were three who claimed to be Germans, one Austrian, one Pole and one Swiss. Monsieur Pichon's view, which he said required confirmation by a person versed in International Law, was that in a Country in military occupation by a Foreign Power it was not the law of the land which prevailed and still less so extra-territorial rights but the law of the occupying army, and even if this were not so the German Consulate could have no right of protection in regard to the Austrian, the Pole and the Swiss. He did not know what Baron von Lancken might have been instructed to say on the subject of the incident, but he intended to tell him that the French Government had called for a full report on it and until it had been received and considered they would not be in a position to discuss the incident.   He might probably give to Baron von Lancken his view of the legal position in a Country in military occupation and point out to him that whatever rights the German Consul might have as regards Germans he could not have the right to receive and aid to escape on board a German vessel persons of other nationalities.   His Excellency stated that he did not regard the matter as very serious.   If however the German Government made much of it he would be inclined to offer to Prince Bülow, who had lately made a speech in favour of arbitration, to refer the question to the Hague Tribunal.

A person who saw Monsieur Clemenceau this morning informed me that he was much irritated at the proceedings of the German Consul at Casablanca, which as far as they were known to him were quite unjustifiable, and said that incidents of that kind produced a state of public opinion which was not conducive to good relations and even endangered peace.   As Minister of War in the absence of General Picquart he had telegraphed to General d'Amade for a full report and my informant gathered that Monsieur Clemenceau did not intend to hurry its receipt.

I have, &c.
FRANCIS BERTIE.

MINUTES.

The French Gov[ernmen]t refuse to discuss the incident until they receive a full report from General d'Amade.   According to what has appeared in the papers the Germans do not seem to have any excuse for their ill-timed action.

G. H. V.
29/9/08.
E. A. C.
Sept. 29.
W. L.

([1]) [The incident occurred on September 25.]

M. Pichon's attitude seems calm and prudent. It is a somewhat complicated question of international law.

C. H.
E. G.

I told M. Poklevski who asked me my opinion, that I thought we should not bother about any British subjects, who had enlisted abroad and taken service with a foreign country.

E. G.

No. 120.

Sir F. Bertie to Sir Edward Grey.

F.O. 371/488.
33797/33655/08/28A.
(No. 370.)
Sir,

Paris, D. *September* 29, 1908.
R. *September* 30, 1908.

With reference to my despatch No. 368 of yesterday's date([1]) on the subject of the attempted escape of six deserters from Casablanca, I have the honour to inform you that the following communiqué appeared in the Press respecting the visit of the German Chargé d'Affaires to Monsieur Pichon, to which I made allusion in my despatch above mentioned.

" . . . . L'entretien a été très courtois, et les dispositions les plus conciliantes ont été manifestées de part et d'autre. Au cours de la conversation Monsieur Pichon a fait observer qu'il fallait, avant de discuter la question au fond, connaître les faits avec précision. Il a déclaré qu'un exposé complet de ces faits avait été demandé télégraphiquement au Général d'Amade."

The press in general comments in a moderate manner on the incident. A leading article in the "Temps" of last night, which I enclose herein,([2]) sets forth the two positions which can presumably be adopted with regard to the matter. It remarks that the intervention of the German Consulate at Casablanca must be considered much more blameworthy if it be proved that some of the deserters were not of German nationality. It expresses the hope however that the two Governments will examine the affair in perfect loyalty, and will be able to arrive at a satisfactory solution.

The "Figaro" remarks that the case presents elements of the most complicated kind, that it is the sort of problem in international law which examiners would be happy to find to puzzle the candidates whom they were examining. It is to be hoped however that means will be found to close the incident in a friendly manner.

Communication has also been made to the press of a telegraphic report from General d'Amade. The General states that he has in his possession an order written by the German Consul by which the clerk (" chancelier ") of the Consulate is directed to assist in the embarcation of six persons. It would appear that of these six deserters one is an Austrian, another a Swiss, and a third a Russian Pole. General d'Amade states that the French sailors did not strike the Consulate officials first. A Moorish employé of the Consulate struck the first blow and the clerk also used violence.

I have, &c.
FRANCIS BERTIE.

([1]) [*v.* immediately preceding document.]
([2]) [Not reproduced.]

No. 121.

Sir F. Lascelles to Sir Edward Grey.

F.O. 371/483.
34273/1013/08/28A.
(No. 434.)   Confidential.   Berlin, D. September 30, 1908.
Sir,   R. October 5, 1908.

Herr Stemrich informed me yesterday that he had been much gratified by the
way in which the German reply to the Franco-Spanish Note on the subject of the
recognition of Mulai Hafid as Sultan of Morocco had been received in Paris, and he
did not anticipate any difficulty in coming to an understanding on the subject upon
which both Governments were agreed in principle.   The recent incident at Casablanca,
in connection with the arrest by French gendarmes of deserters from the Foreign
Legion who were under the protection of the German Consulate was no doubt a very
unpleasant one, but both Governments had the sincere desire to settle it amicably
and he did not think there would be much difficulty in doing so.

I observed that it was somewhat of a surprise to me that the German Government,
who I understood looked upon desertion from military duty as a crime, should seek to
protect even their own subjects from its consequences, to which Herr Stemrich replied
that the German Government were bound to protect their subjects, but that they could
not be expected to have much sympathy with such of them who chose to take service
in the French army.

My French colleague believes that this question will not lead to any complications.
He is under the impression that the German Government feel that their Agents in
Morocco have been in the wrong, and it was significant that although only three of the
six deserters arrested by the Gendarmes were of German nationality, no complaint had
yet reached the French authorities from the Governments of the countries to which
the three other deserters belonged.

I have, &c.
FRANK C. LASCELLES.

No. 122.

Mr. White to Sir Edward Grey.

F.O. 371/488.
35049/33655/08/28.
(No. 248.)   Tangier, D. October 4, 1908.
Sir,   R. October 10, 1908.

No further discussions have taken place in regard to the deserters' incident at
Casablanca between the French and German Ministers.   M. Regnault tells me that
General d'Amade is holding an exhaustive enquiry into the case and will communicate
the full particulars to his Government, when the matter will probably be discussed
between the two Governments direct and not between the Legations here.

M. Regnault stated that it was clear that the German cavass struck the first blow
and that the German Consul gave a pass for the six persons accompanying M. Just, the
clerk of the Consulate, i.e., for an Austrian, a Swiss and a Russian Pole, as well as
three Germans.   He showed me a copy of the pass, the original of which is in General
d'Amade's possession.   Only five deserters however accompanied M. Just when he first
went to the water-port, the sixth appeared later.   It is difficult to explain the action of
the German Consul, M. Luderitz, in this matter as he has hitherto behaved with tact
and comparative moderation considering the difficult position he occupies, and has
maintained friendly personal relations with the French officials.   M. Regnault thinks
that M. Luderitz' hand was forced by M. Just, a newly-arrived official, who is a very

active supporter of the anti-French party, and by M. Ficke, a German merchant and newspaper correspondent, agent of the German Morocco Committee, who has been a thorn in the side of the French officials since the occupation of Shawia. M. Regnault believes that the German Consular officials at Casablanca dare not oppose M. Ficke, for fear of his complaining of them to his influential Committee.

M. Ficke, it appears, has been carrying on a regular desertion propaganda among the soldiers of the Foreign Legion and has assisted them in escaping by providing them with clothes and harbouring them on his premises until they could be embarked on a steamer. The desertions from the Foreign Legion have therefore been numerous, two hundred and seventeen up to date. It was in view of this that General d'Amade determined to adopt measures to put a stop to further desertions.

I have, &c.
HERBERT E. WHITE.

No. 123.

Mr. White to Sir Edward Grey.

F.O. 371/488.
35908/33655/08/28.
(No. 249.)
Sir,

Tangier, D. *October* 7, 1908.
R. *October* 17, 1908.

With reference to my despatch No. 248 of the 4th inst[ant](¹) I have the honour to report that, having occasion to see the French Minister this morning, he reverted again to the Casablanca incident, giving me the photographic copy enclosed herewith(²) of the pass issued by the German Consul for the six deserters, and reading to me the statements of some of the persons who had given evidence at the enquiry instituted by General d'Amade.

The principal facts brought out by this evidence were as follows : The first blow was struck by M. Just, who hit the French sailors with his cane ; the broken cane being in the possession of the French Authorities. The German cavass was not interfered with until he struck the sailors, who pursued and arrested one of the deserters, who attempted to escape. His hands were tied behind his back, as he was a powerful man and could not be restrained otherwise. The young French officer who drew a pocket revolver declared that he did so in self-defence, seeing an infuriated man coming at him with uplifted arm and not wishing to come to blows with him. He states he did not know this man was a German official, as he was in a dishevelled condition after his immersion in the muddy water by the upsetting of the boat.

The Austrian and Swiss deserters declared that they were induced to desert, when they had no idea of doing so, the Austrian stating that he was practically kept a prisoner by the Austrian Vice Consul, who is a German merchant, from the day on which he agreed to desert until the ship arrived and he went down to the beach accompanied by the Austrian Vice Consul.

M. Regnault informed me that some days after the incident the Austrian Vice Consul at Casablanca made a protest in regard to the incident to the French Acting Consul by order of his Government.

Later I was calling upon the German Minister, who also brought up the subject. He stated that an enquiry had been held by their officials and it was clear from the evidence they had received that the French were the aggressors. He ridiculed the idea of M. Just having used any violence, describing him as a very mild little man, who would be the last person to strike any one. He denied that the German Consul

(¹) [*v.* immediately preceding document.]
(²) [Not reproduced.]

had any intention of protecting the deserters, who were not of German nationality, and who were, he stated, two Austrians, sent by their Vice Consul, and a German Swiss. He states that the French Authorities have also in their possession, though they have not produced it, another paper issued by M. Luderitz and shown by M. Just where the number of Germans was given as three.

Baron von Wangenheim, whilst expressing the hope and the belief that the incident would be satisfactorily settled, exhibited a certain amount of irritation, and said his Government would have to insist on reparation being given. He thought that it might perhaps be argued that the French could arrest deserters of foreign nationality in Showia, but they certainly could not in the town of Casablanca, which is not in military occupation nor the field of military operations, but under the French and Spanish police. He added that in any case the action of the French was inexplicable as desertions had been going on for some time and the subject had been spoken of between the two Legations : if the French thought they were entitled to arrest the deserters they should have first discussed the matter here and come to an agreement, instead of taking the law into their own hands and thus giving rise to this regrettable incident.

If, as it would appear, the evidence collected in the enquiry held by the German Authorities conflicts on the main points with that obtained by the French, an awkward situation may arise, especially if the views expressed by Baron von Wangenheim are those of his Government. It is quite possible however that Baron von Wangenheim's assumption of a somewhat uncompromising attitude is in the nature of bluff, as he would reckon on his language reaching M. Regnault, especially as I understand he has used somewhat similar language to a French journalist here.

I have, &c.
HERBERT E. WHITE.

No. 124.

Mr. White to Sir Edward Grey.

F.O. 371/488.
36893/33655/08/28.
(No. 256.)   *Tangier, D. October 16, 1908.*
Sir,   R. *October 24, 1908.*

With reference to my despatch No. 249 of the 7th instant(1) I have the honour to report that I learn from M. Regnault that the Austrian Ambassador at Paris has informed the French Government that the protest made by the Austrian Vice Consul at Casablanca in regard to the arrest of the Austrian deserter from the Foreign Legion was made without the authority of his government, which did not desire to take any notice of the incident.

I have, &c.
HERBERT E. WHITE.

(1) [v. immediately preceding document.]

No. 125.

Sir F. Lascelles to Sir Edward Grey.

F.O. 371/483.
37090/1013/08/28A.
(No. 461.)   *Berlin, D. October 20, 1908.*
Sir,   R. *October 26, 1908.*

The North German Gazette of last evening announces that the French and Spanish Ambassadors in Berlin yesterday presented to Herr von Schoen the draft of a Note which the Doyen of the Diplomatic Corps at Tangier is to present to Mulai Hafid on the subject of his recognition as Sultan of Morocco.(¹)

Meanwhile the German Press, which for the last few days has been fully occupied with the discussion of the situation in the Balkans, has turned its attention now again to the Moroccan question, and especially to the recent Casablanca incident. The Cologne Gazette learns that the reports received by the French and German Governments respectively with regard to the incident of the German deserters at Casablanca are so much at variance that it has been proposed to submit the whole question to the Hague Court of Arbitration. The Cologne organ welcomes such a solution as a dignified and suitable way to deal with a matter about which neither country could possibly desire to go to war. At the same time it is understood that the German Government have not yet received the French official material in the case, which M. Cambon is expected to hand to Herr von Schoen within the next day or two: and until this happens, it is naturally impossible for the German Government to decide whether or not they will submit the question to arbitration.

I have, &c.
FRANK C. LASCELLES.

(¹) [v. supra, pp. 104–5, No. 114, and p. 108, No. 118, note (¹).]

No. 126.

Minutes by Mr. Crowe and Mr. Langley.

F.O. 371/488.
38740/33655/08/28.

(Written on extract of *Alldeutsche Blätter* of October 30, 1908.)

I should not have called attention to this article from the principal Pan-German organ, were it not for a conversation which I had with Herr von Schwabach our consul general at Berlin, yesterday evening.

He assured me that the feeling of irritation against France was intense in Germany. It was considered that by a series of adroit measures, France had practically established herself in Morocco. The behaviour of the French troops in particular was criticized in the most violent manner, and it had become the firm conviction of all Germans, of every class, that there must be a war with France, in order to put an end to her constant and growing menace to Germany, and her provocative attitude, which no German Government could put up with any longer! Herr von Schwabach surprised me by declaring that he in common with every German shared these views, and that a war with France was now only a question of time and opportunity. He is very far from having sympathy with the Pan-German party. That is why the coincidence of his views with those expressed in the present article struck me as significant. Evidently the feeling in Germany is very like what it was in 1875 and 1886 when Bismarck tried to provoke a war with France, and took care to rouse public opinion for the purpose.

I should add that Herr von Schwabach is on intimate terms with Herr von Holstein, and I have no doubt whatever that it is the latter's views which he expressed.

E. A. C.
Nov. 6.

A very wrong-headed and mischievous article. If these are really Herr von Holstein's views, and from his reputation that does not seem improbable, we must hope that they will not prevail at the German Foreign Office.

> W. L.
> C. H.
> E. G.

No. 127.

Mr. White to Sir Edward Grey.

F.O. 371/488.
38674/33655/08/28.
(No. 274.)
Sir,

Tangier, D. *October* 31, 1908.
R. *November* 7, 1908.

With reference to my despatch No. 256 of the 16th inst[ant](1) I have the honour to report that M. Regnault read to me a despatch which had been addressed to him by the Acting French Consul at Casablanca stating that he had received a letter from the Austrian Consul withdrawing, by order of his Government, his two notes protesting against the arrest of the Austrian deserter from the Foreign Legion and requesting that these notes be returned to him and considered as not having been written. The French Consul accordingly returned the notes in question and the Austrian Consul sent him back his letter communicating General d'Amade's reply to the protest.

The incident has thus, so far as the question of the Austrian protest is concerned, been settled to the entire satisfaction of the French Government.

> I have, &c.
> HERBERT E. WHITE.

(1) [*v. supra*, p. 113, No. 124.]

No. 128.

Sir Edward Grey to Sir F. Bertie.

F.O. 371/488.
38577/33655/08/28.
(No. 525.)
Sir,

Foreign Office, *November* 3, 1908.

The French Chargé d'Affaires came to tell me to-day that he had received a telegram from M. Pichon which he wished to communicate to me confidentially.

On October 14th, Herr von Schön proposed to M. Jules Cambon that, as the differences of opinion about the Casablanca incident could not be settled otherwise, they should be referred to arbitration.

M. Cambon accepted arbitration.

On October 16th, Prince Radolin in Paris said that the German Government demanded the immediate release of the German subjects who had been arrested as deserters, and an apology for the violence offered to officials of the German Consulate.

To this M. Pichon had replied that he could not have an apology from French Officers, and that in any case the French Government had already accepted arbitration.

Nothing more was heard till the 1st of November, when Prince Radolin presented formally a demand in writing for the immediate release of the German deserters and an apology, such as he had already spoken about.

M. Pichon had answered that the French Government adhered to their decision to accept arbitration, and that the different points raised by the incident were so connected that they would all be covered by arbitration.

[19656] I 2

M. Pichon thought, however, that it was significant that this demand should have been made formally, in writing, and on a Sunday, which was not a usual day for business. He thought that the demand might have been made as an attempt to divert attention, in Germany, from the stir created by the publication of the interview with the Emperor.([1])

I told the French Chargé d'Affaires that this news seemed to me very important and extraordinary.

He asked whether I had heard anything from Berlin of a nature to cause apprehension.

I told him I had heard nothing of this kind. No word had passed between us and the German Government about the interview with the Emperor. Count Metternich had, indeed, come to see me the day after its publication, but he had come about some trifling matter, and had made no reference to the interview. I had made no reference to it either, because I did not know what to say about it, and I thought it would be an embarrassing subject. Count Metternich had since gone away for a few days, and I had attributed this to the embarrassment caused to the German Government by the publication of the interview.

I had felt that the consequences of the interview, and the difficulties created by it, were bound to cause bad humour in Berlin : none the less because the whole thing was entirely the Germans' own fault. But I had heard nothing whatever that tended to show that the German Government were likely to make trouble.

There was clearly nothing for me to do at present but to wait till I heard what answer the German Government returned to M. Pichon's reply to Prince Radolin's formal demand.

I hoped the French Government would keep me informed of the course of events.

I observed that a comparison of the dates would point to the instructions to Prince Radolin at Paris having been drawn up the same day as the official explanation of the Emperor's interview.

I hardly thought the Germans could force a question on which arbitration had been accepted to the point of a quarrel—it would put the whole opinion of the world against them, which after all counted for something.

[I am, &c.]
E. G[REY].

MINUTE BY KING EDWARD.

App[rove]d.—E.R.

([1]) [For the *Daily Telegraph* interview, *v. Gooch & Temperley*, Vol. VI, pp. 201–226.]

No. 129.

Sir F. Bertie to Sir Edward Grey.

F.O. 371/488.
38437/33655/08/28A.
(No. 440.)   *Paris, D. November 4, 1908.*
Sir,   R. *November 5, 1908.*

The President of the Council who returned to Paris yesterday sent me a message by Mr. Lister, who had called on him to take leave before starting for Tangier, to say that he was not at all satisfied with the attitude of the German Government in regard to the desertion cases at Casablanca and that it might mean mischief. I therefore went to see Monsieur Clemenceau this afternoon after an interview which I had with the Minister for Foreign Affairs.

I will first describe what Monsieur Pichon said to me on the subject, though I was informed by His Excellency that he was keeping you acquainted through the

French Embassy in London with the communications which were passing between the French and German Governments. On the 14th of October Monsieur Pichon received by telegraph from the French Ambassador at Berlin a proposal from Monsieur de Schoen that the Casablanca incident should be referred to Arbitration. He accepted the proposal the next day after consultation with the President of the Council. Hardly had this acceptance been communicated to the German Government, when Monsieur de Schoen informed Monsieur Jules Cambon that there was a matter which Prince Bülow considered should be settled apart from arbitration. It was the assault on the German Consular Officials, for which the French Government should express their regret. M. Pichon replied at once that when he accepted arbitration it was for the whole incident, the question of right in regard to the arrest of the deserters from the French Foreign Legion and the question of the acts which accompanied these arrests. Whether the latter were justified or not depended on what the Arbitration Tribunal decided on the question of the right of arrest, and he could not separate the two questions. The German Government suggested that advantage might be taken of M. Regnault being in Berlin for him to place himself in communication with the Legal Adviser of the German Foreign Office to endeavour to come to an understanding on the divergent statements as to the acts of violence. M. Pichon consented to their discussing the matter, but there was no satisfactory result. On the 1st instant the German Ambassador had an interview with M. Pichon and in the name of the German Government demanded that the French Government should express regret at the acts of violence (voies de fait) committed against German Consular Officials by French Officers and Officials. For the reasons already stated, M. Pichon declined to do this. He stated to Prince Radolin that if the arbitration went against the French contention it might be possible that an expression of regret at the arrests and the manner of their execution might be due, but certainly not before the arbitration. He would, if the German Government so wished, consent to an expression of regret on both sides that the incident should have been accompanied by acts of violence (voies de fait) leaving it undetermined which side was the first assailant and in the wrong, the expression of regret to be recorded either by an exchange of Notes of even date or in the preamble to the Arbitration Agreement or in any other suitable manner. That was the actual state of the case. The French Government had been most conciliatory. Possibly this proceeding on the part of the German Government was intended to divert public attention in Germany from The Emperor's conversations and the endeavour to obtain a cheap triumph at the expense of France, but the French Government were quite determined not to yield beyond the offer that he had made for a mutual expression of regret. They could not, even if they were inclined so to do, apologise for the acts of their army and navy officers. The deserters had tumbled out of a boat into the sea and had been seized and justifiably seized by the French officers and officials, the German Consular officials had intervened and "voies de fait" had occurred. As to who began the acts of violence the German and French Governments were not agreed, but, as the German officials tried to release the prisoners the probability was undoubtedly that they had begun the violence.

M. Pichon said that he would keep His Majesty's Government and the Russian Government informed of all the phases of this fresh difference between Germany and France and he trusted that the French Government would receive their support in resisting the unjustifiable demands of the German Government.

I told M. Clemenceau what M. Pichon had said to me and I asked him whether he really thought that Germany was seeking a pretext of quarrel with France. His Excellency replied that in the present frame of mind of The Emperor and the state of chaos at Berlin it was impossible to say what the German Government wanted. He did not think that they knew themselves. The French Government were however quite determined not to give way beyond the offer made by them that mutual regrets at the acts of violence should be placed on record. The danger was the impossibility to depend on The German Emperor from one day to another. The publication of his conversations in the " Daily Telegraph " was the act of a madman. The *coup* had " manqué," but he might try another to rehabilitate himself in the eyes of his people.

I have, &c.

FRANCIS BERTIE.

MINUTES.

The matter may prove to be extremely serious. Very violent articles are already being published in the Pan-German press. (I am having one of the most characteristic of these translated.)

What the incident means, is I think that Herr von Schoen has been more or less disavowed by Prince Bülow. If the chancellor as the result of the present domestic crisis, acquires greater power over the executive, there are indications that his policy will be largely influenced by Herr von Holstein, by far the ablest, most unscrupulous and most determinedly anti-English of Prussian officials. The legal adviser in whose hands the affair seems to have been placed, since he was charged with the negotiation with M. Renault, is Dr. Kriege, who was Herr von Holstein's right-hand man, and the author of most of the fulminating despatches and communications emanating from the Berlin Foreign Office during the acute stage of the Morocco crisis before Algeciras.

I do not know whether Sir F. Bertie expects H[is] M[ajesty's] G[overnment] to give an answer to the question whether the French gov[ernmen]t could count upon receiving British support in resisting the unjustifiable demands of the German gov[ernmen]t.

Sir E. Grey will no doubt himself consider and decide what action, if any, is to be taken.

E. A. C.
Nov. 5.
W. L.

We have to wait and see the result of the French reply, but it is quite obvious that we must support the French Gov[ernmen]t in endeavouring to obtain a pacific solution through arbitration at the Hague Tribunal.

It is to be hoped that the crisis may not become acute, but if it does, I understand that Sir E. Grey has already practically decided on the line to be followed.

C. H.

The line, if the question becomes acute will have to be decided by the Cabinet; meanwhile I have told the French Chargé d'Affaires that we certainly hold that the matter is one to be referred to arbitration and are ready to express that opinion whenever and in whatever quarter it is likely to be of use.

E. G.

MINUTE BY KING EDWARD.

The position is undoubtedly grave—but it is still to be hoped that something be satisfactorily arranged.

E.R.

No. 130.

Sir A. Nicolson to Sir Edward Grey.

F.O. 371/488.   St. Petersburgh, November 5, 1908.
38554/33655/08/28A.   D. 6·36 P.M.
Tel. (No. 241.)   R. 7 P.M.

Minister for Foreign Affairs is very anxious as to the latest developments of the Casa Blanca question and as to the demands of Germany. He would be grateful if you could let me communicate to him your impressions, as he fears that the question may become a most serious one.

No. 131.

Sir Edward Grey to Sir F. Bertie.

F.O. 371/488.
38578/33655/08/28.
(No. 526.)

Sir,   *Foreign Office, November 5, 1908.*

The French Chargé d'Affaires showed me to-day a telegram from M. Pichon stating that M. Iswolsky had been greatly disturbed by hearing that the Germans had made new trouble about the Casablanca incident : because before M. Iswolsky left Berlin quite recently Prince Bülow had told him that the Casablanca affair was settled except for one or two small details.

M. Iswolsky had gone on to say that he heard from a sure source that Austria was intending to advance upon Belgrade, and that whether she carried out her intention or not would depend upon what passed at the meeting of the German Emperor and the Austrian Heir Apparent.

I told the French Chargé d'Affaires that, after he had given me the previous information about the German attitude towards the Casablanca incident, I had spoken to the Prime Minister. It seemed to us that there was nothing to be done, for the moment, till the German reply was received.

I expressed the opinion, however, that the matter was one which ought to be settled by arbitration, and I said that we were ready to express that opinion whenever, and in whatever quarter, it would be useful. I doubted whether, at the present moment, Germany would be willing to listen to advice from outside.

As France had already accepted arbitration, when this matter became public, there would clearly be but one opinion : that France was in the right.

The French Chargé d'Affaires pointed out that this last development had leaked out first in Berlin.

I observed that this made it seem as if the matter had intentionally been timed for the meeting of the Reichstag, and as if the matter would be arranged as soon as it had served its purpose.

But it was very dangerous to play with things of this kind in public, as it was easy for two countries to drift into a position from which neither of them could recede.

[I am, &c.]
E. G[REY].

MINUTE BY KING EDWARD.

App[rove]d.—E.R.

No. 132.

Sir Edward Grey to Mr. R. McKenna.

Private.([1])

My dear McKenna,   *Foreign Office, November 5, 1908.*

I do not like the way in which the Germans have revived the Casablanca difficulty with France. A fortnight ago, Bülow himself said it was practically settled.

It certainly will not do for us to make any preparations or movements of ships which are noticeable ; that might precipitate a quarrel between Germany and France, which might not otherwise occur ; for any hostile movement on our part would be construed as an unjustifiable menace at this stage, and would influence German opinion.

([1]) [Grey MSS., Vol. 48.]

But I think the Admiralty should keep in readiness to make preparations in case Germany sent France an ultimatum and the Cabinet decided that we must assist France.

I shall be at the House later in the evening.

Yours sincerely,
E. GREY.

No. 133.

Sir A. Nicolson to Sir Edward Grey.

F.O. 371/488.   *St. Petersburgh, November 6, 1908.*
38663/33655/08/28.   D. 1·45 P.M.
Tel. (No. 242.)   R. 4·15 P.M.

My tel[egram] No. 241.([1]) France and Germany.

I should like to supplement my short telegram of last night. M[inister for] F[oreign] A[ffairs] is afraid that demands of German Gov[ernmen]t are formulated with the desire to divert public attention from other matters, and that, if they are not granted he hears that German Ambassador at Paris will proceed on unlimited leave of absence. He told me that German Emperor had recently said he was being ringed in, and that if this continued he would break through and if necessary go to war with all the world. M[inister for] F[oreign] A[ffairs] is much afraid that in the present mood of the Emperor, matters may be pushed to dangerous extreme. He considers the moment the most disadvantageous possible for Germany, as Italy would probably remain neutral and Austria will be occupied with Balkan affairs. He asked what we would do in case matters became acute. I told him I would of course only speak as an individual but I was sure we would do our best to obtain pacific solution and avert a catastrophe, but if war were to break out I would not guarantee what we might not do. In the case of unprovoked war against France I thought it very possible that we should join hands with France. I expressed some doubts whether German public would allow their Emperor to land them in a war.

M[inister for] F[oreign] A[ffairs] is most anxious and I imagine he has received some more disturbing news than has appeared in the papers.

MINUTES.

The alarm of the Russian government appears to have been caused by remarks made by the Emperor. Recent experiences may perhaps permit a doubt how far such remarks can be held to express the deliberate opinion or intentions of the German Government.

It is, at any rate, not impossible that Germany is trying to frighten Russia so as to persuade her to put pressure on her ally France, to yield to German demands.

The present telegram is but an "extender" of what Sir A. Nicolson previously reported of his interview with Mons[ieur] Isvolsky. That interview took place before the indications of a recent "détente" at Berlin have appeared.

E. A. C.
Nov. 6.

Would it be well to repeat this telegram, for confidential information, to Rome, and Berlin
Vienna } with No. 241.([1])
Constantinople

E. A. C.
Nov. 6.

([1]) [*v. supra*, p. 118, No. 130.]

The question as to what we should do if matters became acute has been answered by anticipation in the telegram sent to Sir A. Nicolson.

This telegram which has already been repeated to Paris should I think be repeated to Berlin and Rome with No. 241 and our reply.([2])

W. L.
E. G.

([2]) [v. immediately succeeding document.]

No. 134.

Sir Edward Grey to Sir A. Nicolson.

F.O. 371/488.
38554/33655/08/28A.
Tel. (No. 580.)

Foreign Office, November 6, 1908.
D. 2·30 P.M.

Your telegram No. 241.([1]) My personal opinion is that Casa Blanca question will be arranged : it is hardly conceivable that Germany will on such a pretext force war on France at a moment when this would probably be the signal for a conflict in the Balkans and when the ultimate consequence might be to involve nearly the whole of Europe in war.

But I cannot divine the German motive in reviving the Casa Blanca incident; the advantage of playing with such a question in public for Parliamentary purposes seems too disproportionate to the risk involved. I cannot therefore but feel some degree of discomfort.

France has clearly put herself in the right and Germany has put herself in the wrong by their respective attitudes towards arbitration. I am sure this will be the strong opinion in this country and I expect it to be the same in others.

If contrary to my hope and expectation an acute crisis is reached we might suggest to Russia and Italy to join in a strong appeal to Germany and France in the interests of peace to refer the matter to the Hague or to the mediation of some impartial authority who would command respect and confidence. But this would only be pressed upon Germany as a last resort : to offer advice to her before a conflict was in prospect would probably be resented.

You may tell Iswolsky unofficially that these are my views.

([1]) [v. supra, p. 118, No. 130.]

No. 135.

Sir A. Nicolson to Sir Edward Grey.

F.O. 371/488.
40779/33655/08/28A.
(No. 510.) Confidential.
Sir,

St. Petersburgh, D. November 6, 1908.
R. *November 23, 1908.*

Although a considerable time must necessarily elapse before this despatch reaches your hands, I venture to report, for the purposes of record, the observations which M. Iswolsky made to me yesterday in regard to the differences which have arisen between France and Germany in connexion with the recent incident at Casablanca.

On my visiting M. Iswolsky yesterday to enquire whether he had any news to give me before the departure of my messenger, His Excellency said that he had some very grave news to impart to me, and which was troubling him exceedingly. It appeared that the negotiations which were proceeding between the Governments of

France and Germany had suddenly entered upon an unexpected and serious phase. When he was last in Berlin he had understood that all was proceeding smoothly, and since then he had gathered that both Governments had agreed to submit to arbitration both the legal and the material aspects of the question. There was a divergence of opinion both as to what had actually occurred, and also in regard to various legal points. To his surprise he had now learnt that the German Government had apparently suddenly altered their attitude, and, while being prepared to submit the legal points to arbitration, had demanded that France should apologise for the action of her officers and officials and should liberate the deserters. He had also been informed that the German Government intended, should these demands not be granted, to instruct Prince Radolin to depart from Paris on unlimited leave of absence. M. Pichon, he understood, had replied that the French Government were always ready to submit both parts of the question to arbitration, but until the Arbitration Court had found that the French officials were to blame they were unable to accede to the demands of the German Government.

M. Iswolsky considered that the position in which the question was now placed was an exceedingly serious one; and it appeared to him as if the Emperor was anxious to divert public attention from what might be termed the " Daily Telegraph " incident and to go almost as far as initiating a quarrel with France. His Majesty was no doubt in an irritable mood, and he knew that recently His Majesty had spoken very strongly as to his being hemmed in and encircled and that if this were to continue he would break through even at the risk of war with all the world. At the same time M. Iswolsky was of opinion that the present moment · was, perhaps, the most disadvantageous possible for Germany to enter into a conflict. Since 1902 or 1903 the obligations imposed on Italy by the Triple Alliance had been much restricted, and she was no longer bound to place as heretofore 100,000 men on the Rhine. Her responsibility was not limited to a purely defensive attitude: and in the event of a conflict between France and Germany she would probably remain neutral. Austria Hungary was concerned with Balkan affairs, and if hostilities broke out there would in all probability be a Slav uprising which would largely occupy her attention. What would be the attitude of England, as much would depend on that? Could I tell him?

I said that, of course, I could only speak as a private individual, but I should imagine that if the difference between France and Germany entered upon an acute phase, my Government would do all in their power by diplomatic means to bring about a peaceful arrangement, and to avert a catastrophe: but that if their efforts were to fail, and war were to ensue, I could not answer for what my countrymen might do. I thought it very possible that, if Germany were to enter into what would be considered as an unprovoked conflict with France, my countrymen would range themselves on the side of France, and support her. At the same time I doubted if the German public would permit the Emperor to land them in a war, and although they were a well-disciplined people, they had recently shown that they were not disposed on all occasions to be unduly submissive. I could hardly imagine that the German Emperor would be prepared to face a combination of France, Russia, and possibly England.

M. Iswolsky said that he had the most serious misgivings, and enquired whether I had received any news on the subject. I replied in the negative. He said that he would be much obliged to me if I would tell you that he was much preoccupied with the situation, and that he would be glad if I could ascertain the views of my Government and communicate them to him.

M. de Panafieu, the French Minister, came to see me to-day and told me that under instructions from his Government he had communicated at 11 ·P.M. on the 3rd instant to M. Iswolsky a detailed exposition of the whole affair, and also the demands of the German Government as presented by Prince Radolin, and with the text of which you have doubtless been made acquainted. M. Iswolsky considered that the matter was so serious that he requested the Chief of the Staff to visit him, and both he and General Palitzin proceeded to M. Stolypin's residence where they remained in consultation till 4 A.M. M. de Panafieu thought that no further developments would occur till the return of the German Emperor to Berlin when a final decision would be taken by the German Government.

M. Tcharykow told me this evening that from a telegram which had been received from M. de Nelidoff, it would appear that there were hopes in Paris that the question would receive a pacific solution : and he remarked that it was fortunate that the public was not aware of the text of the demands communicated by Prince Radolin, as they were couched in a form which closely resembled an ultimatum.

I have, &c.
A. NICOLSON.

No. 136.

Sir F. Bertie to Sir Edward Grey.

F.O. 371/488.
38696/33655/08/28A.
(No. 447.) Confidential.
Sir,

Paris, D. *November* 6, 1908.
R. *November* 7, 1908.

I paid a visit to the Political Director at the Ministry for Foreign Affairs this afternoon in order to inquire whether there had been any fresh developments of the difference between the German and French Governments in regard to the Casablanca incident. I informed M. Louis of the statement which you had made to the French Chargé d'Affaires as recorded in your Telegram to me No. 247 of yesterday evening([1]) viz. that the incident seemed to His Majesty's Government to be a matter to be settled by arbitration and that they would be prepared to express that view on whatever occasion and in whatever quarter it might be thought likely to be useful.

M. Louis was glad to know exactly what you had said to the French Chargé d'Affaires. He told me that conversations were taking place between the two Governments to endeavour to settle a formula for an expression of regret by both of them at *voies de fait* having taken place in the course of the incident at Casablanca. The German Government had not yet withdrawn their demand for the surrender of the deserters or for reparation for the acts of violence against the German Consular Official which was made in the Note which the German Ambassador addressed to the French Minister for Foreign Affairs on the 1st instant. The foreign policy of Germany M. Louis said, appeared to be in the hands of so many people of divergent views that it was impossible to know what the German Government really wanted. At one moment it was the Emperor, at another Prince Bülow, at another M. de Schoen, and at another M. de Holstein, who seemed to inspire the communications made to foreign Governments

I have, &c.
FRANCIS BERTIE.

([1]) [Not reproduced as its substance is here quoted. *cp. supra,* p. 119, No. 131.]

No. 137.

Count de Salis to Sir Edward Grey.

F.O. 371/488.
38856/33655/08/28A.
(No. 488.) Confidential.
Sir,

Berlin, D. *November* 6, 1908.
R. *November* 9, 1908.

The excitement created by the publication of the Emperor's Interview in the Daily Telegraph for some days turned the attention of the German press away from the developments of the recent Casablanca negotiations as reported in Sir F. Lascelles' Despatch No. 461 of the 20th ultimo.(¹) During the last day or two, however, the alarmist reports published in the French press have revived the interest here in the Moroccan incident, and the German papers have been publishing long articles of recrimination in answer to the French remarks upon the German Government's unconciliatory attitude. In some quarters it has even been suggested that this sudden renewal of active interest in a foreign incident has been artificially awakened in order to divert attention from awkward subjects nearer home.

This morning's papers adopt a calmer tone and announce that the negotiations between the two Governments are proceeding satisfactorily and will soon lead to an arrangement that will be acceptable to both sides. Meanwhile the following semi-official account is given of the course of the negotiations up to the present time.

On October 14 Herr von Schoen in an unofficial conversation with Mr. Cambon, suggested, among other solutions of the Casablanca difficulty, the possibility of submitting the question to arbitration. On October 15 Prince Radolin reported that Mr. Pichon had informed him that he was ready to agree to the proposal to submit the question to arbitration, as conveyed to him in a despatch from Mr. Cambon. But in the meanwhile Mr. Cambon received a further communication from Herr von Schoen requesting that he would not regard his suggestion as a formal proposal. On the 18th of October accordingly Prince Bülow had an interview with Mr. Cambon in the presence of Herr von Schoen, in which the Chancellor proposed the following solution of the matter.

1. France was to express her regret at the interference of her officials with the prerogatives of the German Consul, by the violent seizure by French officers of various persons who were under the protection and charge of the German Consul.
2. Germany was to express her regret for the incorrect conduct of the German Consul in giving passes to persons who had no right to them.
3. The legal question to be submitted to arbitration.

The French view is understood to be that the facts also should be submitted to arbitration and that no preliminary apology can be required of the French Government.

On my enquiry yesterday as to whether the accounts in the papers were more or less accurate, Mr. Cambon replied that he was fairly sanguine of being able to arrive at a satisfactory settlement; he was however rather hampered by the uncompromising attitude of the French Press. I understood that to another enquirer he added in the strictest confidence " and of Mr. Clemenceau," who would, however, he hoped, ultimately give way to the extent of agreeing to a vague and general expression of regret on the part of both Governments.

I have, &c.
J. DE SALIS.

(¹) [v. supra, pp. 113–4, No. 125.]

No. 138.

Sir A. Nicolson to Sir Edward Grey.(¹)

F.O. 371/488.
38803/33655/08/28A.
Tel. (No. 245.)

St. Petersburgh, November 7, 1908.
D. 1·50 P.M.
R. 2·30 P.M.

Your tel[egram] No. 580.(²)

I communicated your views to Russian M[inister for] F[oreign] A[ffairs] this morning as I knew he was anxious to have them. He had received a telegram from

(¹) [This document has already been printed in Gooch & Temperley, Vol. V, p. 488, No. 433. The minutes there given are not reproduced here as they relate only to the subject of the last paragraph.]

(²) [v. supra, p. 121, No. 134.]

Berlin which held out some hope of a pacific solution but he is still uneasy and will remain so until the matter is finally arranged.

He has received not very satisfactory news from Sofia that the Turkish demands are exaggerated and that Bulgaria is uneasy as to Turkish military preparations; I understand that he has telegraphed to London and Paris on the subject.

No. 139.

Sir F. Bertie to Sir Edward Grey.

F.O. 371/488.
38819/33655/08/28A.
Tel. (No. 86.)

Paris, November 7, 1908.
D. 3·20 P.M.
R. 5·30 P.M.

Casablanca desertions.

Petersburg tel[egram] No. 242 of yesterday.([1])

See my despatch No. 447 of yesterday.([2]) I have seen M[inister for] F[oreign] A[ffairs] this morning.

Question of German Ambassador at Paris going on unlimited leave is not a recent suggestion. At the time of the acute stage of difference Prince Bülow said to the French Ambassador that if two Governments did not come to terms something must be done to satisfy German public opinion and when French Ambassador asked what he meant Prince Bülow replied that he might have to recommend to Emperor to give German Ambassador at Paris an unlimited leave of absence.

There is nothing fresh since yesterday. The latest phase being that whereas French Gov[ernmen]t insist on formula of regrets being in the vaguest terms so as not to prejudge the arbitration and also being mutual to the effect that both Governments regret that the incident should have given rise to "voies de fait." the German Gov[ernmen]t desire that the French declaration shall express regret for acts of violence committed against German consular official by the French authorities. The German counter-declaration would then state that German Government regret that their Consul should have exceeded his functions by extending his protection to those not entitled to it.

Matter is in suspense, pending an answer from German Emperor who is absent from Berlin shooting.

Attitude of French Government remains as stated in my despatch 440 of Nov[ember] 4th.([3])

MINUTES.

The situation remains unchanged pending the receipt of the reply of the German Gov[ernmen]t.

G. S. S.
9/11.

The German demand is so obviously unfair that it is difficult to believe in its " bona fides."

E. A. C.
Nov. 9.

But see Sir F. Bertie's tel[egram] No. 88.([4]) The French Gov[ernmen]t think that Prince Bülow is tiding over until he has got rid of the interpellation on Tuesday.

W. L.

It is to be hoped that this may be the case, and in any case time is valuable so as to allow public opinion in Germany to crystallise in opposition to war.

C. H.
E. G.

([1]) [*v. supra*, p. 120, No. 133.]
([2]) [*v. supra*, p. 123, No. 136.]
([3]) [*v. supra*, pp. 116–8, No. 129.]
([4]) [*v.* immediately succeeding document.]

No. 140.

Sir F. Bertie to Sir Edward Grey.

F.O. 371/488.
38821/33655/08/28A.
Tel. (No. 88.)   *Paris, November 8, 1908.*
   Casa Blanca desertions.
   The French are rather perplexed by the sudden departure from Berlin of
M. de Schoen, who was carrying on, and was to have continued, the conversations
with the French Ambassador on the formula for mutual expressions of regret. They
hope, and are inclined to think, that Prince Bülow is preparing to adopt a new and
more conciliatory attitude. The latest phase is that the French Government are ready
to join with the German Government in mutual expressions of regret that the incident
at Casa Blanca should have occurred, as well as of regret that it should have been
accompanied by acts of violence. The formula would not particularly specify what
the incident was. The French Government think that Prince Bülow will prolong the
conversations till after the interpellation in the Reichstag.

No. 141.

Sir F. Bertie to Sir Edward Grey.

F.O. 371/488.
39270/33655/08/28A.
(No. 454.)   *Paris, D. November 10, 1908.*
Sir,   R. *November 11, 1908.*
   The news telegraphed from Berlin that the Imperial Government have decided
to agree to submit to arbitration the question of facts as well as the question of right
arising out of the incident of the Deserters at Casablanca and have changed their
attitude respecting the form in which the regrets for the incident at Casablanca are
to be expressed, has been received by the French Press with every sign of satisfaction.
Extracts from the official statement in the "North German Gazette" and the semi-
official explanations of the German change of front in the "Cologne Gazette" are
reproduced by the more important Paris papers. M. Lautier, writing in the "Figaro,"
states that he is able to guarantee that the new German Secretary of State for
Foreign Affairs has accepted the formula of regrets proposed by M. Jules Cambon
with the introduction of the word "subalternes," so that it now runs as follows :—
"Les deux Gouvernements regrettent l'incident du 25 septembre qui a amené leurs
agents subalternes à des voies de fait et à de fâcheuses violences." M. de Kiderlen-
Waechter, so M. Lautier states, asked that a second sentence should be added to the
following effect :—" Chacun des deux Gouvernements s'engage à exprimer des regrets
à l'autre, selon la décision de l'arbitre." The two negotiators are to refer to their
respective Governments and M. Lautier anticipates that no further difficulty will arise
in agreeing on a formula satisfactory to both parties.
   The "Temps" publishes a slightly different formula to that given by M. Lautier.
It is as follows :—

   "Les deux Gouvernements regrettant les événements qui se sont produits à
   Casablanca le 25 Septembre dernier et qui ont amené des agents subalternes à des
   violences et à de fâcheuses voies de fait, décident de soumettre l'ensemble des
   questions soulevées à ce sujet à l'arbitrage.
   "D'un commun accord, chacun des deux Gouvernements s'engage à exprimer
   ses regrets sur les actes de ces agents, suivant le jugement que les arbitres auront
   porté sur les faits et sur la question de droit."

The impression gained from a perusal of the French papers this morning is that all sections of opinion are perfectly aware of the fact that the change of front on the part of Germany is in fact a complete retreat from her former position, and constitutes a diplomatic success for the French Government, and a considerable satisfaction for the " amour propre " of France. The Press has shown throughout the discussion of this incident remarkable unanimity in supporting the attitude of the Government and in advocating a calm but firm refusal of the renewed demand put forward by the German Ambassador at Paris that France should express regret for the action of her military authorities while Germany should do the same as regards that of her Consulate at Casablanca. In the course of the past week, the analogy between the situation immediately preceding the retirement from office of M. Delcassé and the present moment has not infrequently been mentioned in the Press, and the attitude adopted by M. Clemenceau is favourably compared to that of the French Cabinet in 1905.

There can be no doubt that M. Clemenceau and M. Pichon have had the cordial approval of public opinion in France and that their attitude has stregthened their position and increased their prestige. It is likely that this fact will be evident in the forthcoming Debate in the Chamber of Deputies on Moroccan affairs which was to have taken place immediately after the reassembly of the Legislature on October 13th, but which was postponed at the request of M. Pichon until a Yellow Book in course of preparation should have been laid before Parliament.

The satisfaction felt in France at the " détente " in the situation and the prospect of a settlement consonant with French dignity is also shewn by a certain disposition to give credit to the German Government for not adopting an unyielding attitude. The " Figaro," for instance, acknowledges that the weight attached by the German Foreign Office to the report communicated to them within the last few days, of M. Dorbé, French Commissioner of Police at Casablanca, and the attention paid to his statements with regard to the occurrences there, are acts " de bonne foi et de bonne volonté " which must be noted with pleasure in France.

I have, &c.
FRANCIS BERTIE.

No. 142.

Sir F. Bertie to Sir Edward Grey.

F.O. 371/488.
39381/33655/08/28A.
(No. 455.)   *Paris,* D. *November* 11, 1908.
Sir,   R. *November* 12, 1908.

In my despatch No. 454 of yesterday(1) I had the honour of transmitting to you two versions of the formula of regrets said to have been agreed on between the French and German Governments. The one published in the " Figaro " under the authority of Monsieur Lautier ran as follows :—

> " Les deux Gouvernements regrettent l'incident du 25 septembre qui a amené leurs agents subalternes à des voies de fait et à de fâcheuses violences. Chacun des deux Gouvernements s'engage à exprimer des regrets à l'autre selon la décision de l'arbitre."

It was evident that if the French had consented as represented by Monsieur Lautier to refer to " leurs agents subalternes " the wording would have included French subordinate Agents and would have been a concession to German demands. The

(1) [*v.* immediately preceding document.]

correct text however is that given in the "Temps" which speaks of "des agents subalternes" which does not necessarily refer to French agents and is as follows :—

"Les deux Gouvernements regrettant les événements qui se sont produits à Casablanca le 25 septembre dernier et qui ont amené des agents subalternes à des violences et à de fâcheuses voies de fait décident de soumettre l'ensemble des questions soulevées à ce sujet à l'arbitrage.

"D'un commun accord chacun des deux Gouvernements s'engage à exprimer ses regrets sur les actes de ces agents suivant le jugement que les arbitres auront porté sur les faits et sur la question de droit."

I congratulated Monsieur Pichon this afternoon on the termination of the difference. He said that it would have been closed some time ago if there had been any direction at Berlin or if the German Embassy had been allowed to settle it with the French Government. It was impossible to know from one day to the other what the German Government wanted. Their attitude was constantly changing.

I have, &c.
FRANCIS BERTIE.

No. 143.

Sir E. Goschen to Sir Edward Grey.

F.O. 371/488.
39836/33655/08/28A.
(No. 491.)   *Berlin,* D. *November* 11, 1908.
Sir,   R. *November* 16, 1908.

With reference to my Telegram No. 65 of yesterday,(¹) I have the honour to report that the following is the text of the agreement with regard to the recent Casablanca deserters incident which was signed at the Foreign Office yesterday.

"The German and French Government regret the events which took place at Casablanca on the 25th of September last, and which gave rise to the exercise of force and to aggressive acts on the part of subordinate officials. They have decided to submit all the questions which have arisen in this connection to a Court of Arbitration. By mutual agreement each of the Governments bind themselves to express their regret at the conduct of these officials, according to the decision which the Arbiter shall give on the question of fact and of law."

The German papers this morning generally express their relief and satisfaction at the announcement of this solution of the incident. The "Berliner Lokal Anzeiger," which is occasionally made use of by Prince Bülow for the purpose of explaining the Government's action or policy, publishes the following apparently inspired account of the final stage of the negotiations from the German point of view.

There was from the very first, the article maintains, a difference between the two Governments regarding the legal aspect of the incident; but since the exchange of the circumstantial reports, it has transpired that considerable differences as to the facts of the case also existed. The original German demand that France should, as a preliminary to arbitration, express her regret at the attack upon the German consular officers was based upon the assumption that the French Government did not deny that such an attack was made. When, however, a perusal of the French case showed them that the facts set forth therein upon this point did not correspond with those stated in the German versions the Imperial Government were compelled to recognise that the

---

(¹) [Not reproduced. It stated that the Arbitration Agreement was about to be signed by the French and German Governments, and summarized its text.]

declaration demanded would in a certain sense prejudice the arbitral decision. The misunderstanding on this point might have been removed sooner, it is added, had the Imperial Foreign Office been placed in earlier possession of the French case.

In view of the desire of the German Government, which was also shared by the French Government, to settle the matter formally as quickly as possible, the two Governments decided to draw up the above-quoted agreement, which, it is hoped, will have proved satisfactory to both parties. The German nation can now await the verdict of the Arbiter with equanimity; whatever form it may take, it will now no longer cast any shadow upon the good relations of the two countries.

I have, &c.
W. E. GOSCHEN.

No. 144.

Sir F. Bertie to Sir Edward Grey.

F.O. 371/488.
41165/41165/08/28A.
(No. 478.)   *Paris,* D. *November* 24, 1908.
Sir,   R. *November* 25, 1908.

The correspondent of the "Matin" at Berlin has telegraphed to his paper an account of an interview which he had yesterday with Herr von Kiderlen-Waechter the German Secretary of State for Foreign Affairs.

Herr von Kiderlen-Waechter is represented to have stated that he considered the Casa Blanca incident as closed. The Arbitration Court would now decide the question, and the two countries would accept its decision. He continued: "But a lesson may be drawn from this incident, namely that matters of this kind should above all be dealt with between diplomatists who are capable of discussing them with the necessary moderation, in order to avoid creating an excitement in the press and public opinion. It seems to me that the French press took this affair *au tragique* it was not one likely in the opinion of the two Governments to have grave consequences. We have never followed an aggressive policy, and yet our good faith is constantly being questioned. You, in France, believed for instance that we wanted to play a double game with Mulai Hafid, that we demanded his instant recognition, whereas we merely expressed the desire that he should be recognized. You must surely admit that it was a natural desire seeing that he was already *de facto* sovereign, and that his recognition assured peace in Morocco." "It is the same thing in the Balkans" continued Herr von Kiderlen-Waechter, "where we are suspected of dark plots, while our action is limited in reality to defending our economic interests, and to giving our allies the support which they are entitled to expect from us. As both Germany and France have only economic interests involved, there should be no divergences between them of a serious nature."

Herr von Kiderlen-Waechter added that the so-called internal crisis in Germany had been greatly exaggerated at home and even more abroad. The question which was for the moment occupying attention was financial reform.

I have, &c.
FRANCIS BERTIE.

[*ED. NOTE.*—The Arbitration Agreement was signed at Berlin on November 24, by Herr von Kiderlen-Waechter and M. Jules Cambon. The Court was to consist of five arbitrators chosen from the members of the Permanent Court of Arbitration at the Hague, and was to meet at the Hague on May 1, 1909. Herr von Kiderlen-Waechter, Acting Secretary of State during the illness of Herr von Schoen, disapproved the latter's handling of the question, and claimed the whole merit of the peaceful settlement. *v. Jäckh*, II, pp. 13 and 16.]

No. 145.

Lord Acton to Sir Edward Grey.

F.O. 372/171.   The Hague, May 22, 1909.
19337/2111/09/28.   D. 6 P.M.
Tel. (No. 5.) Treaty. *En clair.*   R. 7·15 P.M.
    Casa Blanca Arbitration Award, given to-day, is to the following effect :—

Conflict between exclusive Consular jurisdiction established by the Capitulations and exclusive military jurisdiction of an Army of Occupation should, in the present instance, be decided in favour of France, as Casa Blanca was at the time occupied by the French military forces. In view, however, of absence of universally accepted doctrine on subject of concurrent Consular and military jurisdictions, German Consulate was not to blame for protecting deserters at their request. But Secretary to German Consulate committed a fault of manifest gravity in attempting the embarkation on a German steamer of deserters not of German nationality, and in making the Consul sign to that end a safe conduct for six instead of three persons. In signing the safe conduct Consul committed an unintentional fault. Further, under circumstances, German Consulate had no right to grant protections even to deserters of German nationality, though error in so doing cannot be described as a fault either international or the reserve (? reverse). On other hand French military authorities should have confined action to preventing embarkation and have left deserters in custody of German Consulate pending decisions as to competing military and Consular jurisdictions. They should have respected, so far as possible, *de facto* protection exercised by German Consulate, which course would have contributed to maintain prestige of Consular authority in Morocco. Threats made with aid of revolver and blows dealt at Moorish soldier attached to German Consulate, after he had ceased to resist were not justified.
    Text by messenger to-night.

MINUTES.

The award makes no appeal to a sense of strict logic or abstract justice.
Clearly the arbitrators consider the French to have been in the right. But in order that a just verdict may not offend Germany, the wrongful actions of the German agents are declared to have been little, harmless, errors for which they cannot be blamed; and the French authorities are told that although they were in the right, they ought in courtesy to have acted as if they had been in the wrong.
The award satisfactorily settles the dispute. But whether it will inspire confidence in the judicial character of arbitration in general, must be very doubtful.
E. A. C.
May 24.

Verdict for the French, but they should not have defended their rights by force!
W. L.

The main result of the arbitration is satisfactory, but the methods of compromise, and the petty provisos by which it is qualified rather detract from its value as a political pronouncement.
W. E. D.
27.5.09.

[ED. NOTE.—The Casablanca dispute was closed by the following arbitral award :—

Lord Acton to Sir Edward Grey.

F.O. 372/171.
19374/2111/09/28.
(No. 28.) Treaty.   The Hague, D. May 22, 1909.
Sir,   R. May 24, 1909.
    With reference to my telegram No. 5 Treaty of this day's date([1]) I have the honour to transmit, herewith, copies of the French and German texts of the award delivered to-day by the Arbitral Tribunal in the matter of the Casablanca dispute.
I have, &c.
ACTON.

([1]) [v. immediately preceding document.]

PAR CES MOTIFS,

Le Tribunal arbitral

Déclare et prononce ce qui suit :

C'est à tort et par une faute grave et manifeste que le Secrétaire du Consulat impérial allemand à Casablanca a tenté de faire embarquer, sur un vapeur allemand, des déserteurs de la Légion étrangère française qui n'étaient pas de nationalité allemande.

Le Consul allemand et les autres agents du Consulat ne sont pas responsables de ce chef; toutefois, en signant le sauf-conduit qui lui a été présenté, le Consul a commis une faute non intentionnelle.

Le Consulat allemand n'avait pas, dans les conditions de l'espèce, le droit d'accorder sa protection aux déserteurs de nationalité allemande; toutefois, l'erreur de droit commise sur ce point par les fonctionnaires du Consulat ne saurait leur être imputée comme une faute, soit intentionnelle, soit non intentionnelle.

C'est à tort que les autorités militaires françaises n'ont pas, dans la mesure du possible, respecté la protection de fait exercée sur ces déserteurs au nom du Consulat allemand.

Même abstraction faite du devoir de respecter la protection consulaire, les circonstances ne justifiaient, de la part de militaires français, ni la menace faite à l'aide d'un revolver, ni la prolongation des coups donnés au soldat marocain du Consulat.

Il n'y a pas lieu de donner suite aux autres réclamations contenues dans les conclusions des deux Parties.

Fait à *La Haye*, dans l'Hôtel de la Cour permanente d'Arbitrage, le 22 mai 1909.

Le Président: Hj. L. HAMMARSKJÖLD.
Le Secrétaire général : MICHIELS van VERDUYNEN.]

IV.—THE FRANCO-GERMAN AGREEMENT OF FEBRUARY 1909.

[*ED. NOTE.*—The discussions which led to the Agreement were initiated by M. Caillaux, Minister of Finance. in a conversation with Freiherr von der Lancken on December 13, 1908. *v. G.P.*, XXIV, ch. 182, and *Livre Jaune, Affaires du Maroc*, V, (1908–10), pp. 61–86. *cp. Tardieu*, pp. 1–24; and Freiherr von der Lancken : *Meine dreissig Dienstjahre*, (Berlin, 1931), pp. 75–88.

No. 146.

Mr. Lister to Sir Edward Grey.

F.O. 371/695.
1780/1780/09/28.
Tel. (No. 3.)   *Tangier, January* 11, 1909.

Harris has received a private telegram from the "Times" that they understand a *détente* has taken place between France and Germany over Morocco. They instruct him to make inquiries, and, if so, to frame his telegrams accordingly. He has seen French Chargé d'Affaires, who at first declined to admit any great change, but subsequently acknowledged that the way in which Germany had taken occupation of Skrirat was certainly satisfactory. It was no doubt outside French zone, and he had been anxious himself as to what they might say.

German Minister told Harris that attitude of French Legation towards him had undoubtedly been more conciliatory during the last few weeks, and that his instructions were to promote as much as possible the better feeling.

No. 147.

Mr. Lister to Sir Edward Grey.

F.O. 371/695.
2935/1780/09/28.

(No. 12.)   *Tangier,* D. *January* 15, 1909.
Sir,   R. *January* 23, 1909.

I cannot help thinking for a number of reasons, unimportant perhaps in themselves, but all pointing to the same direction, that the desire of Germany for the moment is for a *détente* in her relations with France in Morocco.

I had a long talk to the French Chargé d'Affaires on the 13th instant, and mentioned to him what Mr. Harris had told me, as reported in my telegram No. 3 of that date.(¹) He said that he had certainly been struck by the attitude of Germany with regard to the occupation of the Kasbah of Skrirat* by French troops. · It was undoubtedly outside the French Zone, and he had personally been anxious as to the manner in which the news would be taken in Berlin. He had happened to be on board one of the French men-of-war when the wireless telegram from the German Consul at Casablanca to Doctor Rosen reporting the incident in alarmist and exaggerated terms had been intercepted. He had consequently been prepared for an outburst, and his surprise had been great when he heard that the German Press had been informed at the Wilhelmstrasse that the German Government knew nothing of the incident, and that in any case it did not regard them [*sic*] in any sort of way. He had himself seen the text of the telegram; so that there was no doubt that the incident was known at Berlin, and Doctor Rosen was not the man to minimize it when reporting it. This fact, taken with what Doctor Rosen told Mr. Harris that his instructions were to do all in his power to promote the friendlier feelings, which, he believed, existed between the two Legations, seems to indicate that for the moment Germany does not wish to create difficulties for France in Morocco. It appears to me possible that the instructions to which Doctor Rosen alluded may have been conveyed in the answer sent to his report announcing the occupation of Skrirat.

The account too given by His Majesty's Consul at Casablanca of the attentions shown by the French Authorities to Herr Luderitz, the German Consul there, on the occasion of his departure from that port, which was reported in my despatch No. 11 of the 11th instant, is significant.(²) I also learn that General d'Amade has been entertained by M. Brandt, the German Merchant who acts as Austro-Hungarian Consul, and that the greatest cordiality reigned at the entertainment.

This morning Mr. Harris came to see me again and told me he had had another talk with Doctor Rosen on the subject, who had repeated with even greater emphasis what he had said on Wednesday, and had expressed satisfaction at the change which had taken place in the tone of the "Temps," as evidenced by M. Tardieu's last articles. He had deplored the fact that his strained personal relations with M. Regnault rendered a *rapprochement* between the two Legations more difficult, but expressed the hope that what the two Ministers had failed in bringing about, might be effected by commercial co-operation between the two countries. In this respect the International Mining Syndicate, in which Mr. Harris is taking a prominent part, and which would have his whole hearted support, might render the greatest service to the two countries. (Mr. Harris' personal feelings may possibly have added colour to his report of Dr. Rosen's remarks.) Mr. Harris then inquired as to the truth of a report that two Engineers of the German Firm of Mannesmann, who have been trying for some time to obtain mining concessions in Morocco, were leaving to-day for Fez. Doctor Rosen admitted that the report was correct : he said, however, that he did not consider that M. Mannesmann constituted a danger to the prospects of the

(¹) [*v.* immediately preceding document.]
* About 30 kilometres S. of Rabat. [G. S. S.]
(²) [Not reproduced.]

syndicate. He would not conceal from Mr. Harris that he had telegraphed to his Government recommending that the claims of the Firm should be fully considered by the German group, but that their inclusion would not modify the proportion of participation of the various nationalities. He also authorised Mr. Harris to telegraph to the syndicate renewing his promise of entire assistance.

I have, &c.
REGINALD LISTER.

No. 148.

Sir F. Bertie to Sir Edward Grey.

F.O. 371/666.
4490/4490/09/17.
(No. 53.)   Paris, D. *February* 1, 1909.
Sir,   R. *February* 3, 1909.

I have the honour to enclose herein a memorandum by Mr. Carnegie containing an account, given him by Mr. Saunders, the "Times" Correspondent, of a conversation which the latter had had with M. Clemenceau this morning.

I have, &c.
FRANCIS BERTIE.

Enclosure in No. 148.

Memorandum.

Mr. Saunders, the "Times" Correspondent, called at the Embassy this morning. He said that he had just seen M. Clemenceau whom he had found in a state of considerable nervous irritation. The Prime Minister began by complaining bitterly of the action of His Majesty's Government in regard to financial matters in Turkey. They had, he said proposed that the English and French should co-operate and now had suddenly let the scheme drop. "The English," he exclaimed, "want to get everything in Turkey for themselves." Mr. Saunders remarked that he imagined that what His Majesty's Government wanted was a strong Turkey and that the French Government must want that also, but that he was not much acquainted with the financial question to which M. Clemenceau had referred. M. Clemenceau did not respond with much heartiness in regard to the remark about the similarity of French and British interests in a strong Turkey and said rather excitedly "Go and see M. Pichon, he will tell you all about it, and say to him that I, the Minister President, sent you to him."

M. Clemenceau then exclaimed that he had been much astonished at a proposal which, according to a Mr. Addis, whom he had seen lately, His Majesty's Government had made, that the Germans should be allowed a share in a railway loan in China. He added that he had sent a man to the Foreign Office in London to make enquiries about Mr. Addis and that nothing was known there about him. "There is a cleft in the *entente*," said M. Clemenceau at the conclusion of the interview, "and care must be taken that it does not widen."

Mr. Saunders said he knew nothing about the Railway Loan mentioned above, so I briefly gave him the outlines of the scheme and told him who Mr. Addis is.

Mr. Saunders was to see M. Pichon late this afternoon. In the course of our conversation Mr. Saunders remarked that owing to the comparatively short time he had been in Paris his views on current affairs here were of no great value but from what he had already learnt he had been struck by the prevailing desire of pecuniary gain which seemed common to most classes in France. It appeared to him that French Foreign policy was largely if not wholly influenced by this idea of gain, and, if this view was correct, therein lay a certain danger for the stability of the *Entente*. There was no doubt that England wanted a strong Turkey, but does France? Was she not more likely to benefit financially under a weak and corrupt régime, as in the past, than under a strong and pure administration? It was impossible that Germany viewed the changed conditions in Turkey with favour. There seemed to be a danger therefore that France and Germany might come to some understanding on the subject to the detriment of English interests in Turkey and of Turkey herself. The Prince of Monaco, who was reported to have acted on more than one occasion as a go-between for France and Germany, was now in Paris. He had been received by and had had a long interview with the President and had also seen either M. Clemenceau or M. Pichon (I forget which it was). This might of course mean nothing but still was perhaps worth noting.

LANCELOT D. CARNEGIE.

Paris, February 1, 1909.

MINUTES.

The presence in Paris of the Prince of Monaco lends a certain amount of colour to the idea that France and Germany may be attempting to negotiate some kind of *rapprochement*. It was the Prince of Monaco who conveyed M. Etienne to Kiel in 1907 to have a political interview with the German Emperor, while the same year rumours appeared in the German press that the Emperor and President Fallières would meet at Monaco.

Further the sudden recent modification of Germany's attitude towards France in Morocco—which greatly displeases the pan-Germans—can probably only be accounted for by the fact that the two countries were trying to arrange something between them—and from M. Clemenceau's language to Mr. Saunders an arrangement if made will probably not be such as would commend itself to us.

G. S. S.
3/2.

The *rapprochement* in Morocco has taken the form of a deal about the arms contract. Mr. Saunders has put his finger on the weak spot in French foreign policy.

W. L.

There was also the deal over the drainage works at Tangier and Laraiche.

Ċ. H.
E. G.

No. 149.

Sir F. Bertie to Sir Edward Grey.

F.O. 371/695.
5053/1780/28/09.
Tel. (No. 24.) Confidential.

Paris, February 6, 1909.
D. 3·44 P.M.
R. 5·15 P.M.

Minister for Foreign Affairs tells me that he has instructed the French Ambassador to communicate to you, for your opinion, an Agreement which has been negotiated with the German Government, but not signed, whereby Germany disinterests herself from Moroccan affairs. I asked him what was the *quid pro quo.* He assured me that there was none.

MINUTES.

It is very unlike the Germans to give something for nothing. One cannot help wondering whether the *quid pro quo* is in the nature of some tacit understanding in regard to contracts and commercial affairs in Morocco.

G. H. V.

Germany must certainly have got some *quid pro quo*, the nature of which we must make every effort to ascertain.

G. S. S.
8/2.

Mr. Villiers has perhaps suggested where Germany is to find her *quid pro quo*. We shall find out only too soon if he is right.

W. L.

Politically it is a great advantage that France and Germany should agree not to quarrel about Morocco.

Commercially I fear other people must lose by an *entente* between them, though the open door must be preserved on paper.

As long however as the independence and integrity of Morocco are preserved; the Gov[ern-men]t and condition of that country will be so bad that there will not be very valuable commercial development for anybody.

E. G.

No. 150.

Sir M. de Bunsen to Sir Edward Grey.

F.O. 371/695.
5484/1780/09/28.
Tel. (No. 5.) Confidential.

Madrid, February 9, 1909.
D. 8·40 P.M.
R. 11·30 P.M.

Sir F. Bertie's telegram No. 24.(¹)

French Ambassador read to me to-day in confidence the Franco-German Agreement concerning Morocco, which was to be signed to-day in Berlin. The German Ambassador suggested to his Excellency this morning that they should jointly communicate the text to the Spanish Minister for Foreign Affairs, but the French Ambassador had already done so yesterday.

The Minister for Foreign Affairs remarked to me yesterday evening that the Spanish Government would probably wish to associate themselves in some way with this Agreement, which tended to diminish the existing tension between France and Germany in Morocco, and must therefore be welcomed by the Spanish Government. It did not appear to me, however, that his Excellency was entirely pleased with an understanding which emphasizes the political predominance of France in Morocco.

The French Ambassador learns to-day from the Spanish Minister for Foreign Affairs that the Spanish Ambassador at Berlin has been instructed to propose to the German Government an Agreement with Spain on the lines of an Agreement with France. The Spanish Ambassador at Paris was to inform the French Government of this intention.

(¹) [v. immediately preceding document.]

No. 151.

Mr. Lister to Sir Edward Grey.

F.O. 371/695.
5513/1780/09/28.
Tel. (No. 10.)

Tangier, D. *February 9, 1909.* 9·8 P.M.
R. *February 10, 1909,* 2·30 A.M.

Your telegram No. 11.(¹)

French Chargé d'Affaires informs me that he first (group omitted ? heard) news of Declaration last night by telegraph.

He was instructed to concert with his German colleague and jointly communicate Declaration to the Moorish Government. He accordingly called on Dr. Rosen, who had not as yet received any telegram, and appeared to know nothing of the Agreement. He received the news with bad grace, but subsequently recovered himself, and said that a complete change would now of necessity take place in the attitude of the German Legation, which would correspond far better with his personal feelings.

(¹) [This telegram, despatched on February 8, repeated Sir F. Bertie's Tel. No. 24 of February 6. (v. supra, p. 134, No. 149.)]

He (? subsequently) received his instructions, and the (? two) went together to the Ministry for Foreign Affairs and communicated the Declaration to Guebbas, (? who) professed to be much pleased. This I doubt. The person who will not be pleased is the Spanish Minister, who is shortly starting for Fez, and whose principal trump card was German hostility to France.

No. 152.

Sir Edward Grey to Sir E. Goschen.

F.O. 371/695.
5613/1780/09/28.
(No. 36.)
Sir, *Foreign Office, February 9, 1909.*

I told the German Chargé d'Affaires to-day([1]) that I had heard a few days ago that Germany and France were coming to an agreement about Morocco, but that I should not have spoken about it officially yet had it not been that I was told this afternoon that Reuter had received the text of the agreement from Paris.

I wished to express my satisfaction that an agreement had been come to. I had always felt the danger of difficulties arising between France and Germany about Morocco, and if I had been asked to name what I most desired in Foreign Affairs, one of the things would have been that the difficulties between Germany and France about Morocco should be removed. I assumed that this would be done by the agreement. Our only interest in Morocco was to preserve equal opportunities for commerce, and if these were safeguarded the political effect of the agreement would be excellent.

The Chargé d'Affaires told me that an agreement with France about Morocco had been desired in Berlin for some time. He himself had remarked to Herr von Schön, on the occasion of the German Emperor's visit to England, that the relations between England and Germany could never be permanently improved till the Moroccan question was settled. Till then, there would always be a danger that England and Germany would find their relations disturbed by disputes between Germany and France about Morocco.

I said this was perfectly true. We had our diplomatic engagements with France. They had come into operation, as he knew, during the Algeciras Conference. As long as difficulties were liable to occur between Germany and France about Morocco, these engagements were liable to make difficulties between Germany and us.

This danger was I hoped now removed.

[I am, &c.]
E. G[REY.]

([1]) [For Herr von Kühlmann's report v. G.P., XXIV, p. 494.]

No. 153.

Sir Edward Grey to Sir F. Bertie.

F.O. 371/695.
5715/1780/09/28.
(No. 75.)
Sir, *Foreign Office, February 9, 1909.*

M. Cambon showed me to-day the declaration which he had shown to Sir Charles Hardinge on Saturday 6th, and which was to be exchanged with Germany, with regard to Morocco.([1])

([1]) [v. infra, p. 139, No. 155, encl. 2.]

I told him I was very glad the sun was shining as regards Morocco. I was very pleased that France and Germany had come to terms, for I had always felt that the question of Morocco was one which might at any moment cause great difficulties, and I now considered that the danger had passed away.

As to the details of the agreement, I thought there might be some criticism made upon the last sentence, by which France and Germany undertook to seek to associate their nationals in undertakings for which those nationals obtained concessions. This might be construed to mean that France and Germany would co-operate to secure concessions in such a way as to leave a very poor chance for other countries. It ought to be made quite clear that the intention was not that France and Germany would give each other a preference; in other words, that the sentence was not intended to have an exclusive meaning, or to prejudice the open door.

M. Cambon said that, when he was authorized to communicate the declaration to me officially, he would make it clear that the words in question were not open to this criticism. Some years ago, in Algeria, there had been a concession for mines which necessitated the making of a railway; and for two years the French Chamber had refused to sanction it, because Germans were associated with the enterprise. He understood that the words in question meant that there would now be no opposition to the association of French and German nationals in undertakings in Morocco.

M. Cambon was evidently somewhat puzzled as to the origin of the agreement. His brother at Berlin had written to M. Pichon to say that the Germans were pressing for an agreement. On Friday 5th he had arrived suddenly with the terms of it, which had not then been seen by M. Clemenceau, and which had been approved subsequently.

M. Cambon's own explanation was that Prince Bülow, being in a difficulty and in danger of losing the support of the Reichstag for his financial proposals, and having lost the confidence of the Emperor, saw the risk of finding himself without a friend in Germany, and of being exposed to the attack that by his policy he had left Germany without a friend. Hence Prince Bülow had wished to present the Reichstag with some such arrangement as this; and M. Cambon thought it might be supplemented by some Colonial arrangement with us.

I said that, in other words, this meant that Prince Bülow wished to erect a *façade* of friendship.

So far as we were concerned, Count Metternich had asked me in a general way what we meant to discuss at Berlin. I had replied that if the Germans wished to discuss Near Eastern affairs Sir Charles Hardinge would of course be ready to discuss them. Naval expenditure seemed to me the most important subject at present, but we would not discuss it unless the Germans desired it, we had our own plans and were ready to proceed with them. I had suggested that Lord Crewe should have a talk with Herr Dernburg, who had lately been in South Africa, and discuss with him the various frontier questions we had there. But I had had no indication from Count Metternich that the Germans wished to make any new proposal. I knew they would like an arrangement about the frontier police in South Africa; but our difficulty about all arrangements of this sort was that they had to be made by, and at the expense of, the Colonial Governments.

I observed to M. Cambon that the Spanish Ambassador had questioned me last night about the agreement between France and Germany. I had told the Spanish Ambassador that there was something in prospect, but that I was sure it would contain nothing in any way contrary to the Agreement between Spain and France.

The Spanish Ambassador had seemed very hurt that nothing had been said to the Spanish Government, and I had therefore felt unable to tell him that I had had any communication from M. Cambon. I thought it very natural that the Spanish Government who, like us, had an Agreement with France about Morocco, and who, like us, had supported France at the Algeciras Conference, should expect to be treated in the same way as we were.

M. Cambon said he was sure that a communication had been made to the Spanish Government, for his brother at Berlin had spoken to the Spanish Ambassador there.

[I have, &c.]

E. G[REY].

No. 154.

Sir M. de Bunsen to Sir Edward Grey.

F.O. 371/695.
5625/1780/09/28.
Tel. (No. 6.)

Madrid, February 10, 1909.
D. 5·56 P.M.
R. 9·15 P.M.

My immediately preceding telegram.(¹)

Spanish Ambassador in Berlin telegraphs that German Government raise no objection to Spanish proposal to negotiate an Agreement with Germany similar to one just signed between Germany and France. Minister for Foreign Affairs does not anticipate any difficulty.

French Ambassador would prefer that Spain should simply adhere to Franco-German Agreement, but Spanish Government are a little hurt at the omission of any mention of Spain in that Agreement, and prefer to conclude a separate one.

(¹) [*v. supra*, p. 135, No. 150.]

No. 155.

Sir Edward Grey to Sir F. Bertie.

F.O. 371/695.
5945/1780/09/28.
(No. 80.)

Sir,

Foreign Office, February 10, 1909.

M. Cambon handed me to-day the text of the Franco-German Declaration about Morocco, with a covering Note, copies of which are inclosed herein.

M. Cambon then said that the reception of the King appeared to be good in Berlin, and the speeches were excellent. He thought Germany would now propose something to us, but he did not know what. Possibly it might be about the Bagdad Railway.

I told him we should be quite willing to discuss the Bagdad Railway, on the terms I had previously indicated. I had been approached recently by one or two British financiers who had been in communication with German financiers. They had asked me whether the British Government were prepared to favour negotiations with Germany about the Railway. I had always replied that we were prepared to do so on proper terms, provided there were negotiations *à quatre*, between France, Germany, Russia, and ourselves. The difficulty lay in the Russian Government. I had not, however, had any proposal about anything from Berlin.

M. Cambon said that Naval Expenditure would be a great difficulty. Did I think the Germans would agree to compare Estimates, as I had suggested some time ago, with a view to reduction?

I told him I was afraid the Germans would not do this. We should have to decide what expenditure was necessary to enable us to maintain a sufficient superiority as the German programme of construction advanced, and I thought the Germans ought not to resent this.

[I am, &c.

E. GREY.]

Enclosure 1 in No. 155.

M. Paul Cambon to Sir Edward Grey.

Ambassade de France en Angleterre, Londres
Monsieur le Secrétaire d'Etat,   *le* 10 *Février,* 1909.
J'ai l'honneur de communiquer, ci-joint, à Votre Excellence le texte de la
déclaration Franco-Allemande en date d'hier relative au Maroc.

Comme Votre Excellence le constatera, cette Déclaration est conforme à l'Acte
d'Algésiras et ne porte aucune atteinte aux droits et aux intérèts des autres Nations.

Veuillez, &c.

PAUL CAMBON.

Enclosure 2 in No. 155.

Declaration.

Le Gouvernement de la République Française et le Gouvernement Impérial
Allemand, animés d'un égal désir de faciliter l'exécution de l'Acte d'Algésiras, sont
convenus de préciser la portée qu'ils attachent à ses clauses en vue d'éviter toute cause
de malentendus entre eux dans l'avenir.

En conséquence,

Le Gouvernement de la République Française entièrement attaché au maintien de
l'intégrité et de l'indépendance de l'Empire Chérifien, résolu à y sauvegarder l'égalité
économique et, par suite, à ne pas y entraver les intérèts commerciaux et industriels
Allemands,

et le Gouvernement Impérial Allemand, ne poursuivant que des intérèts
économiques au Maroc, reconnaissant d'autre part que les intérèts politiques
particuliers de la France y sont étroitement liés à la consolidation de l'ordre et de la
paix intérieure et décidé à ne pas entraver ces intérèts,

déclarent qu'ils ne poursuivent et n'encouragent aucune mesure de nature à créer
en leur faveur ou en faveur d'une Puissance quelconque un privilège économique, et
qu'ils chercheront à associer leurs nationaux dans les affaires dont ceux-ci pourront
obtenir l'entreprise.([1])

([1]) [*v. infra,* p. 830, *App.* IV.]

No. 156.

Sir M. de Bunsen to Sir Edward Grey.

F.O. 371/695.
6152/1780/09/28.
(No. 27.) Confidential.   *Madrid, D. February* 11, 1909.
Sir,   *. R. February* 15, 1909.

The French Ambassador's nervousness at the prospect of a Declaration similar
to the Franco-German one concerning Morocco being signed at Berlin between Spain
and Germany does not tend to diminish. His Excellency thinks it very foolish of
Spain to complicate her position in Morocco by making any such Agreement. Unlike
France, she has no special dispute with Germany over the affairs of Morocco. By
simply adhering to the Franco-German Declaration she could secure for herself all
the benefits which may be expected to accrue from the pacifying effects of that
understanding. And this advantage would be hers without the necessity, to which
France was obliged to yield, of promising to encourage partnerships in commercial
enterprises between her own subjects and those of Germany. Such partnerships,
though inconvenient, would offer no particular danger as between France and Germany,
for France is financially the stronger Power. In the case of Spain and Germany
the position would be reversed. The German capitalist would soon drive out his
Spanish partner and remain in sole possession. What Spain claims as her special

sphere of influence would slowly but surely slip from her grasp. It was incredible that Spain should take a step involving such serious possibilities.

In the course of a conversation with the Spanish Foreign Minister yesterday morning I asked him how matters really stood. His Excellency confirmed the information already given me by M. Revoil that negotiations had been opened between the Spanish and German Governments at Berlin. Señor Polo de Bernabé had just telegraphed that Germany had offered no objection. Señor Allendesalazar anticipated no difficulty and said he expected to hear very shortly that a Declaration had been signed. The Spanish Government had thought it necessary to take this course. Simple adhesion, as suggested by France, to a document defining the relations between France and Germany in Morocco, without the faintest allusion to any special interest of Spain in that country, would have had no significance whatever. If France possessed a special political interest in Morocco, so did Spain. This had been fully recognized at Algeciras, and Señor Allendesalazar thought it was only natural that Germany should now be called upon to admit it. I asked His Excellency if he did not think there would be some danger to Spanish interests if Spain undertook, as France had done, to endeavour to associate her nationals with those of Germany in any future concessions that might be secured to them in Morocco. He thought the situation would not be practically affected by any such form of words. It was already open to Spanish concessionnaires to call in foreign capital if they chose. No positive obligation to do so would be created by adopting the French formula.

I believe the Spanish Government to be moved by a sense of wounded pride as much as by any other motive. I gather from various sources that they resented the secret manner in which the Franco-German Declaration was negotiated. It was communicated to them verbally, and in rather an off-hand way, by M. Révoil only 24 hours before signature. It contained no reference of any kind to Spanish interests. It seemed to assert a French predominance over the whole of Morocco which Spain is herself far from being prepared to accept. Spain thinks she sees in it the intention to oust her from the position which for centuries she has occupied on the northern coast.'. . . .(¹)

I have sent a copy of this despatch to His Majesty's Minister at Tangier.

I have, &c.
M. DE BUNSEN.

(¹) [The omitted part of this despatch gives details of commercial enterprises.]

No. 157.

Sir Edward Grey to Sir F. Bertie.(¹)

F.O. 371/695.
5714/1780/09/28.
(No. 74.)

Sir, *Foreign Office, February* 11, 1909.

The French Ambassador stated some days ago in conversation with Sir C. Hardinge that repeated advances had been made by the German Government within

(¹) [This despatch was based on a minute drawn up for Sir E. Grey by Sir C. Hardinge. The minute closed with the following comment, to which Sir E. Grey added the note printed below :—

This development seems a complete vindication of the Anglo-French " entente." The Germans have thrown up the sponge.

C. H.
Feb. 6, 09.

It will need tact and a liberal interpretation to work this agreement and the pledge for French and German co-operation in concessions is ominous for the chances of others, but politically the effect should be excellent, if the bargain really stands by itself.

E. G.]

the preceding fortnight to come to terms with France about Morocco, but that the French Government, while accepting these advances, had replied that it would be difficult to find a formula by which Germany recognised French political interests in Morocco while France could only recognise the equal economic interests of Germany with those of other Powers as guaranteed by the Act of Algeciras.

M. Cambon called again on the 6th instant and under instructions from his Government showed Sir C. Hardinge a copy of a Declaration which the German Minister for Foreign Affairs proposed should be made by the French and German Governments, as well as the drafts of two explanatory letters. The Declaration would be made public but the letters would be kept secret.

The Declaration was in the following sense :—

The French Government being resolved to maintain the independence and integrity of Morocco and the principle of economic equality and not to impede German commercial and industrial interests : and the German Government, for their part, pursuing only economic interests in Morocco and recognising that the special political interests of France are closely bound up with the consolidation of internal peace and being resolved not to impede those interests :

The two Governments declare that they will not pursue nor encourage any measure likely to create in their favour or in that of any Power an economic privilege and that they will endeavour to associate their nationals in affairs for which they are able to obtain a concession.

The letter to be addressed to Herr von Schön by the French Ambassador was in the following sense :

The " désintéressement " of Germany will not affect situations already obtained by their nationals but it implies the non-candidature of Germans to functions of Directors, technical councillors of Moorish public works, posts susceptible of having a political character, or as instructors in such services. It is further understood that in matters where French and German interests are associated French interests in Morocco are more important than the German interests.

Herr von Schön's draft reply is in the following sense :

In acknowledging the French Ambassador's note he signifies his entire concurrence in the interpretation given therein of the joint Declaration.

On M. Cambon asking Sir C. Hardinge for his opinion on this agreement the latter replied that he was much surprised, but that, if there was nothing behind it, it might be regarded as very satisfactory as it placed Germany in the same position as Great Britain towards France in Morocco.

Sir C. Hardinge then enquired what the explanation could be, to which M. Cambon replied that he knew the German Chancellor to be in a very bad position in the Reichstag where he is being strongly attacked as a disturber of the peace. Prince Bülow was anxious therefore to do something to show that he is a pacifist. M. Cambon added that he understood that some proposal was to be made when the King was in Berlin, relating to colonial affairs.

[I am, &c.
E. GREY.]

No. 158.

Sir Edward Grey to Sir F. Bertie.

F.O. 371/695.
6594/1780/09/28.
(No. 87.)
Sir,   *Foreign Office, February* 16, 1909.

In the course of general conversation to-day, M. Cambon said it had been suggested in some quarters that Germany would now ask France for something, as a consequence of the Franco-German Agreement about Morocco, but he did not think she would do so.

It was possible, he thought, that Germany might wish to introduce herself between England and France in commercial matters in Morocco. But, in this case, it would be for England to associate herself with France and Germany in exploiting mines and in other operations of that kind in Morocco.

I told him I quite understood this. I felt that the Franco-German Agreement had removed a stumbling-block between Germany and England : for as long as Germany pursued what M. Cambon had called a policy of *taquinerie* with regard to Morocco, no matter how friendly our relations with Germany might be, they were always liable to be disturbed by disputes between France and Germany about Morocco. But if Germany abandoned this policy, and adopted a smooth one instead, this obstacle was removed.

Political weather, however, was very uncertain, and I thought it desirable to keep the *Entente* between France and England as fresh and vigorous in the sunshine as it had been during the storms of the Algeciras Conference and on other occasions. At the same time, there was no reason why we should not enjoy the sun while it shone.

M. Cambon thought that Germany's desire was to consolidate her own internal politics, and to do this she required a friendly foreign policy.

If this was what Germany wished, I thought we should assist her to display a *façade d'amitié*. And for this reason I should be glad, if M. Iswolsky agreed, to see Germany join with us in negotiations at Vienna. I thought it was only if Germany would co-operate with us in advising at Vienna a policy of moderation and peace that our efforts could be made effective.

[I am, &c.]
E. G[REY].

No. 159.

Sir E. Goschen to Sir Edward Grey.

F.O. 371/695.
6996/1780/09/28.
(No. 56.) Confidential.   *Berlin,* D. *February* 18, 1909.
Sir,   R. *February* 22, 1909.

At his last official reception I congratulated Herr von Schoen on the successful termination of his negotiations with the French Government on the subject of Morocco. His Excellency said that ever since he had been in office it had been his dream to come to an understanding with France upon Moroccan affairs and that he was quite delighted that his efforts had now been crowned with success. He added that the Spanish Government had shown some irritation at having been left out of the arrangement and at not having been apprised from the first that such an arrangement was in contemplation. They had now proposed that a similar understanding should be negotiated between Germany and Spain. This proposal however had not found favour with the Imperial Government for various reasons—the chief one being that they wished the Franco-German declaration to stand by itself as an event of great political importance and not to lose its effect by being made one of other similar agreements.

He had explained to the Spanish Ambassador that Spain and France stood on a wholly different footing as regards their relations with Germany. With France, Germany had been long at variance on many points in connection with Morocco and the relations between the two countries had consequently been subjected to an unpleasant strain on more than one occasion causing considerable anxiety not only to the two countries interested but also to others. Whereas with Spain, Germany had always been on the best of terms, with no question between them to upset the equanimity of either Government. Therefore the Imperial Government thought a special arrangement between the two Countries at the present moment entirely unnecessary, all the more that by adhering to the Anglo-French agreement of 1904, Spain might be regarded as practically adhering to the present Franco-German agreement which was drawn up on similar lines. Herr von Schoen said that he thought he had finally induced the Spanish Ambassador to share this view. It was, he added, entirely a question of Spanish "Amour-propre" and he thought that the choice of the King of Spain as Arbitrator in the Anglo-German dispute with regard to Walfisch Bay had gone far towards smoothing down the somewhat ruffled feathers of the Spanish Government.

I have, &c.

W. E. GOSCHEN.

No. 160.

Sir E. Goschen to Sir Edward Grey.

F.O. 371/695.
7004/1780/09/28.
(No. 64.) Very Confidential.
Sir,
Berlin, D. *February* 19, 1909.
R. *February* 22, 1909.

The congratulatory telegram addressed by the Emperor to Prince Radolin on the occasion of the signature of the Franco-German Declarations respecting Morocco has given rise to great unpleasantness. The Chancellor is said to be exceedingly annoyed that the telegram was despatched without his cognizance and his annoyance, so it is alleged, is not lessened by the fact that his first knowledge of it was through the medium of a French newspaper.

Among Prince Bülow's friends and supporters the affair is looked upon as an attempt on the part of Prince Radolin and the Emperor's immediate circle to rob the Chancellor of the credit which is due to him for having initiated and carried to a successful conclusion the negotiations of which the agreement between the two countries is the result. They maintain, in spite of denials, that it was Prince Radolin who caused the telegram to be published and they suspect, upon no tangible grounds that I can discern except that he is known to be no friend of Prince Bülow, that it was Prince Fürstenberg who inspired the telegram. However this may be, there is no doubt that Prince Bülow is very irritated about the whole affair and it may be safely surmised that he had it in his mind when in his recent speech before the Agricultural Association, he said "I will remain true to my programme as long as I hold my burdensome office, and that may be longer than my opponents think and hope."

Herr von Schoen told the French Ambassador yesterday that Prince Radolin had been called upon for an explanation with regard to the publication of the telegram in the "Matin," and that he had replied that he had had nothing to do with it and that moreover the remarks on the telegram which had been attributed to him by the same paper were a complete and gross fabrication. An official communiqué to this effect was published this evening.

A prominent German personage speaking on this subject said that he could conceive of nothing more calculated to destroy the good effect of the Royal Visit than the prominence given in the Emperor's telegram to the approval of the King. The despatch of the telegram without Prince Bülow's knowledge was an error of judgment, but its publication was no less than a calamity.

The telegram ran as follows :—'' With my best congratulations accept my hearty thanks for having contributed by your labours to the conclusion of the Convention. Its conclusion gave additional cordiality to the Royal Visit, already so successful. The King has congratulated me most warmly upon it. I have conferred upon M. Cambon the Grand Cross of the Red Eagle.''

From these words a certain section of the Press, which has already expressed dissatisfaction with the arrangement with France, finds it possible to deduce that it was made at the bidding of England. So that it is not altogether impossible that the gloomy forecast of the personage whose words I have quoted above may be to a certain extent realized.

The whole affair is most unfortunate.

I have, &c.
W. E. GOSCHEN.

MINUTES.

Another error of judgment! The German Emperor has not yet learnt to abstain from telegrams.

G. H. V.
22/2/09.
G. S. S.
W. L.
C. H.

I hear that Prince Radolin asked that the Emperor should bestow his blessing in some form or another on account of the share he had in the Franco-German agreement (which is said to have been very small), and that this blessing took the form of a telegram.

C. H.
E. G.

No. 161.

Sir M. de Bunsen to Sir Edward Grey.

F.O. 371/698.
22725/22003/09/28.
(No. 118.) Confidential.

Madrid, D. *June* 14, 1909.
R. *June* 18, 1909.

Sir,

The Minister for Foreign Affairs mentioned casually to me in conversation a few days ago that Germany had now recognized, in the form of a written communication, the special political position which Spain claims to occupy in Morocco. He did not offer to show me the document in question, but, by the courtesy of the French Chargé d'Affaires, I have been permitted to read a copy of it, as received by him from Paris.

The original document appears to have been left with Señor Allendesalazar about a week ago by Count Tattenbach, German Ambassador, in the form of a *Note Verbale.* It is to the effect that while unable for various reasons to sign the tripartite Declaration between France, Germany and Spain which had been at first contemplated, the German Government willingly admits that, in signing the Declaration of February 9, 1909, with the French Government, it had no idea of disputing or in any way infringing upon the special political status which is conferred upon Spain by her Treaties with Morocco, and has since been recognized in the General Act of Algeciras. The Spanish reply, drawn up in a similar form, takes act of this fresh recognition of the rights claimed by Spain in Morocco.

I have, &c.
MAURICE DE BUNSEN.

No. 162.

Communication from the Spanish Ambassador, June 21, 1909.

F.O. 371/697.
23222/16224/09/28.
Confidential.   *Spanish Embassy, London, June 16, 1909.*

Con referencia á su carta del 29 de Abril unltimo, á la contestación de Sir Edward Grey de 3 de Mayo siguiente y à la Nota del Foreign Office de 8 del mismo més relativas à la proyectada declaración hispano-alemana sobre Marruecas, el Embajador de España tiene la honra de poner en conocimiento del Muy Honorable Secretario de Estrado de Negocios Extranjeros, en cumplimiento de instrucciones recibidas de su Gobierno, y con caracter confidencial, la solución dada à dicho asunto.

El Ministro de Negocios Extranjeros del Imperio aleman insistió en que no era posible firmar la Declaración sin que el Gobierno de S[u] M[ajestad] Católica se comprometiere à hacer una concesión que no tiene relación alguna con el asunto y que ha sido desde hace tiempo repetidas veces denegada; y manifestó asimismo que tampoco podía sustituirse la declaración hispano-franco-alemana por un canje de notas, porque lo mismo esta que aquella darian seguramente lugar à protestas en las Cámeras y en la opinión pública alemana; y además, dada la actual situación politica en Marruecos, podría interpretasse, aunque infrendadamente, como intromisión de Alemania, dando lugar á nuevas discusiones sobre la politica germánica que el Gobierno del Kaiser desea evitar à todo trance.

Esta manifestación fué hecha par el Embajador de Alemania en Madrid en los terminos que en la copia adjunta se expresan (anejo n°. 1); á la que contestó el Gobierno del Rey, mi Augusto Soberano, encargando á Su Embajador en Berlin que hiciese, à su ver, verbalmente y dejando copia, al Secretario de Estado del Imperio aleman la que en el anejo n°. 2 aparece. En ella se torna acta del reconocimiento hecho una ver mas por parte del Gobierno Imperial de los intereses politicos particulares de España en Marruecos, à interpretandula en este sentido fué acogida la declarición del Conde de Tattenbach en el mismo espiritu de cordialidad que la inspirata.

El Señor Pulo cumplió sur encargo y telegrafió después que el Secretario de Estado del Imperio Alemán habia agradecido vivamente la communicación y hallado correcta la interpretación dada à la declaración del Conde de Tattenbach, autorisandole, con manifestaciones en·extremo amistosas, à declarado así.

Londres, 16 de Junio de 1909.

Enclosure 1 in No. 162.

Communication to German Minister at Madrid from German Government.

Copy.

Je vous prie de déclarer verbalement au Gouvernement Espagnol ce qui suit. Le Gouvernement Impérial, obligé de tenir compte de l'opinion publique en Allemagne et au Maroc, qui pourrait donner à la déclaration proposée une interprétation autre qu'elle ne comporte et par conséquent serait inquiétée, se voit à son grand regret dans l'impossibilité de signer le protocole en question. Vous êtes toutefois autorisé à déclarer expressément, une fois de plus, au Gouvernement Espagnol qu'il va de soi que l'arrangement du 9 février entre l'Allemagne et la France ne touche en aucune façon aux droits de l'Espagne au Maroc. Le Gouvernement Impérial reconnaît, comme il a toujours reconnu, que l'Espagne par suite du développement historique et de l'existence de ses possessions territoriales sur la côte marocaine. possède certains intérêts politiques particuliers au Maroc, sanctionnés d'ailleurs par l'Acte d'Algéciras. L'arrangement du 9 février n'a pour but que d'écarter la possibilité de frictions entre l'Allemagne et la France et d'apaiser, dans l'intérêt général, la situation au Maroc. Il va de soi que cet arrangement n'est d'aucune façon dirigé contre l'Espagne avec qui l'Allemagne désire continuer à avoir les relations les plus amicales.

Enclosure 2 in No. 162.

Note verbale communicated to the German Secretary of State by the Spanish Ambassador at Berlin.

Copy.

El Conde de Tattenbach me hiro el dia dos la Declaración que ese Señor Secretario de Estado había anunciado à v[uestra] E[xcelencia] acerca del alcance del acuerdo de nueve de Febrero ultimo entre Alemania y Francia concerniente à Marruecos. Sin entrar en el exámen de los motivos por los que el Cabinete de Berlin crée hallarse en la imposibilidad de dar al Principe de Radolin instrucciones de firmar la declaración que en un principio se proyectó, el Gobierno de S[u] M[ajestad] torna acto del reconocimiente una ver más, por parte del Gobierno imperial, de los intereses politicos particulares de España en Marruecos. Cuando las Potencias, convocadas por S[u] M[ajestad] Xerifiana, determinaron, hace tres anos, las reformas que en aquel momento reclamata estado de Mogreb, hichos intereses politicos particulares de España fueran tenidos en eventa, entra otras cosas, para atribuir à nuestro pais una participación y un mandato especiales en las reformas de que se trata. El Acto de Algeciras, como el Conde de Tattenbach, en membre de su Gobierno, expresata, sanciono, pues, con aplicación à un aspecto concreto, los intereses aludiales; sin limitár, claro está, sin manifestaciones ulteriores, en relación con otras circumstancias y conceptos, dentro del respeto—que ha sido siempre norma del Gobierno de S[u] M[ajestad] à los dernios intereses legitimos y à los principios que las Potencias han establecido de comun acuerdo por base de su conducta en Marruecos. Interpretandola en este sentido, la declaración del Conde de Tattenbach fué acojida por mi con el mismo espiritu de cordialidad que la inspirata.

V.—THE FRANCO-MOROCCAN CONVENTION, FEBRUARY–MARCH 1910.

[*ED. NOTE.*—After long negotiations between M. Pichon and El Mokri, the Moorish special envoy, an agreement was signed in Paris on January 14, 1910. Since the approval of the Sultan, which was reserved, was not forthcoming, an ultimatum was sent on February 18, demanding ratification within forty-eight hours. The Sultan yielded, and on March 4 the convention was signed. It provided for the conditional evacuation of the Chaouia and Ujda districts, for joint administration of the region adjoining the Algerian frontier, for the raising of a loan of ninety million francs, and for recovery by France of a war indemnity of seventy million francs. The loan contract was signed on March 21. *cp. Livre Jaune, Affaires du Maroc,* V, (1908–10), pp. 309–43; *G.P.,* XXIX, pp. 41–51; and *Tardieu,* (Paris, 1912), pp. 89–101.]

No. 163.

Mr. Lister to Sir Edward Grey.

F.O. 5815/5815/10/28.
(No. 22.) Confidential.

Tangier, D. *February 9,* 1910.
R. *February 19,* 1910.

Sir,

The French Minister told me to-day that there was no doubt that the Sultan had been doing all in his power during the last few months to induce the German Government to save him from the French; in return for this he had gone so far as to offer them a coaling station. The German Government, however, had resisted even that temptation, which must have been a great one, and had told His Shereefian Majesty that by their arrangement with France they had abandoned all political interest in Morocco, and that they had no intention of departing from that attitude.

The Sultan has now sent Ben Azzous, who is the Mannesmanns' right hand man in Morocco, to Berlin, with instructions to do all he can to induce the Press to redouble their efforts on behalf of Mannesmann, and to insist upon the protection of German interests in Morocco, and thus prevent its absorbtion [sic] by France. As a quid-pro-quo he is to hold out hopes of the grant of concessions and economic advantages of all kinds, by means of which German vested interests in the country will become so important that the Government will be obliged to adopt a more active policy.

Ben Azzous was the Ambassador sent to Berlin by Mulai Hafid before his recognition, and he was no doubt able to establish relations with many prominent people during his stay there.

He has also been charged with completing the purchase of four batteries from Krupp: el Mokri had received instructions to order them last spring but he purposely delayed carrying out his instructions at the instigation, I believe, of the French Government.

Ben Azzous has also placed an order for five thousand Mauser rifles and a million cartridges with a Hamburg firm of the name, I believe, of Genschau.

Monsieur Regnault said that these large orders for arms were really rather serious at a moment when the French might be obliged to put on the screw in Morocco!

I have, &c.
REGINALD LISTER

No. 164.

Sir M. de Bunsen to Sir Edward Grey.

Madrid, February 19, 1910.

F.O. 5951/777/10/28.
D. 1·45 P.M.
Tel. (No. 3.)
R. 3·50 P.M.

Moroccan loan.

French Ambassador has informed the Spanish Government that pressure is to be brought to bear on the Sultan to compel compliance with French demands. H[is] E[xcellency] expressed the hope that the Spanish Gov[ernmen]t would show agreement with French Gov[ernmen]t by withdrawing consul and nationals from Fez in the event of the Sultan proving obdurate. Spanish M[inister for] F[oreign] A[ffairs] having asked my opinion I said it was natural that French patience should be at last exhausted; that other countries besides France were interested in the success of the loan; and that Spain should show a front with France in this question. Foreign Minister agreed but said that, in view of Spanish negotiation with Morocco, withdrawal of Spaniards from Fez if found necessary would be represented rather as an act of prudence in case of possible native resentment against Europeans than as a political demonstration against the Sultan.

(Sent to Tangier.)

MINUTES.

In making a similar communication to us, the French gov[ernmen]t hardly went so far as to suggest that we *should* withdraw our consuls and subjects from Fez.

It must be remembered that such withdrawals are both difficult and expensive tor the private traders.

I have already suggested an additional paragraph in our draft tel[egram] to Mr. Lister,(¹, dealing with this subject.

E. A. C.
Feb 19.

It is curious that the communications to ourselves and the Spanish Gov[ernmen]t are not similar.

It is perhaps fortunate for us as we have no wish, unless it is absolutely unsafe for them to remain, to withdraw the Consul or other B[ritish] s[ubject]s.

W. L.

M. Cambon certainly did not ask that we should withdraw our Consul and British subjects. It is probably the desire of the French Gov[ernmen]t to show unanimity of opinion with the Spanish Gov[ernmen]t that has inspired the request made for the withdrawal of the Spanish Consul and subjects.

C. H.

We shall have to join in presenting a common front to Mulai Hafid.

E. G.

(¹) [v. immediately succeeding document.]

No. 165.

Sir Edward Grey to Mr. Lister.

F.O. 5999/777/10/28.   Foreign Office, February 19, 1910.
Tel. (No. 3.) Confidential. R.   D. 10 P.M.

French Ambassador informs me confidentially that French Gov[ernmen]t propose to instruct French Min[ister] at Tangier to write to Sultan giving him 48 hours to approve agreement made with Moorish mission at Paris.(¹) Failing compliance all French officials and citizens will be ordered to leave Fez, when French Gov[ernmen]t would proceed successively to seizure of custom-houses at Casablanca and Rabat, to occupation of Azemur and lastly to seizure of markets on Algerian frontier.

You should consider question whether it would be advisable to make any arrangements for facilitating simultaneous departure from Fez of consul and any British subjects wishing to leave. But such a step should obviously be avoided unless there are imperative reasons for taking it.

(¹) [v. supra, p. 146, Ed. note.]

No. 166.

Mr. Lister to Sir Edward Grey.

F.O. 6742/777/10/28.
(No. 26.) Confidential.   Tangier, D. February 20, 1910.
Sir,   R. February 26, 1910.

His Majesty's Ambassador at Madrid was good enough to repeat to me his telegram No. 3 of yesterday's date.(¹) It reached me last night and this morning early I wrote to the French Minister asking if I could see him. My letter crossed one from him saying that he wished to see me, and would call at the Legation at 9·45 on his way to see the Commissioner for Foreign Affairs. In the meantime I received your telegram No. 4.(²)

(¹) [v. supra, p. 147, No. 164.]
(²) [v. immediately succeeding document. The reference suggests that Mr. Lister's letter was delayed in despatch.]

M. Regnault told me that he had despatched a mounted messenger to Fez yesterday with instructions to M. Gaillard to insist upon the ratification by the Sultan of the various arrangements made and signed by the Moorish Mission in Paris, upon the immediate fulfilment of the provisions which they contained and upon the settlement of various other questions, the most important of which were [sic] the conclusion of the arrangements for the liquidation of the debts of the Maghzen. M. Regnault told me for my private information that M. Gaillard was also instructed to insist upon a full recognition of the position of the French Military Mission, and the dismissal of the Turkish Officers. He asked me, however, to keep this to myself, as the Spanish Government had not been told of it. A period of forty eight hours were [sic] to be given to the Maghzen to agree to these demands: if at the expiration of that time no answer had been received, or one of an unsatisfactory nature were returned, the French Consul was to inform the Moorish Government that he, the French Military Mission, and all the members of the French Colony would leave Fez. No details would be given as to the further steps which the French Government proposed to take, but it would be made perfectly clear to the Maghzen that this was only the beginning.

M. Gaillard had been told to inform his colleagues of the instructions which he had received, and the French Government hoped most earnestly that the Consuls of Great Britain, Spain, and Germany would act with him, and that if M. Gaillard were driven by further obstruction on the part of the Sultan to leave the Capital, his colleagues, with their colonies would leave with him.

I said that I had just received a telegram on the subject from you reporting to me the steps which the French Government proposed to take successively, and informing me of the proposed exodus from Fez in the event of a refusal from Moulai Hafid.(³) I said that you were of opinion that the step should only be taken if there were imperative reasons for doing so.

M. Regnault replied that he considered it imperative that the Sultan should be made to realise that complete solidarity existed amongst the Powers: moreover he thought a general exodus advisable on grounds of prudence, should the Sultan remain obdurate. Were any Europeans to remain in Fez he considered it not improbable that the Sultan might excite popular fanaticism and cause a disaster. In any case he begged me most earnestly to issue instructions to His Majesty's Consul to act in conformity with the French Consul. The French Government, he said, looked to His Majesty's Government for support in this matter. He believed personally that the Sultan would yield in any case when he saw that France was in deadly earnest; but His Majesty was far more certain to do so if he found himself confronted by an absolutely united attitude on the part of the Foreign Consuls.

I asked him what the Spaniards were doing, and told him that I understood that they desired to act in agreement with France, but that they seemed to prefer that, if an exodus proved necessary, it should be based on grounds of prudence: M. Regnault said he would not object to this, though he considered solidarity should be the real reason. He said he was now going to see Cid Guebbas, and that after that he should call on the Spanish and German Ministers.

I saw M. Merry del Val very soon after M. Regnault had left him. He told me that his instructions were to act in unison with France; the Spanish Government did not, nor indeed did he, anticipate any danger, but they were anxious to show their friendship for the French Government and to fall in with their wishes: he was however to reserve final action until he received a further telegram. He had so informed M. Regnault and had reported their conversation to Madrid. He consequently expected to receive very shortly definite instructions to act in the sense desired by M. Regnault. He was anxious to learn what the views of the German Minister were on the subject.

(³) [v. immediately preceding document.]

On my return to the Legation, I found that during my absence M. Maroum the German Interpreter had been sent by the German Minister, who was ill in bed, with a message which he delivered to Mr. White to the effect that the German Legation was sending a special messenger to Fez this afternoon with instructions to Dr. Vassel to act in conformity with the French Consul, and leave Fez should the latter do so.(⁴) He said that Dr. Rosen would be delighted for the messenger to take any communication which I might wish to send to Fez, and asked Mr. White whether I was sending similar instructions to Mr. MacLeod. Mr. White replied that he believed so, but that I was out, and he did not know what was actually decided. He promised to let the German Legation know, should I not be sending such instructions. I then saw M. Regnault who had just returned from the German Legation. He told me that he had discussed the whole question with Dr. Rosen who had regretted that he had not known of the matter rather sooner, as he would then have instructed Dr. Vassel to join M. Gaillard in his representations. The question, he said, was a serious one for Germany, as there were several important German Merchants at Fez, the success of whose business depended upon their personal presence. He had, however, concluded by saying that Dr. Vassel would be instructed " de se solidariser avec ses Collègues et de quitter Fez si le Consul Français se voyait obligé de partir." M. Regnault also read me a telegram which he had received from Paris reporting a conversation between M. Jules Cambon and M. de Schoen, in which the latter assured the Ambassador that Germany would once more show that she was faithful to the spirit of the Franco-German *entente* in Morocco, and that Dr. Vassel's instructions would be satisfactory : the question was being referred to the Chancellor. This seemed to confirm the message given by Maroum, and it appeared to me impossible that I, the Representative of the Power bound by solemn engagement to support France in Morocco, should withhold the support so earnestly asked for by the French Minister when it was being granted by Germany and Spain. I accordingly sent you my telegram No. 10.(⁵) Time pressed, as M. Regnault had begged me to send my instructions to Fez by the German messenger. I was obliged to take a decision and I wrote two despatches to Mr. MacLeod, copies of which I enclose herewith.(⁶)

With regard to the second, it had occurred to me that should the exodus really take place Dr. Verdon and Sergeant Balding would be placed in a very difficult position. They could not well remain on in Fez, at the same time if they left it appeared more than probable that they would lose their post when things returned to their normal position, and they would not have the backing behind them that the French Instructors possessed. I accordingly mentioned the matter to M. Regnault. He fully realized my point and gave me an assurance that their cases should be treated on the same basis as those of the French Instructors. He has written to Paris in this sense.

I asked M. Regnault whether he did not think that the ultimatum would have more effect if, at the time of its presentation, the Sultan were told what the results of its refusal would be, but he said no, and told me that his views had been borne out by the signs of terror of the unknown evinced by Guebbas when he saw him in the morning. The latter had begged to be told what was intended, but M. Regnault replied that it was better for him to remain in ignorance as long as he could, and left the Commissioner only more frightened. Of one thing he told His Excellency he could be certain, and that was that, if the Sultan still remained obdurate, the French intended to stop the entry of all arms and munitions of war destined for the Maghzen no matter whence they came or where they arrived. This, M. Regnault said, he had told no one but himself.

(⁴) [For a telegram from Herr von Schoen to Dr. Rosen, German Minister at Tangier, of February 19, 1910, *v. G.P.* XXIX, p. 46, and for further negotiations, *ib.* pp. 47–54.]

(⁵) [Not reproduced as its tenour is indicated.]

(⁶) [Not reproduced as their tenour is indicated.]

The despatches and a letter from M. Regnault to M. Gaillard reporting his conversation with myself and the German and Spanish Ministers were sent off by the German Rakkas, but I have been somewhat upset by a note from the German Minister, in which the [sic] says that his instructions to Doctor Vassel were to leave Fez with the German Colony if he thought there would be any danger in remaining, or in case all the Consuls with their respective colonies were leaving the Capital.

This was not the message that he sent through Maroum nor was it the impression he had conveyed to the French Minister. I thought it best to try to clear this up with Doctor Rosen, with whom I am on very friendly personal terms, and I bearded him this evening in his sick chamber. He told me frankly that he had not liked to tell the French Minister that the German Consul would only leave if all his colleagues left, not, if only his French colleague left. He thought it would be disagreeable hearing for him. He had merely kept silent and said nothing. I said that he certainly had conveyed the impression to M. Regnault that Doctor Vassel was to be instructed to act with his colleagues, and leave Fez if the French Consul were obliged to go. He answered that he must leave him under that impression: moreover the result would be the same, as if all our Consuls left, the German Consul would be obliged by his instructions to leave also. He regretted that Maroum should not have given his message correctly to White. He realised that he should have gone himself to see me and the Spanish Minister, but he had been too unwell to leave the house! His attitude appeared most cynical, and Mr. White and I are inclined to think that Maroum's message was intentionally misleading.

Doctor Rosen told me in confidence that, with the instructions to Doctor Vassel he had sent a private letter to the Sultan in which he had urged him most strongly to agree to the French demands. He had begun by stating that in thus writing he was breaking one of his rules of conduct, which was never to offer advice to the Sultan, but the gravity of the situation had led him to do so. The Sultan could gain nothing by waiting: on the other hand he might lose everything. His motives in writing were absolutely disinterested, he only wished to warn His Majesty out of friendship of the serious danger he was running were he to continue his resistance. If the contents of the letter were such as Dr. Rosen recounted to me, it may carry weight. I am inclined to share the view which M. Regnault holds most strongly that the Sultan will certainly yield, and that no exodus will prove necessary: I only hope it will turn out so, but, in any case, I do not see how it would have been possible for me to decline to instruct Mr. Macleod in the sense desired by M. Regnault.

I have, etc.
REGINALD LISTER.

No. 167.

Sir Edward Grey to Mr. Lister.

F.O. 5948/777/10/28.
Tel. (No. 4.)   *Foreign Office, February* 21, 1910.
Your telegram No. 10.([1]) (Moroccan loan.)
I agree you should instruct H[is] M[ajesty's] Consul at Fez to support his French Colleague and to leave Fez, with other British subjects, if the Sultan proves obdurate and a similar step is taken by the other Powers.

([1]) [Not reproduced, but *v.* immediately preceding document, note ([5]).]

No. 168.

Mr. Lister to Sir Edward Grey.

F.O. 8566/777/10/28.
(No. 36.)   Confidential.   *Tangier,* D. *March* 5, 1910.
Sir,   R. *March* 5, 1910.

In continuation of my despatch No. 26 Confidential of the 20th ultimo,(¹) 1
have the honour to report that the note addressed by M. Regnault to Si Aissa Ben
Omar, setting forth the various demands made by France, was delivered to the
Vizier for Foreign Affairs by the French Consul at Fez on the 22nd February.
On the following morning M. Gaillard was received by the Sultan, attended by his
Viziers. His Shereefian Majesty expressed great surprise at the despatch of the
note considering that he had already sent orders for the ratification of the various
agreements come to between el Mokri and the French Government in Paris.
M. Gaillard pointed out that this was not sufficient, and that he must insist on
a solemn engagement from the Sultan that he accepted all the various demands
made in M. Regnault's present note. The discussion appears to have lasted more
than two hours, and finally M. Gaillard received assurances from the Sultan that
he would comply with the demands : he promised to send him a written reply within
twenty-four hours. M. Gaillard had a subsequent interview with the Viziers, and
the latter sent in to the Sultan a draft of the reply which they proposed to return,
in the sense of the promises he had given M. Gaillard. In the evening, however,
the Sultan appears to have got much excited with drink, and himself wrote a reply
which was altogether unsatisfactory and none too civil in tone. He made all sorts
of difficulties with regard to the full powers to be given to the Moorish Ambassador
at Paris, and refused to dismiss the Turkish Instructors. M. Gaillard returned the
note, which he felt sure was written under the influence of liquor, and intimated
to the Maghzen that unless the demands of the French Government in their entirety
were complied with at once, he must withdraw from Fez, taking with him the French
Military Mission and all the members of the French Colony. His Majesty's Consul,
who had so far taken no action in the matter, then, after consultation with
M. Gaillard, sent word to the Minister for Foreign Affairs that he desired to see
him as soon as possible; he intended to inform him that he too had received my
instructions to leave with his colony were the French demands not complied with.
This, however, did not prove necessary, as in the meantime a message was sent
to M. Gaillard to the effect that the Maghzen had decided to comply fully with the
French demands, and that an amended note with various letters appended was
being sent to him at once. These documents were examined by M. Gaillard and
proved satisfactory, as I had the honour of informing you in my telegram No. 16
of the 1st March.(²) They were despatched by special messenger to M. Regnault,
and he has been kind enough to communicate to me the translations which have
been made of them, copies of which I have the honour to transmit to you
herewith.(²)

M. Regnault tells me that he considers the various letters quite satisfactory,
and is very much gratified at the successful result of the French action.

Mr. Macleod informs me that there was no sort of excitement at Fez when
the situation became known, the opinion being generally held that the Sultan would
give way. Indeed to the well-to-do classes His Shereefian Majesty has become such
an object of dislike that the predominant feeling was one of satisfaction at his
discomfiture. The merchant class who have so many claims to collect are positively
desirous to have the loan carried through as soon as possible.

In Tangier very general satisfaction prevails, and all the various merchants
after years of anxious waiting, are rubbing their hands at the thought that the end
is in sight.

(¹) [*v. supra,* pp. 148–51, No. 166.]
(²) [Not reproduced.]

It is satisfactory to note that Cid Guebbas has received orders to give effect to article 60 of the Algeciras Act relative to the acquisition of real estate by foreigners. His Excellency has already notified these instructions to the Doyen of the Corps Diplomatique for the information of the Representatives of the Powers.

I have, &c.

REGINALD LISTER.

VI.—THE HISPANO-MOROCCAN CONVENTION, JANUARY–NOVEMBER 1910.

No. 169.

Extracts from Annual Report for Spain for the Year 1910.

[Enclosed in Despatch No. 8 from Sir M. de Bunsen of January 20, 1911, R. January 28, 1911. (F.O. 3284/3284/11/41.)]

I.—FOREIGN RELATIONS.

(A.) *Morocco.*

Spheres of Influence.

1. As in previous years, Morocco continues to hold almost the entire field of Spanish foreign affairs. Ill-understood and unpopular in many quarters, as had been the Melilla campaign of the summer and autumn of 1909, there was no disposition on the part of the Spanish people to loosen its grip on the occupied territory in the Riff. Señor Perez Caballero, the new Foreign Minister, had spoken his mind very plainly (see paragraph 27 of 1909 report). In the eyes of the Liberal, as of the preceding Conservative Government, the southern boundary of Spain lay in Morocco. The problem awaiting solution was to determine the best means of establishing Spanish power and prestige throughout what was claimed as the legitimate sphere of Spanish influence in that country. The line of demarcation between the French and Spanish spheres had been drawn in the secret convention of October 1904. To the north of that line successive Spanish Governments, of varying political hue, have shown so far agreement in resenting interference from the outside. As France steadily developed her influence at Fez, so should Spain develop hers from the mouth of the Muluya to the Atlantic coast. This unswerving purpose is visible throughout the year under review. Both in the Melilla and Ceuta regions it led, in the early part of the year, to strained relations between France and Spain.

Effect of French Ultimatum.

12. The eagerness of Spain to assert herself in Northern Morocco was greatly stimulated by the success of the Franco-Moorish negotiation in Paris. The refusal of the Sultan to ratify the draft convention had been speedily overcome by the threat that failing ratification the French consul and colony would withdraw from Fez. In this demonstration Spain had just consented, reluctantly, to join when the Sultan's timely acquiescence rendered unnecessary any further display of pressure. The Franco-Moorish convention was signed in Paris on the 4th March.([1]) It provided, under conditions, for the eventual evacuation of the Showia and Ujda districts, for joint administration of the region adjoining the Algerian frontier, for the raising of a loan of 90,000,000 fr., and for recovery by France of a war indemnity of 70,000,000 fr. As shown below, the text of this convention, which was published in a French yellow-book in November, was closely followed by the Spanish Government in drafting their new agreement with Morocco.

([1]) [*v. supra*, p. 146, *Ed. note.*]

13.   The Franco-Moorish Loan Agreement, signed in Paris on the 27th March, contained stipulations which strengthened the growing conviction at Madrid that France is gradually establishing something like a proctectorate over Morocco.   The provisions increasing the powers of the French delegate of the holders of the 1904 loan, and placing certain Moorish revenues under the control of this official together with the Sultan's delegate, appointed with the concurrence of the French Government, gave rise to apprehension lest the foreign financial control thus established over the public debt of the Makhzen might prove a serious obstacle to the extension of Spanish influence in Northern Morocco.   Señor Perez Caballero, Minister for Foreign Affairs in Señor Moret's Cabinet, had called Sir M. de Bunsen's attention to this aspect of the question at the end of the year 1909, pointing out that the presence of French agents and tax collectors in the Spanish sphere of influence would place the Spanish Government in an awkward position.   This view was also strongly pressed at Paris in a correspondence between the Spanish Ambassador and M. Pichon.   The Marquis del Muni claimed that the whole tenour of the agreements of October 1904, and of the 1st September, 1905, required that, in the recognised Spanish sphere, the financial agents to be instituted in connection with the new loan should be Spanish subjects.   Especially would this be the case when, at latest, in the year 1919 the Spanish sphere should come entirely under Spanish control, as stipulated in the former agreement.

14.   M. Pichon, in his reply dated the 20th January, 1910, denied that the texts appealed to could be properly interpreted to exclude the employment of French agents in the Spanish sphere.   He gave the assurance, however, that, in organising the new system of financial supervision in Morocco, the French Government would respect the recognised situation of Spain in Morocco under the agreements.   Note was taken by the Spanish Ambassador of this assurance.   The Spanish Government has since sought, by article 14 of the convention with Morocco of the 16th November, to counteract the influence of the contemplated French agents by providing for the appointment of Spanish agents to collect the share of certain mining taxes claimed by Spain under the convention.

15.   Confidential negotiations are understood to have been set on foot by the Spanish Embassy in Paris with a view to an arrangement being reached with the French Government, in virtue of which the Spanish sphere should be reserved as far as possible to the operation of Spanish agents, whether in respect of the 1910 loan or of the collection of the mining taxes.   In return, Spain would withdraw her right to appoint Spanish agents of any kind in the French sphere.   It is to these negotiations that the Spanish Ambassador in London alluded when, in communicating a copy of the convention of the 16th November, he mentioned the desire of his Government " to establish a preliminary and confidential understanding with the Paris Cabinet, so that the organisation of the guarantees of the mining tax, corresponding fully with its economic object, may harmonise in practice, from the political point of view, with the provisions of the previous Franco-Spanish agreement.

Moorish Embassy at Madrid.

19.   El Muaza, special Moorish Ambassador at Madrid since July, 1909, had proceeded in the spring of 1910 to Fez with a set of Spanish demands which he had accepted *ad referendum*.   They were returned by the Sultan with a Shereefian reply showing the extent to which His Majesty was prepared to go in meeting the wishes of Spain.   El Muaza returned to Madrid at the end of August with these counter-proposals which were promptly declared by the Spanish Government to be entirely inacceptable.   Señor Garcia Prieto intimated in plain terms that the mission had long outstayed its welcome.   If El Muaza could not meet Spanish views regarding the war indemnity, and the Ceuta police and custom-house, there was no reason why he should be detained in Madrid any longer.

20. On the 6th September the Spanish Prime Minister told the British Ambassador the situation was becoming critical. The Sultan was only playing with Spain The army was dissatisfied with the state of affairs at Ceuta. The fortress was commanded by the Sierra Bullones heights. Some day these would have to be seized in self defence, and strong pressure was even now being applied by the Spanish generals to induce the Government to consent to a forward movement. Sir Maurice de Bunsen deprecated the use of force, expressing his conviction that both England and France would be ready to lend their good offices to secure a satisfactory arrangement.

21. Meanwhile there was alarm at Tangier. El Mokri was convinced that Spain was meditating an attack on the heights adjoining Ceuta, and perhaps on Tetuan. The French Minister fully shared these fears. Señor Padilla, Spanish chargé d'affaires, accused the Makhzen of desiring to provoke a rupture. On the 10th September, Sir M. de Bunsen was instructed by telegraph to inform the Spanish Government that His Majesty's Government were seriously concerned at the reports which had reached them in regard to the strained relations between Spain and Morocco; that they understood a friendly settlement was desired by the Moorish Government; that they would be ready to do everything in their power to further such a solution; and that they earnestly trusted a rupture, which might have the most serious results, would be avoided. The Spanish Government replied that, though the attitude of the Makhzen was highly irritating, there was no present intention to break off relations or use force, and that they would gladly take advantage of the friendly offers of assistance made by the British Government.

22. Alarmed at the persistent rumours of an impending Spanish attack, and convinced that the Spanish Government were in earnest in demanding a settlement on more favourable terms than those conveyed by the Moorish counter-proposals, the Sultan determined to despatch El Mokri himself, his new Vizier for Foreign Affairs, to Madrid, with extensive powers to effect an arrangement. His Excellency arrived at Madrid at the end of September, being received by the King as Ambassador Extraordinary with the usual ceremony on the 30th of that month. A few hours before, El Muaza had presented his letters of recall. Replying to Mokri's address, King Alfonso expressed his persuasion that both Morocco and Spain would find advantage in an understanding founded on the respect due to treaties and to " the legitimate claims and interests arising out of the circumstances of the time."

23. The negotiation which ensued gave little promise at first of a successful issue. While professing conciliatory intentions, Mokri had declared himself, at Tangier, in private conversations, opposed to concession on the three points to which Spain attached greatest importance, namely : the Melilla war indemnity, the Ceuta frontier police, and the Ceuta custom-house. As it soon became evident that Mokri conducted his negotiations at Madrid under the direct inspiration of the French Embassy, the opinion held on these points in Paris was destined to become the determining factor in the situation. M. Pichon fortunately showed a conciliatory disposition. Though regarding the attitude of the Spanish Government as unreasonable and dangerous, he was prepared to admit (21st October) that something might be conceded in respect of the war indemnity and frontier police. He saw, however, at first no necessity for the establishment of a Ceuta custom-house, or for measures of protection in that region. Subsequently the French chargé-d'affaires at Madrid received authority to make on all points the concessions necessary to prevent a rupture of the negotiations.

24. The first serious crisis that occurred was on the 25th October, when after admitting the principle of a war indemnity and fixing the outside amount which Morocco could pay at 25,000,000 pesetas, Mokri declared that, failing acceptance by Spain, there was nothing more he could do in Madrid, and he must ask for his farewell audience. Señor Garcia Prieto became greatly incensed against the Moorish Ambassador. He regarded the offer as an insult. and prepared to break off relations. In urgent telegrams to Paris and London he announced the intention

of the Spanish Government to seize the Sierra Bullones, overlooking Ceuta, unless an entire change of front were effected immediately by the representative of the Sultan. Spain, having shown her goodwill by reducing her demand from 125,000,000 to 80,000,000 pesetas, the offer of only 25,000,000 pesetas could not be for a moment considered.

25. The British and French Embassies counselled patience, and on the 27th October oil was poured on the troubled waters by Mokri in the form of a letter, in which he set forth, in temperate language, the concessions he had already made on many points of importance. He added an offer to procure a positive undertaking from the Makhzen that points threatening Ceuta should never be fortified or occupied by artillery. As to the Ceuta custom-house he announced his willingness to accept it, subject to the consent of the Powers interested in the 1904 and 1910 loans. Though he could only offer 25,000,000 pesetas as a war indemnity, he was prepared to consent to arbitration if Spain persisted in thinking she was entitled to more.

26. At this stage the Spanish Government took into consideration a suggestion, emanating from Sir Edward Grey, that failing agreement on a money indemnity, the difficulty might be got over by a cession to Spain of territory near Melilla and by a rectification of the frontier zone at Ceuta. Mokri objecting, however, to any form of territorial cession, the negotiation continued on the basis of a pecuniary indemnity.

27. Early in November another crisis occurred in the negotiation. The dispute over the money payment was practically settled when a serious hitch arose over the arrangements desired by Spain in the region adjoining Ceuta. It was a question of the extent to which the authority of the frontier kaïd and his 250 native police, under Spanish officers, should be allowed to penetrate. Spain drew the line from Point Alcazar to Wadi Negro, which would have subjected to the kaïd's influence one of the three main divisions of the Anjera tribe. A nearer line was also drawn from Point Ciris to Wadi Fenidak or Castillejos, to include the more mountainous region by which the security of Ceuta was held to be threatened. Over this nearer zone, which was never to be fortified, Spain demanded that the kaïd and the Governor of Ceuta should exercise a joint authority. On the other hand, Mokri contended that the frontier kaïd and police should be stationed along the existing frontier of Ceuta without authority over any of the country beyond. The British and French Governments suggested that an offer should be made to Spain to extend the existing narrow strip of land constituting the Ceuta neutral zone, so as to include within it the Sierra Bullones range. Spain explained that this would afford no sufficient protection to Ceuta, which was commanded by all the adjacent ranges of mountains, and not by the Sierra Bullones alone.

28. The Spanish negotiators again became very restless, and the talk of a settlement by force revived. At this juncture France consented to the Ceuta custom-house, on terms calculated to safeguard the interests of the holders of the Morocco loans. She also agreed to the Ciris–Fenidak line as defining the limits of the kaïd's authority. Mokri finally consented to fix the war indemnity at 65,000,000 pesetas, including the Casa Blanca military indemnity and other extras. All outstanding difficulties being thus removed, the convention was drawn up in its final shape on the 15th November and signed on the following day.

Hispano-Moroccan Convention.([2])

29. Its main provisions are to the following effect:—

With the object of terminating frontier difficulties and securing fulfilment of treaties, it is agreed that existing conventions be supplemented as follows:—

Articles 2 to 6.—Occupied Riff region and territory lying near the Spanish fortress of Alhucemas and Peñon de Velez to be administered jointly by a Moorish

([2]) [*v. Martens, 3rd Ser.*, (Liepzig, 1913), VII, pp. 94–100.]

and a Spanish High Commissioner. These will appoint subordinate officials, maintain order, and otherwise fulfil conventions of 1894 and 1895. They will have under their orders a native police force of 1,250 men with Spanish instructors. First available contingent of this force is assigned to the neighbourhood of Alhucemas and Peñon de Velez. Remainder, when organised, will gradually occupy the posts now held by the Spanish troops. The whole Spanish occupying force will thus be withdrawn eventually into Melilla. But this cannot take place till the entire police force has been fully organised so that it will be capable of securing observance of treaties, keeping the peace, facilitating trade, and enforcing payment of taxes. Provision is made for paying the police force, at first out of a Spanish advance, and later out of the duties collected by the proposed Moorish custom-house on the Melilla frontier. The High Commissioners may set up markets in places selected by them.

Articles 7 to 12.—Ceuta frontier arrangements. Makhzen engages neither to fortify nor allow to be fortified any point held to threaten the security of the Spanish fortress. A capable Moorish kaïd will settle purely local disputes in concert with the Governor of Ceuta. Appeal to the representatives of Spain and the Makhzen at Tangier in case of disagreement. Kaïd assisted by native police force of 250 men under Spanish instructors, the sphere of his authority extending from 5 to 10 kilom. inland from the Ceuta frontier to a line as defined. Moorish custom-house to be eventually established on the Ceuta frontier, under conditions safeguarding interests of loan holders. Its receipts will pay cost of administration of custom-house, and also the frontier kaïd, officials, and police.

Articles 12 to 16.—Melilla war indemnity of 65,000,000 pesetas, including Casa Blanca expenses, and cost of Moorish and other refugees in Melilla between 1902 and 1907; the whole payable in seventy-five annuities of 2,545,000 pesetas, guaranteed by 55 per cent. of Makhzen share of proposed new mining tax; and, further, by surplus of Ceuta customs. Provisions as to collection of Spanish share of mining tax. Indemnity is exclusive of 1,500,000 pesetas for public improvements in occupied region.

The convention bears the date of the 16th November, 1910, and is subject to approval of the Makhzen within two months. It was signed by Señor Garcia Prieto, Spanish Minister for Foreign Affairs, and Mohammed El Mokri, Moorish Ambassador.

30. Throughout the negotiation both parties kept in close touch with the British Ambassador and the French chargé d'affaires, M. Martin. Mokri was advised at every stage by the French Embassy. The latter was at first disinclined to allow him to concede the points demanded by the Spanish Government in respect of the war indemnity and the desired arrangements at Ceuta. In the end, and as the result of conference between the French and British Governments, the necessary concessions were made, and a Spanish military outbreak prevented. Sir Maurice de Bunsen received from the Spanish Foreign Minister and from Mokri friendly recognition of the assistance rendered by the British Embassy, under instructions from Sir Edward Grey.

31. The convention was well received both in the press and Cortes. Newspapers of all shades of opinion expressed satisfaction at the termination, on honourable terms, of the long-standing controversy. In the Senate all parties combined to congratulate the Government on its success. Similar manifestations were made in the Lower House, where Señor Canalejas held forth on the pacific intentions of Spain and on the civilising task which lay before her in Morocco.

32. Only the provisions relating to eventual evacuation of the occupied territory called forth, in some quarters, a note of criticism. It was easily shown by the Government that the General Act of Algeciras prohibited anything like annexation. There was also the example of France, whose convention of the 4th March, 1910, with Morocco contained almost identical stipulations in respect of the ultimate surrender to the Makhzen of the Showia and Ujda districts.

33. A perusal of the text of the two conventions shows indeed, very plainly, that the appearance of the French original in a yellow-book was very opportune (October, 1910). In the Spanish preamble, in the stipulations concerning administration of the frontier zones, in those relating to the opening of markets, and in the clauses providing for eva‿uation when circumstances permit, it is evident that the earlier convention served as a model for the latter. Spain keeps in view the secret treaty with France of October, 1904. For her, there are already two spheres of influence in Morocco, the southern French, the northern Spanish. Her policy is directed towards securing, within her own sphere, an undisputed preponderance. For every advantage secured by France at Fez, she claims a corresponding favour in the region of the Mediterranean coast. The new convention has, to some extent, secured Moorish as well as French and British recognition of these aspirations. Its provisions seem to foreshadow a more harmonious development of French and Spanish activities in Morocco than in the past. There remains, however, the inherent difficulty of adjusting the respective policies of two Powers so unequal in wealth, enterprise, and power. Perhaps the most that can be expected is a temporary relaxation of the tension which rendered co-operation so difficult during the last few years. The proposal to replace Señor Merry del Val by another Spanish Minister at Tangier, and so to entrust the execution of the convention to hands which have taken no part in the quarrels leading up to it, seems to strengthen the prospect of a better understanding between the Spanish and French Legations.

No. 170.

Sir M. de Bunsen to Sir Edward Grey.

F.O. 6856/6856/10/28.
(No. 16.) Confidential.   *Madrid,* D. *February* 19, 1910.
Sir,   R. *February* 26, 1910.

In the course of a recent visit to H[is] M[ajesty's] Embassy, Señor Canalejas, the new Spanish Prime Minister, touched on the affairs of Morocco. His Excellency said trouble had arisen between the Moorish Governor of Larache and the native police force under Spanish officers which is established at that port. Though he hoped matters would soon be smoothed over, it had been thought well to send the cruiser "Numancia" and a gun-boat to Tangier, whence they could proceed at short notice to Larache in case of necessity. As regards the general situation in Morocco he said that, though the Spanish and French Governments were fairly in agreement, there was a strong disposition on the part of the general public in Spain to resent what it regarded as French encroachments in the region falling properly under Spanish influence. Señor Canalejas did not go into details, but his language showed that he shared the apprehension often expressed in Spanish political circles that the stronger and wealthier of the two foreign nations enjoying a special position in Morocco is not likely to be satisfied with a strict limitation of its influence to the region assigned to it under the Franco-Spanish secret arrangement of October, 1904.

Señor Canalejas showed nervousness as to French aims with regard to Taza, a point which, though within the French sphere of influence, would dominate, if it passed into French hands, the entire Riff region.

I asked him what reason he had to suppose that the French contemplated an advance to Taza. He said there were indications pointing in that direction. He mentioned a French scientific expedition which he had heard of. But his language was vague, and he said he merely wished me to understand that, in his opinion, questions were not unlikely to arise which might put some strain on the Franco-Spanish understanding concerning Morocco, and with regard to which an appeal to the good offices of England might possibly have to be made.

Monsieur Révoil, the French Ambassador, tells me he is not dissatisfied with the assurances he has so far received from the new Spanish Government on these questions. His Excellency has represented to Señor Canalejas and Señor Garcia Prieto the desire of France to interpret her engagements with Spain in a fair and liberal spirit and to abstain from any action showing disregard for the legitimate aspirations of Spain.

I have, &c.
MAURICE DE BUNSEN.

No. 171.

Sir M. de Bunsen to Sir Edward Grey.

F.O. 8462/777/10/28.
(No. 23.)   Confidential.   *Madrid, D. March* 7, 1910.
Sir,   R. *March* 11, 1910.

The steps taken by the French Government to enforce acceptance at Fez of the conditions attached by them to the proposed Morocco loan have been followed with evident nervousness by the Spanish Government. I mentioned in my despatch No. 289 of December 28th last([1]) that the late Foreign Minister, Señor Perez Caballero, had expressed apprehension lest the guarantees demanded by France might involve the invasion of what Spain regards as her own sphere of influence in Northern Morocco by a host of French financial agents charged with the control of certain Moorish taxes. Señor Garcia Prieto, the new Foreign Minister, was much embarrassed by a request made by the French Ambassador that, in the event of the withdrawal of the French Consul and colony from Fez as a means of exercising pressure upon the Sultan, the Spanish Consul and colony should follow suit. As reported in my telegram No. 3 of February 19th,([1]) Señor Garcia Prieto replied to Monsieur Révoil that, if this step unfortunately became necessary, the Spanish withdrawal would be explained to the Makhzen as having been dictated by considerations of prudence in view of a possible native rising against Europeans, rather than by any desire to make a political demonstration on the side of France. The surrender of the Sultan to the French demands has prevented this difficulty from arising. The Government of Señor Canalejas is, however, still feeling very uneasy as regards the progress of events in Morocco. Two conversations which I have held with Señor Canalejas since his accession to office have left me under the impression that His Excellency regards the success of the French negotiation as a decided step towards the establishment of a virtual French Protectorate over Morocco. I reported some of the Prime Minister's remarks in my despatch No. 16 Confidential of February 19th.([2]) He reverted to the subject during a visit which I paid him at his official residence on the 4th instant. He said it was becoming impossible for Spain to make the slightest move in the region of Ceuta, which was undoubtedly within her sphere of influence, without arousing the inquisitiveness and even opposition of the French. Lately some French officers had been in Ceuta disguised as Moors. He could hardly imagine that they could have acted without the knowledge and approval of their superior officers. French influence, he added, was always being employed to set the minds of the Makhzen against the very necessary works which Spain was carrying out on the road from Ceuta to Tetuan.

I said that French vigilance had probably been aroused by the course of events at Melilla. There also "necessary works" were being carried out in the neighbourhood of the town in July last. The inevitable "incident" occurred and within three or four months Spain had been led on to occupy an extensive district beyond

([1]) [Not reproduced as its tenour is indicated.]
([2]) [*v.* immediately preceding document.]

her boundary. I said I presumed that the Spanish Government would adopt all possible precautions to prevent, as they could if they chose, the Tetuan road becoming the scene of a similar incident. Señor Canalejas replied that they would certainly do so, but that, if the neighbouring tribes used violence to stop the works, Spain would of course be compelled to make reprisals.

The French Ambassador had indeed already spoken to me seriously on this subject. M. Révoil is beginning to suspect that a Spanish movement on Tetuan is already in contemplation. Just as the French occupation of the Shawia and Ujda regions led up to the Spanish counterstroke in the Riff, His Excellency fears that the consolidation of the French general position in Morocco as the result of the recent loan negotiation will bring about a similar Spanish movement in the neighbourhood of Ceuta. M. Révoil hears that the Ceuta garrison has been increased since last summer from 6,000 to 10,000 men. He attaches weight to suggestions which are beginning to appear in the newspapers to the effect that something should be done to show that Spain is extending her influence in Morocco as well as France. The Conservative " Epoca " published an article in this sense a few days ago which His Excellency regards as very significant, considering the close understanding now existing between Government and opposition. He fears also that the influence of The King and Army is likely to be exercised in the direction of making another forward movement.

It is to be hoped that more moderate counsels will prevail, but there can be no doubt that Spain notes with apprehension the strengthening of the French hold on Morocco, that, since the conclusion of the Franco-German agreement of February 1909, she has increasingly felt the relative weakness of her own position in that country, and that an attempt to redress the balance by means of a military occupation of Tetuan, evacuated under foreign pressure in 1861, would appeal powerfully to the patriotic sentiments of many Spaniards who felt no enthusiasm for the recent campaign in the Riff region.

I am sending a copy of this despatch to His Majesty's Minister at Tangier.

I have, &c.
MAURICE DE BUNSEN.

MINUTE.

Sir M. de Bunsen should in conversation with M. Révoil point out that while he has given conciliatory advice to Spain the effect of it must depend upon how the French meet requests of Spain about the mining concession and the employment of Spaniards at Laraiche in so far as these are reasonable.([3])

E. G.

([3]) [Repeated to Sir M. de Bunsen in Tel. No. 5 of March 9.]

No. 172.

Sir Edward Grey to Sir M. de Bunsen.

F.O. 12478/727/10/28.
(No. 39.)
Sir,   *Foreign Office, April 11, 1910.*

The Spanish Ambassador called to see me to-day, and dwelt upon the difficulties which Spain experienced with France in Morocco. He told me that there were difficulties with regard to the Mining Companies, the employment of Spaniards in the Spanish sphere, and even with regard to Casablanca, where the Spaniards had a share in the police which they had not desired, but which had been forced upon them at Algeciras, the French were now reorganising the police in the country districts there without saying a word to Spain about it. All these things made the situation very difficult for Spain. He did not wish to ask me to say anything to the French Government at the present moment; but he wished me to know the difficult position in which Spain was, in the hope that if there was a quarrel between France and Spain we should give support to Spain.

I said that we had already expressed to the French Government our hope that the difficulties between the Mining Companies would be settled, and my last information was to the effect that the difficulties were on the point of being satisfactorily settled.

With regard to this, the Ambassador observed that he knew that the Spanish Premier was doing his best in every possible way, but he had not yet heard that an arrangement was about to be effected.

As to the other matters, I said to the Ambassador that we were most anxious that things should go smoothly between France and Spain. I would bear in mind his view whenever I had an opportunity of doing anything to help. It seemed to me that these matters were not worth a quarrel, though no doubt they were troublesome to adjust.

[I am, &c.]
E. G[REY].

No. 173.

Sir M. de Bunsen to Sir Edward Grey.

F.O. 21446/8054/10/28.
(No. 75.)   Confidential.   *Madrid, D. June 13, 1910.*
Sir,   R. *June 16, 1910.*

The French Ambassador again spoke to me a few days ago on the subject of Morocco. It was satisfactory, he said, that an Agreement had been reached with reference to the Riff mines controversy between the French and Spanish interests involved, and to the Ceuta road question. If the Spanish Government had refused to come to terms over the Riff mines, they would have been in an awkward position at the Paris Conference on the proposed Morocco Mining Regulations. At this Conference it had only been possible to make out a Spanish case for the possession of the Riff mines by producing the documents held by Monsieur Massenet on behalf of the French company concerned, which had afforded proof of the purchase of the ground from the native proprietors. Monsieur Révoil added that the Spanish Government were still seeking by every means to extend their influence in the Riff country and in the neighbourhood of Tangier. They were setting up small military outposts along the left bank of the Muluya commanding the roads leading into the Quebdana country from the South. His Excellency did not seem to object to these military movements which he thought were not unconnected with the known intention of the French Government to set up more market places on Moorish territory along the Algerian frontier, and especially at Sidi Melluk, south of the Beni Snassen country, and at Debdu still further south, on the model of those already established at various points under the French treaties with Morocco, and with similar privileges.

Monsieur Révoil states that the Spanish Ambassador at Paris is already beginning to raise the question of the prolongation or renewal of the arrangements made at the Algeciras Conference for the organization of the Morocco Police under French and Spanish officers. The assistance of the foreign police officers was to be rendered to the Makhzen for a period of five years dating from the Ratification of the General Act of Algeciras. This period will expire at the end of the year 1911, or at a later date according as ratification by the Powers or the subsequent ratification by the Sultan be taken as the starting point. Monsieur Révoil fears that Spain will press for a redistribution of the spheres in which the French and Spanish police officers respectively exercise their functions. Her contention seems to be that the police at Casablanca under Spanish officers is [sic] hampered by the continued occupation of that region by the French forces. Spain, M. Révoil believes, is driving at concentration in her own hands of the entire Morocco police force at Tangier, both inside and outside the town. But the French Government, in his opinion, would never allow the control of the roads leading into Tangier to pass under the control of Spanish officers.

I have, &c.
MAURICE DE BUNSEN.

No. 174.

Sir Edward Grey to Sir M. de Bunsen.

F.O. 32863/32656/10/28.   *September* 10, 1910.
Tel. (No. 24.)   D. 1 P.M.

My tel[egram] No. 23.(¹)

H[is] M[ajesty's] Gov[ernmen]t are seriously concerned at rumours of strained relations between Moorish and Spanish Gov[ernmen]ts and at report that latter are considering forcible measures, such as an advance on Tetuan, in connexion with matters in dispute.

From the information they have received from Tangier they are led to believe that the Moorish Gov[ernmen]t are disposed to act reasonably and that the questions at issue at [sic : are] capable of an amicable solution by diplomatic means.

H[is] M[ajesty's] Gov[ernmen]t earnestly trust that the Spanish Gov[ernmen]t will not take any steps likely to lead to a rupture between the two countries. They consider that any repetition of the Melilla incidents would certainly be followed by the most serious results in Morocco and they feel bound to warn the Spanish Gov[ernmen]t of the grave consequences which might arise from any hasty action on their part.

H[is] M[ajesty's] Gov[ernmen]t are ready to do all in their power to forward a settlement and will willingly instruct their Representative at Tangier in this sense.

Y[our] E[xcellency] should make a communication to the Spanish Gov[ernmen]t in this sense as soon as possible.

(¹) [Not reproduced. It repeated Tel. No. 62 of September 9, from Sir F. Bertie, in which he reported on the events described above and stated that M. Louis would be grateful if Sir M. de Bunsen were sent instructions in the sense of the above despatch. (F.O. 32860/32656/10/28.)]

No. 175.

Sir M. de Bunsen to Sir Edward Grey.

F.O. 34172/32656/10/28.
(No. 124.)   *Zarauz,* D. *September* 16, 1910.
Sir,   R. *September* 21, 1910.

On my return to Zarauz this morning from a short absence on the East coast of Spain I read with interest the telegraphic correspondence which has passed between Tangier, Madrid and London on the subject of an apprehended Spanish aggressive movement in the neighbourhood of Ceuta. As stated in my despatch No. 122 of the 2nd instant,(¹) I was aware that extreme dissatisfaction had been caused at Madrid by the Sultan's reply to the Spanish demands arising out of the Melilla campaign. I therefore took the opportunity offered by a conversation with the Prime Minister at Madrid on the 6th instant to ask His Excellency how matters

(¹) [Not reproduced.]

stood. Señor Canalejas said that the difficulty presented by the Morocco problem overshadowed even the very embarrassing circumstances of the Home politics of this country at the present time. Fortunately the press knew very little about it, and the questions at issue had not yet been made the subject of public discussion. But public opinion was very sensitive with regard to Morocco and expected something tangible as the result of the protracted negotiations with the Moorish Mission which arrived in Madrid 14 months ago. The reply received from Fez did not enable a statement to be made which the country could be expected to accept. The Army was chafing at the unceasing growth of French influence in Morocco, and at the refusal of the French, who had spread over a large part of the country, to sanction the slightest corresponding advance on the part of Spain in the Ceuta region. And yet France had signed what amounted to a partition treaty with Spain in respect of Morocco in 1904. That treaty, it was true, prohibited Spain, during the main-tenance of the independence of Morocco, from taking any step of importance in her own sphere of influence without the concurrence of France. But there was no reason why France should veto everything that Spain tried to do to increase her influence in her own sphere. Certainly no extensive military movement should be made while he remained at the head of affairs. The Republican and Labour organizations would be strongly opposed to any such enterprise. But he could not deny that there was a good deal of reason in the dissatisfaction of the Army with the present position of affairs at Ceuta. The fortress was commanded by a spur of the Sierra Bullones. By mounting a few guns there the Sultan could drive the Spanish garrison into the sea. It was impossible for Spain to remain content with the occupation of a position so entirely at the mercy of the Moors. Sooner or later she would be compelled in self defence to seize the heights from which the security of Ceuta was so dangerously threatened. The Generals were already pressing hard for sanction to carry out this very simple military operation, which would only take a few hours. Their wish was perfectly reasonable, and he was finding it difficult to dispute their view that some-thing must be done to secure the position of this Spanish fortress.

His Excellency went on to say that Spain was badly isolated. France was rapidly advancing towards the establishment of a protectorate over Morocco. Germany was delighted to see her becoming more and more involved in a policy which must eventually prove a severe strain on her resources. Austria and Italy stood aloof. England, though sympathetic, would do nothing displeasing to France. Spain was therefore thrown on her own resources. Some day she might be compelled in desperation to make a display of force in defence of her position on the north coast of Morocco.

I disputed His Excellency's hint that His Majesty's Government had been backward in coming to the assistance of Spain in Morocco. At the recent Mining Regulations Conference in Paris I said that strong support had been given by the British Delegate to the proposals of his Spanish colleague. I added that within the last few weeks you had specially instructed the British Chargé d'Affaires at Tangier to use his best endeavours to remove the objections entertained by the French Legation to the Spanish demand for an Electric Light concession. What His Majesty's Government deprecated was a sudden Spanish movement in force in the Ceuta region, such as must inevitably lead to international complications. I begged His Excellency to allow no step of this kind to be taken without previous agreement with the French and British Governments, who, I believed, would willingly lend their good offices to bring about an arrangement with the Makhzen which would secure Spain from any danger of attack on her establishments along the north coast.

Señor Canalejas thanked me for my advice, but repeated that the consolidation of French influence in Morocco constituted a most formidable problem for Spanish Governments of whatever party.

I have. &c.
MAURICE DE BUNSEN.

MINUTES.

The contention of the Spanish Gov[ernmen]t is really quite indefensible. If the Moors were actually threatening to endanger Ceuta by placing guns on the surrounding hills, Spain might plausibly argue that to prevent such an act of hostility, she must as a precautionary measure, occupy and annex the spot herself. But it is not alleged that the Moors have ever contemplated such a thing.(¹) It is as if Great Britain were to claim the right to occupy the heights of Sierra Nevada, because if the Spanish Gov[ernmen]t were to place big guns there, the safety of Gibraltar would be endangered. When some years ago Spain actually made preparations for mounting such guns, H[is] M[ajesty's] G[overnment] strongly protested and no doubt would have felt justified in declaring war, had Spain persisted. She yielded however, and there the matter, rightly ended.(²)

The fact that the Spanish Gov[ernmen]t advances arguments of this kind is a bad symptom. It shows that they really are contemplating aggressive measures. They admit that under the terms of the convention of 1904 they have no right to make encroachments on Moorish territory or to take any political action of importance without the concurrence of France. They then complain that France refuses to concur in a Spanish policy of aggrandizement, and finally declare they have such a grievance on account of that refusal, that they will be unable to restrain the military party from precipitating an incident. This is not playing the game. We are not in a position to do more than warn them, and this we have done. We must now await the result of Mokri's mission to Madrid.

I don't think we need trouble the General Staff as to the position of Ceuta.

The sentence alluding to the secret convention of 1904 should be omitted from the print.

E. A. C.
Sept. 21.

In approving Sir M. de Bunsen, add the first part of Mr. Crowe's minute, as marked.

I expect that it is a question of internal policy. The Gov[ernmen]t cannot afford to have the Church and the Army against them at the same time and the former is probably intriguing with the Generals.

L. M.

Yes, and they also wish for something to divert attention from home troubles, though that would be very risky.

E. G.

(¹) [Despatch No. 111 of September 29, 1910, (F.O. 34172/32656/10/28), to Sir M. de Bunsen, in approving his action, conveyed the sense of this passage. *v.* Mr. Mallet's minute.]
(²) [*v. supra*, p. 1, *Ed. note.*]

No. 176.

Sir Edward Grey to Sir M. de Bunsen.(¹)

F.O. 35982/32656/10/28.
(No. 113.)

Sir,
                                          Foreign Office, October 6, 1910.

The Spanish Ambassador called at this Office a few days ago and had a long conversation with Sir Arthur Nicolson on the subject of Spanish relations with Morocco.

He stated that the French were behaving in a disagreeable manner towards Spain and said that Monsieur Pichon had told the Spanish Ambassador in Paris that El Mokri would decline to agree to the Spanish demands on the following two points.

    (*a.*) The establishment of a customs house at Ceuta.
    (*b.*) The recruiting of a native police force to be organized by Spanish officers for duties in the vicinity of Ceuta.

(¹) [The above draft was based on a memorandum written by Sir A. Nicolson of his conversation with Señor de Villa Urrutia. Sir Edward Grey minuted the memorandum as follows : " If the French speak to us, they will no doubt state why they object to what Spain asks. These particular demands may be undesirable, but it is a pity that the French can never find any opportunity of being agreeable to Spain. E. G."]

H[is] E[xcellency] declared that under no circ[umstance]s would Spain withdraw these demands.

In reply to a question, Señor Villa Urrutia stated that El Mokri had not yet opened discussions and he agreed with Sir A. Nicolson's observation that in that case it would be better before taking any step to wait till he had done so. He only wished me to be cognisant of the question so that if the French Ambassador spoke to me about it I might be aware of the Spanish attitude. If H[is] M[ajesty's] G[overnment] could eventually give their moral support to Spain and say a word in her favour at Paris the Spanish Gov[ernmen]t would of course be very grateful. They were most grateful for all that H[is] M[ajesty's] G[overnment] had already done for Spain and if El Mokri received a hint from the French Gov[ernmen]t to meet the wishes of the Spanish Gov[ernmen]t he would certainly yield as he was entirely under French influence.

Sir A. Nicolson remarked that, in his own personal opinion, to raise police to keep order among the wild tribes round Ceuta was risky and might lead to much trouble. To this the Ambassador agreed and stated that Spain had no aggressive designs but desired the organization of the police force as a moral satisfaction.

He mentioned that his Gov[ernmen]t intended to say a word at Paris as to the recent selection by the Makhzen of a French protégé as governor of the Anjera tribes.

Sir A. Nicolson informed him that in any case nothing could be done until El Mokri opened pourparlers at Madrid.

[I am, &c.
E. GREY.]

No. 177.

Mr. Lister to Sir Edward Grey.

Tangier, October 17, 1910.

F.O. 37793/32656/10/28.　　　　　　　　　　　　　　D. 4·55 P.M.
Tel. (No. 57.)　　　　　　　　　　　　　　　　　　　R. 7·30 P.M.

Sir M. de Bunsen's telegram No. 49.(1)

It may possibly be considered desirable for the purpose of arriving at a settlement for the Moorish Government to recognise the principle of indemnity. At the same time I do not consider there are sufficient grounds for holding them liable, nor can the Spanish case be held to be identic with that of the French at Casa Blanca.

Responsibility of the Melilla incident in my opinion rested entirely with Spaniards who wilfully disregarded protests and warnings of the Moorish Government (see my annual report of last year).(2) A dangerous precedent would be created, and temptation to Spaniards would be almost irresistible to repeat in the neighbourhood of Ceuta, where everything is in readiness, tactics which have proved so successful in the Riff.

Moorish Government would of course be absolutely crippled by any fresh call on their already exhausted resources. (Sent to Madrid.)

(1) [Not reproduced. It referred to a conversation between Sir M. de Bunsen and El Mokri on the payment of an indemnity to Spain by the Moorish Government, and asked for instructions as to the attitude of Great Britain.]
(2) [F.O. 9347/9347/10/28.]

No. 178.

Sir F. Bertie to Sir Edward Grey.

F.O. 37796/32656/10/28.
Tel. (No. 80.)

Paris, *October* 17, 1910.
D. 7·25 P.M.
R. 9 P.M.

Morocco.

French Ambassador has been instructed to speak to you on the subject of the demands made on the Moorish Government by the Spanish Government.

Minister for Foreign Affairs says that they are excessive, the war indemnity being put at 5,200,000*l.*, whereas the French demand for everything was only 3,600,000*l.*, including 80,000*l.*, for international claims. His Excellency hopes that you will advise the Spanish Government to put a good deal of water into their wine, for the Moorish Government cannot produce such a sum and the Moorish envoy is bound to reject such a demand, and if the Moorish Government make an appeal to the Powers, which they will do, the situation will be most injurious to French, British, and Spanish interests, and will profit no one except Germany, who will be pleased to see mischief between the three Powers chiefly interested in Morocco.

MINUTES.

The Spanish position, so far as I could gather from the Spanish Ambas[sado]r, is that Spain does not wish either France or ourselves to intervene. The Spanish Gov[ernmen]t consider that their difficulties are with Morocco alone, and that they should be left to settle those differences without outside interference—though the Ambas[sado]r hinted that his Gov[ernmen]t would not object if either France or ourselves of our own initiative and uninvited approached the Moorish Envoy with a view to inducing him to be more conciliatory. This view, an unfortunate and unreasonable one, in my opinion, I communic[ate]d to M. Cambon yesterday. Spain may be seeking for a pretext for pushing matters in extremities with the Moors. I should have thought that this was a most foolish desire from many points of view—but the Spanish Ambas[sado]r intimated that recourse to extreme measures was not excluded. In view of the above, intervention, or mediation, or friendly advice is a delicate undertaking having regard to the Spanish character.

I should be inclined to instruct Sir M. de Bunsen to initiate a convers[atio]n with the Spanish Min[ister] for F[oreign] A[ffairs] on the Moorish negotiations, and he might, as coming from himself, utilize Mr. Lister's suggestions.([1]) We could inform M. Cambon of this procedure and perhaps the French Ch[argé] d'aff[aire]s at Madrid could be told to follow the same methods and utilize M. Pichon's views.([2]) There would then appear to be no concerted action and no official interference, and both Sir M. de Bunsen and the French Ch[argé] d'Aff[aire]s might intimate to the Spanish M[inister] for F[oreign] A[ffairs] that they would give advice of moderation and conciliation to El Mokri—this to satisfy the Spanish M[inister for] F[oreign] A[ffairs] that we are not taking sides on behalf of the Moor. Would you kindly telegraph if you agree.

A. N.

Since writing the above I have seen both the Spanish and French Ambass[ado]rs. The former tells me that if the Spanish Gov[ernmen]t could obtain a satisfactory arrang[emen]t as to the police and Ceuta Customs they would not make themselves difficult as to the indemnity. He did not *ask* that we should do anything at all—but if we liked *proprio motu* to mention the above to the French and enlist their agreement in so far as that they should make no difficulties as to the police and customs all would probably go well. Spain was most anxious to come to an agreement with Morocco but if the negotiations failed, then public opinion would ask that something serious should be done.

M. Cambon read me a tel[egram] from M. Pichon to the effect that Spanish demands as to the Ceuta customs would injure the interests of French and other bondholders (I doubt if they would materially if at all) and that Spain should restrict the police to the Ceuta frontier—I told M. Cambon of what the Spanish Ambassador had said to me—and I said it would be well if a settlement could be reached. M. Cambon quite agreed that mediation or intervention at Madrid

([1]) [*v.* immediately preceding document.]
([2]) [M. Pichon's views are given in Tel. No. 84 from Sir F. Bertie of October 21, 1910. He there states that M. Pichon concurred in the opinion expressed by Mr. Lister in his Tel. No. 57 (*v. supra*, p. 165, No. 177), and feared that the Spanish Government were contemplating a *coup* at Ceuta which would result in serious complications.]

would have to be very carefully handled. I told him what I had proposed to you as to the procedure at Madrid and he seemed to think that it was quite a possible one, and in fact coincided somewhat with what he had himself privately proposed to M. Pichon.

We might add to my proposed tel[egram] to Sir M. de Bunsen a resumé of what the Spanish Ambas[sado]r said, and repeat the whole tel[egram] to Sir F. Bertie so that he may let the French Gov[ernmen]t know. Sir M. de Bunsen had better be told to take no action till his French colleague has received instructions.

A. N.

Sir A. Nicolson.

I leave this to be handled as you propose, which seems to me to be quite right. The Spanish Ambassador recounted to me the whole situation that I might know the Spanish view. He did not ask for mediation and deprecated it officially : but if I remember rightly Mokri has spoken to Sir M. de Bunsen(³) and his having done so might be a peg on which de Bunsen will hang anything he said at Madrid to the M[inister for] F[oreign] A[ffairs].

E. G.

(³) [Sir M. de Bunsen reports this conversation in his Tel. No. 49 of October 15. *v. supra*, p. 165, No. 177, *note* (¹).]

No. 179.

Sir Edward Grey to Sir M. de Bunsen.

F.O. 37796/32656/10/28.
Tel. (No. 31.)   *Foreign Office, October* 20, 1910, 8 P.M.

Your telegrams Nos. 49(¹) and 50(²). Spain and Morocco.

Official intervention on our part is neither practical nor intended. I see however no reason why you should not discuss matter privately with Spanish M[inister for] F[oreign] A[ffairs] and utilize arguments advanced in Mr. Lister's telegram No. 57(³) as coming from yourself. I am suggesting to French Gov[ernmen]t that your French colleague should also have private conversation with Spanish M[inister for] F[oreign] A[ffairs] and make use of French M[inister for] F[oreign] A[ffairs'] arguments—see Paris telegram No. 80.(⁴) This will avoid appearance of concerted action. At the same time you might both inform Spanish M[inister for] F[oreign] A[ffairs] that you will advise moderation and conciliation to Moorish envoy, and take the necessary steps with El Mokri.

You will see from my telegram to Paris No. 367(⁵) the information given to me by Spanish Amb[assado]r in London on the subject.

You should take no action till your French colleague has received instructions.

The Spanish Ambassador was asked today to endeavour to dissuade the Spanish Gov[ernmen]t from breaking off negotiations on Saturday and now urged that all patience should be exercised in dealing with the Moors.

(¹) [Not reproduced. *v. supra*, p. 165, No. 177, *note* (¹).]
(²) [Not reproduced.]
(³) [*v. supra*, p. 165, No. 177.]
(⁴) [*v.* immediately preceding document.]
(⁵) [In Tel. No. 367 to Sir F. Bertie of October 20, 1910, the following passage occurs : " Spanish Ambassador here states that if his Gov[ernmen]t could obtain a satisfactory arrangement in regard to police and Ceuta Customs they would not make great difficulties as to indemnity. He added that if French Gov[ernmen]t would waive their objections to customs all might possibly go well."]

No. 180.

Sir F. Bertie to Sir Edward Grey.

F.O. 38465/32656/10/28.
Tel. (No. 85.)

Paris, D. October 21, 1910, 10·40 P.M.
R. October 22, 1910, 8 A.M.

Spain and Morocco. My immediately preceding telegram of to-day.(¹)

French Minister for F[oreign] A[ffairs] has reminded the Spanish Ambassador of the stipulations of secret Convention of October 3rd, 1904, by which Spain undertook not to take any action without the consent of France in certain parts of Morocco to which France recognised reversionary claims by Spain,(²) and he informed Ambassador that the French Gov[ernmen]t must hold Spanish Gov[ernmen]t to the observance of that engagement.

(¹) [v. supra, p. 166, No. 178, note (²).]
(²) [v. infra, pp. 210–11, No. 233. For text, v. infra, pp. 826–9, App. IV.]

No. 181.

Sir Edward Grey to Sir M. de Bunsen.

F.O. 38934/32656/10/28.
Tel. (No. 36.)

Foreign Office, October 26, 1910.
D. 6 P.M.

Spanish Ambassador has informed me of views of Spanish Gov[ernmen]t.

I have said that it is not our business to interfere with Spain, but that I regard with great apprehensions consequences of action by Spain in Morocco, which may lead to great disturbance, and spoke generally in sense of 4th paragraph of your telegram No. 53.(¹)

Ambassador maintained that to accept reference to Hague Tribunal would destroy Spanish influence in Morocco for ever and that Moors would give no trouble if it were not for French support. I pointed out that Moors had no support from French in Melilla affair, but gave a great deal of trouble and that this business might be much bigger than Melilla.

(¹) [The fourth paragraph of Tel. No. 53 from Sir M. de Bunsen of October 25, 1910, runs as follows : " I expressed as strongly as I could my regret that his Excellency was seriously proposing to act in direct defiance of warnings I had so frequently expressed in your name against any forcible action from Ceuta. I said that I could not believe that after due reflection Council of Ministers would resort to force on the mere question of amount of indemnity, which the Makhzen had recognised in principle, and as to which a reference to The Hague Tribunal had been formally offered. I deprecated proposed action as likely to lead to complications, and to place Spain in a false position in the eyes of Europe."]

No. 182.

Sir M. de Bunsen to Sir Edward Grey.

F.O. 41945/32656/10/28.
(No. 153.)
Sir,

Madrid, D. November 14, 1910.
R. November 18, 1910.

Throughout the negotiation which El Mokri has been conducting in Madrid with the Spanish Minister for Foreign Affairs I have been repeatedly appealed to by both parties to support the contentions which they have respectively put forward. Your instructions left me in no doubt that, while His Majesty's Government had no intention or desire to interfere officially in the matter, they were ready to contribute as far as possible towards promoting an amicable settlement. I have therefore endeavoured, in friendly conversations, to discourage the extreme pretensions of either side. Thus, at an early stage, I took upon myself to throw doubts, as a personal opinion of my own, on the force of the Moorish argument that Spain had no right to claim any war indemnity whatever in respect of Melilla. Later on, your instruction as to the possible inclusion of the Sierra Bullones within the neutral zone of Ceuta proved to be a wholesome corrective to the Spanish demand for territorial concessions of an extensive character. Your suggestion was eventually adopted by the French Government, and it has now taken the form, with M. Pichon's approval, of an offer by Mokri to the Spanish negotiators that the sphere of the operations of the proposed native frontier police force under Spanish instructors but commanded by the Moorish frontier Kaid, should extend beyond the Sierra Bullones, so as to include the line of heights lying between Point Ciris and Wady Fenidak or Castillejos. Though this offer fell short of the Spanish demand, which sought to include a fraction of the Angera tribe within the territory subject to the authority of the Kaid and of his police, and which would thus have extended the beat of the police under Spanish instructors to the line of Wadis Alcazar and Negro, there seems to be good hope that it or something like it will be accepted by the Spanish Government as a compromise. I supported a settlement on these lines, after having the satisfaction of finding that the French Embassy was equally prepared to recommend it. In doing so I have been obliged to lay stress in my conversations with Señor Garcia Prieto on the objections which I knew were entertained at Tangier generally, and at Paris, to any foreign police intervention in the Angera region.

I trust that, in adopting the general attitude described above, I have been so fortunate as to secure your approval.[1] My fundamental object has been to act in agreement with the French Embassy. Both with regard to the war indemnity and to the Ceuta frontier I have had no difficulty in obtaining the assent of the French Chargé d'Affaires, M. Martin, to the unofficial advice which I have offered, and the latter has successfully urged the Moorish Ambassador to conform to it, as representing equally the views of the French Government. At the same time I have been anxious to show the Spanish Government that the British Government sympathize with their desire to secure an equitable settlement both in respect of the war indemnity and of the Ceuta frontier arrangement to which they attach so much importance.

Señor Garcia Prieto, while abandoning reluctantly some of the extreme points for which he had contended, has been good enough to thank me verbally for my attitude with regard to these questions.

I have, &c.
MAURICE DE BUNSEN.

[1] [In Despatch (No. 135) of November 25, after the signing of the convention, Sir Edward Grey expressed to Sir M. de Bunsen his entire approval of his proceedings.]

No. 183.

Memorandum by Sir A. Nicolson.[1]

F.O. 41889/32656/10/28.

Sir Edward Grey,   *Foreign Office, November 15, 1910.*

The Spanish Ambassador called this afternoon. In the first place he conveyed on behalf of his Gov[ernmen]t their best thanks for the endeavours which you had made towards a satisfactory settlement of the differences between Spain and Morocco: and they quite understood that you could not have done more than you did.

[1] [The substance of this, in shorter form, was sent to Sir M. de Bunsen as Tel. No. 134, of November 21, 1910.]

The matter appears to be on the point of being concluded. The following have been agreed to :—

Indemnity to be 65 millions (including 4 millions for Casablanca indemnity).
Arrangement as to mining tax.
Question of Customs House at Ceuta.

Positions near Melilla to be evacuated on the same conditions as French evacuation (not yet accomplished) near Algerian frontier. The only outstanding point is one relative to the jurisdiction of the Kaid and the police in the vicinity of Ceuta. Spanish M[inister for] F[oreign] A[ffairs] and El Mokri have come to an agreement on it but the sanction of the Cabinet has to be obtained.

I give barest outline of what has been settled as we shall hear in full from Sir M. de Bunsen.

I said I would convey the thanks of Spanish Gov[ernmen]t to you, and I was sure that you would highly appreciate them.

A. N.

We have, I hope, heard the last of this troublesome business.

I hope so too.

E. G.

No. 184.

Sir M. de Bunsen to Sir Edward Grey.

F.O. 42436/32656/10/28.
(No. 156.)   *Madrid,* D. *November* 19, 1910.
Sir,   R. *November* 22, 1910.

The convention between Spain and Morocco which has been under negotiation at Madrid since July of last year was signed on the evening of the 16th instant at the Ministry of State by Señor Garcia Prieto, Minister for Foreign Affairs, and El Mokri, the Sultan's Ambassador.(¹)

When El Mokri took over the negotiation from his predecessor El Muaza on September 30th, the prospects of a successful issue were far from promising. King Alfonso's speech in reply to the Moorish Ambassador's address contained expressions which indicated the likelihood of a severe diplomatic struggle. The progress of the negotiations soon justified this expectation, and on at least two occasions relations between the parties became so strained that a rupture was a not improbable contingency. The first danger point was reached when Mokri took a stand on 25 million pesetas as the utmost that his country could undertake to pay in respect of the Melilla war indemnity. His Excellency had previously been induced with difficulty to admit that any war indemnity at all was payable. Spain having demanded over 100 millions, Señor Garcia Prieto for a moment lost patience, harmony being at length restored by a letter in which, in temperate language, the Moorish Ambassador placed on record the various concessions he had already made, with the addition of an offer to engage that the Makhzen would never allow the heights around Ceuta to be fortified in a manner to threaten the security of that fortress.

At this juncture your suggestion with regard to the possible substitution of some territorial compensation near Melilla, or of a rectification of the frontier near Ceuta, was efficacious in turning the attention of the Spanish negotiators to this alternative to a full money payment of the war indemnity. Spain however pitched

---

(¹) [The text was published by the *Madrid Gazette* on January 14, 1911, together with a declaration signed on January 12 in Paris by Señor Perez Caballero and El Mokri to the effect that the Convention was accepted and ratified by both contracting parties. *cp. infra*, pp. 298–9, No. 335.]

her territorial pretensions so high that Mokri preferred to meet half way the Spanish pecuniary demands, and an agreement was finally reached on the basis of a money indemnity of 65 millions of pesetas. This sum includes the 4 millions exacted by Spain in respect of the cost of the Spanish military contingent at Casablanca, certain works executed in the occupied region of the Riff, compensation for the assault of the neighbouring tribes on Alhucemas and Penon de Velez, and other items. The stipulated sum, bearing three per cent. interest, is payable by the Makhzen in 75 annuities of 2,545,000 pesetas, guaranteed by 55 per cent. of the share accruing to the Makhzen from the contemplated tax on mines.

The second crisis which arose during the negotiation occurred quite recently over the question of the extent of territory within which the Moorish Kaïd or Governor of the Ceuta frontier, and his body of 250 native police under Spanish Instructors, should be allowed to exercise the authority hitherto nominally placed in the hands of the Kaïd of the Angera tribe. On this point the Spanish Government showed great sensitiveness, and I was informed by them that failing a satisfactory arrangement in the region in question, Spain would prefer to drop all the other advantages she had gained and to break off the negotiation altogether. The military authorities had convinced the Government that the due security of Ceuta required nothing less than the extension of the authority of the frontier police over a zone which should include one of the three sections into which the Angera tribe is divided. This would have carried Spanish influence, as exercised by the Spanish Instructors of the Police force, to a line extending from Point Alcazar to the mouth of Wady Negro. The French Government, as well as most of the foreign Representatives at Tangier, being credited with a determined opposition to any police interference with the Angera tribe in its mountain strongholds, it was evident that the Spanish demand in this respect was not one which was at all likely to prevail. It was, however, for a time warmly supported by Señor Garcia Prieto as an irreducible minimum. El Mokri declared from the first that it was entirely inadmissible. He was ready however to concede the line of heights from Cape Ciris to Fenidak or Castillejos as the outside limit of the police authority, and had prepared the Spanish Government for his formal concurrence on this point when a hint from the French Embassy induced him to restrict the concession to which he had made up his mind to a line including only the actual heights of Sierra Bullones and excluding from police operations the more extensive line of heights which he had intended to yield. His altered attitude was the consequence of a telegram received by M. Martin, French Chargé d'Affaires, from M. Pichon to the effect that the French Government were not prepared to agree to a sphere of police influence outside the Ceuta boundary extending beyond the Sierra Bullones. The French Chargé d'Affaires, realising the awkward *impasse* which would be created by insisting on this view, represented the situation by telegraph to the French Government, which accordingly saw fit to withdraw its objection to the Ciris–Fenidak line. At the final meeting of the negotiators before the signature of the Convention Mokri was thus enabled to accept the line in question, and even certain variations of the line to the advantage of Spain which had been put forward by the Spanish Government. The line as finally accepted by Mokri runs from west to east from Wady Rmel to Wady Fenidak, the ulterior valleys being substituted for the mountain summits. In return for this concession, and for the offer by Mokri of an extra million of pesetas bringing up the total indemnity to 65 millions, Señor Garcia Prieto abandoned his demand in respect of police control over a section of the Angera tribe, and declared himself ready to sign the convention, the text of which was now nearly complete.

I have briefly reported in my despatch No. 153 of the 14th instant([2]) the general attitude which, in conformity, as I hope, with your instructions, I have assumed in connection with this negotiation.

([2]) [*v. supra*, pp. 168–9, No. 182.]

Immediately after the final agreement Señor Garcia Prieto, in writing to inform me of the same, included his thanks for what he was pleased to term my "friendly co-operation." From Mokri I received no less cordial acknowledgments, coupled with the request that I would convey to you his thanks for the assistance which he considered that your instructions had enabled me to render.

Mokri had been throughout advised at every stage by the French Embassy, and I venture to think that the latter, by timely concessions where they were needed, and chiefly as regards the war indemnity, the Ceuta Custom House and the police sphere outside Ceuta, rendered possible an agreement which would otherwise have been extremely problematical.

It must be remembered that, throughout the negotiation, the Spanish military authorities, as I was more than once assured by the Foreign Minister, were pressing for forcible assertion of the claims of Spain; that the garrison of Ceuta, at least 10,000 men, is fully prepared for a warlike enterprise; that a demonstration in force could have been made without moving a single man from Spain across the straits; and that the Spanish occupation of Tetuan in 1860 and the successful engagements which led up to that event are still surrounded in the Spanish mind with a halo of legendary glory calculated to arouse, in support of a renewed exhibition of Spanish prowess in the Ceuta region, an enthusiasm which was conspicuously absent during the Melilla campaign.

The Convention, in so far as its main features are realised, has been greeted with a very remarkable chorus of approval in all the leading newspapers of the Capital. Señor Canalejas has briefly explained its purport in both Houses of the Cortes, laying special stress on the pacific character of the policy of Spain in Morocco. His Excellency declared that Spain, equally with France, had a civilising mission to fulfil in that country. The new agreement would greatly promote its accomplishment. Señor Canalejas also alluded gratefully to the assistance rendered during the negotiations by the French and British Governments. In the Senate his speech was responded to by a few words of congratulation in turn from representatives of all the parties in the State, including the Republican, and the Bishop of Jaca expressed the satisfaction of the Church.

The only provision of the Convention which so far has encountered the slightest criticism is that relating to the eventual evacuation of the occupied territory in the Riff, which is provided for under conditions similar to those stipulated in the Franco-Moroccan agreement of March 4, 1910 with regard to the Showia region. The idea that the achievements of last year are not to result in permanent annexation is not yet fully accepted in the Spanish mind. But Señor Garcia Prieto has had no difficulty in explaining that, in view of the plain terms of the General Act of Algeciras as regards the maintenance of the independence and integrity of Morocco, no other course was open to the Spanish Government than to provide for evacuation when the occupied districts can be safely handed over to the native authority.

I am forwarding in a separate despatch an outline of the main features of the Convention so far as they are known here.

I have, &c.
MAURICE DE BUNSEN.

CHAPTER LII.
THE EXPEDITION TO FEZ.

No. 185.

Sir Edward Grey to Mr. Lister.

F.O. 44470/26399/10/28.
(No. 171.)
Sir,   *Foreign Office, December* 12, 1910.

With reference to Mr. White's despatch No. 157 of Aug[ust] 5([1]) last I have to inform you that Messrs. James Power and Co. have enquired, in connection with a recent newspaper report which has since been denied, whether there is any probability of Agadir being opened to international trade in the near future. The firm have been told in reply that H[is] M[ajesty's] Gov[ernmen]t have no information to that effect.

I should be glad to know whether you consider it would be desirable to discuss the matter with your colleagues and to propose collective measures with a view to the opening of Agadir.

[I am, &c.
E. GREY.]

([1]) [Not reproduced.]

No. 186.

Sir E. Goschen to Sir Edward Grey.

F.O. 45392/45128/10/18.
(No. 351.)   *Berlin,* D. *December* 13, 1910.
Sir,   R. *December* 16, 1910.

I have the honour to report that, in the course of yesterday's debate in the Reichstag, the Imperial Secretary of State for Foreign Affairs, Herr von Kiderlen-Waechter, made certain statements with regard to Germany's foreign policy. Speaking of the incident connected with the arrival of a French ship in the harbour of Agadir in Morocco,([1]) Herr von Kiderlen recalled the fact that France and Spain had been entrusted with the task of policing the sea off the south coast of Morocco. The Secretary of State then pointed out that although this mandate did not carry with it the right to enter the so-called closed harbours, the French ship had in the present case been engaged in the exercise of police duties and in the suppression of the smuggling of arms. This was the sole reason for the ship having entered the port. An official statement to this effect had been received from the French Government and the latter had added that there was no question of opening the port. This opportunity had been seized by the German Government to re-affirm their own point of view, which was also shared by the French Government, that the opening of one of the closed harbours could only be carried out by the Sultan with the assent of all the Contracting Powers. It was understood that, were any such action contemplated, fair notice would be given, so that the subjects of any particular Power should not

([1]) [On December 4, the *Kölnische Zeitung* announced that France had occupied the harbour of Agadir.]

be in a position to gain undue advantages. The Secretary of State concluded his remarks on this subject by saying that he regarded the Agadir incident as completely closed. . . . .([2])

I have, &c.
W. E. GOSCHEN.

([2]) [The rest of this despatch gives a further account of the debate in the Reichstag.]

No. 187.

Mr. Lister to Sir Edward Grey.

F.O. 47060/26399/10/28.
(No. 248.)
Sir,

Tangier, D. December 23, 1910.
R. December 31, 1910.

I have received your despatch No. 171 of the 12th Instant([1]) relative to the possible opening of the Port of Agadir, in which you ask me whether I consider it desirable to discuss the matter with my colleagues and to propose collective measures to obtain the same.

As you are aware, the opening of the port of Agadir would mean the destruction of the commerce of Mogador, which is largely in British hands : the firms at present established there would no doubt transfer their business to Agadir, but before taking any steps in the matter I would prefer to have the opinion of His Majesty's Consular Officers at Casablanca and Mogador as to the views of the British merchants themselves. One cannot help feeling that it is almost a pity to raise the question just at the moment that we have succeeded, or may shortly hope to succeed, in obtaining the abolition of the exorbitant road dues which have been strangling the trade of Mogador, but of course we must be guided by the interests of British commerce in the matter.

I have, &c.
REGINALD LISTER.

([1]) [*v. supra*, p. 173, No. 185.]

No. 188.

Mr. Lister to Sir Edward Grey.

F.O. 4133/3288/11/28.
(No. 13.)
Sir,

Tangier, D. January 30, 1911.
R. February 4, 1911.

With reference to my despatch No. 248 of the 23rd Ultimo([1]) relative to the opening of the port of Agadir, I have the honour to transmit to you herewith copies of despatches which I have received on the subject, from His Majesty's Consular Officers at Casablanca and Mogador, and also an extract from a private letter from Mr. Wellesley, who by my instructions made enquiries into the matter at the time of his recent journey down the Coast.

The reports may on the whole be considered favourable to the opening of the port of Agadir.([2]) At the same time, I cannot help thinking that in view of the hypernervousness recently shown by the Germans in the matter, it would be wiser to allow it to drop for the moment.

I have, &c.
REGINALD LISTER.

([1]) [*v.* immediately preceding document.]
([2]) [The reports, being concerned with commercial details, are not printed, with the exception of No. 2.]

Enclosure in No. 188.

Vice-Consul Johnstone to Mr. Lister.

Sir,   *Mogador, January* 21, 1911.

With reference to Your Excellency's despatch No. 20 of the 23rd ultimo, in which I am instructed to furnish you with information relative to the possible opening of the port of Agadir, its effect on British trade, as compared with the trade of other nations and the purchase of land at the locality, I have the honour to report that I have carefully inquired into the matter, and have come to the conclusion that the general opinion here is that the opening of the port would be distinctly beneficial to British trade. From the formation of the country I am informed it would be difficult to establish the N'Zails(³) which are crippling the trade at this port, and the trade of the Sous country could be tapped directly which seems to imply that the trade of Great Britain, which is the most important trade of Mogador, and the greater portion of which finds its way to the South, would be freed from the greatest obstacle which now opposes it.

I am told that land in Agadir has been rapidly changing hands in anticipation of the opening of the port. Of course purchases have been effected through Moors and under Moorish names but I know of five British protected persons who are interested in land at the locality in question and there are probably many more. For the reasons I have given above it appears to me that British trade would profit more than the trade of any other nation but there may possibly occur some failures at this port among the small merchants at the outset owing to the expense of changing headquarters.

The harbour is said to be considerably safer and more convenient for shipping than the harbour at Mogador. Agadir itself is only at present a village overlooking the harbour, and all water has to be carried up to it from the cisterns at Funti on the beach, where if the port is opened the trading town will most probably be established. I have been told that the Germans have been buying land in considerable quantities round Funti but have also been informed that the Mannesmanns have the idea of obtaining interests which may enable them to open a port considerably further South towards Cape Juby, while I have been told confidentially that the Spaniards intend in about 2 months' time to claim a port near Cape Aglou as Santa Cruz de Mar-Pequeña. Thus if two other ports further South than Agadir are opened to commerce of course the value of Agadir would be considerably diminished.

All merchants recognise that the opening of Agadir would mean the death of Mogador as a trading centre but as Mogador has suffered so heavily owing to the N'Zails it would hardly appear to me that the extinction of this town as a trading centre could greatly affect British trade with Southern Morocco.

[I have, &c.]

H. JOHNSTONE.

(³) [Enclosures providing shelter for caravans. They had been made the pretext for the levy of heavy exactions by neighbouring Kaïds. *v.* Mr. White's despatch No. 140 of July 11, 1910.]

No. 189.

Mr. Lister to Sir Edward Grey.

F.O. 4995/4131/11/28.

(No. 18.) Very Confidential.   *Tangier,* D. *February* 5, 1911.
Sir,   R. *February* 11, 1911.

The French Chargé d'Affaires showed me a telegram yesterday which he had received from his Government, saying that the German Ambassador had spoken to M. Pichon on the subject of the desire of the British Merchants of Casablanca that permission might be obtained (as had been done in the past) for the importation of their surplus stock of grain to the Sous, where a severe famine existed, and asking for a report on the matter. M. de Billy said that he had already written at some length on the subject, and read me extracts from his despatch, in one of which he said that the whole incident reminded one irresistibly of certain scenes out of " Much ado about nothing."

M. de Billy told me very confidentially that he personally was convinced that the Germans had come to some arrangement with the Spaniards in connexion with the cession of Ifni, and that they consequently were particularly anxious that no steps should be taken to bring about the opening of the Port of Agadir, which might upset their game, whatever it was, and neutralize any special advantages which they may have secured.

I think that this question of Ifni should be very carefully watched as you will recollect (see Mr. White's No. 223 Confidential of October 28, 1910),(¹) the Treaty of April 26, 1860 ceded Santa Cruz de Pequeña to Spain for " the formation thereon of a fishing establishment similar to that which Spain possessed there in ancient times." The locality was never discovered, and in 1883 Ifni was offered and accepted in its place by the Spanish Government, the Minister for Foreign Affairs declaring that it would be used solely as a fishing station. Any attempt on the part of the Spaniards, backed by the Germans, to enlarge the scope of the cession made to them should in my opinion be resolutely opposed, as any sort of port at Ifni would tap the whole of the Sous district and seriously prejudice the trade of Mogador.

Were the port of Agadir to be opened the importance of a trading station at Ifni would be diminished, and it is possible that M. de Billy is right in his view that it is for this reason that the mere mention of Agadir acts upon the Germans like a red rag to a bull.

I have, &c.
REGINALD LISTER.

(¹) [Not reproduced.]

[ED. NOTE.—On February 8, 1911, Herr von Schoen forwarded from Paris to Berlin a report, dated February 7, of the German Military Attaché, Major von Winterfeldt. In this report he concluded that there had been an exchange of views between French and British military experts, but that binding military engagements had not been formulated, v. G.P., XXIX, pp. 66–8. At the same time there was a debate in the French Senate in which the same subject was mentioned, and there was a discussion in the French Press. cp. Livre Noir, I, pp. 37–8.]

No. 190.

Sir Edward Grey to Sir M. de Bunsen.

F.O. 4608/3980/11/28.
(No. 11.)

Sir, Foreign Office, February 7, 1911.

The Spanish Ambassador called at the Foreign Office on the 2nd inst[ant] and told Sir Arthur Nicolson that the French had asserted that the police force organized by the Spaniards within the walls of Tangier was not sufficient and that the French had consequently supplemented the force by Moorish soldiers under French officers. This was in contravention to the Algeciras Act and was the coping-stone to the edifice of complaints which Spain had to make against French action in Morocco so far as regarded Spanish influence and interests.

The Spanish Gov[ernmen]t had instructed M. de Villa Urrutia to mention the matter here, as if H[is] M[ajesty's] Gov[ernmen]t did not feel in a position to say a word to the French Gov[ernmen]t in a [sic] favour of a stricter observance of the Algeciras Act and of a more conciliatory disposition towards Spanish interests, Spain would be inclined to withdraw altogether from the organization of police forces at Tetuan, Laraiche, Tangier and Casablanca, and leave it to the Powers to decide who should undertake the police duties in those ports.

Sir Arthur Nicolson informed the Ambassador that he had heard nothing as to what had occurred at Tangier but that he would enquire. He also pointed out that if Spain renounced the obligations as regards the police which had been conferred on her at Algeciras she would reopen a question which had proved to be the most difficult and delicate to deal with at the Conference.

The Ambassador also mentioned that Spain intended to take advantage of a promise given by Mulai Hafid in 1908 that he would accept a Spanish military mission, as the Spanish Gov[ernmen]t had learnt that France proposed to send a military mission of some 30 officers to take charge of the Moorish army.

I understand from Mr. Lister's telegram of the 2nd inst[ant](¹) that the question of the Tangier police force has now been settled satisfactorily by negotiations between the French and Spanish representatives.

[I am, &c.
E. GREY.]

(¹) [Not reproduced as its substance is indicated here.]

No. 191.

Mr. Lister to Sir Edward Grey.

F.O. 8955/8955/11/28.
(No. 37.) Confidential.   *Tangier,* D. *March* 5, 1911.
Sir,   R. *March* 11, 1911.

I have received a Cypher Telegram from His Majesty's consul at Casablanca stating that his German colleague has informed him that a German war-vessel will visit Casablanca shortly and remain a few days. I asked the French Chargé d'Affaires whether he had been similarly informed. He replied that he had heard nothing from his Consul, but that Guebbas had been round to see him about the matter and appeared in somewhat of a twitter. The German Minister had, His Excellency said, made a very official notification of the arrival of the vessel to him, and he wondered whether there was more in it than met the eye! It must be remembered that Guebbas is of a very nervous temperament, and M. de Billy thinks that the notification was made specially official by Baron Seckendorff, who is a "formaliste" in the extreme.

I don't see any reason why a German war-vessel should not go to Casablanca, and probably it is thought that its presence may give some form of moral assistance to German commercial and agricultural enterprise in the Shawia, which is particularly active just now under the lead of the Mannesmanns.

I have, &c.
REGINALD LISTER.

No. 192.

Note communicated by M. Paul Cambon, March 14, 1911.

F.O. 9551/2245/11/28.
(Privée et Confidentielle.)

Pour assurer le ravitaillement de nos postes au Maroc, l'autorité militaire Française a l'intention de construire dans la Chaouïa un chemin de fer reliant

Casablanca à Settat et dans la région de l'Est sur la frontière Algérienne un autre chemin de fer reliant Marnia à Oujda et Oujda à Taourirt.

Le Gouvernement Allemand ayant eu connaissance de ces projets fit remarquer au Gouvernement Français par M. de Schoen vers la fin de Décembre dernier que les lignes en question devraient être construites dans les conditions de l'Acte d'Algésiras. Il déclarait ne faire aucune objection à la construction directe par la France, mais sous la condition que tous les étrangers pourraient user des nouvelles lignes dans les mêmes conditions que les Français.

M. Pichon donna à l'Ambassadeur d'Allemagne des assurances à cet effet.

Un peu plus tard, au commencement de Février dernier, M. de Schoen entretint de nouveau notre Ministre des Affaires Etrangères de cette question. Il fit observer que son Gouvernement ne faisait pas d'objection à la construction de lignes militaires dans notre zone d'occupation, mais que la ligne projetée d'Oujda à Taourirt paraissait sortir de cette zone et constituer l'amorce d'une voie de pénétration.

Il rappela que, deux ans auparavant, les deux Gouvernements avaient favorisé la création d'une Société Marocaine des Travaux Publics avec la participation financière de groupes Français, Allemands, Anglais, etc., que, la participation Française étant la plus· importante, la Présidence de la Société Marocaine app[a]rtenait à un représentant du groupe Français et il suggéra que l'autorité militaire Française fût invitée à s'adresser à cette Société pour la construction de ses lignes. Ainsi les travaux seraient confiés à une Société Internationale, la question de savoir si les chemins de fer militaires deviendraient l'amorce de voies de pénétration ne serait pas soulevée et la continuation de ces lignes pourrait être confiée, le moment venu, à la Société Marocaine.

M. Pichon n'avait pas encore répondu à cette suggestion lorsque, le 22 Février dernier, M. de Schoen aborda de nouveau la question en demandant que les projets des futurs chemins de fer fussent établis de façon à ne pas écarter les soumissions Allemandes pour les fournitures de matériel. Le Ministre Français des Affaires Etrangères n'eut pas le temps de poursuivre cette conversation à cause de la crise Ministérielle qui survint à ce moment. Il mit M. Jules Cambon au courant des démarches de M. de Schoen et le chargea de suivre ces pourparlers si M. de Kiederlen [sic : Kiderlen] les continuait. Il se montra disposé à déclarer que le concours de la Société Marocaine serait demandé pour l'exécution des lignes militaires, mais il prescrivit à notre Ambassadeur à Berlin de réclamer du Gouvernement Allemand la promesse de s'abstenir de toute concurrence si notre ligne d'Oujda à Taourirt se contin[u]ait dans la direction de Fez ou de l'Atlantique ou si la ligne de la Chaouïa prenait du développement, à la condition bien entendu d'un traitement égal sur ces voies ferrées pour toutes les Puissances signataires de l'Acte d'Algésiras.

M. de Kiederlen [sic : Kiderlen] reprit en effet la conversation avec M. Jules Cambon et mit en avant diverses suggestions, notamment pour la mise en adjudication d'une ligne de Tanger à Fez. Il ne soulève aucune objection à l'exécution de lignes militaires dans nos zones d'occupation si nos officiers sont invités à se mettre officieusement en rapport avec la société marocaine pour l'exécution des travaux.

Quant aux adjudications publiques qui pourraient éventuellement avoir lieu plus tard, il se déclare disposé à user de son influence pour écarter ceux de ses nationaux qui se proposeraient de faire concurrence à la société marocaine. Il désire seulement qu'il soit expressément stipulé que toutes les voies ferrées à construire au Maroc soient ouvertes aux ressortissants de toutes les Puissances signataires de l'Acte d'Algésiras aux mêmes conditions et spécialement en matière de tarifs.

Les entretiens du Ministre Allemand des Affaires Etrangères et de notre Ambassadeur à Berlin sont récents et M. Cruppi en a reçu la relation il y a moins de 8 jours. Il n'a pas encore répondu, mais il m'a chargé d'informer officieusement et confidentiellement Sir E. Grey de ces suggestions.

J'ignore encore l'opinion de M. Cruppi et il est probable qu'il m'entretiendra de cette question lors de la visite que je dois lui faire dans quelques jours; mais je ne vois, quant à moi, aucun inconvénient à répondre favorablement aux ouvertures qui nous sont faites. Elles n'ont rien de contraire aux dispositions de l'Acte d'Algésiras, elles règlent les rapports de Paris et de Berlin en ce qui touche les chemins de fer au Maroc et elles ne portent atteinte aux droits et aux intérêts d'aucune Puissance. C'est dans ce sens que je m'exprimerai si mon avis est demandé.

14 *mars* 1911.

MINUTES.

We have for some time had indications that the French gov[ernmen]t intended to build small, narrow-gauge, railways both in the Shawia and on the eastern frontier of Morocco, nominally to facilitate the provisioning and the movements of their troops of occupation. In the peculiar circumstances of the case, it would probably be difficult for H[is] M[ajesty's] G[overnment] to object to such a purely military measure.

We also heard from a French Director of the Société Marocaine des Travaux Publics, whom Mr. Norton brought to the F[oreign] O[ffice] last autumn, that the Société was negotiating with the French government with a view to obtain, among other things, the contract for building these railways as part of a general scheme for acquiring a railway monopoly in Morocco.

We now learn for the first time that France has been negotiating with the German government on this question since December last, and has practically come to an agreement with them on lines which, they cannot be unaware, are not acceptable to H[is] M[ajesty's] G[overnment]. They know that we have formally refused to give any support to an international syndicate of which France holds 50%, Germany 30% and Great Britain 5%, and that, in any case, we cannot approve an arrangement which is in direct violation of the Algeciras Act.

Under that act, all railway concessions must be offered to open competition by public tender. We are now asked to consent to a proposal to set aside the requirements of the Act, and to renounce the rights thereunder guaranteed to British trade and enterprise, in favour of a practically Franco-German syndicate.

It is most regrettable that the French government should put H[is] M[ajesty's] G[overnment] into the dilemma of having either to abandon important British treaty rights or to take up an attitude of opposition to the French government, which it is one of the main objects of German policy to bring about. It seems to me impossible for H[is] M[ajesty's] G[overnment] to adopt the former alternative. They would have no defence to a charge made by British traders and financiers that their briefed rights under the Algeciras Act had been taken away from them by the deliberate act of their own government, without any authority.

It is to be feared that the present instance is only a more flagrant example of the vicious policy which the French government are pursuing in Morocco, whereby, trading upon the friendliness of this country, they are ready to make important political bargains with Germany at our expense. I think the time has come when it is wise, if not necessary, to speak an earnest word to the French ambassador, and to warn him that such a policy will lead to the estrangement of the two countries, if persisted in, to the delight and profit of Germany. The attitude of France leaves us no choice but to stand on our treaty rights, and to vindicate them at the price of impairing our attitude of readiness to assist her in every possible way in Morocco, which it will be acknowledged we have loyally proved hitherto.

E. A. C.
Mch. 15.

The French have for months through the Société Marocaine* been trying to get our consent to a monopoly in favour of that Society of all public works in Morocco. We have refused for two reasons : (1) that British participation in the Société is ridiculously small; (2) that we cannot agree to any monopoly and thereby impair the rights of independent British firms under the Algeciras Act to tender for any contracts that are going.

Having failed to get our consent to the principle of a monopoly the French are now under cover of military railways endeavouring to avoid competition for two main lines into the heart of the country, and contracts for material will no doubt follow contracts for construction. If we give way now we shall find the Société Marocaine barring the way at every turn, and some pretext will always be found for excluding independent British competition.

Apart from the principle of the thing which is of the utmost importance we shall have no answer to any British firms when they complain that their rights have been ignored, and in railway construction there would almost certainly be firms, like Pontings, who would wish to compete.

I hope that we shall stand strictly on our rights and insist upon open tender for all lines outside the purely military railways within the districts in French occupation.

W. L.

* The English part of the Syndicate.

There can be no doubt whatever that we must stand on our rights as secured under the Algeciras Act, and that if any British firm tenders for the railways we must give it our support and endeavour to see that it obtains fair play. There is a British firm, Topham Ltd., interested in enterprises in Morocco.

A. N.

I have spoken to M. Cambon and so I think has Sir A. Nicolson.

E. G.

No. 193.

Sir Edward Grey to Sir F. Bertie.

F.O. 9551/2245/11/28.
(No. 99.)

Sir,   *Foreign Office, March* 14, 1911.

M. Cambon gave me to-day a detailed account, for my confidential and private information, of what had passed between the French and German Governments respecting certain railways which the French contemplated making in Morocco, in the first place for military reasons.(¹)

M. Cambon himself saw nothing in the conclusions arrived at between France and Germany that need be unacceptable to us, but M. Cruppi wished us to be informed.

I said that I should have to refer to the Act of Algeciras, to see exactly what was the bearing of all he had told me, and how we stood.

He gave me, privately and confidentially, the accompanying Memorandum.(²)

[I am, &c.]
E. G[REY].

(¹) [*v. Caillaux*, pp. 86–8.]
(²) [*v.* immediately preceding document.]

No. 194.

Sir F. Bertie to Sir Edward Grey.

F.O. 9448/2084/11/28.
(No. 117.)   *Paris*, D. *March* 14, 1911.

Sir,   R. *March* 15, 1911.

With reference to my despatch No. 113 of the 10th instant(¹) I have the honour to transmit to you herewith, extracted from this evening's " Temps,''(²) an official communiqué made to the Press as to the decision come to in regard to Morocco at the Council of Ministers held at the Élysée to-day. It has been decided to send out to Casablanca two battalions of infantry and two sections of mountain artillery to enforce order in the Chaouia district. Note is taken of the engagement entered into by the Sultan to punish those responsible for Lieutenant Marchand's murder and the French Government declare their intention of enforcing the execution of that engagement with the least possible delay. The Council of Ministers moreover approves the Franco-Moroccan financial scheme whereby the Maghzen will be enabled to procure the money necessary for the organisation of a Moorish force to maintain the authority of the Sultan over the tribes, to police the ports during 1912, to execute urgent public works, etc., and to fulfil the engagements entered into before the 30th June, 1909.

I have, &c.
FRANCIS BERTIE.

(¹) [Not reproduced. It refers to the possible despatch of French forces to punish the tribes responsible for the murder of Lieutenant Marchand.]
(²) [Not reproduced.]

No. 195.

Sir Edward Grey to Sir F. Bertie.

Private.([1])

My dear Bertie,   *Foreign Office, March* 16, 1911.

Cambon has communicated to me, for my private and confidential information, what has passed between France and Germany about railways in Morocco.([2]) You will get a copy of this.

I told Cambon to-day that we were always pleased that France and Germany should avoid difficulties about Morocco. It suited both France and us that this should be so. I should, therefore, not do anything to make things more difficult for the French than I could help. But the Act of Algeciras had to be considered. At any moment, a British firm might put in a tender for railways in Morocco, and ask for my support. I should be obliged to give it, and the situation might become embarrassing diplomatically if I had to support the British firm against the " Société Marocaine," which was supported by France and Germany.

Cambon said it was possible that no British firm would appear upon the scene, and he hoped that at any rate I would not encourage any British firm to do so.

I replied that I would not give any encouragement, but British firms were ready enough to come forward without any encouragement. As an example, I mentioned the firm of Pauling, which had pressed for my support for a railway in Manchuria, where I was bound by a previous Agreement with Russia not to promote railways. This firm had come forward not only without any encouragement from me, but also in a way which was very embarrassing to me, for I had been obliged to refuse the support it asked. In the case of Morocco, there would be no Treaty obstacle to the giving of support : on the contrary, British firms would be able to appeal to the Act of Algeciras, which entitled them to demand that we should get fair play for them.

Cambon thought the best solution would be to increase the British share in the " Société Marocaine." It might be possible to eliminate the participation of the Swedes and others, and to arrange that we should have as large a share as the Germans.

Even if this were done we should still be in a difficulty if independent British firms came forward : they would demand their chance according to the Act of Algeciras.

Yours sincerely,
E. GREY.

([1]) [Grey MSS., Vol. 13.]
([2]) [*v. supra*, pp. 177–9, No. 192.]

No. 196.

Sir Edward Grey to Sir F. Bertie.

F.O. 10258/2245/11/28.

(No. 103.)

Sir,   *Foreign Office, March* 22, 1911.

With reference to my despatch No. 99 of the 14th inst[ant]([1]) I have to inform Y[our] E[xcellency] that the French Ambassador called at the F[oreign] O[ffice] on the 16th inst[ant] and discussed with Sir Arthur Nicolson the question of the construction of railways in Morocco.

Sir A. Nicolson told H[is] E[xcellency] that, after examination of the Act of Algeciras it was clear that if any British firms tendered for the construction of railways in Morocco H[is] M[ajesty's] Gov[ernmen]t would be bound to support them.

([1]) [*v. supra*, p. 180, No. 193.]

M. Cambon stated that France and Germany had come or were coming to an arrangement by which a free hand was given to the Société Marocaine; but he quite understood that other countries were at liberty to take any action they desired. He hinted that perhaps the British share in the Société might be increased.

Sir A. Nicolson observed that even in that event H[is] M[ajesty's] Gov[ernmen]t could not recognize the Société as having a monopoly of public works in Morocco and that they would always be obliged to support independent British firms who asked for assistance.

[I am, &c.
E. GREY.]

No. 197.

Question asked in the House of Commons, March 30, 1911.

(Parl. Deb., 5th Ser., House of Commons, Vol. 23, p. 1490.)

Mr. Jowett asked the Secretary of State for Foreign Affairs, if, when he came into office, there was in existence any understanding or undertaking, expressed or implied, in virtue of which Great Britain would be under obligations to France to send troops, in certain eventualities, to assist the operations of the French Army?

Sir E. Grey: The extent of the obligation to which Great Britain was committed was that expressed or implied in the Anglo-French Convention laid before Parliament. There was no other engagement bearing on the subject.[1]

[1] [v. infra, pp. 188–9, Nos. 205–6.]

No. 198.

Mr. Lister to Sir Edward Grey.

F.O. 12941/8457/11/28.
(No. 65.)   Tangier, D. April 2, 1911.
Sir,   R. April 8, 1911.

As I had the honour to report in my telegram No. 15 of March 31st,[1] the small Mehalla in Fez sustained rather a severe reverse on the 26th instant. The Sultan appears to have insisted on sending it out against the advice of Commandant Mangin, who declined all responsibility for what might occur. His view was fully justified. The Ait Yussi have now joined the Beni M'Tir, and the fear is that this success may induce other powerful tribes, such as the Hyaina and the Sheragha, who have hitherto remained loyal in this last revolt, to join the rebels.

Reports reach us from Mequinez that Moulai Sliman, a cousin of the present Sultan, has been proclaimed Sultan, but so far there is no confirmation of this. The reason for the whole movement is undoubtedly hatred of the Grand Vizier, and the determination on the part of the tribes round Fez, who have suffered so cruelly under his exactions, to have him removed. The Sultan is of course very closely associated with him, and appears unwilling to throw him over; in fact Dr. Verdon tells me that the Grand Vizier actually sent in his resignation to the Sultan, who refused to accept it. There appears so far to be no anti-Christian feeling.

The situation is evidently a serious one and Dr. Verdon writes privately to tell me that the Basha of Fez, who is one of his patients, came to ask him what Europe would do in the event of things going worse and Fez being besieged. This is

[1] [Not reproduced as its tenour is indicated.]

significant as showing the views taken by the Moors themselves. At the same time one must always remember that in Morocco situations change with kaleidoscopic rapidity, and it is quite possible that in a few days we may hear that the tribes have submitted or quarrelled amongst themselves, and that the Sultan's position is once more assured.

I have, &c.
REGINALD LISTER.

MINUTE.

It looks as if a change of Grand Vizier might settle the matter.

E. G.

No. 199.

Mr. Lister to Sir Edward Grey.

F.O. 12945/8457/11/28.
(No.69.)   Confidential.   *Tangier,* D. *April* 3, 1911.
Sir,   R. *April* 8, 1911.

As I had the honour to report in my telegram No. 17 of yesterday's date,([1]) the effect produced by the rout of the small body of men sent out by the Sultan on the 26th Instant [March] has been very serious.

The French Consul at Fez, writing on the 27th, reported that all the tribes round the Capital had now joined in the rebellion, and that it appeared more than probable that Fez would be invested. The Sultan had neither money nor men at his disposal. The price of food would go up at once and M. Gaillard considered it quite likely that the Inhabitants, who had no particular love or loyalty for the Sultan, would take the matter into their own hands and capitulate.

The French Chargé d'Affaires sent M. de Beaumarchais round yesterday morning to communicate this news to me. M. de Billy, he said, was of opinion that it was essential to do all in our power to keep the communications open as far as possible in the direction of the Capital. This could best be done by means of the Mehalla under Raisuli's command in the neighbourhood of Alcazar and of the Mehalla which had been operating in the Sherarda, and which had lately been immobilized on account of the heavy rains. The former had received no pay since the month of July, and it was imperative if they were to render any service, to get some money for them. An arrangement had been made with the State Bank for an advance of four hundred thousand francs, and a portion of this was to be sent up at once by Captain Moreau, one of the French Instructors here. A further four hundred thousand was promised, but would not be paid until the 15th April: however, they were in telegraphic communication with Paris on the subject, and it was hoped that the money would be placed at their disposal at once.

M. de Beaumarchais then said that the situation in the Gharb was also very unsatisfactory, and that there appeared considerable danger that the various tribes, hearing of the successes of the Berbers round Fez, might be induced or driven to join the rebellion. This, M. de Billy thought, must be prevented if possible, and he had sent to ask me whether as a great favour I would use my influence with Menebhi and get him to write to any influential friends he might have in the Gharb, and perhaps also to Raisuli, to impress upon them the necessity for maintaining order and keeping open the communications.

M. de Billy was of opinion that if the tribes were made to recognise that the European Powers were determined to take a strong line in the matter they would

---

([1]) [Not reproduced as its substance is here given.]

think twice before they revolted, and with this object in view he asked whether Menebhi might add something to the effect that if the situation grew worse, and the lives of the Europeans at Fez were in danger, it must be remembered that French reinforcements had arrived recently in the Shawia, that the garrisons on the Algerian frontier were very strong, and that it was possible that the French Government might be obliged to march troops up to Fez to ensure the safety of the Europeans. M. de Beaumarchais added that he did not say for one moment that this would be done, merely that M. de Billy thought that the threat or perhaps rather the hint of the possibility of such a measure being taken, would do much to keep the Gharb tribes quiet.

I said I would send for Menebhi at once and talk the matter over with him. He arrived in about an hour's time and said he was quite prepared to write the letters as desired and mentioned the names of four private persons in the Gharb, all of them intimate friends of his own, with whom he was in constant correspondence, and whose influence in the country was really greater than that of the Kaids. The letters of course would be absolutely private and he would make it quite clear that any suggestions or hints that he might make came from him personally. He fully confirmed all that M. de Beaumarchais had said as to the unsatisfactory situation in the Gharb. He had, he said, many friends amongst the tribes, and their position was a very difficult one : they had always been friendly with the Sherarda, and it had required considerable courage on their part not to join in the present movement. He himself had always enjoined upon them the necessity of remaining loyal to the Maghzen, and so far his counsels had prevailed, but they had all suffered cruelly from the exactions of Glawi, and the rapacity, cruelty, and lust of his Khalifa in the Gharb apparently knew no bounds. They had written him desperate letters quite recently saying that they were between the Devil and the Deep Sea and that they would be surely eaten up either by the Maghzen or by the Sherarda, who were furious at what they considered their desertion. So much did they anticipate trouble that many of them had sold all their cattle, etc., and he had now a sum of no less than twenty-eight thousand dollars (about £4000) which they had sent in to him to keep until times got better. It appears that the notorious, Remiki, who now enjoys Spanish protection (see my despatch No. 232 of November 5th, 1910),(²) is once more making trouble. Menebhi tells me that he spoke quite openly on the subject to the new Spanish Minister, and told him that it was disgraceful for a foreign Government to grant protection to so notorious a scoundrel. M. de Villa Sinda had replied that he was new to the post and knew nothing about the matter, but said he would inquire into it. Another Remiki, either a brother or a cousin, enjoys German protection, and is also giving trouble. A blood feud has moreover sprung up lately between two of the greatest families in the Gharb, which is not calculated to conduce to the general tranquillity.

I thought it would be a good thing that M. de Billy should see Menebhi and they met at the Legation in the afternoon and we talked over the whole situation. M. de Billy was most grateful to Menebhi for the prompt response which he had given to his request, and I am not at all sorry that the French should have been once more obliged to come to him for assistance, as indeed they always are when they find themselves in a tight place. It may, I hope, make them a little less inclined to criticise him in future. Menebhi evidently takes a very serious view of the situation. The rising he says is general throughout the country, but so far it is directed entirely against the Grand Vizier. It is however on far too large a scale to fizzle out as smaller movements so often have in this country, and he is convinced that it must entail great changes. He shares the view expressed by M. Gaillard that the inhabitants of Fez will insist upon capitulating if the town is surrounded. They consist mainly of artisans who live by the produce of their daily labour, they have no feelings for Glawi or indeed for the Sultan, in fact they would probably very much prefer to see the former at all events removed, and they have

(²) [Not reproduced.]

no intention of undergoing the misery and horror of a siege which would spell ruin for them. They would, Menebhi said, very soon get hold of the Authorities and insist upon their opening negotiations with the tribes and acceding to their demands. Menebhi does not believe that the tribes will enter the town, or that any of the excesses concomitant with such a victorious entry will take place. The awe inspired by Moulai Idris, the patron saint of Fez, is very great, and the whole town, or at any rate the old part of it, is looked upon as his "sanctuary."

At the same time of course it is useless to attempt to shut our eyes to the fact that the Europeans are in a critical situation, and further news is awaited with anxiety. Fortunately the British, French and German Consuls are all men of proved wisdom and courage, and all work absolutely together.

M. de Billy told me that he had instructed Captain Moreau to be very careful to keep Raisuli's Mehalla, which would now be accompanied by French Instructors outside the limits of the Spanish Sphere, that is to say on the far side of the Lukkus River, and thus avoid the possibility of any protest by the Spanish Government.

I have, &c.
REGINALD LISTER.

No. 200.

Sir F. Bertie to Sir Edward Grey.

F.O. 12612/12612/11/17.
Tel. (No. 25.) Pressing.

Paris, April 5, 1911.
D. 8·20 P.M.
R. 10·30 P.M.

5th April.—Minister for Foreign Affairs has sent me this evening the text of a statement which he proposes to make in a declaration of policy at a meeting of the Senate to-morrow at 2·30 P.M. It is as follows:—

"Mon accord avec l'Angleterre (? a) apporté naguère une solution satisfaisante à des questions importantes demeurées trop longtemps en suspens. Nous sommes disposés à résoudre dans le même esprit les questions d'ordre secondaire, dont le règlement apportera aux deux pays intéressés un avantage réciproque. Quand la communauté des intérêts(? s') affirme ainsi entre deux nations sur des faits positifs on peut être certain qu'elles resteront amies et unies en présence de toute éventualité et on peut s'en remettre à leurs Gouvernements respectifs du soin de donner le moment venu une forme précise à leur entente."

French Minister for Foreign Affairs would like to have your opinion on it if possible to-morrow morning.

I have written him a private letter saying that, in my opinion, the remainder of the statement after the words "amies et unies" might give rise to inconvenient questions in the House of Commons.

No. 201.

Sir Edward Grey to Sir F. Bertie.

F.O. 12612/12612/11/17.

Foreign Office, April 6, 1911.

Your telegram No. 25.(¹)

I entirely agree with view expressed in last paragraph of your telegram. The last words of proposed statement by M[inister for] F[oreign] A[ffairs] are sure to give rise to inconvenient demands for more precise explanation of their meaning. They had much better be omitted.

(¹) [*v.* immediately preceding document.]

No. 202.

Sir A. Nicolson to Sir F. Bertie.

Private.(¹)

My dear Bertie,   *Foreign Office, April* 6, 1911.

Many thanks for your letter of yesterday's date.

[M. Paul] Cambon came to me two days ago(²) to inform me that unless there was an improvement in the serious situation round Fez the French Government might possibly find it necessary to take military measures for the protection of Europeans in the capital. He said he imagined that should it be found necessary to do so a column would be despatched from Algeria to Fez. As you know by our agreement with France we could not possibly make any objections to any measures which she may see necessary to take for the preservation of order and tranquillity. I pointed out to Cambon, as my own personal opinion, that I feared that if the news of an advance of French troops over the frontier became widely known in Morocco it might create a fierce agitation in that country and possibly precipitate a general catastrophe. Moreover if the tribes really did enter Fez and the lives of Europeans were exposed to serious dangers the advent of the column might be too late to avert the catastrophe. From a remark which he let drop I rather gathered that one of the objects of the French forces might be to assist in retaining the present Sultan on his throne. I said that if such were the case and the French troops were to be despatched with the object of keeping the Sultan on his throne it was clear that they would never be able to leave the country and in fact that what was intended merely as a temporary measure to meet an urgent need might develop into a more permanent and far-reaching proceeding. He considered that it would be impossible for the French to remain with folded arms while the lives of Europeans were in danger. I quite admitted this and said that I merely put before him certain other considerations which I thought might be taken into account. He was careful to explain to me that no decision had at all been arrived at and that he was merely foreshadowing what might possibly take place. I recorded a summary of my conversation with him which, I believe, will be embodied in a despatch to you : of course, only for your own information.(³) Cambon told me that the French Gov[ernmen]t are consulting with Spain on the subject—but it appears they have not yet done so, and have spoken both to us and Germany without saying a word to Spain. This is tactless. I am not clear exactly as to how matters stand between the French and Spaniards at the present moment. It seems to me that the French are a little hard upon the Spaniards. I suppose you will receive the memorandum which was left by the Spanish Ambassador here three or four days ago. The Spaniards were much pleased at the observations which you were requested to make to the French Government that they should go easy with Spain and not take any measures which were incompatible with the Act of Algeciras.

Your pressing telegram of yesterday arrived last night and we were very pleased that you lost no time in intimating to the Foreign Minister the inconvenience of the last part of the statement which he proposed to make to the Senate to-day.(⁴) I must say that the words which he proposed to employ would have caused great comment here as they would almost give the impression that something very serious was impending and that the two Governments had come to a definite understanding as to the action which they would take.

(¹) [Carnock MSS., Vol. II of 1911.]

(²) [M. Jules Cambon on the same day (April 4) held similar language to Herr von Kiderlen-Waechter at Berlin, and wrote him a report of the conversation on the 5th; the latter returned a reply in writing on the 7th, attempting to dissuade France from military action. *v. G.P.*, XXIX, pp. 78–81; *v.* also *Livre Noir*, II, p. 478.]

(³) [Not reproduced as it is the same in substance as the above letter.]

(⁴) [*v. supra*, p. 185, No. 200.]

I hope that Grey's telegram this morning arrived in time.([5])

I quite agree with the French as to the imprudence of publishing the Secret Treaty—and I told Villa Urrutia so.

A. N.

([5]) [v. immediately preceding document.]

No. 203.

Sir E. Goschen to Sir A. Nicolson.

Private and Secret.([1])

My dear Nicolson,   Berlin, April 7, 1911.

My private Secretary is ill—so I must write this letter instead of having it typed. I hope you won't mind and that you will be able to read it.

I took the opportunity offered by the exchange of the Ratifications of the Protectorates Extradition Treaty to communicate to Kiderlen Sir E. Grey's remarks with regard to the paragraph in the German Press to the effect that a positive Understanding between England and Germany was on the point of being concluded. I pointed out that there was nothing in what Sir Edward had said to the French and Russian Ambassadors which could possibly furnish grounds for such a statement. I told him again that all Sir Edward had said to them was that the unbinding pourparlers, of which the Chancellor had publicly spoken, were about to be renewed and that those Pourparlers would probably include the discussion of the Bagdad and Persian questions.([2]) He had also, I said, alluded in very general terms to a discussion of Naval matters, but that of course he had not shown them either the Chancellor's Memo[randum]([3]) nor the one he had sent in reply.([4]) I added that Sir Edward saw no objection whatever to his making a communication to the Austro-Hungarian and Italian Governments within similar limits should he think fit to do so. Kiderlen thanked me civilly for my communication but made no remarks whatever about it. In the course of conversation afterwards, as he seemed in a fairly communicative mood, I asked him what the Portuguese had done to annoy the Imperial Government. He then gave me the information which I telegraphed.([2]) He used rather strong language, called the Portuguese Gov[ernmen]t a set of 'Chenapaus' and said that they wanted bringing to their senses. He said that he had not yet spoken to the Chancellor about sending a ship, but that he should advise it very strongly as the Imperial Government had been very patient and had met with nothing but evasive and contumelious answers. However no step of that nature would be taken without England and France being informed. He repeated this to Cambon on the following day.

The latter tells me that things are not going very well between France and Germany at the present moment. On returning from Paris he had addressed a note to the Imperial Government asking them whether they had any objection to French troops occupying Rabat temporarily for the purpose of punishing a certain tribe who had murdered a French national, and who drew their supplies from Rabat. Kiderlen at once came round and gave a very stiff and categorical refusal, saying at the same time that the answers might have been different if France had not been recently showing anything but a friendly spirit towards Germany. Cambon told him that that was rather a strong remark for the Secretary of State for Foreign Affairs to make to an Ambassador who had always endeavoured, not, he had hoped, without success, to treat affairs in the friendliest possible way. What complaint had the Imperial Government to make against France? Kiderlen replied, in much

([1]) [Carnock MSS., Vol. II of 1911.]
([2]) [v. Gooch & Temperley, Vol. VI, pp. 602–3, Nos. 447–8.]
([3]) [v. Gooch & Temperley, Vol. VI, pp. 524–5, No. 400. encl.]
([4]) [v. Gooch & Temperley, Vol. VI, pp. 598–600, No. 444, encl.]

the same language as that to which *we* are accustomed, that Germany found France opposed to her everywhere : and he instanced the support which France was giving to England in the Bagdad Railway question. 'What was the reason' he asked 'for this blind support? What did France expect to get from England?' Cambon replied that France supported England because she was her friend. Had not Germany supported Austria for the same reason, even when d'Aehrenthal had brought Europe within two fingers of war? Kiderlen said that in any case Germany could not consent to France occupying Rabat, as it would be against the Act of Algeciras and would, moreover have a very disturbing effect upon German Public opinion. Kiderlen added that, provided France was ready to give some little *quid pro quo* of a commercial nature, the Imperial Government would raise no objection to a French punitive expedition going into the adjacent country inhabited by the tribes, but they must not occupy Rabat. Cambon asked him whether he was to take this refusal as final, to which Kiderlen replied that he had not as yet consulted the Chancellor and that he would give him (Cambon) the official answer in a few days. Cambon told me all this in the strictest confidence, so, please, this is only for your, and of course Sir Edward Grey's *private* information. Cambon has promised to let me know as soon as he receives the official answer which he hopes may be modified by the Chancellor.

Yours very sincerely,
W. E. GOSCHEN.

No. 204.

Sir F. Bertie to Sir Edward Grey.

(By Post.)

F.O. 13059/8457/11/28.　　　　　　　　　　　　　　Paris, D. *April* 8, 1911.
Tel.　(No. 30.)　　　　　　　　　　　　　　　　　　　R. *April* 9, 1911.

Morocco. Madrid telegram No. 8 of 7th April.([1])

French Minister for Foreign Affairs, who had just seen Spanish Ambassador, told me that latest news from Fez showed an improvement in the situation, at all events for the moment. His interview with Spanish Ambassador had been satisfactory.

I reminded him of the danger, if France got entangled in a military expedition to Fez, of Germany taking advantage of it for her own purposes. His Excellency said that French Government will do all they can to avoid an expedition, but it might become necessary, and in that case Germany could not reasonably object, but he would be watchful.

([1]) [Not reproduced.]

No. 205.

Sir F. Bertie to Sir Edward Grey.

Private and Confidential.([1])

My dear Grey,　　　　　　　　　　　　　　　　　　Paris, *April* 9, 1911.

Cruppi was in a pessimistic state yesterday. I think that in a great measure he spoke the words of the Quai d'Orsay instilled into him by his Chef de Cabinet M. Herbette. He said that your statements have an influence and carry conviction above those of all others and he regretted that you had found it necessary to repudiate so strongly the existence of any unknown Agreement([2]) between England and France for your repudiation had had a regrettable effect in certain Parliamentary

([1]) [Grey MSS., Vol. 13.]
([2]) [v. supra, p. 182, No. 197.]

circles. He knew what had passed between the Departments of the two Governments for he had seen the dossier. He would have preferred that there should have been a suspicion that an understanding did exist for possible eventualities. He threw out a hint that there might be a change of disposition within the Cabinet in regard to foreign policy and that perhaps this accounted for your statement. My impression is that he may have been led to believe that there is an inclination towards Germany. I do not think that the matter is worth noticing unless he returns to the subject.

Yours sincerely,
FRANCIS BERTIE.

No. 206.

Sir Edward Grey to Sir F. Bertie.

Private.(¹)

My dear Bertie,   *Foreign Office, April* 10, 1911.

There w[oul]d be a row in Parl[iamen]t here if I had used words which implied the possibi'ity of a secret engagement unknown to Parl[iamen]t all these years committing us to a European war. But I send you a copy of the question and of my answer.(²) I purposely worded the answer so as not to convey that the engagement of 1904 might not under certain circumstances be construed to have larger consequences than its strict letter.

But Parl[iamen]t would have under these circ[umstance]s to put its own construction upon it. At the time of the Algeciras Conference if Germany had fastened a quarrel upon France I think the agreement of 1904 w[oul]d have been construed by public opinion here as entailing in spirit the obligation to help France. An absolute engagement on the other hand is more I think than Parl[iamen]t is prepared for.

[E. GREY.]

(¹) [Grey MSS., Vol. 13.]
(²) [*v. supra*, p. 182, No. 197.]

No. 207.

Sir F. Bertie to Sir Edward Grey.

F.O. 13955/39807/11/28.

(No. 168.) Secret.   *Paris, D. April* 13, 1911.

Sir,   R. *April* 15, 1911.

At an interview which I had yesterday with the Minister for Foreign Affairs, I asked him what reply he intended to make to the renewed representation from the Spanish Government that the Franco-Spanish Secret Convention of 1904 should be published.

M. Cruppi said that no such representation had reached him. I thereupon informed him of what I had heard from His Majesty's Ambassador at Madrid (see his Telegram to you No. 10 of yesterday.(¹) His Excellency stated that he would give the most categorical refusal to an application for publication and the Secret Convention could not be published without the assent of the French Government.(²) He was, he said, losing patience with the Spanish Government. They were acting in an underhand manner. His conviction was that the German Government were

(¹) [In his telegram No. 10 of the 11th instant (F.O. 13718/3980/11/28), Sir M. de Bunsen stated that Señor Garcia Prieto had addressed a further note to M. Geoffray urging the publication of the Franco-Spanish Secret Convention of 1904, but that M. Geoffray, feeling sure of German opposition to the arrangements contemplated in the Secret Treaty, was fundamentally opposed to its publication.]

(²) [For M. Isvolski's views *v. Livre Noir*, I, pp. 63–4.]

advising them in regard to Morocco in the hope of bringing about a misunderstanding between the Spanish and French Governments. This M. Cruppi would do his utmost to avoid, but the Spanish Government were acting in a very provocative and foolish manner and he trusted that His Majesty's Government would use their great influence with the King and his Government to persuade them to be calmer and more reasonable. The publication of the Convention at the present moment would be most unadvisable, and might cause serious complications.

Having heard from a fairly reliable source that at the General Staff of the War Department there was considerable anxiety in regard to Germany at the present moment, I asked M. Cruppi whether, when he spoke of possible complications, he had any ground for thinking that the German Government intended to make difficulties. His Excellency said that he did not attribute any such intention to the German Emperor or the Imperial Government. He thought that they were sincerely desirous to maintain peace, but he was very anxious in regard to the tone adopted by the German Mercantile world and a portion of the German Press always referring to the omnipotence of Germany and to the necessity that every matter should be settled in accordance with German ambitions and amongst such matters was the question of Morocco. This created a dangerous atmosphere. This condition I reminded M. Cruppi rendered it very necessary that the French Government should act with the greatest caution in Morocco so as not to give the German Government any opportunity to make objections and difficulties. His Excellency said that the French Government would be most careful in that respect and ought to be assisted by the Spanish Government in avoiding German representations, instead of which the Madrid Cabinet were creating difficulties and by their actions and suggestions helping to bring in Germany into a discussion of the question of Morocco.

M. Cruppi then referred to the objection which you had made to a part of the declaration of policy which he had proposed to make to the Senate.([3]) He said that he quite understood and appreciated your objection. He felt however that having regard to the inflammable state of the political atmosphere in and out of Europe and the attitude of the German Mercantile world and the Press, a crisis might come on at any moment and quite unexpectedly and that it behoved the French and British Governments to carry matters further as regards possible co-operation in certain eventualities than had hitherto been done. He did not mean a formal Convention but an understanding which would not bind the two Governments to act but which would define what the joint action should be in case they had to co-operate. To defer such a definition until the crisis came would be very bad policy, for if unfortunately war came it might be too rapid in its progress to await the conclusion of the arrangements which would be necessary for effective co-operation. M. Cruppi said that he intended to confer with M. Paul Cambon on the subject when he next came to Paris, which he was expected to do in a few days' time.

I have, etc.

FRANCIS BERTIE.

MINUTES.

The friction between France and Germany is increasing, and it is difficult not to believe, with M. Cruppi, that Spain is drifting into the arms of Germany.

Germany is very successfully working for associating the strong military forces of Turkey with the triple-alliance-policy of vetoing any independent foreign policy on the part of other countries on any question in which Germany has her own ambitions, and of multiplying dissensions between the Entente-Powers and third States.

In the face of this situation, the French suggestion that some closer agreement, in whatever form, between England and France respecting the eventuality of an armed conflict with Germany, is desirable, deserves the most careful consideration.

E. A. C.
Apl. 15.

([3]) [v. supra, p. 185, Nos. 200 and 201.]

We have instructed Sir M. de Bunsen about the publication of the Secret Convention, and he has warned the Spaniards against ill-considered action in regard to Tetuan. Spain appears bent on making difficulties for France in Morocco, whether at Germany's instigation or not we do not know, but we may at any rate be sure that if Germany does not take advantage of the circ[umstance]s to make further trouble she will exact a price for not doing so.

W. L.
E. G.

No. 208.

Sir E. Goschen to Sir A. Nicolson.

Private and Secret.(1)

My dear Nicolson,   *Berlin, April 14*, 1911.

Many thanks for your letter received last night. I have nothing to tell you in return because everyone is away for Easter and I have heard nothing. [M. Jules] Cambon is coming to see me this afternoon and perhaps he may have something to tell me as he has been very busy with Kiderlen during the past week. He *has* been to see me and has told me some interesting details which enable me to supplement my letter 'Private and Secret' of last week.(2)

It appears that after having reflected and seen the Chancellor, Kiderlen became more reasonable. He brought to Cambon a draft answer (to the latter's note)(3) in which it was stated that the German Government realized that circumstances might arise which might render it necessary for France to send an expedition to Fez; but that they must ask that before doing so the French Government would communicate to the Imperial Government all particulars of this proposed expedition : viz. the date of its departure for Fez and the force of which it would be composed &c. I understood from Cambon that as regards Rabat the note made much the same stipulation, introducing at the same time certain observations with regard to Casablanca and the troubles which had arisen there in consequence of former French action. After a good deal of argument Cambon persuaded Kiderlen to modify these observations as serving no purpose and being likely to embitter discussion and arouse the susceptibilities of the French Government. As regards Fez Cambon pointed out that certainly no expedition would be sent unless such a step was rendered absolutely necessary by pressing danger to Europeans. If they bound themselves to keep back the expedition until they had communicated with the German Government, and in that case of course with other Powers also, the psychological moment would in all probability be lost, and the expedition would run the chance of arriving at Fez too late to save the Europeans from massacre. To make a long story short the German note, as amended by Cambon, practically raised no objection to the French going both to Fez and Rabat should circumstances render such a step absolutely necessary. So much for the official part of their conversation. In a more private conversation which followed Kiderlen gave Cambon to understand that the Imperial Government was not particularly satisfied with the wording of the Act of Algeciras, and that they were of the opinion that it was hardly suitable to present circumstances. Therefore they thought that it might be as well one of these days to submit it to a little revision. Cambon, who smelt a rat, said nothing in reply and turned the conversation.(4) But in sending home the German note he mentioned Kiderlen's idea with regard to revision and, reminding his Government that while the Algeciras Act was 'perpetual' the Mandate for policing duty was not, warned them that when

---

(1) [Carnock MSS., Vol. II of 1911.]

(2) [*v. supra*, pp. 187–8, No. 203.]

(3) [These are apparently the communications of M. Jules Cambon on the 5th, and of Herr von Kiderlen-Waechter on the 7th, quoted in *G.P.*, XXIX, pp. 78–81. The French account is in *Caillaux*, pp. 94–6.]

(4) [cp. *Caillaux*, p. 95.]

the latter came up for renewal, this idea of revision would very probably be mooted by the German Government and, also probably, be supported by Spain. In view of this contingency he recommended his Government to be *very* careful and to *avoid* sending an expedition either to Fez or Rabat unless absolutely forced to do so. They should, in his opinion, confine themselves to punishing the offending Tribe in some way or another without going near Rabat—for to this the German Government had raised no objection. Cambon hinted that the Germans always had a sea port in their eye and that it was for that reason that the Act of Algeciras was beginning to pall upon them. As for Spain she was, at all events in Moroccan affairs getting too intimate with Germany for his taste. He had a very strong feeling that she (Spain) would be very glad to see troubles arise in Morocco which might eventually lead to a partition of the country, in which she, according to previous arrangements, would get a share. Germany was fully aware of Spain's feelings on this subject and had an accurate knowledge (imparted by Spain) of all the arrangements, secret and otherwise, made between Spain and other Powers, and he felt convinced that Germany was using this knowledge to egg on Spain to take such action as would cause as much trouble as possible.

You know Cambon as well, or better, than I do. . . . .([5]) Don't you think he is taking rather an exaggerated view of Germano-Spanish intrigues? I do, but at all events he seems to me to have given very sound advice to his Government with regard to Fez and Rabat.

It is rather characteristic of German methods that while Kiderlen is hinting at the necessity of revision, the semi-official Press is quoting the Act of Algeciras daily as an instrument which must be upheld at all costs!

Yours very sincerely,
W. E. GOSCHEN.

([5]) [A few words are omitted here for personal reasons.]

No. 209.

Sir Edward Grey to Sir M. de Bunsen.([1])

F.O.13379/13379/11/28.
(No. 25.)
Sir,   *Foreign Office, April 15, 1911.*

The Spanish Ambassador called at the Foreign Office on the 8th inst[ant] and informed Sir Arthur Nicolson that if France found it necessary to occupy Taza and Fez, Spain would be compelled to take certain measures in her sphere in Morocco. He said that the Spanish Gov[ernmen]t had told the French Gov[ernmen]t that they were ready to act in unison with them either materially or morally in any measures which the latter might deem necessary to take for the protection of European interests in Morocco, but that the French Gov[ernmen]t had replied that they preferred to act independently, leaving to Spain liberty of action in the Spanish sphere. If France advanced to Taza and Fez and occupied them it would be impossible for Spain, were such an occupation to become in any way of a permanent character, to abstain from occupying Tetuan and, the Ambassador was understood to say, Laraiche also.

Sir A. Nicolson observed that he did not follow the Spanish Ambassador's reasoning. The French Gov[ernmen]t had said that in order to protect Europeans

---

([1]) [Sir A. Nicolson recorded the above conversation in a brief memorandum upon which the above draft was based. Sir Edward Grey minuted the memorandum as follows: " I entirely approve of what you said. Precautionary measures are wise : but unnecessary advance by Spain will force the pace of France. E. G.'']

they *might* have to send a column to Fez, but they would not take that measure unless the need was urgent and the danger imminent. Why should Spain take any active measures in her sphere where there was at present no need and no danger? Señor de Villa Urrutia replied that if France moved troops there would be effervescence all over Morocco. Sir A. Nicolson observed that possibly this might be so, possibly not; but that so far as he recollected the French military action in the Shawia had left the greater part of Morocco indifferent and quiet. In any case Spain could wait till the effervescence had shown itself.

The Ambassador said that Spain might do this, but that there would be no harm in taking precautionary measures such as the strengthening of the garrison at Ceuta. Sir A. Nicolson replied that there would be no objection to that; what he did see objection to was that, if France advanced to Fez to protect Europeans Spain should reply by advancing to Tetuan where Europeans were not endangered. H[is] E[xcellency] remarked that he contemplated an occupation nominally provisional, but developing into permanence, of Fez. Señor Canalejas had consulted the leaders of all parties and there was unanimity that in such an event Spain, in defence of her vital interests, would have to reply by the occupation of certain localities in her sphere. .

The Ambassador explained that he was speaking unofficially and he left with Sir A. Nicolson an official memorandum giving the substance of the Spanish reply to the French communication. A translation of this memorandum is enclosed herewith.

[I am, &c.]
E. G[REY].

Enclosure in No. 209.

Memorandum communicated by Señor de Villa Urrutia.

(Translation.)

The Madrid Cabinet having been warned by the Paris Cabinet of the necessity in which France may find herself, if the situation becomes worse, of undertaking military operations to protect European interests at Fez, declared that it will as always be on the side of France on the basis of the Spanish-French Agreement and the Act of Algeciras and that as events at Fez react and may react more in future on other districts Spain must anticipate the consequences of the same and is occupied with the measures called for by the circ[umstanc]es within the limits of perfect prudence in regard to the northern ports and the vicinity of her possessions.

No. 210.

Sir F. Bertie to Sir Edward Grey.

F.O. 14802/8457/11/28.
(No. 175.) Confidential.   *Paris, D. April* 19, 1911.
Sir,   R. *April* 21, 1911.

There are various signs that efforts are being made here to accustom French public opinion to the idea of an expedition to Fez. The " Temps " of yesterday evening, for instance, discussed in its leading article, *à propos* of the despatch of four battalions of Colonial Infantry to Casablanca, whether or not an advance on Fez—which France had the right and might feel it her duty to effect—should take place from the Atlantic sea-board. The article observed that there was no difficulty in getting to Fez, the military problem would be how best to secure communications with the base, and that, when there was a choice between a maritime base and a continental one, the latter was always preferable. Hence an advance from the Algerian frontier and not from Rabat or Casablanca would commend itself.

[19656]   ()

The " Matin," which is frequently directly inspired by the Quai d'Orsay, gives prominence to a statement this morning on the subject of Morocco. This statement gives a short résumé of the present situation. The Shereefian troops, 2000 in number commanded by Lieutenant Colonel Mangin, are shut up in Fez and are probably short of ammunition and supplies. Another Shereefian force of 3000 men under Major Brémond has been recalled to Fez from the Sherarda country but was fortunately first able, owing to the energy of the French Consul at Alcazar, to receive supplies from Tangier. The route from Fez to Tangier is no longer open and the French instructors and the Europeans at Fez are exposed to danger. It is the duty of the French Government to come to their assistance and this eventuality is being considered. It would seem preferable to employ for this purpose African rather than European troops as the former would be less likely to stir up the fanaticism of the Moors. For the moment, the statement in the " Matin " continues, it is impossible to predict the turn of events, but France will not hesitate, if need be, to send an expedition to succour those besieged in Fez. The expedition would leave " sans aucune arrière-pensée," as all the foreign Governments know that French policy in Morocco is open and loyal and that France will not disregard her treaty engagements.

The above extracts from the " Temps " and the " Matin " are only two examples of the way in which various leading French papers are now expressing themselves on the subject of active intervention in Moroccan affairs, but it will be seen from them that the question now discussed is not so much whether an expedition should be sent to Fez, but how it should be done. Nothing is said, except in the Socialist papers, as to the dangers attendant on interfering with what M. Clemenceau once called the " Moroccan Wasps' Nest," or the objections to having French forces locked up in the interior of Morocco for an indefinite time. The only voice of any weight which has of late been raised against such a policy is that of M. Ribot in the Senate on the 7th instant (reported in my despatch No. 159 of the 8th instant),[1] when he criticised the idea of an expedition to Fez and of France attempting to maintain order throughout the whole of Morocco which morally meant undertaking the conquest of that country. It may, in fact, be said that the point of view in France as regards intervention in Morocco is undergoing a complete change. M. Pichon's policy, in which he was actively supported by M. Clemenceau and presumably also by M. Briand, although the latter Minister made few public utterances on foreign policy, was non-intervention in the intestine quarrels of the Moors. M. Pichon was much attacked in 1908 for not actively supporting Abd-el-Aziz against Mulay Hafid, who at that time was supposed to be the German candidate for the throne. The French Government, however, persisted in their policy of abstaining from openly taking sides against the revolting tribes who were seeking to raise Mulay Hafid to power, although it was obvious that the fall of Abd-el-Aziz was viewed with great anxiety by them as likely to be harmful to French interests. The French Government at this time were evidently afraid of being drawn into complications in Morocco and the question of an expedition to Fez was never mooted in any responsible quarter. M. Pichon, in one of the last public utterances made by him on Moroccan affairs, explained his line of policy as follows : " Notre programme n'est pas toujours d'une exécution facile. Il a contre lui ceux qui, de parti pris, sont hostiles au développement traditionnel de notre politique africaine, et ceux qui lui reprochent, au contraire, d'être trop modeste . . . .[2] Il se heurte aux impatients et aux timorés. Mais il correspond, j'en suis sûr, à ce que commande l'intérêt de la France, à ce qui est compatible à la fois avec le souci de notre situation européenne. Rien ne serait plus facile pour nous que le succès de telle ou telle opération militaire, nos troupes nous y ont accoutumés, mais c'est l'opération elle-même qui, étant pour le moins inutile, serait condamnable dans son principe."

[1] [Not reproduced.]
[2] [Thus in original.]

There has always been a strong party in France advocating a forward policy in Morocco, and the Nationalist papers who pretend to represent the interests of the Army frequently in the past abused M. Pichon for holding back the generals either on the Algerian frontier or in the Shawia district. The "Temps" has also advocated a more forward policy than what former French Cabinets would sanction, and was one of the first papers to mention, when the present Sultan's military difficulties became apparent, the possibility of an advance on Fez.

M. Cruppi apparently adopted the view that an expedition to Fez might become necessary, and his declaration in the Senate on the 7th April (reported in my telegram No. 27 of April 8(^{3})) to the effect that, if the security of the European Colonies at Fez were menaced, it would be the duty of France to endeavour to relieve them, gave a great impetus to the desire of the Forward Party for energetic action. A "dash to Fez," as it is called is now to all appearance eagerly anticipated by the latter and would doubtless be highly popular with the Military authorities on the Algerian frontier. The fact of the Chamber having adjourned until the 23rd May frees the Government from the contingency of embarrassing debates in Parliament should they decide on a military advance on Fez. As far as the effect of such a step on French public opinion is concerned, it may be said with certainty that the Government would carry it with them if it appeared that the lives of French officers were endangered by the capture of Fez by the revolting tribes. Since the practice of allowing the French Instructors to command the Sultan's Mehallas in the field has prevailed, the French Government have run the risk of being placed in the dilemma of either abandoning these officers, in the case of defeat, to the mercy of the tribes, or of rescuing them. This danger was pointed out by M. Jaurès in the Chamber, and he urged that instructions should be sent to them to restrict themselves to training the Sultan's troops and not to take command in operations against the revolting tribes.

A telegram to the "Matin" from Blida near Algiers dated yesterday states that a battalion of Algerian troops has received orders to mobilize for service in Morocco.

I have, &c.
FRANCIS BERTIE.

(^{3}) [Not reproduced as its substance is here given.]

No. 211.

Sir F. Bertie to Sir Edward Grey.

F.O. 14805/8457/11/28.
(No. 178.)
Sir,

Paris, D. *April* 20, 1911.
R. *April* 21, 1911.

M. Raymond Recouly, Foreign Editor of the "Figaro," who is in touch with Government circles, publishes this morning the inclosed statement(^{1}) which gives an explanation of the intentions of the French Government in arranging for the despatch of a Mehalla commanded by French officers and strengthened by a few companies of French troops from Casablanca viâ Rabat into the interior.

The presence of this Mehalla on the lines of communication between Fez and the coast will, so M. Recouly states, act as a counter-irritant and relieve the pressure round the capital. The French Government, he declares, do not desire to undertake, at the present moment, an expedition to Fez, and are aware of the numerous objections to such a proceeding. They are anxious to avoid it while, at the same time, taking measures to assist those besieged in Fez. A march on Fez would only be sanctioned if circumstances imperatively demanded it.

(^{1}) [Not reproduced.]

It appears likely that the French Government have been glad of the opportunity afforded them by the message sent from the Sultan through the French Consul at Fez to adopt a middle course between ordering an advance of French troops on Fez, and maintaining an attitude of inaction. The strengthening of the French forces on the Algerian frontier, however, clearly shows that they are ready to take military measures on a larger scale if circumstances render it in their eyes advisable.

I have, &c.
FRANCIS BERTIE.

No. 212.

Sir F. Bertie to Sir Edward Grey.

F.O. 14939/8457/11/28.
Tel. (No. 38.)

Paris, April 21, 1911.
D. 2·17 P.M.
R. 4 P.M.

Your telegram No. 62 of yesterday.(¹)

The information in my telegram No. 37 of April 20th(¹) is what I understood French M[inister for] F[oreign] A[ffairs] to have said.

French General Staff when asked by Military Attaché whether any French contingent would accompany Shawia mehalla which is to march on Fez would not deny possibility but stated that it could not make any definite answer as situation kept on changing.

In my opinion there is no doubt that the mehalla will not be dispatched into the interior without a stiffening of French troops of some sort with it or in support. I will enquire further at the Ministry for Foreign Affairs.

MINUTES.

There is apparently a certain amount of indecision and perhaps of reluctance to admit facts on the part of the French government. This sufficiently explains the contradictory nature of their several communications.

E. A. C.
Ap. 21.

We must wait.

F. A. C.
21.4.
A. N.

(¹) [In his telegram No. 62 of April 20, 1911, Sir Edward Grey stated that M. Daeschner had informed him that at the special request of the Sultan an entirely Moorish force was being organized for the relief of Fez. He further inquired whether the information contained in Sir F. Bertie's telegram No. 37 of April 20, which stated that a French force was leaving for Fez, was derived from an official communication from the French Government.]

No. 213.

Sir Edward Grey to Sir F. Bertie.

F.O. 14926/8457/11/28.
(No. 138.)
Sir,

Foreign Office, April 21, 1911.

The French Minister called yesterday and showed to Sir A. Nicolson a telegram from the French M[inister for] F[oreign] A[ffairs] to the effect that, in view of the situation at Fez which was daily becoming more critical, and at the urgent request of the Sultan, orders had been sent to French agents in Morocco to assist in the formation of a Mehalla in the West (Shawia), which should proceed to the Capital. A French column would also be prepared to advance for the protection of Europeans should the necessity arise.

M. Daeschner laid stress on the fact that it was a purely Moorish Mehalla which was being formed and that it was at the request of the Sultan that the French would assist in the formation thereof. He was unable to give any information as to how the men for the mehalla would be recruited, and how they would be assembled together; but he recognised that some time must necessarily elapse before the force could be got together, and that the country to be traversed from the Shawia to Fez was by no means easy.

Sir A. Nicolson enquired if the French Gov[ernmen]t had acquainted the German Gov[ernmen]t with the above information; and M. Daeschner replied that the telegram he had received appeared to be a circular.

[I am, &c.
E. GREY.]

No. 214.

Sir F. Cartwright to Sir Edward Grey.

F.O. 15097/13911/11/28.
Tel. (No. 31.) Secret.
Morocco.

Vienna, April 22, 1911.
D. 5·30 P.M.
R. 6·30 P.M.

I learn most confidentially that German Chancellor has informed Austrian Ambassador at Berlin that, in the opinion of German Government, should French Government occupy Fez and render position of Sultan one of absolute dependence upon France, basis upon which Treaty of Algeciras was founded would have disappeared, and that thereby whole of Moroccan question would be reopened. German view is that Algeciras Act starts with assumption that the Sultan of Morocco shall be independent. On the Austrian Ambassador enquiring of German Chancellor whether he had made this view of the Moroccan (question) clear to the French Ambassador in Berlin, Chancellor replied that M. Cambon, if he liked, could have interpreted the language used by Chancellor to him in that sense.[1]

I gather from what French Ambassador here tells me, that French Ambassador at Berlin seemed (? after) his interview with Chancellor to hold somewhat optimistic views with regard to Germany's attitude in the Moroccan question.

From what I learn here I am inclined to believe that Germany is trying to frighten Spain by telling her that France will " tuni[si]fier " Morocco, but will maintain shadow of a Sultan in order to deprive Spain of benefits of secret agreement, namely, division of Morocco into spheres of influence in the event of collapse of Moorish Government. To the Austro-Hungarian Government German Ambassador asserts that France intends as soon as possible to abolish open door and equal chances in Morocco.

Acting Minister for Foreign Affairs here declares that he understands nothing about Moroccan question, and apparently nothing will be done with regard to it until the return of Count Aehrenthal to Vienna in the middle of May.

MINUTES.

The situation is likely to become serious rapidly. Germany's game is to repeat what she tried to do before and at the Algeciras conference : Frighten France by threatening armed intervention; urge England to abandon France; stir up Spanish vanity and feeling against

[1] [This is apparently the interview reported by Herr von Bethmann Hollweg to Herr von Schoen on April 19, *v. G.P.*, XXIX, pp. 85–6.]

France; press Austria, Italy and the smaller Powers concerned (Holland and Sweden) to follow a German lead; and so create the maximum of mischief and friction at no expense whatever to herself.

We may expect that the occasion will be improved by special activity at Constantinople, and that Germany will urge upon us that, in view of the situation in Turkey, Persia, Morocco, &c., it behoves Great Britain to come to a friendly understanding with Germany,—such understanding being then used at Paris and Petersburg further to undermine the position of the triple entente.

E. A. C.
Ap. 24.

I am doubtful as to the expediency or prudence of " *warning* " either the French or Spanish Gov[ernmen]ts, though I agree in the main with the views of Sir E. Crowe. I would suggest a tel[egram] to Sir F. Bertie as follows(²) :—

"Very Conf[identia]l—Sir F. Cartwright's tel. No. 31 Secret.

You might take an opportunity of informing very confidentially the French Gov[ernmen]t without mentioning the source of substance of information contained in the first para[graph] : and it would be interesting to ascertain whether French Amb[assado]r at Berlin has reported any similar inform[atio]n. I understand that the French Gov[ernmen]t are in full and frank communic[atio]n with the Spanish Gov[ernmen]t."

(Repeat Berlin, Vienna, Madrid.)

A. N.
M.

(²) [This telegram was sent to Sir F. Bertie as Tel. No. 67 of April 24, 1911.]

No. 215.

Sir M. de Bunsen to Sir A. Nicolson.

Private.(¹)

My dear Nicolson,   *Madrid, April* 22, 1911.

I let the last bag go to you without a letter to you— an ungrateful return for the very interesting one you wrote me on April 5, for which indeed many thanks. I hope I have sufficiently kept you informed on Spanish action in connection with the troubles at Fez. However fully justified, and indeed inevitable, a French advance on Fez may be, Spain cannot look on unmoved while France is strengthening her grasp in Morocco—at least so her government seems to think. Hence the military preparations. If France occupies Taza on her way to Fez, Spain will find it difficult to resist army pressure clamouring for a move on Tetuan. Similarly Larache would be the set off to Rabat. France occupying Rabat Spain will occupy Larache. This is what my French colleague expects would happen. How the Powers not in with the Franco-Spanish arrangements of 1904 would regard such moves as these, it is hard to say. My line has been to say that I do not understand why a necessary French advance should involve an unnecessary Spanish advance. To this Garcia Prieto replies no move will be made unless required to put down disturbances in the Spanish sphere with which Spain could not allow any one else to deal.

There has been a good deal of anti-French talk in the Spanish Press, but Geoffray thinks he has now given explanations which will improve the tone of the Press, and that the Gov[ernmen]t are beginning to understand that they can only hope to get what they want—or a part of it—by securing the goodwill of France. . . . .(²)

Yours ever,
MAURICE DE BUNSEN.

(¹) [Carnock MSS., Vol. II of 1911.]
(²) [The closing remarks are of a purely personal kind.]

[*ED. NOTE.*—On April 22 a Wolff telegram stated that the situation in Fez was worse, and that the Sultan of Morocco had sought refuge in the French consulate. The Emperor William II, who was then in Corfu, telegraphed to Berlin that he thought that Germany ought not to prevent the French from restoring order, that Spain could be left to protest, and that Germany need not send a battleship. Herr von Bethmann Hollweg replied discrediting the Wolff rumour. *v. G.P.*, XXIX, pp. 89–90.]

No. 216.

Sir F. Bertie to Sir Edward Grey.

Paris, April 25, 1911.

F.O. 15494/13751/11/28.
Tel. (No. 42.)

D. 6 P.M.
R. 9·15 P.M.

(?) France and Morocco.

Vienna telegram No. 31, Secret, of 22nd April.([1])

I have seen French Minister for Foreign Affairs.

German Chancellor has held language to the French Ambassador([2]) from which it may be inferred that if a French occupation of Fez were followed by a change in the position of the Sultan, depriving him of independence, the question of Morocco and of Treaty of Algiers would no longer be the same as now. German Government have not made any objection to the French preparations for the relief of Fez with the assistance of French troops. On the contrary, Chancellor has said that the revolted tribes ought to be well punished.

French Minister for Foreign Affairs does not apprehend any direct opposition from the German Government to the French action, but he was aware that they were endeavouring to stir up the Spanish Government and the Austrian Government against the French Government. He does not think that they are at all likely to succeed with the Austrian Government. He is in full and frank communication with the Spanish Government through the French Embassy at Madrid and the Spanish Ambassador here, and as French Government intend strictly to observe the provisions of the Algeciras Act and of other conventional arrangements with Spain, England, and Germany, Spanish Government will have no cause for remonstrance or complaint. There are, however, parties in Spain who desire to take advantage of the present state of affairs in Morocco and the necessity in which the French Government find themselves for sending a relief force to Fez to bring into force or partly act on secret convention between Spain and France. To this French Government cannot consent. They desire to preserve independence of Sultan of Morocco such as it has been hitherto under the Algeciras Act, and the relief expedition to Fez has no ulterior political object. He has seen Spanish Ambassador, who is recovering from a severe operation, and has fully explained to him situation and the attitude of the French Government, and their determination to strictly observe their treaty engagements. Spanish Ambassador asked whether French troops would be sent to Tazza, implying that, in such a contingency, Spanish Government would be justified in dispatching troops to Tetuan. Minister for Foreign Affairs told him that he could not say whether it would be necessary to send French troops to Tazza, but such a proceeding would not justify Spanish Government in making a move on Tetuan, and the French Government could not consent to it. French Government had only the obligation of giving notice to the Spanish Government when they contemplated action within the French sphere, but the Spanish Government were bound to obtain the consent of the French Government to Spanish action in the Spanish sphere.

([1]) [*v. supra*, pp. 197–8, No. 214, *min.*]
([2]) [*cp. supra*, p. 197, No. 214.]

French Minister for Foreign Affairs hopes that His Majesty's Government will continue to use their influence at Madrid to prevent Spanish Government from listening to bad advice and committing imprudences. It has already succeeded in causing the Spanish Government to abandon proposal to publish Franco-Spanish secret convention. It would be of the greatest benefit if the King of Spain could be shown through British counsels that those who give out that the intention of the French Government is the "tuni[si]fication" of Morocco are misrepresenting French policy. France is bound to Spain and England by agreements which she is firmly resolved to observe.

No. 217.

Mr. Rattigan to Sir Edward Grey.

F.O. 15474/8457/11/28.

Tel. (No. 35.) *En clair.* *Tangier,* D. *April* 25, 1911.

Special courier dispatched from Alcazar last night has just arrived with letters from Consul Macleod and Sergeant Balding. Former states Fez still quiet on 20th, and tension relieved by arrival of grain and cattle. Indecisive fighting took place round town on 19th. Balding states mehalla moved short distance on 21st, but was at once attacked by rebels in force, who occupied position just vacated by army. They were driven off but Balding states army is completely surrounded by hostile tribes and ammunition badly needed. French Consular Agent left Alcazar with convoys for army few days ago but Carleton hears he is having great difficulty in getting through.

No. 218.

Sir M. de Bunsen to Sir Edward Grey.

F.O. 16148/13751/11/28.

(No. 53.) Confidential. *Madrid,* D. *April* 25, 1911.

Sir, R. *May* 1, 1911.

I mentioned in my telegram No. 13 of to-day([1]) that the French Ambassador at Madrid is now not dissatisfied with the position which Spain seems disposed to take up in respect of events in Morocco. When it was first realised that the French Government were preparing to take military action in response to the Sultan's appeal from Fez for assistance, the Madrid press assumed a tone of bitter hostility towards France, implying that the disturbances round Fez had been engineered to provide a pretext for the establishment of a French protectorate. Some papers clamoured for a simultaneous Spanish advance on Fez, and others for the immediate military occupation of strategic points within the Spanish sphere, such as Tetuan, Larache and Alhucemas. The former suggestion no longer finds supporters but there is still a remarkable concensus of opinion in the Press in favour of a strict reservation of the entire Spanish sphere of influence to the exclusive action of Spain. The extent of that sphere is only vaguely realised, but all are agreed that it extends southwards beyond Alcazar, and that within its limits it behoves Spain alone to provide for the maintenance of order. The independent "Correspondencia" stands alone in proclaiming that nothing abnormal is happening in Morocco and that there is no likelihood of Spanish intervention being called for. The "Manana," though a Government organ, is conducting a vigorous campaign in favour of an undertaking

([1]) [Not reproduced. It gives a shorter account of the Spanish attitude to events in Morocco.]

with Germany, which it seeks to prove would be more useful to Spain than a continuance of the *entente* with France. Señor Canalejas has disavowed this proposition, and judging from the more recent declarations of Spanish statesmen there is no present reason to apprehend a departure from the avowed policy of proceeding in the development of affairs in Morocco hand in hand with France.

This policy is again asserted in a semi-official letter from the Minister for Foreign Affairs dated the 20th of April and written in reply to a notification from M. Geoffray that the French Government intended to take military measures. M. Geoffray has had the goodness to allow me to read this communication which disclaims any jealousy of French action for the relief of Fez, provided the French forces and Moorish Mahallas under French direction are kept outside the regions in which Spain has a special interest, as defined in Article 2 of the Secret Treaty of October 1904.([2]) It concludes with the expression of a confident belief that, should events compel France to assume a more extensive control over the government of Morocco than is at present contemplated, she will first come to a full understanding with Spain as regards the new situation which would thus be created.

M. Geoffray considers this letter fairly satisfactory. He continues to be an advocate of a settlement of the Morocco question on the basis of the above-mentioned Secret Treaty. If he opposes its publication, it is because he believes that thereby the whole Morocco question would be reopened, and that the result would be a set of new arrangements less favourable than the present ones to both countries. So long as the secret Treaty remains unpublished, it is open to France and Spain to apply its terms in so far as they are not manifestly at variance with the general act of Algeciras. His Excellency desires to continue acting as long as possible on the assumption that the general Act of Algeciras still holds good. At the same time he often expresses to me his view that this assumption can only be maintained by putting a considerable strain on the theory which underlies it, namely that of the existence of an independent Sultan, assisted by a strong Makhzen.

In reality M. Geoffray considers that the above theory has long since broken down. For some time both Sultan and Makhzen have been prompted by France, and have owed to her the very limited authority they have been able to exercise. Before long it will be impossible, in His Excellency's opinion, to resist the admission that the above relation amounts to a French protectorate, and it will then become necessary to arrive at some fresh international understanding which will recognise the new order of things.

I have, &c.
MAURICE DE BUNSEN.

([2]) [*v. Gooch & Temperley*, Vol. III, pp. 49–52, No. 59.]

No. 219.

Question asked in the House of Commons, April 25, 1911.

(*Parl. Deb.*, 5th Ser., House of Commons, Vol. 24, p. 1601.)

Major Archer-Shee: I beg to ask the Secretary of State for Foreign Affairs whether he can inform the House as to the number of British subjects residing in Fez at the present time, and what steps the Government propose taking to safeguard British interests in that part of Morocco?

Mr. McKinnon Wood: The number of British subjects residing at Fez on 27th March, 1911, apart from persons of Moorish parentage, was ten. Of these, six were women and two were children. His Majesty's Government do not contemplate any active measures. They consider that the arrangements being made under French supervision will afford the necessary protection of British subjects at Fez. No special measures appear to be called for to safeguard British interests in that part of Morocco.

Mr. Dillon: Has the Government any information which would give them cause for believing that there is any danger to Europeans?

Mr. McKinnon Wood: No; we have no such information.

No. 220.

Sir F. Bertie to Sir Edward Grey.

F.O. 15745/13911/11/28.
(No. 188.) Confidential.   *Paris, D. April 26, 1911.*
Sir,   *R. April 28, 1911.*

M. Cruppi told me to-day that the news from Morocco were [*sic*] neither good nor bad. Preparations were being completed for the relief of Fez. He trusted that it would not be necessary for French troops to go as far as that city. He hoped that the relief column would get into touch with Major Brémond's mehalla to the West and North-West of Fez and furnish him with the necessary supplies to enable him to get the better of the revolted tribes, but if the relief could not be thus effected the French troops would have to go to Fez itself.

On my asking whether he had any reason to suppose that the German Government would raise any question in regard to French action in Morocco, M. Cruppi said that although the German Government were endeavouring to instil distrust into the mind of the Spanish Government he hoped that they would not succeed, and he felt that His Majesty's Government could be of great assistance in dissuading the King of Spain from listening to the evil counsels of those who were endeavouring to persuade him that France was playing false to Spain. He had no proof that His Majesty was being influenced that way but he could not help thinking that there might be an inclination to listen to such advice. He could assure me that the policy of the French Government was perfectly straightforward. They had no hidden designs. The relief of Fez was a duty to humanity and to the honour of France. They were resolved to keep strictly to the terms of the Algeciras Act and within the limits of their rights and their engagements to England, Spain and Germany, and to action within those rights and engagements Germany could have no right or ground for objection.

I have, &c.
FRANCIS BERTIE.

No. 221.

Sir Edward Grey to Sir M. de Bunsen.

F.O. 15711/13751/11/28.
(No. 28.) Confidential.
Sir,   *Foreign Office, April 26, 1911.*

The Spanish Ambassador called at the Foreign Office to-day, and Sir A. Nicolson took the opportunity of giving H[is] E[xcellency] the substance of the assurances which M. Cruppi had communicated to Sir F. Bertie in regard to French action in Morocco,([1]) and remarked that those who stated that the French Government intended to *tuni[si]fier* Morocco were misrepresenting French policy, and that France was firmly resolved to observe her agreements with Spain and Great Britain.

([1]) [*cp. supra,* pp. 199–200, No. 216.]

Sir A. Nicolson added that he trusted that Spain would close her ears to any whisperings in a contrary sense, and enquired whether Germany, for instance, had been speaking at Madrid on the subject.

The Ambassador observed that Germany had informed the Spanish Government that she had stated to the French Government that she considered that there was no necessity for French troops to proceed to Fez: and that if French troops did advance to the capital there would arise not only the danger of serious troubles occurring throughout Morocco, but there would also be a *répercussion* in Europe affecting the political situation there.

H[is] E[xcellency] added that if France occupied Fez it was clear that she would remain there, whatever she might say to the contrary, and that therefore the Sultan and the Moorish Government would be completely under French influence, and the Sultan would very soon be in the same position as the Bey of Tunis. In these circumstances Spain would consider that the independence of the Sultan had vanished, and that she would be fully justified in putting into operation the clauses of the secret Treaty which empowered Spain to take over certain districts in Morocco.

Sir A. Nicolson remarked that this would amount to a partition of the country and would open up the whole Morocco question, which was most undesirable. Señor de Villa Urrutia said that this might be so, but it would be impossible for Spain to acquiesce passively in the establishment of French domination at Fez over the Sultan and his Government: it was all very well for the French to say that they were merely going to relieve the capital and succour Europeans for, once there, they would not be able to leave. Spain had explained her point of view very clearly at Paris, and though she did not, for the moment, intend to do more than make the necessary preparations, she would probably be compelled to take further action if the situation were to develop on the lines he had indicated. H[is] E[xcellency] doubted whether it would even be to the interest of England to have a French colonial empire extending from Tunis to the Atlantic seaboard, although for the present British relations with France were amicable. Were France to establish herself on the Moorish coast opposite to Spain either directly or through a vassal Sultan, it could not be to the advantage of England and would of course be quite inacceptable to Spain. There could be no possible danger to British interests were a weak Power like Spain to be at Tetuan, Laraiche, etc.

Sir A. Nicolson observed that in any case it would be necessary to wait and see how the situation developed, and that H[is] E[xcellency]'s arguments afforded food for reflection. He trusted, however, that Spain would take no hasty action, and that she would confide in the sincerity of the French Government.

[I am, &c.
E. GREY.]

No. 222.

Sir E. Grey to Sir M. de Bunsen.

F.O. 15494/13751/11/28.   *Foreign Office, April 27,* 1911.
Tel. (No. 19.)   D. 1·30 P.M.

Sir F. Bertie's tel[egram] No. 42 of Ap[ril] 25th. Morocco.(¹)

Y[our] E[xcellency] can take such action as you consider prudent in the sense of last paragraph.

(Repeat Paris, Tangier, Berlin, Vienna.)

(¹) [*v. supra,* pp. 199–200, No. 216.]

No. 223.

Sir F. Bertie to Sir Edward Grey.

F.O. 15713/8457/11/28.
Tel. (No. 43.)

Paris, *April* 27, 1911.
D. 2·25 P.M.
R. 3·45 P.M.

French M[inister for] F[oreign] A[ffairs] sent for me this morning to tell me that besides information communicated to Sir A. Nicolson by the French Embassy he has received further disquieting news from Morocco. Colonel Mangin writing on April 19th begged Major Brémond to hasten to the rescue and Major Brémond under date of April 21st states that he has been violently attacked by tribes and that the whole country is in revolt. Consul Boissord who had got as far as Douaf has retired to Souk-el-Arish Arba and Major Brémond has been obliged to retire to Malek.

Mequinez is reported to be in the hands of the rebel tribes and they are said to be debating as to declaring the Sultan's brother Moulai-el-Zin Sultan.

No. 224.

Sir F. Bertie to Sir Edward Grey.

Private and Confidential.([1])
My dear Grey,

Paris, *April* 27, 1911.

Cruppi has no certain proof of German intrigues, but he feels convinced that Spanish action in Morocco is prompted by German Agents. He holds that the German Government play on Spanish susceptibilities telling the Spaniards that France is playing them false. They hope that an incident will bring the Spanish army into the field of action that Spain will proceed to occupy portions of Moroccan territory and that then the German Government will come forward and say that the state of affairs has rendered the Algeciras Act inapplicable and will suggest to the French Government : " causons ensemble " for a share of spoil to Germany. He will do all he can to avert this and will ménager the Spaniards as much as possible, but he finds them very unreasonable. He hopes that you will keep them straight.

Yours sincerely,
FRANCIS BERTIE.

([1]) [Grey MSS., Vol. 13.]

No. 225.

Sir F. Bertie to Sir Edward Grey.

F.O. 15874/13911/11/28.
Tel. (No. 45.) Confidential.

Paris, *April* 28, 1911.
D. 4·55 P.M.
R. 7·15 P.M.

French Minister for Foreign Affairs called at the embassy this morning to make the following communication :—([1])

He learns from Morocco that military preparations are active at Ceuta for, it is thought, an occupation of Tetuan. He hears from the French Ambassador at Madrid that the King has expressed to him the most friendly sentiments for France and his desire to work in concord with the French Government; but M. Geoffray also reports that Spanish Government intend to make, or have made, representa-

([1]) [An important summary of the situation to date was sent to St. Petersburgh by M. Isvolski on this day. *v. Livre Noir*, I, pp. 101–4.]

tions to His Majesty's Government that the march of the French general on Fez and the state of anarchy in Morocco bring into operation the secret Franco-Spanish agreement, or, alternatively, the assembly of a conference.

French Minister for Foreign Affairs, comparing this report with statements in a portion of the German press, cannot avoid suspicion that there have been suggestions from Germany to the Spanish Government, or pourparlers of some sort between them.

French Minister for Foreign Affairs is to see Spanish Ambassador this afternoon, and he expects to have from him a communication to the same effect as that contemplated to you. He intends to say to his Excellency that the sole object of the advance on Fez is a rescue of the Europeans there, and the furnishing of relief to the Sultan to enable him to deal with the revolted tribes, and that there is no intention on the part of the French Government to remain permanently at Fez or to take advantage of the state of affairs for territorial purposes; that he cannot admit that there is a state of anarchy in Morocco, and particularly not in the Spanish sphere; that the French Government have kept the Spanish Government informed of their intentions as bound to do by the Algeciras Act, and that the Spanish Government are precluded by the Act from taking any military or other measures within the Spanish sphere except with the concurrence of the French Government.

If in the judgment of the Spanish Government there are circumstances bringing into operation the secret agreement, what are they? He will not lay much stress on the march of Captain Obilo with his tabor from Laraiche to El Kasar, though it was not called for and was dangerous (group undecypherable), on their proceedings at Ifni, and the mission to Marakesh for the alleged purpose of purchasing horses, all of which were likely to provoke incidents. He will put these aside for the purpose of considering without prejudice what the Spanish Government desire. Above all it is essential to avoid a condition of affairs between France and Spain giving opportunity for the intervention of Germany or the raising of a European question.

In these circumstances, French Minister for Foreign Affairs will suggest that the Spanish and French Governments should confer with the British Government as an intermediary to see what are the grievances of the Spanish Government, and how far they can be met without a departure from the provisions of the Algeciras Act and of the secret Franco-Spanish, Anglo-French, and Anglo-Spanish agreements.

French Minister for Foreign Affairs says that in this Morocco question it is urgent that France, England, and Spain should work together in complete accord. I am sending by post a communication (from) Spanish Ambassador to the French Minister for Foreign Affairs which the latter has given me confidentially.

No. 226.

Sir Edward Grey to Sir F. Bertie.

F.O. 15977/13911/11/28.   *Foreign Office, April 28, 1911.*
Tel. (No. 76.) Confidential.   D. 7·45 P.M.
We were informed by Spanish Ambassador to-day that German and Austrian Ambassadors at Paris had received instructions to tell French Minister for Foreign Affairs that their Governments would view with displeasure an advance of French troops to Fez, as such a measure might lead to a conflict at Fez and possibly to a holy war throughout Morocco.

(Repeated to Berlin, No. 51, and Vienna, No. 11.)

No. 227.

Sir E. Goschen to Sir Edward Grey.

F.O. 15873/13911/11/28.
Tel. (No. 20.)

Berlin, *April* 28, 1911.
D. 8·22 P.M.
R. 10 P.M.

Morocco.

French Ambassador to-day communicated to Secretary of State for Foreign Affairs assurances of French Government with regard to object and scope of expedition, laying stress on their intention that the expedition should retire directly its objects were secured.

His Excellency said that he received these assurances with satisfaction, and gave Ambassador to understand that no difficulties would be raised by Imperial Government with regard to expedition. His Excellency expressed at the same time considerable doubt as to whether French Government would be able to realise their intention of retiring at an early date, all the more that it was always a very difficult matter to decide exactly when order was restored. He added that in any case French Government must bear in mind that an indefinitely prolonged occupation would mean the end of the Act of Algeciras, in which case Germany would resume her entire liberty of action.

The Chancellor held much the same language, but was even more sceptical as to the ability of the French Government to carry out their stated intentions.

No. 228.

Sir M. de Bunsen to Sir Edward Grey.

F.O. 15912/13751/11/28.
Tel. (No. 15.) R.

Madrid, D. *April* 28, 1911, 8 A.M.
R. *April* 29, 1911, 10·25 P.M.

Paris telegram No. 44 of 27th April.(¹)

Minister for Foreign Affairs assured both French Ambassador and myself to-day that no movement of Spanish troops in Morocco is at present contemplated, and that Spanish Government would be glad to avoid disagreeable and expensive necessity of sending troops. They feel bound, however, to have a force ready, for no one can tell what will come of the French movement on Fez, and Spain must be prepared to act within her own sphere if disturbances arise.

I took the opportunity to inform his Excellency, as authorised by your telegram No. 19,(²) that French Minister for Foreign Affairs had given the British Ambassador at Paris the most positive assurances as to the intention of the French Government to respect the Algeciras Act and other conventions, and not to follow Tunis precedent. I begged his Excellency to communicate the above to the King of Spain as from myself, when he sees His Majesty to-morrow.

Minister for Foreign Affairs promised to do so, saying that he did not doubt good intentions of France, but events might be too strong for her.

(Repeated to Paris and Tangier.)

(¹) [Not reproduced. It refers to the landing cf Spanish officers and non-commissioned officers at Laraiche, and to Captain Obilo's expedition described in Tel. No. 45, *v. supra*, pp. 204–5, No. 225.]

(²) [Not reproduced as its tenour is indicated.]

No. 229.

Sir E. Goschen to Sir Edward Grey.

F.O. 16099/16083/8457/11/28.
(No. 112.) Very Confidential. *Berlin, D. April* 28, 1911.
Sir, R. *May* 1, 1911.

M. Jules Cambon, my French colleague, came to see me yesterday and talked to me for some time on the subject of Morocco. He told me that at the outset of the present situation he had found Herr von Kiderlen difficult to deal with and inclined to take a rather high and blustering line. After he had talked the matter over with the Chancellor however he had modified his tone considerably and discussed the subject of the expedition quite reasonably but always with a note of warning in his remarks. Then the Easter Holidays had come and both Herr von Kiderlen and the Chancellor had gone away. During their absence he, M. Cambon, had by instructions from his Government informed the Under Secretary in charge of the Imperial Foreign Office that it had been definitely decided owing to the news from Morocco, that the expedition should be sent. M. Cambon had subsequently received instructions to communicate to the Imperial Government the objects and scope of the expedition, and to inform them at the same time that the expedition would be withdrawn as soon as its object, namely to secure the lives and property of Europeans and to restore order, had been attained. He was also to give the Imperial Government every assurance that nothing would be done contrary to the Act of Algeciras,(¹) or which might in any way affect the commercial and trade interests of other Powers. Owing however to Herr von Kiderlen having prolonged his leave of absence he had not yet been able to deliver this message, and M. Cambon gave me to understand that although he had written to the Chancellor to say that he would like to see him, His Excellency had not shown any alacrity to see him before Herr von Kiderlen's return. M. Cambon said that in his opinion the dilatory proceedings on the part of the Chancellor and the Secretary of State reflected the whole German attitude on this question, which was one of premeditated silence, in fact the same sort of attitude as that adopted by the German Government in 1904. He could not help thinking that they were hanging back in the hope that something might occur which would give them an excuse for interfering and turning the situation in some way or another to their own advantage. I asked M. Cambon what the Chancellor had said when he had first spoken to His Excellency about the expedition. M. Cambon told me that the Chancellor had pointed out that any action such as the occupation of Fez which resulted in a change in the position of the Sultan and the loss of his independence, would necessarily alter the basis on which the Algeciras Act was founded and lead to the reopening of the whole Morocco question. In answering the Chancellor, M. Cambon laid before His Excellency the reasons which rendered an expedition absolutely necessary, and expressed his conviction, especially in view of the great responsibility which might under certain circumstances rest upon those who delayed, or caused to be delayed, the despatch of the expedition, that His Excellency would raise no objection to the action which France was bound both by her position and her engagements to take in this matter. The Chancellor had replied: "I raise no objection, but neither do I encourage you in your action." His Excellency had added that while he was sure that the French Government were acting with the best possible motives, experience told him that when a relieving or expeditionary force once got into a place, reasons were nearly always found to render the date of its departure extremely difficult to fix. From this conversation M. Cambon gathered that the Imperial Government did not intend to raise any objections to the French preparations for the relief of Fez, but that they were watching events, and especially the attitude of Great Britain

(¹ [*v. A. & P.* (1906), CXXXVI, (*Cd.* 3087), pp. 331-88.]

and Russia, very narrowly, and would not show their hands until the situation was further developed.

To-day M. Cambon called on me again and told me that Herr von Kiderlen had returned and that he had communicated both to him and subsequently to the Chancellor, the assurances of the French Government to the effect that there was no question of the expeditionary force remaining in Fez a moment longer than was necessary, that its only object was to secure the lives and property of the European residents, and to restore order, that no action would be taken contrary to the act of Algeciras or the agreement of 1904,(2) and that in no case would anything be done which could in any way affect the commercial interests of Germany or any other Power.

Herr von Kiderlen in reply had said that the Imperial Government received these assurances with satisfaction and would make no difficulties with regard to the despatch of the expedition, although, he must confess, it had not escaped their notice that the expedition was now on a very much larger scale than when it was first mooted. He was absolutely sure that the assurances of the French Government were made in good faith, but he could not conceal his doubts whether they would be able to carry out their intention of leaving Fez as soon as possible. They might wish to leave, but what with public opinion and other forces behind them, he doubted their ability to do so. He sincerely hoped everything would go right and that the French Government would be able to fulfil their assurances, but if the contrary occurred and the occupation became indefinitely prolonged, that would mean the end of the Act of Algeciras and the consequent resumption by Germany of her full liberty of action.(3)

M. Cambon told me that the Chancellor, whom he saw immediately afterwards held similar language, though, if anything, he was a little more sceptical even than Herr von Kiderlen with regard to the prompt withdrawal of the expedition after the attainment of its primary objects.(4)

I have the honour to enclose, herewith, a summary which has been prepared by Mr. Chilton, of the articles published by the chief Berlin newspapers upon the present phase of the Morocco question.(5)

Up to the last few days their reticence on the subject was remarkable.

I have, &c.
W. E. GOSCHEN.

(2) [v. Gooch & Temperley, Vol. II, pp. 404-5, App.]
(3) [v. G.P. XXIX, pp. 97-8, and already referred to p. 206, No. 227; v. also p. 209, No. 230, note (3).]
(4) [The Emperor William II's sentiments of April 22 were repeated on April 30, v. G.P., XXIX, p. 101.]
(5) [Not reproduced.]

No. 230.

Minute by Sir A. Nicolson.

Secret.
Lord Morley.(1)   Foreign Office, April 28, 1911.

The French Ambass[ado]r called this afternoon. He told me he had dined en petit comité with M. Cruppi and the Min[iste]r of War the evening before last, and they had explained confidentially to him the French plans.

A Moorish column under French Officers was marching from Casablanca to Salbe and would proceed thence towards Fez with the object of reinforcing and revictualling Major Brémond's column. This Moorish column would be followed closely by a French flying column—but the latter would halt at a place about 50 miles distant from Fez, whence it would be able to assure the safety of the lines of communication with the coast. This column would be in wireless communication

(1) [Carnock MSS., Vol. II of 1911.]
(2) [Lord Morley was in temporary charge of the Foreign Office.]

with the base. There was no intention for any *French* column to enter Fez unless something quite unexpected occurred. The above-mentioned Moorish column, after joining hands with Major Brémond, would advance and relieve Fez—and there remain to re-establish the authority of the Sultan and to protect Europeans. This would be the plan if all went well. There were two possibilities on the other side to consider.

1. The Moorish column might arrive too late to assist Major Brémond. The latter might have been surrounded and destroyed. In that case the Moorish column, assisted possibly by the French column, would punish the tribes who had destroyed Major Brémond's force. But such punishment would in no wise call for an advance of the French column to Fez. The destruction of Major Brémond's force would have necessarily occurred in a certain area distant from Fez and punitive operations could be circumscribed to that area.

2. The other danger was that the gates of Fez might be opened to the rebels, who might massacre Europeans, upset Sultan &c. In that event the French might have to advance to Fez. But the Gov[ernmen]t were unwilling to enter Fez if it could possibly be avoided, being well aware that once there it would be difficult to leave; and also because their presence there might give rise to insurrections throughout the country necessitating expeditions from Algeria, tantamount to a war of conquest.

The French Gov[ernmen]t did not intend to tell anyone of their intention not to advance to Fez; but he had received special authority from M. Cruppi to tell me most confidentially, but he begged that the information should be kept strictly to Sir E. Grey and myself—Such was the Moorish side of the question.

As to the European side. The German Gov[ernmen]t were as yet correct—raising no difficulties—but waiting on events and not committing themselves one way or the other. M. Jules Cambon, however, reported from Berlin that he was convinced the line of German policy was as follows: to instigate Spain to raise difficulties to France as far as she could; and in the event of French troops entering Fez Germany would indicate that the Algeciras Act had been violated, and must be subjected to a revision; that an entirely new situation was created, rendering obsolete the Algeciras Act and the 1909 Franco-German agreement, and that a new order of things must be set up. By that new order of things Germany must have compensations, probably Mogador on the Atlantic seaboard, and possibly also a port on the Mediterranean. This was the forecast of M. Jules Cambon derived from his observation and suppositions.([3]) All the above M. Cambon commun[icate]d to me in strict confidence.

I thanked him. I told him that I thought the French Gov[ernmen]t had taken a wise decision in halting the French column at a distance from Fez, and in restraining themselves, unless absolutely compelled to take another course, from any occupation of Fez. Should it be possible to relieve the capital and succour the Europeans by means of the Moorish column alone, Spain would have to remain passive and Germany also—and further complications would be avoided. Supposing the worst and that the rebels entered Fez, upset the Sultan &c—perhaps the French Government might negotiate with a new Sultan, though I admitted that a new Sultan would be brought in on an anti-European wave—and if Europeans were massacred the French would have to punish the rebels, and this would necessarily lead to an occupation of Fez. On the whole the line sketched out by his Gov[ernmen]t seemed most reasonable, and we must hope that it could be successfully carried through.

A. N.

([3]) [*cp. G.P.*, XXIX, pp. 97–8. Herr von Kiderlen-Waechter in his report of an interview with M. Jules Cambon of April 28 says that he told him that, if the Sultan could only rule in Fez by the aid of French bayonets, Germany would regard the Act of Algeciras as annulled " et reprendre entièrement notre liberté d'action." *cp. supra*, p. 208, No. 229.]

No. 231.

Minute by Sir A. Nicolson.

F.O. 16326/13751/11/28.

Lord Morley,
April 28, 1911.

The Spanish Ambas[sado]r informed me this afternoon that the German and Austrian Ambas[sado]rs in Paris had told the Spanish Ambas[sado]r there that they had received instructions to tell M. Cruppi that their Gov[ernmen]ts would view with displeasure an advance of French troops to Fez as such a measure might produce a conflict at Fez and probably a holy war throughout Morocco.

The Spanish Ambas[sado]r added that he wished to assure me that his Gov[ernmen]t were not exchanging views with Berlin either as to Moorish affairs or a conference. All that had passed were certain conversations with the Spanish Ambas[sado]r at Berlin of quite an informal character. The Spanish Gov[ernmen]t intended to work as far as possible with France and with us.

A. N.

Seen.

E. G.
1.5.11.

No. 232.

Sir F. Bertie to Sir Edward Grey.

Paris, *April* 29, 1911.

F.O. 16014/13911/11/28.
D. 3·7 P.M.

Tel. (No. 47.) Confidential.
R. 4·30 P.M.

Morocco.

Your telegram No. 76 Confidential, of yesterday evening.([1])

I have seen French Minister for Foreign Affairs. He is sending French Embassy in London a telegram which should reach them this evening at about 7 o'clock, containing for your information a long account of interviews which French Ambassador at Berlin has had with the German Minister for Foreign Affairs and the Chancellor. The assurances given by the Ambassador have apparently satisfied them for the moment, but the German Government will observe an expectant attitude to see how far the French Government can fulfil their declared intentions, and they state that if the French occupation of Fez be more than quite temporary, and the situation be in any way altered by the revolt against the Sultan and the French intervention, they will consider that the Algeciras Act has lost its force, and the German Government will resume their liberty of action.

French Minister for Foreign Affairs has not received any communication from the German or Austro-Hungarian Ambassadors. I shall see him at midday tomorrow.

([1]) [*v. supra*, p. 205, No. 226.]

No. 233.

Sir F. Bertie to Sir Edward Grey.

Paris, *April* 29, 1911.

F.O. 16015/13751/11/28.
D. 4·25 P.M.

Tel. (No. 48.) Confidential.
R. 6·15 P.M.

Morocco.

Your telegram No. 76, Confidential, of 28th April([1]) and my telegram No. 47, Confidential, of to-day.([2])

([1]) [*v. supra*, p. 205, No. 226.]
([2]) [*v.* immediately preceding document.]

Minister for Foreign Affairs has also sent to French Embassy in London, for communication to you, a long account of an interview which, as I informed you in my telegram No. 45 of 28th April,([3]) he was to have with the Spanish Ambassador. Spanish Ambassador's language was to following effect : State of revolt in Morocco round Fez and the troubles elsewhere and the advance of French troops on Fez has brought into operation Franco-Spanish secret convention, and the Spanish Government propose to act on it, in the event of French opposition to denounce it, and, if necessary, appeal to another Power, which he did not name, result of which would be to raise a question to be settled by Europe.

When French Minister for Foreign Affairs suggested that Spanish and French Governments should concert with the British Government as to the situation and Spanish desire or proposals the Ambassador was much embarrassed, and proceeded to criticise the attitude of His Majesty's Government in an unfriendly manner.

French Minister for Foreign Affairs held the language which he informed me (see my telegram No. 45 of 28th April) he intended to hold to the Spanish Ambassador, who was very uncompromising.

French Minister for Foreign Affairs has information that the German Ambassador has been advising the Spanish Ambassador to advise the Spanish Government to act on the rights of Spain under the Franco-Spanish secret agreement of 1904, or to appeal to the Powers so that the Morocco question may be reconsidered. when Germany will support the Spanish claims.

MINUTES.

Sir Eyre Crowe, whom I saw on Saturday, was strongly of opinion that we should make an energetic representation at Madrid, and that failure on our part to do so would almost inevitably lead to a crisis in Europe, which it is in our power to avert.

A. P.
May 1st, 1911.

I think this is practically the language we have held both at Madrid and here, but it may be useful that Sir M. de Bunsen should make such a representation under direct and explicit instructions from His Majesty's Government.

Q[uer]y. Draft a telegram.

F. A. C.
1.5.

I will speak to the Secretary of State.([4])

A. N.
E. G.

([3]) [v. supra, pp. 204–5, No. 225.]
([4]) [Tel. No. 33 of May 1st contained instructions for Sir M. de Bunsen to act in this sense.]

No. 234.

Sir E. Goschen to Sir A. Nicolson.

Private.([1])

My dear Nicolson,   Berlin, April 29, 1911.

I have been laid low during nearly the whole of the week with this beastly Flu cold, and even now I feel awfully slack and seedy. [M. Jules] Cambon left for Paris last night " pour calmer les esprits " he said and give his impressions. I don't think that in his heart of hearts he much approves of this expedition, but as it has to be he has worked like a Beaver at getting the Germans to take a reasonable view of it. When the Chancellor was hanging back about it he asked him whether he had read Lord Cromer's book and reminded him of the responsibility

([1]) [Carnock MSS., Vol. II of 1911.]

which had been thrown on Gladstone for the arrival of the British column too late to save Gordon. He said "the same responsibility may attach to you if you make difficulties and delay the Expedition!" In discussing the matter with Kiderlen he mentioned to the latter that the expedition for relieving Europeans and restoring order was covered by the 1909 agreement. Kiderlen said: "Oh, the 1909 Agreement! that was a piece of Schön's work—we needn't talk about that." Cambon reminded him that the document was signed by the Secretary of State acting for his Gov[ernmen]t—"besides, mon ami, you seem to forget that it was you and I who negotiated that agreement, and that at the time you were not at all pleased that you had done all the work and that others had got the credit." I think Kiderlen must have seen that he was not likely to get much change out of Cambon in a war of words because he afterwards became much more pleasant and amiable.

Cambon attaches great importance to the present attitude of England and Russia, but especially England. He thinks, and I believe rightly, that Germany is watching that attitude very narrowly, and that if she sees that France will at the present juncture receive the same support from those Powers as she did at Algeciras, then she will hold her hand and not make trouble. If on the contrary she sees any likelihood of that support being withdrawn or given grudgingly she will at once proceed to make trouble and turn the situation to her own advantage. M. Cambon says that notwithstanding the utterances of certain English newspapers *he* himself feels quite easy in his mind and quite certain that G[rea]t Britain will remain loyal to her friendship with France; but he is rather afraid that the German Government think otherwise—and he told me that at the Press Bureau a French journalist had been told that G[rea]t Britain and Germany were getting nearer to each other every day; that the visit of the Emperor was expected to improve matters still further and that there was every likelihood that the present *détente* would shortly be turned into an *entente!* (The same journalist told de Salis this too.) Cambon said that this looked as if at the Wilhelm Strasse they had hopes that France would not receive much support from Great Britain in the present situation, but he thought that they forgot that the same statesman was at the British Foreign Office who had been there when the Act of Algeciras was concluded and that the man who had borne the brunt of the negotiations at Algeciras was his second in command. He hoped that nothing would be said or done in England to make the Germans believe that there was any change in England's attitude, as that would be disastrous for France. He left for Paris last night, otherwise I think he would be glad to see a Reuter's tel[egram] reproduced in the German Press this morning to the effect that the necessity of sending an expedition is realised in English official circles.

Cambon told me one amusing thing which was that Schebeko told him that he was certain he could rely on Russia's fidelity and support but that he felt rather doubtful whether England was entirely trustworthy.

No time for more, as it [is] only since yesterday afternoon that I have felt up to writing at all.

Yours very sincerely,
W. E. GOSCHEN.

No. 235.

Sir M. de Bunsen to Sir Edward Grey.

F.O. 16369/13911/11/28.
(No. 55.)   *Madrid,* D. *April* 29, 1911.
Sir,   R. *May* 2, 1911.

Speaking to me yesterday of the recent developments of events in Morocco, the Spanish Minister for Foreign Affairs claimed some credit for having used his influence to prevent, or at least postpone, the despatch of a contingent of troops to Morocco. The Government, though very unwilling to intervene were strongly urged from many quarters to do so, and public opinion in Spain would not forgive them if they failed to uphold, during the complications which were only too likely to occur, the claim of this country to exercise a preponderant influence in what is commonly called the Spanish sphere of influence.

To my remark that all seemed very quiet in that region, he replied that there were signs, here and there, of incipient trouble. The cruiser " Rio de la Plata " had been sent to Laraiche to obtain accurate information concerning affairs in Laraiche and Alcazar districts, in which it was only too likely that the effervescence in the Gharb would be increasingly felt. The report of the persons charged to make this enquiry had not yet been received, but information was daily reaching the Government which showed that robbery and violence were rife in the country lying between Ceuta and Tetuan, and that the concentration of the French forces on the right bank of the Maluya was already causing some agitation among the tribes of the Riff. The Military Governors of Ceuta and Melilla had been instructed to do all they could to prevent the agitation spreading, and especially to avoid any semblance of provoking an incident which might call for repressive measures. At Ceuta much self-restraint was required to abstain from inflicting immediate and summary punishment on the marauders, and the difficulty of the Governor's position was increased by the non-existence of the police force, which, under the terms of the Convention between Spain and Morocco of Nov[ember] 16, 1910, was to maintain order within a specified radius of the Spanish fortress. His Excellency thought that in view of the incapacity of the Makhzen to keep its engagements in this respect Spain would be fully justified in herself taking what steps might be necessary to provide for the safety of the region affected. He said he expected that he would shortly have to make some announcement on this point.

As already reported in my telegram No. 15 of the 28th instant,([1]) I took the opportunity to inform Señor Garcia Prieto of the upshot of the explanations concerning French policy in the present crisis which His Majesty's Ambassador in Paris reported to you as having been made to him by the French Minister for Foreign Affairs on the 25th instant. In view of Mr. Cruppi's clear and straight-forward declarations to Sir F. Bertie,([2]) I said that it was impossible to doubt that the French Government were only yielding to a most unwelcome and inconvenient necessity in despatching an armed force to the relief of the Sultan and of the European inhabitants of Fez, and that they were resolved to observe strictly the requirements of the general Act of Algeciras without forgetting their special convention with Spain. As France was often accused in the Spanish Press of harbouring the desire to convert Morocco into a second Tunis, I was glad, I said, to be able to inform His Excellency that M. Cruppi had in express terms denied having any such wish or intention.

I added that I hoped King Alfonso was under no misapprehension as to the true character of French policy. Señor Garcia Prieto was good enough to promise that he would to-day convey to His Majesty my account of what the French Minister for Foreign Affairs had said to the British Ambassador in Paris. He assured me, however, that there was no disposition on the part of the King or of the Spanish Government to question the good faith of France. She would no doubt desire to escape as soon as possible from the hornet's nest of Fez. But His Excellency said that it was impossible to resist the reflection that events might occur which would compel her to maintain, however unwillingly, a hold on the Moroccan Capital. The little that even now remained of the independent authority of the Sultan would in any case tend to diminish, almost to vanishing point, as the result of the measures taken by France to keep him on the throne. Morocco would become a French

([1]) [v. supra, p. 206, No. 228.]
([2]) [v. supra, pp. 199–200, No. 216.]

Protectorate in all but the name, nor would it be long possible to disguise the evident fact by protestations of fidelity to the arrangements of Algeciras.

I have, &c.
MAURICE DE BUNSEN.

No. 236.

Sir F. Bertie to Sir Edward Grey.

F.O. 16350/13911/11/28.
(No. 195.) Confidential.
Sir,

Paris, D. *April* 29, 1911.
R. *May* 2, 1911.

The Austro-Hungarian Ambassador, Count Szecsen, whom I knew well at Rome when he was Ambassador accredited to the Vatican, came to see me yesterday afternoon. After some preliminary conversation of no importance he plunged into the real object of his visit, viz., enquiries as to the position of the French in Morocco, what they might be expected to do and not to do, and how their probable acts as he anticipated them would be regarded by Spain and the other Powers more or less interested in Morocco. According to Count Szecsen French intentions—those announced—had been unimportant at first, but they had increased as time went on and now instead of a Moroccan force under French instructors it was a French column which was advancing on Fez. If French troops occupied that city they would probably remain to maintain in power the Sultan whose support by foreign troops would render him still more unpopular than he was already. The whole country was in revolt and it seemed impossible that the present Sultan could hold his own except with the military aid of France. This would prolong the French occupation of Fez and it seemed doubtful that the French troops would be withdrawn whatever might be the present intentions of the French Government. This would entirely change the aspect of the Morocco question. It would become a matter for European discussion. If the French became dominant in Morocco they might close the open door stipulated in the Act of Algeciras. The Spanish Government were alarmed at the proceedings of the French in Morocco and seemed to contemplate action of some sort in that country. Count Szecsen asked me what my opinion was on the subject of the assurances which the French Government had given as to their intentions and their ability to carry them out if those intentions were genuine.

You will remember that Sir Fairfax Cartwright (in his telegram No. 31 secret of April 22nd)([1]) informed you that he learnt that the German Government in their communications with the Austro-Hungarian Government attributed to the French Government the intention to put an end to the open door and equality of chances in Morocco; and that according to the Spanish Ambassador in London the German and Austro-Hungarian Ambassadors had instructions to inform the French Minister for Foreign Affairs that their Governments would view with displeasure an advance of French troops to Fez, a proceeding which might lead to a Holy War in Morocco. M. Cruppi had not when I saw him this morning received any such communication from those Ambassadors. There had been conversations between the French Ambassador and the German Minister for Foreign Affairs and the German Chancellor of which M. Cruppi had informed me and I reported to you, but there had been no representation from the Austro-Hungarian Government. It is I think probable that the instructions which were sent to those Ambassadors were not of so positive and accentuated a character as the Spanish Ambassador intimated to you and the Spanish Government desired, and that whereas a short time since it was Germany who prompted Spain to assert herself in Morocco, it is now Spain who is hoping to make use of Germany to offer opposition to France in the interest of Spain.

([1]) [*v. supra*, p. 197, No. 214. For Count Szécsen's account of this interview, *v. Ö.-U.A.* III, No. 2529.]

In replying to the several enquiries which Count Szecsen had made I told him that what I might say must be taken by him as my personal opinions and that they were given to him as a friend and not as to the Ambassador of Germany's ally and if he accepted them in that spirit I would speak freely and without reserve. Count Szecsen said that he would like me to express my opinions without reserve and he would regard them as personal and privately imparted to him. What I thereupon said to Count Szecsen was to the following effect : The French Government had given assurances that they had no desire to send French troops to Fez, they hoped that the Mehalla under Major Brémond might be sufficient to rescue the Europeans and with fresh supplies of all sorts to enable the Sultan to re-establish his authority. If however the relief of Fez could not be effected without the aid of French troops and their entry into Fez, the occupation of that city would be only for such a brief period as might be absolutely necessary to put the Sultan on his legs again. The French Government had no ulterior object in view in the action which they were taking. They intended strictly to conform themselves to the Act of Algeciras and their other treaty engagements and they desired to avoid raising any European question. I believed in these assurances for it was to the interest of France that they should be observed. What constituted a danger was the tone of a portion of the German Press which urged the German Government to take advantage of the present state of affairs in Morocco to upset the Algeciras Act, and the retorts of the French Press. A public opinion might be created in Germany which might push the Government further than it was at present intended to go in its objections to French action in Morocco. If I were a German I should be glad to see a state of affairs which would enable me to hope that the Morocco question might be reopened with a possible opportunity to get something for Germany, and I quite understood the anxiety of the Pan-Germanic Press that there should be dissensions between Spain and France. Germany had created a great navy but her want was coaling stations and Count Hatzfeldt had once made suggestions to Lord Salisbury in regard to Morocco which might have provided in some measure for the deficiency, but the suggestions were not entertained. If the Morocco question were now reopened Germany might hope to profit by it. In 1905 it had brought Germany and France to the verge of war. I believe that had it not been for the conviction in Germany that France would receive material support from England, Germany would have attacked France. Luckily for the peace of Europe Germany and France were afraid of each other at the present time. Count Szecsen interposed saying that he did not think that Germany feared France. What she regarded with apprehension was what might be the after-effects of a successful war against France. When I suggested that in talking of war between Germany and France it must be remembered that Russia was France's ally, Count Szecsen shrugged his shoulders and observed that Russia did not count for much.

With regard to the fear which Count Szecsen had expressed that France might close the open door in Morocco I said that I had no such apprehension in present circumstances for such a proceeding on the part of France would alienate the sympathies of the British public and lose her the support of His Majesty's Government, and whatever might be the desire of the French Government in regard to the door they could not afford to break their engagements and so to isolate themselves by closing it in the face of England, and to raise a European question in which they would be opposed by her as well as by Germany and others.

As to the re-establishment of the authority of the Sultan Mulai Hafid and his maintenance in his position by French arms as Count Szecsen appeared to apprehend I said that Moroccan tribes assembled for revolt and dissolved when goods to be pillaged and supplies ran short in an unaccountably rapid manner. Harvest time was approaching and the hostile tribes might for one reason or another disappear from around Fez. I thought that if the French Government found that the present Sultan was quite unacceptable to the bulk of the people of Morocco and that he could not maintain himself when set on his legs they would be ready to recognize some other Sultan preferred by the Moors. Mulai Hafid was to be given an opportunity of re-establishing his authority but there was in my opinion no idea on the part of the French Government of forcing him on the country.

Count Szecsen thanked me for having spoken freely to him and after some further conversation on other matters of no importance he left me to pay a visit, he said, to the Spanish Ambassador. My impression is that Count Szecsen has been made fully acquainted with the views of the German Government and their communications to the Austro-Hungarian Government and that he has been instructed to ascertain if he can what are the real intentions of the French Government in regard to Morocco and how far they are likely to give way to German objections, but that he has not yet received directions to make any representations to the French Government.(²)

As indicative of the opinions professed at the Embassy of Germany's ally I may mention that at a luncheon party to-day where everyone except Colonel Fairholme was a subject of the Emperor Francis Joseph an Austrian Secretary of the Austro-Hungarian Embassy observed to him with some asperity that the troubles in Morocco had been entirely brought about by French interference; that had they not interfered the tribes would not have revolted to such an extent, and that he was convinced that if Major Brémond and the other French officers were to offer to clear out they would be given a free pass and be allowed to proceed unmolested to the coast, and the tribes would then accept the authority of the Sultan.

I informed M. Cruppi to-day of my conversation with Count Szecsen and he thanked me for what I had said to the Ambassador. I also acquainted His Excellency with the information which I had received from His Majesty's Ambassador at Madrid (see his telegram No. 15 of yesterday)(³) that with your authority Sir Maurice de Bunsen had informed the Spanish Minister for Foreign Affairs that I had received the most positive assurances from the French Government of their intention to respect the Algeciras Act and their other Treaty engagements in regard to Morocco and not to follow the precedent of Tunis, and that the Spanish Minister had undertaken to communicate to King Alphonso that information on behalf of Sir Maurice de Bunsen; and that M. Garcia Prieto had said that he did not doubt the good intentions of the French Government, but he thought that events might be too strong for them. M. Cruppi expressed his gratitude at the communication which Sir Maurice de Bunsen had made by your authority.

I have, &c.
FRANCIS BERTIE.

P.S. April 30th. I have seen M. Cruppi this evening. He has not received any representations from either the German or Austro-Hungarian Ambassadors. He does not think that the German Government will make any further objections than those communicated to the French Ambassador at Berlin or that the Austro-Hungarian Government will make representations of any importance. He has no official confirmation of the reports that Major Brémond has reached Fez with his relief Mehalla. He is greatly satisfied at the reply which Sir Arthur Nicolson has informed the French Ambassador has been made on your behalf to the communication on the subject of Morocco made to His Majesty's Government by the Spanish Ambassador analogous to the one made to the French Government by the Spanish Ambassador at Paris.

FRANCIS BERTIE.

(²) [In his telegram No. 154 of May 8, Sir Edward Grey entirely approved the language held by Sir F. Bertie to Count Szécsen.]
(³) [v. supra, p. 206, No. 228.]

No. 237.

Sir F. Cartwright to Sir Edward Grey.

F.O. 16322/13911/11/28.
Tel. (No. 33.)
Morocco.

Vienna, May 1, 1911.
D. 1·30.
R. 3.

Though official opinion continues to feign indifference Austro-Hungarian point of view is gradually being disclosed through unofficial sources. An undoubted though unavowed emissary of the Ministry of Foreign Affairs has paid repeated visits to the French Embassy to discuss Morocco question. In the course of these conversations great stress has been laid on the probability of displeasure at Berlin on the one hand and of continued good will at Vienna on the other. This goodwill even goes so far as to encourage France to proceed undaunted on her own independent course.

Natural inference is that A[ustro]-H[ungarian] government desire to see difficulties arise between Germany and France in order to obtain the reward which will fall to the intermediary. This reward is nothing less than the French market for A[ustro]-H[ungarian] armament loans. Whether this step has been taken in connivance with Berlin is difficult to say but it may be that as the latter requires money from Paris for the Bagdad Railway they are combining in this process of blackmail. When it was hinted at French Embassy that it would be more fitting that St. Petersburgh should act as intermediary between Berlin and Paris, the reply came promptly that Germany and Russia were so thick since the Potsdam meeting that there was not the slightest hope of assistance from that direction.

No. 238.

Sir Edward Grey to Sir M. de Bunsen.([1])

F.O. 16438/13379/11/28.
Tel. (No. 33.)

Foreign Office, May 1, 1911.
D. 5·20 P.M.

You should inform M[inister for] F[oreign] A[ffairs] that in my opinion it would be quite premature for Spain to act as if independence and integrity of Morocco was threatened by action, which French are taking. Something is necessary to assure safety of Europeans at Fez and French expectation is that in a short time emergency will have passed, a settlement will have been made with the tribes and order will have been restored. Any French force at or near Fez will then be withdrawn. It is only if these expectations fail to be realized that Spain will have ground for claiming execution of secret agreement. It would be most unwise for Spain to force partition of Morocco: the political consequences would be deplorable.

([1]) [This telegram was repeated to Sir F. Bertie.]

No. 239.

Mr. Rattigan to Sir Edward Grey.

F.O. 16355/16355/11/28.
Tel. (No. 47.) Confidential.

Tangier, D. May 1, 1911, 8·50 P.M.
R. *May 2, 1911, 8 A.M.*

Secretary of Austrian Legation let slip yesterday in conversation with me that Germany would like to obtain Mogador. I told French Chargé d'Affaires who said that he had always had the idea that Germany would make Mogador and possibly Ifni price of her (gr[ou]p undec[ypherable]) to Spain in reopening Moorish question. I therefore venture to report statement for what it is worth.

No. 240.

Sir A. Nicolson to Sir E. Goschen.

Private.(¹)
M~ ^lear Goschen,   *Foreign Office, May 1, 1911.*
    Many thanks for your letter of the 29th.(²) I trust that you will now soon be quite recovered as affairs with regard to Morocco seem to be warming up rather. I have had several conversations both with [M. Paul] Cambon and the Spanish Ambassador and so far as I can gather, the situation is as follows :—

    The German Government seem to be quite correct in their language at Berlin to the French. They hold in reserve the attitude which they may take should the French be compelled to occupy Fez, and they seem to intimate in a somewhat vague way that they will then have to consider the whole question of Morocco, as they assume that the French occupation of Fez if it is to assume more than a very temporary character, will set up an entirely new situation which will require revision by all the signatories of the Algeciras Act. On the other hand it is clear that the Germans, so far as our information goes, are holding unofficially different language in Madrid and probably elsewhere, and have been endeavouring to encourage Spain to raise difficulties with France. Here they have not whispered a word either unofficially or officially. So far as I can see Spain at the outset was desirous of taking some active action towards Tetuan and perhaps Laraiche. We strongly deprecated any action of this character so long as matters remained calm in those regions, and I think from the latest news which we have received from Madrid that our advice has been taken by her. The Spanish Foreign Minister has said that he has no desire whatever to [? see] unnecessary action being taken in Morocco and that all that the Spanish Government are doing is to take some precautionary measures so as to be prepared for any eventuality. The French, however, are not quite satisfied with the Spanish assurances and desire that we should do what we can to bring Spain to act entirely in harmony with France and ourselves. The Spanish Ambassador assures me that there has been no interchange of views, properly so-called, between Madrid and Berlin, although certain remarks have been dropped by the German Representatives as to the grave situation which might be produced by the French settling down in Fez. The Spanish Ambassador informed me on Friday, as you will probably have seen from a telegram, that both the Austrian and German Ambassadors in Paris have been instructed to inform the French Government that their Government would view with displeasure any advance of the French troops to Fez. This information was derived from the Spanish Ambassador at Paris. So far as I have been able to ascertain neither the German nor Austrian Ambassador has yet moved in Paris. The Spanish Ambassador in Paris, whom I knew well in Algeciras, is a very hot-headed and impulsive man, and I think he goes very much further in his language than his Government desire him to do. I quite agree with you that it is of the utmost importance that we should support France as far as we possibly can in the action which she is undertaking. Of course I mean merely diplomatic support, for by the 1904 agreement we have given her a mandate for preserving order in Morocco, and naturally we ourselves can take no measures of any character whatsoever. There is a question to-morrow in the House of Commons as to French intervention in Morocco, and I hope that we shall then make it perfectly clear that we have no objection to the steps which France is

(¹) [Carnock MSS., Vol. II of 1911.]
(²) [*v. supra*, pp. 211–12, No. 234.]

taking. This I think will be the best means of letting it be known to the world what our attitude really is. I have hopes that the Moorish column which is advancing towards Fez will be able to relieve that town without the necessity of calling upon the French column which is following it to enter Fez, and it will greatly simplify the situation if Fez can be relieved and succoured by Moorish troops alone, but owing to the extent to which the rebellion appears to have spread, I rather doubt if order can be re-established without the active intervention of French troops. I feel quite convinced that the French have no desire whatever to do more than is actually necessary, as they do not wish to be drawn into a general pacification of Morocco. It will be a very serious enterprise and would undoubtedly lead to certain complications in Europe. Our news from Fez is very sparse and not very clear, and it does not seem to be quite certain whether Major Bremond's column has been able or not to reach Fez.

Grey returns this morning and I am anxious that he should go fully into the whole question with Cambon and perhaps also with the Spanish Ambassador. I think there seems to be little doubt that if the French have to occupy Fez or to take more extended measures in Morocco that Germany will put rather a high price on her consent being obtained to these measures. I have heard from more than one quarter that she desires to obtain in such an eventuality the cession of Mogador and possibly even a port in the Mediterranean, though personally I much doubt if she would care to claim the latter concession. . . . .([3])

[A. NICOLSON.]

([3]) [The omitted paragraphs refer to the European situation in general terms.]

No. 241.

Sir M. de Bunsen to Sir Edward Grey.

Madrid, May 2, 1911.

F.O. 16354/13751/11/28.
Tel. (No. 17.)

D. 12·20 A.M.
R. 8 A.M.

My tel[egram] No. 16.([1])
I saw Spanish Prime Minister this afternoon and spoke to him generally in the sense of your telegram No. 33([2]) since received. I will however communicate it at once to the M[inister for] F[oreign] A[ffairs] and the observations contained in your telegram. French Amb[assado]r having had interview with the M[inister for] F[oreign] A[ffairs] to-day my remarks will be used to confirm his warning and form another proof of the identity of the views held by the British and French Gov[ernmen]ts with regard to the critical anarchy (in) Morocco. Spanish Prime Minister holds the prevailing Spanish view that France is proceeding to Fez without due cause and means to stay there. I think that I produced some impression on him. He assured me of his decision to work harmoniously with France and England notwithstanding all that was being said to the contrary.

French Ambassador is replying to last two semi-official letters that he has received from Spanish M[inister for] F[oreign]A[ffairs] rejecting proposal tc

([1]) [Not reproduced. It stated that, though Señor Garcia Prieto had given satisfactory assurances to M. Geoffray, there was still considerable Spanish opposition to French action in Morocco. M. Geoffray desired to act in as conciliatory a manner as possible and to be associated with Sir M. de Bunsen in his discussions of the situation in Morocco. The French Government, while unable to consent to a general modification of the Franco-Spanish Secret Convention, were prepared to discuss any points on which the Spanish Government desired to receive satisfaction. (F.O. 16070/13751/11/28.)]

([2]) [*v. supra*, p. 217, No. 238.]

modify secret treaty but offering on behalf of the French Gov[ernmen]t to receive and discuss jointly with H[is] M[ajesty's] Gov[ernmen]t and in the most friendly spirit any reasonable proposals which Spanish Gov[ernmen]t may have to make with regard to action which may be desirable in the Spanish sphere.

(Repeated to Paris.)

No. 242.

Sir Edward Grey to Sir M. de Bunsen.

F.O. 16866/13911/11/28.
(No. 32.)
Sir,   *Foreign Office, May 2, 1911.*

The Spanish Ambassador came to see me to-day, and I impressed upon him that the intention of the French Government was not to disturb the political *status quo* in Morocco. Their hope and expectation was that their expedition would result in communications being kept open with Fez, the place would be saved from starvation, a settlement with the tribes would be come to, and then the French troops could be withdrawn. It was most important that the Spanish Government should not regard what was being done as upsetting the Act of Algeciras, and that they should do nothing which would precipitate a crisis.

The Spanish Ambassador said that he was instructed to tell me what had passed in Paris. There had been a conversation between the German Ambassador there and the Spanish Ambassador. The German Ambassador had said that Germany, having declared to France that she had no political interest in Morocco, could not object to the French expedition to Fez; but that a French occupation of Fez would have a repercussion on the politics of Europe, and he feared there would be grave complications. The German Ambassador was convinced that the French intended to go ahead in Morocco, and were concealing their real intentions. He then gave as his personal opinion that, if France and Spain could come to an agreement for keeping order in Morocco and for its pacification, and would guarantee liberty of trade, Germany and other Powers would accept a proposal to that effect from France and Spain.

The Spanish Ambassador then told me what had passed between M. Cruppi and the Spanish Ambassador in Paris. M. Cruppi had advised the Spanish Government to express their wishes in London, and make them known to us. The Spanish Government were in doubt as to what this meant. Either it meant that the French Government expected the British Government to take the French side entirely, in which case Spain would get nothing, and would only be wasting her time and ours by consulting us; or else it might mean that France thought it might be easier to make some concessions to Spain if we advised them.

It appeared to the Spanish Government that the suggestion made by the German Ambassador in Paris would, if confirmed by the German Government, provide a golden opportunity for putting an end to all difficulties. France and Spain would first come to a full agreement, and then they would informally arrive at an agreement with us and Germany, so as to include all four countries. The Spanish Government were enquiring in Berlin whether the German Government endorsed the opinion of their Ambassador in Paris. They would not do anything until they heard what the German Government said about this, nor would they do anything then until they knew what we thought of the proposal.

He then explained that, under the Secret Agreement,(¹) Spain was in an inferior position to France, inasmuch as France had liberty of action, whereas Spain was obliged to consult France before taking any action in the Spanish sphere. In any

(¹) [*v. Gooch & Temperley*, Vol. III, pp. 49–52, No. 59; also *v. infra*, pp. 826–9, *App.* IV.]

agreement with France, Spain would require a guarantee that the action of France, military, financial, or otherwise, would not extend to the Spanish sphere; and that, in the Spanish sphere, it would be Spain who gave advice and support to the Sultan. She would also require the arrangement about Tangier to be made quite clear: it was rather ambiguous as the agreement now stood.

I said that this proposal of the German Ambassador in Paris was new to me, and I must have time to consider it. Meanwhile, I must again impress upon the Spanish Government that they should give time to see how things went in Morocco, as well as for the consideration of what they had now put before me; and that they should not do anything which would precipitate a crisis.

The Spanish Ambassador repeated with emphasis what he had already said: that his Government would not do anything pending the result of the enquiries which were being made in Berlin and here.

He also told me that while Spain had listened to what Germany had to say Spain had not in return made communication to the German Gov[ernmen]t of her views and intentions.

[I am, &c.]
E. G[REY].

No. 243.

Sir Edward Grey to Sir R. Rodd.

F.O. 16798/13911/11/28.
(No. 67.)
Sir,   *Foreign Office, May 2, 1911.*
The Italian Ambassador sounded me to-day about Morocco.

I said that I was sure the French did not wish to magnify the trouble there, or to alter the *status quo*, and it was most undesirable that any Power should construe their action as being contrary to the Act of Algeciras. I felt certain that France did not wish to re-open the question of Morocco, and I agreed that it was very desirable not to raise it: for if it was reopened, we should have over again all the trouble which there was at the time of the Algeciras Conference.

[I am, &c.]
E. G[REY].

No. 244.

Sir F. Cartwright to Sir Edward Grey.

                                                 Vienna, May 3, 1911.
F.O. 16648/13911/11/28.   D. 7·50 P.M.
Tel. (No. 34.)   R. 8·30 P.M.
Morocco.
Acting Minister for Foreign Affairs intimated to me to-day that as Austria-Hungary had practically no interests to defend in Morocco she would try to avoid being drawn into Morocco question unless France committed a palpable breach of the Algeciras Act, such as a prolonged occupation of Fez. From Acting Minister for Foreign Affairs' language, I gather that Germany will likewise only act in similar case.

No. 245.

Sir Edward Grey to Sir F. Bertie.

F.O. 16801/13911/11/28.
(No. 150.)

Sir,

Foreign Office, May 3, 1911.

I told M. [Paul] Cambon to-day of the advice which I had pressed upon the Spanish Ambassador yesterday with regard to Morocco, urging that Spain should not precipitate a crisis.

I then told him that the Spanish Ambassador had informed me that M. Cruppi had advised the Spanish Government to make their wishes known in London. The Spanish Government were of opinion that, if M. Cruppi thought we should side with France and therefore Spain would get nothing, it would be a waste of the Spanish Ambassador's time and of mine to pursue this course; but if, on the other hand, M. Cruppi had advised this because he thought it might be easier to make a compromise with Spain in this way, the Spanish Government were quite willing to do as he suggested.

I went on to tell M. Cambon that the German Ambassador in Paris had told the Spanish Ambassador there that his own personal opinion was that, if France and Spain would come to an agreement with each other as to the policing and pacification of Morocco, Germany and other Powers would accept this in return for a guarantee of liberty of commerce. The Spanish Government were enquiring in Berlin whether the German Government endorsed this view of their Ambassador. The Spanish Government would take no step until they heard from Berlin and until, if the German Government endorsed their Ambassador's view, they knew what we thought of it. If the German Government really meant what their Ambassador in Paris had said, the Spanish Government thought that this would be a way out of all difficulties.

I observed to M. Cambon that if the German Government were prepared to say definitely that liberty of commerce was all they required in Morocco, as the German Ambassador had said, this was a very important fact.

As for Spain, her fear was that the increase of French influence at Fez, the centre of government, would mean increased French influence in the Spanish sphere, while the hands of Spain would remain tied, because the Sultan would still be nominally independent, though really obliged to do everything under French influence. Moorish officials in the Spanish sphere would be nominally those of the Sultan, but actually those of France. I thought that it should be possible for M. Cruppi to discuss this difficulty with Spain, and to reassure her.

M. Cambon said that Spain thought it necessary to do something every time that France did anything. This was a policy of vanity on the part of Spain, but one had to take her as she was. Personally, he thought that an agreement could be come to with her. The arrangements for policing the ports of Morocco expired at the end of this year, and the discussion for the renewal of these arrangements might be made the occasion for satisfying Spain. This was his personal opinion, but he asked me whether he might say to M. Cruppi that I thought it would be wise for France to embark on a policy of this kind with Spain.

I replied that certainly he might say that. I saw no other way of getting over the difficulties.

M. Cambon showed me a telegram from the French Ambassador in Madrid, recounting what Sir Maurice de Bunsen had told him of a conversation with Señor Canalejas, in which the latter had spoken most bitterly of French unfriendliness to Spain. Sir Maurice de Bunsen had succeeded in calming him, but had carried away from the interview an unpleasant impression.

I said that this conversation had not yet been reported to me.

[I am, &c.]

E. G[REY].

No. 246.

Sir M. de Bunsen to Sir Edward Grey.

F.O. 17301/13751/11/28.
(No. 57.)   Confidential.   *Madrid,* D. *May* 3, 1911.
Sir,   R. *May* 8, 1911.

In continuation of my previous despatch No. 56 Confidential of the 2nd instant,(¹)
I have the honour to furnish the following account of a conver[s]ation which I held
with the Spanish Prime Minister on the 1st instant.(²)

I saw Señor Canalejas by appointment, and found His Excellency in the nervous
and agitated frame of mind to which he has been brought by the increasing difficulty
of his political position at home and by the serious embarrassment caused by the
turn which events are taking in Morocco.   After thanking me for my visit and
adding that, as the conversation was to be regarded as a confidential one, he would
speak with entire frankness, he proceeded to declare that without doubt France
was the implacable enemy of Spain.   The fair words of M. Cruppi in Paris did not
alter the fact that the attitude from day to day of the French agents in Morocco
was of unconcealed hostility to everything Spanish.   These gentlemen showed no
regard whatever for the feelings of the Spanish Community, and they persistently
ignored the rights claimed by Spain under existing Treaties.   I asked His Excellency
if he could give me instances to prove what he alleged.   He said the French
representative at Tangier—presumably M. de Billy the Chargé d'Affaires, as
M. Regnault has been absent for some time,—had been slow to return the visit of
the new Spanish Minister and had avoided anything like a frank exchange of views
with him, such as would be useful under the present circumstances.

Señor Canalejas had that very day received the officer whom he had recently
sent in the cruiser " Rio de la Plata " to report on the state of aff[a]irs in the
region of Larache.   One officer had found at Alcazar, a place within the Spanish
sphere, a number of French Military instructors, who were rapidly turning the town
into a base of military operations.(³)   The Prime Minister said he was tired of the
whole question.   It would almost be better for Spain that the matter should now
come to a point.   She would then be compelled to strain every nerve to assert her
rights.   She would of course be defeated as she had been defeated in Cuba.   But
she would have upheld her honour and could retire behind the walls of her fortresses
on the Morocco coast with her honour intact.

I begged His Excellency to look upon the facts in a calmer spirit.   He had
spoken as if France were already firmly established at Fez, with the Sultan under
her wing, and the Government of Morocco in her sole grasp.   In reality she was
only at the beginning of an expedition, undertaken very unwillingly, and destined
perhaps to produce its effect without Fez being even entered.   At all events it was
obviously premature to proceed as if a French protectorate had been already
proclaimed and the Algeciras arrangements suspended.   The object of France I
understood to be to make those arrangements more secure and permanent than
they appeared at the present moment to be.   It was early days to assume that she
would fail.   When she did so, it would be time enough to consider how Spain would
be affected by the altered situation.   Even then it was by a friendly understanding
with the other countries most concerned, that is with France and England, that
she was most likely to secure the objects she had in view.

(¹) [Not reproduced.   It contained information that M. Geoffray, the French Ambassador,
had sent to Señor Garcia Prieto on May 1 a reply to his two letters of April 20 and April 28.
This reply is described as having set forth the French reasons " for considering that the time had
not yet come for modifying existing arrangements," and further that, while deprecating the
independent action which Spain desired to take, the French Government were ready to consider
any reasonable Spanish demands.   (F.O. 17300/13751/11/28.)]

(²) [Sir M. de Bunsen's language was " entirely approved " by Sir Edward Grey in his
despatch No. 40 of May 15.   (F.O. 17301/13751/11/28.)]

(³) [Marginal comment by Mr. Villiers : " This is not the case."]

At the present stage it would be supremely unwise for Spain to precipitate events, for I could assure His Excellency that, from all I had heard, there was now every readiness at Paris to make allowances for the natural aspirations of Spain in Morocco. It would be at all events the height of unwisdom to employ force to obtain privileges or positions which might be equally well secured, for ought he knew, by friendly negotiations. The local bickerings to which he had alluded probably reached his ears in an exaggerated form and they would certainly not be diminished by Spain taking the law into her own hands. If only the Spanish Government would say frankly what it was they wanted I believed there was a fair prospect of matters being arranged to the satisfaction of all concerned. It was at all events worth trying.

I spoke also of the treaties and conventions by which Spain continued to be bound, and I expressed regret that there should be a disposition to break away from them. Very different had been the spirit which presided over the meeting of our two Sovereigns at Cartagena less than four years ago, when an exchange of Notes was negotiated showing the closest community of views between Spain, England and France as regards the continuing of the *status quo* in the territories adjoining the Mediterranean and Atlantic.

Señor Canalejas said he was quite ready to admit the force of these considerations. They were, indeed, always present to his mind, and as regarded the attitude of France, he was glad to hear that I was able to describe it as not unfavourable to an harmonious understanding with Spain. He promised to give full weight to all I had said, and terminated the interview with the most friendly acknowledgment of the assistance Spain had often derived from the counsels of the British Government.

Before doing so he had given me an indication of the kind of action which, if allowed, Spain would be likely to make in the early future.

Tetuan, he said, was of course in every patriotic Spaniard's thoughts. He had resolutely opposed, however, till then, the course often pressed upon him of ordering a military occupation of that important town, which was already policed under Spanish instructors. What he felt it would not long be possible to resist, was the very reasonable demand of the Ceuta Authorities that Spain should take measures to put a stop to the frequent robberies by which the neighbourhood of Ceuta was being rendered daily a more dangerous region to traverse. It was with that object in view that the contemplated frontier police under a Moorish Kaïd had been assigned, in the convention between Spain and Morocco of November 16, 1910, a sphere of operations extending some distance beyond the present limits of Spanish jurisdiction. But the frontier police force it seemed impossible to call into being while the Sultan continued a prisoner in Fez and the Makhzen paralysed. Spain would be fully justified under the circumstances, His Excellency thought, in sending herself a force to perform these very necessary police duties, and also to occupy, in a manner rendering them secure from attack, the heights from which Ceuta could be easily destroyed if they fell into the hands of the enemy.

I said I thought an arrangement to facilitate the policing of the country behind Ceuta might easily be come to.

Another object occupying the mind of the Prime Minister was the strengthening of the native police force under Spanish instructors which is stationed at Larache. He said His Government would much like to transfer thither from Casablanca which lay beyond their sphere, the Spanish instructed police of the latter port. Casablanca would thus be left entirely in French hands and much friction avoided.

On this point I merely remarked that the plan of a divided police force at Casablanca had been carefully devised at Algeciras, with the object, probably, of discountenancing the theory of a partition of Morocco into spheres of influence.

Any modification of it would therefore require the assent of the signatory Powers.

But on both the points His Excellency had mentioned, I said that it seemed to me that arrangements could be made without much difficulty to meet Spanish views consistently with the General Act of Algeciras, if Spain would only abstain from adopting hasty measures in disregard of treaty engagements.

Since my conversation with the Prime Minister I have had the honour to receive your telegram No. 33 of the 1st instant,(⁴) directing me to inform the Spanish Government of the manner in which their present attitude is regarded by His Majesty's Government. I lost no time in communicating its purport to Señor Garcia Prieto who must thus be convinced that you view the Spanish claim to exercise independent action in Morocco in precisely the same light as the French Government.

I have, &c.

MAURICE DE BUNSEN.

MINUTES.

There is a false ring about the grievances. Sir M. de Bunsen's language which was very judicious may have done some good.

W. L.

I should hardly say that Spain had not some justifiable complaints ag[ain]st France in the past—fairly remote and also recent—but the grievances she now cites are not serious or well-founded. We must hope that the approaching discussions will have good results.

A. N.

Sir M. de Bunsen spoke very well.

E. G.

(⁴) [v. supra, p. 217, No. 238.]

No. 247.

Sir E. Goschen to Sir Edward Grey.

Berlin, May 4, 1911.

F.O. 16793/13911/11/28.
Tel. (No. 21.) Confidential.
D. 2.
R. 2·30.

Morocco.

Russian Chargé d'Affaires tells me that he has been instructed to inform Imperial Government that in view of assurances given by French Ambassador at St. Petersburg the Russian Government see no objection whatever to measures which French Government have found it necessary to take in Morocco and are in complete agreement with them on the subject. He is also to express the hope that the German Government share those views.

No. 248.

Mr. Lister to Sir Edward Grey.

Tangier, May 4, 1911.

F.O. 16804/8457/11/28.
Tel. (No. 51.)
D. 2·45 P.M.
R. 5·45 P.M.

My telegram No. 49.(¹)

German consul, in reporting arrival of Brémond's army in splendid condition, states that there is no possibility now of Fez being taken, and that Europeans are in no danger. He added that he could not answer for their safety were French

(¹) [This telegram of May 3 announced that the Sheraida Mehalla entered Fez on the 26th.]

relief column to be sent. German Minister has telegraphed this to his Government(²) and informed French chargé d'affaires. From latest hurried note (? from) German Minister I derive the impression that he has no anxiety as to the safety of Europeans or Fez. Under these circumstances it appears to me that French column should not continue its advance; in this way all danger of difficulties with Germany would be avoided. Moorish harkas under Amrani would of course proceed to Fez, where their presence would be very useful.

I gather that French chargé d'affaires personally holds this view, but he seems nervous lest other counsels should prevail in Paris.

MINUTES.

I imagine Mr. Lister thinks it might be advisable for us to communicate with the French Gov[ernmen]t in this sense. But would it not be better to leave it alone? The French must of course be fully aware of the circumstances at Fez and they are the best judges as to whether the mehalla should or should not advance.

? No action.

G. H. V.
5.4.11.
A. P.

The French Gov[ernmen]t, who are perfectly aware of the dangers of an advance, will have had this information from their Chargé d'Affaires and it seems unnecessary for us to offer any advice for the present at any rate.

W. L.

If M. Cambon comes here he may be told it verbally, but it is better not to make an express communication.

E. G.

Nothing should be said of the last paragraph.

(²) [A memorandum by Herr von Kiderlen-Waechter dated May 3 recommending a firm attitude was read by the Chancellor to the Emperor William II on May 5. *G.P.*, XXIX, pp. 101–8.]

No. 249.

Sir Edward Grey to Sir M. de Bunsen.

F.O. 16866/13911/11/28.   *Foreign Office, May 4,* 1911.
Tel. (No. 40.)   D. 5·45 P.M.

I have been informed by Spanish Ambassador here that in the opinion of German A------ssador at Paris, if France and Spain came to an agreement for policing and pacification of Morocco, Germany and other Powers would accept it if liberty of commerce were guaranteed. I understood from Spanish Ambassador that Spanish Gov[ernmen]t were enquiring at Berlin whether this was view of German Gov[ernmen]t, and that if so Spain and France might come to an agreement with each other, with which England and Germany could be associated afterwards. Information of French Gov[ernmen]t is that Spain proposes at once a discussion between the four Powers. This is a difficult thing and undesirable. On the other hand what Spanish Ambassador here suggested to me is a course, which might result in clearing up some difficulties. In my opinion France would be willing to come to an arrangement, which would reassure Spain on the chief points on which Spanish Gov[ernmen]t have expressed dissatisfaction and anxiety. You should impress this view upon M[inister for] F[oreign] A[ffairs].

No. 250.

Sir Edward Grey to Sir F. Bertie.

F.O. 17133/13751/11/28.
(No. 156.)
Sir,
                                        Foreign Office, May 4, 1911.
The French Ambassador informed me to-day that his Government heard that Spain was proposing an immediate discussion between England, France, Germany, and Spain for the settlement of the question of Morocco, and that in this settlement Spain would require that the policing of Tangier should be regulated. M. Cruppi viewed with great apprehension the bringing of Germany into the discussion, and also the way in which Spain was apparently working to bring Germany in.

I said that this information of the French Government was clearly one version of a communication which the Spanish Ambassador had made to me the other day, but there was an important difference in the proposed procedure. The Spanish Ambassador had been quite explicit that the first step was for Spain to make sure at Berlin that the German Government demanded nothing but liberty of commerce in return for their assent to an agreement between France and Spain. The next step would be a discussion between France and Spain to reach an agreement with each other; and not till that agreement had been reached would England and Germany be associated with it.

M. [Paul] Cambon then expressed his own personal opinion that France might give Spain guarantees that, if French troops occupied Fez, and the occupation was prolonged, Spain would not be prejudiced in her sphere of Morocco. Discussion might be opened at once with Spain for a new arrangement as to the policing of the ports, seeing that the present arrangement expired at the end of this year, and the opportunity might be taken to give some satisfaction to Spain. Spain complained of the inferior position in which she was placed under the Secret Agreement which she had with France as to Morocco, by the provisions of which Spain might not take any action in her sphere without previously coming to an agreement with France, whereas France was not under a corresponding restriction in her sphere. The French Government might discuss this difficulty with the Spanish Government. The question of Tangier was the only one on which M. Cambon thought it might be impossible to come to terms with Spain. The most difficult tribes were in the country round Tangier. If the whole policing was given up to Spain, there would be a breakdown, and European interests in Tangier were so considerable that there would certainly be cause for intervention by other Powers.

I suggested that the question of Tangier might be reserved until an agreement had been come to on the other points which M. Cambon had mentioned. If an agreement was reached with regard to these, Spain might perhaps be induced to agree that it was necessary to continue Tangier as an exception, because of its special position, and that an agreement on the other points should not be upset by insisting upon the exclusive policing of Tangier and its district by Spain.

I told M. Cambon that I would see the Spanish Ambassador to-morrow, and explain to him the difference between the method of procedure which he had suggested to me, and that which the French Government heard was advocated by the Spanish Government.

                                        [I am, &c.]
                                          E. G[REY].

No. 251.

Sir E. Goschen to Sir Edward Grey.

Berlin, May 5, 1911.

F.O. 16960/8457/11/28.
Tel. (No. 23.)

D. 11·55 A.M.
R. 4·45 P.M.

Morocco.

Secretary of State for Foreign Affairs on being questioned by one of my colleagues as to his views on the present situation in Morocco said he had nothing further to say on the subject and that German point of view was known to everyone. He was now going on leave for a month. In the course however of some further conversation he said that under ordinary circumstances time was on the side of the French but that if they were now imprudent and precipitated matters situation would be changed and it would be Germany who would reap the advantage.

A Madrid Telegram has been published here stating that a party of German engineers and traders have landed at Mogador and are purchasing land at high prices. I hear that Press Bureau have informed an inquiring journalist that the Government have no knowledge as to the truth of the report but that Mannesmann firm were very active people and that there was no knowing what they might be doing.

No. 252.

Sir Edward Grey to Sir F. Bertie.

F.O. 17064/13751/11/28.
Tel. (No. 95.)

Foreign Office, May 5, 1911.
D. 6 P.M.

General purport of my conversations with French and Spanish Ambassadors this week is that Spain would be ready to come to an agreement with France if she can be fairly met on certain points. The most important are : (1) To find some means of assuring Spain that if French control Fez this will not strengthen French control in Spanish sphere. Spain fears that with a Sultan dependent on France every Moorish official in Spanish sphere will be a French nominee looking to France for support. (2) Spain is dissatisfied with her inferior position under secret agreement with France, which restricts action of Spain in her sphere.

I think it is important that France should discuss these points with Spain, and find some means of assuring her that situation in Morocco will not be altered to her disadvantage, and have said so to French Ambassador, who then expressed personal opinion that this is not an impracticable course.

Spain also wants to get exclusive police of Tangier and district. There are objections to this ; but other points might be discussed first.

Latest news from Fez points to improvement there, and if French troops can, after all, avoid entering Fez, the situation will be easier ; but I am convinced that it is very desirable for French Government to find some means of reassuring Spain on points (1) and (2).

(Repeated to Madrid, No. 44, and Berlin No. 67.)

No. 253.

Sir E. Goschen to Sir A. Nicolson.

Private.([1])

My dear Nicolson,   *Berlin, May* 5, 1911.

. . . .([2]) *Morocco.* The attitude of the German Government and most of the German Press is so correct that it is almost alarming. But I suppose that they are playing some deep game with Spain, and that the latter is falling, a not too unwilling victim, into Germany's tenacious clutch. Judging from the telegrams and despatches I have read the Spanish tongue is somewhat forked on this question, for the Spanish Premier and the Spanish R[epresentatives] abroad seem to vary their language according to the nationality of the persons to whom they talk. Polo de Bernabé seems to hold fairly sound views. He says Spain is not 'carrying on' with Germany and that she does not want to quarrel with France, *only* the latter *must* show a little more consideration for Spanish interests and wishes. " As long as Spain and France are at loggerheads" he says "on Moroccan questions, the interests of both countries must suffer and Germany will reap the advantage. Therefore it is foolish for France and Spain to quarrel. One of the chief reasons for disagreements and unpleasantness is the system of mixed police. Under this system there must always be ructions and in such ructions Spain, as the weaker Power, always has to go to the wall and thus her prestige and influence suffer. The Police part of the Act of Algeciras lapses at the end of this year and why shouldn't France and Spain come to a new arrangement by which France should have the entire policing of Casablanca and Spain that of Tangier? Such arrangement would do away with a fruitful source of unpleasantness between the two Countries." I can quite fancy that such an arrangement would suit Spain and possibly France, but I can also imagine that other people might not be so happy at the idea of Tangier being entirely policed by Spain.

I must tell you that Kiderlen received the communication from the Russian Government, about which I telegraphed yesterday, very amiably.([3]) Schébéko was rather nervous about how it would be received, but I hear that he found Kiderlen most cordial and pleasant. The latter said that he quite understood the attitude of the Russian Government, that the German Government also had perfect confidence that the French assurances had been given in good faith, and that their only fear was that circumstances might drive France beyond the point where it was her wish and her intention to stop. I have not been able to report this officially as I have not seen Schebeko yet and my information though correct, is only second hand. I hope that the more satisfactory news now received from Tangier will enable France to reduce the scope of her expedition, and that her Government will not allow themselves to be pushed into playing into Germany's hands by any foolish idea that people will say that they stopped short of their intentions for fear of Germany. The Pan-Germans are already beginning to exploit this idea and to rub it in, but I am glad to say that their views of the duties of the German Gov[ernmen]t in the Moroccan question are not shared by the bulk of public opinion. They, the Pan Germans are now beginning a campaign against the renewal of the Police Mandate, and are urging the Government to oppose it tooth and nail. They say that as long as it exists troubles in Morocco will never cease, as the Sultan will continue to be the tool of France and consequently an object of hatred and execration throughout his dominions : that this means that Morocco will gradually become a French dependency in which case good-bye to the Open door and equal opportunities for Trade &c. The French instructors also come under their ban and they maintain that until these disappear there is no hope for any improvement in Moroccan affairs.

([1]) [Carnock MSS., Vol. II of 1911.]
([2]) [The opening remarks are of a personal nature.]
([3]) [For the same information as to Russia's attitude, *v. G.P..* XXIX, p. 112, *note, v.* also *supra*, p. 225, No. 247.]

The rest of the Press is cautious and prudent and not in the least provocative. It reflects in fact Kiderlen's attitude. The latter has, chiefly through his careful manipulation of the Press, already great influence in the Country. It is lucky in some ways that he has such a clever and well-balanced solid mind. Otherwise the adulation of the Press and its continual references to his strong and vigorous hand, and to the delight of the country at having at *last* a strong man in charge of its Foreign Affairs, might turn his head and make him too anxious to make 'coups.' This danger does of course exist and one can't help thinking of it, but up till now he has shown himself to be a man who is fairly impervious to either praise or blame, a man who has a *very* clear idea of what he wants and allows nothing to draw him aside from the course he marks out. That is at all events my present opinion of him. Of course with such a man at the Foreign Office the Chancellor has now very little to say to Foreign Affairs. . . . .(⁴)

Yours very sincerely,
W. E. GOSCHEN.

(⁴) [The closing paragraphs of this letter refer to personal and general matters.]

No. 254.

Sir Edward Grey to Sir M. de Bunsen.

F.O. 17141/13911/11/28.   *Foreign Office, May 9,* 1911.
Tel. (No. 54.)   D. 1·15 P.M.

My immediately preceding telegram.(¹)
You should in the manner which you think most advisable and appropriate intimate to the Spanish M[inister for] F[oreign] Affairs that we shall fully maintain the 1904 Agreement with France and shape our attitude in accordance with that which we adopted at Algeciras in 1906.(²)

(¹) [Not reproduced.]
(²) [*v. Gooch & Temperley,* Vol. III, pp. 204–349, *passim.*]

No. 255.

Mr. Lister to Sir Edward Grey.

Tangier, May 9, 1911.
D. 1·30 P.M.
R. 4·45 P.M.

F.O. 17616/8457/11/28.
Tel. (No. 59.) R.

I have received letter from Mulai Zin announcing his proclamation as Sultan. He says he desires to maintain friendship which has always existed between his ancestors and Great Britain and as proof of this he has chosen as Minister for Foreign Affairs Mikwar who has always exerted himself on behalf of British interests. Zin has also written to German Minister and to Abd-el-Aziz. I am communicating a copy of my letter to my colleagues. I do not propose to reply.

Reports which reach me from all sources, European and native alike, throughout the country all show depth of unpopularity of Hafid, and the French will have a most serious task before them if they intend to maintain him. French chargé d'affaires seems to have realized this.

I am assured that Fez would have surrendered before this had not leading Sherifs dreaded possibility of harm befalling Europeans. I believe that negotiations are in progress between them and Zin, and, provided safety of Europeans could be assured, situation might be simplified were they to succeed. Task of French would be undoubtedly facilitated were Hafid to be deposed before arrival of column. This cannot be expected for a fortnight, as great difficulties are being experienced in landing stores etc. Two convoys have already been attacked and five French soldiers killed.

No. 256.

Sir Edward Grey to Sir F. Bertie.

F.O. 17678/8457/11/28.   *Foreign Office, May 9, 1911.*
Tel. (No. 107.) R.   D. 6·30 P.M.

I told M. Cambon of the instruction sent to Sir M. de Bunsen to-day.(¹)

While admitting that in view of the situation at Fez the French must relieve the place by the quickest possible route, I observed that the revolt of the tribes was apparently against the extortion and misrule of Mulai Hafid and Glawi. If so, it would be a pity for the French to make it their object to force these bad rulers upon the Moors; to do so would turn the revolt into an anti-French or anti-foreign channel, it would not recommend itself to public opinion, and it would make it impossible for the French to withdraw.

When the French officers got into touch with the tribes, if they found that a pacific settlement could be made and all difficulties dissipated by a change of Sultan or Grand Vizier or both, it would be well not to miss the opportunity.

M. Cambon thanked me cordially for what I had told him of the communication to Madrid, and said he would tell M. Cruppi my view of the situation in Morocco. Personally he thought it probably indispensable that Glawi should be dismissed, and Mulai Hafid might himself have to go if he would not concede that.

(Repeated to Berlin, No. 79; Madrid, No. 55; and Tangier, No. 33.)

(¹) [*v. supra*, p. 230, No. 254.]

No. 257.

Sir M. de Bunsen to Sir Edward Grey.

                                 Madrid, May 9, 1911.
F.O. 17622/13751/11/28.   D. 7 P.M.
Tel. (No. 23.) Confidential.   R. 9·45 P.M.

Spanish occupation of heights near Ceuta.

French Ambassador, after having informed Spanish Minister for Foreign Affairs yesterday that French Government had no objection to offer, is now instructed to make it clear to his Excellency that any Spanish advance beyond line defined in article 8 of Spanish convention with Morocco of 16th November, 1910,(¹) would be dangerous, and that French Government would not consent to it.

As I understand that the French Government are requesting you to instruct me in the same sense, I venture to hope that latitude may be left to me to make this communication in terms which will not give unnecessary offence.

French Ambassador agrees with me in thinking that unless a little rope is given to Spain in the present crisis she will be tempted to break away from her natural allies and seek support elsewhere. If French Government are not prepared to resist by force such a move as a Spanish occupation of Tetuan, French Ambassador doubts wisdom of using strong language. He thinks that Spain can only be kept in the

(¹) [*v. Martens, 3rd Ser.:* (Leipzig 1913), VII, pp. 94–100.]

Anglo-French orbit by delicate handling and by not opposing off-hand everything she may want to do to assert position assigned to her under the secret convention. This, indeed, was the object in view in inviting the Spanish Government to submit a statement of their demands as regards Spanish sphere of influence. His Excellency intends postponing his communication to the Spanish Government until I have received instructions. If you think it sufficient, I would propose merely to say to Minister for Foreign Affairs that His Majesty's Government consider that Spanish Government acted with wisdom in restricting operations to the above-mentioned line.

(Repeated to Paris.)

No. 258.

Sir M. de Bunsen to Sir Edward Grey.

F.O. 17734/13911/11/28.
Tel. (No. 24.)

Madrid, May 10, 1911.
D. 12·40 P.M.
R. 4·50 P.M.

Your Tel[egram] No. 53 Secret.([1])

Though French Ambassador and I have no reason to think that German Ambassador here is encouraging Spanish Government to make themselves disagreeable, it is of course evident that Spanish Government look at situation much as the Germans do and think that Germany is not likely to object to their taking up a stiff position in Morocco which would limit French influence there.

I had long conversation with German Ambassador yesterday. H[is] E[xcellency] holds the same language as the German Government at Berlin. France must not establish her influence at Fez in a way to destroy principle laid down at Algesiras. If she does, situation reverts to the *status quo ante*. German Ambassador thinks it quite natural that Spain should occupy Ifni if she means to do so, as she has occupied heights near Ceuta. Both actions are justified by the failure of the Maghzen to assist her in carrying out convention of November 16, 1910.([2]) From what King of Spain tells him he does not think that Spain intends to take any further forcible action at present. But if the French entered Fez he would think it natural that Spain should respond by occupying Tetuan. On my pointing out how different the circumstances would be [he] admitted that there is nothing at Tetuan calling for Spanish intervention, but added that French intervention at Fez is also unjustified judging by reports of the German consul at Fez who stated that Major Bremond's column had returned in good condition. German Ambassador has been engaged in an acrimonious discussion with the Spanish Government over a dispute which has arisen in the Riff between Spanish mining company and German called Natter, who states that, after occupying for many months a mining site which he had purchased in neighbourhood of the Spanish mines, he has been forcibly ejected by the Spanish military authorities who claim that the site is included in the territory belonging to Spanish company. The latter, whose principal shareholder is Mr. Macpherson of Cadiz, claiming to be a British subject, have appealed to me for support.

(Repeated to Paris.)

([1]) [Not reproduced.]
([2]) [*cp. supra*, pp. 156–8, No. 169; and pp. 170–2, No. 184. *v. also Martens, 3rd Ser.*: (Leipzig 1913), VII, pp. 94–100.]

No. 259.

Sir Edward Grey to Sir M. de Bunsen.

F.O. 17622/13751/11/28.   *Foreign Office, May* 10, 1911.
Tel. (No. 56.)   D. 7·30 P.M.
Your telegram No. 23.(¹) The views expressed by French Ambas[sado]r appear to be sound—and it would be well to avoid offending Spanish susceptibilities. I quite agree with the language which you propose to hold to M[inister for] F[oreign] A[ffairs]. It seems to me essential for France to give Spain some latitude of action, if she is to be kept with us.
(Repeat above to Paris.)

(¹) [*v. supra*, pp. 231–2, No. 257.]

No. 260.

Sir Edward Grey to Sir F. Cartwright.

F.O. 17745/13911/11/28.
(No. 28.)
Sir,   *Foreign Office, May* 10, 1911.
The Austro-Hungarian Ambassador asked me to-day whether I had any news from Morocco.(¹)
I said that the news from Fez was bad : the town was cut off from supplies; the people inside were getting short of ammunition, and food also was running short. With the revolted tribes outside and approaching starvation inside, it was obvious that the only thing for the French to do was to relieve Fez by the quickest possible route. When this had been done, I hoped that some settlement might be made by the French which would restore the normal order of things; but at present the first thing to do was to relieve Fez as soon as possible. In Parliament here, we had been pressed as to the danger to British subjects in Fez. There were not many there, but they were people who deserved sympathy; and if the French had not been taking measures to relieve the place, we should have had to ask them to do so. As it was, the French subjects in danger in Fez were more numerous than the British subjects, they included French officers—and the French had therefore been bound to act promptly upon their own initiative.

[I am, &c.]
E. G[REY].

(¹) [Count Mensdorff's report has not been traced in *Ö.-U.A.*]

No. 261.

Sir M. de Bunsen to Sir Edward Grey.

                                                    Madrid, May 11, 1911.
F.O. 17915/13751/11/28.   D. 4·45 P.M.
Tel. (No. 25.) R.   R. 6·45 P.M.
My telegram No. 21.(¹)
Minister for Foreign Affairs has communicated to me a copy of memorandum(²) sent yesterday to French Ambassador, containing demands of Spain as regards her

(¹) [Not reproduced. It stated that M. Cruppi approved M. Geoffray's suggestion that the Spanish Government should express their desires respecting the Spanish sphere, and that he hoped Sir M. de Bunsen would join in the ensuing discussions. *cp. supra*, pp. 219–20, No. 241, and note (¹).]
(²) [*cp. infra*, pp. 238–9, No. 266. The memorandum is not printed there as an adequate summary is given in the covering despatch.]

sphere of influence in Morocco. Memorandum is accompanied by draft declaration and protocol setting forth the manner in which Spanish Government consider that they should be allowed to exercise their influence. (End of R.)

These proposals go far beyond anything that could be conceded, but French Ambassador agrees with me in thinking that some of them may form reasonable basis for discussion, and that good effect has already been produced by French offer to take Spanish demands into consideration.

(R.) Draft declaration is drawn up in name of France, Spain, and England. and Minister for Foreign Affairs states that he sends me these papers " in order that from the beginning you may be in a position to take part with French Ambassador and myself in work of conciliation and good understanding upon which we are entering, and of the happy result of which I cannot doubt."

I have replied that I shall be happy to use my good offices and to tender friendly advice, but that I have no authority to take part in a tripartite negotiation as apparently contemplated by Spanish Government. I hope to be able to furnish an abstract in a few days.

(Repeated to Paris and Tangier.)

MINUTES.

It was to be expected that the Spanish demands would be stiff.

G. H. V.
12.5.11.

The Spaniards have taken a leaf out of the German book which contains as one of the most important principles of international conduct the rule to create or help to create difficulties and embarrassments for other Powers and then, when those Powers are in difficulties, to demand political concessions from them as the price of refraining from further unfriendliness.

These are the ethics and the spirit against which all pacifist talk and arbitration propaganda are at present, and are likely to remain for some time, altogether powerless.

E. A. C.
May 12.

No action necesssary.

W. L.
A. N.
E. G.

No. 262.

Sir F. Cartwright to Sir A. Nicolson.

Private.([1])
My dear Nicolson, *Vienna, May* 11, 1911.

The Morocco question continues to largely occupy the attention of a certain section of the Vienna press—the pan-German section of it,—and a great deal is written about the shifty conduct of France. The general public, however, take but a languid interest in the matter, and the "Ballplatz" assumes an air of perfect calm and of disinterestedness with regard to this question. Pallavicini repeated to me yesterday that Austria practically washed her hands of the Moroccan question, and he threw cold water upon the accuracy of statements which have recently appeared in some of the newspapers here to the effect that Austrian trade in Morocco considerably exceeded in value that of Germany, and that therefore Austria-Hungary ought not to neglect to protect her growing interests in that country. Pallavicini professes to be thoroughly bored with the Moroccan question, and he said to me that in his eyes the only merit of that question was that as the European Powers could only look at one question at the time, it was to the advantage of Austria that their attention was now turned towards Morocco instead of towards the Balkans : this was evidently a great relief to the Ballplatz. Pallavicini asserted to me yesterday that official circles in Berlin were at present viewing the situation calmly, but it

([1]) [Carnock MSS., Vol. II of 1911.]

seems to me that all the while the German press is allowed unchecked liberty of abusing France and of keeping alive among the German public a feeling of distrust of that country, and of uncertainty as to the real issues of the Moroccan question. The German Government evidently desire to keep up public excitement, both in Germany and in Austria-Hungary, by means of the press with regard to Morocco until they can see more clearly what advantages they may draw for themselves by any mistake which may be committed by France. I have told Crozier, the French Ambassador here, that he had better not lead his Government to put too absolute a trust in the apparent indifference of the Austrian Government in Moroccan affairs. Here they certainly do not desire to go out of their way to pick a quarrel with France, but if the French go to Fez and stay there for any time, Germany will bring such pressure to bear upon this Government that the Ballplatz will reluctantly be compelled to throw in their lot with Germany and make the show of a united front of the two allies against the other Powers. All the same I feel sure that Aehrenthal will do his best to moderate German action if an acute crisis should arise between Germany and France over Morocco, in the first place, because he does not want to help to bring about a European conflagration, and secondly, because the French Government are just beginning to be a little more amiable about the floating of Austro-Hungarian loans on the French market. Crozier yesterday announced to Pallavicini that the French Government would give their consent to the quotation on the French Bourses of certain small Hungarian commercial loans, amounting to about 150 million franks [sic: francs]. Pallavicini was profuse in his thanks to Crozier for this concession, and as still more French money is wanted here, we may be sure that the Austro-Hungarian Government will abstain from doing anything disagreeable to France, except under the greatest pressure from Berlin.

Yesterday in his conversation with me Pallavicini showed himself very eager that the French should not go to Fez, at least that they should not stay there any time. I pointed out to him that if the French retired to the coast with the European residents, it was quite possible that the Sultan might ask to be taken away as well, and that then anarchy would follow throughout Morocco, every tribe acting for themselves [sic] in complete independence. Pallavicini intimated that the European Powers could put up with that for a time, and that they might wait and see what would happen. He thought that before long some chief of character would little by little assert his authority and so, step by step, acquire the position of a Sultan. Pallavicini evidently hopes that France will do everything in her power that is possible to prevent Germany from calling upon Austria-Hungary for diplomatic support, on the ground that a clear breach of the Algeciras Act has been committed by France; that would produce a situation extremely distasteful to the " Ballplatz."

It may be worth while letting you know that I note in the great majority of newspaper articles which appear here—inspired from Berlin—that their sting is against Delcassé's presence in the French Cabinet, and that it looks as if Germany intends to use the Moroccan question as a means of making herself so nasty to France, that public opinion in that country will grow alarmed to such an extent that Delcassé's chances of forming the next Cabinet will be entirely eliminated. Most of the pan-German newspapers of Vienna publish from the Berlin " Kreuz Zeitung " a serious warning to France, which amounts to this that if Germany's interests in Morocco are injured by French military expeditions, she will ask for compensation not from the Moroccan Government, but directly from the Government of the Republic. . . . .(²)

Yours truly,
FAIRFAX L. CARTWRIGHT.

(²) [The rest of this · long letter gives details on the Balkan situation, the crisis in Constantinople, and the Austro-Hungarian internal situation.]

No. 263.

Sir A. Nicolson to Sir F. Bertie.

Private.(¹)

My dear Bertie,   *Foreign Office, May* 11, 1911.

     . . . .(²) It is hardly necessary for me to go into any details in regard to the
Morocco question. I think our telegrams to you will have kept you fully informed
of our attitude. I am strongly of opinion myself that it would be a great mistake
if the French were to persist in supporting the present Sultan at any cost, as I
am sure that such a course would force them permanently to occupy Fez and would
probably also lead to their having to undertake a conquest of Morocco. I do not
see why they should not select a Sultan who would be agreeable to the majority
of the tribes, as by this means they would free themselves from a great responsibility.
I hope that we have succeeded in restraining Spain from taking any precipitate or
hasty action, and I do think that the French should do all in their power not to
wound Spanish susceptibilities. The future attitude of Germany is somewhat
mysterious and the Spanish Ambassador told me yesterday that Kiderlen had
informed the Spanish Ambassador at Berlin that he was going away to Kissingen
for a six weeks' cure as he felt that he could do so now with safety, and he was
sure that by the time the six weeks had elapsed, a very serious situation would have
developed which would necessitate his presence in Berlin. I expect that Germany
calculates that in that time France will have plunged herself up to her neck in
Moorish affairs and that the moment will have arrived for Germany to step in and
demand her price. It is essential that we should not waver in the very slightest
in our support of France, as I think that if Germany is aware that both Russia and
ourselves intend to strongly support France throughout this question, there will be
less chance of any European complications arising.

                                                        [A. NICOLSON.]

     (¹) [Carnock MSS., Vol. II of 1912.]
     (²) [The omitted paragraphs refer to Anglo-French financial co-operation in Turkey.]

No. 264.

Mr. Lister to Sir Edward Grey.

                                                    Tangier, May 13, 1911.

F.O. 18229/8457/11/28.   D. 1·20 P.M.
Tel. (No. 65.)   R. 8 P.M.

     My telegram No. 58.(¹)

     Meeting of all fractions [*sic :* factions ?] of the Anjera tribe called for to-day to
discuss the question of opposing the Spaniards. Harris has written to Valiente to
impress upon him the necessity of extreme caution. French chargé d'Affaires informs
me that the Spaniards have now occupied point 10 miles from Tetuan. Their action,
in my opinion, was by no means warranted by the state of the country, and may lead
to serious disturbances in districts bordering on Tangier.

     (¹) [This telegram of the 8th instant stated that a Spanish Riffian force had been stationed at
Fanideek, in Moorish territory. The Spanish Government announced their intention of maintaining this force on a permanent basis unless the Moorish police force, provided for in the
convention, was at once established.]

No. 265.

Sir F. Cartwright to Sir Edward Grey.

F.O. 18232/13911/11/28.
Tel. (No. 43.) Most Confidential.
Morocco.

Vienna, May 13, 1911.
D. 8·40 p.m.
R. 10·15 p.m.

I have been informed in strict confidence by person who wrote article alluded to in my telegram No. 39(¹) that, after he had received verbally from the German Ambassador lines on which article was to be written, he proceeded to the Austro-Hungarian Foreign Office to take advice as to the desirability of publishing it. He was there told that he could proceed with the matter, as, in the opinion of Foreign Office, it would tend to awaken Austrian public opinion to the dangers into which German policy might lead her ally, and would therefore probably act as a check on German *intransigeance.*

Writer of the article tells me that the language of the German Ambassador to him was much toned down in the article. Ambassador said that the real Spanish view of the Moroccan question was good, but the Spanish Government were afraid to carry out that view from fear of France starting a revolution in Spain. The Ambassador also declared that if the French entered Fez the German Government would send peremptory demand for them to withdraw, and that in his opinion the French Government were steering straight for a new Fashoda.

My informant believes the Ambassador to have given expression to the real views of the German Government, communicated to the Ambassadors for their guidance but not for publication.

I learnt confidentially a few days ago that the German Ambassador complained to the Acting Minister for Foreign Affairs about the intrigues of certain Ambassadors (naming the French Ambassador and myself) influencing the Austro-Hungarian press in a sense adverse to Germany. The German Ambassador professed to have nothing to do with the article above mentioned. Editor of the Foreign Office organ here tells me that he will publish on Monday in another paper an inspired article not more favourable to France than is thought advisable to express in semi-official organ. The editor explained to me that the difference in the attitudes of the Austro-Hungarian and German Governments was as follows :—

Austro-Hungarian Government accepts in a benevolent spirit the assurances given by France ; Germany accepts them officially in a malevolent spirit.

MINUTES.

It would, I think, be well to be prepared to find that the course foreshadowed by Herr von Tschirschky will be followed. It is quite in harmony with Germany's usual procedure at first to display indifference and suddenly, at a critical moment favourable to her action, to turn round and categorically demand material concessions as the price of keeping quiet. This was the course actually pursued on the occasions of the Anglo-French Agreement of 1904, of the Algeciras Conference in 1905–6, and of the Franco-German further understanding about Morocco in 1909. Nothing is likely to be done in this direction before the conclusion of the Emperor's London visit.

E. A. C.
May 15.

Germany may be relied upon to get their compensation if the French give her half a chance of demanding it.

W. L.
A. N.
E G.

(¹) [*v. infra,* p. 464, No. 491 (b).]

No. 266.

Sir M. de Bunsen to Sir Edward Grey.

F.O. 18712/13751/11/28.
(No. 63.)
Sir,

Madrid, D. *May* 14, 1911.
R. *May* 16, 1911.

In my despatch No. 58 Confidential of the 5th instant,(¹) I gave some account of the correspondence which has recently passed between the French Ambassador and the Spanish Minister for Foreign Affairs in connection with events in Morocco. The correspondence closed with a letter, dated May 2nd, at the conclusion of which M. Geoffray suggested, with the approval of his Government, that the Spanish Government should state frankly the nature of their grievances so that a discussion might take place between the two Governments " with the object of arriving, in concert with the British Government, at the best way of applying, in the territory of Morocco, the principles set forth in the Conventions of 1904 and in the Act of Algeciras.''

The quotation in inverted commas is translated from the Spanish version of the text.

In the course of the conversations which M. Geoffray and myself held on Friday May 5th with Señor Garcia Prieto the latter informed both of us that the Spanish Government proposed to act on the above suggestion and that a memorandum would be drawn up accordingly.

The promised memorandum reached the French Ambassador on the night of the 10th instant.

Señor Garcia Prieto was good enough to send me a copy, under cover of a private letter which concluded as follows;—"I send you the accompanying documents so that, from the first, you may be in a position to take part, with M. Geoffray and myself, in the work of conciliation and good understanding upon which we are entering, and of whose happy result I cannot doubt.''

In acknowledging this communication I was careful to make it clear that, as instructed in your telegram No. 49 of the 8th instant,(²) my co-operation, which I said I should be happy to afford, must be limited to good offices and friendly advice. and that I was not at present authorized to enter into a formal negotiation or to sign new conventions.

I have the honour to forward herewith an abstract of the Spanish memorandum(²) together with a translation of a Draft Declaration and protocol by which it is accompanied.

The Spanish Government contend, in the memorandum, that the Secret Convention of 1904 has been unfairly applied.

Experience shows that :—1). France has concluded financial arrangements with Morocco affecting the Spanish sphere of influence, and exceeding the maximum period of fifteen years mentioned in Article 2 of the Convention, without consulting Spain. The resources of the Spanish sphere have been pledged as security for loans contracted in the general interest or in the exclusive interest of France. The Spanish sphere is thus financially crippled.

2). The distribution of the police requires readjustment. The stipulated expansion of the Casablanca native extra-urban police under Spanish instructors has been rendered impracticable by the terms of the last Franco-Moorish Convention. France monopolises military instruction of the native troops throughout Morocco.

3). In the Morocco Public Works department the proper position and authority of the Spanish engineer has never been recognized. Spain has been thwarted over the Draft Mining Regulations. She is insufficiently represented in the State Bank and other institutions.

(¹) [Not reproduced as its substance is here given. *cp. supra*, pp. 233–4, No. 261, and *note* (¹).]

(²) [Not reproduced as its tenour is indicated.]

4). It is not sufficiently recognized that Tangier notwithstanding its "special character" forms part of the Spanish sphere of influence.

5. The Spanish share in loans etc. is insufficient.

6. The Spanish language has been improperly excluded from employment, equally with the French language, in proclamations etc.

In conclusion it is argued that an occupation even temporary of Fez by the French must inevitably affect the position of the Sultan and the existing régime, in a manner compelling Spain to secure her rights. The best way to meet the new situation would be to admit that circumstances have brought into action the provision contained in the Secret Convention allowing Spain under certain contingencies full liberty to do what she pleases in her own sphere; and, further, to publish the Secret Treaty. But, as France sees objections to publication, the Minister for Foreign Affairs suggests, as an alternative, a form of Declaration for signature by the Spanish Government and the French and British representatives at Madrid, and also a Protocol, which latter is drawn up in a form permitting it to be communicated to the Powers while the Declaration remains secret.

The Draft Declaration contains six articles :—

1). The first period of the Secret Treaty being ended, Spain enjoys free action in her sphere of influence.
2. Franco-Moorish financial arrangements of March 1910 not to be secured on the resources of the Spanish sphere. France and Spain will come to an agreement concerning the construction of a Tangier–Fez railway passing through Arzila, Larache and Alcazar.
3. Annexed Protocol, for communication to the Powers, sets forth measures jointly agreed to for restoring order and re-establishing the Sultan's authority.
4. The French and Spanish engineers at the head of the Moorish Office of Works shall each advise and assist the Makhzen in relation to the sphere of influence of his country.
5. Each Government shall support the action of the other in the respective spheres of influence.
6. Spanish language to be on a footing of equality with the French in Proclamations etc.

British Ambassador to take act of the foregoing, which remains secret as long as the Secret Convention remains so. If the Sultan loses his independence, Spain declares herself to be at liberty to determine by herself the legal status of her sphere of influence.

The Protocol is divided into two parts. The first provides that French instructed troops shall not operate in the Spanish sphere; that if foreign officers be required to instruct the native forces in the Spanish sphere, they shall be taken from the Spanish instructors of native police; that it is expedient that the police mandate exercised by France and Spain in Morocco be renewed under specified new conditions as to distribution etc; and that Spain will introduce into the Riff country and the regions south of Wady Mesa, which form the frontier of the Ifni district, the régime contemplated in Article 3 of the Hispano-Moorish Convention of November 16th 1910.

Part 2 of the Protocol aims at the immediate repayment of the holders of the 1904 and 1910 loans of that portion of their contributions which is secured on certain Moorish revenues in the Spanish sphere. It further contemplates arrangements in virtue of which the ceded revenues in the French and Spanish spheres of influence shall be administered by agents of the French and Spanish Governments respectively.

M. Geoffray is sending M. Martin, Councillor of the French Embassy, to-day to Paris to lay these papers before the French Government and explain personally their full purport.

In the conversation which His Excellency has already held with the Spanish Minister for Foreign Affairs, since the receipt of the memorandum, he has confined himself to stating that, although the latter displays a profound divergence of view between the two Governments, he is glad to have before him a concrete statement of the full extent of the Spanish demands, and is not without hope that it will provide a basis for useful discussion, in view of the understanding which is so desirable in the interest of the peaceful development of affairs in Morocco.

M. Geoffray had confided to me that, in his opinion, such an understanding might be sought in an arrangement meeting to some extent the Spanish claims in respect of the non-penetration of French instructed troops into the Spanish sphere. He thinks that some redistribution of the police of the open ports might be considered, if the other Signatory Powers of the Algeciras Act saw no objection, but he holds that the demand for the elimination of the French instructed police from Tangier, and the desired recognition of that port as constituting a portion of the Spanish sphere of influence, are outside the range of possible discussion.

His Excellency does not think it would be possible for France to recede from the financial arrangements concluded with Morocco in the convention of March 1910; nor, in his opinion, would any interference with the constitution of existing organisms, such as the State Bank, Public Works Department, etc., be at all admissible, in the manner suggested by Spain.

M. Martin is instructed to represent as forcibly as he can to the French Minister for Foreign Affairs M. Geoffray's view that something substantial must be yielded to Spain if she is to be prevented from breaking away from her present allies.

I have, &c.
MAURICE DE BUNSEN.

Enclosure 1 in No. 266.

Draft Declaration.

(Translation.)
The Governments of Spain, France and Great Britain, animated equally by the desire to maintain and confirm this understanding between them concerning the Morocco question, and recognizing that it would be useful to enquire jointly, in view of the events which are taking place in that Empire, what would be the most appropriate way of applying existing Conventions, have conferred this task respectively on the Minister of State of His Catholic Majesty and on the Ambassadors of the French Republic and of His Britannic Majesty at Madrid. As the result of this enquiry the two first-mentioned, duly authorized thereto, have agreed as follows :—

1. The first period of the application of the Convention of October 3, 1904 is declared to be at an end, Spain remaining therefore free to exercise her action within her sphere of influence as recognized in the said agreement.

2. The financial convention of the   [*sic*] of March last between France and the Makhzen having reached neither ratification by His Imperial Majesty nor examination by the State Bank, the Paris Cabinet will cause it to be modified in such a manner as to place it in agreement with the principle stated in the foregoing paragraph, that is to say so that it may not be secured on the resources of the Spanish Sphere of Influence. The Governments of His Catholic Majesty and of the French Republic will come to an understanding with a view to the construction of an [*sic*] Tangier–Arzila–Larache–Alcazar–Fez Railway, in conformity with the new situation.

3. Since it is expedient to bring into harmony with the stipulations of Paragraph 1 the situation created by previous events, and to secure the concordance of the action respectively of Spain and France as between themselves and in relation

to the Act of Algeciras, the arrangements concerning which the two countries are in agreement, as regards the method of the gradual restoration of order, the re-establishment of the Shereefian authority and the financial measures required by these objects, have been set forth in the annexed special Protocol, which may be communicated to the other Signatory Powers of the said Act. It is understood that, though in the said Protocol no allusion is made to spheres of influence, it is the intention of both countries that its stipulations should be applied within the limits fixed by the Franco-Spanish Convention of 1904 and 1905, the said limits not being either directly or indirectly modified.

4. The Spanish and French Legations at Tangier shall inform Messrs. Porché and Llorens that the two Governments desire that, in matters falling within the competence of the Office of Public Works of the Makhzen, including mines, the advice and assistance to be given to the Sultan and to native agents shall emanate from the Spanish official when the matter in hand concerns the Spanish Sphere of Influence. If, for the adequate application of this principle, the Madrid Cabinet should consider an administrative division useful, a proposition to that effect shall be made forthwith to the Makhzen.

5. Independently of what is set forth in the annexed Protocol, both Governments will instruct their agents in Morocco to the effect that, in all matters requiring the intervention of the diplomatic body or of special commissions or organisations, the representatives or delegates of either country shall extend their support to those of the other in all that refers to the respective spheres of influence. As far as their means permit, both Governments will contrive that the same course should be pursued in the Administrative Councils etc of the State Bank and of other Societies in which capital belonging to different countries is invested. It is agreed that, if in future the two Governments should consider that it would be expedient to favour the constitution of these groups or societies in such a way as to avoid, in concrete cases, the inconvenience of competition in matters in which competition is legally admissible, Spanish capital shall enjoy, within the Spanish sphere of influence, the predominance which is due to it.

6. The Government of the Republic will not oppose the use of the Spanish language, on a footing of equality with the French, in the promulgation of the Notices issued by the Makhzen and by the administrative offices of Morocco and in dealings between the administration and private individuals.

For his part, the Ambassador of His Britannic Majesty, duly authorized, takes act of the foregoing in the letter and spirit of Article 8 of the Franco-British Declaration of April 8, 1904.

The text of the present agreement shall not be published until the Franco-Spanish convention of October 3, 1904 is published. Its application, which aims at securing the integrity of the Empire, shall cease if the authority of the Sultan ceases, as foreseen by Article 3 of the Convention of 1904, or if it should diminish to the point that it could no longer be regarded as independent, in which case Spain shall have full and absolute liberty to determine the legal status of her sphere of influence.

Enclosure 2 in No. 266.

Protocol.

The Governments of Spain and France, being in accord since October 3, 1904 concerning the extent of the rights and the guarantee of the interests of their respective countries in Morocco and having in mind the expediency of now defining, in view of the events which are now taking place in that Empire, the most efficacious manner of exercising those rights and securing those interests, in harmony with the principles and stipulations set forth at the International Conference of Algeciras, have agreed on the following provisions :—

I.

The measures which the Government of the French Republic may consider it necessary to take in order to restore the authority of the Sultan, by putting an end to the violence and disorder which prevail in Moorish territory, shall not be applied in Larache nor in the neighbourhood of Alcazar, to the north of the River Lucus, which fall within the Spanish sphere. Spanish officers are charged with the duty of organizing the police in the said port of Larache and at Tetuan, of taking part in the organization of the Tangier police, and of adopting the precautions and taking the measures which they hold to be necessary in order that the peace may not be disturbed and that the authority of His Imperial Majesty may be strengthened in this part of the Empire. If to this end the intervention of foreign officers to pay, instruct or organize the forces of the Sultan should be necessary, it shall be undertaken by the Spanish instructors of police.

Both Governments shall forthwith propose to the other Signatory Powers of the Act of Algeciras and in due course to the Government of the Swiss Confederation and to the Makhzen, the renewal of the mandate of the instructors and Inspector General of the police of the Morocco ports, on the conditions laid down in that agreement, supplemented by the following :—

In view of the circumstances in which Casablanca is placed, the *cadre* of the police in that place shall not be mixed but French. Similarly the *cadre* of the Instructors at Tangier shall not be mixed but Spanish. Provision shall be made to set on foot a police force of 100 men in each of the cities of Arzila, Alcazar, and Azemur, the *cadre* of the officers being Spanish in the first two places and French in the third. The Regulations Commission shall make the alterations which may seem to be expedient in the numbers of the contingents of the different ports, always within the Act of Algeciras.

In the Riff (to be interpreted as including also the Gomara region) and in the southern portion of the Empire, beyond the River Mesa, which will in fact be the frontier of Ifni owing to the establishment of Spain in that place, the Government of His Catholic Majesty intends to cause the Makhzen to apply a régime analogous to that which is set forth in Article 3 of the Hispano-Moorish Convention of the 16th November, 1910.([2])

II.

Since it is necessary that the Makhzen should have the means required to apply the measures contemplated by the preceding Article, the Government of the French Republic will exert its influence over the holders of the 1904 and 1910 loans, notwithstanding any of the clauses of their contracts, with a view to their accepting immediate reimbursement of that portion of their contributions which is secured on the Customs receipts and property of the Makhzen, on the Sultan's share of the Urban Tax, Mostafadet and Sakat, etc in the ports of Tetuan, Tangier and Larache. The Government of His Catholic Majesty will come to an understanding with the Makhzen concerning the manner of providing it with funds for this reimbursement, either directly or by means of some loan to be guaranteed by the Spanish State, so that the annuities for interest and amortization being less than they now are, something may remain over which could be applied to the above objects.

The Government of the French Republic, for its part, concedes to the Government of His Catholic Majesty the security and the rights which have been conceded

([2]) [*cp. supra*, pp. 156–8, No. 169; and pp. 170–2, No. 184. *v.* also *Martens, 3rd Ser.*: (Leipzig 1913), VII, pp. 94–100.]

to it by the Makhzen over the said revenue, in the financial agreement of the 21st March, 1910. As compensation the Government of His Catholic Majesty concedes to the Government of the Republic the security and the rights belonging to the former over the mines revenue of the Makhzen in the regions to be determined by common agreement.

The Government of His Britannic Majesty takes act of the foregoing in the letter and spirit of Article 8 of the Franco-British Declaration of April 8, 1904.(³)

And the undersigned, duly authorized, holding it to be expedient that the above Protocol be communicated to the Cabinet of Berlin and to the other Signatories of the Act of Algeciras, agree that this shall be done jointly by the Representatives of the three countries accredited to each of the said Powers.

MINUTES.

The object of the Spaniards is, and always has been perfectly clear : they want an absolutely free hand to do exactly what they like without any interference in their sphere, which includes Tangier, Tetuan, Laraiche and Alcazar, besides large mineral wealth and a big forest. The French are to have no say at all in anything that concerns this sphere. They want to divide up Morocco, *like [sic] we and the Russians have divided Persia,*(⁴) with the ultimate object of incorporating their sphere in the Spanish dominions. Of course this cannot be allowed; and the great difficulty, not to say insuperable objection, to meeting most of the present Spanish demands, is that the Spaniards are totally unfitted to manage their sphere owing to the incompetence and corruption of their agents.

In Sir M. de Bunsen's valuable summary the Spanish demands are divided into six heads :

1. Financial arrangements. The Spanish grievance is justified.
2. Police. This could be arranged, except as regards Tangier, and the French are ready to meet Spanish wishes.
3. Engineers. The difficulty is chiefly due to the personality of M. Llorens who is utterly useless. It will be a difficult thing to say so to the Spaniards. The Spanish pretension that the Algeciras Act meant the two engineers to be equal is absurd, as the Act talks of a " principal " and " assistant " engineer. The mining regulations were accepted and signed by Spain.
4. Tangier must remain " international." The Spanish claim cannot be entertained for a moment.
5. Loans. We have the same grievance as Spain. It could be remedied in the future, but not in the past.
6. Spanish language. The French will no doubt agree to this. (I doubt this. E. A. C.)

M. Geoffray is pro-Spanish and very anxious to meet their demands, but he thinks the greater part of them quite impossible. If this is M. Geoffray's view the French Gov[ernmen]t are hardly likely to be more " coulant " and the outlook is not good.

M. Geoffray expects to get his instructions on Monday next and we shall no doubt hear what they are. Till then we are hardly called upon to express any opinion; after all, we have never yet said we would consent to being officially concerned in any written instrument published or unpublished such as the Spanish Gov[ernmen]t now propose.

G. H. V.
18/5/11.

It is impossible to believe that France will accept the proposed Declaration or any substantial part of it. We had better hold back with any expression of opinion.

E. A. C.
May 19.

We can only wait to hear what the French have to say about these proposals.

They have been very greedy about the financial arrangements and may be able to do something towards removing the Spanish grievance in that respect.

(³) [*v. Gooch & Temperley*, Vol. II, p. 405, *App.*]

(⁴) [Marginal comment by Sir Eyre Crowe : " No. We have not divided Persia in that way. Nor do we claim or exercise any of the rights of administration and military advice which Spain exercises and wishes to extend. E. A. C."]

Meanwhile it might be useful to have Mr. Lister's observations upon the effect which these proposals if accepted would have upon British interests, more especially at Tangier and on the south-west coast.

W. L.

There is a good deal to be said on many of the points raised in this memo[randum], but it is hardly worth while analysing it in detail, as the final agreement will doubtless have modified it greatly.

A. N.

No. 267.

Count de Salis to Sir Edward Grey.

F.O. 18556/16083/11/28.
(No. 139.)   Berlin, D. May 14, 1911.
Sir,   R. May 16, 1911.

I have the honour to transmit to you, herewith, translation of a communiqué which has appeared in the "Norddeutsche Allgemeine Zeitung," contradicting a statement made by the "Wiener Allgemeine Zeitung" that steps had been taken by the Russian Government at Berlin with a view to bringing about a *détente* between France and Germany in the Morocco question.

You will observe the acrimonious tone in which it has been thought necessary to deny that the Russian Government have taken any step of this kind on behalf of the French.

I have, &c.
J. DE SALIS.

Enclosure in No. 267.

Extract from the "Norddeutsche Allgemeine Zeitung" of May 13, 1911.

(Translation.)

The Press campaigns respecting the Morocco question which were lately sharply criticised are continued by a new incorrect announcement in the "Wiener Allgemeine Zeitung." The paper now announces that the Russian Government have taken a mediatory step in Berlin to bring about a *détente* in the Morocco question, basing their action on their treaty obligations towards France. To this statement the following answer has been sent to the "Kölnische Zeitung" from Berlin:— This statement constitutes a mischievous distortion of the simple fact that the Moroccan question has lately formed the subject of several friendly conversations both between other Cabinets and between the German and Russian Governments. There has been no question of a mediatory step on the part of the Russian Government, as there has been no cause for mediation on the Moroccan question between Berlin and Paris. Nor has there been any cause for attention to be drawn to Russian Treaty obligations towards France in the Moroccan question, and this has in fact not been done. Both Governments have received communications as to the French intentions in Morocco which as far as we know, were in the main identic and were accepted in both quarters with the same confidence in the loyalty and sincerity of the French Government. Clear expression has, as we have reason to believe, been given to this feeling of confidence in the conversations between German and Russian statesmen. Moreover the point of view of the German Government was recently so clearly and openly expressed that it should be regarded as all the more satisfactory in view of the fact that neither the general situation nor the attitude of the German Government towards it have in any way changed since then. It is regrettable that the 'Wiener Reichspost' has also joined these speculations, and in a Berlin letter has dealt with the Moroccan question in some rather strange observations from the point of view of the German-Austrian-Russian relations. Such discussions are, to say the least, pointless. Combined with the sensational rumours mentioned above they make it difficult for the Press to maintain a moderate tone in dealing with the Moroccan question as should be done in dealing with so important a subject no less by serious papers than in official quarters.''

No. 268.

Sir F. Bertie to Sir Edward Grey.

F.O. 18530/13911/11/28.
(No. 215.)   Confidential.   Paris, D. *May* 14, 1911.
Sir,   R. *May* 16, 1911.

I have had the honour to report to you in another despatch of this date(¹) the anxiety which M. Cruppi feels in regard to the state of affairs in the Ottoman Empire and the predominance of German counsels and interests at Constantinople. His fears on the subject of German influence are not confined to the Ottoman Empire. He says that the German Government are egging on the Spanish Government to make unreasonable claims in regard to the position of Spain in Morocco so as to create a situation giving an opportunity for Germany to hope to obtain something for herself out of the trouble which the German Agents may succeed in bringing about and Spain is foolishly playing into Germany's hands and aspires to undertake matters for which Spaniards are quite unfit. His Excellency is quite ready, he says, to make reasonable concessions to Spain within the provisions of the Act of Algeciras and the Secret Agreements of 1904 but there seem to be no means of satisfying the Spaniards without imperilling French and British interests. He is very grateful for what you have done at Madrid in the way of restraining the Spanish Government from precipitate action; but if the German Government were convinced by some way or another of the determination of England to uphold the Act of Algeciras and the Secret Agreements regarding Morocco, they would probably abstain from encouraging Spain to advance unreasonable claims and complications would be avoided. He is willing that Spain should have a freer hand in the neighbourhood of Ceuta, but he objects to a Spanish occupation of Tetuan for which there is no reason and he cannot think that it would be consistent with British interests that Germany who by favour of the Turks is to have a privileged position at the Eastern end of the Mediterranean, viz., at Alexandretta, should gain a footing at the Western end of that sea opposite to Gibraltar by a permanent Spanish occupation of Tetuan, for assuredly if the Spaniards remained there it would be with German acquiescence and for German purposes. These are the views which I gather from a conversation with M. Cruppi yesterday that he holds in regard to the position which may be created by the attitude of Spain if persisted in with Germany at her back.

With regard to some observations which you have made to the French Ambassador in London on the subject of the Sultan Mulai Hafid and the extent of the support which the French Government may be inclined to give to him in view of his unpopularity in Morocco M. Cruppi stated to me that he does not fully share your views. He considers that Mulai Hafid and his brothers, Pretenders to the throne of Morocco, are all much alike when in power and when not. They are unreliable and though generous in promises of reform, when Pretenders, neglect, when in power, to fulfil them. So also of the Grand Viziers. If the French Government did not support the authority of the recognized Sultan at the present moment they would be open to the charge of disregarding the *status quo*, and Germany would proclaim the fact. It had become the duty of France to go to Fez for the succour of the French and other Europeans there. I remarked that the fear you had was

(¹) [Not reproduced.]

that if the French troops entered Fez it would become difficult for them to come away unless they entirely subdued the revolted tribes and such an undertaking might require a long stay and bring Germany out of her present expectant attitude. I asked M. Cruppi whether, if after the relief of Fez it should be found that the greater part of the country would not accept Mulai Hafid, the French Government would continue to support him, His Excellency said, but rather hesitated in his reply, that in such case the French Government would reconsider the position. He evidently attached great importance to the Sultan having applied to the French Government for their aid for he referred to the fact several times. Probably he feels that a successor or substitute to the present Sultan might not follow the same course. His Excellency ignores the fact that it is only the desperate situation of Mulai Hafid in regard to his own people which causes him to appeal to France. I have heard indirectly that it has been intimated to the Spanish Government on the part of the French Government that a Spanish occupation of Tetuan for no other reason than the French advance to Fez might be very inconvenient to Spain, for the Spanish troops would be expected to evacuate Tetuan as soon as the French troops withdraw from Fez.

I have, &c.
FRANCIS BERTIE.

MINUTES.

We have directed Sir M. de Bunsen to make the desired intimation to the Spanish Government. The telegram (No. 54) was sent on May 9,(1) and was repeated to Paris at the time. It seems curious therefore that Sir F. Bertie did not mention this in reply to M. Cruppi's remark.

Since then we have instructed Sir M. de Bunsen to make a further representation on the subject of the dangers involved in any Spanish move towards Tetuan—and this instruction has also been repeated to Paris.

With the general remarks of M. Cruppi respecting the attitude and policy of Germany it is impossible not to agree. But it is also certain that the danger of German interference will be proportionate to the degree to which France will allow herself to be entangled at Fez. It is difficult to follow or assent to the argument that the present Sultan must be backed up. Nor is it quite true to say that he differs in nothing from his brothers. He has some qualities which distinguish him favourably from them : his energy and determination. But as a ruler he has been a failure owing to his cruelties and rapacity, in which he seems clearly to surpass all possible rivals.

The French would probably do wisest to let the Moors themselves settle whom they will accept as Sultan.

E. A. C.
May 16.

M. Cruppi, as we know through the French Ambassador, wishes us to make a communication not to the Spaniards but to the Germans.

The conduct of Mulai Hafid and El Glawi has been intolerable and makes the support of the French difficult to justify.

W. L.

We must not forget that the south of Morocco whence El Glawi comes will doubtfully accept what the north may agree to. The French should not tie themselves to Muley Hafid and they may find it useful to let Muley Zin mount the throne if accepted by Ulema etc., but for the present we have said enough to the French and should await development of events.

A. N.

It was not regarded as a change in the *status quo* in Morocco when Abdul Aziz was deposed and Mulai Hafid took his place and I do not see why another change of Sultan made at the instigation of the tribes should have any effect on the political *status quo*.

E. G.

(1) [v. supra, p. 230, No. 254.]

No. 269.

Sir F. Bertie to Sir A. Nicolson.

Private and Confidential.(¹)

My dear Nicolson,   *Paris, May* 14, 1911.

. . . .(²) Cruppi is generally alarmed all round. He says that the composition of the new Turkish Cabinet is very unsatisfactory. Hakki Pasha and the new Finance Minister being entirely pro-German. The Government by the Committee of Union and Progress cannot continue much longer and there will probably soon be trouble in the Balkans. The Yemen revolt still continues and the Turkish soldiers sent thither will die of fever. The Grand Shereef shows signs of shaking off the Turkish yoke. Spain is foolishly playing into Germany's hands and aspires to undertake jobs for which she is quite unfit. · Germany is on the watch to see what she can grab out of any trouble that she can create by her intrigues and England is so occupied by her unfortunate internal difficulties that Germany may think that she is a "quantité negligeable." If only the understanding between France and Russia and England could be made more active and evident the danger from Germany of troubling the peace of Europe would be averted for the German Government would hesitate to try the game of bluff. He is very grateful for what Sir Edward Grey has said at Madrid. He would like the German Government to be convinced of the determination of England to uphold the Act of Algeciras and the secret agreements. He is quite ready to make reasonable concessions to Spain within the provisions of those engagements, but there seem to be no means of satisfying the Spaniards without imperilling French *and* British interests. Caballero is *intransigeant*. Cruppi is willing that they should have a freer hand in and about Ceuta, but he objects to their establishing themselves at Tetuan and he cannot think that it would suit England that the Germans who are going to have a privileged position at the Eastern end of the Mediterranean at Alexandretta by favour of the Turks should gain a footing behind the Spaniards at Tetuan at the Western end of that sea opposite to Gibraltar for assuredly if the Spaniards remained there it would be for German purposes.

As to Mulai Hafid and the Pretenders to the throne of Morocco Cruppi considers them all alike whether in or out of power. If the French Government dropped Mulai Hafid at the present moment they would be open to the charge of departing from the *status quo* and Germany would proclaim the fact. The French must go to Fez to succour the besieged. I said that what Sir Edward feared was that the French Government might find it difficult if they entered Fez to get away unless they entirely subdued the revolted tribes which might be a long job and bring Germany out of her attitude of watching. I asked him whether if after the relief of Fez it should be found that the people [of] the greater part of the country would not accept Mulai Hafid, the French Government would continue to support him. Cruppi rather hesitated but said that in such case the French Government would reconsider the position. He insisted a good deal on the Sultan having appealed to the French Government for their aid. Probably he does not feel that his successor or substitute would do the same. He ignores the fact that it is only the desperate situation of Mulai Hafid that causes him to appeal to France.

You will see that Cruppi was in a despondent state. What he, Jules Cambon and I suppose Paul Cambon also and many others hanker after is something more visible to Germany and useful to France than the existing *Entente* between England and France. The French Government have found it very useful in restraining Spain, but they do not feel sure how far they could rely on it if Germany became threatening

----

(¹) [Carnock MSS., Vol. II of 1911.]

(²) [The omitted paragraphs refer to Franco-Belgian relations and Anglo-French financial policy in Turkey.]

or bluffed. This feeling is useful to us as a security against France committing imprudences in her discussions with Germany, but it is also a danger as France might if hard pressed give us away in a question important to British and not to French interests, as Sazonow gave away at the Potsdam interviews both France and England. I quite understand and appreciate the difficulty for H[is] M[ajesty]'s Government to anticipate events by a formal and binding agreement in furtherance of the *Entente* with France, but everything military and naval ought to be arranged unofficially to meet the contingency of British and French forces *having* to act together. Otherwise in these days of quick locomotion we might arrive a day too late for the fray and find our essential interests already compromised. Perhaps those arrangements *have* been made.

Yours ever,
FRANCIS BERTIE.

No. 270.

Sir F. Bertie to Sir Edward Grey.

F.O. 18528/8457/11/28.
(No. 213.)   *Paris*, D. *May* 15, 1911.
Sir,   R. *May* 16, 1911.

I have the honour to transmit to you, herewith, a report which I have received from Colonel W. E. Fairholme, Military Attaché to this Embassy, relating to the military situation in Morocco and the progress of the French expedition.

I have, &c.
FRANCIS BERTIE.

Enclosure in No. 270.

Note by Colonel Fairholme on the Situation in Morocco and Progress of the French Expedition.

---

1. *On the Casa Blanca Side.*

Partly owing to the rough weather which has impeded the landing of stores, troops, and animals at Mahedieh, General Moinier's preparations for the dispatch of the relief column have taken a good deal longer than had been anticipated in France, and the column, under Colonel Brulard, only left El Knitra on the morning of the 11th May.

The latest news of it, unofficial from Tangiers, dated the 14th, states that it had passed the latitude of Lalla Ito, and that it had been caught up by Colonel Gouraud's supporting column on the 12th, the latter force being then 1,500 strong.

If all goes well the relief column is expected to reach Fez on the 20th or 21st. The exact route to be followed depends on the state of the roads and the attitude of the tribes, but that viâ Sidi Gueddar, Jebel Telfat, and Sidi Malek is spoken of as likely to be adopted.

A force of about 600 tribesmen, both mounted and on foot, was encountered a few miles from El Knitra, but was easily dispersed by artillery fire. Serious opposition was expected to be met with at Mechrat-er-Remla.

Colonel Brulard's column numbers about 3,000 men, and is reported to be composed as follows:—

1 battalion of colonial infantry.
1 battalion of Senegalese Rifles.
1 field battery, 2 sections mountain artillery.
½ squadron chasseurs, ½ squadron spahis.
A light field ambulance.

The Goum of the Shawia, consisting of 800 infantry and 200 horsemen, divided into six self-contained sections.

In support of Colonel Brulard's column is a detachment of all arms, commanded by Colonel Gouraud, which numbers about 1,800 men. Its mission is to secure the communications of the column with its base near Rabat. This body of troops had arrived at El Knitra by the 9th May; there were then encamped at that place some 8,000 French troops of all arms.

The total of French troops, white and black, in the Shawia and on their way to Fez now amounts to about 20,000, including the original garrison. Some 15,000 reinforcements have been dispatched to the Shawia and to Algeria since the 18th April, when the General Staff first got orders to prepare for an expedition; 2,000 mules were purchased in Algeria and shipped to the Shawia.

As might have been expected, the enforced delays and the consequent inactivity of the French troops at El Knitra have been taken as a sign of weakness by the tribesmen, who have become bold and enterprising, and have carried out a series of successful raids on convoys passing between Mahedieh, Rabat, and El Knitra, while on the 7th instant they even dared to attack the camp at the latter place. The attacks on the convoys were facilitated by the cover afforded by the forest of Mamora, close to which the road hitherto followed by the convoys passes. On the 6th and 7th the Moors captured 149 camels and 60 mules in this manner, and killed or wounded several French officers and men.

The escorts of the convoys are now being strengthened, and a safer road employed.

2. *On the Algerian Side.*

So early as the 30th April it was reported that some 12,000 men had been concentrated in the Taourirt region.

General Toutée, who commands the Oran division, was on the 8th May at Merada, a village on the eastern bank of the Mouloya, with a force of about 3,000 men and twenty-four field and two mountain guns.

His instructions apparently precluded him from crossing the river, but this did not prevent his shelling the village of Guersif on the western bank on the 9th May to punish the inhabitants for harbouring the murderers of a French subject, an inn-keeper named Mul.

Next morning a strong contingent of tribesmen crossed the ford at Guersif and advanced with great determination to attack General Toutée's camp at Merada. A force of about 2,500 men of all arms was sent out to meet them, and after a sharp engagement, during which the Moors suffered heavily, drove them in disorder across the Mouloya. The tribesmen left thirty-four of their dead lying on the battle-field, and are reported to have received a severe lesson.

It is stated that General Toutée's instructions are to be ready to throw a bridge over the Mouloya, but not actually to construct it without further orders.

The French Government has been severely criticised in various quarters for not undertaking the relief of Fez from the Algerian frontier side, but we know that General Toutée's forces are not equipped with the necessary transport for operations at a long distance from railhead.

Spanish susceptibilities have also to be considered, as the Taza route would bring the French rather nearer to the Spanish sphere of influence than is considered desirable.

3. *Situation at Fez.*

Official news was received from the French consul at Fez, dated the 6th May. The situation is apparently becoming more critical. The town had been attacked on the 4th by forces estimated to number 10,000, which is 3,000 more than the figures spoken of in connection with previous attacks. The attack is said to have only been repulsed with difficulty.

The news of the dispatch of the relief expedition seems, however, to have raised the spirits of the defenders of Fez.

The Sultan has renewed his appeal to the French Government for help, and the latter has now confirmed General Moinier's previous instructions to expedite the dispatch of the relief expedition to raise the siege of Fez, which town it is only to occupy for as long a time as may be strictly necessary.

A message from the British consul at Fez, dated the night of the 7th to 8th, describes the situation as extremely precarious.

4. *The Gharb Region.*

The situation is becoming strained in the El Ksar district, where a small mehalla under a French officer, Captain Moreau, supported by the horsemen of the Kaïd Cherkawi, is having difficulty in keeping order.

The market of Souk-el-Arba was threatened on the 10th May with an attack by the Beni-Ahsen and Sherarda tribes.

5. *Spanish Activity near Ceuta.*

An official telegram from Melilla announces that a Spanish column commanded by General Larrea has arrived at the Quebdana tribe, near the Mouloya River.

W. E. FAIRHOLME, Military Attaché.

Paris, May 15, 1911.

No. 271.

Minute by Sir A. Nicolson.

F.O. 18712/13751/11/28.
Sir Edward Grey,   *May* 16, 1911.

The important passage in the enclosed letter from de Bunsen is that which refers to the intention of Spain to occupy Tetuan if the French occupy Fez. We know that the latter intend to carry out the latter measure, temporarily, and as they have now informed the Cabinets officially of this intention we may expect any moment to hear that the Spaniards are advancing on Tetuan. It is not difficult to appreciate the importance and possible consequences of such action. We sent a tel[egram] to Madrid yesterday counselling prudence and caution &c, and I am afraid it would not be of much avail to repeat these counsels at Madrid, but perhaps Villa Urrutia might be asked to come down to the F[oreign] O[ffice] tomorrow and have some friendly advice tendered to him.

A. N.

Ask him to come. I will see him tomorrow afternoon.

E. G.
16.5.11.

Enclosure in No. 271.

Sir M. de Bunsen to Sir A. Nicolson.

Private.
My dear Nicolson,   *Madrid, May* 14, 1911.

I am sending the Spanish statement of grievances u[nder] f[lying] s[eal] to Bertie, having a safe opportunity tonight. It is some good, I think, having a concrete set of demands before us in black and white, instead of the vague generalities the Spaniards generally deal in. Geoffray thinks it will do as a base of discussion. What can of course never be admitted is the restriction of Tangier to Spanish influence exclusively, as they want. Otherwise it would be well if the French could make a few concessions. In the long run, however disagreeable to our Colonies in Morocco, I suppose it *is* in our interest that Spain should establish her influence along the north coast of Morocco. If not, why did we insist on France squaring matters with Spain, as a condition of our assenting to the entente of April 1904? France did so, and is now being held to her secret engagement. If she pleads the Act of Algeciras, Spain will say the Act has ceased to exist in practice, for the French hold on the Showia and on the Ujda, Tourirt, Debdu region is never likely to be relaxed.

There was a theatrical performance at the French Embassy last night—very good Paris performers who came for the occasion, and all beautifully done—for the King and Queen and all the Royalties. I suppose the French Gov[ernmen]t thought it worth while to give the show, for the Geoffrays could hardly have paid for it out of their private means. The King spoke both to Geoffray and myself in the most friendly way, saying he had backed up the idea of a frank discussion of the situation with France and thought it ought to lead to a practical result. Whether it does or not, the French offer to hear what Spain had to say has done some good. The tone of the Government communiqués to the Press is quieter than it was, and I think they are holding their hand to see what happens.

But France, and we too, must be prepared for a dash on Tetuan if France goes either to Fez or Taza. Canalejas again told me last night this move would be inevitable if either of those things happened. I said I could not see how Spain w[ou]ld be able to justify such a breach of the principle of the integrity of the Empire, which she professed to uphold. At this he smiled, and mentioned Tourirt, Ujda, and Debdu—in French occupation already, and not likely to be ever abandoned. I don't think Geoffray himself would care two straws if Spain *did* take Tetuan. He is a strong anti-Colonial and hates the Regnault policy. He always says the Cambons agree with him, especially Jules Cambon who " voit noire," and would be very glad to keep out of Fez. I mentioned in one of my telegrams that Prince Ratibor spoke to me at length in the sense that it would be quite natural for Spain to respond to the " unnecessary " occupation of Fez by the equally unnecessary occupation of Tetuan. No doubt he expresses the same opinions to the Spanish Government. This makes it difficult for France and England to say to Spain *you shall not go to Tetuan,* unless we are prepared to prevent her *effectively.*

Meanwhile I have told the Spanish Gov[ernmen]t we mean to stick to the 1904 Treaty with France and to the Algeciras Act.

Martin, the French Conseiller, goes to Paris tonight with the Spanish Memorandum and is to tell M. Cruppi that his chief thinks some concessions must be made. He is also taking my despatch to be left at our Embassy in Paris.

I am grateful for the instructions I have received on the present situation.

If no complications occur making it desirable I sh[oul]d stay here, I am proposing to go on leave about the end of the month, and hope to see you soon after. My wife has not been well lately, and I shall be glad to take her away for a change. Except for the King's funeral I have not been in England for 17 months.

Yours ever,

MAURICE DE BUNSEN.

No. 272.

M. Paul Cambon to Sir A. Nicolson.

F.O. 18711/8457/11/28.   *Ambassade de France, Londres,*
Cher Sir Arthur,   *le 16 mai,* 1911.

Je vous répète, comme vous m'en avez prié, ce que je vous ai dit tout à l'heure sur les intentions de mon Gouvernement au maroc.

Les dernières nouvelles du maroc montrent la situation à Fez comme compromise et le sultan réclame la prompte coopération de nos troupes. Le Gouv[ernemen]t Français a prescrit au Général Moinier de presser la marche de la colonne de secours pour débloquer Fez et même pour l'occuper le temps strictement nécessaire.

En me chargeant de porter cette décision à la connaissance de Sir Ed[ward] Grey, M. Cruppi me prie de lui déclarer que le but de notre action est toujours d'assurer la souveraineté du Sultan, l'intégralité du territoire et la liberté des transactions commerciales intimement liées au maintien de l'ordre et de la sécurité.

Votre sincèrement dévoué,
PAUL CAMBON.

No. 273.

Sir R. Rodd to Sir Edward Grey.

F.O. 19193/13911/11/28.
(No. 80.) Secret.   *Rome, D. May 16, 1911.*
Sir,   R. *May 20, 1911.*

I have the honour to report that I endeavoured this afternoon to sound the Minister for Foreign Affairs on the subject of Morocco and to ascertain whether he had any suspicion of the intentions with which Germany has been credited, by observing to him that there seemed to be a great discrepancy between the reports as to the actual condition of things at Fez emanating from German and French sources respectively, which suggested that the reports in question were rather inspired by political motives than the actual facts of the case. The Marquis di San Giuliano said that having no agent on the spot he had no first-hand information; he gathered however, from the reports he had received from Berlin that the French Ambassador had been quite satisfied with the attitude of the German Minister for Foreign Affairs. Italy is, however, as has on more than one occasion been admitted to me here, not consistently taken into the confidence of her partners in the Triple Alliance.

On the other hand it has come to my knowledge that the King of Italy, who is generally the best informed man in the country, has expressed considerable anxiety as to the probable attitude of Germany on the Moroccan question and has confessed to an apprehension that France may receive a sudden warning to halt, which, if it did not lead to the gravest issues, might create a feeling of bitter resentment and disturb the international situation for a considerable period to come.

I have, &c.
RENNELL RODD.

No. 274.

Sir Edward Grey to Sir M. de Bunsen.

F.O. 18911/13751/11/28.   *Foreign Office, May 17, 1911.*
Tel. (No. 61.) R.   D. 10·15 P.M.

I have urged on Spanish Ambassador the danger of Spain occupying Tetuan, representing to him that we desire two objects. (1) That French when they get to Fez should restore peace by a settlement with the tribes and come away as soon as possible without altering the political status of Morocco. This is French intention and we have expressed to them the hope that they will adopt line of least resistance to effect it. (2) That certain concessions should be made by France to Spain guaranteeing Spain against prejudice in her sphere and meeting her complaint of inferiority of her position under secret Franco-Spanish agreement.

If these objects are attained diplomatic difficulties as regards Morocco will disappear, and position of Spain will be better off than it has been before.

Occupation of Tetuan or unnecessary action by Spain in Spanish sphere will create new trouble, especially with Anjera tribes, will widen area of disturbance in Morocco and make attainment of these objects difficult if not impossible.

If these objects are made impossible, partition of Morocco will be ·forced, European complications will ensue and it is uncertain how anyone will come out of it.

Ambassador said he would report my views to his Government. Latter might wait for the present, but if French stayed at Fez no Gov[ernmen]t could live in Spain unless it occupied Tetuan.

I said if French stayed in Fez a new situation would arise, which would be considered then; but this did not make it necessary for Spain to move to Tetuan when French reached Fez.

Ambassador asked that you should be authorized to take part in discussion à trois; it was not a new treaty or convention that was under discussion and we were in a sense a party to existing agreements between France and Spain.

I promised to authorize this, and you can do it. This will, I understand, also be agreeable to French.

(Repeated to Paris and Tangier.)

No. 275.

Sir A. Nicolson to Sir F. Bertie.

Private.(¹)

My dear Bertie :—   *Foreign Office, May 17, 1911.*

. . . .(²) As regards the Morocco question you will have seen from the telegrams that we are doing our best to restrain Spain from taking any precipitate action, and Sir Edward Grey is seeing the Spanish Ambassador this afternoon and will repeat to him what Bunsen has already said at Madrid. In the letter from de Bunsen which you forwarded to me yesterday he says that we must be prepared for the Spaniards moving on to Tetuan in the event of France going either to Fez or Taza. and that Canalejas informed Bunsen on the 13th that such a move on the part of Spain would be inevitable in the case of France occupying either of the above two places. This is rather a serious matter as it is clear that the French column will in all probability be compelled to enter Fez. Cambon assures me that France will not keep her troops there a moment longer than is absolutely necessary. This I have no doubt is her present intention, but I am still sceptical as to whether she will find it easy to leave Fez once she has entered it, as she appears determined to maintain the present Sultan on his throne, in any case for the present. I think the French are making a mistake in giving support to the present Sultan but they consider, so far as I can judge from what Cambon says, that they are morally bound to afford him assistance as he has made such urgent appeals for it. There is no justification whatever for Spain wishing to occupy Tetuan; so far as our information goes all is quite tranquil in those regions, but the Spaniards state instigated thereto I daresay by the Germans that there is equally no necessity for France to go to Fez. They adopt the opinion of the Germans that all is quite tranquil in the capital and that the French have greatly exaggerated the dangers of the situation. The reports which we have received from our Consul and from Dr. Verdon entirely corroborate the information which the French Consul, who I know to be a very calm and cool-judging man, has sent to his Government. We have received the

(¹) [Carnock MSS., Vol. II of 1911.]

(²) [The first paragraph of this letter refers to Anglo-French co-operation in Constantinople.]

Spanish memorandum stating their grievances and desires: we will examine it as soon as it has been printed. I imagine that the French will be in Fez within a very few days. Although they may have some fighting I presume that they will have no great difficulty in clearing away the tribes from the city. It will then, however, be by no means the end of our difficulties, but it is useless to attempt to forecast what the developments may be.

We were a little puzzled at first by your telegram in regard to Cruppi's anxiety respecting our negotiations concerning the Bagdad Railway, but we now see that he was under the impression that we were negotiating at Berlin, which is not the case. We have not yet replied to the Turkish proposals and we have not said a word at Berlin as yet on the subject. Cruppi can remain quite assured that we should not give our consent to the four per cent. increase without having first consulted the French Government.

Grey had a conversation last evening with the German Emperor after dinner. The Emperor talked chiefly on indifferent subjects and the only reference which he made to political matters was the attitude at Montenegro in regard to the Albanian troubles. He did not mention a word as to Morocco and therefore, very naturally, Grey did not feel himself able to drag in that question. We are only waiting for a favourable opportunity of letting Berlin know that we intend to loyally adhere to the agreement of 1904. I dare say that Metternich will give us an opening to say something. The Emperor is making himself exceedingly amiable with everyone whom he meets and I expect he will carefully abstain from touching upon politics. However as his visit does not terminate until Saturday, he may before then emerge from his present reserve. Your long letter of the 14th[3] was shown by Grey to the Prime Minister and he had a talk with the latter in regard to extending our present 'entente' with France. I have my doubts whether it will be found possible to go as far as the French apparently desire us to do. [You can quite understand that there is considerable hesitation here to binding ourselves to any definite course of action in view of possible eventualites. Personally I should wish that some arrangement in the nature which you indicate could be made. I gather that there has been a certain amount of desultory talk between our military authorities and the French military authorities but nothing definite seems to have been laid down], and I have my doubts whether a concerted plan of action will ever be settled. [To my mind this is unfortunate and I quite agree with you that if a crisis does arise it will be sudden and probably unexpected.][4] However these are my personal opinions which I give to you for your own information only.

[A. NICOLSON.]

[3] [v. supra, pp. 247–8, No. 269.]
[4] [The sentences enclosed in square brackets are quoted in Nicolson, p. 351.]

No. 276.

Sir A. Nicolson to Sir M. de Bunsen.

Private.[1]

My dear de Bunsen:— *Foreign Office, May* 17, 1911.

Many thanks for your letter of the 14th.[2] We received the Spanish memorandum[3] last night and have naturally not yet had time to examine it carefully. I do not at all like the present outlok as it is clear now that the French will enter Fez and I am much afraid that this will lead to a counter move on the part of Spain towards Tetuan. I feel quite sure that you will do all that you possibly can to restrain the ardour of the Spaniards. They will no doubt be urged to take some action, not only by their own public opinion, but I daresay also at the instigation of

[1] [Carnock MSS., Vol. II of 1911.]
[2] [v. supra, pp. 250–1, No. 271, encl.]
[3] [cp. supra, pp. 238–43, No. 266, and encls.]

Germany. I am sorry that the French consider it necessary to uphold the present Sultan, even provisionally. It is clear that he is intensely unpopular and that he can only be retained upon his throne by military support. This will mean a somewhat prolonged stay of the French at Fez, even if it did not also carry with it expeditions into various parts of the country for the repression of disorder and for the protection of Europeans. We have given as strong a hint as was possible to the French that it might be prudent for them to acquiesce in the establishment of a Sultan who was more likely to win the approval of the tribes. They consider themselves morally bound to support the present man owing to his having made such urgent appeals for assistance. Grey is seeing the Spanish Ambassador this afternoon and will repeat to him what you have already said at Madrid. I do not think that we can go much further than we have done in the way of giving advice of a sober and restraining character. The whole situation is very delicate and unsatisfactory and will, I am afraid, become still more so. Probably at a later date when France is plunged deeply into troubles at Fez and elsewhere and when Spain has also begun to occupy places which she thinks it is essential for her to do, we shall then have Germany stepping forward and declaring that the Algeciras Act and all Conventions have gone by the board and that she herself must receive compensation, and I imagine that the compensation which she will require will be a pretty large one. So far as I can gather from Cambon's language I think that the French will be disposed to be conciliatory towards the Spaniards so far as they can and I quite agree with you that it would be quite impossible to admit Spain to an exclusive influence in Tangier. We might perhaps prefer to see Spanish influence in the North coast of Morocco to that perhaps of any other Power, as she is and will continue to be, a weak State which would not be particularly menacing to us. But what we do object to is that she should unnecessarily hasten the partition of Morocco, and if she occupies Tetuan, which she threatens to do immediately the French enter Fez, such an act would render it still more difficult for the French to evacuate. I think that there would be more likelihood of France leaving Fez within a reasonable time if Spain remains quiescent. There is no doubt that in the case of the occupation of Tetuan France would lay down as a condition for her departure from the capital that the Spaniards should also retire from the places which they had occupied. . . . .(⁴)

[A. NICOLSON.]

(⁴) [The concluding paragraphs refer to personal and general matters.]

No. 277.

Sir M. de Bunsen to Sir Edward Grey.

Madrid, *May* 18, 1911.

F.O. 18988/13379/11/28.
Tel. (No. 27.)

D. 9·50 P.M.
R. 10 P.M.

Your telegram No. 61.(¹)

I have communicated to the Minister for Foreign Affairs purport of your conversation with the Spanish Ambassador explaining the objects desired by His Majesty's Government and warning the Spanish Government against precipitate action.

(¹) [*v. supra*, pp. 252–3, No. 274.]

His Excellency was very grateful, but said that he was engaged in a daily struggle with the Prime Minister and Minister of Marine and Minister of War, who thought immediate occupation of Tetuan already justified in view of the action taken by France. He urges an early settlement of the Spanish demands.

(Repeated to Paris and Tangier.)

No. 278.

Sir Edward Grey to Sir E. Goschen.

F.O. 19139/13911/11/28.
(No. 115.)
Sir,   *Foreign Office, May 18, 1911.*

The German Ambassador asked me to-day([1]) whether I had any news from Morocco.

I said that the information we had had was that the state of things in Fez gave rise to great anxiety: as must necessarily be the case with all communications cut, the price of food rising, and the revolted tribes all round the town. I had been pressed in the House of Commons as to the possible danger to British subjects. I could not give a reassuring account of the state of things; but of course the situation was worse for the French, who had more subjects in Fez, including French Officers. The French clearly had no choice but to do what they were doing. I asked Count Metternich what the view of his Government was.

He replied that the French had given loyal assurances of their intention, and his Government quite believed that they did not desire to stay in Fez, or do more than they had said. If they were forced by circumstances to go further and make the Sultan a mere puppet in their hands, a new situation would have arisen, inconsistent with the Algeciras Act. In that case, the hands of the other Powers would of course be freed; but this situation might never arise.

I said that I hoped it would not arise; but, if it did, I hoped it would not stir up political difficulties. We did not wish to have the state of things of the Algeciras Conference over again, and I had hoped that the Agreement between Germany and France as to Morocco had removed any possibility of this recurring. The question of Morocco was one in regard to which some of us were bound by Treaty engagements, which would of course come into operation if difficulties arose. It was not like a general question in which there were no special engagements.

[I am, &c.]
E. G[REY].

([1]) [This conversation referred also to the Bagdad Railway question, and Sir Edward Grey's despatch upon this subject is printed in *Gooch & Temperley,* Vol. VI, p. 630, No. 466. *cp.* also *ib.,* p. 631, No. 467, and *note* ([2]).]

No. 279.

Sir F. Bertie to Sir Edward Grey.

Tel. Private.([1])   *Paris, May 18, 1911.*

The French Minister for Foreign Affairs told me to-day, under a promise of secrecy, with reference to the Spanish objections to the French going to Taza and to supposed German changed attitude if the French troops should remain more than a brief period at Fez, that he has resisted pressure from the French militant military party for an advance to Fez from the Algerian side, and has given instructions that an entry of the French troops into Fez should if possible be avoided, and native troops only be sent into the city.

([1]) [Grey MSS., Vol. 13.]

No. 280.

Sir M. de Bunsen to Sir Edward Grey.

F.O. 19177/13751/11/28.   *Madrid,* D. *May* 19, 1911, 10 P.M.
Tel. (No. 29.) R.   R. *May* 20, 1911, 8 A.M.

Your telegram No. 61.(¹)

Minister for Foreign Affairs is much pleased with report he has received from the Spanish Ambassador of your conversation with him showing the efforts you are making to bring about an understanding between France and Spain. Your warning about Tetuan has been noted, and the Minister for Foreign Affairs told me to-day that he would do his best to prevent a rash movement in that direction. (End of R.)

He also spoke with satisfaction of the first offer mentioned in Paris tel[egram] No. 59,(²) which the French Ambassador had just brought to his knowledge. Minister for Foreign Affairs is anxious about Alcazar, where, he says, neighbouring tribes are threatening disturbances in consequence of passage of El Amrani's column through the Gharb country. He claims that, if necessary, the Laraiche police, and not the French force, must be employed to protect Alcazar.

I said this was an excellent opportunity for the French and Spanish consuls at Alcazar to concert measures.

(Repeated to Paris.)

(¹) [*v. supra*, pp. 252–3, No. 274.]
(²) [Not reproduced. Tel. No. 59 from Sir F. Bertie of May 18, 1911, states that M. Cruppi had made two offers with a view to placating the Spanish Government. The first was to promote the French Consul at Tetuan, whom the Spaniards disliked, to another post; the second, that the French and Spanish Consuls at Alcazar should concert measures to avoid friction.]

No. 281.

Sir F. Bertie to Sir A. Nicolson.

Private and Confidential.(¹)
My dear Nicolson,   *Paris, May* 19, 1911.

At my interview with Cruppi yesterday on his mentioning that the attitude outwardly of the Germans was satisfactory I said that I had heard on pretty good authority that the German Minister for Foreign Affairs has stated that he would not regard the occupation of Fez as provisional if it lasted longer than three weeks, and that if that were his point of view a longer occupation might be followed by a German demand for a conversation and compensation. It was on this that Cruppi told me of the secret instructions sent to the French General to avoid if possible the entry of French troops into Fez and to send in the native ones if that would suffice. He said that every care would be taken to avoid giving to the German Government any opportunity to raise a question of a change in the *status quo*, and he felt confident of succeeding in that intention.

Yours ever,
FRANCIS BERTIE.

(¹) [Carnock MSS., Vol. II of 1911.]

No. 282.

Sir F. Bertie to Sir Edward Grey.

Paris, May 20, 1911.

F.O. 19272/13751/11/28.   D. 9·25.

Tel. (No. 61.)   R. 10·12.

Madrid Tel. No. 28 of May 18th.([1])

I met French M[inister for] F[oreign] A[ffairs] last night. He is not prepared to reduce period of fifteen years prescribed in the Secret Convention of 1904 and to give Spain now the free hand which the Spanish Government desire, nor to alter the Tangier police arrangements. He hopes that you will point out to the Spanish Government that the result of complying with their demands in those respects would be to alter the status quo and bring into question and discussion the Algeciras Act, and that you will use your influence to dissuade them from persisting in such demands. In other matters he is ready to make concessions to the Spanish Government.

MINUTES.([2])

Sir Edward Grey,   *May* 22, 1911.

I told M. Cambon today that I had submitted my d[ra]ft tel[egram] to Bunsen to you, and that you thought that it would greatly ease the situation with Spain if the French, instead of mentioning vaguely that the question of the Spanish sphere would be discussed later, were to fix a definite date—say the commencement of next year, when Spain would be freed from her *Etat d'infériorité*. M. Cambon personally saw no objection to this and said that he would submit it to M. Cruppi.

In these circumstances we might hold back our telegram to Bunsen (see 19272) till M. Cambon hears from M. Cruppi?

A. N.

I am very glad M. Cambon personally saw no objection to my proposal. It is one which we can urge Spain to accept. The vague proposal the Spaniards would have regarded as an attempt to put them off with nothing. They may not be satisfied with the mere definite offer but it is a fair one.

E. G.

([1]) [Not reproduced. It reported discussion of the policing of Morocco and the recognition of end of Secret Convention of 1904, between Señor Garcia Prieto, M. Geoffray, and Sir M. de Bunsen.]

([2]) [These minutes follow a series of others by Sir Eyre Crowe, Mr. W. Langley, Sir A. Nicolson and Sir Edward Grey. In the first of these Sir Eyre Crowe gives the draft of a telegram which he suggested might be added to Sir F. Bertie's telegram when repeating it to Sir M. de Bunsen. The draft was not sent, as the above minutes indicate.]

No. 283.

Sir M. de Bunsen to Sir Edward Grey.

Madrid, May 20, 1911.

F.O. 19344/13379/11/28.   D. 8·20 P.M.

Tel. (No. 30.) R.   R. 10 P.M.

Prime Minister declared to representatives of the press yesterday that there was no truth in story of an impending occupation of Tetuan.

The King of Spain said the same to me this morning, but spoke as if he hoped that occupation would take place a few months hence.

(Repeated to Paris and Tangier.)

No. 284.

Minute by Sir Edward Grey.([1])

F.O. 20058/20058/11/28.

May 22, 1911.

The French and Spanish Ambassadors have given me these separately. They must each have an answer.

E. G.

Enclosure in No. 284.

Le Gouvernement de la République Française et le Gouvernement de Sa Majesté le Roi d'Espagne, considérant qu'il serait utile de renouveler, pour une nouvelle période d'un an, le mandat qui leur a été conféré par Sa Majesté le Sultan du Maroc, pour empêcher la contrebande des armes sur les côtes de l'Empire Chérifien, l'Ambassadeur de la France serait heureux de savoir si le Gouvernem[en]t de Sa Majesté Britannique ne verrait pas d'objection au renouvellement de ce mandat. dans les mêmes conditions générales.

Ambassade de France, Londres,
    le 22 *mai,* 1911.

MINUTES.

I suppose that we must renew this mandate, though it is almost an impertinence of the French to ask it in view of their attitude towards the Arms Traffic in the Persian Gulf.

W. L.
A. N.

I have told the French Ambassador verbally that we consent and in doing so have made a reference to the Persian Gulf. The written assent can be communicated now to both Ambassadors.

E. G.

([1]) [This was answered by a note of June 3, addressed both to M. Paul Cambon and the Spanish Chargé d'Affaires, *mutatis mutandis*, in which Sir Edward Grey formally agreed to the renewal of the mandate to the French and Spanish Governments, down to the end of the year 1911.]

No. 285.

Sir Edward Grey to Sir F. Bertie.

F.O. 20049/13751/11/28.
(No. 177.)

Sir,   *Foreign Office, May* 22, 1911.

In speaking to M. Cambon to-day of his conversation with Sir Arthur Nicolson,([1]) in which he stated that the French Government proposed that an offer should be made to Spain to discuss at some future date her position under the Secret Agreement, while negativing her request that the period during which her liberty of action was restricted should be regarded as having now come to an end, I said that I thought this would not be an offer satisfactory to Spain. Spain would be sure to urge that, after France had sent troops to Fez and restored order, and after the possibility of complications with Germany had passed away and things had reverted to their normal condition in Morocco, she would then be met with the reply that, as everything in Morocco had reverted to its normal condition, it was unnecessary to alter

([1]) [*v. supra,* p. 258, No. 282, *min.*]

the Secret Treaty. It would be difficult to reassure her on this point, and she must get something out of the present situation if she was to be kept with us. I had therefore suggested that Spain should be promised that she should get her corresponding liberty of action on the 1st January next. If this were done, I should be prepared to tell her that the Secret Agreement must not be altered while the crisis in Morocco continued, and that she ought to be content with the near and certain prospect of obtaining the advantage which she desired.

M. Cambon personally raised no objection to this proposal. He would communicate it to M. Cruppi. He asked me whether I thought Spain ought to be promised her liberty of action from the 1st of January, or only that on the 1st of January France would negotiate with her to arrange this.

I said that, if it could be done, it would be better to promise liberty of action upon that date.

As regards Tangier, I said that I should be prepared to urge upon Spain that to alter the situation there would be to alter the situation created by the Act of Algeciras, and that Tangier was in an exceptional position and must remain so.

[I am, &c.]
E. G[REY].

No. 286.

Sir M. de Bunsen to Sir Edward Grey.([1])

Madrid, May 23, 1911.

F.O. 19794/13379/11/28.
Tel. (No. 32.) R.

D. 9·30 A.M.
R. 2·30 P.M.

Spanish Ambassador has probably informed you of the action taken this morning by the Governor of Ceuta in establishing a post of Spanish "Police" at a point on the road to Tetuan called Ponte Negron well beyond Police boundary fixed in Convention with Morocco of November 16th, 1910.

The pretext is an alleged assault on a Spanish fishing boat in that neighbourhood for which reparation could not be obtained from the Governor of Tetuan. It was no doubt more accurately described to-day to French Ambassador by Under Secretary of State for Foreign Affairs as "a little sop to public opinion." U[nder]-S[ecretary of] S[tate] for F[oreign] A[ffairs] said that the Spanish Government were trying to avoid occupying Tetuan.

(Repeated to Tangier and Paris.)

([1]) [Sir Edward Grey's telegram No. 64 of May 23, D. 11·15 p.m., reported a conversation with the Spanish Ambassador in which Sir Edward Grey "urged strongly that Spain should do nothing beyond what is described in your tel[egram] No. 32 which is already done." He said further that "some anticipation of date was open to discussion, though alteration of policing of Tangier was out of the question. Spain should keep quiet in Morocco and concentrate attention on the negotiations with France. It was not impossible that some points in these might be re-adjusted to her advantage which would be clear gain to her, for when present crisis was over she would have improved her position without risking money or anything in Morocco." F.O. 19794/13379/11/28]

No. 287.

Sir Edward Grey to Sir M. de Bunsen.([1])

F.O. 20522/13751/11/28.
(No. 46.)   Secret.
Sir,

Foreign Office, May 25, 1911.

The Spanish Ambassador complained to me to-day that the French answer to Spain made concessions only on trivial points, and was absolutely silent as to anticipating the date of putting Spain on an equality in her sphere.

I observed that this answer of the French had probably been drawn up before I last spoke to him. I had since impressed upon M. Cambon the importance which the Spanish Government attached to this point, and how impossible it would be to come to an arrangement at all if the Secret Agreement between Spain and France remained entirely unmodified respecting the terms of years. I was sure that the matter was still open for discussion, but the French might not yet have made up their minds as to what proposal they could make with regard to it.([2])

[I am, &c.]
E. G[REY].

([1]) [Also sent to Sir F. Bertie as No. 183, Secret.]
([2]) [M. Isvolski reports an interview with M. Cruppi on May 24 dealing with the Franco-Spanish situation, *v. Livre Noir*, I, pp. 105–8.]

No. 288.

Sir Edward Grey to Sir F. Bertie.

F.O. 20725/13751/11/28.
(No. 187.)
Sir,

Foreign Office, May 25, 1911.

I congratulated M. Cambon to-day on the arrival of the French at Fez.([1]) To have arrived there, to have found everything safe, and to have relieved the place without any fighting was a great success. It would complete the success if the French found that they were able to make a peaceful settlement, and leave soon. On the merits of the case, and from the point of view of public opinion, it was very desirable that one result of the settlement should be to redress the grievances and prevent the extortion and abuses from which the tribes had suffered. I hoped this would be achieved. It was a thing which I was sure would appeal to public opinion in France as well as elsewhere. In connection with this, I read to M. Cambon Mr. Lister's telegram no: 77.([2])

M. Cambon said that he had no information, but he saw in the Press that an amnesty was already a part of an arrangement. Of course, what the French had done would consolidate the power of the Sultan.

M. Cambon then observed to me that he was afraid Spain still had designs on Tetuan.

I told him in general terms the substance of my last conversation with the Spanish Ambassador, in which I had urged that the Spanish Government should do nothing beyond establishing the police post, which was already a *fait accompli*, and should concentrate their attention upon negotiations with the French Government. They would get some concessions, and they would get them for absolutely nothing.

([1]) [On the 21st May, *v.* immediately succeeding document.]
([2]) [This telegram of May 24 reported that Commissioner for Foreign Affairs at Tangier believed that the tribes would disperse if a general amnesty were guaranteed.]

I also told M. Cambon what the Spanish Ambassador had said about the importance of anticipating the date when Spain would be put upon an equality in her sphere.

M. Cambon said that he had not yet had an answer from M. Cruppi as to the suggestion which I had made about this.(³) Spain, by her action with regard to the police post, had already violated the Secret Agreement.

I observed that, however soon the French left Fez and however well everything went, one result would of course be that French influence would be much strengthened at Fez, and Spain would expect some compensation out of the situation.

[I am, &c.]
E. G[REY].

(³) [v. supra, p. 258, No. 282, min.]

No. 289.

Mr. Lister to Sir Edward Grey.

Tangier, May 26, 1911.
D. 4·50 P.M.
R. 9·15 P.M.

F.O. 20344/8457/11/28.
Tel. (No. 80.) Confidential.

I received cypher message from His Majesty's consul at Fez, dated 21st May, reporting arrival of French column. He adds that "Sultan and Mangin from vengeance and uselessly had about twelve villages of Ulad Jama raided and burnt this morning by Fez troops in contravention of assurances given me by French consul with regard to policy of pacification. Foreigners, except French, indignant. Much pressure may be required to prevent repetition of such useless destruction of property, much of which belongs to foreigners and protected persons." Special war correspondent of the "Times" with the column telegraphed in the same sense.

I drew serious attention of French chargé d'affaires to the matter this morning, which must, I said, produce a very bad impression. He agreed with me, but said he had heard nothing of it. The column, he knew, had shown special leniency on the march, which consuls rather feared might be interpreted as weakness by Moors.

I gathered from M. de Billy's attitude that there was no chance of any repetition of such action now that General Moiner had arrived. He read me instructions which he had just received from Paris for M. Gaillard. Latter is to have sole charge of negotiations with Sultan, but will of course consult general. In return for dispatch of column at Sultan's request he is to insist on reforms which may prevent repetition of abuses which have created the present situation. Measures are to be taken concerning assessment and collection of (? taxes) and for keeping strict account of all State revenues and expenditure on reorganisation of army and creation of a department for immediate examination and settlement of foreign claims.

M. Gaillard is further to consult Sultan as to modification of the personnel of the Government necessitated by situation. He is throughout to bear in mind necessity "de ménager la possibilité" of a prompt evacuation of Fez district by the French troops. M. de Billy had not been authorised to communicate these instructions to me, and begged that I would treat information as strictly confidential.

No. 290.

Sir M. de Bunsen to Sir Edward Grey.

F.O. 20509/13751/11/28.
(No. 73.)
Sir,

Madrid, D. May 26, 1911.
R. *May 29, 1911.*

With reference to my despatch No. 67 of the 19th instant(¹) I now have the honour to forward herewith a copy of a memorandum which the French Ambassador handed on the 24th instant to the Spanish Minister for Foreign Affairs.(²) It contains, under five headings, the concessions which the French Government are prepared to make to that of Spain in respect of the demands put forward by the latter in the confidential Memorandum and draft Declaration and Protocol, as transmitted in my despatch No. 63 of the 14th instant.(³)

The principal points are as follows :—

(1.) Satisfaction is given to Spain as regards the course of the proposed Tangier–Al Cazar Railway.
(2.) Moorish Department of Public Works to be recommended to employ preferentially Spanish engineers in connection with Public Works in and around Laraiche and Tetuan and especially on the Ceuta–Tetuan road.
(3.) French and Spanish Legations at Tangier will concert together with a view to settling questions that arise in the spirit of the Convention of 1904.
(4.) Provision is made for the employment of the Spanish language in certain cases.
(5.) French military instructors will not lend their services to set up permanent native military organizations within the Spanish sphere of influence; native troops accompanied by French military instructors will not operate so as to conflict with troops or police employed by Spain in virtue of the Act of Algeciras and her conventions with the Makhzen. Definition of duties of French officers at Tangier.

M. Geoffray explained to Señor Garcia Prieto that the question of a redistribution of the police forces now stationed in the eight open ports of Morocco was largely a financial question, and that it was therefore being carefully considered in Paris in consultation with the French Minister of Finance. There was every desire to meet the wishes of Spain on this point, except in respect of Tangier, which must retain its special character as the seat of the diplomatic body and other international institutions.

M. Geoffray informs me that his Government will firmly resist the Spanish demand for an advancement of the period when, under Art[icle] 2 of the secret convention, Spain would be invested in her sphere of influence with a greater degree of liberty than that which she at present enjoys.(⁴) I agree with His Excellency in thinking that the present French offer, if supplemented by a satisfactory rearrangement of the port police, will afford evidence of a sincere desire on the part of the French Government to meet the legitimate grievances of Spain.

A second meeting will now no doubt shortly take place between the Spanish Foreign Minister, the French Ambassador and myself in order to discuss in detail the new French proposals.

I have, &c.
MAURICE DE BUNSEN.

(¹) [Not reproduced. It reported the first informal discussion between Señor Garcia Prieto, M. Geoffray, and Sir M. de Bunsen.]
(²) [Not reproduced, as it is here summarized.]
(³) [v. supra, pp. 238–43, No. 266, and encls.]
(⁴) [cp. supra, p. 258, No. 282, and mins.]

No. 291.

Sir F. Bertie to Sir Edward Grey.

(By Post.)

F.O. 20340/8457/11/28.   *Paris,* D. *May* 27, 1911.
Tel. (No. 69.) Confidential.   R. *May* 28, 1911.

Morocco. Your despatch No. 177 of 22nd May.([1])

French Minister for Foreign Affairs spoke to me this evening about his negotiations with Spanish Government. He says that he quite appreciates force of your and M. Cambon's arguments in favour of giving Spain, on 1st January next, free hand which she desires.([2]) He cannot, however, decide such an important question without bringing the matter before the Cabinet, and for the last week, owing to Ministerial crisis resulting from aeroplane accident, it has been impossible to consider question. He has informed French Ambassador at Madrid that he will consult his colleagues on Tuesday, 30th May. He admits the danger of throwing Spain into the arms of Germany if concessions be not made to Spain, but he fears that if Spain be given free hand, which would have to be by a formal note, there may be danger of the German Government thereupon coming forward and saying that *status quo* contemplated by Act of Algeciras is non-existing and demanding a discussion, for he knows that everything that passes between the French and Spanish Governments is communicated to German Government by the Spanish Government.

French Minister for Foreign Affairs draws a great distinction between French informal consent or abstract objection to various Spanish proceedings and a formal recognition by France that a date named in secret agreement is to be anticipated by seven years. He thinks that inevitable result of such recognition would be the publication of secret agreement and possibly a serious European question.

([1]) [*v. supra,* pp. 259–60, No. 285.]
([2]) [*cp. supra,* p. 258, No. 282, *min.*]

No. 292.

Sir M. de Bunsen to Sir Edward Grey.

F.O. 21122/13751/11/28.
(No. 80.)   *Madrid,* D. *May* 27, 1911.
Sir,   R. *June* 1, 1911.

I proceed to give as connected and intelligible an account as I am able of the conversation which took place at His Majesty's Embassy this afternoon between the Minister for Foreign Affairs, the French Ambassador and myself. It had been agreed between us that we should meet once more, before the receipt by Monsieur Geoffray of his definite instructions which are expected in a few days, in order to talk over the preliminary counter-proposals which His Excellency had been authorised by telegraph to submit to the Spanish Government a few days ago, as reported in my despatch No. 73 of May 26.([1])

I knew from what Señor Garcia Prieto had let fall in conversation at his usual diplomatic reception yesterday afternoon that His Excellency was far from satisfied with the French offer. It had produced, he told me, a deplorable effect not only on himself but, in a marked degree, on the King and Señor Canalejas, the Prime Minister. I expressed surprise and said I had myself regarded the French proposals as indicating much good-will on the part of the French Government, which would

([1]) [*v. supra,* p. 263, No. 290.]

no doubt continue to discuss the further suggestions which Spain might have to offer in the same friendly spirit. But Señor Garcia Prieto harped on the point of the advancement of the second period mentioned in the Secret Convention and repeated what he had said so emphatically at our first meeting à trois, namely that failing compliance with this demand it would be mere waste of time to continue the discussion.

Our conversation to-day was opened by Señor Garcia Prieto who read us a telegram he had just received from the Spanish Ambassador in Paris giving an abstract of to-day's article in the "Temps" on the Morocco question. Monsieur Geoffray said the "Temps" was now the organ of the Colonial Party and therefore an opposition newspaper. The Foreign Minister replied that he saw little opposition between the words of the "Temps" and the actions of the French Government. France was now installed at Fez and Morocco was at her feet. Monsieur Geoffray protested against the implied rejection of all the assurances which France had given to the world as regards her intention to withdraw her troops from Fez the moment peace was restored and the Sultan's authority re-established. I said His Majesty's Government has frankly accepted these assurances, and I read to Señor Garcia Prieto the categorical statements made on these points by the French Consul at Fez to His Majesty's Consul, as forwarded to you by Mr. Lister in his telegram No. 78 of May 25(²). Señor Garcia Prieto replied that Spain had also accepted the French assurances, but that the entry of the French troops into Fez was nevertheless an event of a very disturbing character.

Turning to the French counter-proposals, His Excellency began by remarking that no notice was to be found in them of the all-important point of the advancement of the date when the second period of the 1904 Convention will begin to take effect. Monsieur Geoffray said that his Government had already stated its objections to any departure on this point from the terms of Article 2 of the Convention in question. He proceeded to argue that the desired anticipation of the date of 1919 would in practice be less advantageous to the Spanish Government than the proposals now made by France. His point was that the present proposals go beyond anything that France would be compelled to concede even if the second period were in full operation. There was nothing, for instance, in the General Act of Algeciras to compel the Sultan to restrict the action of his Mehallas within the Spanish sphere, or to select Spanish Engineers to design and execute Public Works at Tetuan and Larache. Yet France now freely offered her influence to secure these concessions for Spain. The same might be said of the other French concessions. They related to matters which would not be affected by the greater or less liberty of action enjoyed by Spain in her sphere, for her liberty of action, whether in the 1st or 2nd period, would continue to be restricted by the exercise of the Sultan's authority within the four corners of the Algeciras Act. Spain would lose and not gain by endeavouring to force on the 2nd period. She would obtain much better terms by friendly agreement with the French Government, which was naturally in a better position than ever before to influence the decisions of the Sultan. To concede the 2nd period would be to open the door to endless misunderstandings.

Señor Garcia Prieto replied, in excited language, that Spain took precisely the contrary view. Only by France acknowledging that circumstances had changed would she be able to obtain the elbow room which had so long been denied to her in her own sphere. France should yield on the point of the 2nd period, and, having done so, should use her influence with the Sultan to bring about the settlement desired by Spain, namely, the acceptance of the general principle that in the sphere subject to Spanish influence administrative and military acts should be performed through the agency of Spaniards. There would be nothing in this contrary to the Act of Algeciras, and it was extremely unlikely that Germany or any other country would protest. In angry tones His Excellency went on to say

(²) [Not reproduced.]

that, if the second period was refused, Spain would declare that the 3rd period of the 1904 Convention had arrived, the period namely which was contemplated in Article 3 of the Secret Convention. Who, in truth, could now honestly contend that the political *status quo* of Morocco still subsisted, or that the Sultan had not amply demonstrated his impotence to preserve the peace within his dominions? The conditions which Article 3 had in view were now manifestly fulfilled, and in the Spanish reading of the article there was nothing to require that Spain should abstain from proclaiming that patent fact until she could secure the concurrence of France. Señor Garcia Prieto repeated the argument on this point contained in the concluding portion of the Memorandum of Spanish demands. The French Ambassador said his Government interpreted the article differently, holding that the words "d'un commun accord" referred to all the conditions mentioned in the Article.

I here remarked that the French must be assumed to be the best interpreters of their own language, but that the point was not of great importance since it was obviously to the advantage of all concerned that no important decisions affecting the *status quo* in Morocco should be taken without a previous understanding between the three Powers chiefly interested. This observation provoked an extraordinary outburst on the part of the Foreign Minister. I am quite disposed, he said, to admit that what you say is true. We should be better off in the end if we took your good advice. But Spain lives largely on sentiment, and when impelled by sentiment she acts recklessly, without counting the cost. Call us, if you like, a nation of madmen. We are mad sometimes. We were mad to go to war with America. We are quite capable of committing a similar act of madness now. Very likely we should suffer for it. We should not mind, if we felt we were striking a blow to uphold our rights.

I appealed to His Excellency to discuss dispassionately the French proposals, and the remainder of the conversation passed off more peacefully.

His Excellency commented adversely on the several French suggestions for a settlement. In his opinion the share offered to Spain, both in the matter of the Tangier–Alcazar railway and in that of the employment of Spanish Engineers in certain places, was entirely inadequate. Some discussion followed between His Excellency and the French Ambassador on the subject of the duration of the Algeciras arrangements concerning the police of the ports. As Señor Garcia Prieto promised to recast his observations in the form of a written counter project, it seems unnecessary to trouble you with further details at present.

Monsieur Geoffray and myself remain under the impression that little progress has yet been made in these conversations towards a practical issue. The points of view are too widely divergent. Spain considers that the artificial fabric raised at Algeciras has broken down, and that the arrangements made in 1904 revive in their integrity. France has more in mind what she has accomplished since the Berlin Agreement of February 9, 1909, and she is endeavouring to prove that the present *de facto* situation is not inconsistent with the Algeciras Act. It is difficult at present to see how these opposing contentions can be harmonised.

I have, &c.
MAURICE DE BUNSEN.

No. 293.

Sir M. de Bunsen to Sir Edward Grey.

F.O. 20787/13911/11/28.
(No. 78.)   *Madrid*, D. *May* 27, 1911.
Sir,   R. *May* 30, 1911.
I take the liberty of forwarding a Memorandum in which I have endeavoured
to explain the grounds, as I understand them, of the present attitude of the Spanish
Government as regards Morocco.

I have, &c.
MAURICE DE BUNSEN.

Enclosure in No. 293.

Memorandum by Sir M. de Bunsen.

The main difficulty in adjusting the pretensions respectively of France and
Spain in Morocco arises from the different conceptions which have been formed from
time to time of the régime which it is desirable to set up in that country.   Three
distinct solutions of the problem have been successively devised, and consciously
or unconsciously embodied in international conventions.   The first was partition
into French and Spanish spheres of influence; the second internationalization; and
the third a more or less disguised French Protectorate.   In all three cases it was
provided that the independent authority of the Sultan and the integrity of the Empire
should be maintained.
1). Partition pure and simple into spheres of influence was the basis of the
Franco-Spanish draft Treaty of 1902.   Its terms were never published, and signature
was prevented by the refusal of Señor Abarzuza, then Spanish Minister for Foreign
Affairs, to be a party to an attempt to settle the Morocco question without the
ascertained concurrence of England.   There is reason to believe that the northern
portion of Morocco, reserved under this still-born arrangement to the influence of
Spain, included both Fez and Taza.
Partition, with the door left open to commerce, was also the idea underlying
the *entente* between England and France.   By the Declaration of the 8th April,
1904,([1]) England recognised that " it appertains to France, more particularly as
a Power whose dominions are conterminous for a great distance with those of
Morocco, to preserve order in that country, and to provide assistance for the purpose
of all administrative, economic, financial, and military reforms which it may
require."   But the existing Spanish establishments on the north coast were not to
be interfered with, and England secured from France the engagement to come to
an understanding with the Spanish Government with regard to the interests which
Spain " derived from her geographical position and her territorial possessions on the
Moorish coast of the Mediterranean."
On the strength of these provisos, Spain accepted, in the published Franco-
Spanish Declaration of October 3rd, 1904([2]) the arrangements contemplated by the
Declaration quoted above.   France carried out the bargain made with England in
respect of Spain by concluding with the latter country on the same date the Secret
Convention fixing " the extent of the rights and the guarantee of the interests "
possessed by Spain in Morocco.   By this instrument French and Spanish spheres
of influence were established on the lines of the abortive 1902 convention.   The line
of separation was drawn, however, a good deal further to the North, excluding both

([1]) [*v. Gooch & Temperley*, Vol. II, pp. 404–5, *App.*]
([2]) [*v. infra*, pp. 826–9, *App.* IV.]

Fez and Tazza from the Spanish sphere. It was also stipulated that Tangier should retain its special position as the seat of the Diplomatic body and various other mixed institutions.

France at this time seems to have accepted unreservedly the idea of partition, subject to the nominal maintenance of the Sultan's authority, and the integrity of his Empire. Spain was to exercise within her sphere precisely the same powers as those recognised by England in the Declaration of April 8, 1904, as appertaining to France throughout the whole country. According to the Marquis de Muni, Spanish Ambassador in Paris, and one of the negotiators of the secret Convention, there was at first no idea of assigning to Spain in her sphere a position inferior to that reserved to herself by France in the French sphere.

The restrictions finally embodied in Article 2 of the Secret Convention, which place a limit on the exercise of Spanish rights during the first period of the existence of the Convention, was inserted, as His Excellency asserts, in consequence of the unwillingness of the Spanish Government to accept entire responsibility for the maintenance of order within the Spanish sphere. France, in view of the Spanish hesitation on this point, reserved to herself the right of intervention in the Spanish sphere during a period which could not exceed 15 years (i.e., till 1919). Within the same period Spain was only to take action in her sphere after securing the assent of France. But notwithstanding these limitations the northern region of Morocco was to constitute from the date of the signature the sphere of influence of Spain (Article 3). Morocco from October 3, 1904, onwards, was to consist of two defined spheres of influence. The Convention of that date was communicated to His Majesty's Government, who offered no objection, the Convention thus becoming, as it were, part and parcel of the Anglo-French Declaration of April 8, 1904, which it rounded off and completed. In a further Convention, concluded in the following year but not communicated to His Majesty's Government, arrangements were made between France and Spain concerning the policing of their respective spheres of influence.

2. The visit of the German Emperor to Tangier in 1905([3]) struck a blow at the theory of the two spheres of influence, the effects of which continue to be felt. In 1906 the Conference of Algeciras, summoned under pressure from Germany, asserted the equal rights in Morocco of all the Powers. Thenceforward the theory of internationalization has held the field. A special position was assigned to France and Spain only as regards the frontier zones adjoining respectively the French Algerian possessions and the Spanish presidios. Within the frontier zones, the extent of which has remained undefined, matters relating to customs and contraband of arms were to be settled directly between the Makhzen and Spain or France as the case might be. A native police force was also formed in the eight open ports under French or Spanish instructors. In all other respects the position of the different Powers was held to be equal. Morocco was internationalized, and to a considerable extent remains so to the present day, as proved by the fact that Holland, one of the lesser signatory Powers of the Algeciras Act, was able recently to offer effective opposition to the adoption by the Diplomatic Body at Tangier of the Draft Mining Regulations laboriously drawn up by the four Powers principally interested in Morocco.

The dramatic circumstances under which the Algeciras Conference assembled and the publicity given to its resolutions, have caused the General Act which issued from its deliberations to become the chief constitutional charter of the Empire. It was however provided in its concluding article that " all the Treaties, Conventions, and arrangements of the signatory Powers with Morocco remain in force," the provisions of the General Act prevailing in cases of conflict.

Under this stipulation, Spain has continued to assert, as far as allowed, the prevailing rights which both France and England recognised in the 1904 Conventions

([3]) [v. Gooch & Temperley, Vol. III, v. index, sub William II.]

as belonging to her within the defined region. Her policy has been manifestly directed towards the rehabilitation of the theory of Spheres of influence, subject only to the fundamental requirements of the General Act as regards the independence of the Sultan and the integrity of the Empire. The former requisite has assumed gradually a more and more shadowy character. The latter was not held by Spain to be infringed by her conquest and occupation of the Riff. Her presence in the occupied region was said to be only temporary and terminable on the day when the Sultan should be in a position to exercise his own authority there. Spain holds that her rights under the Secret Convention were openly disregarded by the French when they proceeded to send military instructors to Tangier; to increase largely the French military Mission at Fez, thus getting into their hands, to the exclusion of Spain, the control of the entire military forces of the Sultan; and to allow Morocco to negotiate loans on easy terms at Paris, which loans are secured on Moorish revenues in the Spanish as well as in the French sphere of influence; an arrangement which, if carried out, will cause a swarm of French collectors of taxes to settle in the Spanish sphere, without provision being even made for their withdrawal after 1919 when the first period of the Secret Convention will expire. A great grievance was the provision made in the Paris loan arrangement of 1911 for a railway to cross the Spanish sphere of which no notice whatever was given to Spain. The part played by M. Porché, the French Chief Engineer on the Board of Public Works in thwarting the Spanish demands to be allowed to construct in concert with the Makhzen a road from Ceuta to Tetuan was also deeply resented at Madrid. Within the last two months Spanish complaints have been mainly directed against the employment of Alcazar as a basis of military operations for the relief of Fez. Alcazar being within the Spanish sphere it was contended that military assistance should have been drawn, if needed, from the neighbouring police force at Larache, or, if the latter were insufficient, from Spain and not from France.

On all these points, and many others, Spain contends that her just claims have been flouted by France which has thus continued to extend her own influence to an unjustifiable extent within the sphere which she agreed in 1904 should be reserved to Spain. In order to render French encroachments on the Spanish sphere less easy in the future Spain is now pressing for recognition of her contention that the first period of the Secret Convention during which her action was restricted in the manner described above should be held to have elapsed, and that the régime henceforward applicable in the Spanish sphere is one of unrestricted Spanish action so far as France is concerned and subject, of course, to the provisions of the Algeciras Act.

3. This aspiration conflicts, however, with the last of the three solutions of the Morocco question mentioned above, namely that of a French Protectorate. France, it is true, has repeatedly disavowed any intention of establishing a Protectorate over Morocco, or, in other words, of applying to that country the system which she has so successfully set up in Tunis. Spain admits the sincerity of this disavowal but doubts the ability of France to resist the natural tendency of events which, she contends, is impelling France to assume a control over the Sultan and Makhzen which amounts to a Protectorate in all but the name. Even Germany, according to this argument, has abandoned her championship of internationalization. By her agreement with France, of February 9, 1909 she disclaimed all but an economic interest in Morocco, and recognized that France has special political interests there which are closely bound up with the consolidation of internal tranquillity. Not a word is said of any concurrent Spanish interest, the inference being clear, as Spain further contends, that by this instrument Germany allows France to proceed unmolested to the consolidation of her political influence at Fez, so far as the Algeciras Act will allow; for liberty to take measures to keep the peace among insurgent tribes involves inevitably, in the hands of a strong Power the consequence that the Sultan becomes a mere puppet in the hands of his preserver. That the Makhzen, indeed, has long been entirely subservient to French influence was

clearly shewn during the negotiations which El Mokri conducted at Madrid with the Spanish Government in the autumn of 1910. El Mokri, as was well known to the Spanish Government, was in constant touch with the French Embassy, which inspired from day to day, in concert it is true with the British Embassy his replies to the demands of the Spanish Government. The Sultan's last struggle for independence was his refusal to accept at the beginning of the year 1910 the Draft of the Convention with France. The French ultimatum brought him to his knees and the Convention of March 4, 1910, confirmed triumphantly the ascendency of France. Since that date the Sultan has exercised no independent power. The first to repudiate his authority were the tribes surrounding Fez. He was only enabled by the skilled assistance of the French military mission to hold out against his rebellious subjects till the day of the entry of a French army into Fez. His future position, and that of his successors, must be equally dependent on French support. Nothing, in short, but a French protectorate, avowed or disavowed, will hence-forward keep a Moorish Sultan on his throne. The above is the drift of the arguments employed by Spaniards to justify their fear that, if they fail now to secure recognition of their claims under the 1904 Convention they will be deprived for ever of the field of expansion in Morocco to which their eyes have been turned since the loss of the Spanish colonies. France, they do not doubt, will then gradually force them back into their presidios, and spread herself over the regions which had been formerly assigned to Spain. It would be too late then to appeal to the conventions of 1904 or to the German assurance, somewhat grudgingly given in June 1909, that Germany continued to recognize the special political interests which Spain possesses in Morocco, and that the agreement with France of February 9, 1909 was in no sense directed against Spain.

Great pressure has been brought to bear on the Government to settle the question off hand by a forcible occupation of Tetuan and Larache. Under strong persuasion from London and Paris this course has been for the present rejected in favour of an effort to obtain satisfaction by means of a friendly discussion with France and England. If this fails, it may become a difficult task to restrain the Spanish Government from taking independent action.

The problem is how to reconcile the fundamental arrangements of 1904 with those which supervened at Algeciras in 1906 and especially with those which would seem to be the natural consequence of the all important Franco-German Convention of 1909.

I have, &c.
MAURICE DE BUNSEN.

MINUTES.

A very clear statement of the Spanish position.

The difficulty is however that the Spanish aim of finding in Morocco territorial compensation for the lost Spanish colonies cannot at present be realized except by repudiating the Franco-Spanish convention. It is true that Spain declares she does not desire to repudiate, but is willing to proceed by way of an amicable revision of that convention in her favour. But at the same time she threatens that if her wishes for a modification of the treaty are not met, and that at once, she will herself lay hands on what it is her ambition to acquire.

Spain's attitude somewhat resembles that of the United States in the matter of the repudiation of the Clayton–Bulwer treaty, which Great Britain formally consented to abrogate when the U[nited] S[tates] declared that if we did not consent, they would repudiate it.

E. A. C.
May 30.

The memo[randa] give a very clear account of Spanish aims and show equally clearly how incompatible they are with French policy and the situation created by the Algeciras Act.

W. L.

Sir M. de Bunsen should be thanked for his clear statement.

A. N.

It is very helpful of Sir M. de Bunsen to have sent this Memorandum.

E. G.

No. 294.

Sir M. de Bunsen to Sir A. Nicolson.

Private.(¹)

My dear Nicolson,   *Madrid, May* 27, 1911.

A few lines before the bag is made up to answer your very welcome letter of the 17th.(²) It is a great comfort to me to feel so thoroughly in touch with the Foreign Office and your kind expressions about my work here are very encouraging. I am sometimes almost embarrassed by the eagerness which both the Spanish Foreign Minister and the French Ambassador display to have me on their side. This after all is natural enough, considering that it was England that gave France her opening in Morocco on the express condition that France should come to an agreement with Spain. So both Powers appeal to England when questions arise as to the interpretation of the bargain. Fortunately I have found no difficulty in working in full agreement with Geoffray. He has been fairer to the Spaniards than his predecessors, Jules Cambon and Révoil. Just now he is annoyed with them, and I confess I am too, for the childish impatience and petulance displayed by Garcia Prieto in our present *pourparlers.* The French propositions seem to me perfectly fair, as a beginning, and Geoffray thinks them quite capable of further expansion. Instead of recognising the goodwill shown by France, Garcia Prieto yesterday raked up all the old accusations, threatened independent action, and behaved generally more like a naughty boy than a responsible statesman. Geoffray was good enough to tell me afterwards that he thought I had cut in at the right moments and been of some use in leading the discussion into peaceful channels. I do not feel, however, that much has been gained beyond keeping the Spaniards out of Tetuan at least till France had got into Fez. Geoffray thinks if Spain does now occupy Tetuan it will not so much matter. Meanwhile we both kept our tempers and showed every willingness to receive and consider the written comments on the French proposals which Garcia Prieto at last promised he would send in. So Spain cannot say she was compelled by *our* attitude to look after herself. If she kicks over the traces and does something foolish it will be an attempt to satisfy the very strong (though perhaps, ignorant or at least only half instructed) body of opinion which has formed itself in Spain on the Morocco question: France, as the argument runs, has long exercised a virtual Protectorate over the Sultan and his Empire. The entry into Fez has rivetted the chain. Enormous slices of Moorish territory have passed into French hands. Even if the Shawia be evacuated, it is to be re-occupied immediately by a native force under the French military mission. The French frontier has been shifted, without anybody's leave being asked, from the Kis to the Muluya. Spain is in occupation of the Riff. How then can anybody seriously talk of the independence of the Sultan and the integrity of Morocco? These expressions will not serve much longer even as a useful *façade.* The *façade* is fast crumbling to pieces, exposing the reality behind. That reality is a French Protectorate. If Spain does not speedily grab what she can, the Protectorate will soon be extended to the walls of her Presidios, and France will close her in on the south as completely as she does in the north.

Now supreme wisdom for Spain would of course be to show patience and rely on England to see her through and to prevent all these dreadful things happening. But the Government and country are weak and proud, and not blessed with a calm temperament. As matters stand, a dash on Tetuan would, I believe, be highly popular.

I think our cue is to continue endeavouring with France to bring about a fair settlement, failing which Spain must be allowed like a naughty boy to go and break a window if she is determined to be mischievous. As she only has the strength

(¹) [Carnock MSS., Vol. II of 1911.]
(²) [*v. supra,* pp. 254-5 No. 276.]

of a child she will perhaps not do much harm. But we shall give her no excuse for breaking away: and if she does she will be responsible for the consequences, which will probably not turn out to her advantage.

I am of course glad to put off my leave till it becomes evident that there is nothing I can usefully do by staying on.

Yours ever,
MAURICE DE BUNSEN.

No. 295.

Mr. Lister to Sir Edward Grey.

F.O. 20643/8457/11/28.
Tel. (No. 81.)

Tangier, *May* 29, 1911.
D. 11·50 A.M.
R. 2·30 P.M.

My Tel[egram] No. 78.(¹)

French Consul at Fez reports that Sultan wishes immediate advance to Mekinez and that no pity should be shown to Mulai Zin and his Government. General refuses to move until arrival of Gourauds column. He and French Consul both favour policy of leniency but I have pointed out to French Chargé d'Affaires that there can be no option in the matter after the positive assurances given by French Consul to H[is] M[ajesty's] Consul and transmitted by latter to Mekinez in a letter submitted and approved by Monsieur Gaillard. As assurances were actually conveyed by our Consul we should be placed in a very false position if they were disregarded.

(¹) [Not reproduced. It reported the French assurances that French troops would be withdrawn when peace was restored and the Sultan re-established.]

No. 296.

Sir Edward Grey to Sir F. Bertie.

F.O. 20643/8457/11/28.
Tel. (No. 131.)

Foreign Office, *May* 29, 1911.
D. 10·30 P.M.

Tangier telegram No. 81.(¹)

H[is] M[ajesty's] Gov[ernmen]t assume there is no danger of their being placed in false position indicated by Mr. Lister but it would be well to get this view confirmed; to carry out a policy of vengeance at instigation of Mulai Hafid would destroy all the prestige of the expedition to say nothing of extended operations, which it might entail.

(¹) [v. immediately preceding document.]

No. 297.

Sir F. Bertie to Sir Edward Grey.

(By Post.)

Private.(¹)
Tel. Private and Secret.

Paris, D. 9 A.M., *May* 30, 1911.
R. 9 A.M., *May* 31, 1911.

(? M[inister for] F[oreign] A[ffairs]) told me in strict confidence this evening that as he could not do anything in derogation of the secret agreement of 1904 without consulting its author and signatory he had spoken to M. Delcassé and found him

(¹) [Grey MSS., Vol. 13.]

strongly opposed to anticipating the term of restriction and giving the Spaniards the free hand which they desire.

French M[inister for] F[oreign] A[ffairs] is to see the President of the Council this evening. He is most anxious to meet your wishes in regard to concessions to the Spaniards as far as may be possible, but he finds himself in a very difficult situation. It would be no satisfaction to the amour propre of the Spaniards to make to them concessions unless they could announce them and if they were in derogation of the Algeciras Act Germany might intervene on their publication.

No. 298.

Sir Edward Grey to Sir M. de Bunsen.

F.O. 21078/13751/11/28.   Foreign Office, May 30, 1911.
Tel. (No. 70.)   D. 6 P.M.
 Madrid.

French Ambassador observes that Spanish Gov[ernmen]t ask that date fixed in Secret Convention for termination of first period restricting Spanish action in their sphere should be anticipated by a Protocol communicated to all Powers party to Act of Algeciras. I agree that this is impossible. Franco-Spanish secret convention is not part of Act of Algeciras and if modified it must be done by arrangement between Governments, who are parties to it and not as if it was an alteration of Act of Algeciras. If Spanish Gov[ernmen]t can get some satisfaction in substance I conclude they will not stand out for an impossible form.

(Repeat to Paris No. 132.)

No. 299.

Sir Edward Grey to Sir F. Bertie.

F.O. 21422/8457/11/28.
(No. 196.)
Sir,   Foreign Office, May 30, 1911.

I asked M. Cambon to-day whether he had any news from Fez. It was reported that the Sultan was very anxious for a policy of vengeance.

M. Cambon said that the Sultan was already committed to an amnesty, which included even Mulai-Zin, who had been proclaimed Sultan at Mekinez.

             [I am, &c.]
               E. G[REY].

No. 300.

Sir Edward Grey to Sir F. Bertie.

F.O. 20058/20058/11/28.
(No. 200.)
Sir,   Foreign Office, May 30, 1911.

In telling M. Cambon to-day that we agreed to the renewal for a year, under the same general conditions, of the mandate to France and Spain to suppress the contraband trade in arms in Morocco,(1) I asked him what answer I should give if I

(1) [cp. supra, p. 259, No. 284.]

[19656]   T

were pressed in Parliament as to why we gave this consent as regards Morocco, when the French did not consent to the suppression of the arms traffic in the Persian Gulf.

M. Cambon observed that the question of Muscat was one to be settled by compensation.

I replied that it would appear to people in Parliament that the suppression of the contraband arms traffic in Morocco could fairly be set off against the suppression of that in the Persian Gulf, without raising the whole question of French rights in Muscat.

M. Cambon said that we had no real interest in the arms traffic in Morocco.

I observed that the question of arms traffic in the Persian Gulf might be raised, and not altogether unfairly, in connection with that on the coast of Morocco.

[I am, &c.]
E. G[REY].

No. 301.

Mr. Lister to Sir Edward Grey.

Tangier, May 31, 1911.

F.O. 21101/8457/11/28.
Tel. (No. 84.) R.

D. 3·55 P.M.
R. 8·30 P.M.

Detailed reports from His Majesty's consul at Fez received to-day show that action of Moorish troops in raid of 21st was even more brutal than at first appeared.(¹) Some fourteen villages were burnt and pillaged. Real culprits had all fled; remainder, consisting principally of old men, were killed or taken prisoners. About eighty women and girls were brought into Fez and publicly sold into slavery by soldiers.

No respect was paid to the aman granted by Moorish Government and by French military authorities. I protested very strongly to French chargé d'affaires, and pointed out to him that result of such proceedings would be to range British public opinion with that of Germany against France.

He fully admitted justice of what I said, and seemed much upset at news, but hopes that instructions have now reached Fez giving full powers to French consul. This seems probable, as His Majesty's Consul at Fez reports that raiding was to have recommenced on following day, but order was cancelled by general, and a three days' grace, extended to eight, was proclaimed for insurgents to come in.

(Repeated to Paris.)

(¹) [v. supra, p. 262, No. 289.]

No. 302.

Sir F. Cartwright to Sir Edward Grey.

Vienna, June 1, 1911.

F.O. 21253/13911/11/28.
Tel. (No. 53.)

D. 12·30.
R. 2·45.

Morocco.

I found it impossible yesterday to obtain from Count von Aerenthal [sic: Aerhenthal] any definite expression of his views with regard to present state of Morocco question. He declared that one must wait and see what may happen now that the French have reached Fez and how they will deal with situation there. He expressed a hope that Act of Algeciras would not be torn up. To the French Ambassador he did not allude to Morocco at all even though it was their first meeting since the latter's return to the Foreign Office, so French Ambassador did not raise the question.

My personal opinion is that Austro-Hungarian Government would regret to be compelled to assume any attitude which might be disagreeable to the French Government owing to some mistake committed by the latter. They should therefore be very careful not to do anything which might be interpreted by Germany as a clear breach of Algeciras Act.

No. 303.

Sir M. de Bunsen to Sir Edward Grey.

F.O. 21259/13751/11/28.
Tel. (No. 39.)

Madrid, June 1, 1911.
D. 4·15 P.M.
R. 7·45 P.M.

French Ambassador will inform the Spanish Government to-day that the French Government agrees to a rearrangement of the Casa Blanca police, and proposes that the French contingent be distributed between Mazagan and Rabat and the Spanish contingent between Laraiche and Tetuan. The two Governments would come to an agreement as to the duration and financial basis of the new arrangements, which would then be submitted to the Algeciras signatory Powers.

As regards advance of second period mentioned in the secret agreement of 1904, the Spanish Ambassador at Paris was informed yesterday by the French Minister for Foreign Affairs that the French Government cannot consent to an alteration of the convention, but is determined to carry it out as it stands in such a way as to allow Spain to exercise (? at once) the full economic influence to which she is entitled in her own sphere. When the criticism caused by the relief of Fez has subsided the Minister for Foreign Affairs promises further that the French Government will be prepared to discuss amicably with the Spanish Government the question of political influence (? as) claimed within her sphere.

French Minister for Foreign Affairs informs the French Ambassador that the Spanish Ambassador seemed satisfied with above declaration. Spanish Ambassador at Paris is due to-day in Madrid.

(Repeated to Paris.)

No. 304.

Sir Edward Grey to Sir F. Bertie.

F.O. 21101/8451/11/28.
Tel. (No. 133.)

Foreign Office, June 1, 1911.

In view of facts reported in Mr. Lister's tel[egram] No. 84,(¹) H[is] M[ajesty's] G[overnment] are unable to receive a Moorish special mission on occasion of His Majesty's Coronation. You should inform El Mokri.

(Sent to Tangier.)

(¹) [v. supra, p. 274, No. 301.]

No. 305.

Sir Edward Grey to Sir F. Bertie.

F.O. 21625/21625/11/28.
(No. 202.)
Sir,

Foreign Office, June 1, 1911.

I spoke to M. Cambon to-day about the accounts which had appeared in the Press of the barbarities committed by the Sultan's troops near Fez. They were

[19656]

T 2

sure to make a great stir in this country, and a telegram from Mr. Lister received to-day confirmed them generally.([1]) It was impossible for me, after having defended in Parliament the necessity of the French expedition, to refuse to give any information; and I hoped that the French Government would make the facts known as soon as possible. If, as I supposed, their information was the same as that supplied by our Consul, I should then be able to say that what we had heard confirmed their account.

I added that it was clear that the Sultan wished to commit the French to very disagreeable things. I assumed that the responsibility for these barbarities was solely upon the Sultan and his troops; and we were telegraphing to say that a Moorish Mission could not be received at the Coronation.

M. Cambon said that he was going to Paris, and that he would get the fullest information for me from M. Cruppi.

[I am, &c.]
E. G[REY].

([1]) [v. supra, p. 274, No. 301.]

No. 306.

Sir E. Goschen to Sir Edward Grey.

F.O. 21734/4451/11/18.
(No. 152.)   Secret.
Sir,

Berlin, D. June 1, 1911.
R. June 6. 1911.

Shortly after my arrival from England on the 25th ultimo I called upon the Imperial Chancellor and had some conversation with him both on the visit of the Emperor and Empress to London and other subjects. . . . .([1])

By a very natural train of thought the Chancellor asked me what I had heard of the Morocco question when I was in London. I said that I had had the advantage of some conversation with you on this subject and that it was your view that in the face of the reports received from Fez the French Government could not have acted otherwise than they had done and that full confidence could be placed in their assurances that after they had restored order the French force would leave Fez as soon as possible. You were moreover strongly of the opinion that every allowance should be made for the difficulties of the situation, and that in view of their avowed intention to do nothing which could be regarded as contravening the Act of Algeciras, no pressure of any sort should be brought to bear upon them from any quarter which might result in their leaving their difficult task unfinished. I added that you hoped above all that no political discussions of an international character would arise out of the situation, as in that case England would have to abide by her treaty engagements and the grouping of the Powers would, you presumed, be the same as at the time of the Algeciras Conference. The Chancellor replied that the Imperial Government, while not encouraging the French expedition as, from the reports they had received from Fez, they had failed to see that there was any very special or urgent necessity for it, had raised no objections whatever, and, as I could not have failed to perceive, had observed the calmest and most correct attitude possible. This attitude they would continue to maintain and it was far from their thoughts to object to the French troops remaining at Fez for a reasonable time for the purpose of restoring order. They had however always thought, and still thought, that circumstances would be too strong for the French and that they would be unable to carry out their assurances, which he was convinced had been given in perfect good faith.

([1]) [The omitted paragraphs give details of the visit of the Emperor and Empress to London (May 15–20), and refer to the negotiations for the exchange of naval information and a general understanding. They add nothing of importance to the information already printed in *Gooch & Temperley*, Vol. VI, pp. 577–665, *passim*.]

I asked His Excellency what he considered to be a "reasonable time"; but to that question I neither obtained, nor did I expect to obtain, any answer.

My Italian colleague tells me that he has put the above question to nearly everybody in the Imperial Foreign Office from the Chancellor downwards and has never obtained the slightest inkling of what the Imperial Government considers to be a reasonable time for the French to remain in Fez. Herr von Kiderlen had indeed given him an answer though not a direct one: he had said:

"When France contented herself with peaceful penetration, time was on her side and the game was in her hands. By precipitating matters she has lost her advantage and the game now bids fair to be in our hands."

The Chancellor concluded the conversation with these words:—

"There is one thing I can tell you which is that the situation in Morocco does not cause me the very slightest feeling of anxiety."

I have, &c.
W. E. GOSCHEN.

MINUTES.

The Chancellor's reference to Morocco was quite satisfactory and M. Kiderlen's was significant.

W. L.
A. N.

No. 307.

Sir Edward Grey to Sir F. Bertie.

Private.([1])
My dear Bertie,   *Foreign Office, June 1, 1911.*
I am afraid that, unless Spain can be put in a more equal position in her sphere as regards France, we shall not be able to hold her.

The French have enormously strengthened their position in Morocco by what they have done, and Spain will expect to have her position strengthened in her sphere. But I think that the *demand of Spain that this should be done by a political communication sent to the Powers of the Algeciras Act([2]) is illogical and unreasonable. It should be done by a modification of the Secret Agreement between France and Spain; and the Spanish Government must get what public credit they can by some general statement that they are satisfied that their liberty of action in Morocco will not be prejudiced by French influence, and that this has been the outcome of communications which have passed between the two Governments.

I am very sorry that Delcassé opposes any thing of the kind, because we cannot hold Spain unless she gets some thing substantial out of the situation. I should have thought that it was surely better to run the future risk of Spain being foolish in her sphere on her own responsibility rather than to increase the immediate risk of political complications in Europe in connection with the present crisis.

If things calm down and the French get away from Fez, it will be much more difficult for Spain to take any action which would precipitate an international crisis than it is at the present time. We are already skating on very thin ice, in maintaining that the Act of Algeciras is not affected by all that has happened, and every week that the French remain at Fez the ice will get thinner.

([1]) [Grey MSS., Vol. 13.]
*Cambon tells me this is what Spain has asked, but de Bunsen does not know of it.
[E. G.]
([2]) [*cp. supra*, p. 273, No. 298.]

If the Act of Algeciras does go by the board, the partition of Morocco between France and Spain will ensue. I do not suppose that it would be impossible to get Germany's consent to this; but it would be necessary to pay a price for the consent: though that price need not necessarily be anything in Morocco.

Yours sincerely,

E. GREY.

No. 308.

Sir E. Goschen to Sir Edward Grey.

F.O. 21741/13911/11/28.
(No. 159.)
Sir,

Berlin, D. *June* 2, 1911.
R. *June* 6, 1911.

In the course of a short conversation which I had with Herr Zimmerman to-day, the subject of Morocco came up and I repeated to him more or less what I had said to the Chancellor a few days previously, namely that you hoped that the situation would lead to no discussions of a political nature.(¹) Herr Zimmermann said that he hoped so too and that he did not anticipate there would be anything of the sort provided of course that France did what she had to do " within a reasonable time " and did not change the whole political situation by remaining at Fez indefinitely. He added that the German Government were as anxious as anybody that no political discussions should take place as in that case he presumed that Germany and England would again find themselves, so to speak, in opposite camps. This would, particularly under present circumstances, be highly disagreeable to Germany and her Government was anxious to do everything possible to avoid such an eventuality. I said that such a situation would be also disagreeable to His Majesty's Government, therefore I hoped that when he spoke of a reasonable time he meant time sufficient for France to have a chance of restoring order and effecting some good after the great trouble and expense to which she had been put by her necessary expedition. He said that whether the expedition had been actually necessary or not was a matter of opinion, but the German Government certainly did not wish to add to her difficulties by pressing her to retire prematurely. I then asked Herr Zimmermann what he considered to be a reasonable time for the French to remain at Fez, taking into consideration the difficulties with which he had admitted they had to cope. He replied that he thought a month or six weeks would give them ample time to do all that they had to do. He added that that was only a personal opinion and that he could not say what the views of the Imperial Government were upon the matter.

The greater part of the German Press is exercising quite as much reticence as the Government on the subject of Morocco and contents itself for the most part with reporting the movements of the French troops and the more salient features of the situation as they occur day by day. The pan-German Press on the other hand is extremely violent and calls loudly for the Government to take some action and change their " Sphinx-like " attitude. It is not necessary that I should trouble you with long translations of these diatribes; it is sufficient to say that in papers like the " Post " and the " Hamburger Nachrichten " all the stories about French barbarity, the selling of women and children in the Fez bazaars, the burning of villages belonging to inoffensive tribes, and particularly the reports as to the request of the Sultan that France should at once assume the Protectorate of Morocco, are raked together and put forward as reasons why Germany should take action at once. They say that one of the consequences of the apathy of the German Government

(¹) [*v. supra*, pp. 276–7, No. 306.]

is that the public is beginning to lose confidence in the hitherto much belauded Secretary of State for Foreign Affairs and that another consequence is that people abroad are gradually coming to the conclusion that Germany has made a bargain of some sort with France.

The "Post" states at some length that it is not at all sure that this latter idea is not correct and affects to have heard that France has offered in return for a free hand in Morocco, either to give Germany all she wants in the matter of the Bagdad Railway, or to hand over to her French Congo. As regards the Bagdad Railway the "Post" says that it is a commercial undertaking, for which a German Company holds the concession, and for the successful carrying out of which Germany has ample funds at her disposal, adding that Germany is not the least disposed to make the slightest concession for the admission of German securities to the Paris Bourse.

As regards the handing over to Germany of French Congo, the "Post" observes that Germany has already as much as she can stand of unhealthy tropical colonies. What Germany wanted and had not got was subtropical territory where Germans could live and work; Morocco was just such a country. "What Algeria is for France to-day," it adds, "Morocco can in 40 years be for Germany. A hundred thousand Germans could well settle there and prosper. Morocco produces everything we want and offers enormous possibilities for our manufactures, our merchants and our artisans. Moreover it lies only three or four days' journey from Hamburg. Such countries are not to be found in dozens on the face of the globe, and it is ridiculous to offer us as compensation for our share in such a country an unhealthy bit of tropical country like French Congo.

In conclusion the article from which I am quoting says that all such sort of compensation must be summarily rejected, that for Germany the partition of Morocco into spheres of influence was the only thing.

"We have in the meanwhile confidence that our Foreign Office really takes the same view and will look to it that Germany's sphere of interest when such a partition takes place will correspond in extent to her effective strength, her need for fresh territory and the stake in Morocco which her force represents."

These quotations will, I think, be sufficient to show you the line taken by the Pan-German Press on the Morocco question.

I have, &c.
W. E. GOSCHEN.

No. 309.

Sir F. Bertie to Sir Edward Grey.

(By Post.)

F.O. 21653/21615/11/28.
Tel. (No. 73.) *En clair.*

Paris, D. *June* 3, 1911.
R. *June* 4, 1911

Morocco.

Your telegram No. 133 of 1st instant,(¹) my private telegram to Sir A. Nicolson of the 2nd, and his reply of that date.(²)

I read to M. Cruppi this afternoon Tangier telegram No. 84 of 31st May(³) down to "military authorities," and I said that in the circumstances described His Majesty's Government could not receive a Moorish special mission for the Coronation. Would he therefore so inform El Mokri, who, he had requested me to inform you, had been appointed to represent the Sultan Mulai Hafid?

M. Cruppi, who has seen M. Cambon this morning on the subject, earnestly begs you to suspend your final decision in the matter until he has had time to

(¹) [*v. supra*, p. 275, No. 304.]
(²) [Not reproduced.]
(³) [*v. supra*, p. 274, No. 301.]

receive replies to telegrams which he dispatched to the French consul at Fez and to General Moinier on 1st June, calling for reports as to the real facts. He is informed that there were no sales of women and girls, and he is led to believe that the raiding and burning of villages and ill-treatment of their inhabitants, which he greatly deplores, were reprisals for their torturing and killing of the Sultan's messengers on their way from Fez to Tangier, some having had their eyes put out, others having been crucified or having been hung up by their feet, and others killed.

M. Cruppi has given instructions that the Sultan is to be warned that such acts as are attributed to him cannot be permitted by the French Government. He says that the refusal to receive a Moorish mission at the Coronation will be a great blow ("une atteinte sérieuse") to the position of the Sultan, whose sovereignty it is the policy of the French Government to support as the ruler of Morocco. He admits that Mulai Hafid is a barbarian, but he does not think that he is worse than his predecessors, and to diminish his position at the present moment may have serious consequences to French policy as showing a divergence between the French and British Governments, and giving an opportunity to the German Government for mischief.

MINUTES.

I understand Sir E. Grey has definitely decided that the Moorish Mission will not be received.

G. H. V.
6/5/11.

But of course if it should turn out that we were misinformed as to the facts, the matter will have to be reconsidered. We must wait and hear what the French consul at Fez reports. But meanwhile it would be well to repeat this telegram to Tangier and to request Mr. Lister to inform Consul McLeod that the French gov[ernmen]t seem inclined to discredit the report as to the sale of slaves. Mr. McLeod should report fully and with some precise detail both what happened and on what authority he has relied for his statements.

E. A. C.
June 6.

There is still time to allow El Mokri to come if the reports are contradicted as he is in Paris. At present there is nothing to show that the French have, as requested, warned him that we cannot receive the Mission.
Q[uer]y. Telegraph to Mr. Lister as suggested.

W. L.

Reports, since these minutes were written, have been received from Mr. Mcleod which leave no doubt as to facts. Unnecessary therefore to telegraph to Mr. Lister.

A. N.
E. G.

Sir A. Nicolson,
We cannot reverse the decision not to receive a Moorish Mission. The Sultan's rule has admittedly been cruel and brutal and the facts are notorious. The news of the recent vindictive brutalities is confirmed by our Consul at Fez as we know from a telegram from Mr. Lister.

I can defend French policy here much better by saying that France will stop the brutality of the Sultan, than by condoning it as I should have to do if the Mission was received.

E. G.
5.6.11.

No. 310.

Sir F. Bertie to Sir Edward Grey.

(By Post.)

F.O. 21654/13751/11/28.　　　　　　　　　　　　　　Paris, D. *June* 3, 1911.
Tel. (No. 74.) Confidential. *En clair.*　　　　　　　　R. *June* 4, 1911.

M. Cruppi gave me the following information this afternoon :—

He saw on the 31st ultimo the Spanish Ambassador, who was starting for Madrid. He had a long conversation with him, and found him much calmer than hitherto. He told the Ambassador that the French Government could not possibly consent to alter the secret agreement of 1904, or other conventional arrangements regarding Morocco, for to do so would reopen the whole question and cause grave complications; but the French Government would be ready to make to Spain, without derogation to treaty agreements, the greatest possible concessions financially and in matters of police and otherwise within the Spanish sphere.

MINUTES.

It is to be hoped that there will not be a repetition of the arrangement by which British commercial interests are sacrificed in order to conciliate Spanish (as formerly German) demands. Commercial Dep[artmen]t.

E. A. C.
June 6.

The " otherwise " is disquieting.

W. L.
A. N.
E. G.

No. 311.

Sir F. Bertie to Sir Edward Grey.

(By Post.)

F.O. 21655/13751/11/28.   *Paris, D. June 3, 1911.*
Tel. (No. 75.) Confidential.   R. *June 4, 1911.*

I again suggested to the French Minister for Foreign Affairs this afternoon that, unless he made large concessions to Spain, she might make use of Germany to gain her ends. His Excellency said that so long as the French Government pursued the policy, which they fully intended to do, of observing their treaty engagements, the German Government could have no ground to make objections to French proceedings, of which they had received proper notice. The French troops were not in Fez, and they would withdraw from the vicinity of it as soon as possible. The instructions to General Moinier were to that effect, and he was directed to do nothing contrary to the Algeciras Act or the independence of the Sultan, but to arrange with him for the re-establishment and maintenance of order and the institution of reforms, and to organise posts of Moorish soldiers with French instructors to keep up communications between Fez and the coast.

No. 312.

Sir A. Nicolson to Sir F. Bertie.

Private.(¹)
My dear Bertie :—   *Foreign Office, June 8, 1911.*

I am glad to see by the telegram which we have received this morning that Monsieur Cruppi does not intend to make difficulties in regard to our refusal to receive the Moorish Special Mission, and that he has appreciated the position in which we are placed. You will receive the despatches from our Consul at Fez which put beyond all manner of doubt the facts which were summarized in Lister's telegram on which we took our decision to decline to receive the Mission.(²) Had they arrived here there would in all probability have been demonstrations in some sections of public opinion and undoubtedly questions asked in the House of

(¹) [Carnock MSS., Vol. II of 1911.]
(²) [*v. supra*, p. 274, No. 301.]

Commons, and it would have been exceedingly inconvenient and embarrassing for us to have given a proper answer to them. By refusing to receive the Mission the question of the acts of the Sultan will be forgotten and no comments will be made. It would also have been somewhat difficult for us to have avoided criticisms being made as to the participation of the French military instructors in what occurred. On the whole I am quite sure that we have taken a right line and one which will enable us to co-operate in the future as we have done in the past in the French line of policy. I do not think that it looks very probable that the French will be able to withdraw to the coast so soon as they anticipated, but hitherto the Germans are remaining quiescent, and from the last conversation which Goschen had with the German Foreign Office,(³) it would seem that they are ready to give the French a month or six weeks in which to re-establish some kind of order in Fez and the neighbourhood, and if we can contrive in restraining the Spaniards, I daresay gradually we shall be able to get the Moorish question into smoother and easier paths.

We shall answer the memorandum which Cruppi sent you,(⁴) and I think we shall be able to show him that he is in error in the strictures which he passes on the conduct of the British protected subjects and especially on that of Menebhi; the latter in reality used what influence he has in furtherance of the requests which were made to him, through us, by the French Legation in Morocco, and I think it is unjust to accuse him of having fermented [*sic :* fomented ?] trouble.

I suppose you will be coming over here very shortly so I will not trouble you with a longer letter.

[A. NICOLSON.]

(³) [*v. supra*, pp. 278–9, No. 308.]
(⁴) [Not reproduced. In it M. Cruppi justified the action of the Shereefian forces in the Lemta region; expressed his regret that Menehbi and other British-protected persons should have acted in a hostile manner towards the Moorish Government and the policy pursued by France; and stated that the French Government had no intention of carrying out a policy of vengeance at the request of the Sultan, or of undertaking extended military operations.]

No. 313.

Sir E. Goschen to Sir A. Nicolson.

Private.(¹)
My dear Nicolson,   *Berlin, June 9, 1911.*

It was very kind of you to write me such a long letter when you are so busy. All you told me about the French in Morocco was most interesting. Their policy is indeed rather difficult to understand, but their job is so difficult altogether and the Spaniards seem determined to complicate matters still further. Polo de Bernabé, perhaps one of the most sensible of his race, is also now on the high horse and the other day he gave me the benefit of a long tirade on the subject of the French iniquities and the want of consideration shown by the French Gov[ernmen]t for Spanish interests and susceptibilities. He gave me the impression that his people in Madrid were rather disappointed to find de Bunsen taking up the cudgels for France so warmly. I told him that they were much mistaken if they thought that de Bunsen was in this matter either pro-French or anti-Spanish. He was, I knew, working in the best interests of Spain, to whom he was warmly attached, and that he was only anxious she should not lose by precipitate and ill-considered action the advantages she would be pretty sure to get if she met France half-way and in a conciliatory spirit. But he was not convinced. I agree with you, and it is the opinion

(¹) [Carnock MSS., Vol. II of 1911.]

of the Imperial F[oreign] O[ffice] who certainly ought to know, that it looks at the present moment as if Spanish action and the fact that France is entangling herself in punitive actions were likely to lead to the re-opening of the whole of the Morocco question. . . . .(²)

Yours very sincerely,
W. E. GOSCHEN.

(²) [The rest of this letter refers to general matters.]

No. 314.

Sir Edward Grey to Sir F. Bertie.

Private.(¹)

My dear Bertie,   *Foreign Office, June 9, 1911.*

There would have been a row here about the reception of a Moorish Mission after what appeared in the Times about the conduct of the Sultan's troops.

With Macleod's despatches in my possession I cannot palliate what has occurred; and if I were to attempt to condone it the result would be to disgust people here and make them feel that support of French policy took us into nasty places.

The only possible course for me is to admit the facts, and mark our opinion of them by a step which attributes the responsibility to the Sultan. I can say with truth that the Sultan's career of vengeance and barbarity was stopped as soon as General Moinier knew what was going on. The disagreeable feature is that the French officers in the employment of the Sultan were possibly, if not probably, with the Sultan's troops, and I fear the French Consul at Fez will not have moral courage enough to report the truth to Cruppi. I hope Cruppi will suspect this and understand that the real facts are in Macleod's despatch to me and that the only way for me to support French policy is to condemn the excesses of the Sultan's troops and emphasize the fact that Moinier stopped them.

I am afraid the French have got too deeply in to get out and they will have to go through with a partition of Morocco, in which there will be some difficult and rough water to navigate, and some price to be paid. But if the disagreeable day can be put off so much the better.

Yours sincerely,
E. GREY.

(¹) [Grey MSS., Vol. 13.]

CHAPTER LIII.

THE SPANISH LANDING AT LARAICHE AND ALCAZAR AND ITS RESULTS.

[ED. NOTE.—The following documents supplement the account of the events of June 1911, given below in the Annual Report, pp. 307–09, No. 335.

As shewn there, the Spanish troops landed at 7 P.M. on June 8 at Laraiche, and 500 of them were sent at midnight to Alcazar.]

No. 315.

Mr. Lister to Sir Edward Grey.

F.O. 22485/8755/11/28.   *Tangier*, D. *June* 9, 1911, 9·5 P.M.
Tel.   (No. 101.) R.   R. *June* 10, 1911, 8 A.M.

My immediately preceding telegram.([1])

Spanish Minister has just informed me of Spanish landing : he only knew bare fact but had sent torpedo-boat back for precise details. He appeared to think that force sent to Alcazar was composed of police possibly strengthened by soldiers.

He gave me definite assurance that measure was one of police and precaution and purely provisional in character. Panic had reigned in Alcazar for several days and appeals for help were being daily received from Spaniards there of which he said there were 30 with wives and children. Spanish Gov[ernmen]t had been obliged to take some action but were determined that that action should be on smallest possible scale ; (?) great respect would be shown for Moorish authorities—nothing was further from wishes of Spanish Gov[ernmen]t than to do anything which could violate Algeciras Act.

He was very nervous and official at first and then in a burst of confidence asked me what I thought of the whole thing. I replied that I certainly thought that (group omitted) ? situation had been seriously complicated by Spanish action but that I was glad of his assurances which I would at once communicate to you.

(Repeated to Madrid.)

([1]) [Not reproduced.]

No. 316.

Communication by Spanish Chargé d'Affaires.([1])

                                        Embajada de España en Londres,
F.O. 22563/8755/11/28.   *June* 10, 1911.

Señor Prieto to Señor de Villa Urrutia.

Tel.   *Madrid, June* 8, 1911.

Consejo Ministros examinó hoy noticias Larache Alcázar que confirman asesinato protegido español Benmalec y dos de sus hijos por gentes del pretendiente Fayza, las cuales habiendo apresado à aquellos en cabila Mesnuda hace varios dias y reclamado por su rescate veinte mil duros, les dieron muerte y maltrataron sus cadaveres paseando las cabezas por las tribus como tropeo y para excitar à los

([1]) [For M. Isvolski's views of June 6, *v. Livre Noir*, Vol. I, pp. 117–8.]

indigenas contra lo extranjeros. Semejante hecho ha causado en colonia y protegidos la mas honda impresión y pasividad del Gobierno ante tan bárbaro atropello, precipita la hora en que dos buques guerra españoles estacionandosé frente à Larache, seria interpretado como un abandono de los deberes de protección que al Gabinete Madrid incumben. Deseoso cumplir esos deberes, dentro del más escrupuloso respeto à Acta Algeciras, Gobierno de S.M. se limitará por el momento á poner en tierra parte dotacion de los buques, dando á este desembarco mas bien el carácter de una demostracion. Si medidas adoptadas por las Autoridades Jèrifianas para reparar atentado y castigo autores, resultasen suficientes, como es de esperar, Gobierno S.M. no necesitaria llevar mas adelante su acción. Las disposiciones mencionadas además contriburán, en el caso en que el estado del tiempo y las malas condiciones del fondeadero de Larache obliguen á los buques á retirarse, à dejar al Tabor, que es muy reducido en número, mayor libertad de movimiento y á levantar los ánimos de las colonias, especialmente en Alcazar ciudades abiertas donde el temor aumenta cada dia, á causa de la probabilidad de que el pretendiente rehaga sus fuerzas en la montaña, de que el cabecilla Uldelfa cumpla ser amenaza de mezclarse à la lucha con los contingentes que recluta en el Jemas y de que el desorden que ha sido y a causa robos y excesos en las inmediaciones de la localidad aumente.

GARCIA PRIETO.

MINUTES.

I understand the Spanish ambassador verbally asked for an expression of the views of H[is] M[ajesty's] G[overnment] on this communication.

If an answer is given, it will presumably be done verbally. In that case it might be said that H[is] M[ajesty's] G[overnment] have received this news with the greatest surprise in view of the fact that they were assured only recently that troops would not be landed. Their surprise is all the keener as even the assurance contained in the present communication has been at once belied by the Spanish authorities. The telegram says that action will be confined to a demonstration by landing at Larache. In fact however the landing force appears immediately to have marched to and occupied Alcazar.

The reports received by H[is] M[ajesty's] G[overnment] do not confirm the allegation that serious unrest exists at Alcazar, and they would recall that some time ago the Spanish reports from that place, which at the time spoke of the presence of large French military force, were found to be absolutely devoid of foundation.

H[is] M[ajesty's] G[overnment] had not expected that the Spanish gov[ernmen]t would openly violate the terms of the Franco-Spanish agreement of which H[is] M[ajesty's] G[overnment] at the time of its conclusion were requested to take formal note. They fear that the action of the Spanish gov[ernmen]t is likely to lead to the gravest political complications both in Morocco and in the general relations of the European Great Powers, and H[is] M[ajesty's] G[overnmen]t must leave to the Spanish gov[ernmen]t the full responsibility for the serious consequence which their ill-advised policy will surely bring about.

E. A. C.
June 10.

The Spanish Chargé d'Affaires brought in these telegrams yesterday. We had not at the time he gave me them had any reports from Tangier—and so I naturally thought that all that was contemplated was to land a small force at Laraiche—but I had no idea that the force would be 500 strong and would march on to Alcazar. I wish to give these explanations as had I been in possession of all the facts my language would have been different.

The Ch[argé] d'Aff[aire]s said he had been instructed to ask for an opinion. I said I could give him none as I had no data except those which he had furnished to me—and I did not see why a force should be landed at Laraiche because a Spanish protégé had been murdered by some tribes somewhere—nor did I see how the Moorish Gov[ernmen]t could be expected in present circ[umstance]s to arrest and punish the guilty parties. The Ch[argé] d'Aff[aire]s pressed for an opinion. I said I would give only as a personal opinion " that I regretted that the Spanish Gov[ernmen]t thought that a case had arisen which necessitated the disembarkation of a force at Laraiche." I said I would communicate the papers to you.

Since this interview we have heard that the force has been landed and marched on to Alcazar. There is no indication in the tel[egram]s communicated by the Ch[argé] d'Aff[aire]s that such a step was contemplated—and it is a most serious step. I would propose to wait till

Tuesday when you will be here, and the Spanish Ambas[sado]r will have returned and we shall have had fuller and further inform[atio]n, and we can then speak very seriously to the Spaniards.

A. N.

I will see the Ambassador on Tuesday. If pressed before that Sir A. Nicolson can speak as suggested in these minutes.

E. G.

No. 317.

Sir E. Goschen to Sir Edward Grey.

Berlin, June 11, 1911.
D. 7·20 P.M.
R. 7·30 P.M.

F.O. 22607/13911/11/28.
Tel. (No. 31.) Confidential.

French Ambassador communicated to Chancellor to-day French statement on Morocco affairs.

Chancellor received it in a very friendly manner, and said that it was very opportune in view of Spanish action; he gave, however, no indication of what he thought of the latter. My French colleague expressed hope that German Government would not take Spain's impulsive step too seriously, all the more that they would see from the communication just made that the French Government were not inclined to let it interfere with their intention to do their work as quickly as possible and then retire. M. Cambon took the opportunity to impress on the Chancellor that, whereas France had acted in accordance with the wishes of the Sultan and after informing Algeciras Act Powers, Spain had followed contrary course.

No. 318.

Minute by Sir A. Nicolson.

F.O. 23618/13911/11/28.
Sir Edward Grey,

Foreign Office, June 12, 1911.

The Spanish Ambassador called to-day. As you will see him to-morrow I need not go into detail as to what he said to me nor what I said to him, as the remarks to be made are pretty obvious.

There were, however, one or two points which came out in conversation which I should like to record. In the first place he said that in the early days of French intervention, France let it be understood that she would not seriously object to Spain going to Tetuan. Another point was, and this is more important, that France was offering Germany to come to terms with her and was intimating that France had much to offer in many quarters. Germany ostensibly and officially announced that no discussions were proceeding with France, and that she (Germany) thoroughly relied on France's word that the troops would be withdrawn as soon as possible: but she let Spain know that France was knocking at her door and trying to placate her. "A highly placed German" said to Spain, "La France commence à vouloir se ficher de nous: depuis longtemps elle s'est fichée de vous: mais l'Allemagne est assez forte de ne pas se laisser prendre." What troubles Spain is that France and Germany should come to an agreement and leave her out in the cold. This and much more the Ambassador will doubtless repeat to-morrow to you.

A. N.
E. G.

No. 319.

Sir Edward Grey to Mr. Rennie.

F.O. 23593/8755/11/28.
(No. 60.)
Sir,   *Foreign Office, June 13, 1911.*

I saw the Spanish Ambassador to-day, and told him that orders had been sent to General Toutée to withdraw to the Algerian frontier from Melilla. I expressed great apprehension as to the consequences of the Spanish action at Alcazar, which was not justified by any local circumstances; and I urged that the Spanish troops should at least be withdrawn from Alcazar to Laraiche.

The Spanish Ambassador said that this was absolutely impossible. Satisfaction must be given for the murder of the Spanish "protégé."

I observed that this "protégé" was a man of bad character, who had been rejected by the Germans, and who had been killed, I understood, in the French sphere. Was it really the case that, if compensation was paid, the Spanish troops would be withdrawn from Alcazar?

The Spanish Ambassador admitted eventually that the troops could not be withdrawn while French activity in Morocco continued. Spain must obtain some improvement in the situation in her sphere. France had refused to anticipate the date of the second period of Spanish liberty of action in the Spanish sphere. She had promised to discuss the matter later on, but Spain felt that she would have no chance of getting later on, when things in Morocco were quiet, what France was unwilling to give at the present moment. Spain was sure that France had already entered into communications with Germany to make a settlement as to Morocco, and if Spain had done nothing she would have been left out altogether. As for the protest of the Moorish Gov[ernmen]t against the Spanish action, this was purely formal (Guebbas had in conversation admitted as much); it was done at the dictation of France, and was merely another instance of the subordination of the Moorish Government to France.

I said that Spain was running two dangers. In the first place, she might throw into unrest the north of Morocco, which was now quiet; and she would then have imposed upon herself a very difficult task, such as she had in the case of Melilla, that would be very inconvenient to her. In the second place, she might precipitate a European crisis which would lead to the partition of Morocco; a price would have to be paid, and no one could say what the result might be for Spain.

The Ambassador said that, if there was a partition of Morocco, he thought Germany would be quite willing that Spain should occupy her sphere as an "enclave" in French influence.

I observed that no one could say what price would have to be paid, or what the outcome would be. Spain was playing with fire. I regarded the future with anxiety, and I would strongly urge his Government to be very careful what they did.

[I am, &c.]
E. G[REY].

No. 320.

Sir Edward Grey to Sir F. Bertie.

F.O. 23592/8755/11/28.
(No. 227.)
Sir,   *Foreign Office, June 13, 1911.*

M. Cambon spoke to me to-day of the grave consequences of the action which Spain had taken in occupying Alcazar and Laraiche. He said that if France took a severe line with Spain it would lead to a rupture, but we were in a stronger position; and in effect he said that it depended upon us to save the situation.

I told him what had passed with the Spanish Ambassador this afternoon, and said that the conclusion to which I had come was that it would be impossible to get Spain out of Alcazar until she obtained some satisfaction out of the situation. It might be possible to prevent her doing more than she had already done, and occupying other places; but if I pressed her too hard it would only throw her into the arms of Germany. It seemed to me from what the Spanish Ambassador had said that the view of Spain with regard to a partition of Morocco was that France, who would get the larger share, would have to pay some price; but that Germany would not be unwilling to see Spain have her sphere, and would not ask for a price from her.

M. Cambon then said that, if Spain looked to an agreement with Germany, France would naturally ask why she herself should not make an agreement with Germany without considering Spanish interests. Spain had practically torn up the Secret Agreement with France: and France need no longer recognise at all any Spanish zone in Morocco.

M. Cambon added that the friendship of Germany could not really be worth as much to Spain as the friendship of France and England. . . . .([1])

I said that the sentiment in Spain as to Morocco was undoubtedly strong. The Spaniards had lost all their Colonies, and they looked upon their sphere in Morocco as all that was left to them. As for their being children, children were never inclined to sit still; and when the result of their sitting still might be insurrection in their own house, they were still less inclined to do so. The only argument which I could think of using with the Spanish Ambassador was that, if Spain precipitated a political crisis, a settlement as to Morocco would be come to that would in fact be arranged by France and Germany, with the cognizance of England: and it might be that Spain would be left out of account.

[I am, &c.]
E. G[REY].

([1]) [A passage of a personal nature is here omitted on grounds of international courtesy. It contained nothing affecting the historical value of the document.]

No. 321.

Sir Edward Grey to Sir M. de Bunsen.

F.O. 22565/13911/11/28.
(No. 54.)
Sir,   *Foreign Office, June 14, 1911.*
    The Spanish Chargé d'Affaires called at the F[oreign] O[ffice] on the 8th inst[ant] and enquired, by instructions from his Gov[ernmen]t, whether it was true that H[is] M[ajesty's] Gov[ernmen]t and the German Gov[ernmen]t had exchanged views on the question of Morocco and that a document embodying these views had been transmitted to Paris.

    The Chargé d'Affaires was informed by Sir A. Nicolson that the report was pure fiction. It was quite possible that in regard to a question playing for the moment so prominent a part allusions were made to the subject at Berlin and here; but there had been no exchange of views and the only Powers with whom H[is] M[ajesty's] Gov[ernmen]t were exchanging views were France and Spain.

                                                        I am, &c.
                                                        E. GREY.

No. 322.

Sir Edward Grey to Mr. Rennie.

F.O. 23533/8755/11/28.
(No. 57.)

Sir,   *Foreign Office, June* 14, 1911.

I told the Spanish Ambassador to-day the substance of Mr. White's telegram no. 107,(¹) giving an account of the Moorish protest to the "doyen" of the Diplomatic Corps at Tangier respecting the action of the Spanish Government in occupying Alcazar. I pointed out that this protest brought the question one step nearer to becoming a European question, and to a Conference and perhaps the partition of Morocco. I again urged the risk to which Spain was exposed by her action.

The Ambassador reiterated that Spain could not possibly withdraw from Alcazar now : all the concessions offered to Spain by France were of no importance as long as France refused to anticipate the date of the second period of the secret convention, but he informed me, quoting from a telegram from his Government, that she would not go an inch beyond Alcazar. She had done her best to smooth over the incident of the protest of the Commissioner of Foreign Affairs at Tangier to the Spanish Minister there, and she was anxious not to make things more difficult. On the other hand, she heard that some of the extra police from Tangier, with French Officers and artillery, were moving towards Alcazar; and that a Moorish mehalla, presumably with French Officers, was advancing to the Lucus.

I said that my reason for urging that it was a risk for Spain to precipitate a Conference or a partition of Morocco was that she had now put France in a position to say that Spain had directly violated the Secret Convention, and that it therefore no longer existed. Then, if a partition took place, France and Germany might come to terms without any reference to the Convention which had previously existed between Spain and France.

The Ambassador contended that France had indirectly violated the spirit of the Convention, though she had been more clever than Spain in the manner she had done so. In any case, as the desire of France was, not a partition, but a protectorate over the whole of Morocco, the Secret Convention would be of no use to Spain. He asked me whether, if the French had ignored the Convention, and come to an arrangement with Germany, we should have stood by Spain?

I replied that, as long as the Secret Convention continued, we could not be a party to any arrangement which ignored it; and as long as it remained in full force it was a guarantee that, if partition took place, Spain would have her sphere. But if she put France in a position to say that the Convention no longer existed, there was no certainty as to what the result might be. That was why I wished to reinforce the point which I made yesterday, and to urge that it was not in the interest of Spain to take action in Morocco in direct contravention of the Secret Convention, and so to precipitate partition.

The Ambassador referred to the assurance which he had already given me, that Spain would not move an inch beyond Alcazar. He made it plain that, in the event of a partition, Spain relied upon our preferring in our own interest to see her, rather than a stronger Power, in possession of the Mediterranean coast of Morocco.

I replied that, if the Secret Convention disappeared, there was no saying what the outcome of negotiations about Morocco might be.

[I am, &c.]
E. G[REY].

(¹) [Not reproduced as its tenour is indicated.]

No. 323.

Sir Edward Grey to Mr. Rennie.

F.O. 23533/8755/11/28.   *Foreign Office, June 15, 1911.*
Tel.   (No. 76.)   D. 3·15 P.M.

I have urged strongly upon Spanish Ambassador here that occupation of Alcazar without even notice to France beforehand is a violation of the Secret Agreement between France and Spain, and that if Spain by tearing up the secret agreement with France forces a partition of Morocco there is no certainty that her zone will be recognized.   Ambassador maintains it is impossible for Spain to withdraw from Alcazar under present circumstances, but has assured me that she will not go an inch beyond Alcazar.

Spain should at least make a declaration to the Powers about Alcazar parallel to that which France has made about Fez and say that her occupation of Alcazar will not be prolonged beyond what is required to secure order.

No. 324.

Sir Edward Grey to Sir F. Bertie.

F.O. 23534/8755/11/28.
(No. 228.)
Sir,   *Foreign Office, June 15, 1911.*

I informed M. Cambon to-day of the substance of my conversation of yesterday with the Spanish Ambassador respecting Morocco (see my despatch to Mr. Rennie No. 57 of 14th instant([1])).

M. Cambon urged that Spain, if she would not withdraw from Alcazar now, should at least make a declaration that she would withdraw when order was secured. There should be no difficulty about this; she would be the judge of the time and it would correspond to what the French had themselves said about Fez.

I said there could be no objection to this and I would urge it on Spain.   I had not done so before because it meant the abandonment of my request to withdraw from Alcazar immediately.

You will see from my telegram to Mr. Rennie No. 76 of June 15,([2]) that I have acted as suggested by M. Cambon.

I am, &c.
E. GREY.

([1]) [*v. supra*, p. 289, No. 322.]
([2]) [*v.* immediately preceding document.]

No. 325.

Mr. Rennie to Sir Edward Grey.

                                                         Madrid, June 16, 1911.
F.O. 23595/13751/11/28.   D. 3·45 P.M.
Tel.   (No. 49.) R.   R. 7·5 P.M.
    Morocco.

My telegram No. 48 (   ).([1])

Reply of Spanish Minister for Foreign Affairs to French representations has now been received.   It repeats intention of Spanish Government to act in close accord

([1]) [Not reproduced.   It reported that M. Geoffray had sent a written representation against the occupation of Laraiche and Alcazar to the Spanish Government.   This stated that as military measures did not appear to have been justified, the French Government were unable to give their consent; and continued that in the report of the conversation between M. Pichon and Señor Caballero of June 10th, communicated to the Madrid press, M. Pichon was represented as having only asked for further information, while no reference was made to his having referred to the responsibility Spain was incurring by her unjustifiable action.]

with France and expresses regret that circumstances which occasioned Spanish action at Alcazar and Laraiche are not clearly understood. In order that French Minister for Foreign Affairs may fully appreciate reasons, Spanish Ambassador at Paris has been instructed to communicate detailed report of events at Alcazar. In any case the Spanish Government consider that no French interests have suffered, and that Spanish Government have acted within their rights and within agreements as interpreted by seven years' experience.

As regards omissions in account of interview between French Minister for Foreign Affairs and Spanish Ambassador, communicated to Madrid Press, conversation had been fully reported by Spanish Ambassador, but, French Minister for Foreign Affairs having asked for supplementary information regarding landing of troops, it was thought that account of conversation, as communicated, was for the moment sufficient. Moreover, it seemed inexpedient to publish anything that might allow it to be supposed that there were even a temporary divergence of opinion between the two Governments.

As regards conversations between the two Governments at Madrid, in the opinion of the Spanish Government it was in the present circumstances more than ever necessary that the two Governments, in concert with His Majesty's Government, should endeavour to come to an understanding regarding application of existing agreements.

Communication of Spanish Minister for Foreign Affairs ends by calling attention to the presence of MM. Boisset and Moreau with the forces of the Makhzen within the Spanish zone of influence near Alcazar. Reasons for their presence are difficult to explain, and French Minister for Foreign Affairs is requested to issue instructions to prevent such excessive display of zeal on the part of French agents.

(Repeated to Paris.)

No. 326.

Mr. Rennie to Sir Edward Grey.

F.O. 24410/13379/11/28.
(No. 105.)
Sir,

Madrid, D. *June* 18, 1911.
R. *June* 24, 1911.

The President of the Council made a statement yesterday to the representatives of the Press regarding the situation in Morocco which is reproduced in most of this morning's papers, and is to the following effect.

He began by protesting against the rumour first started by the "Matin" that Spain would take Tangier on June 27th; the international character of that town was sufficient proof of the absurdity of this *canard*. As regards the recent debate in the French Chamber concerning Morocco, he concurred in the general lines of Monsieur Cruppi's speech: had he himself had to speak, he would not have said otherwise. All reports to the effect that Spain was going to move on Tetuan, Argila or Tangier were ridiculous. He had already declared in the Cortes, as clearly as he was able to do, and he would again repeat his statement—that Spanish action in Morocco had in view three objects, viz: to secure an expansion of Ceuta in order to guarantee security in the zone outside the fortress; to guarantee the same security at Melilla, and to take steps so that within the zone of Spanish influence, the Spanish police at Larache and Alcazar should be in a position to perform its duties. It was the firm resolve of the Spanish Government that their action should confine itself to the limits necessary for policing the Ceuta–Tetuan district, and up to the Muluya–Kert line which was necessary for the Melilla district. The expansion in these two directions as well as the reinforcement of the Larache police were obviously measures only of a provisional character.

Señor Canalejas went on to say that, in order to avoid creating alarm, the only troops that had been sent to Larache belonged to the Marine Infantry which formed part of the crews of men-of-war. He then went on to state that in spite of the explicit declarations that had been made, stories were current that 10,000 troops were about to be sent to Morocco, whereas, as a matter of fact, the number of men mobilised did not amount to 1,400. Nothing except rations, munitions and other necessaries were now being sent to Larache. After the police system had been reconstituted and when affairs in Morocco returned to a normal state, the Spanish Government would adopt the necessary attitude. It was true that a protest had been lodged by the Sultan, but this protest was merely a theoretical one and of little importance. He considered that the Government had merely performed a duty and he was in no way afraid of having acted as he had done. He felt, however, called upon to dissipate the state of alarm that was continually being fostered by the French press. As regards the stories current in the foreign press regarding an alliance with Germany, he remarked that the "German international policy was well-defined, and that when that country had a duty to perform, it performed it."

I have, &c.

ERNEST A. RENNIE.

[*ED. NOTE.*—On June 22, M. Isvolski summarised the French attitude towards the landing. *v. Livre Noir*, Vol. I, pp. 125–6.]

No. 327.

Communication by Señor de Villa Urrutia.

F.O. 24163/8755/11/28.   Spanish Embassy, June 20,(¹) 1911.

Declaracion verbal.

Para marcar bien naturaleza y alcance medidas tomadas Larache y Alcazar, el Gobierno de S.M. cree útil reiterar lo que desde un principio manifestó, á saber que aquellas responden á necesidad obtener reparacion por el asesinato protegido español Benmalek y sus hijos y castigar culpables así como asegurar tranquilidad Comarca. Una vez alcanzado este objeto y conseguida garantía eficaz para órden y normalidad, tales medidas provisionales cesarán.

20 *Junio*, 1911.

MINUTES.

The Spanish Amba[ssador] handed me the enclosed June 19.(¹) I told him that if the Spanish troops were to remain at Alcazar till *all* the conditions were fulfilled their stay would hardly be a provisional one. I asked him whether in any case the troops would not be withdrawn when the French withdrew from Fez. He said he doubted if this would be possible as the French would only retire to the Chaowia, and by their recent action at Fez and Maquinas and their undertaking the organisation of the Moorish army they would be complete masters over the Sultan who would be a puppet in their hands and he repeated much more in that strain. I concluded by saying that the best thing would be to resume the discussions at Madrid.

Today (June 20) M. Cambon came to see me. I read to him the enclosed doc[umen]t which he did not think would at all satisfy M. Cruppi. The object of M. Cambon's visit was to say that M. Cruppi was seriously alarmed at the outlook. But they had information that the Spaniards intended to reinforce their Alcazar garrison up to 4,000 men—and to establish military posts

---

(¹) [There seems to be some confusion about the date of this document. The Spanish memorandum is dated June 20, as it is here reproduced. In his minute on the memorandum, however, Sir A. Nicolson refers to it as having been handed to him on June 19. In No. 331, *encl.*, it is referred to as being of June 20, and in No. 332 as being of June 19.]

between Alcazar and Ceuta. Moreover at Madrid they were letting it be thought that M. Villa Urrutia was reporting that England was indifferent and not really objecting seriously to Spanish action (I contested this by repeating what had been said to M. Villa Urrutia here). M. Cruppi feared that he would soon be placed in the dilemma (1) of taking strong exception to the Spanish action thus producing very possibly a rupture or (2) of tacitly accepting the situation and practically carrying out a partition of Morocco—when naturally Germany (who still maintained silence) would step in and take her share—M. Cambon thought it would be well to resume discussions at Madrid but he did not think the " verbal declaration " afforded a good basis. He was puzzled what to suggest to M. Cruppi and he thought that the situation was unsatisfactory and ominous.

A. N.

I will deal with this tomorrow morning.

E. G.
20.6.11.

No. 328.

Count de Salis to Sir Edward Grey.

Berlin, June 21, 1911.
D. 7·30 P.M.
R. 10·30 P.M.

F.O. 24390/8755/11/28.
Tel. (No. 38.) Confidential.
Morocco.

I learn confidentially that the Spanish Ambassador made a formal declaration today to Acting Sec[retary] of State for F[oreign] A[ffairs] to the effect that recent Spanish action was taken to obtain reparation for an outrage on a Spanish protégé and punishment of the guilty, but that when order is restored and things had resumed their normal course, the temporary measures taken will cease.

Acting Sec[retary] of State is understood to interpret this communication in the sense that the Spaniards will evacuate places occupied as soon as French leave Fez.

MINUTES.

This formal declaration is shorter and better than the one communicated by the Spaniards to us.(1) But probably this is a summary only of the declaration made at Berlin.

E. G.

(1) [v. immediately preceding document.]

No. 329.

Sir Edward Grey to Mr. Rennie.

F.O. 24163/8755/11/28.
Tel. (No. 77.) R.   *Foreign Office, June 21, 1911.*

Spanish Ambas[sado]r has communicated the verbal declaration(1) which Spanish Gov[ernmen]t have made in regard to the presence of their troops at Alcazar.

You should inform the M[inister for] F[oreign] A[ffairs] that it appears to H[is] M[ajesty's] Gov[ernmen]t that the conditions enumerated in it would require an extended time to fulfil and that the declaration holds out little prospect of an early withdrawal. H[is] M[ajesty's] Gov[ernmen]t would be glad if the Spanish Gov[ernmen]t would state that if order is maintained in the district at Alcazar the force will be withdrawn to Laraiche, leaving the settlement of the other questions mentioned for subsequent treatment by the usual diplomatic means. You should

(1) [v. supra, p. 292, No. 327.]

inform the M[inister for] F[oreign] A[ffairs] confidentially that after the declarations of M. Cruppi in the French Chambers, it is evident that the French Gov[ernmen]t desire to withdraw their forces from Fez as soon as possible and that the expression of a similar desire on the part of the Spanish Gov[ernmen]t would facilitate greatly the resumption of discussions at Madrid, which it is in the general interest should not be interrupted.

No. 330.

Sir Edward Grey to Mr. Rennie.([1])

F.O. 23997/8755/11/28.
(No. 63.)
Sir, *Foreign Office, June 27, 1911.*

The Spanish Ambassador called at the Foreign Office on the 16th instant and was informed by Sir A. Nicolson of the suggestion which I instructed you in my telegram No. 77 of 21st inst[ant]([2]) to make to the Spanish Government namely that they should make a declaration to the Powers similar to that which had been issued by France. His Excellency intimated that he did not think that his Government would make any difficulty on this point, as they had already stated that the measures which they were taking were simply police measures and purely provisional.

Señor de Villa Urrutia observed that M. Cruppi was showing a very conciliatory disposition and was anxious that the recent protests of the Makhzen should not lead to the Morocco question being brought before the Powers. M. Cruppi apparently considered that the protest was ill-timed and not couched in happy terms, and he seemed to think that the French agents in Morocco were too zealous.

No trouble would, in the Ambassador's opinion, be caused at Alcazar by the tribes, who were well disposed and tranquil; moreover the Spanish authorities were in excellent relations with Raisuli who was a quieting element. The danger lay in the presence of the mehalla under Captain Moreau at Alcazar and in the activity of the French Vice-Consul there. These two officers might create trouble between the mehalla and the Spanish forces, or stir up the tribes; and his Excellency hinted that it would be well if H[is] M[ajesty's] G[overnment] could say a word to the French as to instructing their military and Consular officers at Alcazar to be quiet and careful. The Spanish Government would no doubt be glad to see the withdrawal of the mehalla from the neighbourhood of Alcazar.

His Excellency remarked in conclusion that he would like to rectify an error. The Spanish gov[ernmen]t were reproached for having taken under their protection a man who had been discarded by the Germans. Confusion had been made between two individuals. The man discarded by the Germans was Abdala ben Malec. The murdered man was a Spanish protégé named Ahmed ben Malec el Mesmudi.

[I am, &c.
E. GREY.]

([1]) [This despatch was drafted from a minute written by Sir A. Nicolson on his interview with Señor de Villa Urrutia. Sir Edward Grey added the following comment: " Of course the French will not listen to a request to withdraw the mehalla after Spain has refused to listen to a request to withdraw her forces. If the mehalla move it will only be on the initiative of the French themselves or on condition that the Spaniards withdraw from Alcazar. E. G.'']

([2]) [v. immediately preceding document.]

No. 331.

Mr. Rennie to Sir Edward Grey.([1])

F.O. 25399/8755/11/28.
(No. 111.)   *Madrid,* D. *June* 27, 1911.
Sir,   R. *June* 30, 1911.

With reference to my despatch No. 109 of June 24th,([2]) I have the honour to enclose herewith a copy and translation of a communication which I have to-day received from Señor Garcia Prieto regarding the intentions of the Spanish Government as to the occupation of Alcazar.

In the course of my conversation on June 23rd, I had left with His Excellency a personal *aide-mémoire*([3]) in order that there should be no doubt as to the nature of the statement which His Majesty's Government would be glad to receive. The reply now forwarded is marked "personal" and is enclosed in a private letter from the Minister with the request that it should be communicated to you.

I have, &c.
ERNEST RENNIE.

Enclosure in No. 331.

Señor Prieto to Mr. Rennie.

(Translation.)
(Personal.)

The Powers having made no observations on the first declarations of the Spanish Government, the latter, in making their statement of June 20,([4]) were inspired by the desire to be agreeable to His Majesty's Government in whose opinion it appeared useful that a fresh statement should be made of Spanish intentions to attribute a purely provisional character to the measures taken at Alcazar. The declaration was adapted to this spirit, and to the position assumed from the beginning by the Cabinet of Madrid: it makes the limits of those measures dependent on steps, which will not require an extended period for application, provided the Makhzen are animated by sincere feelings of friendship. On the hypothesis, never positively put forward by the Spanish Government, of an analogy between Spanish action at Alcazar and French action at Fez, it is evident that the French Government would not conclude their action without full and positive guarantees for the establishment of normal conditions. If the Makhzen, instead of assisting towards a settlement, has adopted an attitude that makes it increasingly difficult for the Spanish Government to withdraw from their legitimate attitude, and if the French Government consider it necessary to suspend the conversations at Madrid, which since the beginning of May the Spanish Government have urged should be held, no blame should be attributed to Spain, who is always ready to serve the general interests by showing a conciliatory spirit.

MINUTES.

M. [Paul] Cambon spoke to me yesterday (June 30) as to this document, which he considered obscure but as having for its object to throw all the blame on France. He asked what notice we proposed to take of it—and I told him we would wait for the full text. He is pretty sure to return to the question. I see no other course open but to suggest that the conversations be resumed at Madrid, though the French do not appear to be desirous of doing so after the recent Spanish action. M. Cambon had also been instructed to enquire whether we had suggested

([1]) [The contents of this despatch were sent in shorter form and with less accurate translation as Tel. No. 53 of June 27, received the same day.]
([2]) [Not reproduced. This reports a conversation between Señor Garcia Prieto and Mr. Rennie when the latter communicated the substance of Sir Edward Grey's telegram No. 77, (*v. supra,* pp. 293–4, No. 329), and asked for a more precise indication of the Spanish Government's intentions. Señor Garcia Prieto replied that this would be forthcoming shortly and added that he hoped the conversations between himself and the British and French Representatives would be renewed. (F.O. 24968/13751/11/28.)]
([3]) [This personal *aide-mémoire* embodied the substance of Sir Edward Grey's telegram No. 77 of June 21, 1911 (*v. supra,* pp. 293–4, No. 329).]
([4]) [*v. supra,* p. 292, No. 327.]

to the Spaniards that they should withdraw from Alcazar only—without referring to Laraiche. I replied that this had been the case, as it seemed to us that it would be better to proceed step by step and deal first with Alcazar which was inland. Our suggestion, even limited as it was, had, as he knew, not led to any result. M. Cambon appeared to be satisfied.

A. N.

We need not trouble about this now that the Germans have raised the whole question.

E. G.

[ED. NOTE.—A *modus vivendi* for the Alcazar district to prevent the recurrence of fresh incidents in the Spanish zone was arranged by an exchange of views between France and Spain on July 26, and the Press was informed that a satisfactory solution had been reached. *cp. infra,* p. 310, No. 336, and p. 401, No. 422.]

No. 332.

Sir Edward Grey to Mr. Rennie.

F.O. 24163/8755/11/28.
(No. 64.)

Sir, *Foreign Office, June 27, 1911.*

The Spanish Ambassador called at the Foreign Office on the 19th instant and handed to Sir A. Nicolson a memorandum, a translation of which is enclosed herewith,(¹) respecting the action taken by the Spanish Government at Laraiche and Alcazar.

Sir A. Nicolson observed that, if the Spanish troops were to remain at Alcazar until the conditions stated in the memorandum were fulfilled, their stay would hardly be a provisional one. He also enquired whether in any case the Spanish troops would not be withdrawn when the French withdrew from Fez.

Señor de Villa Urrutia doubted whether this would be possible, as the French would only retire to the Shawia. Their recent action at Fez and Mequinez and their intention to undertake the organization of the Moorish army would render them complete masters over the Sultan, who would be a puppet in their hands.

Sir A. Nicolson stated, in conclusion, that the best thing would be to resume the discussions at Madrid.

I am, &c.
E. GREY.

(¹) [Not reproduced. For the original v. *supra*, p. 292, No. 327.]

No. 333.

Mr. White to Sir Edward Grey.

Tangier, June 28, 1911.
D. 5·25 P.M.
R. 8 P.M.

F.O. 25264/8755/11/28.
Tel. (No. 117.)

British consular agent at Alcazar reports that squadron of Spanish cavalry, under Colonel Silvestre, had ridden out towards Gibel Sarsar ostensibly to fetch wood. He expresses the opinion that these cavalry reconnaissances will cause trouble.

On 25th June he reported that cavalry had created great excitement by riding through town with drawn swords, and had made reconnaissance towards hill tribes. I then mentioned matter to the Spanish Minister, pointing out danger of provoking an incident. He replied that he had been informed that reconnaissance had had good effect, but he promised to write to Colonel Silvestre on the subject.

(Repeated to Madrid.)

No. 334.

Mr. White to Sir Edward Grey.

F.O. 25382/8755/11/28.
Tel. (No. 118.) Confidential.

Tangier, June 29, 1911.
D. 4·45 P.M.
R. 8 P.M.

French chargé d'affaires is much put out at the Spanish activity at Alcazar. Captain Moreau, who has just returned to Tangier, told him that Colonel Silvestre in his march, reported in my telegram No. 117,([1]) crossed to the south side of the River Lukkos, and passed close to Moreau's camp. He said Spanish troops marched through standing crops, which incenses natives, and he expects trouble.

(Repeated to Madrid.)

([1]) [*v.* immediately preceding document.]

No. 335.

Extract from Annual Report for Spain for the Year 1911.([1])

[Enclosed in Despatch No. 60 from Sir M. de Bunsen of April 24, 1912, R. April 29, 1912. (F.O. 17898/17898/12/41.)]

I.—FOREIGN RELATIONS.

(a.) *Morocco.*

King's Visit to Melilla.

1. Early in the year it became apparent that Morocco was destined to occupy, even to a greater extent than before, the attention of the Spanish Government. On the 6th January, King Alfonso, attended by Señor Canalejas, Prime Minister, and the Ministers of War and Marine, proceeded to Melilla to inspect the Spanish positions. Though delayed by storms and hampered by torrential rains, His Majesty was escorted by General Arizon, Governor of Melilla, to the scenes of the most striking episodes of the war of 1909. General Toutée was deputed by the French Government to present their respects to the King of Spain at Melilla, and friendly speeches were exchanged. The King was received by his troops with enthusiasm. On the 15th January he proceeded to Almeria and next day to Madrid. His Majesty's Morocco trip was treated at home as an important event. On the King's name-day (the 23rd January) the national aspirations were expressed in exaggerated language by Señor Montero Rios, president of the Senate. In the course

([1]) [This Annual Report may conveniently be divided into two parts (for the second half *v.* immediately succeeding document), corresponding roughly to the two political phases of 1911; the Spanish Government was only indirectly concerned with the second phase.]

of the customary address, his Excellency said that, as when the Romans, Goths, and Moors successively held sway in Spain, so at the present day Spain still regards the Atlas Mountains, and not the Straits of Gibraltar, as forming her southern boundary. She must continue to fulfil her destiny in Morocco, and King Alfonso, the first Spanish Sovereign since Charles V to set foot on African soil, might well come to live in history as "Alfonso Africanus."

Incident at Tangier.

2. The "Madrid Gazette" of the 14th January published the text of the Hispano-Moorish convention, signed at Madrid on the 16th November, 1910[2] (paragraph 29 of 1910 report), together with a declaration signed in Paris on the 12th January by Señor Perez Cabellero and El Mokri, to the effect that the convention was accepted and ratified by the high contracting parties. The beneficial effects, however, which this agreement was expected to produce on the relations between French and Spanish agents in Morocco, showed as yet no sign of making themselves felt. At Tangier especially the bickering continued uninterruptedly. In January a disagreeable incident occurred. The shopowners of Tangier had been led, by the increasing insecurity of the streets, to petition for some night-watchmen. The British Minister suggested that the required duty might well be performed by the native police force, which acts, within the town limits of Tangier, under Spanish instructors. At the instigation, however, of the French Minister, a small detachment of Makhzen police, directed by a French officer, proceeded to occupy the street in question. As no notice had been given to the Spanish Minister, there was real danger of a conflict with the Spanish instructed police. Though nothing of the kind happened, great offence was given to the Spaniards, and, though Sir R. Lister successfully exerted his influence to procure the withdrawal of the detachment, the Spanish Government began to put forward actively their demand for more considerate treatment on the part of the French officials in Morocco.

Spanish Proposal to French Government.

3. With this end in view, pressure began to be applied in Madrid to the French Embassy with a view to obtaining the consent of the French Government to the advancement of the date at which, under the secret convention of October 1904, a more effective control over the Spanish sphere of influence in Morocco would pass into the hands of Spain. King Alfonso, the Prime Minister, and the Foreign Minister urged this course strongly upon M. Geoffray as the most practical means of putting an end to the friction at Tangier. It was pointed out that the 1904 convention contemplated three successive régimes in the Spanish sphere. Of these, the first two were to co-exist with the *status quo* in Morocco, *i.e.*, with the independence and integrity of that country. The third would follow on the extinction of the *status quo*. Under the first régime, France might act within the Spanish sphere on merely giving Spain notice of her intention, but Spain could only take action there after obtaining the consent of France. Under the second régime (that is, after the year 1919, but the *status quo* continuing) France could only take action in the Spanish sphere with the consent of Spain, but Spain could take action there without French consent. Under the third régime, *i.e.*, when the *status quo* should have passed away, which might be before or after 1919, France would no longer be able to claim any right of action in the Spanish sphere even with the consent of Spain, and Spain would acquire complete freedom of action. It was the second of these régimes which Spain now desired to bring into operation, without waiting till it would naturally take effect in the year 1919. Though animated by the most friendly sentiments towards Spain and desirous of meeting her wishes on many points the French Ambassador deprecated such a completely new departure as the one proposed. He pointed out that to accept it would involve a modification of the

convention of 1904; it would involve also the publication of the convention; and the whole Morocco question would thereby be raised.

Views of French and British Governments.

4. His Majesty's Government took a similar view. Every effort was made to avoid reopening questions which the Franco-German Convention of February 1909 was understood to have finally settled on the basis of French political preponderance in Morocco within the limits of the Algeciras settlement. On the other hand, M. Geoffray favoured the conclusion of an understanding with Spain sufficiently liberal to forestall military action on her part. He feared that, failing wide concessions to her demands, she would break loose from Ceuta, occupy the heights by which that fortress is surrounded, and quite probably push on to Tetuan.

France tightens her Hold on Morocco.

5. These fears were far from being unfounded. France, whether designedly or by the force of events over which she had little control, was steadily tightening her military and financial hold on Morocco. The Sherarda tribes were already up in arms (February) against the Sultan. A hostile native confederation contrived in a few weeks to envelop Fez on all sides. Colonel Brémond was dispatched with an Imperial mehalla to join hands with the French military mission at Fez, which was operating under Colonel Mangin against the tribes. Meanwhile it leaked out that a negotiation was actively proceeding in Paris between the French Government and El Mokri. A new loan, complementary to those of 1904 and 1910, was to be issued to enable the Sultan to set up an organised native force, armed under modern conditions, and capable, under French direction, of reducing to obedience insurgent tribes and refractory taxpayers. The loan, like its predecessors, was to be secured on certain revenues accruing in the Spanish as well as in the French sphere of influence. One of the items of the draft treaty provided for a railway traversing the Spanish sphere from Tangier to Alcazar. There were also arrangements concerning the payment of the foreign-officered port police force after the 1st January, 1912, when the provision made for it at Algeciras would expire. No attempt was made to secure the concurrence of Spain in matters so deeply affecting her interests. At Paris, Señor Perez Caballero, the Spanish Ambassador, was kept completely in the dark. At Tangier it never occurred to M. Porché, the French engineer in charge of the Moorish Department of Public Works, who drew up the railway scheme, to consult the Spanish assistant engineer with regard to its details, or even to allow him to know that it was being taken in hand. On the 15th March the "Temps" published the official announcement of the approval of the draft loan convention by the French Council of Ministers. The draft convention had been communicated two days previously to the Spanish Ambassador.

Spanish Dissatisfaction at Franco-Moorish Loan Convention.

6. The news produced in Madrid profound dissatisfaction. No one doubted that France had designedly ignored the 1904 convention. Under the pretext that she was investing the Sultan with power to maintain his independence she was adopting measures rendering impossible, if they should be carried out, the realisation of Spanish aspirations in Morocco. She was acting as if the words "spheres of influence" had never found a place in the engagements of the two countries concerning Morocco. The Spanish Government turned instinctively to England, but nothing was known in London of the loan convention. Sir F. Bertie was directed to remark on the inconvenience arising from this absence of trustworthy information on a matter of such importance. M. Cruppi then furnished a copy of the convention. He explained that, on acceding to office, he could only proceed with a work initiated

by the preceding French Government. Spain was over-suspicious and anxious. He would do his best, however, to conciliate her interests with those of France.

Representation by Spanish Ambassador in Paris.

7. The Spanish complaint was put in a concrete form in a long instruction from Señor Garcia Prieto to the Spanish Ambassador in Paris, Señor Perez Caballero. A copy was communicated to Sir Edward Grey by the Spanish Ambassador in London on the 20th March. It urged that French action in respect of loans and their guarantees, exclusive instruction of the Shereefian army, port police, and execution of public works, as manifested in the loans convention, constituted a breach of the convention of October 1904, and of the stipulations of the General Act of Algeciras. It laid stress on the one-sided action of the French Government in making these new arrangements behind the back of Spain, although they could not but affect profoundly her power to administer effectively in the future the zone assigned to her by treaty. The French Government were asked for explanations. These were furnished in a French note dated the 3rd April, but failed to satisfy the Spanish Government.

Suggestions of French Ambassador in Madrid.

8. Meanwhile M. Geoffray, French Ambassador in Madrid, was doing his best to induce his Government to make some concession to Spain. There was danger otherwise, he pointed out, that Spain would throw herself into the arms of Germany. He received on the 22nd March a letter from the Spanish Minister for Foreign Affairs, expressing a desire to consult with France as to the publication of the secret convention of 1904. While not directly supporting this proposal, which the French Government subsequently rejected, he suggested various courses, which might tend to conciliate the susceptibilities of Spain. She might be told, for instance, that the Alcazar railway scheme would not be unduly pressed; that she might increase her police force at Tetuan and Larache; that French-directed Makhzen troops would not penetrate into the Spanish zone without Spanish consent; and that, within that zone, only Spanish agents should be employed to collect the taxes assigned as security to the loans. Sir Francis Bertie was desired to speak to the French Government in the same conciliatory spirit (Foreign Office telegram, No. 49, to Paris, of the 27th March). M. Cruppi, who had made a friendly declaration regarding Spain in the Chamber of Deputies on the 24th March, promised the British Ambassador that, though a firm hand would be needed, he would do his best to avoid wounding the feelings of the Spaniards. The latter, however, rendered such an attitude rather difficult by their own behaviour. His Excellency alluded especially to alleged Spanish intrigues with the Sultan with a view to the establishment of a Spanish military mission at Fez, side by side with the one which France had maintained there since 1877.

French Advance on Fez impending.

9. Early in April the impending contingency of a French advance on Fez, in order to protect the lives of Europeans and to secure the Sultan upon his throne, began to loom large on the political horizon. M. Geoffray warned his Government that Spain would be likely to retaliate by making a corresponding demonstration in her zone. On the 4th April M. Cruppi gave friendly assurances to the Spanish Ambassador in Paris. If the advance took place, the French Government desired that it should be in agreement with Spain, who, if she liked, might take any necessary measures for the protection of her fortresses in Morocco. Señor Garcia Prieto gave out at Madrid that, if disturbances arose, Spain must insist on her right herself to maintain order within her zone. On the 11th April his Excellency again fruitlessly pressed the French Government to allow the publication of the secret

treaty of 1904. The British Government agreed that publication was inexpedient, and would make a bad impression on the Moors. In London the Spanish Ambassador was warned that Spanish military action, if taken merely to set off French action and without real necessity, would only force the pace, and should be avoided if possible.

Debates in the Cortes.

10. On the 8th April the Morocco question was made the subject of ministerial statements in both Houses of the Cortes. Señor Garcia Prieto spoke in the Senate. Spain, he said, had offered to act jointly with France, if intervention at Fez became inevitable. Thus the spirit of the General Act of Algeciras would be observed. Speakers belonging to the various parties promised their support. In the Chamber of Deputies Señor Canalejas, Prime Minister, declared the policy of the Government to be the strict observance of treaty rights and obligations. Spain would shrink from no sacrifice to assert her undoubted rights within the zone recognised as hers. If French action elsewhere reacted on the Spanish zone, Spain would not hesitate to take the necessary measures. Representatives of the different sections of the Opposition offered unqualified support, with the exception of the republican and socialist leaders. Señor Azcarate denied that there was any call for Spain to act separately from all the other Powers signatory of the Algeciras Act. Señor Pablo Iglesias hinted darkly at the renewal, if Spain embarked on fresh adventures in Morocco, of the revolutionary propaganda employed by the anarchists and socialists in 1909.

Spanish Explanations in London.

11. On the same day Señor Villa Urrutia explained the Spanish view of the situation to Sir Arthur Nicolson at the Foreign Office. Spain felt that the nominally provisional occupation of Fez, which France seemed to contemplate, would be bound to develop into a permanent occupation. This would compel Spain to occupy certain localities in her sphere.

French Advance on Fez begins.

12. Meanwhile the circle of hostile tribes closed round Fez. Colonel Mangin's 2,000 Shereefian troops within the capital had been with difficulty reinforced by the 3,000 commanded by Major Brémond. Communications with Tangier and Casa Blanca were completely cut off. On the 20th April the French consul at Fez transmitted to the French Government a request from the Sultan for armed assistance from the coast. Public opinion in Paris had by this time become accustomed to the idea of an advance on Fez. First a purely Moorish relief force was spoken of. A French stiffening was soon found necessary. In the end the French contingents headed the advance.

Feeling in Spain.

13. Spain responded by pouring troops into Malaga, Algeciras, and Cadiz for use wherever they might be required. Señor Garcia Prieto explained that this might be either in the Gharb, where Spain could not allow any other Power to intervene for the protection of El Kasr, or in the neighbourhood of Ceuta, which was ill-defended against any sudden raid. France watched the Spanish preparations with evident uneasiness. M. Cruppi assured Sir F. Bertie that she had no intention of following the Tunis precedent or of evading in any way the fulfilment of her treaty obligations towards Spain, and he suggested that the King of Spain should be reassured on these points by the British Ambassador at Madrid. Sir Maurice de Bunsen spoke to the Spanish Minister for Foreign Affairs in the desired sense on

the 25th April, Señor Garcia Prieto promising to convey the message to the King next day, though he added that there was no present intention to move Spanish troops into Morocco.

Discussions between France and Spain.

14. On the same day an unpleasant interview took place between M. Cruppi and Señor Perez Caballero, Spanish Ambassador in Paris. The latter took up the position that the French advance amounted to an alteration of the *status quo* in Morocco; that article 3 of the secret treaty had thereby become operative; that Spain would now act as she chose in her zone; and that, if she encountered opposition, she would simply denounce the treaty and appeal to another Power. M. Cruppi denied that the state of anarchy presupposed by article 3 could be said to exist in Morocco, and especially in the Spanish zone; he pointed to the danger of German intervention in the event of dissensions arising between France and Spain; and he suggested that Spain should frankly state to the French and British Governments what her grievances were, so that they might be taken into account as far as possible consistently with existing treaties. Señor Caballero would not hear of the situation being discussed with England. His intemperate language gave great offence to the French Government. On M. Geoffray making complaint of it, he was assured by Señor Garcia Prieto that it had already been disavowed, and Señor Caballero called to order in a telegram from Madrid. Though Señor Canalejas, the Spanish Prime Minister, continued to show irritation at the action of France, the communications which passed between the Foreign Minister and the French Ambassador were framed in friendly terms. Thus, in a letter dated the 20th April, Señor Prieto disclaimed any jealousy of the steps being taken for the relief of Fez, provided the Spanish zone was not infringed upon by the French forces or by mehallas under French command. Should France be compelled to assume a more extensive control over the Government of Morocco than was at present contemplated, he relied on a full understanding being previously come to with Spain.

England urges Agreement between France and Spain.

15. The advice given by His Majesty's Government to Spain was that she should accept French assurances as to the temporary character of the French march on Fez and abstain from forcible action such as could only precipitate the partition of Morocco. She was warned that the political consequences of any unwarranted intervention on her part would be deplorable. In a further telegram Sir Maurice de Bunsen was directed to support the idea, said to have originated in Berlin and to be not unwelcome in Paris, that France and Spain should come to an agreement on the chief points causing anxiety in Spain. He was to advocate a direct agreement between them, and not one in which England and Germany should also take part. A communication in the above sense was made by the British Ambassador to the Spanish Foreign Minister on the 5th May. The French Ambassador also spoke to the latter to the same effect. Señor Garcia Prieto promised to send M. Geoffray a memorandum embodying the Spanish demands. M. Geoffray now put forward the suggestion that Sir Maurice de Bunsen should be authorised to take part in the impending discussions. In this way it would be made clear that France entirely rejected the contention of Señor Perez Caballero that England was not concerned in the question at issue between the two countries. The frequent intercourse of the Spanish and German Ambassadors at Paris about this time had roused suspicion of a secret understanding between Spain and Germany. The French Government feared that a bargain might be struck between them in virtue of which Germany would obtain Mogador or some other port on the Atlantic, Spain establishing herself at once firmly in her sphere of influence under German protection. It was to counteract German influences in the councils of Spain that the idea of a tripartite discussion between France, Spain, and England was favoured at Paris.

Spanish Sympathy with Attitude of Germany.

16. It may here be remarked that the suspected intrigue with Germany has since been persistently denied by the Spanish Government and by the King of Spain. No evidence in support of it could be gathered from the attitude of the German Ambassador at Madrid. It is true that about this time Spain began to display intense uneasiness in face of the hole-and-corner loan negotiations at Paris, and the preparations for a French advance on Fez. The Spanish consul at Mogador paid a mysterious visit to Ifni; Major Silvestre, chief of the Spanish officers at Casa Blanca, proceeded to Marakesh on the pretext of a mission to buy horses; at dawn on the 7th May three strategic positions on the line of heights overlooking Ceuta were occupied by a body of Riff sharpshooters and other troops from the neighbouring fortress; complaints began to be freely made by the Spanish Government of the action of France in using El Kasr, a place within the Spanish zone, as a military base in connection with her forward movement; the occupation of Larache or Tetuan was freely urged in the press as a step which could not be much longer delayed. But these signs of Spanish restlessness were easily explained without the supposition of an agreement with Germany. Spain was only continuing to do what she had done ever since the conference of Algeciras. When France moved, Spain moved also. The French occupation of Ujda in 1907 was followed by the Spanish occupation of the Restinga (Mar Chica) in February 1908, and of Cap de l'Eau in the following month. The rapid extension of French influence throughout 1908 in the Shawia region, and in the councils of the Sultan at Fez was followed by the Riff war in 1909. The French treaty with Morocco in 1910, including exaction of a war indemnity, was followed by a similar Spanish treaty with Morocco. To every French action there was a Spanish counterpart. It was too much to expect that so far-reaching a movement as the one for the relief of Fez should be taken as if it were a matter of indifference to the Spanish zone. The French advance was from the first regarded at Madrid with intense suspicion and apprehension. It was felt that, whatever France might say, the status of Morocco was being fundamentally changed. The fiction of the continued survival of the Algeciras settlement was scornfully rejected. Spain resolved to take material guarantees to ensure that, when the final break-up took place, her claims should secure attention. Thus she regarded events in Morocco in a frame of mind not dissimilar from that of Germany. Germany would only have been spurring a willing horse, if she had urged Spain to take the steps she was only too ready to take without any incentive.

Reliance on Support of England.

17. On a review of circumstances, it seems reasonable to ascribe the evident leaning of the Spanish Ambassador in Paris towards a Spanish understanding with Germany rather to his personal sympathy with the utterances of a portion of the Spanish press and with the sentiments of one or two influential subordinates in the Spanish Foreign Office, than to any direct inspiration from the responsible spokesmen of the Spanish Government. But, however this may be, it is a fact that from the beginning of May onwards, Señor Garcia Prieto (Marquis of Alhucemas), Minister for Foreign Affairs, adopted a policy of reliance on the guidance of Great Britain. At every crisis he appealed to the fundamental treaties, by which the acquiescence of His Majesty's Government in the political preponderance of France in Morocco had been rendered conditional on the recognition by France of the claims of Spain in that country. On the other hand, Sir Maurice de Bunsen, under instructions, informed his Excellency that His Majesty's Government would fully maintain the Anglo-French Agreement of 1904, and that their attitude would be shaped in accordance with that which they adopted in 1906 at Algeciras.

Tripartite Discussion begins at Madrid.

18. In accordance with the above-mentioned suggestion of M. Geoffray, and with a request from the Spanish Ambassador in London, Sir Maurice de Bunsen was authorised to take part in the proposed discussion between France and Spain. With the object, mainly, of eliminating the injudicious action of the Spanish Ambassador in Paris, Madrid was fixed upon as the place in which the discussion should be held. A correspondence between Señor Garcia Prieto and M. Geoffray was already in progress. The former had followed up his above-mentioned letter of the 20th April by another dated the 28th April, in which he urged that the expedition towards Fez and the collapse of the Sultan's authority had already produced the conditions contemplated by article 3 of the secret convention as justifying the demand that Spain should exercise her full and unhampered influence in the recognised Spanish sphere. After consultation with Paris, the French Ambassador replied to both the above communications on the 2nd May. Though the French Government, he wrote, were compelled to deprecate the independent action which Spain desired to exercise in her sphere, they were quite ready to consider in a friendly spirit any reasonable demands which she might wish to put forward. He was himself authorised to discuss the questions at issue with Señor Garcia Prieto, and, he added, with Sir Maurice de Bunsen, as representing the other Power whose consent was indispensable to any alteration of the *status quo*. The object of the discussion was defined as being that "of arriving, in concert with the British Government, at the best way of applying, in the territory of Morocco, the principles set forth in the conventions of 1904 and in the Act of Algeciras."

Spanish Memorandum, Draft Declaration, and Protocol.

19. In response to this invitation the Spanish Foreign Minister drew up a memorandum embodying the Spanish demands. A copy was communicated to Sir Maurice de Bunsen on the 10th May[3] under cover of a private letter from Señor Garcia Prieto, stating that "I send you the accompanying documents so that from the first you may be in a position to take part, with M. Geoffray and myself, in the work of conciliation and good understanding upon which we are entering, and of whose happy result I cannot doubt." The memorandum contended that the secret convention of 1904 had been unfairly applied in respect chiefly of the loan conventions with Morocco, by which France had pledged the customs and other revenues of the Spanish as well as the French zone to the service of the loans and war indemnity for a period of seventy-five years; and, further, in respect of the distribution of the police, the execution of public works, and the language question. In conclusion, it argued that an occupation of Fez by the French, even if temporary, must inevitably affect the position of the Sultan and the existing régime in a manner compelling Spain to secure her rights. It ought to be admitted, then, that circumstances had brought into action the provision contained in the secret convention, allowing Spain, under certain contingencies, full liberty of action in her zone. Also the secret convention ought to be published. But, France objecting to publication, a draft declaration and protocol were submitted. The former declares that the first period of the secret convention is at an end; that Spain enjoys free action in her zone; that the Spanish zone shall be rendered free from the lien of the loans and war indemnity; that satisfactory arrangements shall be come to in respect of a Fez–Tangier railway, public works, &c. The protocol excludes French-instructed Makhzen troops from operating within the Spanish zone. It provides for partial repayment of the holders of the 1904 and 1910 loans, and suggests new arrangements concerning police and other disputed questions. The memorandum was accepted by the French Ambassador as affording a basis for useful discussion,

[3] [cp. supra, pp. 238–43, No. 266, and encls.]

and he urged his Government to make a few substantial concessions such as would be likely to retain Spain within the orbit of her present allies.

Meetings at British Embassy.

20. Three meetings were subsequently held at the British Embassy (18th and 27th May([4]) and the 6th June) between Señor Garcia Prieto, Minister for Foreign Affairs, and the French and British Ambassadors. The documents discussed were the above-mentioned memorandum of the 10th May, the French counter-proposals of the 24th May, the Spanish counter-proposals of the 29th May, and a revised version of the French counter-proposals submitted early in June. The principal points were :—

(1.) The Tangier–El Kasr, or, as Spain preferred to call it, the Tangier–Fez Railway. Spain claimed that it should pass through Arzila, and that the length lying within her zone should be entirely under her control. M. Geoffray promised that a conciliatory formula should be drawn up in Paris.

(2.) Public works : Spain pressed for employment of only Spanish agents in the Spanish zone, whereas France sought to restrict this privilege to Larache and Tetuan, the neighbourhood of those places, and the regions occupied by Spanish troops.

(3.) Co-operation between the French and Spanish Legations at Tangier with the object of settling, in harmony with the Franco-Spanish conventions of 1904, all matters arising before the diplomatic body and the commissions subject to its control. On this there was agreement.

(4.) Spanish language to be placed on an equality with French. An agreement was practically reached.

(5.) Employment of French-instructed native troops in Spanish zone. Spain sought to exclude this entirely. An understanding seemed within reach.

(6.) Police question : Spain made various proposals in the direction of an increase of the port police at Larache, creation of a similar police force at El Kasr and Arzila, and the exchange of the positions respectively by the French and Spanish-instructed police at Tangier, Spain taking thenceforth the outside position and France the inside.

(7.) Spain continuing to demand the advancement of the second period of the secret convention, so that she might forthwith enjoy freedom of action in her zone, M. Geoffray could only repeat that his Government could not consent to this at present. He added, however, that they would be willing, when matters settled down, to discuss the question of the political status of the Spanish sphere of influence. Meanwhile, they desired to give full scope to the economic development of Spain within her zone.

Attitude of Spanish Foreign Minister.

21. In the course of these discussions the Foreign Minister displayed various moods, betraying at one time by his uncompromising language and agitated demeanour a desire to break off all further conference, and, at another, the desire to meet France half way. In the end the latter tendency prevailed, and, although the occupation of El Kasr and Larache and the departure of the British Ambassador for the coronation in London served as a pretext for the discontinuance of the conversations, there was a tacit understanding that they should be resumed in due course.

([4]) [v. supra, p. 263, No. 290, note ([1]); and pp. 264–6, No. 292.]

x

General attitude of Spain.

22.   Meanwhile the French advance on Fez was watched at Madrid with a complete distrust of the assurances repeatedly given from Paris, and, to some extent supported from London, to the effect that only a temporary occupation was in view, that the independence of the Sultan would be thereby confirmed, and a state of affairs produced under which the intentions of the General Act of Algeciras would for the first time be realised to their full extent.   Spain held firmly to the view that the Sultan had long ceased to be independent; that he would now become more than ever the puppet of France; and that France, though her good faith was not disputed, would find it impossible to withdraw her protecting hand from the capital of the Empire.   The *status quo*, in short, of the year 1904 had already ceased to exist.   Though France would not yet recognise the patent fact, it behoved Spain to take action upon it.   Only by occupying certain strategic positions could she make sure that, when the final break-up of Morocco came, she would be able to make good her claim to administer her zone.   The text of the 1904 treaty might be ignored by France on the ground that Spain had infringed it, and that it therefore held good no longer.   France might come to terms with Germany and divide up Morocco on a totally different plan.   England, although so well-disposed towards Spain, might not see her way to thwarting French designs in this direction.   In any case the future was obscure.   Everyone must look out for himself.   The only course open to Spain was to assert her claims by a series of overt acts.   She must take the risk of possible expulsion from the newly occupied posts.   But this was risk in which she never seriously believed.   She felt that, in the last resort, England, and if not England, then Germany, would intervene on her behalf.   It would suit everybody better that she, rather than France, should hold the northern coast-line of Morocco.

Spain proposes Military Co-operation with France.

23.   Before, however, making any strategic move in her sphere, Señor Perez Caballero, Spanish Ambassador in Paris, made to the French Government the formal proposal that, following the Casa Blanca precedent of 1908, a Spanish force should co-operate with the French relief force just starting for the Moorish capital.   The suggestion was that a mixed Franco-Spanish column, starting from Tangier under the command of a Spanish general, and dropping on its way through the Spanish zone a chain of Spanish detachments charged with the occupation of this part of the country, should proceed from the point at which it entered the French zone onwards to Fez under French command, the mixed force having by that time become almost exclusively French.   Thus each of the two nations would become responsible for the defence and tranquillity of its own particular zone.   The French Ambassador at Madrid had no knowledge of this design until some months later he saw the correspondence at the Quai d'Orsay.   It was rejected without hesitation by the French Government, and Spain was thrown back on the alternative policy of taking independent action in her zone.   To sit still and do nothing was out of the question.

Spain occupies Heights near Ceuta and other Points.

24.   At first her eyes were turned mainly on Tetuan.   Spanish activity in the Ceuta region had always been regarded with suspicion at Tangier; every effort to establish communications between the fortress and the country lying behind had been nipped in the bud; the Ceuta–Tetuan road project had been severely suppressed; by the Treaty with the Makhzen, of the 16th November, 1910, an extension of the police zone of Ceuta from 5 to 10 kilom. inland had with difficulty been secured. But owing to the prevailing anarchy it was impossible to bring the treaty into force. Ceuta was therefore as unprotected as ever.   A Moorish mehalla under French instructors might any day seize one of the heights commanding the fortress.   The

Spanish garrison could then be easily driven into the sea. In a conversation held with Sir Maurice de Bunsen on the 1st May, Señor Canalejas, Prime Minister, had foreshadowed the employment of a Spanish force from Ceuta to occupy the heights in question, and to perform generally the police duties which should have been exercised, according to the treaty with Morocco, by a Moorish kaïd. At dawn, on the 7th May, this operation was successfully carried out. The points occupied were Cudia Frederico, commanding Wady Marsa; Cudia Fajana, commanding Wady Fenidak (or Castillejos); and the heights de la Condesa, commanding a portion of the road to Tetuan. All three were strategic positions along the line of heights overlooking Ceuta. The pretext was the evident inability of the Makhzen to undertake its treaty obligations. The Spanish advance was, in reality, the first countermove to the French advance on Fez. France offered no objection.

About the same time the wells of El Zayo, overlooking the lower valley of the Muluya, in the Quebdana country, were occupied by a Spanish column.

On the 21st May the French relief force entered Fez.([5])

On the 22nd May Monte Negron, an elevated position near the coast, lying about half way between Ceuta and Tetuan, was seized by a body of Riff rifles supported by two companies of engineers, under orders from the Governor of Ceuta.([6]) This point lay some 8 kilom. beyond the new Ceuta police zone as established by the convention with the Makhzen of the 16th November, 1910. The shadowy pretext was an assault on a Spanish fishing-boat. The Basha of Tetuan was requested by the Spanish consul to see that the peace was kept along the remaining portion of the road to that place. It was in reality Spain that now undertook the policing of the entire road. She did not, however, attempt to occupy Tetuan itself, though Spanish officers were frequently seen there. She had in fact been headed off from doing so by the repeated representations of the British and French Ambassadors. Her attention had been specially called by them to the danger of a rising of the Angera tribes if Spain should extend still further the sphere of her military activity in the neighbourhood of Ceuta.

Occupation of Larache and El Kasr.

25. Whether impressed by these arguments or moved by other considerations, it is certain that from the date of the actual occupation of Fez by the French troops Spain began to turn her attention towards Larache and El Kasr. Señor Garcia Prieto expressed nervousness regarding the situation in that region. There were reports of an incipient agitation among the neighbouring tribes. If disturbance should ensue, his Excellency claimed for Spain the right and duty to put it down in this portion of her sphere. Early in June two Spanish ships, with marines on board, were despatched to Larache. On the 8th June a landing was effected. A Spanish protected Moor had been murdered near El Kasr. The Powers were informed that, if the Shereefian authorities inflicted punishment and preserved order, there would be no need for further action. Otherwise, in view of the threatening attitude of a new local pretender, Spain must herself see to the safety of El Kasr.([7]) In point of fact an advance was immediately made to that place. It was at first occupied by a small force of between 400 and 500 marines and Larache police. But reinforcements soon arrived from Spain and the south-west corner of the Spanish sphere of influence was brought completely under Spanish control. Spain contended that the move was justified, both under the 1904 convention, which gave her a free hand on alteration of the *status quo* in Morocco, and under the Algeciras Act, which confided to her·the task of instructing the police at Larache, and implicitly that of maintaining order in the whole region in the same way as France had done in the

([5]) [*v. supra*, p. 262, No. 289.]
([6]) [*v. supra*, p. 260, No. 286.]
([7]) [*v. supra*, p. 284, No. 315.]

Shawia region on the similar pretext of having been entrusted, jointly with Spain, with the policing of Casa Blanca.

Comments in London.

26. The action of Spain was resented at Paris and disapproved in London. Sir Edward Grey expressed to the Spanish Ambassador on the 13th June great apprehension as to the consequences.([8]) Would not the Spanish troops be withdrawn, he asked, on payment of compensation for the murdered protégé? Señor Villa Urrutia finally admitted that the true motive of Spain lay deeper. Her troops would remain where they were while French activity in Morocco continued. France had shewn in the Madrid conversations that she was still quite indisposed to grant the demand of Spain for liberty of action in her zone. The Spanish Government had reason to know that France and Germany were trying to settle the Morocco question between them. Spain would be left out in the cold if she did not look after her own interests. Sir Edward Grey pointed out the two dangers which Spain was provoking —a disturbed northern zone in Morocco, and perhaps a European crisis leading to partition, without much consideration for Spain herself.

Comments in Paris.

27. In Paris a conversation took place between M. Cruppi and the Spanish Ambassador on the 10th June. Señor Perez Caballero was told that Spain was incurring responsibilities; that France could not acquiesce in a course of action which she regarded as uncalled-for and contrary to the 1904 agreement and to the General Act of Algeciras; and that the conversations at Madrid had now better be suspended till Sir M. de Bunsen's return from leave. The language, however, held by France never amounted to a peremptory protest of the kind which it was after-wards contended had been addressed by her to Spain on this occasion. M. Geoffray's communications, on the contrary, were framed in the most friendly words. France made her reserves, she did not protest. She explained, through her Ambassador in London, why it was that France could not well take a severe line with Spain. That would lead to a rupture which might be dangerous. But she urged England to step in on the strength of the stronger position which she occupied as the friend of both parties.

English Advice.

28. Sir E. Grey accordingly urged upon the Spanish Ambassador that the occupation of El Kasr without even previous notification to France was a violation of the 1904 agreement, and that, if Spain could not be induced to evacuate. she should at least make a declaration to the Powers on the same lines as the communication made by France respecting Fez, and say that the occupation would not be continued longer than was necessary to restore order. To this hint the Spanish Prime Minister responded by a statement made on the 17th June to the representatives of the press.([9]) He said that there would be no move on Tetuan, Arzila, or Tangier; Spanish policy had three objects, namely: expansion of Ceuta to make the fortress safe; equal security for Melilla; reinforcement of Larache police to enable them to perform their duties. These measures were of a provisional character. When Morocco returned to a normal state, the Spanish Government would act accordingly. Mr. Rennie, His Majesty's chargé d'affaires, was directed to press for a more explicit statement to the effect that when France should withdraw from Fez, Spain would withdraw her troops from El Kasr and Larache. Señor Garcio Prieto replied in a vaguely worded letter (27th June).([10]) The action of Spain would depend

([8]) [v. supra, p. 287, No. 319.]
([9]) [v. supra, pp. 291–2, No. 326.]
([10]) [v. supra, p. 295, No. 331, encl.]

on that of the Makhzen. France was not likely to leave Fez without full and positive guarantees. The best course was to resume the Madrid conversations. On the 19th June Señor Villa Urrutia had communicated to the Foreign Office a memorandum stating that the provisional measures taken at Larache and El Kasr would cease when their purpose was attained, namely, punishment of the murderers and tranquillity of the district.([11]) The formal assurance desired by His Majesty's Government was thus evaded.

Moorish Protest.

2º. On the 12th June Sid Guebbas sent a written protest to the diplomatic corps at Tangier, in the name of the Sultan against the action taken by Spain. The Spanish Minister refused to take act of it, and it was regarded by the Spanish Government as merely a further proof that the Sultan had become the docile instrument of France.

([11]) [v. supra, p. 292, No. 327.]

No. 336.

Extract from Annual Report for Spain for the Year 1911.

[Enclosed in Despatch No. 60 from Sir M. de Bunsen. D. April 24, 1912. R. April 29, 1912. (F.O. 17898/17898/12/41.)]

Attitude of Germany.

30. The French march on Fez and the consequent Spanish occupation of Larache and El Kasr afforded Germany her opportunity of striking a bargain. If Morocco was to be partitioned she must have her share or compensation elsewhere. Informal conversations to this effect had been taking place for some time at Berlin and Kissingen. At the latter place the idea of compensation in the French Congo had been put forward by Herr von Kiderlen on his becoming convinced that France was determined to exclude Germany from Morocco.([1]) The stages by which this suggestion eventually bore fruit in the shape of the Franco-German agreement of the 4th November, 1911, are well known.([2]) Though France had shown no unwillingness to proceed with the discussion, Germany thought fit to administer a touch of the spur. The "Panther" arrived at Agadir on the 1st July.([3]) Spain indulged in the most extravagant expressions of delight. Here was the greatest of continental Powers taking a leaf out of her book. The move to Larache and El Kasr was now fully explained and justified. Germany equally with Spain had been unable to bear the swallowing up of Morocco by France. The Madrid press made no effort to conceal its satisfaction. The impression already prevailing abroad that Spain was bound to Germany by a secret understanding appeared to be fully confirmed. It is possible, however, that the Spanish denials were true. As explained above, the attitude of Spain can be easily accounted for without pre-supposing more than a similarity of views between Spain and Germany. At Madrid there was no sign of a stimulus having been applied by the German Ambassador. The sympathy, moreover, which Spain at first displayed with German action was short-lived. It was soon replaced by a feeling of dread lest Spain should be left out in the cold as the result of an agreement between Germany and France. Spain came to mistrust Germany as much as France. Though England had openly blamed her recent action, it was on England that she again placed her reliance at this juncture. Only England, she felt, could help her to enter upon her inheritance in Morocco. She knocked, indeed,

([1]) [v. infra, p. 322, Ed. note; and pp. 353–7, No. 373.]
([2]) [v. infra, pp. 615–8, No. 626, and pp. 831–4, App. IV.]
([3]) [v. infra, p. 322, Ed. note.]

at the door both in Berlin and Paris for admittance to the Franco-German conferences. In both places she met with a refusal. Compensation was the basis of the discussions. If Spain had no compensation to offer, she had better keep away. In London she was told that her fears seemed unfounded. France was only trying to find out what Germany wanted. She would then no doubt remember her engagements with Spain, and that England was likewise interested in their observance.

Incidents at El Kasr.

31. Though somewhat relieved, Spain continued to strengthen her hold on El Kasr and Larache. By the middle of July her force in those places rose to over three thousand men. Regarding herself as being in full military occupation, she naturally fell foul of existing arrangements, under which certain buildings were held and services performed by the Makhzen troops. The latter were nominally under the orders of the Khalifa of Raisuli, the Sultan's representative at Arzila. French military instructors, at first Captain Moreaux and later Lieutenant Thiriet, commanding a Moorish mehalla on the left bank of the Lucus, also claimed authority over them. Colonel Silvestre, commanding the Spanish forces, forbade any patrols by armed native troops and took possession of the buildings used by the latter as barracks. No unauthorised persons bearing arms were admitted within the Spanish lines. Two serious incidents arose. On the 17th July, M. Boisset, French vice-consul at El Kasr, was arrested for entering the town under arms. He was immediately released, but an apology was exacted by France, and reluctantly offered by the Spanish Ambassador in Paris, as well as personally to M. Boisset by the local Spanish authorities. A few days later Lieutenant Thiriet, crossing the Lucus on his way to El Kasr, had an altercation with a Spanish detachment, which he accused of harbouring deserters from the mehalla. Blows were exchanged, and Lieutenant Thiriet, on being confronted with Colonel Silvestre, is said to have behaved in an unseemly manner. The French and Spanish accounts of these incidents naturally differed, but in the case of Lieutenant Thiriet the French Government did not think the circumstances warranted a fresh demand for an apology.

Modus Vivendi of July 26.

32. In apprehension, however, of more serious conflicts arising, a verbal *modus vivendi* was concluded on the 26th July between the French Ambassador and the Spanish Foreign Minister at San Sebastian. It provided that the Moorish troops and French officers in the service of the Makhzen should keep to the south side of the Lucus, and the Spanish troops to the north side; that Spain should abstain from enrolling deserters from the mehalla; that deserters should be mutually surrendered; and that French travellers passing between Fez, El Kasr, Larache and Tangier should be furnished with a French diplomatic or consular pass, establishing their destination and identity. The *modus vivendi* was regarded by the Spanish Government as a recognition by France of their contention that El Kasr and Larache lay within the Spanish zone. It was in any case effective in preventing for some time the recurrence of regrettable incidents. It thus paved the way to a resumption of the conversations, interrupted since the beginning of June, concerning the relations between the French and Spanish spheres of influence in Morocco. A proposal to that effect was put forward by Señor Garcia Prieto on the 7th August. The following day an interview took place in London between the King of Spain and Sir Edward Grey. His Majesty was assured that, notwithstanding all that had happened at Larache and El Kasr, Spain might still reckon on the friendly sentiments of England. It was held, however, both in Paris and London, that the Franco-Spanish conversations had better stand over till something had been settled at Berlin.

New French Draft Convention.

33. The French Government, meanwhile, prepared a draft convention for submission in due course to the Spanish Government. It was accompanied for the first time by the French demand that Spain should make some territorial concession as compensation for the enormous sacrifices which Germany was exacting from France in the French Congo. Spain, as well as France, would profit by the elimination of Germany from Morocco. It was only fair therefore that Spain should pay a portion of the price. M. Geoffray was authorised to acquaint the Spanish Government with the purport of the draft convention. He was not to communicate the text. Acting on this instruction he handed to the Foreign Minister on the 2nd September at San Sebastian a short memorandum, putting in at the same time a demand for the cession of the Ifni district. Señor Garcia Prieto was taken aback, and said Ifni was about to be occupied in accordance with the undoubted treaty right of Spain. Sir Maurice de Bunsen was present at this and the following interviews. A day or two later the French Ambassador informed the Foreign Minister that France would require Spain to cede the whole of her southern zone in Morocco, otherwise the favourable terms just offered as regards the administration of the northern Spanish zone would be withdrawn. On the 5th September the King of Spain expressed to Sir Maurice de Bunsen his painful surprise at this peremptory demand, so humiliating to Spanish pride. His Majesty hoped France might be induced to accept in lieu of Ifni an area equivalent, approximately, to her sacrifice in the French Congo, and taken from another part of the Spanish southern zone. Meanwhile, under French pressure, the Spanish Government abandoned the projected occupation of Ifni. On the 8th September a further meeting was held between M. Geoffray, Señor Garcia Prieto, and Sir Maurice de Bunsen. The Foreign Minister expressed a general concurrence with the French proposals regarding the Spanish zone, but said that Spain could never cede Ifni and the coast lying opposite the Canaries. His Excellency having admitted, nevertheless, the principle that some compensation was due to France, he was invited to formulate an offer. M. de Selves, the French Foreign Minister, was informed on the 13th September by Sir Francis Bertie that His Majesty's Government approved generally the draft convention with Spain, and especially the article providing for the special position of Tangier, a point to which they attached great importance. The Spanish Council of Ministers, meeting at Madrid, failed to devise a concrete offer of the kind demanded by France. What security had they that, after buying off France, Spain would not be required to buy off Germany as well? Spanish Guinea had been placed by the French negotiation at Berlin at the mercy of Germany. Spain must be guaranteed against the danger of a double exaction. This point was elucidated by Señor Garcia Prieto at a further meeting held with M. Geoffray and Sir Maurice de Bunsen at San Sebastian on the 14th December. What, he asked, was the precise extent of the sacrifice about to be made by France to Germany in the French Congo? Could France guarantee Spain against a German demand for compensation in exchange for German recognition of the Spanish sphere of influence? Failing an answer to these questions, there was no solid ground on which to formulate a counter-proposition.

No answer was forthcoming. The San Sebastian conversations were accordingly dropped. Before the end of September the Foreign Minister returned to Madrid, followed within a few days by the French and British Ambassadors.

Question of Spain giving Compensation to France.

34. In reply to enquiries from the Spanish Ambassador in London, His Majesty's Government declared on the 28th September that they considered the provisions of the treaty of 1904 between France and Spain as still in force; that they had no indication that the French Government desired in any way to depart

from those provisions; but that if, owing to French concessions to Germany, the Powers signatory to the Algeciras Act disinterested themselves politically in Morocco. it would be right that Spain should give France some reasonable compensation, or the latter would have paid the whole price of acquiring liberty of action for Spain in the Spanish sphere. From this time onwards the question of the amount of territorial compensation to be paid by Spain became a principal obstacle in the way of a speedy understanding between France and Spain. The problem offered many other difficult points for solution.

French Proposals.

35. M. de Selves, French Minister for Foreign Affairs, inclined at first to seek a settlement on the basis of the session to Spain of certain portions of Morocco in absolute' sovereignty (Paris, No. 451, Confidential, of the 19th October).([4]) The idea was worked out in a "projet d'accord hispano-marocain," handed by M. Regnault, French Minister in Morocco, to Sir Francis Bertie on the 19th October. By this document, Spain received in sovereignty only the portion of the Moorish coast districts watered by the rivers running into the Mediterranean. France took under her protectorate the coast watered by the rivers running into the Atlantic. The Spanish strip ran eastwards from Cape Alcazar, a point to the east of Tangier, to the Muluya. Tangier was administered under the sovereignty of the Sultan by a municipal body, having an international character, as defined by a " déclaration française," likewise communicated by M. Regnault to the British Ambassador in Paris. Sir Francis Bertie at once pointed out the wide discrepancy existing between these documents and the treaties of 1904. About the same time the Spanish Ambassador in London gathered from his French colleague that the French proposals, approved in September by Sir Edward Grey, but only presented in outline to the Spanish Government, were regarded by France as being no longer in existence.([5]) The French press assuming a menacing tone towards Spain, and demanding the evacuation of Larache and El Kasr, the Spanish Government let it be known that they would only be induced by overwhelming force to relinquish these places (Madrid, No. 182, of the 28th October).([6])

Effect of Franco-German Treaty.

36. On the 4th November the Franco-German agreement was signed at Berlin.([7]) In communicating it to the Spanish Government, M. Geoffray stated that the French Government had not lost sight of the fact that they must come to a special arrange- ment with Spain concerning her position in Morocco. That such an arrangement must be based on the 1904 treaty, and not on the recent suggestions put forward by M. Regnault, was made clear to the French Foreign Minister by Sir Francis Bertie on the 2nd November.([8]) Sir Edward Grey's instructions on this point were categorical. The French Government must understand that the establishment of a strong naval Power on the Atlantic coast in the place of Spain would strike at one of the fundamental conditions of the *entente* with France. M. de Selves returned a conciliatory answer, disclaiming any intention to act in disaccord with England. M. Caillaux, Prime Minister, on the other hand, assumed an entirely uncompromising attitude. He persisted in his determination to present the Regnault project at Madrid. He knew nothing of any earlier project. Spain had incurred the just resentment of France. She had violated the 1904 convention and must be made to fall in with French demands, though the *entente* with England might be strained thereby.

([4]) [*v. infra*, p. 576, No. 593: and *cp.* pp. 583–7, No. 598.]
([5]) [*v. infra*, p. 593, No. 605.]
([6]) [*v. infra*, pp. 595–6, No. 609.]
([7]) [*v. infra*, pp. 615–8, No. 626, and pp. 831–34, *App.* IV.]
([8]) [*v. infra*, pp. 599–601, No. 614.]

Spanish Interests in Morocco.

37. Meanwhile the Spanish Government had replied to the French and German request for adherence to the Berlin agreement that they must first obtain security for their political and special interests in Morocco, which had been ignored in the recent negotiation (*note verbale*, London, 7th November).(⁹) What these interests were was for the first time fully realised by the French public on the appearance in a Paris newspaper of the full text of the secret convention of 1904.(¹⁰) A few days later the press divulged the text of the unsigned treaty of 1902, and that of the Franco-Spanish agreement of 1905.(¹¹) France, it became clear from the documents, was to receive a Morocco cut off from the Mediterranean. But had not Spain broken the secret convention by occupying Larache and El Kasr? On the 9th November M. de Selves was asked before the Commission for Foreign and Colonial Affairs of the Chamber of Deputies whether the French Government had protested against the occupation. He replied there had been no protest as far as he was aware. In point of fact, M. Geoffray had made his "reserves" at the time, in letters to the Spanish Government couched in friendly terms. The reasons for the absence of a more formal objection were given by M. Paul Cambon to Sir Edward Grey in the month of June (see paragraph 27). M. de Selves, however, informed the commission on the following day that he had been mistaken. France, he said, had, after all, duly entered her "protest." A French press campaign, urging a radical revision of the 1904 treaty, was immediately set on foot, under the leadership of the "Temps" and "Matin." M. de Selves, however, adopted an attitude favourable to a friendly settlement with Spain on the basis of the 1904 treaty.

French Demands.

38. In a conversation held with Sir Francis Bertie on the 26th November(¹²) he said he was prepared to relinquish the demand for the evacuation of Larache and El Kasr. Only a slight rectification of the boundary line south of the River Lucus would be demanded of Spain as far as her northern zone was concerned. Territorial compensation would be sought by France exclusively in the southern Spanish zone, and in such a way as to leave a strip including Ifni in Spanish hands. A draft convention on these lines was left with Sir Francis Bertie by M. Geoffray on the 30th November.(¹³) It omitted, however, the Tangier question (reserved for an annexe), and it implied a French claim to the possession of the entire southern Spanish zone. On the following day M. Geoffray communicated a draft regulation concerning Tangier. It was regarded as unsatisfactory in London. On the 6th December Sir Francis Bertie informed M. de Selves that His Majesty's Government, without giving a definite opinion on the draft convention, were ready to give a general support to it as the basis of discussion with the Spanish Government.(¹⁴) M. de Selves had just informed the Spanish Government that the French Government had no objection to the British Ambassador at Madrid taking part in the negotiations—and, indeed, would welcome his doing so. Sir Maurice de Bunsen received instructions accordingly.

Conversations at Madrid.

39. During the remainder of the month of December three meetings were held at Madrid between Señor Garcia Prieto, Minister for Foreign Affairs, and M. Geoffray, French Ambassador. Sir Maurice de Bunsen was present throughout. The French draft convention was considered inacceptable, on the ground mainly—

(⁹) [*v. infra*, p. 620, No. 629.]
(¹⁰) [*v. infra*, pp. 826–9, *App.* IV.]
(¹¹) [The plan of 1902 was confidentially communicated to the British Ambassador on February 13, 1903, *v. Gooch & Temperley*, Vol. II, p. 279, No. 336; *cp.* also *ib.*, Vol. III, p. 30, No. 30, and *note*, and *infra*, pp. 676–7, No. 675, and *note* (³). For the agreement of 1905, *v. Gooch & Temperley*, Vol. III, pp. 136–7, No. 176.]
(¹²) [*v. infra*, pp. 721–3, No. 716.]
(¹³) [*v. infra*, pp. 742–4, No. 725, *encl.*]
(¹⁴) [*v. infra*, pp. 756–7, No. 737.]

(1) that it reserved to the Sultan—*i.e.*, to the French protecting Power—the right to frame " general regulations " for the whole country . . . . an arrangement amounting, in the Spanish view, to an extension of the French authority over the Spanish zone ; (2) that the irksome control of the Moorish Board of Customs—a body directed by M. Guiot, representative of the French holders of the 1904 and 1910 loans—would be maintained by it in the custom-houses of Larache and Tetuan ; and (3) that the proposed scheme for the construction of a railway from Tangier to Fez by a single company would tend to place the control of the entire railway in French hands.

A counter-draft was accordingly drawn up embodying the Spanish contention that the general regulations should be framed in each zone separately ; that the credit of Spain should be substituted for that of the custom-houses in the Spanish sphere of influence, as a guarantee of the loans and French war indemnity ; and that the Spanish and French portions of the projected line should be kept distinct.

M. Caillaux, French Prime Minister, showed firmness in maintaining the French standpoint ; and a new French draft, following the main lines of the old one, was prepared in Paris. Meanwhile Spain laid down the principle that the question of territorial compensations should not be discussed till the régime of the Spanish zone, whatever it might be, had been clearly determined. The Foreign Minister failed to elicit any information as to the progress of the discussions which were understood to be proceeding between London and Paris in respect of the all-important question of Tangier.

Situation at End of Year.

40. By the end of the year there was little prospect of a settlement being reached. Spain regarded the French proposals as being designed to keep a strong French control over the Spanish zone. She felt humiliated by the suggestion, put forward by the French press, that the northern zone would be merely leased to Spain, under conditions depriving her of the free action which she claimed to exercise in it under article 3 of the convention of October 1904.

Riff Mines.

41. During the year the Spanish Riff Mining Company, though anxious to commence exporting its iron ore, was unable to do so (except a single cargo) owing to the opposition of Messrs. Mannesmann. This firm, though disavowed by the German Government, received considerable indirect German support, and endeavoured to induce the Spanish company either to take it into partnership or buy out its opposition by a substantial payment. The Spanish company refused, but realised that if it attempted to dispose of the produce of its mines, Messrs. Mannesmann would be strong enough to prevent the shipment of the ore. The Spanish Government, also fearing a German protest, prohibited export pending settlement of the questions at issue respecting mining rights in Morocco. The mining company, meanwhile, were compelled to make terms with another German firm, Messrs. Natter, which demanded the surrender of a piece of land claimed by the company as having been always included among its possessions. The German Embassy adopting a threatening attitude, the Spanish company agreed to the appointment of a mixed commission to investigate the conflicting claims. The result was a convention signed on the 16th August, 1911, by which Messrs. Natter and Navarrete received a portion of the piece of land claimed by them, besides the promise of the first 20,000 tons of ore which should be extracted from the other portion. The Spanish company thus bought off in 1911 one of their German rivals, as they bought off in 1910 their French rival, M. Massenet, manager of the Compañia del Norte (see 1910 report, paragraphs 2–4). They did not, however, succeed thereby in disarming Messrs. Mannesmann, who continued to press for similar favours. Fortunately, the losses of the Compañía Española del Riff, in respect of blackmail and denial of permission

to export its ore, were to some extent made good by the profitable services of its line of railway, which proved exceedingly useful to the Spanish army of occupation in the Riff.

No. 337.

Extract from Annual Report for France for the Year 1911.

[Enclosed in Despatch No. 544 from Sir F. Bertie. D. December 31, 1912, R. March 3, 1913. (F.O. 10060/10060/13/17.)]

Spain.

Franco-Spanish Negotiations respecting Morocco.

67. At the end of August M. de Selves gave to me for perusal the draft of a convention for regulating the position between France and Spain in Morocco, on the hypothesis of the conclusion of an agreement with Germany by which, so far as the German Government were concerned, France would obtain an entirely free hand politically in Morocco.([1]) There was no mention in it of the Spanish sphere, in which Ifni is situated, and the stipulation in regard to Tangier was not very definite. On the 1st September I called M. de Selves's attention to these points, and remarked that although the proposed convention was to take the place of the secret agreement of 1904 between France and Spain, which would consequently be abrogated, France and Spain would still be bound in regard to the non-fortification of the portion of the Moroccan coast in which Tangier was situated, mentioned in the Anglo-French declaration of 1904 respecting Morocco, which was adhered to by Spain.

68. As to Ifni, M. de Selves said that, as Spain had allowed fifty years to elapse without entering into the occupation of the zone granted to her by the treaty of 1860 with Morocco, it was supposed that she could not attach much value to it; and he hoped that, although it was recognised by the agreement of 1904 as a Spanish zone, the Spanish Government might be willing to make over the rights of Spain to France in recognition of the fact (which it would be if the Berlin negotiations succeeded) that it would be France that found the compensations to Germany which had enabled the French Government to settle with the Spanish Government the position of Spain in Morocco on well-established lines. M. de Selves wished to have your observations on this draft, which was not to be regarded as a definitive document, and particularly in regard to article 13, relating to the part of the coast of Morocco in which England was specially interested. You saw no objection to it from the British point of view, and it appeared to you to be an honest attempt to remove Spanish grievances. In order to provide against the possibility of its being argued that Spain's adherence to the Anglo-French declaration had lapsed you suggested the insertion in the new convention of an article in the same terms as article 1 of the Franco-Spanish convention of 1904, *i.e.:* "L'Espagne adhère, aux termes de la présente convention, à la déclaration franco-anglaise du 8 avril, 1904, relative au Maroc et à l'Égypte."([2]) You concurred in the provisions of article 13 of the new convention relative to Tangier, but in case any question should arise about it in future years you desired to place on record that His Majesty's government consider it essential that Tangier should maintain its special international position with a zone of 15 kilom.

69. With regard to the arrangements to be made with Spain after the conclusion of the Franco-German negotiations, M. de Selves suggested (18th October)([3]) as a solution of the difficulties which might arise in relation to the Sultan in matters concerning the Spanish zones that Spain might have the absolute cession in full

([1]) [*v. infra*, pp. 494–7, No. 525, and *encl.*]
([2]) [*v. Gooch & Temperley*, Vol. III, p. 49, No. 59. *v.* also *infra*, p. 827, *App.* IV.]
([3]) [*v. infra*, p. 576, No. 593.]

sovereignty of certain portions of Morocco. M. Regnault brought to me on the following day(⁴) the drafts of an agreement between Morocco and Spain and of a French declaration respecting Tangier, the question of police and the non-fortification of the coast. The effect of these documents would have been that the north-west corner of Morocco in the Spanish zone would be transferred to the French protectorate. Tangier was to be administered under the sovereignty of the Sultan by a municipal body of an international character. The French Government in order to ensure the free passage of the Straits of Gibraltar were to guarantee that neither fortifications nor strategical works should be constructed anywhere between Cape Alcazar and the heights dominating the right bank of the River Sebou. I stated to M. Regnault that His Majesty's Government would certainly not consent to the substitution of France for Spain on the Atlantic coast of Morocco. Two days later M. de Selves told me that the proposals were only a sketch for your consideration, and that he would not put them forward without your concurrence. You informed the French Ambassador that His Majesty's Government could not support any negotiations with Spain unless based on the agreements of 1904 to which England was a party. To treat them as if they did not exist would be to drag the *entente* in the mud, and would have the most disastrous effect on public opinion in England. On the 2nd November,(⁵) I informed M. de Selves by your direction that you and the Prime Minister were preoccupied at the prospect of the situation which would be created if M. Regnault's project were put before the Spanish Government, who were irritated and alarmed at the reports of the demands to be made by the French Government which would deprive Spain of some of the advantages secured to her by the 1904 agreement. His Majesty's Government admitted that some compensation was due to France for the improved position which Spain would occupy owing to French sacrifices in the Congo. To convert a Spanish zone on the Mediterranean coast of Morocco into a sovereign possession would probably raise questions with other Powers, and Germany might demand compensation. The substitution of France for Spain on the north-western coast of Morocco would not be consistent with the British interests which Lord Lansdowne had in view when he negotiated the 1904 agreement. To put pressure on Spain to accept such proposals as it was credibly reported to be the intention of M. Caillaux to do would throw her into the arms of Germany, which would be injurious to British and French interests. M. Regnault's project was not one that could commend itself to M. de Selves, for it contained elements of danger to the foreign policy of France if the *entente* was intended to continue its task of preserving peace whilst protecting the solid interests of France and England. All this M. de Selves admitted, and he-stated that it was because he felt from his conversations with me that His Majesty's Government might object to the project which was of M. Regnault's making that he had sent it to me for your consideration, for he desired to act in unison with His Majesty's Government in the questions which must arise with Spain in Morocco. M. de Selves undertook to prepare M. Caillaux for the communication which I had been instructed to make to him of the views of His Majesty's Government. I recommended M. de Selves to abandon altogether M. Regnault's project and to revert to His Excellency's earlier proposals communicated to me at the end of August, and to insert in it a prohibition to Spain to alienate in any form her rights in the territories comprised in her zones in Morocco. To his enquiry as to where French compensations from Spain might be found, I suggested that they might be sought in the south of Morocco. Information had reached the German Government, so the German Ambassador informed you, that M. Caillaux meditated being hard on Spain and holding out the threat of internal troubles which would endanger the Spanish throne if the Spanish Government were not accommodating.

70. I had my interview with the President of the Council on the 3rd November,(⁶)

(⁴) [v. infra, pp. 583–7, No. 598, and encls.]
(⁵) [v. infra, pp. 599–601, No. 614.]
(⁶) [v. infra, pp. 603–4, No. 618.]

and urged on him the considerations which I had put to M. de Selves. The "projet" Regnault was, I had good reason to know, concocted by that gentleman in consultation with the President of the Council, and His Excellency showed for it the affection of a parent. He gave no sign of any intention to adopt a conciliatory attitude. He held forth at great length on the grievances which France had against Spain, stated that the Spanish Government had intrigued with the German Government, and relying on German support had bearded France in every way, and their conduct had become intolerable. If His Majesty's Government supported the Spanish Government, in refusing satisfaction to French claims, French public opinion would be greatly irritated, and "il y aurait danger que la France et l'Angleterre se brouillent." I replied that the French public had shown great common sense in all the difficulites with Germany, and that I did not suppose that they would be foolish enough to quarrel with England on account of the question of what compensation would be reasonable for Spain to give to France in Morocco.

71. On the following day (4th November)([7]) I had a further conversation with M. Caillaux, but I did not succeed in moving him from his declared intention to press on the Spanish Government the Regnault project, and when I suggested to him that in view of the engagements of France under the 1904 agreements she could not make war on Spain for the possession of the coveted zone . . . .([8]) He reproached me for my constant references to the 1904 agreements, which he contended had been broken by the Spaniards, and were not properly applicable in the changed circumstances in Morocco. To my reply that the agreements in question were the basis of the position which France had occupied in Morocco, and must be the basis for the negotiations with the Spanish Government in which British interests were involved, M. Caillaux answered that friendship with England would cost dear to France if her legitimate aspirations were to be opposed by England. He spoke of the great sacrifices made to Germany by France, the little support which France could expect from the British army owing to its limited strength, and he said that it was a question whether France could not have come to more satisfactory terms with Germany without the *entente*. After refuting his insinuations against the *entente* as hampering France, I asked him whether he really meant that, in his opinion, it would be advantageous to France that it should not exist, as in such case I would so report to you. He replied that he did not mean that, but he thought that it was being made to work to the disadvantage of French interests.

72. Notwithstanding M. Caillaux's intractable attitude, I had the impression that His Excellency on further reflection, and finding that he would get no assistance at Madrid from His Majesty's Government in support of his inclinations, would reconsider his position, for I had reason to believe that the French Cabinet was by no means unanimous in support of his proposed mode of treating with the Spanish Government, and from a conversation which I had on the same day with the President of the Republic, I ascertained his views to be that the word of France being engaged by the agreements of 1904 they must form the basis of the negotiations.

73. On the 8th November the secret Franco-Spanish convention of 1904 was published in the "Matin."([9]) Two days later there appeared in the "Figaro" the secret treaty negotiated but not signed between France and Spain in 1902, and the "Temps" produced the secret Franco-Spanish treaty of 1905, and two of the secret articles of the Anglo-French convention of 1904. These disclosures were a surprise and great disappointment to the French press and public, who were more disposed to ponder over what might have been than to consider what was possible. M. Delcassé was much abused by his political and newspaper enemies for not having

---

([7]) [*v. infra*, p. 619, No. 627.]

([8]) [A passage of a personal nature is here omitted on grounds of international courtesy. It contained nothing affecting the historical value of the document.]

([9]) [Some correspondence took place earlier in the year on the subject of the publication of this Convention and is printed *infra*, p. 321, *Ed. note. v.* also *infra*, pp. 826–9, *App.* IV.]

gone through with the arrangements of 1902 with Spain so favourable to French ambitions. Little or no consideration was given to the difficulties which would have arisen with England if an attempt had been made to carry them out.

74. On the 9th November M. de Selves stated to the Chamber Commission for foreign affairs, on information given to him by M. Bapst, the Political Director, who was by his side, that the French Government had neither protested nor made any reservations on learning of the Spanish occupation of Larache and Alcazar (M. Cruppi being at that time Minister for Foreign Affairs). The next day he corrected himself, saying that M. Cruppi had protested on three occasions, but that M. Bapst, being then at Biarritz, was not aware of the protests. M. de Selves told me that the protests were not technically protests, for they had been oral and not written, and that he had made the correction to the commission without giving any details, in order to save the face of his colleague, M. Cruppi, who had become Minister of Justice. M. Bapst was made a scapegoat by being given unlimited leave of absence, M. Louis, the ambassador at St. Petersburgh, temporarily taking his place at the Quai d'Orsay.

75. On the 16th November the President of the Republic gave a dinner in honour of the King of Servia, and in the course of the evening MM. Ribot, Delcassé, Cruppi, Etienne, and Pichon spoke to me on the subject of the negotiations with Spain. On the 18th at the Opera, where there was a gala performance for the King of Servia, M. Caillaux, addressing me in a loud voice at the buffet in the President's ante-room before a number of people, said : " Ah, M. l'ambassadeur, homme terrible, vous faites une campagne. Cela a produit une grande commotion parmi ces hommes politiques auxquels vous avez parlé. Prenez garde, c'est très dangereux." This referred to the conversations at the Elysée. I replied equally loudly as M. Caillaux had spoken : " Je ne fais ni campagne ni intrigues. Je n'ai pas cherché ces hommes politiques dont vous parlez. Ce sont eux qui m'ont posé des questions auxquelles j'ai cru devoir répondre. J'ai exprimé mes opinions, voilà tout " ; and on M. Caillaux suggesting that it was not necessary to reply to those who had made enquiries of me at the Elysée, I stated that " Garder le silence aurait donné une fausse impression de la situation et de la politique de mon pays." M. Caillaux then changed his tone, and said very quietly : " Il faut qu'un arrangement se fasse. Il faut que nous en causions." Yes, I replied, " Mais en tout cas pas le projet Regnault." To this he replied, " Proposez donc quelque chose d'autre." This closed the conversation.

76. On the 20th November,([10]) being apprehensive lest the French Government meditated a departure from their treaty engagements in regard to Tangier, you instructed me to endeavour to obtain satisfactory assurances on the subject of those engagements. France had given an undertaking to Spain in regard to the internationalisation of Tangier, which, in accordance with the Anglo-French declaration of 1904, had been communicated by the French Government to His Majesty's Government, who had thus become parties to the undertaking. If the French Government contemplated a departure from the policy thus defined, His Majesty's Government must reconsider their position. I had an interview with M. de Selves on the 26th November,([11]) and on my referring to conversations which I had had with M. Caillaux on the 18th and with M. Cruppi on the 20th of the month, of which I had given an account to M. de Selves, His Excellency informed me that since those conversations the situation had changed. He had made proposals to the Cabinet for the negotiations with Spain which his colleagues had accepted, and the President of the Republic had approved. They were that the engagements of 1904 with England should be the basis for the negotiations with Spain in regard to such modifications in the Franco-Spanish agreement as might be considered by the British Government admissible, with the object of giving compensation to France for her sacrifices to Germany so far as Spain had derived profit from them in Morocco. No

([10]) [v. infra, pp. 705–6, No. 700.]
([11]) [v. infra, pp. 721–3, No. 716.]

compensation would be required from Spain in the north of Morocco. There would merely be a slight rectification of the boundary line in order to obviate disputes in the vicinity of Alcazar. France would claim the Spanish southern zone, Ifni, with some surrounding territory, being left to Spain. Tangier and its immediate vicinity would be internationalised and a Tangier–Fez railway would be constructed by the French Government in co-operation with the Spanish Government. M. de Selves further suggested that the Sultan might appoint a commissioner to represent him for the treatment of all questions between the Spanish authorities and the Makhzen. M. de Selves said that in making these proposals he had been guided by the desire to act in union with His Majesty's Government and to preserve intact the *entente* with England, which for both France and England was so necessary for the mutual protection of their general interests. In reply to His Excellency's enquiry whether I thought that his proposals would meet with your concurrence, I told him that I felt confident that you would consider the bases for the negotiations as satisfactory.

77. The " grande commotion " which M. Caillaux said that my conversations at the Élysée had caused, was due to my having stated undeniable facts as to the engagements of France under the 1904 agreements which had been made public, and as to the interests of England which they protected, and to my having stated to M. Étienne in reply to his suggestion of our interests on the Mediterranean coast of Morocco being secured, and of there being no British objection to France being on the Atlantic coast of Morocco : " Éloignez-vous de la côte de l'Atlantique aussi bien que de la Méditerranée." M. de Selves had been so alarmed at the possible effect on the *entente* of M. Caillaux's language to me, of which I had kept him informed, that he had spoken of it to the President of the Republic and to some Senators who shared his alarm, and remonstrances were thereupon made to M. Caillaux, who, through M. Cruppi, endeavoured to explain them away to me.

78. The French Ambassador at Madrid communicated to me unofficially on the 30th November the drafts of the convention proposed by M. de Selves.([12]) You considered it a fair basis for discussion with the Spanish Government, and one to which you could give a general support, and by your desire I expressed to M. de Selves your satisfaction at the intention of the French Government to negotiate on the basis of the 1904 agreements.([13])

79. The French draft regulations for the administration of Tangier, which were communicated to me by M. Geoffray on the 1st December for submission to His Majesty's Government for their observations, did not meet with their approval, and on my communicating to M. de Selves their objections, and pointing out to him that the French draft would make the Makhzen *alias* the French Government supreme at Tangier, which would not be internationalisation, His Excellency reminded me that the French draft was merely an " avant-projet," and he said that he would have the memorandum of your objections examined with the view of considering in what measure your observations and suggestions could be adopted. The demarcation line for the Tangier district made a long loop so as to include within it a belt along the Atlantic coast. This digression from M. de Selves's assurances was due to M. Regnault, who, being on the drafting commission, had reinserted some of his views which had the support of the President of the Council, who expounded to me his views on the evening of the day on which M. Geoffray had communicated to me the draft annexes, viz. : that, out of deference to His Majesty's Government, the French Government waived their demand for Larache and Alcazar, and out of regard for Spanish susceptibilities Ifni would be excluded from the compensation which France would require in the south, but it would be absolutely essential that the 1904 line in the Lukhos district should be altered, and guarantees must be given for the security of the Tangier–Alcazar railway, and for French commercial enterprise within the Spanish zone. In the course of the conversation

([12]) [*v. infra*, pp. 741–5, No. 725, and *encl.*]
([13]) [*v. infra*, p. 748, No. 727.]

M. Caillaux accused the Spanish Government of intriguing and negotiating with the German Government, and the Spanish Ambassador in Paris of intrigues with French political persons and the press. I reminded M. Caillaux that he was in error in talking of French concessions to Spain, for any compensations to France would be derogations from the rights of Spain under treaty arrangements with France; we did not deny, I said, that compensations were reasonably due, and we were ready to use our influence to obtain the consent of the Spanish Government, but the compensations must be found where they would not be inconsistent with the important interests of Spain and England secured by the 1904 agreements.

80. At the request of the Spanish Government, fully concurred in by the French Government, His Majesty's Ambassador at Madrid took a part in the negotiations between the Spanish Minister for Foreign Affairs and the French Ambassador.

81. In the debate in the Chamber on the Franco-German convention (14th December)([14]) M: de Selves stated that the negotiations with Spain were inspired with two ideas, viz., to ask for some compensation for French sacrifices from which Spain would benefit, and to have regard for Spanish feelings and dignity, for a great country like France should never take advantage of its strength. M. Caillaux's statement was that in the negotiations which were based on the 1904 agreement France intended to respect the dignity of Spain, but at the same time to safeguard her own interests. A fortnight later (28th December) M. Caillaux complained to me of the attitude of the Spanish Government. He had, he said, out of regard for His Majesty's Government made the French "projet" as moderate as possible, and quite expected it to be accepted practically as it stood. The Spanish counter-project was unacceptable, for it would be impossible to carry out some of its provisions, and others would amount to the annexation of the Spanish zone. He hoped that you would use your influence at Madrid to bring the Spanish Government to a reasonable frame of mind. He also expressed the desire that the negotiations at Madrid should be expedited so as to close the question, for it was important that it should not continue to be the subject of parliamentary debate. He was, he said, being attacked on all sides, by some on the plea that he was putting unwarrantable pressure on Spain, a weak power; by others on the score that he was not exacting from Spain all that France had a good claim to expect. He hoped that you would assist him out of this dilemma.

Arrest of French Consul at Alcazar.

82. On the 16th July the French consul at Alcazar, M. Boisset, was arrested by some Spanish soldiers at that place and taken before Colonel Silvestre, who was in command of the Spanish troops stationed in the district. French public opinion was much incensed by this incident, and the French Ambassador at Madrid was instructed to demand an immediate apology at Paris through the Spanish Ambassador, and also an apology at Alcazar through Colonel Silvestre.

83. On the 19th July M. Pérez Caballero, Spanish Ambassador at Paris, conveyed an expression of regret from the Spanish Government for the arrest of the French consul. The Spanish Government intended, so M. Caballero stated, to instruct Colonel Silvestre to apologize to M. Boisset as soon as it was in possession of the facts connected with his arrest. The Spanish Government further undertook to instruct the officer in command at Alcazar to refrain from enlisting soldiers from the shereefian mehallas, and to return to the Moorish Government the arms and horses brought in by various deserters. Three days later a somewhat similar incident occurred, when Lieutenant Thiriet was hustled by some Spanish soldiers at Alcazar.

([14]) [v. infra, pp. 806–20, App. II.]

84.   M. de Selves told the Spanish Ambassador that measures would have to be taken at once to prevent such incidents.   In consequence, the Spanish Government forbade the enlistment of deserters from the shereefian mehallas.   M. de Selves gave orders that the French officers in command of mehallas should avoid contact with the Spanish officers and troops.

[*ED. NOTE.*—The following documents relate to the publication of the Secret Franco-Spanish Convention of October 3, 1904.   They are printed together here in order that the narrative should not be interrupted.

Sir M. de Bunsen to Sir Edward Grey.

F.O. 13718/3980/11/28.
Tel.   (No. 10.)   Confidential.

Madrid, April 12, 1911.
D. 11·15 A.M.
R., 1 P.M.

Notwithstanding French refusal reported in my telegram No. 4(15) Spanish M[inister for] F[oreign] A[ffairs] has again written to French Ambassador urging the expediency of publishing Secret Franco-Spanish Convention of 1904, on the ground that it is not inconsistent with the Algeciras Act, and that European opinion has become accustomed to idea of partition of Morocco into spheres of influence between France and Spain.   French Ambassador is most strongly opposed to publication, believing that Germany would never consent to arrangement contemplated in Secret Treaty.

(Repeated to Paris and Tangier.)

Sir F. Bertie to Sir Edward Grey.

F.O. 13729/3980/11/28.
Tel.   (No. 33.)   Confidential.

Paris, April 12, 1911.
D. 7·40 P.M.
R. 8·50 P.M.

Morocco.   Madrid telegram No. 10 of to-day.(16)

Minister for Foreign Affairs had not at 6 o'clock this evening received any fresh application from the Spanish Government for publication of the secret Franco-Spanish convention of 1904. He will refuse his consent most categorically, and he hopes that you will support such a refusal and strongly advise Spanish Government to desist from urging publication, as it would certainly raise an embarrassing question with Germany.

Sir Edward Grey to Sir M. de Bunsen.

F.O. 13729/3980/11/28.
Tel.   (No. 8.)

Foreign Office, April 13, 1911.
D. 2·15 P.M.

Sir F. Bertie's telegram No. 33.(16)

If a favourable opportunity occurs you should let the Spanish Gov[ernmen]t know verbally that, in my opinion, the publication of the secret convention of 1904 would be a grave mistake, and certain, among other consequences, to have a deplorable effect upon the Moors.]

(15) [Not reproduced.]
(16) [*v.* immediately preceding document.]

CHAPTER LIV.

THE SENDING OF THE "PANTHER" TO AGADIR
AND ITS EFFECTS, JULY 1-21, 1911.

[*ED. NOTE.*—The German decision to send an armed vessel to Agadir has been the subject of much controversy. But Herr von Kiderlen-Waechter was the originator of the scheme. (*v. Jäckh*, Vol. II, pp. 122–3.) Discussion took place between M. Jules Cambon and the Chancellor at Berlin on June 20, and on June 21 between M. Jules Cambon and Herr von Kiderlen-Waechter at Kissingen. M. Cambon stated that he was not authorized to make proposals, only to give assurance as to an early evacuation of Fez. For other details *v. Caillaux*, pp. 99–101; *G.P.* XXIX, pp. 177–8, *notes*; and *infra*, pp. 353–7, No. 373. On the 26th Herr von Kiderlen-Waechter went to Kiel and obtained the Emperor's consent. On the 27th orders were given to the German Admiralty, and the gunboat "Panther" was sent to Agadir where she arrived on July 1. The available evidence as to the movements of the "Panther" and those of the light-cruiser "Berlin" and the gun-boat "Eber" is given in full, *infra*, pp. 846–7, *App.* VI. For Sir Edward Grey's views as to the motives underlying the despatch of the "Panther," *v. Twenty-Five Years*, Vol. I, pp. 238–41; for Sir Arthur Nicolson's views, *v. Nicolson*, pp. 341–51.]

No. 338.

Aide-mémoire communicated by Count Metternich, July 1, 1911.

F.O. 25641/25641/11/28.

Des Maisons allemandes, établies au sud du Maroc et notamment à Agadir et dans ses environs, se sont alarmées d'une certaine fermentation parmi les tribus de ces contrées que semblent avoir produite les derniers événements dans d'autres parties du pays. Ces maisons se sont adressées au Gouvernement Impérial pour lui demander protection pour leur vie et leur biens. Sur leur demande le Gouvernement a décidé d'envoyer au port d'Agadir un bâtiment de guerre, pour prêter, en cas de besoin, aide et secours à ses sujets et protégés ainsi qu'aux considérables intérêts allemands engagés dans les dites contrées. Dès que l'état de choses au Maroc sera rentré dans son calme antérieur, le bateau chargé de cette mission protectrice aura à quitter le port d'Agadir.

MINUTE.

I have read it to the Cabinet; in view of future possibilities copies of telegram conversations and such papers as this and M. Cambon's letter(¹) should be kept ready so that they could be printed and circulated with little delay if need be.

E. G.

(¹) [*v. infra*, pp. 323–4, No. 340; *v.* also *Nicolson*, pp. 341–2.]

No. 339.

Minute by Sir A. Nicolson.(¹)

F.O. 25641/25641/11/28.

Sir Edward Grey,   *Foreign Office, July 1, 1911.*

The German Ambassador called this morning and said he had been instructed to make a verbal communication, which is recorded in the annexed Aide-Mémoire.(²) A similar communication was, Count Metternich said, being made to the French

(¹) [Printed in *Twenty-Five Years*, Vol. I, pp. 221–2. The postscript there given is missing from the original draft in the Foreign Office file, but appears in the *Confidential Print*. Count Metternich's instructions and account of the interview are in *G.P.* XXIX, pp. 155–7. *v.* also Count Benckendorff's account in *Siebert*, p. 590.]

(²) [*v.* immediately preceding document.]

and Spanish Gov[ernmen]ts by the German Ambassadors at Paris and Madrid. I merely remarked that Agadir was not an open port, and that I was unaware that any German or foreign subjects resided there or in its neighbourhood.

Count Metternich continued by saying that he wished to make an explanatory statement: the advance of France to Fez, in regard to the necessity of which German reports differed from those of the French, and also the establishment both by France and Spain of military posts in various parts of Morocco, had created a new situation, and one which rendered the provisions of the Act of Algeciras illusory. By that Act France and Spain were only authorized to organize police forces in certain open ports. The German Gov[ernmen]t had no desire to pass any criticisms on the above action of France and Spain, but they were bound to lend an ear to the requests of German subjects and protected subjects in districts in the south where no organized police forces existed. It was the duty of the German Gov[ernmen]t to afford the necessary protection to the lives and properties of their subjects in the south, and to continue to afford such protection until a condition of normal peace and tranquillity had been re-established. The German Gov[ernmen]t were ready to endeavour to find with the French and Spanish Gov[ernmen]ts a definite solution of the Morocco question. They were well aware that there were difficulties in the way of reaching a solution : but owing to the friendly relations between Germany, France and Spain they did not consider that such difficulties were insurmountable. If the British Gov[ernmen]t were ready to assist the German Gov[ernmen]t towards this end their aid would be gladly welcomed.

I said that I would repeat to you as faithfully as possible what he had said to me. He could understand that the communication was one of great importance and would have to be very carefully considered.

A. N.

No. 340.

M. Paul Cambon to Sir Edward Grey.

F.O. 25883/25883/11/28.
(Confidentielle.)
Cher Sir Edward,

Ambassade de France à Londres,
1er *Juillet*, 1911.

Monsieur de Selves a reçu aujourd'hui la visite de l'Ambassadeur d'Allemagne à Paris qui lui a remis le memorandum suivant :

" Des maisons allemandes établies au Sud du Maroc notamment à Agadir se sont alarmées de la fermentation parmi les tribus de ces régions. Elles se sont adressées au Gouvernement Impérial pour réclamer protection de leur vie et de leurs biens. Sur leur demande le Gouvernement Impérial a décidé d'envoyer au port d'Agadir un bâtiment de guerre pour prêter en cas de besoin aide et secours à ses sujets et protèger les importants intérets allemands engagés dans ces contrées. Dès que l'état de choses au Maroc sera rentré dans son calme antérieur, le bateau chargé de cette mission protectrice aura à quitter le port d'Agadir."[1]

En remettant ce document, M. de Schoen a dit que la situation du Maroc rendait nécessaire à bref délai une conversation entre les deux Gouvernements, qu'il n'y avait pas lieu d'examiner si l'envoi d'un bâtiment de guerre à Agadir était conforme à l'Acte d'Algésiras, cet Acte ayant reçu trop d'atteintes pour être allégué avec autorité, que l'opinion allemande était très nerveuse au sujet du Maroc et que l'envoi d'un navire de guerre avait en grande partie pour but de la calmer, que cette mesure de précaution ne devait pas influer sur les relations des deux Gouvernements et qu'il importait de ne pas laisser la presse en dénaturer la caractère.

[1] [*cp. supra*, p. 322, No. 338, where there are some slight differences of wording. The text sent to Paris with instructions on June 30 for communication to the French Government is given also in *G.P.* XXIX, pp. 153–4. The text there is identical with that given *supra*, p. 322, save for punctuation and capitalisation.]

Monsieur de Selves a exprimé à M. de Schoen ses vifs regrets de la décision du Gouvernement Allemand.([1]) Il s'est déclaré convaincu de l'utilité d'une conversation sur les affaires marocaines, mais l'envoi à Agadir d'un bâtiment allemand modifiera la situation et l'opinion publique en France sera difficile à persuader de la réalité du motif allégué par le Gouvernement Allemand.

En me priant de Vous faire connaitre l'acte de ce Gouvernement, Monsieur de Selves me charge de Vous demander comment Vous l'envisagez et quel moyen Vous parait possible d'adopter pour en restreindre la portée. Il ajoute que nous pouvons être amenés à envoyer de notre côté un navire à Mogador et il demande si Vous seriez disposés à envoyer vous-même un navire dans les eaux marocaines de l'Océan Atlantique.

Je reçois toutes ces indications trop tard pour Vous en saisir autrement que par cette lettre et je Vous serais obligé de me faire connaître Vos vues par l'intermédiaire du Foreign Office.

Votre sincèrement dévoué,
PAUL CAMBON.

([1]) [cp. G.P. XXIX. pp. 156–7; 159–62; and Caillaux, pp. 106–7.]

No. 341.

Mr. White to Sir Edward Grey.

F.O. 26615/13379/11/28.
(No. 197.)   Tangier, D. July 1, 1911.
Sir,   R. July 8, 1911.

With reference to my despatch No. 179 of the 24th instant([1]) I have the honour to report that Mr. Harris informs me that, at an interview he had with him yesterday evening, the Spanish Minister stated that the articles that had been appearing lately in the "Times" had done much harm to the Spanish cause, and that they very much regretted the change of policy in that influential paper, from which they had expected support.

Mr. Harris replied that there had been no change on the part of the "Times," or of himself as its correspondent here. He had no desire to write anything unpleasant about Spain, but when the Spanish Government adopted the policy of attempting to shut all non-Spanish enterprise out of the Moorish districts adjoining their possessions he was bound to take up the cudgels on behalf of the Union des Mines, and in the same manner he had to write about the recent action of the Spanish Government at Laraiche and Alcazar. . . . . .([2])

I have, etc.,
HERBERT WHITE.

([1]) [Not reproduced. It refers to Franco-Spanish relations in Morocco, but adds no information to that recorded elsewhere.]
([2]) [Here follows detailed account of a discussion on the mining question.]

No. 342.

Count de Salis to Sir Edward Grey.

                                         Berlin, July 2, 1911.
F.O. 25648/16083/11/28.   D. 1·27 P.M.
Tel. (No. 42.) En clair.   R. 1·56 P.M.

The "Norddeutsche," which appeared last night, publishes following statement :—

"The German firms interested in South Morocco have drawn the attention of the Imperial Government to the dangers which threaten German interests there in view of the possible spread of the disorders prevailing in other parts of the country, and have begged for steps for the protection of the lives and property of Germans and German protected subjects. With this object Imperial Government have decided to send 'Panther' to harbour of Agadir, and have so informed Powers. At the same time the Moroccan notables in the district have been informed that the appearance of a German war-ship does not betoken any unfriendly intention either towards Morocco or its inhabitants."

No. 343.

Count de Salis to Sir Edward Grey.

Berlin, July 2, 1911.

F.O. 25649/25641/11/28.   D. 8·30 P.M.
Tel. (No. 43.) Confidential.   R. 9 P.M.

My immediately preceding telegram.(¹)

I gather from a confidential source that in the course of an interview between the Spanish Ambassador and the Acting Secretary of State the latter declared that the motives which had prompted the dispatch of a German man-of-war to Agadir were the following :—

1. German interests menaced by agitation of El Glawi in order to avenge his disgrace. An outbreak of this agitation was to be feared at any time.
2. Public opinion, which would not allow German Government to stand by while other Powers were dividing up country.

Acting Secretary of State added that stay of German ship at Agadir would depend on France and Spain, which were both violating the Algeciras Act. There were two solutions, either a return to the *status quo*, which was improbable, if not impossible, or an arrangement between the three Powers.

The Spanish Ambassador was further informed, in reply to his enquiry, that the extent of German pretensions had not yet been decided, but that it was not for Berlin to make proposals. It was, however, very desirable that the matter should be settled promptly. Meanwhile the " Panther " would remain at Agadir.

MINUTES.

The sting is in the last paragraph. Germany reserves to herself the right to follow up her action by any and every kind of further and other proceedings that may commend itself to her.

The really serious aspect of the whole incident is this :—

It is hardly conceivable that Germany would have taken this step without considering the possible contingency of her policy leading to a war in which France and England would be ranged against her. However much such a contingency may have been discounted at Berlin as improbable in view of the general attitude of France and England in relation to questions of war and peace, no prudent government would fail, before embarking on a policy of aggression, to provide for the emergency, which cannot be put aside as an impossibility.

The fact that Germany has made the plunge, must give rise to the supposition that she now considers herself in a position to face the danger of an armed Franco-British opposition to her.

If this should prove to be the case, as I think it likely to be, we are now face to face with a pressing and immediate danger, against which it is of vital importance to be prepared. For the sole danger of an Anglo-German conflict consists in the possibility of Germany feeling confident of being able successfully to wage war against us.

In view of the care which Germany is taking to remain perfectly unfettered as to further action, it appears to me that H[is] M[ajesty's] G[overnment] would act most prudently, if they on their part refrained at this stage from giving to Germany any clear indication of their

(¹) [*v.* immediately preceding document.]

real views or of the attitude they may have to adopt. If the German Ambassador makes any enquiry, it would be well to say that H[is] M[ajesty's] G[overnment] do not at present express any opinion : They have received a communication of grave import and they will have to consider it in all its bearings, which are clearly manifold and complex. The longer we can maintain this attitude towards Germany, the better will be our chance of not prematurely or hastily committing ourselves to any line which subsequent developments may make it inconvenient for us to follow.

E. A. C.
July 3.

I quite agree with Sir Eyre Crowe. And we should certainly not give the German Gov[ernmen]t any indication as to what line we may follow—beyond letting them know that we shall send a ship to Agadir and that they have created a situation which requires careful consideration and delicate handling. More we should not say at this juncture.(²)]

A. N.
E. G.

(²) [For further reference to the proposal to send a British ship to Agadir, v. infra, p. 331, No. 351 and note.]

No. 344.

Count de Salis to Sir Edward Grey.

Berlin, July 2, 1911.
D. 8·30 P.M.
R. 9 P.M.

F.O.25650/25641/11/28.
Tel. (No. 44.) Confidential.
My telegram No. 43.(¹)
I understand that, in view of what he has been told here, the Spanish Ambassador is confident that conversations *à trois* will now be resumed, only third party will in future be Germany instead of England.

MINUTES.

It is very difficult to believe that the German action was taken without some previous communication with the Spanish government. The attitude of the latter, in provocation of France, is easily explained on the hypothesis that they could count on German intervention.

We shall have to make it plain at Madrid that we do not accept the rôle of having nothing to say in Morocco and remaining passive spectators of a territorial division between the three other Powers.

E. A. C.
July 3.

It is naturally essential that we should participate in any discussions regarding Morocco.
A. N.

Certainly we must have our say.

E. G.

(¹) [v. immediately preceding document.]

No. 345.

Sir F. Bertie to Sir Edward Grey.

F.O. 25790/16083/11/28.
(No. 307.)
Sir,
Paris, D. July 2, 1911.
R. July 3, 1911.

I have the honour to inform you that the news which was only generally known this morning in Paris that the German Government had decided to send a warship to Agadir has created a great sensation in Paris.

All the papers devote a large space to commenting on this event, which was quite unforeseen by French public opinion. The "Matin" protests against it as contrary to German engagements towards France. It observes that of late certain German papers have been declaring that France owed to Germany some compensation for not having made opposition to the French expedition to Fez. At the beginning of last month M. Jules Cambon and M. de Kiderlen-Waechter had two interviews at Kissingen([1]) at which the desire was expressed that the relations between their respective countries should be as satisfactory as possible, and with that end in view, that a conversation should take place between the two Governments. The despatch of a warship to Agadir would appear to be in the nature of a notice to France that Germany has something to offer in a negotiation.

M. Calmette, Editor of the "Figaro," declares that when the three principal departments of a country (viz., for Foreign Affairs, War and Marine) are disposed of at the caprice of one man or at the dictation of coteries, a country is at the mercy of any provocation and of any surprise.

M. Jaurès, writing in the "Humanité," says that what he has never ceased to foretell has unfortunately come to pass. Germany, after Spain, has followed the example set by France of intervening in Morocco on the classical excuse of protecting her subjects. She has entered by the door criminally opened by the French Colonial party. A protest against German action as being contrary to the Act of Algeciras is absurd on the part of France, for if this Act be violated by an intervention to protect German subjects, it follows that France has also violated it herself and her protest cannot be effective.

The "Eclair" observes that France instinctively understands from the departure of the gunboat Panther for Agadir that Germany, while her attitude continues for the present to be correct, has *arrière-pensées* which are less innocent. She has fixed her choice on territory which would establish her on the Atlantic within reach of French stations. She would in this way have the means of counteracting French influence and of raising up numberless difficulties for France. A frontier with Germany on one continent is enough; France does not want an African frontier with her also.

"L'Action" remarks that between Germany and France no *casus belli* should be allowed to arise in regard to the affairs of Morocco. These affairs are essentially international, it is the duty of all Europe to settle a difference of this sort, if a difference arises.

"La Petite République" declares that the act of the German Government recalls proceedings of Prince Bülow, when he affirmed in 1904 that the Anglo-French agreement did not injure any German interests in Morocco and when he all the same induced the Emperor William II to make the famous journey to Tangier in March 1905, which was to be the prelude of the most serious crisis which France and the peace of Europe have experienced since the scare of 1875 and the Schnoebelé incident.

The correspondent of the "Matin" at Berlin telegraphs to his paper that he has learnt in quarters with which the Mannesmann Brothers have relations that one of the firm was captured two years ago by the Moors in the "hinterland" of Agadir, in the Souss district, and that during his captivity there, which lasted three months, he discovered that it was extremely rich in copper. He subsequently made large purchases of land there.

The general impression derived from the Press this morning is that the action with regard to Agadir on the part of Germany has occasioned mingled feelings of astonishment and indignation in France, comparable with what was felt at the time of the visit of the German Emperor to Tangier in 1905.

The fact that the German action should have taken place at a time when a new Minister for Foreign Affairs, without previous experience of the conduct of

([1]) [*v. supra*, p. 322, *Ed. note.*]

foreign affairs, has just taken over that department increases the unpleasant impression in Paris.

M. de Selves, according to present arrangements, is to leave Paris to-morrow for Holland in attendance on the President of the Republic.

I have, &c.

(for the Ambassador),

L. D. CARNEGIE.

No. 346.

Mr. O'Beirne to Sir Edward Grey.

F.O. 25881/25641/11/28.
Tel. (No. 139.) Confidential.

St. Petersburgh, July 3, 1911.
D. 11·50 A.M.
R. 1·30 P.M.

Spanish Chargé d'Affaires mentioned to me yesterday that the intended despatch of German ship of war to a Moorish port was known several days to the Spanish Government and that they had reason to believe German Government meant to act energetically in Morocco.

No. 347.

Sir Edward Grey to Count de Salis.

F.O. 26033/25641/11/28.
Tel. (No. 127.) Confidential.

Foreign Office, July 3, 1911.
D. 5·45 P.M.

I have told Count Metternich that I have seen the Prime Minister this morning, and that we regard the situation created by the German move to Agadir as so important that it must be considered at a Cabinet. Till that had been done I would say nothing more, but I wished the German Government to know without delay that we regarded the situation as new and important. It was also very delicate, and, in my personal opinion, if an atmosphere favourable to a satisfactory and peaceful discussion was to be created, public opinion here and elsewhere must not be inflamed. The German action was very abrupt, and had excited public opinion here.

Count Metternich repeated reasons for this action and what he had said to Sir A. Nicolson. I said that British commercial interests were, I thought, considerably larger than German in Morocco, and reasons given for German action would apply at least as strongly to us. We could not remain passive spectators of a new settlement made between Germany, France, and Spain to take the place of the Act of Algeciras. We must take part in such a discussion. Count Metternich urged that a favourable development would depend greatly upon whether or not we made France feel that we would support her against Germany. I replied that at the moment I was preoccupied rather with purely British interests than with obligations to France. The situation might develop so as to affect British interests directly.

(Repeated to Paris for Sir F. Bertie's confidential information, No. 165.)

No. 348.

Mr. Russell to Sir Edward Grey.

F.O. 25945/25641/11/28.

Tel. (No. 64.) Confidential.

Vienna, *July* 3, 1911.
D. 6·50 P.M.
R. 8·40 P.M.

Morocco.

Count von Aehrenthal informed French Ambassador this afternoon that he had no previous warning of the dispatch of German ship to Morocco. The first he heard of it was on Saturday, when the German Ambassador made the announcement at the same time as it was made to press. Count von Aehrenthal said that he had received the communication in the same manner as he had received similar communications from French and Spanish Governments,([1]) that is to say, that he committed himself to no opinion, and merely took act of statement.

German action is, I think, not unwelcome here, as it is hoped that it may distract German attention from Albania and prevent any interference in that quarter.

([1]) [The report of Herr von Tschirschky of July 1 does not seem quite the same as this. *v. G.P.* XXIX, p. 158.]

No. 349.

Communication from Count Benckendorff of July 3, 1911.

Traduction d'un Télégramme de M. Neratov au Comte de Benckendorff du 2 Juillet.

F.O. 27150/25641/11/28.
(Confidentiel.)

D'ordre de son Gouvernement l'Ambassadeur de France m'a entretenu de la situation créée par la décision du Gouvernement Allemand d'envoyer un navire de guerre à Agadir pour la protection de ses sujets et des intérêts Allemands.([1])

Le Gouvernement de la République se rend compte de la gravité de la mesure adoptée et hésite sur les décisions à prendre. J'ai cru devoir signaler quelques côtés de la situation méritant une attention particulière. Du moment que l'Allemagne a informé toutes les Puissances de sa décision, il ne peut pas espérer qu'elle y renonce. Il y a lieu de considérer sa décision comme un fait accompli. Le côté militaire de la question ne paraît avoir qu'une importance secondaire; sa portée est diplomatique, assurer les intérêts politiques de l'Allemagne en présence de l'infraction déjà accomplie aux formalités de l'acte d'Algeciras; le désir de l'Allemagne est probablement d'entamer de nouvelles négociations avec la France au sujet de la question Marocaine en s'appuyant sur un fait accompli. Il résulte de mes explications avec M. Louis que la France se déciderait peut-être à envoyer un batiment de guerre à Mogador à proximité d'Agadir afin de répondre à la mesure militaire de l'Allemagne par une mesure militaire, en justifiant celle-ci par la nécessité de renforcer la police à Mogador en conformité avec l'acte d'Algeciras.

Pour le côté diplomatique de la question M. Louis, s'est exprimé dans le sens d'un caractère international à donner aux négociations (et je me suis rangé à cette opinion) et non dans le sens de négociations franco-allemandes, qui selon moi seraient moins propice à une solution pacifique.

Il faut donc s'attendre à ce que le Cabinet de Paris prenne comme base de sa réponse à l'Allemagne les actes internationaux et qu'il fasse part de cette réponse

([1]) [*v.* Count Pourtalès' account of his interview with M. Neratov of July 1, *G.P.* XXIX, pp. 158–9; and M. Neratov's instructions to Count Benckendorff of July 2. *Siebert*, pp. 588–9.]

par communications ultérieures à toutes les autres Puissances engagées par les actes en question. M. Louis n'est pas favorable à l'éventualité d'une Conférence.

Le Gouvernement Britannique étant touché par la présente question de plus près que nous, il est désirable de conformer avec soin les points de vue Anglais et Russes.

Veuillez Vous informer de la manière de voir du Cabinet de Londres et nous télégraphier d'urgence.

No. 350.

Mr. Rennie to Sir Edward Grey.

F.O. 26266/25641/11/28.
(No. 116.)   Madrid, D. July 3, 1911.
Sir,   R. July 6, 1911.

The news of the despatch of a German Man-of-war to Agadir appeared in the Press of the evening of July 1st and is commented on at length by yesterday's and to-day's papers which during the past week have been showing considerable reserve on the Morocco question.

The general tone of the newspapers of all shades of opinion seems to be one of expectant excitement mingled with almost undisguised pleasure at the embarrassment that it is expected will be caused to France by this latest development of events. Attention is called to the fact that it is the French sphere that is to be the scene of the German move. It is also pointed out with a show of satisfaction that the despatch of the German warship is merely analogous to the late Spanish action at Alcazar, which now thus finds its justification. The key to the question is held to be the attitude which will be adopted by His Majesty's Government.

(Confidential.) The German Ambassador whom I saw this morning told me that on the receipt of his instructions the day before yesterday he had gone to see Señor Garcia Prieto and had conveyed to him the notification in the form of a *pro-memoriâ*, which His Excellency had received without comment, merely stating that he would communicate it to the Cabinet. The interview seems to have been of a brief description. Prince Ratibor said that the news had come to him as a surprise and that he knew nothing of what had occurred at Agadir beyond the statements contained in the telegram from his Government.

I have, &c.
ERNEST RENNIE.

No. 351.

Sir Edward Grey to Sir F. Bertie.

F.O. 26236/25641/11/28.
(No. 260.)
Sir,   Foreign Office, July 3, 1911.

I told M. Cambon to-day that we regarded the situation created by the German move to Agadir as very serious. I had seen the Prime Minister, and a Cabinet was to be held to-morrow morning. Till that was over I could not say anything which would commit the Government.

M. Cambon told me that Herr Zimmerman, the Acting Minister at the German Foreign Office, had told the Spanish Ambassador in Berlin that the German Government had sent a ship to Agadir not only to protect their own subjects, but because German opinion demanded that the Government should show that they were not disinterested in Morocco. When the Spanish Ambassador asked how long the ship would stay, Herr Zimmermann had said that it must stay until things had returned to their previous normal state : a solution which he did not think possible, or until a settlement had been come to by conversation " à trois " between France, Spain, and Germany. In saying this, he had added that the conversation must be " à trois seulement.''

I told M. Cambon that, though pending the Cabinet I could not say anything, except to express my own personal opinion, I thought it was necessary that we should make it quite clear that we were interested in a settlement of the Moroccan question. We had both commercial and strategic interests to consider. As long as only France and Spain, who were charged with special functions in Morocco, were dealing with the situation there, there was no need for us to take any step. But now that Germany had taken special steps on her own account, it would be natural that we should take special steps to protect our own interests.

I was therefore considering whether, having regard to the suggestion in his communication of sending a ship to Mogador, we should not send a ship to Agadir. Agadir was not an open port, though the question of its being opened had been discussed, and we should require a report on the situation. If we did take separate steps to protect our interests, as we had recognised by the Agreement of 1904 that it belonged specially to France to take measures of pacification in Morocco, I should recall this in any announcement I made, and say that any measures which we would take on our own behalf would be taken in consultation with the French Government.

M. Cambon expressed strongly his personal view that we should send a ship to Agadir. He said that the French Government also might send a ship.([1])

I observed that it was a question, if France sent a ship, whether it should not go to some other place than Agadir so as to avoid the umbrage which might be given by putting a French ship and a British ship one on each side of a German ship at a particular spot.

M. Cambon readily agreed that there was force in this consideration.

I informed him that I was going to see the German Ambassador this afternoon, but only for the purpose of telling him that we regarded the question as serious, and were going to have a Cabinet to discuss it to-morrow. I thought it desirable that the German Government should know as soon as possible that their action made it necessary for us to consider British interests.

[I am, &c.]
E. G[REY].

([1]) [cp. supra, pp. 323–4, No. 340. According to Caillaux, pp. 109–11, this proposal was subsequently disavowed by the French Government. In fact, Great Britain declined to send a ship, v. infra, pp. 333–4, No. 355, and cp. infra, p. 337, No. 359; v. also Twenty-Five Years, Vol. I, p. 220. Other references are given in G.P. XXIX, p. 162, note.]

No. 352.

Count de Salis to Sir Edward Grey.

Berlin, July 4, 1911.

F.O. 26081/25641/11/28.
Tel. (No. 45.) Confidential.
    Morocco. ·

D. 2·10.
R. 2·40.

Spanish Ambassador tells me confidentially that, in conversation with him yesterday, Chancellor affected to minimize importance of step taken by despatching vessel to Agadir, declaring that matter would easily be settled either by a return to *status quo* or far more probably by arrangement between the three interested powers. In reply to Ambassador's enquiries Chancellor insisted that he did not anticipate difficulties on the part of England who was not directly interested. Moreover German relations with England were now excellent and he had every reason to believe dispositions of England towards Germany were most friendly.

Spanish Ambassador betrayed great satisfaction that affairs in Morocco would now be discussed in conversations in which France would necessarily be in a minority.

MINUTES.

The remarks of the German Chancellor show clearly that it is the intention of the German government to make use of the " excellent relations " he has established with England, in order to detach England from France. Herr von Bethmann-Hollweg clearly believes that the political understanding between Germany and England which, according to his scheme was to give Germany a free hand to deal with France, does actually exist: he counts firmly on England standing aside.

Point is given to this aspect of the situation by the manifest co-operation of Spain with Germany, unblushingly avowed by the remark of the Spanish ambassador at Berlin.

I think it must now be doubtful whether we can hope to maintain Spain loyal to her understanding with us and France by mere humouring of the Spanish government. It might be worth the effort, to make a very sharp communication to Spain, pointing out that her co-operation with Germany in opposition to France might compel England to reconsider her policy towards Spain.

E. A. C.
July 4.

It is difficult to understand why England is less interested than Germany!

W. L.

I think that the Chancellor will soon be aware that England does not intend to stand aside in any discussions which may take place. And also that we intend to remain loyal to our obligations to France.

A. N.

I have made a communication to Count Metternich which will counteract this.([1])
The Spanish Ambassador should be asked to come to see me to-morrow.

E. G.
4.7.11.

([1]) [v. infra, p. 334, No. 356.]

No. 353.

Sir F. Cartwright to Sir Edward Grey.

Trieste, July 4, 1911.

F.O. 26096/25641/11/28.
Tel. Unnumbered.
Morocco.

D. 4·8 P.M.
R. 10 P.M.

French Ambassador yesterday enquired from Count von Aehrenthal what he thought of German action in Morocco. Count von Aehrenthal replied that it did not surprise him, as he had been expecting a *coup de main* from Germany in that direction for some time, but he assured him that he had no previous knowledge of German action, which was first announced to him on Saturday last by the German Ambassador. Count von Aehrenthal declared that he had made no observation to German Ambassador, but had merely taken note of German statement that occupation of port in Morocco was only temporary.

No. 354.

Sir A. Nicolson to Sir Edward Grey.

Private.(¹)

My dear Grey,   *Foreign Office, July 4, 1911.*

In case I do not see you before the Cabinet meeting, I write a line to say that M. Cambon looked in on me after his visit to you(²) and expressed the strong hope that we would send a vessel to Agadir. I sincerely trust that we shall do so if only to ascertain what the Germans are doing there. The vessel need only stay a short time and then proceed to the nearest port whence she could communicate by telegraph. I am not sure that the Canaries would not be the nearest. From what Metternich let drop to you it looks as if the Germans wished to repeat their Algeciras tactics and endeavour to detach us from France. I feel confident that they will on this occasion be as unsuccessful as they were at Algeciras.

Y[ou]rs sincerely,
A. NICOLSON.

(¹) [Grey MSS., Vol. 54.]
(²) [*v. supra*, pp. 330–1, No. 351.]

No. 355.

Sir Edward Grey to Sir F. Bertie.

F.O. 26228/85641/11/28.
(No. 261.)

Sir,   *Foreign Office, July 4, 1911.*

I told M. Cambon to-day that we had decided not to send a ship to Agadir at present, because if we sent one at all it must be with instructions to remain as long as the Germans remained : we could not send a ship, and then remove it before the German ship went.

M. Cambon enquired whether, if the Germans landed a force, or sent a stronger naval force to Agadir, we would send a ship.

I replied that, if new circumstances arose, we should reconsider the question of sending a ship.

I then informed him that I was authorised by the Government to say that our attitude would be to fulfil our Treaty obligations to France in the diplomatic discussions which were now inevitable, and which, in our opinion, must be discussions *à quatre*, between France, Germany, Spain, and ourselves, and not *à trois* without us. Before entering upon such discussions, it was essential to settle the solution which we wished to attain in the discussions. We ought, therefore, to know what France would consider a reasonable and practicable solution from the point of view of French interests; for instance : the restoration of the previous *status quo* by the withdrawal of Germany from Agadir, and of Spain from Alcazar and Laraiche, as well as of France from Fez and the posts in the interior.

M. Cambon here observed that the French force had already been withdrawn from Fez. The French instructors were left there, but they had been there from a period anterior to the Algeciras Act. Their continued presence in Fez was not, therefore, a disturbance of the *status quo ante*.

To this I of course agreed.

M. Cambon explained that the only posts established had been for the purpose of victualling the French column, and these would naturally be withdrawn.

I then suggested that a new arrangement might be preferred by France, consolidating her position in Morocco, and giving Germany compensation either in Morocco or elsewhere to secure her recognition of the new arrangement. In such an event, we should have to consider what conditions we should require on the part of Germany, to secure British interests.

I also informed M. Cambon of what it had been decided to say to the German Ambassador as to our attitude towards Morocco, and told him that I intended to carry out this decision this afternoon.(¹)

[I am, &c.]
E. G[REY].

(¹) [v. immediately succeeding document.]

No. 356.

Sir Edward Grey to Count de Salis.(¹)

F.O. 26235/25641/11/28.
(No. 147.)
Sir,   *Foreign Office, July 4, 1911.*

I informed Count Metternich to-day, on behalf of His Majesty's Government, that I must tell him that our attitude could not be a disinterested one with regard to Morocco. We must take into consideration our Treaty obligations to France and our own interests in Morocco. We were of opinion that a new situation had been created by the despatch of a German ship to Agadir. Future developments might affect British interests more directly than they had hitherto been affected, and therefore we could not recognise any new arrangement which was come to without us.(²)

Count Metternich asked me whether he might take down the exact words. I therefore dictated them to him, observing however that he must take this as a conversation and not as a written communication.

He remarked that the new situation had been created by French and Spanish action.

I said I understood the view of the German Government to be that the French and Spanish action had made it necessary for them to calm German public opinion by showing that Germany was not disinterested in the question of Morocco. They had taken the overt step of sending a ship to Agadir. We had not taken any overt step, though our commercial interests in Morocco were greater than those of Germany. It was therefore the more incumbent upon us to make it clear that we, no more than Germany, could let things develop without taking an interest in them.

Count Metternich then said that the attitude of our Press towards the sending of a German ship to Agadir was not likely to foster that favourable atmosphere for discussion for which I had expressed a wish in conversation yesterday. The German Press, on the other hand, had been very calm.

I said that I had stated yesterday that the action of Germany in sending a ship to a closed port, where it was not known that commercial interests existed, was sure to excite the Press here and elsewhere. If we, instead of the German Gov[ernmen]t, had sent a ship to Agadir, while the German Gov[ernmen]t did nothing, the German Press would have been equally excited.

In commenting upon the communication which I had made, Count Metternich said that he was sure the German Government would understand that it was natural for us to take an interest in the question.

[I am, &c.]
E. G[REY].

(¹) [*Twenty-Five Years*, Vol. I, pp. 222–3, quotes this and states that the communication was made '' after consultation in the Cabinet.'' *v. Siebert*, pp. 590–2.]

(²) [For Count Metternich's report, *v. G.P.* XXIX, p. 167. This gives the sense of this and the two preceding sentences, but in slightly different words. For comment *v. Churchill*, p. 44.]

No. 357.

Sir Edward Grey to Sir G. Buchanan.

F.O. 26698/25883/11/28.
(No. 181.)
Sir,
                                            Foreign Office, July 5, 1911.

I told Count Benckendorff to-day, in answer to his enquiry as to our attitude with regard to Morocco, what I had said to the German Ambassador yesterday.([1])

He asked whether I thought of suggesting a Conference.

I said that I thought it would be desirable that the four Powers most interested : France, Spain, Germany, and ourselves, should come to an understanding before any Conference met, in order to avoid the wranglings which there were at the Algeciras Conference. But France was the Power which had the greatest interest in this question, and I should not propose a Conference or anything of that sort, but leave it to her to say what she wished in that respect.

[I am, &c.]
E. G[REY].

([1]) [v. immediately preceding document.]

No. 358.

Sir Edward Grey to Mr. Rennie.

F.O. 26699/25641/11/28.
(No. 72.)
Sir,
                                            Foreign Office, July 5, 1911.

I observed to the Spanish Ambassador this afternoon that the consequences which I had feared from the Spanish action at Alcazar had come to pass. I now had recent reports that more and more Spanish troops were being sent to Alcazar, whereas the French had withdrawn theirs from Fez. I urged that the situation had become one which made it necessary to be very careful.

The Ambassador said that he had not heard of the despatch of any reinforcements to Alcazar since what he had said to Sir Arthur Nicolson a few days ago; but all the Spanish couriers and post between Alcazar and Laraiche had lately been robbed.

The Ambassador assured me that his Government did not know beforehand of the German intention to send a ship to Agadir, though they had known for some time that Germany intended to do something.

His Government were not now having conversations with anyone; but they had gathered that the view of the German Government was that an appeal by France to the juridical effect of the Franco-German Agreement about Morocco and of the Algeciras Act would not facilitate a peaceful solution. The French had fooled others by going to Fez.

I asked whether the German Government meant that the action of the French in going to Fez had not been straightforward?

The Spanish Ambassador confirmed this.

I said that, if that was so, then the action of the German Government had been anything but straightforward. When they received the news of the French expedition to Fez, they had expressed confidence in the loyalty of the French assurances, and they had not deprecated the expedition. Though they had expressed apprehensions that the French might be forced to stay in Fez longer than was expected, they had given all of us to understand that, if the French expectations of speedy withdrawal were realised, there would be no complaint. The moment when the French were carrying out the withdrawal even more rapidly than had been anticipated was not the time to accuse them of want of straightforwardness.

The Ambassador said that the French expedition had led to other punitive expeditions in the interior. He then went on to say that the French must not suppose that, by delaying their withdrawal while the Germans stayed at Agadir, a solution of the question could be reached. Germany was determined to have a settlement of the Moroccan question. The settlement might perhaps be a return to the *status quo ante*: but this was difficult, if not impossible, seeing that by the fact of the French expedition to Fez(¹) the Sultan had been placed practically under French protection, and that a return to the *status quo* would entail the withdrawal of the French not merely from Fez, but also from Casablanca, where the presence of a French force was a breach of the Algeciras Act. The German Government therefore thought that there would have to be a new arrangement: in fact, a partition of Morocco.

I said that it was useful to know what the view of the German Government was. The only comment I would make upon it for the moment was that a communication which I had made to Count Metternich yesterday, in which I had stated that we could not recognise any new arrangement which was come to without us, was even more timely than I had realised at the moment.

The Spanish Ambassador said that, of course, the arrangement would have to be between the four Powers most interested, of which we were one.

I observed that British interests were now likely to be affected in a more direct way than had hitherto been the case, and that the situation was too serious for me to make further comment upon it at the moment.

[I am, &c.]
E. G[REY]

(¹) [*v. supra*, pp. 173–283, *passim*.]

No. 359.

Sir A. Nicolson to Lord Hardinge of Penshurst.

Private.(¹)

My dear Hardinge,   *Foreign Office, July* 5, 1911.

Many thanks for your letter of June 9th. . . . .(²)

We are at this moment entirely preoccupied with the German move in respect to Morocco, and it was evidently a carefully thought out plan, and, as is usual with the Germans, was sprung suddenly upon us. I imagine that after the visit of the Emperor here(³) and the activity of the Anglo-German Friendship Society, the Emperor was convinced that our attitude had changed and that he would succeed in detaching us from France. The communication was made to me by Metternich last Saturday and I saw that he was extremely nervous during its delivery.(⁴) I merely remarked that Agadir was not an open port and that I was quite unaware that any German or foreign subjects of any nationality could be at a place where there was no trade. To this he replied that he was only instructed to communicate the fact and that he himself was quite unaware as to the conditions of Agadir. He then gave me verbally an explanatory statement as to the reasons which had induced the German Government to take the step of sending a warship to Morocco. He stated that the advance of the French to Fez, as to the necessity of which the German reports differed widely from those of the French, and also the establishment by the French and the Spaniards of military posts in various parts of Morocco, had created a new situation, which rendered the provisions of the Act of Algeciras illusory. The German Government had no wish to pass any criticisms on the act of France and Spain, but it was clear that a return to the *Status Quo ante* was out of the question

(¹) [Carnock MSS., Vol. III of 1911.]

(²) [The opening remarks of this letter are entirely personal.]

(³) [The Emperor visited London on May 15–20 for the unveiling of the memorial to Queen Victoria. *cp. Gooch & Temperley,* Vol. VI, p. 631, No. 467, and *note* (¹).]

(⁴) [As Sir Edward Grey was out of town, Sir Arthur Nicolson received the communication, *v. supra,* pp. 322–3, Nos. 338 and 339. *v. also G.P.* XXIX, p. 157, and pp. 164–5.]

and that the German Government were compelled to listen to the requests of their subjects and protected subjects in the South where no police forces existed for protection to their lives and properties. The German Government were therefore compelled to afford such protection, and to continue to afford such protection, until a normal state of peace and tranquillity was re-established in Morocco. The German Government were quite ready to enter into a discussion with the French and Spanish Governments with the view of endeavouring to find a definite solution of the Morocco question. They were well aware that there were great difficulties in the way of such a solution, but in view of the friendly relations which existed between Germany, France and Spain, they did not consider that such difficulties were insurmountable. If the British Government were disposed to assist towards such a solution their aid would be gladly welcomed. I told Count Metternich that naturally all that I could say at the present moment was that I should repeat to Sir Edward Grey as faithfully as possible what he had said to me, and that he must understand that I considered that the communication which he had made was one of grave importance. Since then there has been a Cabinet Council, and Sir Edward Grey has seen both Metternich([5]) and Monsieur Cambon.([6]) I was exceedingly anxious, and so were the French, that we should at once send a ship to Agadir,([7]) if only for the purpose of ascertaining what was really passing there, as naturally we are, and shall continue to be, without any information as to what the Germans may be doing in that locality. Unfortunately, the Cabinet did not see their way to sending a vessel, but they have empowered Grey to make a very stiff communication to the German Government.([8]) We have in substance informed the Germans that our attitude is to safeguard British interests and to observe our treaty obligations to France and that their act having created a new situation it is essential that we should take part in any discussions which may take place between France, Spain and Germany. From conversations which the German Chancellor has had with the Spanish Ambassador at Berlin, it is clear that he was under the impression that we should be quite willing to stand aside and subscribe to any terms to which the three Powers might agree. I think the fact that the German Government desired to ignore us entirely in the matter and to take for granted that our relations with Germany were of so friendly a nature that we should raise no difficulties in the matter, has considerably stirred up our authorities here, and has by no means made a favourable impression upon them. This is all to the good, and I am most anxious that we should not at all weaken in our support of France. We are now waiting to hear from Paris what line they propose to follow. It seems to me that there are only two courses open,—either to endeavour to restore the state of things which existed before the French advanced to Fez, and which would entail the withdrawal of the French from Fez and the interior, as well as the retirement of the Spanish troops and necessarily also the withdrawal of the German vessel from Agadir. This combination is, however, an extremely improbable one and there remains the other alternative, which would be to arrange what would practically be a partition of Morocco. In these circumstances if Germany were permitted to have a share we ought certainly to lay down our conditions. I do not suppose that we ourselves require or could well claim any portion of the Moorish territory, but I think we might lay down—and here Grey entirely agrees with me—a set of conditions to our consent to a division of Morocco into spheres of influence. These four conditions would be : (1) the internationalisation of Tangiers and its neighbourhood, to be detached from the Moorish Empire, and to be administered by an international municipality; (2) a treaty pledge that no ports on the Morocco coast, either Atlantic or Mediterranean, should be fortified; (3) that Germany should not endeavour to acquire a port on the Mediterranean coast; and (4) the maintenance of the open-door. The above four conditions are, I think,

([5]) [v. supra, p. 334, No. 356.]
([6]) [v. supra, pp. 333–4, No. 355.]
([7]) [v. supra, pp. 330–1, No. 351; and p. 333, No. 354.]
([8]) [The communication of July 4, v. supra, p. 334, No. 356.]

the very minimum which we could demand and on which we ought certainly to insist. Before this reaches you the question will doubtless have further developed, and I have only given you above a rough sketch of how matters at present stand. I am not at all sorry that the incident has occurred as I think it will open the eyes of all those who have been so clamorous of late for an understanding with Germany and I hope that it will postpone indefinitely any further negotiations for a political understanding with that country. . . . .(⁹)

[A. NICOLSON.]

(⁹) [The rest of this letter refers to the Balkan situation, the Bagdad Railway, the Arbitration Treaty with the United States, and other subjects not connected with this volume.]

No. 360.

Sir Edward Grey to Sir M. de Bunsen.

F.O. 26243/8755/11/28.   *Foreign Office, July* 6, 1911.
Tel. (No. 80.)   D. 6 P.M.
 Mr. White's No. 123.(¹)
 You should inform Spanish Minister for F[oreign] A[ffairs] that the action of the Spanish auth[ori]ties in Morocco at this moment is calculated, in the opinion of H[is] M[ajesty's] Go[vernmen]t, seriously to endanger all prospects of finding a satisfactory solution by amicable agreement among the Powers primarily interested. H[is] M[ajesty's] G[overnment] confidently hope that the Spanish authorities will be instructed to abstain from any forward military movements, which if persisted in may create grave European complications.

(¹) [Colonel Silvestre had been reported as having written to Raisuli to say he would come to visit him at Arzila, and that his cavalry would remain one hour's march distant from the town.]

No. 361.

Sir F. Bertie to Sir Edward Grey.

F.O. 26390/16083/11/28.
(No. 315.)   *Paris,* D. *July* 6, 1911.
Sir,   R. *July* 7, 1911.
 I have the honour to report that the French Press, after the first shock of surprise and indignation at the news of the despatch of a German gunboat to Agadir, has, generally speaking, had the appearance of obeying a *mot d'ordre* that the German action had better be minimised and regarded as a temporary move to induce the French Government to hasten negotiations with Berlin and to make some offer to Germany, not necessarily in Morocco, as an offset to the extended action of France in Morocco.
 The "Bureau de la Presse" at the Ministry for Foreign Affairs has during the last 2 or 3 years been reorganized and managed on different lines with the object of enabling the Ministry to induce the Press, or at any rate, the chief organs which write with authority on Foreign Affairs, to present a unanimous front in any crisis of foreign policy. In the affair of the Casablanca deserters,(¹) the Ministry for Foreign Affairs expressed their satisfaction at the manner in which the French Press had obeyed the indications given them as to how to deal with the demands

(¹) [*v. supra,* pp. 109–31, *passim.*]

of Germany. The treatment of the Agadir incident is to all appearance another example of the relative readiness of the chief Paris papers to conform their utterances to an indication given them from official quarters.

The " Matin " this morning believes that the German attitude may be expressed by the sentence " Que m'offrez-vous? " It adds that the French Government, however, do not mean to make a definite answer as to what they are ready to offer as the German Government would be sure to declare that they were not offered enough and would ask for more.

Satisfaction is shown by the papers at the attitude of the French Government in delaying any action in reply to the German move until they have consulted the British and Russian Governments.

I have the honour to transmit to you herewith(²) an article from the " Temps " of to-day's date, which states that everything leads to the conclusion that the German demonstration at Agadir is a summons to France to enter upon a negotiation of some kind. The article observes that it is therefore of interest to review what has been realised or attempted of late in the way of recent Franco-German agreements on economic questions. It enumerates those dealing with the " Union des Mines Marocaines," the " Société Marocaine de Travaux Publics," the Société Française du Gabon," (a negotiation in which the Ngoko Sangha Company were involved, see my despatch No. 39 Africa of the 3rd instant(³)); the Moorish Railways, and the Cameroon–Congo Railway.

The article concludes that it is not difficult for France and Germany to talk over matters. They have only to continue with increased activity conversations already begun.

Little or nothing is said in the French Press as to the possibility of Germany establishing herself at Agadir or as to the objections from the point of view of naval strategy which such an eventuality might entail. The impression given is that the French feel that Great Britain would be more affected than France thereby and that His Majesty's Government can be counted upon to prevent Germany from obtaining an undue advantage on the Atlantic coast-line.

I have, &c.

(For the Ambassador),

L. D. CARNEGIE.

(²) [These extracts are not reproduced. For Count Benckendorff's views on this day v. Siebert, p. 592.]
(³) [Not reproduced.]

No. 362.

Sir V. Corbett to Sir Edward Grey.

F.O. 26834/25641/11/28.
(No. 29.) Confidential.   Munich, D. July 6, 1911.
Sir,   R. July 10, 1911.

In the course of a conversation which I had with Count Podewils to-day I asked him if he could tell me anything which might help me to reconcile the divergent explanations I had seen given in the press for the despatch of a German ship of war to Agadir.

His Excellency replied that the whole matter was very simple. German merchants were constantly complaining that their overseas interests were neglected by the Government and that German Representatives abroad would give them no help lest it might provoke diplomatic complications. As long as two years ago, when Baron Schoen was still Foreign Secretary, the question of the protection of German interests at Agadir had been raised by Messrs. Mannesmann and the Foreign Affairs Committee of the Federal Council (of which he himself is ex officio

Chairman,) had agreed that, if menaced, they were worthy of protection. The condition of Morocco had lately called for European intervention in other provinces and nothing could be more natural than that Germany should send a gun-boat to Agadir to see that the interests of her nationals were not imperilled.

In answer to my question as to whether there were many German subjects in the Sus valley and in what their interests consisted, His Excellency said rather vaguely that Messrs. Mannesmann certainly had large interests in those regions. He added that their group had lost considerable sums of money, and that they were inclined to ascribe the fact to the insufficient Government backing they had received. He did not however pretend that anything particular had recently occurred in those regions to call for exceptional precautions.

I observed that it seemed to be generally accepted by public opinion that the despatch of the " Panther" implied a new political departure, intended to lead up either to a modification of the Algeciras Convention or to some kind of negotiation in which Germany would be able to obtain what was termed " compensation." Count Podewils assured me that there had been no new departure. If any change of policy had been contemplated he would have been informed whereas he had just received a letter from Count Lerchenfeld telling him that there was no fear that the despatch of the " Panther" would lead to any political complications, that the Emperor had already left for Norway and that the Imperial Chancellor was just off on his holiday.

As I was leaving, His Excellency referred me to what he said was an interesting article on the subject which had appeared in to-day's edition of the Munchener Zeitung. He had not himself had time to read it as the paper had only just arrived, but from what he had been told about it, it seemed to very fairly interpret the German attitude. The article in question which has all the appearance of an authoritative statement, is as follows :—

> " The Morocco question affords no ground for serious alarm. Germany's action at Agadir took place and had to take place because disturbance and excitement had manifested themselves in South Morocco, a part of the country unvisited by either French or Spanish troops, and might endanger German interests there. Germany has however no intention of remaining permanently at Agadir or of establishing herself at all in South Morocco. She will certainly quit the harbour of Agadir as soon as France and Spain withdraw their troops from the country. Germany's withdrawal will follow *pari passu* on the retreat of the two Powers, since her standpoint continues afterwards as it was before, to be based on the Convention of Algeciras by which the integrity of the Shereefian Kingdom was established. Germany is now waiting quietly for France to approach her with proposals for settling matters in Morocco. All the Chanceries of Europe are however convinced that out of the Morocco Question no conflict can arise calculated to lead to complications dangerous to the peace."

The impression left on my mind was that Count Podewils was not entirely ingenuous in his statement. He particularly insisted that the German action had been dictated by anxiety for German commercial interests only and had no reference to the action of any other country whereas the article above quoted, to which he referred me, argues an intimate relation between the action of Germany and that of France and Spain.

I do not know what rôle the Foreign Affairs Committee (which as you will remember, only came into being after the famous " Daily Telegraph " interview,([1])) fills and as it has, I believe, held no sitting for more than six months, it is probable enough that Count Podewils is not very precisely informed of Herr von Kiderlen's views or intentions.

([1]) [The sentence in brackets was crossed out in the despatch by Sir Eyre Crowe, who commented in the margin " No. This is quite wrong. Omit from print."]

The most generally accepted opinion here seems to be that the recent French expedition to Fez and the apparently wanton descent of the Spaniards on Laraiche made it incumbent on this Government to do something which would look like an assertion of German influence. The existence, real or imaginary, of German interests at Agadir suggested a demonstration at that place, the policing of which does not, I believe, come under the Act of Algeciras. Such action might never have been taken if it had not been for the measures taken by Spain, and, while not intended to provoke an immediate crisis, is nevertheless in the nature of pegging out a claim for the time which it is anticipated is not far distant when the whole situation in regard to Morocco will have to be reviewed.

My French Colleague, who has several times spoken to me on this subject, has repeatedly insisted on the perfect good faith of his Government in their desire to carry out both the letter and the spirit of the Algeciras Convention, but he has been equally emphatic in declaring his belief that the German Government, while ready to admit a French sphere of influence in Morocco, were determined, as the price of their benevolent attitude to obtain compensation "there or elsewhere." In making both these statements I have reason to believe that he is only echoing the words of his late chief, Monsieur Cruppi.

I have, &c.
VINCENT CORBETT.

No. 363.

Sir Edward Grey to Sir F. Bertie.

F.O. 26700/25883/11/28.
(No. 276.)
Sir, *Foreign Office, July 6, 1911.*

M. Cambon informed me to-day that he had a communication from M. Caillaux, who was taking charge of Foreign Affairs in the absence of M. de Selves, that M. Jules Cambon had been instructed to say at Berlin that, as Germany had expressed a wish to converse on the subject of Morocco, it was for her to express her views. M. Jules Cambon had been instructed to ask for explanations. M. Caillaux expressed his satisfaction at the statement made by me to M. Cambon the day before yesterday. He wished to know whether I had any positive views as to the compensation to be given to Germany. It would not be well to suggest compensation in Morocco.

M. Cambon proceeded to discuss the matter on the assumption that under no circumstances could Great Britain agree to any territory being given to Germany in Morocco, and that therefore any compensation of that sort must be found outside. He thought as Germany's interests in Morocco were understood to be economic, she should be asked what it was that she required to satisfy them. Our interests, M. Cambon assumed, consisted of our Treaty obligations to France and our commercial interests.

I said that we should have to consider our strategic interests also, if there was any question of fortifying a naval base on the flank of our trade routes.

M. Cambon said this was exactly why it was impossible for Great Britain to agree to any territorial compensation to Germany in Morocco.

I said it would be preferable that whatever Germany received, in return for giving France a free hand in Morocco, should be outside Morocco; but from our own point of view, though it was difficult, it was not impossible to find something for her in Morocco. An open commercial port, for instance, would not be irreconcilable with our interests, though no doubt we should wish to have some compensation from Germany for seeing her established in Morocco.

M. Cambon urged that a commercial port might at any moment become a fortified one.

I replied that, if there was an international agreement that it was not to be fortified, we could always interfere to prevent its fortification, and if necessary we would do so. I agreed, however, that France should find out what Germany wanted. When this has been ascertained, France could consider whether it was reconcilable with her interests; and we could consider whether it was reconcilable with ours.

In reply to further arguments on M. Cambon's part, to the effect that we should lay it down as absolutely impossible that Germany should have any territorial sphere in Morocco, I said it would be preferable that anything Germany had should be outside Morocco, but that though difficult it was not impossible for us to conceive conditions under which she could get some compensation in Morocco in return for a politically free hand in France. I would not, however, suggest anything which France regarded as irreconcilable with her interests, and I merely wished M. Cambon to understand that we did not, from our point of view, wish to shut the door in advance upon any possible solution. I asked him what the French view would be as to giving Germany anything in Morocco.

He replied that he did not know.

[I am, &c.]
E. G[REY].

No. 364.

Question asked in the House of Commons, July 6, 1911.

(Parl. Deb. 5th Ser., House of Commons, Vol. 27, p. 1341.)

Mr. Balfour: Perhaps the Prime Minister will redeem his promise and carry out what he led the House to believe he would be able to do to-day, that is make a statement to the House as to the present aspect of affairs in Morocco?

The Prime Minister: Recent events are causing discussion between the Powers most interested in Morocco, and at this stage I can say little of the negotiations which are passing between them. But I wish it clearly to be understood that his Majesty's Government consider that a new situation has arisen in Morocco in which it is possible that future developments may affect British interests more directly than has hitherto been the case. I am confident that diplomatic discussion will find a solution, and in the part that we shall take in it we shall have due regard to the protection of those interests and to the fulfilment of our treaty obligations to France, which are well known to the House.(¹)

(¹) [For Count Mensdorff's comment, *v. Ö.-U.A.*, III, No. 2557.]

No. 365.

Sir Edward Grey to Mr. Rennie.(¹)

F.O. 26227/8755/11/28.
(No. 73.)
Sir,   *Foreign Office, July 7, 1911.*

The Spanish Ambassador called at this office on the 1st inst[ant] and the following are the chief points touched on by H[is] E[xcellency] in the conversation which ensued.

(¹) [This draft was based on a memorandum by Sir A. Nicolson describing his interview with Señor de Villa Urrutia on July 1. The memorandum closes as follows: " All the above has in reality been superseded by the German communication,(²) which was made subsequent to my conversation with the Spanish Amba[ssado]r. A. N." Sir Edward Grey added as a minute: " Yes: we may tell the Spaniards now that these are details with which we cannot take up time now that the large question has been raised. E. G."]

(²) [*v. supra*, p. 322, No. 338.]

He said it was reported that the Maghzen, instigated thereto by the French, were contemplating the appointment of a new Governor at Alcazar, in place of Raissuli who was represented there by a deputy. The Spaniards could not admit the installation of a new Governor, who would probably arrive with a Mehalla, and they would have to consider their position were such a new Governor sent.

H[is] E[xcellency] stated that El Mokri was being requested by the Spanish Ambassador at Paris to explain to the Sultan the nature of the measures recently taken by Spain, and to protest against the menace of the Moorish Government to disavow all engagements taken in regard to the Riff being carried into effect. If a satisfactory reply were not received from the Maghzen within a reasonable delay, Spain "would find it necessary to adopt certain measures."

M. de Villa Urrutia finally enquired whether it would not be possible for a discussion to take place here in regard to the police question, i.e., between himself, M. Cambon, and the F[oreign] O[ffice].

I am, &c.
E. GREY.

No. 366.

Sir F. Bertie to Sir Edward Grey.

(By Post.)

F.O. 26874/25883/11/28.   *Paris*, D. *July* 9, 1911.
Tel. (No. 92.)   R. *July* 10, 1911.

I had a long interview this morning with M. de Selves, in the course of which he gave the most formal assurances of the desire of himself and M. Caillaux's Ministry to continue the policy of free and confidential communication with His Majesty's Government so that their interests being identic on all great questions they may be able to co-operate and support each other's interests. He is quite aware that the German *coup* at Agadir is for the purpose of testing the solidity of the *entente* between England and France, which the German Government hoped had lately been weakened, and partly to have something in hand to keep if resistance were not strong or to give up for a consideration elsewhere in the course of conversations.

M. de Selves gave me the following account of his interviews with the German Ambassador.

On Saturday July 1st M. de Schoen sent a secretary to the Quai d'Orsay to ask for an appointment to see M. de Selves on a very pressing matter. When M. de Selves received M. de Schoen the Ambassador was very embarrassed in his manner, saying that he regretted to begin his relations with the Minister which he hoped would be most cordial for the benefit of Germany and France, by a communication which M. de Selves might not think quite agreeable. Representations had been made to the German Government by Germans having interests at Agadir and the Sus country that there was agitation in the district and their interests were endangered. The German Government had consequently determined to send a vessel of war to Agadir to protect those interests. He then handed the circular communication to M. de Selves who after reading it asked whether the determination was irrevocable for if not he would suggest that the ship should not be sent for it would not be viewed by French public opinion as a *bon procédé* preliminary to a discussion as to the need of a vessel at Agadir where, so far as he knew there were no disturbances or excitement. On the Ambassador stating that the vessel was already at Agadir and that the German Government were quite ready to consider any proposals that the French Government might have to make M. de Selves said that he took note of the communication made by the Ambassador. It was however a matter which did not seem to be consistent with the Act of Algeciras and was much too serious for him to make observations on it as Minister for Foreign Affairs until he had brought the subject before the Cabinet and the President of the Republic whom he had arranged to accompany to Holland on the Monday, on an official visit to the Queen. He therefore begged that M. de Schoen would obtain from Berlin further particulars as to the precise object of the despatch of the vessel. M. de Schoen having then said that the German Government desired to have conversations (causer) with the French Government but professing not to know about what Monsieur de Selves speaking not as Minister to Ambassador, but as one man of the world to another asked whether the despatch of a ship to Agadir did not seem to be an unusual mode of beginning a friendly conversation, but he begged the Ambassador to obtain instructions from the German Government to enable him to discuss the matter with the French Minister for Foreign Affairs on his return from Holland.

The next day at a garden party at the Elysée, M. de Selves bantered the Ambassador (blagué) on the new system of beginning conversations which he did not think very "élégant," for even in a duel the adversaries began by saluting each other and not by one giving the other a sword thrust in the stomach, nor when one person desired a conversation with another did one generally begin by a blow with the fist.([1])

On the day of M. de Selves' return from Amsterdam (Friday July 7th) M. de Schoen called on M. de Selves and stated that M. de Kiderlen-Waechter considered that as there had been conversations between himself and the French Ambassador at Kissingen([2]) they had best be continued between them at Berlin. Those conversations M. de Selves told me had only been on general subjects such as were usual between diplomats after dinner over a cigar and there had been nothing precise or important so far as he knew. M. de Selves stated to M. de Schoen that he had no objection to conversations between the French Ambassador and the German Secretary for Foreign Affairs regarding any matter which the German Government might desire to bring before the French Government but that he (M. de Selves) was not going to give up the reins to anyone else and he must reserve to himself the right to discuss any such questions with the German Ambassador who should seek instructions from his Government for the purpose.

The German Ambassador called again on M. de Selves yesterday and in reply to an enquiry of the previous day by M. de Selves as to what it was that the German Government had in mind in referring to conversations between M. de Kiderlen-Waechter and M. Jules Cambon stated that the Congo had been discussed by them. This surprised M. de Selves and he has telegraphed to M. Jules Cambon to report by telegraph whether there were any and if so what conversations concerning the Congo.

At this last interview with the German Ambassador M. de Selves told him that the German Government if they had any idea of a permanent stay on the Morocco coast they must put it away from their thoughts for it would be entirely inconsistent with great French interests and would raise again the whole question of Morocco.

M. de Selves concurs in your opinion that it will not be advisable for the present to send French and British ships to Agadir but he is inclined to think that it may become necessary and to invite the Spanish Government to do the same if the German force be increased or remain too long. He considers that the question of Germany and Morocco must not be allowed to drag on so that the German Government may by procrastination await another and perhaps more favourable opportunity of asserting themselves, such as complications in the East. The French Govern-

([1]) [v. G.P. XXIX, p. 159.]
([2]) [v. supra, p. 322, Ed. note.]

ment cannot acquiesce in the establishment of Germany on the coast of Morocco in any way, not even in the form of a so-called free port. He has no doubt that there has been an understanding though perhaps not a written one between Germany and Spain. He has reliable information that the German Government have applied to the Spanish Government for facilities for using Spanish Ships of War and Stations for passing on wireless telegraph communications from German ships in Morocco waters, but he does not know what answer the Spanish Government have made to the application.

M. de Selves will keep you informed of all that passes between the French and German Governments and he will agree to nothing without full consultation with His Majesty's Government. He feels sure that you will equally consult with him on all communications which you may receive from the German Government. He will not consent to discussions to be restricted to Germany and France or to the two with Spain added.

No. 367.

Sir E. Goschen to Sir Edward Grey.

Berlin, July 10, 1911.

F.O. 27021/25883/11/28.　　　　　　　　　　　　D. 8·35 P.M.
Tel. (No. 47.) Secret.　　　　　　　　　　　　　R. 10·10 P.M.
Morocco.

My French colleague had a long conversation yesterday with the Minister for Foreign Affairs.([1]) It appears to have been very stiff at first, but to have resulted in the admission on both sides that an understanding might be arrived at on the following basis :—

Germany would renounce the idea of obtaining a territorial or political footing in Morocco on the condition that France would give her compensation outside Morocco, *e.g.*, a satisfactory rectification of the Congo frontier.

Secretary of State for Foreign Affairs said. that before making any definite engagement in this sense he must have time to consult the Minister of the Colonies and others. He added that it seemed to him impossible that any third Power should join in the negotiations, having for their object an understanding on the above basis, as firstly, compensation outside Morocco would be a matter entirely between the two Governments; and secondly, if one Power joined in the conversations all the other Algeciras Powers, including smaller Powers, would feel entitled to take part in them.

My French colleague told me that he had expressed agreement with the Minister for Foreign Affairs on this point for the following reasons :—

Firstly, because it appeared to him that England would in such a case not wish to interfere, as she would obtain what she wanted without any trouble to herself, and, secondly, because a general conversation would render it more difficult for Germany to abandon her pretensions in Morocco as she now seemed disposed to do. If, however, as was unfortunately quite possible, the idea of outside compensation fell through, and Germany insisted on a sphere of influence in Morocco, Great Britain would always have time to insist on having her say. M. Cambon finally declared to the Secretary of State that France meant to remain absolutely faithful to her understandings with Great Britain, and would of course keep His Majesty's Government informed of any conversations which might take place on the above or any other basis.

([1]) [*v. G.P.* XXIX, pp. 173–7; *v.* also, *Jäckh.* Vol. II, pp. 123–6.]

My French colleague attributes the present attitude of the Secretary of State for Foreign Affairs almost entirely to the Prime Minister's statement in the House of Commons.

He begged that the French Government might not be informed of his having communicated his conversation with the Secretary of State to me.

No. 368.

Sir Edward Grey to Sir F. Bertie.

F.O. 27186/25883/11/28.
(No. 279.)
Sir,   *Foreign Office, July 10, 1911.*

M. Cambon showed me to-day two communications which he had received from M. de Selves yesterday. The German Ambassador in Paris had informed M. de Selves that, in his opinion, Germany did not entertain any territorial designs on Morocco, and wished to talk about the Congo. M. de Selves would like to know whether we saw any objection to the discussion of this subject with Germany.

I said that I assumed it was the French Congo which was meant.

M. Cambon confirmed this.

I then said that I did not see how there could be any objection on our part.

M. Cambon told me that M. de Selves feared that Germany was going to ask something of France that would put her interest and ours in opposition.

I repeated that I did not see how any such objection could arise in connection with the French Congo.

M. Cambon also told me that M. de Selves would like us to join with France and Russia in making a representation in Berlin to the German Government to withdraw their ship from Agadir. If Germany refused, he thought that we and France ought to send ships to Agadir and Spain might be asked to send one too.

I replied to this that the moment did not seem to me to be opportune for sending ships to Agadir. It would be better to wait and see what answer was given to the French Ambassador in Berlin, who had been instructed to enquire whether what the German Ambassador had said in Paris about the French Congo represented the view of the German Government. The sending of ships now to Agadir would prejudice the opening of the conversation. Further, I did not see any object in asking Germany to withdraw her ship at this moment. She would certainly say that she could not withdraw her ship until order had been restored in Morocco : which meant, until she had secured some settlement. No doubt, as we were the stronger naval Power, we could turn German ships out of Agadir, and prevent any others from being sent there : but this would be an act of war, and the situation did not demand it. If the conversations as to Morocco resulted in a settlement, the situation at Agadir would solve itself.

M. Cambon informed me very definitely that under no circumstances could the French allow Germany to establish herself in Morocco. It would be an *enclave* on the flank of the French possessions, and constant trouble would be made from it.

I said that, as far as we were concerned, though public opinion here would expect guarantees from Germany and some compensation for her being established in Morocco, we did not mind an open port on the west coast of Morocco. We thought that it would be physically very difficult for Germany to turn it into a naval base, and that if she attempted to do so, so long as we had the stronger Fleet, we could prevent its being done. But if France was decided that it was irreconcilable with her interest that Germany should be established in Morocco, there remained two solutions : one was to get back to the *status quo* of the Algeciras Act, which was difficult, because it would raise the question of the French force at Casablanca and every change made since the Algeciras Act; the other was that Germany should concede to France the same position in Morocco as we had conceded, but she could not be expected to do this without some compensation. Germany's argument had always been that we had received compensation for conceding this position to France, and that as Germany also had interests in Morocco she should also receive something.

I said that of course the French Gov[ernmen]t would keep us informed of what Germany said and M. Cambon said this would be done.

[I am, &c.]
E. G[REY].

No. 369.

Sir F. Bertie to Sir Edward Grey.

F.O. 27343/25883/11/28.   *Paris*, D. *July* 11, 1911, 6·50 P.M.
Tel. (No. 93.) R.   R. *July* 12, 1911, 8·20 A.M.

French Minister for Foreign Affairs sent for me this morning. He read to me the reports by telegram and despatch from French Ambassador at Berlin of his interview([1]) with the German Minister for Foreign Affairs, which were as follows:—

After the usual exchange of compliments and an enquiry by the French Ambassador why so soon after the conciliatory conversations at Kissingen a German ship had appeared at Agadir without apparent reason, there were some recriminations, fencing, and *gestes* which it is not necessary to repeat. German Minister for Foreign Affairs first stated that German interests in the district were endangered, but when asked to indicate the dangers he shifted his ground and said that the German Government had gone to Agadir for the same reasons as the French Government had gone to Fez, for there were equal interests to protect, but he then went on to say that public opinion in Germany required such a demonstration, for the French Government had not carried on in the spirit of their engagement of 1909. M. Cambon reminded the German Minister for Foreign Affairs that there was also a public opinion in France, which had been much surprised at what the German Government had done, and German Minister for Foreign Affairs, when asked to specify breaches of the engagement of 1909, stated in the matter of railways nothing had been done except to construct French military railway—to which M. Cambon reminded him that the German Government had made no objection when informed of its proposed construction. This the German Minister for Foreign Affairs admitted, but he contended that the French were monopolising everything and keeping Germans out of all undertakings in Morocco, and it was necessary to come to an understanding before matters went further and to "causer."

M. Cambon then said that the French Government were quite ready to "causer." What had the German Minister for Foreign Affairs to propose? The answer was "nothing." M. Cambon gave the same reply to an enquiry by the German Minister for Foreign Affairs as to what the French Government had to propose. After a long pause the German Minister for Foreign Affairs said that he would be prepared to negotiate in regard to Morocco with M. Cambon at Berlin, but there must be no third party. The matter of an arrangement between Germany and France did not concern England. If she were brought in Spain would claim to join in the negotiations and then Russia and Austria, and there would be a renewal of the Algeciras Conference, which might lead to complications.

M. Cambon replied that the French Minister for Foreign Affairs was quite ready to converse with the German Government, but he must reserve to himself right of conversing through German Ambassador at Paris as well as through the French Ambassador at Berlin, and he must reserve to himself the right of keeping the

([1]) [This is apparently that of July 9, v. *G.P.* XXIX, pp. 173–8.]

British Government informed of the communications with the German Government, for France had engagements regarding Morocco with England, who had interests there, and also with other countries and with Spain, and though for the moment there was a divergence of views with Spain, the French Government were fully determined to adhere to their agreements with England and Spain, between whom there were also engagements regarding Morocco.

M. Cambon noticed that the German Minister for Foreign Affairs was surprised, "ému," and "atteint" at the attitude taken up by the British Government and public opinion in England.

German Minister for Foreign Affairs, after speaking for some time on the interests of Germany in Morocco, expressed his readiness to renounce all German political interests in Morocco in exchange for compensations elsewhere. When M. Cambon asked where and of what kind, German Minister for Foreign Affairs replied that Germany had all she required in the East. It was in the Congo that she would desire her compensations. He expressed surprise at M. Cambon's not having instructions on the subject, as the Congo had been mentioned in Kissingen conversations, and at M. Cambon's saying he must refer matter to Paris; and when he asked for some particulars German Minister for Foreign Affairs stated that he must wait a few days for return to Berlin of the Minister of Colonies, whom it would be necessary to consult.

M. Cambon has come to conclusion from attitude of German Minister for Foreign Affairs and what he hears at Berlin that there was a conviction there, resulting from impressions produced by exchange of civilities between Sovereigns of England and Germany and the visit of Crown Prince of Germany to London for Coronation and by reports made to German Government, that England disinterested herself entirely concerning Morocco, and that Germany might squeeze France without raising any question with England. In these circumstances she would have remained permanently at Agadir and elsewhere on Atlantic coast of Morocco. M. Cambon thinks that a few days' delay for return of Minister of Colonies is really for time to communicate with Emperor.

French Minister for Foreign Affairs intends to instruct French Ambassador that there can be no question of territorial concessions to Germany in Morocco either by occupation of a port, even as a commercial one or otherwise, but that he is prepared to consider any suggestions that German Government may desire to make for compensation in return for renunciation by Germany of all political interests in Morocco. He gathers from French Ambassador in London that there would not be objection on the part of His Majesty's Government to concessions being made to Germany in regard to Congo. I told him I could not say, as, Congo being of great extent, it was impossible, until German desires were made known, to judge how British interests might be affected by their being granted. With respect to how you (group undecypherable) establishment of Germany on Atlantic coast of Morocco, even if there were a French Government prepared to acquiesce in such an arrangement, British Government would never consent to it for it would be contrary to vital interests of England, and the supposition that Germany had such an intention raised a strong feeling in country, as must have been evident to German Government from English news. French Minister for Foreign Affairs said that French Government could not for a moment think of such a thing as to consent to establishment of Germany anywhere in Morocco. It would be contrary to essential interests of France as well as of England.

After completion of negotiations with Germany, French Ambassador proposes to enter into negotiations with Spanish Government and His Majesty's Government for giving satisfaction, as far as may be possible and reasonable and in large spirit, to Spain. He trusted that meanwhile you will exert your influence at Madrid to restrain Spanish Government from foolish actions such as they have recently committed in Morocco, and appear bent on continuing. French Minister for Foreign Affairs would be glad to have your views on situation, as described to me by him.

MINUTES.

This throws a flood of light on the action of the German government. I have no doubt as to the correctness of the diagnosis made by M. Jules Cambon that the Emperor thought he had "captured" the sympathies of England to a sufficient extent to justify the belief that he could fall upon France alone and neglect any British feeling in the latter's favour. It would be well if it were carefully noted and pondered, not only by H[is] M[ajesty's] G[overnment] but also at the Court, for what purposes the Imperial visits to London and to India, and the demonstration in aid of Anglo-German friendship by Inter-parliamentary and other committees are in reality organized : it would be something gained if it were at last understood that all these things are part of the armour of the German government, brought into use for the one and sole purpose of bringing about the political isolation of this country and its dependence on Berlin. There is a generous tendency here to neglect these German manœuvres. I venture to think that this neglect is not without danger. The actions of German governments, sovereigns, princes, ambassadors, and committees are *never* separable from political aims. Their methods have time and again been shown to be the contrary of straightforward and ingenuous, it is therefore right and advisable always to consider the political effect intended.

Germany may now be counted upon to continue her well-tried policy of blackmailing. For the present France is the victim. She has twice before (at Algeciras and in 1909) paid a price for German good-will in Morocco. She is now called upon to pay once more for Germany's "renouncing all political interests in Morocco." I am afraid France is not in a position now to refuse payment. But it is quite certain that whatever price she pays now, will not prevent Germany from further extortions of exactly the same nature before long. Nothing will stop this process except a firm resolve, and the strength, to refuse, and, if necessary, to fight over it. This is the real lesson, not only for France, but also for us. If we had consented to a German port in Morocco, we should have had to be prepared for further demands presented in the same manner.

I am very sceptical as to Herr von Kiderlen's assurance that he will accept a rectification of the Congo frontier as a settlement of the present account, and I think we should continue to be on our guard. Germany is still at Agadir, and until she has left it, there is no surety whatever that she has any intention of leaving. It is more probable that she will stay, and insist on "compensation" elsewhere as well. It is ominous that she does not say what she wants. She has made certain that neither France or England mean to fight. It is this which regulated her conduct and nothing else. Her demands will therefore certainly go as far as can safely be done without touching a point where the two Powers will fight. A rectification of frontiers is a long way this side of the line.

Sir F. Bertie states my view that it is at least premature for Great Britain to "disinterest herself" formally in any question of compensation on the Congo. I trust we shall commit ourselves to no line until we know what the German demands are.

I think we should do all we can to maintain a footing in these negotiations. The mere fact that Germany wants to exclude us, should be a warning to us. "Divide et impera" has always been a favoured German maxim. Moreover it will be quite impossible to exclude the subject of Morocco itself from any settlement, and on that subject we ought to insist not only on being heard ourselves but on bringing in the other treaty Powers, whose interests would certainly not be served by German ambitions.

E. A. C.
July 12.

I agree that we ought to know what exactly the Germans want in the Congo, and that, I understand, is what the French are finding out.

Germany does seem to be playing the same game with France in regard to Morocco as she played with us in regard to Egypt, and will probably continue to do so till a firm stand is made.

W. L.

I entirely agree with Sir Eyre Crowe's observations.

A. N.

No. 370.

Sir Edward Grey to Mr. Rennie.

F.O. 26364/25641/11/28.
(No. 74.)

Sir, *Foreign Office, July* 11, 1911.

The Spanish Ambassador called at this office on the 3rd instant, and stated that his Government were taken completely by surprise by the recent communication from the German Gov[ernmen]t.(¹) He asserted most positively that there had been no previous communications between Berlin and Madrid on the subject.

(¹) [*v. supra*, p. 322, No. 338.]

H[is] E[xcellency] also reiterated his previous assurances that Spain had not been " pushed " by Germany to take the action she had done at Laraiche and Alcazar.

Sir A. Nicolson replied that, while he fully believed these assurances, he was not so sure that Spanish action at Laraiche and Alcazar had not " pushed " Germany to Agadir.

In answer to a question, M. de Villa Urrutia stated that M. Garcia Prieto had simply replied to the German communication regarding Agadir that he would " take note " of it, and that he would have to submit it to the King and Cabinet.

H[is] E[xcellency] stated that the Spanish Government were naturally desirous of ascertaining the views of the British and French Gov[ernmen]ts before definitely replying to Germany, and was informed by Sir Arthur Nicolson that the subject would be considered at a meeting of the Cabinet.

I am, &c.
E. GREY.

No. 371.

Sir F. Cartwright to Sir A. Nicolson.

Private.(¹)

My dear Nicolson,   Vienna, July 11, 1911.

I returned yesterday morning from Trieste, where I have been for a few days to receive the detachment of the Mediterranean Fleet under Admiral Poë. Our men were very well received and there were the usual official dinners and sympathetic speeches, and everything went off very well.

Soon after my arrival here yesterday, I was received by Count Aehrenthal with whom I had a long conversation. Talking of Morocco, he said to me that for some time he had been expecting a move from Germany which would prove disagreeable to France. He had had no previous knowledge as to what shape that move would take, but he knew that they were restless in Berlin to do something. The intimation that the " Panther " was to be sent to Agadir was made to him on the 1st instant, apparently at the same time as it was made in Paris and in London.(²) He had received it calmly and had taken note of the German declaration that the vessel was sent to the Moroccan port merely temporarily, and that no idea existed of permanently occupying that place. Count Aehrenthal said to me that in his opinion the French Government had made a mistake in concluding the arrangement with Germany of 1909, and as it proved, it had only led them into a fool's paradise, inducing them to believe that they were now secure from the side of Germany and that they were at liberty to do what they pleased in Morocco. Dr. Szeps of the " Fremdenblatt " tells me that immediately after the conclusion of the 1909 arrangement, Tschirschky, the German Ambassador here, said to him that he thought that the French would regret the arrangement they had just made. Aehrenthal also observed yesterday to me that he thought the French had made a mistake in forcing their way to Fez, for that had given the Germans the excuse for taking the action they had now done at Agadir. Aehrenthal asked me whether I could explain to him the meaning of Mr. Asquith's statement in the House of Commons that the Agadir incident had created a new situation in Morocco. Were these words to be interpreted to mean that His Majesty's Government considered the Algeciras Act as a dead letter? I told him that I had no official information on this point, but my own personal belief was that the words in question meant that we had retired from direct interference from Moroccan affairs in favour of the French, but not of the Germans, and that the appearance of Germany on the scene would liberate our hands and thereby create the new situation in Morocco. Aehrenthal expressed a hope that we would hold to the Algeciras Act, and he said that he was

(¹) [Carnock MSS., Vol. III of 1911. For Count Aehrenthal's account, v. Ö.-U.A., III, No. 2561.]

(²) [v. G.P. XXIX, p. 158. Count Szögyeny's telegram from Berlin seems to have been received on July 2; v. Ö.-U.A., III, No. 2550.]

very satisfied to observe that the Agadir incident had been taken with reasonable calm in England, and that we had made no unnecessary fuss about it.

Dr. Szeps, the editor of the "Fremdenblatt," visited me this morning, and he has given me some interesting information as to how the German action is viewed here. Soon after the news reached Vienna of the sending of the "Panther" to Agadir, a *communiqué* was published in his newspaper in which it was said that Austria-Hungary, while expressing sympathy with the German action, reserved her judgment, but hoped that the incident would tend to clarify the present involved Moroccan situation, and bring things back to the state of affairs established by the Algeciras Act. Dr. Szeps tells me that Tschirschky complained bitterly, both to him and to Aehrenthal, of the wording of the communiqué, and that Aehrenthal sent for Szeps on the 8th instant and had a long conversation with him on Austria's position with regard to Moroccan events. Aehrenthal appears to have said that Tschirschky demanded that he, Aehrenthal, should take an immediate opportunity for making some public declaration of "Austria's shining armour fidelity to Germany."(3) but that he had absolutely declined to do so. According to Szeps, Aehrenthal judges the Moroccan question from an entirely different point of view than is done in Berlin. Two months ago, both Germany and Austria, after exchanging views, decided to accept in good faith the assurances of France that the expedition to Fez would only be of a temporary nature, and that therefore neither Austria-Hungary nor Germany would protest against it. Aehrenthal told Szeps that he could admit that Germany might see fit to declare that since those declarations were made, her interests in Morocco had been touched by the insecurity produced in certain districts by the French action at Fez, and that therefore she might see fit to suddenly act in defence of these menaced interests. But according to Aehrenthal, Austria was not in the same position as Germany; her interests had not been threatened, the French were about to retire from Fez, and it was not decently possible for her to make a sudden "volte-face," and to withdraw the confidence with which she had received the assurances made by France some time ago, merely because Germany wished her to do so. Szeps said to me that Germany was working to bring matters back to a period anterior to the Algeciras Conference :— Aehrenthal was determined to do his utmost to maintain the Algeciras Act intact, as far as possible, admitting, however, that small alterations might be made in it after due negociations between the Powers. Hence a certain amount of coolness seems to exist between Kiderlen-Waechter and Aehrenthal with regard to Morocco which may have the effect of restraining Germany from acting with too much "intransigeance" in that direction.

Dr. Szeps assures me that at the Ballplatz it is known that Metternich has for some time past been sending reports to Berlin that a Germanophile current was beginning to run somewhat strongly among certain political sections in Great Britain. He also says that the Kaiser returned from his recent visit to London impressed by the friendly feeling which seemed to exist on all sides in England towards Germany. Dr. Szeps asserts that the politicians of Berlin thought that the moment had come when something could be done to squeeze France, as they did not apprehend that Great Britain would give her anything more than lukewarm support in any dispute which might arise between France and Germany.

Such is the opinion prevailing at the Ballplatz where the desire seems to exist that means may be found for settling the Moroccan question amicably by a deal over an extended line of minor questions. . . . .(4)

Yours truly,
FAIRFAX L. CARTWRIGHT.

(3) [*v.* Wickham Steed : *Through Thirty Years*, (1924), Vol. I, pp. 335-7.]
(4) [The closing sentences contain a general reference to Albanian and Macedonian affairs.]

No. 372.

Sir F. Bertie to Sir Edward Grey.

F.O. 27474/85641/11/28.
(No. 323.)   *Paris*, D. *July* 12, 1911.
Sir,   R. *July* 13, 1911.

I had the honour to receive yesterday evening your Despatch No. 276 (26700/11)(¹) of the 6th instant recording a conversation which you had had that day with the French Ambassador on the subject of Morocco. I was not previously aware of the possibility of His Majesty's Government acquiescing in the establishment of Germany on the coast of Morocco. My fear was that the French Government if hard pressed by the German Government might prefer to consent to Germany obtaining a footing on the Atlantic Coast of Morocco, which would be more injurious to British than to French interests, and thus cast on His Majesty's Government the whole odium of opposing the fulfilment of objects which Germany was anxious to obtain and France might not be entirely resolved to refuse. When therefore in the course of my interviews with the French Minister for Foreign Affairs on the 9th and 11th, which are reported in my Telegrams Nos. 92 and 93 of those two dates,(²) I learnt that he had informed the German Ambassador on the 8th instant that if the German Government had any idea of a permanent stay on the Morocco Coast they must put it away from their thoughts, for it would be entirely inconsistent with great French interests, and when he informed me that the French Government could not acquiesce in the establishment of Germany on the Coast of Morocco in any way, not even in the form of a so-called free port, I encouraged him in that view by reminding him of the case of Batoum and the falsified assurances given in 1878 by Russia.

At the interview of yesterday Monsieur de Selves expressed the intention to instruct the French Ambassador at Berlin that there can be no question of territorial concessions to Germany in Morocco either by the occupation of a port, even as a commercial one, or otherwise. On this I observed to Monsieur de Selves that even if there were a French Government prepared to acquiesce in the establishment of Germany on the Atlantic Coast of Morocco the British Government would never consent to it, for it would be contrary to the vital interests of England, and the supposition that Germany had such an intention had raised a strong feeling in England, as must have been evident to the German Government from the English newspapers. Monsieur de Selves replied to this observation that the French Government could not for a moment think of such a thing as to consent to the establishment of Germany anywhere in Morocco. It would be contrary to the essential interests of France as well as of England.

In saying what I did to Monsieur de Selves, I had in mind what occurred in regard to the assurances given by Russia in 1878 respecting Batoum. By Article 59 of the Treaty of Berlin the Emperor of Russia declared his intention to constitute Batoum a free port essentially commercial. Eight years later the Russian Ambassador in London delivered to the Earl of Rosebery a notice announcing the intention of the Emperor of Russia to terminate that arrangement, but stating that Batoum would preserve in the future the character of a port essentially commercial. Lord Rosebery instructed His Majesty's Ambassador at St. Petersburg to inform the Russian Government that His Majesty's Government could not consent to recognize or associate themselves in any shape or form with this proceeding, and that they were compelled to place on record their view that it constituted a violation of the Treaty of Berlin, unsanctioned by the Signatory Powers. So far as I can recollect no other Power signatory of the Berlin Treaty made any like protest, and Batoum became a fortified port. I did not suppose, judging by the history of our

(¹) [*v. supra*, pp. 341–2, No. 363.]
(²) [*v. supra*, pp. 343–5, No. 366, and pp. 347–8, No. 369.]

relations with the German Government, that any assurances in regard to the character of a port in their possession or occupation could be relied on to be observed by them beyond such period as they might consider necessary in their own interests. They might adhere in the letter to assurances that the port would remain a free port and a commercial port and yet accumulate at it for future use a store of guns and make other military preparations for converting it at short notice and at a favourable opportunity, first by earthworks and later on by more formidable defences, into a fortified Naval base, and so create a danger to British interests.

I have, &c.
FRANCIS BERTIE.

MINUTES.

There is another case presenting an even closer analogy than Batoum, and that is Bizerta.

When the French first seized this port and there were rumours of its being adapted for naval purposes, our Admiralty firmly declared that there was no objection to this at all from a naval point of view. All the old arguments about an enemy weakening himself by scattering its [*sic*] forces, were produced, and it was urged, as now respecting Agadir, that we had the command of the sea and could always take Bizerta whenever we liked, and also prevent its ever being turned into a naval base.

Not many years afterwards, other naval officers occupying the Admiralty buildings declared the fortification of Bizerta to be the greatest danger to British powers in the Mediterranean. The Foreign Office was urged to make threatening representations to France. Representations were made. They were of course perfectly futile. Bizerta became, contrary to previous naval opinion, an exceedingly formidable naval base (at the price of considerable expenditure) and remained a thorn in our side all the time our relations with France were unfriendly.

I am afraid the casual opinions, given verbally by naval lords, never carry weight with their successors, and are in fact often belied by subsequent events. What is wanted is a considered, written, statement explaining the grounds on which the *Board of Admiralty*, acting under their responsibility for the naval policy of the country, arrive at certain definite conclusions, with an examination of all the circumstances, including the historical and political aspect of the case.

E. A. C.
July 13.

In this case the French are willing to take the chestnuts out of the fire for us and there seems no reason why we should deprive them of the pleasure.

W. L.
A. N.

I quite agree as to having the opinion of the Admiralty recorded and I have already stipulated for that.([3])

Bizerta is an instance more in point than Batoum; though it would I imagine be more easy for us to control German action at Agadir and cut her off from it than it was to do the same as regards France at Bizerta.

The history of Bizerta as described by Sir E. Crowe is nevertheless instructive.

E. G.

([3]) [*cp. infra*, p. 358, No. 375.]

No. 373.

Sir E. Goschen to Sir Edward Grey.

F.O. 27849/25883/11/28.
(No. 194.) Very Confidential.   Berlin, D. *July* 12, 1911.
Sir,   R. *July* 17, 1911.

My French Colleague has kindly communicated to me, confidentially, all that has passed between him and Herr von Kiderlen both at Kissingen on the 20th ultimo and at Berlin since his return from Paris.

It appears that it was at Kissingen, in the course of conversation, that Monsieur Cambon first pointed out plainly to Herr von Kiderlen that there was one thing to which, in the face of public opinion, the French Government could not possibly assent, namely, that Germany should obtain a political or territorial footing in Morocco. To this Herr von Kiderlen replied that German public opinion must also be taken into account, that in German commercial and industrial circles much resentment was felt at the manner in which France had neglected to carry out the provisions of the 1909 agreement([1]) from which they had hoped so much, and that this resentment would be extended to the Imperial Government if the latter sat still with folded arms while France was doing what she liked with Morocco. Monsieur Cambon appears to have admitted that in some respects, particularly as regards certain projected railways, the German expectations under the 1909 agreement had not been entirely realized. This has been the fault of circumstances, but not the result of any want of good faith on the part of the French Government. If, as appeared from what Herr von Kiderlen had said, the German Government felt aggrieved in this respect, he thought that his Government would be ready to give some satisfaction, always presupposing that territorially and politically speaking Germany would disinterest herself from Morocco, and seek such satisfaction as might be justifiable outside, and not in, that country. After a conversation of considerable length Herr von Kiderlen said that as France seemed determined to exclude Germany from Morocco, and as Monsieur Cambon had given him to understand that in the present state of feeling in France no Government could stand who took an opposite view, he supposed that he must make the best of it and seek the satisfaction to which Germany was clearly entitled in some other quarter. He thought he would be justified in asking for some colonial advantages such as it was in the power of France to give, and suggested that a rectification of the Congo frontier in a manner favourable to German interests might be acceptable. Perhaps Germany might also ask for something in the East (dans l'Orient). Monsieur Cambon must at this point have shown some sign of interruption, because Herr von Kiderlen added quickly, " Well! that will probably not be necessary, as after all we have all we want there! "

Finally Herr von Kiderlen begged Monsieur Cambon to lay the above suggestion before the French Government, and this Monsieur Cambon, in the idea that a declaration on the part of Germany of disinterestedness as regards Morocco was worth a considerable sacrifice, promised to do.

Thereupon Monsieur Cambon left for Paris and arrived there to find the Ministry fallen. He was therefore unable for the moment to report his conversation with Herr von Kiderlen. In the meantime he received a letter from his Naval Attaché dated from Kiel, saying that the Emperor had been particularly gracious to him and had again and again assured him of the friendly feelings felt by both Him and His Government for France and of their lively desire that the question of Morocco should be settled without any friction between the two Governments. The letter, which was apparently written on the very day when the fall of the French Government had been announced, added that the Emperor had said that it would facilitate matters very much if the personage chosen to succeed Monsieur Cruppi were a statesman thoroughly acquainted with international affairs and accustomed to deal with them : such a man for instance as Monsieur Delcassé, who would seem indicated for the post. On the day following the receipt of this letter Monsieur Cambon called upon the President of the Republic and after communicating to him the substance of the Kissingen conversation, backed his opinion of the hopefulness of the outlook by producing the letter from Kiel and reading to the President the Emperor's gracious and friendly words. The President, according to Monsieur Cambon's account, did not attach much importance to the Emperor's language, in fact rather the contrary, but he seemed to think that the Kissingen conversation opened the door to an amicable arrangement. On the next day came the news of the despatch of a German warship to Agadir. Monsieur Cambon, after a further interview with the President, went straight to Herr von Schoen and, after informing him of what had passed at Kissingen, told him in the strongest possible language what he thought of Herr von Kiderlen's proceedings.([2]) Herr von Schoen asked him whether he should repeat

([1]) [v. supra, p. 139, No. 155, encl. 2.]

([2]) [According to Herr von Schoen this interview was on the 6th, but there may have been two, v. G.P., XXIX, pp. 171–2.]

his language to Herr von Kiderlen and Monsieur Cambon replied "Certainly! I beg you to do so."

After receiving his instructions which, he said, were of a vague nature, Monsieur Cambon returned to Berlin and at once called upon Herr von Kiderlen.([3]) He found the latter naturally somewhat embarrassed and ill at ease. Herr von Kiderlen asked him whether he had any proposal to make with regard to Morocco. Monsieur Cambon replied in the negative, and in putting the same question to Herr von Kiderlen received a similar answer. A silence ensued which lasted for quite an appreciable period. Monsieur Cambon debated with himself whether he should let the interview rest there and take his leave, but decided that after all it would be better to stay and have the matter out. He therefore reminded Herr von Kiderlen of the Kissingen conversation and asked whether he was prepared to renew it. On Herr von Kiderlen signifying his assent Monsieur Cambon said that before any discussion could take place there were certain things which required explanation, as the situation had been changed by the sudden despatch, after Herr von Kiderlen's friendly language, of a German warship to Agadir. "I had barely time," Monsieur Cambon said, "to reach Paris, a bearer of what I was entitled to regard as a friendly and conciliatory message from you, when the news of the extraordinary action of the Imperial Government reached me." Monsieur Cambon added that he was all the less able to understand this sudden move on the part of the Imperial Government as only the day before the news had reached him he had received a letter from a member of his staff at Kiel saying that, amongst other gracious utterances, the Emperor had assured him of His friendly sentiments towards France and of the fervent hope both of Himself and His Government that nothing would occur in Morocco which could possibly give rise to any friction between the two countries. Surely the Imperial Government must have been aware that nothing was more likely to excite public opinion in France than the despatch of a German warship to a closed port without any obvious reason!

Herr von Kiderlen replied that there was a public opinion in Germany as well as in France and that enormous pressure had been brought upon him to send a ship to Agadir for the protection of German subjects and of Germany's important interests in the South of Morocco. He added. that he had received hundreds of letters from German firms of the greatest influence and importance pointing out the dangers to which German subjects and employés were exposed and demanding that some steps should be taken by the Government to protect their lives and property. These demands it had been impossible for him to ignore. Monsieur Cambon said that he had never heard that Germany had interests in South Morocco of such magnitude as to render it necessary to send a ship to Agadir for their protection but that as Herr von Kiderlen said that they existed he was bound to believe it. Nevertheless it had been a strong and a sudden step and it seemed to him to require a little more explanation. What rendered the step most inexplicable, and he must return to that point, was that it had been taken only four days after he, Herr von Kiderlen, had given him to understand that Germany would, on certain conditions, be prepared to disinterest herself of Morocco. He, Monsieur Cambon, had on that occasion expressed the opinion that the French Government would not be averse to making the sacrifices entailed by the conditions suggested, but before he could even report the conversation the German ship had been sent to Agadir. The treatment he had received in this matter was certainly not calculated to impress the French Government with a sense of security in any future conversations which might take place.

Herr von Kiderlen then again alluded to the grievances felt in German industrial and commercial circles with regard to the 1909 agreement and the systematic manner in which their interests had been disregarded by France : but Monsieur Cambon having eased his mind of some of the resentment which he felt against Herr von

([3]) [On July 9, v. G.P. XXIX, pp. 173–8, and cp. supra, pp. 347–8, No. 369.]

2 A 2

Kiderlen's proceedings and which he had put in far stronger language than I have ventured to write, suggested that they should put the past on one side, drop recriminations and devote themselves to discussing the present situation and to an endeavour to find a solution satisfactory to both countries. From this point on the conversation assumed a more friendly tone and, from the account given to me by Monsieur Cambon was more or less a repetition of what had been said already at Kissingen.

The end of it was that Herr von Kiderlen said "Vous voulez donc que nous faisions notre deuil du Maroc," and on Monsieur Cambon replying that as a matter of fact that was what France desired, Herr von Kiderlen said that in that case they must see what could be done elsewhere. He personally still held the opinion that a rectification of the Congo frontier offered a solution, but before engaging himself in any way he would have to consult the Minister of the Colonies and others. Herr von Kiderlen also expressed the opinion that any negotiations on the lines suggested should be conducted by the two Governments alone. Monsieur Cambon told me that he had concurred in this view, making it at the same time clear to Herr von Kiderlen that his concurrence in this respect only extended to conversations which had for their basis disinterestedness on the part of Germany as regards Morocco and satisfaction for Germany in some quarter where the interests of other Powers were not involved. He had also, he said, pointed out that if their negotiations for such outside satisfaction failed and Germany made claims for territory or political influence in Morocco it was perfectly certain, from what the British Prime Minister had said that England would insist upon having her say in the matter. It was, he had added, absolutely necessary that the substance of all their conversations should in any case be communicated to Great Britain and Spain. This closed the conversation. I did not understand from Monsieur Cambon that up to the present any allusion had been made on either side to the duration of the stay of the German ship at Agadir.

Having occasion to see Herr von Kiderlen with regard to some minor matters I called upon His Excellency yesterday. As, from what Monsieur Cambon had told me, I gathered that things were going fairly smoothly as regards Morocco and making for a settlement which might prove satisfactory to His Majesty's Government, I abstained, on Herr von Kiderlen making some general reference to the Morocco question, from making any remarks which might disturb his equanimity. I only said that the attitude of His Majesty's Government had been made absolutely clear both by your observations to Count Metternich([4]) and Mr. Asquith's statement in the House of Commons.([5]) He would have gathered from those utterances that in the new situation caused by the despatch of a German ship to Agadir His Majesty's Government were determined to watch matters very closely. I added that there had at one time been some mention of a "conversation à trois" between Germany, France, and Spain. He would, I was sure, readily understand that such a conversation would not coincide with the views of His Majesty's Government and that they would not be able to recognize any new arrangement arising out of it, particularly such as might affect British interests.

Herr von Kiderlen said that there had never been any idea of such a "conversation à trois"; no member of the German Government had ever made such a suggestion; rumours to that effect had, he believed, appeared in the French Press, but they were utterly untrue and he hoped that I would write in that sense to my Government. As a matter of fact both the Chancellor and Herr Zimmermann made the suggestion to the Spanish Ambassador, but as this fact had been communicated by the latter to this Embassy in strict confidence, I did not pursue the subject. Herr von Kiderlen then told me that he had had very friendly conversations on the subject of Morocco with my French colleague. They had done their best to avoid

([4]) [v. supra, p. 334, No. 356.]
([5]) [v. supra, p. 342, No. 365.]

all recriminations and to find a *modus vivendi*. He had strong hopes that they would succeed but it was too early to speak with any certainty on the subject.

I have, &c.
W. E. GOSCHEN.

MINUTES.

I confess to being, for the moment, altogether nonplussed, and can find no answer to the question : " What is Germany really driving at? " Herr von Kiderlen's behaviour seems almost inexplicable.[6]

The only point which, I think, emerges with more and more clearness, is that whatever was the initial German design, it was unexpectedly (to them) frustrated by the attitude of England, and that, in consequence of this, a new course had suddenly to be steered, with the result, perhaps, that Germany herself finds it now difficult to explain either to France or even to herself what she originally set out to do and how much she can still hope to do in the altered circumstances. We must restrict ourselves to carefully watching events. It is to be hoped that the French government will keep us informed of what is passing with Germany. Herr von Kiderlen will, on the other hand, do his best to persuade France that one condition of his discussing the whole matter amicably must be that the discussions remain secret and are not revealed to third parties. It will be remembered how anxious the German gov[ernmen]t were at the time that their political discussions with us should be kept secret. In either case the motive is obvious.

E. A. C.
July 17.
A. N.
W. L.
E. G.

(6) [cp. infra, p. 795, Ed. note.]

No. 374.

Sir G. Buchanan to Sir Edward Grey.

F.O. 27838/25641/11/18.

(No. 200.)   *St. Petersburgh*, D. *July* 12, 1911.

Sir,   R. *July* 17, 1911.

The French Ambassador tells me that he has every reason to be satisfied with the attitude adopted by the Russian Government with regard to the dispatch of the German gunboat " Panther " to Agadir. The Acting Minister for Foreign Affairs had, Monsieur Louis said, replied to the first communication made to him on the subject by the German Ambassador by stating that Russia had a double interest in this question, as, in the first place she was the ally of France, and in the second she was a signatory of the Act of Algeciras. Monsieur Nératow had ever since continued to give him every assistance in his power and had collaborated with him in endeavouring to solve the problem as to what were the real objects and intentions underlying Germany's action.

From the conversations which I have had both with Monsieur Louis and Monsieur Nératow I gather that neither has yet succeeded in finding a solution that entirely satisfies him, and that while the latter is inclined to look on the Agadir incident as merely a fresh move made by Germany in the Moroccan game, the former believes that it has a much wider significance. Though the immediate object of this sudden display of the German mailed fist is, in his opinion, to obtain concessions in Morocco by exercising pressure on France, the policy which dictated the dispatch of the " Panther " is, he thinks, part and parcel of Germany's general foreign policy and he considers that there is an intimate connexion between the Albanian and Moroccan questions, which indicates collusion between Berlin and Vienna.

In the first conversation which I had with Monsieur Nératow after my return from London, His Excellency told me that the German Ambassador had just been to see him and had made a second communication, in answer apparently to the explanations which His Excellency had asked for on the receipt of the first. Count Pourtalès had now assured him that there was no question at present of disembarking troops; that the German Government did not contemplate the occupation of any portion of Moroccan territory; and that their ship would be withdrawn as soon as order was restored. These assurances, His Excellency said, had given him satisfaction, as they went further than what had been said in the original communication. In speaking of the withdrawal of the "Panther" as soon as order was restored, Count Pourtalès had omitted the words "in Morocco"; and he interpreted this omission to mean that the "Panther" would leave as soon as calm once more reigned at Agadir.

I remarked that His Excellency seemed to me to be taking too optimistic a view, as I did not think that Count Pourtalès' words necessarily bore the interpretation which he had put on them and on calling on Monsieur Nératow two days later I found that he had been undeceived. He had, he said, made enquiries at Berlin and had found that the language which was being held there and in some other capitals did not confirm what the German Ambassador had said to him. He supposed therefore that Count Pourtalès had made the communication in somewhat milder terms than he had been authorised to do by his instructions. The French Ambassador, however, explains this discrepancy by the fact that the German Foreign Office often adapts the language which its Representatives abroad are instructed to hold in the place and person to whom a communication is to be made, and that consequently the same communication may be couched in different language at different capitals.

I have, &c.

GEORGE W. BUCHANAN.

No. 375.

Sir Edward Grey to Sir F. Bertie.

Private.([1])

My dear Bertie,   *Paris, July* 12, 1911.

I discussed the question of Germany getting a port on the West Coast of Morocco with McKenna and Sir Arthur Wilson, the First Sea Lord, a little time ago. Wilson regarded it with equanimity. I was told there was no place there that could easily be made a naval base, and I understand that the Admiralty would be perfectly satisfied with an arrangement that included an undertaking not to fortify any port in Morocco. We should then have a Treaty right as well as the Sea Power (which we have now) to prevent it.

But the opinion of the Government is that, though in view of the Admiralty opinion we need not and cannot be irreconcilable about the West Coast of Morocco, there would be a great fuss here at seeing Germany share in a partition of Morocco, and we should require something from her elsewhere.

This being so I cannot let the French place upon us the whole burden of keeping Germany out of Morocco at all costs, though I think it is undesirable to let Germany in, and a settlement that did not let her in would be infinitely preferable.

Wilson's opinion was that on no account must Germany get a footing in the Mediterranean.

Yours sincerely,

E. GREY.

Since writing this I have seen your despatch No. 323([2]) and your letter to Nicolson.([3]) Batoum was not on the ocean and so at the mercy of our fleet as an Atlantic port would be, nor was the question of its fortification of much strategic importance to us.

E. G.

([1]) [Grey MSS., Vol. 13.]
([2]) [*v. supra*, pp. 352–3, No. 372.]
([3]) [*v.* immediately succeeding document.]

No. 376.

Sir F. Bertie to Sir A. Nicolson.

Private and Confidential.([1])

My dear Nicolson,   Paris, July 12, 1911.

Many thanks for your letter of the 10th which arrived by the bag yesterday evening.([2]) I received at the same time the record of the interview between Sir E. Grey and the French Ambassador July 6 (see F.O. No. 276 of that date([3])). I have not any record of a subsequent interview if there was one, but your letter shows me that there is hesitation and a desire in some quarters to ignore dangers and inclination to believe in assurances which would last just as long as might be necessary for the convenience of Germany. This readiness to believe may be unfortunate in its results. It cannot exist in any one having experience of German ways. If the French get to think that we are ready to give way to Germany we shall help to throw them into the Teuton embrace. I am convinced that the German Government made sure from their information from England that we should not stand by the French in the Morocco question and that the favourable moment had arrived to assert themselves. I felt equally confident that the German Government if we join with the French in refusing to agree to the establishment of a German port, call it what you may, on the Atlantic Coast of Morocco, may bluster, but there will be nothing else.

If the Germans increase their naval force at Agadir and land men I think that we ought to do so also with the French and also the Spaniards whom we can I believe drag along with us.

Yours ever,
FRANCIS BERTIE.

I inclose a copy of a despatch which I have written today.([4])

([1]) [Carnock MSS., Vol. III of 1911.]
([2]) [Not reproduced.]
([3]) [v. supra, pp. 341–2, No. 363.]
([4]) [v. supra, pp. 352–3, No. 372.]

No. 377.

Sir Edward Grey to Sir F. Bertie.

F.O. 27343/25883/11/28.   Foreign Office, July 13, 1911.

Tel. (No. 174.)   D. 3 P.M.

Your telegram No. 93.([1]) It appears *prima facie* as if a settlement by which in return for compensation in French Congo Germany ceased to make difficulties in Morocco would be very satisfactory and without prejudice to British interests. But I cannot of course express final opinion without knowing precisely what Germany intends to ask and to give. It is at any rate infinitely preferable to any basis for negotiations that included compensation to Germany in Morocco.

As regards Morocco we should think anything that gave Germany a footing on Mediterranean absolutely irreconcilable with British interests. A footing on West coast regarded solely from British point of view is not vital, so long as no port is fortified. We should require binding engagement to that effect and could rely upon our own sea power to prevent fortifications. But to reconcile British opinion to seeing Germany obtain political or territorial footing in Morocco we should have to

([1]) [v. supra, pp. 347–8, No. 369.]

obtain something from her elsewhere, and it is the least desirable form that settlement could take. I understand from French Ambassador that it would be in highest degree objectionable to France and if that is so it seems unnecessary to discuss question of bringing it into negotiations.

No. 378.

Sir Edward Grey to Sir E. Goschen.([1])

F.O. 27622/13911/11/28.   *Foreign Office, July* 13, 1911.
Tel. (No. 148.) R.   D. 10 P.M.

Italian Ambassador having asked my opinion about Morocco I said that Germany had opened the question in the worst possible way. Having given it to be understood that her interests were only commercial, she had gone to a port which was closed commercially : she had thus made it clear that commercial interests were only a pretext. Agadir happened also to be the port most suitable for a naval base. Germany had thus at the outset mobilized the whole of British public opinion and made it certain that our interests would be engaged on the side of France.

It is now for Germany if she wishes to make conversations easy to do so by removing first impression created by her action.

We do not wish to impede a settlement between her and France, but we must wait to know what Germany's object is before we can decide whether British interests require us to intervene in discussions.

You should adapt your language to these views when the occasion demands it or if it becomes necessary to repeat or supplement what I said to German Ambassador on July 4.([2])

([1]) [Printed in *Twenty-Five Years,* V,ol. I, pp. 234–5.]
([2]) [*v. supra,* p. 334, No. 356.]

No. 379.

Sir Edward Grey to Sir F. Bertie.

F.O. 27479/25883/11/28.
(No. 283.)
Sir,   *Foreign Office, July* 13, 1911.

The French Ambassador called on Sir A. Nicolson on the 8th instant and read to him a telegram from M. de Selves stating that he had asked the German Ambassador to call at the Quai d'Orsay, and had explained to him that the French Gov[ernmen]t desired to ascertain in a friendly manner what were the desiderata of the German Gov[ernmen]t and to discuss matters amicably. The German Ambassador had replied that he had no instructions on the subject, and that he thought the conversations between the French and German Gov[ernmen]ts should take place at Berlin. To this M. de Selves had demurred, and he had requested the German Ambassador to telegraph to his Gov[ernmen]t and urge that the discussions should be proceeded with at Paris.

Sir Arthur Nicolson told M. Cambon that he did not quite comprehend M. de Selves's procedure, as he had been under the impression that the British and French Gov[ernmen]ts were, in the first place, to come to an understanding as to what line was to be followed with Germany, and that they would then address themselves together to Berlin. M. Cambon agreed, but said that it was necessary, before taking any step, to ascertain what Germany actually wanted. When Germany had formulated her requirements the moment would then arrive to tell her, as indeed had already been done, that the French Gov[ernmen]t must consult with

H[is] M[ajesty's] G[overnment], and M. de Selves might repeat this to the German Ambassador at their next meeting. The French Gov[ernmen]t were at present only endeavouring to ascertain what Germany wanted, but it was their intention to fall in with the British view that they should explain clearly to the German Gov[ernmen]t that France would not enter into discussions without the participation of H[is] M[ajesty's] G[overnment].

M. Cambon then read a second telegram in which M. de Selves expressed the hope that H[is] M[ajesty's] G[overnmen]t would associate themselves with the French Gov[ernmen]t in requesting the German Gov[ernmen]t, with the view of rendering the discussions easier, to withdraw their ship from Agadir. While expressing doubts whether the German Gov[ernmen]t would agree to do this, Sir A. Nicolson replied that he would refer the point to me.

M. Cambon again laid stress on the fact that whatever compensations might eventually be accorded to Germany, they must on no account be given in Morocco. This was, for the French Gov[ernmen]t, a condition *sine quâ non*. H[is] E[xcellency] added that this was as much in the interests of Great Britain as of France.

[I am, &c.
E. GREY.]

No. 380.

Sir Edward Grey to Sir F. Bertie.

F.O. 27568/25883/11/28.
(No. 285.)
Sir,   *Foreign Office, July* 13, 1911.
The French Ambassador called at the Foreign Office on the 11th inst[ant] and read to Sir A. Nicolson a telegram from Berlin giving an account of the conversation respecting Morocco between the German Minister for Foreign Affairs and M. Jules Cambon, the French Ambassador there. The latter had emphasized with M. de Kiderlen that France must keep both H[is] M[ajesty's] Gov[ernmen]t and Spain fully informed of what passed and consult both Powers as to any arrangements. Sir A. Nicolson observed that he was glad to hear Spain had been so specifically mentioned, as the Spanish Ambassador had recently expressed some uneasiness lest Spain should be left out in the cold until all had been practically settled; and he gave M. Paul Cambon a short account of what had passed between M. de Villa Urrutia and himself on the preceding day.

H[is] E[xcellency] said it was now necessary to wait to hear what Germany wanted and he seemed to be somewhat perplexed as to what she would claim as an equivalent to giving France a free hand in Morocco.

He asked if Sir A. Nicolson had noticed reports in the press as to a secret treaty between Mulai Hafid and France. The facts were that last year the Sultan had suggested

1. that France should guarantee him in possession of his throne.
2. that he should be given a money advance.
3. that in return he would promise always to employ French military instructors and
4. to give France the preference in any concessions.

France had refused to enter into any such engagements.

M. Cambon observed more particularly that, as regards No. 1 the responsibilities would be too great; that as regards No. 3 the French had military instructors already; while No. 4 was contrary to the Act of Algeciras.

[I am, &c.
E. GREY.]

MINUTE.([1])

A record of what M. Cambon said should be drawn up for circulation to the Cabinet, omitting any reference to the telegram from Sir E. Goschen which has not been circulated but kept secret as the French Ambassador requests.

E. G.

([1]) [This minute was written on Sir A. Nicolson's memorandum of the conversation upon which the above draft was based.]

No. 381.

Sir F. Bertie to Sir Edward Grey.

Paris, July 14, 1911.

F.O. 27630/25883/11/28.
Tel. (No. 99.) R.

D. 2·30
R. 5·25

French M[inister for] F[oreign] A[ffairs] informs me that the French Ambassador had another interview yesterday with the German M[inister for] F[oreign] A[ffairs] who stated that Germany has no intention to establish herself in Morocco (prendre pied au Maroc), that German Gov[ernmen]t realized that Sultan cannot of himself re-establish his authority. German Gov[ernmen]t are therefore prepared to recognize that task of preventing disorder and anarchy and restoring authority of the Sultan properly devolves on France. In return for this recognition it would be necessary that there should be some rectifications of frontier between the Cameroon and the French Congo which the German M[inister for] F[oreign] A[ffairs] did not specify. He further said that German metallurgic industry has mining interests in the Sus country and the German Gov[ernmen]t would wish to know what guarantee to that interest French Gov[ernmen]t would be prepared to give.

MINUTE.

I think we should put in a caveat about economic concessions. There should be none that are inconsistent with our 1904 agreement with France. I will discuss this with Sir A. Nicolson and Mr. Langley on Monday.

E. G.
16.7.11.

No. 382.

Sir F. Bertie to Sir Edward Grey.

Paris, July 14, 1911.

F.O. 27639/8755/11/28.
Tel. (No. 100.) R.

D. 3·11 P.M.
R. 6·30 P.M.

I brought unofficially to the notice of the Minister for Foreign Affairs this morning complaints made to Sir A. Nicolson by Spanish Ambassador respecting the proceedings of certain French agents at Alcazar.

French Minister for Foreign Affairs said that complaints were pretexts on the part of Spanish authorities for sending artillery and reinforcements to Alcazar. He had interview on 12th July with Spanish Ambassador, who had made several such complaints. He told him that French Government desired very much to spare the susceptibilities of Spain, and at proper-moment to come to an understanding with Spain, but proceedings of Spanish officers rendered position very difficult, and they appeared to regard districts which they have occupied without the authority of the Sultan as conquered territory, and they forbid Moorish authorities from carrying out their duties. France is acting at the request of the Sultan. Spain is acting contrary to his wishes. The action of French officers has for its object maintenance or re-establishment of the authority of the Sultan, whereas proceedings of the Spanish authorities appear to be directed to its destruction. In order to obviate friction and probable conflicts between mehallas under French officers and Spanish troops he has impressed on French commanders the advisability of avoiding as much as possible going into neighbourhood of Spanish troops and of observing greatest tact when they come into contact with or relations with Spanish officers.

Spanish Ambassador takes line of argument that Spanish troops have been obliged to act as they have done, and the occupation of the country must be taken as an existing fact and be considered from that point of view.

No. 383.

Sir E. Goschen to Sir Edward Grey.

Berlin, July 14, 1911.

F.O. 27637/25883/11/28.
Tel. (No. 48.) Confidential.

D. 6 P.M.
R. 7 P.M.

Morocco.

It appears that both here and at Paris Spanish Government have formally asked to take part in conversations between French and German Governments. German Secretary of State objected to this, and suggested that French and German Governments should refuse in more or less identic terms. He himself drew up an answer, which he has given to Spanish Ambassador here, and which I understand French Minister for Foreign Affairs has given to Spanish Ambassador at Paris.

(Secret.)

Secretary of State told M. Cambon that if Spanish Government continued to press matter he shall tell them that France proposes to make some colonial sacrifice in return for German disinterest in Morocco, and ask whether Spain is prepared to do likewise, and, if so, what she has to offer, adding that, unless she desires to offer something of a similar nature, there can be no possible reason for her to take part in the conversations.

MINUTES.

But if Spain is excluded, we probably shall be too, and this will not suit us. The present position is that the French are enquiring what the Germans want, and when this has been ascertained we ought to come in to the discussions. It is very unlikely that the Germans *only* want a Congo rectification and it might be advisable to make it quite clear at Berlin as well as in Paris, that we insist on having a say in any settlement of the Morocco question. The expediency of excluding Spain from these conversations seems very doubtful.

G. H. V.
14/7/11.

The " compensation " which France may offer to Germany, in return for a free hand in Morocco, elsewhere, is one thing. It is quite possible that it will take a shape which will not give H[is] M[ajesty's] G[overnment] a footing for interference.

On the other hand, the object of any such compensation must be a resettlement of the international position in Morocco, in which Great Britain is directly concerned, and from which it is not in the power, even if it is the wish, of Germany to exclude us. If we can rely on France telling us frankly and fully what goes on between her and Germany, there is no reason for us to stir until the German aims and demands are disclosed. Previous experience should however put us on our guard against too implicit reliance on French openness in matters of this nature. There is a grave risk of British economical interests in Morocco being bartered away surreptitiously by France to Germany before we are told of what is going on. I think a hint to M. Cambon at some opportune moment, with a reference to past objectionable transactions, might be useful.

As for Spain, it is difficult to understand the rebuff administered to her by Germany and France except on the hypothesis that these two Powers are in fact agreed to settle the Morocco question between them in a sense entirely satisfactory to France. Otherwise, Germany would not be so foolish as to throw away the chance of worrying France by encouraging Spain. On the hypothesis stated, and assuming further that Germany is really going to be content with a little concession on the Congo, the German game may possibly be explained by the determination to separate France and England at any cost. With this view, the first move was a step which it was expected would leave England unmoved, and allow Germany to deal a blow at France. This expectation having been defeated, the next attempt is to show to France that whilst Germany has it in her power to make herself exceedingly objectionable to her, there is no real desire to do so. Germany really wants to come to a definite friendly settlement with France so that France and Germany may in future freely work together. True, a small price must be paid by France by way of concession, but if France will only shape her policy in general agreement with Germany, she will find an accommodating neighbour and a staunch friend against other people, whose ambitions are, after all, very inconvenient both to France and Germany (*i.e.*, England and America).

This would be a return to the policy of Bismarck at the time of Jules Ferry, and would signify a determined bid for a Franco-German coalition against England. That this idea is not foreign to the German mind is proved by the articles published from time to time in the German press and periodicals, notably a strong plea for such a policy recently put forward by M. Harden in the " Zukunft."

Whether France would fall into the trap, is another matter. I do not think it likely at present. But in the long run it would be rash to say that French politicians might not be found to swallow the German bait, just as England did for a long period of years, when she also was " induced " by very similar manœuvres, to pay a " small price " for a rapprochement with Germany, which in the end, by too much repetition of the process, led to the complete estrangement of the two countries.

For the moment, all we can do is to keep our eyes and ears wide open and remain on our guard.

E. A. C.
July 15.

It would be a good thing if this douche were administered to Spain but the German M[inister for] F[oreign] A[ffairs] will probably do nothing of the sort.

W. L.

There is no necessity for us to move at present. And we should trust France to keep us fully informed of what passes. M. Jules Cambon informed M. de Kiderlen that the French Gov[ernmen]t, when they were acquainted with German desires, would have to consult or inform both the British and Spanish Gov[ernmen]ts. I think that if France succeeds in inducing Germany to disinterest herself in Morocco, it will then remain for France to arrange matters with Spain— and subsequently to obtain consent of all the Powers to what undoubtedly will be a new situation in Morocco. But till the situation is more fully and more clearly developed a reserved attitude on our part is the best position to assume.

A. N.
E. G.

No. 384.

Sir E. Goschen to Sir Edward Grey.

F.O. 27851/25883/11/28.
(No. 196.) Very Confidential.   *Berlin, D. July 14, 1911.*
Sir,   R. *July 17, 1911.*

With reference to my despatch No. 194 of the 12th inst[ant],(¹) I have the honour to report that my French colleague has given me the following account of a further conversation which he has had with Herr von Kiderlen-Waechter on the subject of Morocco. Herr von Kiderlen said that he had had some conversation with the Minister of the Colonies on the subject of the proposed rectification of the Congo frontier. The Minister had not shown himself averse to a settlement of the nature proposed, but his ideas of colonial expansion, inherited doubtless from his predecessor, were, in Herr von Kiderlen's opinion, rather too large for present purposes, and he had seemed to require rather more than France could be expected to give. Herr von Kiderlen however thought that the Minister could be induced to modify

(¹) [*v. supra*, pp. 353–7, No. 373.]

these ideas, and, if not, he had no doubt that some arrangement of a give and take nature could be made which would satisfy the German Colonial Authorities and at the same time not render the conditions too onerous for France. The great point was to satisfy public opinion on both sides and the Secretary of State thought that there was no insuperable difficulty in the way of attaining that result. M. Cambon without laying too great a stress on the point said that he thought matters would be simplified and their conversations rendered easier if the Imperial Government could see its way to removing the direct cause of the present feeling of uncertainty in France and elsewhere. Herr von Kiderlen however avoided any discussion on that point and turned the conversation to the demand which had just been formally put forward by Spain that she should be admitted to the conversations now proceeding between France and Germany. He said that he was entirely against Spain taking part in these conversations and proposed that as Spain had made their demand simultaneously at Berlin and Paris the two Governments should give a polite refusal to the Spanish Government in more or less identic terms. On this he produced a draft answer which M. Cambon telegraphed to Paris and which I believe was adopted by M. de Selves and which Herr von Kiderlen has since addressed to the Spanish Ambassador at Berlin. In continuing his conversation with M. Cambon, Herr von Kiderlen said very characteristically that if the Spanish Government persisted in their demand he should tell the Spanish Ambassador that if his Government insisted upon sacrificing a portion of their colonial possessions in order to secure German disinterest in Morocco, he would be glad to know what they had to offer, that if on the contrary Spain had nothing to offer, there was no point in her taking part in a conversation which had colonial sacrifice as its basis.

M. Cambon thinks that up till now the outlook for a satisfactory settlement is favourable, but says that he will not feel quite at ease until he has Germany's renunciation of all territorial and political aggrandizement in Morocco down in black and white.

I have, &c.
W. E. GOSCHEN.

No. 385.

Mr. White to Sir Edward Grey.

F.O. 28917/25641/11/28.
(No. 223.) Confidential.   *Tangier,* D. *July* 16, 1911.
Sir,   R. *July* 24, 1911.

No further news has been received from Agadir. The correspondents of several newspapers have left Mogador for that place, some by sea and others by land, so direct news should be received before long.

The report has been spread amongst the Kaïds of the South that they are to be dispossessed by Kaïd M'tougi, and others appointed in their place. The Vice-Consul at Marrakesh expresses the opinion that if M'tougi sends a force into the Sus there will probably be fighting and that an opportunity would thus be afforded to the Germans for landing, should they desire to do so. I understand however from M. de Billy that instructions of a tranquillizing nature have been sent to the southern kaïds with a view to preventing any disturbances. The kaïd of a district near Mogador informed Mr. Vice-Consul Johnstone early this month that he had been dispossessed by M'tougi and appealed for protection. This Kaïd is one of the "Conseillers Indigènes" of the Union des Mines and as such would receive the good offices of the French Legation. M. de Billy, however, did not know that this Kaïd was a Conseiller Indigène and informed me this morning that he had heard he had appealed to the Germans for protection.

His Majesty's Consul at Fez reports, in a private letter, an unconfirmed rumour that the Sultan has formally protested, through Dr. Vassel, against the action of Germany in sending a cruiser to Agadir. M. de Billy, to whom I mentioned the report, is inclined to discredit it, as he had, under instructions from Paris, advised Mulai Hafid not to make any protest. He tells me that the Sultan said to M. Gaillard that some time since, a German agent, probably one of the Mannesmanns, had told him that the German Government had been given an undertaking by Mulai Hassan that if ever any cession of territory was made to another Power, Germany should receive a cession in Sus. M. de Billy supposes this undertaking, if really given, must have been obtained by Count Tattenbach on his mission to the Court in 1890, when the German treaty was negotiated. He considers however, that this arrangement is in any case abrogated by the terms of the Act of Algeciras, and could not now be held to be binding upon Mulai Hafid.

At the time of Count von Tattenbach's mission there were persistent rumours that some sort of a promise of a cession of territory had been obtained by Germany, but, as was the case when similar rumours were current a few years earlier, it was believed to be in the North. As however was reported in Sir W. Kirby Green's despatch No. 56 of the 6th July, 1890, Count von Tattenbach positively denied the report. At later dates there have been rumours of a desire of Germany to obtain a footing in the Sus, but I have no recollection of any report having reached this Legation of any undertaking in this respect having been given by Mulai Hassan.

I have, etc.

HERBERT E. WHITE.

No. 386.

Sir F. Bertie to Sir A. Nicolson.

Private.([1])

My dear Nicolson,   *Paris, July* 16, 1911.

Sir Edward Grey has in a private letter (July 12)([2]) given the reasons why H[is] M[ajesty's] Government would not object to Germany having a port on the Atlantic Coast of Morocco provided that it were stipulated that it should not be fortified; and pointing out with reference to a despatch from me (No. 323)([3]) that Batoum is not on the ocean and so at the mercy of our fleet as an Atlantic port would be and the question of its fortification was not of much strategic importance.

My despatch was not intended as a criticism of the failure on the part of the Government of the day to prevent the fortification of Batoum. It was meant as a reminder that Russia falsified her Treaty assurances and that we alone of all the signatories of the Treaty protested.

The same thing might happen again if Germany were allowed now to have a commercial port on the Atlantic Coast of Morocco. No Treaty engagements would be likely to dissuade Germany from preparing to fortify a port in Morocco. Should we do more than protest at the preparations? I doubt it. We might be fully occupied with other matters when the conversion into a fortified port was taking place. We might be alone in our objections to fortification. France having been silenced or placated and public opinion in England might not be in a state to support strong measures against Germany. As it is now it seems to me that it is to our interest that France should object to Germany having even a commercial port in Morocco. Public opinion has been outraged in England at the brigand-like proceedings of the Germans; and they appear to be surprised and alarmed "surpris, emus and atteints," which is a state of mind to be encouraged. If they learn that we

([1]) [Carnock MSS., Vol. III of 1911.]
([2]) [*v. supra*, p. 358, No. 375.]
([3]) [*v. supra*, pp. 352–3, No. 372.]

have no unalterable objection to their having a commercial port, and in these days there are no limits to indiscretions, they may squeeze the French. Selves was very much taken aback by the change of attitude which Cambon found or thought he noticed in H[is] M[ajesty's] Government as regards a German port on the Atlantic Coast of Morocco. . . . .(⁴)

Yours ever,
FRANCIS BERTIE.

(⁴) [This letter closes with some purely general remarks.]

No. 387.

Sir Edward Grey to Sir F. Bertie.

F.O. 27630/25883/11/28.
Tel. (No. 178.) R.   *Foreign Office, July* 17, 1911.
    Your telegram No. 99.(¹) In conversation with M[inister for] F[oreign] A[ffairs] you can stipulate as regards economic concessions generally that we should know what they are in order that we may be sure that principles of commercial equality are not infringed : as regards mining concessions in particular they should be consistent with provisions of Article 58 of Mining Regulations signed at Paris in 1910.(²)

(¹) [*v. supra*, p. 362, No. 381.]
(²) [Not reproduced.]

No. 388.

Sir Edward Grey to Sir E. Goschen.

F.O. 27743/25641/11/28.
(No. 157.)
Sir,   *Foreign Office, July* 17, 1911.
    The German Ambassador called at the Foreign Office on the 12th inst[ant] and talked to Sir A. Nicolson on the subject of Morocco.(¹)
    After observing that the question of Agadir was "en bonne voie," H[is] E[xcellency] recapitulated France's action in Morocco. He referred firstly to her occupation of the Shawia; to which Sir A. Nicolson replied that that was ancient history. Next he alluded to the French advance on Fez. Sir A. Nicolson remarked that France was obliged to relieve Fez, which was isolated, and had been asked to do so by the Sultan. Count Metternich then said that by the 1904 agreement England was bound to leave France a free hand, but Germany was not. Sir A. Nicolson replied that by the 1909 agreement(²) Germany also had recognized the political interests and predominance of France in Morocco. H[is] E[xcellency] observed that France had in the same 1909 agreement engaged to respect and maintain the sovereignty of the Sultan, but she had gone to Fez notwithstanding. Sir A. Nicolson pointed out that it was with this very object that France had gone to Fez.

(¹) [Sir A. Nicolson's memorandum of this conversation, on which the draft was based, closes with the remark : " I doubt if Germany will be satisfied with a mere rectification of a Congo frontier. A. N." Sir Edward Grey has added the following minute : " In case Count Metternich calls on me I should like to have the record of what the Germans said about accepting as satisfactory the assurances of the French Gov[ernmen]t when they announced their expedition to Fez. E. G." For the German acceptance of the French assurances, *v. supra*, p. 208, No. 229, and *cp. supra*, p. 256, No. 278.]
(²) [*v. infra*, p. 830, *App.* IV.]

Count Metternich continued by saying that Germans were in danger in the south and that therefore a ship had been sent to Agadir. To Sir A. Nicolson's remark that he was unaware of there being any Germans or foreigners at Agadir H[is] E[xcellency] said that there were German houses in the hinterland. Sir A. Nicolson replied that it was news to him that there were any German residents in the Sus. The Ambassador admitted there were none, but there were German interests. However, conversations had now begun with France, and H[is] M[ajesty's] Gov[ernmen]t must not think that Germany ever intended to exclude England from any discussion in which the future of Morocco was concerned. Sir A. Nicolson replied that he understood H[is] M[ajesty's] Government would maintain a reserved attitude until they knew what Germany's aims and desires were; at present they were completely ignorant of both.

Count Metternich then remarked that forty years ago Germany waged a successful war, since when she had attained her unity and developed enormously her force and power. In that time France, the vanquished country, had added greatly to her colonial possessions, and England had added hundreds of thousands of square miles to her vast Empire. Germany had merely received a few small portions practically of little value. If the matter were looked at impartially it was clear that Germany had a right to more, and if she received more, this would not mean the break-up of the British Empire.

Sir A. Nicolson replied that the British Empire would probably survive for some time longer, and that to anyone who studied the last forty years, the history of that period was interesting and instructive reading.

[I am, &c.
E. GREY.]

No. 389.

Sir Edward Grey to Mr. Rennie.

F.O. 27768/13751/11/28.
(No. 78.)
Sir,   *Foreign Office, July 17, 1911.*

The Spanish Ambassador informed Sir A. Nicolson on the 10th inst[ant](¹) that the French M[inister for] F[oreign] A[ffairs] had stated to the Spanish Ambassador in Paris that the French Gov[ernmen]t must first converse with the German Gov[ernmen]t on the question of Morocco before discussing matters with Spain. The Spanish Gov[ernmen]t were in consequence much exercised in their minds and feared that France would come to some arrangement with Germany and then present Spain with a *fait accompli.* It was clear, M. de Villa Urrutia remarked, that France would have to give compensation of some kind to Germany, either in Morocco or elsewhere. By the agreement of May 16, 1907,(²) respecting the maintenance of the territorial *status quo* in the Mediterranean and the East Atlantic Ocean, France was bound to communicate with Spain in regard to any change in the *status quo* in " that part of the Atlantic Ocean which washes the shores of Europe and Africa," so far as France's maritime or insular possessions were affected France was not therefore at liberty to cede any port to Germany on the African coast without discussing the matter with Spain. Should she nevertheless do so, it would be

(¹) [Sir Edward Grey wrote the following minute on the memorandum of the above conversation which Sir A. Nicolson drew up as a basis for the draft despatch : " M. Cambon should be told of this conversation (except the last sentence). I should have it by me, when next he calls— or Sir A. Nicolson can tell him, if he sees him before I do; the engagement must be kept, and nothing has yet been done contrary to it. E. G."]

(²) [*v. supra*, p. 33, No. 41.]

open to Spain, in order to secure Germany's recognition of Spanish claims in Morocco, to offer her compensation on her own account, without consultation with France; and H[is] E[xcellency] observed that Spain had useful cards in her hands with which to bargain.

Sir A. Nicolson told the Ambassador he had no reason whatever to believe that France would settle matters with Germany independently of Spain and that the fears of the Spanish Government seem to him unfounded. France at present was merely endeavouring to find out what precisely it was that Germany wanted, and she could not usefully converse with Spain until she had ascertained this. The Ambassador remarked that he did not trust France.

[I am, &c.
E. GREY.]

No. 390.

Sir Edward Grey to Sir M. de Bunsen.

F.O. 28233/13751/11/28.
(No. 79.)
Sir,   *Foreign Office, July* 17, 1911.

The Spanish Ambassador informed me to-day that his Government were ready to propose a *modus vivendi* with the French Government, under which his Government would agree not to send a single soldier more to Alcazar, if the French Government would undertake to make no trouble there. He was very much disturbed by hints which had been dropped that the French might order the Moorish mehalla to attack the Spaniards, and also that the French might settle the Moroccan question with the Germans and us, leaving the Spaniards altogether out of account. He asked me whether I would support with the French the *modus vivendi* which he had proposed; and whether, in the event of France coming to an arrangement with Germany that ignored the agreements between France and Spain, we would maintain that Article 8 of our Convention with France still held good.

I said that I had warned him, in one of our conversations after the Spaniards had gone to Alcazar, that the result of the Spanish action might be to precipitate a crisis in Morocco, leading to conversations between France and Germany, and that then no country would be able to tell how its own interests might eventually be affected. This was the situation which had actually come about. Until we knew the outcome of the conversations between France and Germany, we ourselves could not tell how British interests were likely to be affected, or what action it might be necessary for us to take. Spain seemed to be in a similar position.

The Ambassador asked whether Spain might not still rely upon our good-will; if Spain could get no support from her old friends she must make the best terms she could independently. I said that Spain had not been ready to take the advice of her old friends but I was genuinely anxious that, whatever settlement was reached, it should not result in an alteration of the grouping of the Powers and I would do my best to secure that there should be no cause for this. I should not at all like a breach between Spain and France, and I should like still less a breach between Spain and us. At the moment, however, the only thing for Spain to do was to keep as quiet as possible at Alcazar. If the rumours as to expeditions beyond her sphere had proved to be true, the situation would have become impossible.

The Ambassador said that it was out of the question that there should be such expeditions. But he urged that a settlement might be made which would not affect British interests, though it would be adverse to Spanish interests. The Spaniards were in Morocco, while we were not; and, as Germany had made it clear that she was going to insist upon a final settlement of the Moroccan question, Spanish interests were bound to be affected, though we might be able to stand aside.

I said that Spain had been in closer relations with Germany than we had, and we had not had such an expression of the German view about Morocco. The Ambassador himself had hinted, after the Germans went to Agadir, that a tripartite partition of Morocco between Germany, Spain, and France was the settlement which the Germans had in view. I could conceive such a settlement which might not be adverse to Spanish interests, but might be so to British interests; just as he could conceive a settlement which might be adverse to Spanish interests, but not to ours. Until the situation had developed, I could not say either what we might have to do, or what we could do. Meanwhile, the best thing for Spain to do was to remain as quiet as possible, and to come to an arrangement with France if she could. The language of the French Minister for Foreign Affairs to Sir Francis Bertie had given no indication whatever that France intended to abandon the agreement she had made with Spain; nor, so far as I was aware, had anything taken place hitherto in the conversations at Berlin that was inconsistent with that agreement.

The Spanish Ambassador expressed apprehension that France might say that Spain had broken the secret agreement with France by going to Alcazar and might on this pretext set the agreement aside.

I reminded the Ambassador that I had deprecated Spanish action at Alcazar as weakening the force of the secret agreement: this was just what I had had in mind at the time. But France had not yet taken up this position: it was not a point that we should raise and till France did so it was unnecessary to anticipate it.

[I am, &c.]
E. G[REY].

No. 391.

Sir F. Bertie to Sir Edward Grey.

Private.([1])
My dear Grey,   *Paris, July* 17, 1911.

I do not know what your views will be of the German idea of rectifications of frontier between the Cameroons and the French Congo. I think that these excessive requirements of the Germans viz: the French Congo from the river Sangha to the ocean are known by them to be impossible of acceptance and are intended to reconcile the French to the establishment of Germany on the Morocco coast in a non military guise. How would it suit us to have the Germans at Libreville on the estuary of the Gaboon and at Brazzaville? Selves and Paul Cambon whom I saw together this morning of course give prominence to the injury which such a cession as the Germans ask for would do to British interests as well as to those of France. Cambon says that the aim of Germany is to have a port on the Atlantic, that if she succeeded in exacting from France the French Congo as asked for, she would soon add to it the Spanish settlement between it and the Cameroons and also absorb the Portuguese Possessions at and in the vicinity of the mouth of the Congo River. You will remember that Germany in the Secret Agreement with us of 1898 pegged out a reversionary claim to Portuguese territories there. Cambon also says that Germany as the Congo riverain Power in the place of France would claim to stand in her shoes and have the right of preemption when the Congo Free State is for disposal which it will most probably be before long.

Selves has instructed Jules Cambon to inform the German Government that he is painfully surprised at the excessive pretensions which the so-called rectifications of frontier have assumed, that the French Minister for the Colonies being absent from Paris, the French Government cannot send definite instructions to their

Ambassador at Berlin, but that he (Selves) considers the requirements of the German Government as inadmissible.

Selves is anxious to have your views on the situation as soon as possible. Paul Cambon remains here until Monday next July 24th.

Yours sincerely,
FRANCIS BERTIE.

No. 392.

Sir F. Bertie to Sir Edward Grey.

Paris, *July* 18, 1911.

F.O. 28138/25883/11/28.
Tel. (No. 103.) Very Urgent.

D. 12·13 A.M.
R. 8 A.M.

French M[inister for] F[oreign] A[ffairs] sent for me this morning in order to give to me an account of a further interview which the French Ambassador at Berlin had had with the German M[inister for] F[oreign] A[ffairs] on the evening of Saturday July 15.(¹) French Ambassador at London was present most of the time during my interview and gave explanations and made observations and suggestions.

Following is a summary of French Ambassador at Berlin's report of his conversation with German M[inister for] F[oreign] A[ffairs] which French M[inister for] F[oreign] A[ffairs] read to me.

German M[inister for] F[oreign] A[ffairs] began conversation with a long harrangue [*sic*] on the grievances of Germany. France had made arrangements with England and Spain and even Italy to compensate them for their concurrence in French designs in Morocco. Germany who had interests in Morocco got nothing. Since the Algeciras Conference there had been Franco-German Agreement of 1909,(²) but it had proved illusory to Germany. She had been excluded from her proper share in concessions and railway schemes. French Gov[ernmen]t had gone to Fez without coming to preliminary understanding with the German Gov[ernmen]t which they ought to have done. If France wished Germany to forgo her political interests in Morocco and to withdraw from Agadir, French Gov[ernmen]t must give proper compensation for such a sacrifice of interests.

French Ambassador at Berlin reminded German M[inister for] F[oreign] A[ffairs] that notice had been given to the German Gov[ernmen]t of the rescue expedition to Fez and told him that political conditions of Morocco had prevented full effect being given to Franco-German Agreement of 1909 which the French Gov[ernmen]t fully intended to strictly observe. There ensued some mutual recriminations after which M. Cambon asked what were rectifications of frontier between the Cameroons and the French Congo which the German Gov[ernmen]t would suggest as compensation for resignation of interests in Morocco and withdrawal from Agadir.

German M[inister for] F[oreign] A[ffairs] said that he had conferred with German Minister for the Colonies and he had proposals to make for the bases for negotiations. He then took a map and indicated in it that France should cede to Germany all the territory of the French Congo lying between river Sangha and the sea in return for which Germany would concede to France some rectifications in North Cameroons, would renounce political interests in Morocco and would withdraw from Agadir after obtaining guarantees in regard to mining interests in the Suss country.

M. Cambon told German M[inister for] F[oreign] A[ffairs] that he supposed that German Gov[ernmen]t made such suggestions in order to ensure failure of the negotiations and he pointed out that the remnant of the Congo to be left to France

(¹) [*v.* G.P. XXIX, pp. 184–6, abridged in *Jäckh*, Vol. II. p. 126. *cp. Mermeix*, pp. 100–1.]
(²) [*v. supra*, p. 139, No. 155, *encl.* 2, and *infra*, p. 830, *App.* IV.]

2 B ?

would be cut off from the sea. To this objection German M[inister for] F[oreign] A[ffairs] replied that Germany would guarantee to France Railway access to the sea through the territory to be ceded by her.

M. Cambon who told German M[inister for] F[oreign] A[ffairs] that he considered German suggestions as quite inadmissible but undertook at request of German M[inister for] F[oreign] A[ffairs] to refer them to French Gov[ernmen]t and to ask for their instructions on them.

French Ambassadors at Berlin and London and French M[inister for] F[oreign] A[ffairs] are of opinion that great aim of German Gov[ernmen]t is to obtain a port on the Atlantic. They would probably prefer to establish themselves on the Moroccan coast in order to create whenever it suited them a fermentation among the tribes and to pose as their protectors against the French. They have therefore made these unacceptable demands.

French M[inister for] F[oreign] A[ffairs] also read me a telegram from French Chargé d'Affaires at Tangier reporting that parties from German ship at Agadir land increasing numbers up to 40 men and make expeditions into the country around, spreading agitating rumours among the tribes and apparently with the intention of provoking incidents as pretexts for establishing a permanent landing party to be gradually increased.

In the course of conversation on the German pretensions which ensued French Ambassador at London enlarged on injury to British interests which, if acceded to, they would involve. Germany would have in (? her) possession Libreville, a port on the Atlantic which would detract from British interests. She would soon add to what she had taken of the French Congo the Spanish settlement between it and the Cameroons and also absorb the Portuguese possessions at (word omitted) and in the vicinity of the (?) E[ast] Congo River. Germany as the successor to France on the lower part of the Congo River and the riverain neighbourhood of the Congo State would claim to stand in the place of France with preemption over rights (*sic*) when the Congo State is, as M. Cambon considers it probably will be before long, for disposal.

As to Agadir, French Ambassador at London thinks that the German Gov[ernmen]t if they fail to obtain excessive compensation elsewhere, are minded to create incidents there and gradually to increase their force there, landing men permanently, and remain without giving any guarantees in regard to status of the port; in the absence of British and French ships no definite information will be obtainable as to German proceedings. French M[inister for] F[oreign] A[ffairs] wishes to have your views on the situation created by excessive demands of German Gov[ernmen]t, as soon as possible.

MINUTES.

We begin to see light. Germany is playing for the highest stakes. If her demands are acceded to either on the Congo or in Morocco, or—what she will, I believe, try for—in both regions, it will mean definitely the subjection of France. The conditions demanded are not such as a country having an independent foreign policy can possibly accept. The details of the terms are not so very important now. This is a trial of strength, if anything. Concession means not loss of interests or loss of prestige. It means defeat, with all its inevitable consequences.

The defeat of France is a matter vital to this country. Therefore it will be of little use for H[is] M[ajesty's] G[overnment] to consider in detail the particular conditions which might or might not be put up with, before deciding the larger and dominant question whether England is prepared to fight by the side of France if necessary. This is the question to be wisely considered and firmly decided. On the decision everything else depends. The rest is detail, not unimportant, and certainly full of difficulties, but impossible to handle except from the firm ground of the determination that England is, in the last resort, either determined not to prevent German aggression by force, and risk the consequences, or decided to resist it with all her energies and, again, take the consequences.([3])

E. A. C.
July 18

([3]) [cp. infra, p. 795, Ed. note.]

The German Gov[ernmen]t were sure to open their mouths very wide at first, but the present proposal does look as if they intended to wreck the negotiation and stay at Agadir. They can hardly believe that a French Gov[ernmen]t could accept their terms and stay in office.

W. L.

We have arrived at a critical moment. France naturally cannot make the cession demanded of her. Germany *may* modify her Congo demands but in that case she will remain at Agadir—and this would be equally unacceptable to France. We are, therefore, face to face with a very serious situation. H[is] M[ajesty's] Gov[ernmen]t will have to decide whether they will remain true to their engagements to France and maintain the present grouping of Powers, so essential to the preservation of peace, or whether they will leave Germany to settle matters with France. I cannot imagine that the latter would be the course adopted. The only hope of keeping the peace is for us to range ourselves alongside of France, as we did in 1905 and 1906, and show a united front to German demands, the character of which it is superfluous to specify. If Germany saw the slightest weakening on our part her pressure on France would become intolerable to that country who would have to fight or surrender. In the latter case German hegemony would be solidly established, with all its consequences immediate and prospective.

A. N.

The answer we give to France is critical and I have sent the telegram this morning to the Prime Minister and to Mr. McKenna.

E. G.

No. 393.

Sir Edward Grey to Sir F. Bertie.

F.O. 28288/25883/11/28.
(No. 295.)

Sir,   *Foreign Office, July 18, 1911.*

M. Cambon informed me on the 13th instant that the German Ambassador in Paris had seen M. de Selves, and had said that, now France had agreed to discuss the question of the Congo, a settlement of the question of Morocco ought to be easy. M. de Selves had reminded the German Ambassador that it was he himself who had brought the Congo into the discussion, and that as this had been done at Germany's request, it was for Germany to make her views clear.

M. Cambon reminded me of what the view of the Admiralty had been with regard to a port at Agadir, as communicated to M. Delcassé six years ago.

I said that I was aware of what had passed then. But as in any case it was infinitely preferable on general grounds that a settlement should be made which did not give Germany a footing in Morocco, and as conversations were proceeding on the basis of a Congo settlement, it seemed unnecessary to discuss the Admiralty point of view now as to ports on the west coast of Morocco.

[I am, &c.]
E. G[REY].

No. 394.

Sir Edward Grey to Sir R. Rodd.

F.O. 28289/13911/11/28.
(No. 113.)

Sir,   *Foreign Office, July 18, 1911.*

The Italian Ambassador informed me on the 13th inst[ant] that the Franco-Italian Agreement made it impossible for Italy to oppose French political action in Morocco. But the Italian Government could not be disinterested in eventual consequences which might affect the equilibrium in the Mediterranean or the international situation, owing to the action of France or any other Power. Such action might cause a state of things affecting serious Italian interests, political as well as economic. Italy therefore wished to make her voice heard in time. The Ambassador added, on his own part, that if there was to be a general upset, Italy could not be left in the lurch. He then said that this attitude of the Italian Government appeared to be much the same as that of the British Government, and he invited my opinion.

I said that Germany had opened the question in the worst possible way. After giving it to be understood that her interests were only commercial, she had gone to a port which was commercially closed. She had thus made it clear that commercial interests were only a pretext. Agadir happened also to be the port most suitable for a naval base. Germany had thus at the outset mobilised the whole of British public opinion, and if she had been in any doubt as to what our attitude would be she had by her own action removed that doubt, and made it certain that our interest would be engaged on the side of France. If Germany wished conversations to be easy, it was now for her, having charged the atmosphere with electricity, to do something to calm it.

The Italian Ambassador observed that Germany would be certain to keep a ship at Agadir until a settlement was reached.

I said that it was desirable that Germany should not keep a ship there too long, as that might end in our also sending a ship.

The Ambassador asked whether we did not intend to be a party to any negotiations which might take place. He understood that negotiations were proceeding between Germany and France alone.

I told him that at present there were no negotiations, but only conversations to ascertain on what basis negotiations could take place.

[I am, &c.]
E. G[REY].

No. 395.

Sir A. Nicolson to Sir E. Goschen.

Private.(¹)

My dear Goschen :— *Foreign Office, July* 18, 1911.

. . . .(²) I had a curious conversation with Metternich last Friday.(³) He came to see me ostensibly on a very trivial matter which certainly did not call for a visit on his part. After having disposed of this question, he meditated for some time, as is his wont, and then dilated at some length upon the action of France in Morocco and the manner in which they had contravened their engagements and also the Algeciras Act. I need not trouble you with what he said in this respect as it was merely a repetition of what has constantly been said recently by Germany. I met his arguments one by one, somewhat to his annoyance. He then plunged into a reflective mood for some minutes and then stated that forty years ago Germany had waged a successful war and had won a victory at great sacrifices. Since that date Germany had consolidated her unity and had developed enormously her resources and was now a powerful and homogeneous country. During the past 40 years France, the vanquished one, had added greatly to her colonial possessions, and England has also increased her already vast Empire by hundreds of thousands of square miles. Germany, on the other hand, powerful and victorious as she had been, had acquired nothing but a few isolated localities of little or no value, and to anyone who viewed

(¹) [Carnock MSS., Vol. III of 1911.]
(²) [The first part of this letter is printed, *infra*, pp. 623–4, No. 633.]
(³) [*i.e.*, the 14th. It seems probable, however, that the reference is to the conversation of the 12th described in Sir Edward Grey's despatch of July 17 (*supra*, pp. 367–8, No. 388). No trace has been found in the British archives of a conversation between Count Metternich and Sir A. Nicolson on July 14. Count Benckendorff, writing on the 19th, gives an account of an interview (described as taking place a few days earlier) which had been related to him by Sir A. Nicolson. *cp. Siebert*, pp. 592–4.]

the matter impartially, it was clear that Germany had every claim to a great deal more than she had received, and no one could with justice dispute her receiving large concessions. He did not think that whatever she might obtain would mean the disruption of the British Empire. Having terminated this homily, he rose and took his leave. Metternich, as a rule, very rarely launches into political disquisitions with me, and this new departure on his part left me under the impression that the concessions or compensations which Germany intended to demand from France, would be of a wide and comprehensive character. I told Cambon, who came to see me immediately afterwards, of the substance of Metternich's remarks, and he agreed with me that .coming from the quarter which they did, that they were certainly ominous. My forebodings have been amply carried out by the telegram which we have received this morning from Bertie,([4]) and which gives the substance of the demands which were made to your French colleague at Berlin. As I have no doubt that Jules Cambon will have given you a full account of what passed between him and Kiderlen last Saturday, it is unnecessary for me to go into details. I have only just received the advance copy of the telegram and have not had time to examine the question, but it is clear that what the Germans were pleased in the first instance to characterize as a rectification of the frontier, has developed into acquiring—as I had already foretold to Grey—practically the whole of the French Congo. I imagine that the Germans do not suppose that the French will accede to these demands, and the result will no doubt be that the Germans will settle themselves permanently at Agadir which will be equally unacceptable to France. I trust that our Government will not be beguiled into admitting the harmlessness of the establishment of a large German settlement on the Atlantic Coast, for whatever engagements the Germans may give as to the innocuous character of such a settlement and of its purely commercial and peaceful intentions, there is no doubt that whenever they thought it desirable, they would convert a commercial port into a naval base, and we must not forget that such a naval base is within easy access of the Canaries, which they could seize at any moment by a *coup de main* or by negotiations with the Spaniards. I happened the other day to be looking through the Memoirs of the late Lord Granville and I came across the passage where Munster suggested to him that England might concede Heligoland to Germany for the purpose of establishing a harbour of refuge to German and British North Sea fishermen. The idea of converting Heligoland for any other purpose was naturally scouted as out of the question but the Government of that day declined to enter into the proposals in any shape or form. Now that they have got Heligoland into their hands, the innocent harbour of refuge has been converted into a very formidable fortress. There is no reason to doubt that a similar procedure will be followed in regard to any port which she might be able to acquire on the Atlantic Coast.

We are now entering into a critical phase of this Morocco question. To my mind it is more than ever essential that France and ourselves should show a united front. It is only by this means that we can hope that Germany will moderate her demands or keep them within reasonable limits, for were she to detect the slightest wavering or indifference on our side, she would no doubt press France with extreme rigour and the latter would either have to fight or surrender.

I will not go into the Albanian question with you, although this is a matter which is also causing us considerable anxiety, and it looks by no means improbable that the Rebellion will assume before long such dimensions as may lead it to spread beyond the borders of Albania.

I have one or two letters to write this morning, so I will close now. If, before this letter leaves, anything of serious importance arises, I will add a postscript.

[A. NICOLSON.]

(⁴) [*v. supra*, pp. 371–2, No. 392.]

No. 396.

Sir Edward Grey to Sir F. Bertie.([1])

F.O. 28138/25883/11/28.   , *Foreign Office, July* 19, 1911.
Tel. (No. 180.)   D. 3·30 P.M.

Your telegram No. 103.([2])

German demands being more than France can concede the obvious course seems to be for France to make counter proposals stating what she can concede in French Congo. There is no reason for us to object to any concessions there which French Gov[ernmen]t does not consider unreasonable.

A further telegram will follow as to possible developments of situation should Germany refuse to modify her demand about French Congo.

                                            E. G.

([1]) [This telegram is paraphrased in *Twenty-Five Years*, Vol. I, p. 232.]
([2]) [*v. supra*, pp. 371–2, No. 392.]

No. 397.

Sir Edward Grey to Sir F. Bertie.

F.O. 28138/25883/11/28.   *Foreign, Office, July* 19, 1911.
Tel. (No. 181.) Urgent.   '   D. 7·45 P.M.

Your telegram No. 103.([1]) German demands on French Congo may foreshadow breakdown of negotiations with France, Germany thus remaining at Agadir.

H[is] M[ajesty's] Gov[ernmen]t might then on their own initiative propose to Germany a Conference of Powers signatory of Algeciras Act, intimating that in case of refusal H[is] M[ajesty's] Gov[ernmen]t must take action to protect their own interests.

Germany would in reply probably stipulate that basis and scope of conference should be defined.

It is therefore essential before H[is] M[ajesty's] Gov[ernmen]t make any proposal or intimation of this kind to Germany that they should know not only whether France would like the proposal to be made, but whether in a conference she would exclude under all circumstances any idea of a settlement that gave Germany a foothold in Morocco.

H[is] M[ajesty's] Gov[ernmen]t do not consider it vital to their interests to exclude Germany from getting any foothold in Morocco provided satisfactory conditions are obtained from her. They cannot therefore make any admission of Germany into Morocco a *casus belli* unconditionally, though they could not suggest it or deal with it except in concert with France and on conditions satisfactory to France.

If a settlement based on compensation to Germany in French Congo proves impracticable it will not be possible to exclude Germany from Morocco and place France in possession without a resort to war. Only alternatives would therefore be a return to *status quo* of Algeciras Act or consolidation of position of France in Morocco by some compensation to Germany in Morocco and it is essential before H[is] M[ajesty's] Gov[ernmen]t take any step involving serious consequences that they should know final view of France as to latter alternative in principle.

It would be desirable to know this before Cabinet meets again Friday morning.

                                            E. G.

([1]) [*v. supra*, pp. 371–2, No. 392.]

No. 398.

Sir F. Bertie to Sir Edward Grey.

F.O. 28392/28247/11/28.
(No. 333.)
Sir,

Paris, D. *July* 19, 1911.
R. *July* 20, 1911.

In conversation with Monsieur de Selves this afternoon I suggested that possibly Monsieur de Kiderlen Wächter had put forward the excessive proposals in regard to the French Congo with the object of bringing the French Government to prefer that Germany should establish herself at Agadir rather than that France should have to make such extensive concessions to Germany in the Congo.

Monsieur de Selves said that if Germany was to be allowed to remain permanently at Agadir in breach of the Act of Algeciras there would be no reason why any other Power Signatory of the Act should not, on some pretext as shallow as the one the German Government had put forward, establish itself on the Coast of Morocco. The German and Spanish proceedings were as much as to say that Treaty engagements were only binding so long as they suited an individual State signatory of the Treaty.

Monsieur de Selves informed me that he had sent for the Spanish Ambassador and had called his attention to the arrest of the French Consul Monsieur Boisset by Spanish soldiers. He told the Ambassador that if the facts were as they had been reported, and he had no reason to doubt the information which he had received, the matter was very serious and required explanations and an apology from the Spanish Government. The French Ambassador had left for Madrid to place himself at once in communication with the Spanish Government on the subject.

Monsieur Caballero said that he could not believe that the facts had been correctly reported. He admitted that if they were so they called for explanations and on that supposition he expressed the regret which he felt and the Spanish Government would undoubtedly express.

I have, &c.
FRANCIS BERTIE.

No. 399.

Sir Edward Grey to Mr. Asquith.

Private.([1])
My dear Asquith,

Foreign Office, July 19, 1911.

It is now 15 days since I made Metternich the communication that the Cabinet authorized.([2]) We have not had since from the German Government any indication that they recognize our position in the matter or that our communication has impressed them in any way.

They will assume that we know the demand they have made upon France and, if we give no sign, their attitude will stiffen; all chance of their settling with France about the French Congo will disappear and there will be further developments at Agadir that will make it more difficult to draw back and to accept reasonable terms.

There is talk of having the F[oreign] O[ffice] vote in the House next Tuesday [July 25] and whether that be so or not I do not know how to meet a question, whether we know what is happening at Agadir. We do not know and our long ignorance and silence combined must lead the Germans to imagine that we don't very much care. We shall drift into a situation that will render it more and more

([1]) [Grey MSS., Vol. 61.]
([2]) [*v. supra*, p. 334, No. 356.]

difficult both for us and for France to come to terms with Germany and more and more difficult for us to remain inactive. I think therefore it is essential that I should on Friday [July 21] be authorized to make some communication to Germany to impress upon her that, if the negotiations between her and France come to nothing, we must become a party to a discussion of the situation and that as Agadir is a closed port, where we have no means of obtaining information, we must, unless we are kept informed by Germany, of any new developments there, send ships ourselves to see that our interests are not prejudiced. This is not unreasonable in view of the fact that judging by the trade figures of Mogador our commercial interests in that region of Morocco are greater than those of Germany.

This is on the assumption that we have not by Friday received a reply from France that will enable us to take a more definite line. I found it difficult today to resist the decision of the Cabinet not to commit ourselves to the proposal of a Conference, till we know whether France would insist upon excluding any idea of admitting Germany to any part of Morocco on any terms, but I fear lest irreparable harm may have been done by continued silence and inaction.

Yours sincerely,
E. GREY.

No. 400.

Sir F. Bertie to Sir Edward Grey.

Paris, July 20, 1911.

F.O. 28514/28247/11/28.   D. 1·30 P.M.
Tel. (No. 105.) R.   R. 3·10 P.M.

I have communicated to French M[inister for] F[oreign] A[ffairs] contents of your telegram No. 181 Urgent,(¹) of yesterday evening respecting Morocco negotiations. He will see me again this evening on the subject.

His Excellency told me that Spanish Government apologized yesterday evening through French Ambassador at Madrid and their Ambassador here for treatment of French Consul, M. Boisset, and have directed Spanish Colonel to apologize to him.

French M[inister for] F[oreign] A[ffairs] also told me that a delegate sent to Agadir by the French Legation in Morocco was well received by German Senior Naval Officer and was by him informed that Germany has rights on Morocco coast from Saffi to Agadir.

(¹) [v. supra, p. 376, No. 397.]

No. 401.

Sir F. Bertie to Sir Edward Grey.

F.O. 28524/25883/11/28.   Paris, D. July 20, 1911, 9·35 P.M.
Tel. (No. 106.) R.   R. July 21, 1911, 8 A.M.

Morocco. My tel[egram] No. 105 of this morning.(¹)

Following is translation of memo[randum] given to me by M[inister for] F[oreign] A[ffairs] at 7 this evening in reply to memo[randum] in which I communicated to H[is] E[xcellency] this morning contents of your telegram No. 181 Urgent of yesterday evening.(²)

(¹) [v. immediately preceding document.]
(²) [v. supra, p. 376, No. 397.]

M[inister for] F[oreign] A[ffairs] received this afternoon a tel[egram] from French Ambassador reporting that M[inister for] F[oreign] A[ffairs] at Berlin had invited him to come to him in order to renew conversations which had been suspended since Saturday last.

(Memo[randum] begins.) The negotiations proceeding between French and German Gov[ernmen]ts in regard to Equatorial Africa have not broken down: and according to all appearances they will last for some time.

In the event of these negotiations failing, French Gov[ernmen]t would not put aside the idea of H[is] M[ajesty's] Gov[ernmen]t taking not only *vis-à-vis* to the German Gov[ernmen]t but also *vis-à-vis* to all Gov[ernmen]ts signatory of the Algeciras Act, the initiative of proposing a Conference; and in their opinion it would be preferable that the British Gov[ernmen]t, when taking such an initiative, should themselves indicate programme of that conference.

British Gov[ernmen]t by the Agreement of 1904, recognised to France and Spain alone spheres of political influence in Morocco and consequently denied to other Powers all political pretensions over that country. To allow the German Gov[ernmen]t now to create a State establishment on any point whatever of Moroccan territory would be contrary to the agreement of 1904 as well as to the official declaration made by Germany to France in Feb[ruary] 1909. The French Gov[ernmen]t could not therefore admit that the Conference which might be held could be called upon to consider the concession in any form (à un titre quelconque) of a portion however small of Moorish territory; but the French Gov[ernmen]t, faithful to the principles laid down in the Algeciras Act, as well as in special agreements with the Powers, are quite ready to recognise the rights of foreign Powers to all economic advantages compatible with the above-mentioned Acts. (Memo[randum] ends.)

I am sending by post to-night French text of M[inister for] F[oreign] A[ffairs'] reply.

No. 402.

Sir Edward Grey to Sir F. Bertie.

F.O. 28138/25883/11/28.
Tel. (No. 183.)   *Foreign Office, July 20, 1911.*

Your telegram No.: 103.([1])

If Belgian Congo was ever for sale I cannot think France would want to add the whole of that to her already very extensive African possessions. Neither France nor we can reasonably expect to increase what we have and keep Germany who has much less out of everything.

It occurs to me therefore that admission of Germany to a share in French pre-emption rights of Belgian Congo might be a possible element of bargain, if Germany would withdraw her excessive demand about French Congo.

This would have to be without prejudice to rights of Belgium as long as she desired to retain them, and if Congo State was for sale there are parts contiguous to existing British possessions that we might desire to purchase and conditions that we might want as to means of through communication, but our desires would be so modest that we could no doubt easily arrange them with Germany in return for our acquiescence in what she took.

([1]) [*v. supra*, pp. 371–2, No. 392.]

We do not desire to acquire more tropical territory in Africa on any extensive scale, and prefer to concentrate on development of what we have. France I should think is in the same condition, but essential point is that France should be clear in her own mind as to how much it is worth her while to give Germany in return for a stronger position in Morocco than the Algeciras Act gives her at present.

No. 403.

Sir F. Bertie to Sir Edward Grey.

F.O. 28529/25883/11/28.
(No. 336.)   *Paris, D. July 20, 1911.*
Sir,   *R. July 20, 1911.*

With reference to my telegram No. 106(¹) marked pressing of this evening I have the honour to transmit to you herewith copies of the memorandum which in consequence of the instructions contained in your telegram No. 181 Urgent of July 19th,(²) I communicated to Monsieur de Selves this morning and of the French text of the Memorandum which His Excellency gave to me this evening in reply thereto in regard to the Franco German negotiations on the subject of Morocco.

                                    I have, &c.
                                      FRANCIS BERTIE.

Enclosure 1 in No. 403.

Memorandum communicated to M. de Selves by Sir F. Bertie.

Sir Edward Grey informs me that there will be a meeting of the Cabinet to-morrow Friday morning and that before then he would wish to know the definite views of the French Government in regard to the situation as hereunder set forth.

The demands put forward by the German Government in regard to the French Congo may foreshadow the breakdown of the negotiations with the French Government, and Germany remaining at Agadir.

In such event His Majesty's Government might thereupon on their own initiative propose to the German Government that there should be a Conference of the Powers Parties to the Algeciras Act intimating to the Berlin Cabinet that in the case of a refusal on their part to accept the proposal His Majesty's Government will be obliged to take action to protect British interests. The reply of the German Government would probably be a stipulation that the basis and scope of the Conference should be laid down. It is consequently essential before any such proposal or intimation is made that His Majesty's Government should be made acquainted with the views of the French Government not only in regard to whether the proposal for a Conference would be agreeable to them but whether in such a Conference France would in all circumstances exclude any solution that would give a foothold in Morocco to Germany. The British Government do not regard the exclusion of Germany from any such foothold as vital to British interests provided always that satisfactory conditions be obtained from her. They are therefore unable to treat as an unconditional *casus belli* any such admission, though they could not, except in concert with France and on conditions satisfactory to her suggest or deal with it.

Failing a settlement on the bases of compensation in the French Congo on such a solution being regarded as impracticable by the French Government it will not be possible to exclude Germany and place France in possession of Morocco without a resort to war. It might be possible as an alternative to return to the *status quo* established by the Act of Algeciras or as an alternative, by some compensation to be awarded to Germany in Morocco in order to obtain the consolidation of the

(¹) [*v. supra*, pp. 378–9, No. 401.]
(²) [*v. supra*, p. 376, No. 397.]

position of France in that country. It is essential that His Majesty's Government should be made acquainted with the final view in principle of the Government of the Republic on the alternative just mentioned (viz., some compensation in Morocco to Germany) before any step envolving '[*sic*] serious consequences can be taken by His Majesty's Government.

Paris,
July 20th, 1911.

Enclosure 2 in No. 403.

Memorandum communicated to Sir F. Bertie by M. de Selves.([3])

Les pourparlers engagés entre le Gouvernement Français et le Gouvernement allemand au sujet de l'Afrique Équatoriale française ne sont pas rompus; et selon toute apparence ils se prolongeront durant quelque temps.

Si ces pourparlers venaient à échouer, le Gouvernement français n'écarterait pas l'idée que le Gouvernement britannique prît, non seulement vis à vis du Gouvernement allemand, mais vis à vis de tous les Gouvernements signataires de l'Acte d'Algésiras, l'initiative d'une Conférence; et, d'après lui, il serait préférable que le Gouvernement britannique, en prenant cette initiative, traçât lui-même le programme de cette Conférence.

Le Gouvernement anglais, par l'accord de 1904, a reconnu à la France et à l'Espagne, seules, des sphères d'influence politique au Maroc et a, par conséquent, dénié aux autres Puissances toute prétention politique sur ce pays. Laisser aujourd'hui le Gouvernement allemand créer un établissement d'Etat sur un point quelconque du territoire marocain serait contraire à l'accord de 1904, ainsi, d'ailleurs, qu'à la déclaration officielle faite par l'Allemagne à la France au mois de février 1909. Le Gouvernement français ne pourrait donc admettre que la Conférence éventuelle puisse être appelée à envisager la concession à un titre quelconque au Gouvernement allemand d'une portion, si petite soit-elle, du territoire marocain; mais fidèle aux principes posés dans le préambule de l'Acte d'Algésiras, comme dans ses accords particuliers avec les Puissances, il est tout prêt à reconnaître à des Puissances étrangères, et notamment à l'Allemagne, tous les avantages économiques qui seraient compatibles avec les Actes susrappelés.

Paris, le 20 juillet, 1911.

([3]) [Sir A. Nicolson's comments on this memorandum are given *infra*, p. 386, No. 409.]

No. 404.

Sir Edward Grey to Sir F. Cartwright.

F.O. 29234/13911/11/28.
(No. 47.)
Sir,
Foreign Office, July 20, 1911.

As Count Mensdorff asked me to-day about Morocco, I spoke to him in the same sense as I had previously spoken to the Italian Ambassador([1]) as to the effect of the way in which Germany had opened the question, by sending a ship to Agadir.

Count Mensdorff expressed the hope that the question would all be settled satisfactorily.

I said that a settlement depended upon Germany, and it rested with her to give things a satisfactory turn. Other people were not disposed to be unreasonable in coming to a settlement, and as Germany had put things in a bad way by her opening, it was for her to get them right.

[I am, &c.]
E. G[REY].

([1]) [*v. supra*, pp. 373-4, No. 394. Count Mensdorff's report of this interview has not been traced in *Ö.-U.A.*]

No. 405.

Sir Edward Grey to Sir F. Bertie.

Private.(¹)

My dear Bertie,   *Foreign Office, July* 20, 1911.

The French have drifted into difficulties without knowing which way they really want to go.

We are bound and prepared to give them diplomatic support, but we cannot go to war in order to set aside the Algeciras Act and put France in virtual possession of Morocco. It she can get that for herself we are bound not to stand in her way or to claim more rights than we are entitled to under the Anglo-French Agreement of 1904; but if we go to war it must be in defence of British interests. An attempt by Germany to humiliate France might affect British interests so seriously that we should have to resist it, but there is no case for that at present. France, Spain, and Germany have all stepped outside the Algeciras Act together. France perhaps is less wrong technically because she went to Fez at the request of the Sultan, but in effect she has turned Morocco into a French protectorate.

If one looks at a map of Africa and considers the large amount coloured British and coloured French, much larger each of them than all that Germany has, it is obvious that neither France nor we can put more of our own colour on the map without Germany getting some substantial addition to her share.

As to British interests it really doesn't matter to us who owns tropical territory that we do not want for ourselves. Our trade is as well off in German as in French possessions.

As to ports, we have by secret agreement given Angola to Germany, if Portugal parts with it;(²) Germany will get all that coast some day and Lobito Bay with it, a better place I should think for a naval station than Libreville is, and when she has Angola it wouldn't make any difference to us if she had French Congo coast too.

Of course I see that Germany is asking more than France can give in the French Congo and that these negotiations may come to nothing. If so there is only one way of getting Germany out of Agadir and that is a Conference demanding a strict return to the *status quo* of the Algeciras Act.

The other alternative is to let Germany stay on conditions that will satisfy France in Morocco and us elsewhere.

We, *i.e:* Great Britain, can no doubt turn Germany out of Agadir by force, but we should be able to make a deal with her about it, and it isn't worth our while to fight her unless she was unwilling to deal.

If therefore we make a move and Germany proposes a deal we shall be in a false position. If we deal with Germany about Morocco without France being a party we shall be betraying France; if we refuse to deal and go to war with Germany we shall be fighting to turn Germany out of Morocco solely in order to please France.

The best solution would be a deal between France and Germany based upon some concession in the French Congo.

The next best would be a tripartite partition of Morocco between France, Spain, and Germany. France would get the lion's share and we should want some compensation from Germany which we should look to ourselves to obtain.

But if France won't have that, there may be nothing for it but a return to the *status quo* of Algeciras: a cumbrous troublesome and temporary expedient.(³)

Yours sincerely,

E. GREY.

(¹) [Grey MSS., Vol. 13.]
(²) [*v.* Secret Anglo-German Convention of August 30, 1898, printed in *Gooch & Temperley*. Vol. I, p. 73, No. 91, *encl.*]
(³) [*v. infra*, pp. 383–4, No. 407, *note* (³).]

No. 406.

Sir F. Bertie to Sir Edward Grey.

Paris, *July* 21, 1911.
F.O. 28696/25883/11/28.   D. 3·35 P.M.
Tel.   (No. 107.)   R.   R. 6 P.M.

French Minister for Foreign Affairs has given me this morning following account of interview between French Ambassador at Berlin and German Minister for Foreign Affairs yesterday.

German Minister for Foreign Affairs said that it seemed to be impossible to have conversations (" causer ") with French Government, as they were communicated to French press.(¹)

He complained specially of an article in " Écho de Paris " of yesterday's date. It is stated that it is not a question of negotiations but of bargaining (" marchandage "), and it gives account of a conversation between French Minister for Foreign Affairs and the German Ambassador, in which former was stated to have not treated as serious the German proposals in regard to French Congo.

German Minister for Foreign Affairs appears to be much ruffled at word " marchandage," and any proposals made by him being regarded in that light. He was, he said, not in the habit of making proposals that were not serious. He would be ready to renew conversations on condition that nothing should be communicated to press that had not jointly between himself and French Ambassador been approved.

French Minister for Foreign Affairs has replied that he has not communicated nor has he authorised the communication to French press of any of the conversations referred to, and that he is quite ready, as far as he is concerned, to give undertaking for which German Minister for Foreign Affairs asks as a preliminary to further conversations.

Minister for Foreign Affairs says that there seems leakage at Berlin quite as much as at Paris, and he can not be responsible for surmises and deductions made by newspapers on scraps of information which they somehow find means of obtaining. I am sending you article in " Echo de Paris."

(¹) [*v. Mermeix*, p. 109; quotations from the *Matin* of the 19th are given there on pp. 114–5, and from the *Echo de Paris* of the 20th on pp. 116–7.]

No. 407.

Sir F. Bertie to Sir Edward Grey.

Private and Confidential.(¹)
My dear Grey,   Paris, *July* 21, 1911.

I received late last night your telegram No. 183 of yesterday(²) and this morning by messenger your two private letters of yesterday.(³)

I went this morning to see Selves to ask what had passed yesterday between Jules Cambon and M. de Kiderlen Wächter. He gave me the account which I telegraphed to you in my No. 107 of today of which for convenience of reference I inclose a copy.(⁴) He then went on to wonder what the real objects and intentions of the Germans might be. I thought it advisable not to frighten him by imparting to him what you say in your telegram and the first of your two private letters.

(¹) [Grey MSS., Vol. 13.]
(²) [*v. supra*, pp. 379–80, No. 402.]
(³) [For the second of these, *v. supra*, p. 382, No. 405. The first letter asked Sir F. Bertie to come to London to discuss the situation and said that Sir Edward Grey was sending the second letter, " which may be of some use to you in helping the French to clear their minds."]
(⁴) [*v.* immediately preceding document.]

I think that it will be better for our relations with France that whatever concessions may be necessary to prevent an open quarrel between France and Germany should be either in compliance with demands by Germany or offers from France. I therefore took advantage of the discretion which you left to me by your second private letter.

I said that I was going to London to see you and it would be useful to me to know the back of the mind of the French Government so as to be able to judge whether there would be any probability of giving effect to the chief desire of the French Government viz. to get the Germans out of Morocco. If there were a Conference the Germans would contend and with some reason that the Morocco of today is not the Morocco of the Algeciras Act. The French Government would maintain and also with reason that they had gone to Fez at the request of the Sultan whose authority they desire to uphold, but would the French Government be ready to return to the *status quo* of the Algeciras Act? To this Selves replied "yes after we have by reorganizing the Sultan's Army placed him in a position to maintain himself. It devolved on us to prevent anarchy and restore order." I said that the Germans would probably not be satisfied with an undertaking on the part of the French Government to withdraw at a date not specified and it might in the opinion of the majority of the Powers not be possible to revert to the old "status quo." I quite appreciated the impossibility from the French point of view of handing over to Germany the portion of the French Congo demanded by M. de Kiderlen Wächter. Would it be possible to satisfy the Germans by some other means? There was an atlas on a desk in the room and we went to it. I then described to him how we had had ambitions for an all British Railway from the Cape to Cairo, for which purpose we had acquired from the Congo Free State in 1894 the lease of a narrow band of territory connecting Lakes Tanganika and Albert Edward. The German Government who evidently had ambitions in the Congo State had intervened and under German pressure we had to surrender our lease. Judging from the attitude of Germany on that occasion I had always been of opinion that she would never quietly acquiesce in the exercise by France of the right of preemption over the territories of the Congo State which she had acquired by Convention with that State and later on with Belgium. The occasion for preemption might never arise but if it did France would probably have to come to an arrangement with Germany whose ambition no doubt is to extend her possessions from the East Coast of Africa right into and if possible across the Congo to the Atlantic. Would it be possible for France by foregoing a part of her rights of preemption [to] go some way towards reducing the demands of Germany in the French Congo and persuade her to waive her pretensions in Morocco? I added that England possesses territories of which the interests would be affected by the exercise of the preemptive rights of France over the Congo. I also said that those rights have never been officially recognized by either Germany or England. Of course the proceedings of Germany at Agadir were indefensible. It might be better described as "chantage" than as "merchandage," but it was not likely that she would renounce her political claims in Morocco unless she were paid for such renunciation. The question was what price would France be prepared to pay.

I thought that all this had better be said as coming from me than from you. I think that if we talked *now* of a partition of Morocco between France, Spain and Germany as a settlement which would be acceptable to us we should alarm the French Government. They might feel that they were about to be deserted by us for the benefit of Germany.

M. de Selves said that he would reflect on what I had said and that he would when next we met show me the instructions which he had sent to the French Ambassador at Berlin regarding possible concessions to Germany in the Northern portion of the French Congo.

Yours sincerely,
FRANCIS BERTIE.

No. 408.

Sir F. Bertie to Sir Edward Grey.

Private and Confidential.(¹)

My dear Grey,   *Paris, July* 21, 1911.

Since I wrote to you this afternoon on the subject of my interview this morning with M. de Selves(²) I have seen the President of the Council. I told him that I was going to London and I asked whether he had any views which he wished to be brought before you in regard to Morocco. He inquired whether I desired that he should speak quite frankly and on my saying certainly, he said that he could not comprehend British policy if it was to be judged from the Memorandum which I had communicated to M. de Selves(³) and which had been passed on to him. The British Government seemed to be now indifferent to the establishment of Germany on the Atlantic coast of Morocco. In this matter they had changed their mind and their attitude. He could not understand why. I told him that the Naval Authorities do not consider that an unfortified Agadir in German possession would be a danger to British interests. To this M. Caillaux replied: Your Admirals are always thinking of the water and how they can deal with an enemy's ships. The Government in England should bear in mind that in the event of a war between France and Germany, supposing England to be on the side of France, if Germany were established at Agadir or anywhere on the coast of Morocco she would have penetrated into the interior and have established relations with the natives and by that means would be in a position to create such fermentation amongst the tribes in Morocco and Algeria as to make it impossible for France to transfer to Europe for use against Germany the Algerian troops. This impossibility would be an injury to British as well as to French interests. As to Agadir remaining an unfortified port, it would be ridiculous to suppose that any engagement given by Germany that it should remain so would be observed. An undertaking had been given by the French Government when Tunis was taken under French protection that Bizerta would not be fortified. It is fortified. Nobody endeavoured to stop it. The same would be the case in regard to Agadir.

As to French interests M. Caillaux said that he could not at any price consent to Germany establishing herself in Morocco. By the Anglo-French Agreements of 1904 France had waived her rights in Egypt and recognized the political claims of England there. England has reciprocated by waiving any political claims in Morocco and recognizing the special position of France there to the exclusion of all other Powers except Spain. How in such circumstances could His Majesty's Government suggest to the French Government that they should admit Germany to a territorial and consequently a political position in Morocco? It would be inconsistent with the Agreement of 1904. If France was to be deserted (*lachée*) by England and left to face Germany alone in the controversy it would be a serious blow to the Entente between France and England, a great shock to French public opinion and the consequences might be very serious. France might have to submit to onerous conditions. It would be quite contrary to his policy and his wishes but he might be forced to make great sacrifices to Germany in order to keep her out of Morocco which would be a matter of supreme importance for France. The consequent feeling of resentment in France at being what would be regarded as deserted by England would be deep and lasting.

Yours sincerely,

FRANCIS BERTIE.

P.S. M. Caillaux came to see me early this morning to ask me to impress on you that it is quite impossible for France to admit Germany to a footing in Morocco. I showed him this letter which he said correctly expressed his views.

July 22, 1911.   F. B.

(¹) [Grey MSS., Vol. 13.]
(²) [*v.* immediately preceding document.]
(³) [*v. supra*, p. 381, No. 403, *encl.* 2.]

[19656]   2 c

No. 409.

Minute by Sir A. Nicolson.

Private.(¹)
Sir Edward Grey.   *Foreign Office, July* 21, 1911.

On reading through again Sir F. Bertie's tel[egram] No. 106,(²) I think that it would be advisable at the present juncture not to reply to it. I do not consider that we should advance matters by sending a reply, and it would be well to have a talk both with Sir F. Bertie and M. Cambon early next week on the situation and not to enter into any discussions with France by telegraph as to the scope and interpretation of the 1904 agreement, which might assume a controversial character.

To my mind the moment may arrive when we shall have to deal with the situation on far broader grounds and from a higher standpoint than are offered by the wording of existing agreements or by the relative values of ports or districts on the western coast of Africa. We do not know what turn negotiations between France and Germany may take, and we should now await the further developments of these negotiations patiently and watchfully.

In the meantime we should not, in my opinion, give France any grounds for believing that our adhesion to the Triple Entente is in any way weakening. Were she to come to distrust us, she would probably try to make terms with Germany irrespective of us, while Germany who would soon detect our hesitation would be inclined to impose far harder terms than may be the case at present. In any case France would never forgive us for having failed her, and the whole Triple Entente would be broken up. This would mean that we should have a triumphant Germany, and an unfriendly France and Russia and our policy since 1904 of preserving the equilibrium and consequently the peace in Europe would be wrecked. Our naval position in the Mediterranean and elsewhere would be quite altered, necessitating increased naval estimates, while the cessation of our intimate relations with Russia would render our position in Central Asia unstable and insecure. We should even be brought to that position which the Emperor William recently outlined, and be going cap in hand to Berlin to ask what we could do to please him.

I indicate the above as showing to my mind the necessity of dealing at the present moment very carefully with France and of looking rather at the wider than at the more limited questions. I consider that since 1906 we have not had so serious and delicate a situation, or one which requires more cautious and careful treatment.

A. N.
E. G.

(¹) [Grey MSS., Vol. 54.]
(²) [*v. supra*, pp. 378–9, No. 401.]

CHAPTER LV.

MR. LLOYD GEORGE'S SPEECH OF JULY 21, AND ITS RESULTS.

[ED. NOTE.—Lord Grey in *Twenty-Five Years*, Vol. I, pp. 224–5, gives the following account of the origin of Mr. Lloyd George's speech :

" On the afternoon of July 21 I was suddenly told that Lloyd George (then Chancellor of the Exchequer) had come over to the Foreign Office and wanted to see me. He came into my room and asked me if the German Government had given any answer to the communication I had made on behalf of the Cabinet on July 4 (*v. supra*, p. 334, No. 356). I said that none had reached me, but, to make sure, I had enquiry made in the Office whether anything had come that day which had not yet reached me. There was nothing. Lloyd George then asked me whether it was not unusual for our communication to be left without any notice, and I replied that it was. He told me that he had to make a speech in the City of London that evening, and thought he ought to say something about it; he then took a paper from his pocket and read out what he had put down as suitable. I thought what he proposed to say was quite justified, and would be salutary, and I cordially agreed. I consider that there was nothing in the words Germany could fairly resent. Lloyd George spoke as he had proposed that evening . . . . .

The speech was entirely Lloyd George's own idea. I did nothing to instigate it, but I welcomed it. The effect was much greater than any words of mine could have been."

The salient part of the speech is quoted below (pp. 391–2, No. 412). For a further discussion of the speech and its effects, *v. Churchill*, pp. 47–50.]

No. 410.

Sir E. Goschen to Sir Edward Grey.

F.O. 28924/25883/11/28.
(No. 203.)   Berlin, D. *July* 21, 1911.
Sir,   R. *July* 24, 1911.

I have the honour to report that my French colleague and Herr von Kiderlen-Waechter met yesterday for the first time since Saturday last the 15th instant. From M. Cambon's account the conversation consisted almost entirely of complaints on the part of Herr von Kiderlen of the way everything that passed between them was given by the French Minister of Foreign Affairs to the French Press. I did not gather from M. Cambon that the conversation was very pleasant or that any progress was made in the " compensation " negotiations.

I saw Herr von Kiderlen to-day for a few moments. He did not say anything to me about either the French or English Press, but he said that the negotiations were rendered very difficult by the rapacity of the Imperial Colonial Office, which made somewhat large demands and were very disinclined to give anything in return. I asked His Excellency whether that meant that they were averse to the principle of Germany disinteresting herself from Morocco. He said that what he meant was that if France handed over to Germany a large slice of her colonial possessions in return for what already practically existed namely the preponderance of French influence in Morocco, something, he thought, must be done, for the sake of reconciling French colonial public opinion, in the way of giving up some small slice of German colonial territory to France. This idea, he said, the Imperial Colonial Office seemed utterly unable to grasp. His Excellency then talked about public opinion in Germany, and said that whereas before Agadir he had received nothing but eulogies from the press, he was now, though still having the confidence of the best newspapers, subjected to a perfect fire of criticism from the Pan Germans, who threatened him with the direst consequences if he gave up the smallest fraction of what Germany considered to be her rights in Morocco.

He said that he received a pile of anonymous letters every day to that effect. He added however that he did not care in the least for such rhodomontades as long as he could get what he wanted, namely a fair settlement with France, which would settle their differences over the Morocco question once for all.

What he wanted to avoid was little bits of territory here and little bits of territory there; that meant a multiplicity of frontiers and frontiers meant friction.

The following are some of the German Press comments on the present state of the Morocco question :—

The " Frankfurter Zeitung " in a long leading article in its Tuesday evening edition, says : " No one who pretends to know anything about politics can declare that Germany would regard with indifference the annexation of Morocco by the French. On the contrary it is greatly to her interest that Morocco should not become French. Should this, however, be proposed, Germany's compensation must be proportionate. She cannot be put off with a slice of the Congo or the swampy Lake Chad. More than this would however probably cause the French Government serious obstacles with the people. The ' Temps,' the principal organ of Colonial policy, has already declared that there never could be any question of the diminution of French colonial possessions. This points to very unfavourable prospects for the result of the ' compensation ' negotiations. We can only imagine one possibility whereby Germany could leave Morocco to the French with small or even no colonial compensation, and that would be if France would renounce her secret enmity against Germany, if she would accept the hand of friendship which has been offered to her for so long, and enter into genuine co-operation with Germany. French capital and German power for work would work wonders of progress, welfare and peace, not only for the good of the two nations, but for the whole of mankind, and before this glorious future the whole of the Morocco conflict would vanish like shadows before the sun."

The " National-Zeitung " of the 19th instant says that people here are astonished by the discussion of " compensations " in the French Press. It maintains that compensations can either be given or required only if the other party is willing to renounce previous rights and that there can be no question of Germany abandoning the rights which belong to her by treaty in Morocco.

The " Kölnische Zeitung " rebukes the " Temps " for publishing what purports to be the chief points of the conversations between M. Cambon and Herr von Kiderlen. It states that it has already drawn attention to the fact that nothing whatever is known concerning the nature of the negotiations between the two Powers and that it is therefore superfluous for the " Temps " to try to show that these negotiations are following a definite direction corresponding with the wishes of France.

Professor Schiemann in his weekly article on foreign politics in the " Kreuz-his endeavour is to have a definite understanding on the question of the African Zeitung " draws attention to the fact that Herr von Kiderlen has openly shown that interests of France and Germany. The Professor declares that such an understanding cannot be arrived at without sacrifice on both sides. He goes on to say that in patriotic circles it is desired that Germany should establish herself in Southern Morocco, but, in his opinion, this desire will never be fulfilled if the idea is adhered to that the aim of the present negotiations must be the adjustment of German and French interests in Africa. " If we relinquish the pursuit of an alluring prospect in Southern Morocco," Professor Schiemann says, " and thus of a position which would without doubt imperil the North African Empire of France, some considerable African compensation must be found in another place, so that both Powers may be satisfied and the African question once and for all removed from the Franco-German account-books. How this is to be accomplished, it is no task of ours to discuss, nor in our opinion is it the task of the newspapers at all."

The " Tageszeitung " thinks that the question of compensation should not be put aside until it is known what is going to become of Morocco.

The " Münchener Neueste Nachrichten," in quoting the English writer, Mr. Cunninghame Graham, as having said that Germany had rendered a service at Agadir both to the Moors and to the world in general, says that Germany has shouted "Catch the thief!" with such energy that Europe has been compelled to listen. England has now an opportunity of giving up her earlier egoistical foolishness towards Germany and to give her friendship by a similar "rapprochement" as that made by her with France.

The "Berliner Tageblatt" devotes a leading article, entitled "The Nessus Shirt," to blaming the French press for its attitude, and to pointing out the advantages of compensation inside, and not outside, Morocco. It says that the silence observed by M. Cambon and Herr von Kiderlen leads to the most divergent rumours as to the progress of the Moroccan negotiations. Thus the Pan-German Press speaks of "Germany's splendid retreat," while a part of the French press complains as to Germany's extravagant claims, which, should they cause the failure of the present negotiations, will, according to the "Temps" of the 19th instant, necessitate the Morocco question being laid before the other Signatory Powers of the Algeciras Act.

The "Berliner Tageblatt" then proceeds to contest the statement made by certain French newspapers to the effect that Germany's interference was unjustified and that she had no more right than the other Algeciras Powers to claim compensation. It says that Germany is, on the contrary, considerably interested in such an important transfer of territory as is constituted by the incorporation of Morocco into the French Colonial Empire. History shows that the acquisition of territory by one Power has always led to claims for compensation by other interested Powers, and France recognized this standpoint in her treaty of April 8, 1904, with England. The policy of compensation is supported, the article says, by those in Germany who desire good relations with France, chiefly because it removes once and for all this bone of contention. To this, somewhat remarkable, view the "Berliner Tageblatt" remarks that the policy in itself is sound enough, but it should have been adopted before the Algeciras Conference.

The article proceeds to speculate and comment on the various territories which might be offered in compensation. It protests against a rectification of the Cameroon frontier on the score of the utter uselessness of the district, "which, according to an expert opinion, may be of some value after the third glacial period." It mentions, without comment, the "Matin's" statement that Germany is demanding the whole of the French Congo Coast, and then says that the "virgin soil of Agadir with a little bit of Hinterland, as yet not soaked with European blood" would be the cheapest and best form of compensation, because, though it might infringe the interests of other Powers, it would at least not offend them from any sentimental considerations.

The writer overrules Herr Harden's suggestion that France should pay nothing, but should merely guarantee friendship to Germany. He points out that the value of such a guarantee cannot be ensured by a written undertaking, and that a proud and independent people like the French cannot be forced into a friendship. In the opinion of the "Berliner Tageblatt" the advent of better relations between the two countries can best be ensured by some such issue to the present negotiations as will leave no feeling of bitterness in France, nor of disappointment in Germany.

In conclusion the article says that Herr von Kiderlen's already difficult task is rendered far harder by the ever impending threat, at each step he takes, that the other signatories of the Algeciras Act will be called in. It would perhaps have been better, the writer says, if Germany had consulted the more important Algeciras Powers before taking action. In any case the greatest obstacle remains "this wretched Algeciras Act" which German diplomacy threw over its own body, as Hercules did the Nessus shirt. The negotiations may result in nothing, and in that case, the writer says that the French newspapers will have contributed to this result on the one side, and on the other the Pan Germans can console themselves with the thought that, by their enthusiasm about the Algeciras Conference, they helped Germany on with the Nessus shirt.

I have, &c.
W. E. GOSCHEN.

No. 411.

Sir Edward Grey to Sir E. Goschen.

F.O. 29130/13911/11/28.
(No. 164.)
Sir,   *Foreign Office, July* 21, 1911.

I told Count Metternich to-day([1]) that, though I had no formal communication to make to him, I wished it to be understood that our silence must not be interpreted as meaning that we were not taking any interest in the Morocco question which had been indicated by our original statements.

We knew that a rectification of the frontier of the French Congo had been proposed as a basis for negotiations with France. We thought it quite possible that a settlement might be come to between Germany and France on this basis which would not affect British interests. We should be very glad if that happened, and in the hope that it would happen we had hitherto stood aside. But I had been made anxious by the news which appeared yesterday as to the demands which the German Government had made upon France : demands which were in effect, not a rectification of the frontier, but a cession of the French Congo, and which it was obviously impossible for France to concede. I understood that negotiations were still proceeding, and I still hoped that they might lead to a satisfactory result. But, if not, it must be understood that a very embarrassing situation would arise.

I pointed out to Count Metternich that the Germans were at Agadir, a closed port, that according to native rumours they were landing and negotiating with the tribes, and might be acquiring concessions there, for all that we knew. It might even be that the German flag had been hoisted at Agadir, a port which for all those on that coast was the most suitable for a naval base. We could not say to what extent the situation might be altered to our disadvantage, and if negotiations with France came to nothing we should be obliged to do something to watch over British interests, and become a party to a discussion of the situation. The longer the Germans remained at Agadir, the more risk there was of their developing a state of affairs which would make it more difficult for them to withdraw, and more necessary for us to take some step to protect British interests.

I wished to say all this now, while we were still waiting in the hope that the negotiations with France would succeed, for if I did not say this now, and the time came when we had to assert ourselves, it would cause more resentment if Germany had been led to suppose by our previous silence that we did not take an interest in the matter.

Count Metternich was not in a position to give me any information. He deprecated my assuming that what I had sketched as the possible damage to British interests was accomplished. He was sure that Germany had no intention of acquiring commercial monopolies, and unfairly prejudicing our interests.

To this I replied that the fact that Germany remained in occupation of a closed port involved at least a monopoly of commercial opportunities.

Count Metternich then said, on the situation generally, that we had made our bargain with France about Morocco, but Germany was not under the same obligations. Her Agreement with France in 1909 had been based on the independence and integrity of Morocco, which had since been destroyed by French action. Germany had the right to take steps to protect her own interests, and as the situation in Morocco had been upset, she must take steps.

I observed that this was not really relevant to the point which I had raised, which was the way in which British interests might be affected by the change in the situation. What Count Metternich was saying was relevant to a discussion of how the situation had come to be changed, and what the conditions of the Act of

([1]) [For Count Metternich's report, *v. G.P.* XXIX, pp. 199–203.]

Algeciras required, but that was not the point. The point was the impossibility of our standing aside, and disinteresting ourselves, if the changes in the situation developed adversely to our interests, and Germany did not come to any arrangement with France.

Count Metternich urged that what Germany had done in Morocco was infinitely less than the military operations which France had carried out.

I said that, at any rate, whatever France had done had been known to the world. She had not occupied a closed port from which she could operate without anyone else knowing what was happening. Everyone had known everything that France was doing. I still hoped that the negotiations between France and Germany would result in a settlement. I thought this might be done without affecting British interests, though, if economic arrangements in Morocco were a part of the settlement, we should have to know what they were before we could express a final opinion upon them.

I again impressed upon Count Metternich that my object in speaking to him this afternoon was to make it clear that we must join in a discussion of the situation if it continued without any settlement with France being reached; and that the fact that the Germans remained at Agadir, where no one could know besides themselves what they were doing, must result in a very embarrassing situation.

[I am, &c.]
E. G[REY].

No. 412.

Extract from Speech of Mr. Lloyd George on July 21, 1911, at the Mansion House.

[Quoted from the *Times* of July 22.]

The Lord Mayor gave a banquet at the Mansion House last night to the Chancellor of the Exchequer, the Governor and Directors of the Bank of England, and bankers and merchants of the City of London. The references by the Chancellor of the Exchequer to the position of international affairs and to the necessity of maintaining the prestige of Great Britain among the Great Powers at all hazards were loudly cheered. . . .

[Extract from the speech of the Chancellor of the Exchequer.]

PEACE AND BRITISH PRESTIGE.

But I am also bound to say this—that I believe it is essential in the highest interests, not merely of this country, but of the world, that Britain should at all hazards maintain her place and her prestige amongst the Great Powers of the world. (Cheers.) Her potent influence has many a time been in the past, and may yet be in the future, invaluable to the cause of human liberty. It has more than once in the past redeemed Continental nations, who are sometimes too apt to forget that service, from overwhelming disaster and even from national extinction. I would make great sacrifices to preserve peace. I conceive that nothing would justify a disturbance of international good will except questions of the gravest national moment. But if a situation were to be forced upon us in which peace could only be preserved by the surrender of the great and beneficent position Britain has won by centuries of heroism and achievement, by allowing Britain to be treated where her interests were vitally affected as if she were of no account in the Cabinet of nations, then I say emphatically that peace at that price would be a humiliation intolerable for a great country like ours to endure. (Cheers.) National honour is no party question. (Cheers.) The security of our great international trade is no party question; the peace of the world is much more likely to be secured if all nations realize fairly what the conditions of peace must be. And it is because I have the conviction that nations are beginning to understand each other better, to appreciate each other's points of view more thoroughly, to be more ready to discuss calmly and dispassionately their differences, that I feel assured that nothing will happen between now and next year which will render it difficult for the Chancellor of the Exchequer in this place to respond to the toast proposed by you, my Lord Mayor, of the continued prosperity of the public purse. (Cheers.)[1]

(1) [According to the Editors of *G.P.*, XXIX, p. 203, *note*, the verbal text of this speech was not known in Berlin on the 22nd and was requested by telegraph. When, on the 23rd, Herr von Kiderlen-Waechter instructed Count Metternich to reply to Sir Edward Grey, he had not yet had the full text before him, *ib.*, pp. 203–5. For his comments on the 24th *v. ib.*, pp. 210–1.]

No. 413.

Sir F. Bertie to Sir Edward Grey.

F.O. 28903/16083/11/28.
(No. 340.)   *Paris, D. July 22, 1911.*
Sir,   *R. July 24, 1911.*
     With reference to my despatch No. 337 of yesterday's date(1) I have the honour to acquaint you that the Berlin correspondent of the "Echo de Paris" telegraphs to that journal that the negotiations between M. de Kiderlen-Wächter and M. Jules Cambon are being hindered by the Press campaign in England and by the indications on those negotiations which have been given by certain French newspapers.
     "This," the correspondent adds, "is at the present moment the most important point, and I have no hesitation in declaring that, if those indications were to continue the negotiations might suddenly be interrupted."
     Meanwhile the following notice has been issued to the press by the Ministry for Foreign Affairs :—

     "Certains journaux parisiens publient depuis quelques jours des informations ou des comptes rendus de conversations diplomatiques au sujet des négociations franco-allemandes.
     "Nous sommes autorisés à déclarer que toutes ces informations ou comptes rendus ne reposent sur aucune communication et n'engagent que leurs auteurs."
                             I have, &c.
                           FRANCIS BERTIE.

(1) [Not reproduced. It forwarded a copy of an article in the *Echo de Paris* on the Franco-German negotiations. *cp. supra*, p. 383, No. 406, and *note* (1).]

No. 414.

Minute by Sir A. Nicolson.(1)

Sir Edward Grey,   *Foreign Office, July 22, 1911.*
     M. Daeschner read to me some telegrams relative to the discussions between France and Germany. We have had the main points from Sir F. Bertie. One or two further details may be mentioned. M. de Kiderlen said that if France did not come to terms Germany would take her stand and was ready to go "jusqu'au bout." M. Cambon replied that France would be ready to accept the "coup" and was prepared to go as far if not further than Germany. M. de Kiderlen mentioned that what had been proposed by Germany was seriously meant and represented "*le fond*

(1) [Grey MSS., Vol. 54.]

des idées Impériales"—that he had spent three hours trying to bring his "Colonials" to reason and that what he would propose would be considered fair by sensible men. The conversation had no further results.

M. de Selves has instructed M. Jules Cambon to be prepared to offer rectification of Congo–Kameroon frontier between 3° and 11° N. Lat. Such rectification does not face on the sea board.

A. N.
E. G.

No. 415.

Sir F. Bertie to Sir Edward Grey.

Private.([1])
My dear Grey,   *Paris, July 22, 1911.*

I have seen Selves this afternoon. He has explained to me three alternative rectifications of frontier between the Cameroons and the French Congo which he has authorized the French Ambassador at Berlin to negotiate with M. de Kiderlen Wächter. He says that nothing will induce the French Government to consent to the Germans taking a territorial footing in Morocco. No Ministry would survive such a settlement of the difference with Germany. He has given me a memorandum and map showing what the rectifications are. I take them with me to-morrow.

Yours sincerely,
FRANCIS BERTIE.

([1]) [Grey MSS., Vol. 13.]

No. 416.

Mr. White to Sir Edward Grey.

F.O. 29981/25641/11/28.
(No. 232.)   *Tangier, D. July 23, 1911.*
Sir,   R. *July 31, 1911.*

With reference to my despatch No. 224 of the 18th instant,([1]) I have the honour to report that on the 17th instant the French Chargé d'Affaires came to see me and stated he had received serious news from Agadir. Kaïd Guelouli had informed the French Consul at Mogador that the Germans were seeking to provoke an incident, that whereas at first not more than 15 men landed at a time from the "Berlin"([2]) and only visited the town of Agadir, they now landed in parties of 40 men "en armes" and made short marches ("exécutent des marches") into the country, causing excitement in the district. It subsequently however appeared from a letter received by Cid Guebbas from Kaïd Guelouli that the expeditions referred to were for purposes of sport. Baron von Seckendorff mentioned the subject to me the other day and said the German officers had been well treated at Agadir, and are shooting in the neighbourhood of the town. I observed that at a place like Agadir, where the people are not accustomed to Christians, there was always a chance of a fanatical attack on some of the officers when out shooting, and that it would be better to run no risks. Baron von Seckendorff replied that he was not in communication with the commander of the "Berlin," who communicated direct with his Government, and he could not therefore interfere in the matter. If, as Kaïd Guelouli states, the Germans land in parties of about 40 and all are armed, the officers must be accompanied by guards of their own men, as there are only about a dozen officers on board and not many of them would be allowed on shore at the same time.

([1]) [Not reproduced. It referred to increased German activities at Mogador and Agadir.]
([2]) [*cp. supra,* p. 322, *Ed. note.*]

A few days later M. de Billy showed me a radiogram he had received from his Consul at Mogador, reporting that Kaïd Kourimi's delegate had returned from Agadir on the 18th instant : he had been well received by the captain of the " Berlin " who had told him that " L'Allemagne a des droits sur la partie du Maroc comprise entre Saffi et Agadir." I subsequently received a radiogram from His Majesty's Vice-Consul at Mogador that he had been told by his French colleague that the captain of the " Berlin " had said that " he was in charge of the coast-line of Morocco from Saffi to Agadir." It seems to me probable that this is the more correct version of what the captain said, but M. de Billy feels confident that the original version is the correct one as the radiogram from his Consul at Mogador is quite clear on the point, and it was only from him that Mr. Vice-Consul Johnstone received his information.

The German Vice-Consul at Mogador has for some time been active in extending protection to the principal men in the south. M. de Billy told me that Hadj Thami Glawi had shown the French Vice-Consul at Marrakesh a letter he had received from the German Vice-Consul at Mogador asking him to go to Agadir and have an inter-view with the captain of the " Berlin," from which nothing but good could come to him. Hadj Thami, however, did not go.

The Kaïd of Kourima, a powerful Governor, who has always been at enmity with Kaïd M'tougi, applied a few weeks since to Mr. Vice-Consul Johnstone for British protection, which of course, could not be granted to him. Shortly after he entered into communication with the German Vice-Consul, and then sent an emissary to Agadir, as stated above. On the return of this emissary, the German Vice-Consul at Mogador, according to the report of the French Consul at that place, sent to Kaïd M'tougi insisting that he should revoke his order depriving Kaïd Kourimi of his territories, and recommended the latter to resist by force any attempt to dispossess him. In order to avoid any disturbances, the French Consul advised the Governors who were to receive portions of Kaïd Kourimi's territories to make no attempt to take possession of them, and to take no steps until the receipt of further orders from the Sultan.

I have, &c.
HERBERT E. WHITE.

No. 417.

Sir Edward Grey to Sir E. Goschen.

F.O. 29384/25641/11/28.
(No. 167.)
Sir, *Foreign Office, July* 24, 1911.

Count Metternich asked to see me to-day, and when he came informed me that he had fully reported to his Government what I had said to him on Friday, the 21st.([1]) He was now instructed to make a communication to me. It was as follows :([2])

From the beginning, the German Government had sent a ship to Agadir in order to protect German interests, and for no other reason. The special cause was the attack of natives on a German farm.

At this point I observed that I had not, I thought, heard of this attack before. I had understood that the despatch of the ship had been due to apprehension as to what might happen, not to what had actually happened.

Count Metternich remarked that he had not been told of it before.

---

(1) [*v. supra,* pp. 390–1, No. 411.]
(2) [This despatch is quoted in *Twenty-Five Years,* I, pp. 226–8, and the communication is also given in *G.P.* XXIX, pp. 203–5; the interview is described by Count Metternich, *ib.,* pp. 211–2.]

He then proceeded to say that so far nothing had happened to give reason for thinking that the German intentions were changed. Not a man had been landed; and he could inform me, though this was very confidential, that the German Commander had strict orders to land men only in case of extreme necessity, when the lives of Germans were menaced.

I observed that I thought there were no Germans in this region, and that I supposed, therefore, the term German must mean German protected persons.

Count Metternich said that he had no information on this point.

He went on to say that his Government regretted the credence which was given to insinuations as to the intentions of Germany that came from hostile quarters. Germany never had thought of creating a naval port on the Moroccan coast, and never would think of it. Such ideas were hallucinations. She had no intentions on Moroccan territory, but demanded that France should keep strictly to the Act of Algeciras, or else come to explanations with Germany. The German Government thought that the latter course would be more in the interests of France, and they had proposed quite generally that Germany should be given compensation in Colonial matters, in order that she might give up her right to object to French action in Morocco. Negotiations had been begun with France, and both parties had promised to keep the strictest secrecy. On the German side this had seriously been done: not even the allies of Germany were informed of what had passed. France, on the contrary, to Germany's regret, had given partial information to the Press, and also to her friends; the information being incorrect and incomplete, and calculated to mislead as to the intentions of Germany.

Herr von Kiderlen had declared to M. Jules Cambon that he could not go on with negotiations and make positive and detailed proposals, (a thing which he had not done hitherto), until secrecy was guaranteed. In order to avoid misrepresentation, he had proposed that information should be given, when mutually agreed upon, to mutual friends, and to the Press. M. Jules Cambon's answer to this was expected yesterday.

If the German demands were rather high, Germany was ready to make concessions in Morocco as well as in Colonial matters. But the chauvinistic tone of the French and part of the British Press, menacing Germany with the interference of the friends of France, did not tend towards a settlement. Should the present negotiations be wrecked, even then Germany would have no designs upon Moroccan territory; but she would have to demand from France, with determination and emphasis, that the Algeciras Act should be fully carried out, in spirit as well as in letter. Germany could not, as one of the Great Powers, let the French presume to encroach upon her rights contrary to written Treaties. Germany still hoped that things would not come to that point, and that a friendly exchange of opinions à deux would avoid this. If, however, France should not wish to come to an understanding on the basis proposed, Germany would have to demand a return to the status quo ante in Morocco, and in doing so would count on the support of the other Powers who were parties to the Algeciras Act, and especially of England.

Count Metternich told me confidentially that his Government had made no demand as to the right of pre-emption in the Belgian Congo.

I said that I would communicate this statement to the Prime Minister. But, as I was likely to be asked in Parliament what was happening at Agadir, I should like to know whether I might say that the German Government had informed me that not a man had been landed.

Count Metternich requested that I should make no public statement with regard to this conversation until he had had time to communicate with his Government.

I further observed that the question of what was the status quo ante was a matter of interpretation, in which I assumed that all the Powers who signed the Algeciras Act would have a say, and if so what Germany had said seemed to me to point to a conference in the last resort.

Count Metternich said that no doubt there were sometimes in Treaties dark points which it was difficult to interpret, but there were other points which were clear. In this case it was very clear that France ought to withdraw from any occupation of Morocco extending beyond what was contemplated by the Algeciras Act: and the question was not one to be submitted to a vote, nor was it open to serious discussion. Germany, he repeated, hoped for our support.

I observed again that the question as to the *status quo ante* was a matter for interpretation, and it would have to be discussed if the time came to raise it.(³)

[I am, &c.]
E. G[REY].

(³) [Count Benckendorff reported to M. Sazonov in a letter of August 1, 1911, an interview with Sir Edward Grey of July 25 at which he was informed of this conversation with Count Metternich. *v. Siebert*, pp. 594–5.]

No. 418.

Sir A. Nicolson to Sir F. Cartwright.

Private.(¹)

My dear Cartwright,   *Foreign Office, July* 24, 1911.

. . . .(²) The situation which German action in Morocco has produced is, to my mind, a very serious one. I may tell you confidentially that the French will not under any circumstances whatsoever consent to Germany obtaining a foothold in Morocco. They are of opinion that if Germany were to establish herself in Morocco she would be in a position, in case of war or strained relations between herself and France, to stir up most serious trouble on the Algerian frontier and in Algeria itself, thereby compelling France to retain a large force of what she says are her best troops in Algeria, and consequently to weaken herself very considerably in Europe. France is, I think, prepared to make certain reasonable and moderate concessions to Germany in equitorial [*sic* : equatorial] Africa, though not of that scope which Germany demanded in the first place. To my mind the difficulty will be to enable Germany to retire from the position which she has taken up without losing too much prestige. Germany evidently quite miscalculated this country after the visit of the German Emperor in May. He was convinced that he had got this country entirely on his side, and I believe that he was also under the impression that the current in favour of Germany was running far more strongly than that in favour of France. He considered therefore that he was in a position to deal as he liked with the latter country without any risk of raising a protest or difficulty on the part of England. I presume that he has now been quite undeceived and is able to see clearly that we have no intention whatever of abandoning France. The German Government will therefore, except they wish to push matters to an extremity—which I can hardly think is their desire—have to moderate very considerably the demands they have made, and will have to content themselves with the reasonable concessions which France is prepared to offer in return for German evacuation of Agadir and a complete recognition by Germany of France's special position in Morocco. This will be by no means an easy task to fulfil, but it will have to be done if we wish to prevent affairs being pushed to extremes. The speech of Lloyd George which, I may tell you, was no sudden inspiration but a carefully thought out one, has produced a considerable impression in Berlin and also in Paris—impressions which I may say are of an entirely different character. Coming from him it will probably carry more weight than from any other member of the Cabinet, and it was certainly delivered at a most opportune moment.

(¹) [Carnock MSS., Vol. III of 1911.]

(²) [The first two paragraphs of this letter relate to the situation in Albania. A similar private letter to Sir E. Goschen, of the same date, is quoted in *Nicolson*, p. 350.]

The discussions between Cambon and Kiderlen at Berlin are not making much progress. I have hopes that this week they will come to close quarters and I daresay that the French will feel themselves able to communicate at least a portion of the concessions which they are disposed to grant, and then we shall be able to see what reception is accorded to them by Kiderlen. The latter pretends that he himself has the most moderate views and would be quite ready to come to a settlement on the most reasonable terms but that he is much pushed by the Colonial Minister who wishes to lay down the most exacting demands, and he slipped out on one occasion that the demands which had been made represented the substance of the Imperial ideas. I don't believe for one moment that Kiderlen is exercising the moderating influence which he desires us to believe, and I am pretty sure that he thought he saw an opportunity for playing a big card and improving his reputation. Now that he has got into a dilemma he is anxious to lay the blame on the shoulders of others. It is curious but I believe that this is the third occasion after an Imperial visit to London that something disagreeable has arisen. I imagine that the warmth of the reception which is always undoubtedly accorded to the Emperor in England completely misleads him as to its real purport and meaning, and he goes away with the firm conviction that he had got us comfortably in his pocket. . . . .([3])

[A. NICOLSON.]

([3]) [The rest of this letter refers to Persian affairs and matters of topical interest.]

No. 419.

Sir Edward Grey to Sir E. Goschen.([1])

F.O. 29439/25641/11/28.
(No. 168.)
Sir, *Foreign Office, July 25, 1911.*
    The German Ambassador came to see me to-day, and, in reply to my question of Monday as to whether I might make use in Parliament of the information which the German Government had given that no men had been landed at Agadir,([2]) he gave me the answer of the German Government.

    The information was confidential, and they must request me to treat it as such. They could not consent to its being used in Parliament after the speech of the Chancellor of the Exchequer.([3]) That speech had been interpreted without contradiction as having a tone of provocation for Germany, and the German Government could not let the belief arise that, in consequence of the speech, they had made a declaration of intentions about Morocco.

    I observed that I must say at once that the fact that the Chancellor of the Exchequer's speech, which seemed to me to give no cause for complaint, had created surprise was in itself a justification of the speech : as it could not have created surprise unless there had been some tendency to think that we might be disregarded.

    The German Ambassador said that he had a further communication to make about the speech, but meanwhile he went on to say that, if an understanding with France fell through owing to French resistance, Germany must demand that the Treaty of Algeciras be kept, and the *status quo ante* be restored, whether that were agreeable to France or not.

    ([1]) [This despatch is quoted in *Twenty-Five Years*, Vol. I, pp. 228–31. Tel. No. 153, despatched at 1·10 P.M. on July 26 (F.O. 29439/25641/11/28) conveyed the same information in shorter form.]
    ([2]) [*v. supra*, pp. 394–6, No. 417.]
    ([3]) [For Herr von Kiderlen-Waechter's instruction of July 25, *v. G.P.* XXIX, p. 212; for Count Metternich's account of the whole interview, *v. ib.*, pp. 213–4; and for the comments of Herr von Kiderlen-Wächter, *v. ib.*, pp. 214–8.]

The German Government did not think that a Conference would be necessary. Germany, as one of the Signatories of the Treaty of Algeciras, was entitled by herself to vindicate the rights of the Treaty. If, in that endeavour, Germany found the support of third parties, it would be very welcome, and would facilitate her action. But if, after the many provocations from the side of France and her free and easy manner in Morocco, as if neither Germany nor a Treaty existed, France should repel the hand which was proffered to her by Germany, German dignity as a Great Power would make it necessary to secure by all means, and if necessary also alone, full respect by France for German Treaty rights.

This communication was read to me by Count Metternich, and he then proceeded to read to me a further communication.

The text of the speech of the Chancellor of the Exchequer had given rise, in part of the British Press and in nearly the whole of the French Press, to attacks on Germany. The German Foreign Secretary could not say how far this was intended by the British Government. The effect of the speech had made a bad impression in Germany as, owing to utterances made by me to Count Metternich, the effect of the speech could not have been unforeseen.

Negotiations were in progress with France, to put an end to the difficulties which had arisen owing to the free and easy way in which she had thought it right to disregard the obligations of Algeciras. Germany had explicitly and repeatedly declared that she would like, without recriminations on the past, to come to a peaceful and amicable understanding directly with France. France had accepted this, and had agreed to carry on negotiations for the time being secretly. Germany had made propositions to France that seemed to the German Government quite loyal and acceptable. Those propositions concerned territories in which English interests were neither directly nor indirectly engaged.

If, notwithstanding that, England thought that she ought to express some wishes, it might have been expected that these wishes would have been transmitted to Germany in the usual diplomatic channel. Instead of this, the British Government had, through one of their members, given public declarations which, to say the least, *could* have been interpreted as a warning to Germany's address, and which, as a matter of fact, had by the British and French Presses been interpreted as a warning bordering on menace.

Germany could not see by what reasons the British Government had been guided. The British Government could not have been in any doubt that, by that proceeding, the friendly understanding between Germany and France could not be furthered. Considering the tone which for some time had been adopted by part of the British Press and by the whole of the French Press, the British Government could hardly doubt what effect the speech of the Chancellor of the Exchequer would have. If the British Government, assuming this as a hypothesis, should have had the intention to embroil the political situation and lead towards a violent explosion, they could not have chosen a better means than the speech of the Chancellor of the Exchequer, which took so very little into account, with regard to Germany, the dignity and place of a Great Power, which the Chancellor of the Exchequer claimed for England in that speech.

I said that I could only repeat what I had already said about the speech of the Chancellor of the Exchequer. The speech had not claimed anything except that we were entitled to be considered as one of the great nations. It had claimed no pre-eminence, and it had not even indicated that there was a crisis. It had dealt in general terms with remote contingencies. The German Government had said that it was not consistent with their dignity, after the speech of the Chancellor of the Exchequer, to give explanations as to what was taking place at Agadir. I felt that the tone of their communication made it not consistent with our dignity to give explanations as to the speech of the Chancellor of the Exchequer.[3]

[3] [cp. Churchill, p. 48.]

This, however, I could genuinely say. It was not intended by anything that had been said or would be said to embroil Germany's negotiations with France. On the contrary, we sincerely desired that they should succeed. The Foreign Office Vote was to be taken in the House of Commons the day after to-morrow, and I would then make this clear. But the tone of the German communication was very unfavourable also as regards France, and made it more than ever evident that a very difficult situation would arise if the German negotiations with France did not succeed.

Further conversation of a less formal and more discursive kind took place, in the course of which I observed that the German objection appeared to be to the Press comments on the speech rather than to the speech itself.

From this Count Metternich did not dissent.

[I am, &c.]
E. G[REY].

No. 420.

Consul-General Sir F. Oppenheimer to Sir E. Crowe.

F.O. 29370/25641/11/28.
Confidential.   *Frankfort-on-the-Main*, D. *July* 25, 1911.
Dear Sir Eyre,   R. *July* 26, 1911.

After my recent return from London I took an early opportunity of meeting a gentleman from whom I have already on former occasions gathered interesting information and naturally the conversation quickly drifted to the subject of Morocco. It appears that the gentleman in question has not been in Berlin during the last ten days or so and perhaps some of the Berlin views he expressed and which are hereafter set out have since been modified; yet it is hardly likely that far-reaching changes have taken place in the German attitude, because no doubt the quarters from which the original information had come would then have found it in their own interest to supplement or modify the information previously supplied.

It would appear that the Port of Agadir was seized with the intention of forcing the French into making a plain, authoritative statement to Germany of their intentions in Morocco. It was seized as a guarantee of their good-will to come to a satisfactory understanding with Germany. Failing that, it was the German Emperor's intention that Germany should convert Agadir into a permanent naval base. The Emperor was, however, turned from his original intention by very strong pressure exercised by Admiral von Tirpitz and by Kiderlen-Wächter himself.

Kiderlen-Wächter made it clear from the first that he did not desire a renewal of the Act of Algeciras, though he has expressed it as his conviction that if Germany insisted she must succeed in enforcing its terms. He also let it be understood that Germany would decidedly prefer not permanently to remain at Agadir.

Kiderlen-Wächter's views were expressed in an article written under his supervision and which appeared in the Kölnische Zeitung; I enclose a printed reference thereto.(¹) You will remember the stir this inspired article created also in Germany because it for the first time revealed the possibility that Germany would be satisfied with compensations outside Morocco. The "All-Deutschen," who seem particularly anxious that Germany should acquire some territories in Morocco, took a strong stand in opposition to the intentions expressed in the said article, but this opposition Kiderlen-Wächter is inclined to disregard.

The German demands were formulated as follows:

1. Mining rights in Morocco must be capable of acquisition also by non-French subjects.
2. The exports of minerals from Morocco to remain absolutely free, *i.e.*, no export duty to be levied on ore from Morocco.

Germany to acquire territorial compensations outside Morocco.

(¹) [Not reproduced.]

The territory which Germany wants is the French Congo. To save the French prestige, Germany has expressed her willingness that the German acquisition should take the form of an exchange (this "concession," though I have so far found it stated in no paper, is authentic), so that Germany should acquire the French Congo and cede some territory elsewhere to France. Concerning the German cession no definite suggestion had then been made, but, of course, it was insisted that the territorial part of the bargain was to be a make-believe exchange only : the territories which Germany would eventually cede must be much less valuable, at least from the German point of view, than the land of the French Congo which Germany strongly desires to receive. The suggestion, reprinted in several papers, that Germany is also asking for the cession by France of her right of pre-emption of the Belgian Congo was absolutely denied by my informant.

In Germany it is generally believed that the negotiations with France can be satisfactorily concluded and that in spite of the opposition of the "All-Deutschen" against any compensation outside Morocco, Kiderlen-Wächter will eventually find a majority in the Reichstag to sanction an agreement on the above lines. It is, moreover believed that with the ratification of such an agreement Morocco as such will cease to exist and will become a French colony. My informant regarded the latter fact as the probable secret of the attitude taken up by Great Britain, and which he described as incomprehensible unless indeed Great Britain realised that it had nothing to gain from a Franco-German agreement on the above lines and that from a strategical point of view it preferred the permanent occupation by Germany of Agadir and Sus—the alternative to the German proposals—for the very reason which induced Tirpitz to dissuade the German Emperor from his original intention.

Yours sincerely,
FRANCIS OPPENHEIMER.

No. 421.

Sir Edward Grey to Mr. Carnegie.

F.O. 29440/25883/11/28.
(No. 305.)
Sir,   *Foreign Office, July* 25, 1911.

M. Cambon came to see me to-day on his return from Paris.

I told him some of the substance of my conversation with Count Metternich on the 21st of this month.([1]) I explained that I had impressed upon Count Metternich that we had remained silent since our first communication to him only in the hope that a settlement would be come to with France; and that, as the German demands seemed likely to destroy this hope, for they were demands which France obviously could not concede, I thought it better to say—though without making a formal communication—that, if the conversations with France did not succeed, we should have to become a party to a discussion of the situation.

I also told M. Cambon that, in reply to what I had said on the 21st, Count Metternich had, on the 24th, made a communication to me from the German Government.([2]) There were two principal points in this communication : (1) Germany would waive her objections to French action in Morocco if she could receive compensation as the result of negotiations which must be carried on *à deux*; and (2) if these negotiations failed, Germany would have to demand from France that the Algeciras Act should be fully carried out in spirit as well as in letter. With regard to this second point, I had observed to Count Metternich that the *status quo* was a matter of interpretation, on which all the Powers which had signed the Act were entitled to have a say, and that what Germany suggested seemed to point to a Conference in the last resort. Count Metternich had expressed the opinion that some things in the interpretation of the Act were too clear to admit of serious discussion.

M. Cambon told me that the remark which I had made to Count Metternich as to a return to the *status quo* implying the need of a Conference appeared to him perfectly right, and was in accordance with the views of M. de Selves. He said, however, with regard to our suggestion that we might initiate the proposal for a Conference, that this was a thing on which we should fall back only in the last resort.

I said that I entirely agreed with this. It would be preferable to secure a settlement by means of the negotiations now proceeding. We had made the suggestion only because we were considering the situation which might arise if diplomacy failed to make a settlement. We were anxious not to occupy ground diplomatically which we were not prepared to defend by measures more than diplomatic, if need be.

M. Cambon said that, if such a point as that was reached, it would be necessary for France and England to discuss it. But he himself was not pessimistic about the diplomatic situation.

M. Cambon also informed me that the French Ambassador in Berlin had had with Herr von Kiderlen a conversation too long to report by telegraph. He expected to receive a report of it to-morrow morning, and, if so, he would come to see me in the afternoon.

[I am, &c.]
E. G[REY].

No. 422.

Mr. Rennie to Sir Edward Grey.

Zarauz, July 26, 1911.
D. 5·30 P.M.
R. 9·45 P.M.

F.O. 29448/13751/11/28.
Tel. (No. 63.) R.

My telegram No. 62 (of July 25).([1])

Spanish Minister for Foreign Affairs and the French Ambassador this morning exchanged verbal declarations in the sense of the draft *modus vivendi*.([1]) I understand (? that this) (? form of) exchange was considered preferable to written arrangement, in view of the provisional nature of the occupation of Alcazar and consequently temporary character of agreement.

(Repeated to Paris.)

([1]) [Not reproduced. It stated that a draft *modus vivendi* for the Alcazar district had been drawn up by the French and Spanish Governments. The details are summarized in the Annual Report for Spain for 1911, quoted *supra*, p. 310, No. 336.]

No. 423.

Sir E. Goschen to Sir Edward Grey.

Berlin, July 26, 1911.
D. 7·58 P.M.
R. 9·45 P.M.

F.O. 29447/25883/11/28.
Tel. (No. 52.)

Morocco.

My French colleague has received instructions to inform the Imperial Government that their demands are too exorbitant, and such as no French Government could entertain. He tells me that he has telegraphed to Paris that, as such a communication would almost certainly cause the conversations to be broken off, he would be glad to know if that was the last word of the French Government. He says that he has done this in order to gain time and in the idea that the recent discussions in London, of which he had heard nothing, might have perhaps modified the decision. He is depressed, and thinks that premature disclosures in Paris press have made it difficult for Germany to reduce demands. Secretary of State for Foreign Affairs told me this afternoon that the indiscretions of the French Government in communicating between the two Governments, and the menacing language of particularly the French military papers, had had the effect of rendering it impossible for the German Government to modify those demands. Speech of the Chancellor of the Exchequer, though doubtless not meant as a menace to Germany, had unfortunately been regarded as such in both Germany and France, and had thus also contributed to the above effect. He complained also that, while the French papers had been duly informed of the German demands, nothing had apparently been told them with regard to territorial compensations offered by Germany to France.

MINUTES.

The German " demand " for the cession of a large French colony is not one of which the refusal could possibly justify Germany even before German public opinion to compel enforcement by resort to war. Even therefore if Germany were bent on war she would have to find some other pretext. In these circumstances there seems no reason why France should yield. No doubt she will now put forward her counter proposals.

E. A. C.
July 27.

The German Gov[ernmen]t cannot allow the world to suppose that they are unable to dictate terms to France.

W. L.
A. N.
E. G.

No. 424.

Sir E. Goschen to Sir Edward Grey.

F.O. 29783/25883/11/28.
(No. 205.)   Confidential.   *Berlin, D. July 26, 1911.*
Sir,   *R. July 29, 1911.*

Having occasion to see Herr von Kiderlen on various matters I called upon His Excellency this afternoon. Having transacted my business with him I was taking my leave when he said that he would like to say a few words to me about Morocco. He said that Count Metternich had also had some conversation with you and had pointed out to you, by instruction, that Germany had no intention whatever of making any effort to get a foot of Moroccan territory, still less of acquiring a military or naval port on the Moroccan Coast. He, Herr von Kiderlen, knew perfectly well that any attempt to acquire or establish such a port would meet with the strongest opposition on all sides. But what he did think was this: by disinteresting herself from Morocco Germany practically handed over the protectorate of Morocco to France. The latter had squared England by giving her a free hand in Egypt, Italy by an arrangement certainly of no great value, concerning Tripoli, Spain by a sphere of influence in Morocco. Neither Russia nor Austria were likely to place any difficulties in the way of France, and the only Powers left who might have something to say were Holland, Belgium and Sweden, whom she could more or less disregard. Therefore if Germany retired from the field France would remain all powerful in Morocco. Surely the acquisition of this enormous advantage was worth some considerable sacrifice on the part of France. Besides other Powers interested in Morocco had been paid for leaving France alone. Why therefore should not Germany also receive compensation?

I said that I had understood that France had not been unwilling to make some sacrifice, but that if what had been stated in the French Press was correct the sacrifice asked from France was too big. The greater part if not the whole of French Congo, and that was what I understood had been asked, was a large price for Germany to ask. Practically speaking a whole French colony was asked for in return for a renunciation of certain ideas and ambitions. Herr von Kiderlen said that one of the things he complained of was that the French Government, though really bound to secrecy at the commencement of the negotiations, had communicated to their Press all the German demands and at the same time had withheld all information as to what Germany had proposed to give in exchange, namely Togoland and a strip of territory in the Cameroons. I asked His Excellency whether he had proposed that France should hand over the whole of the French Congo. He answered in the affirmative adding that it was not all of great value to Germany but that he disliked the idea of having bits of territory and a multiplication of frontiers. I repeated that I thought it was a great deal to ask of France to give up a whole French Colony. He answered that he was prepared to do the same in giving up Togoland, and that I might be certain that if ever the bargain was made he would be reviled (conspué) by nearly the whole German Press. That contingency however he could have faced with comparative equanimity if he could have succeeded in making an arrangement which would remove a continual source of friction between Germany and France.

He went on to say that the extent of the compensation he demanded from France was a matter of opinion. He thought it fair and France thought it extravagant. It had been, and ought to have remained, a subject of friendly discussion; this however had been rendered impossible by the premature and indiscreet disclosures of the French Government; the latter had denied any indiscretion, but as a matter of fact he had seen in the French Press statements which corresponded word for word with what he had said to M. Cambon. In any case these indiscretions had resulted in such threatening language in the French papers and especially those which, like "La France Militaire," represented French military opinion, that now it was absolutely impossible for him to modify his demands. If he did so there would, he said, be an outcry through all Germany that the Imperial Government had yielded owing to menaces from France and England. "For," he said, "there can be no doubt that the language of Mr. Lloyd George, though, I am quite willing to believe, not meant as a threat to Germany, has been regarded as such both here and in France and thus has contributed in no small degree to the inability of the Imperial Government to modify their demands." I said that I regretted very much that Mr. Lloyd George's words should have been regarded as a threat to Germany; personally I could not see how they could bear that interpretation; I knew that the Pan-German papers had adopted that point of view, but I had been glad to see that the more moderate papers had been at pains to show that there was no threat to Germany implied. I had not heard from you on the subject, but, speaking for myself, I felt pretty sure that all that was meant was that it must not be thought that because domestic affairs were engaging the attention of His Majesty's Government, they disinterested themselves from anything which might touch their interests abroad. That under the circumstances appeared to me a very natural and useful observation to make. Herr von Kiderlen said that he was more concerned with the effect which Mr. Lloyd George's statement had evidently had than with the motive which had inspired it, and he could not conceal from me that it had added considerably to the difficulties of the situation. I said that notwithstanding all difficulties, I hoped that his conversations with M. Cambon would lead to some definite and satisfactory result. He said that he hoped so too, but while he had been prepared for a certain amount of bargaining and even haggling, because naturally in negotiations everyone wished to get the best of them if possible, he had not been prepared for indiscretions, and the resulting threatening language of the French Press and the violence of French public opinion had upset all idea of mutual concessions and rendered it impossible for him to modify what he had proposed as compensation. If France refused to entertain his proposals it would be the worse for her, as the whole Morocco question would have to be reopened and she would have to be called to account for her breaches of the Act of Algeciras, such as her expedition to Fez, her action at Casablanca, and other doubtful proceedings, and also for the marked manner in which she had neglected to carry out the provisions of the 1909 agreement with Germany. I said that as regards the expedition to Fez, he would remember that it had been undertaken at the request of the Sultan and also in order to safeguard the lives and property of Frenchmen and other foreigners at Fez. Their object had been to strengthen the authority and sovereignty of the Sultan, and this on the invitation of the latter. Moreover the French Government had informed the Powers of their contemplated action, and I had always understood that the German Government had raised no objection to that action, and had contented themselves with pointing out the difficulty France would have in doing, within a reasonable period, what she had undertaken to do. The action which the Imperial Government had thought fit to take subsequently had neither been invited by the Sultan nor had any notice been given to the Powers before its completion. Without taking any notice of this remark Herr von Kiderlen observed that the idea that the French had been asked by the Sultan to restore order in Morocco was not worth a moment's discussion and could not be taken seriously. The Sultan had merely said what the French had told him to say, and Germany could have afforded herself the same luxury had she thought it worth while to do so and to pay for it. Times out of number the Sultan had appealed to Germany behind the backs of the other Powers to do things which might have been considered contrary to the Act of Algeciras, but she had always loyally refused to be led astray however advantageous the proposals had been. But France wanted everything. That she could not have unless Germany was cleared out of the field, and for that advantage she would have to pay. If she refused, Germany would regain full liberty of action and the whole Morocco question would probably have to be reopened, much, as he had said before, to the disadvantage of France. I repeated that I hoped the conversations with the French Government would lead to some definite result and that I was sure that there was nothing my Government desired more than that a settlement should be arrived at satisfactorily to both countries and by which British interests were not affected.

Whether Herr von Kiderlen intends really to refuse all abatement of his demands will be known very shortly, as I believe that my French colleague has instructions to inform His Excellency that the French Government cannot possibly negotiate on the basis of the German demands.

Both Herr von Kiderlen and M. Cambon seem to be be depressed at the turn things have taken, and both are equally annoyed at the indiscretions of the French Government and the violent tone of the French Press.

I have, &c.
W. E. GOSCHEN.

No. 425.

Sir Edward Grey to Mr. Carnegie.

F.O. 29560/25883/11/28.
(No. 312.)

Sir, *Foreign Office, July 26, 1911.*

M. Cambon showed me to-day what had passed between Herr von Kiderlen and the French Ambassador in Berlin.

Germany had held to a demand for such a cession of the French Congo as would bring the Kamerouns to the Congo River, but she had considerably increased her offers of territorial compensation to France elsewhere in West Africa, and had promised France an absolutely free hand in Morocco.

The French Ambassador had observed that France would, in any case, be able to remain in Morocco, subject to the Algeciras Act; and that Germany could not give away Morocco, because it did not belong to her. But Herr von Kiderlen had replied that they must deal with facts, and that if Germany did not object to a free hand for France in Morocco no other country would object. Germany would, however, require certain guarantees that no export duties would be placed on minerals, and that taxation would be kept low.

The opinion of the French Government was that all that would be left of the French Congo would be worthless if they gave Germany what she asked; and that it would be only betraying Germany if they promised to give this, because a cession of territory could not be made without the consent of the French Parliament, and this consent could never be obtained for so large a cession as Germany wished to have. Nevertheless, the French Ambassador in Berlin had been much impressed by the change of tone on the part of Herr von Kiderlen, which pointed to a genuine desire on his part to come to a settlement.

After reading the record of what had passed, I observed that it indicated a real desire to come to a settlement, and also a very strong wish to get a position on the Congo.

M. Cambon said that, amongst other objections to the cession of Libreville or any other place on the French Congo coast to Germany, it was urged in France that we would regard British interests as having been betrayed.

I assured him emphatically that, as regards any concessions which France thought it reasonable to make in the French Congo, I should be prepared to say that we had known of them when they were being made, and had informed the French Government that there was nothing in them prejudicial to British interests. This would make it clear to public opinion here that the French Government had done nothing in this respect to impair the *entente* with us.

I then showed M. Cambon the records of my last three conversations with Count Metternich about Morocco, those of the 21st, 24th, and 25th instant.([1]) I impressed on him that the fact that Germany had made a complaint about the speech of the Chancellor of the Exchequer must be kept secret; but I thought it important that the French Government should know the language which Germany had held to us about France. This indicated that, if the negotiations with France came to nothing, Germany would not be content to remain quietly at Agadir, but would present France with a demand amounting practically to an ultimatum that France should withdraw from all military occupation of Morocco, in order to restore the *status quo.* If a Conference of the Powers of the Algeciras Act were suggested, Germany would refuse to entertain the proposal, and would act alone. It might be possible for us, as one of the Signatory Powers of the Algeciras Act, then to make to Germany a demand that she should withdraw from Agadir, just as she had demanded that France should withdraw from military occupation in Morocco. Germany would probably reply that her withdrawal from Agadir would take place when France withdrew to the coast.

[I am, &c.]
E. G[REY].

([1]) [*v. supra*, pp. 390–1, No. 411; pp. 394–6, No. 417; pp. 397–9, No. 419.]

No. 426.

Statement by Mr. Asquith in the House of Commons.([1])

July 27, 1911.

The Prime Minister: I think I said two days ago, in answer to an inquiry by the right hon[ourable] Gentleman opposite (Mr. Balfour), that I thought it would be more convenient, instead of answering a question across the floor of the House, that we should take the occasion of this Vote to make a statement as to a question which very largely and generally, if it does not absorb, at any rate excites public attention. I mean the question which has arisen in the international sphere in regard to Morocco, and I think it will be of general interest, as well as for the convenience of the House, that I should make that statement at once before any debate or discussion has arisen. It is obvious that this Moroccan question has reached a point at which it will become increasingly difficult, embarrassing, and anxious unless a solution is found. Too close an analysis at the present moment of causes and antecedents might provoke in more than one quarter recrimination and retorts, which it is on every ground desirable to avoid. I propose, therefore, simply to state to the House what is the actual situation to-day. Conversations are proceeding between France and Germany. We are not a party to those conversations. The subject matter of them may not affect British interests. On that point, until we know the ultimate result, we cannot express a final opinion. But it is our desire that these conversations should issue in a settlement honourable and satisfactory to both the parties, and of which His Majesty's Government can cordially say that it in no way prejudices British interests. We believe that to be quite possible; we earnestly and sincerely desire to see it accomplished. The question of Morocco itself bristles with difficulties, but outside Morocco, in other parts of West Africa, we should not think of attempting to interfere with territorial arrangements considered reasonable by those who are more directly interested. Any statements that we have so interfered to prejudice negotiations between France and Germany are mischievous inventions, without the faintest foundation in fact. But we have thought it right from the beginning to make it quite clear that, failing a settlement such as I have indicated, we must become an active party to discussion of the situation. That would be our right as a signatory to the Treaty of Algeciras; it might be our obligation under the terms of our agreement of 1904 with France; it might be our duty in defence of British interests directly affected by further developments. There have been times when we were not sure how far this was fully understood. I am glad to say we are now quite satisfied that that is not the case. The statement which I made here at this table more than three weeks ago,([2]) and the speech since made elsewhere by my right honourable friend the Chancellor of the Exchequer([3]) have, I hope and believe, made it perfectly clear that we claim not any predominant or pre-eminent position, but that of one party interested in possible developments and in seeing a solution of the present difficulties. Sir, in our judgment, it would have been a grave mistake to let such a situation drift till an assertion of our interest in it might, owing to previous silence, cause surprise and resentment at the moment when this assertion became most necessary. That, I trust, we have sufficiently guarded against by the statements already made. I repeat that we earnestly desire a successful issue of the conversations now in progress, and I would venture, in the general interest, to make a strong appeal to the House, not on the present occasion to enter into further details or open up controversial ground.

([1]) [*v. Parl. Deb.*, *5th Ser.*, House of Commons, Vol. 28, pp. 1827–8. *cp.* also *G.P.* XXIX, pp. 223–5.]

([2]) [*cp. supra*, p. 342, No. 365.]

([3]) [*cp. supra*, pp. 391–2, No. 412.]

No. 427.

Sir Edward Grey to Sir G. Buchanan.

F.O. 29568/13911/11/28.　　　　　　　　*Foreign Office, July 27, 1911.*
Tel. (No. 386.)　　　　　　　　　　　　　　　　　D. 5·30 P.M.

I told Count Benckendorff yesterday that the German Government had indicated to us quite clearly that, if the negotiations with France did not result in a settlement, they would demand that France should retire from all military occupation of Morocco, and observe strictly the "status quo" of the Algeciras Act.

A Conference of the Powers who had signed the Algeciras Act might then be proposed, but Germany had made it plain that she might refuse to entertain the idea of a Conference, and would proceed by herself with her demand upon France.

I thought that the Russian Government ought to know in advance what had been said by Germany, in order that they might decide how they would deal with such a situation if it arose.

No. 428.

Sir E. Goschen to Sir Edward Grey.

F.O. 29784/16083/11/28.
(No. 206.)　　　　　　　　　　　　　　*Berlin, D. July 27, 1911.*
Sir,　　　　　　　　　　　　　　　　　　R. *July 29, 1911.*

Mr. Lloyd George's speech has aroused a certain amount of excitement in Germany. Many of the papers at first began by calling it a "warning to Germany" but refrained from any comments, but the indignant tone of the Press has increased in the last few days.

The "Kölnische Zeitung," in a telegram from its Berlin correspondent on Saturday evening thinks that in spite of its "peaceful ending" the speech is meant as a warning or even a threat addressed to Germany, but it adds that the same speech, with its statement of principles applicable to the Great Powers, could have equally well been delivered by any non-English statesman and that similar truths have also been uttered from the tribune of the Reichstag without anyone discovering in them warlike tendencies or menaces against another country.

In its evening edition of the 24th instant, the same paper publishes a leading article suggesting that the simplest solution of the problem would seem to be that France should withdraw her troops, except the police, from Morocco, throw open the door for international trade and give guarantees that she will not regard Morocco as a French colony. Then there would be no doubt that Germany, having secured her economic interests in the Sus, would withdraw her ships from Agadir.

The "Kölnische Zeitung" of yesterday now says that German economic interests in Morocco are, without doubt, not the chief difficulty in the Berlin negotiations. France does not dispute them and all that has to be done is to prevent them from being subjected to the rough treatment to which, as experience has shown, foreign trade is exposed in the French Colonies and spheres of interest. The chief point, however, the "Kölnische Zeitung" thinks, is what compensation Germany can claim for the increase of power which France is about to get in Morocco.

The same paper in an article headed "Imponderabilien" points out that the actions of France and Spain in Morocco are allowed to go unchallenged and that the French Press sees in them only a safeguard of the respective interests of those two countries, while the German action in sending a ship to Agadir to protect Germans there causes paroxyms in the French Press which declares that the Act of Algeciras is violated. The article continues:—"As matters stand at present it would be a useless work to show that Germany has from the very beginning never placed her own advantages in the Morocco question in the foreground. Many people in Germany think that our Foreign Office has not pushed German interests in Morocco enough, but Germany's action in sending a ship to Agadir has received the unreserved assent of public opinion in this country. Members of Parliament of all political opinions and newspapers have considered this step as absolutely justified and even defended it as deliverance from a bann, and consequently the appearance of England on the scene is all the more acutely felt. It reminds us of the famous ' Hands off! ' which Gladstone flung at Austria-Hungary in 1878 when she occupied Bosnia and Herzegovina. We thought the time was past when British statesmen could use such language to another country. In any case the German people is not inclined to allow its hand to be forced by Foreign Powers whose history has taught us that a State can only exist if it is ready to defend to the utmost its rights and its claims. Prince Bismarck spoke more than once of the ' doubtful factors in politics which have often a far more powerful influence than questions of material and direct interests and the importance of which cannot be over estimated.' In London and Paris care must be taken not to interfere with the doubtful factors which are now the motives of German policy.''

The '' Frankfurter Zeitung '' of the 24th instant also devotes a leading article to Mr. Lloyd George's speech, the language of which it thinks is most serious and almost menacing, all the more so as the Chancellor of the Exchequer is not one of those statesmen who would for choice make a patriotic appeal to the country. The paper complains that German aims and German need of expansion are not understood in England. If they were England and Germany might, it thinks, arrive at an agreement or even perhaps an alliance. The journal cannot see why England should object to Germany getting compensation outside Morocco and cannot understand why England makes so great a distinction between Germany's recent action at Agadir and the advance of the French to Fez and the Spaniards to Alcazar— or again between the German action in Morocco and the Russian action in Persia. The article continues :—'' It is really not easy to satisfy the men who rule in England to-day. England ought to realize the danger of hemming in the rapidly growing population of Germany. She must of course try to maintain her own position but people in London should see that it will not do to force a great nation which possesses a larger population than England and which increases by a million inhabitants yearly, from all places where it seeks an opportunity for national expansion.''

The '' Münchener Neueste Nachrichten '' says :—'' We deprecate most strongly good advice conveyed in the tone of a threat. It will be well to remain calm and see what the British Government not only has to say, but thinks of doing and that is the business not of the Chancellor of the Exchequer, but of the Prime Minister.''

The '' Post,'' the organ of the Imperial Party, asserts that France never intended that the negotiations should be brought to a successful issue and it 'maintains that it knows for a fact that the French Embassy in Berlin is responsible for the leakage in connection with the negotiations. Germany has been absolutely loyal in complying with the agreement that the negotiations should be secret.

The popular '' Lokalanzeiger '' says that it is not possible to derive from Mr. Lloyd George's words the belief that he was desirous of criticising Germany's policy. Any statesman of an independent Empire has the right to speak as Mr. Lloyd George has spoken and it would seem absurd to remonstrate with him about it. It would, the paper continues, be hardly admissible to suggest that Mr. Lloyd George intended to interfere in the Franco-German negotiations.

The '' Börsen Courier '' interprets Mr. McKinnon Wood's statement in the House of Commons on Tuesday[1] as another English threat. Germany's best reply is to be calm in the consciousness that the '' Panther '' was after all sent to Agadir only to protect German interests and not to violate the rights of others.

[1] [cp. Parl. Deb., 5th Ser., House of Commons, Vol. 28, p. 1439.]

The "Hamburger Nachrichten" is convinced that neither France nor England will risk war for the sake of Morocco, France because not even the successful support of the British fleet would save her from the danger of defeat on land and England on account of the disturbance to her commerce which must necessarily be produced by an Anglo-German naval war.

The "Berliner Tageblatt" in a leading article to-day says: "Rumour has it that in the last few days the Franco-German negotiations have reached a very difficult stage, and excitable persons are already speaking of a European war. All sorts of ridiculous rumours are being spread, for example that Herr von Kiderlen has drawn up an ultimatum and that the British fleet is preparing for war. The German Press, having itself no news, is unable to impart any information to the 60 million souls who are naturally clamouring to know how matters stand.

"While these 60 millions remain in perfect ignorance of the real state of affairs Herr von Kiderlen and M. Cambon are negotiating behind closed doors. We do not know in what sense Herr von Kiderlen has been negotiating, and the only tangible piece of news was the statement published in the 'Matin' to the effect that Germany was demanding the coast of the French Congo. Herr von Kiderlen has as yet had no opportunity of showing his metal in any action of first class importance. Consequently criticisms of his ability are widely divergent. He is supposed to be a pupil of Bismarck's although the Bismarckian press is loud in its denunciation of his present policy. He is also an intimate friend of the extreme Junkers. According to regulations the Secretary of State has discussed foreign affairs with the Chancellor, 'whose name is Bethmann Hollweg.' We naturally presume that these two have done the cleverest and most prudent thing that was to be done, and have not rushed into an *impasse*. We presume so, but we know nothing and the 60 millions know just as little as we do.

"When the German cruiser was sent to Agadir we pointed out that the desire to negotiate with France about Morocco and to dismiss this problem once for all by means of compensations was sound and reasonable, but that it was better to reserve all expressions of gratification till it was seen 'how the trip continued.' To-day—three weeks later—the end of the trip is not in sight and it looks as if, once again, the uncompromising attitude of England had come as a surprise. We say 'once again' because the situation was very similar at the beginning of 1904 before the conclusion of the *entente cordiale*, as well as before and during the Tangier journey when the Emperor first heard of England's true intentions during His stay at Lisbon. The situation was again similar during the Algeciras Conference when, on March 11, 1906, a German official organ wrote 'France's resistance at Algeciras has isolated her and driven the more important neutral states, especially Russia, the United States, Italy and even England over to Germany.' On this occasion too it seems that a little too much confidence has been placed in the friendliness of court intercourse since the view that Lloyd George only spoke as a private individual must be regarded as a very doubtful evasion.

"We do not believe for a moment that the discussion about Congo or Agadir will end in a European war, and we do not attach the slightest importance to all the alarm rumours. There is nothing to show that the official circles in Berlin have lost their *sang froid*, and if only a few personal resentments can be overcome there will be a way out of the dilemma. The negotiations between M. Delcassé and Lord Lansdowne lasted 4 months and constantly came to a deadlock, and it is the same story every time two nations negotiate as to territorial concessions. France has just as great an interest as Germany in arriving at an understanding which would give her the incalculable advantage of a free hand in Morocco. She is moreover interested in not appearing to the world as the protégée of England. The only possibility of any danger arising would be if the British Government, having regard to the critical nature of the internal situation, were still further to increase the severity of their utterances. But they will hardly do this and we may look forward to Mr. Asquith's statements to-morrow being diplomatic and not warlike. Should we be disappointed in this, Germany will know how to adopt a calm attitude in face of the lamentable consequences. But cool consideration leads us to deny the possibility of any but a favourable result of Mr. Asquith's speech.

"All this excitement and these gruesome rumours would be quite impossible if the Governments would emerge from the mists in which they are hiding. It is surely wrong that the world should be again waiting for the approval of England, who already occupies rather a large part of the earth's surface, and that, in this Franco-German question the eyes of the whole of humanity should be fixed on Mr. Asquith. This mystery making has always produced a feeling of irritation, and it is not enough for statesmen to preach confidence to grown up nations and to say nothing of their actions or their motives. Public opinion is not very exacting, but surely it might be supplied with that to which it has a just claim. Both Herr von Kiderlen and M. Cambon are famed for their literary style, and it should not be very difficult for them to tell us as much as they can tell us. All allowances must be made for the German Government in their delicate position, but some allowance must be made for the 60 millions too."

I have, &c.
W. E. GOSCHEN.

No. 429.

Sir E. Goschen to Sir Edward Grey.

F.O. 30654/8457/11/28.
Private.   *Berlin,* D. *July* 27, 1911.
My dear Grey,   R. *August* 3, 1911.
    Many thanks for your letter and for sending to me the intensely interesting Metternich conversations.(¹) They came in the nick of time as Cambon expects to see Kiderlen to-morrow morning, and he was very glad to know of the language held by Metternich in London and of the replies you had made to him : with which, I need hardly say, he was delighted. He promised me that he would show no knowledge that the German Government had complained of Mr. Lloyd George's speech, and altogether to be very careful with regard to the papers which you had kindly allowed him to see.

    I am sending by the Messenger who brought them an account of a conversation which I had with Kiderlen yesterday.(²) I wish very much I had had the advantage of reading your conversations before I saw him, as there are one or two things I should not have said or perhaps put differently. But after all I was only speaking my own views in a very informal conversation and by no means as the mouthpiece of His Majesty's Government. In any case I avoided argument as much as possible as I did not wish to excite him and make Cambon's delicate task still more difficult. The atmosphere is in a highly electrical state and until the negotiations are either broken off or get into a more tranquil groove, one cannot be too careful here.

    Kiderlen's point, on which he harped the whole time, is that while he thinks his demands for compensation not extravagant in view of the enormous advantages which would accrue to France in the event of Germany disinteresting herself from Morocco, still he had originally proposed them not as hard and fast demands, but as material for discussion and bargaining : but that now owing to the menacing language of the French Press, to which fresh life had been given by Mr. Lloyd George's speech, those demands have become hard and fast and it has been taken out of his power to modify them. "Germany" he said "is too great and too powerful to yield to threats and public opinion would stand no Foreign Minister

(¹) [*v. supra,* pp. 390–1, No. 411; pp. 394–6, No. 417; pp. 397–9, No. 419.]
(²) [*v. supra,* pp. 402–4, No. 424.]

who had even the appearance of doing so.'' With the exception of one or two outbursts like this, which were, I should think, designed for conveyance to France viâ England, Kiderlen's tone was quite quiet and even friendly, and he made no mention whatever of the language you had held to Metternich.

Cambon has been very depressed during these last days owing to his instructions which he said must have the effect of breaking off the conversations. He has been trying to gain time by asking his Government for certain explanations : and he has now gained it, because today he received fresh instructions which he says give him a more free hand. He does not believe that Kiderlen, who is palpably ill at ease and bothered, will be quite as stiff as he gives himself out to be, and he thinks that there is still a chance of a more moderate deal. He intends to try and get Kiderlen to spin out the conversations as long as possible so as to give time for the various Presses to become more moderate and for the present seething excitement to subside.

He is very anxious for two things : first that you should make it clear to the French Government, not through his brother Paul, but through Bertie, that His Majesty's Government would be *glad* (Mr. Asquith's speech(³) has not made this *quite* clear) to see France come to an arrangement with Germany. Secondly, if the conversations break down, that it will be made equally clear that England will go '' solidly '' with France.

This latter point is evidently pre-occupying his mind very much as he is always impressing on me and his Government, that no time should be lost in making some definite agreement as to what the Powers should do in the event of Germany holding to her full demands and the conversations being broken off. He is in fact haunted with the idea that France, if things go wrong, will be left in the lurch and have to face Germany alone.

I am afraid this letter is very badly written—but it is difficult to do anything properly with the thermometer standing at over 90° in the shade !

Yours very sincerely,
W. E. GOSCHEN.

P.S.—*July* 28.

I have just had time before sending off this letter to glance over the German morning papers : and I find Mr. Asquith's speech has had an excellent effect. But I have only seen two papers namely the Chauvinistic '' Post '' and the liberal '' Tageblatt.'' . . . .(⁴)

W. E. G.

(³) [*v. supra*, p. 406, No. 426.]
(⁴) [Here follow brief summaries of the favourable comments of the two papers.]

No. 430.

Sir Edward Grey to Sir E. Goschen.

F.O. 29711/13911/11/28.
(No. 172.)
Sir, *Foreign Office, July* 27, 1911.
Count Metternich made to me to-day the following communication :—(¹)

'' We trust that Sir Edward Grey, by our very open and candid communication,(²) has gathered the conviction that our pourparlers with France at the moment do not touch British interests. We trust to the Minister's great loyalty, that he has so often shown, that he will find it possible to state this fact in Parliament, without however giving any details of our confidential communica-

(¹) [*v. G.P.* XXIX, pp. 214–5.]
(²) [*v. supra*, pp. 394–6, No. 417.]

tion. We acknowledge with pleasure that the Minister has stated that he desires an agreement between Germany and France, and feel quite convinced that this will prove most helpful to the progress of the negotiations.

"But, having in view the wish expressed by Sir Edward, we cannot quite see how he can in the present state of the pourparlers describe our demands as obviously impossible, without knowing what we on our side have the intention to offer to France in the political and *Colonial* territorial field. It is not possible, in regard of the formal pledge of secrecy we have given, to go into details; but as the territories to be eventually exchanged are exclusively German and French we do not believe that special English interests could be touched, and that it seems advisable to leave it to the two parties immediately concerned to form an estimation of the value of the objects to be eventually exchanged.

"Adverse criticism from the English side must obviously render the negotiations more difficult. On the other hand, a public statement that England would be pleased to see a successful conclusion of the Franco-German pourparlers would have a most beneficial influence on an auspicious result, for which we most earnestly hope. We most seriously wish to diminish any points of friction we have with France in the Colonial sphere, especially in Africa, and hope it may eventually be possible to make them disappear entirely : we could not look forward, even if this was done, to establishing intimate relations with France; but we believed that it would do away with a cause of frequently recurring tension. If the wishes of England are in the same direction, the best way to help to bring about this result would be by having a calming influence on public opinion in France, which just now, by half-truths and inaccurate statements, has been brought to considerable excitement."

I expressed appreciation of the friendly tone in which the communication was couched. I thought that perhaps I had better not make much comment upon it, at any rate until the statement on Morocco had been made by the Prime Minister this afternoon. Count Metternich would then be able to see how far what was said met the German desire that the negotiations should be facilitated.

Count Metternich began to say something as to previous utterances on our part not having had that effect.

But I expressed the hope that we might take this last German communication as a new point of departure, and not go back upon things which must lead to mutual recrimination.

Count Metternich then pressed me to say whether we should regard the cession of the part of the French Congo from the Sango River to the sea as affecting British interests.

I said that I must leave him to infer how far this point was covered by the statement to be made in Parliament this afternoon.

He urged that, in French opinion, there was the impression that such a cession was impossible from the point of view of British interests.

I replied that it would be a mistake to suppose that my use of the words "obviously impossible," as applied to the German demands upon France as they appeared in the newspapers last week, meant that I had gone to the French and expressed the opinion that they must not make concessions in the French Congo, because of British interests. On the other hand, it must not be expected that we could suggest to France concessions which no French Government could possibly present for the approval of the French Parliament. Count Metternich said this was certainly not expected of us.

I also observed to Count Metternich that the French Government ought to be free to inform us of the course of negotiations. We could not tell what might come into these beyond the present basis of discussion, and our desire to facilitate them was so genuine that we should certainly not make use of any information which we received in order to impede negotiations where British interests were not affected.

In the course of further informal conversation Count Metternich expressed some regret at the way in which our public opinion had rushed to adverse conclusions about German action.

I asked what else could have been expected when Germany suddenly sent a ship to Agadir, a closed commercial port, but said to be the place most suited for a naval base on the west coast of Morocco? Of course that mobilized British public opinion. And from the time of the Cabinet communication that I made to Count Metternich on July 4,([3]) there had been no communication to us from the German Gov[ernmen]t till the 24th of July([4]) and then what was said about a naval base was in a form that I could not use. But I suggested again that we should not pursue these points now.

[I am, &c.]
E. G[REY].

([3]) [v. supra, p. 334, No. 356.]
([4]) [v. supra, pp. 394–6, No. 417.]

No. 431.

Sir E. Goschen to Sir A. Nicolson.

Private.([1])

My dear Nicolson,   Berlin, July 27, 1911.

Things are not going very well and Cambon is both depressed and rather excited. He is furious with his Government for their indiscretions, which he considers have ruined all the chance he had of making an acceptable settlement. These indiscretions, he maintains, were not made by de Selves, but by one of his underlings who hates him (Cambon) and would stick at nothing to do him a bad turn. He is also rather aghast at the effect which Mr. Lloyd George's speech has had on the French Colonial Chauvinists. A good deal of his talk comes from the fact that the thermometer is about 90°—a temperature which is not suitable for carrying on worrying and delicate negotiations.

There is no doubt, I think, that Kiderlen is not at all at his ease and one feels when conversing with him that he is talking "big" in order to cover up his own errors and miscalculations; it was an error for instance to begin a series of what were to be friendly conversations by kicking his fellow negotiator . . . . ;([2]) and his estimate of the probable attitude of H[is] M[ajesty's] G[overnment] was obviously miscalculated. This serious miscalculation was in all probability, and I have heard it from many sides, due to what he heard from the Emperor, and especially the Crown Prince respecting their visits to London. Of course the Crown Prince talked to a lot of irresponsible people in London, who were only too anxious to say what might be agreeable to him. He probably accepted their remarks as expressions of British public opinion and conveyed them to Kiderlen as such. That the latter should have accepted them as such seems scarcely credible, but there is every appearance that he did. The amicable Chancellor may have had something to do with it. In any case I *think* that Kiderlen now feels that the negotiations were not started very happily and I have every hope that these feelings will lead him sooner or later into a more conciliatory groove.

July 28. Since writing the above Mr. Asquith's speech has been made and telegraphed.([3]) It has, as far as I am able to judge, had an excellent effect here and I feel that it will give Kiderlen a much desired opportunity to climb down a little. Cambon's spirits have risen enormously and he is going to see Kiderlen

([1]) [Carnock MSS., Vol. III of 1911.]
([2]) [A few words only are here omitted.]
([3]) [v. supra, p. 406, No. 426.]

tonight hoping to find him in a softened mood. He is also in better spirits because he managed by various devices to delay carrying out his instructions (those wh[ich] in his opinion would have broken off the conversations)—until he received others giving him practically a free hand. Now he is quite hopeful again. . . . .([4])

Yours very sincerely,
W. E. GOSCHEN.

([4]) [The rest of this letter contains unimportant details of the negotiations, and summarizes various Press reports.]

No. 432.

Sir E. Goschen to Sir Edward Grey.

F.O. 29785/29785/11/28.
(No. 208.)   *Berlin,* D. *July* 28, 1911.
Sir,   R. *July* 29, 1911.
    I have the honour to forward, herewith, a despatch, as marked in the margin, which I have received from Colonel Russell, Military Attaché to this Embassy, relating to the existence or absence of military preparations in Germany.

I have, &c.
W. E. GOSCHEN.

Enclosure in No. 432.

Lieutenant-Colonel Russell to Sir E. Goschen.

(No. 16.) Confidential.
Sir,   *Berlin, July* 27, 1911.
    I think that it is desirable that I should record my impressions at the present juncture with regard to the existence, or absence, of any unusual preparations of a warlike nature in this country.
    I believe that a number of alarmist reports have recently appeared in French newspapers, chiefly referring to German military operations near the frontier and the alleged calling out of a large number of additional reservists.
    With regard to the former contention it must be conceded that manœuvres are now in progress in the neighbourhood of Metz, but this is the season of the year in which large bodies of troops are normally brought together for purposes of training. The report regarding the calling out of additional reservists does not in my opinion rest on any solid foundation of fact. The orders for the calling out of reservists for their autumn training were issued in March last, were not in any sense abnormal and have not, I am convinced, been altered since that date.
    It is impossible to predict in a situation like the present what the future may bring forth, but I think it may fairly be said that no indications of any unusual military activity are observable at this moment.
    The time of year, no doubt, is an eminently favourable one for a sudden mobilization. The navy is fully armed and manned for the Manœuvres. In the Army the youngest soldiers have nearly completed their first year's training and have thus been fully competent for some time past to take their places in the ranks. The reservists who are to be called for training this year are about to join their units. These are, however, quite normal phenomena.
    On the other hand I have heard indirectly that no proceedings of any unusual character are to be noted on the railways. To my knowledge a number of officers holding important appointments here, among whom I believe may be included the Chief of the General Staff, are absent on leave at the present time. There is less than the usual activity to be observed in and about the building of the Great General Staff, if one may judge by casual external evidence.

My French colleague who has just returned from a tour in Eastern Prussia, assures me that he was received by his German brothers in arms with the greatest cordiality and perhaps with almost excessive conviviality.

He further states that the numerous French officers on leave in Germany, with whom [he] is in touch, do not inform him of any unusual proceedings.

This normal state of affairs may, however, of course change at a moment's notice. In the German scheme for mobilization no uncertainty exists, nor is there any need for undue haste. Everything which human forethought can provide for beforehand, has already been accomplished.

> I have, &c.
> ALICK RUSSELL,
> *Military Attaché.*

No. 433.

Sir Edward Grey to Sir F. Bertie.

F.O. 30103/13911/11/28.
(No. 318.)

Sir,
                                                            Foreign Office, July 28, 1911.

M. Cambon informed me to-day that he had sent to his Government the communication of the German attitude and intentions towards France, which I had received on Monday, and that M. de Selves wished to ask me one or two questions.

In the event of the negotiations between France and Germany breaking down, would we propose a Conference, even though Germany had indicated that she would not accept a Conference?

I replied that I could give only a personal opinion. It could not be final as regards myself personally, and it could not commit the Government: for even if the negotiations did fail, no definite decision could be come to until we knew what was the actual situation when the failure took place. The situation then might be different from what we had been led to expect. But with this reservation, and speaking personally, I thought that a conference should be proposed. It was the natural, reasonable, and justifiable proposal to make when the Act of Algeciras was broken. Germany might agree to a Conference and then break it up: but there would at least be some gain of time, and in any case I thought that, if Germany refused to let a settlement be secured by a Conference, the fact should be made known.

M. de Selves also wished to know whether, supposing that Germany refused to agree to a Conference, and remained at Agadir and proceeded to land men, we should think that some observations should be made to Germany, and that ships should be sent to Agadir by ourselves France and if possible Spain.

I said that, in my opinion, we ought not to send a ship to Agadir unless we were prepared to regard this as possibly the first step in a war. We could not contemplate such a step without being able to take into full consideration all the circumstances which might exist at the time.

I went on to say to M. Cambon that if the Franco-German negotiations broke down the present situation could not be allowed to continue without some solution. I would suggest that if Germany declined a Conference all the Signatory Powers of the Algeciras Act, without being invited to a Conference, should be asked to express their views as to what the situation required.

I then told M. Cambon that I wished to make to him a suggestion which had occurred to me personally, but which I did not desire to go beyond himself, unless he thought that there was something in it. The difficulty in which the French Government were placed was, I understood, that any concessions of territory which they might wish to make would have to be submitted for the approval of the French

Parliament. Any concession of a part of the French Congo would to some extent change the colour of the map of Africa : for a certain part, large or small, which was at present coloured French would then be coloured German. But there would be no corresponding change in the colour of Morocco on the map if all that happened was that Germany gave France a free hand in Morocco : for France would still be bound by the Algeciras Act. I thought that, possibly, the French Government might be able to offer larger concessions if it was arranged that their bargain with Germany was made subject to its being confirmed by a Conference. This Conference would be composed of the Signatory Powers of the Algeciras Act, it would recognise the protectorate of France over Morocco, and Morocco would then be coloured French on the map of Africa. This would counterbalance the alteration in colour made elsewhere. The consent of the Conference to the bargain could be secured in advance : for Germany could obtain the agreement of her Allies, Austria and Italy; while Russia and we should agree with France, who would of course make her own arrangements with Spain with whom she had special agreements. There would, therefore, be no reason why Germany should not be willing to have such a Conference into which she would go in agreement with France and both together assured of a majority for their views ; and it might then be possible for the French Government to propose larger concessions to the French Parliament. There were certain reservations which would have to be made with regard to Tangier and economic liberty, but these were details which could be considered later.

M. Cambon said that he thought the idea was a good one, and worth considering, but the proposal that France should give up the whole of the French Congo from Sanga to the sea was one that France could not accept : the district in question was larger than the whole of Morocco ; besides, all Morocco to the south of the Atlas Mountains was a desert, and it was only a comparatively small part to the north of these Mountains that was really valuable.

[I am, &c.]

E. G[REY].

No. 434.

Sir Edward Grey to Sir F. Bertie.

Private.([1])

My dear Bertie,   *Foreign Office, July* 28, 1911.

To get Morocco as she has Tunis would be a great step for France. It is worth her while to pay a good price for it. But though a free hand from Germany might, as Kiderlen urged, give Morocco to France *in fact*, it would be difficult to put it before the French Chamber as the complete gain that it really would be.

If the French Government want an out and out bargain so drawn up that the gain to France and Germany is in appearance as well as in fact equally balanced, they could with Germany's consent get this at a Conference.

What I mean is this : France can and does in effect say to Germany at present that cession of territory held by her in fee simple is not in pari materiâ with a free hand to her from Germany in Morocco. But France might raise her terms offered to Germany conditionally upon Morocco being given at a Conference as her exclusive sphere of action. In other words, France and Germany may strike a bargain that we and Russia as friend and ally of France : Austria and Italy as allies of Germany should all agree to support at a Conference. Germany would not refuse a Conference into which she went agreed with France and both assured in advance of a majority.

([1]) [Grey MSS., Vol. 13.]

I only suggest this for you to use in conversation if you think it desirable or opportune. The French difficulty is with their Chamber, and it seems to me that in this way they might be able to put their bargain in a better light to the Chamber.

I do not forget that Spain has her own bargain with France, but that must be adjusted between them.

Tangiers (unless it went to us) must remain an international place as it is now; but these are details; and so are the economic arrangements for which we should stipulate. The general principle would be that a new Conference cancelled the Act of Algeciras, and painted Morocco in French colour on the map of Africa.

Yours sincerely,

E. GREY.

CHAPTER LVI.

THE APPROACH TO THE CRISIS, JULY 24-AUGUST 21, 1911.

No. 435.

Vice-Consul Johnstone to Consul Madden.([1])

F.O. 31024/25641/11/28.
(No. 90.)
Sir,

Mogador, July 24, 1911.

With reference to my despatch No. 86, of the 21st instant,([2]) relative to the presence of the German Men-of-War at Agadir, I have the honour to report that Mr. G. Broome has informed me that on Saturday evening, the 22nd instant, he received a native messenger from Agadir, in whom he places confidence and who told him that during last week, probably Wednesday, the German Naval Officers had an interview with the Chiefs of the tribes surrounding the port. Tents had been prepared for the reception, on shore and the spokesman on the German side is said to have informed the Kaids that the Germans had come, as one independent people to another people, equally independent, in order to ascertain whether it was a fact that the inhabitants of the " Sus " country wished the Europeans to open a port on their coast. The Germans, the spokesman is said to have stated, would in no way interfere in matters of Government or Religion, all that was wanted was that land might be sold to Europeans (Nasrani) from round Agadir to Wad Massa, and that the safety of the Trade Roads should be assured by the Native Chiefs. The Chiefs are said to have replied that they were ready to accept the German proposals, as long as they incurred no expense whatever in the matter. A paper is then said to have been drawn up and signed by the Kaids and the German Ship (presumably the " Panther ") despatched a radiogram. A feast was offered to the Chiefs, and they were received on board the Ship, a salute being fired upon their arrival and departure.

On Saturday, I was told by natives that only one German Man-of-War was at Agadir, and that was the " Panther," but to-day I hear there is a second one, so that possibly the " Ebor " [*sic :* " Eber "] has arrived.([3])

The French Consul tells me that the Germans are insisting that the local authorities give preference to German Subjects in the purchase of land.

Mr. G. V. Forrest has arrived in this town from near Suk-el-Hud, in Mramar, in the North of Kerima. He reports that the tribesmen are very unsettled and excited, and that small parties of armed men are patrolling the country in case of invasion by Kaid M'Tuggi's men. He states that the Natives seem to believe that Kaid Anflus will help Kaid Koraimi, and that the Germans will come to his assistance against M'Tuggi. The road from Mogador to Mramar was open and peaceful when Mr. Forrest passed over it on Friday and Saturday.

I have received no confirmation of the news which Mr. Broome communicated to me yesterday.

I have, &c.
H. B. JOHNSTONE.

([1]) [This despatch was enclosed in Mr. White's despatch to Sir Edward Grey, No. 244, of July 30.]
([2]) [Not reproduced. It was enclosed in Mr. White's despatch No. 240 of July 27. It refers to rumours of the disembarkation of men from the " Berlin," *cp. supra,* p. 393, No. 416.]
([3]) [For an examination of the movements of the German warships here mentioned, *v. infra,* pp. 846-7, *App.* VI.]

No. 436.

Sir A. Hardinge to Sir Edward Grey.

F.O. 30008/29348/11/28.
(No. 122.)   Africa.   Confidential.   *Brussels,* D. *July* 28, 1911.
Sir,   R. *July* 31, 1911.
M. Davignon alluded in conversation with me yesterday to the anxious international situation created by the German *coup* at Agadir and asked what was thought
of it in London.   I told him that I had had no opportunity of learning anything
on the subject beyond what had appeared in the papers, and enquired if His Excellency
had heard any particulars himself about the alleged German proposals with regard
to the French right of pre-emption over the Belgian Congo.   He said he had not,
but his own view was that any transfer or abandonment of such right by France
would require the assent of the Belgian Government.   The right has been given
by King Leopold in return for a consideration and was not a proper object of barter
between France and another Power without reference to Belgium.   It had moreover
no longer any *raison d'être,* as the prospect of the sale of the territory of the old
Independent State, which was intelligible so long as it was the property of a single
individual, had passed out of the region of practical politics now that it was
administered, as an integral part of her dominions, by a solvent and progressive
country such as Belgium.   I am inclined on this particular point to agree with
M. Davignon, and I do not know why M. Cambon imagines, as he appears to do
by a recent despatch published in the confidential print, that a sale by Belgium of
the Congo is likely in the near future.   She might have refused to take it over from
the late King, and perhaps would not have done so if a referendum of the electors
could have been taken on the question two or three years ago, but having once
annexed and paid for it, she will, I think, stick to it, even at the cost of heavy
financial sacrifices, unless of course, she is ruined, or her international status
modified, as the result of an European war.
M. Davignon added that the Belgian Ministers at the great European capitals
were very guarded as to the probable result of the Franco-German negotiations, and
was evidently himself by no means free from anxiety on the subject.   The King also
adverted to it in conversation with me at the evening party given yesterday at the
Palace in honour of the Queen of Holland.

I have, &c.
ARTHUR H. HARDINGE.

No. 437.

Sir F. Bertie to Sir Edward Grey.

Paris, July 29, 1911.
F.O. 29890/25883/11/28.   D. 1·5.
Tel.   (No. 111.)   Confidential.   R. 2·30.
Urgent.   Morocco.
French M[inister for] F[oreign] A[ffairs] begs for definite views of H[is]
M[ajesty's] G[overnment] in regard to cession of French islands to Germany may
be communicated to him at once as Franco-German negotiations are approaching
a crisis and the French Ambassador who had an unsatisfactory interview with German
M[inister for] F[oreign] A[ffairs] yesterday is to see him again on the 31st of July.

MINUTES.

I understand that the Admiralty consider that no objection exist[s] to the cession of these
islands (presuming them to be French) to Germany, from the point of view of our naval interests.
Yet some time ago the Admiralty were keen to acquire one of those very islands for this country.
Both those views can hardly be correct.

There is a further point : At the Imperial Conference Sir E. Grey gave a very definite pledge that on questions of foreign policy in which the Dominions were interested, they would in future be consulted before H[is] M[ajesty's] G[overnment] were committed definitely. It is hardly possible to ignore the fact that the New Zealand and Australian governments have in the past shown themselves exceedingly jealous as to any arrangements concerning the Pacific groups of islands. Perhaps the Admiralty's wish to obtain the one island above referred to, was based on considerations affecting the naval forces of the Dominions? In any case we must realize that an unfavourable view *may* be taken in the Dominions if it becomes known that H[is] M[ajesty's] G[overnment] gave a formal consent to France ceding an island to Germany, which France refused to cede to us,—quite apart from the position of the other islands.

It seems to me that we must either consult the Dominions, or ask the French not to consult us but act on their own responsibility, in which latter case, a private assurance might perhaps be given to the effect that H[is] M[ajesty's] G[overnment] will recognize the " fait accompli."

E. A. C.
July 29th.
A. N.
E. G.

No. 438.

Sir E. Goschen to Sir Edward Grey.

Berlin, July 29, 1911.

F.O. 29899/25883/11/28.
Tel. (No. 54.)

D. 1·49.
R. 3·10.

Confidential. Morocco.

Yesterday's conversation between my French colleague and Secretary of State for Foreign Affairs([1]) very unsatisfactory.

M. Cambon laid before Secretary of State terms which France was prepared to discuss. Latter used same language as he had held to me and Count Metternich to you([2]) and said that dignity of Imperial Gov[ernmen]t did not allow him in face of threats from English and French press to abate his demands. My colleague said that was not negotiation irrespective of imposition of conditions,([3]) and he presumed it meant that the conversations should drop. Was this so? The answer was " We shall see." Secretary of State was then asked what position he proposed to take up and answered that he took his stand on the Act of Algeciras. My colleague asked how about 1909 agreement and the reply was that the Imperial Gov[ernmen]t now regarded that as non-existant [*sic*]. Finally Secretary of State said that his own opinion was that German demands should be upheld in their entirety, but that he would see the Emperor today and give decision of Imperial Gov[ernmen]t on Monday.

Private. My French colleague has sent full account of conversation to his brother by our bag to-day, and it will doubtless be communicated to you at once. He prefers that it should not be known at Paris that he has communicated it to me.

([1]) [Apparently that given, *infra*, pp. 421–2, No. 440.]
([2]) [*v. supra*, pp. 397–9, No. 419.]
([3]) [Sir A. Nicolson has here written in the margin : " I do not know what this means. A. N." The words " irrespective of " were corrected before circulation to " but ".]

No. 439.

Sir F. Cartwright to Sir Edward Grey.

F.O. 29905/25641/11/28.
Tel. (No. 83.) Very Confidential.
  Morocco.

Vienna, July 29, 1911.
D. 2 P.M.
R. 4·50 P.M.

    . I learn in strict confidence from the editor of the organ of the Ministry for Foreign Affairs that he saw German Ambassador a few days ago, who told him that if Great Britain and France sent ships to Agadir German Government had decided to answer such action by mobilising two army corps in Alsace-Lorraine. Editor enquired whether he was authorised to hint at this decision of the German Government in his newspaper. German Ambassador begged him not to do so, as the German Government had decided to take no action during course of present conversations between France and Germany.

    I beg to recall declaration made by German Ambassador to the same person reported in my telegram No. 43 (   ).([1])

(1) [*v. supra*, p. 237, No. 265.]

No. 440.

Sir F. Bertie to Sir Edward Grey.

F.O. 29973/25883/11/28.
Tel. (No. 110.) Urgent. Confidential.

Paris, July 29, 1911.
D. 6·15 P.M.
R. 9·15 P.M.

    Minister for Foreign Affairs sent for me this morning to give me an account of interview of yesterday between the French Ambassador at Berlin and German Minister for Foreign Affairs.([1]) Latter found the three combined offers of territory in the French Congo (see map which I communicated to you) quite insufficient. He again complained of communication to the press in France, but was constrained to admit that indiscretion regarding suggested exchange of Togoland for French territory must have come from German sources, though not communicated from official quarters. He found fault with Chancellor of the Exchequer's Mansion House speech, and said that French Government did not seem disposed to come to an arrangement with the German Government.

    French Ambassador at Berlin reminded German Minister for Foreign Affairs that Germany had by the 1909 agreement declared that she had only economic interests in Morocco and recognised the special political interests of France, and had said that she would not put obstacles ("entraver") in their way. French Government, nevertheless, were offering considerable cessions of French territory for a fresh and more definite renunciation by Germany of political interests in Morocco. French Ministry would be severely criticised at home for what they had offered, and public opinion and the French Parliament would certainly not consent to cessions suggested by German Government. Could German Minister for Foreign Affairs make other suggestions? He replied that there was public opinion in Germany as well as in France. Agreement of 1909 was dependent in its terms on the Algeciras Act, which had been infringed and in some respects entirely disregarded by the French Government, so that Germany could not consider her hands bound by agreements which had not been observed by France. French Government should have come to an understanding with the German Government before the expedition to Fez. French Ambassador at Berlin suggested that interpretation of the Algeciras Act was a matter which concerned all the signatories, and not only Germany and France.

(1) [*cp. Mermeix*, pp. 123–9. The Editors of *G.P.* XXIX, p. 304, *note*, state that there is nothing in their archives about this important interview. It is given in *Livre Jaune: Affaires du Maroc*, VI, pp. 432–3.]

German Minister for Foreign Affairs said that German Government were quite able to judge for themselves whether the Algeciras Act had been properly observed or not; that personally he had no suggestions to make other than those put forward. The pourparlers, which ought to have been kept secret, having become subject of discussion of the press in France and England in a manner still (group undecypherable), he did not consider it to be consistent with her dignity to abate her requirements, but he would consult German Chancellor and the Emperor on the subject of further discussions, and he would see French Ambassador on Monday next. 31st July.

French Minister for Foreign Affairs was in a very agitated state. He expressed himself as most anxious to come to terms with the Germans, and for that purpose he would be ready to make great sacrifices, but there were limits beyond which neither he nor any French Minister for Foreign Affairs can go. No Ministry would survive a consent by it to the cession of French Congo demanded by Germany, nor, he is convinced by enquiries he has made in experienced quarters, would Chambers sanction cession of Libreville, and he is not prepared to make to Germany, in return for a free hand to France in Morocco, more than the three combined alternatives depicted on map which he communicated to me and which I left with you; but if Togoland, in addition to Bec du Canard in the North Cameroons be ceded to France as well as a free hand in Morocco, French Government will make the following additions to their concessions to Germany (see map communicated to you), namely, the territory comprised within a line from Fort Archambaut between 8th and 10th north parallel along River Bamingui to the conventional line marked in purple between 6th and 8th north parallel, and following that conventional line to the junction of red and green on the map, and, in last extremity of negotiation, the further cession of territory which would be added to the German Cameroons by a straight line drawn from Ekododo near to and north of Libreville to Ouesso. This would give to Germany a port near Libreville. These cessions are the utmost that France can make, with perhaps the addition of an island or two, as to which he is anxiously awaiting your views, as the French Government could not think of making any offer in regard to them without the concurrence of His Majesty's Government. I have telegraphed to you separately on this subject. If the German Government reject these offers and insist on their demands for French Congo, French Minister for Foreign Affairs will discontinue conversations with German Government.

French Minister for Foreign Affairs, after giving this account of conversation, said that it seemed impossible to satisfy Germans. They appeared, or at all events German Minister for Foreign Affairs seemed, to desire humiliation of France, but the French Government cannot accept such a position, and it will be necessary to consider what should be done if the conversations cease. I am to see him this evening, and I will telegraph again after my interview.

MINUTES.

Anything that we can do to make the French keep a cool head, will be useful. I do not think that Herr von Kiderlen's attitude of insistence on his original demands need be treated as a new and unexpected factor in the situation. He was not likely to offer concessions before he need, certainly not before he has seen the Emperor.

Herr von Kiderlen's repudiation of the 1909 agreement is nothing more or less than a piece of bad faith.

E. A. C.
July 31.

The only possible excuse for any demand by Germany is that the Algeciras Act has been infringed and that the 1909 Agreement being dependent on that Act falls to the ground.

W. L.

It is quite arguable that the French advance to relieve Fez at the request of the Sultan does not constitute a breach of the Algeciras Act. I don't know to which article of that Act it w[oul]d run counter.

A. N.
E. G.

No. 441.

Sir F. Bertie to Sir Edward Grey.

F.O. 29900/25883/11/28.
Tel. (No. 112.) Confidential. R.

Paris, July 29, 1911.
D. 9 P.M.
R. 11·15 P.M.

My telegram No. 110 of to-day.(¹)

French Minister for Foreign Affairs, in discussing situation which might arise if conversations between German Minister for Foreign Affairs and French Ambassador were broken off, asked whether, if Germans increased their naval force at Agadir or landed men, His Majesty's Government would be prepared to join with French Government, and possibly with Spanish Government, in sending ships to Agadir to do just whatever the Germans might do, and whether, if German Government made a demand on French Government to withdraw militarily from Morocco, you would propose a conference of the Powers signatories of the Algeciras Act to consider question of its interpretation and application.

I said that you would certainly be prepared to call a conference whenever French Government had finally resolved that they could not make any further concessions to Germany with a view to obtaining a free hand in Morocco, but that to send French and British ships to Agadir would constitute a proceeding from which it might be difficult to withdraw, and might be treated as a provocation by Germany, and it therefore would require consideration if Germany rejected a proposal for a conference. I further said that personally I thought that if French Government had determined not to make further concessions to Germany than those he had indicated to me this morning it would be best that conversations should be broken off by German Minister for Foreign Affairs rather than by French Ambassador, or, if former rejected final offers but did not break off conversations, that French Ambassador should say that he must refer to Paris for further instructions. This might give time for French Government to inform His Majesty's Government of the rejection of the final French offers and for you to propose to German Government a conference before presentation of any ultimatum by German Government, from which it might be difficult for them to recede. If Germany refused to join conference she would place herself in the wrong in the public opinion of Europe, which would be an advantage to France.

French Minister for Foreign Affairs said that procedure which I had suggested might be advantageous. He then observed that having regard to view expressed by German Minister for Foreign Affairs and the exponents of German opinion on the subject of the interpretation of the agreement of 1909 and of Algeciras Act, any fresh undertakings given by Germany could not be taken as very reliable, and he had been warned by senators and deputies that France might be duped if she came to an arrangement with Germany and made cessions of French territory for a free hand in Morocco. German Government, in two or three years' time, as in case of 1909 agreement, might declare that the fresh agreement was not applicable in new circumstances and might make further claims for compensation.

Minister for Foreign Affairs says that he is by no means pessimistic, and that he hopes for successful issue to negotiations, but he wishes to be prepared for surprises and to concert with His Majesty's Government as to what should be done. I expressed to Minister for Foreign Affairs the opinion that danger lies, in any case, in German Minister for Foreign Affairs' personal position being involved. His failure to bring off his first great *coup* might bring about his dismissal, and he might therefore do his utmost by misrepresentations to persuade Emperor to insist on extreme German demands.

(¹) [v. immediately preceding document.]

No. 442.

Sir F. Bertie to Sir Edward Grey.

F.O. 29901/25883/11/28.

Tel. (No. 113.) Confidential.

Paris, *July* 29, 1911.
D. 8·50 P.M.
R. 10·30 P.M.

Your private letter of (? 28th July).(¹)

In the course of conversation with French Minister for Foreign Affairs reported in my telegram No. 112(²) of this evening, I suggested to him that if Germany consents to a conference it might be possible for France before it met to come to terms with Germany which would give her all that she could require in Morocco and have agreement so far as it concerned that country confirmed by Powers parties to Algeciras Act.

Germany might not [*sic*] be more reasonable than she now is when she found the majority of them to be against her.

I added that it would be for France to come to an agreement with Spain.

(¹) [*v. supra*, pp. 416–7, No. 434.]
(²) [*v.* immediately preceding document.]

No. 443.

Sir Edward Grey to Sir F. Bertie.

F.O. 29890/25883/11/28.

Tel. (No. 187.) R.

Foreign Office, *July* 30, 1911.

Your tel[egram] No. 111. Urgent.(¹)

Following communic[ate]d to M. Cambon last night.

I recognize right of French Gov[ernmen]t to make what proposals they please respecting these islands. Having consulted naval authority I find there is no *primâ facie* objection on strategic grounds to cession of any of these islands; without further time for consultation I cannot say more. But in view of urgent state of negotiations between France and Germany, I cannot ask for further delay. And if in order to secure favourable issue of negotiations with Germany French Gov[ernmen]t propose at once cession of any of these islands to Germany I shall regard French Gov[ernmen]t as having acted with perfect loyalty to the *Entente* in having consulted us.

(¹) [*v. supra*, p. 419, No. 437.]

No. 444.

Sir Edward Grey to Sir F. Bertie.

F.O. 29900/25883/11/28.

Tel. (No. 188.)

Foreign Office, *July* 31, 1911.
D. 8·40 P.M.

Your telegram No. 112.(¹) I approve your language. It is very desirable that the French should secure an agreement with Germany as the result of a Conference failing such agreement, may be simply to restore *status quo* of Algeciras Act which now satisfies nobody. On the other hand a conference called to confirm an agreement between France and Germany would probably cancel Algeciras Act and recognize

(¹) [*v. supra*, p. 423, No. 441.]

a free hand to France in Morocco permanently. This would secure France against apprehensions expressed by M[inister for] F[oreign] A[ffairs] in last paragraph but one, of your telegram and would justify substantial concessions elsewhere on the part of France. But if conversations with Germany break down we shall be ready to propose a Conference. It is very desirable however that it should be Germany and not France that breaks them off.

No. 445.

Sir R. Rodd to Sir Edward Grey.

F.O. 30690/13911/11/28.
(No. 116.) Confidential.   Rome, D. July 31, 1911.
Sir,   R. August 4, 1911.

I have the honour to report that I saw the Minister for Foreign Affairs, for the first time for some weeks, this afternoon as he was passing through Rome on his way from the baths to the mountains, and I took the opportunity to ask him what was actually the position of Italy in relation to the Morocco question. I knew, I said, that by an arrangement with France Italy was pledged not to oppose any action of the former in Morocco, as France was pledged not to oppose any political action of Italy in Tripoli. What however was her position as regards Germany, if an actual partition of Morocco should be proposed?

The Marquis di San Giuliano replied that Italy's membership of the Triple Alliance naturally connoted obligations of benevolence to her ally, but there was nothing in the alliance which compelled her to disinterest herself in Morocco in favour of Germany, or to renounce her right to be consulted as a signatory of the Treaty of Algeciras. As regards France such an obligation existed as I had referred to, and as far as Morocco itself was concerned Italy would have no right to question French annexations of Moroccan territory. She would however have every right to consider how far her interests and the balance of power in the Mediterranean would be affected by such an annexation and how far she might not be obliged to contemplate redressing the balance by some definite step in Tripoli. He did not know how the negotiations were going on and what the probabilities were of a solution which would end in the handing over of a large portion of Morocco to France, and the attitude of Italy could only be guided by circumstances as they arose.

The reference to Tripoli in this portion of our conversation should, I have the honour to submit, be read in connection with the observations of His Excellency reported in my immediately following despatch.([1])

                                                           I have, &c.
                                                           RENNELL RODD.

([1]) [This despatch will be reproduced in a later volume.]

No. 446.

Sir Edward Grey to Sir F. Bertie.

F.O. 30324/25883/11/28.
(No. 321.)
Sir,   Foreign Office, July 31, 1911.

M. Cambon came to see me this morning, and gave me the same information as was contained in your telegram No. 110 of the 29th([1]) instant. He was not sanguine as to the issue of the negotiations.

([1]) [v. supra, pp. 421–2, No. 440.]

I said that there was to be a Cabinet this afternoon, and to-morrow I should be able to let him know whether, in the event of the Franco-German negotiations breaking down, we should propose to all the Powers of the Act of Algeciras a Conference to decide in what respects there had been departure from the Act of Algeciras and what a return to the *status quo* required and whether the Algeciras Act should be altered.

⌈I am, &c.⌉
E. G⌈REY⌋.

No. 447.

Sir F. Bertie to Sir Edward Grey.

Private.(¹)
My dear Grey,   *Paris, July* 31, 1911.

The Prime Minister has just been to see me and I have only a few minutes to catch the bag.

He says that he is most anxious to come to terms with the Germans, but that he cannot cede Libreville or Brazzaville. No French Ministry could do so. His unofficial information from Berlin is that the German Government will not accept anything less than what they demanded, but he is inclined to think that they are bluffing and will do so to the last possible moment and that they may then say we will return to the Algeciras Act. In order to prepare for possible surprises he has sent orders this morning to the Generals and Admirals concerned in mobilisation to have everything ready. He says that the German Government have sufficient spies to learn these secret orders which may open their eyes to the fact that France cannot be pushed further. I suggested that perhaps the German Government might regard the orders as intended to be known to them and bluff.

He will ask the German Government to suggest other conditions than the French Congo for the consideration of the French Government if the German Government reject the latest French offers.

I impressed on M. Caillaux the great importance of it being Germany and not France that ceases the conversations

Yours sincerely,
FRANCIS BERTIE.

(¹) [Grey MSS., Vol. 13.]

No. 448.

Sir E. Goschen to Sir Edward Grey.

Berlin, August 1, 1911.
F.O. 30374/25883/11/28.   D. 6·27 P.M.
Tel. (No. 55.)   R. 7 P.M.
Morocco.

Secretary of State, having returned from Swinemünde, asked my French colleague to-day what proposals he had to make. French Ambassador communicated to his Excellency what France could offer. Secretary of State said that the French proposals formed an acceptable basis for discussion.

MINUTES.

This is what we expected. Germany is seeking the way for retreat.

E. A. C.
Aug. 2.
W. L.

I do not agree that this necessarily means that Germany is retreating—though it is quite possible she is changing her ground.(¹)

A. N.
E. G.

(¹) [Some general comments on the situation on August 1 are made in a private letter of that date from Sir A. Nicolson to Sir G. Buchanan, quoted in *Nicolson*, p. 345.]

No. 449.

Sir Edward Grey to Sir F. Bertie.

F.O. 30548/25883/11/28.
(No. 329.)

Sir,   *Foreign Office, August* 1, 1911.

In the course of some general conversation with M. [Paul] Cambon to-day I observed that, though it might not be helpful in the difficulties of the moment, I was sure that in future the German desire for expansion in Africa could be met if the Portuguese Colonies or the Belgian Congo were offered for sale.

M. Cambon said he understood that we had a Treaty with Germany as to the Portuguese Colonies.

I replied that there was a Secret Treaty,(¹) and that we should therefore have no trouble with Germany as to those Colonies. With regard to the Belgian Congo there was the French right of pre-emption to be considered; but I did not suppose that France would wish to purchase the whole of that State. We did not desire further expansion for ourselves in Africa, though if they were for sale we should like to purchase some comparatively small pieces of territory adjoining British possessions; we should not therefore stand in the way of German expansion. Unfortunately, these Colonies in Africa could not be useful at present, as they were not ours to give away.

I also took this opportunity to refer to the apprehension expressed by M. de Selves that any arrangement come to with Germany by France now might later on be put aside by Germany, as the latter had already done in the case of the Franco-German Agreement of 1909 as to Morocco :(²) so that an arrangement with Germany would be only temporary as regards Morocco, though the concessions which France might make elsewhere to secure the arrangement would be permanent. I pointed out to M. Cambon that this apprehension would be removed if the bargain between France and Germany was confirmed by a Conference which put an end to the Act of Algeciras. It was somewhat cynical on the part of Germany to offer to sell the Act of Algeciras to France behind the backs of the other Powers : and this was in effect what Herr von Kiderlen was doing when he proposed to give France, for a consideration, a free hand in Morocco, and said that none of the other Powers would be likely to raise objections afterwards. It would therefore be not only politic, but also right, that a bargain between France and Germany should be confirmed by a Conference of the Signatory Powers of the Act of Algeciras, at which France should be freed from the provisions of that Act. France would then have a much better case to put before her Chamber, and Germany would not be able to reopen the question later on.

M. Cambon said that he had already put this view before his Government, after my previous conversation with him.

[I am, &c.]
E. G[REY].

(¹) [v. *Gooch & Temperley*, Vol. I, pp. 71–5.]
(²) [v. *supra*, p. 139, No. 155, *encl.* 2, and *infra*, p. 830, *App.* IV.]

No. 450.

Sir Edward Grey to Sir F. Bertie.

F.O. 30549/25883/11/28.
(No. 330.)
Sir, *Foreign Office, August* 1, 1911.

M. [Paul] Cambon told me to-day that M. de Selves concurred in the suggestion which I had made as to the grounds on which a Conference might be suggested if the conversations between France and Germany broke down.

I told M. Cambon that the Government had considered the matter, and that if the conversations did break down we should be prepared to propose a Conference of the Powers that were parties to the Act of Algeciras, "to decide in what respects there has been a departure from the Act of Algeciras, and what the situation requires." We thought that some general words of this kind would be best, at any rate in the first instance. But if the time came to propose a Conference, I would consult with the Prime Minister as to the actual wording.

[I am, &c.]
E. G[REY].

No. 451.

Sir F. Bertie to Sir Edward Grey.

F.O. 30516/25883/11/28.
Tel. (No. 114.) *Paris,* D. *August* 2, 1911.
(by Post.) R. *August* 3, 1911.

At the interview yesterday between the French Ambassador at Berlin and the German Minister for Foreign Affairs latter began by stating that the Emperor was greatly displeased at the insinuations in the French newspapers that he and his Ministers were not in accord. The Ambassador replied that nobody could regret the insinuations more than M. de Selves.

M. de Kiderlen Waechter then asked whether the French Government had any fresh proposals to make. M. Jules Cambon said that the French Government could not cede the French Congo from the Sangha to the sea, but, in return for a free hand in Morocco, the Bec du Canard and access to the river Benue, France would give some islands in Oceania and Polynesia in addition to the rectifications of frontier already offered. M. de Kiderlen Waechter said that in view of the offer of islands he would not insist on the cession of the French Congo from the Sangha to the sea, but he spoke of a cession to Germany of a piece of coast north of Libreville and he stated that Germany must insist on having a band of territory bringing her to the river Congo. The Ambassador said that he would refer M. de Kiderlen's proposals to the French Government and with regard to Morocco and the free hand which France was to have and with reference to the word "Protectorat" which had been mentioned by M. de Kiderlen Waechter he enquired how the German Government proposed that the consent of the Powers parties to the Algeciras Act should be obtained. The Minister said that he thought that it would be difficult to use the word "Protectorat" in any formal document but that he would guarantee the consent of the Powers to France having the free hand which she desired and the French Government should draft the necessary document. M. de Selves having told me that there appeared to be no longer any question of the cession of Togoland to France I pointed out to him that M. de Kiderlen Waechter appeared to have got wind of the readiness of the French Government in the last extremity to make the cession of territory abutting on the coast near Libreville in return for Togoland. He said that he had no idea how the German Government came to know of it, and he supposed that M. de Kiderlen's intention is to surround by German territory Spanish Guinea and obtain its cession to Germany.

M. de Selves is more hopeful of an understanding but he cannot say what the view of the French Government will be of the requirement of the German Government for a band of territory to the river Congo.([1]) No information has been given as to its locality or extent.

([1]) [*cp. G.P.* XXIX, pp. 308–9, and *notes.*]

No. 452.

Sir F. Bertie to Sir Edward Grey.

F.O. 30540/30540/11/28.

(No. 356.)　　　　　　　　　　　　　　　　　　　*Paris,* D. *August* 2, 1911.

Sir,　　　　　　　　　　　　　　　　　　　　　R. *August* 3, 1911.

I have the honour to transmit to you herewith copy of Monsieur de Selves' reply to the communication which I made to His Excellency in accordance with the instructions contained in your Telegram No. 178 of the 17th ultimo([1]) with regard to the principles of commercial equality and to mining concessions in Morocco.

I shall be glad to learn what reply I am to make to Monsieur de Selves.

I have, &c.

FRANCIS BERTIE.

Enclosure in No. 452.

M. de Selves to Sir F. Bertie.

En réponse à la note de l'ambassade britannique en date du 19 de ce mois, le ministre des affaires étrangères a l'honneur de faire connaître à Son Excellence Sir Francis Bertie que le Gouvernement de la République est résolu à maintenir, dans les négociations engagées avec le gouvernement allemand, le principe de l'égalité commerciale, pour toutes les parties de l'Empire marocain.

En ce qui concerne les mines, le gouvernement français considère toujours qu'il y aurait lieu d'appliquer l'organisation définie par le projet de règlement minier qu'ont préparé les délégués techniques des quatre Puissances principalement intéressées en cette matière. Il va faire de nouvelles démarches pour obtenir l'adhésion à ce texte du gouvernement des Pays-Bas, qui était seul à en demander la modification, et il serait tout disposé à s'entendre avec celui-ci pour faire lever les objections du Cabinet de la Haye par un amendement transactionnel. Il serait obligé au gouvernement anglais de lui faire connaître s'il adopte ce point de vue, et dans ce cas, s'il veut bien appuyer ces efforts auprès du gouvernement néerlandais.

Paris, le 31 *juillet* 1911.

([1]) [*v. supra,* p. 367, No. 387.]

No. 453.

Sir Edward Grey to Sir F. Bertie.

F.O. 30806/25883/11/28.
(No. 334.)
Sir,   *Foreign Office, August 2, 1911.*

M. [Paul] Cambon told me to-day that the French Ambassador in Berlin had had an interview with Herr von Kiderlen yesterday.(¹)

Herr von Kiderlen had asked what the Ambassador had to propose. The Ambassador had spoken of certain French islands, as regards which France might be prepared to concede something to Germany as an element in the bargain. In reply to the statement of the French Ambassador that, at most, France could give only a very thin strip of the French Congo, reaching to the sea, Herr von Kiderlen had said that territorial access to the river Congo was essential for Germany. In return for this, Germany would concede to France access on the French Congo to the River Benoue, [and] a free hand in Morocco. It might be difficult to mention the word "protectorate" in a document which was to receive the assent of the other Powers who were parties to the Act of Algeciras, but that was virtually what was implied, as regards Morocco and the description of it was a question of drafting.

The matter had been referred to M. de Selves, and apparently the position now was this : Germany would admit France to access to the Benue river, while France conceded to Germany a strip of territory from the Kamerouns to the river Congo, but the strip could in no circumstances be west of the River Sanga. It looked as if a proposal of this sort might become an agreed basis of negotiation.

M. Cambon observed that, in this event, France would wish to have the same access up the Niger and Benue to the east as she now had up the Niger to the west through Nigeria.

I said that I assumed this meant free navigation of the river.

I then observed that, if what was virtually a French protectorate was to be established in Morocco, provision would have to be made for the exceptional position of Tangier, and for economic rights.

M. Cambon said that the arrangement that he contemplated was one in which the position of the Sultan in Morocco would remain, but France would have the right of police and of financial control. Economic liberty and equal rights of commerce would be preserved. The position of Spain in her sphere would be similar to that of France in hers, and a special arrangement would be made for the exceptional position of Tangier.

Herr von Kiderlen had laid great stress upon keeping any of these proposals from public knowledge at present.

[I am, &c.]
E. G[REY].

MINUTE BY KING GEORGE.

App[rove]d.
G.R.I.

(¹) [*cp. G.P.* XXIX, pp. 308–9; also *Livre Jaune : Affaires du Maroc,* VI, p. 437; and *Caillaux,* pp 171–4. M. Caillaux gives on pp. 162–71 an account of previous private negotiations from July 25 onwards in which Herr von Lancken was concerned. For later reference to M. Caillaux, *v. G.P.* XXIX, pp. 310–1, 314–5, and *notes; v.* generally, *Mermeix,* pp. 190–308.]

No. 454.

Sir F. Bertie to Sir Edward Grey.

F.O. 30679/25883/11/28.
(No. 357.) Secret.
Sir :—

Paris, D. *August* 3, 1911.
R. *August* 4, 1911.

From the interview which I had with the Minister for Foreign Affairs yesterday and of which I gave an account in my telegraphic message No. 114 of that day([1]) I derived the impression that he personally would be disposed to consent to M. de Kiderlen Waechter's demand that Germany should have territorial connection with the River Congo through the French Congo provided that the breadth of the connecting-band be moderate and its locality be not greatly injurious to French interests and that in other respects and particularly in regard to a French Protectorate or a free hand in Morocco the terms of the German Government be acceptable to France and be properly secured.([2]) I think however that he foresees and dreads opposition from the French Colonial Department and Party to the concessions required by M. de Kiderlen Waechter and that he is not confident of the consent to them of the majority of his colleagues. Another difficulty which will arise supposing that the German and French Governments come to terms will be how the acquiescence of the other Powers parties to the Algeciras Act is to be obtained either in a Conference or without one. Germany may be able to answer for Austria-Hungary and perhaps Sweden and possibly but not probably Italy. France can make sure of Russian and British consent, but who is to answer for the United States of America, Belgium, Holland and Portugal. Will they require compensations on the principle and example instituted by Germany and if so who is to provide them. There remains the case of Spain. If Germany, as suspected by M. de Sélves, is to acquire Spanish Guinea as the price of the recognition as far as she is concerned of Spanish pretensions in Morocco, the German Government will have succeeded in permanently estranging Spain and France, an estrangement which probably will not be confined to the question of Morocco.

Having derived these impressions as to the feelings and apprehensions of the Minister for Foreign Affairs, partly inspired I have no doubt by representations made to him by the permanent staff of his Department, I paid a visit this morning to the President of the Council in order to ascertain his views on the state of the negotiations. M. Caillaux expressed himself as satisfied with their progress. There had he said been a change in the attitude of M. de Kiderlen Waechter. He no longer demanded the cession of the French Congo down to the sea. Provided that France obtained a practical protectorate or control over the administration of Morocco, a free hand under whatever form it might be given, and that France were not required to cede Libreville or Brazzaville he (M. Caillaux) would not reject the demand that Germany should have a band of territory to bring her to the Congo River. With regard to the acquiescence of the Parties to the Algeciras Act to a French Protectorate or control over Morocco it would be for Germany to obtain their acquiescence. Germany might perhaps acquire Spanish Guinea in return for German recognition of the Spanish occupations made in Morocco, but M. Caillaux felt confident, he informed me, of being able to come to an arrangement with Spain. I asked His Excellency whether he expected opposition from the Colonial Party to the concessions required by Germany in return for a recognition by her of French control over Morocco. He made light of any such opposition saying that there was such a desire in France to obtain the control that the sacrifices required would be readily made.

I have, &c.
FRANCIS BERTIE.

([1]) [*v. supra*, pp. 428–9, No. 451.]
([2]) [But see account of Herr von Schoen of the views of M. de Selves on August 2. *G.P.* XXIX, p. 309.]

No. 455.

Sir F. Bertie to Sir Edward Grey.

Private.([1])

My dear Grey,   *Paris, August 3, 1911.*

After the conversation with the President of the Council on the subject of the Morocco negotiations which I have reported in my secret despatch of to-day he said that even if France come to terms with Germany in the question of Morocco which he fully expects, Germany is sure before long to raise other questions disturbing to peace. He is anxious to effect a general interchange of Colonial interests between France and England so as to remove every cause of difference between the two countries. He foresees in the not distant future a conflict in which France and England and Russia will be fighting against Germany and any allies that she may have in addition to Austria. He says that the French officers who have lately been at Aldershot have brought back a very high opinion of the British soldier Infantry and Cavalry. He thinks that the French Artillery is superior to the English Artillery. There are however not British soldiers enough. If England were at war in Europe would Japanese troops be sent to assist? He talked for some time to this effect. I did not encourage him in regard to a war, but I said that as concerned a colonial arrangement the French Government had in previous negotiations not behaved well in the matter of the Arms Traffic in the Persian Gulf. They would not meet our views so the Conference on that question failed with the result that there was a trade in arms carried on by a French firm and also by Germans and English arms also reached the Afghans who came to the coast for purchases. M. Caillaux evidently knew little about the matter, but he said: "if the question is one in which Muscat is concerned I am quite ready to come to an arrangement." He talked rather wildly but his wild talk may be useful in negotiations with the Quai d'Orsay and the French Colonial Department of which latter Office he has no high opinion.

Yours sincerely,

FRANCIS BERTIE.

([1]) [Grey MSS., Vol. 13.]

No. 456.

Sir E. Goschen to Sir Edward Grey.

                                                        Berlin, August 4, 1911.

F.O. 30827/25883/11/28.   D. 7·8 P.M.

Tel. (No. 57.) *En clair.*   R. 7·29 P.M.

Following official communiqué published this afternoon :—

"There has been a rapprochement in the conversations between French Ambassador and Herr von Kiderlen on matters of principle. The elaboration of the details requires, however, careful study, on which the competent authorities are now engaged. The result is then to be submitted by the Chancellor to the Emperor."

No. 457.

Sir E. Goschen to Sir Edward Grey.

F.O. 31044/25883/11/28.

(No. 213.)   *Berlin, D. August 4, 1911.*

Sir,   R. *August 8, 1911.*

There was a marked change in Herr von Kiderlen's manner and tone after his return from Swinemuende. As you are aware, before his visit to the Emperor His Excellency told Monsieur [Jules] Cambon that the dignity of the German people would not allow him to bate one jot of his demands. On his return he adopted quite a different tone. Monsieur Cambon asked him how he had found the Emperor. His Excellency replied that His Majesty was very annoyed and particularly so at the way in which the French Press had dragged him into the Morocco discussions. Monsieur Cambon at once assured him that both Monsieur de Selves, the French Government and he personally, all regretted extremely that the French Press had made such unjustifiable references to His Majesty. Herr von Kiderlen said that he was sure that the Emperor would be very pleased to hear that the French Government dissociated themselves from the unfortunate attitude of the French Press in this particular instance and at once asked whether Monsieur Cambon had any proposals to make on behalf of his Government. Thereupon Monsieur Cambon informed His Excellency of what France proposed to offer, adding that further than those offers the French Government would be unable to go. They constituted in fact the maximum of the sacrifices that France was ready to make. You have probably been informed by the French Government of the extent and scope of these offers so I will not repeat them here : in any case, Herr von Kiderlen said that they appeared to him to provide an acceptable basis of discussion.

In giving me this information Monsieur Cambon said that though he probably still had a hard time before him, he hoped that the worst was now over.

Herr von Kiderlen also told me that things were going better, adding that they need never have gone otherwise than well, if he had not been put into such a difficult position by the French and English Press. I ventured to state that the German Press had not contributed very much to the tranquillity necessary for difficult negotiations. He admitted this but said that it had remained fairly quiet until goaded into strong language by the attitude of its foreign confrères. "Anyhow" he added, "I am tired of writing *démentis* every morning and I have given strict orders to the Press Bureau to give nothing to the Press and to take no notice of what it says."

The German Press is therefore supposed now to be left to its own devices and as it receives no information from head-quarters it contents itself chiefly, especially that part of it which represents Pan-German opinions, with inditing violent articles against France and England and with pointing out the utter mendacity of the French Press as regards the information it supplies with regard to the negotiations.

The statement in the French Press that the Imperial Government is willing to cede Togoland is quoted as an instance of its mendacious inventions!

The "Hamburger Nachrichten," which has on the whole set its face against the violent language of its contemporaries says that it is entirely out of the question that Togoland should be made the subject of barter : and the "Koelnische Zeitung," while noting with satisfaction a tendency on the part of the French Government to wring the neck of the numerous *canards* which are now on the wing in France, says, with regard to the cession of Togoland, that it would be well if the French Press would exercise a little self-control and cease altogether from indulging in flights of fancy.

The "Frankfürter Zeitung," referring to the articles in the French Press in which hopes were expressed that the return of the Emperor from his northern cruise would bring about a change in the situation favourable to France, points out that these hopes have not been realised, and that what passed at Swinemuende made it on the contrary quite clear that all attempts, "direct or indirect" to intimidate Germany must be given up once for all. It adds that if the "Swinemuende days" have brought this truth home to France, then it is possible to regard those days as having brought about a change for the better. "For recent utterances in the French Press," it says, "show that it is slowly but surely dawning upon France that concessions must be made and that the sooner she comes to an understanding with Germany the better."

There appears to me to be no doubt that the secrecy which is being observed at all events here, with regard to the negotiations is tending to make public opinion rather nervous—and during the last few days all sorts of rumours have been rife as to what is going to happen. One of these rumours, for which, as far as I know, there is not the slightest foundation, is that Herr von Kiderlen, finding himself without the support he anticipated, intends to send in his resignation. Another is that the Chancellor has put off his journey to Gastein owing to the critical state of affairs. The truth of this rumour is, however, doubted by the "Tageblatt" which states that if the Chancellor has deferred his journey it is rather because the end of the negotiations is in sight and he wishes to be in Berlin to give the finishing touches.

The papers are beginning to discuss the idea of a conference and are doing all they know to point out to France how dire the results would be for her should one take place. One paper puts the matter thus: "Herr von Kiderlen should lose no time in placing before Monsieur Cambon the preliminary conditions of the new conference desired by France, viz., the definite return to the stipulations of the Act of Algeciras: the removal of all French and Spanish troops from the interior and the coast towns: the complete evacuation of the Shawia district: the exact geographical delimitation of the Morocco frontiers: the reduction of the numbers of French instructors and strict control of all matters connected with finance customs and public works. Herr von Kiderlen should make it clear that unless France agrees to these conditions beforehand there will be no conference." The paper adds that until this is clearly understood in Paris and London there will be no end to the campaign of bluff carried on by the Colonial wirepullers in both countries.

The epitome of public opinion in Germany would not be complete without a brief reference to the constant endeavours of the Pan-German newspapers to persuade France that Great Britain will confine her assistance to words and advice only and will in no eventuality give her military support. "England," they say, "never fights except for her own hand, and France would do well to remember this before she goes too far in her opposition to Germany's just requirements."

Professor Schiemann takes the soundest view, as he expresses the opinion that as long as the conversations continue the least said in the Press the better.

Since writing the above a communiqué, the contents of which I had the honour to telegraph to you this day,(1) has been published stating that there has been a rapprochement in the conversations between the Secretary of State for Foreign Affairs and Monsieur Cambon as far as questions of principle are concerned. It added that the working out of the details is now in the hands of the competent Imperial Authorities who are giving the matter their closest attention and that the result of their deliberations will be communicated by the Chancellor to the Emperor.

Monsieur Cambon appeared to me to think this communication was rather premature, but Herr von Kiderlen expressed so much anxiety to have it published that Monsieur Cambon waived his objection. Herr von Kiderlen said that the German newspapers were getting so impatient and spreading such fantastical, not to say mischievous, rumours, that he thought it best to let them know that the conversations were following a normal and not unfriendly course.

I have, &c.
W. E. GOSCHEN.

(1) [v. immediately preceding document.]

No. 458.

Sir A. Nicolson to Sir Edward Grey.

F.O. 30962/25883/11/28.
My dear Grey,

53, *Cadogan Gardens, S.W.,*
August 4, 1911.

M. Cambon came to my house this afternoon having received a telegram from M. de Selves, who makes the following enquiry.

Germany desires a territorial access to the Congo—there are various routes by which this access can be provided. Among others one which would lead through

Ubangi-Sharia, and which would bring Germany to the confines of the Bahral Ghazul, in other words to our southern Soudan. M. de Selves would like to know as soon as possible whether we would have any objection to this route—for if so he would eliminate it from consideration.

Perhaps you would kindly let Mallet have your reply tomorrow, as M. Daeschner will come to the F[oreign] O[ffice] to see him.

Yours sincerely,
A. NICOLSON.

Perhaps a telegram to Mallet would be the best.([1])

([1]) [v. immediately succeeding document.]

No. 459.

Sir Edward Grey to Mr. L. Mallet.([1])

Fallodon, August 5, 1911.
D. 10·45 A.M.
R. 1·48 P.M.

F.O. 30962/25883/11/28.
Tel.

I don't think we need or can object to route described in Nicholson's [*sic*: Nicolson's] letter of yesterday.([2])

([1]) [The substance of this telegram was communicated to M. de Fleuriau by Mr. Mallet on August 5.

Mr. L. Mallet to M. de Fleuriau.

F.O. 30962/25883/11/28.
Dear M. de Fleuriau,   *Foreign Office, August 5. 1911.*
I have just rec[eive]d a telegram from Sir E. Grey to the effect that he would not offer objection to this route in the proximity of the Eastern Sudan described by M. Cambon to Sir A. Nicolson in his interview with Sir A. Nicolson yesterday (4th).

Yours truly.
LOUIS MALLET.]

([2]) [v. immediately preceding document.]

No. 460.

Sir F. Bertie to Sir Edward Grey.

Paris, August 5, 1911.
D. 4·53 P.M.
R. 6·30 P.M.

F.O. 30962/25883/11/28.
Tel. (No. 115.) R.

Minister for Foreign Affairs gave me this morning following information :—

Minister for Foreign Affairs received on evening of 3rd August despatch from French Ambassador at Berlin dated 2nd August asking for instructions as to offers to be made to Germany.

M. de Selves replied yesterday that Ambassador was to negotiate with a view to restricting as much as possible the territory to be conceded to Germany, in lieu of previous rejected offers, within extreme limits of parallels 7 and 3 north of the Equator and following the conventional line (marked purple on map in your possession) as little to the east as possible. This would bring concession down south so as to include a port on the coast near Libreville. He might also negotiate in regard to some islands, but he was to refer home for further instructions as to those islands.

[19656]   2 F 2

French Ambassador at Berlin saw German Minister for Foreign Affairs yesterday. The latter said that Bec du Canard might be given to France but not Togoland. Germany did not want any islands except Comoro Islands, but wanted the French Congo territory from parallel 2 north-eastwards to Ubanghi, down that river to its junction with the Congo, and down that River to Alima, and up that river westward to River Ogowe, and thence to the sea at a point between Libreville and the Muni.

Minister for Foreign Affairs is determined not to concede these demands. He will not give anything below Sangha River except strip of territory referred to in my telegram No. 110, Confidential, of 29th July,(¹) namely, from Ekododo, north of Libreville, to Ouesso. He is not prepared to give up Comoro Islands.

In the course of conversation between French Ambassador at Berlin and German Minister for Foreign Affairs, the latter alluded to the possible disappearance of the Congo State, but only in a vague way and as an uncertain event. He, however, proposed to acquire by secret treaty with France the pre-emptive rights which she has by secret treaty with Spain over Spanish Guinea.

As Germans may demand an extension eastward of the territory which French Minister for Foreign Affairs is prepared to offer them between parallels 7 and 3, which would bring them into proximity in territories connected with Egyptian Soudan, he has instructed French Ambassador in London to consult you on the subject.

MINUTES.

The attached note communicated by M[onsieur] de Fleuriau yesterday(²) relates to the same phase of the negotiation. Even between these two versions it is difficult to understand the exact position. I have endeavoured to trace the French and German proposals with red and blue pencil respectively on the French map attached to paper 28951.(³) It will be seen that the German proposal, although it would leave the coast from Libreville to the south in the hands of France, would practically reduce the French Congo to a small enclave entirely cut off from the interior. It is intelligible that the French should refuse this. But it is not clear to what extent the original French proposals concerning the territories due east of the Cameroons still hold the field.

The correspondence, which I attach hereto, between M[onsieur] de Fleuriau and Mr. Mal[l]et(⁴) shows that some secret negotiation is going on of which the department is in absolute ignorance. In these circumstances it is quite useless to offer any opinion.

It seems a pity that Sir F. Bertie on his part offers no comment on the foreshadowed proposal to cede to Germany territory that would bring her on to our Sudan frontier. He is so fully cognizant of the complicated history of the partitioning of Africa in recent years, that his opinion on the effects of such an arrangement would have been particularly valuable. If it is not too late, I would suggest that he be asked for his observations on the point.

E. A. C.
Aug. 8.

Sir E. Crowe since this minute was written has seen the minute from Sir A. Nicolson,(⁵) and knows that the point was considered and an answer given to the French on Saturday.

W. L.

(¹) [v. supra, pp. 421–2, No. 440.]
(²) [v. infra, pp. 442–3, No. 466.]
(³) [Not reproduced.]
(⁴) [This refers to Mr. Mallet's letter of August 5, v. supra, p. 435, No. 459, note (¹), and the acknowledgment sent by M. de Fleuriau on the same day.]
(⁵) [v. supra, pp. 434–5, No. 458.]

No. 461.

Sir Edward Grey to Mr. L. Mallet.

F.O. 30962/25883/11/28.   Fallodon, Christon Bank,
My dear Mallet,   Northumberland, August 5, 1911.

I do not think it matters very much whether we have Germany or France as a neighbour in Africa. It is no doubt preferable to have the weaker power as a neighbour, but we cannot press this preference to the embarrassment of negotiations between France and Germany.

So I sent you a telegram([1]) on these lines today.

I shall be up Monday morning.

Yours sincerely,
E. GREY.

([1]) [v. *supra*, p. 435, No. 459.]

No. 462.

Mr. Palairet to Sir Edward Grey.

F.O. 31033/16083/11/28.

(No. 128.)

Sir,

Vienna, D. August 6, 1911.
R. *August 8, 1911.*

I have the honour to report that the negotiations now proceeding between Monsieur [Jules] Cambon and Herr von Kiderlen Waechter in regard to the Morocco question are followed with the closest interest by the Viennese Press. The reports, often conflicting, from Paris and Berlin regarding the progress of these negotiations are reproduced here with appropriate comments, varying in accordance with the optimistic or pessimistic tone of the latest news. Among the articles published on the subject there have been few of sufficient note to deserve more than a passing mention : but during the last few days three have appeared to which I venture to draw your attention as being of some interest.

The Christian Socialist "Reichspost," in an article of yesterday's date, takes England severely to task for her anti-German attitude and for her unreserved and violently expressed support of France. It warns England that Germany, though still calm, will not tolerate any dictation as to the terms acceptable to her. It assures Germany that Austria will "stand shoulder to shoulder" with her—an assurance which would carry more weight if it conveyed anything more than the "Reichspost's" own opinion.

The "Tageblatt," on the other hand, always more friendly to England, devotes a leading article to a hearty welcome of Mr. Haldane's speech on the desirability of good relations between England and Germany. This paper, unlike the "Reichspost," is able to appreciate with fairness the attitude of Great Britain in the Morocco question, and speaks with approval of her evident desire to see the Franco-German negotiations reach a successful conclusion, so long as her own interests are not endangered.

The most illuminating comment is, however, that made by the London correspondent of the "Wiener Allgemeine Zeitung," who telegraphed yesterday the following communication to that paper :—

"London, August 5th. In political circles here general satisfaction has been felt at the announcement made yesterday by the Bureau Wolff, as the conviction is now held that the danger of an international complication on account of the Morocco question is at an end.

"It is maintained here that German policy was not correctly informed in regard to England's attitude, and that this error was the cause of Germany's latest action in the Morocco question by sending the 'Panther' to Agadir.

"The Emperor William was, during his recent visit to London, the object of marked demonstrations of popularity, and on this occasion there reappeared the strong sympathy which is felt in England for the person of the German monarch. The Emperor was persuaded by his advisers that these demonstrations of the English people were not directed at the person of the Emperor alone, but also at German policy. The Emperor was confirmed in this view by the reports of the German Ambassador in London, Count Wolff-Metternich, who stated that there was an increasing pro-German current in Great Britain, and who gave it as his opinion that the moment was now opportune for an attempt by Germany to separate England from France. It cannot indeed be denied that a feeling more friendly to Germany was actually beginning to make itself felt in England. This current was, however, not so strong as Count Metternich imagined—as was shown by later events.

"Immediately after the despatch of the 'Panther' to Agadir a leading English statesman stated that in his view Germany's principal object in this action was to feel the pulse of England.

"The course of events shows, however, that German policy was insufficiently informed as to the feeling in England. The pro-German feeling of the English nation was not yet strong enough to separate England from France, which was very clearly shown, first by Mr. Asquith's declaration, and then still more clearly by Mr. Lloyd George's speech and the second declaration of the Premier. From that moment there could be no more doubt that England stood under all circumstances behind France.

"The most recent phase of the Morocco question is here attributed to the recognition by Germany of this fact. It is generally considered that the German Emperor desires to avoid as far as possible a conflict with England, and, after convincing himself that German policy had not been correctly informed as to England's attitude, has entered upon a path, in agreement with the Chancellor and with Herr von Kiderlen Waechter, which permits an agreement on the Morocco question to be regarded as almost certain."

This article should do much to enlighten Austrian readers as to the real facts of the question. It is, so far as I am aware, the first reference in any Austrian newspaper to a connection of the German Emperor's visit to England with Germany's subsequent action in Morocco.

I have, &c.
(For His Majesty's Ambassador).
MICHAEL PALAIRET.

No. 463.

Sir E. Goschen to Sir Edward Grey.

F.O. 31337/16083/11/28.
(No. 218.)   *Berlin, D. August* 6, 1911.
Sir,   R. *Augus*: 9, 1911.
Two days ago an article appeared in the "Post" entitled "Crisis and Retreat" which exceeded in recklessness of statement and Chauvinistic bombast all the bellicose articles to which that paper has recently treated its readers. I do not propose to trouble you with a full translation of this article, which was apparently written, without any accurate knowledge of the real position of affairs in the questions pending between France and Germany, nor of the intentions of the Imperial Government. As it has, however, formed the subject of a strong protest in the semi-official "Norddeutsche Allgemeine Zeitung," a few extracts from it will be sufficient to explain the stir it has made and the reasons for which an official protest was deemed necessary.

The immediate cause of the "Post's" outburst was the communiqué announcing that there was a *rapprochement* between Herr von Kiderlen Waechter and Monsieur [Jules] Cambon as regards the questions of principle which are involved in their negotiations.

The article opens with the following statement :—

" This communiqué has come upon us like a flash of lightning in a dark sky. Oh! would that they had been spared this moment, this moment of unspeakable shame, of deep national ignominy, far deeper than that of Olmütz ! ''

The writer then, after the usual references to Bismarck, says that he is convinced that Herr von Kiderlen, as an honourable man and one conscious of his responsibility before the nation as director of Imperial Foreign Affairs, will not subscribe to this national humiliation, and, rather than give way in a vital question affecting Germany's position as a world Power, will sacrifice his own person and send in his resignation.

" Herr von Kiderlen's resignation, as well of course as that of the Chancellor may therefore be counted upon with the greatest certainty, if not to-day or to-morrow, at all events at the close of the negotiations.''

The writer then draws a picture of the scene after Olmütz, and relates how the King and Prince William were prostrate with grief, how the Ministers went almost mad with despair and how Count Brandenburg actually died of a broken heart, " thus by his death he expiated his shame, which only death could expiate.''

Then comes the outrageous passage against which the " Norddeutsche Allgemeine Zeitung,'' and, be it said, most of the respectable papers, protest.

" And now? Has Prussia so changed? Is the old Prussian feeling dead? Have we become a nation of women—governed in the interests of a group of alien financiers? Are we dead to all feelings of national honour, have we lost all sense of political responsibility, or political foresight? Has Germany become a mere object of ridicule for foreign nations to laugh at? What has happened to the Hohenzollerns, who count among their ancestors a Great Elector, a Frederick William I, a Frederick the Great and an Emperor William I? Are we to regard our Emperor as the strongest support cf France, a support worth more than 50 French divisions? Are we to look upon him as the hope of France? We dare not and will not believe that such is the case. Neither will we believe that the French and English papers are right when they say, as they have been saying for the last week, ' Only wait till your Emperor returns from abroad, then the retreat will be sounded and Germany will yield.' Guillaume le Timide, le Valeureux Poltron! Brandenburg died of a broken heart. But we! We console ourselves for the present humiliation of the Fatherland with tea parties, dinners, suppers, travels, inspections and functions of every sort, and we earn thereby cheap praise from abroad—with contempt behind it.''

The protest of the Government organ against this outburst runs as follows :—

" The ' Post,' which in this case we do not recognize as the organ of the Free Conservatives, has published an article, in which, without any knowledge whatever of the present position of the Morocco negotiations, it indulges in flights of imagination and speaks of a moment of unspeakable shame, of the humiliation of Germany, of the retirement of the Chancellor and of the Secretary of State for Foreign Affairs and of a new Olmütz. We should have paid no attention to these figments of an overheated brain, if the ' Post' had not in the last part of its article had the presumption to drag in the name of the Emperor and accuse His Majesty, in the cowardly form of rhetorical questions, of political weakness and of favouring foreign nations at expense of German interests. In holding this language, the ' Post' utters, and makes its own, thoughts which we are only accustomed to find in abusive articles in the foreign Press. Its attempt to disseminate, under the mask of patriotism, such unworthy statements in the German Press deserves the sharpest rebuke and protest.''

To this the "Post" replied as follows: "We readily admit that the 'Norddeutsche Allgemeine Zeitung' is right in thinking that we did not write the article in question in our capacity as the organ of the Free Conservative party. But we can assure the 'Norddeutsche Allgemeine Zeitung,' in case it is not aware of the fact, that we know ourselves to be in complete accord with the great majority of patriotic Germans.

"The Government organ would be astonished if it knew whose sentiments we were expressing in our article, written, we may admit, under intense excitement in one of the gravest moments of our internal and external political life. We honour the men who as Servants of their Sovereign, cover Him with their person—we understand their attitude and would probably in their place not have done otherwise. We will therefore say nothing with regard to the uncivil language in which their protest is couched.''

The "Tageblatt," commenting on the above, says "Thus the 'Post' still clings to its determination to hold the Emperor responsible for the 'National humiliation' which, it is not necessary to state, exists only in its own imagination.''

As regards the allegations in the "Post" and other Pan German papers respecting the retirement of Herr von Kiderlen, the "Kölnische Zeitung" publishes the following communiqué :—

"Wild reports were circulated yesterday pointing to the imminent rupture of the negotiations and the probable resignation of Herr von Kiderlen, who is represented as preferring to give up his office rather than to modify his Morocco programme. These rumours have no foundation whatever and are pure invention. The negotiations are following a normal course and there is no question of Herr von Kiderlen's resignation.''

The "Norddeutsche Allgemeine Zeitung" also publishes a communiqué in its issue of to-day to the following effect :—

"With regard to the progress of the Franco-German negotiations it was stated officially on Friday last that a *rapprochement* had taken place with regard to the principal lines on which they should be conducted, and that the details were forming the subject of close study and mutual consultation. Therefore the two Governments must until further notice refuse to give publicity to their deliberations. To do so would, as the 'Westminster Gazette' aptly observes, endanger the result of the negotiations. We can hardly endorse the advice given by the English newspaper to await that result patiently. It may, however, be fairly stated that the German press, as far as the great newspapers of the non-Socialist parties are concerned, has shown calmness and confidence in spite of the numerous efforts made abroad to disturb its equanimity.''

The Pan-German newspapers are naturally excluded from this official eulogy.

I have, &c.

W. E. GOSCHEN.

No. 464.

Sir F. Bertie to Sir A. Nicolson.

Private.(¹)

My dear Nicolson;   *Paris, August 6, 1911.*

I can understand that H[is] M[ajesty's] Government should wish to divert the German land hunger from British Possessions of which I have not noticed any readiness to divest ourselves. I quite appreciate the anxiety that France should on the present occasion give morsels to keep away the wolf from an attack on the fold in which we should have to be shepherd dogs, but people who are nervous as the French are become suspicious and suggestions concerning the pre-emptive rights of France over the Congo State as a possible asset in satisfying Germany are a mistake. The French will suspect that we hope that if we persuade them to make over some of those rights to Germany we may ourselves have a deal with her.

It is unfortunate for Germany that she arrived late for the feast of spoils in Asia, America and Africa and has got no or small helps. I cannot see that it would be an advantage to us that a powerful Germany should stand in the shoes of a weak Belgium in the Congo State in whole or in part. German officers might possibly be more humane towards the natives than the mixed crew employed by Belgium, but we know of examples of German brutality. What advantage would it be to us that Germany should have an African Empire extending over an enormous portion of that Continent and from sea to sea. In such a climate the surplus population of Germany could not live to stay and breed so as not to be lost to the Empire. They would still have to go to America, Australia, &c. Germany has pegged out claims by the secret Agreement of 1898(²) to much the greater part of the Portuguese Possessions in Africa and as we now know she is minded to acquire Spanish Guinea and as much of the French Congo as she can squeeze out of the present negotiations. If she can get to the Upper waters of the Congo she will become a neighbour of small potentates who at her instigation and with her assistance might give us trouble in the Egyptian Soudan.

The Germans say that they don't want any French islands(³) that have been offered except the Comoros which the French now won't give them. Our present Naval Authorities seem not to have seen objection to the Germans having them I suppose on the theory that we could blow the Germans out of the water, but that might be a costly remedy in lives and money. I wonder whether Botha was consulted.

I see in the Confidential Print a reference to a conversation with Metternich about the Portuguese Possessions in Africa.(⁴) Are we endeavouring or going to endeavour to bring about the break up of those Possessions? At present by the ancient Treaties which oblige us to defend Portugal and her Possessions against all comers she is bound to be with us in any war in which we may be engaged and we have the right to use all Portuguese ports including Oporto. In the Boer war we preferred to exempt Portugal from that obligation in regard to Lourenço Marquez through which we might have attacked the Transvaal, for Germany might have taken part against us. She would have done so if she could have persuaded France to join her, but the German offers were not acceptable. In a European war the use of Oporto might be of great advantage to us. Would the Portuguese willingly admit us as belligerents if we had deprived them of their Colonial Possessions?

Yours ever,

FRANCIS BERTIE.

(¹) [Carnock MSS., Vol. III of 1911.]
(²) [*v. Gooch & Temperley*, Vol. I, pp. 71–5, Nos. 90–2, and *encls.*]
(³) [*cp. G.P.* XXIX, pp. 308–9.]
(⁴) [This subject will be treated in a later volume.]

No. 465.

Sir M. de Bunsen to Sir Edward Grey.

F.O. 30964/13751/11/28.

Tel. (No. 65.)

Zarauz, August 7, 1911.
D. 10·40 A.M.
R. 3 P.M.

French Ambassador has received a letter from the Spanish Minister for Foreign Affairs suggesting that he and I should fix a convenient day (? groups omitted) with his Excellency concerning relations between France and Spain in Morocco, which were interrupted early in June. Minister for Foreign Affairs hears from Spanish Ambassador at Paris that French Minister for Foreign Affairs has no objection. French Ambassador has no information to that effect, and is requesting instructions.

French Ambassador is personally in favour of meeting the wishes of the Spanish Government without waiting to know the result of the Berlin negotiation. He thinks it important to ascertain present attitude of Spain, and is hopeful of reaching an agreement if (?) his Excellency will continue negotiations from the point reached when they were broken off.

Do you agree to my taking part in discussion at San Sebastian in the event of the French Government consenting?

(Repeated to Paris.)

MINUTES.

M. Daeschner has just communicated the annexed note, from which it appears that, contrary to the statement of the Spanish ambassador at Paris, the French gov[ernmen]t do not consider that a resumption of the conversations at Madrid would be desirable before some sort of settlement is arrived at with Germany.

In these circumstances, I would suggest a different telegram to Sir M. de Bunsen.

E. A. C.
August 8th.

[*Note communicated by M. Daeschner.*]

Le Gouvernement Espagnol ayant demandé à reprendre les pourparlers engagès au mois de Juin au sujet de l'application de l'accord franco espagnol sur le Maroc, M. de Selves a pensé que la conversation ne pourrait être utilement reprise tant que la conversation avec l'Allemagne ne sera pas terminée.

Il a invité M. Geoffray a ajourner la demande du Ministre d'État.

M. de Selves serait heureuse si Sir Maurice de Bunsen s'exprimait dans le même sens à Madrid.

No. 466.

Communication from Monsieur de Fleuriau, August 7.

F.O. 30962/25883/11/28.

Le 4 Août au matin, M. de Kiderlen avait mandé M. J. Cambon afin de lui parler d'un communiqué à faire à la Presse, et l'Ambassadeur de France en a profité pour demander au Ministre allemand quelle solution il envisageait aux négociations pendantes.

M. de Kiderlen ne s'est pas exprimé d'une manière très-précise.

Il a dit qu'après avoir consulté l'Amirauté et le Département des Colonies allemands, il n'attachait pas d'importance à la cession des îles françaises du Pacifique et de l'Océan Indien, sauf peut-être à celle des Comores. C'est en Afrique que le Gouvernement allemand désire obtenir des compensations.

M. de Kiderlen ne demanderait plus la côte du Gabon et du Congo français; il demanderait un territoire ayant directement accès au fleuve Congo et dont la limite méridionale suivrait la rivière Alima, tributaire du Congo, et le cours de l'Oghoné pour rejoindre la côte de l'Atlantique entre la colonie espagnole du Rio Muni et Libreville.

M. J. Cambon s'est élevé contre ces prétensions et a demandé au Ministre allemand s'il maintenait son offre primitive du Togoland. M. de Kiderlen a répondu négativement en donnant pour prétexte que la France ne lui offrait pas d'avantages suffisants pour compenser la perte du Togoland et du bec de canard du Cameroun. L'Ambassadeur de France a fait observer que son Gouvernement était disposé à se montrer très laye dans ses cessions de territoire à l'est du Cameroun.

Au moment où M. Jules Cambon sortait, M. de Kiderlen lui a soudain parlé des droits de préemption de la France sur le Rio Muni espagnol, ainsi que de la disparition *possible* de l'État Libre du Congo; cette disparition parait à M. de Kiderlen trop incertaine pour que l'on puisse en tenir compte; mais il désirerait acquérir de la France ses droits sur le Rio Muni (convention du 27 Juin 1900, art[icle] VII).

No. 467.

Sir E. Goschen to Sir Edward Grey.

F.O. 31728/16083/11/28.
(No. 219.)   *Berlin,* D. *August* 8, 1911.
Sir,   R. *August* 12, 1911.

The " Post's " attack on the Emperor, which I had the honour to bring to your notice in my immediately preceding despatch of the 6th instant([1]) has met with the strongest disapproval from nearly the whole of the German Press. Even the Pan-German papers admit that the castigation it received from the Government was richly deserved. While deploring however the offensive tone of the " Post's " article they consider that some excuse for it is to be found in the neglect of the Government to take any steps to check the wild rumours which have recently been spread both in the German and the Foreign Press on the subject of the negotiations.

Herr Harden in the last number of the " Zukunft " has an article which is just as strong as that of the " Post " but being much more cleverly written it has been treated by the Government and the Press with comparative leniency.

He opens fire on the Emperor for having gone off to Norway after having upset the equanimity of Europe by the dispatch of a warship to Agadir, and, attributing His Majesty's apparent nonchalance to the events of 1908, he put the following words into the Emperor's mouth : " The self restraint which at that time I was desired to exercise for the future shall now be put into practice and we will see how you will like it. I allowed Bethmann-Hollweg after considerable pressure to lodge a flea in his great coat (in the shape of Kiderlen) little foreseeing that he would produce him in such a short time as a National Hero. Well if that German formalist has more confidence in the snarling Kiderlen than in me he must work out his own salvation. I won't interfere, I will wait and see how far they get and if things go badly they will have to make several appeals to me before I help them to drag the cart out of the mud."

He then describes how the Chancellor and Herr von Kiderlen went to Swinemünde to make their report, and how, what with tea parties and dinners it was four and twenty hours before they could succeed in doing so. He then wonders whether by these proceedings His Majesty meant to show, as was believed in France and England, that Agadir was not a burning point in his policy, that he considered it an event of minor importance and that it was far from his wish to have it regarded as a vital matter of State which might bring him within measurable distance of war with the Western Powers. If this was in His Majesty's mind, Herr Harden says, then it would have been better if he had given expression to his wishes sooner. Had

---

([1]) [*v. supra,* pp. 438–40, No. 463.]

he done so the Empire would have been spared much abuse and the Emperor much praise; praise which must make him wince. "Now," Herr Harden adds, "it is too late! The General who throws the flag of his country over the wall of an enemy's fortress has no choice left. He must guard that flag from ridicule and dishonour and must follow it up. If he does not do this he loses the confidence of army and people. If William has recognized this danger, the gravest of his reign, he will act as it is his duty to act. In any case it is the duty of the Chancellor to see that he does recognize the danger. He should say 'That Your Majesty should exercise self restraint is praiseworthy in the extreme, but your self restraint should not be carried to a point where it may cause misunderstanding. Your Majesty approved my intention to make up for lost opportunities, to come to an unavoidable settlement with the French without further delay, and to obtain for our increasing population an outlet on habitable territory. As the Supreme Power in the land you ordered that a warship should be sent to Agadir. That could only mean that Germany was resolved that the sword should obtain for her those legitimate rights which the tongues of others have disputed. This is how our action has been understood everywhere: nowhere has it been given another interpretation. If we now represent it as a harmless step, only meant to protect the lives and property of a few apocryphal German subjects we shall lose the last shadow of the respect which we have hitherto enjoyed. I shrink from no responsibility either for action or for inaction, as one or the other may serve the State. But at the present moment any retreat from our standpoint, should such be decided upon would inflict the greatest injury upon the Empire, and no feeling of loyalty could make me cover it with my responsibility. Would your Majesty not rather be reviled as a hotspur than be regarded as a timid mannikin shivering inside a coat of shining armour at the very idea of a bloody encounter? This question sounds mortifying. But I dare to put it because I am sure of the answer. Because I know that my King and Emperor could not possibly show the slightest sign of faint heartedness in a matter which is before the European Court of Honour. If an Emperor were so unwarlike as not to lay his hand on the sword at even an attempt to humiliate his Empire the German people would take matters into its own hands and forge its own destiny. And the most loyal Monarchist could not but applaud such a decision.'"

After a long but interesting analysis of Herr von Kiderlen's character and career, he asks what points there are in that career to justify the confidence placed in him by a large portion of public opinion. "His first unsuccessful bluff (the Russian treaty not yet signed): his crude ignorance of the laws of acoustics (*i.e.*, his refusal to listen to the British proposals for the limitation of armaments); the consolidation of the Edwardian coalition; so stands the balance which is to incline us to blind belief in his direction of affairs! Has anyone the face to maintain that Germany's affairs are to-day in a more comfortable state than they were before the arrival of this Messiah from Swabia? As a matter of fact the reverse is the case. It is time that this fulsome adulation of the Foreign Secretary should cease. A man who does nothing and only smiles is far less dangerous to the State than a man of conspicuous ability who stirs up trouble in the hope of gaining personal prestige. Herr von Kiderlen should study the psychology, the history and the language of Great Britain and pack away the odds and ends of a Balkan diplomat into a camphor-box: perhaps then he will learn to take wider views and to understand the ways of Western Powers."

Herr Harden then turns to the Chancellor, for it is he, he says, who is responsible to the Emperor and the nation and not Herr von Kiderlen. After stating his disqualifications for an office which he should never have undertaken, he comes to his handling of the present situation. He points out that at the time of Mr. Lloyd George's speech the Chancellor should have at once asked through the German Ambassador in London whether the British Government accepted responsibility for that speech. "He did nothing of the sort and on the contrary allowed newspapers under his influence to represent that piece of international impertinence as a harmless piece of rhetoric not in the least directed against Germany: he allowed the same thing to happen with Mr. Asquith's speech which practically said 'We will not suffer Germany to occupy territory in Morocco, but as far as West Africa is concerned we will object to no settlement which does not affect British interests.' This arrogant assumption of censorial power is quite intolerable, and the nation who bows before it will be justly despised by Great Britain. The Chancellor will have to see to it that intercourse with a Government which has meddled in such an unseemly manner with German affairs is confined to what is strictly necessary, and that German Princes and notables receive strict instruction to make no further bids for cousinly love on the other side of the Channel.''

Herr Harden adds that the impression left by the failure of the Chancellor to take up Mr. Asquith's and Mr. Lloyd George's utterances is that there has been a gentle hint of intervention on the part of Great Britain before which Germany yielded. ''No compensation,'' he says, ''could ever wipe out such a humiliation.''

After a few remarks about the ''compensations,'' in the course of which he said that any man who suggested that Togoland should be handed over to France was nothing more or less than a traitor and deserved to be hounded out of Germany, he concludes his article with the words:—''and we read in the paper that at Swinemünde the Chancellor looked in excellent spirits!''

This article will undoubtedly be widely read, and it cannot fail to do considerable harm, and lead public opinion to regard the negotiations askance. His opinions carry some weight and, though people may, and do, find fault with the tone of his articles, his language is such that it remains in their minds. It is therefore to be feared that if he continues, as he has done now in two successive articles, to hammer away on the theme that Germany is yielding to British pressure, not only will the negotiations be rendered more difficult, but, in the event of their leading to a settlement, the relations between Germany and Great Britain will remain anything but pleasant for some time to come.

In this connection I may mention that the ''Tageblatt,'' hitherto an ardent supporter of friendly relations with Great Britain, uses in its issue of this morning, language which would appear to show that Mr. Harden's words have not fallen upon barren ground :—

''If we may venture to express a wish,'' it says, ''it is that Germany will not, after all this trouble is over, take Great Britain back into her affections too soon nor too quickly pass the sponge of reconciliation over Mr. Lloyd George's challenge or the malicious little pin pricks of Mr. Asquith. The most peaceful Anglophil amongst us will have this time found the English tobacco a little too strong, and it would be advisable not to show too much enthusiasm on the occasion of the unveiling of the King Edward Memorial at Homburg.''

I have, &c.

W. E. GOSCHEN.

No. 468.

Sir Edward Grey to Sir M. de Bunsen.

F.O. 30964/13751/11/28.

Tel. (No. 84.)   *Foreign Office, August 9, 1911.*

Your tel[egram] No. 65 (of August 7).([1])

According to communication received from French embassy here French government consider that conversations at Madrid could not usefully be resumed so long as the discussions in Berlin are not concluded. I concur in this view.

([1]) [*v. supra*, p. 442, No. 465.]

No. 469.

Sir M. de Bunsen to Sir Edward Grey.

F.O. 31981/13751/11/28.
(No. 143.)   Confidential.   *Zarauz*, D. *August 9, 1911.*
Sir,   R. *August 14, 1911.*

As stated in my telegram No. 66 of to-day,(¹) Monsieur Geoffray, French Ambassador, has been invited by his Government to favour them with his opinion as to the nature of the arrangements which will have to be made with Spain in the event of a settlement, agreeable to the remaining signatory Powers of the General Act of Algeciras, being reached between France and Germany.

His Excellency has replied that, in this eventuality, he can only suppose that it will be necessary to fall back on the Secret Franco-Spanish Convention of October, 1904, the 3rd Article of which is sure to be invoked by Spain as being applicable to the altered condition of affairs created by the presumed German recognition of what would amount to a French Protectorate, and therefore to an undoubted alteration of the *Status quo* in Morocco.   In other words, His Excellency is of opinion that it will be necessary to recognize that, within the Spanish sphere as defined by Article 2, Spain must be left at liberty to exercise her influence free from any restraining action on the part of France.

I gather from the conversation which I held with Monsieur Geoffray at San Sebastian this morning that His Excellency is fully conscious of the extreme difficulty of devising a settlement with Spain which will secure her free action within the Spanish sphere consistently with the maintenance, which he considers absolutely necessary, of the unity of the Sultan's administration throughout the whole of Morocco.   In his view, the Makhzen must necessarily become more and more the passive instrument of the French Government.   It is to be feared that, Spanish agents, in the Spanish sphere, will regard every action of the Makhzen as inspired by France, and that they will endeavour to thwart such action, and substitute for it their own independent authority.   Monsieur Geoffray feels, however, that unless France is prepared to repudiate her signature and incur the charge of acting in bad faith, she has no alternative but to give the régime contemplated by Article 3 of the Secret Convention at least a trial.   It would be hopeless to seek to replace that régime by a Franco-Spanish condominium at Fez.   The expulsion of the Spaniards from northern Morocco without war would be also surely impracticable.   To resort to force for such a purpose would almost inevitably produce European complications. If Spain found that England no longer objected to her elimination from northern Morocco, she would be only too likely to seek support at Berlin.   There remains therefore only a partition into spheres of influence, and the attempt must be made to assimilate, as far as possible, the administration of the French and Spanish spheres.

The French Ambassador believes that the logical result of the recognized French ascendency at Fez will be the transference of the Diplomatic Body from Tangier to Fez.   He recognizes that, whatever happens, arrangements will have to be made to preserve the special international position of Tangier.

The foregoing paragraphs state, as accurately as I am able, the personal views expressed to me in confidence by the French Ambassador this morning.   His Excellency was careful to explain that they were provisional and subject to the aspect which the question would assume when the precise terms of the assumed Franco-German settlement became known.

Meanwhile Monsieur Geoffray is instructed to intimate to the Spanish Government that the moment has not yet arrived for resuming the interrupted conversations.

I have, &c.
MAURICE DE BUNSEN.

(¹) [Not reproduced, as its substance is recorded in fuller form in the present despatch.]

No. 470.

Sir Edward Grey to Sir M. de Bunsen.

F.O. 31677/13751/11/28.
(No. 88.)
Sir,   *Foreign Office, August* 10, 1911.

The Spanish Ambassador explained to me to-day the desire of his Government to continue now the discussions with France about Morocco. France, they thought, would be easier to deal with now than after she had reached a settlement with Germany; and in the event of the conversations between France and Germany not going well, it would be desirable for France to have Spain on her side : which she could not expect unless she came to an agreement with Spain about Morocco.

I said it appeared to me that a further agreement between Spain and France could be made only as an advance towards a partition of Morocco.. I did not see how this could be negotiated when at any moment Germany might break off the conversations with France, and stipulate for a strict observance of the Algeciras Act. In fact, it might impede the conversations if, at the very time when Germany was contending that Morocco must not be partitioned unless she was satisfied, France was-negotiating with Spain for a partition.

The Ambassador seemed to recognise that the subject was one of some difficulty. He said that he would not ask me to press France to continue the discussions with Spain; but if France of her own accord proposed, or agreed, to continue the discussions, he would like me to authorise you to take part in them.

This I promised to do.

We had some further conversation about Morocco, much on the lines of that which I had already had with the King of Spain.

[I am, &c.]
E. G[REY].

No. 471.

Sir F. Bertie to Sir Edward Grey.

Paris, August 12, 1911.
F.O. 31826/25883/11/28.   D. 3 P.M.
Tel. (No. 117.) Confidential. R.   R. 6 P.M.

Negotiations are proceeding between the French Ambassador at Berlin and the German Minister for Foreign Affairs on bases of Germany ceding Togoland and the Bec du Canard and giving entirely free hand to France in Morocco, and France ceding to Germany strip of territory south of Spanish Guinea already mentioned, the territory marked green on the map which I left with you, and the territory north and north-east of the Sangha up to and along the conventional line marked in purple reaching to Egyptian Soudan.([1]) Matter is under consideration of the Emperor. French Minister for Foreign Affairs foresees great difficulties in arranging the questions affecting concessions to commercial companies if these bases be accepted.

([1]) [*v. G.P.* XXIX, pp. 320–3.]

No. 472.

Sir F. Bertie to Sir Edward Grey.

F.O. 32110/25883/11/28.
Tel. (No. 120.) Confidential. R.
Morocco.

Paris, *August* 14, 1911.
D. 3·45 P.M.
R. 7·45 P.M.

My telegram No. 117 of 12th August.([1])

French Ambassador at Berlin had an interview with the German Minister for Foreign Affairs yesterday. The latter, on supposition of the cession of the Bec du Canard and Togoland to France, returned to his demand described in my telegram No. 115 of 5th August([2]) for the French Congo territory from parallel 2 north-eastward to Ubanghi, down that river to the Alima, and up that river westward to the River Ogowe, and thence to the sea at a point between Libreville and the Muni.

French Ambassador at Berlin expressed surprise at the German Minister for Foreign Affairs renewing this demand, which the French Government, as he had informed the German Minister for Foreign Affairs, would not in any circumstance concede. Discussion then turned to the question of the cession to Germany of Ubanghi–Shari (see my telegram No. 117 of 12th August).([1]) and French Ambassador at Berlin desiring to preserve accession for France to the River Ubanghi, German Minister for Foreign Affairs said that territory to be ceded might stop at Banghi or Fort Possel, but in such a case Germany must have (added to the strip north of Libreville conterminous with Spanish Guinea already agreed on) the territory within a line from either Banghi or Fort Possel to navigable part of the Ogowe River.

French Minister for Foreign Affairs will consult with the Minister of the Colonies to-day on these demands.

M. Cambon reports that the Chancellor and the German Minister for Foreign Affairs are to have a consultation with the Minister concerned on 16th August, the result of which is to be submitted to the Emperor at Wilhelmshöhe on the 17th August by the Chancellor and German Minister for Foreign Affairs, who will remain there for dinner to be given on 18th August for the birthday of the Emperor of Austria. German Minister for Foreign Affairs will then go to Marienbad for five or six days' rest before returning to Berlin for the resumption of the negotiations.

([1]) [*v.* immediately preceding document.]
([2]) [*v. supra*, pp. 435–6, No. 460.]

No. 473.

Sir Edward Grey to Sir F. Bertie.

F.O. 32255/25883/11/28.
(No. 348.)
Sir,

Foreign Office, *August* 14, 1911.

M. [Paul] Cambon informed me to-day that M. de Selves was considering the basis of an agreement with Germany, under which the Germans would put France in the same position in Morocco as she had been placed by our Agreement, while the French would make to Germany the concessions in the French Congo of which I was aware. But French opinion was very sensitive about giving Germany territory which would cut the French Congo in half, and the French Government were therefore trying to get Togoland.

The French Ambassador in Berlin had had a short interview with Herr von Kiderlen on the 11th.([1]) The latter had spoken of going away soon for eight days or so, and there was to be another interview on the 16th.

([1]) [*v. G.P.* XXIX, pp. 322–3.]

M. Cambon then showed me the telegrams which had been sent to him, giving news of the trouble at Taroudant. The Austrian Consul was interested in the matter, as one of the Europeans there was an Austrian; the other was a German, both were employés of Mannesmann. The Austrian had suggested the intervention of Kaïd M'Tougi, which would probably lead to disorder on a large scale in the Suss.

He told me that it was stated that the Germans were considering the landing of troops at Agadir. He thought that such action would make it essential to send ships to Agadir. He was, therefore, anxious to know what I thought should be done in the event of German troops being landed.

I said that it would be difficult to come to a decision before we knew what th circumstances were.

[I am, &c.]
E. G[REY].

No. 474.

Sir F. Bertie to Sir Edward Grey.

F.O. 32285/25883/11/28.
Tel. (No. 122.) R.

Paris, August 15, 1911.
D. 2·18 [P.M.]
R. 4·20 [P.M.]

Morocco.

French M[inister for] F[oreign] A[ffairs] gave me following information this morning.

German M[inister for] F[oreign] A[ffairs] sent for French Ambassador yesterday([1]) evening and told him as a result of a consultation with the German Chancellor that owing to public opinion in Germany Togoland could not be ceded, and reconsidered German requirements would be a cession of French territory to include both banks of the River Sangha and the liberty to use Brazzaville railway for conveyance of German troops for embarkation on Congo River. All the territorial proposals hitherto made were left vague.

M. [Jules] Cambon informed German M[inister for] F[oreign] A[ffairs] that the French Government could not entertain any proposal for a cession of both banks of the Sangha River and that as Togoland was not to be ceded great reductions must be made in proposed cessions of French territory. M. Cambon also expressed the opinion that if territorial arrangements were to come to anything they should be settled before German M[inister for] F[oreign] A[ffairs] left Berlin so that immediately after his return the question of arrangements regarding Morocco should be discussed.

M. Cambon is to have further interview with German M[inister for] F[oreign] A[ffairs] to-morrow.

French M[inister for] F[oreign] A[ffairs] suspects sinister motive for frequent changes in demands of German Government.

([1]) [*cp. G.P.* XXIX, pp. 328–9, and Russian report in *Siebert*, pp. 597–9.]

[19656]

No. 475.

Sir Edward Grey to Sir F. Bertie.

F.O. 32285/25883/11/28.
Tel. (No. 192.)

Foreign Office, August 16, 1911.
D. 11·30 p.m.

French Ambassador has shown the reports of conversations at Berlin described in your telegrams Nos. 120 and 122.([1]) Report of latter conversation is rather more favourable to prospect of a settlement.

I have said that if Germans land temporarily at Agadir for some good reason such as death of German at Tarudant now said to be in real danger I think no immediate action should be taken. If landing is prolonged there would be two alternatives.

1. To propose a Conference.
2. To send ships as proposed by French M[inister for] F[oreign] A[ffairs].

But I said that this latter step might be followed by a mobilization of German Army on French frontier. Nothing should therefore be done at Agadir without being prepared for this possible reply on the part of Germany and without being agreed beforehand as to what should be done if it happened.

I said that this was only my personal opinion as I had not yet consulted the Prime Minister.

([1]) [v. supra, p. 448, No. 472, and p. 449, No. 474.]

No. 476.

Sir E. Goschen to Sir Edward Grey.

F.O. 32839/8457/11/28.
(No. 230.) Secret.
Sir,

Berlin, D. August 16, 1911.
R. August 21, 1911.

I have the honour to report that on Friday evening last I proceeded to Homburg von der Hoehe to be present at the unveiling by His Majesty the German Emperor of the King Edward memorial in that town.([1]) I was unfortunately prevented by a mishap from attending the ceremony. I had, however, the honour of meeting the Emperor at luncheon afterwards when He showed me a telegram which He had received from the King and expressed to me the great pleasure He had derived from His Majesty's charmingly expressed and cordial message. I had also the honour of dining at Friedrichshof in the evening. After dinner the Emperor took me aside and spoke to me at great length and not without some heat on the subject of Morocco. His Majesty told me that as early as May last France had offered Germany the Congo, Madagascar and He did not know what in return for a free hand in Morocco. Everything was being discussed in the friendliest possible manner and an arrangement appeared in sight when Mr. Lloyd George made his speech and everything was changed. I ventured to remind His Majesty that in the interval He had sent a ship to Agadir. That step had consolidated public opinion in England. Whatever might have been the differences of opinion between the various parties of the State with regard to Home politics there had been no two opinions with regard to the gravity of that step for which no adequate reason could be discovered. The very fact that Germany and France had been discussing the Morocco question amicably rendered the despatch of a German warship at that moment to Agadir all the more incomprehensible to British public opinion. The Emperor said that then He could only say that British public opinion was very easily alarmed if they could be

([1]) [v. account by the Emperor William II, &c. G.P. XXIX, pp. 227–30.]

perturbed by His sending a little ship with only two or three little pop guns on board to the coast of Morocco. I said that I could not see that the size of the ship made any difference : it carried the German man-of-war ensign and it was what the ship represented and not its size which public opinion in England regarded as important. "What could the public think," I ventured to remark, "when a warship was sent to a closed port, where, as far as was known, no German commercial interests existed, and which appeared to offer a convenient roadstead and facilities for the establishment of a naval base." His Majesty denied that such facilities existed and added that, however that might be, He had had good reasons for sending the ship and had let His intentions with regard to Morocco be known in London; if the Government and public opinion had not been informed of those intentions it was not His fault. I asked His Majesty if I was to understand that He had spoken in London of His intention to send a ship to Agadir. His Majesty did not answer that question but went on to say that the result of Mr. Lloyd George's speech was that He had never known German public opinion so excited against England as it was now, for it was convinced that England was endeavouring to prevent Germany from coming to an arrangement with France and was in fact endeavouring to thwart Germany's natural desire for expansion in every possible way. I said that I thought Mr. Asquith's speech had finally disposed of that idea. His Majesty replied that that speech had come too late and that it had not been able to do away with the ill effects of Mr. Lloyd George's speech. I asked His Majesty what after all the latter had said? He seemed to me to have said what had been said in Germany very often, viz., that a powerful nation could not be left out of discussions which might affect its interests. His Majesty said that He knew the speech by heart and that it meant a good deal more than that. In any case it had thoroughly upset people in Germany and had gone far to undo all the work He had done to bring about good relations between the two countries. "Now," His Majesty said, "What is going to happen? I do not want any territory in Morocco whatever, but if I give France a free hand there I must have proper compensation. I have laid my demands on this head before the French Government, and if they do not accept them I will have the *status quo* after Algeciras, and see that every French soldier in the interior and coast towns and the Shawia district is turned out of Morocco, and if I can't get them out by peaceable means I will turn them out by force."

I said that I was of course unaware of what His Majesty's demands exactly were, but that I trusted they were such as a French Government could see its way to accepting. There were of course certain sacrifices which no French Government would be allowed by French public opinion to accept. His Majesty said that as He interfered as little as possible with the negotiations He did not know what the French Government had recently offered, in fact He had heard nothing of the negotiations for a fortnight. "But," He added, "my patience which has been very great has its limits."

He then reverted to what His Majesty called British interference. He said that we had only one friend in Europe and that was Himself, and yet we did everything to be disagreeable to Him and to thwart Him. He had made every effort to be friends with us and He could say with confidence that two straighter and more sincere men than He and His Chancellor did not exist. And now because they had sent a little ship to Agadir the whole British nation rose against them. They had not been able to avoid sending the ship. Some Hamburg firms of high standing not those " rascally Mannesmanns " with whom He had not the slightest sympathy, had written to say that owing to the French proceedings at Fez, the tribes in the Hinterland of Agadir were assuming a very threatening attitude, and that therefore they, the Hamburg firms, must urgently demand that a ship should be sent for their protection. What could He do? Of course He had to send a ship and he was sure that His Majesty's Government would have done the same.

His Majesty then went over a lot of old ground, going back to the old grievance of how the assurances given by His Government about German shipbuilding had been disbelieved and of how we took no notice of what other nations were doing in the way of increasing their naval strength and directed all our discontent and annoyance against Germany. He mentioned besides many other grievances with which you are only too familiar and which I need not therefore repeat here. But the great grievance which ran through the whole of the conversation was that He had wanted to come to an understanding with France both as regards Morocco and all other questions and that Great Britain, who He thought had shown signs of a more friendly spirit towards Germany and of a desire to be on good terms with her, had done all in her power to thwart His wishes. "Why on earth," His Majesty said, "are you always against me, me the grandson of Queen Victoria, and your only real friend in Europe? Personally I have no reason to complain, because everyone in England always gives me the heartiest of welcomes, but you have an expression in England 'Love me, love my dog'; and I say 'Love me, love my nation.'"

You will have noticed that His Majesty spoke with some emphasis of His intentions if the French Government refuse to fall in with His demands. Such utterances coming from the Supreme Head of the State in a moment of great international anxiety cannot, even allowing for His Majesty's impulsive nature, but make a somewhat unpleasant impression. It is, however, my opinion that the Emperor sincerely desires an arrangement and that the outburst I have recorded above was the result of passing irritation caused by the charges of timidity and hesitation which have been so freely brought against Him by the Pan-German papers. I may mention that except during His long conversation with me, when He worked Himself into a certain amount of excitement, His Majesty appeared to be in excellent spirits.

I have, &c.
W. E. GOSCHEN.

No. 477.

Sir Edward Grey to Mr. A. Chamberlain.([1])

Private.

My dear Chamberlain,   *August* 17, 1911.

I hear from Lloyd George that you have asked about the Morocco question.

The position is this: the negotiations between France and Germany go very slow; they are a little nearer each other than they were; we are kept informed fully by the French; the Germans make a great point of secrecy. I don't want to hinder the negotiations by any stiff language about Germany as long as there is a prospect of a settlement between her and France on reasonable terms; at the same time I don't want to say any soothing words that might be interpreted in Germany as a weakening of our attitude.

I think therefore that as far as the Government is concerned it would be as well for us not to say anything.

Yours very truly,
E. GREY.

([1]) [Grey MSS., Vol. 67.]

No. 478.

Sir E. Goschen to Sir Edward Grey.

F.O. 32639/25883/11/28.
Tel. (No. 60.) Confidential.

Berlin, August 18, 1911.
D. 1·49 P.M.
R. 2·50 P.M.

Morocco.

S[ecretary] of S[tate] for Foreign Affairs told me yesterday that the negotiations were not going well, (? and) that France had not only reduced her first offers but was asking for more in return. He said that if the negotiations failed it would be entirely the fault of the French Government whose Press indiscretions had rendered most difficult any modification of German demands. For the moment the way did not seem clear to any satisfactory arrangement. It appears that his depression was due to somewhat heated di[s]cussion between French M[inister for] F[oreign] A[ffairs] and the German Ambassador at Paris.

In the afternoon Secretary of State saw my French colleague and things seem to have gone more smoothly though not much progress was made in the geographical negotiations. S[ecretary] of S[tate] for Foreign Affairs still refused Togoland but seemed not disinclined to consider suggestion made by French Ambassador that Germany should cede strip of Togoland which might be called rectification of frontier. French Ambassador then turned conversation to Morocco and said that if the French Gov[ernmen]t knew exactly what Germany meant by "freehand" it might ease colonial compensation negotiations. In course of ensuing conversation Secretary of State agreed to definition of Morocco as stated by French Ambassador viz.:— including Suss country: to secret act acknowledging the French protectorate: to non-interference in any negotiations between France and Spain: and to thirty years as period for which any mutual agreement as to commercial liberty should be binding.

My French colleague seemed fairly satisfied with conversation.

Secretary of State left yesterday for Wilhelmshöhe having arranged with the French Ambassador who is leaving for Paris not to return before the 28th instant.

No. 479.

Sir F. Bertie to Sir Edward Grey.

(By Post.)

F.O. 32646/25883/11/28.
Tel. (No. 125.)

Paris, D. *August* 18, 1911.
R. *August* 19, 1911.

At the interview yesterday between the French Ambassador at Berlin and M. de Kiderlen-Waechter the former asked whether the latter had any fresh proposals to make in view of the fact that Germany was not prepared to cede Togoland, for without that cession France could not maintain all her offers. M. de Kiderlen-Waechter said that public opinion would not permit the cession of Togoland. He dropped the acquisition of Ubanghi-Shari but he revived the demand for the Alima frontier. M. Cambon reminded him that the French Government had already refused to entertain that proposal. M. de Kiderlen-Waechter said that the Bec du Canard was a valuable concession, and that the French Government did not seem disposed to come to terms. M. Cambon denied this, and the conversation then turned on what Germany was to renounce in Morocco supposing that the territorial arrangements could be agreed on.

In the discussion M. Jules Cambon elicited from M. de Kiderlen-Waechter that Germany would agree to disinterest herself as regards Spain in Morocco and leave it to France to come to an arrangement with Spain; that Germany would require a recognition of the right to export minerals, but would accept the thirty years provided for in the Anglo-French agreement of 1904.

M. Jules Cambon enquired, as Togoland could not be ceded, whether there could be a rectification of frontiers which might reconcile French public opinion to some cessions of French territory elsewhere than south of the Sangha. M. de Kiderlen-Waechter replied that he did not say either yes or no; he would reflect on the suggestion. He must absent himself from Berlin for ten days if possible, as he required rest, and he suggested that the French Government should consider what offers they could make other than those already put forward, and that there should be another meeting not sooner, he hoped, than the 28th.

The French Ambassadors at Berlin and London are to come to Paris to consult with the French Government on the situation.

No. 480.

Sir F. Bertie to Sir Edward Grey.

(By Post.)

F.O. 32647/25641·/11/28.
Tel. (No. 126.) Very Confidential.   *Paris, August* 18, 1911.
  Morocco.

My immediately preceding telegram (   ).(1)

French Minister for Foreign Affairs' impression of the situation is that Emperor will remain pacific unless the Pan-Germanists manage to persuade him that by not insisting on German demands he will act contrary to the traditions of the Hohenzollerns, and that it will be so held by public opinion in Germany.(2) He believes that originally German Minister for Foreign Affairs intended to establish Germany permanently in a portion of Morocco, but that, in view of unexpected attitude of England and Russia in favour of France, he would endeavour to obtain such large concessions from France as would reconcile German public opinion to getting nothing in Morocco.

French Minister for Foreign Affairs attributes German Minister for Foreign Affairs' procrastination to the desire to see how much strikes and disturbances in England are likely to hamper her action in foreign affairs.

(1) [*v.* immediately preceding document.]
(2) [For a report of M. Caillaux's attitude on this day, *v. G.P.* XXIX, pp. 331–2.]

No. 481.

Sir E. Goschen to Sir Edward Grey.

F.O. 32841/25883/11/28.
(No. 232.)   *Berlin, D. August* 18, 1911.
Sir,   R. *August* 21, 1911.

  I had a short conversation with the Secretary of State for Foreign Affairs yesterday just before he saw Monsieur Jules Cambon. His Excellency complained very much of the manner in which the French Government continually shifted their ground and said that now they were reducing the offers which at one time they had been ready to make and at the same time were increasing their own demands. He pointed out to me again how the whole situation had been affected by the early French indiscretions and how difficult it was for him to modify the German demands once they had been given to the public. He also complained bitterly of the French military Press which he said was deliberately inciting to war. I said that I had read some articles in the German newspapers which seemed to me also to go rather far in that direction. He said that he fully admitted it, but that they were the result of the French articles particularly those in "la France militaire" which were outrageous. He added that in consequence of these articles on both sides the excitement in Germany was growing and he really could not see how a satisfactory agreement was to be reached. He then alluded to the incident at Aix les Bains of which he had just heard and said that though he did not attach much importance to it himself, it would, he feared, have a deplorable effect on public opinion. I may mention at once that later on in the day the French Ambassador called on him and explained to him, by Monsieur de Selves' instructions, that an enquiry into the affair had shown that it had been greatly exaggerated and that no French officers had been concerned in it. Monsieur Cambon told me that Herr von Kiderlen had seemed intensely relieved by the explanation. His Excellency had at once ordered a communiqué to be sent at once to the papers and had instructed the Press Bureau to do all in its power to prevent the false reports from being repeated. It would seem therefore that Herr von Kiderlen is sincerely anxious to avoid anything which might add to the difficulties of the situation.

Immediately after I had left the Imperial Foreign Office my French colleague was received by Herr von Kiderlen. Monsieur Cambon told me that he also had found Herr von Kiderlen depressed and not very well disposed : and he attributed this depression to his having just received the report of a somewhat acrimonious discussion between Monsieur de Selves and the German Ambassador in Paris.

But after a little mutual recrimination they seem to have got to business and to have made some progress, if not with the exchanges to be made in Equatorial Africa, at all events with that part of the negotiations which concerns Morocco.

I have had the honour to telegraph to you what appeared to me to be the main points of the discussion, as related to me by my French colleague, and as you will doubtless receive a full account of the conversation from Paris, I will not trouble you by going into them again. I may mention, however, that Monsieur Cambon, who had been rather anxious as to whether Herr von Kiderlen would make difficulties with regard to the Sus country, was very relieved to find that he accepted quite readily the French definition of Morocco, namely, from the Algerian frontier down to the Spanish colony of Rio de Oro. In fact Herr von Kiderlen seems to have agreed to everything that Monsieur Cambon suggested with a view to making it clear what France was to receive in return for her colonial sacrifices in Equatorial Africa.

As regards Monsieur Cambon's suggestion that, if the German Government found it absolutely impossible to hold to their former offer of Togoland, a strip of that country might be ceded in the form (for the public) of a rectification of frontier, Herr von Kiderlen said that he would not say "Yes" neither would he say "No," but that it might offer a solution and he would think over it. In any case the whole of Togoland was quite out of the question.

At the close of the conversation Herr von Kiderlen suggested that they should both go on leave and return to Berlin on the 28th instant. "When we meet then," Herr von Kiderlen said laughingly, "we will decide whether it shall be peace or war."[1]

I have, &c.
W. E. GOSCHEN.

[1] [Herr von Kiderlen-Waechter left Berlin on August 17 and reported to the Emperor William II at Wilhelmshöhe on August 18; he afterwards went to South Germany and Switzerland, returning to Berlin on the 29th. v. G.P. XXIX, p. 337, note; Jäckh, II, p. 138 sqq. M. Jules Cambon left for Paris on August 21 and returned to Berlin on the night of August 30–1.]

No. 482.

Sir Edward Grey to Sir E. Goschen.

F.O. 32100/4451/11/18.
(No. 196.)
Sir :—   *Foreign Office, August 18, 1911.*

Count Metternich called on the 3rd instant and in course of conversation remarked that up till 1900 the policy of Great Britain had been to lean towards Germany, and to act in concert with her without actually becoming a member of the Triple Alliance. But since 1900 this policy had undergone a change, and we had ranged ourselves with France and Russia.

In reply Sir A. Nicolson declared that no change in our policy had taken place and that it was the same now as had existed for centuries. He said that we had always been and were still in favour of maintaining the equilibrium of Europe. Up till 1900 we had not unfortunately been on very good relations either with France or Russia, and had regarded them in some sense as dangerous and aggressive Powers. It was true therefore that we had inclined to shape our course with that of the Triple Alliance. Sir A. Nicolson continued that since 1900 we had settled our differences with both France and Russia, and the course of events had insensibly led to a fresh grouping of the Powers destined to maintain the equilibrium and peace. Count Metternich remarked that we had exchanged a weak adversary for a strong one.

Sir Arthur Nicolson demurred to the term "adversary" and showed that in former days Russia was by no means a weak adversary to us, as she could put great military pressure upon us on some of our weak points.

Count Metternich then said that since 1900 Germany had always found England in her way.

Sir A. Nicolson expressed disagreement with this view and said that in recent events Germany could have no grounds of complaint against England, for our attitude had been quite natural and logical.

Count Metternich did not assent to this conclusion.

I am, etc.,
[E. GREY].

No. 483.

Sir E. Goschen to Sir A. Nicolson.

Private.([1])
My dear Nicolson,   *Berlin, August 18, 1911.*

Many thanks for your letter from which I was glad to learn, amongst other things that your cure is doing you good. I was much interested in your conversation with Metternich.([2]) He ought to know by this time that our "preliminary canters" with Germany in bygone times were not of a nature to make us too anxious to take her permanently into wedlock. The Emperor always harps on the same subject : "Why on earth did you choose France and Russia instead of Me : they both hate you like poison, while I am and have always been your friend." That is what He has said to me hundreds of times. The balance of Power theory does not appeal to the German mind. I had, as you will see from a despatch I have written on the subject, a very animated conversation with His Majesty the other night after dinner at Friederichshof.([3]) Of course I have left out of that despatch heaps of His remarks as I don't want to make more mischief than I can help; but I must say that He used very strong language about many people. H[is] M[ajesty] talked far more about

([1]) [Carnock MSS., Vol. III of 1911.]
([2]) [It is not certain to which conversation this refers, but possibly it is the one recorded in the immediately preceding document.]
([3]) [*v. supra*, pp. 450-2, No. 476.]

our iniquities than about the French—in fact he said that He did not know how the negotiations were going on as he had heard nothing about them for a fortnight! But the one remark he did make about the French was rather strong. He said that if the negotiations came to nothing He would have every French soldier out of Morocco, and if they didn't withdraw peaceably He would turn them out by force. Those were his very words, and they are strong considering they were addressed by the Head of the State to an Ambassador representing a country friendly to, and more or less acting with, France, and at a moment of general International unrest. They were, I presume, intended to impress upon my mind that He is not the timid ruler which the Pan Germans represent him to be. Of course he must be very irritated by all the attacks which have been made upon Him by the Pan Germanic lower Press, and He must have to hold himself very tightly in hand. I think H[is] M[ajesty] exaggerates when He says that He has never known German public opinion so excited against Germany [sic: ? England] as at the present moment. Kiderlen says so too; but, from what I hear, there is a by no means inconsiderable section of Public Opinion who are, on the contrary, annoyed with Kiderlen for having estranged England and for having placed Germany in a false position from which it may be difficult for her to emerge with credit.

You will notice (when you read my despatch) that when I mentioned that the Agadir Episode had intervened between the time when He said that Germany and France had nearly come to terms, and Mr. L. George's speech, He said very hotly that when in England He had stated his views on the Morocco question very plainly and had mentioned what he intended to do. "If," he added, "the Government was not informed that was not my fault." He did not answer my question as to whether He had stated in England that he was going to send a ship to Agadir— but went on to explain that the sending of the ship was in order to show that Germany was not to be disregarded. He must have forgotten this afterwards because He told me later that He had been obliged to send a ship in consequence of an urgent appeal from Hamburg Firms of high standing, "not those d——d rascals the Mannesmanns, but respectable and influential people." I suppose I was right in telling Him how the incident was regarded in England. He didn't take much notice of my remarks beyond saying that it was all Mr. Lloyd George's fault that English Public Opinion had become excited on the subject. But I told Him that there were no two opinions about it. Government and people, Liberals, Radicals and Conservatives all thought alike. I must confess that the Emperor's language, and Kiderlen's depression, when I saw the latter on my return from Homburg, gave my optimism a slight shock— and I could not help feeling that if by any chance Germany wanted war the moment when the United Kingdom is dislocated by strikes must appear rather tempting; but I have now recovered as Cambon's conversation with Kiderlen went fairly well yesterday and I feel more than ever that Kiderlen wants a settlement. Cambon was fairly satisfied with the conversation but he told me that he had had some difficulty in getting Kiderlen into a good humour as the latter had been considerably put out by some remarks made by de Selves to Schön. Cambon himself was not very pleased about it and seems to think that there are too many cooks at work on the negotiations.
. . . .(⁴)

In haste,
W. E. G.

(⁴) [The rest of this letter is omitted because it adds no information of importance.]

No. 484.

Sir F. Bertie to Sir Edward Grey.

F.O. 32791/25883/11/28.
Tel. (No. 127.) R.

Paris, August 19, 1911.
D. 3·20 P.M.
R. 7 P.M.

Berlin telegram No. 60 of 18th August : Morocco.([1])

French Minister for Foreign Affairs says that it is not true that French Government have not only reduced their first offers but are asking for more from Germany. As to press indiscretions, there seem to be more indiscretions at Berlin than at Paris (*vide* "Lokalanzeiger," "Cologne Gazette," and "Frankfurter Zeitung" and other German newspapers). The adjournment of discussions between German Minister for Foreign Affairs and French Ambassador is caused by desire of the former to absent himself for ten days on the plea of ill-health; and advantage of this adjournment is to be taken by M. [Jules] Cambon to come to Paris on 21st August to consult with French Government.

French Minister for Foreign Affairs says that he has not had any somewhat heated discussion with German Ambassador. He had not seen German Ambassador for a fortnight past until 16th August. Ambassador pleaded illness as reason for his absence. French Minister for Foreign Affairs expressed to him regret which he felt at small progress made in discussions, and said that withdrawal of Togoland from bargain to be made would naturally greatly modify situation, and that French Government must take that into account in offers of French territory, and that frequent changes in demands made by Germany, which he cited to the Ambassador, rendered negotiations very difficult.

German Ambassador shared regret expressed by French Minister for Foreign Affairs, and said that public opinion in Germany rendered cession of Togoland impossible. French Minister for Foreign Affairs reminded him that public opinion in France had to be considered by French Government in question of cessions of French territory. The conversation of German Ambassador was, French Minister for Foreign Affairs states, most placid ("des plus calmes"), and he does not believe that German Ambassador can have reported otherwise to German Minister for Foreign Affairs, who, having put forward impossible pretensions, is trying to save his face by misrepresenting attitude of French Government and endeavouring to throw blame for situation on them.

([1]) [*v. supra*, p. 453, No. 478.]

No. 485.

Sir F. Bertie to Sir Edward Grey.

F.O. 32792/25883/11/28.
Tel. (No. 128.) Secret.

Paris, August 20, 1911.
D. 4·40 P.M.
R. 6·50 P.M.

At the request of the President of the Council I went to see him this afternoon.([1]) He wishes to know whether, if in order to placate Germany it be necessary to make such concessions of territory as will cut off the northern part of the French Congo from direct communication with the sea, His Majesty's Government will entertain proposals for an exchange of territories by which France would obtain a cession of territory in Northern Nigeria which would give her access to the Bec du Canard (to be acquired by her) from her northern Congo territory to her possessions in Northern

([1]) [*cp.* Herr von Schoen's report of M. Caillaux's views on August 18, *G.P.* XXIX, pp. 331–2.]

Nigeria. President of the Council states that if Germans land men at Agadir or increase their naval force there, whether on the pretext of German life and property or not, French Government will send ships to Mogador and Saffi to do whatever Germans do at Agadir. He hopes that His Majesty's Government will join in such action. I said that action of His Majesty's Government would, I thought, depend upon circumstances on account of which Germans might make further demonstrations at Agadir.

No. 486.

Sir V. Corbett to Sir Edward Grey.

F.O. 33180/25883/11/28.
(No. 45.) Confidential.   *Munich,* D. *August* 20, 1911.
Sir,   R. *August* 22, 1911.

The feeling of profound disappointment at the course, so far as it is known to the public, of the Moroccco negotiations continues to find expression in the German press of all shades.

When the " Panther " first sailed to Agadir, it was taken for granted that the move would be crowned with the same decisive effect as followed the German intervention at Petersburg in 1909. Two months have now passed and the situation has not improved. The negotiations which it was expected would bring about the definite recognition of Germany's right to " a place in the sun " are still dragging on infructuously and the French Government so far from giving way, is understood to be stiffly maintaining its ground with the moral support of England and Russia. That England in the throes of a momentous constitutional struggle, to say nothing of her labour troubles, should still take an active interest in Moroccan affairs and that Russia despite the fair words of the Potsdam interview([1]) should remain faithful to her ally, are facts as surprising as they are disconcerting to the German mind.

It seems to me to be ominous that both in France and Germany the eventuality of war is beginning to be spoken of as a contingency regrettable but possibly unavoidable. That some persons, and those not the least influential in France believe that the French military and naval forces will if not to-day, at least in a few months' time be sufficiently strong to justify the Government in risking an appeal to arms, is, I believe, an open secret. The renewal of the French propaganda in Alsace Lorraine points the same way. In Germany the colonial party and those in touch with them are profoundly dissatisfied; it would require very little to fan their discontent into a blaze.

War may not be imminent—I believe it is not—but unless the present German grievance that they have no room for expansion be removed, I feel convinced that sooner or later the force of internal interests will compel a recourse to arms. Should this unhappily be the case, domestic differences will be forgotten and the German nation will march as one man to make a final bid for the hegemony of the world. . . . .([2])

I have, &c.
VINCENT CORBETT.

([1]) [This subject will be treated in a later volume.]
([2]) [Sir V. Corbett here illustrates the first part of this despatch by the quotation of various public utterances in which the value of Moroccan territory is emphasized, and the importance to Germany of retaining rights there.]

No. 487.

Sir Edward Grey to Sir F. Bertie.

F.O. 32792/25883/11/28.
Tel. (No. 195.) R.   Foreign Office, August 21, 1911.
    Your tel[egram] No. 128, Secret.([1])
    Proposals in first part will receive careful consideration of H[is] M[ajesty's]
G[overnmen]t, but in view of the present delicate state of negotiations I trust that
French Government will not take so decisive a step as the sending of ships to
Mogador and Saffi without further consideration and before I have had an
opportunity of discussing matter with the French Ambassador.
    Such action might be open to objections pointed out in penultimate paragraph
of my tel[egram] no. 192.([2])
    Despatch of French ships to two open ports would be no real set off to presence
of Germans at Agadir, while it would inevitably be considered by Germans as
provocative and must render negotiations more difficult.

    ([1]) [v. supra, pp. 458-9, No. 485.]
    ([2]) [v. supra, p. 450, No. 475. There had been some very sharp private discussion between
M. Caillaux and the German Government on the question of France or England sending ships to
Agadir, v. G.P. XXIX, pp. 314-9. This is not mentioned in Caillaux.]

No. 488.

Sir F. Bertie to Sir Edward Grey

F.O. 33055/25883/11/28.
(No. 372.) Secret.   Paris, D. August 21, 1911.
Sir,   R. August 22, 1911.
    As I had the honour to inform you by my telegram No. 128 secret([1]) I had an
interview with the President of the Council yesterday. His Excellency began the
conversation by expressing great satisfaction at the termination of the strikes in
England and at the firmness with which His Majesty's Government had met the
dangerous situation which had been created by them. He then went on to say that
he hoped that the cessation of internal trouble in the United Kingdom would have a
good effect on the Franco-German negotiations concerning Morocco. M. de Kiderlen
Waechter had got himself into an awkward position. He had utilized the German
Press to excite public opinion in his support and the Pan-German public was getting
out of hand, and the danger was that though the German Emperor was, M. Caillaux
believed, not in favour of pressing impossible demands, and of incurring the risks of
war, the personal reputation of M. de Kiderlen Waechter was involved in the question
and he might have difficulty in persuading the public that he was demanding and
obtaining what he had led them to expect. The suspension of the conversations
at Berlin on the pretext of M. de Kiderlen Waechter requiring ten days' rest was
for the purpose of awaiting the result of the strikes in England so that he might
judge how far the action of His Majesty's Government in matters of foreign policy
would be likely to be hampered or modified thereby. Now that the danger of internal
troubles in the United Kingdom had disappeared the German Government might
become more reasonable, but an agitation was being got up by the Pan-Germanists
and the Emperor and his Government might be forced to adopt a menacing attitude.
M. Caillaux had no information that the German Government contemplated an

    ([1]) [v. supra, pp. 458-9, No. 485.]

increase of their naval force at Agadir or a landing of men there, but disturbances in the Sus district which German Agents were endeavouring to promote or the protection of German life and property might possibly be made the pretexts for an increase of their naval force or a landing of men.(²) The French Government had determined that in either of those events they would send ships to Mogador and Saffi to act at those ports in the same way as the German ships at Agadir. M. Caillaux said that he hoped that His Majesty's Government would join in such action by also sending ships to those ports. I reminded His Excellency of a recent conversation which you had had with the French Ambassador who had asked you what you thought as to sending French and British ships to Agadir in the event of there being a landing of German troops there and I expressed the opinion that His Majesty's Government would require to be acquainted with the circumstances for which the Germans had landed men at Agadir before they came to a decision in regard to sending British ships to Mogador and Saffi. M. Caillaux requested me to submit the question to you. He said that for the satisfaction of public opinion in France it would be absolutely necessary to make a demonstration at Mogador and Saffi if the Germans took further action at Agadir, and he earnestly trusted that His Majesty's Government would join in such a demonstration.

The President of the Council then turned to the territorial questions between the German and French Governments. He said that except for the strip of the Congo abutting on Spanish Guinea and running from the coast near Libreville to Ouesso the French Government were not prepared to make any cessions of territory to Germany south of the Sangha river. How much they would cede north of that river and to the east of the German Colony of the Cameroons would depend upon whether Germany gave up Togoland or part of it as a "rectification of the frontiers" in addition to the Bec du Canard in the Cameroons. All this M. Caillaux indicated on a map and he requested me to enquire of you whether in the event of it becoming necessary in order to placate the German Government and preserve peace, to make such concessions of French territory as would cut off the Northern part of the French Congo from direct access to the sea His Majesty's Government would entertain proposals for an exchange of territories by which France would receive a cession of territory in the North of British Nigeria which would give to her Northern Congo Colony access through the Bec du Canard to her possessions north of Nigeria.

M. Caillaux then spoke of the state of public opinion in France and the question of war. He said that he did not think that either the German Emperor or the majority of his people desired war and certainly neither the French Government nor the French people desired it, but in France an opinion was gaining ground that Germany was putting upon France and there was consequent irritation. There was not now the same fear of Germany as there was some years ago. The French army was quite different now to what it was in 1870. As was then proved, the German Army was vastly superior to the French Army. Now however the French army was in a highly efficient state and the people had confidence in it and the men had confidence in their officers and in themselves. The result of battles was always doubtful and he trusted that war would not ensue from the question of Morocco but if it did come the chances in favour of France would he believed be good.

I have, &c.

FRANCIS BERTIE.

(²) [cp. *supra*, p. 322, *Ed. note;* and pp. 393–4, No. 416.]

No. 489.

Sir F. Bertie to Sir Edward Grey.

(By Post.)

F.O. 33051/25883/11/28.
Tel. (No. 129.)   *August 21, 1911.*

Morocco. I have communicated to the President of the Council your telegram No. 195 of to-day.([1]) He wishes me to convey to you his grateful appreciation of the willingness of His Majesty's Government to consider the question of a possible exchange of territories to give to France access from her northern Congo Colony to her possessions north of Nigeria.

M. Caillaux attaches the greatest importance to your opinion and he will do nothing in regard to sending ships to Mogador and Safi until after the matter has been discussed with you by the French Ambassador whom he has seen this morning on the subject.

([1]) [*v. supra*, p. 460, No. 487.]

No. 490.

Note by Sir John French.([1])

1911.

The Emperor arrived at Altengrabow to inspect troops at 6 A.M. on Wednesday August 2nd.

He rode at once on parade, and after riding down the line and speaking to the German Officers, he sent for me to speak to him. He began by giving me a very hearty welcome, and said that he wished me to see everything that there was to be seen. He added these words:—"Remember the French are now your allies, and whatever you may tell your own people, I trust to your honour to see that nothing that transpires here is reported through you to France."

At luncheon I was placed on His Majesty' right and he spoke very freely on the Political situation and Military affairs generally. The Emperor strongly deprecated Mr. Lloyd George's speech at the Mansion House, describing it as provocative, encouraging France to resist him, and dangerous to the peace of Europe. He said he was the more surprised at our attitude in the Morocco question, because he had himself told the King (when in England in May) the action he had intended to take, and which he actually did take. He gave me to understand that the British Government also knew beforehand that he intended to send a warship to Agadir.

The Emperor told me that in his opinion the action of the French in Morocco had completely wiped out the Treaty of Algeciras, and had left the signatory Powers an absolutely free hand.

He said that personally he deplored the differences between Germany and England but that they were none of his making, and that if we interfered in the affairs of Germany, we must take the consequences. He said we had always fought shoulder to shoulder, and were natural Allies.

He further expressed the opinion that great wars of the future would be "Racial," hence his reason for wishing all Europe to be as strong as possible against such possible contingencies as the "Yellow Peril."

I talked a good deal to him on technical matters, and took notes of what he said. They are not of importance from a political point of view, and so I am not

([1]) [Grey MSS., Vol. 68. The typescript, which is undated, is endorsed in the hand of Sir Edward Grey, "Given to me by Sir John French."]

including them in this precis. On Thursday August 3rd, I sat opposite the Emperor at luncheon and he talked quite freely to me across the table. He had previously presented me with his photograph, saying in a jocular manner :—" Here is your Arch Enemy ! here is the disturber of the peace of Europe !! "

His Majesty said he considered his Army was as efficient a machine of war as any Army could possibly be made, and he implied that it was superior to any in the world. He explained the system by which the Army is under his sole command and control. The War Minister has only to provide the money and deal with certain details of administration. He said that all *Officers'* reports came direct to him, and were dealt with altogether in his Military Cabinet. Thus every Officer understands that his future prospects depend upon the Emperor alone.

His Majesty further remarked upon the necessity for being able to " Support one's politics with the Sword," and of keeping the " Sword sharp." He told me that I had seen how sharp the sword of Germany was in my experience at Altengrabow and assured me that each separate arm was just as efficient as the Cavalry. He added words to this effect " Remember those who run up against that sword will find it very sharp indeed " and further " I don't mean to interfere with you nor do I mean you to interfere with me and if you do you will find how sharp the sword is." (*note* I can't vouch that every word is accurate but the sense is absolutely as stated)

Speaking of France the Emperor said he had no fear but that he could over-run her whenever he liked. He said her soldiers were brave and good but he didn't think the French Army was well led or that their discipline was high. He did not think France would ever fight him unless egged on and supported by us and our press. He particularly mentioned Harmsworth and The Daily Mail also the late Moberly Bell of the Times as being most hostile to Germany and doing much harm.

The Emperor said his Policy was not understood in England. That he had made proposals to Lord Rosebery when P[rime] M[inister] some 13 or 14 years ago, to occupy Coaling Stations conjointly with England but that he had met with nothing but rebuffs. He said he had afterwards concluded similar arrangements with Russia.

CHAPTER LVII.
THE RUSSIAN DÉMARCHE.

[*ED. NOTE.*—The Russian attitude in the Morocco question was first defined in the following two telegrams :—

No. 491.

(*a.*)

Sir E. Goschen to Sir Edward Grey.　　　　　*Berlin, May 4,* 1911.

F.O. 16793/13911/11/28.　　　　　　　　　　　　　　　　D. 2.
Tel. (No. 21.)　　　　　　　　　　　　　　　　　　　　R. 2·30.

　　Confidential. Morocco.

　　Russian Chargé d'Affaires tells me that he has been instructed to inform Imperial Government that in view of assurances given by the French Ambassador at St. Petersburg the Russian Government see no objection whatever to measures which French Government have found it necessary to take in Morocco and are in complete agreement with them on the subject. He is also to express the hope that the German Government share those views.

(*b.*)

Sir F. Cartwright to Sir Edward Grey.　　　　　*Vienna, May 5,* 1911.

F.O. 16965/13911/11/28.　　　　　　　　　　　　　　　D. 5·20 P.M.
Tel. (No. 39.)　Most Confidential.　　　　　　　　　　R. 7·30 P.M.

　　I learn most confidentially from French Ambassador that about a week ago French Ambassador at St. Petersburgh informed Acting Russian Minister for Foreign Affairs that France desired to know clearly what attitude of Russia would be should the Morocco question assume wider dimensions. As a result of this action Acting Russian Minister for Foreign Affairs showed French Ambassador draft of a telegram addressed to Russian Ambassador at Berlin, which he would submit to the Emperor, substance of which was that Russian Ambassador could intimate to the German Government that Russia would stand by France. Acting Minister for Foreign Affairs added to the French Ambassador that in all grave questions France could rely on support of Russia, *especially* in any dispute which might arise with Germany.

　　Two days ago a violent anti-French article, professing to represent Germany's views as to French action in Morocco, appeared in a leading Vienna newspaper. This article, I learn most confidentially from the editor, was inserted at the direct request of German Ambassador here after a conversation with the editor. The article which caused annoyance here has now been semi-officially repudiated by "Cologne Gazette." It seems to me possible that Russian and Austrian representations at Berlin may have had some effect in moderating Germany's official attitude in regard to Morocco (see my telegram No. 34(¹)).

　　I am inclined to doubt accuracy of the language attributed (in Sir F. Bertie's telegram No. 53(²)) to the Austrian Ambassador in Paris. Spanish Ambassador in Paris is a man to be mistrusted, and he may have wished to frighten French Foreign Office by intimating that Spain was sure of Austrian support.

　　On May 5 M. Neratov informed M. Isvolski at Paris (*Siebert,* p. 585, and *note*) that friendly remonstrances at Berlin, asking for the fullest consideration to France, had produced a very satisfactory answer. On May 7, having received information as to German views on the lines of the Kiderlen–Cambon interview of April 28 (*v. supra,* pp. 207–8, No. 229) Russia returned a vague reply to Berlin (*v. G.P.* XXIX, pp. 112, 117). On June 6 M. Isvolski reported from Paris that the French plan as regards Fez was " sans reproche " but she might be unable to execute it without international complications (*v. Livre Noir,* I, p. 119).

　　On July 2, after the despatch of the " Panther " to Agadir was known, M. Neratov sent instructions to Count Benckendorff " we should like to conform our attitude to that of England." Count Benckendorff informed Sir Edward Grey accordingly on July 3 (*Siebert,* pp. 588–9; *v.* also *supra,* pp. 329–30, No. 349). According to *Caillaux,* pp. 142–4, M. Isvolski sought him out at some date between July 20–31 (probably the 25th) and expressed his astonishment that France should resist the territorial concessions demanded by Germany. Russia could not fight for the Congo. M. Caillaux states that, in consequence, he took the matter up at St. Petersburgh. The Emperor Nicholas II counselled prudence to M. Louis, but stated that he would keep the terms of the Dual Alliance.]

　　(¹) [*v. supra,* p. 221, No. 244.]
　　(²) [Not reproduced. It stated that the Austro-Hungarian Ambassador at Paris had been urging the Spanish Ambassador to make difficulties as to French action in Morocco.]

No. 492.

Sir G. Buchanan to Sir Edward Grey.

St. Petersburgh, July 30, 1911.

F.O. 29907/13911/11/28.

D. 8·8 P.M.

Tel. (No. 168.)

R. 10 P.M.

In speaking to me yesterday of the Moroccan question Acting Minister for Foreign Affairs said that Russian Ambassador in London had telegraphed on Friday that he had been told by the Prime Minister that a further communication had been made to you by the German Ambassador on Thursday that somewhat toned down the earlier one which, as Acting Minister for Foreign Affairs supposes, had prompted you to speak to Russian Ambassador. His Excellency did not therefore quite understand how things actually stood at present.

I said that I knew nothing beyond what you had told me in your telegram No. 386 (   ),([1]) of which I gave him a summary.

His Excellency subsequently said that he did not believe that Germany would push matters to extremes, as she knew a war could not nowadays be tête-à-tête. Before taking any decision as to our future action it would be well to await result of German Minister for Foreign Affairs' audience with the German Emperor, as now that he had returned to Germany His Majesty's influence would be more directly felt.

Acting Minister for Foreign Affairs seems to fear that, if Germany obtains large compensation in the Congo or elsewhere in return for renunciation of all political claims in Morocco, other Powers such as Austria and Italy may be tempted to put forward similar demands.

(Confidential.)

French Ambassador tells me that he is perfectly satisfied with diplomatic support so far given him by Acting Minister for Foreign Affairs, but that Russian official circles are inclined to take too optimistic a view of Germany's intentions. He is evidently convinced that France will be able to count upon Russia's material support should Germany push matters too far, but says that until Emperor of Russia returns from Finland Acting Minister for Foreign Affairs will not be in a position to make any declaration with regard to future eventualities.

([1]) [Thus in original. *v. supra*, p. 407, No. 427.]

No. 493.

Sir A. Nicolson to Sir G. Buchanan.

Private.([1])

My dear Buchanan,

Foreign Office, August 1, 1911.

Many thanks for your last letter. We are, as you may imagine, entirely preoccupied with the crisis which has arisen over the Moorish affairs and which has created a very serious situation. It has had the advantage of showing a perfect unanimity of feeling amongst all sections of the public here, and the Government is firm and quite united. We are waiting to know what will be the result of the conversations which are being held at Berlin and which so far as they have gone do not hold out much promise of a satisfactory solution. I have every belief that the maintenance by us of our present attitude—and I am quite convinced that there will be no flinching on our side—may eventually render Germany more compliant and reasonable. I think that the position which we have assumed has come as a complete surprise to Germany for even among the extreme Liberal sections there

([1]) [Carnock MSS., Vol. III of 1911.]

ıs a determination to stand very firmly by the side of France. I am quite sure that Russia will do the same and Germany will see that the Triple Entente is not so weak a combination as she apparently imagines. She has, in fact, committed a great blunder and I think she will have great difficulty in extricating herself from it without losing considerable prestige. We were given to understand that after the interview which Kiderlen had with the Emperor at Swinemünde he would give the French Ambassador in Berlin a decided reply as to what Germany's final demands will be, but as we have heard nothing either from Paris or Berlin, I presume that Kiderlen has not yet spoken to the French Ambassador on the subject. I do not know whether this silence is ominous or favourable, and as they are continually shifting their ground at Berlin it is difficult to make any forecast. They come down here one day to make disagreeable communications and twenty-four hours later completely change their tone and become most suave and amiable.

Although not much has been said in our Press there is a very determined feeling here which is most satisfactory, though naturally no one wishes to push matters to extremities, I do not think that there will be any wavering were we compelled to take a more pronounced attitude. . . . .(²)

[A. NICOLSON.]

(²) [The rest of this long letter refers to the Bagdad Railway question, Persian affairs, and the situation in Albania.]

No. 494.

Sir Edward Grey to Sir G. Buchanan.

F.O. 31669/25883/11/28.
(No. 219.)
Sir,   *Foreign Office, August 9, 1911.*
I observed to Count Benckendorff to-day that I was not quite easy as to the negotiations between France and Germany. Herr von Kiderlen was evidently not in a hurry. It might be, and probably was, the case that all he wished was to get time during which to move away from the extreme position which he had at first taken up. But it was just possible that he might wish to keep the conversations alive, in order that he might choose his own moment for giving a brusque and unfavourable turn to the situation. If so, much would depend upon what Russia was prepared to do at such a time, and what Germany thought that Russia would do.

Count Benckendorff agreed that this was very important, especially what Germany thought that Russia might do. Owing to the terms of the Russian Alliance with France, he thought it was pretty clear what Russia would do. As a matter of fact, in one of the first conversations between the Acting Minister for Foreign Affairs and the German Ambassador in St. Petersburg, the former had told the Ambassador that Germany must remember that France and Russia were Allies.

[I am, &c.]
E. G[REY].

[*ED. NOTE.*—On August 16, when Sir Edward Grey held a grave conversation with M. Paul Cambon (*v. supra*, p. 450, No. 475), Count Benckendorff reported that Sir Edward Grey asked him(¹) " ' What would you do in the case of complications? ' I told Sir Edward that I had not the right to give an official answer; *the Treaty Alliance between France and Russia existed in its full compass; war would certainly be a great misfortune for Russia; personally, however, I had not the slightest doubt but that the terms of the Treaty would be strictly carried out.*" On the

(¹) [*Siebert*, p. 598, *italics* are in original. No record of this conversation has been found in the F.O. archives or private papers.]

same day Herr von Kiderlen-Wächter acknowledged the correctness of Russia's attitude hitherto and suggested that the negotiations would be greatly facilitated " *if France would only cease threatening Germany with her Alliances, and would be more careful in preserving the stipulated secrecy of the negotiations. It was desirable that France should realize this, or that her friends should point it out to her.*"([2]) This appears to have been the origin of the so-called " *démarche* " made by M. Isvolski to M. de Selves on September 1. *v. infra*, pp. 471–2, No. 499.]

([2]) [*Siebert*, p. 597.]

No. 495.

Sir F. Bertie to Sir Edward Grey.

F.O. 33424/25883/11/28.
(No. 376.)   Most Confidential.   *Paris*, D. *August* 23, 1911.
Sir :—   R. *August* 25, 1911.

In the course of the interview with the Minister for Foreign Affairs, of which I had the honour to give you an account in my telegram No. 130 Confidential of yesterday,([1]) I pointed out to His Excellency that if the French Government occupied Mogador, Saffi and other parts of Morocco as a counter stroke to a German landing at Agadir or an increase of the German naval force there such action by the French Government might be taken by the German Government as a throwing down of the gauntlet and a defiance to Germany. It might put a stop to all further negotiations, make it certain that Germany would refuse a Conference and bring on an immediate conflict.

M. de Selves said that neither the present Ministry nor any French Ministry could survive a quiescent acceptance of such a situation as was contemplated as possible at Agadir, and the Ministry had fully and carefully considered the question before coming to the decision of which he had informed me.

To-day was M. de Selves' reception day. I found on my arrival in the ante-room the German, Russian and Spanish Ambassadors. They were discussing the Morocco question in a general way. I took no part in the conversation. Baron de Schoen's observations were to the effect that, in his opinion, matters would be arranged, the suspension in the conversations at Berlin would give time for reflection and consideration of the questions at issue, the essential thing would be to devise a formula which, without mentioning the word " Protectorat " would give to France all that she could require in Morocco and would secure Germany's economic interests. His Excellency then left and the *huissier* announced to the Russian Ambassador that M. de Selves was ready to receive him.

I was then alone with the Spanish Ambassador who spoke to me of the grievances of Spain and the desirability of the Spanish Government joining in the Berlin conversations; otherwise later on when Germany and France had come to terms Spain might have difficulties with France. No doubt Germany would be quite ready to recognize the legitimate claims of Spain but that alone would not suffice. I asked M. Caballero whether the German Government had shown any desire to acquire Spanish Guinea or Fernando Po as a price for the recognition of Spanish claims in Morocco in the same way as they asked for cessions of territory in the French Congo for a recognition of the claims of France. The Ambassador said that no such pretensions had been advanced by the German Government. The conversation was stopped by the return to the Ante-room of the Russian Ambassador who remained with me after M. Caballero left it to see M. de Selves.

M. Isvolsky spoke to me to the effect that it would be deplorable that there should be a war on account of Morocco; that he could not see what harm the Germans at Agadir and in the Sus country could do to France supposing that the

([1]) [*v. infra*, pp. 482–3, No. 510.]

French Government could not get them out of Agadir by compensations elsewhere. A German occupation of Agadir might affect British interests but not those of France. I observed that the French Government did not see things in that light and would not accept the establishment of Germany in Morocco. As to British interests, an unfortified Agadir would not injure them, but, as he knew, engagements not to fortify did not hold good long as had been shown by Bizerta and, I added, by Batoum. This he admitted. I asked him whether if there were war he thought that Austria would take the field in support of Germany. His answer was that it was impossible to say for the exact terms of the Triple Alliance were not known except to the Parties to it. All the European Alliances being so far as was known defensive in their terms who was to decide as to which was the attacked party so as to entitle it to the armed support of its ally? If, however, war began between France and Germany, it would almost certainly cause a general European War.

The language of the Russian Ambassador being strange for the Representative of the Ally which had, the French Minister for Foreign Affairs had informed me, given assurances to the French Government of support to the cause of France in Morocco, I asked M. de Selves when my turn to see him came whether there was any change in the attitude of the Russian Government, for M. Isvolsky's conversation had given me the impression that the Russian Government might wish the French Government to make greater sacrifices to Germany than they were prepared to do and notably at Agadir. M. de Selves with a smile said he knew what the Russian Ambassador's views were for he had expounded them not only to him but to a journalist, but they were not those of the Russian Government as he had ascertained by inquiry at St. Petersburg. The reply of the Russian Government which had been kept fully informed of the discussions with the German Government was entirely satisfactory. It was that Russia would give to France her full support as her Ally. I next referred to the apprehensions of the Spanish Ambassador, and M. de Selves told me that M. Caballero had just expressed to him the desire of the Spanish Government to resume the discussions concerning Morocco and to join in the conversations at Berlin. M. de Selves had, he said, replied to the Ambassador that he would be happy to resume the discussions at the earliest opportune moment and would give the requisite instructions to the French Ambassador at Madrid, but the time had hardly yet come considering that it was impossible at present to foresee what the issue of the conversations at Berlin would be, and as to a Spanish participation in those conversations, it was the German Government which had declined to admit the participation in them of any other Power than France. Whenever matters had been settled between France and Germany, the French Government would be prepared to discuss with the Spanish Government the claims and wishes of Spain with every desire to gratify them as far as might be reasonably possible.

After these references to the Russian and Spanish Ambassadors I mentioned to M. de Selves the sanguine language of the German Ambassador and I asked whether M. de Schoen could be taken as knowing and expressing the views of the German Government. M. de Selves said that from the conversation which he had just had with the Ambassador, he discerned the possibility of a change at Berlin. He had expressed the regret which he felt that the Ambassador had not been authorized to fully discuss with him the question of Morocco for he felt that with M. de Schoen's conciliatory disposition an agreement might soon have been come to. The Ambassador had thereupon said that he now had the requisite authority and would discuss the matter with him very shortly.

Monsieur de Selves is inclined to think that it is possible that the German Emperor and his Chancellor feeling that M. de Kiderlen-Waechter has been too exacting desire to take advantage of his being absent on a holiday, a holiday which may be prolonged according to circumstances, intend to endeavour to come to an understanding with the French Government through His Majesty's Ambassador at Paris.

M. de Selves was not able to show to me in detail the cessions of territory, mentioned in my despatch No. 372, of August 21st([2]) which the French Government are prepared to make to Germany in return for an absolutely free hand in Morocco, for he had not received from the Colonial Department the maps to illustrate them. He said that unless the formula for the renunciation by Germany of all political claims in Morocco and for her recognition of a French Protectorate if later on desired by France, be perfectly clear and be concurred in by the other Parties to the Act of Algeciras he will find great difficulty in reconciling the French Chambers to the great sacrifices of French territory which the French Government contemplate as the price of a free hand for France in Morocco.

I have, &c.
FRANCIS BERTIE.

([2]) [v. supra, pp. 460–1, No. 488.]

No. 496.

Sir G. Buchanan to Sir Edward Grey.

St. Petersburgh, August 24, 1911.

F.O. 33414/13911/11/28.
Tel. (No. 190.)

D. 3·16.
R. 4·55 P.M.

Very Confidential.

Your despatch No. 219.([1])

French Ambassador tells me that Russian Gov[ernmen]t have recently given formal assurance that France may count upon both their diplomatic and military support. H[is] E[xcellency] could not say however whether they had let Germany know this. H[is] E[xcellency] said that Acting M[inister for] F[oreign] A[ffairs] was no longer so optimistic as he had been at first when he thought that it was a mere matter of bluff on Germany's part.

([1]) [v. supra, p. 466, No. 494.]

No. 497.

Sir F. Bertie to Sir Edward Grey.

F.O. 34382/25883/11/28.
(No. 384.) Most Confidential.
Sir :—

Paris, D. August 29, 1911.
R. September 1, 1911.

I went to the Quai d'Orsay this morning to see the Minister for Foreign Affairs on the subject of the recognition of the Portuguese Republic. . . . .([1])

M. de Selves further informed me of a conversation which he had had yesterday with the Russian Ambassador who had asked for an interview. M. Isvolsky enquired as to the state of the negotiations with Germany. Whilst M. de Selves was describing to him their position, he noticed that M. Isvolsky evidently had something which he desired to say and yet found difficulty in saying, which M. de Selves observed to me was not to be wondered at, for the Ambassador, after some observations as to the horrors of war and how disastrous it would be if the negotiations at Berlin failed and a conflict became a possibility, asked whether in such a deplorable contingency the French Government would accept arbitration. M. de Selves whilst deploring such a contingency stated that the French Government were doing and would do

([1]) [Here follow further details on the same subject, and the Spanish aspect of the Morocco question is discussed.]

everything that was reasonably possible to avoid it, and that as to arbitration, Russia would not be likely to offer her arbitration and the French Government would certainly not ask her to set aside her proper position as the Ally of France to assume that of Arbiter in a question in which the interests of France were deeply involved. M. Isvolsky admitted that in the particular circumstances Russia might not be a suitable arbitrator, but he asked whether the Emperor of Austria might not be such a one. M. de Selves observed to the Russian Ambassador that, much as he respected the great experience and impartiality of the Aged Monarch he hardly thought that His Majesty would be a suitable arbitrator in such a case, as M. Isvolsky must realize if he would reflect on the situation. M. de Selves then went on to make some observations to His Excellency on the state of public opinion in France which he said must probably have been noticed by the Ambassador when he read the newspapers and in the course of his conversations with the many French public and private persons with whom he came in contact. France ardently desired a pacific solution of the questions at issue with Germany and the French Government would go to the utmost limit of reasonable concessions to effect such a settlement, but France of the present day was not the France of ten years ago and of the Morocco crisis of 1905. The French people desired peace but an honourable peace. There were limits in the way of concessions to Germany beyond which they would not permit the Government to go even if they were so disposed, which they were not. M. Isvolsky must have observed how calm and collected public opinion was. It was so because it had reliance on the determination of the Government to maintain the legitimate rights and interests of France, and confidence in the ability of the French Army to defend them, if the need arose, from the unreasonable pretensions of Germany. In such circumstances Russia would, as M. de Selves had the assurance from the Russian Government, give to her Ally the support which France had the right to expect.

I have, &c.
FRANCIS BERTIE.

No. 498.

Sir F. Bertie to Sir Edward Grey.

Private and Confidential.(¹)

My dear Grey,   *Paris, August* 29, 1911.

Isvolsky will not be long for this Parisian world if he continues to make such suggestions not only to the French Government but to many others as admission of Germany to a share in the Morocco cake, and the reference to Russia or the Emperor of Austria as Arbitrator of the differences between France and Germany. He does these things not only without authority but knowing, so Selves says, that they are contrary to the intentions of the Russian Government.

Yours sincerely,
FRANCIS BERTIE.

(¹) [Grey MSS., Vol. 13.]

No. 499.

Sir F. Bertie to Sir Edward Grey.

F.O. 34484/25883/11/28.
Tel. (No. 141.) R.

Paris, *September* 1, 1911.
D. 6·45 P.M.
R. 10·15 P.M.

I had an interview with Minister for Foreign Affairs this evening. He had received information this morning in a private letter from French Embassy at Berlin that Herr Zimmermann, Under-Secretary at German Foreign Office, had begged Sir E. Goschen to request His Majesty's Government to use their influence at Paris with a view to prevailing on French Government to be conciliatory in conversations which were about to be resumed at Berlin for a settlement of the Morocco question. The same request had, the letter stated, been made to Russian Government.

Russian Ambassador asked for an appointment, and saw French Minister for Foreign Affairs this morning. He brought with him some notes, which he said were made from telegraphic instructions which he had received, and he consulted them during the interview from time to time. The communication which he made was, French Minister for Foreign Affairs informed me, to the following effect: Russian Government, and especially Emperor of Russia, were perturbed at state of relations between France and Germany. They trusted that cessions of territory which French Government would be ready to offer to Germany would be sufficient to satisfy her. The extent of cessions of colonial territory to be made by France could not be of importance to her when it became, as it might, a question of avoiding war. A war would be a great danger to recently established liberal institutions in Russia, and it would be difficult to make Russian people realize necessity of war for a few kilometres more or less of colonial territory. Though Russian army had been greatly improved by recent reforms, it was not yet quite perfected ("à point"). What would happen if the German Government rejected the offers of the French Government and there were a rupture of the negotiations? Could not France in such an event accept arbitration of Emperor of Austria? French Minister for Foreign Affairs told me that he did not quite make out whether an arbitration by the Emperor of Austria was a suggestion from the Russian Government or a revival of a personal one of M. Isvolsky.

French Minister for Foreign Affairs' observations to Russian Ambassador were, he informed me, that he was surprised, and he might even say "peiné," at Ambassador's communication.([1]) It led him to think that Russian Government could not have been kept accurately informed of the course of Franco-German conversations and liberal spirit of conciliation in which they had been carried on by French Government, of the very liberal proposals which, as M. Isvolsky knew, had been made, and the still greater sacrifices which they were prepared to offer to German Government when conversations were renewed, which they would be in a few days' time. German Ambassador had admitted to French Minister for Foreign Affairs that they were conceived in a most liberal spirit. As German Government were not yet fully acquainted with the extent of those sacrifices it was impossible to know whether they would satisfy German Government or not. There could therefore be no question of considering or even talking of arbitration at the present moment. He would therefore discard it altogether from conversation. If sacrifices which French Government offered to Germany did not satisfy German Government it would mean that they did not wish the negotiations to succeed. It could not be foreseen what the next step of the German Government might be. They had begun the conversations which they announced that they desired to have with the French Government by sending a ship of war to Agadir on pretext of there being there German lives and interests which required protection. If conversations, which French Government had accepted and had conducted in a most liberal and pacific

([1]) [*v. Livre Noir*, I, pp. 132–4.]

spirit, failed to bring about an arrangement, and the German Government thereupon took further action, it would show that German Government desired to humiliate France in the eyes of the French people and of the world. It would mean the publication to the world that whatever Germany might demand of France or any other nation must be accorded. France could not accept such a position. No self-respecting nation could do so. He therefore begged Russian Ambassador correctly to inform his Government of the situation, and to remind them of the assurances which they had given French Government that Russia would stand by France as her ally. French Minister for Foreign Affairs says that request made by German Government to Russian and British Governments for counsels of conciliation to French Government is obviously an endeavour to separate England and Russia from France by making out—contrary to the truth—that French offers of territory are quite insufficient for reasonable compensation to Germany, and to throw the blame for possible ulterior complications on France. He has instructed French Ambassador at St. Petersburgh fully to explain the situation to the Russian Government, to repeat to them the observations which French Minister for Foreign Affairs made to M. Isvolsky, and to ask for an audience of the Emperor of Russia in order correctly to acquaint His Majesty with the situation, and to express to him the confidence felt by French Government that Russia will adhere as in the past to her part of faithful ally of France.

French Minister for Foreign Affairs is telegraphing to French Embassy in London to inform you of the situation.

No. 500.

Sir F. Bertie to Sir Edward Grey.

Paris, September 2, 1911.

F.O. 34659/25883/11/28.

Tel. (No. 143.) Confidential. R.

D. 3·48 P.M.
R. 5·45 P.M.

See my telegram No. 141 of yesterday.([1])

Minister for Foreign Affairs has shown me to-day a telegram from French Ambassador at St. Petersburgh, dated yesterday. It states, with reference to some guarded remarks which the Ambassador reported as having been made to him by Russian Minister for Foreign Affairs in regard to the possibility of a threatening of war and of a Russian mediation to avert it, that he is convinced that any instructions which Russian Ambassador may have received and on which he founded his communication to French Minister for Foreign Affairs were inspired by M. Isvolsky himself, M. Nératof's late chief, and were not due to any change of attitude on the part of the Emperor, and that the considerations urged by M. Isvolsky and the arguments which he used in support of them, and suggestion that Emperor of Austria would be a fitting arbitrator, were his own.

French Ambassador at St. Petersburgh further states that from language of entourage of Emperor, of the Grand Dukes, and of the generals there can be no doubt that His Majesty intends faithfully to adhere to assurances of support of Russia as France's ally which by his orders were lately given to French Government. Having regard to these circumstances, French Ambassador proposes not to ask for a special audience to bring to Emperor's notice the strange communication made to French Minister for Foreign Affairs by Russian Ambassador, but to take an opportunity of speaking to the Emperor on the subject just before His Majesty leaves for the Crimea, when he will receive French Ambassador.

([1]) [*v.* immediately preceding document.]

No. 501.

Sir G. Buchanan to Sir Edward Grey.

St. Petersburgh, September 3, 1911.

F.O. 34653/25883/11/28.

Tel. (No. 196.)

D. 7·50 P.M.

R. 9·40 P.M.

Sir F. Bertie's telegram No. 141 (   ).(¹)

French Ambassador is not greatly perturbed by Russian communication, which was probably inspired by M. Isvolsky. Russia, he thinks, naturally wishes to avert war, and there may be two currents of opinion as to the policy to be pursued; but he is confident that she will do her duty as France's ally should there be a rupture of negotiations. In support of this view he cites the categorical assurances she has already given; the fact that on the very day when Russian Ambassador made his communication to French Minister for Foreign Affairs Russian and French Chiefs of the Staff were conferring here on the future plan of campaign should war break out; and the terms in which the Grand Duke Nicholas, the probable commander-in-chief of the Russian forces, drank to the health of the army of Russia's ally at a dinner given a few days ago to the French military delegation.

He hopes to be received in audience by the Emperor in the course of the next few days before His Majesty leaves for the Crimea, and he does not seem nervous as to the result. Russian Government, he says, have been kept informed day by day as to the course of the negotiations.

At the dinner in honour of the King of Servia last Friday at which I was the only Ambassador present, the Emperor gave me no opportunity of speaking to him, and only shook hands as he was leaving with the King. Whether this was done intentionally in order to avoid a political conversation I cannot say, but it rather gave me that impression.

President of the Council, with whom I had a long conversation the same evening, said that he did not believe in war and that Germany was only bluffing. I did not question him as to Russia's attitude, as after what French Ambassador had told me (see my telegram No. 190 (   ))(²) I did not think it was an open question. Acting Minister for Foreign Affairs also held very optimistic language, but I will sound him again at an interview I am to have with him to-morrow.

MINUTES.

M. Louis has telegraphed to M. de Selves in this sense—see Sir F. Bertie's tel. No. 143 [34659].(³)

It seems unnecessary to repeat this to Paris.

G. H. V.
4.9.11.
A. P.

General Wilson told me that the Russian Army was not yet in a position to render great help to France: in a few years time, however, the Russian Army reforms would so far have progressed that the Russian Army would be in a position to render France decisive aid in a war with Germany.

Thus, he said, Germany had a delicate problem to solve as to the most favourable moment to strike.

From a naval point of view she had much better wait a few years.

From a military point of view she had far better act at once.

A. P.
Sept. 4, 1911.
W. L.
E. G.

(¹) [v. supra, pp. 471–2, No. 499.]
(²) [v. supra, p. 469, No. 496.]
(³) [v. immediately preceding document.]

No. 502.

Sir G. Buchanan to Sir Edward Grey.

F.O. 35648/25883/11/28.
(No. 255.)   St. Petersburgh, D. September 6, 1911.
Sir,   R. September 11, 1911.

At a dinner at Court, to which I was invited last week, I sat next to the President of the Council, who spoke to me, among other matters, on the Moroccan question. He did not, he said, believe that there was any serious danger of war. Germany had from the very outset been playing a game of bluff and, though he admitted that this was a game which exposed those who engaged in it to a considerable risk, he did not apprehend a rupture of Franco-German relations. He had never, he must confess, been able to make out what Germany really wanted; but he had been much struck by the fact that German public opinion was at present more incensed against England than against France.

I remarked that the German press was accusing us of trying to prevent an amicable arrangement and of inciting France to resistance. There was not a word of truth in this; and I could assure him that His Majesty's Government were most anxious that the negotiations now proceeding should be brought to a speedy and satisfactory termination. The situation otherwise would become most critical. So far from creating difficulties we had all along done everything in our power to facilitate a settlement. Germany, unfortunately, had been under the impression that we should look on as disinterested spectators while she imposed her terms on France and, now that she had discovered her mistake she was indulging in every sort of abuse of us. I personally, however, believed that the firm attitude adopted by His Majesty's Government at the outset had made for peace, as, had we shown the slightest sign of vacillation, Germany might have gone too far and we should have drifted into war. Monsieur Stolypine agreed, adding that the recent outburst of Anglophobia in Germany was no new departure. It was but the frank expression of sentiments which Germany had long cherished. Nevertheless he did not think that she would push matters to extremities. I replied that if the German Government realised that Russia and England would, in such an eventuality, stand by France she would probably pause before she went too far. His Excellency tacitly admitted this, but did not commit himself to saying what Russia would do should the negotiations break down and as I had already been informed by my French Colleague of the categorical assurances which his Government had received on the subject I did not press His Excellency further.

On receiving Sir F. Bertie's telegram No. 141 of the 2nd instant,([1]) I called on the French Ambassador and enquired what view he took of the communication which the Russian Ambassador at Paris had just made to Monsieur de Selves.

Monsieur Louis replied that it had not caused him any serious preoccupation and that, as Monsieur Iswolsky had already spoken some ten days ago in a somewhat similar sense on his own account, the step, which he had now taken under instructions from his Government, had in all probability been inspired by him and need not necessarily be imputed to German instigation. It was, he thought quite natural that Russia should wish to avert the danger of war and it was quite possible that there were at the present moment two currents of opinion as to the course, which she ought to pursue; but he believed that the Emperor, the Court and the Government were all firm supporters of the Alliance with France. Russia, he remarked, knew quite well that, were she to fail France now, she would never be able to count on French support in the future and that the whole fabric of the Alliance, built up by Alexander III, would be destroyed. He was, therefore, confident that, were there to be a rupture of the negotiations, Russia would do her duty as France's ally.

([1]) [v. supra, pp. 471-2, No. 499. It was of the 1st inst.]

I remarked that the Russian Court was a sealed book whose secrets it was very difficult to penetrate, but that I had always imagined that there were many German sympathisers in the immediate entourage of the Emperor. Monsieur Louis replied that this might be the case when it was a question of an Anglo-Russian as against a Russo-German understanding, but that the French Alliance had taken a deeper root and was now generally accepted as a permanent institution. There, were, moreover, specific grounds for the confidence which he placed in Russia's loyalty to her Ally at the present crisis. The Russian Government who had been kept informed day by day of the course of the negotiations had given France the most categorical assurances of both her diplomatic and military support. On the very day, moreover, on which Monsieur Iswolsky had made his communication to M. de Selves, the Chief of the General Staff of the French Army was conferring at St. Petersburg with the Chief of the General Staff of the Russian Army on a joint plan of campaign in the event of war. It was also a significant fact that at a moment like the present, when peace and war were hanging in the balance, the Grand Duke Nicholas Nikolaievitch, who in all probability would be the Commander in Chief of the Russian forces, should, at a dinner given a few days ago to the French Military delegation, have toasted the Army of Russia's Ally.

On my asking Monsieur Louis whether he had thought that the Russian Army was a match for the Austrian, His Excellency replied in the affirmative. The Russian Army had greater cohesion and tenacity than the Austrian and it would be certainly to France's advantage that they should both take part in the war, on their respective sides, than that they should both stand aloof. The French Army, he believed, could be mobilised as rapidly as the German and, though mobilisation in this country would proceed at a slower rate, no long interval would elapse before the Russian Army was in a position to take the offensive.

Owing to a series of Court functions, which His Excellency was obliged to attend, it was not till this afternoon that the Acting Minister for Foreign Affairs was able to see me and that I could speak to him on the subject of Morocco. He told me that there was no truth in the report, mentioned in Sir F. Bertie's telegram No. 141 of September 2, that the Russian Government had been asked by Germany to give counsels of moderation at Paris. The instructions sent to Monsieur Isvolsky had been prompted by the desire to impress on the French Government the grave consequences which would ensue should they fail to approach this final and critical stage of the negotiations in a conciliatory spirit. France was at the present moment inclined to be too impatient and to expect an immediate and definite answer from Germany to the proposals which Monsieur Cambon had been instructed to make. This was not at all likely to happen and it would be contrary to German diplomatic methods. A war on account of Morocco—a country in which Russia was in no way interested—would be most unpopular in this country, and, even if successful, would predispose Russian public opinion in the future against the French Alliance.

I remarked that from all I knew of the negotiations counsels of moderation were more needed at Berlin than at Paris. I was afraid, moreover, that if Germany heard that representations were being made to the French Government she would think that Russia was wavering in her loyalty to her Ally and would in consequence adopt a more *intransigeant* attitude.

Monsieur Nératow replied that there was no danger of this and that counsels of moderation would be useful in both capitals. Russia had throughout held a very firm language at Berlin and Germany perfectly understood that if there was war the war would be a European one.

As his Excellency then proceeded to refer to the attacks made against England in the German press and to the strong feelings of resentment entertained for us in Berlin, I thought it well to repeat to him what I had said to Monsieur Stolypine on the subject and to express my regret that I had not had an opportunity of assuring the Emperor at the Dinner at Peterhof last Friday how utterly unfounded were the accusations brought against us. His Excellency said that he would inform His Majesty of what I had told him and then went on to tell me that he had just heard that France had addressed what virtually amounted to an ultimatum to Spain. He could not, he said, conceive how at a moment like the present France could have taken so rash and ill-advised a step. It would not fail to encourage Germany to raise her demands and if war did break out, it might place France at a serious disadvantage.

My French colleague, whom I had just seen, tells me that he was received in Audience by the Emperor this afternoon. He was able, he said, to give His Majesty a true and succinct account of the whole history of the Moroccan question and to assure him of the earnest desire of the French Government to come to an amicable understanding with Germany. Monsieur Louis is entirely satisfied with the result of his audience. The Emperor, while expressing the natural wish for the exercise of prudence on the part of France in order to avert the calamity of war, did not hint that the French Government could do more than they were doing, but said that his own impression was that Germany was ready to treat. His Majesty repeated the assurances already given that, in the case of necessity France can count on both the diplomatic and military support of Russia. His language on the point was quite firm and Monsieur Louis is convinced that His Majesty will never refuse to honour the signature which His Father the Emperor Alexander III affixed to the Franco-Russian Alliance.

Monsieur Louis tells me that he knows nothing of a reported French ultimatum to Spain and says that the Emperor did not mention the subject to him.

I have, &c.
GEORGE W. BUCHANAN.

No. 503.

Sir F. Bertie to Sir Edward Grey.

Private.(1)
Tel.   *Paris, September 6, 1911.*

I have received this morning your private telegram of last night, but not the private telegram of the previous day therein referred to. Perhaps you intended to refer to your private letter of the 4th, which reached me last night.(2)

Before acting on directions given in your letter of September 4, I propose to endeavour to ascertain from French M[inister for] F[oreign] A[ffairs] this afternoon the views of the French Government in regard to the position of the negotiations at Berlin, and what are the objections to concessions to Germany of the line of the Alima, and to report them to you for consideration.

If I were to make such a communication as you suggest to the French M[inister for] F[oreign] A[ffairs] and the President of the Council without your having such knowledge, I should be placing you and H[is] M[ajesty's] G[overnment] in the same position as M. Iswolsky and the Russian Government, when it was imagined by the French Government that the advice which he was giving them as to increasing their offers of territorial cessions was by order of the Emperor of Russia, and not merely a tentative communication inspired by M. Iswolsky. As you know from my despatch no: 384, most confidential, of August 29,(3) and my telegrams nos: 141 and 143 of September 1 and 2 respectively,(4) M. Iswolsky's advice was greatly resented by the French Government.

(1) [Grey MSS., Vol. 13.]
(2) [In a private telegram to Sir F. Bertie of September 6, Sir Edward Grey states that the reference should have been to the letter of September 4, *v. infra*, pp. 503–4, No. 531.]
(3) [*v. supra*, pp. 469–70, No. 497.]
(4) [*v. supra*, pp. 471–2, Nos. 499–500.]

M. Jules Cambon has either suggested to the French Government to increase their offers and his advice has been rejected, or he is afraid to give such advice knowing it will not be accepted. It may be that there are objections, Parliamentary or other, which he does not appreciate.

I think that before the French Government will consider *finally* German territorial demands they will require to be assured that they will obtain their idea of a free hand in Morocco, and that does not appear to be certain yet. Supposing that the Convention for that purpose were later on to be repudiated by Germany, as has been the Agreement of 1909, and it came out that it was under pressure from H[is] M[ajesty's] G[overnment] that the price for the Convention had been increased, public opinion in France would hold England responsible for the deception.

No. 504.

Sir G. Buchanan to Sir Edward Grey.

F.O. 35316/25883/11/28.
Tel. (No. 201.)

St. Petersburgh, September 7, 1911.
D. 8·30 P.M.
R. 10·45 P.M.

Sir F. Bertie's telegram No. 141 ( ).([1])

Acting Minister for Foreign Affairs told me this afternoon that Russian Government had had no request from Germany to preach moderation at Paris. M. Isvolsky had been instructed to point out grave consequences that would ensue were France to approach this final stage of the negotiations in an unconciliatory spirit. 'War on account of Morocco would, his Excellency said, be most unpopular in this country, and would, even if successful, indispose public opinion against the French alliance.

I remarked that I thought there was at the present moment more need to counsel moderation at Berlin than at Paris, and that if Germany heard that representations were being made at Paris she might think that Russia was wavering in her support of her ally and become more *intransigeant*. His Excellency replied there was no danger of this. Counsels of moderation would be useful in both capitals, and Russia had throughout held very firm language at Berlin. Germany, he remarked, was quite aware that if war broke out it would be a European one.

As his Excellency referred to the attacks made on England in the German press, I said that I regretted I had not had an opportunity of assuring the Emperor last Friday how utterly unfounded were the accusations brought against us. His Majesty's Government were deeply anxious that the negotiations should succeed, and had from the outset done all they could to facilitate a settlement.

His Excellency said he would inform His Majesty of what I had told him, and went on to say that he had just learnt that France had addressed what virtually amounted to an ultimatum to Spain. He could not conceive how she could have been so ill-advised as to take such a step at the present moment. It would encourage Germany to raise her demands, and, if war did break out, would place France at a disadvantage. He feared that French were in a very nervous and excitable state.

([1]) [*v. supra*, pp. 471–2, No. 499.]

No. 505.

Sir G. Buchanan to Sir Edward Grey.

F.O. 35317/25883/11/28.

Tel. (No. 202.) Very Confidential.

St. Petersburgh,
D. *September* 7, 1911, 8·30 P.M.
R. *September* 8, 1911, 8 A.M.

My immediately preceding telegram (of 7th September).([1])

French Ambassador tells me he was received in audience by the Emperor this afternoon, and laid the whole situation before His Majesty. He was entirely satisfied with the result.

Emperor, while expressing natural wish that France should exercise prudence so as to avert war, never hinted that French Government could do more than they were doing. He expressed the opinion that Germany desired to treat. He also repeated the assurances already given that in case of necessity France could count on Russia's diplomatic and military support. His language on this point was quite firm, and Ambassador is convinced that His Majesty will carry out his engagements under the Franco-Russian alliance.([2])

French Ambassador knows nothing of the reported French ultimatum to Spain, nor did the Emperor mention it to him.

([1]) [*v.* immediately preceding document.]
([2]) [*Siebert–Benckendorff*, II, p. 166, reports (in a communication to St. Petersburgh of the 12th) an interview with Sir Arthur Nicolson on September 11, when the latter said that he was fully satisfied with the words used by the Emperor Nicholas II to M. Louis.]

No. 506.

Sir G. Buchanan to Sir A. Nicolson.

Private.([1])

My dear Nicolson, *St. Petersburgh, September* 7, 1911.

The démarche which the Russians made last Friday at Paris came on me as a complete surprise.

Neratow has never shown much inclination to discuss the Moroccan question; but, whenever I have referred to it in the course of our conversations, he has always expressed himself very optimistically as regards the eventual issue of the negotiations and has never hinted that the French were not liberal enough in their offers of compensation to Germany. Louis had, moreover, told me that he was perfectly satisfied with the attitude of the Russian Government so that my mind was quite made easy on the subject. It is curious that on the very day on which Iswolsky made his communication to de Selves I should have noticed a difference in the Emperor's manner towards myself. It may have been quite unintentional on His Majesty's part; but the way in which he avoided speaking to me was rather marked.

I had seen the Emperor only ten days previously when Prince Arthur of Connaught arrived at Peterhof. On that occasion he was most friendly and pleasant and came up twice to talk to me. At the dinner, however, given to the King of Servia, to which I was asked on account of Prince Arthur, the Emperor, I thought. looked worried and rather "gêné." When we left the Dining Room Benckendorff the Ambassador's brother, asked me to move forward to where the Emperor and the King of Servia were standing. After a few minutes the latter called up one of the Russian Ministers and the Emperor advancing into the room passed me by without a sign. The Minister of the Court, Baron Freedericksz, apparently noticed it as he came up and asked me to stand in another part of the room where His Majesty was

([1]) [Carnock MSS., Vol. IV. of 1911.]

about to pass, but again the Emperor did not speak to me; and it was only as the two Sovereigns went away together that the Emperor shook hands with me for the first time in the evening. I trust that it was only an oversight, but as I was the only Ambassador invited and had sat directly opposite him at dinner, he must have been aware of my presence; and the impression made on me was that His Majesty wished to avoid a political conversation.

Louis is not nearly so perturbed by Iswolsky's communication as de Selves appears to be. He remarks quite justly that it is but natural that the Russians should wish to avert a war about Morocco, which would excite no enthusiasm in the country, upset their finances and lead to a recrudescence of the revolutionary movement, should the Russian Army meet with reverses. He is also quite confident that Russia will not back out of the categorical assurances, which she has given, and that, if the negotiations break down, she will come to France's assistance. I fancy that Iswolsky and Kokovtzoff have been the chief inspirers of the step now taken; but I personally think that nothing is more likely to lead to war than to let Germany suspect that Russia is vacillating in the support of her ally. . . . .(²)

Ever yours,
GEORGE W. BUCHANAN.

(²) [The rest of this letter treats of general matters.]

No. 507.

Sir Edward Grey to Sir G. Buchanan.

F.O. 35990/25883/11/28.
(No. 245.)
Sir, *Foreign Office, September 8, 1911.*

The Russian Ambassador came to see me to-day,(¹) and I again asked him whether he had any news from St. Petersburgh as to Morocco.

He told me that his Government were rather disturbed by what seemed to be the brusque attitude of the French in Madrid.

I explained that there seemed to have been some misunderstanding about this.

I then asked him whether he had heard of the suggestion which M. Iswolsky had made in Paris for arbitration by the Emperor of Austria.

He said that he had heard of it, but not from his Government. He explained how natural it was that the Russian Government, who had no interest in Morocco, though they were prepared to stand by their Alliance with France, should wish to suggest every possible means of avoiding war, precisely because if war came they would be engaged in it.

I told him that I also had been suggesting every thing of which I could think to keep the peace between France and Germany, but one could not expect France to submit to the arbitration of Germany's Ally. This seemed to me to be out of the question. I added, however, that I thought the principle of arbitration or mediation should not be dismissed as an impossible suggestion in the last resort, though it might be difficult of application.

[I am, &c.]
E. G[REY].

(¹) [*Siebert*, p. 604, records Count Benckendorff's views reported to St. Petersburgh this same day, and conversations with M. Paul Cambon and Sir Edward Grey. Count Benckendorff interpreted M. Isvolski's attitude, as due to the difficulty of interesting public opinion in Russia in the Morocco question. The last passage of this document is to be found in *Siebert–Benckendorff*, II, pp. 159–60. An interview with Sir Arthur Nicolson on September 11, is referred to on p. 478, No. 505, *note* (²). On September 20, (*Siebert–Benckendorff*, II, pp. 169–70), Count Benckendorff reported that he had left Balmoral the day before and found everyone from the King downward anxious for the Berlin negotiations to lead to a happy result.]

No. 508.

Sir E. Goschen to Sir A. Nicolson.

Private.([1])

My dear Nicolson,   *Berlin, September 8, 1911.*

The Russian attitude as regards Morocco seems to be on the queer side. When Cambon was in Paris the other day Iswolsky went to see him and in the course of conversation said that France could naturally not expect that Russia would do more for her than France and England had done for Russia at the time of the Bosnian crisis. Cambon told him that that was a very serious statement to make and that it did not harmonize with previous assurances given by the Russian Government. After a few caustic remarks from Cambon about the Bosnian crisis and what had taken place at Buchlau, Iswolsky dropped the point of Russian military assistance and suggested that Russia should mediate. Cambon said that he quite appreciated the goodwill implied by the suggestion, but that, as Russia was France's ally and bound under certain circumstances to march with France, he did not see how the suggestion could possibly be adopted. Iswolsky then suggested that the good offices of the Emperor Francis Joseph might be invited. To this Cambon replied that it was quite true that the Emperor was now advanced in age and that he was naturally very averse to another war during His reign, but that He was after all Germany's ally and also bound under certain circumstances to march with Germany, so that as regards mediation He was in exactly the same position as the Emperor of Russia. Iswolsky said that these were only private ideas of his own actuated by his fervent desire that the peace between Germany and France should not be disturbed. As, however, Cambon seemed to think his ideas impossible he would say no more on the subject. Cambon at once went to Selves and recounted their conversation and shortly afterwards Iswolsky called on de Selves too and made the same suggestions which he made to Cambon. De Selves gave him Cambon's answers over again and then telegraphed to Louis to ask Neratow whether the views held by Iswolsky were those of the Russian Government. The answer was that Iswolsky must have expressed his own private opinions, as the Russian Government abided by their assurances to give France full support in the question now at issue between her and Germany.

This was how the matter was related to me by Cambon, so I was rather surprised to gather from the last telegram sections that the Russian Government was rather shaky on the subject of the support they propose to give to France.

In the meantime I do not believe that at present at all events anything will happen as far as the negotiations are directly concerned that will call for either our or Russia's armed support. But at the same time it cannot be denied that the atmosphere is highly electric and that things want careful handling. Cambon said to me only to-day, even after he had read the German counter-project and pronounced it to be quite inacceptable, that, given a decent amount of prudence on the part of de Selves' surroundings, he is sure that an arrangement will be effected. Kiderlen, I believe, is also of that opinion.

The greater part of public opinion here is wholly against a fight with France on the subject of Morocco. In serious military circles the same feeling exists, but it seems to me that they would all like to have a slap at England if they could. We are held, both by public opinion and by the Press, to be responsible for the whole trouble, and even by personal friends I am asked what our object is in exciting the French and making them so difficult to deal with. This idea has got such a tight hold of the German mind that it is difficult to eradicate it. . . . .([2])

Yours very sincerely,

W. E. GOSCHEN.

([1]) [Carnock MSS., Vol. IV of 1911.]
([2]) [This letter closes with general comment on the European situation.]

CHAPTER LVIII.

THE CRISIS AND ITS SETTLEMENT, AUGUST 21-NOVEMBER 4, 1911.

No. 509.

Mr. White to Sir Edward Grey.

F.O. 33785/25641/11/28.
(No. 269.)   *Tangier, D. August 17, 1911.*
Sir,   R. *August 28, 1911.*

The action taken by Germany at Agadir has made a considerable impression on the native population throughout the country and has in some measure brought to life the false hopes raised by the dramatic visit of the Kaiser to Tangier in 1905.

When in trouble the Moors now again turn to Germany for assistance and protection, and this is the case even at Tangier, the German Minister being sometimes embarrassed by the appeals that are made to him.

A few days ago a large deputation of Moors—over two hundred I am informed—representing two districts of the town, waited upon the German Minister to expose their grievances. They stated that they paid the new house tax, but that, whilst the roads outside the town were being relaid, their own streets and drains were still in the same state as before the institution of the tax. They also complained that Moorish masons etc. were not employed on the works in progress.

The German Minister suggested that they should address themselves to the Doyen of the Diplomatic Body, but they replied that their appeal was to the German Minister, that they pinned their faith on the German Emperor, who had visited Tangier and had given them the fullest assurances of His Majesty's good-will and interest in their behalf, and they insisted on Baron von Seckendorff's bringing their appeal to His Majesty's notice, to which he had to assent. The deputation went away satisfied and are now patiently awaiting the results of His Majesty's intervention on their behalf.

The house tax has as yet been only levied for one year, and half of the net proceeds is taken by the Makhzen, therefore the amount available for expenditure on the town is comparatively small; it was paid over to the Commission d'Hygiène, and, together with the amount collected by private subscriptions, is being expended on the scavenging service, lighting and repairing the streets, etc. The works to which the deputation referred are those put up to tender by the Adjudications Committee and paid for out of the proceeds of the special tax of two and a half per cent. on imports, to which the districts represented by the deputation pay nothing. The labour employed by ten contractors is principally native, though the superintendents are Europeans.

I have, &c.
HERBERT E. WHITE.

No. 510.

Sir F. Bertie to Sir Edward Grey.

(By Post.)

F.O. 33199/25883/11/28.   *Paris, D. August* 22, 1911.
Tel. (No. 130.) Confidential.   R. *August* 23, 1911.

M. de Selves sent for me this evening in order to give me an account of the situation in regard to Morocco, which is as follows :—

There was a conference this morning, at which were present the President of the Council, the Minister for Foreign Affairs, the Ministers for War, Marine, Colonies, and Justice, and the French Ambassadors at Berlin and London.([1]) M. Jules Cambon informed the conference of the state of feeling in Germany. He stated that there was great excitement in military circles incited by the Pan-German press, which had accused the Emperor of cowardice, thereby causing the entourage of His Majesty to assume an anti-French attitude.

M. Jules Cambon does not think that the Emperor is inclined for war, nor that M. de Kiderlen-Waechter is, but unless he obtain what will be regarded as a success by the German public his personal position will be seriously affected. These circumstances constitute dangers to the maintenance of peace, and it seems doubtful that M. de Kiderlen-Waechter wishes the negotiations for territorial arrangements with France to succeed. The French Ministers, after considering the situation, have resolved to make to Germany offers of territory in French Congo which are very large and adequate considering that the German Government will not cede Togoland or any part of it, and will only give France the Bec du Canard.

M. de Selves will give me a detailed description to-morrow of the territory which the French Government propose to cede in addition to the strip abutting on Spanish Guinea from near Libreville to Ouesso. From his cursory description I gather that it would be the territory north and east of the Sangha, bounded on the east by the Ubanghi to a point south of Bangi, where that river is navigable, and thence in a north-westerly direction towards the Bec du Canard, which will become French. This arrangement would place Northern French Congo in communication with the sea by the Rivers Ubanghi and Congo.

The French Government are of the opinion that if the German Government do not accept these proposals it will mean that they do not desire to come to an arrangement with the French Government.

M. de Selves asked me what I thought the German Government would do if the territorial negotiations fell through. I said that I did not think that they would summon France to evacuate Morocco as had been talked of, but they might remain at Agadir. His Excellency stated that such was the conclusion at which the French Ministers had arrived, and if the German Government landed men at Agadir or increased their naval force there a situation would be created which would require France to take action. No Ministry could survive the acceptance of such a situation, and the French Government have resolved in either of such events at Agadir to send ships to Mogador and Saffi and to occupy other parts of Morocco territory. M. de Selves asked what would be the attitude of His Majesty's Government in such circumstances.

I suggested to M. de Selves that if there was a landing of Germans at Agadir it might be for some specified reason, such as the protection of German life and property. It might be a pretext, but if the French Government immediately thereupon occupied Mogador and Saffi and other parts of Morocco territory, it would give colour to the assertions of the German press that France was taking possession

----

([1]) [*v.* the account in *Caillaux*, pp. 179–84, where it is stated that these conclusions were adopted by the Cabinet as a whole on August 24. M. de Selves gave an account to Herr von Schoen on August 23. *v. G.P.* XXIX, pp. 340-1.]

of Morocco without justification, no French lives or property being endangered, and it was most important that France should not give an opening to an accusation of bringing on a conflict.

M. de Selves replied that the French were prepared to make the great sacrifices of territory which he had mentioned to me, but it would be quite impossible for them not to take action such as he had described if there were a change in the *status quo* at Agadir increasing the position of Germany there. What, therefore, it would be most important to obviate would be any such change in the *status quo*. He had no information that the German Government were meditating a landing or an increase of naval force, but would it be possible for His Majesty's Government to convey to the German Government in some indirect manner, and not in any way as a French menace, that a landing or increase of force would inevitably complicate matters and render negotiations for an amicable arrangement impossible, as French public opinion would be such as to render it unavoidable for the French Government to take some action?

M. Paul Cambon has left this afternoon for London in order to put the situation before you and to enquire what the attitude of His Majesty's Government will be, supposing that the territorial offers of the French Government be refused by the German Government, a refusal which the French Government consider will mean that Germany does not desire to come to an arrangement with France.

No. 511.

Sir Edward Grey to Sir F. Bertie.

F.O. 33413/25883/11/28.   *Foreign Office, August* 23, 1911.
Tel. (No. 200.)   D. 9·45 P.M.

French Ambassador informs me that French Gov[ernmen]t have decided, if Germans land a force at Agadir, to send ships to Mogador and Saffi and troops to Marakesh. He asks that we should also in that event send ships to Mogador and Saffi. I have replied that in our opinion a Conference on lines previously suggested by me([1]) should be proposed before we take any active step and that we should be ready to propose a Conference.

Ambassador asked what we should do if a Conference was refused; I replied that I could not say without consulting Prime Minister and my colleagues. Personally I thought if a Conference was refused we should be on much stronger ground in taking any active step.

([1]) [*v. supra*, p. 450, No. 475.]

No. 512.

Sir Edward Grey to Sir F. Bertie.

F.O. 33413/25883/11/28.
(No. 355.)
Sir,   *Foreign Office, August* 23, 1911.

The French Ambassador came to see me to-day, and showed me the *projet* of a Convention between France and Germany, drawn up in Paris, of which he could not give me a copy, as it was not yet definitive.

I read it, and observed that it amounted to a veiled protectorate for France over Morocco, with a guarantee for economic equality similar to that which had been put in our Agreement with France. The proposed Convention seemed to me to go beyond this Agreement in one respect only : it contemplated a cession of Consular jurisdiction on the part of Germany.

[19656]   2 I 2

M. Cambon said that of course this would be a matter for a separate arrangement. I told him that I saw nothing to object to in the proposed Convention, in principle.

M. Cambon informed me that the part of French Congo offered to Germany North East of the Sanga river was equal to the whole of France in superficial area: if Germany did not accept this she could not be satisfied. In any case the French Ambassador at Berlin was instructed not to break off negotiations. If they were broken off it must be by Germany.

M. Cambon then told me that his Government had decided that it would be absolutely necessary for them to take some step if Germany landed troops at Agadir. In this event they would send ships to Mogador and Saffi, and some troops to Marakesh, and would inform Germany that she would retire from these places when Germany left Agadir. He was charged to ask me whether we also would send ships to Mogador and Saffi. The French Government felt quite certain that, if Germany thought we were going to side with France, there would be no conflict; and they were most anxious to have our moral support.

I replied that it was not certain that there would be no conflict if Germany thought that we would side with France. Germany might be quite prepared to take the risk of war against a combination. I had discussed this matter with the Prime Minister and my Colleagues, and we had come to the decision that we ought not to take any active step before a Conference had been proposed. Therefore, if the situation which the French Government contemplated arose, we should be ready to propose a Conference on the lines which I had previously suggested.(¹)

M. Cambon said that Germany would probably refuse to accept the proposal of a Conference, and he asked what would happen then.

I replied that I had not discussed that contingency with the Prime Minister and my Colleagues, so that I could give him only my personal opinion. It seemed to me that if Germany refused to go to a Conference, we should be on much stronger ground with public opinion in any step which it might then be necessary to take.

M. Cambon observed that, in the case of Bosnia and Herzegovina, a Conference had been proposed and refused, and the matter had been allowed to go by default.

I said that the case of Bosnia and Herzegovina was no parallel to the case of Morocco. We had not actually proposed a Conference, and had simply said that we could not give our consent to the alteration of an international Treaty until the other Powers who were parties to it, and especially the Powers who had a more direct interest in it than we had, had also given their consent. We had let it be understood that we made no conditions of our own, and that when other people were satisfied we also would be satisfied. But if Germany remained indefinitely at Agadir, landed a force, and occupied a part of Morocco, it would amount practically to a partition of Morocco. We could not allow that to happen without having our say in the matter.

[I am, &c.]

E. G[REY].

(¹) [v. supra, pp. 415–7, Nos. 433–4; p. 427, No. 449; p. 428, No. 450; p. 450, No. 475; p. 483, No. 511.]

No. 513.

Sir F. Bertie to Sir Edward Grey.

(By Post.)

F.O. 33451/25883/11/28.   Paris, D. *August* 24, 1911.
Tel. (No. 132.) Confidential. R.   R. *August* 25, 1911.

My despatch No. 376 of 23rd August.(¹)

Minister for Foreign Affairs has shown to me this evening on maps the several cessions of territory which the French Government would be ready to offer in

(¹) [v. supra, pp. 467–9, No. 495.]

succession to Germany in return for a free hand in Morocco.(²)   Firstly, from junction of Sangha with Congo River northward to Ibenga on Ubanghi and then in a north-westerly direction to north of conventional line (passing Carnot, which would remain French) to Cameroons frontier.   Secondly, starting from between Ibenga and Mongumba in a north-westerly direction, and including Carnot in territory to be ceded to Germany.   Thirdly, starting from same point but keeping to north-east of River Bali and crossing due north the conventional line and including a piece of Ubanghi as far as non-navigable part of River Logune.   Fourthly, the same as thirdly, but reaching to Lai on navigable part of River Logune.

(²) [For Herr von Schoen's account of a similar interview, *cp. G.P.* XXIX, pp. 340–1.]

No. 514.

Sir F. Bertie to Sir Edward Grey.

(By Post.)

F.O. 33452/25883/11/28.   Paris, D. *August* 24, 1911.
Tel. (No. 133.)   Confidential.   R. *August* 25, 1911.
My despatch No. 376 of yesterday.(¹)
M. de Selves gave to me this evening the following information :—

The German Ambassador called on him this morning,(²) and after expressing his anxiety to facilitate an understanding enquired the nature of the free hand which the French Government desired in Morocco, for it would be difficult to put the word protectorate into a formal paper.   M. de Selves replied that it would be immaterial to the French Government what the protectorate might be called provided that it was equivalent to one.

Baron de Schoen then asked what were the ideas of the French Government in regard to commercial and industrial matters and mines.   M. de Selves answered to the effect of the draft convention which the French Ambassador communicated to you yesterday,(³) and said that there would be no export duty on iron ore, that the construction of railways, telegraphs would, like public works and other undertakings, be by adjudication, but their working (" exploitation ") must be in the hands of the Morocco Government, or in those of the companies to which the Government might grant a working concession.

M. de Schoen then said that Germans had obtained considerable mining interests in the Sus country, and it would be desirable that the working of any railways as well as their construction should be in German hands, great importance being attached in Germany to the Sus country as rich in minerals.   M. de Selves told the Ambassador that he did not see how the German Government could, whilst giving a free hand in Morocco to France, expect such a reservation as M. de Schoen had suggested.

The conversation then turned to the question of territorial cessions, and M. de Selves indicated on a map the alternative cession described in my immediately preceding telegram as " firstly."(⁴)

M. de Schoen, whilst disclaiming any authority from the German Government to negotiate, said that M. de Selves' offer would be quite inadequate, and he indicated a line running from the extreme point of the Bec du Canard in a south-easterly direction to the Ubanghi River as the one within which all the French

(¹) [*v. supra*, pp. 467–9, No. 495.]
(²) [*cp. G.P.* XXIX, pp. 340–1.   There were apparently two interviews—a short one on the 23rd, and a longer one on the 24th when M. de Selves showed the places on the map.]
(³) [*cp. supra*, pp. 483–4, No. 512.]
(⁴) [*v.* immediately preceding document.]

territory between it and the Cameroons and down to the Sangha River had already been offered by M. Jules Cambon. M. de Schoen also said that it would be necessary that Germany should have south of the Sangha the line of the Alima.

M. de Selves reminded M. de Schoen that the French Government had already refused to concede the line of the Alima, that the offers made on behalf of the French Government by their Ambassador at Berlin had been on the supposition that Togoland, or a part of it, would be ceded to France, which now was not the case, and that he had certainly never made the extreme offer which M. de Schoen attributed to him. M. de Selves would, however, ask M. Jules Cambon, who was waiting to see him, to come in and explain himself. M. de Schoen was very much taken aback. M. Jules Cambon came and denied *in toto* having made any such offer himself. The line described by M. de Schoen was something like one which M. de Kiderlen-Waechter had suggested and he (M. Jules Cambon) had rejected. Such a line would bring into contact French and German frontier officials, which it had been his endeavour to avoid by having as far as possible river boundaries.

M. de Schoen will telegraph to Berlin for instructions, and will see M. de Selves again to-morrow.

M. de Selves says that the German Government shift their ground so frequently that he can hardly believe that they wish negotiations for an arrangement to succeed

---

No. 515.

Sir F. Bertie to Sir Edward Grey.

F.O. 33477/25883/11/28.
Tel. (No. 134.) Confidential.

Paris, D. *August* 24, 1911, 11·20 P.M.
R. *August* 25, 1911, 8 A.M.

Morocco. My despatch No. 376 most confidential of yesterday and your telegram No. 200 of last night.(¹)

French M[inister for] F[oreign] A[ffairs] showed to me this evening M. Cambon's report of his conversation with you yesterday. I asked him whether he could not persuade his colleagues in the Cabinet not to precipitate matters by a hurried occupation of Mogador, Saffi and Marakesh on Germany taking further action at Agadir. He said that he would bring question before the Cabinet to-morrow with the considerations which you had put to M. Cambon, but Germany might, if France did not take immediate action, occupy Mogador in addition to Agadir.

(¹) [*v. supra,* pp. 467–9, No. 495; p. 483, No. 511.]

No. 516.

Sir F. Bertie to Sir Edward Grey.

F.O. 33559/25883/11/28.
Tel. (No. 135.) Confidential.

Paris, August 25, 1911.

Morocco. Your despatch No. 355 of August 23.(¹)

French M[inister for] F[oreign] A[ffairs] whom I have seen this evening quite appreciates reasons which you gave to the French Amb[assado]r for not taking any action pending a proposal for a conference.

(¹) [*v. supra,* pp. 483–4, No. 512.]

The Cabinet held this morning has given full discretion to the President of the Council and the M[inister for] F[oreign] A[ffairs] to decide what action if any shall be taken in the event of an alteration in the *status quo* at Agadir. I do not think that they will do anything without consultation with H[is] M[ajesty's] Gov[ernmen]t.

[*ED. NOTE.*—On August 24 the French grand manœuvres were announced as cancelled (*v.* also p. 634, No. 641). The Emperor William II telegraphed to the Chancellor on August 28 that this cancellation enabled the French troops to be concentrated in their stations, and that the negotiations must be prolonged until September 24 when the German manœuvres would be over. *v. G.P.* XXIX, p. 345. The British manœuvres were abandoned on alleged cause of drought *(v. Times,* August 19 and 22), as also the Belgian (*v. Times,* August 8, early edition).]

No. 517.

Sir F. Bertie to Sir Edward Grey.

(By Post.)

F.O. 33572/25883/11/28. *Paris,* D. *August 25, 1911.*
Tel. (No. 136.) *En clair.* R. *August 26, 1911.*

M. de Selves informed me this evening that the German Ambassador, with whom he had an appointment for 3 o'clock, had written to him saying that, as the President of the Council had asked to see him, perhaps M. de Selves would like to fix some other time for the interview. M. de Selves after ascertaining from M. Caillaux that there must be some misapprehension, for it was not he who had asked to see the German Ambassador but it was the Ambassador who had asked to see him, wrote to M. de Schoen to say that he did not desire to change the appointment and that he should expect him at 3 o'clock, at which hour the President of the Council would be at the Ministry for Foreign Affairs on other business than Morocco and the Ambassador could see him if he so desired.

The interview was between the three.(¹) The German Ambassador at first showed a disposition to again claim the line of the Alima, saying that he understood that the French Government might be disposed to concede it. M. Caillaux flouted the idea, and stated that the Cabinet had unanimously decided against it. There was some general but vague discussion, and without definite result. M. de Schoen's tone was, however, more moderate than at his previous interview with M. de Selves.

(¹) [*v. G.P.* XXIX, pp. 342–3.]

No. 518.

Sir E. Goschen to Sir Edward Grey.(¹)

F.O. 33774/25883/11/28.
(No. 241.) Confidential. *Berlin,* D. *August 25, 1911.*
Sir, R. *August 28, 1911.*

I had to-day some conversation with Herr Zimmermann on the subject of Morocco and particularly on the subject of the despatch of the "Panther" to Agadir. He complained bitterly about Mr. Lloyd George's speech(²) which he said had done untold harm both with regard to German public opinion and the negotiations. I said that for what had done most harm one must go back a little further than Mr. Lloyd George's speech, namely to the despatch of the German warship to Agadir. He said that he had never understood why public opinion in England had been

(¹) [Printed in *Twenty-Five Years,* I, pp. 236–7.]
(²) [*v. supra,* pp. 387–417, chap. LV, *passim;* an extract from the *Times* report of the speech is given there, pp. 391–2, No. 412.]

upset by that event. " When we informed Sir Edward Grey that we were going to send a ship to Agadir." I here interrupted and said, " You mean that you *had* sent a ship to Agadir." He acquiesced in my interruption and, continuing, said, " when we informed Sir Edward Grey that we had sent a ship to Agadir he took the news quite quietly and we had no idea that there was going to be all this trouble about it." I said that it was in my recollection that you had spoken strongly to Count Metternich on the subject. He said " Well at all events we had no idea that public opinion would feel so strongly about it, and Mr. Lloyd George's speech came upon us like a thunderbolt." He added that the whole trouble arose from the fact that it was not recognized in England that the despatch of a ship to Agadir, which had been the Emperor's idea, was really meant to make it easier for the French Government to defend any compensation they might be ready to give, and which they had expressed readiness to give, before the French Parliament. I could not help saying that it seemed to me to be a somewhat dubious method of facilitating the negotiations and that I could scarcely fancy a French Minister of Foreign Affairs standing up in the French Parliament and saying that he had had to yield to German demands for compensation because Germany, as a hint that she meant business, had sent a warship to a closed Moroccan port. Besides, I added, I thought that the " Panther " had been sent to protect the lives and property of the employés of certain Hamburg merchants. " Ah ! " said Herr Zimmermann, " that was the primary reason, and the reason for the urgency which prevented us from informing the Powers of our intention. But it was thought all the same that it would have a good effect on the negotiations in the way I have just stated." I am bound to say that even Herr Zimmermann smiled when I mentioned the Hamburg merchants. I said that I was glad to know the real reason why the ship had been sent to Agadir, but I thought, if he would allow me to say so, that it might have been wiser if, before Monsieur Cambon left Kissingen, he had been consulted as to whether the despatch of the " Panther " would have the salutary effect on the negotiations which the Imperial Government anticipated. To this Herr Zimmermann replied that he was not at Berlin at the time or perhaps——. Here he broke off his sentence which would seem to imply that he agreed with me.

Herr Zimmermann went over a lot of old ground, and spoke at some length as to the disappointment Germany had felt at our attitude, the growing excitement in German public opinion, the irritation of the Emperor and many other things which you have repeatedly heard from Count Metternich, and which I have reported as having been said by the Emperor. I need not therefore trouble you with the rest of his observations.

The reasons, however, which he gave me for the despatch of a ship to Agadir are, as far as I am aware, quite new and therefore may be of some interest.

I have, &c.
W. E. GOSCHEN.

MINUTES.

A further comment that I made upon the despatch of a ship to Agadir was that authorized by the Cabinet and Count Metternich at his own request took it down in writing.([3])

E. G.

26033 (No. 127, telegraphic)([4]) and the record of the conversation in which I conveyed to Count Metternich the statement authorized by the Cabinet should be circulated with this to the Cabinet for convenience of reference.

E. G.

([3]) [*v. supra*, p. 334, No. 356.]
([4]) [*v. supra*, p. 328, No. 347.]

No. 519.

M. Paul Cambon to Sir Edward Grey.

Private.([1])   146, *Boulevard Haussmann. VIII*E.
Cher Sir Edward,   *le 26 août*, 1911.

M. de Kiderlen ne rentrera pas à Berlin avant le jeudi 31 c[ouran]t. Le 1 et le 2 septembre étant conservés pour tous les fonctionnaires Allemands aux fêtes commémoratives des évènements de 1870, il ne peut y avoir d'entretien entre mon frère et M. de Kiderlen que le 3 ou le 4 septembre.

D'ici là nous ne pouvons rien augurer. Cependant on paraît croire ici à une conclusion des pourparlers et l'on fait tout ce qu'on peut pour y arriver.

Aussitôt que je connaîtrai la date de la reprise des conversations de Berlin, je vous en ferai part.

Croyez, cher Sir Edward, à mes sentiments les plus cordialement devouès.

PAUL CAMBON.

([1]) [Grey MSS., Vol. 13.]

No. 520.

Mr. White to Sir Edward Grey.

                                           Tangier, August 27, 1911.
F.O. 33703/31824/11/28.   D. 4·30 P.M.
Tel. (No. 147.) R.   R. 6·20 P.M.

A few days ago Sid Guebbas informed German Minister that he had heard from the Governor of Mogador that Europeans at Tarudant were in danger, and he requested that they be instructed to return to the coast under escort. German Minister, after consulting his Government, has replied that captain of cruiser at Agadir reports Tarudant quiet; that the German Government expect the Makhzen to assure safety of Germans at that town so that German Government should not be obliged themselves to take necessary steps to ensure their safety.

French chargé d'affaires thinks that this reply is intended to induce the French Government to hasten to accept German terms.

No. 521.

Sir M. de Bunsen to Sir Edward Grey.

F.O. 34784/13751/11/28.
(No. 151.)   *Zarauz, D. August* 30, 1911.
Sir,   R. *September* 4, 1911.

Monsieur Geoffray, French Ambassador, had the goodness to read to me to-day the text of the draft Convention with Spain concerning her sphere of influence in Morocco, which it is proposed to submit to the Spanish Government in the event of the Berlin negotiation leading to a satisfactory settlement between France and Germany.

The draft Convention was to be communicated to-day to Sir Francis Bertie, and Monsieur Geoffray expressed the hope that, if it should meet with your concurrence, you would furnish me with instructions to support him in urging the Spanish Government to acquiesce in the proposed arrangements which seemed to him to constitute a perfectly fair adaptation of the terms of the Secret Convention of October 1904 to the present condition of Morocco. Meanwhile His Excellency is authorised to speak to the Spanish Government generally in the sense of the draft Convention, withholding however the full text until the issue of the Berlin negotiation is known.

The draft Convention provides that, subject to the maintenance of the Sultan's authority throughout Morocco, Spain shall be entrusted with the task of administering her own sphere of influence in that country. The limits of her sphere of influence are those laid down in Article 2 of the Secret Convention, except as regards the region of Wazan and Wady Lucus where a slight modification of the line hitherto claimed by Spain is proposed. Spain is further required to abandon to France the region of Ifni as delimited in Article 4 of the Secret Convention. France and Spain renounce reciprocally, each in the sphere of influence of the other, the right of protection over natives. When Spain shall set up Courts of Justice to supersede, within her sphere, the existing exterritorial [sic] jurisdiction, France will recognize the new Courts, her nationals enjoying the same rights and privileges as those of Spain. Spain may employ troops and police for the maintenance of order. The revenues of her sphere are assigned to be spent within that sphere, except as regards a sum to be set apart annually for Imperial needs, and a further sum representing the share of the interest of existing loans which may fairly be held to fall upon the Spanish sphere. The principle of the open door is maintained in respect of adjudication for Public Works, as also the present special position enjoyed by Tangier, (including a radius of 15 kilometres round) in virtue of her Municipal and Sanitary institutions. The working of existing organic institutions such as Customs, State Bank, etc., to be determined by means of mixed commissions appointed respectively by France and Spain.

The foregoing arrangements, which I merely quote in outline and from memory, appear to me to meet fairly enough the Spanish contention that the status of Morocco has changed and that she is entitled therefore, under Article 3 of the Secret Treaty, to "exercise her action freely" within her recognized sphere of influence. Scarcely any limits indeed are placed upon her freedom of action except such as necessarily arise from the maintenance of the sovereign authority of the Sultan and from the need which obviously exists to provide contributions towards the Imperial expenses of the State and towards the service of existing loans.

The surrender of Ifni to France is likely, no doubt, to prove, if granted, a very unpopular concession. Though the possession of this region would be of doubtful advantage to Spain, it represents in the mind of the people the only material achievement of the Tetuan campaign of 1860, beyond a slight expansion of the Ceuta zone. You may possibly consider, however, that from a purely British point of view, its acquisition by France would offer no objection. In the hands of a strong Power it may perhaps be said that the danger of the possible development of Ifni in the interests of another nation would be largely eliminated.

Monsieur Geoffray has already intimated verbally to the Spanish Minister for Foreign Affairs that France desires to include Ifni within her sphere of influence in Morocco. He pointed out that if Spain had taken part in the Berlin negotiation she would no doubt have been required by Germany to make, as France will have to do, a large territorial concession. The Berlin negotiation, if successful, would redound to the benefit of Spain as well as France. It was only fair then that Spain should make good, by the small sacrifice now demanded of her, a portion of the serious loss which France is incurring in the interests of both countries.

Señor Garcia Prieto, as Monsieur Geoffray informs me, seemed somewhat staggered by the French demand. He informed the French Ambassador that the Spanish Government were in communication with that of Morocco, through El Mokri in Paris and El Guebbas in Tangier, as well as through the Spanish Consul at Fez, with a view to the appointment of a Moorish Commissioner to meet the Spanish Commissioner designated to proceed jointly with him to a delimitation of the Ifni region as required by the Convention between Spain and Morocco of November 16, 1910. These *pourparlers* were far advanced and it was possible that El Muaz, who preceded El Mokri as Moorish Ambassador for the negotiation of the said Convention at Madrid, would be shortly delegated by the Sultan to proceed to Ifni. Señor Garcia Prieto did not, however, take up an uncompromising attitude. He merely said that the matter was one of great importance to Spain, and that it would be discussed in all its bearings at the Cabinet Councils due to be held this week in Madrid in the presence of the King.

I have, &c.
MAURICE DE BUNSEN.

No. 522.

Sir M. de Bunsen to Sir Edward Grey.

F.O. 34342/13751/11/28.
Tel. (No. 70.)

Zarauz, August 31, 1911.
D. 10 A.M.
R. 3 P.M.

My tel[egram] No. 67.(¹)

French Ambassador has now suggested text of draft convention concerning Spanish sphere of influence in Morocco, which, if you concur, will be submitted to Spanish Gov[ernmen]t in the event of Berlin negotiations leaving France with a free hand in Morocco.

French Ambassador is anxious that I should receive instructions to support him in urging Spanish Government to accept proposed settlement. H[is] E[xcellency] is authorised to speak to Spanish Gov[ernmen]t in the general sense of draft Convention without waiting for issue of Berlin negotiations, and he has already intimated to the M[inister for] F[oreign] A[ffairs] that France will expect Spain to renounce her claim to Ifni, M[inister for] F[oreign] A[ffairs] was greatly startled by this announcement and he informed French Ambassador that measures for the early occupation of Ifni in concert with the Commissioner to be deputed by the Sultan were already far advanced.

Matter will be fully discussed at the Cabinet Councils to be held at Madrid during next few days. Although Ifni could be of little real use to Spain its surrender will no doubt be unpopular. In other respects draft convention which was to be communicated yesterday to H[is] M[ajesty's] Ambassador in Paris appears to me to meet very fairly the demands of Spain in respect of her sphere of influence.

(Repeated to Paris.)

(¹) [Not reproduced. It reports the French intention of increasing the numbers of the French military mission at Fez, and the wish to retain Ifni under French influence.]

No. 523.

Sir E. Goschen to Sir Edward Grey.

F.O. 37403/25883/11/28.
(No. 251.)
Sir,

Berlin, D. August 31, 1911.
R. *September* 4, 1911.

A meeting of several thousand Pan Germans was held in Berlin yesterday to consider the Morocco question. The main characteristics of the meeting were the comparatively friendly tone of the speakers towards France and a note of strong animosity against England.

All the speakers stated that the object of the meeting was not to protest against the action of the Government, but to claim protection for German political and commercial interests and they all without exception demanded, for various reasons, territorial compensation, the general idea running through the various speeches being that Germany should have a piece of Morocco, but failing that a compensation in territory equal in value to the enormous increase of power accruing to France. In any case, whatever territory was eventually ceded to Germany it must, in order fully to compensate her, include a strip of coast.

The resolution passed at the conclusion of the meeting and unanimously accepted was to the following effect :—

" The action of France in Morocco, by which the Algeciras Act has been infringed, effects [sic: affects] Germany's important political and economic interests in such a way that the emphatic safeguarding of those interests becomes the duty of our Government. To guard these interests France must be required to return to the Act of Algeciras. Should this solution not be selected, Germany must ensure for herself the same rights and the same influence in West Morocco as France claims in any other part of Morocco. In no case must we allow France to increase her army from the population of Morocco, as such action would constitute a threat to Germany and would force us to increase our armaments. We must quietly but decisively reject interferences on the part of any other State in the Franco-German Morocco dispute."

I have, &c.
W. E. GOSCHEN.

No. 524.

Sir E. Goschen to Sir Edward Grey.

F.O. 34704/33698/11/28.
(No. 252.)   Secret.   *Berlin, D. September* 1, 1911.
Sir,   R. *September* 4, 1911.

I have the honour to forward, herewith, a despatch, as marked in the margin, which I have received from Colonel Russell, Military Attaché to this Embassy, relating to a conversation with H[is] M[ajesty] the German Emperor.

I have, &c.
W. E. GOSCHEN.

Enclosure in No. 524.

Lieutenant-Colonel Russell to Sir E. Goschen.

Conversation with the Emperor.

(No. 20.)   Secret.
Sir,   *Berlin, September* 1, 1911.

At the conclusion of the annual autumn parade of the Guard Army Corps on the Tempelhofer Feld, which was held to-day, His Majesty the Emperor called me to his side.

His Majesty began by expressing regret that it had been found impossible to make arrangements at this late hour for the 3 British officers whose attendance at the manœuvres had been asked for by the British Government. The Emperor explained that the manœuvre area was only sparsely populated and the accommodation was limited and primitive. His Majesty much regretted the matter, but hoped that the names of the British officers in question might be recorded for attendance at the German manœuvres next year.

I was at a loss to understand which 3 officers His Majesty was referring to, as permission had been asked, but had not yet been received, for 8 British officers to attend manœuvres in various parts of Germany this year. (An unofficial affirmative had till then only been given in the case of 3 officers.) I, therefore, asked the Emperor if he did not intend to allow any British officers to attend manœuvres in Germany this year. His Majesty replied that he thought permission had already been given for the usual contingent of British officers. I assured His Majesty that though the usual application for 8 British officers had reached the German Foreign Office some time ago, no official reply had as yet been given to it. The Emperor seemed surprised at what I said and stated that he had imagined that the three officers he had been speaking about were over and above the usual contingent of British Officers. His Majesty also suggested jokingly that 8 was rather a large number, but I protested that it was the same as in former years. His Majesty then said that he would attend to the matter. (A few hours after the above conversation a message was received from the German Foreign Office that permission would be given for all the 8 British officers, for whom application had been made, to attend the manœuvres.)

Assuming then a distressed but by no means irate tone, His Majesty exclaimed: "What in Heaven's name does your ambassador in Vienna mean by the dreadful statements he has made. The German people were already somewhat irritated over the Moroccan question and Lloyd George's speech had not tended to improve matters. I had just done my best to smooth matters over, when now this comes on the top of everything. My people are furious (with great emphasis) about it; I cannot tell you how angry they are."

I assured His Majesty that the statements which had appeared in the press had been officially contradicted, and that it was of course impossible for Sir Fairfax Cartwright to have uttered the words which had been attributed to him in the newspapers.(1) His Majesty, however, said that he was very well instructed, and was convinced that those were the views of our Ambassador in Vienna. "I know him well," the Emperor continued. "He has a dreadful hatred of Germany. No one dislikes us as he does. When he was in Munich he wrote terrible things about this country. He and Maxse are the greatest enemies Germany has. Your ambassador in Vienna has also said insulting things about me, which are very difficult for me to get over. He knows me too and played as a child with members of my family. I should have thought he would have remembered that. The way he has behaved is not worthy of a responsible diplomatist."

The Emperor then promised me that he would go into the matter of the British officers attending the manœuvres, shook hands and wished me good-bye in a cordial manner. In doing so His Majesty charged me to inform you, Sir, of what he had said to me.

The Emperor's manner during the conversation recorded above, was calm and friendly. He appeared to be more distressed than angry, when referring to the British ambassador in Vienna.

I cannot vouch absolutely for the words His Majesty made use of in the cases where I have endeavoured to give them. I think, however, that I have recorded them correctly and am convinced that I have rendered the sense at all events quite faithfully.

I have, &c.
ALICK RUSSELL,
Lieutenant-Colonel.

(1) [v. infra, pp. 837–45, App. V.]

No. 525.

Sir F. Bertie to Sir Edward Grey.

F.O. 34506/13751/11/28.

(No. 386.) Confidential.   *Paris,* D. *September* 1, 1911.

Sir,   R. *September* 2, 1911.

Monsieur de Selves gave to me two days ago for perusal the draft of a Convention for regulating the position between France and Spain in Morocco on the supposition that the Berlin conversations result in an agreement by which so far as the German Government are concerned France will obtain an entirely free hand politically in Morocco.

I noticed that there is no mention in it of the Spanish sphere in which Ifni is situated and that the stipulation in regard to Tangier is not very definite. I called Monsieur de Selves' attention to-day to these points remarking however that although the proposed Convention was to take the place of the Secret Agreement of 1904 between France and Spain, which would consequently be abrogated, France and Spain would still be bound in regard to the non-fortification of the portion of the Moroccan coast in which Tangier was situated, mentioned in the Anglo-French declaration of 1904 respecting Morocco, which was adhered to by Spain.

As to Ifni, M. de Selves said that as Spain had allowed 50 years to elapse without entering into the occupation of the zone granted to her by the Treaty of 1860 with Morocco it was supposed that she could not attach much value to it and he hoped that although it was recognized by the Agreement of 1904 as a Spanish zone the Spanish Government might be willing to make over the rights of Spain to France in recognition of the fact, (which it would be if the Berlin negotiations succeeded) that it would be France that found the compensations to Germany which had enabled the French Government to settle with the Spanish Government the position of Spain in Morocco on well established lines.

M. de Selves has authorized me to forward to you which I now do the Draft, but he begs me to inform you that it is by no means a definitive document and that he would be glad to have any observations that you may wish to make on it and particularly in regard to Article XIII relating to the part of the coast of Morocco in which England is particularly interested.

I asked M. de Selves whether any communication had been made to him by the Spanish Ambassador in consequence of the French Ambassador at Madrid having mentioned to the Spanish Government the desire of the French Government to acquire Ifni. M. de Selves had not received any communication of the intention of the Spanish Government to occupy Ifni such as was made to you yesterday by the Ambassador. When I told him of it he said that he regretted that the Spanish Government should have come to such a decision.

I have, &c.

FRANCIS BERTIE.

Enclosure in No. 525.

Draft of Franco-Spanish Convention.

Le Gouvernement de la République française et le Gouvernement de Sa Majesté le Roi d'Espagne considérant en raison des modifications qui se sont produites dans la situation politique du Maroc au cours des dernières années il y a lieu de préciser et de modifier en tant que de besoin, les engagements réciproques qui y ont fait l'objet de la Convention du 3 octobre 1904, se sont mis d'accord sur les dispositions ci-après :

ARTICLE I.

Le gouvernement français et le gouvernement espagnol déclarent garantir les droits souverains de Sa Majesté chérifienne sur le Maroc.

Le gouvernement français, sous cette réserve, reconnaît au gouvernement espagnol le droit d'administrer le territoire marocain compris dans les limites ci-après :

partant de l'embouchure de la Moulouya, la limite remontera le Thalweg de ce fleuve jusqu'à l'alignement de la crête des hauteurs les plus rapprochées de la rive gauche de l'Oued Defla. De ce point, la limite gagnera directement à l'Ouest, la ligne de faîte séparant le bassin de la Moulouya, puis ceux de l'Oued Inaouen et de l'Oued Sebou qui sont dans la zone française, des bassins de l'Oued Kert et de l'Oued Ouergha ; elle suivra cette ligne de faîte jusqu'au mont de Moulaï bou Chta. Delà, elle remontera vers le Nord en suivant une distance de 25 km. à l'Est jusqu'à sa rencontre avec le Loukkos, la route orientale de Fez à El Ksar par Ouezzan, puis elle descendra le Loukkos jusqu'à une distance de [?] kilomètres en aval du passage de cette rivière par la route occidentale d'Ouezzan à El Ksar, de manière à laisser dans la zone espagnole la route de Larache à El Ksar, et de là elle gagnera par une ligne droite la côte de l'Atlantique.

ARTICLE II.

Dans l'étendue de leurs zones respectives et d'accord avec le gouvernement marocain, le gouvernement français et le gouvernement espagnol procèderont aux occupations militaires qu'ils jugeront nécessaires au maintien de l'ordre public et à la sécurité des transactions commerciales. Ils pourront exercer dans leurs zones toute action de police sur terre et dans les eaux territoriales.

ARTICLE III.

Le gouvernement espagnol n'apportera aucune entrave au passage des officiers et gradés français entrés au service chérifien, qui se rendront de Tanger à Fez, ou inversement, non plus qu'au passage de leurs armes et bagages. Il n'apportera de même, aucune entrave aux convois de ravitaillement envoyés de Tanger à Fez pour les besoins des troupes chérifiennes commandées par des instructeurs français.

ARTICLE IV.

Le gouvernement français et le gouvernement espagnol s'engagent à assurer chacun dans sa zone respective, la liberté et la pratique extérieure de tous les cultes existant au Maroc.

ARTICLE V.

Le gouvernement français et le gouvernement espagnol déclarent que, fermement attachés au principe de la liberté commerciale au Maroc, ils ne se prêteront à aucune inégalité pas plus dans l'établissement des droits de douane, impôts et autres taxes que dans l'établissement des tarifs de transport par chemin de fer. Le gouvernement français s'entendra avec le gouvernement espagnol pour que ces droits et tarifs soient les mêmes dans tout le Maroc.

ARTICLE VI.

Les revenus de toute nature des régions administrées par l'Espagne seront affectés aux besoins de ces régions, à leur administration et aux améliorations qui seront jugées nécessaires.

Toutefois il sera prélevé annuellement dans des conditions à déterminer avec le contrôle de la Dette marocaine une somme à déterminer qui constituera la part des régions administrées par l'Espagne dans le Service et l'amortissement des emprunts de l'Etat marocain conclus avant le présent accord.

Une somme à déterminer sera également versée chaque année au trésor marocain comme contribution des régions administrées par l'Espagne aux dépenses générales de l'Etat marocain.

L'Espagne conserve sa créance sur le gouvernement marocain telle qu'elle résulte de l'accord du 16 novembre 1910, mais elle renonce à sa part de 55% sur la redevance minière dans le reste du Maroc.

Article VI *bis*.

Les gouvernements français et espagnol conviennent que les monnaies d'argent française et espagnole seront librement introduites au Maroc et y jouiront de la même valeur libératoire que la monnaie marocaine.

Article VII.

Les hautes puissances contractantes veilleront à ce qu'il ne soit perçu aucun droit d'exportation sur le minerai de fer exporté des ports marocains. Les exploitations de minerai de fer ne subiront aucun impôt spécial. Elles ne seront assujetties qu'aux impôts généraux et aux redevances domaniales qui atteindront toutes les entreprises minières.

Article VIII.

Le gouvernement français s'entendra avec le gouvernement espagnol pour faire régler par des commissions techniques nommées par moitié par le gouvernement français et par moitié par le gouvernement espagnol, le fonctionnement dans les régions administrées par l'Espagne des différents organismes financiers et administratifs existant aujourd'hui au Maroc.

Article IX.

Le gouvernement français et le gouvernement espagnol s'engagent à veiller chacun dans sa zône respective à ce que les travaux et fournitures nécessités par les constructions éventuelles de routes, chemin de fer, ports, etc., soient octroyés par le gouvernement chérifien suivant le système de l'adjudication. Mais l'exploitation de ces grandes entreprises sera réservée à l'Etat ou librement concédée par lui.

Article X.

Le gouvernement français renonce à exercer aucun droit de protection sur des sujets marocains dans les régions administrées par l'Espagne. Le gouvernement espagnol renonce de même à exercer aucun droit de protection sur des sujets marocains dans le reste du Maroc.

Article XI.

Le gouvernement français et le gouvernement espagnol s'entendront avec le gouvernement marocain pour qu'il appartienne au gouvernement espagnol de couvrir de sa protection dans les pays étrangers les sujets marocains originaires des régions administrées par lui.

Article XII.

Lorsque des organisations judiciaires marocaines régulières auront été créées par l'Espagne et que l'Espagne aura décidé de leur transférer la juridiction des tribunaux consulaires espagnols, le gouvernement français transférera également à ces mêmes tribunaux la juridiction des tribunaux consulaires français, étant entendu que les ressortissants français jouiront des mêmes garanties légales et réglementaires que les ressortissants espagnols. Une entente entre les Gouv[ernemen]ts Français et Espagnol réglera l'entrée en vigueur de la nouvelle organisation.

ARTICLE XIII.

La ville de Tanger avec un périmètre de 15 kilomètres gardera le caractère spécial que lui donnent ses institutions municipales et sanitaires que l'Espagne s'engage à respecter. La Municipalité de Tanger assurera la police dans la ville et son périmètre.

ARTICLE XIV.

Les hautes puissances contractantes sont chargées chacune dans leur zone de la surveillance et de la répression de la contrebande des armes sur terre et sur mer. Elles établiront d'un commun accord les règles à observer pour cette répression.

ARTICLE XV.

Les Français et les Espagnols continueront à jouir dans les eaux et ports marocains du droit de navigation et de pêche.

ARTICLE XVI.

Le gouvernement français s'engage à respecter dans sa zone les écoles et établissements espagnols. Le gouvernement espagnol prend le même engagement en ce qui concerne les écoles et établissements français dans la sienne. Il s'engage en outre à ne pas faire opposition à la cession à un clergé de nationalité française du ministère paroissial exercé aujourd'hui par le clergé espagnol dans la zône française.

ARTICLE XVII.

Après avoir pris connaissance de la convention intervenue le [?] entre la France et l'Allemagne au sujet du Maroc l'Espagne déclare y adhérer et considère comme abrogées dans l'avenir toutes les stipulations des traités, conventions ou accords de toute nature qui seraient contraires aux précédentes stipulations.

MINUTES.

. . . . (1) Sir F. Bertie called M. de Selves' attention to an important point. Article VII of the Anglo-French Declaration respecting Egypt and Morocco lays down that no fortifications or strategic works are to be erected on the coast of Morocco comprised between but not including Melilla and the heights which command the right bank of the River Sebou; but this does not apply to the Spanish presidios. Spain's adherence to the Anglo-French declarations forms Art. 1 of the Franco-Spanish 1904 secret convention; and if this latter convention is now to be superseded it might be argued that Spain's adherence to the Franco-British convention has lapsed.(2) Would it not be possible to insert in the new Convention an article in the same terms as Art. 1 of the old Convention, *i.e.*, " L'Espagne adhère, aux termes de la présente Convention, à la Déclaration Franco-Anglaise du 8 avril 1904 relative au Maroc et à l'Egypte."

The last paragraph of Sir F. Bertie's despatch is significant.

G. H. V.
2.9.11.

I think it might be well to consult Sir R. Lister, if he has not left England, about the draft.

A. P.
Sept. 2, 1911.

I have read the proposed Franco-Spanish Convention. I have always been of opinion that on broad political grounds it is most desirable that France should make all such concessions as she possibly can to Spanish *amour propre*, although, as one who has lived in Morocco and become acquainted with Spanish inefficiency, I cannot but pity the districts which are to be administered by Spaniards. Spain will by this Convention practically become mistress in her own sphere : she ought to have no further grievances against France, and therefore less temptation

---

(1) [The first part of this minute is omitted as being merely a summary of the above draft.]

(2) [Marginal comment by Mr. Parker: " Sir F. Bertie apparently assumes that this would not be so : but Mr. Villiers' suggestion seems a good one. A. P."]

to throw herself into the arms of Germany : in any case a great deal of f[r]iction will undoubtedly be saved.

I think it might be advisable for safety's sake to make the insertion proposed by Mr. Villiers.

I suppose that as the French recognized the right of Spain to have a fishing station at Ifni, they cannot now object to it : at the same time it appears to me quite irregular that the Spaniards should occupy the place with soldiers, as I understand they intend to do, in view of the arrangement made between the Spanish M[inister for] F[oreign] A[ffairs] and El Mokri last autumn (see my despatch No. 44 Conf[identia]l of March 11, 1911).(³) At all events it is most unfortunate and inconsiderate of them to choose the present moment for taking this step after waiting more than 50 years! The idea when I left Morocco was that a Mixed Moorish and Spanish Delegation was to be sent to make the necessary arrangements.

The special position of Tangier must of course be maintained.

I see no objection to the police being placed under the Municipality : at the present moment it is Spanish inside the gates and French just outside, an arrangement which gives rise to a considerable amount of jealousy and ill feeling.

R. LISTER.
2.9.11.

? Write to Paris saying we have no objections to draft Convention but suggesting insertion of article as proposed in above minute. (—and state our view definitely as to Tangier so that it may be on record in case any question about it arises in future years.)(⁴)

G. H. V.
4.9.11.

I agree.

As far as we are concerned the important provisions are that there shall be no differentiation in Customs dues or railway rates, and that Tangier should maintain its special position with a zone of 15 miles. Tangier itself will gain by getting rid of the Spanish Police.

W. L.
E. G.

(³) [Marginal note : " Annexed." Not reproduced. It is a lengthy discussion of the problem and very general in character.]

(⁴) [The sentence in brackets was added by Sir Edward Grey.]

No. 526.

Sir E. Goschen to Sir Edward Grey.

Private.(¹)

My dear Grey, *Berlin, September* 1, 1911.

. . . .(²) From what you tell me and from what I have heard from the French Chargé d'Affaires during Cambon's absence there seems to be considerable doubt whether things will go as well as at one time I thought they would. It *ought* to depend upon what the Germans mean by giving France a free hand in Morocco. If they give really satisfactory written assurances to France on this head, then I think the French may fairly be expected to make a pretty big sacrifice in West Africa. But will they? Cambon always tells me that all the *sensible* men in the French Government take this view, but he fears that others, not so sensible and more under the influence of the Colonial party, do not realize the enormous advantages of a free hand in Morocco and will do their best to reduce the French offers to the narrowest possible limit.

(*Later.*) Since writing the above I have seen Cambon who telephoned to me that he would like to see me. He showed me a draft convention.(³) There are one or two things in the Morocco part of it which I think Kiderlen is sure to kick at and which it appeared to me it would be wiser to leave out. Cambon agreed but he said that unfortunately he was not a free agent. He rather grumbled that in all previous

(¹) [Grey MSS., Vol. 23.]

(²) [The opening sentences of this letter are of a general nature.]

(³) [Apparently that on pp. 511–21, No. 539.]

negotiations which he has brought to a successful termination he has been given a free hand more or less (*ad referendum* of course) and just in these, the most important of all, he is hampered at every step. Then he came to the point which I was just mentioning to you when he telephoned to me. He said that they do not seem to realize in France the *enormous* advantage of a free hand in Morocco—nor the fact that in order to get what they want they must pay *handsomely* for it : and he added his opinion *that they (the French) were not offering enough.* He begged me to ask you whether it would not be possible for you to see your way to instructing Bertie to see both M. de Selves and M. Caillaux and impress upon them that you would be glad to see the matter settled and that, in view of the big stake they were playing for in Morocco, it would be wise for them to be very generous in their territorial offers and at all events make such proposals as there would be some chance of the Germans accepting. Coming from you, he said, direct through Bertie (who might, he observed with a smile, be depended upon to put it forcibly) such advice would have considerable effect, much more than if it came through his brother Paul, whom they regard as his (Jules') double and mouthpiece. He begged and prayed me to lay this suggestion before you—as he is of the opinion that there is but little chance of Kiderlen's accepting what is now proposed in the way of compensation. He considers it in fact idiotic to hesitate about making a really big sacrifice in the Congo in view of the paramount importance to France of " une action directrice " in Morocco. " In my own personal opinion " he added " that is worth the whole of the French Congo ! " In the meantime by means of mass meetings and Press articles great pressure is being brought to bear on the German Government either to secure a sphere of influence in Morocco or failing that, to make it quite clear to the French Government that Germany will not recede one inch from the position which she has taken up, that she will accept no territorial compensation less than she originally demanded, and that the most binding guarantees must be given that German Commercial and Industrial interests in Morocco will be properly and effectively safeguarded.

Kiderlen is not the man to pay much heed to public opinion unless it suits his purposes to do so. The difficulty is to know what his purposes are. Personally I think that he would prefer a settlement, but I see from the print that the French have considerable doubts on that head.

The only thing which is *quite* certain for the moment is that there is a wave of ill-feeling against England which has increased in volume since the Article in the " Neue Freie Presse."(4) Nothing in the world will convince them here that the Article was not written by Cartwright. I have done my best with Kiderlen who spoke to me, quite goodhumouredly I must say, on the subject, and I said everything I could, but he only grinned and said that the words may have been those of Dr. Münz but the sentiments were those of Cartwright! It has been distasteful to me, for many reasons, to have to write about the article and what is said here about it—but I have not seen my way to avoid doing so as I am here, after all, to keep you informed as to Public opinion in Germany, and the indignation against the article and the personage to whom they attribute its inspiration has been, and is, so great that I could not pass it over in silence.

Yours very sincerely,
W. E. GOSCHEN.

(¹) [*v. infra*, pp. 837–45, *App.* V.]

No. 527.

Sir M. de Bunsen by Sir Edward Grey.

F.O. 35067/13751/11/28.
(No. 152.)   *Zarauz, D. September* 3, 1911.
Sir,   R. *September* 6, 1911.

As already reported in my telegram No. 71 of yesterday,([1]) I was present yesterday morning at a meeting held at San Sebastian between Señor Garcia Prieto, Spanish Minister for Foreign Affairs, and M. Geoffray, French Ambassador, in continuation of the conversations *à trois* concerning Morocco which were held between us in May and June last.

Both Señor Garcia Prieto and M. Geoffray had requested me to attend the meeting, but the late hour at which I received the invitation on Friday evening precluded me from obtaining your concurrence before accepting it. I ventured to think that you would desire me to comply with the wish expressed by Their Excellencies, who quite understand that I took part in the meeting without formal instructions.

M. Geoffray opened the conversation by reading to the Foreign Minister an abstract of the principal provisions of the draft Convention, the text of which has, I understand, been already communicated to Sir Francis Bertie and, doubtless, through His Excellency to yourself.

Señor Garcia Prieto said that he would reserve his observations on this important paper but I gathered from his demeanour while it was being read to him that he was generally satisfied with its contents. I may here state that the draft Convention, as it now stands, is more favourable to the demands of Spain than was the original outline of the Convention, which M. Geoffray was good enough to show me some weeks ago. The latter, which was drafted by M. Herbette of the French Ministry of Foreign Affairs, contained a paragraph creating within the Spanish sphere of influence a large neutral zone, extending from the meridian of Tangier to the Atlantic coast. Within this zone, which included the whole of the Western portion of the Spanish sphere, Spain was to be prohibited from employing troops or interfering in any way in the administration of the neutralized territory. The intention was to eliminate Spanish authority entirely from the line of communication between Fez and the Straits of Gibraltar. This and several other provisions which the Spanish Government would have been obviously unable to accept were withdrawn by the French Government in accordance with advice tendered by M. Geoffray, and the revised text of the Convention may now, I think, be said to constitute a perfectly fair offer on the part of France and one which seeks to interpret as well as present circumstances permit the terms of article 3 of the Secret Convention of October 1904 conceding a free hand to Spain in certain eventualities.([2])

M. Geoffray proceeded to make an announcement which, though it was no news to the Spanish Minister for Foreign Affairs was received by him with marks of extreme surprise. France, said the French Ambassador, was being called upon to surrender to Germany vast regions in one of the French colonies, in exchange for the recognition of a new order of things in Morocco by which Spain as well as France would profit. It was only fair that Spain should make some corresponding sacrifice. France would expect her to cede to the French sphere of influence in Morocco the whole of the Ifni region, or, in other words the whole of the territory defined in Articles 4 and 5 of the Secret Convention as falling to the share of Spain. As Spain had allowed fifty years to pass since the date of the Treaty with Morocco which ceded to her a fishing station at Santa Cruz de Mar Pequeña, since declared to be identical with Ifni, M. Geoffray thought it was not unfair to conclude that this territory offered no very great attraction to Spain and that the sacrifice involved in

---

([1]) [Not reproduced as it is in the same sense as the above despatch.]
([2]) [*v. infra*, pp. 827–8, *App.* IV.]

its surrender would be light in comparison with that which would have to be made by his own country to satisfy Germany. His Excellency added that without being able to point to some proof of the willingness of Spain to assist France in bearing the loss imposed by Germany the French Government would never be able to persuade the Chamber of Deputies to accept the proposed Convention regarding the Spanish sphere of Influence.

Señor Garcia Prieto expressed his personal opinion that the Spanish Government would be unable to agree to make the required sacrifice. He admitted, however, that France might fairly expect some concession from Spain and his language seemed to imply that he would formulate in concert with the rest of the Cabinet a counter-proposition. Meanwhile he could only say that Spain attached to the territory in question the highest importance. It lay opposite the Canary Islands whose inhabitants would bitterly resent its possession by any other Power. Without its occupation the Rio de Oro country, lying immediately to the South could never be properly developed. It was true that Spain had long neglected to occupy it in accordance with her undoubted right but ever since the beginning of French activity in Morocco she had not ceased to press the Moorish Government to complete the stipulated cession. Arrangements for this purpose were concerted between Señor Garcia Prieto and El Mokri simultaneously with the conclusion of the Convention of November 16, 1910,[3] and embodied in a document since published in a Spanish Red Book (See my despatch No. 48 of April 13 last).[4] Negotiations with the Makhzen, with a view to the appointment of a Moorish Commissioner to proceed to Ifni in order to make, in concert with the Spanish Commissioner already named, the necessary delimitation on the spot, had been in progress for some time. The Makhzen was adopting its usual dilatory tactics and it had now become necessary for Spain to act single-handed. Orders indeed had already been issued for the occupation of Ifni on the 3rd or 4th September.

M. Geoffray said he could only repeat what he had said before. If Spain wished to enjoy the benefits of the draft Convention, she would have to surrender Ifni to France. He begged that the question might be immediately considered in Cabinet Council and that, pending a decision, no act of occupation should be allowed to take place at Ifni. Otherwise a hostile French press campaign would certainly ensue to the detriment of the present negotiations. He hoped within a few days to be able to submit the actual text of the Convention. Meanwhile it would be deplorable if Spain took a step calculated to render the present situation more difficult than it already was.

Señor Garcia Prieto said that he hoped to be able to persuade the Prime Minister to order the suspension of the proposed act of the occupation of Ifni at least for a few days.

From a few words dropped by His Excellency in private conversation with myself after the departure of the French Ambassador, I gathered that the French demands, which had been already known to the Spanish Government for some days, were regarded as being exorbitant and entirely inadmissible. Spain had an indisputable treaty right to the territory in question and when the French requisition became known it would give rise, His Excellency thought, to a burst of popular indignation which it would be extremely difficult for any Spanish Government to resist.

I have, &c.
MAURICE DE BUNSEN.

[3] [v. Martens, 3rd Ser.: (Leipzig 1913), VII, pp. 94–100.]
[4] [Not reproduced.]

No. 528.

Sir E. Goschen to Sir Edward Grey.

F.O. 34904/25883/11/28.
Tel. (No. 67.)

Berlin, September 4, 1911.
D. 8·25 P.M.
R. 9 P.M.

Morocco.

Negotiations were resumed to-day. French Ambassador communicated draft of convention(¹) to Secretary of State, who took it away for submission to the Chancellor. Answer at next meeting on Wednesday. Secretary of State raised objections to articles 5 and 6 and to last article respecting German protégés in Morocco. As regards territorial compensations in Congo, Secretary of State maintained that they were insufficient in view of what France would gain in Morocco. He refused rectification of Togoland frontier as proposed by France, but French Ambassador declined to accept refusal as final answer, and begged that it might be reconsidered.

Tone of conversation was friendly, and, on the whole, French Ambassador seemed not dissatisfied.

(¹) [For text, v. infra, pp. 511–21, No. 539, and G.P. XXIX, pp. 361–4.]

No. 529.

Sir Edward Grey to Sir G. Buchanan.(¹)

F.O. 35283/25883/11/28.
(No. 242.)
Sir,

Foreign Office, September 4, 1911.

The Russian Ambassador asked me to-day what I thought of the prospects of the conversations between France and Germany.

I said that the outcome was very obscure. The Germans had changed their ground so often that it was very difficult to form an opinion. There would certainly not be war unless Germany intended to have it. If the conversations came to a deadlock, everything would depend upon what Germany did. If she took some action to rush matters, either by landing a force in Morocco or by sending to France a communication in the nature of an ultimatum about the Algeciras Act, such as Count Metternich had foreshadowed in a conversation with me some weeks ago, it would of course mean that she intended war. But otherwise some settlement would be patched up. I said that I understood the Russian Government were being kept informed of everything, and I asked whether he had any news from St. Petersburg.

He replied that he had none.

I told him that Sir Fairfax Cartwright had not been cognisant of the article in the '' Neue Freie Presse '';(²) and the attacks upon him had been worked up from German sources. There must have been some object in this. It might be that Germany intended to make a settlement with France, and to explain that this settlement was not satisfactory owing to the action of England. The German Government might intend to cover their retreat by giving this explanation to German public opinion. It might be one way of securing peace, though it would tend to an increase of naval expenditure.

I observed that the whole matter might have been settled if the Germans had gone to the French when the latter reached Fez, and told them quietly that

(¹) [Printed in Twenty-Five Years, I, pp. 235–6.]
(²) [v. infra, pp. 837–45, App. V.]

Germany must have a settlement. But when the Germans opened the proceedings by sending a warship to Agadir, they mobilised public opinion here, in France, and in Germany. The Germans were now hampered by the public feeling which they had themselves created.

Count Benckendorff expressed himself very decidedly to the effect that the sending of a German warship to Agadir was very unfortunate, and indeed immoral.

[I am, &c.]

E. G[REY].

No. 530.

Sir Edward Grey to Sir M. de Bunsen.

F.O. 35282/13751/11/28.
(No. 93.)
Sir,   *Foreign Office, September* 4, 1911.

The Spanish Ambassador told me to-day that he had reported to his Government that he personally shared my view that no settlement could be come to between Spain and France about Morocco until the outcome of the conversations between France and Germany was known. However, the French Ambassador in Spain had opened a conversation, based upon the giving up of Ifni by Spain.(¹) The Spanish Ambassador said that Spain could never give up Ifni, and in fact could not postpone her occupation of it for more than a few days. There was no reason why Spain should give compensation to France for a settlement with Germany.

I said that I could not agree with this principle. If the result of the negotiations between France and Germany were that France and Spain obtained a free hand to divide Morocco, subject to economic liberty, Spain could not expect to make no sacrifice herself, while France paid the whole price.

The Ambassador said he understood that France would get from Germany a free hand in her own sphere only, and Spain could not be expected to pay both France and Germany.

I said that of course Spain could not be expected to pay both. I had spoken on the assumption that Germany had asked nothing from Spain. The Germans changed their ground so often that it was impossible to say what the outcome would be of the conversations between France and Germany; and any discussion of a settlement between Spain and France seemed to me, therefore, to be academic at the present moment.

[I am, &c.]

E. G[REY].

(¹) [*v. supra*, pp. 500–1, No. 527.]

No. 531.

Sir Edward Grey to Sir F. Bertie.

Private.(¹)
My dear Bertie,   *Paris, September* 4, 1911.

I enclose a quotation from a letter of Goschen to me written on September 1.(²)

I agree entirely with Jules Cambon's views. Apparently what the Germans now ask for is the line of the Alima: this does not mean any more sea-coast than the French are offering north of Libreville; it means a triangle of internal territory

(¹) [Grey MSS., Vol. 13.]
(²) [*v. supra*, pp. 498–9, No. 526.]

more than the French offer; the base of the triangle being a line from Wesso to the Alima. Assuming (I admit all depends upon this assumption) that the Germans are really prepared to concede to France a clean bargain in Morocco, it is sheer unreason to make the difference between peace and war depend upon the Wesso–Alima triangle.

There are three choices plain before the French:

1. A bargain in which France practically gets Morocco, subject to economic liberty.
2. A retreat in Morocco to within what the letter and spirit of the Algeciras Act may be held to require.
3. War.

1. is infinitely preferable, and I am sure must be worth many times everything that lies between Wesso and Alima.

I know that it is a delicate matter to say this to Caillaux and de Selves; but the situation is serious, and the extent to which British support is forthcoming, if trouble is ahead, must depend upon its being clear that France has had no reasonable and honourable way of avoiding it.

I shall be glad if you will take any moment that you consider to be opportune for letting Caillaux and de Selves know my view.

Yours sincerely,
E. GREY.

No. 532.

Sir Edward Grey to Sir F. Bertie.(¹)

F.O. 35547/25883/11/28.
(No. 374.)

Sir, *Foreign Office, September 5,* 1911.

M. [Paul] Cambon showed me to-day a telegraphic summary of the conversation of yesterday between the French Ambassador [M. Jules Cambon] and Herr von Kiderlen in Berlin.(²)

Herr von Kiderlen had, after some discussion, accepted in principle the project for what was virtually a French protectorate over Morocco. He had made difficulties about the limitation of economic equality to thirty years; about the French protectorate over Moorish subjects abroad; and about the judicial organisation; and he had protested against the proposals about German *protégés.* He was, however, ready to agree to a secret understanding as to the establishment later on of a French protectorate, really and technically. He had said that the Germans could not give anything in Togoland, and that he must refer all the proposals to the Chancellor.

M. Cambon asked me what I thought of this.

I said that I expected Herr von Kiderlen would reply that what was offered in the French Congo was not enough. Personally, it seemed to me that, geographically, climatically, and generally, Morocco was of so much greater importance to France than the French Congo, that it would be a pity for France not to increase her offer of territory in the French Congo if necessary, and if she could get a clean and definitive arrangement as to Morocco. Could she not, for instance, give the triangle for which Germany asked up to the River Alima?

M. Cambon said that this was impossible. He said it must be remembered that, after the experience of the arrangement with Germany of 1909, the French Parliament would be apt to say that what was given up in the French Congo was

(¹) [Printed in *Twenty-Five Years,* I, pp. 232–3, *et sqq.* for further discussion.]
(²) [*cp. supra,* p. 502, No. 528.]

solid, while nothing was being obtained from Germany except a bit of paper which might be worth nothing.

I remarked that any cessions of territory in the French Congo might be made dependent upon the agreement with Germany being accepted by all the other Powers who were parties to the Act of Algeciras. This would give France an assured position in Morocco.

I observed how important it was that if there was trouble it should be quite clear that it was Germany who forced it. I hoped therefore that the French would not break off the negotiations. M. Cambon replied that the French Ambassador at Berlin was fully aware of the importance of this.

[I am, &c.]
E. G[REY].

No. 533.

Sir F. Bertie to Sir Edward Grey.

F.O. 35195/25883/11/28.
Tel. (No. 144.) R.

Paris, D. September 6, 1911.
R. *September* 7, 1911, 8 A.M.

Morocco.

French Minister for Foreign Affairs told me to-day that he had seen Russian and German Ambassadors, and that M. Isvolsky [*sic*] did not revert to question of additional cessions of territory to Germany, or to suggestion of arbitration.(¹) German Ambassador, whom he had questioned on economic advantages which Germany would expect to obtain in Morocco, said that some time since when he was kept informed of Morocco business there was, he knew, a memorandum on the subject which French Minister for Foreign Affairs had mentioned, but that he did not know whether German Minister for Foreign Affairs' views were now the same or not. German Ambassador appeared to be mortified at being kept in complete ignorance of views of German Government.

(¹) [*v. supra*, pp. 476–7, No. 503; pp. 469–70, No. 497, *et sqq.*]

No. 534.

Sir F. Bertie to Sir Edward Grey.

Private.(¹)
Tel.

Paris, September 7, 1911.
D. 12·45 A.M.
R. 8 A.M.

My private telegram of September 6.(²)

It being M[inister for] F[oreign] A[ffair]'s reception day, I could pay him a visit without an appointment or any particular reason, and I did so this afternoon.

I asked him whether he had any news as to the result of the conversation between the French Ambassador and the German M[inister for] F[oreign] A[ffairs].

He said that the news was neither good nor bad. The Ambassador had communicated the draft Convention respecting Morocco to the German M[inister for] F[oreign] A[ffairs], who had taken it ad referendum for the consideration of the German Chancellor, after making some observations on some minor points in it, and stating that territorial cessions offered by France were insufficient for what she was asking in Morocco. The question of territorial cessions however would, the French M[inister for] F[oreign] A[ffairs] observed, only be discussed when the

(¹) [Grey MSS., Vol. 13.]
(²) [*v. supra*, pp. 476–7, No. 503.]

French Government had received the formal assurance that they would obtain the main points of what they desired in Morocco, as set forth in the draft Convention.

I then read to the M[inister for] F[oreign] A[ffairs] in French Sir E. Goschen's telegram no: 67 of September 4,(³) and stated that, as I had forwarded to you the copy of the draft Convention which he had given me, I should be glad if he would show me Articles 4 and 6 of the last Article referred to by Sir E. Goschen.

This he did. He then observed, with reference to the German M[inister for] F[oreign] A[ffair]'s statement that the territorial cessions were insufficient, that he did not know what more the Germans could want, for the French Government were offering the greater part of the French Congo.

I asked the French M[inister for] F[oreign] A[ffairs] whether he could explain the continuation of the desire of the German Government to obtain the line of the Alima. What would be its special value to Germany, what was its particular value to France?

The French M[inister for] F[oreign] A[ffairs] said that he supposed Germany desired to have territory conterminous with the Congo State for as long a stretch as they could obtain. There might also be reasons of commerce of which he was not aware : but he thought that chief reason might be to extract from France what she had refused, and to show that she was obliged to yield to German demands, and so humiliate her. He asked me what I thought of the situation.

I told him that I had seen a friend who had arrived this morning from Germany. He had found there a very bombastic and warlike spirit, and preparations were being made there for war, and I thought it possible that the German Government, having excited public opinion, and the appetite for territory, might perhaps be carried away and press their demands to the point of covert menaces of war. In such an event, would the French Government refuse further concessions?

The M[inister for] F[oreign] A[ffairs] replied that he did not think the French Government would concede more than the extreme offers which they were making, and not in any case did he believe they would concede the line of the Alima ; and he reminded me that, at the Conference between the President of the Council, himself, the French Ambassador at Berlin, and the German Ambassador, it had been absolutely refused, (see my telegram 133, confidential, of August 24).(⁴) The French M[inister for] F[oreign] A[ffairs] further expressed his conviction that, if the French Government made any further cessions of territory, it would not be the line of the Alima. It would have to be elsewhere, but he considered that it would be difficult enough to reconcile the French Parliament and French public opinion to the offers which the French Government were making. He did not believe that any French Ministry could survive further concessions such as the line of the Alima. It would leave to France very little of her valuable Congo Colony.

Sir E. Goschen, in his private telegram of September 4 to you,(⁵) which you have repeated to me, expresses the opinion that, if the French Government can be induced to make a really acceptable offer, (viz. : the line of the Alima), it would strengthen the hands of H[is] M[ajesty's] G[overnment] both as regards public opinion in England and in any subsequent conversations with the German Government.

To be of such utility in conversations with the German Government, it would be necessary that they should know that the line of the Alima had been conceded under the pressure or by the advice of England. The French Government might learn this by intention or accident, and H[is] M[ajesty's] G[overnment], though they might possibly obtain advantages in their dealings with Germany for the concession made by France, would most certainly incur the odium of French public for having, as would be thought, urged on the French Government a sacrifice to Germany for the benefit of British interests.

(³) [v. supra, p. 502, No. 528.]
(⁴) [v. supra, pp. 485–6, No. 514.]
(⁵) [Not reproduced ; contents indicated above.]

No. 535.

Sir E. Goschen to Sir Edward Grey.

Berlin, September 8, 1911.

F.O. 35432/25883/11/28.   D. 11·40 A.M.

Tel. (No. 69.)   R. 12·30 P.M.

Morocco.

Secretary of State for Foreign Affairs at meeting yesterday evening showed French Ambassador rough draft of German counter project of Convention. He considers German pretentions [*sic*] as regards railways and their exploitation excessive and as denoting the intention to exclude all other powers from participation. He also said that in some points German project places the two powers on the same political plane.

German draft convention which in rough state cannot reach French Gov[ernmen]t before day after to-morrow if then so there will be probably no discussion of it here for another week.

Territorial compensations were not touched upon in conversation.

Under Secretary of State told the Italian Ambassador that they intended to be very stiff about economic guarantees which were very far from being satisfactory in the French proposals.

No. 536.

Sir Edward Grey to Sir F. Bertie.

F.O. 35451/25883/11/28.   *Foreign Office, September 8, 1911.*

Tel. (No. 230.)   D. 7 P.M.

French Ambassador has informed me of interview between French Ambassador at Berlin and German M[inister for] F[oreign] A[ffairs] yesterday. German M[inister for] F[oreign] A[ffairs] has apparently shifted ground of difficulty completely from French Congo to economic interests in Morocco. French Ambassador here observed that it was satisfactory that Germany practically accepted first four articles of French draft conceding the principle of French position in Morocco, but that it would be impossible to concede to German subjects or German commerce a privileged position. I expressed this view also, as Franco-German arrangement would have to be accepted by other Powers parties to Algeciras Act. It appears that text of German counterdraft will not be ready for a day or two and it seems as if negotiations were entering upon very tedious but less dangerous ground.

(Repeat to Sir E. Goschen.)

No. 537.

Sir F. Bertie to Sir Edward Grey.([1])

F.O. 35515/25883/11/28.   *Paris,* D. *September* 8, 1911.

Tel. (No. 147.) Confidential. R.   R. *September* 9, 1911.

Berlin telegram No. 69 of to-day.([2])

I have seen French Minister for Foreign Affairs this evening. He says that, from French Ambassador at Berlin's telegraphic report—which he read to me—of his interview with German Minister for Foreign Affairs yesterday, there is a complete

([1]) [The original decypher of this telegram cannot be traced, the above copy of the decypher being taken from the Confidential Print.]

([2]) [*v. supra*, p. 507, No. 535.]

change of front on the part of the German Government, for whereas hitherto they have expressed their readiness to accord France, so far as Germany is concerned, a practical protectorate of Morocco under the guise of some other form of words, and their expectation that there would be no difficulty in negotiations provided that their economic interests were respected, and they have made a great point of obtaining large territorial concessions in French Congo, they now lay great stress on what are political matters in Morocco, and do not seem to attach the same importance to territorial compensations. Moreover, whereas they formerly said that it would be for France to settle matters with Spain, they now propose that besides Spanish possessions in Morocco being excluded from a definition of Morocco territory, the subject of proposed Franco-German convention, any parts of Morocco which may be recognised by France as within Spanish zones of influence shall likewise be excluded, thus reserving such parts for dealings between German and Spanish Governments, and enabling former to extract advantages from latter as consideration for a German recognition of special position of Spain in those parts of Morocco. French Minister for Foreign Affairs is wholly unable to appreciate whether this change of front is due to German Emperor and his Chancellor not concurring in German Minister for Foreign Affairs' line of negotiations or to a desire to cause negotiations to be fruitless.

French Minister for Foreign Affairs has given me a copy of French draft convention communicated to German Minister for Foreign Affairs last Monday (3rd September), and I have forwarded it to you by post to-day.([3]) French Ambassador at Berlin gathers from his conversation with German Minister for Foreign Affairs, and from latter's sketch of provisions of German counter-draft, which is to be communicated to French Ambassador in Berlin to-morrow or the next day, that as to French draft, German Government maintain that various administrative, economic, financial, and military reforms contemplated in article 1 must be on initiative of Moorish Government, and not on that of French Government; that, similarly, any military occupation of Morocco territory and the policing on land and in territorial waters by France provided for in article 2 must be at instance of Moorish Government. As to article 3, German Government require that period for complete equality in customs, taxation, tariffs, and railway transport shall not be limited to thirty years.

German Government do not object to French diplomatic and consular representation in Morocco and her interests abroad provided for in article 5, but they claim that, if Germany is to be precluded from entering into any engagement with Morocco without previous concurrence of France, French Government must give a like undertaking not to enter into any such engagement without German concurrence.

As to article 6, German Government require that any courts of justice to be established in Morocco in lieu of consular courts must be on model of Egyptian mixed tribunals. In regard to 7, German Government claim that in cases where construction of a railway has been adjudicated to a certain nationality, such nationality shall have a share in working (" exploitation ") of such railway.

As to article 9, German Government claims to exclude from definition of Morocco territory any zones which may be recognised by France as within Spanish sphere of influence.

German Government decline to give up right, as stipulated in article 14, to grant protection in Morocco to Moorish subjects.

([3]) [v. infra, pp. 511–21, No. 539.]

No. 538.

Sir E. Goschen to Sir Edward Grey.

F.O. 35614/25883/11/28.
(No. 265.)   Berlin, ·D. September 8, 1911.
Sir,   R. September 11, 1911.

As I had the honour to state in my telegram No. 67 of the 4th instant,(¹) last Wednesday was the day fixed by Herr von Kiderlen for giving Monsieur [Jules] Cambon the reply or counter project to the French draft Convention.(²) On that day, however, the Secretary of State for Foreign Affairs intimated to the French Ambassador that, as the Chancellor would not arrive in Berlin till the evening, he must defer their meeting till the next day at 11 A.M. When that hour arrived, however, Herr von Kiderlen sent a message that he was not yet ready but that he would be glad to see the French Ambassador at 6·30 P.M. Monsieur Cambon, who did not augur well from these delays, called upon him at that hour and was shown, and allowed to take away, for telegraphing purposes, a very rough draft of the German counter project of convention.

There was but little time for any discussion, as Herr von Kiderlen had another engagement at 7. He promised, however, that he would have the draft corrected and typed in time for Monsieur Cambon to transmit it to his Government on Saturday next.

Monsieur Cambon told me in the evening that he had not been sorry that the interview was so short as he wished to be in possession of the views of his Government before entering into any discussion respecting the German counter project with the Secretary of State for Foreign Affairs. He said that his own impression was that it was quite inacceptable and that if the demands made by Germany were acceded to there would be absolutely no reason for giving her any territorial compensation whatever.

As regards railways in Morocco, their exploitation, and the supply of material for their construction, the German project provides that Germany should participate to the extent of 30%, the remaining 70% going to France.(³) Monsieur Cambon pointed out to Herr von Kiderlen that this provision would appear to exclude other Powers from all participation and that that was hardly in accordance with the principle of the "Open Door," by which Germany set so much store : it would moreover have the effect of giving Germany a certain measure of the political influence for the renouncement of which she was claiming territorial compensation. Herr von Kiderlen, however, remarked that he had no time on the present occasion to go into the matter; he would explain the ideas of the Imperial Government on the subject at their next meeting.

Monsieur Cambon also gave me to understand that the German project retained the French article with regard to diplomatic representation, but stipulated for reciprocity, namely that if at any time France on her side contemplated making a fresh treaty with Morocco the fact should be duly notified to the German Government. This sentence, Monsieur Cambon maintained, appeared to place the two Governments on practically the same political plane and it was out of the question that it should be accepted.

As far as I can see, both parties seem to think that the convention proposed by the other is quite inacceptable. In any case there can be no further discussion on the subject here until the French Government have considered the German proposal and furnished Monsieur Cambon with instructions. That can scarcely be at the earliest before the end of next week. My French colleague seems to be confident that they will eventually arrive at an arrangement, but he thinks that the discussions will extend over at least a month. He is of the opinion that Herr von

(¹) [v. supra, p. 502, No. 528.]
(²) [v. infra, pp. 511–21, No. 539.]
(³) [v. infra, pp. 515–6, No. 539, Art. 7; and p. 534, No. 557, note (¹).]

Kiderlen desires a settlement and will do what he can to facilitate matters, but that His Excellency is greatly hampered by the rapacity of the Bureaux, and more particularly of the Colonial Department.

The Under Secretary of State for Foreign Affairs, Herr Zimmermann, in conversation with the Russian Chargé d'Affaires, declaimed violently against the French proposals which he said scarcely offered even a basis for discussion. He used much the same language to my Italian colleague adding that it was evidently very distasteful to the French Government to give guarantees that Germany should receive fair treatment in the field of commerce and industry in Morocco, but that the Imperial Government had fully made up their minds to be very stiff on that subject and to make arrangements such as would not share the fate of the assurances given by France in the arrangement of 1909.([4])

I have, &c.
W. E. GOSCHEN.

MINUTES.

The negotiations are reaching a point where we begin to be concerned in them. Whatever the French may do, we cannot agree to any provisions which give Germany a privileged position as regards commerce in Morocco. We must have exactly the same rights and position as she does. The German railway proposal is preposterous. Would it not be advisable to instruct Sir F. Bertie to make the point quite clear in an official communication to M. de Selves? There really may be some danger of a Franco-German deal to our detriment.

The last paragraph does not augur well.

G. H. V.
11.9.11.

We have, except as regards the percentage claimed in railways by Germany, fuller information in Sir F. Bertie's tel[egram] No. 147 of Sept[ember] 8([5]) as to the nature of the German reply.

M. Cambon hits the nail on the head when he says ''if the demands made by Germany were acceded to there would be absolutely no reason for giving her any territorial compensation whatever.''

A. P.

Copy to Paris and tell Sir F. Bertie to point out that the proposal by which the supply of railway material would be confined to France and Germany would be a violation of the Treaty rights of this and other countries which we could not admit.

This might strengthen French hands, and, as Mr. Villiers says above, might usefully be put on record.

F. A. C.
11.9.

I hardly think it is necessary at this juncture to put in any caveat. The French are quite alive to the fact that we and others would naturally demur to a Franco-German monopoly. This despatch was written on first impressions of a '' very rough draft '' of the German counterproject. A closer examination of the full text will show greater encroachments on the political sphere by Germany—France has not only to '' notify '' to Germany any accord with Morocco—but to '' come to a previous understanding with her.''

A. N.

Wait till the French have the text and we know what it is.

E. G.

([4]) [Herr Zimmermann's views as expressed to Herr von Schoen on September 10 are in *G.P.* XXIX, pp. 374-6.]

([5]) [*v.* immediately preceding document.]

No. 539.

French and German Draft Conventions, September 4–8, 1911.(¹)

F.O. 36565/25883/11/28.

French Text.	*German Text.*

A la suite des troubles qui se sont produits au Maroc et qui ont démontré la nécessité d'y poursuivre, dans l'intérêt général, l'œuvre de pacification et de progrès prévue par l'Acte d'Algésiras, le Gouvernement de la République française et le Gouvernement Impérial allemand ont jugé nécessaire de préciser et de compléter l'accord franco-allemand du 9 février, 1909. Ils sont convenus à cet effet des dispositions ci-après :—

A la suite des troubles qui se sont produits au Maroc et qui ont démontré la nécessité d'y poursuivre, dans l'intérêt général, l'œuvre de pacification et de progrès prévue par l'Acte d'Algésiras, le Gouvernement de la République française et le Gouvernement Impérial allemand ont jugé nécessaire de préciser et de compléter l'accord franco-allemand du 9 février, 1909. Ils sont convenus à cet effet des dispositions ci-après :—

ARTICLE 1ᵉʳ.

ARTICLE 1ᵉʳ

Le Gouvernement Impérial allemand, *dont les intérêts au Maroc ont un caractère exclusivement économique,* déclare qu'il n'entravera pas l'action *directrice* de la France en vue de prêter son assistance au Sultan pour l'introduction de toutes les réformes administratives, économiques, financières et militaires dont il a besoin pour le bon gouvernement de son Empire, comme aussi pour tous les règlements que ces réformes comportent.

En conséquence, il donne son adhésion aux mesures de réorganisation, de contrôle et de garantie financière que, de concert avec le Gouvernement marocain, le Gouvernement français croira devoir prendre à cet effet, sous la réserve que l'action *directrice* de la France sauvegardera au Maroc l'égalité économique entre les nations.

Au cas où la France serait amenée à préciser et à étendre ces droits de contrôle et de protection, le Gouvernement Impérial

Le Gouvernement Impérial allemand déclare qu'il n'entravera pas l'action de la France en vue de prêter son assistance au Sultan pour l'introduction de toutes les réformes administratives, économiques, financières et militaires dont il a besoin pour le bon gouvernement de son Empire, comme aussi pour tous les règlements que ces réformes comportent.

En conséquence, il donne son adhésion aux mesures de réorganisation, de contrôle et de garantie financière que, *sur la demande et* de concert avec le Gouvernement marocain, le Gouvernement français croira devoir prendre à cet effet, sous la réserve que l'action de la France sauvegardera au Maroc l'égalité économique entre les nations.

Au cas où la France serait amenée à préciser et à étendre son contrôle et sa protection, le Gouvernement Impérial allemand, reconnaissant au Maroc pleine liberté d'action à la France, sous la

(¹) [The table here given is taken from the *Confidential Print*. The italics and a black line at the side denote the differences in the French and German texts. The French text was presented by M. Jules Cambon to Herr von Kiderlen-Waechter on September 4. It was forwarded by Sir F. Bertie in his despatch No. 400 of September 8 (F.O. 35449/25883/11/28). It is quoted in *G.P.* XXIX, pp. 361–4. The German counter-draft was handed to M. Jules Cambon, in " very rough " form for telegraphic purposes, on September 8, and a corrected version was given him on the 10th. The basis of the text is described in *G.P.* XXIX, pp. 365–72, p. 373, *note.* A copy was forwarded by Sir F. Bertie as an enclosure in his despatch No. 405 of September 12, 1911, *v. infra,* p. 524, No. 545.]

allemand, reconnaissant au Maroc pleine liberté d'action à la France, sous la réserve que la liberté commerciale prévue par les traités antérieurs sera maintenue, n'y apportera aucun obstacle.

Article 2.

Dans cet ordre d'idées, il est entendu que le Gouvernement Impérial ne fera pas obstacle à ce que la France, d'accord avec le Gouvernement marocain, procède aux occupations militaires du territoire marocain qu'elle jugerait nécessaire au maintien de l'ordre et de la sécurité des transactions commerciales, et à ce qu'elle exerce toute action de police sur terre et dans les eaux marocaines.

Article 3.

Le Gouvernement français déclare que, fermement attaché au principe de la liberté commerciale au Maroc, il ne se prêtera à aucune inégalité pas plus dans l'établissement des droits de douane, impôts et autres taxes que dans l'établissement des tarifs de transport par chemin de fer.

Cet engagement est valable pour une période de trente ans. Faute de dénonciation expresse faite au moins une année à l'avance, cette période sera renouvelée de cinq ans en cinq ans.

réserve que la liberté commerciale prévue par les traités antérieurs sera maintenue, n'y apportera aucun obstacle.

Il est entendu qu'il ne sera apporté aucune entrave aux droits et à l'action de la Banque d'État du Maroc stipulés dans l'Acte d'Algésiras.

Article 2.

Dans cet ordre d'idées, il est entendu que le Gouvernement Impérial allemand ne fera pas obstacle à ce que la France, *sur la demande et* d'accord avec le Gouvernement marocain, procède aux occupations militaires du territoire marocain qu'elle jugerait nécessaire au maintien de l'ordre et de la sécurité des transactions commerciales, et à ce qu'elle exerce toute action de police sur terre et dans les eaux marocaines.

Article 3.

Le Gouvernement français déclare que, fermement attaché au principe de la liberté commerciale au Maroc, il ne se prêtera à aucune inégalité pas plus dans l'établissement des droits de douane, impôts et autres taxes que dans l'établissement des tarifs de transport par voie de chemin de fer, *de navigation fluviale ou toute autre voie de transport et notamment dans toutes les questions de transit.*

Le Gouvernement français s'emploiera également auprès du Gouvernement marocain afin d'empêcher tout traitement différentiel entre les sujets des différentes nations, et, notamment, il s'opposera à toute mesure qui pourrait différencier les marchandises d'une Puissance par des ordonnances administratives sur les poids, les mesures, le jaugeage et le poinçonnage.

Le Gouvernement français s'engage à faire prévaloir son influence sur la direction de la Banque d'État afin que celle-ci confère aux membres de sa direction à Tanger à tour de rôle les postes de délégué à la Commission des Valeurs douanières et de délégué au Comité permanent des Douanes dont elle dispose (articles 96 et 97 de l'Acte d'Algésiras).

French Text.

ARTICLE 4.

Le Gouvernement français veillera à ce qu'il ne soit perçu au Maroc aucun droit d'exportation sur le minerai de fer exporté des ports marocains. Les exploitations de minerai de fer ne subiront aucun impôt spécial. Elles ne seront assujetties qu'aux impôts généraux et aux redevances domaniales qui atteindront toutes les entreprises minières.

ARTICLE 5.

Dès à présent, si Sa Majesté le Sultan du Maroc venait à confier aux agents diplomatiques et consulaires de la France la représentation et la protection des sujets et des intérêts marocains à l'étranger, le Gouvernement Impérial déclare qu'il n'y fera pas d'objection.

Le Gouvernement Impérial déclare, d'autre part, qu'il ne contractera aucun accord quelconque avec le Gouvernement marocain sans s'être entendu au préalable avec le Gouvernement de la République française.

ARTICLE 6.

Lorsque des organisations judiciaires *marocaines* régulières auront été créées au Maroc et que la France aura décidé de leur transférer la juridiction des tribunaux consulaires français, le Gouvernement Impérial allemand transférera également à ces mêmes tribunaux la juridiction des tribunaux consulaires allemands, étant entendu que les ressortissants allemands jouiront des mêmes garanties légales et réglementaires que les ressortissants français.

ARTICLE 7.

Le Gouvernement de la République française s'engage à veiller *pendant la période prévue à l'article 3* à ce que les travaux et fournitures nécessités par les constructions éventuelles de routes, chemins de fer, ports, &c., soient octroyés par le Gouvernement chérifien suivant

[19656]

German Text.

ARTICLE 4.

Le Gouvernement français veillera à ce qu'il ne soit perçu au Maroc aucun droit d'exportation sur le minerai de fer exporté des ports marocains. Les exploitations de minerai de fer ne subiront aucun impôt spécial. Elles ne seront assujetties qu'aux impôts généraux et aux redevances domaniales qui atteindront toutes les entreprises minières.

ARTICLE 5.

Dès à présent, si Sa Majesté le Sultan du Maroc venait à confier aux agents diplomatiques et consulaires de la France la représentation et la protection des sujets et des intérêts marocains à l'étranger, le Gouvernement Impérial déclare qu'il n'y fera pas d'objection.

Les deux Gouvernements s'engagent à se faire connaître les engagements sur lesquels ils pourraient s'entendre avec le Gouvernement marocain.

ARTICLE 6.

Lorsque des organisations judiciaires régulières auront été créées au Maroc *à l'instar des tribunaux mixtes d'Egypte* et que la France aura décidé de leur transférer la juridiction des tribunaux consulaires français, le Gouvernement Impérial allemand, *dès que les autres Puissances signataires en feront autant,* transférera également à ces mêmes tribunaux la juridiction des tribunaux consulaires allemands, étant entendu que les ressortissants allemands jouiront des mêmes garanties légales et réglementaires que les ressortissants français.

ARTICLE 7.

Le Gouvernement de la république s'engage à veiller à ce que les travaux et fournitures nécessités par les constructions éventuelles de routes, chemins de fer, ports, &c., soient octroyés par le Gouvernement chérifien suivant les règles de l'adjudication.

2 L

les règles d'adjudication. *Toutefois, l'exploitation de ces grandes entreprises sera réservée à l'Etat **ou** librement concédée par lui.*

Le Gouvernement français usera également de son influence auprès de la Banque d'Etat afin que celle-ci confère aux membres de sa direction à Tangier, à tour de rôle, le poste de délégué à la Commission générale des Adjudications et Marchés.

De même, le Gouvernement français amènera le Gouvernement marocain à conférer un des postes de délégué chérifien au Comité spécial des Travaux publics à tour de rôle à des candidats qui seront présentés par les quatre Puissances autorisées par l'Acte d'Algésiras à nommer les censeurs auprès de la Banque d'État.

Le Gouvernement français s'engage à user de son influence auprès du Gouvernement marocain dans ce sens que, pour la nomination des fonctionnaires et ingénieurs auxquels sera confiée l'exploitation des grandes entreprises, il sera tenu compte de la nationalité des constructeurs dans la proportion de leur participation.

Les deux Gouvernements s'entendront sur la construction des chemins de fer au Maroc, selon les principes établis dans l'Acte d'Algésiras.

Annexe au dernier alinéa de l'Article 7.

Le Gouvernement Impérial allemand ne fera pas d'objection à la construction d'un chemin de fer militaire d'Oujda par Taourirt à la rive droite de la Moulouya et d'un second chemin de fer militaire de Casablanca par Settat à la rive droite de l'Oum-er-Rebia.

Le Gouvernement français, de son côté, s'engage à se mettre d'accord pour la construction de ces deux chemins de fer avec la Société marocaine de Travaux publics.

Pour ces deux lignes, il devra être employé un matériel (rails, traverses, matériel roulant, &c.) tel qu'aucune industrie ne soit exclue de la possibilité de faire des offres.

Le Gouvernement français s'engage à obliger le Gouvernement marocain de charger l'ingénieur du Makhzen à procéder immédiatement aux démarches nécessaires pour faire mettre en adjudication dans le cours d'une année un chemin de fer de Tanger par Larache à Méquinez et Fez.

L'exécution des travaux de ce chemin de fer devra nécessairement et en toutes circonstances précéder la construction de lignes quelconques dans la partie du Maroc qui se trouve au nord du Tensift.

Dans le cas où, à l'occasion de la mise en adjudication publique du chemin de fer Tanger–Larache–Méquinez et Fez, un entrepreneur français ou une société française seraient déclarés adjudicataires, le Gouvernement français userait de son autorité auprès d'eux pour qu'ils mettent à la disposition des intéressés allemands 30 pour cent du capital ainsi que des travaux.

Les certificats que les concurrents sont tenus de demander en vertu des deux règlements pour les adjudications fourniront une occasion pour prévoir cette nécessité à temps.

D'autre part, dans le cas où un entrepreneur allemand ou une société allemande serait déclaré adjudicataire du chemin de fer susindiqué, le Gouvernement allemand fera valoir son influence pour qu'une participation de 70 pour cent soit offerte à des intéressés français.

De la même manière, la construction de tous les chemins de fer au nord du Tensift sera réglée.

Le Gouvernement français s'engage à obliger le Gouvernement marocain de charger l'ingénieur du Makhzen de procéder aux démarches nécessaires pour faire mettre en adjudication publique une jonction par chemin de fer de Taroudant et de Marrakech avec l'Océan Atlantique, conformément aux projets que les experts lui fourniront et dès que ces projets seront remis entre ses mains.

Dans le cas où, à l'occasion de la mise en adjudication publique de la jonction de Taroudant et Marrakech avec la côte, un entrepreneur allemand ou une société allemande serait déclaré adjudicataire, le Gouvernement allemand s'engage à faire prévaloir son autorité sur l'adjudicataire pour que celui-ci fasse participer des intéressés français à raison de 30 pour cent.

De même, dans le cas inverse, le Gouvernement français obligera les entrepreneurs ou la société française ayant été déclarés adjudicataires de la construction des chemins de fer susindiqués, à en mettre 70 pour cent à la disposition des intéressés allemands.

La même obligation s'appliquera à tous les chemins de fer qui seront à construire à l'avenir au sud du Wadi Tensift et au nord du Wadi Draa.

ARTICLE 8.

Les deux Gouvernements signataires renoncent à se prévaloir de tout accord ayant un caractère international qui serait contraire aux précédentes stipulations.

[Suppressed.]

ARTICLE 9.

Le territoire marocain sur lequel s'exerceront les dispositions résultant de la présente convention comprend, à l'exception des possessions espagnoles, les régions situées entre l'Algérie, l'Afrique occidentale française et la colonie espagnole de Rio de Oro, selon les stipulations des traités et accords conclus par le Maroc.

ARTICLE 8.

Le territoire marocain sur lequel s'exerceront les dispositions résultant de la présente convention comprend, à l'exception des possessions espagnoles *et des districts dans lesquels l'influence espagnole sera reconnue*, les régions situées entre l'Algérie, l'Afrique occidentale française et la colonie espagnole de Rio de Oro, selon les stipulations des traités et accords conclus par le Maroc.

ARTICLE 10.

Les précédents articles de la présente convention seront communiqués aux autres Puissances signataires de l'Acte d'Algésiras, *près desquelles les deux Gouvernements s'engagent à se prêter mutuellement appui pour obtenir leur adhésion.*

ARTICLE 9.

Les précédents articles de la présente convention seront communiqués aux autres Puissances signataires de l'Acte d'Algésiras.

ARTICLE 11.

Comme suite et comme conséquence des dispositions ci-dessus, les deux Gouvernements contractants sont convenus de procéder aux rectifications et échanges territoriaux suivants dans leurs domaines coloniaux :—

I. *Pour l'Allemagne :*

L'Allemagne cède à la France :

1. Sur la frontière Togo–Dahomey—

(*a*.) L'Ile Bayol ;

(*b*.) Le territoire compris entre le méridien Bayol et le Mono de

[Article 11 of French text not yet examined by the German Government:]

French Text.   *German Text.*

telle façon que la frontière suive
le méridien Bayol jusqu'à son
intersection avec la Rivière
Mono ;

(c.) Entre le 7ᵉ et le 9ᵉ degré de
latitude nord :
Le secteur Tohoun–Tado vers
Agouma ;
Le secteur Cabolé Bédou ;
Le secteur traversé par la route
Bassila–Pénésoulou tels que ces
trois secteurs sont définis sur le
croquis ci-joint.(⁴)

D'autre part, il est entendu qu'à partir
du 10ᵉ degré de latitude nord la frontière
Togo–Dahomey se dirigera directement
sur un point situé dans le village de
Gando appelé aussi Djé, à 30 kilom. à
l'est de Sansanné–Mango et sur le
parallèle passant par cette ville ; et que
le territoire des différents villages
formant l'agglomération de Pougno,
attribuée à la France par la convention
de 1897, s'étendra au sud du 11ᵉ degré
de latitude nord de façon à englober les
villages de Timanga, Nanison, Banangadi,
Pilpodi, Sankoti, Tamfiégou et Timouri.

2. La partie de la colonie du Cameroun
située au nord de la Bénoué et du Mayo-
Kébi.

II. *Pour la France :*

La France cède à l'Allemagne—

1. Une bande de territoire située au
sud de Cameroun et définie ainsi qu'il
suit : la frontière partira du côté de
l'Atlantique d'un point de la rive
orientale de la baie de Monda située sur
le parallèle   La frontière se
dirigeant vers l'est longera la frontière
de la Guinée espagnole et la frontière
actuelle du Cameroun en laissant à la
France les sources des Rivières N'Kan
Lara et Okano, et à l'Allemagne les
sources des Rivières Wollen et N'Tem.
Elle coupera la Rivière Ivondo à son
confluent avec la Karagoua, rejoindra de
là en ligne droite le poste de Sembé, qui
sera à l'Allemagne, et suivra depuis ce
point les Rivières Sembé et N'Koko
jusqu'au confluent de cette dernière avec
la Sangha.

(⁴) [Not reproduced.]

2. Un territoire situé à l'est du Cameroun et défini ainsi qu'il suit : la frontière partira du confluent de la N'Goko et de la Sangha et suivra le cours de cette dernière rivière jusqu'au confluent du bras le plus oriental de celle-ci avec le Congo, de manière à laisser à la France les postes de Ouesso Bongha et Loukoléla—français. Elle remontera ensuite le cours du Congo et de l'Oubanghi jusqu'à Bétou (qui sera à [?]). De là, elle suivra le Loubagai pour rejoindre le Lobay au point où confluent le Bali et le Baéré ; elle remontera le Bali jusqu'à hauteur de Kedé puis empruntera le cours des Rivières Lélé, Baba, Ouaham et Bahr Sara jusqu'au confluent de cette dernière avec le Bali. Elle remontera le Bali puis descendra le Som et le Logone oriental jusqu'à Lai (qui reste à la France) ; enfin remontera le Logane occidental et la Membéré jusqu'à la frontière actuelle du Cameroun.

Le Gouvernement Impérial cède à bail au Gouvernement français aux fins et conditions à déterminer dans un acte spécial, un terrain à choisir d'un commun accord en bordure sur l'Oubanghi entre Bétou et Desbordeville. Ce terrain d'une longueur de 400 mètres au plus aura une superficie qui ne pourra excéder 50 hectares.

Dans un délai d'un an à compter de l'échange des ratifications de la présente convention il sera procédé d'un commun accord à l'abornement des frontières décrites ci-dessus.

ARTICLE 12.

Les présents échanges de territoire sont faits dans les conditions où ces territoires se comportent, c'est-à-dire à charge par les deux Gouvernements de respecter les concessions publiques ou particulières qui ont pu être consenties.

[See article 15 of German text.]

ARTICLE 13.

Le Gouvernement allemand n'apportera aucune entrave au passage de troupes françaises et de leur matériel de ravitaillement par le Congo, l'Oubanghi,

[See article 16 of German text.]

French Text. *German Text.*

le Bénoué et le Mao-Kébi; il ne mettra aucun droit sur les marchandises françaises transitant au travers du territoire concédé à l'Allemagne à l'est de la Sangha. Un accord conclu entre les deux Gouvernements déterminera les conditions de ce transit et les points de pénétration.

ARTICLE 14.

[See article 17 of German text.]

Le Gouvernement français et le Gouvernement allemand cesseront, du jour de la ratification de la présente convention, d'exercer aucune sorte d'autorité ou de protection sur les indigènes des territoires respectivement cédés par eux. *Le Gouvernement allemand renonce en outre à exercer au Maroc aucun droit de protection sur des sujets marocains.*

ARTICLE 10.

Le Gouvernement français s'engage à obliger le Gouvernement marocain à adjoindre à tous les services de transport des censeurs analogues à ceux qui ont été prévus pour la Banque d'État du Maroc par les articles 51–53 de l'Acte d'Algésiras. Chaque censeur aura le droit de veto.

ARTICLE 11.

Pour éviter autant que possible les réclamations diplomatiques, les plaintes des sujets allemands qui ne seront pas réglées par l'intermédiaire des deux consuls dans les districts où l'action réformatrice de la France remplacera de fait l'administration marocaine ou exercera sur cette dernière une influence autoritative, seront soumises à des commissions spéciales, sur la composition et la compétence desquelles les deux Gouvernements s'entendront.

ARTICLE 12.

En cas de modifications à apporter aux traités internationaux de Maroc, le Gouvernement français veillera à ce qu'il ne soit pas porté atteinte aux droits actuels des pêcheurs des Etats signataires de faire la pêche de long de la côte

marocaine et de profiter des occasions
qu'elle leur offre pour la navigation,
la pêche et leurs besoins professionnels.

ARTICLE 13.

Dès la mise en vigueur du présent
traité, les Gouvernements allemands et
français demanderont simultanément au
Gouvernement marocain l'ouverture du
port d'Agadir. Ils procéderont de même
si plus tard l'ouverture d'autres ports de
la côte atlantique du Maroc paraissaient
désirable. Quant aux ports situés entre
le Tensift et le Draa, le Gouvernement
français se conformera aux désirs du
Gouvernement allemand, qui, de son
côté, soutiendra les désirs français relatifs
aux ports situés au nord du Tensift.

[See Article 11 of French text.]

ARTICLE 14 [French text, Article 11].

(Not yet examined by the German
Government.)

[See Article 12 of French text.]

ARTICLE 15.

Les présents échanges de territoire
sont faits dans les conditions où ces
territoires se comportent, c'est-à-dire à
charge par les deux Gouvernements de
respecter les concessions publiques ou
particulières qui ont pu être consenties,
*et que les Gouvernements se communi-
queront.*

[See Article 13 of French text.]

ARTICLE 16.

Le Gouvernement allemand n'apportera
aucune entrave au passage des troupes
françaises et de leur matériel de ravitaillement par le Congo, l'Oubanghi, la
Bénoué et le Mao-Kébi; il ne mettra
aucun droit sur les marchandises
françaises transitant au travers du territoire concédé à l'Allemagne à l'est de la
Sangha.
*La France également n'apportera
aucune entrave au passage des troupes
allemandes et de leur matériel de
ravitaillement par la colonie du Gabon.*
Un accord conclu entre les deux
Gouvernements déterminera les conditions de ce transit et les points de
pénétration.

French Text.   *German Text.*

[See Article 14 of French text.]   ARTICLE 17.

Le Gouvernement français et le Gouvernement allemand cesseront du jour de la ratification de la présente convention d'exercer aucune sorte d'autorité ou de protection sur les indigènes des territoires respectivement cédés par eux.

No. 540.

Sir Edward Grey to Sir F. Bertie.

Private.(¹)
My dear Bertie,   *Paris, September* 8, 1911.

I think you have acted with wise discretion about the line of the Alima. I never contemplated letting Germany know that we had said anything to the French about it.

It is essential that before war comes (if it does come) it should be clear that Germany has meant war and has forced it: unless that is so, I could not be sure of what the force of public opinion here would be, and if the Government has to take a decision for war it must have the strongest possible case to put before Parliament.

With this object I stipulated that a Conference should be proposed if the negotiations between France and Germany come to a deadlock. If Germany accepts, war is one remove further off; if she refuses, she appears as the person who prefers war.

I have the authority of the Cabinet to propose a Conference formally to the Powers if need be, and so far so good: and the French have agreed to that.

But I foresee now that in some way or another it will become known that Taft is ready to offer mediation or arbitration: or if it is not known it will be suggested.(²)

I do not think the Germans will accept it: any impartial arbitrator would say, looking at the 1909 Agreement of Germany with France, that Germany's interests in Morocco are confessedly only economic, and Germany would get less than she is claiming now. It would be very desirable, however, that France should be willing to let Taft arbitrate or mediate if the situation becomes acute. The French are so sensitive about Iswolsky's absurd suggestion(³) that France should submit to an arbitration by Germany's Ally, that it would hardly do to mention Taft yet: but I foresee that before we go to extremes, if extremes are to come, I shall have to suggest this.

I am waiting to hear Cambon's news to-day.

Yours sincerely,
E. GREY.

(¹) [Grey MSS,, Vol. 13.]
(²) [*v. infra*, pp. 523–4, No. 544.]
(³) [*v. supra*, pp. 464–80, chap. LVII, *passim.*]

No. 541.

Sir M. de Bunsen to Sir Edward Grey.

F.O. 35570/13751/11/28.   *Zarauz,* D. *September* 9, 1911, 6 P.M.
Tel. (No. 74.) R.   R. *September* 10, 1911, 8 A.M.

French Ambassador and I had another conversation with Minister for Foreign Affairs at San Sebastian this morning. Minister for Foreign Affairs said that

Spanish Government have carefully considered offers and demands of the French Government on the understanding that they were dependent on issue of Berlin negotiations. The proposal respecting Spanish sphere of influence, though satisfactory on the whole, would require modification on certain points. As to required surrender of the whole of the zone on which Spain had counted, Spanish Government had been glad to hear from Spanish Ambassador in Paris that this demand need not be regarded as an ultimatum, and that French Government would be open to an offer, otherwise it would have been impossible to pursue the negotiations. Spain could not cede coast lying opposite Canary Islands, including Ifni. She was, however, prepared to consider a cession of territory corresponding to cession France was about to make in French Congo.

French Ambassador invited Spanish Minister for Foreign Affairs to formulate a reply to French Government on these lines. Minister for Foreign Affairs promised to do so.

(Repeated to Paris.)

No. 542.

Sir F. Cartwright to Sir Edward Grey.

Vienna, September 10, 1911.

F.O. 35571/25883/11/28.
Tel. (No. 94.) Very Confidential.
Morocco.

D. 7·30 P.M.
R. 10·15 P.M.

Count von Aehrenthal sent for French Ambassador yesterday, and, after many amiable phrases for French Government, said that Morocco question, as far as it affected Morocco alone, did not interest Austria, for she had full confidence in French assurances that the "open door" would be maintained there. The Morocco question, however, was assuming wider dimensions, and seemed likely, if left open much longer, to put a serious strain on the relations between certain of the great European Powers. For this reason Austro--Hungarian Government desired ardently that an amicable settlement should be promptly arrived at between France and Germany. In this dispute Austria asked nothing for herself, and all she desired was that peace of Europe should not be threatened. He understood Germany was prepared to give France a free hand in Morocco, and in Count von Aehrenthal's opinion this would prove so great an advantage to France that he ventured in the most friendly manner to express the hope that she, like a *beau joueur*, would not hesitate to show a generous spirit in meeting German reclamations.

Count von Aehrenthal read French Ambassador the draft of a telegram he was sending to the Austrian chargé d'affaires in Paris instructing him to speak in the above sense to the French Minister for Foreign Affairs.([1])

Throughout conversation Count von Aehrenthal showed himself most friendly to France. French Ambassador is of opinion Count von Aehrenthal may have acted spontaneously so as to be able to meet request of Germany for Austrian intervention in Paris by being able to say that he has already done all that is possible to meet the situation. French Ambassador hears that financial situation in Germany is very critical and that Germany is desperately desirous of coming to an arrangement with France which may not be described as a humiliation for her.

([1]) [Ö.-U.A. III, No. 2619, gives the text of telegram referred to; v. also No. 2613.]

No. 543.

Sir Edward Grey to Sir F. Bertie.

F.O. 34506/13751/11/28.
(No. 376.)
Sir,   *Foreign Office, September* 11, 1911.

I have given my careful consideration to the draft Franco-Spanish Convention respecting Morocco which is enclosed in Y[our] E[xcellency]'s despatch No. 386 of the 1st inst[ant],(¹) and I see no objection thereto from the British point of view. It appears to me indeed to be an honest attempt to remove Spanish grievances and a great deal of friction will undoubtedly be saved when it has come into force.

I observe that you called M. de Selves' attention to the provisions of Art[icle] VII of the Anglo-French Declaration of 1904 in regard to the non-fortification of the Morocco Coast opposite Gibraltar.(²) Spain's adherence to the Anglo-French Declaration forms Art[icle] I of the Franco-Spanish Convention of the same year(³); and if this latter Convention is now to be superseded it might possibly be argued that Spain's adherence to the Anglo--French Declaration has lapsed. It would be well to provide against this possibility and the difficulty could be met by the insertion in the new Convention of an article in the same terms as Art[icle] I of the old Convention, *i.e.,* " L'Espagne adhère, aux termes de la présente Convention, à la Déclaration Franco-Anglaise du 8 avril 1904 relative au Maroc et à l'Egypte." I should be glad if you would urge upon M. de Selves the desirability of inserting an article to the above effect in the draft Convention.

I entirely agree with the provisions of Art[icle] XIII of the new Convention relative to Tangier and in case any question should arise about it in future years I desire to place on record that H[is] M[ajesty's] Gov[ernmen]t consider it essential that Tangier should maintain its special international position with a zone of 15 kilometres.

[I am, &c.
E. GREY.]

(¹) [*v. supra,* pp. 494–7, No. 525, and *encl.*]
(²) [*v. Gooch & Temperley,* Vol. II, pp. 390–1, No. 417.]
(³) [*v. infra,* p. 827, *App.* IV.]

No. 544.

Sir Edward Grey to Sir F. Bertie.

F.O. 35797/25883/11/28.
(No. 378.)
Sir,   *Foreign Office, September* 11, 1911.

I transmit to Y[our] E[xcellency] herewith a memorandum of a conversation with Mr. G. Paish respecting the readiness of the President of the U[nited] S[tates] of] A[merica] to act as arbitrator between France and Germany in the Morocco question.

[I am, &c.
F. A. CAMPBELL.]

Enclosure in No. 544.

Confidential.

Mr. G. Paish called at the F[oreign] O[ffice] this afternoon. He said that he had reason to know that if matters came to a deadlock between France and Germany as regards territorial compensation President Taft was willing and ready to act as Arbitrator.

He had received this information from Senator Burton, a friend of his, a prominent member of the Senate foreign affairs Committee, and in close personal relations with President Taft. Senator Burton was the man who gave expression to President Taft's views in the Senate with regard to the reciprocity Treaty.

He said that President Taft was anxious to act as arbitrator, as his position in American politics would be much strengthened thereby, and that if it was thought difficult for either France or Germany to suggest arbitration, from fear of being considered to be shewing weakness, President Taft might be willing to offer his services spontaneously.

He suggested that Senator Burton, who is going to France tonight and will stay there some time might be used as an unofficial channel of communication with the President, if and when the psychological moment arrived, as he appreciated that it might be difficult for us to put forward the suggestion officially to France.

He added that he was rather disturbed at the heavy selling by German houses of American and other easily marketable securities which has been, he said, a feature of the last two or three days.

No. 545.

Sir F. Bertie to Sir Edward Grey.

F.O. 35951/25883/11/28.
(No. 405.) Confidential.   *Paris, D. September* 12, 1911.
Sir,   *R. September* 13, 1911.

In compliance with a request from M. de Selves I called on him this morning. His Excellency showed to me the German counter proposals in reply to the French Projet de Convention which had been communicated to M. de Kiderlen Waechter by the French Ambassador. I sent to you a summary of the German counter proposals as described to me by M. de Selves on the 8th instant in my telegram No. 147 Confidential of that date.(¹) M. de Selves was good enough to allow me to send a Secretary to the Quai d'Orsay this afternoon to make a copy of the German communication as it was too detailed for me to remember its contents sufficiently from His Excellency reading it to me to enable me to report it to you as fully as I wished. I have the honour to transmit to you a copy of the document herewith.(²)

The French Projet de Convention has been taken as a basis but it has been completely changed in all its essential provisions from the French point of view and much to the detriment of the position which the French Government aspire to obtain in Morocco. The German Government do not admit that they have only exclusively economic interests in Morocco and they refuse to acknowledge the "action directrice" of France in Morocco. There are provisions in regard to the construction and working of railways which I have not time to describe before the departure of the messenger with this despatch.

I have, &c.
FRANCIS BERTIE.

MINUTES.

The most important points to be noticed are—

1. Suppression of admission that Germany has only economic interests in Morocco.
2. France being obliged to abstain from any measures of reorganisation, military or financial, unless requested by the Sultan.
3. Suppression of " action directorée " of France.
4. The serious modification introduced into Art[icle] 5.
5. The railway concessions.
6. Art[icle] XIII—whereby Germany is to decide what ports are to be opened between the Tensift and the Draa.

(¹) [*v. supra*, pp. 507–8, No. 537.]
(²) [*v. supra*, pp. 511–21, No. 539.]

In general Germany would have a large indirect participation in the political field and has apparently ear-marked a large portion of the south of Morocco as a special economic preserve. These remarks are made after rather a cursory reading of the counter proposals.

A. N.

We must wait for the French view.

E. G.

No. 546.

Sir A. Nicolson to Sir G. Buchanan.

Private.(¹)

My dear Buchanan, *Foreign Office, September* 12, 1911.

I am much obliged to you for your letters by last Bag. I heard nothing, when at Balmoral last week, as to the projected marriage to which you refer, though I can hardly imagine that the young man would have gone so far as he did unless he had first obtained the consent of the Head of the family.

I hope that your Military Attaché will send us information as to what is taking place in Russia in regard to military affairs, and also if he can ascertain whether any serious preparations are being quietly made in the event of hostilities breaking out. The French, we learn, are thoroughly prepared and a most excellent spirit permeates all ranks of the army. Our military experts are of opinion that the French Army has never been better organized or in a fitter state to undertake a campaign, but at the same time, I cannot imagine that war will break out. It is difficult to conceive that Germany would be prepared to face as strong a combination as would be formed by France, Russia and ourselves. Austria—though, of course, she will have to fulfil her part of her Treaty—will not do so with any enthusiasm; and Italy, I believe, will stand on one side. The risks therefore which Germany will incur would be exceedingly great, and if she were not to succeed, the results will certainly ruin her for a generation or two, and may possibly produce serious internal trouble in the country. At the same time, I cannot understand why the German Government do not make every effort to arrive at a speedy settlement with France. The counter project, so far as one is able to gather from the telegraphic summaries which we have received, must be perfectly unacceptable to France. In fact, Germany, as you will have seen from Bertie's telegram,(²) has completely shifted her ground, and put forward pretentions and demands which no French Government could possibly accept. We have not yet heard what reply the French Government intend to make to the German communication, but Paul Cambon—who is at present in Paris—returns to London to-morrow or the next day, and will doubtless give us full information on the subject. Should negotiations fall through, I do not anticipate that war will necessarily ensue. I presume that we should very likely then propose a Conference to which Germany would not refuse her consent, provided that matters in Morocco were put back exactly on the same footing as stipulated by the Act of Algeciras, that is to say, France and Spain should evacuate the districts which they occupy in Morocco. Failing such steps on their part—it is pretty clear that neither country will feel inclined or be able to take these steps—Germany will presumably announce that she will continue to maintain her ships at Agadir. The situation would then be exceedingly embarrassing, and is one which I imagine could not well be prolonged for any length of time, and war might eventually be developed out of it. . . . .(³)

[A. NICOLSON.]

(¹) [Carnock MSS., Vol. IV of 1911.]
(²) [*v. supra*, pp. 507–8, No. 537.]
(³) [The omitted paragraphs of this letter are of a general character.]

No. 547.

Sir F. Bertie to Sir Edward Grey.

F.O. 36169/13751/11/28.

(No. 408.)
Sir,

Paris, D. *September* 14, 1911.
R. *September* 15, 1911.

I have the honour to report to you, with reference to your despatch No. 376 of the 11th instant(¹) that I informed Monsieur de Selves yesterday that His Majesty's Government entirely agree with the provisions of Article XIII of the Draft Convention which His Excellency proposes to negotiate with the Spanish Government in regard to Morocco on the supposition that the French and German Governments come to terms in their present discussions on the subject of that country, for His Majesty's Government consider it essential that Tangier should maintain its special international position with a zone of fifteen kilometres.

I further informed M. de Selves that the Convention appears to you to be a genuine endeavour to remove Spanish grievances and a great deal of friction would undoubtedly be avoided if it came into force, and from the British point of view you see no objection to the Convention; but that if it is to supersede the Franco-Spanish Convention of 1904 it might possibly be argued that the adherence of Spain therein given to the Anglo-French Declaration of that year concerning Morocco has consequently lapsed. It would therefore be well to provide against this possibility in regard to the non-fortification of the Morocco coast opposite Gibraltar, which was provided for by Article VII of the Anglo-French Declaration; and the doubt might be met by inserting in the new Convention an Article in the same terms as Article I of the superseded Convention, viz.: "L'Espagne adhère, aux termes de la présente Convention, à la Déclaration Franco-Anglaise du 8 avril 1904 relative au Maroc et à l'Égypte."(²)

Monsieur de Selves, with whom I left a Memorandum, of which a copy is herein enclosed,(³) reminded me that the draft convention which he had communicated to me confidentially for your consideration was only a sketch and had not been submitted to the French Cabinet. His Excellency said that he was glad that you had formed a favourable opinion of its terms and that he would certainly insert in it an Article to make provision for the non-fortification of the Coast referred to in the Anglo-French Declaration of 1904.

I have, &c.
FRANCIS BERTIE.

(¹) [*v. supra*, p. 523, No. 543.]
(²) [*v. infra*, p. 827, *App.* IV.]
(³) [Not reproduced as its substance is given above.]

No. 548.

Sir F. Cartwright to Sir A. Nicolson.

Private.(¹)
My dear Nicolson,

Vienna, *September* 14, 1911.

. . . .(²) The Morocco question is beginning to attract a little more attention here than it has hitherto done, and this because it is becoming more and more an international question which, if it is not soon settled satisfactorily, may prove a menace to the peace of Europe. A few days ago Aehrenthal, who is still in the country, came into Vienna to attend the Requiem Mass on the anniversary of the Empress' death, and he has since left Vienna again and will not be permanently back

(¹) [Carnock MSS., Vol. IV of 1911.]
(²) [The opening paragraphs of this letter refer to the anonymous article published in the *Neue Freie Presse* attributed to Sir F. Cartwright. *v. infra*, pp. 837–45, *App.* V.]

till the end of the month. During his short stay in Vienna he sent for Crozier, the French Ambassador, and he had a talk with him on the Moroccan situation. He began by saying many pleasant things about France and throughout the conversation he maintained a most friendly tone towards the Ambassador. He informed Crozier that he had instructed the Austro-Hungarian Chargé d'Affaires in Paris to take an early opportunity of speaking to the French Foreign Minister in the following sense :—Austria-Hungary has nothing to complain of as to the attitude of France with regard to Morocco; the Dual Monarchy had no special favour to ask for herself in that country; she merely wanted the principle of the "open door" maintained and of equal opportunities as guaranteed to her by the Algeciras Act. He— Aehrenthal—had no wish to enter into any criticism of French action in going to Fez; he was quite satisfied with the assurances France had given on undertaking that expedition. What caused him, if not anxiety, at least preoccupation, was the prospect of France and Germany being perhaps unable to come to an amicable arrangement with regard to Morocco. That would create a situation in Europe which might be fraught with danger to her peace, and he therefore in the most friendly spirit ventured to express a hope that France might see her way "de se rendre un peu coulante en l'affaire des compensations à offrir à l'Allemagne." . . . .(³)

Yours truly,
FAIRFAX L. CARTWRIGHT.

(³) [The omitted paragraphs are of a general character.]

No. 549.

Sir E. Goschen to Sir Edward Grey.

Berlin, September 15, 1911.

F.O. 36270/25883/11/28.
Tel. (No. 71.)

D. 8·25 P.M.
R. 10·8 P.M.

Morocco.

French Ambassador communicated French answer to the German counter-project to the Secretary of State for Foreign Affairs this afternoon. Latter has promised answer on Monday.

French Ambassador seemed satisfied with his interview, and said that he had found the Secretary of State fairly reasonable.

No. 550.

Sir G. Buchanan to Sir Edward Grey.

St. Petersburgh, September 15, 1911.

F.O. 36269/25883/11/28.
Tel. (No. 213.) Confidential.

D. 8·50 P.M.
R. 10·30 P.M.

Acting Minister for Foreign Affairs told me to-day that the German chargé d'affaires had yesterday made an official communication to the effect that Germany was not seeking for any economic privileges in Morocco, and that all she desired was equality of treatment with guarantees to ensure this.(¹)

(¹) [cp. a somewhat similar declaration by M. Neratov reported by Herr von Lucius to Berlin on September 13, 1911. G.P. XXIX, pp. 376–7, and p. 373, note.]

His Excellency has instructed the Russian Ambassador at Paris to inform the French Government of this communication, as he thinks that, after Germany has placed this interpretation on the demands which she had put forward in her counter-project, she can hardly refuse to modify the text of that document so as to bring it into harmony with these declarations.

German chargé d'affaires had at the same time given his Excellency further explanations as regards recall of the German reservists. It is only reservists belonging to a German particular class who are being summoned to join the colours from all foreign countries alike, wherever they may reside, and not all the reservists resident in Russia and Holland as stated in my telegram No. 207 (   ).[2]

[2] [Sic. Not reproduced, as its tenour is indicated.]

No. 551.

Sir M. de Bunsen to Sir Edward Grey.

Zarauz, September 16, 1911.

F.O. 36437/13751/11/28.   D. 10·45 A.M.
Tel. (No. 75.)   R. 2·30 P.M.

At a further meeting with M[inister for] F[oreign] A[ffairs] on Thursday French Ambassador and I were informed that before agreeing to abandon any portion of territory claimed by Spain in southern Morocco Spanish Gov[ernmen]t wish to be assured that in the event of their making the desired sacrifice for the benefit of France they will not be called upon subsequently to pay a price to Germany or any other Power in exchange for recognition of Spanish sphere of influence in Northern Morocco. French Ambassador is requesting instructions.

(Repeated to Paris.)

No. 552.

Sir E. Goschen to Sir Edward Grey.

F.O. 36458/25883/11/28.
(No. 275.)   Berlin, D. September 16, 1911.
Sir,   R. September 18, 1911.

As I was not able to have more than a few minutes' conversation with Monsieur Jules Cambon yesterday evening, I am not in a position for the moment to give you any further information with regard to the conversation between His Excellency and Herr von Kiderlen-Waechter beyond that contained in the telegram which I had the honour to address to you last night; namely that Herr von Kiderlen-Waechter's tone had been more conciliatory than had hitherto been the case, that he had shown himself ready to give way on certain not unimportant points and that M. Cambon considered the conversation to be fairly satisfactory and to promise well for the future course of the negotiations.

M. Cambon also told me that he considered that, unless something totally unexpected should occur, there was no likelihood of any grave complications arising out of the present situation.[1]

The Lokal-Anzeiger publishes the following statement this morning:—

" Herr von Kiderlen-Waechter received yesterday afternoon at 5 o'clock at his private residence the visit of M. Cambon, the French Ambassador. We

(1) [A long memorandum of this date by M. Jules Cambon is quoted in G.P. XXIX, pp. 380–2. v. also Livre Jaune, Affaires du Maroc, VI, p. 519 et sqq. Herr von Kiderlen-Waechter replied on the 17th, v. G.P. XXIX, pp. 383–4.]

understand that as a result of their conversation, which lasted till 6·30, it was found that on some important points the French Government have adopted the views of the German Government. In regard to a few other points, only some questions of wording remain to be settled, and it appeared that there exists a difference of opinion merely in regard to certain questions and guarantees. In view of the good-will with which both diplomatists have been and are still animated in their discussions, it is to be hoped that an agreement may be reached without difficulty even in regard to these last differences. It has further resulted that certain indiscretions committed in Paris, such as those which have found their way into the French Press, have not facilitated the negotiations, and the principle has again been enunciated by the negotiators of the two Governments that no further communication in regard to the details of the negotiations shall be made to the Press under any circumstances until the negotiations have been completely terminated.''

As this statement gives it to be understood that M. Cambon expressed his readiness to accept some of the German counter-proposals, and as Herr von Kiderlen-Waechter, on his side, according to M. Cambon's account, showed a disposition to drop some of his demands, it would seem as if the negotiations had entered upon a more satisfactory phase.

The only point on which Herr von Kiderlen-Waechter showed some annoyance was the action of the French Government in imparting to the Press matters which should, until settled, remain strictly between the two Governments. These continued indiscretions, he said, placed him in an embarrassing situation, and he hoped that M. Cambon would urge upon his Government the necessity of being more reticent. M. Cambon, who shares Herr von Kiderlen's views on this subject, replied that he would not fail to telegraph to his Government in the sense desired.

I have, &c.

W. E. GOSCHEN.

No. 553.

Communication from M. Paul Cambon of September 16, 1911.

M. de Selves to M. Jules Cambon.

F.O. 36940/25883/11/28.   *Paris, le* 13 *septembre,* 1911.

Le gouvernement français a examiné avec le plus grand désir d'entente le contre-projet que vous a remis vendredi Monsieur de Kiderlen, et qui représente les vues du gouvernement allemand touchant le règlement de nos situations respectives au Maroc.

Malheureusement, ce contre-projet s'écarte sur de trop nombreux points du principe même que nous croyions accepté par l'Allemagne comme devant dominer toute négociation. L'Allemagne, avions-nous dit, et Monsieur de Kiderlen depuis le début de vos entretiens n'y avait jamais contredit, n'a à faire valoir au Maroc aucun intérêt politique et, d'autre part, la France, libre d'agir sur le gouvernement marocain pour l'introduction des réformes dont celui-ci a besoin, s'engage à respecter et à faire respecter par ce gouvernement la double condition de la liberté et de l'égalité commerciale. Nous nous inspirions, en parlant ainsi, des intérêts de toutes les autres Puissances signataires de l'Acte d'Algésiras qui ont le droit indiscutable de demander que, au Maroc, la porte soit ouverte au commerce de tous, sans restrictions, comme sans privilèges.

Le projet que, par ordre du gouvernement français, vous aviez été chargé de soumettre au gouvernement impérial avait été rédigé d'après ces principes. Mais le gouvernement impérial a jugé que notre texte(¹) ne donnait pas de garanties suffisantes pour mettre hors de toute atteinte la liberté et l'égalité commerciale et il a détaillé un certain nombre de conditions nouvelles qui lui paraissent nécessaires pour la sauvegarde de ses intérêts.   Toutes celles de ces conditions qui sont de nature commerciale, nous les acceptons volontiers, afin que personne ne puisse douter de notre ferme et sincère propos de tenir nos engagements.

Ainsi, à l'article 1er, nous consentons à spécifier que la Banque d'Etat continuera d'exister et de fonctionner selon les conditions fixées par l'Acte d'Algésiras.   A l'article III, nous augmentons les garanties que nous avions déjà offertes contre l'établissement d'un régime différentiel quelconque et nous supprimons, bien que Monsieur de Kiderlen l'eût accepté vis à vis de vous, la limitation à une période de trente ans du régime de l'égalité.   Nous insérons un article nouveau qui reconnaît aux ressortissants étrangers le maintien de leurs droits de pêche dans les eaux et les ports du Maroc.   Nous promettons enfin à l'article XII l'ouverture au commerce international de nouveaux ports marocains.

Ces amendements que nous apportons sur le désir d'Allemagne à notre projet montrent éloquemment avec quelle sollicitude nous entendons exécuter dans la pratique notre engagement de respecter la liberté et l'égalité commerciale.   Mais nous avons le regret de voir que, en face de notre bon vouloir, le gouvernement impérial paraît disposé à se départir de ses déclarations et à revendiquer un droit d'action politique au Maroc.

Ainsi, nous notons que, dans son contre-projet, il biffe à l'article 1er l'affirmation qu'il nous avait pourtant donnée dès 1909 que l'Allemagne ne possède au Maroc, que des intérêts exclusivement économiques, et dans la suite des articles il réclame des droits qui sont de nature essentiellement politique et dont l'exercice lui permettrait une ingérence continuelle dans l'administration, sinon dans le gouvernement même du pays.   C'est ainsi qu'à l'article V il prétend obliger le gouvernement français à lui donner communication des "engagements que la France pourrait conclure avec le gouvernement marocain"; à l'article VII il s'attribue le droit de participer à l'établissement du plan général des voies ferrées au Maroc; à l'article X, il se donne un droit de veto sur l'exploitation de ces voies ferrées et de tous les autres services de transport; à l'article XIII, il prétend intervenir dans les ouvertures futures de ports marocains; et, enfin, surtout, dans ce même article XIII, comme dans l'article VII, il se taille dans le sud du Maroc toute une zone où son influence politique prévaudrait sur celle de la France aussi bien dans l'exploitation des chemins de fer que dans les questions d'ouverture de ports.

Le gouvernement français considère que toutes ces conditions d'ordre purement politique sont inadmissibles; leur insertion dans le texte de notre accord altérerait profondément la nature de celui-ci, la situation qui devait nous être faite au Maroc constituant un avantage que des compensations territoriales auraient balancé; il fait [sic] donc que l'avantage promis ne disparaisse pas, que même il ne soit pas diminué.

Mais le Gouvernement allemand ne se borne pas à rechercher des bénéfices politiques; dans l'article VII et l'annexe à cet article, il réclame catégoriquement, à l'exclusion des autres Puissances, un privilège que la France fidèle au principe des engagements internationaux ne saurait consentir.(²)

Le texte revisé que je vous envoie vous montrera que nous avons encore quelques objections, d'un caractère, il est vrai, plus particulier, à formuler contre certaines stipulations proposées par le gouvernement allemand.   Il nous avait dit qu'il nous appartiendrait de régler avec l'Espagne la situation de celle-ci au Maroc.   Pourquoi, dès lors, mentionne-t-il dans son article VIII les districts où l'influence espagnole sera reconnue?

Pourquoi aussi, à son article X supprime-t-il la clause relative à l'appui mutuel que devaient se prêter les deux gouvernements pour faire approuver leur accord par les

(¹) [v. supra, pp. 511–21, No. 539.]
(²) [v. supra, pp. 513–6, No. 539.]

Puissances étrangères intéressées au Maroc? Il importe, à ces deux articles, de rétablir notre texte.

Le gouvernement français, au contraire, consent à laisser tomber l'article qu'il avait proposé pour la réforme judiciaire, il consent, en outre, en ce qui touche la protection sur les indigènes, à une rédaction transactionnelle. Il y a là de notre part une marque nouvelle de notre désir d'entente, car personne n'ignore les embarras que la multiplicité des protégés étrangers et leur qualité de justiciables des tribunaux consulaires causent sans cesse aux autorités marocaines. Depuis longtemps, je vous avais prié de signaler à Monsieur de Kiderlen cette source d'embarras.

Je vous serai obligé de faire part le plus tôt possible de ces considérations au secrétaire d'Etat en les recommandant à son esprit d'équité; il me paraît impossible que le gouvernement impérial persiste à réclamer de nous au Maroc des stipulations qui porteraient atteinte aux droits des Puissances dont nous devons tous être également soucieux et qui, d'autre part, constituerait pour lui un droit de constante intervention politique en contradiction avec le principe même qui a présidé à l'ouverture de la présente négociation.

No. 554.

Sir F. Bertie to Sir Edward Grey.

Private.(¹)

My dear Grey,   *Paris, September 17, 1911.*

. . . .(²) Isvolsky is playing an odd part here. He gives Society people to understand that aid cannot be expected from Russia. He paid a visit to the Political Director at the Quai d'Orsay in the absence of Selves and told him that he had had a conversation with the German Ambassador and he had come to the conclusion that the German requirements were merely commercial and might well be accepted by the French Government. He did not go so far as this to Selves whom he saw later in the day (last Wednesday Sept[ember] 13). To him he admitted that the German demands were somewhat excessive. As the French Government receive through their Ambassador at Petersburg comforting assurances of support and aid they do not attach to Isvolsky's sayings the same importance as formerly.

Selves told me yesterday that the German Ambassador had shown to the Spanish Ambassador the latest German proposals, and had laid stress on the exclusion of the Spanish zones from the Morocco to be recognized by Germany as under French protection or influence, as indicating the interest felt by the German Government in Spanish welfare adding " nous n'allons pas vous lâcher comme les Anglais l'ont fait."

Selves has lately asked me what I thought H[is] M[ajesty's] Gov[ernmen]t would do if the Germans landed or increased their force at Agadir or did both for he thought France must in such eventuality do something. I have said that I did not know, but that I thought that it would depend on the circumstances of the moment in which such a proceeding on the part of the German Government took place. I think that he may before long inquire again of you.

Yours sincerely,
FRANCIS BERTIE.

(¹) [Grey MSS., Vol. 13.]
(²) [The earlier part of this letter deals with the question of American arbitration, and is omitted, as the subject is already covered by Sir Edward Grey's despatch No. 378 of September 11, *v. supra*, pp. 523–4, No. 544, and *encl.*]

No. 555.

Sir E. Goschen to Sir Edward Grey.

Berlin, *September* 19, 1911.
D. 6·50 P.M.
R. 8·45 P.M.

F.O. 36866/25883/11/28.
Tel. (No. 72.)

Morocco.

My French colleague tells me that Secretary of State for Foreign Affairs has abandoned chief points in his counter-project which tended to create special position for Germany in Morocco, namely, share in the exploitation of public works, and 30 per cent. participation in railway construction. French Ambassador thinks, therefore, that, as far as Morocco is concerned, France has obtained more or less all that she can require, and that now there are only questions of detail to be arranged.

As regards Congo, a very violent campaign is being conducted in the French press against the concession demanded by Germany and even against concessions which would find their full value in the advantages gained by France in Morocco. My French colleague regards this as the only point of danger ahead, and he considers that it would be a pity if what has been gained as regards Morocco should be lost through unwillingness to make necessary sacrifices in Congo.

Secretary of State has spoken strongly on the subject of French press to another of my colleagues. He fears that if it persists in its violent language a counter-campaign in German press will inevitably follow such as will seriously affect negotiations and render his own personal position most difficult.

No. 556.

Sir F. Bertie to Sir Edward Grey.

(By Post.)

F.O. 36867/25883/11/28.
Tel. (No. 153.) *En clair.*

Paris, D. *September* 19, 1911.
R. *September* 20, 1911.

M. de Selves has shown to me this evening a telegram from the French Ambassador at Berlin, stating that he has derived a favourable impression as to the disposition of M. de Kiderlen-Waechter from a conversation of two hours with him. The reply of the German Government, prepared by M. de Kiderlen-Waechter, will not be given to M. Jules Cambon until to-morrow, for it has to be submitted to the Chancellor and the Emperor.

If M. de Kiderlen's recommendations, as described by him to the French Ambassador, be confirmed, the German Government will modify article 1 of the French draft([1]) in a way not to change the sense of it desired by the French Government. The German Government renounces any share in the working ("exploitation") of railways and commercial undertakings ("entreprises"); consents to withdraw the German article 7 regarding the nomination of engineers and functionaries for railways and other undertakings; withdraws demand (article 10) for censors; withdraws the addition to article 7 in regard to the 30 per cent. and 70 per cent. participations in railways;([2]) asks for a secret engagement promising that the construction of a railway from Tangier to Fez shall be the first to be undertaken; and, further, asks that the owners of mines and industrial concessions shall be allowed to construct railways to connect their works with the main railway lines.

M. de Kiderlen-Waechter wishes, out of regard for Spain, not to refer in the public agreement to the limits of Morocco, and proposes to have an exchange of secret notes with the French Government on the subject. He also wants a secret agreement in regard to the early opening of the port of Agadir in lieu of the undertaking required by the German article 13 as to that and other ports. Instead of

([1]) [*v. supra*, pp. 511–21, No. 539.]
([2]) [*v. infra*, p. 534, No. 557, *note* ([1]).]

German amendment to French article 14, M. de Kiderlen wants a secret note undertaking to revise, in concert with the Powers, the question of foreign-protected Moors.

M. de Kiderlen-Waechter also wishes for a promise that the Moorish Government will view with favour French and German tenders.

M. Jules Cambon's telegraphic report has not yet been submitted to the Cabinet. M. de Selves is opposed to secret agreements and secret notes because, he says, their existence becomes known and their purport frequently leaks out, or if it does not it is misrepresented to the public. Personally, he sees no objection to the Tangier–Fez railway being one of the first to be constructed, nor to the connecting lines for mines and commercial works. He cannot consent to the Spanish zones being excluded from the definition of Morocco which must appear in the public agreement. He has no. objection to the early opening of Agadir, nor to the revision of the question of foreign-protected Moors in concert with the Powers. He will refuse to comply with the suggestion that there shall be a promise to view with favour French and German tenders, as it would mean to regard with disfavour the tenders of other nationalities, which would be contrary to equality of treatment.

M. de Selves expects M. Jules Cambon's report by despatch to-morrow night. He will receive me on Thursday evening, by which time he hopes to know whether the German answer is in conformity with M. de Kiderlen's conversation.

MINUTES.

It is easy to appreciate the French objection to an exchange of secret notes about such an essential point as the definition of the limits of Morocco. The German Gov[ernmen]t have virtually denounced the 1909 agreement—if they act thus in regard to a formal international treaty they will have little hesitation in disregarding what may merely have been recorded in an exchange of notes.

It is also easy to appreciate the French objection to secret compacts in the present instance. The French Gov[ernmen]t will have to secure the consent—which is only too likely to be reluctant—of the French Chamber to a cession of territory equal in area to two thirds of France : to do this they must be able to demonstrate publicly that they have received in Morocco some substantial and well-secured *quid pro quo*.

The Spanish " zones " are of undefined extent (see map attached to the agreement of 1904 between France and Spain) and Germany's wish to exclude them from the public agreement can hardly arise, whatever M. de Kiderlen may say, out of regard for Spain : it is, in the light of Germany's conduct with regard to Morocco during the past seven years, far more likely to be due to the hope or intention of securing some further advantage in future in the Spanish " zones."

On the surface, the situation described in this telegram may perhaps appear more hopeful : but French public opinion is becoming mistrustful and exasperated, and unless the negotiations are speedily terminated it may be that those *imponderabilia*, which have so often been referred to in the " Cologne Gazette " as likely to influence the policy of Germany, may begin to operate in France, and that the prospect of a lasting settlement without war will be looked upon as illusory.

A. P.
September 20th, 1911.

Anyhow this is the first time that officially things have looked really better.

F. A. C.
20.9.
A. N.
E. G.

No. 557.

Sir F. Bertie to Sir Edward Grey.

F.O. 37068/37068/11/28.

(No. 414.)   *Paris, D. September* 19, 1911.

Sir,   *R. September* 22, 1911.

I thought that it would be well that Sir Reginald Lister, who is in Paris, should see the Minister for Foreign Affairs : I therefore suggested to Monsieur de Selves that it might be interesting to him to have some conversation with His Majesty's

Minister at Tangier. His Excellency readily accepted the suggestion. Monsieur de Selves received him this morning.

I recommended Sir Reginald Lister to speak very frankly to Monsieur de Selves regarding the differential treatment of British enterprise in Morocco. I have the honour to transmit to you herewith a copy of a Memorandum by him on his interview with His Excellency.

I have, &c.
FRANCIS BERTIE.

Enclosure in No. 557.

Memorandum by Sir R. Lister.

I saw the French Minister for Foreign Affairs this morning, and had a long conversation with him on the subject of Morocco.

In discussing the various proposals and counter-proposals, M. de Selves alluded to the German demand that no less than 70% should be granted to German capital in certain enterprizes.([1]) The demand, he said, was outrageous : it was not in the power of France to grant it at all, and it was hardly likely that she would grant to the Germans, especially after their recent behaviour, what she would be obliged to refuse to the English, her friends. This gave me the opportunity which I desired. I said that the one point on which I sometimes experienced difficulty at Tangier was the commercial question. As he knew, British commerce in Morocco was very considerable and very old established. In the past the relations between our two countries had been very different, and the British merchants in Morocco, many of whom had been born and bred in the country, had been brought up to look upon France as the rival, and to suspect her of always seeking to injure their trade. After the conclusion of the *Entente* there was a good deal of grumbling, and the old feeling undoubtedly subsisted. During the three years that I had been at Tangier, I had done all in my power to overcome or at all events to diminish it, and I could fairly say that I had been in a great measure successful. I recognized that I had been much assisted in my efforts by the attitude of the French officials in the *contrôle* of the Customs, whose impartiality and courtesy had won the respect and praise of the most recalcitrant. At the same time cases cropped up from time to time which gave colour to the view of the British Commercial Community that the French intended to oust them where they could, and to open trade routes and start commercial enterprizes from which they might be excluded, or in which at all events they would only be allowed to participate to a very small extent. I could not but deplore this, and, if weighed in the balance, the maintenance of the friendly spirit appeared to me so far more important than the petty advantages which French commerce might thus obtain.

M. de Selves said that he absolutely agreed in my view : that, as he had told His Majesty's Ambassador, he was prepared to give every guarantee that might be asked to ensure the maintenance of complete commercial equality, and that, as I had no doubt observed, he was insisting upon all works, etc. being put up to adjudication. If ever I had reason to believe that British commercial interests were being in any way sacrificed to French, he begged me to speak at once on the matter to the French Representative at Tangier, and that, knowing his views, I might be certain that my representations would receive the most favourable consideration. I thanked M. de Selves and told him that I had always spoken quite openly on such matters to M. Regnault, with whom I was on the best and friendliest terms, and should always continue to do so. I was however much pleased to have received his assurances which gave me an extra guarantee for the future.

M. de Selves asked me, as one who had been in Morocco at the time, what my

---

([1]) [*v. supra*, Franco-German Draft Conventions of 4–8 September, Article 7, *annexe*, pp. 514–6, No. 539. *cp.* also *supra*, pp. 509–10, No. 538; p. 530, No. 553; pp. 532–3, No. 556.]

real opinion was with regard to the situation at Fez, at the time of the despatch of the French relief column. I said that I considered that the situation was one which could not possibly be allowed to continue : the capital was practically blockaded, all ordinary communication with the coast was cut and the lives of Europeans were in danger. It could not possibly have been allowed to continue. People who said the contrary were merely misinformed or wilfully blind.

He alluded to his proposals for an arrangement with Spain, and asked me what I had thought of them. I gave him the gist of the minute I had written at the Foreign Office on the 2nd September.([2]) He said that he was prepared to make as large concessions as were possible to Spanish *amour propre*, though he shared my view as to the sad prospect for the zones to be placed under Spanish influence : all that he must have was some sort of apparent concession on the part of Spain ("une concession de façade") which he could present to French public opinion, and thus obtain its acquiescence in the very real concessions which France was making to Spain [*sic*].([3])

Paris, September 19, 1911.

([2]) [*v. supra*, pp. 497–8, No. 525, *min.*]
([3]) [Sir E. Grey added the following minute : " ? Should not the last word be ' Germany ' and not Spain '? E. G." It was so corrected for circulation.]

No. 558.

Sir F. Bertie to Sir Edward Grey.

F.O. 37069/36824/11/28.
(No. 415.)   *Paris, D. September* 19, 1911.
Sir,   R. *September* 22, 1911.

By my telegram No. 129 of the 21st ultimo([1]) I had the honour to inform you that I had communicated to the President of the Council the contents of your telegram No. 195 of the same date([2]) stating that His Majesty's Government were prepared to consider proposals from the French Government for an exchange of territories by which France would obtain a cession of part of Northern Nigeria which would give her access direct from North French Congo through the Bec du Canard to her possessions north of Nigeria instead of by the circuitous route which would otherwise be necessary.

When I saw M. de Selves this evening he handed me a memorandum, of which I enclose a copy, containing alternative proposals for the cession to France of certain portions of Nigeria and the Gold Coast Colony and stating the compensation which the French Government were prepared to give in return. His Excellency informed me that the only portion of British territory the acquisition of which he desires is the north-eastern part of Nigeria, which would give direct communication between Zinder, where there was a military post, and north French Congo. The territories mentioned in the memorandum are marked in the enclosed map,([3]) which M. de Selves gave me.

I have, &c.
FRANCIS BERTIE.

([1]) [*v. supra*, p. 462, No. 489.]
([2]) [*v. supra*, p. 460, No. 487.]
([3]) [Not reproduced.]

Enclosure in No. 558.

Note.

L'Angleterre céderait :

    a.) un secteur de la Nigéria déterminé par la ligne idéale Porto-Novo–Zinder,
    b.) un secteur de la Nigéria déterminé par la ligne idéale Zinder–Yola.

Ces cessions présenteraient, pour la France, les avantages suivants :

    a.) la cession du secteur ouest élargirait le bas Dahomey region riche en palmiers à huile, très peuplée et très commerçante. Elle nous donnerait, en outre, l'accès du bief inférieur du Niger, c'est-à-dire au sud des rapides de Boussa qui marquent la limite de navigabilité du fleuve ; enfin, en troisième lieu, cette opération nous donnerait le Sokoto, dont la valeur est comparable à celles des autres parties de la bouche du Niger.
    b.) la cession du secteur Est nous donnerait des territoires dont la valeur économique est négligeable sous réserve cependant des richesses minérales dont l'existence a été affirmée. Mais cette cession aurait l'inappréciable avantage de souder nos territoires militaires de Zinder et du Tchad, de coordonner par suite notre politique du centre africain et de faciliter les mouvements de troupe de l'Afrique Occidentale française vers le Kanem, le Ouadai et éventuellement le Borkou-Tibesti.

Pour compenser ces cessions, la France pourrait abandonner toute la partie du Haut-Oubangui comprise, d'une part, entre la frontière actuelle franco-anglaise et, d'autre part, la rivière Kotto. Ce territoire est concédé en entier à la Société franco-belge des Sultanats du Haut-Oubangui. La valeur économique de ces territoires est négligeable, leur valeur politique est à peu près nulle, enfin il ne faut point se dissimuler que dans un avenir peu lointain la voie d'accès normale de cette partie de notre possession de l'Afrique Equatoriale française sera le Haut-Nil.

Au cas où ce premier accord serait trop difficile à négocier, on pourrait se borner à demander à l'Angleterre la cession du secteur Est de la Nigéria.
En échange de ce secteur, on pourrait abandonner :

    a.) nos prétentions sur Cheikh-Saïd,
    b.) nos prétentions sur Mascate.

Ces compensations semblent devoir être suffisantes puisque Yola, qui constitue le seul centre important de la région dont la cession est à envisager, resterait à l'Angleterre.
Au cas cependant où il faudrait envisager des compensations complémentaires, on pourrait céder soit quelques îles de l'Océan Indien (Kerguelen, St. Paul, Amsterdam), soit la cession de quelques îles de la Polynésie (notamment Mangareva dans l'archipel des Gambier).
Il convient de remarquer cependant que si la cession de l'île Mangareva était décidée, nous ne pourrions considérer comme suffisante la cession du secteur Yola-Zinder et nous devrions demander en outre la cession de la Gambie, exception faite pour Bathurst. D'après les renseignements que possède d'ailleurs le ministre des colonies, l'Angleterre aurait suggéré, en 1906, la cession de la Gambie (exception faite de Bathurst) contre l'île Mangareva.
Enfin, une troisième solution pourrait être étudiée sur les bases suivantes :

L'Angleterre céderait :

    a.) le secteur Yola-Zinder de la Nigéria ;
    b.) la partie de la Gold Coast au nord de la Volta Noire.

La France céderait :

> *a.*) ses prétentions sur Cheikh Saïd :
> *b.*) ses prétentions sur Mascate.
> *c.*) l'île Mangareva, dans le groupe des Gambier, ou le Haut Oubangui jusqu'à le Kotto.

MINUTES.

This seems to go considerably beyond what was proposed in Sir F. Bertie's tel[egram] No. 128(⁴) of August 20th, viz., that we should cede to France such territory in N.W. Nigeria (Bornu) as would give, through the Bec du Canard, access to her from her northern Congo territory (to be cut off from the sea by the proposed cessions to Germany) to her territory beyond Northern Nigeria. Our cession to France was to be on the basis of an exchange which was not then specified. Our reply was to the effect that the proposals of the French Gov[ernmen]t would receive careful consideration. Mr. Langley saw Sir J. Anderson of the Colonial Office, but all communications between them were private and the Dep[artmen]t have no knowledge of what passed.

It will perhaps be convenient to analyse here the several proposals contained in the French memorandum.

French Proposal Number 1.

G[rea]t Britain to cede the whole of Bornu in North East Nigeria, and about.twice as much as Bornu in West Nigeria. (Both these districts are coloured blue on the map.)(⁵)

France, in return, proposes to cede to us a bit of territory adjoining the Bahr-el-Ghazal, and coloured red on the annexed map.

The surface area of what France proposes to cede to us is considerably less than half of what we are invited to cede to her. This proposal appears grotesque when the French inform us that the value of the " red " territory is economically " négligeable " and politically " nulle ", whereas the cessions it is proposed that we should make in the East and West of Nigeria are described in the French memorandum as politically desirable to France, and as possessing in one case mineral possibilities and in the other great commercial prosperity.

French Proposal Number 2.

This proposal really consists of two alternatives, which, for facility of reference, I denote as " Y " and " Z " respectively.

Under " Y " we should cede Bornu in North East Nigeria, but not anything in West Nigeria. France, in return, offers to abandon her claims on Sheikh Said (near Aden) and on Muscat.

Sheikh Said. The place was originally purchased from an Arab Sheikh by two Frenchmen in 1869, but the Sublime Porte denied the validity of the sale, and the Sheikh declared that it was void by reason of the purchase money not having been paid. H[is] M[ajesty's] G[overnment] have always maintained that Sheikh Said belongs to Turkey, who has repeatedly made to the French Gov[ernmen]t reservations in regard to her claims on the place, and appears to have maintained a garrison there intermittently for years. On the other hand there are the remains of some huts erected by the French. H[is] M[ajesty's] G[overnment] have more than once informed the would-be owners (Frenchmen) that they consider the place to be Turkish territory. The French Gov[ernmen]t, however, have never agreed to recognise it as such.

If, now, France abandons her claims on Sheikh Said it may benefit Turkey, but it is somewhat doubtful if, in the present state of political combinations, it would really benefit us. Turkey might conceivably cede* or lease the place to Germany, which would be highly inconvenient, as it has been described as " the veritable Gibraltar of the Red Sea ", and in this respect it is important to recall the opinion expressed in April 1893 by the British Resident at Aden :—

> " I am of opinion that it would be most detrimental to permit the French to gain a permanent footing at Sheikh Said, for, irrespective of the neighbouring hills being capable of being strongly fortified and completely commanding the small strait and dominating the island of Perim, the French would almost certainly make the place an entrepôt for the arms traffic."

(⁴) [*v. supra*, pp. 458–9, No. 485.]

(⁵) [Not reproduced, but *v. infra*, p. 538 : *French proposal*, No. 3.]

* I find on further research that Sheikh Said is in the Subaihi territory, and, in connection with the Boundary Agreement of 1905 resp[ectin]g Aden, (Procès Verbal of April 20th, 1905), the Turkish Gov[ernmen]t have undertaken never to alienate to a third Power the Subaihi territory lying between Husn Murad and Kudam, in which Sheikh Said is situated. This was however kept from the French Ambassador by Lord Lansdowne. A. P.

As we have repeatedly informed Turkey that we consider the place to be Turkish, we could not really object if Turkey (perhaps at the instance of Germany) were to fortify it; we certainly could not occupy it ourselves if France abandoned her claims; and it seems to me that the best course we can adopt is merely to inform France, in regard to this point, that we should prefer to leave Sheikh Said out of the negotiations altogether, but that in doing so we should refrain from mentioning again our opinion that the place really belongs to Turkey.

Muscat. On this point it may be recalled that, in August 1908, we proposed, as one of the returns to be made to us by France for the cession of the Gambia, that France should abandon her Treaty of 1844 with Muscat, agree to the abrogation of the Anglo-French declaration of 1862 respecting Muscat and Zanzibar, and thus allow full liberty of action to G[rea]t Britain in Muscat, and put an end to certain privileges enjoyed by French citizens and protégés in Zanzibar. (Zanzibar and Muscat were formerly under the same Sultan and it was considered by the Committee which sat in 1908 under Sir C. Hardinge that it was important to secure the cessation of French privileges in Zanzibar as well as in Muscat.)

It cannot be denied that the abandonment of French claims at Muscat is very desirable. The report of Sir C. Hardinge's Committee is annexed (29453) 1908.([6])

If further compensations are necessary in return for the cession of Bornu (North East Nigeria) France is ready to abandon to us certain islands in the Indian Ocean (Kerguelen, St. Paul, Amsterdam).

The second alternative " Z " of the French proposal Number 2 is as follows :—

Great Britain to cede to France Bornu (North West Nigeria) and the Gambia with the exception of Bathurst. France to abandon her claims on Sheikh Said and Muscat, and to cede certain islands in Polynesia, notably Manga Reva (in the Gambier group).

The French memorandum contains a statement that, according to the information in the possession of the French Colonial Office, G[rea]t Britain suggested, in 1906, to cede the Gambia, with the exception of Bathurst for the island of Mangareva.

The African Dep[artmen]t will be able to say whether there is any foundation for this statement, but, on the face of it, it appears inaccurate, since in 1908 we proposed to France that she should, in return for the Gambia, give us a large number of compensations, of which a coaling station in the Pacific (probably Mangareva) was only one amongst several.

With regard to Manga Reva, the following extract from the report of Sir C. Hardinge's Committee of 1908 is of importance :—

" It is of the highest importance, from an Imperial point of view, to look forward to the naval situation which will be created by the successful completion of the Panama Canal, of which there can now be no doubt. It will then be necessary for H[is] M[ajesty's] G[overnment] to possess a good coaling station on the direct route between the Panama Canal and Australia and New Zealand, but it may not be easy at a later date to acquire it, save at prohibitive cost, whereas the present occasion offers an opportunity for so doing at a reasonable price.

The British possession nearest to the direct route and most suitably placed as regards distances, is Pitcairn Island, but it unfortunately possesses no anchorage . . . .([7]) There is, however, an island belonging to France, Manga Reva, which promises to fulfil these conditions. It is of substantial area, elevated, and there is reason to believe that it possesses a sufficiently good harbour, though this cannot be definitely ascertained until a survey has been made.

It would accordingly seem desirable to ask for the cession of an island in the Pacific on the direct route between Panama and Australia, having the necessary conditions for the establishment of a coaling station, leaving it to subsequent enquiry to determine the suitability of Manga Reva."

The last proposal of France is described as a third possible solution to be studied; it is as follows :—

French proposal Number 3.

G[rea]t Britain to cede to France Bornu (North East Nigeria) and the part of the Gold Coast Colony north of the River Volta (coloured blue on the annexed map).

France to abandon her claims on Sheikh Said, her claims in Muscat. and either the island of Mangareva or the bit of territory adjoining the Bahr el Ghazal and coloured red on the attached map, and of which the economic value is described by the French as " négligeable " and the political value as " nulle."

On reading the French demands, and what they suggest in return, one cannot help recalling what Canning said about the Dutch in his famous despatch :—

" In matters of commerce the fault of the Dutch
" Is giving too little and asking too much."

which seems to apply to the French in the present instance.

([6]) [Not reproduced. For the Muscat question *v. Gooch & Temperley*, Vol. I, pp. 209–14, which does not treat the subject in 1908. This will be dealt with in a later volume.]

([7]) [Thus in original.]

But although on the surface the French proposals seem inacceptable, there are certain concessions which, as set forth in the attached report of Sir C. Hardinge's Committee, we are very anxious to get from France, and it may be possible to reach an agreement beneficial to both countries. We are desirous of getting a coaling station in the Pacific, of securing the final abandonment of certain French rights in Newfoundland, and only this month Lord Hardinge has telegraphed pointing out that no settlement should be accepted by us which does not include the Cession of Chandernagore (one of the French Loges in India) and of French rights in Muscat.

I would suggest therefore that we should propose to the India Office and Colonial Office, and perhaps to the Board of Trade and War Office and Admiralty, that an Interdepartmental Committee should meet at an early date to discuss the French proposals and any alternative proposals which can be made in reply if, as seems probable, the French proposals as they stand are considered impracticable.

Eastern Dept.
African Dept.

A. P.
September 23rd, 1911.

I should say there were the elements of a satisfactory deal in these proposals, and the suggestion for consideration by an Inter-Dep[artmenta]l Committee seems the most practical plan of dealing with them.

F. A. C.
23.9.

An early meeting of an Interdepartmental Committee seems eminently desirable. *Inter alia* the French Gov[ernmen]t wish to facilitate movements of troops towards Wadai. I should think in any negotiations the Wadai-Darfur question should also be treated. The Sirdar is anxious on this subject.

A. N.

These proposals will not do at all : there is no equivalent territorial concession for Bornu or for any solid territorial concession on our part.

An interdepartmental Committee should meet at once to settle what reply we should make. It will be sufficient if the Committee is composed of Representatives of the F.O., C.O., I.O. and Admiralty. The latter Dep[artmen]t must come in as Mangareva is involved.

E. G.

Proceed accordingly.

A. N.

No. 559.

Sir M. de Bunsen to Sir Edward Grey.

F.O. 37077/13751/11/28.
(No. 155.)   *Zarauz, D. September 19, 1911.*
Sir,   R. *September 22, 1911.*

In my telegrams Nos. 74 and 75 of the 9th and 16th instants respectively([1]) I have recorded briefly the result of the two last meetings held at San Sebastian between the Spanish Minister for Foreign Affairs, the French Ambassador and myself, with a view to the settlement of the questions at issue between France and Spain in Morocco. M. Geoffray and I attended both these meetings at the written request of Señor Garcia Prieto. M. Geoffray is instructed generally that, although it would perhaps be preferable to suspend these conversations until the conclusion of the Berlin negotiation, there is no objection to his hearing what Señor Garcia Prieto has to say and reporting the same to Paris.

At the meeting held on the 8th instant, the Foreign Minister began by laying stress on the enormity of the sacrifice which the French Government was inviting Spain to make. He said that the proposals relating to the Spanish Sphere of Influence in Northern Morocco which M. Geoffray had outlined at the previous meeting already contained serious limitations of the absolutely free hand which Spain considered she would have a right to claim in that region as a set-off to the virtual French Protectorate in the South of Morocco. Thus Spain was to be deprived in her

([1]) [*v. supra*, pp. 521–2, No. 541;￬and p. 528, No. 551.]

sphere of the right to levy an export tax on the produce of the mines. She was to be compelled to permit at all times the passage across her sphere of troops and stores destined for the use of the Sultan at Fez. Her independent action would be hampered in many other ways which His Excellency did not precisely specify. It had come therefore as a surprise that France should have demanded, in addition to these restrictions, the abandonment by Spain of an enormous extent of territory in Southern Morocco. The zone claimed by Spain in that portion of Morocco extended from the Wady Mesa in the North to the Southern boundary of Morocco as fixed in Article 6 of the Secret Convention of October, 1904,([2]) namely, to Latitude 27·40 North. The limits of the zone inland were also fixed by the Secret Convention. No Spanish Government, His Excellency said, would be likely to consent to the relinquishment of the whole of this zone. Ifni itself and the coast-line opposite the Canary Islands must in any case be retained. As to the rest His Excellency did not despair of inducing the Cabinet to consent to the surrender of a piece of territory corresponding to the region which it was understood that France would yield to Germany in the French Congo. Señor Garcia Prieto promised to lay the matter fully before the Cabinet Council which he was about to attend in Madrid, and to communicate the result to M. Geoffray and myself immediately after his return to San Sebastian.

M. Geoffray contested Señor Garcia Prieto's opening argument to the effect that a sacrifice was already involved in the limitations sought to be imposed upon the exercise of Spanish authority in Northern Morocco and that therefore to call for an additional sacrifice of a territorial character was a very exacting demand. He dwelt on the benefits which must accrue to Spain as well as to France as the result of the Berlin negotiations and he argued that it was only right that Spain should contribute something to make good the loss which France was about to incur. Moreover M. de Selves had clearly intimated that he would be unable to secure the consent of the French Cabinet to the favourable settlement which he had offered with regard to the Spanish Sphere of Influence in Northern Morocco, unless he could inform them that Spain was prepared to make a large territorial concession to France.

Señor Garcia Prieto admitted in the end that the French demand was not unreasonable in principle. He thought it, however, very excessive in extent.

After an absence of only two whole days in Madrid, His Excellency returned to San Sebastian on the morning of September 14th. We met again the same afternoon. Señor Garcia Prieto was not yet prepared to make a counter-proposition. The Cabinet, he said, had found difficulty in formulating an offer to France. Before doing so, they felt that it was only fair to themselves to ask for information on two essential points :—1) What was the extent of the sacrifice about to be made by France to Germany in the French Congo and 2) What guarantee could be given to Spain that, after making a corresponding cession in her South Morocco zone for the benefit of France, she would not subsequently be called upon by Germany or some other Power or Powers to make a further territorial sacrifice elsewhere in exchange for the recognition of her sphere of influence in Northern Morocco?

M. Geoffray said he would submit these questions to his Government.

Señor Garcia Prieto has since confided to me that he had in mind more particularly the case of Spanish Guinea. This colony, according to forecasts freely made by the press, was likely before long, as the result of French concessions, to be enclosed on all its land sides by German territory. The Spanish Government felt that, by consent or under compulsion, Spanish Guinea was only too likely to be absorbed eventually into the German colony of the Cameroons. If this happened, Spain would have had to pay a heavy price first to France and then to Germany, for the enjoyment of a position in Morocco to which she had a clear treaty right. She preferred to know the worst at once and this was her reason for hesitating to make a deal with France on the lines suggested by M. de Selves.

([2]) [v. infra, p. 828, App. IV.]

His Excellency speaks with some bitterness of the exclusion of Spain from the Berlin negotiation which affected so largely her own interests. He is particularly upset by a telegram received a few days ago from the Spanish Ambassador at Berlin. Señor Polo de Bernabé reported that M. Jules Cambon had obtained from the German Foreign Minister an agreement that Morocco should be held to extend southwards as far as the Northern line of the Spanish territory of Rio de Oro. But Article 6 Paragraph 3 of the Secret Convention of 1904 had clearly laid down that the territory South of Latitude 27·40 was to be regarded by France and Spain as lying outside the limits of Morocco and that Spain was to enjoy complete freedom of action in the territory intervening between that Latitude and the Rio de Oro region. Thus, without consulting Spain, France was endeavouring to shift the Southern boundary of Morocco in a manner restrictive of the conventional rights of Spain.

M. Geoffray has pointed out to Señor Garcia Prieto that the object of France is no doubt mainly to exclude Germany from any portion of the Atlantic coast of Morocco. M. Jules Cambon is therefore pressing very naturally for German recognition of the most Southerly boundary line obtainable for Morocco. But any arrangement which France may have come to with Germany in this respect would be powerless to affect the existing agreement between France and Spain as to the complete freedom of action of Spain in the region in question. In M. Geoffray's opinion that region is not included in the Spanish South Morocco zone, the surrender of which by Spain has been demanded by his Government.

I have, &c.
MAURICE DE BUNSEN.

MINUTES.

From this despatch it is clear that neither M. Geoffray nor Sir M. de Bunsen urged, as the Spanish Ambas[sado]r here has continually asserted, the Spanish Gov[ernmen]t to come to an agreement without delay on the ground that if such agreement is postponed until after the Berlin discussions the conditions will be far harder on Spain than would be the case at present.

A. N.

It shows too how impossible it is to settle the Franco-Spanish question till the Franco-German question is settled.

E. G.

No. 560.

Sir A. Nicolson to Sir Edward Grey.

Private.([1])
My dear Grey,   Foreign Office, September 20, 1911.

I enclose a private telegram which I have received from Goschen.([2]) Cambon came to see me early this morning, and skirted round the question of the French Press. He said that a portion of it was undoubtedly opposed to territorial concessions, but that the Gov[ernmen]t had no influence over the papers and would only make matters worse were they to intervene. It is clear that we cannot interfere in the sense suggested by Jules Cambon—any observations made by Bertie would probably become known and would be resented. We had far better keep out of such intervention, and let the French Gov[ernmen]t manage, if they can, their own Press.

([1]) [Grey MSS., Vol. 54.]
([2]) [This telegram of the 19th is in the same sense as Sir E. Goschen's Tel. No. 72 of the same date (v. supra, p. 532, No. 555). In it he reports, however, that M. Jules Cambon "thinks that it would be highly useful if Sir F. Bertie in conveying the satisfaction of H[is] M[ajesty's] Gov[ernmen]t at the encouraging news from Berlin respecting Morocco could express the hope that the French press might now be induced to moderate its language about the Congo and not spoil a satisfactory arrangement by urging too stiff an attitude."]

From what I hear and from what Cambon told me there is very great mistrust in France of Germany. The manner in which the latter country has treated the 1909 agreement has destroyed confidence that she would better observe a 1911 agreement—and there is a growing feeling in France that the French are asked to make up territorial concessions to obtain engagements which may be ignored as was the 1909 convention. This feeling may lead the French Chambers to refuse to ratify the territorial concessions. Moreover the French public are becoming weary of these continual bickerings and worries with Germany, and feeling united and strong, are quite ready to have done with the matter and fight it out. This is a dangerous phase of feeling, and I have some fears lest Germany may manoeuvre so as to throw the odium and responsibility for a rupture on France. I am not sure that Kiderlen is not playing for this. In the Monday conversation he practically beat a retreat nearly all along the line—and if he holds to his proposals, France, so far as Morocco is concerned, will have obtained all she wants—or nearly so. A German press campaign may be started against the French press, and relations will soon be embittered and a serious situation produced. The fault for this could ostensibly be laid on the French, and Germany could point to the very conciliatory disposition she had shown on the Morocco question.

If the reports be true that Germany is making military preparations, and especially if it be confirmed that the VIII Army Corps has been concentrated at Malmedy, it would look as if she were expecting a conflict or perhaps was ready to precipitate one. At the same time I quite understand the hesitation of the French to place absolute confidence in Germany's engagements even if consigned to paper, and duly signed and sealed. I am afraid we have troublesome times ahead, and we should not slacken in our preparations.

Y[ou]rs sincerely,
A. NICOLSON.

No. 561.

Sir Edward Grey to Sir F. Bertie.

Private.([1])
My dear Bertie, *Foreign Office, September* 20, 1911.

We should (if Franco-German negotiations fail) propose a conference without saying anything about arbitration or waiting for anything.

I should not in any case be the medium of conveying Taft's offer.([2]) There is of course much force in all you say about the difficulty of arbitration, but if Taft made an offer and France accepted it and Germany refused it the moral advantage would be great and very material support to France if war followed, would be certain.

If Germany accepted I think she would come out of the arbitration second best.

However all this depends upon Franco-German negotiations failing, conference being refused by Germany, and Taft making his offer; till this triple contingency has been realized the question will not arise, and meanwhile I shall not say anything about it.

[Yours sincerely,]
E. GREY.

([1]) [Grey MSS., Vol. 13.]
([2]) [*v. supra*, pp. 523–4, No. 544, and *encl.*]

No. 562.

Sir F. Bertie to Sir Edward Grey.

F.O. 37201/25883/11/28.
Tel. (No. 154.) R.

Paris, September 22, 1911.
D. 2·40 P.M.
R. 5 P.M.

Morocco.

Last paragraph of my telegram No. 153 of 19th September.([1])

French Minister for Foreign Affairs, having to be at Rambouillet, was not able to receive me yesterday. He tells me this morning that the situation is as follows :—([2])

German Chancellor has concurred in German Minister for Foreign Affairs' views as expressed to French Ambassador.

French Minister for Foreign Affairs has instructed French Ambassador at Berlin not to mention French territorial compensations to German Minister for Foreign Affairs until there is complete agreement between the two Governments regarding question of Morocco. He recognises that the German Government cannot be expected to consent to Germans being in a less advantageous position than other foreigners as regards tribunals, and he admits that the question of foreign-protected Moors, regarding which there have been great abuses, must be reconsidered by all the Powers interested. What he requires is an assurance from German Government that whenever courts shall have been established giving guarantees of justice analogous to those in France they will join with French Government in applying to other Governments concerned for their consent to abolish their rights of consular jurisdiction. He will not accept any system of mixed tribunals such as exists in Egypt. German Minister for Foreign Affairs represented to French Ambassador that H[is] M[ajesty]'s Government([3]) would be opposed to any other system than that of mixed courts. German Government must also undertake to support French Government in bringing about a reconsideration of the question of protection. Means must also be devised for including in an agreement with Germany the Spanish zones in Morocco, leaving it to France to come to an agreement with Spain on the subject.

French Minister for Foreign Affairs will submit to Cabinet to-morrow a project to embody his views for communication to the German Minister for Foreign Affairs. He will give me information on the subject on 25th September.([4])

([1]) [*v. supra*, pp. 532–3, No. 556.]
([2]) [A summary of the situation between September 17 and 22 is given in *G.P.* XXIX, p. 385, *note.*]
([3]) [In the original decypher the words "the German Gov[ernmen]t" appeared instead of "H[is] M[ajesty's] G[overnment]." The correction was made by Sir F. Bertie in his telegram No. 157 of September 27.]
([4]) [*v. infra*, pp. 549–52, No. 566.]

No. 563.

Sir M. de Bunsen to Sir Edward Grey.

F.O. 37504/13751/11/28.
(No. 158.)
Sir,

Zaraus, D. September 22, 1911.
R. September 25, 1911.

With reference to my despatch No. 155 of the 19th instant,([1]) I have the honour to state that the conversations between the French Ambassador and the Spanish Minister for Foreign Affairs concerning Morocco in which I have recently taken part have not been renewed since our interview on the 14th instant.([2]) Señor Garcia Prieto

([1]) [*v. supra*, pp. 539–41, No. 559.]
([2]) [*v. supra*, p. 528, No. 551.]

informs me in a private letter that, having received as yet no reply from M. Geoffray with regard to the points which he thought it necessary to raise on that occasion, and as the French Government seem to be in no hurry to continue the discussion, he does not propose to summon M. Geoffray and myself to another meeting before leaving for Madrid to-morrow evening.

I intend following the Minister for Foreign Affairs to Madrid in the course of next week. The French Ambassador is also returning to the capital within a few days. Meanwhile M. Geoffray informs me that he has received no answer from Paris on the subject of the enquiries made by the Spanish Government with regard to the extent of the territorial concessions about to be made by France to Germany and to the guarantee required by Spain that she will not have to pay twice over for recognition of her sphere of influence in Northern Morocco. His Excellency is under the impression that, in the present state of the negotiation at Berlin, the guarantee in question is not one which it would be easy for France to give.

I have, &c.
MAURICE DE BUNSEN.

No. 564.

Sir E. Goschen to Sir A. Nicolson.

Private.([1])

My dear Nicolson,   *Berlin, September* 22, 1911.

Many thanks for your long and interesting letter. The German optimism to which you referred was official and evidently meant to prevent the occurrence of another fall on the Bourse.([2]) I am sending a despatch on the subject which, amongst other things, quotes a semi-official statement with regard to the stability of German Finance. This statement mentions that the losses caused by the fall of last week have been already nearly recouped. If this is so, which I very much doubt, it must be owing to the fact that the Government has been purchasing stock to a very large extent. One thing is clear namely that there has been a panic and that the Banks were greatly in need of the tranquillizing assurances which have been so liberally served out to them. These assurances have been fairly justified by the turn now taken by the negotiations. I think that the Emperor and Cassell are right in maintaining that the German Financial position is strong: but I doubt whether it is strong enough to resist many such knocks as it received last week. Forty millions of pounds sterling are no mean sum and many such losses would affect the strongest position. This was at all events the view of the Chief Berlin Bankers or else they would not have pointed out the danger of a repetition of the panic to the Imperial Government. It has been foolish of the French Press to brag about the share France had in bringing about the Berlin "crach" but the French Press is hopeless.

The negotiations as regards Morocco seem to be approaching their termination. One can scarcely blame the Germans for insisting (if they had only stopped at that) on strict guarantees for the "Open door." Both Kiderlen and Zimmermann have at various times said to me that if they had been negotiating with England the Imperial Government would not have been so stiff as experience has shown that when we talk of the "Open door" we mean what we say: (Stemrich used not to take this view when he talked about our proceedings in Persia): whereas experience had also shown that France always wanted everything for herself and, except under great

([1]) [Carnock MSS., Vol. IV of 1911.]

([2]) [As a result of a despatch sent by Sir Edward Grey on September 23, an elaborate report on the financial crisis in Germany was prepared which is printed *infra*, pp. 796–805, *App.* I.]

pressure would always endeavour to evade any promises she might give with regard to equal facilities for trade for other people. I may be wrong, but I am always inclined to mistrust France in Financial matters and am always a little afraid of their doing things behind our backs. I have all along been suspicious of the pre-Agadir negotiations in May, which Cambon never mentioned—but which the Emperor told me had nearly resulted in an understanding both about Morocco and other matters. I often wonder whether a promise of financial help and general support in the Bagdad Railway question was not one of those "other matters." There was a hint to that effect in one of the leading German Newspapers the other day, only a hint but it set me thinking. . . . .(³)

Cambon is still rather preoccupied about the Congo negotiations. He says "Kiderlen va me demander la line," and, while admitting that the German demands will have to be cut down, he, Cambon, is very anxious that adequate and even generous concessions should be made by France. He says that no stone will be left unturned by the Colonial party in France and people financially interested in the Congo, to influence the French Gov[ernmen]t in the direction of cutting-down the concessions to the narrowest possible limit. He *hopes* that the Government will realize the immense advantages they will have gained in Morocco and will have the courage to resist outside influence. He thinks that Caillaux and Delcassé are sound on this point and realize the situation; but he thinks that de Selves wants stiffening, and he never sees me without begging that Bertie may be instructed to say that now that France has got more or less what she wants in Morocco, H[is] M[ajesty's] G[overnment] *presume* that the French Government will finish off the whole question by showing a certain amount of generosity in the Congo. I told Cambon that I would give his message but that I could not guarantee in any way whether H[is] M[ajesty's] G[overnment] would see their way to acting upon it. . . . .(⁴)

Yours very sincerely,
W. E. GOSCHEN.

(³) [The omitted paragraphs refer to the minor questions of Protected Subjects and Tribunals in Morocco.]
(⁴) [The closing paragraphs of this letter refer to British and German naval expenditure and the relations between the two countries.]

[*ED. NOTE.*—The reference made by Sir E. Goschen in the immediately preceding document to the Emperor's account of pre-Agadir negotiations between France and Germany (*cp. supra*, pp. 450–2, No. 476), led Sir Edward Grey to suggest an enquiry of M. Jules Cambon as to the truth of the question. This enquiry and the result are described below in two private letters from the Grey MSS.

Sir Edward Grey to Sir E. Goschen.

Private.(¹)
My dear Goschen,   *September* 27, 1911.
It seems to me on reading your letter to Nicolson of September 22(²) that you might say something to Jules Cambon about the alleged negotiations between France and Germany in May.

If I remember rightly (I am quoting from memory only) the German Emperor said to you "In May France was ready to give us the Congo, Madagascar and I do not know what besides in exchange for a free hand in Morocco."

This statement is absurd and incredible, but I do not see why you should not tell Jules Cambon of it and ask him what is the truth. We are being accused everywhere in Germany of having interfered to prevent France making concessions to Germany that but for us France would voluntarily have made. The Emperor and the German Government are fostering this statement, and what the German Emperor has alleged will provide a convenient opportunity of bringing the German Government to book on this point, if as I imagine the Emperor's statement is untrue.

I daren't press the French more about the Congo. If I do so we may eventually get the odium in France for an unpopular concession and the whole entente may go. Besides I doubt

(¹) [Grey MSS., Vol. 23.]
(²) [*v.* immediately preceding document.]

whether the Morocco bargain is going to be so clear and clean in favour of France as to warrant a larger territorial concession in the Congo than the French have offered : though I agree with Jules Cambon that Morocco in fee simple would be worth all the French Congo.

When the French get rid of Consular jurisdiction in Morocco without Mixed Tribunals, we shall certainly want their consent to abolition or modification of Capitulations in Egypt.

E. GREY.

Sir E. Goschen to Sir Edward Grey.

Private.(3)
My dear Grey,   *Berlin, October* 6, 1911.

You were quite right in your recollection of what the Emperor said to me at Homburg, and you quoted the exact words he used. When Cambon came to see me yesterday with a very long face after his last talk with Kiderlen we had a long conversation about the negotiations generally. So it was easy for me to ask him what the Emperor meant by the words you have quoted.(4) Cambon said that the Emperor couldn't have known what he was talking about; because the subject of compensations for Morocco was never mentioned until he (Cambon) had gone to see Kiderlen at Kissingen in consequence of hints thrown out by the Chancellor a day or two before. The first time that Compensations on the Congo or elsewhere outside Morocco had been actually discussed was when Kiderlen said to him at Kissingen " You want us to ' faire notre deuil du Maroc.' Well, if we consent to disinterest ourselves politically from Morocco you must give us something in return. A rectification of frontiers in Equatorial Africa or a slice of your Congo or something of that description." Before Kiderlen had said this there had been no negotiations on the subject of compensations whatever, and that was the beginning of those which were being carried out at present. This conversation at Kissingen took place, as you know, towards the latter end of June. The Emperor is, I say it with due respect, a somewhat loose talker, and he probably said ' May ' in order to give emphasis to a passing impression in his own mind, and which he wished to convey to me, that the negotiations had been going on for ages and were approaching a settlement, when we stepped in and stopped it. If Cambon's account is correct, and I suppose it is, the Emperor in talking to me magnified the conversation of one day into a month's negotiation and looked upon Cambon's promise to report Kiderlen's proposal to the French Government as justifying Him in saying that Germany and France were on the point of coming to a settlement. . . . .(5)

Yours very sincerely,
W. E. GOSCHEN.]

(3) [Grey MSS., Vol. 23.]
(4) [The wording, as given on p. 545, slightly differs from Sir E. Goschen's report at the time. *cp. supra*, p. 450, No. 476.]
(5) [The last few sentences of this letter deal with matters of a personal character.]

No. 565.

Communication from M. Paul Cambon of September 28, 1911.

Copy of Despatch from French Minister for Foreign Affairs to M. Jules Cambon, and Draft Notes to be exchanged between M. Jules Cambon and Herr von Kiderlen-Waechter.

F.O. 37970/25883/11/28.

(a)

Le Ministre des Affaires Étrangères à Monsieur Jules Cambon, Ambassadeur de la République française à Berlin.

Très Confidentiel.   *Paris, le* 22 *septembre,* 1911.

Il a été très agréable au gouvernement de la République de constater, d'après vos dernières communications, qu'il est à peu près d'accord avec le gouvernement impérial sur le futur statut du Maroc. Il est désormais acquis que le gouvernement impérial nous reconnaît le droit d'exercer dans ce pays une influence politique prépondérante, en acceptant toutes les conséquences qui écoulent logiquement de ce droit; et nous, de notre côté, nous affirmons notre ferme volonté de maintenir au Maroc la liberté et l'égalité économique la plus entière.

Aussi bien toute notre discussion s'est, dès le début inspirée de ce double principe et je suis heureux de voir que le gouvernement allemand appréciant nos efforts de conciliation n'est plus divisé avec nous que sur quelques points. Nous consentons, d'ailleurs, bien volontiers à réduire de nous-mêmes le nombre de ceux ci, ainsi nous acceptons, conformément au désir du gouvernement allemand, de stipuler dans la lettre qui sera jointe à notre futur accord, 1° que le chemin de fer de Tanger à Fez sera un des premiers chemins de fer dont la construction sera poursuivie par le gouvernement marocain, et, 2° que le port d'Agadir sera ouvert au commerce international.

Nous acceptons de même d'insérer à l'article 6 de notre projet d'accord toutes les dispositions que désire le gouvernement allemand pour mieux préciser en matière d'adjudication et de transport l'égalité de droits établie entre les ressortissants des diverses puissances ; et nous ajoutons un article spécial prévoyant l'établissement de chemins de fer d'exploitation industrielle.

Enfin, tenant compte des motifs que nous a présentés Monsieur de Kiderlen pour écarter du corps de l'accord une délimitation explicite du territoire marocain, le gouvernement français reporte à la lettre annexe l'indication de cette délimitation.

La dernière demande de l'Allemagne a été présentée au nom de Monsieur le Chancelier de l'Empire : Monsieur de Bethmann Hollweg voudrait que les quatre censeurs de la Banque d'Etat fussent chargés de rédiger à tour de rôle un rapport annuel sur l'exploitation des services de transport et sur les observations auxquelles elle aurait donné lieu de la part des divers intéressés. Je ferai observer au sujet de cet amendement que les censeurs de la Banque d'Etat appartiennent à quatre nationalités déterminées et que chacun d'eux est nommé par une banque privilégiée avec l'agrément de son gouvernement : il y aurait donc, si la proposition de Monsieur de Bethmann Hollweg est adoptée, un léger avantage économique à consentir à quatre puissances à l'exclusion des autres. Toutefois, le gouvernement français, tenant compte du désir du Chancelier, consent à substituer au texte qu'il avait présenté un texte que vous trouverez à l'article VIII. Je me plais à espérer que le gouvernement allemand verra dans cette substitution une preuve nouvelle de nos sentiments de conciliation.

La rédaction que nous avions soumise au gouvernement allemand en vue du règlement des rapports futurs du gouvernement marocain avec les puissances étrangères pouvait paraître trop rigoureuse, nous avons adouci notre formule et nous espérons que dans sa teneur actuelle elle ne contient plus rien qui puisse froisser les sentiments d'un grand pays.

De même, nous ne méconnaissons pas que le texte proposé par nous au sujet des protégés pouvait être interprété comme plaçant l'Allemagne et nous mêmes à un certain point de vue d'ordre économique, dans une situation d'inégalité vis-à-vis des autres puissances. La rédaction nouvelle que nous apportons, ne peut pas encourir cette critique, puisqu'elle vise une convention internationale dont la modification ou l'abrogation ne peut être obtenue que par l'accord de toutes les puissances signataires.

La réforme judiciaire est une des réformes qui s'imposent le plus fortement dans l'Empire marocain ; elle est d'ordre es[s]entiellement politique, car il faut dans un pays bien organisé que le pouvoir exécutif soit assuré de trouver à côte de lui un pouvoir judiciaire qui réprime les infractions à la loi. Le gouvernement impérial ne saurait se montrer insensible à cette considération et puisqu'il nous reconnaît sans réserve le droit d'exécuter au Maroc les réformes politiques nécessaires, il ne peut nous refuser celui d'y exécuter les réformes judiciaires qui en sont le corollaire obligatoire.

Le gouvernement allemand nous a suggéré l'idée de l'établissement de tribunaux mixtes au Maroc, cette idée ne saurait être accueillie par nous, elle tend, en effet, à l'internationalisation d'un grand rouage politique et un tel résultat serait en discordance avec le principe accepté par l'Allemagne de l'influence politique prépondérante de la France au Maroc. Nous offrons de doter ce pays d'une organisation judiciaire, constituée sur le mode de celle de France ; une telle organisation, dont on voit l'analogue en Tunisie, assure toutes les garanties de bonne justice et exclut d'avance les appréhensions qui auraient pu faire hésiter les puissances à supprimer leurs juridictions consulaires.

[19656]   2 N 2

Je ne doute pas que, lorsque vous aurez fait valoir ces raisons auprès de Monsieur de Kiderlen il n'en reconnaisse le bien fondé et que le gouvernement allemand ne consente volontiers à nos demandes. Nous aurions alors à rechercher sans retard et d'un commun accord l'adhésion des autres puissances.

(b.)

Projet de Lettre de l'Ambassadeur.

Très Confidentiel.

Mon cher Secrétaire d'Etat :—

J'ai l'honneur d'accuser réception à Votre Excellence et de prendre note de la lettre de ce jour par laquelle Elle veut bien me faire connaître que, dans l'hypothèse où le gouvernement français croirait devoir assumer le protectorat du Maroc, le gouvernement impérial n'y apporterait aucun obstacle et donne cette portée à la nouvelle convention du   1911.

Vous voulez bien ajouter que l'adhésion du gouvernement allemand accordée d'une manière générale au gouvernement français par l'article 1 de ladite convention s'applique notamment à toutes les questions donnant matière à réglementation visées dans l'Acte d'Algésiras.

D'autre part, je suis autorisé par mon gouvernement à vous donner l'assurance que dans le cas où l'Allemagne désirerait acquérir de l'Espagne la Guinée espagnole, l'île Corisco et les îles Elobey la France renoncerait en sa faveur à exercer les droits de préférence qu'elle tient du traité du 27 juin 1900 entre la France et l'Espagne. Il est entendu d'autre part que l'Allemagne n'interviendra en aucune façon dans les accords particuliers que la France et l'Espagne croiront devoir faire entre elles au sujet du Maroc, étant convenu que le Maroc comprend toute la partie de l'Afrique du Nord s'étendant entre l'Algérie, l'Afrique Occidentale française et la colonie espagnole du Rio de Oro.

Le gouvernement allemand renonçant à demander la détermination de parts à faire à l'industrie allemande dans la construction des chemins de fer, je puis vous assurer que le gouvernement français verra toujours volontiers des associations d'intérêt se produire entre les nationaux de nos deux pays.

La construction du chemin de fer de Tanger à Fez devra être l'une des premières entreprises poursuivie par le gouvernement marocain. L'ouverture du port d'Agadir au commerce international sera demandée.

(c.)

Projet de Lettre de M. de Kiderlen-Waechter.

Très Confidentiel.

Mon cher ambassadeur :—

Pour bien préciser l'accord qui vient d'être signé en vue de définir la portée de notre déclaration du 9 février 1909, je crois devoir faire connaître à Votre Excellence que dans l'hypothèse où le gouvernement français croirait devoir assurer le protectorat du Maroc, le gouvernement impérial n'y apporterait aucun obstacle et donne cette portée à la nouvelle convention du   1911.

J'ajoute que l'adhésion du gouvernement allemand accordée d'une manière générale au gouvernement français par l'article I de ladite convention s'applique à toutes les questions donnant matière à réglementation visées dans l'Acte d'Algésiras.

Vous avez bien voulu me faire connaître, d'autre part que, dans le cas où l'Allemagne désirerait acquérir de l'Espagne la Guinée espagnole, l'île Corisco et les iles Elobey, la France serait disposée à renoncer en sa faveur à exercer les droits de préférence qu'elle tient du traité du 27 juin 1900 entre la France et l'Espagne. Je suis heureux de prendre acte de cette assurance et d'ajouter que l'Allemagne n'interviendra en aucune façon dans les accords particuliers que la France et l'Espagne croiront devoir faire entre elles au sujet du Maroc, étant convenu que le

Maroc comprend toute la partie de l'Afrique du Nord s'étendant entre l'Algérie, l'Afrique Occidentale française et la colonie espagnole du Rio de Oro.

Le gouvernement allemand renonce, ainsi que nous l'avons dit, à demander la détermination préalable de parts à faire à l'industrie allemande dans la construction des chemins de fer, mais il espère que le gouvernement français verra toujours volontiers des associations d'intérêt se produire entre les nationaux des deux pays.

Il compte également que le chemin de fer de Tanger à Fez qui intéresse toutes les nations sera l'un des premiers dont la construction sera poursuivie par le gouvernement marocain et que le port d'Agadir sera ouvert au commerce international.

MINUTES.

These notes and instructions have now gone off and cannot be altered I imagine, but M. Cambon might be told that we understand that all the interested Powers will be on the same footing as regards industrial enterprise, and that the words " verra toujours volontiers des associations d'intérêt se produire entre les nationaux de nos deux pays " should be so understood.

F. A. C.
29/9.

A. N.

The comment should be made as Sir F. Campbell suggests.

E. G.

No. 566.

Sir F. Bertie to Sir Edward Grey.

F.O. 37635/25883/11/28.

(No. 417.) Confidential.   *Paris*, D. *September* 25, 1911.

Sir,   R. *September* 26, 1911.

I had an interview with Monsieur de Selves this morning and he showed to me the amended French Projet which, after it had been approved by the Cabinet and the President of the Republic, was sent on the 23rd instant to the French Ambassador at Berlin for communication to-day to M. de Kiderlen Waechter.

M. de Selves was good enough to allow me to send a Secretary of the Embassy to take a copy of the Projet and I have the honour to transmit it to you herewith.

M. de Selves informed me that it is proposed that there shall be an exchange of notes with the German Government leaving it to the French Government to come to an understanding with the Spanish Government in regard to the future position of Spain in the parts of Morocco reserved to her as Spanish zones.

I have, &c.

FRANCIS BERTIE.

Enclosure in No. 566.

Troisième Texte Français.

A la suite des troubles qui se sont produits au Maroc et qui ont démontré la nécessité d'y poursuivre, dans l'intérêt général, l'œuvre de pacification et de progrès prévue par l'Acte d'Algésiras, le gouvernement de la République française et le gouvernement impérial allemand ont jugé nécessaire de préciser et de compléter l'accord franco-allemand du 9 février 1909. Ils sont convenus, à cet effet, des dispositions ci-après :

ARTICLE I.

Le Gouvernement impérial allemand déclare que, ne poursuivant au Maroc que des intérêts économiques, il n'entravera pas l'action de la France en vue de prêter son assistance au Gouvernement marocain pour l'introduction de toutes les réformes administratives, judiciaires, économiques, financières et militaires dont il a besoin pour le bon gouvernement de l'Empire, comme aussi pour tous les règlements nouveaux et les modifications aux règlements existants, que ces réformes comportent. En conséquence, il donne son adhésion aux mesures de réorganisation, de contrôle et de garantie financière que, après accord avec le gouvernement marocain, le gouvernement français croira devoir prendre à cet effet sous la seule réserve que l'action de la France sauvegardera au Maroc l'égalité économique entre les nations.

Au cas où la France serait amenée à préciser et à étendre son contrôle et sa protection, le gouvernement impérial allemand reconnaissant au Maroc pleine liberté d'action à la France, et sous la réserve que la liberté commerciale prévue par les traités antérieurs sera maintenue n'y apportera aucun obstacle.

Il est entendu qu'il ne sera porté aucune entrave aux droits et action de la Banque d'Etat du Maroc tels qu'ils ont été définis par l'Acte d'Algésiras.

Article II.

Dans cet ordre d'idées, il est entendu que le gouvernement impérial ne fera pas obstacle à ce que la France, après accord avec le gouvernement marocain, procède aux occupations militaires du territoire marocain qu'elle jugerait nécessaire au maintien de l'ordre et de la sécurité des transactions commerciales, et à ce qu'elle exerce toute action de police sur terre et dans les eaux marocaines.

Article III.

Le gouvernement français déclare que, fermement attaché au principe de la liberté commerciale au Maroc, il ne se prêtera à aucune inégalité pas plus dans l'établissement des droits de douane, impôts et autres taxes que dans l'établissement des tarifs de transport par voie ferrée, voie de navigation fluviale ou toute autre voie et notamment dans toutes les questions de transit.

Le gouvernement français s'emploiera également auprès du gouvernement marocain afin d'empêcher tout traitement différentiel entre les ressortissants des différentes Puissances; il s'opposera notamment à toute mesure, par exemple à la promulgation d'ordonnances administratives sur les poids et mesures, de jaugeage, de poinçonnage, &c...(¹) qui pourrait mettre en état d'infériorité les marchandises d'une Puissance.

Le Gouvernement français s'engage à user de son influence sur la Banque d'Etat pour que celle-ci confère à tour de rôle aux membres de sa direction à Tanger les postes de délégué dont elle dispose à la Commission des valeurs douanières et au Comité permanent des douanes.

Article IV.

Le gouvernement français veillera à ce qu'il ne soit perçu au Maroc aucun droit d'exportation sur le minerai de fer exporté des ports marocains. Les exploitations de minerai de fer ne subiront aucun impôt spécial. Elles ne seront assujetties qu'aux impôts généraux et aux redevances domaniales qui atteindront toutes les entreprises minières.

Article V.

Dès à présent, si Sa Majesté le Sultan du Maroc venait à confier aux agents diplomatiques et consulaires de la France la représentation et la protection des sujets et des intérêts marocains à l'étranger, le gouvernement impérial déclare qu'il n'y fera pas d'objection.

Il ne fera, d'autre part, pas d'objection à ce que les représentants de la France auprès du gouvernement marocain soient chargés par celui-ci d'être son intermédiaire auprès des représentants au Maroc des Puissances étrangères.

(¹) [Thus in original.]

Article VI.

Le Gouvernement de la République française s'engage à veiller à ce que les travaux et fournitures nécessités par les constructions éventuelles de routes, chemins de fer, ports, télégraphes, &c....(²) soient octroyés par le gouvernement chérifien suivant les règles de l'adjudication.

Il s'engage également à veiller à ce que les conditions de ces adjudications, particulièrement ce qui concerne les fournitures de matériel et les délais impartis pour soumissionner, ne placent les ressortissants d'aucune Puissance dans une situation d'infériorité.

L'exploitation des grandes entreprises mentionnées ci-dessus sera réservée à l'état marocain ou librement concédée par lui à des tiers qui pourront être chargés de fournir les fonds nécessaires à cet effet. Le gouvernement français veillera cependant à ce que, dans l'exploitation des chemins de fer et autres moyens de transport comme dans l'application des règlements destinés à assurer celle-ci, aucune différence de traitement ne soit faite entre les ressortissants des diverses puissances qui useraient de ces moyens de transport.

Le Gouvernement de la République usera de son influence sur la Banque d'Etat afin que celle-ci confère à tour de rôle aux membres de sa direction à Tanger le poste dont elle dispose de délégué à la Commission générale des adjudications et marchés.

Article VII.

Le gouvernement français s'emploiera auprès du gouvernement marocain pour que les propriétaires de mines et d'autres exploitations industrielles sans distinction de nationalité et en conformité des règlements qui seront édictés en s'inspirant des principes de là législation française sur la matière puissent être autorisés à céder des chemins de fer d'exploitation industrielle destinés à relier leur centre de production aux lignes d'intérêt général ou aux ports.

Article VIII.

Il sera présenté tous les ans un rapport sur l'exploitation des chemins de fer au Maroc qui sera établi dans les mêmes formes et conditions que les rapports présentés aux assemblées d'actionnaires des sociétés de chemins de fer françaises. Le gouvernement de la République chargera un des administrateurs de la Banque d'Etat de l'établissement de ce rapport qui sera communiqué aux censeurs puis rendu public avec, s'il y a lieu, les observations de ces derniers.

Article IX.

Pour éviter autant que possible les réclamations diplomatiques, le gouvernement français s'emploiera auprès du gouvernement marocain afin que celui-ci défère à un arbitre désigné d'un commun accord par le gouvernement français et le gouvernement intéressé les plaintes portées par des ressortissants étrangers contre les autorités marocaines et qui n'auraient pu être réglées par l'intermédiaire du consul français et du consul du gouvernement intéressé.

Cette procédure restera en vigueur jusqu'au jour où aura été institué un régime judiciaire s'inspirant des règles générales de l'organisation de la justice française et permettant ainsi la suppression des tribunaux consulaires, suppression dont les deux gouvernements acceptent d'ores et déjà le principe.

Il est d'ailleurs expressément entendu que les ressortissants étrangers seront régis sous ce nouveau régime. par les mêmes règles de procédure et bénéficieront des mêmes garanties légales que les ressortissants français.

(²) [Thus in original.]

Article X.

Le Gouvernement français veillera à ce que les ressortissants étrangers continuent à jouir du droit de pêche dans les eaux et ports marocains.

Article XI.

Le gouvernement français s'emploiera auprès du gouvernement marocain pour que celui-ci ouvre au commerce étranger de nouveaux ports au fur et à mesure des besoins de ce commerce.

Article XII.

Pour répondre à une demande du gouvernement marocain les deux gouvernements s'engagent à procéder à la revision, sur la base de la convention de Madrid, de la situation des protégés étrangers et des associés agricoles au Maroc.

Ils sont également d'accord pour poursuivre auprès des Puissances signataires l'abrogation de cette convention, étant entendu toutefois que celle-ci continuera à produire ses effets jusqu'au jour où fonctionnera l'organisation judiciaire prévue à l'article IX.

Article XIII.

Les deux gouvernements signataires renoncent à se prévaloir de toute clause d'accord, convention, traité ou règlement qui serait contraire aux précédentes stipulations.

Article XIV.

Les précédents articles du présent accord seront communiqués aux autres puissances signataires de l'Acte d'Algésiras près desquels les deux gouvernements s'engagent à se prêter mutuellement appui pour obtenir leur adhésion.

No. 567.

Sir F. Bertie to Sir Edward Grey.

F.O. 38006/38006/11/28.
(No. 422.)   Confidential.   *Paris, D. September* 28, 1911.
Sir,   R. *September* 29, 1911.

As the Naval Advisers of His Majesty's Government would see great objection to the establishment of a German fortified naval base on the Atlantic coast of Morocco, and the friends of to-day may be the enemies of to-morrow I conclude that they would also see objection to a French fortified naval base on that coast.

The restriction in regard to fortifications contained in Article VII of the Anglo-French Declaration of April 8 1904 respecting Egypt and Morocco, and later on adhered to by Spain as provided for in one of the secret articles([1]) attached to the Declaration, applies only to the portion of the coast of Morocco comprised between, but not including, Melilla and the heights which command the right bank of the river Sebou, and not to the places then in the occupation of Spain. In the negotiations preliminary to the Declaration of 1904 the Marquess of Lansdowne endeavoured to include the whole coast of Morocco as far South as Mazaghan, and at all events to and inclusive of Rabat.([2]) To this the French Government with obvious ultimate intention but not on any plausible plea objected and Lord Lansdowne ultimately desisted from pressing the point. His Lordship, in a letter to M. [Paul] Cambon, dated October 1st, 1903, wrote " a second condition which His Majesty's Government regard as essential

---

([1]) [v. Secret Article III, *Gooch & Temperley*, Vol. II, pp. 393–4.]
([2]) [cp. *Gooch & Temperley*, Vol. II, pp. 312–3, 333–4.]

is, we understand, also readily accepted by the French Government. It has reference to the greater portion of the Moorish littoral, upon which both Governments desire that no Power should be allowed to establish itself or to erect fortifications or strategical works of any kind. That portion ought, in the view of His Majesty's Government, to comprise the whole seaboard now in the possession of Morocco from the Algerian frontier to Mazaghan including that seaport." In the record of a conversation which took place a few days later (see to Sir E. Monson No. 503 Secret of October 7th 1903)(³) Lord Lansdowne stated that " M. Cambon expressed general agreement with regard to our proposals as to Spain but told me that we had assigned to that country far too extensive a proportion of the Moorish coast-line. Should the ' liquidation ' of Morocco ever take place, it would never do for France to find herself enveloped by a strip of Spanish territory reaching from Mazaghan to the Algerian frontier. I said that I should be prepared to discuss the geographical question with him whenever he was ready to do it, but that there seemed to me to be great advantages in neutralizing as much of the Moorish seaboard as possible. Moreover, there were scarcely any important ports between the points named."(⁴)

The French Ambassador in a letter of October 26th, 1903(⁵) proposed to Lord Lansdowne that in order to guarantee the free passage of the Straits of Gibraltar the two Governments should undertake not to fortify or allow the fortification of any part of the coast of Morocco between Melilla and the heights commanding the right bank of the Sebou (an arrangement subsequently provided for by the Declaration of April 8th, 1904). Lord Lansdowne in reply to this suggestion stated (to M. Cambon November 19th, 1903) that " In order to meet M. Delcassé's wishes we are prepared to consent to a modification of our original proposal and to agree that the portion of the Atlantic coast thus neutralized shall extend from Melilla as far as Rabat, including the port of that name which is about 20 miles South of the Sebou River."(⁶)

On the 20th November 1903 M. Cambon informed Lord Lansdowne (see to Sir E. Monson No. 586 Confidential),(⁷) that he thought that His Majesty's Government might as well not have insisted on neutralizing the Moorish coast-line beyond the mouth of the Sebou. Lord Lansdowne in a despatch to Sir E. Monson of December 9th, 1903 stated that the French Ambassador had informed him that " M. Delcassé saw serious objections to extending the neutral strip beyond the heights bordering the mouth of the Sebou on its right bank. The difference in point of extent was not great, but Rabat was a port where it was of importance that French action should have a free hand, being the outlet of a plain which would probably be crossed later on by a railway. Rabat must therefore remain open to French influence."(⁸)

M. Cambon on a subsequent occasion (see Lord Lansdowne to Sir E. Monson No. 626 A Secret of December 11th, 1903)(⁹) again objected to the inclusion of Rabat in the portion of Moorish territory which was not to be fortified on the ground that " should a ' liquidation ' of Morocco ever become inevitable the neutralized area would probably fall to Spain, and it would be most inconvenient that a French line should have its terminus in Spanish territory." His Excellency added that " France had certainly no idea of fortifying Rabat."

The question which I desire to submit to the consideration of His Majesty's Government is whether advantage might not now be taken of the proposals made by the French Government for the exchange of French and British territories in Africa (reported to you in my despatch No. 415 of the 19th instant)(¹⁰) in consequence of the contemplated change in the position of France in Morocco, as a result of the Berlin

(³) [v. Gooch & Temperley, Vol. II, pp. 317–8.]
(⁴) [v. ib., Vol. II, p. 318.]
(⁵) [v. ib., Vol. II, p. 320.]
(⁶) [v. ib., Vol. II, pp. 324–5.]
(⁷) [v. ib., Vol. II, p. 328.]
(⁸) [v. ib., Vol. II, p. 329.]
(⁹) [v. ib., Vol. II, pp. 333–4.]
(¹⁰) [v. supra, pp. 535–7, No. 558, and encl.]

negotiations, in order to obtain from the French Government a formal undertaking that no part of the Atlantic coast of Morocco South of the River Sebou shall ever be fortified. Such a statement as the one made to Lord Lansdowne by M. Cambon that France had certainly no idea of fortifying Rabat cannot be regarded as an engagement followed as it was by a withdrawal by Lord Lansdowne of his insistence on its inclusion in the coast not to be fortified, and any more formal but voluntary assurance given now might not be lastingly observed as has been exemplified by the cases of Batoum and Bizerta; but an engagement not to fortify in consideration of some concession would give His Majesty's Government the right to make representations to the French Government if any preparations to fortify were made later on, and such preparations would be evidence that the French Government no longer attached value to the now existing *entente* between France and England and would justify His Majesty's Government in taking overtly precautions in consequence.

M. Paul Cambon suggested to Lord Lansdowne on October 26, 1903, that "les deux gouvernements s'engageront à maintenir sauf les conséquences du présent accord, le *statu quo* territorial dans un rayon de cinq cents milles autour dudit détroit"([11]) (viz., the Straits of Gibraltar). Lord Lansdowne declined to enter into such an engagement on the ground that such an area would include the greater part of Spain and part of the desert of Sahara as well as the Balearic Islands and that an arrangement of that sort seemed to His Majesty's Government to be altogether outside the scope of the proposed agreement which was intended to be limited to questions at issue or likely to be at issue between Great Britain and France (see Lord Lansdowne to Sir E. Monson, No. 626 Secret of December 11th, 1903).([12]) However, three years later, by the so-called Spanish notes the British, French and Spanish Governments declared their policy to be directed to the maintenance of the territorial status quo in the Mediterranean and in that part of the Atlantic Ocean which washes the shores of Europe and Africa and they declared that in pursuance of that policy they were firmly resolved to preserve intact their rights over their insular and maritime possessions in those regions.

I beg leave to submit for your consideration that an opportunity should be taken to remind the French Government of the policy declared by France, England and Spain in the notes of 1907([13]) and that it should be suggested that the same policy should be adopted in respect to any parts of the coast of Morocco coming under the protectorate or authority of either France or Spain as a result of the negotiations now being carried on at Berlin between the French and German Governments; and further that it should be intimated to the French Government that His Majesty's Government consider that the fortification of any part of the coast of Morocco would create a material change in the status quo and in the relative naval position of the three Powers parties to the agreement of 1907.

I have, &c.
FRANCIS BERTIE.

MINUTES.

It may reasonably be assumed that a French and a Spanish protectorate in Morocco are within measurable distance. There can be no question but that such protectorates are "circumstances . . . . which would alter or tend to alter the existing territorial *status quo*" and we are therefore justified in approaching both the French and the Spanish Gov[ernmen]ts on the basis of the Anglo-Spanish and Anglo-French Notes of May 1907. I annex copies of these notes herewith. It will be remembered that Sir F. Bertie has already raised the question of the maintenance of the existing Franco-Spanish engagement not to fortify the coast between Melilla and the mouth of the R[iver] Sebu, some miles north of Rabat: and that the French Gov[ernmen]t will see that the engagement is maintained in any new Franco-Spanish agreement. Sir F. Bertie now suggests that we should obtain an engagement from the French not to fortify *any* point on the Moorish coast. I am having a search made in the 1904 archives to see whether there are minutes, &c., showing why Lord Lansdowne abandoned his original position, *i.e.*, no fortifications as far as Mazagan.

([11]) [*v. Gooch & Temperley*, Vol. II, p. 320.]
([12]) [*v. Gooch & Temperley*, Vol. II, pp. 333–4.]
([13]) [*v. supra*, pp. 32–4, Nos. 39, 40, 41.]

Sir F. Bertie seems to contemplate two alternatives :—

(1) that we should obtain such an engagement from France as part of the proposed territorial deal.
(2) that we should approach the French Gov[ernmen]t on the basis of the so-called Mediterranean notes.

If we act on No. 1 presumably we shall have to give some concession on our side; and it may be observed *en passant* that the French are already asking more than we can possibly give for what they offer.   No. 2 seems to be a better plan and I would suggest that such an engagement might be made the condition on which we consent to the Franco-German convention, which practically amounts to an abrogation of the Algeciras Act to say nothing of the Madrid Convention.

In the first instance([14])
? copy to War Office and Admiralty asking for their reasoned opinion from the strategical point of view of an engagement by France and by Spain not to fortify any point on the Moorish coast.

G. H. V.
29/9/11.
E. A. C.
Sept. 30.

I would certainly have the proposed territorial deal with France alone.   It will be a longish time, if ever, before we come to an agreement; and we have good grounds for approaching the French on the 1907 notes.

To W[ar] O[ffice] and Admiralty in first instance as proposed.

F. A. C.
3/10.

The question of mutual exchange of any territories between us and France should be treated by itself—and apart from that of engagements not to fortify ports on the Moorish coast.   This latter question, it seems to me, could be dealt with more appropriately when we are approached for our consent being given to the Franco-German Agreement.   We shall then have to see that proper arrang[emen]ts are made as to internationalising Tangier and that other securities for our interests are obtained.   I think that it is too early to deal with the points raised by Sir F. Bertie though there would be no harm in our requesting the views of the War Office and the Admiralty.

A. N.

Obtain views of War Office and Admiralty as to importance of obtaining this guarantee against fortification.

E. G.

(14) [Thus in original.]

No. 568.

Sir F. Bertie to Sir Edward Grey.

F.O. 38007/25883/11/28.
(No. 423.)   Confidential.
Sir,

Paris, D. September 28, 1911.
R. September 29, 1911.

With reference to my telegram No. 159 of to-day's date,(1) I have the honour to transmit to you herewith a copy of a memorandum which has been drawn up this afternoon at the Quai d'Orsay by one of the Secretaries to His Majesty's Embassy, showing the modifications which the French Ambassador at Berlin has reported that the German Government desire to introduce into the latest French proposals respecting Morocco, a copy of which was enclosed in my despatch No. 417 confidential of the 25th instant.(2)

I have, &c.
FRANCIS BERTIE.

(1) [Not reproduced.   It is in the same sense as the above despatch and states that full particulars are being forwarded.]
(2) [*v. supra*, pp. 549–52, No. 566, and *encl.*]

Enclosure in No. 568.

Memorandum.

Preamble accepted by German Government.

Article I accepted by the German Government with the omission of the words "au Maroc" in the second paragraph. Second paragraph therefore runs as follows :—

Au cas où la France serait amenée à préciser et à étendre son contrôle et sa protection, le Gouvernement impérial allemand reconnaissant pleine liberté d'action à la France &c.

Article II accepted by the German Government.
Article III accepted by the German Government.
Article IV to be as follows :—

Le gouvernement français veillera à ce qu'il ne soit perçu au Maroc aucun droit d'exportation sur le minerai de fer exporté des ports marocains. Les exploitations de minerai de fer ne subiront aucun impôt spécial ni sur leur production ni sur leurs moyens de travail. Elles ne seront assujetties qu'aux impôts généraux et aux redevances domaniales qui atteindront toutes les entreprises minières et sont prévus par le projet de firman minier.

Le gouvernement français veillera à ce que la taxe superficiaire prévue à l'article 35 du projet de firman minier soit régulièrement perçue et il ne tolérera pas que remise soit faite sous un prétexte quelconque du total ou d'une partie de cette taxe.

Article V. First paragraph accepted by the German Government. Following to be substituted for second paragraph :—

Si d'autre part Sa Majesté le Sultan du Maroc confiait au représentant de la France près du Gouvernement Marocain le soin d'être son intermédiaire auprès des représentants étrangers, le Gouvernement allemand n'y ferait pas d'objection.

Article VI accepted by the German Government with the following addition :—

De même le Gouvernement français amènera le gouvernement marocain à conférer un des postes de délégué chérifien au comité spécial des travaux publics à des candidats qui seront présentés, à tour de rôle, par les quatre Puissances autorisées par l'Acte d'Algésiras à nommer les censeurs auprès de la Banque d'Etat.

Article VII to be modified as follows :—

Le gouvernement français s'emploiera auprès du gouvernement marocain pour que les propriétaires de mines et d'autres exploitations industrielles ou agricoles sans distinction de nationalité soient autorisés à céder des chemins de fer d'exploitation industrielle destinés à relier leur centre de production aux lignes d'intérêt général ou aux ports.

Article VIII accepted with the following addition :—

" sur les rapports et sur les demandes ou plaintes qui leur seraient adressées par les ressortissants des différentes Puissances."

German Government proposes following text for Article IX. Pour éviter autant que possible les réclamations diplomatiques le gouvernement français s'emploiera auprès du gouvernement marocain afin que celui-ci défère à un arbitre désigné ad hoc pour chaque affaire d'un commun accord par le Consul de France et le Consul intéressé et à leur défaut par leurs deux gouvernements, les plaintes portées par des ressortissants étrangers contre les autorités et qui n'auraient pas été réglées par l'intermédiaire du Consul de France et du Consul du Gouvernement intéressé. Cette procédure restera en vigueur jusqu'au jour où aura été institué, avec le consentement des Puissances, un régime judiciaire destiné à remplacer les tribunaux consulaires.

Articles X and XI accepted by the German Government.

German Government proposes that Article XII should run as follows: Article XII. Pour répondre à une demande du gouvernement marocain les deux gouvernements s'engagent à provoquer d'accord avec les autres Puissances, sur la base de la Convention de Madrid et par application des articles VIII et XVI de cette Convention la revision de la situation des protégés étrangers et des associés agricoles au Maroc.

Ils sont également d'accord pour poursuivre, le moment venu, auprès des autres puissances des modifications à apporter à ladite Convention.

German Government proposes following text for Article XIII. Les dispositions des traités antérieurs contraires à la présente Convention sont et demeurent abrogées.

Article XIV accepted by the German Government.

No. 569.

Sir Edward Grey to Sir M. de Bunsen.

F.O. 37969/13751/11/28.
(No. 99.)
Sir, *Foreign Office, September* 28, 1911.

The Spanish Amb[assado]r called at the F[oreign] O[ffice] on the 25th inst[ant] and observed that he had noticed in the French press and in some telegrams from Paris to English newspapers an inclination on the part of some sections of the French public to maintain that the Franco-Spanish Treaty of 1904(¹) had lapsed owing to the creation of a new situation; and that it was asserted that the rights of Spain should be limited to her actual possessions in Morocco. H[is] E[xcellency] enquired whether H[is] M[ajesty's] G[overnment] considered that Spain was entitled to the exercise of the rights accorded to her under the treaty of 1904 and whether they would so inform the French Gov[ernmen]t.

Sir A. Nicolson replied that H[is] M[ajesty's] G[overnment] had no indication that the French Gov[ernmen]t desired in any way to depart from the provisions of the treaty which H[is] M[ajesty's] G[overnment] certainly considered as existing and in force.

In the above reply Sir A. Nicolson correctly expressed my view, subject to the reservation that if owing to French concessions to Germany the Powers signatory to the Algeciras Act disinterest themselves politically in Morocco, Spain must give France some reasonable compensation or the latter will have paid the whole price of acquiring liberty of action for Spain in the Spanish sphere.

[I am, &c.
E. GREY.]

(¹) [*v. infra*, pp. 826–9, *App.* IV.]

No. 570.

Sir E. Goschen to Sir A. Nicolson.

Private.(¹)

My dear Nicolson,   *Berlin, September* 28, 1911.

I thought I had made it clear in my letter that what Jules Cambon wanted was not that Bertie should complain about the French Press but that while congratulating de Selves on having got what he wanted in Morocco he might add that he presumed now that they would not make many difficulties about the Congo. I must say that I can see no earthly reason why this should not have been done, as after all if the French Government through pressure from interested persons and their Press are stingy in their concessions and a grave situation is created, *we* shall have to join in paying the piper, so I think we have every right to show an interest in the question and even advise. Nobody could be a stronger supporter of the entente than I, but I confess I should be sorry to see British lives and money sacrificed in the interests of a few French financiers and people who are so short sighted that they cannot see the handsome way in which their bread has been buttered in Morocco. . . . .(²)

Yours very sincerely,

W. E. GOSCHEN.

(¹) [Carnock MSS., Vol. V of 1911.]
(²) [The closing paragraphs of this letter give details as to the Franco-German negotiations and Italian action in Tripoli.]

No. 571.

Sir Edward Grey to Sir F. Bertie.

F.O. 37769/25883/11/28.

(No. 404.)

Sir,   *Foreign Office, September* 30, 1911.

I have received your Excellency's telegram No. 157 of the 27th ult[imo],(¹) calling attention to the error in your telegram No. 154(²) as printed in the telegram sections of Sept[ember] 22nd, 23rd.

I should be glad if you would inform the French Gov[ernmen]t that the German M[inister for] F[oreign] A[ffairs] had no authority for the statement that H[is] M[ajesty's] Gov[ernmen]t would be opposed to any judicial system in Morocco other than that of mixed courts, but that of course if consular jurisdiction were abolished in Morocco H[is] M[ajesty's] G[overnment] would expect some revision of the existing state of things in Egypt.

[I am, &c.

E. GREY.]

(¹) [*v. supra*, p. 543, No. 562, *note* (³).]
(²) [*v. supra*, p. 543, No. 562.]

No. 572.

Sir F. Bertie to Sir Edward Grey.

(By Bag.)

F.O. 38601/25883/11/28.   *Paris, D. October* 2, 1911.

Tel. (No. 162.) *En clair.*   R. *October* 3, 1911.

Morocco.

My telegram No. 159 of 28th September and projet in my despatch No. 423, Confidential, of same date.(¹)

(¹) [*v. supra*, pp. 555-7, No. 568 and *encl.*, and *note* (¹).]

M. de Selves has informed me this evening that the questions at issue in regard to Morocco are in a fair way of settlement.

Article 4. M. de Kiderlen-Waechter, confronted with the fact that at a conference on the mining laws the German delegate had adhered to proposals for a surface tax and output tax on mines, explains that he has been misunderstood, and meant to refer to exportation tax.

M. de Kiderlen-Waechter gives way on article 5 in regard to French representatives being the medium of communication between the foreign representatives and the Moorish Government.

Article 7. M. de Kiderlen-Waechter withdraws his amendment, the French Government agreeing to add agricultural undertakings on a large scale to the permission to be given to mines and industrial undertakings to link themselves up with railways or ports.

M. de Kiderlen-Waechter withdraws the stipulation in Article 9, that " cette procédure restera en vigueur jusqu'au jour où aura été institué, avec le consentement des Puissances, un régime judiciaire destiné à remplacer les tribunaux consulaires " ; and the French Government substitute European in the place of French system of justice in their article 9.

The questions on which there is not yet agreement are those of protégés and " associés agricoles " and the Madrid Convention.

No. 573.

Sir F. Bertie to Sir Edward Grey.

F.O. 38770/16083/11/28.
(No. 429.)   *Paris, D. October 3, 1911.*
Sir,   R. *October 4, 1911.*

It is generally known in Paris that the Franco-German negotiations are about to turn from Morocco to the Congo, and as the moment approaches for a discussion of the compensation to be given to Germany in that quarter, endeavours are being made to arouse public opinion on the subject and to bring pressure to bear on the French Government to curtail the extent of the territory to be ceded to Germany.

The sentimental and patriotic chord has been touched by a public letter addressed to the President of the Republic by Madame de Brazza, the widow of the African explorer who planted the French flag in the Congo hinterland.

M. Hanotaux has written a long article in the " Revue Hebdomadaire " which is widely quoted in the Press and in which he strongly opposes what are believed to be the concessions which the French Government are ready to make in the Congo. In this article, he goes beyond the questions actually at issue, and throws doubt on the wisdom of the French line of policy which was inaugurated by the agreements of 1904 with England and Spain.

M. Joseph Reinach, the well-known and influential Republican Deputy, writes an article in the " Figaro " of to-day's date in which he declares that a concession, such as has been proposed, of the middle French Congo as far as the Ubangi and the frontier of Belgian Congo, is entirely inadmissible. He states that he himself will vote against such an arrangement were it brought before the Chamber and that the Deputies who take his view are numerous. Public opinion, he declares, is daily becoming more resolutely hostile to the idea.

The above are instances of the attitude which is being taken in certain influential quarters respecting the further course of the negotiations. As was to be expected, still more energetic protests are being raised by extremists who see an occasion for damaging the Ministry on the score of weakness in defending French interests. The

French Ambassador at Berlin comes in for a large share of criticism and is accused of being too pliant in respect of the German demands. I enclose herein copies of M. Hanotaux's article extracted from the " Revue Hebdomadaire " and of that of M. Reinach from the " Figaro."(¹)

I have, &c.
FRANCIS BERTIE.

(¹) [Not reproduced.]

No. 574.

Sir F. Bertie to Sir Edward Grey.

F.O. 38931/38931/11/28.

(No. 430.)   *Paris,* D. *October* 4, 1911.
Sir,   R. *October* 5, 1911.

I had the honour, in my Despatch No. 429 of yesterday's date,(¹) to report to you the declaration of M. Hanotaux against the cession of a large portion of the French Congo Colony reaching to the Ubangi River and the frontier of the Belgian Congo, and a similar declaration on the part of M. Reinach, coupled with the statement that he and numerous other Deputies would vote against the ratification of a Treaty containing provision for such a concession. It is of interest to note in this connection that M. Marcel Sembat, one of the authorized spokesmen of the unified Socialist Party in the Chamber, has written an article in the " Humanité " to the effect that his party intends to vote in favour of an Agreement to be come to by the French Government, in order to put an end as soon as possible to the existing state of tension between France and Germany.

As the Unified Socialist Party numbers 75 Members, its support, should the Ministry encounter serious opposition from certain other quarters in the Chamber, as is anticipated, may be of considerable value from the Ministerial point of view.

The Socialist Leader, M. Jaurès, is not yet back from South America, whither he went to give a series of lectures.

I have, &c.
FRANCIS BERTIE.

(¹) [*v.* immediately preceding document.]

No. 575.

Sir F. Bertie to Sir Edward Grey.

F.O. 38932/38932/11/28.

(No. 431.)   *Paris,* D. *October* 4, 1911.
Sir,   R. *October* 5, 1911.

I had the honour to receive last night your despatch No. 404 (37769)(¹) of the 30th ultimo instructing me to inform M. de Selves that M. de Kiderlen Waechter had no authority for the statement that His Majesty's Government would be opposed to any judicial system in Morocco other than that of Mixed Courts, but that of course if consular jurisdiction were abolished in Morocco His Majesty's Government would expect some revision of the existing state of things in Egypt.

I saw M. de Selves this afternoon and I reminded him of the statement made by M. de Kiderlen-Waechter. I spoke to His Excellency in the above sense and I gave him the memorandum in French of which a copy is enclosed herein.

M. de Selves said that the view of His Majesty's Government appeared to him to be quite reasonable.

I have, &c.
FRANCIS BERTIE.

(¹) [*v. supra,* p. 558, No. 571.]

Enclosure in No. 575.

Sir F. Bertie to M. de Selves.

Paris, October 4,, 1911.

Le 22 septembre M. de Selves a informé Sir Francis Bertie que M. de Kiderlen Waechter avait représenté à l'Ambassadeur de France à propos des Capitulations au Maroc que le Gouvernement de Sa Majesté Britannique serait opposé à l'établissement par le Gouvernement français de Tribunaux qui n'auraient pas le caractère de Tribunaux Mixtes.

Sir Francis Bertie a été invité par Sir Edward Grey de déclarer à M. de Selves que le Ministre des Affaires Etrangères allemand n'était nullement autorisé à faire une représentation pareille des vues du gouvernement britannique.

Dans le cas où la juridiction consulaire au Maroc serait abolie le gouvernement britannique se regarderait en droit à un changement dans le système judiciaire actuel en Égypte analogue à celui adopté au Maroc, et compte sur le concours et l'appui du gouvernement français à cette fin.

No. 576.

Sir Edward Grey to Sir F. Bertie.

F.O. 37970/25883/11/28.
(No. 409.)
Sir,   *Foreign Office, October 4, 1911.*

The French Ambassador in London has communicated to me confidentially a copy of the despatch which the French M[inister for] F[oreign] A[ffairs] addressed to M. Jules Cambon on the 22nd ult[imo] on the subject of the Franco-German negotiations respecting Morocco. Annexed to the despatch are draft notes to be exchanged between the German M[inister for] F[oreign] A[ffairs] and the French Ambassador in Berlin dealing with certain points not specified in the proposed Franco-German Convention. Copies of these papers will reach Y[our] E[xcellency] in the Morocco print sections.([1])

In the draft note from M. Jules Cambon to Herr von Kiderlen the following passage occurs : " Le gouvernement allemand renonçant à demander la détermination des parts à faire à l'industrie allemande dans la construction des chemins de fer, je puis vous assurer que le gouvernement français verra toujours volontiers des associations d'intérêt se produire entre les nationaux de nos deux pays." As this passage may possibly give rise to misunderstandings in the future I should be glad if Y[our] E[xcellency] would inform M. de Selves that H[is] M[ajesty's] Gov[ernmen]t understand that by the new Franco-German Convention all the Powers will be on the same footing as regards industrial enterprises in Morocco and that the words " verra toujours volontiers des associations d'intérêt se produire entre les nationaux de nos deux pays " should be so construed.

[I am, &c.
E. GREY.]

([1]) [*v. supra*, pp. 546–9, No. 565.]

No. 577.

Sir F. Bertie to Sir Edward Grey.

(By Post.)

F.O. 39275/25883/11/28.
Tel. (No. 166.) *En clair.*

Paris, D. *October 6, 1911.*
R. *October 7, 1911.*

Morocco.

My telegram No. 162 of 2nd October.([1])

M. de Selves, whom I have seen this morning, informs me that there are still divergences between the German and French Government on the following subjects: Madrid Convention; protégés; and taxes on minerals. The French Government desire the abrogation with the concurrence of the Powers interested as incompatible with the status of a protectorate of those parts of the Madrid Convention which relate to protégés and "associés agricoles." M. de Kiderlen Waechter wishes to limit the projet de convention with France to a stipulation for a modification of those provisions which M. de Selves argues would be an admission that the system is to be continued in some form.

M. de Kiderlen-Waechter desires in the case of iron ore to limit the tax on it to 3 per cent. *ad valorem.* M. de Selves points out that though article 49 of the projet de règlement agreed on by the delegates at Paris in 1910 fixed the tax or royalty at that rate, the protocol of the conference signed by the German delegate expressed the opinion that such tax might be increased for certain purposes therein indicated, inclusive of providing means for the development and security of the country, in which the mining industry is specially interested (see Confidential Print, "Affairs of Morocco," part 41, 1910, p. 181, article 35, p. 184, article 49, and protocol of conference, p. 175, Roman number III, observation No. 3).

M. de Kiderlen-Waechter finds fault with the indiscretions and tone of the French press, which, he says, make it difficult for the German Government to make concessions to French views, and he complains that the French Government are always starting fresh hares, and have produced five successive projets de convention. M. de Selves has replied that there have been indiscretions in the German press which are embarrassing to the French Government, that the hares are hunted ones, and that if the German Government had acted up to their original attitude, viz., that in regard to Morocco they would accept a French protectorate in all but a name, provided that there were economic equality for all nations and free exportation of iron ore, there would only have been one French projet, viz., the first one, and that the four subsequent versions have been necessitated by the endeavours of the French Government to satisfy so far as possible the objections, observations, and demands from time to time made by M. de Kiderlen-Waechter in the course of the conversations at Berlin.

There was not time at yesterday's Cabinet Council to consider the last German objections. M. de Selves will submit them to his colleagues to-morrow.

([1]) [*v. supra,* pp. 558–9, No. 572.]

No. 578.

Sir E. Goschen to Sir Edward Grey.

F.O. 39452/25883/11/28.
(No. 309.) Secret.
Sir,

Berlin, D. *October 6, 1911.*
R. *October 9, 1911.*

On Tuesday last the Secretary of State for Foreign Affairs received the Ambassadors for the second time in the last two months. M. [Jules] Cambon attended the reception and after conversing with Herr von Kiderlen on the subject of the Italo-Turkish war, said that he hoped to see His Excellency again in a day or two when he would be in a position to communicate to him the result of the latest deliberations of the French Government on the subject of Morocco. Herr von Kiderlen replied that M. Cambon need hardly trouble himself to come for that purpose as he (Herr von Kiderlen) had already read the latest proposals of the French Government in the French press. Upon this, he handed to M. Cambon a number of French newspapers and the latter had to admit that as a matter of fact the statements in the newspapers corresponded exactly with the telegraphic summary which he had received, but which had not yet been confirmed in writing. Herr von Kiderlen said that these were the strangest negotiations in which he had ever been concerned, and that it was an unheard of thing that proposals should have been given to the French Press some days before they had been communicated to the Government to whom they were addressed, and before even their full text had reached the hands of the French representative who was conducting the negotiations.

In telling me of this my French colleague admitted that he had nothing to say in reply and that he had had nothing to do but beat a retreat as soon as he conveniently could, stating that in any case he would bring the text of the French answer as soon as it reached him and that he hoped it might, notwithstanding what Herr von Kiderlen had said, meet with a favourable reception.

M. Cambon received his written instructions on the 4th instant and immediately communicated them to Herr von Kiderlen. He came to see me on the following day, yesterday, and told me that Herr von Kiderlen had rejected the proposals contained in the French answer, saying that even if he had felt inclined to accept them, he could not do so as they had already been unfavourably discussed in the German Press. If he now accepted them he would be accused on all sides of sacrificing German interests and yielding to foreign pressure. "I have," he said to M. Cambon, "as I am sure you will admit, given way on many points and every time I make a concession you come back to me with some further demand. Several times we have both thought that everything was arranged and that only minor points and questions of *rédaction* remained, only to find that your Government was not yet satisfied. This cannot go on for ever, and the negotiations have already lasted far too long."

The result of the conversation was that Herr von Kiderlen refused to accept the latest proposals and even, in one case, so M. Cambon said, withdrew a concession which he had already made.

M. Cambon, in giving me this account of the conversation, said that he could not help feeling that there was a certain amount of justice in Herr von Kiderlen's remarks, and he added that he had reported in that sense to his Government.

My French colleague was rather depressed, but he seemed to have no doubts in his own mind but that an arrangement would finally be effected.

I asked M. Cambon whether he thought that the Tripoli question had in any way reacted unfavourably on the negotiations and contributed to Herr von Kiderlen's stiffness with regard to the latest French proposals. He said he thought not, as Herr von Kiderlen was too intelligent a man to be influenced by foolish Press talk to the effect that Italy's Tripoli undertaking had been instigated by England and France. His idea was that Herr von Kiderlen did not like the latest proposals and that their premature publication in the French Press had given him an opportunity to plead their unfavourable reception by German public opinion as a reason for rejecting them.

The report of the conversation as telegraphed to Paris by M. Cambon would seem to have had some effect; as to-day the Berlin newspapers, who have all along complained of Herr von Kiderlen's reticence with regard to the negotiations, are making it a grievance that the French Press has published nothing with regard to the outcome of the latest conversation between the two negotiators.

I have, &c.
W. E. GOSCHEN.

No. 579.

Sir V. Corbett to Sir Edward Grey.

F.O. 39726/25883/11/28.
(No. 62.) Confidential.   *Munich,* D. *October* 6, 1911.
Sir,   R. *October* 10, 1911.

The Bavarian Prime Minister and Minister for Foreign Affairs, Count Podewils has returned to Munich after a long holiday. I attended his first reception yesterday.

His Excellency informed me that he had had several letters from the Imperial Chancellor who seemed confident that the negotiations with France were in a fair way to a satisfactory issue as far as Morocco was concerned. I asked him if he thought that the compensations to be accorded to Germany would also be settled without undue difficulty. He said that as far as the two Governments were concerned, he thought that they would be but the question would then arise of their ratification by the French Chamber. The pourparlers had lasted so long that every man in the street in France now thought that he understood the whole African question and he feared that a considerable concession of French territory would encounter determined opposition.

He was naturally very guarded in what he said of the Imperial Foreign Office but in the course of a longish conversation I gathered that he thought Herr von Kiderlen had been precipitate in his action and had miscalculated the magnitude of the task before him. He had imagined that France could be rushed into an agreement and had been met by a calm consciousness of strength for which he was unprepared.

This is certainly the general opinion here and to the firmness of the French Government which is ascribed to the backing they receive from England, is no doubt due the bitterness of the present anti-British press campaign.

My French colleague told me confidentially yesterday that he had received a letter from M. Herbette, the Secretary-General to Monsieur de Selves, part of which he read out to me. Monsieur Herbette said that he anticipated the greatest difficulties when the Congo discussion came on, as nearly every French statesman of mark—and he cited some dozen of the most prominent names—had declared against any undue surrender of territory and especially against any attempt to cut off one half of the French central African possessions from the other.

Before leaving Count Podewils I said a few words on the subject of the forged report of Mr. McKenna's speech.([1]) It was deplorable, I observed, that absolute fabrications of this kind should be scattered broadcast throughout Germany. That journalists should give a false colouring to the utterances of those to whom they were antagonistic, was perhaps natural if disingenuous, but when it came to absolute barefaced forgeries, one was forced to believe that there was some central agency at work with the definite purpose of embroiling the two nations. I asked him if he thought that these false reports emanated from Berlin and he did not deny that it might be so. I said that as far as I knew, there was no natural ill-feeling against England in Bavaria but that it was not to be expected that the constant attacks of the "Münchener Neueste Nachrichten" and indeed of most of the South German papers could go on from day to day without producing some effect, among the most regrettable of which was that they goaded the English papers into making retaliatory attacks. Count Podewils said that he heartily agreed with me and that newspaper polemics were the curse of the age.

Whether in consequence of my conversation or of a spontaneous assertion of the editorial conscience I cannot say but the "Münchener Neueste Nachrichten" of this evening in allusion to a garbled version of Mr. McKinnon Wood's([2]) speech, observes :

> "The defective reporting of the speeches of English Ministers is gradually becoming a real danger in the way of preserving good relations between Great

([1]) [*v. infra*, pp. 648–55, Nos. 654–61.]
([2]) [At Glasgow, on September 29.]

Britain and Germany, of which a further example is afforded in the Wolff telegram concerning the speech delivered on Friday by the Under Secretary of State for Foreign Affairs.''

I have, &c.
VINCENT CORBETT.

No. 580.

Sir Edward Grey to Sir F. Bertie.

F.O. 39205/25883/11/28.
(No. 417.)

Sir,   *Foreign Office, October* 6, 1911.

The French Ambassador told me that the Vth Draft Agreement with Germany about Morocco had now been drawn up and he promised to send me a copy confidentially. It was expected that Herr von Kiderlen would accept it. I said that would dispose then of all the difficulties about the Morocco portion of the negotiations. Monsieur [Paul] Cambon assented but said there would remain the Congo question and a very strong feeling was growing up in France against large concessions to Germany and against anything that would cut the French Congo in two. This was rather embarrassing to the French Government but they hoped when it was made clear that they had got a good bargain in Morocco French public opinion would be calmed. I said I was sure public opinion here would be surprised if, when the French Government had virtually acquired a protectorate over Morocco, they were to refuse a considerable concession in the Congo. The general impression was that it was Germany who had got the worst of the negotiations and had been foiled in her object. Germany had made it appear as if she had aimed at a slice of Morocco. If the upshot of the negotiations was not only that Germany was excluded from Morocco but that France got beyond the Act of Algeciras and gained control over Morocco it would appear that Germany came second best out of the negotiations even if France did make a considerable concession in the French Congo; but I added that of course if Germany were now to spring upon France the demand for all the French Congo from the Sanga to the sea, which had been rejected long ago, everyone would suppose that Germany had repented of the Morocco part of the bargain now concluded and wished to upset it. The impression that Germany was getting less than she had expected was increased by the irritation and anger of the German press against England who were all writing as if Germany would have got much more from France had it not been for the attitude of England; indeed the idea was fostered in Germany that at the moment of the Chancellor of the Exchequer's speech Germany was on the point of concluding a bargain with France, though this was absolutely untrue. Monsieur Cambon said it would appear from what I had said that people thought Morocco worth more than the Congo. I said I thought in the public mind it was something like that.

[I am, &c.
E. GREY.]

No. 581.

Foreign Office to Admiralty.

F.O. 38006/38006/11/28.

Sir,   *Foreign Office, October* 6, 1911.

In Article VII of the Anglo-French Declaration of April 8th, 1904,(¹) to which Spain subsequently adhered, it is laid down that '' In order to secure the free passage of the Straits of Gibraltar the two Governments agree not to permit the erection of any fortifications or strategic works on that portion of the coast of Morocco comprised

(¹) [*v. Gooch & Temperley*, Vol. II, pp. 373–98, No. 417.]

between, but not including, Melilla and the heights which command the right bank of the River Sebou. This condition does not however apply to the places at present in the occupation of Spain on the Moorish coast of the Mediterranean."

The Franco-German negotiations now being conducted at Berlin will probably modify the existing state of things in Morocco and it has been suggested to Sir E. Grey that it might be advisable, in connection with these negotiations, to endeavour to obtain from the French Gov[ernmen]t a formal undertaking that no part of the Atlantic coast of Morocco south of the Sebou River shall ever be fortified.

Before taking a definite decision in the matter Sir E. Grey requests that he may be favoured with the reasoned opinion of the Lords Commissioners of the Admiralty on the value and importance to this country of any such undertaking on the part of France.

A similar letter has been addressed to the War Office.

[I am, &c.

F. A. CAMPBELL.]

No. 582.

Sir F. Bertie to Sir A. Nicolson.

F.O. 38006/38006/11/28.
Private.

My dear Nicolson,   *Paris, October* 7, 1911.

In your letter of the 5th([1]) which I received yesterday evening you say *à propos* of my despatch No. 422 of September 28th([2]) that you think that " we should keep the question of any territorial exchanges as a question by itself and not to hang on to it any discussions in regard to fortifications on the Morocco coast. An opportunity of speaking to France on the latter question would, I think be more appropriately offered when they submitted for our consent their agreement with Germany, and when we should have to see that certain questions, such as the internationalisation of Tangier, and other matters of interest to us, were properly arranged."

The French have kept us informed, and very fully so, of their negotiations at Berlin. If we see objection to any of the concessions which they are receiving from the Germans or are making to them in Morocco we should speak now and not put off our observations until the conclusion of the negotiations and after the signature of the Agreement with Germany. Moreover unless in such Agreement there be anything to the advantage of France beyond what has been contemplated and provided for in our 1904 Declarations we shall not be able to withhold our concurrence in whatever may have been agreed to between Germany and France. Therefore if, when our concurrence is asked, we endeavour to extract from the French an undertaking not to fortify any part of the Morocco Coast and the French refuse or demur we shall have no means of pressure; whereas if it were a matter of bargain in the territorial exchanges we could refuse the cession which they particularly desire in Nigeria to link up their territory North of that British Possession with their North Congo Colony, unless they agree amongst other undertakings and concessions not to fortify the Morocco Coast.

Yours ever,

FRANCIS BERTIE.

([1]) [Not reproduced.]
([2]) [*v. supra*, pp. 552–4, No. 567.]

No. 583.

Sir V. Corbett to Sir Edward Grey.

F.O. 39727/16083/11/28.
(No. 63.)   *Munich,* D. *October* 8, 1911.
Sir,   R. *October* 10, 1911.

The occult agency whose object it is to breed bad blood between Germany and England by perverted reports of the public utterances of British officials has not been idle during the last week. Mr. McKinnon Wood for instance is represented as saying that "foreign journalists had heedlessly reproached England for adopting an attitude of hostility towards the Secret Agreement between Germany and France."

With regard to Mr. Winston Churchill's speeches which seem to have been reported with tolerable accuracy the "Münchener Neueste Nachrichten" observes :

"English Ministers in union with the Press are seeking with remarkable assiduity to efface the evil and lasting impression, we might say the embitterment, which was called forth in Germany by the interference of Great Britain in the Germano-French Morocco negotiations. These effects of the British policy may perhaps be felt to be particularly disagreeable at the present moment in view of the conflict over Tripoli. Politicians behave suddenly as though England had never troubled the waters to the least degree and desired nothing more earnestly than that Germany and France should clasp one another to their arms in thoroughly brotherly fashion."

Further on with reference to the same subject it says :

"This defence of the British policy, which evades notorious facts with inimitable grace and in a word presupposes on our side an unpardonably bad memory, will be received in Germany with the cool reserve that is due. No supplementary assurance of loyalty, be it ever so fine, will be able to rob us of the conviction that a lasting Germano-French agreement, should one come into existence, will have been achieved rather in defiance of than thanks to the policy of Sir Edward Grey."

Sir Frank Lascelles's friendly words are reported generally without special comment. The "Münchener Zeitung" however after reporting the speeches of Sir Frank and of the Home Secretary adds the following sympathetic sentence :

"In spite of this recognition matters will hardly change, for the campaign of lies carried on by the English and French Press against Germany will never cease."

I have, &c.
VINCENT CORBETT.

No. 584.

Sir F. Bertie to Sir Edward Grey.

F.O. 39707/38932/11/28.
(No. 437.)   *Paris,* D. *October* 8, 1911.
Sir,   R. *October* 10, 1911.

I have the honour to transmit to you herewith, with reference to my despatch No. 431 of the 4th instant,([1]) copy of a communication from Monsieur de Selves in which His Excellency states that, in accordance with Article II of the Secret Anglo-French Agreement of 1904, the French Government will, when Consular jurisdiction

---

([1]) [*v. supra,* pp. 560–1, No. 575, and *encl.*]

shall have been abolished in Morocco, give their support to His Majesty's Government for the adoption of a similar reform in Egypt.

I have, &c.
FRANCIS BERTIE.

Enclosure in No. 584.

Note communicated to Sir F. Bertie by M. de Selves.

Le Ministre des Affaires Étrangères remercie Son Excellence Sir Francis Bertie de la communication qu'il a bien voulu lui faire le 4 de ce mois et aux termes de laquelle le gouvernement de Sa Majesté britannique n'est pas opposé à l'établissement au Maroc par le gouvernement français de tribunaux qui n'auraient pas le caractère de tribunaux mixtes, mais réclame le concours du gouvernement français pour opérer, quand la juridiction consulaire aurait été abolie au Maroc, un changement analogue en Egypte.

En réponse à cette communication, M. de Selves a l'honneur de faire savoir à Son Excellence l'Ambassadeur de Grande Bretagne que, conformément au deuxième des articles secrets de la Convention franco-anglaise du 8 avril 1904,(2) le gouvernement français, le jour où la juridiction consulaire serait abolie au Maroc, prêterait son concours au Gouvernement britannique pour l'introduction en Egypte d'une réforme semblable.

Paris, le 7 octobre, 1911.

(2) [v. Gooch & Temperley, Vol. II, pp. 373–98, No. 417.]

No. 585.

Lord Granville to Sir Edward Grey.

Berlin, October 9, 1911.
D. 1·35 P.M.
R. 2·50 P.M.

F.O. 39688/25883/11/28.
Tel. (No. 82.)
Morocco.

French Ambassador had two conversations with S[ecretary] of S[tate] for Foreign Affairs yesterday. Provided French Government agree to very slight modification, which he thinks certain, he considers Morocco agreement concluded. He expects answer of his Government to-morrow.

No. 586.

Sir F. Bertie to Sir Edward Grey.

(By Post.)

F.O. 39882/25883/11/28.
Tel. (No. 168.) *En clair.*

Paris, D. October 10, 1911.
R. October 11, 1911.

My Telegram No. 166 of the 6th instant.(1)

M. de Selves has informed me this evening that the French Ambassador at Berlin reports that M. de Kiderlen Wächter is prepared to state in a Note with regard to the "modification" of the Madrid Convention that the German Government will not oppose its abrogation if the Powers are in favour of such abrogation. M. de

(1) [v. supra, p. 562, No. 577.]

Kiderlen Wächter further consents to a revision of the lists of protégés and associés agricoles, and he gives way on the other points at issue.

M. de Selves has instructed M. Jules Cambon to obtain written confirmation of M. de Kiderlen Wächter's assurances and if they be forthcoming they will be submitted to the French Cabinet and he hopes that the controversy in regard to the Morocco part of the negotiations may be considered as at an end.

No. 587.

Lord Granville to Sir Edward Grey.

F.O. 40002/25883/11/28.
Tel. (No. 86.) R.
Morocco.

Berlin, October 11, 1911.
D. 6·50 P.M.
R. 8 P.M.

French Ambassador and Secretary of State for Foreign Affairs signed this morning, *ne varietur*, final draft of the Morocco convention, which French Ambassador assures me amounts to giving France the protectorate. (End of R.)

(Secret.)

French Ambassador has shown me the signed text in strict confidence, and asked, me not to report more than the above, as he had no instructions to show it to me, and he was very anxious that his Government should not know that he had done so. So far as I could judge by reading it once, there seems [*sic*] to be but few and unimportant changes from the text given in Sir F. Bertie's despatch No. 417.(¹)

French Ambassador is now drafting form of secret notes to be exchanged regarding reference to Hague Arbitration Court "and other points." He is entirely satisfied with final text.

(¹) [*v. supra*, pp. 549–52, No. 566.]

No. 588.

Sir F. Bertie to Sir Edward Grey.

F.O. 40614/37068/11/28.
(No. 444.) Confidential.
Sir,

Paris, D. October 15, 1911.
R. *October 16, 1911.*

I had an interview with M. de Selves yesterday afternoon in order to carry out the instructions contained in your Despatch No. 409 of the 4th instant(¹) which I had the honour to receive on the evening of the 6th : I deferred acting on those instructions until yesterday as the papers referred to in them did not reach me until the evening of the 13th.

I said to His Excellency that I knew it to be the intention of the French Government that there should be complete commercial equality in Morocco, but there was a passage in the Note which it was proposed that the French Ambassador at Berlin should address to the German Minister for Foreign Affairs and which had been communicated to you by the French Embassy, which might give rise to misunderstandings in the future. I then showed to M. de Selves the passage in question viz : " Le Gouvernement allemand renonçant à demander la détermination de parts à faire à l'industrie allemande dans la construction des chemins de fer, je

(¹) [*v. supra*, p. 561, No. 576.]

puis vous assurer que le Gouvernement français verra toujours volontiers des associations d'intérêt se produire entre les nationaux de nos deux pays." The French Government of course meant thereby to convey what His Majesty's Government understand the new Franco-German Convention to intend viz. : that all the Powers shall be on the same footing as regards industrial enterprises in Morocco, but it would be well that there should be no doubt about it.

M. de Selves reminded me that M. de Kiderlen Wächter had endeavoured to obtain from the French Government acquiescence in a species of Franco-German Condominium. He had refused. M. de Kiderlen had then proposed that in the exchange of Notes there should be a declaration that "les deux Gouvernements s'accorderont pour qu'il y aient des associations d'intérêt entre les nationaux des deux pays." M. de Selves had regarded this formula as an obligation for the two Governments to combine for the establishment of such association and he had rejected it. He had informed the French Ambassador that the French Government would offer no opposition to such combinations if French financiers desired to form them but the Government would not take upon itself to establish them or bring them about. It must be left to the financiers to do as they might deem advisable. The passage to which I had called his attention had been drafted with the view of carrying out that intention. There was no purpose of favouring German enterprise in preference to that of any other nationality.

I suggested to M. de Selves that the best way of obviating any question in the future as to the proper interpretation of the passage would be for him to address to me an explanatory Note in reply to the Memorandum which I gave to him and of which I inclose a copy herein. This His Excellency said he would willingly do and I have the satisfaction of transmitting to you herewith a copy of the Note which M. de Selves has, in accordance with his promise, addressed to me to-day.

I have, &c.
FRANCIS BERTIE.

Enclosure 1 in No. 588.

Memorandum.

The French Ambassador in London communicated confidentially to Sir Edward Grey a copy of the despatch which Monsieur de Selves addressed to M. Jules Cambon on the 22nd ultimo on the subject of the Franco-German negotiations respecting Morocco.([2]) Annexed to this despatch are draft Notes to be exchanged between M. de Kiderlen-Waechter and M. Jules Cambon dealing with certain points not specified in the proposed Franco-German Convention.

In the draft Note from M. Jules Cambon to M. de Kiderlen-Waechter the following passage occurs :—

"Le Gouvernement allemand renonçant à demander la détermination de parts à faire à l'industrie allemande dans la construction des chemins de fer, je puis vous assurer que le Gouvernement français verra toujours volontiers des associations d'intérêt se produire entre les nationaux des [sic] deux pays."([3])

Sir Edward Grey has instructed Sir Francis Bertie to inform M. de Selves that, as the passage quoted above may possibly give rise to misunderstandings in the future, His Majesty's Government understand that, by the new Franco-German Convention, all the Powers will be on the same footing as regards industrial enterprizes in Morocco, and that the words "verra toujours volontiers des associations d'intérêt se produire entre les nationaux de nos deux pays" are to be so construed.

British Embassy, Paris, October 14th, 1911.

([2]) [*v. supra*, pp. 546–9, No. 565.]
([3]) [*v. supra*, pp. 548–9, No. 565. In M. Jules Cambon's note the wording was " *nos* deux pays"; in Herr von Kiderlen-Waechter's note, " *des* deux pays."]

Enclosure 2 in No. 588.

M. de Selves to Sir F. Bertie.

M. l'Ambassadeur,   *Paris, le 15 Octobre* 1911.

En réponse à la note de Votre Excellence en date d'hier, j'ai l'honneur de Vous faire savoir que le texte communiqué à Sir Edward Grey par M. Paul Cambon ne doit pas être interprété comme impliquant une inégalité quelconque dans la situation des ressortissants des diverses Puissances en regard des entreprises industrielles au Maroc.

Les lettres échangées entre M. de Kiderlen et M. l'Ambassadeur de France à Berlin ne comportent de la part du Gouvernement français, en ce qui concerne la construction des chemins de fer au Maroc, aucun autre engagement que celui de ne point mettre obstacle aux projets des entrepreneurs ou concessionnaires français qui désireraient prendre pour associés des sujets allemands. La liberté pour ces mêmes entrepreneurs ou concessionnaires de choisir des associés de toute autre nationalité reste entière.

Je m'empresse de vous donner cette assurance, en vous priant de la transmettre à Votre Gouvernement.

Agréez, &c.
J. DE SELVES.

No. 589.

Sir F. Bertie to Sir Edward Grey.

F.O. 40798/25583/11/28.
(No. 449.)   Confidential.   *Paris,* D. *October* 16, 1911.
Sir,   R. *October* 17, 1911.

I have the honour to transmit to you herewith a copy, which M. de Selves allowed to be taken by a Secretary of this Embassy, of the latest, the sixth, edition of the portion of the Franco-German Convention which relates to Morocco now in course of negotiation at Berlin between the French Ambassador and the German Foreign Secretary.

I have, &c.
FRANCIS BERTIE.

Enclosure in No. 589.

Sixth French Text of Portion of Franco-German Convention.

A la suite des troubles qui se sont produits au Maroc et qui ont démontré la nécessité d'y poursuivre, dans l'intérêt général, l'œuvre de pacification et de progrès prévue par l'Acte d'Algésiras, le gouvernement de la République française et le gouvernement impérial allemand ont jugé nécessaire de préciser et de compléter l'accord franco-allemand du 9 février 1909. Ils sont convenus, à cet effet, des dispositions ci-après :

ARTICLE I.

Le Gouvernement impérial allemand déclare que, ne poursuivant au Maroc que des intérêts économiques, il n'entravera pas l'action de la France en vue de prêter son assistance au Gouvernement marocain pour l'introduction de toutes les réformes administratives, judiciaires économiques, financières et militaires dont il a besoin pour le bon gouvernement de l'Empire, comme aussi pour tous les règlements nouveaux et les modifications aux règlements existants, que ces réformes comportent. En conséquence, il donne son adhésion aux mesures de réorganisation, de contrôle et de garantie financière que, après accord avec le gouvernement marocain, le gouvernement français croira devoir prendre à cet effet sous la réserve que l'action de la France sauvegardera au Maroc l'égalité économique entre les nations.

Au cas où la France serait amenée à préciser et à étendre son contrôle et sa protection, le gouvernement impérial allemand reconnaissant pleine liberté d'action à la France, et sous la réserve que la liberté commerciale prévue par les traités antérieurs sera maintenue n'y apportera aucun obstacle.

Il est entendu qu'il ne sera porté aucune entrave aux droits et action de la Banque d'Etat du Maroc tels qu'ils ont été définis par l'Acte d'Algésiras.

Article II.

Dans cet ordre d'idées, il est entendu que le gouvernement impérial ne fera pas obstacle à ce que la France, après accord avec le gouvernement marocain, procède aux occupations militaires du territoire marocain qu'elle jugera nécessaire au maintien de l'ordre et de la sécurité des transactions commerciales, et à ce qu'elle exerce toute action de police sur terre et dans les eaux marocaines.

Article III.

Dès à présent, si Sa Majesté le Sultan du Maroc venait à confier aux agents diplomatiques et consulaires de la France la représentation et la protection des sujets et des intérêts marocains à l'étranger, le gouvernement impérial déclare qu'il n'y fera pas d'objection.

Si d'autre part, Sa Majesté le Sultan du Maroc confiait au représentant de la France près du Gouvernement marocain le soin d'être son intermédiaire auprès des représentants étrangers, le gouvernement allemand n'y ferait pas d'objection.

Article IV.

Le Gouvernement français déclare que, fermement attaché au principe de la liberté commerciale au Maroc, il ne se prêtera à aucune inégalité pas plus dans l'établissement des droits de douane, impôts et autres taxes que dans l'établissement des tarifs de transport par voie ferrée, voie de navigation fluviale ou toute autre voie et notamment dans toutes les questions de transit.

Le Gouvernement français s'emploiera également auprès du gouvernement marocain afin d'empêcher tout traitement différentiel entre les ressortissants des différentes Puissances; il s'opposera notamment à toute mesure, par exemple à la promulgation d'ordonnances administratives sur les poids et mesures, de jaugeage, de poinçonnage &c....([1]) qui pourrait mettre en état d'infériorité les marchandises d'une Puissance.

Le Gouvernement français s'engage à user de son influence sur la Banque d'Etat pour que celle-ci confère à tour de rôle aux membres de sa direction à Tanger les postes de délégué dont elle dispose à la Commission des valeurs douanières et au Comité permanent des douanes.

Article V.

Le gouvernement français veillera à ce qu'il ne soit perçu au Maroc aucun droit d'exportation sur le minerai de fer exporté des ports marocains. Les exploitations de minerai de fer ne subiront ni sur leur production ni sur leurs moyens de travail aucun impôt spécial.

Elles ne supporteront en dehors des impôts généraux qu'une redevance fixe calculée par hectare et par an et une redevance proportionnée au produit brut de l'extraction. Ces redevances qui seront assises conformément aux articles 35 et 49 du projet de règlement minier annexé au Protocole du 7 juin 1910 de la Conférence de Paris seront également supportées par toutes les entreprises minières

([1]) [Thus in original.]

Le gouvernement français veillera à ce que les taxes minières soient régulièrement perçues sans que des remises individuelles du total ou d'une partie de ces taxes puissent être consenties sous quelque prétexte que ce soit.

ARTICLE VI.

Le Gouvernement de la République française s'engage à veiller à ce que les travaux et fournitures nécessités par les concessions éventuelles de routes, chemins de fer, ports, télégraphes, &c....(¹) soient octroyés par le gouvernement marocain suivant les règles de l'adjudication.

Il s'engage également à veiller à ce que les conditions de ces adjudications, particulièrement en ce qui concerne les fournitures de matériel et les délais impartis pour soumissionner, ne placent les ressortissants d'aucune Puissance dans une situation d'infériorité.

L'exploitation des grandes entreprises mentionnées ci-dessus sera réservée à l'état marocain ou librement concédée par lui à des tiers qui pourront être chargés de fournir les fonds nécessaires à cet effet. Le gouvernement français veillera à ce que, dans l'exploitation des chemins de fer et autres moyens de transport comme dans l'application des règlements destinés à assurer celle-ci, aucune différence de traitement ne soit faite entre les ressortissants des diverses Puissances qui useraient de ces moyens de transport.

Le gouvernement de la République usera de son influence sur la Banque d'Etat afin que celle-ci confère à tour de rôle aux membres de sa direction à Tanger le poste dont elle dispose de délégué à la Commission générale des adjudications et marchés.

De même le gouvernement français s'emploiera auprès du gouvernement marocain pour que, tant que restera en vigueur l'article 66 de l'Acte d'Algésiras il confie à un ressortissant d'une des Puissances représentées au Maroc un des trois postes de délégués chérifiens au Comité spécial des travaux publics.

ARTICLE VII.

Le gouvernement français s'emploiera auprès du gouvernement marocain pour que les propriétaires de mines et d'autres exploitations industrielles ou agricoles sans distinction de nationalité et en conformité des règlements qui seront édictés en s'inspirant de la législation française sur la matière puissent être autorisés à créer des chemins de fer d'exploitation destinés à relier leur centre de production aux lignes d'intérêt général et aux ports.

ARTICLE VIII.

Il sera présenté tous les ans un rapport sur l'exploitation des chemins de fer au Maroc qui sera établi dans les mêmes formes et conditions que les rapports présentés aux assemblées d'actionnaires des sociétés de chemins de fer françaises.

Le gouvernement de la République chargera un des administrateurs de la Banque d'Etat de l'établissement de ce rapport qui sera avec les éléments qui en seront la base communiqué aux censeurs puis rendu public avec s'il y a lieu les observations que ces derniers croiront devoir y joindre d'après leurs propres renseignements.

ARTICLE IX.

Pour éviter autant que possible les réclamations diplomatiques le gouvernement français s'emploiera auprès du Gouvernement marocain afin que celui-ci défère à un arbitre désigné *ad hoc* pour chaque affaire d'un commun accord par le Consul de France et par celui de la Puissance intéressée ou, à leur défaut, par les deux Gouvernements les plaintes portées par des ressortissants étrangers contre les autorités marocaines ou les personnes agissant en tant qu'autorités marocaines et qui

(¹) [Thus in original.]

n'auraient pu être réglées par l'intermédiaire du consul français et du Consul du Gouvernement intéressé.

Cette procédure restera en vigueur jusqu'au jour où aura été institué un régime judiciaire inspiré des règles générales de législation des Puissances intéressées et destiné à remplacer après entente avec elles les tribunaux consulaires.

Article X.

Le Gouvernement français veillera à ce que les ressortissants étrangers continuent à jouir du droit de pêche dans les eaux et ports marocains.

Article XI.

Le gouvernement français s'emploiera auprès du gouvernement marocain pour que celui-ci ouvre au commerce étranger de nouveaux ports au fur et à mesure des besoins de ce commerce.

Article XII.

Pour répondre à une demande du Gouvernement marocain les deux Gouvernements s'engagent à provoquer la révision d'accord avec les autres Puissances et sur la base de la Convention de Madrid des listes et de la situation des protégés étrangers et des associés agricoles au Maroc dont parlent les articles 8 et 16 de cette convention.

Ils conviennent également de poursuivre auprès des Puissances signataires toutes les modifications de la Convention de Madrid que comportera le moment venu le changement du régime des protégés et associés agricoles.

Article XIII.

Toutes clauses d'accord, convention, traité, ou règlement qui seraient contraires aux précédentes stipulations sont et demeurent abrogées.

Article XIV.

Le présent accord sera communiqué aux autres Puissances signataires de l'acte d'Algésiras près desquelles les deux Gouvernements s'engagent à se prêter mutuellement appui pour obtenir leur adhésion.([2])

([2]) [A minute by Mr. Villiers was written on this draft convention. It is not reproduced as it is little more than an analysis of the convention, and is referred to and its substance given *infra*, p. 608, No. 619, *min.* and *note* ([6]).]

No. 590.

Minute by Sir A. Nicolson.

F.O. 41801/13751/11/28.

Sir Edward Grey, *Foreign Office, October 18, 1911.*

M. [Paul] Cambon called this afternoon. He said that the opposition in France in regard to the Congo question was very considerable, but nevertheless he thought that an arrangement with Germany would be reached in two or three weeks time.

He told me that M. de Selves had spoken to him as to the arrangement which would have to be subsequently made with Spain. It seemed to M. de Selves that a curious and unprecedented situation would be created by the Sultan being nominally overlord of Morocco, two portions of which would be under the protectorate of two different foreign countries. He foresaw that there would be great difficulty in arranging so that there should be no friction and overlapping between the French and Spanish administrations of the respective spheres. M. de Selves thought that the simplest plan would be to hand over entirely to Spain in absolute tenure her sphere : in short let her annex it. M. Cambon thought that the Sultan would never consent to such a cession. What did I think?

I told him that it was difficult to give a reply without reflection, but I had a priori some doubts as to whether the Sultan would be quite intractable on the point. He would, I thought, not very clearly distinguish between a Protectorate and an abandonment of a portion of his country, his sovereignty would he might consider in reality, suffer almost as much in the one case as in the other. Moreover the Spanish zone was situated in great part in a portion of Morocco over which the authority of the Sultan was rather shadowy. But I could not answer his enquiry off hand, there were the tribes to consider and also other Powers. At the same time I could quite see the inconveniences of two foreign protectorates in one country and under one nominal sovereign.

A. N.

Annexation would put an end to consular jurisdiction in the Spanish sphere. We could not give that up unconditionally.

E. G.

No. 591.

Sir F. Bertie to Sir Edward Grey.

(By Post.)

F.O. 41081/25883/11/28.   *Paris,* D. *October* 18, 1911.
Tel. (No. 175.) *En clair.*   R. *October* 19, 1911.

M. de Selves informs me this evening that the negotiations at Berlin have not made much progress.([1]) M. de Kiderlen-Waechter is very uncompromising. He says that owing to public opinion in Germany he cannot cede the whole of the Bec du Canard, and he presses for the " coupure " in the French Congo, which was offered only on the supposition that the French Government were to obtain the Bec du Canard and a rectification of frontier at the expense of German Togoland ; and that France was to have the free hand in Morocco contemplated in the early edition of the French projet de convention, from which there have since been derogations at the instance of the German Government.

([1]) [His views were also recorded by Herr von Schoen on this day, *v. G.P.* XXIX, p. 400.]

No. 592.

Sir E. Goschen to Sir Edward Grey.

Berlin, October 19, 1911.

F.O. 41209/25883/11/28.   D. 7·20 P.M.
Tel. (No. 90.) Confidential.   R. 9 P.M.

Morocco.

After four days of apparently hopeless negotiations, French Ambassador made a personal suggestion on his own initiative yesterday morning which would give Germany point of contact on the Ubanghi and Congo. Secretary of State for Foreign Affairs consulted the Chancellor and accepted it late last night. French Minister for Foreign Affairs has telegraphed to-day that this seems a possible basis for negotiations, and that he will submit it to the Cabinet to-morrow. M. Cambon expects considerable further negotiations, but hopes that with basis thus formed agreement will be reached.

No. 593.

Sir F. Bertie to Sir Edward Grey.

F.O. 41224/13751/11/28.
(No. 451.) Confidential.   *Paris,* D. *October* 19, 1911.
Sir,   R. *October* 20, 1911.

After M. de Selves had given me the information in regard to the negotiations at Berlin concerning the cessions to be made to Germany in the French Congo which I reported to you in my telegram No. 175 of yesterday evening,(¹) His Excellency said that he had thought much over the arrangements to be made with Spain after the conclusion of the French negotiations with the German Government supposing that they had a successful issue which he earnestly hoped. If lines defining the limits of the Spanish zones in Morocco were negotiated, what would be the position of the Spanish Government in relation to the Sultan? If Morocco came under the protectorate of France it would be for the French Government to advise him: and in matters relating to the parts of his dominions within the Spanish zones the advice tendered to His Majesty by the French Government might, in the opinion of the Spanish Government, not be in accordance with Spanish interests and in any case for the Spanish authorities to have to carry out measures suggested to the Sultan by French advisers might be hurtful to Spanish *amour propre*. It had been suggested that a Spanish Commissioner might be appointed to advise the Sultan on matters concerning the Spanish zones, but this would hardly be consistent with the position of Morocco under the protectorate of France, and her consequent responsibility to foreign Powers. These were only instances of the many difficulties which would be caused by Spain occupying the position of a species of *succursale* in the French protectorate of Morocco. It had therefore, M. de Selves said, occurred to him that a solution of these difficulties might be that Spain should have the absolute cession of and sovereignty over certain portions of Morocco to be defined by Convention supposing the Sultan could be persuaded to consent to such an arrangement. M. de Selves said that he would not propose it if His Majesty's Government would object, but he would be glad if I could ascertain their views on the subject.

I told M. de Selves that I had no idea what His Majesty's Government might think of such a solution of the undoubted difficulties in a definition of the position in relation to the Sultan of a Spanish occupation and administration of portions of Morocco, but I had noticed that in the draft convention to be discussed with the Spanish Government which he had been good enough to communicate to me(²) there was no stipulation, as there had been in the Franco-Spanish Convention of 1904, that no part of the Spanish zones were to be in any way alienated to a foreign power. M. de Selves replied that this was an omission of which he had been made aware and which would be corrected. The draft Convention had been sent to the French Ambassador for his information only. It had not been communicated to the Spanish Government. His Excellency asked me to receive M. Regnault to explain what his ideas were in regard to possible and satisfactory arrangements with Spain. I am to see M. Regnault to-day.

I have, &c.
FRANCIS BERTIE.

MINUTES.

Clearly we must await further particulars. I am rather doubtful whether the proposed cession by the Sultan to Spain in full sovereignty could be negotiated without considerable difficulty, especially at Berlin. On the other hand there would, I conceive, be no difficulty in our obtaining from Spain binding engagements not to alienate or to fortify the coast, and not to impose differential treatment on British commerce.

The particular difficulties which have impressed M. de Selves do not appear to me to be inherent in a Spanish protectorate as against Spanish annexation. It might be possible to follow

(¹) [*v. supra*, p. 575, No. 591.]
(²) [*v. supra*, pp. 494–7, No. 525, *encl.*]

the precedent of Cyprus and allow Spain to " occupy and administer " the regions comprised within their sphere. This would absolutely exclude any interference whatever on the part of the Sultan with the occupied territory. There might also be other possible solutions. In any case it must remain doubtful whether Spain would be content to accept a mere strip on the Mediterranean coast. She will be most reluctant to leave Alcazar and Laraiche.

E. A. C.
Oct. 20.

We could no doubt obtain from Spain engagements as to alienation, fortification and differentiation, but these might not satisfy Germany, and a Protectorate in name with freedom to administer as she chooses would appear to be a less risky solution for Spain. It would of course suit France to cut down the Spanish zone to the narrowest limits, but it will be surprising if Spain agrees.

W. L.
A. N.

Annexation by Spain raises the questions of the open door and consular jurisdiction. I do not suppose Spain would agree to maintain either if she annexed and we and I suppose other Powers should demand a *quid pro quo* for giving up one or both of these.

Mr. Langley's suggestion may provide a solution.

E. G.

No. 594.

Sir M. de Bunsen to Sir Edward Grey.

F.O. 41711/13751/11/28.
(No. 173.)   Confidential.   *Madrid, D. October 19, 1911.*
Sir,   R. *October 23, 1911.*

The French Ambassador received a few days ago a telegram from Paris instructing him to inform the Spanish Government that, as the negotiations at Berlin are still proceeding, the French Government do not consider that the time has yet come to resume negotiations with Spain. This communication will no doubt cause disappointment to Señor Garcia Prieto, who was encouraged by reports received from the Spanish Ambassador in Paris to hope that negotiations would be opened at Madrid as soon as M. Jules Cambon and Herr Kiderlen-Waechter had come to terms concerning Morocco, and without waiting for the signature of the complete arrangements between France and Germany.

M. Geoffray is inclined to think that the hesitation of the French Government to embark on fresh negotiations with Spain is due, to a great extent, to the existence of divided counsels at Paris as to the nature of the arrangements to be made with this Government. M. de Selves himself is believed by His Excellency to be still disposed to offer a settlement on the lines of the Draft Convention, a copy of which was forwarded to you by Sir Francis Bertie in his despatch No. 386 Confidential of the 1st ultimo.(¹) On the other hand the French Ambassador gives me to understand that certain members of the French Cabinet have been won over to the views of the French Colonial Party, which desires to reduce the Spanish sphere of influence in Northern Morocco to much narrower limits than those marked out in the 1904 Convention. The French Minister of War is said to go as far as to advocate the complete exclusion of Spanish influence from Morocco, except within the limits of the ancient Spanish Presidios.

A new draft Convention seeking apparently to conciliate the views of the anti-Spanish group in the French Cabinet with those which were tentatively put forward by M. de Selves in the earlier draft, has now been received by M. Geoffray from the French Ministry for Foreign Affairs. It is, however, unaccompanied by any despatch, and His Excellency is left in doubt as to its paternity and as to the amount of support, which it is likely to receive from the French Cabinet as a whole.

(¹) [*v. supra,* pp. 494–7, No. 525, *encl.*]

[19656]   2 P

His Excellency had the goodness to allow me to read the document in question, which is to the following effect.

France and Spain, each within her zone, will assist the Moorish Government in the introduction of all necessary reforms, whether administrative, judicial, economic, financial and [sic] or military. But the regulations relating to such reforms are to be drawn up by the Makhzen itself; they will be of a general character, applicable to the whole of Morocco; no special arrangements relating to one or the other zone can be made without the previous consent of the Power exercising influence in that zone. The Regulations will be applied by the authorities of the Makhzen, under the control of French or Spanish agents according to the zone. The foregoing does not apply to the region adjoining the Algerian frontier, or to those near Melilla or Ceuta, in all of which the existing Conventions between Morocco, France and Spain respectively hold good. The line dividing the French and Spanish zones is drawn as in the Secret Convention of 1904, with a few unimportant variations. South of this line, the whole of Morocco falls within the French zone. With the consent of the Makhzen, either Power may send troops or police to any point within its zone, to maintain order and protect commerce. There are articles prohibiting new fortifications in the Spanish zone, and preserving the international character of Tangier. Existing French and Spanish schools, consulates and other establishments are to be reciprocally respected. Freedom of worship is guaranteed, as is also free passage between Tangier and Fez for all Moorish troops and convoys, for Moorish and foreign officials, and for all travellers bearing proper papers of identification. French and Spanish protection, Diplomatic and Consular, is accorded abroad to Moors hailing respectively from the French or Spanish zone. Neither Power will issue any fresh papers of protection to Moors. They agree to revise their lists of protected Moors in the spirit of the Madrid Convention of 1880. Eventually Consular jurisdiction will be surrendered in favour of a new Moorish judicial organisation. There shall be no interference with the service of control over the collection of revenues assigned to the 1904 and 1910 loans. Taxes and Customs surplus, after paying service of Debt and annuity due to the French Treasury, are assigned by the Moorish Minister of Finance to the separate budgets of the two zones, under the following headings :—

1. Sum for the Maintenance of the Sultan's Court and the central administration of the Makhzen, fixed at six millions of pesetas Hassani, 30% falling on the Spanish zone.
2. Sum for payment of the administrative and judicial personnel, as fixed by the Central Moorish Finance Department, on reports sent in by the local administrations.
3. Military expenses.
4. Public works. Credits fixed by the Moorish Minister of Public Works, according to the existing regulations.

All French and Spanish agents are selected and appointed by the Makhzen from lists of candidates submitted by the French and Spanish Governments respectively.

The $2\frac{1}{2}$ per cent. supplementary customs duty remains in the hands of the French Chief Engineer, who will delegate the Spanish Assistant Engineer to supervise Public Works in the Spanish sphere.

Customs and fiscal unity to be preserved throughout the Empire, with complete economic liberty and adherence to Articles 4, 5, 6, and 7 of the new Franco-German Convention. Railways and Telegraphs are to be under the Minister of Public Works, the Tangier–Fez Railway having the first claim to be constructed.

The present agreement supersedes all others.

Comparing this draft with the former one, it is clear that the new draft seeks to invest the central Government at Fez with full powers of administration over both the French and Spanish zones. The detailed financial arrangements are evidently designed to place the final decision with regard to public expenditure in either zone in the hands of the Moorish Minister of Finance, who will be in a position to accept or reject any of the proposals made to him by the local French or Spanish authorities. Obviously the result must be that the French Government, which will exercise its protectorate over the Sultan, would dictate to the latter the reply he should give to all representations emanating from the Spanish zone. Although, therefore, there is in these new proposals an appearance of equality between the administrative and controlling powers to be exercised by France and Spain in their respective zones, it is more than probable that, in practice, Spain would find herself, within her own zone, to be as much under the protection of France as the French officials in the French zone would be.

This, at all events, is the light in which the anonymous project which he has received from the Quai d'Orsay strikes M. Geoffray and he has reported accordingly to his Government. I agree with him in thinking that it would be rejected by the Spanish Government, whereas the earlier draft, of which, subject to an addition regarding fortifications, you have expressed your approval to the French Government, would very likely commend itself to the Spanish Government as forming a possible basis of the future relations between the French and Spanish zones in Morocco.

The question is, however, one of extraordinary difficulty. If the unity of Morocco is to be maintained, the action of the Central Government at Fez must necessarily extend to all parts of the Empire. But the Central Government cannot be exercised independently of the protecting influence of France. Thus French protection must indirectly pervade the whole country—the Spanish portion as well as the French portion. But no Spanish Government could recommend to the Cortes an arrangement by which there would be even an appearance of the Spanish zone in Morocco forming part of the French protectorate. Señor Garcia Prieto expressed to me his opinion a few days ago that the problem could only be solved by placing at Fez a Spanish agent whose advice concerning all matters in the Spanish zone the Sultan would be as much bound to take as the Khedive is bound to take the advice offered by the British Agent at Cairo. Or, he added, the Spanish Agent could be placed at Tangier on the understanding that the Sultan's representative at that port should be completely under his control. In either case, it seems to me that the Spanish and French zones would be under separate administrations; there would be two distinct Protectorates in Morocco, and the unity of the Empire would practically cease to exist.

I lately had some conversation on these questions with Señor Moret, the predecessor as Prime Minister of Señor Canalejas.

Señor Moret thinks it will be impossible to devise an arrangement under which France and Spain could get on peacefully side by side in Morocco, under the Franco-Moorish administration such as seems to be contemplated. He feels also that the Spanish sphere as defined in the 1904 Convention is much too large to be administered by Spain without an expenditure of money and energy which is beyond the resources of this country. He disapproves therefore of the Spanish occupation of Larache and Alcazar and would prefer to restrict the Spanish zone to a strip extending along the coast from Ceuta to the Muluya. But, as he can see no way of satisfactorily adjusting the relations between a zone of Spanish influence and a zone of French influence, he is convinced that the only practical solution of the difficulty would be for Spain to occupy her restricted zone in full possession and to govern it as a Spanish province, as France governs Algeria. By including Tetuan in the Spanish strip, His Excellency thinks that the bitterness of the withdrawal of the Spanish troops from Larache and Alcazar, which he holds to be necessary, would be to some extent counteracted. Tangier and its neighbourhood would, of course, remain internationalized.

Señor Moret's scheme in short is to extend over the whole of the said strip of coast the Spanish Sovereignty which has been exercised for centuries over certain strategic points within that strip. It should not be difficult, in his opinion, to draw a line inland which would give to Spain a reasonable amount of hinterland.

His Excellency has also spoken to the French Ambassador in this sense. To both of us, however, he added that his opinion could now be of no value, as his influence with the present Government is too slight to enable him even to put his views before them. In this I think His Excellency is right. Though there is wisdom in his suggestions, it is, I am afraid, out of the question that the Government of Señor Canalejas, which is so deeply committed to the occupation of Alcazar and Larache should entertain proposals for the evacuation of those places or for any material limitation of the long accepted limits of the Spanish zone.

Since writing the above, I have seen, by the courtesy of M. Geoffray, a telegram addressed yesterday to His Excellency by M. de Selves, stating that the French Government will now shortly send him instructions to resume negotiations with Spain, but that, before doing so, they propose to consult with His Majesty's Government as to the precise proposals which, under present circumstances, it would be expedient to make to the Spanish Government, the opinion of the French Government being that a proposal framed on the lines of the solution favoured by Señor Moret would best meet the existing situation. I have briefly reported the upshot of M. Geoffray's instructions in my telegram No. 79 of to-day.([2])

M. Geoffray has, I believe, replied that Señor Moret's scheme would certainly be rejected by Señor Canalejas; that neither the King nor the Spanish Army could accept it; that it would provoke, if put forward, a burst of indignation throughout the country; and that its immediate effect would probably be to cause Spain to appeal to Germany for protection against what she would describe as an act of spoliation. His Excellency still thinks that the wiser course is to concede to Spain the stipulated zone of influence; to submit to her a *modus vivendi* more or less in the terms of the Draft Convention first proposed by M. de Selves and accepted by you; and to leave it to time and experience to demonstrate to Spain the expediency of gradually restricting her action beyond the Straits of Gibraltar within narrower limits than those laid down in the Convention of 1904.

Meanwhile the failure, which is becoming more and more apparent, of the recent military operations on the Kert, has placed the Government of Señor Canalejas in a difficult position, and the blow which Spanish prestige has sustained in the Riff region is likely to make it more difficult than ever for the Prime Minister to consent to what he would regard as the further humiliation of a retreat from Alcazar and Larache.

The question of the proposals which should now be made by France to Spain is complicated by the fact that nothing definite is yet known as to the extent of territory in Southern Morocco to which Spain would consent to abandon her claims in consideration of a free hand in Northern Morocco. On this point Señor Garcia Prieto has only confided to me that, while accepting the principle of making some territorial sacrifice to France, the Spanish Government could not, in his opinion, surrender their treaty right to Ifni and the adjoining coast-line.

I have, &c.
MAURICE DE BUNSEN.

([2]) [Not reproduced.]

No. 595.

Sir M. de Bunsen to Sir Edward Grey.

F.O. 42494/13751/11/28.
(No. 175.) Confidential.
Sir,

Madrid, D. October 19, 1911.
R. *October* 28, 1911.

As the future arrangements concerning the status of Tangier are a matter of such great importance to His Majesty's Government, I have kept a copy of the articles relating to Tangier contained in the new draft Franco-Spanish convention, which forms the principal subject of my despatch No. 173 Confidential of to-day.(¹)

I have already reported that the French Ambassador was good enough to give me an opportunity of examining the document in question, which reached him without a covering despatch, but which His Excellency is disposed to regard as representing the views of at least a portion of the French Cabinet.

I have the honour to forward herewith copy of the articles in point.

I have, &c.
MAURICE DE BUNSEN.

Enclosure in No. 595.

Articles relating to Tangier contained in new Draft Franco-Spanish Convention.

ARTICLE VI.

Ne se trouve comprise dans aucune des deux zones la ville de Tanger, qui, conformément aux principes posés dans les accords de 1904 et 1905, sera administrée par une municipalité ayant un caractère international. Le territoire compris entre la mer, Sidi Kassem, Gouerch, Zinet, Merbon el Aich et la pointe Altarès sera déclaré territoire municipal de Tanger et placé également en dehors des deux zones.

La loi municipale de Tanger sera établie par le Makhzen d'accord avec les représentants des Puissances étrangères au Maroc.

Le délégué du Sultan à Tanger sera de droit le Président de la Municipalité. La police de la ville et du territoire municipal sera assurée par les forces actuelles de la police shérifienne, qui resteront composées, instruites et administrées d'après le règlement du [?] établi d'accord avec le Makhzen et le corps diplomatique.

Les frais d'armement, d'équipement, et d'entretien de cette force et des officiers, qui l'instruisent, seront prélevés sur le produit des impôts perçus à Tanger et sur le territoire municipal; le surplus sera partagé entre le budget municipal de Tanger et le Makhzen suivant les prescriptions du firman constituant la municipalité. Au cas où ces ressources se trouveraient insuffisantes pour pourvoir à l'entretien de la police, le déficit constaté serait imputé en fin d'exercice sur les disponibilités générales du Makhzen, et, à défaut, avancé par la Banque d'Etat du Maroc, sur le reliquat des perceptions douanières du port de Tanger, après toutefois que le service de la Dette marocaine aura été assuré.

ARTICLE VII.

La ville et le territoire municipal sont déclarés neutralisés et placés sous la garantie des deux Puissances signataires, qui, dès à présent, acceptent que cette garantie de neutralité soit partagée par l'Angleterre.

Il ne sera apporté à Tanger et dans les limites du territoire municipal sans l'assentiment préalable des Puissances signataires de la convention du 31 Mai, 1865, aucune modification au régime des phares et des feux intéressant la navigation.(²)

(¹) [*v.* immediately preceding document.]
(²) [Mr. G. H. Villiers wrote a long minute on this paper about the question of guaranteeing the internationalisation of Tangier, but Mr. W. Langley and Sir Arthur Nicolson declined to discuss it, " as it is not the proposal before us."]

No. 596.

Lord Granville to Sir Edward Grey.

F.O. 41581/25883/11/28.
(No. 331.) Confidential.   *Berlin,* D. *October* 20, 1911.
Sir,   R. *October* 23, 1911.

As I had the honour to report in my telegram No. 90 of yesterday,(¹) the French Ambassador informed me that the first four days' negotiations on the question of compensation for Germany in the French Congo had seemed absolutely hopeless; he

(¹) [*v. supra,* p. 575, No. 592.]

and Herr von Kiderlen had stood *nez à nez* and there did not appear to be any means of reconciling the views of the two Governments. At last on Wednesday morning M. [Jules] Cambon, on his own initiative, took a pencil and sketched on the map a rough outline which would give Germany a narrow strip running down to the Ubanghi and another to the Congo; Herr von Kiderlen agreed to submit this to the Imperial Chancellor and, when he again received M. Cambon late on Wednesday evening, he expressed his willingness to accept this solution. M. Cambon of course had to emphasize again the fact that the suggestion had only been his own and that his Government had not even seen it. His Excellency telegraphed it to M. de Selves that night and received an answer in the course of yesterday to the effect that his suggestion would be submitted to the Conseil des Ministres to-day and and that it seemed to form a possible basis for negotiations. M. Cambon considers that the possession by Germany of a few kilometres of the shores of the Ubanghi and Congo can hardly be looked upon, even by the extreme Colonial Chauvinists, as cutting off the upper part of the French possessions from the lower part and the sea. He is full of hope that the basis thus found will enable him to bring the negotiations to a successful conclusion, but he expects that his Government will hesitate a good deal and make further proposals before finally agreeing to this one.

There is very little worth reporting in the German Press. Rumours are printed as to the progress, or rather want of progress, of the negotiations, a few quotations are given from French newspapers, and the fact is insisted on that Germany cannot accept anything but very extensive compensation in the Congo. The Pan-German "Post" prints a fiery article maintaining that the Government are making a bad bargain in any case as no territory in tropical Africa, however extensive, is worth a share of Morocco : but if Morocco is to be given up entirely Germany ought to demand the whole of the French Congo, Dahomey and Madagascar; short of that the only solution which could be considered acceptable would be that Germany should receive from France the whole Congo Colony, including the Lake Chad and Ubanghi districts, together with France's right of pre-emption of Belgian Congo, and that she should at once arrange with Belgium for the purchase of the country North and East of the Congo, and that she should also at last obtain from Portugal the execution of the Delagoa Treaty. Otherwise the Reichstag should refuse the whole thing and Germany should return to the standpoint of insisting either on the withdrawal of all French and Spanish troops from Morocco or on the division of that country between France, Spain and Germany.

I have, &c.
GRANVILLE.

No. 597.

Sir F. Bertie to Sir Edward Grey.

(By Post.)

F.O. 41526/25883/11/28.   Paris, D. October 21, 1911.
Tel. (No. 177.) Confidential.   R. October 22, 1911.

M. de Selves informs me that an arrangement to get round the difficulty of the "coupure" is probable. A band of territory 4 kilom. wide would be conceded to Germany across French territory to the navigable part of the Ubanghi, in the vicinity of Bangui. This is to enable Germany to construct a railway from the Cameroons to the river, and the French could keep up communication between the two parts of French Congo by the river. It is thought that the German aim is to build a railway through the northern part of Belgian Congo to German East Africa.

A give-and-take arrangement, involving exchanges of territory, is probable in regard to the Bec du Canard.

The Germans are to have both banks of the Sangha, and a small piece of territory south of it at one point.

All these questions are to be further discussed between the French Ambassador at Berlin and M. de Kiderlen-Waechter this evening.

No. 598.

Sir F. Bertie to Sir Edward Grey.

F.O. 41549/13751/11/28.

(No. 455.) Confidential.   *Paris,* D. *October* 21, 1911.

Sir,   R. *October* 23, 1911.

I have the honour to inform you with reference to my despatch No. 451 confidential, of the 19th instant([1]) that M. Regnault, the French Minister in Morocco came to see me on that day, in order to describe to me a scheme which M. de Selves thought might be a satisfactory solution of the problem of settling the respective positions of France and Spain in Morocco supposing that Morocco later on as a result of the present negotiations with Germany became a French Protectorate.

M. Regnault brought with him two documents of which I enclose copies herein. The first of these is entitled " Projet d'Accord Hispano-Marocain " and the other " Déclaration Française." Some of the articles in the Hispano-Moorish agreement are only in outline, but their general object is that Spain should have the absolute cession of and sovereignty over certain portions of Morocco, in return for which she would consent to renounce any pretensions to exert her influence over any other portion of the Sultan's dominions. M. Regnault left with me two maps illustrating the French proposals, which I have the honour to forward to you herewith.([2]) These proposals are based on the idea that the Spanish possessions in Morocco should be delimited not by conventional lines such as were laid down for the Spanish zones by the Franco-Spanish agreement of 1904, but by the natural lines of the water-parting between the Mediterranean and Atlantic. Roughly speaking under the new proposals the basins of the rivers which flow into the Mediterranean with the exception of the upper valleys of the Moulouya, which are to remain under the sovereignty of the Sultan, will belong to Spain, while the Moorish Government or, in other words the French Government will have exclusive control over the basins of all rivers flowing into the Atlantic. The effect of this would be that the North-West corner of Morocco which has hitherto been in the Spanish zone, from a point south of Larache to Cape Al Kazar East of Tangier on the straits of Gibraltar, would come under the Protectorate of France.

Article I of the draft Hispano-Moorish Agreement defines the territory of the Mediterranean coast which the Sultan of Morocco is to cede to Spain. The frontier is to follow the left bank of the Moulouya from its mouth to the ford of Mechra-Sefa. From that point, the want of geographical knowledge of the mountainous Riff region and the insecure state of the country prevent an exact frontier line being laid down at the present time. The two Governments therefore adhere to the principle that the frontier shall follow the line of the water-parting in a westerly direction between the Mediterranean and Atlantic basins. After reaching the Fondak of Ain-Djedida the frontier line turns northward and follows the watershed between the Oued--Khemis, which flows into the Mediterranean, and the Oued-el-Kebir which flows into the Atlantic, and continuing along the watershed between the basins of the Oued Kazar and the Oued Lian reaches the shores of the straits of Gibraltar at Cape Al Kazar.

Article II stipulates that the town and territory of Tetuan shall remain subject to the Sovereignty of the Sultan. They are to be administered jointly by a Spanish High Commissioner and a Shereefian High Commissioner whose powers are to be

([1]) [*v. supra,* p. 576, No. 593.]
([2]) [Not reproduced.]

settled in accordance with the general principles of the Hispano-Moorish Treaty of November 17, 1910 (see confidential print "Affairs of Morocco" Part 41 p. 328). The territory in question is indicated in green on the map A accompanying this despatch.(³)

By article III the Sultan of Morocco cedes territory to Spain, to be delimited subsequently, consisting of a strip of coast between Oued Bou Cedra and Oued Kchich. This territory is indicated in red on map B which accompanies this despatch.(²)

By article IV Spain engages neither to alienate nor to cede in any form, or even temporarily, her rights over the whole of or in any portion of the territories mentioned in the preceding articles.

Article VI. In order to ensure the free passage of the straits of Gibraltar, Spain agrees not to allow any fortifications or strategical works of any kind, other than those already existing, to be erected on the part of the coast of Morocco between Melilla and Cape Al Kazar. The zone in question begins from a point on the coast 30 kilometers South-East of Melilla.

The "Déclaration Française" deals primarily with the question of Tangier. The first article lays down that the city of Tangier, in accordance with the Franco-Spanish Convention of 1904, shall be administered under the Sovereignty of the Sultan, by a municipal body having an international character. The Sultan's delegate at Tangier will be President of the body *ex officio*.

Articles II, III, and IV deal with the question of the police in Tangier and in the surrounding zone, the extent of which is to be determined by the firman by which the municipal organisation will be established.

Article V provides for the free passage through the district of Tangier of convoys destined for the Makhzen or for the Shereefian troops and of all foreigners who are provided with papers of identity.

By article VI the French Government undertakes, in order to ensure the free passage of the straits of Gibraltar to see that neither fortifications nor strategical works of any kind shall be constructed between Cape Al Kazar and the heights which dominate the right bank of the river Sebou.

M. Regnault after enlarging on the difficulty of carrying out in their entirety the arrangements contemplated in the Franco-Spanish Convention of 1904 gave me a summary description of the proposals set forth in the enclosed documents.

When I asked him what he thought would be the view taken by the Spanish Government of the scheme, he replied that Spain must be expected to make sacrifices to France in return for the improved position which she would occupy in Morocco through the territorial compensations to be given to Germany by France.

M. Regnault then enquired what I thought would be the view taken by His Majesty's Government of the proposals which he had described. I told him that I could not say what view His Majesty's Government would take of them, but in my personal opinion they would not be likely to concur in the substitution of France for Spain on the Atlantic Coast of Morocco. In reply to his enquiry as to my reason for the opinion which I had expressed, I observed that France was a first class naval power which Spain was not. He thereupon suggested that the Atlantic Coast in the occupation of Spain might be detrimental to British interests if Spain were in alliance with Germany. I replied that the British fleet came between Germany and Spain. M. Regnault did not pursue the subject. I told him that I would, as I had undertaken to M. de Selves, communicate the suggestions to you for your consideration.

This morning I saw M. de Selves for a few minutes on the subject of the Congo negotiations. He mentioned to me M. Regnault's communication and asked me what I thought of it and what I thought you would think of it. I said that I supposed that the suggestions were rather the ideas of M. Regnault than his own proposals and that they seemed to me to be a very great departure from the intentions of the 1904 arrangements which would be a large pill for His Majesty's Government to swallow. M. de Selves, without admitting that the suggestions were M. Regnault's

(³) [Not reproduced.]

ideas said that the proposals were only a sketch for your consideration. He would not put them forward without your concurrence for he desired to act entirely in unison with His Majesty's Government.

I have, &c.
FRANCIS BERTIE.

Enclosure in No. 598.

Projet d'Accord Hispano-Marocain.

ARTICLE 1er.

Le Sultan du Maroc cède à l'Espagne, sous la réserve indiquée à l'article 2, les Territoires du littoral de la Méditerranée limités par la ligne indiquée ci-après :—

La frontière suit la rive gauche de la Moulouya depuis son embouchure jusqu'au gué de Mechra-Sefa. A partir de ce point, l'absence de connaissances géographiques sur la région montagneuse du Rif et l'état d'insécurité du pays ne permettant pas de préciser, dès maintenant, un tracé, les deux Gouvernements s'en tiennent à ce principe, que la frontière gagnera par le parallèle du point et suivra la ligne de partage des eaux entre le bassin de la Méditerranée d'une part, et d'autre part, les vallées de la Moulouya, de l'oued Msoum, de l'oued Innaouen, du Sebou, du Lokkos, de leurs affluents et des bassins côtiers de l'Atlantique. Cette ligne aboutit au Fondak d'Aïn-Djedida.

Elle se dirige ensuite vers le nord en suivant la ligne de faîte entre les bassins de l'oued Khemis, sur le versant Méditerranéen, et celui de l'oued-el-Kebir sur le versant Atlantique; puis elle se continue par la ligne de faîte entre le bassin de l'oued Kazar d'une part et celui de l'oued Lian, d'autre part pour aboutir à la pointe Al Kazar sur le littoral du détroit de Gibraltar.

ARTICLE 2.

La ville et le territoire de Tetouan resteront soumis à la Souveraineté du Sultan. Ils seront administrés par un Haut Commissaire espagnol et un Haut Commissaire chérifien. Leurs pouvoirs seront déterminés d'après les principes généraux du traité Hispano-Marocain du 17 novembre 1910.

Ce territoire est délimité au Nord par une ligne partant du Cap Negro suivant la ligne de faîte des Montagnes Condia-Taïfou, Condia-bou-Zeguelet, pour aboutir au point le plus méridional du cours de l'oued-Smir et gagner par le parallèle de ce point le cours supérieur de l'oued-el-Khemis.

Elle descendra ensuite le thalweg de cette rivière jusqu'à son confluent avec l'oued Martil ou rivière de Tetouan. De ce point, elle remontra le thalweg de l'oued-el-Hayra jusqu'à son confluent avec l'oued-el-Nahla ou des Beni-Hassen.

Elle suivra ensuite jusqu'à la mer la ligne indiquée sur la carte ci-annexée,(⁴) de l'Etat-Major espagnol, comme étant la limite méridionale de la tribu des Beni-Hozmar.

ARTICLE 3.

Le Sultan du Maroc cède, en outre à l'Espagne un territoire qui sera délimité ultérieurement et qui comprendra une partie du littoral entre l'oued Bou-Cedra et l'oued Kchich. A l'intérieur du pays, cette possession s'étendra jusqu'au cours supérieur de l'oued Moul-el-Achar et de l'oued Asif-N'baga. Elle rejoindra de là le cours supérieur de l'oued bou-Cedra, conformément à la carte ci-annexée du service géographique de l'armée française.(⁴)

ARTICLE 4.

L'Espagne s'engage à n'aliéner ni à céder sous aucune forme, même à titre temporaire, ses droits dans tout ou partie des territoires indiqués aux articles précédents.

(⁴) [Not reproduced.]

Article 5.

Afin d'assurer le libre passage du détroit de Gibraltar, l'Espagne convient de ne pas laisser s'élever de fortifications ou d'ouvrages stratégiques quelconques, autres que ceux déjà existants sur la partie de la côte marocaine comprise entre Melilla et la pointe Al Kazar. La zone visée ci-dessus commence sur la côte à 30 kilomètres au sud-est de Melilla.

Article 6.

Il ne sera apporté aucune entrave sur la partie du territoire espagnol entre Tanger et Tetouan à la libre circulation des convois destinés au Maghzen, des fonctionnaires chérifiens ou des voyageurs de toute nationalité, avec leurs armes et bagages et munis de pièces d'identité, à la condition pour eux de se conformer au règlement chérifien sur le permis de port d'armes. Ils pourront être accompagnés d'escortes et de domestiques.

Article 7.

Le Gouvernement espagnol adhère pour ce qui concerne les territoires visés aux articles 1 et 3 du présent accord, aux dispositions des articles 4, 5, 6, 7 et 12 du projet d'accord franco-allemand.

Article 8.

Disposition à rédiger relative aux tarifs de douane qui, dans les territoires visés au présent accord devront rester fixés à 10% ad valorem et temporairement à $2\frac{1}{2}\%$ pour la Caisse spéciale.

Article 9.

Dispositions à rédiger relatives à l'affectation du produit des douanes, des droits miniers, et des impôts perçus dans les territoires visés au présent accord, à l'amortissement de l'indemnité prévue par les articles 13 et 14 de l'accord hispano-marocain de 1910.

Article 10.

Disposition a rédiger rela[t]ive à la répression réciproque de la contrebande douanière et de la contrebande des armes ou marchandises prohibées.

Article 11.

Les crédits ouverts par l'article 6 de l'Acte d'Algésiras pour la police des ports devant être épuisés au 1er janvier 1912, le Gouvernement marocain sera tenu d'assurer à partir de cette date, par ses propres moyens, la protection des ports. Il s'entendra avec l'Espagne en ce qui touche Tetouan et le territoire de cette ville pour l'organisation d'un corps de police marocain conformément aux principes généraux de la police des ports. L'effectif de cette troupe sera fixé à 300 hommes. Les frais d'armement, d'équipement et d'entretien en seront imputés sur le produit des impôts perçus dans le territoire soumis à l'action de la police.

Article 12.

Disposition à rédiger abrogeant les clauses contraires des traités, conventions, et accords antérieurs.

Enclosure 2 in No. 598.

Déclaration Française.

I.

La ville de Tanger, conformément à l'article [?] de l'accord franco-espagnol de 1904, sera administrée sous la souveraineté du Sultan, par une municipalité ayant un caractère international. Le délégué du Sultan, à Tanger, en sera de droit le Président.

II.

Il appartiendra à la municipalité de Tanger d'exercer la police de la ville et de l'agglomération urbaine, dont le périmètre sera déterminé par le firman constitutif de l'organisation municipale.

III.

Quant à la région extérieure comprise entre les limites du périmètre municipal et une ligne passant au Sud, par Arzila, Souk-el-Had-Rarbia, Fondak-el-Ihoudi, l'oued El-Hericha, le fondak d'Aïn-Djedida, et à l'est par la frontière du nouveau territoire espagnol, et aboutissant au cap d'El-Kçar-el-Skrir, sur le détroit de Gibraltar, la police continuera à en être assurée par les contingents marocains et les cadres qui composent le tabor extra-urbain de Tanger.

Cette force dont l'effectif sera porté à 600 hommes sera administrée, instruite et commandée suivant les principes actuellement en vigueur. Les frais d'armement, d'équipement, de casernement et d'entretien de cette force, seront à la charge du Trésor chérifien.

IV.

Si, dans la région indiquée à l'article précédent, il venait à se produire des troubles qui ne pourraient être réprimés par la police, le gouvernement marocain serait tenu de lui prêter main-forte, mais il ne pourrait intervenir qu'avec les troupes de l'armée chérifienne, et sans recourir à des forces étrangères. Des garnisons de l'armée chérifienne seront, exclusivement de toutes autres, installées à Larache et à El-Kçar-el-Kébir.

V.

Les convois de ravitaillement destinés au Maghzen et aux troupes chérifiennes, circuleront sans entrave sur le territoire municipal de Tanger et dans la région déterminée à l'article 3. Il en sera de même des fonctionnaires étrangers ou chérifiens, ou des voyageurs de toute nationalité munis de pièces d'identité, qui se rendront à Fez, ou inversement avec leurs domestiques, armes et bagages, à la condition, toutefois, pour eux, de se conformer au règlement chérifien sur le permis de port d'armes.

VI.

Afin d'assurer le libre passage du détroit de Gibraltar, le gouvernement français veillera à ce que des fortifications ou des ouvrages stratégiques quelconques ne soient pas élevés entre la pointe d'El-Kçar-el-Skrir et les hauteurs qui dominent la rive droite du Sebou, exclusivement.

VII.

Il ne sera apporté à Tanger et dans le détroit de Gibraltar, sans l'assentiment préalable des Puissances signataires de la Convention du 31 mai 1865, aucune modification au régime des phares et des feux intéressant la navigation.

MINUTES.

Sir F. Bertie has put the finger on the weak spot of the proposed arrangement: the strategically important coast-line from Cape Spartel to Ceuta would become French instead of Spanish. It is impossible not to agree with Sir F. Bertie that this would be a large pill for England to swallow. It would falsify one of the most important features of the agreements of 1904.

Under the proposed agreement, Spain would lose what is probably the most important portion of her present sphere of interest, including Alcazar and Laraiche. She would not even gain Tetuan, as that is to remain Moorish. In fact she would practically remain in possession of what she already holds in the Riff country, with the added obligation of keeping order in the turbulent hinterland.

I doubt whether Spain will be ready to accept this position; and I doubt whether we ought to do so either.

Qu : Invite the opinion of the General Staff and of the Admiralty in the first instance, in strict confidence.

E. A. C.
Oct. 23.

When their views have been obtained it will, I suppose, be time enough to consider upon what terms we can agree to the Sovereignty of Spain over the Northern strip and the disappearance of our Consular jurisdiction, &c.

W. L.

I do not gather that the coast between C. Spartel and Ceuta would become French. From Arzila to Pt. Alcazar I understand it w[oul]d be under the Tangier Municipality—and Pt. Alcazar eastwards w[oul]d be Spanish. No part of the Straits w[oul]d be French according to my reading. However the matter should be carefully examined by the Adm[iralt]y and General Staff.

A. N.

It would be Moorish, except the "municipal" territory of Tangier, of which the proposed limits are not indicated. I have, for the purpose of the present discussion, taken Moorish to be equivalent to French.

E. A. C.
Oct. 25.

Refer to Admiralty and General Staff and ask for their opinion quickly.(⁵)

E. G.

(⁵) [v. supra, pp. 565–6, No. 581; also infra, p. 610, No. 620, and note (²).]

No. 599.

Lord Granville to Sir Edward Grey.

Berlin, October 22, 1911.

F.O. 41525/25883/11/28.
D. 12·15 P.M.

Tel. (No. 92.) Confidential.
R. 3·40 P.M.

My telegram No. 90 (   ) : Morocco.(¹)

French Ambassador received his instructions yesterday morning, and saw Secretary of State for Foreign Affairs in the evening. Everything is now settled except question of Duck's Beak. Germans refuse to give beyond line of the Logone, while French demand rich mountain country to the west. Secretary of State for Foreign Affairs is to give his final answer to-morrow.

(Confidential.)

I gather that French Government are very anxious to finish, and may probably give up their extra demands if German final answer is in the negative.

(¹) [v. supra, p. 575, No. 592.]

No. 600.

Lord Granville to Sir Edward Grey.

F.O. 42687/25883/11/28.

(No. 334.) Confidential.
Berlin, D. October 22, 1911.

Sir,
R. October 30, 1911.

I had an interesting conversation yesterday with the Netherlands Minister who only returned from leave a few days ago. We walked away together from the funeral of the late Herr Stemrich and he at once began to tell me of a long talk he had had with Herr von Kiderlen, who is an old friend and colleague of his. Herr von Kiderlen told him that his own views were and always had been absolutely pacific;

people said he had at the beginning of the Morocco business at least, been very warlike and "intransigeant" till he was pulled up short by the Emperor, but the facts were really almost the reverse; of course in the early stages he had had to take a strong and perhaps warlike attitude *vis à vis* of the French Ambassador, but he had never really meant it and considered it would have been both foolish and criminal to fight for Morocco. He was being severely blamed for his alleged weakness and he received letters by every post from every part of Germany abusing him for his concessionary attitude and urging him to be firm—but he did not care : he was doing what he considered to be his duty and what he thought right, and his shoulders were broad enough to stand the abuse. But there were people in higher positions who thought otherwise : the Crown Prince had spoken to him the other day and said that the "Fürst" (Bismarck) would never have given in to the French as he had done and so on, to which Herr von Kiderlen had merely replied that he would never, out of respect for the memory of all the "Fürsten" in the world, make a "Lieutenant's war." Baron Gevers said Herr von Kiderlen had not referred to the Chancellor at all and I was not able to make out whether the "people in higher positions" included the Emperor as well as the Crown Prince.

In the course of conversation I remarked tentatively that I presumed no other country, such as the Netherlands for instance, would make any difficulties when the Franco-German Agreement was concluded and published. Baron Gevers replied that he thought probably not : in the annual Orange Book on foreign affairs this year there had only been a few lines about Morocco, in which M. de Swinderen mentioned that negotiations in regard to Morocco were in progress between France and Germany, that the Dutch Government had not been allowed to take part in the negotiations and were not cognizant of their terms and that when an agreement between those two countries was concluded the Dutch Government would have to examine it carefully and make sure that Dutch interests were properly safeguarded. I said I supposed that referred to the open door and equal treatment of all nations and Baron Gevers said he supposed so.

We agreed that public opinion both in France and Germany might probably show some disapproval of the agreement, and I said the worst of it was, from our point of view, that the Germans appeared to be convinced, and I feared honestly convinced, that our influence in the matter had been injurious to the negotiations and that we had urged on the French to take an unyielding attitude, whereas I believed, in so far as we had interfered at all, we had used our influence in the direction of moderation. Baron Gevers preserved a chilly silence and obviously did not believe me, but, on the other hand, when I made the same remark to the Austrian Ambassador this afternoon he said he thought the serious and well-informed Germans now realized that that was the case.

I have, &c.
GRANVILLE.

No. 601.

Sir Edward Grey to Mr. Carnegie.

F.O. 42095/25883/11/28.
(No. 443.)
Sir, *Foreign Office, October* 23, 1911:

M. [Paul] Cambon informed me to-day that the negotiations with Germany about Morocco would very soon be finished, and it was very happy that it was so.

I replied that I was exceedingly glad to hear this. If a settlement had not been reached the consequences would have been enormous, and no one could forsee what the end of them would have been.

[I am, &c.]
E. G[REY].

No. 602.

Sir V. Corbett to Sir Edward Grey.

F.O. 42424/38119/11/28.
(No. 68.) Confidential.   *Munich*, D. *October* 24, 1911.
Sir,   R. *October* 27, 1911.

Now that the part of the Berlin negotiations directly connected with Morocco has been brought to a successful termination, it may be worth while to consider what has been the effect on German relations with Great Britain.

In the earlier part of the year I had the honour to report that the press comments on British policy were less hostile than they had been for some time past, which I attributed to the self-complacency engendered by the Potsdam interviews which public opinion here had accepted as the beginning of a rapprochement with Russia and the thin end of the wedge which was eventually to split up the Triple *Entente*. A further step in this direction was taken when the "Panther" was sent to Agadir, in order to force a solution of the Morocco question. It was thought that if friendly working agreements could be patched up both with France and Russia to which Great Britain would be no party, an effective breach would have been made in what the Germans call the "hemming-in policy of King Edward."

Whether the Emperor and his Government ever really hoped, as did a large section of the public, to obtain a slice of Southern Morocco, it is hard to say though it would seem extremely probable if only because it must have been urged by powerful financial interests. Such idea, if it ever existed, was speedily dispelled and the German Government found themselves obliged to acquiesce in the treatment of the question as one of securities in Morocco and compensations elsewhere.

Here, however, two unexpected factors came to light. In the first place it appeared that Russia would maintain the treaty obligations to France in spite of what Monsieur Sazonow may have been trapped into saying at Potsdam, and secondly that the French Government were keeping in touch with that of Great Britain and that the latter did not propose to remain disinterested spectators of negotiations in which British interests might be involved. The last point was made clear by the Chancellor of the Exchequer's speech at the Mansion House.

With the publication of Mr. Lloyd George's words the German house of cards built on the contemplated ruin of the Triple *Entente* fell to the ground and the effect was to inaugurate a press campaign against England which with very brief intermissions has been kept at fever heat ever since.

The Chancellor's speech was in no way provocative and had it been delivered by the Prime Minister or the Secretary of State for Foreign Affairs, would probably have been received with relative calmness. But a Chancellor of the Exchequer, especially one who is occupied with great and far-reaching measures of social reform, must be supposed to be the last member of the Cabinet to desire foreign complications. It was argued therefore that if the Chancellor—*ex officio* the least bellicose member of the Cabinet—spoke as he did, his colleagues in other departments must be prepared to go a good deal further.

In this part of Germany and I believe I shall not be far wrong if I say in all Germany, exclusive of Prussia, there is no natural hostility towards Great Britain except among those who are our trade rivals. The *Particularismus* which is alleged to have prompted the Grand Duke of Hesse to rejoice in 1870 at the prospect of a war which, in the anticipated event of a French triumph would enable him to acquire a portion of the territories of his "hated neighbour," the Grand Duke of Baden, may be vanishing but it has not yet vanished. The Bavarian in a general way dislikes the Prussian and even the Württemberger more than he does the Englishman. It is no uncommon thing to hear a Bavarian declare that the Emperor is no King of his and that his loyalty and allegiance are to his own Royal House alone, indeed, among the higher classes allusions to the Emperor are often resented much in the same way that Norwegians used to be annoyed if one talked of the King of Sweden.

Nor is this at all surprising when one sees the small, though by no means negligible part that Bavaria now plays in the Empire as compared to what was hoped for at a time when it was seriously suggested that the Imperial Crown should alternate between the Houses of Hohenzollern and Wittelsbach.

This does not in the least imply that every Bavarian would not join heart and soul to defend the Empire from aggression or indeed to support it in an aggressive attack on others. The deeply emotional character of the German, and especially of the Southern German, would not for an instant resist a national appeal. (Whether, if at some future date it should come to pass that the German-speaking provinces of Austria were united to Germany, a movement to break off from Prussia might not be conceivable, is, I think, less certain.)

Given the state of feeling the only point of interest as far as we are concerned, is whether the events of the last few months have conduced to make Great Britain more popular or less so in those parts of Germany which are not naturally or inevitably unfriendly to us. To this question I fear there can be but one answer. The high hopes with which the Agadir demonstration was welcomed have been frustrated. If the French Government have conducted the negotiations with moderation, they have also exhibited a firmness for which the Germans were quite unprepared. Their attitude is attributed directly to the backing of the British Government. It is in vain that you yourself or other Ministers of the Crown have declared that the British Government had no other wish than to see an amicable agreement arrived at. These declarations are flouted by a press inspired from Berlin and consequently are not credited by the public. The hard and disconcerting fact has been realized that the Franco-British *entente*, so far from having been undermined by the Morocco question, has been cemented by the trial. In two words the Morocco affair is believed to be about to end in a diplomatic defeat and that defeat is ascribed to the interested support given to France by Great Britain. Among those with whom I have the opportunity to converse I have noticed a difference of tone since the beginning of the year, and a reluctance on the part of those who formerly confessed to British sympathies to parade them now. I imagine that the experience of His Majesty's Representatives at other German posts cannot have been very different.

It must I fear be admitted that the outcome of the Morocco negotiations has been to render us more unpopular where we were unpopular before and to tend to estrange the sympathies of those who formerly had no particular grievance against us.

In the reports which I have had the honour to address to you I have from time to time sought to minimize the significance of the German press attacks on the ground that Germany, as an expanding commercial community, has valid and indeed flattering reasons to be jealous of us. Taken in connection with the sensitiveness to criticism, to which I ventured to call attention in a previous despatch it is inevitable that this feeling, which is fostered by financial interests which desire to see a more energetic commercial policy, by the Pan-Germanists and by the Ultra-Clericals, should occasionally find violent expression in the newspapers. Under existing circumstances a little newspaper abuse more or less need not be considered as symptomatic of anything more than the pardonable jealousy of a youthful and self-conscious community.

During the last few months however a really lamentable part has been played by the press of both nations. Venomous criticisms of British policy and grossly garbled reports of the speeches of British statesmen have lately been of almost daily occurrence. But it is not to be denied that the British press is in this respect as much to blame as the German. Only the other day when it was stated that German troops had been landed at Hankau, the " Daily Mail " published a most impertinent leader on the subject, which was of course quoted in the German papers. Nothing definite was known about the matter and it would have been only decent to assume, until there was proof to the contrary, that the Germans had acted within their rights, the more especially as our own gunboats were at that moment hurrying to the scene of trouble. Instead of this what might, for all we knew, have been a perfectly justifiable action was made the peg for an anti-German article and gibes at the "mailed fist." This is only one example out of many. It is too much to expect that such articles will not be resented here and give rise to reprisals. Perhaps there is little to choose between the "Daily Mail" and the "Münchener Neueste Nachrichten," neither of which is taken seriously by educated people, but they and their associated papers are widely read by a public a large percentage of whom believe that whatever appears in print must be true. It is to be regretted that the English papers like the "Manchester Guardian," "Chronicle," and "Westminster Gazette" which plead for a better understanding with Germany should so constantly accompany the expression of the hope with an attack on His Majesty's advisers. They are quoted in the German papers with approval but they are accepted as voices crying in the wilderness opposed both to the sentiments of the nation and the policy of the Government.

I have, &c.
VINCENT CORBETT.

No. 603.

Sir M. de Bunsen to Sir Edward Grey.

F.O. 42207/41847/11/28.   Madrid, D. October 25, 1911, 8·45 P.M.
Tel. (No. 82.)   R. October 26, 8 A.M.
My telegram No. 80 (   ).(¹)
French Ambassador has now addressed a stiff letter to the Spanish Minister for Foreign Affairs protesting, in accordance with instructions from French Government, against the attitude taken up by Colonel Silvestre regarding the payment of troops under Raisuli's command, and adding that Spain's action at (word omitted), if approved by the Spanish Government, might have serious consequences, as to which French Government declined all responsibility.

If you approve, I will support the French warning by pointing out that the demands put forward by Colonel Silvestre are singularly inopportune at the present moment, and that unless withdrawn they will seriously hamper His Majesty's Government in supporting the claims as regards her sphere of influence.

(Repeated to Paris and Tangier.)

(¹) [Sir M. de Bunsen's telegram No. 80 of October 24, 1911, referred to the demands made by Colonel Sylvestre to Raisuli, and stated the opinion of the French Ambassador that a French protest would have no effect.]

No. 604.

Sir M. de Bunsen to Sir Edward Grey.

F.O. 42208/42208/11/28.   Madrid, D. October 25, 1911, 8·45 P.M.
Tel. (No. 83.) Confidential   R. October 26, 1911, 8 A.M.
Minister for Foreign Affairs declared to me today very categorically in course of conversation that nothing short of overwhelming force would induce Spain to withdraw her troops from Alcazar and Laraiche.

Threatening language of the French press had caused the Spanish Government to submit the question again to the King, Council of Ministers, and chief Conservative opposition, all of whom fully confirmed the above decision.

(Repeated to Paris and Tangier.)

No. 605.

Sir Edward Grey to Sir M. de Bunsen.

F.O. 42266/13751/11/28.
(No. 108.)
Sir,   *Foreign Office, October 25, 1911.*

The Spanish Ambassador complained to me to-day that the French Government had not kept their word with the Spanish Government about the negotiations concerning Morocco. The French Government had promised that, as soon as the Morocco part of the bargain was concluded with Germany, they would continue negotiations with the Spanish Government. The Morocco part had long been concluded with Germany, and now all the Spanish Ambassador knew was that the French Ambassador informed him that the draft submitted some time ago by France to Spain existed no longer.

I remarked that the Congo part of the negotiations between France and Germany had been very delicate, and had entailed great responsibility upon the French Government, who would have to recommend to the French Chamber the bargain which they made. They had no doubt felt it to be impossible to conduct at the same time delicate negotiations with the Spanish Government, entailing a further responsibility.

The Ambassador expressed his apprehension that the French Government would take the view that the Agreements with Spain had been torn up and superseded, and that Spain should have in Morocco only what France considered that she could spare her. Some of the French Press had already taken this view. The Ambassador pressed me to say whether I would support the view that the Franco-Spanish Agreements must be carried out.

I said that, after France had paid the whole price of buying off the German claims in Morocco, it was only reasonable that Spain should concede something to France. The important question was whether the French proposals on this point would be reasonable.

The Ambassador said that Spain could not pay both Germany and France.

I agreed entirely, but pointed out that I assumed that Germany was being paid by France for the whole of Morocco, and could not ask to be paid twice over for part of it. I could not say anything about French proposals until they were made; but meanwhile I took note of the views which the Spanish Ambassador had expressed to me, and I asked him not to think that, because I said little at the moment, I did not realise the importance of the question.

[I am, &c.]
E. G[REY].

No. 606.

Sir M. de Bunsen to Sir Edward Grey.

F.O. 42275/41847/11/28.
Tel. (No. 84.) R.

Madrid, October 26, 1911.
D. 12·45 P.M.
R. 3·30 P.M.

My telegram No. 82.(¹)

Reply of Spanish Government to French Ambassador's letter denies altogether French version of facts. Colonel Sylvestre's conversation with Raisuli had no other than [*sic*] that of securing tranquillity in region, and although question of providing for regular payment of native troops was discussed, Colonel Sylvestre made no

(¹) [*v. supra*, p. 592, No. 603.]

demand to pay them himself nor did he require troops to be assembled for that purpose as stated. M[inister for] F[oreign] A[ffairs] declares in short that Colonel Sylvestre's language and intentions have been entirely misrepresented and that it never entered into plans of Spanish Government to occupy Arzila.

I propose nevertheless to warn M[inister for] F[oreign] A[ffairs] against danger of any action being taken at present which might cause unnecessary irritation in Paris.

Correspondence follows by post.

(Repeated to Paris and Tangier.)

MINUTE.

I informed M. Cambon of all but the last paragraph of this telegram and he expressed himself quite satisfied.

E. G.

No. 607.

Sir Edward Grey to Sir M. de Bunsen.

F.O. 42207/41847/11/28.   *Foreign Office, October* 26, 1911.
Tel. (No. 95.) R.   D. 7 P.M.

Your telegrams Nos. 82 and 84.([1])

It is unnecessary that we should associate ourselves with any threats as to what may be consequences of Spanish action, but you are authorized to support your French colleague by pointing out to Spanish gov[ernmen]t in friendly way that it would be clearly inadvisable in the general interest of harmony between France and Spain in Morocco if Spain should proceed to make a material change in the *status quo* just at the moment when negotiations for a friendly settlement are to begin.

([1]) [*v.* immediately preceding document, and *supra*, p. 592, No. 603.]

No. 608.

Lord Granville to Sir Edward Grey.

F.O. 42697/25883/11/28.
(No. 345.)   Confidential.   *Berlin*, D. *October* 27, 1911.
Sir,   R. *October* 30, 1911.

When I despatched my telegram No. 92 to you on the 22nd instant,([1]) on the strength of information given to me by the Councillor of the French Embassy, I hoped to be able to report before this the final settlement of the Morocco and Congo negotiations. These are however still dragging on and the French Ambassador told me the night before last that he rather fancied Herr von Kiderlen was purposely delaying matters in order to avoid the conclusion of the agreement before the Reichstag's adjournment this evening. I saw Herr von Kiderlen on Tuesday immediately after he had had a meeting with M. [Jules] Cambon, and His Excellency told me with some amusement that he had succeeded with enormous difficulty in squeezing a piece of territory out of the Colonial Office only to find that there had been a misunderstanding and that it was an entirely different piece which the French demanded. When I repeated this to M. Cambon he said that one had to be extremely careful in negotiating with Herr von Kiderlen as, whether intentionally or through carelessness, the latter was very apt to make little mistakes of this sort and to repudiate one day what he had agreed to the day before.

([1]) [*v. supra*, p. 588, No. 599.]

I have not thought it necessary to trouble you with any Press comments on the negotiations—there have been plenty of them, abusing the Government, defending the Government, attacking the French, stating the minimum of what Germany could possibly accept etc.—but there has been nothing very new, and premature comments on an agreement which we may hope will very soon be published do not seem to present much interest.

The Cologne Gazette of yesterday published a telegram from Berlin stating that, according to English reports at least, there was some anxiety in Belgium in connection with the access to the Congo to be granted by France to Germany, lest Germany might cherish designs on the Congo State. These English reporters had suggested, as a means of warding off such a danger, that Great Britain should recognize the annexation of the Congo, and the telegram remarks that England's action in that regard was a matter of supreme indifference to Germany who had herself recognized the annexation and thereby bound herself to respect Belgian territory.

I have, &c.
GRANVILLE.

No. 609.

Sir M. de Bunsen to Sir Edward Grey.

F.O. 42947/8755/11/28.
(No. 182.)
Sir,

Madrid, D. *October* 28, 1911.
R. *October* 31, 1911.

The continued insistence of certain organs of the French press on the contention that the evacuation of Alcazar and Laraiche by the Spanish forces is the necessary preliminary to any satisfactory settlement of outstanding questions in Morocco between France and Spain has considerably alarmed the Spanish Government, and Señor Garcia Prieto, the Minister for Foreign Affairs, loses no opportunity of repeating both to the French Ambassador and to myself that this demand is one which, if really supported by the French Government, would meet in Madrid with the most determined resistance. His Excellency again spoke to me on the subject yesterday. He assured me that no conceivable Spanish Government could peacefully surrender a position deliberately occupied by Spain on the strength of the decision adopted by the Conference of Algeciras that the native police force at Larache should receive its organization and instruction from Spanish officers. In the same way as France had assumed responsibility for the peace of the Shawia region on the strength of the similar duty which had been assigned to her, jointly with Spain, at Casablanca, so Spain had been much more justified by the task confided exclusively to her in respect of the Larache Police, in taking the measures which appeared to her necessary in view of securing the peace and tranquillity of Alcazar and the surrounding country which lay behind Larache. Señor Garcia Prieto disputed the argument put forward in some of the French newspapers that the Spanish occupation of Alcazar constituted a breach of the Secret Convention with France of 1904.[(1)] If there had been any infraction of the letter of that convention, it would be easy, he said, to point to many worse infractions on the part of France. Moreover France had not denounced the convention when the alleged infraction took place. On the contrary, she had signed with Spain at the end of July a *modus vivendi*, implying a recognition of the continued existence of the Secret Treaty.

After remarking that, as the French Government had as yet put forward no demand of the kind apprehended by His Excellency, it seemed premature to discuss these questions in detail, I asked him what was the real value of the Alcazar country to Spain and whether it was a rich district capable of being profitably developed by

(1) [*v. infra*, pp. 826–29, *App.* IV.]

[19656]

2 Q 2

Spanish enterprise. He replied that this was a point which did not at present enter into his calculations. In adopting the very determined resolution to hold fast to the occupied region, the Spanish Government had in view the entirely disastrous effect which evacuation would inevitably produce on public opinion in Spain. The national sentiment would be thereby profoundly humiliated; the loyalty of the army would be subjected to a severe strain; and an internal situation would be created in Spain which would not be without danger to the stability of the existing institutions.

Señor Garcia Prieto added that Señor Maura the opposition leader was animated by sentiments which on these points were not a whit less resolute than those entertained by the Government of Señor Canalejas. Indeed Señor Maura was strongly opposed to any concession whatever being made to France by ceding a portion of the Southern Spanish zone in Morocco. In this particular Señor Garcia Prieto, as already reported, is disposed to meet as far as possible the French demand.

Señor Canalejas's special organ in the press, the *Diario Universal*, published last night a statement to the following effect :—

Commenting on an article in the Figaro, it remarks that the new Franco-German Treaty will affect Spanish interests in Morocco much more than those of Germany, and that the treaty cannot become operative without the consent of Spain, as one of the signatory Powers of the General Act of Algeciras. The establishment of a French protectorate at Fez implies a change in the *status quo* of Morocco, by which full effect will be given to the Franco-Spanish Agreement cf 1904. That agreement gives Spain full liberty of action in certain regions, which include Alcazar and Larache as well as the Riff and the southern zone. On the strength, then, of the 1904 agreement, and of her concurrence in the modification of the Algeciras Act, Spain will be entitled to exercise her action freely, not only in the Riff, at Tetuan and in the extreme South, but also, at Larache and Alcazar. To offer her the former districts in exchange for her abandonment of the latter is to evade openly the observance of the agreement. Irresponsible persons—an allusion no doubt to Señor Moret, who was recently quoted by the " Times " as advocating a restricted Spanish zone in Northern Morocco—may put forward a suggestion to that effect, but no responsible Spanish Government could place itself in such a position. Larache and Alcazar are not necessary to France to enable her to keep up communications between Fez and the Mediterranean, or between Fez and the Atlantic. If France had a great interest in holding Larache and Alcazar, Spain has a still greater one, as a glance at the map will show. France admitted this when she signed the Agreement of 1904. Spanish public opinion is quite clear on this point. Even if Spain had never occupied those places, the country would demand their retention by all the means at its command. But Spanish troops being actually in possession, the claim founded on interest and treaty rights becomes one in which the prestige and honour of the nation are involved.

I have, &c.
MAURICE DE BUNSEN.

No. 610.

Sir Edward Grey to Mr. Carnegie.

F.O. 43246/25883/11/28.
(No. 457.) Confidential.
Sir,

Foreign Office, October 28, 1911.

M. [Paul] Cambon informed Sir Arthur Nicolson this afternoon that he had just received a telegram from M. de Selves announcing that at the last moment Herr von Kiderlen had requested that M. Jules Cambon should address him a secret letter declaring that if in certain eventualities the question of taking over the Belgian

Congo were to arise, the French Government would take no steps without first consulting with the German Government.

M. de Selves held this demand to be quite inadmissible, and said that the signature of the Morocco agreement would consequently be postponed, and that the request of the German Government might lead to a rupture of the negotiations.

M. Cambon asked that this information might be treated as quite confidential.

[I am, &c.
E. GREY.]

No. 611.

Sir Edward Grey to Mr. Carnegie.

F.O. 43089/13751/11/28.
(No. 455.)
Sir,   Foreign Office, October 30, 1911.
I told M. [Paul] Cambon to-day that, when the negotiations with Germany were concluded, we should not be able to support any negotiations between France and Spain unless they were based on the Agreements of 1904. We were parties to those Agreements. To treat them as if they had no existence would be to drag the *Entente* in the mud, and would have the most disastrous effect on public opinion here. I was instructing Sir Francis Bertie, who was returning to Paris the day after to-morrow, to speak very strongly on this point to M. de Selves and M. Caillaux.

[I am, &c.]
E. G[REY].

No. 612.

Sir Edward Grey to Mr. Carnegie.

F.O. 43247/25883/11/28.
(No. 458.) Confidential.
Sir,   Foreign Office, October 30, 1911.
Referring to what he had told Sir Arthur Nicolson of Herr von Kiderlen's([1]) demand at the last moment for a secret assurance that France would discuss with Germany the right of pre-emption over the Belgian Congo if ever it came to be exercised, M. [Paul] Cambon informed me to-day that M. de Selves was thinking of suggesting the following formula :—

" Dans le cas où le status territorial du bassin conventionnel du Congo viendrait à être modifié du fait de l'une ou l'autre des puissances contractantes, celles-ci devront en conférer entre elles comme aussi avec les autres puissances signatrices de l'Acte de Berlin du 26 février 1885."

I said that I could see no objection to this.

M. Cambon said that it went without saying that, if the Congo was ever for disposal there would have to be conversations between the Powers interested, and he did not see that this formula took things further forward. He discussed whether a more explicit formula could not be given, which would make an actual mention of the right of pre-emption and of the Belgian Congo.

([1]) [A survey of the whole situation from the point of view of the German Colonial Office is to be found in a Memorandum by Herr von Lindequist (German Colonial Secretary) of October 31 in *G.P.* XXIX, pp. 403–12.]

I observed that any actual mention of these things at this moment might arouse apprehensions in Belgium that France, Germany, and perhaps England were dividing her Colony between them, and intended to force her to sell it. This would have a very undesirable political effect. I felt, however, that it was perfectly reasonable that, if ever Belgium voluntarily disposed of her Colony, Germany should have an opportunity of acquiring some considerable portion of it, and the matter might then on its merits become a fair subject of negotiation.

[I am, &c.]
E. G[REY].

No. 613.

Sir Edward Grey to Sir E. Goschen.

F.O. 43272/13751/11/28.
(No. 252.)
Sir,   *Foreign Office, October* 31, 1911.

Count Metternich spoke to me to-day very confidentially about the prospect of negotiations between France and Spain respecting Morocco.

Information had reached him through a friend of M. Caillaux that the latter was disposed to press Spain very hard, and that he would not negotiate with her on the basis of the Agreement of 1904, but wished her to be content with the Riff, and to renounce her claims in southern Morocco. M. Caillaux had observed that Spain had better be conciliatory, or else she would have internal difficulties. He had said that the revolt of the Kabyles was not a pure hazard, and might spread in such a way as to endanger the Spanish Throne. M. Caillaux's view was that, in order to avoid a shared protectorate between France and Spain, Spain should annex the Riff, and give compensation to France, including perhaps the Canary Islands,— though it was not clear whether the suggestion as to the Canary Islands had been made by M. Caillaux or only by his friend.

The German Government felt that, if France treated Spain in this way, the Spanish Monarchy would be endangered, and this was their only reason for calling my attention very confidentially to the information which had reached them.

I replied that I had always assumed that the negotiations between France and Spain would be on the basis of the 1904 Agreement. I knew, however, through the Spanish Ambassador, that the Spaniards had been very restless and apprehensive, owing to the delay in beginning the negotiations. When the Spanish Ambassador had approached me on the subject, I had pointed out to him how difficult it was for France to carry on negotiations with Spain before the negotiations with Germany were concluded; and I had said that, till the negotiations with Germany reached a conclusion, I could not press France to make definite proposals to Spain. It seemed to me impossible that the proposals of France to Spain should take any definite form before the end of the negotiations with Germany, but my assumption had always been that the negotiations with Spain would be conducted on the basis of the Agreement of 1904.

As to the communication which Count Metternich had made to me, I could only observe that either M. Caillaux had been very indiscreet, or he had a very indiscreet friend.

[I am, &c.]
E. G[REY].

No. 614.

Sir F. Bertie to Sir Edward Grey.

F.O. 43769/13751/11/28.
(No. 490.) Confidential.
Sir :—

Paris, D. *November* 2, 1911.
R. *November* 6, 1911.

I returned to Paris last night and I had an interview with M. de Selves this evening. After some general conversation he asked me what opinion you had expressed to me when I was in London on the " Projet de Convention " for settling the respective positions of France and Spain in Morocco, communicated to me by M. Regnault, copy of which was enclosed in my despatch No. 455, Confidential, of the 21st ultimo.(¹)

I replied that you and the Prime Minister were preoccupied at the situation which would be created between Spain and France if the Projet in question were communicated to the Spanish Government who were in a state of irritation and alarm at reports which had reached them of demands which were likely to be made by the French Government depriving them of parts of the advantages which the Franco-Spanish Agreement of 1904 had promised them and to which they attached very great importance. His Majesty's Government admitted that some sacrifice was due to France for the improved position which Spain would naturally occupy in Morocco through the compensations in the French Congo which were to be given to Germany in return for her recognition of a French Protectorate of Morocco; but to convert a Spanish zone on the Mediterranean coast of Morocco into full possession and sovereignty would probably raise questions with Germany and perhaps other Powers. Germany might demand compensation for a recognition of Spanish sovereignty. To substitute France for Spain in the Zone on the Western coast of Morocco which had been allotted to Spain by the 1904 arrangements would be a very great and serious departure from those arrangements to which England had been a party. Such substitution would not be consistent with the protection of British interests which Lord Lansdowne had had in view when he negotiated the 1904 Agreement. I had pointed this out to M. Regnault when he communicated to me the Projet, but I had heard that he had described me as thinking that it might be acceptable to His Majesty's Government though I had not, he is alleged to have stated, expressed any decided opinion on it myself. M. de Selves interposed that when on M. Regnault's return from his interview with me he had asked him what I thought of the Projet, M. Regnault had stated that I had said that I would refer it to His Majesty's Government and that I appeared to be in doubt as to my own opinion in regard to the view which would be taken of it by His Majesty's Government.

M. de Selves indicated with his hand the hovering of the hawk before making up its mind. I observed that M. Regnault must have an odd idea of interpreting the " jamais " which I had said to him in regard to the acceptability of the Projet, for I had given him my reasons for considering the substitution of France for Spain on the Atlantic Coast of Morocco as inacceptable to H[is] M[ajesty's] Government, viz: that it would be the substitution of a first class naval Power for one that was not so, and when M. Regnault had suggested to me that it would be contrary to British interests that Spain, who might be in alliance with Germany, should be in occupation of the Atlantic coast of Morocco, I pointed out to him that Great Britain and the British fleet came between Germany and Spain.

M. de Selves reminded me that when asking me the day after my interview with M. Regnault what I thought of the Projet, he had stated on my expressing great doubt of it being acceptable to His Majesty's Government that it was only a projet for your consideration and that he would not put it forward without your concurrence for he desired to act in unison with His Majesty's Government. I told him that I had so reported to you but when in London I learnt that it had been represented to

---

(¹) [*v. supra*, pp. 583–7, No. 598, and *encl.*]

the Prime Minister that M. Caillaux had adopted the proposals contained in the Projet and meant to press them on the Spanish Government. I had consequently been instructed by the Prime Minister and yourself to inform the French Government that not only would any such proceeding have a detrimental effect on public opinion in England in regard to the *Entente* but that His Majesty's Government could not give such a policy support at Madrid. Their view was that the negotiations with the Spanish Government must be on the basis of the 1904 Agreements with such deviations as might be required for reasonable compensation to France for the improved position which Spain was entitled to expect from a recognition by the Powers of a French Protectorate over Morocco. To put pressure on Spain to accept the drastic proposals of the Projet would be to throw her into the arms of Germany which would be injurious to the interests of England and France. Spain would never willingly consent to give up her zone on the west coast. Monsieur Regnault and some of the Colonial party including perhaps some of the members of the French Cabinet had persuaded Monsieur Caillaux of the advantages and feasibility of Monsieur Regnault's scheme for I had no doubt that it was his projet and not one that could recommend itself to the Minister for Foreign Affairs for it contained elements of danger to the Foreign policy of France if the *Entente* was intended to continue its task of preserving peace whilst protecting the solid interests of France and England.

Monsieur de Selves admitted the reality of the dangers which I had indicated and it was because he felt from his conversations with me that His Majesty's Government might object to the Projet that he had sent it to me for your consideration as he desired to act in unison with His Majesty's Government in the questions which must arise with Spain in Morocco.

At my suggestion Monsieur de Selves undertook to prepare Monsieur Caillaux whom he was to see to-morrow morning at a meeting of the Cabinet for the communication which I am to make to him of the views of His Majesty's Government.

Monsieur de Selves then discussed with me the arrangements to be made with Spain on the basis that the questions of the annexation to Spain of the Mediterranean zone and the substitution of France for Spain in the Western zone from the vicinity of Tangier Southward and Westward to the Atlantic coast shall be dropped. He said that the report which I mentioned to him as being current in London that the French Government were meditating a demand on the Spanish Government to withdraw from Larache and Alcazar was a myth. He thought however that Spain might well be asked to waive her rights on Alcazar so that French communications might be kept up through there, as a French protected place, with Tangier and Fez, Compensations to France must be sought elsewhere than on the coast between Tangier and Larache. The Spanish Government held to the retention of Ifni on account of the Canaries and he recognised the validity of their objection to a European Power being established opposite to those Spanish Islands. Monsieur de Selves then enquired where I thought that compensation could be sought to which Spain might not make strong objection and to which England would recommend Spain to consent. I said that I thought that such compensation might be found in the South of Morocco where Spain had something that she might give up and I recommended Monsieur de Selves to abandon altogether Monsieur Regnault's projet and to revert to the scheme which he had communicated to me at the end of August([2]) for the consideration of His Majesty's government and to insert in it a prohibition to Spain to alienate in any form her rights in the territories comprised in her zones in Morocco. There was such a prohibition in the Regnault projet. It had been forgotten or omitted when the earlier projet was drafted at the Quai d'Orsay. Monsieur de Selves said that he would confer with the President of the Council and point out to him the objections of His Majesty's Government to the Regnault scheme. Monsieur de Selves further stated that though the Spanish Government had in his opinion acted impetuously and unwisely in Morocco he made allowance for the excitable temperament and

([2]) [*v. supra*, pp. 494–7, No. 525, *encl.*]

touchiness of the Spanish people and he desired to avoid so far as might be possible hurting their susceptibilities. He admitted that it would be a mistaken policy to run the risk of throwing Spain into the arms of Germany in this particular case or of treating her in a manner to alienate her from co-operation with her neighbour France in general questions.

I have, &c.
FRANCIS BERTIE.

No. 615.

Sir Edward Grey to Sir M. de Bunsen.

F.O. 43241/13751/11/28.
(No. 114.)
Sir, *Foreign Office, November 2, 1911.*
The Spanish Ambassador called at the Foreign Office on the 28th ult[imo] and said that the Spanish Gov[ernmen]t understood that the French Gov[ernmen]t would lay down as a preliminary basis of their approaching negotiations with Spain that Alcazar and Laraiche should be evacuated. The Ambassador stated that it would be impossible for any Spanish Gov[ernmen]t to take such a step and if the French Gov[ernmien]t maintained this demand it would be quite useless to commence any discussions. The Spanish Gov[ernmen]t wished that H[is] M[ajesty's] Gov[ernmen]t should inform the French Gov[ernmen]t accordingly. H[is] E[xcellency] also said that his Gov[ernmen]t had "reason to believe" that the German Gov[ernmen]t would require some concessions from Spain and though Spain was disposed to give some compensation to France she could not be expected to pay twice over.(¹)
[I am, &c.
E. GREY.]

(¹) [This draft is based on a minute of the interview written by Sir A. Nicolson. Sir Edward Grey has added the following comment: "The latter point is quite just. E. G."]

No. 616.

Sir Edward Grey to Sir M. de Bunsen.

F.O. 43639/13751/11/28.
(No. 115.)
Sir, *Foreign Office, November 2, 1911.*
I recalled to-day, in conversation with the Spanish Ambassador, the apprehension which he had expressed to me a short time ago in connection with the line taken by the French Press, to the effect that the Agreement of 1904 between France and Spain must be treated as non-existent.
I said that I adhered to the view that it was unreasonable to press the French Government to define their proposals to Spain before their negotiations with Germany were concluded. I had therefore not pressed the French Government. But I had discussed the matter with Sir Francis Bertie, who was shortly returning to Paris, and in the conversations which I had here with M. Cambon, and in such official conversations as Sir Francis Bertie had in Paris, it had been assumed, and would continue to be assumed, that the Agreements of 1904 would be the basis and starting-point for negotiations between Spain and France as to Morocco. I asked the

Ambassador whether he had noticed the line taken by the "Journal des Débats," as reported in yesterday's "Times."

He replied that he had noticed it. It was satisfactory, and all that he could wish.

I said that I thought it significant that this line had been taken in a paper of some importance.

The Ambassador thanked me for what I had told him. He again impressed upon me the impossibility of a Spanish withdrawal from Alcazar and Laraiche as a preliminary to negotiations with France. Even if these places were subsequently restored to Spain, the withdrawal would leave a bad feeling. He said that the Spanish Press was showing a moderate and conciliatory spirit.

I observed that I hoped the Spaniards would do all they could, during the present interval, to avoid incidents in Morocco that might disturb French feeling.

[I am, &c.]

E. G[REY].

No. 617.

Minute by Sir A. Nicolson.

F.O. 45802/8457/11/28.

Sir Edward Grey,   *Foreign Office, November* 2, 1911.

In conversation to-day with M. Cambon respecting the hitch which has occurred in the Franco-German negotiations, I mentioned that I believed that on a former occasion he had repeated to me the language which he had held at Paris in respect to the possible attitude of England in the event of a break occurring between France and Germany.

M. Cambon replied as follows " I told M. Caillaux and all the Ministers very clearly that it would be exceedingly difficult for any British Government to take any action which was not supported by British public opinion : that in the event of Germany attacking France or wilfully breaking off the negotiations British public opinion would side with France and would enable the British Gov[ern]ment to support France. British public opinion was impetuous and did not reason very deeply, but it had an instinctive sympathy with the party attacked and an instinctive mistrust and dislike of an aggressive and bullying Power. All British history proved this. But if France were to place herself in the wrong, and were to attack Germany or wilfully break off the negotiations, British public opinion, in any case at the outset, would not be on the side of France, and the British Gov[ernmen]t would not, therefore, be able to assist France at the commencement, whatever they might do later. As British aid would be required immediately and at the outset, the result would be that France would not be able to count on British support."

A. N.

M. Cambon states the position quite accurately.

E. G.

I read the whole of this to the Cabinet yesterday. It should be kept for reference.

E. G.

16.11.11.

No. 618.

Sir F. Bertie to Sir Edward Grey.

F.O. 43770/13751/11/28.
(No. 495.) Confidential.   *Paris,* D. *November* 3, 1911.
Sir,   R. *November* 6, 1911.

With reference to my Despatch No. 490 of yesterday([1]) I have the honour to inform you that I had an interview with the President of the Council this evening on the subject of the arrangements to be made to settle the respective positions of France and Spain in Morocco. I urged on him all the considerations which I had put to the Minister for Foreign Affairs as reported in my despatch of yesterday.

M. Caillaux showed no signs of any intention to adopt a conciliatory attitude in the matter. He mentioned a series of grievances which France had against Spain, many of them, as I observed to him, not being pertinent to the question of Morocco. He said that the Spanish Government had intrigued with the German Government and relying on German support they had bearded France in every way, and their conduct had been intolerable.

Spain had broken her engagements by the occupation of Alcazar and other such acts in Morocco and the French Government would have been justified in denouncing the Convention of 1904. France had by great sacrifices in the Congo Colony obtained from Germany a recognition of the claims of France in Morocco. Was Spain not to compensate France for the position which the French Government were ready to concede to Spain in Morocco? There was a public opinion in France as well as England and there were no public men of any prominence, except M. Clemenceau, who did not insist with him that the compensation to be required from Spain should be ample and such as to be in proportion to the French sacrifices. I observed to him that His Majesty's Government did not question the claim of France for some concessions from Spain for the improved position which she had a right to expect from the terms of the Convention of 1904, but they must not be exaggerated. M. Caillaux replied that the compensation he asked for was set forth in the Regnault Projet. I said that His Majesty's Government could not support such a claim at Madrid and the possession by France of the zone in the North West of Morocco which had been allotted in certain contingencies to Spain by M. Delcassé's Convention of 1904 and marked out on the map accompanying that Convention would not be consistent with British interests. M. Caillaux asked where I suggested that compensation should be sought. I said in the South of Morocco. M. Caillaux rejected such an idea. That part of Morocco was worthless and Spain would be as unwilling to part with any portion of her so-called possession of Rio del Oro, which she had never occupied, as she would no doubt object to waiving any of her claims under the 1904 Convention. . . . .([2])

I admitted that the Spaniards had acted impetuously and foolishly in proceeding to the occupation of portions of Morocco, but that was not a good reason for carrying resentment to the point of estranging Spain and throwing her into the arms of Germany. It would be a serious matter in case of war with Germany for France to have a hostile Spain in her rear. I reminded him that the late King of Spain had promised the German Emperor that if war broke out between Germany and France he would place 100,000 men on the Franco-Spanish frontier. The present King had refused to renew this promise. Was it not important to encourage His Majesty to maintain his good disposition towards France? . . . .([2])

I then put it to him that in the event of a war with Germany in which Italy, Austria and Turkey were allied with her, it would be a serious drawback to France

([1]) [*v. supra,* pp. 599–601, No. 614.]
([2]) [A passage of a personal nature is here omitted on grounds of international courtesy. It contained nothing affecting the historical value of the document.]

and England, if those two Powers were acting together, to have a hostile Spain with her ports closed to their ships.

M. Caillaux did not discuss this point. . . . .(³)

I asked M. Caillaux why he desired to withdraw from Spain one of the zones promised to her by the Delcassé Convention? France would, thanks to the support of England, have a magnificent domain without it. Why was he bent on offending Spain and public opinion in England by making exaggerated claims?

M. Caillaux answered that if His Majesty's Government supported Spain in refusing satisfaction to the French claims, French public opinion would be greatly irritated and there would be a danger of France and England falling out. ("et il y aurait danger que la France et l'Angleterre se brouillent.")

To this I said that Frenchmen were much less excitable than formerly, and had shown great common sense in all the difficulties with Germany and I did not suppose that they would be foolish enough to quarrel with England on account of the question of what compensation would be reasonable for Spain to give to France in Morocco.

M. Caillaux said that it might not be a quarrel but that there would not be the same French good-will to England in all parts of the world and on all questions as now.

The conversation then turned again to the question of the Atlantic zone in Morocco. I asked him what he regarded as essential for French interests. He said that he must have railway communication from Tangier viâ Alcazar to Fez free of all possibility of Spanish authority or interference and this could only be ensured by carrying out the Regnault Projet. He knew nothing of any other earlier scheme such as I had mentioned to him as having the concurrence of His Majesty's Government. One Projet only had been communicated to him by M. de Selves, who was then accompanied by M. Regnault, and he had approved that Projet.

M. Caillaux observed during our interview that France, as regarded the so-called Spanish zone in the North West of Morocco, was only under Treaty obligation to England for the non-fortification of the coast. I disputed this view, for, as I reminded him, the Delcassé Convention of 1904 with the accompanying maps on which the Spanish zones were delineated had been officially communicated by the French Government to His Majesty's Government, who had accepted them as a satisfactory settlement.

I requested M. Caillaux to reflect on all that I had said, and I observed that I would renew our conversation to-morrow at the President's shooting party at Rambouillet where he and I were to meet.

M. Caillaux said that he would reflect but that he could not change his mind.

I have, &c.
FRANCIS BERTIE.

(³) [A passage of a personal nature is here omitted on grounds of international courtesy. It contained nothing affecting the historical value of the document.]

No. 619.

M. Daeschner to Sir Edward Grey.

F.O. 43587/25883/11/28.   *Ambassade de France, Londres,*
Monsieur le Secrétaire d'État,   *le 3 novembre,* 1911.

J'ai l'honneur de transmettre, ci-joint, à Votre Excellence le texte de la Convention récemment conclue entre mon Gouvernement et celui de Berlin au sujet du Maroc.

En notifiant cet accord au Gouvernement de Sa Majesté le Roi, je suis chargé de lui demander son adhésion aux stipulations de la dite convention et je serais heureux si Votre Excellence voulait bien me faire parvenir sa réponse dans le plus bref délai possible.

Veuillez, &c.

E. DAESCHNER.

Enclosure in No. 619.

Convention Franco-Allemande concernant le Maroc.([1])

A la suite des troubles qui se sont produits au Maroc et qui ont démontré la nécessité d'y poursuivre dans l'intérêt général l'œuvre de pacification et de progrès prévue par l'Acte d'Algésiras, le Gouvernement de la République Française et le Gouvernement Impérial allemand ont jugé nécessaire de préciser et de compléter l'accord franco-allemand du 9 Février 1909.([2]) Ils sont convenus, à cet effet des dispositions ci-après :

ARTICLE 1ᵉʳ.

Le Gouvernement Impérial Allemand déclare que, ne poursuivant au Maroc que des intérêts économiques, il n'entravera pas l'action de la France en vue de prêter son assistance au Gouvernement marocain pour l'introduction de toutes les réformes administratives, judiciaires, économiques, financières et militaires dont il a besoin pour le bon gouvernement de l'Empire, comme aussi pour tous les règlements nouveaux et les modifications aux règlements existants que ces réformes comportent. En conséquence, il donne son adhésion aux mesures de réorganisation, de contrôle et de garantie financière que, après accord avec le Gouvernement marocain, le Gouvernement français croira devoir prendre à cet effet sous la réserve que l'action de la France sauvegardera au Maroc l'égalité économique entre les deux nations.*

Au cas où la France serait amenée à préciser et à étendre son contrôle et sa protection, le Gouvernement impérial allemand reconnaissant pleine liberté d'action à la France, et sous la réserve que la liberté commerciale prévue par les traités antérieurs sera maintenue, n'y apportera aucun obstacle.

Il est entendu qu'il ne sera porté aucune entrave aux droits et actions de la Banque d'Etat du Maroc tels qu'ils sont définis par l'Acte d'Algésiras.

ARTICLE 2.

Dans cet ordre d'idées, il est entendu que le Gouvernement impérial ne fera pas obstacle à ce que la France, après accord avec le Gouvernement marocain, procède aux occupations militaires du territoire marocain qu'elle jugera nécessaires au maintien de l'ordre et de la sécurité des transactions commerciales et à ce qu'elle exerce toute action de police sur terre et dans les eaux marocaines.

ARTICLE 3.

Dès à présent, si Sa Majesté le Sultan du Maroc venait à confier aux agents diplomatiques et consulaires de la France la représentation et la protection des sujets et des intérêts marocains à l'étranger, le Gouvernement impérial déclare qu'il n'y fera pas d'objection.

Si, d'autre part, Sa Majesté le Sultan du Maroc confiait aux représentants de la France près du Gouvernement marocain le soin d'être son intermédiaire auprès des représentant[s] étrangers, le Gouvernement Allemand n'y ferait pas d'objection.

([1]) [*v. infra*, pp. 615–18, No. 626.]

([2]) [*v. supra*, p. 139, No. 155, *encl.*, and *infra*, p. 830, *App.* IV. *cp. Gooch & Temperley*, Vol. VI, p. 230, *Ed. note.*]

* In the text received from the German Embassy (see despatch to Sir E. Goschen, No. 263 of the 6th November) the word " deux " is omitted. [The foregoing note is entered on the *Confidential Print*. Sir E. Goschen's despatch is printed *infra*, pp. 619–20, No. 628. The word " deux " was withdrawn by M. Daeschner, *v. infra*, p. 615, No. 626, *note* ([1]).]

ARTICLE 4.

Le Gouvernement Français déclare que, fermement attaché au principe de la liberté commerciale au Maroc, il ne se prêtera à aucune inégalité pas plus dans l'établissement des droits de douane, impôts et autres taxes, que dans l'établissement des tarifs de transport par voie ferrée, voie de navigation fluviale ou toute autre voie, et notamment dans toutes les questions de transit.

Le Gouvernement Français s'emploiera également auprès du Gouvernement marocain afin d'empêcher tout traitement différentiel entre les ressortissants des différentes Puissances; il s'opposera notamment à toute mesure, par exemple à la promulgation d'ordonnances administratives sur les poids et mesures, le jaugeage, le poinçonnage, etc....(³) qui pourrait mettre en état d'infériorité les marchandises d'une Puissance.

Le Gouvernement Français s'engage à user de son influence sur la Banque d'Etat pour que celle-ci confère à tour de rôle aux membres de sa direction à Tanger les postes de délégué dont elle dispose à la Commission des Valeurs douanières et au Comité permanent des douanes.

ARTICLE 5.

Le Gouvernement Français veillera à ce qu'il ne soit perçu au Maroc aucun droit d'exportation sur le minerai de fer exporté des ports marocains. Les exploitations de minerai de fer ne subiront sur leur production ou sur leurs moyens de travail aucun impôt spécial. Elles ne supporteront en dehors des impôts généraux qu'une redevance fixe, calculée par hectare et par an, et une redevance proportionnée au produit brut de l'extraction. Ces redevances qui seront assises conformément aux articles 35 et 49 du projet de règlement minier annexé au protocole du 7 Juin 1910 de la Conférence de Paris(⁴) seront également supportées par toutes les entreprises minières.

Le Gouvernement Français veillera à ce que les taxes minières soient régulièrement perçues sans que des remises individuelles du total ou d'une partie de ces taxes puissent être consenties sous quelque prétexte que ce soit.

ARTICLE 6.

Le Gouvernement de la République Française s'engage à veiller à ce que les travaux et fournitures nécessités par les concessions éventuelles de routes, chemins de fer, ports, télégraphes, etc....(³) soient octroyés par le Gouvernement Marocain suivant les règles de l'adjudication.

Il s'engage également à veiller à ce que les conditions des adjudications, particulièrement en ce qui concerne les fournitures de matériel et les délais impartis pour soumissionner, ne placent les ressortissants d'aucune Puissance dans une situation d'infériorité.

L'exploitation des grandes entreprises mentionnées ci-dessus sera réservée à l'Etat Marocain ou librement concédée par lui à des tiers qui pourront être chargés de fournir les fonds nécessaires à cet effet. Le Gouvernement Français veillera à ce que, dans l'exploitation des chemins de fer et autres moyens de transport comme dans l'application des règlements destinés à assurer celle-ci, aucune différence de traitement ne soit faite entre les Ressortissants des diverses Puissances qui useraient de ces moyens de transport.

Le Gouvernement de la République usera de son influence sur la Banque d'Etat afin que celle-ci confère à tour de rôle aux membres de sa direction à Tanger le poste dont elle dispose de Délégué à la Commission Générale des adjudications et marchés.

De même, le Gouvernement Français s'emploiera auprès du Gouvernement Marocain pour que, durant la période où restera en vigueur l'Article 66 de l'Acte d'Algésiras, il confie à un ressortissant d'une des Puissances représentées au Maroc un des trois postes de Délégué Chérifien au Comité spécial des Travaux Publics.

(³) [Thus in original.]
(⁴) [Not reproduced.]

ARTICLE 7.

Le Gouvernement Français s'emploiera auprès du Gouvernement Marocain pour que les propriétaires de mines et d'autres exploitations industrielles ou agricoles, sans distinction de nationalité, et en conformité des règlements qui seront édictés en s'inspirant de la législation française sur la matière, puissent être autorisés à créer des chemins de fer d'exploitation destinés à relier leurs centres de production aux lignes d'intérêt général et aux ports.

ARTICLE 8.

Il sera présenté tous les ans un rapport sur l'exploitation des chemins de fer au Maroc qui sera établi dans les mêmes formes et conditions que les rapports présentés aux assemblées d'actionnaires des sociétés de chemins de fer françaises.

Le Gouvernement de la République chargera un des Administrateurs de la Banque d'Etat de l'établissement de ce rapport qui sera, avec les éléments qui en seront la base, communiqué aux censeurs, puis rendu public avec, s'il y a lieu, les observations que ces derniers croiront devoir y joindre d'après leurs propres renseignements.

ARTICLE 9.

Pour éviter, autant que possible, les réclamations diplomatiques, le Gouvernement Français s'emploiera auprès du Gouvernement Marocain afin que celui-ci défère à un arbitre désigné *ad hoc* pour chaque affaire, d'un commun accord, par le Consul de France et par celui de la Puissance intéressée ou à leur défaut, par les deux Gouvernements, les plaintes portées par des ressortissants étrangers contre les autorités marocaines ou les agents agissant en tant qu'autorités marocaines, et qui n'auraient pu être réglées par l'intermédiaire du Consul de France et du Consul du Gouvernement intéressé.

Cette procédure restera en vigueur jusqu'au jour où aura été institué un régime judiciaire inspiré des règles générales de législation des Puissances intéressées et destiné à remplacer, après entente avec elles, les tribunaux consulaires.

ARTICLE 10.

Le Gouvernement Français veillera à ce que les ressortissants étrangers continuent à jouir du droit de pêche dans les eaux et ports marocains.

ARTICLE 11.

Le Gouvernement Français s'emploiera auprès du Gouvernement Marocain pour que celui-ci ouvre au commerce étranger de nouveaux ports au fur et à mesure des besoins de ce commerce.

ARTICLE 12.

Pour répondre à une demande du Gouvernement Marocain, les deux Gouvernements s'engagent à provoquer la revision, d'accord avec les autres Puissances et sur la base de la Convention de Madrid, des listes et de la situation des protégés étrangers et des associés agricoles au Maroc dont parlent les articles 8 et 16 de cette Convention.

Ils conviennent également de poursuivre auprès des Puissances signataires toutes les modifications de la Convention de Madrid que comporterait le moment venu le changement du régime des protégés et associés agricoles.

ARTICLE 13.

Toute clause d'accord, convention, traité ou règlement qui seraient contraires aux précédentes stipulations, sont et demeurent abrogées.

Article 14.

Le présent accord sera communiqué aux autres Puissances signataires de l'Acte d'Algésiras près desquelles les deux Gouvernements s'engagent à se prêter mutuellement appui pour obtenir leur adhésion.

MINUTES.

With the exception of two verbal changes this text is the same as that sent to us by Sir F. Bertie on Oct[ober] 16th, Paper No. 40798.([5]) In my minute on that paper([6]) I analysed the Convention and tried to show that except as regards commercial matters Morocco will become in due course a French possession just as much as Algeria.

The French now ask for our adhesion. As far as I am aware we are prepared to give it, subject to two considerations, which have not yet been settled :

1. Corresponding modifications in the régime in Egypt. Minutes are being written in the Eastern Dep[artmen]t on this subject.

2. The undertaking which it is proposed to obtain from the French not to fortify the Atlantic coast of Morocco south of the Sebu R[iver]. We have asked the War Office and the Admiralty for their opinion on the value of such an undertaking and the latter, who are primarily concerned, have not yet replied.

Till these two points are settled I do not think there is anything more to be said.

G. H. V.
4.11.11.

I have omitted another point on which it would be as well to be quite sure, viz., the internationalisation of Tangier. The French are it is understood quite ready to agree to this, though it is not mentioned in the final text of the Convention.

G. H. V.
6.11.11.

See separate minute herewith.

E. D.

Franco-German Convention respecting Morocco.

Article I is much the same as Article II of the 1904 Declaration. It treats in addition of judicial reform, but this point is covered by Secret Article II of the Anglo-French agreement of 1904, to which we have recently drawn the attention of the French. We ought to stipulate that we shall have the same economic equality as is given to Germany by this article (only France and Germany are specifically mentioned).

The latter part of Article I and Articles II and III foreshadow a French Protectorate over Morocco, and Germany pledges herself not to object. I do not think we could object, or attach conditions to our consent, even if we wished to.

In Article II of the 1904 Declaration the French Government stated that they did not intend to alter the political status of Morocco, that in the secret article I a declaration was made that if either Government found themselves constrained by force of circumstances to modify their policy in respect to Egypt or Morocco, Articles 4, 6 and 7 of the Declaration would remain intact.

It is clear that this foreshadowed a French Protectorate over Morocco on the one side and a possible annexation of Egypt on the other, and, it seems to me, that we practically gave our consent to the Protectorate beforehand, provided Articles 4, 6 and 7 of the Declaration remained in force.

If this is so, we have no treaty grounds for imposing any conditions on the French in return for our recognition of their Protectorate.

We might however call their attention to the Secret Article, and obtain from them a secret assurance that they will attach no conditions to their consent, if ever we wished to annex Egypt.

Article 4 safeguards commercial equality and is applicable to all the Powers.

Article 5 deals with the working and export of iron ore.

Article 6. *Paragraphs 1 and 2.*

Public works as defined in Article 106 of the Algeciras Act are to be put up to tender according to the rules of adjudication.

Doubtless these are the rules made under the Algeciras Act, but perhaps it would be wiser to get an assurance from the French Government that such is definitely the case.

Paragraph 3 introduces a new condition. It states that the exploitation of certain public works, such as roads, railways, &c., will be reserved to the Moroccan State, or freely conceded to third parties, who may be charged with the provision of the necessary funds.

This is, I think, contrary to Article 4 of the 1904 Declaration, in which it is stated that concessions are only to be granted on such conditions as will maintain intact the authority of the State over these great undertakings and (public works), and also to Articles 105 and 106

([5]) [*v. supra*, pp. 571–4, No. 589.]

([6]) [This minute is not reproduced, but its tenour is here indicated.]

of the Algeciras Act, the latter of which practically repeats the phraseology of the 1904 Declaration while the former states that in no case shall the rights of the State over the public services of the Shereefian Empire be alienated for the benefit of private interests. In practice however these conditions were unworkable in Morocco, as, owing to the State having no available funds, it was not possible to undertake any public works and the development of the country was stopped. As however the latter part of paragraph 3 provides against any discrimination in rates, &c., and as the building of railways and roads in Morocco is to our advantage commercially, I do not think that by agreeing to the new stipulation we should lose anything of practical value. It does however give us a peg on which we could hang any small request we may wish to make to the French in connexion with this agreement. I would suggest that Articles 4, 5, 6 and 7 should be sent to the Board of Trade, and their opinion taken as to whether our commercial equality is fully safeguarded by them, though I have no doubt this is the case.

As regards the rest of the Articles I agree with what Mr. Villiers has written.

It is suggested that in return for our adherence to the agreement we should ask the French for :—

    (1) an undertaking not to fortify *any part* of the Moroccan Coast.
    (2) the internationalization of Tangier.
    (3) corresponding modifications in the Egyptian judicial régime.

As regards 3 the French are bound by secret article 2 of the 1904 Declaration to agree, as soon as they definitely undertake the abolition of consular jurisdiction in Morocco, which is however only foreshadowed in paragraph 2 of Article 9. We have already drawn the attention of the French Government to this point.

As regards 2 Tangier has in practice already a special position, and it ought not to be difficult to secure French assent to its definite internationalization. No mention is made of Tangier in the present agreement, though we understand that the position of the town will form one of the subjects of discussion when the Franco-Spanish negotiations progress.

If the Diplomatic body move to Fez, the regulations for Tangier might be placed in the hands of the consular corps at the latter place and reference made to the diplomatic body only in cases of disagreement.

(3) The assurance as regards the non-fortification of any part of the Moroccan coast seems to me to be on a different footing.

We should certainly be justified in view of the change that is taking place in Morocco in approaching the French Gov[ernmen]t under the Mediterranean (1907) notes, but we have, as far as I can see, no reason to expect that the French will give us such an assurance, nor any treaty right to adduce in support of our request.

If my reading of the Secret Article I of the 1904 Declaration is correct, we are already bound to give our assent to their Protectorate, provided articles 4, 6 and 7 of the Declaration are adhered to, and what we *now* propose to ask for is an amplification of article 7, a request which we put forward in vain in 1904 (see Sir F. Bertie's despatch No. 422, Confidential, of September 28).([7])

If the French refuse we have no means of enforcing our wish, and I venture to suggest that the mere putting forward of such a request at this time would, were it to become known, have an unfortunate effect on French public opinion. It would appear that we wished to impose conditions incompatible with complete control on the territory newly acquired by the French, for which they have paid a considerable price.

The War Office (see their letter of November 3) do not seem to think it in any way vital for us to get such an assurance, and unless the Admiralty are very decided as to its necessity (in which case we shall probably have to pay elsewhere in order to secure it), it would appear wiser not to mention it to the French Government at any rate at present.

It might be considered later whether it should form one of the subjects of the probable future negotiations.

Although under Article 14 the two Governments engage to give each other mutual support in obtaining the adhesion of the signatory Powers of the Algeciras Act to the present agreement, it should be noted that we have not yet received the agreement from the German Gov[ernmen]t nor in any way been approached by them.

E. D.
6.11.11.

I entirely agree.

We can at once refer to the Board of Trade, and meanwhile stir up the Admiralty.

We should I think in any case not express our formal acceptance of the Franco-German agreement until it has been comm[unicate]d to us by Germany as well as by France.

E. A. C.
Oct. 6.

Since Sir E. Crowe's minute was written the letter from the Admiralty has been received and sent in with the letter from the W[ar] O[ffice].([8])

    ([7]) [*v. supra*, pp. 552–4, No. 567.]
    ([8]) [*v.* immediately succeeding document, and *note* (²).]

We must remember to communicate eventually to the Censor the provisions respecting the Banque d'Etat.

As regards the internationalisation of Tangier we may get what we want through the Franco-Spanish negotiations, as the Spaniards have always been very jealous of French interference there.

I agree with Mr. Drummond that we cannot claim the extension of Art[icle] 7 of the 1904 Declaration unless we adopt Sir F. Bertie's suggestion and make it a plank in our general negotiations with the French. In these, however, we shall have much to ask and little to give.

W. L.

I should like to obtain some written assurance as to the internationalization of Tangier before or when we announce our consent to the Convention—and not wait for the outcome of the Franco-Spanish negotiations which lies in the laps of the gods—I attach great importance to this matter—and it is one which should be settled—As to fortifications I still am of opinion that we should obtain a declaration from France that she maintain the engagements entered into with us under the secret 1904 agreement. I hardly think we can ask that this engagement should be extended to the whole of the Atlantic coast of Morocco. It is doubtful when we shall conclude a general arrang[emen]t with France as to territorial exchanges—the French will now not be in a hurry.

The Board of Trade could be consulted on the points in which our trade is interested.

Is it necessary to await the formal communic[atio]n by Germany? I do not know what is the custom in these matters.

A. N.

The German Ambassador made the communication on Monday.

I will discuss these minutes with Sir A. Nicolson this afternoon.

E. G.
8.11.11.

No. 620.

Admiralty to Foreign Office.

F.O. 43880/38006/11/28.
Confidential.

Sir,
Admiralty, November 3, 1911.

In reply to your letter No. 38006/11 of the 6th ultimo([1]) respecting Article VII of the Anglo-French Declaration of April 1904,([2]) I am commanded by my Lords Commissioners of the Admiralty to acquaint you, for the information of the Secretary of State for Foreign Affairs, that it is considered desirable that the formal undertaking suggested in your letter that no part of the Atlantic coast of Morocco south of the Sebou River should ever be fortified, should be obtained from the French Government if possible.

2. If the Franco-German negotiations result in France being given a free hand in Morocco, the responsibility for making suitable arrangements for the development and opening up of the country will devolve upon her. The want of a port on the West Coast will sooner or later be felt and the construction of a harbour will then be a question of money only. It will undoubtedly be to the advantage of this country if such a port be of a purely commercial nature and not fortified.([3])

I am, &c.
O. MURRAY.

([1]) [v. supra, pp. 565–6, No. 581; p. 588, No. 598, min.]
([2]) [A letter was also sent by the War Office to the Foreign Office on November 3, 1911, conceived in somewhat similar terms. (F.O. 43515/38006/11/28.)]
([3]) [v. infra, pp. 691–2, No. 687.]

No. 621.

Sir M. de Bunsen to Sir Edward Grey.

F.O. 43660/25883/11/28.
Tel. (No. 85.)

Madrid, November 4, 1911.
D. 3·5 P.M.
R. 5·30 P.M.

French Ambassador communicated last night to the Spanish Government the Franco-German agreement concerning Morocco. His Excellency expressed at the same time the hope that Spanish Government would adhere to the agreement. He added that, although agreement related to the whole of Morocco, it was of course understood by the French Government that special arrangements would have to be made by them with the Spanish Government with regard to acknowledgment of claims of Spain in Morocco. German Ambassador had not received last night his instructions to communicate agreement, but he told the French Ambassador that he was expecting them hourly.

No. 622.

Sir E. Goschen to Sir Edward Grey.

F.O. 44082/25883/11/28.
(No. 364.)
Sir,

Berlin, D. November 4, 1911.
R. *November* 7, 1911.

I have the honour to inform you that the Franco-German Agreement regarding Morocco and the Congo(1) was signed this afternoon at five o'clock by Monsieur [Jules] Cambon and Herr von Kiderlen-Waechter. It is announced that the text intended for the French Government will be despatched to-night to Paris, and that after its arrival there the Agreement will be published simultaneously by the two Governments.

I have, &c.
W. E. GOSCHEN.

(1) [For text, *v. infra*, pp. 615–18, No. 626, and pp. 831–4, *App.* IV.]

No. 623.

Sir Edward Grey to Sir M. de Bunsen.(1)

F.O. 44063/13751/11/28.
(No. 116.)
Sir,

Foreign Office, November 4, 1911.

The Spanish Ambassador called at the Foreign Office to-day and stated that the Moroccan agreement had been communicated to the Spanish Gov[ernmen]t, and that the latter had been informed that the German Gov[ernmen]t had treated Morocco as a whole, but that the French Gov[ernmen]t had not lost sight of the fact that they must come to a special arrangement with Spain as to the position which the latter should hold in Morocco.

(1) [This despatch is based on a memorandum by Sir A. Nicolson of his interview with Señor de Villa Urrutia. Sir Edward Grey has added the following minute: "This is all that we could expect the French Gov[ernmen]t, knowing what we do of M. Caillaux's views, to say to begin with. E. G."]

[19656]

2 R 2

The Ambassador said that his Government did not iike this wording, as no allusion was made to special Treaties or to the position which Spain already held in Morocco.

[I am, &c.

E. GREY.]

No. 624.

Herr von Kiderlen-Waechter to M. Jules Cambon.(¹)

F.O. 45870/25883/11/28.

Mon cher Ambassadeur,   *Berlin, le 4 novembre,* 1911.

Pour bien préciser l'accord du 4 novembre 1911 relatif au Maroc et en définir la portée, j'ai l'honneur de faire connaître à Votre Excellence que dans l'hypothèse où le Gouvernement français croirait devoir assumer le protectorat du Maroc, le Gouvernement impérial n'y apporterait aucun obstacle.

L'adhésion du Gouvernement allemand, accordée d'une manière générale au Gouvernement français par l'article 1 de ladite convention, s'applique naturellement à toutes les questions donnant matière à réglementation et visées dans l'Acte d'Algésiras.

Vous avez bien voulu me faire connaître d'autre part que, dans le cas où l'Allemagne désirerait acquérir de l'Espagne la Guinée espagnole, l'île Corisco et les îles Elobey, la France serait disposée à renoncer en sa faveur à exercer les droits de préférence qu'elle tient du traité du 27 Juin 1900 entre la France et l'Espagne. Je suis heureux de prendre acte de cette assurance, et d'ajouter que l'Allemagne restera étrangère aux accords particuliers que la France et l'Espagne croiront devoir faire entre elles au sujet du Maroc, étant convenu que le Maroc comprend toute la partie de l'Afrique du Nord s'étendant entre l'Algérie, l'Afrique Occidentale française et la Colonie espagnole du Rio de Oro.

Le Gouvernement allemand, en renonçant à demander la détermination préalable de parts à faire à l'industrie allemande dans la construction des Chemins de fer, compte que le Gouvernement français sera toujours heureux de voir des associations d'intérêt se produire entre les ressortissants des deux pays pour les affaires dont ils pourront respectivement obtenir l'entreprise.

Il compte également que la mise en adjudication du Chemin de fer de Tanger à Fez, qui intéresse toutes les nations, ne sera primée par la mise en adjudication des travaux d'un autre chemin de fer marocain et que le Gouvernement français

---

(¹) [Copies of this letter (No. 624) and of the following document (No. 625) were communicated to Sir Edward Grey by M. Daeschner on November 17, 1911, with the following covering letter :

M. Daeschner to Sir Edward Grey.

Ambassade de France à Londres.

D'ordre de son Gouvernement, le Ministre de France a l'honneur de communiquer officiellement, ci-joint, au Secrétaire d'Etat pour les Affaires Etrangères le texte des lettres explicatives qui ont été échangées entre l'Ambassadeur de la République à Berlin et le Secrétaire d'Etat Allemand pour les Affaires Etrangères à la suite de la conclusion de l'Accord du 4 Novembre relatif au Maroc.

M. Daeschner est chargé de faire observer à cette occasion que les documents en question ne sont communiqués aux Parlements Français et Allemand que sous la forme verbale et à titre confidentiel.

Albert Gate House,
     ce 17 *Novembre,* 1911.]

proposera au Gouvernement marocain l'ouverture du port d'Agadir au commerce international.

Enfin, lorsque le réseau des voies ferrées d'intérêt général sera mis à l'étude, le Gouvernement allemand demande au Gouvernement français de veiller à ce que l'administration marocaine ait le plus réel souci des intérêts économiques du Maroc, et à ce que, notamment la détermination du tracé des lignes d'intérêt général facilite dans la mesure du possible la jonction des régions minières avec les lignes d'intérêt général ou avec les ports appelés à les desservir.

Votre Excellence a bien voulu m'assurer que, le jour où aura été institué le régime judiciaire prévu par l'article 9 de la Convention précitée et où les tribunaux consulaires auront été remplacés, le Gouvernement français aura soin que les ressortissants allemands soient placés sous la juridiction nouvelle exactement dans les mêmes conditions que les ressortissants français. Je suis heureux d'en prendre acte et de faire connaître en même temps à Votre Excellence que, au jour de l'entrée en vigueur de ce régime judiciaire, après entente avec les Puissances, le Gouvernement allemand consentira à la suppression, en même temps que pour les autres Puissances, de ses tribunaux consulaires. J'ajoute que, dans ma pensée, l'expression "les changements du régime des protégés" portée à l'article 12 de la Convention du 4 Novembre 1911 relative au Maroc, implique l'abrogation, si elle est jugée nécessaire, de la partie de la Convention de Madrid qui concerne les protégés et les associés agricoles.

Enfin, désireux de donner à ladite Convention le caractère d'un acte destiné non seulement à écarter toute cause de conflit entre nos deux pays, mais encore à aider à leurs bons rapports, nous sommes d'accord pour déclarer que les différents qui viendraient à s'élever entre les parties contractantes au sujet de l'interprétation et de l'application des dispositions de la Convention du 4 Novembre et qui n'auraient pas été réglés par la voie diplomatique, seront soumis à un tribunal arbitral constitué dans les termes de la Convention de La Haye du 18 Octobre 1907. Un compromis devra être dressé, et il sera procédé suivant les règles de la même convention, en tant qu'il n'y serait pas dérogé par un accord exprès au moment du litige.

Veuillez, &c.

[von KIDERLEN-WAECHTER.]

No. 625.

M. Jules Cambon to Herr von Kiderlen-Waechter.

F.O. 45870/25883/11/28.

Mon cher Secrétaire d'Etat, *Berlin, novembre 4, 1911.*

J'ai l'honneur de prendre acte de la déclaration que Votre Excellence a bien voulu me faire que, dans l'hypothèse où le Gouvernement français croirait devoir assumer le protectorat du Maroc, le Gouvernement Impérial n'y apporterait aucun obstacle, et que l'adhésion du Gouvernement allemand, accordée d'une manière générale au Gouvernement français par l'article 1er de l'accord du 4 novembre 1911 relatif au Maroc s'applique naturellement à toutes les questions donnant matière à réglementation visées dans l'Acte d'Algésiras.

D'autre part, j'ai l'honneur de vous confirmer que dans le cas où l'Allemagne désirerait acquérir de l'Espagne, la Guinée espagnole, l'île Corisco et les îles Elobey, la France est disposée à renoncer en sa faveur à exercer les droits de préférence qu'elle tient du traité du 27 juin 1900 entre la France et l'Espagne. Je suis heureux par ailleurs de recevoir l'assurance que l'Allemagne restera étrangère aux accords particuliers que la France et l'Espagne croiront devoir faire entre elles au sujet du Maroc, étant convenu que le Maroc comprend toute la partie de l'Afrique du Nord s'étendant entre l'Algérie, l'Afrique Occidentale française et la colonie espagnole du Rio de Oro.

Je me plais aussi à vous informer que, le Gouvernement alle and renonçant à demander la détermination préalable de parts à faire dans l'industrie allemande dans la construction des chemins de fer, le Gouvernement français sera toujours heureux de voir des associations d'intérêt se produire entre les ressortissants des deux pays, pour les affaires dont ils pourront respectivement obtenir l'entreprise.

Vous pouvez également tenir pour certain que la mise en adjudication du chemin de fer de Tanger à Fez qui intéresse toutes les nations, ne sera primée par la mise en adjudication des travaux d'aucun autre chemin de fer marocain et que le Gouvernement français proposera au Gouvernement marocain l'ouverture du port d'Agadir au commerce international.

Enfin, lorsque le réseau des voies ferrées d'intérêt général sera mis à l'étude, le Gouvernement français veillera à ce que l'administration marocaine ait le plus réel souci des intérêts économiques du Maroc et à ce que notamment la détermination du tracé des lignes d'intérêt général facilite dans la mesure du possible la jonction des régions minières avec les lignes d'intérêt général ou avec les ports appelés à les desservir. Votre Excellence peut également compter que le jour où aura été institué le régime judiciaire prévu par l'art[icle] 9 de la convention du 4 novembre 1911 relative au Maroc, et où les tribunaux consulaires auront été remplacés, le Gouvernement français aura soin que les ressortissants allemands soient placés sous la juridiction nouvelle exactement dans les mêmes conditions que les ressortissants français.

Je suis heureux d'autre part de prendre acte, qu'au jour de l'entrée en vigueur du nouveau régime judiciaire après entente avec les Puissances, le Gouvernement allemand consentira à la suppression, en même temps que pour les autres Puissances, de ses tribunaux consulaires. Je prends acte également que dans la pensée de votre Excellence, l'expression '' le changement du régime des protégés '' portée à l'article 12 de la convention précitée implique l'abrogation, si elle est jugée nécessaire, de la partie de la convention de Madrid qui concerne les protégés et associés agricoles.

Enfin désireux de donner à la convention du 4 novembre 1911 relative au Maroc le caractère d'un acte destiné non seulement à écarter toute cause de conflit entre nos deux pays, mais encore à aider à leurs bons rapports, nous sommes d'accord pour déclarer que les différends qui viendraient à s'élever entre les parties contractantes au sujet de l'interprétation et de l'application des dispositions de ladite convention et qui n'auraient pu être réglés par la voie diplomatique, seront soumis à un tribunal arbitral constitué dans les termes de la convention de La Haye du 18 octobre 1907. Un compromis devra être dressé et il sera procédé suivant les règles de la même convention en tant qu'il n'y serait pas dérogé par un accord exprès au moment du litige.

Veuillez, &c.

[JULES CAMBON.]

MINUTES.

The notes deal with ten points:

1. A French protectorate over Morocco.
2. French pre-emption rights over Spanish Guinea.
3. German '' désintéressement '' in Franco-Spanish negotiations.
4. The sea-frontiers (extent) of Morocco—from Algiers to Rio del Oro.
5. Formation of '' Associations d'Intérêt.''
6. Tangier–Fez railway (primacy of—).
7. General railway policy in Morocco.
8. Suppression of Consular Courts.
9. Abrogation of Madrid Convention.
10. Machinery for arbitration.

It does not appear to me necessary for us to raise any questions on the notes, or to make any reservations.

1. A French protectorate we should be practically bound to recognize under the convention of 1904.

2 and 3 are points with which we are not concerned.

4. It is satisfactory that the usually recognized frontiers of Morocco are acknowledged.

5. We have already made a representation to the French gov[ernmen]t, and received assurances which we must accept as satisfactory. (See Sir F. Bertie's No. 444 of Oct[ober] 15, (No. 40614) annexed hereto.)([1])

6 and 7 give rise to no criticism.

8. The suppression of consular jurisdiction (capitulations) is governed, so far as we are concerned, by one of the secret articles of the Anglo-French Declaration of 1904. Our consent to the withdrawal of our jurisdiction in Morocco will automatically involve the corresponding abolition of French jurisdiction in Egypt. I see no need to recall attention to this, especially if the secret clauses are to be published shortly.

9. The abrogation of the Madrid Convention will require our formal assent. We shall presumably have no objection to it on conditions acceptable to all the treaty Powers.

10. I have already expressed the opinion that we stand to gain by the arbitration clause.

Qu[ery] Thank for communication of notes and say H[is] M[ajesty's] G[overnment] have duly taken note of them.([2])

E. A. C.
Nov. 18.

The Spaniards have always feared that they might have to pay the Germans and the provision about Spanish Guinea, &c., looks as if their fears may be justified.

W. L.
A. N.
F. D. A.
E. G.

([1]) [v. supra, pp. 569–70, No. 588, encl. 1 and 2.]
([2]) [A note to this effect was sent to M. Daeschner by Sir Edward Grey on November 24, 1911.]

No. 626.

Convention entre la France et l'Allemagne relative au Maroc.([1])

F.O. 46809/25883/11/28.

Le Gouvernement de la République Française et le gouvernement de Sa Majesté l'Empereur d'Allemagne, à la suite des troubles qui se sont produits au Maroc et qui ont démontré la nécessité d'y poursuivre, dans l'intérêt général l'œuvre de pacification et de progrès prévue par l'Acte d'Algésiras, ayant jugé nécessaire de préciser et de compléter l'accord franco-allemand du 9 février 1909,([2]) ont résolu de conclure une convention à cet effet. En conséquence, M. Jules Cambon, ambassadeur extra-ordinaire de la République française auprès de Sa Majesté l'Empereur d'Allemagne et M. de Kiderlen-Waechter, secrétaire d'Etat des Affaires étrangères de l'Empire d'Allemagne, après s'être communiqués leurs pleins pouvoirs, trouvés en bonne et due forme, sont convenus des dispositions ci-après :

ARTICLE 1er.

Le gouvernement impérial allemand déclare que, ne poursuivant au Maroc que des intérêts économiques, il n'entravera pas l'action de la France en vue de prêter

([1]) [A copy of the convention was communicated to Sir Edward Grey by M. Daeschner on November 23, 1911, with the following covering letter :—

Ambassade de France, Londres,
le 22 novembre, 1911.

Monsieur le Secrétaire d'Etat,

Pour faire suite à ma lettre du 3 de ce mois,([3]) j'ai l'honneur de faire parvenir ci-joint à Votre Excellence une copie de la Convention franco-allemande sur le Maroc, telle qu'elle a été signée à la date du 14 Novembre.([4])

Comme vous le constaterez, ce nouveau texte comporte par rapport à celui que je vous ai précédemment communiqué, une légère différence dans l'article 1er. Il est dit, en effet, à la fin du 1er paragraphe de cet article que l'action de la France sauvegardera au Maroc l'égalité économique, non pas " entre les *deux* nations," mais " entre les nations."

Ce point avait précédemment fait l'objet d'une des observations formulées dans la note de Votre Excellence du 14 de ce mois.([5])

Veuillez, &c.
E. DAESCHNER.]

([2]) [v. infra, p. 830, App. IV.]
([3]) [v. supra, p. 604–8, No. 619, and encl.]
([4]) [In the French text the date is given here as " 14 Novembre," evidently an error, as the convention was signed on November 4, infra, pp. 618, 831, 834.]
([5]) [v. infra, pp. 689–90, No. 685.]

son assistance au gouvernement marocain pour l'introduction de toutes les réformes administratives, judiciaires, économiques, financières et militaires dont il a besoin pour le bon gouvernement de l'Empire, comme aussi pour tous les règlements nouveaux et les modifications aux règlements existants que ces réformes comportent. En conséquence, il donne son adhésion aux mesures de réorganisation, de contrôle et de garantie financière que, après accord avec le gouvernement marocain, le gouvernement français croira devoir prendre à cet effet, sous la réserve que l'action de la France sauvegardera au Maroc l'égalité économique entre les nations.

Au cas où la France serait amenée à préciser et à étendre son contrôle et sa protection, le gouvernement impérial allemand, reconnaissant pleine liberté d'action à la France, et sous la réserve que la liberté commerciale, prévue par les traités antérieurs, sera maintenue, n'y apportera aucun obstacle.

Il est entendu qu'il ne sera porté aucune entrave aux droits et actions de la Banque d'Etat du Maroc, tels qu'ils sont définis par l'Acte d'Algésiras.([6])

ARTICLE 2.

Dans cet ordre d'idées, il est entendu que le gouvernement impérial ne fera pas obstacle à ce que la France, après accord avec le gouvernement marocain, procède aux occupations militaires du territoire marocain qu'elle jugerait nécessaires au maintien de l'ordre et de la sécurité des transactions commerciales, et à ce qu'elle exerce toute action de police sur terre et dans les eaux marocaines.

ARTICLE 3.

Dès à présent, si Sa Majesté le Sultan du Maroc venait à confier aux agents diplomatiques et consulaires de la France la représentation et la protection des sujets et des intérêts marocains à l'étranger, le gouvernement impérial déclare qu'il n'y fera pas d'objection.

Si, d'autre part, Sa Majesté le Sultan du Maroc confiait au représentant de la France près du gouvernement marocain le soin d'être son intermédiaire auprès des représentants étrangers, le gouvernement allemand n'y ferait pas d'objection.

ARTICLE 4.

Le gouvernement français déclare que, fermement attaché au principe de la liberté commerciale au Maroc, il ne se prêtera à aucune inégalité pas plus dans l'établissement des droits de douane impôts et autres taxes que dans l'établissement des tarifs de transport par voie ferrée, voie de navigation fluviale ou toute autre voie et notamment dans toutes les questions de transit.

Le gouvernement français s'emploiera également auprès du gouvernement marocain afin d'empêcher tout traitement différentiel entre les ressortissants des différentes puissances; il s'opposera notamment à toute mesure, par exemple à la promulgation d'ordonnances administratives sur les poids et mesures, le jaugeage le poinçonnage etc....([7]) qui pourraient mettre en état d'infériorité les marchandises d'une puissance.

Le gouvernement français s'engage à user de son influence sur la Banque d'Etat pour que celle-ci confère à tour de rôle aux membres de sa direction à Tanger les postes de délégué dont elle dispose à la Commission des valeurs douanières et au Comité permanent des douanes.

ARTICLE 5.

Le gouvernement français veillera à ce qu'il ne soit perçu au Maroc aucun droit d'exportation sur le minerai de fer exporté des ports marocains. Les exploitations de minerai de fer ne subiront sur leur production ou sur leurs moyens de travail aucun impôt spécial. Elles ne supporteront, en dehors des impôts généraux, qu'une

([6]) [The text is printed in A. & P. (1906), CXXXVI (Cd. 3087), pp. 331–388.]
([7]) [Thus in original.]

redevance fixe, calculée par hectare et par an, et une redevance proportionnée au produit brut de l'extraction. Ces redevances, qui seront assises conformément aux articles 35 et 49 du projet de règlement minier annexé au Protocole de la Conférence de Paris du 7 juin 1910 seront également supportées par toutes les entreprises minières.

Le gouvernement français veillera à ce que les taxes minières soient régulièrement perçues sans que des remises individuelles du total ou d'une partie de ces taxes puissent être consenties sous quelque prétexte que ce soit.

ARTICLE 6.

Le gouvernement de la République française s'engage à veiller à ce que les travaux et fournitures nécessités par les constructions éventuelles de routes, chemins de fer, ports, télégraphes, etc.... soient octroyés par le gouvernement marocain suivant les règles de l'adjudication.

Il s'engage également à veiller à ce que les conditions des adjudications, particulièrement en ce qui concerne les fournitures de matériel et les délais impartis pour soumissionner, ne placent les ressortissants d'aucune puissance dans une situation d'infériorité.

L'exploitation des grandes entreprises mentionnées ci-dessus sera réservée à l'Etat marocain ou librement concédée par lui à des tiers qui pourront être chargés de fournir les fonds nécessaires à cet effet. Le gouvernement français veillera à ce que, dans l'exploitation des chemins de fer et autres moyens de transport comme dans l'application des règlements destinés à assurer celle-ci aucune différence de traitement ne soit faite entre les ressortissants des diverses puissances, qui useraient de ces moyens de transport.

Le gouvernement de la République usera de son influence sur la Banque d'Etat afin que celle-ci confère à tour de rôle aux membres de sa direction à Tanger le poste dont elle dispose de délégué à la Commission générale des adjudications et marchés.

De même, le gouvernement français s'emploiera auprès du gouvernement marocain pour que, durant la période où restera en vigueur l'article 66 de l'Acte d'Algésiras, il confie à un ressortissant d'une des puissances représentées au Maroc un des trois postes de délégué chérifien au Comité spécial des travaux publics.

ARTICLE 7.

Le gouvernement français s'emploiera auprès du gouvernement marocain pour que les propriétaires de mines et d'autres exploitations industrielles ou agricoles, sans distinction de nationalité, et en conformité des règlements qui seront édictés en s'inspirant de la législation française sur la matière, puissent être autorisés à créer des chemins de fer d'exploitation destinés à relier leurs centres de production aux lignes d'intérêt général ou aux ports.

ARTICLE 8.

Il sera présenté tous les ans un rapport sur l'exploitation des chemins de fer au Maroc qui sera établi dans les mêmes formes et conditions que les rapports présentés aux assemblées d'actionnaires des sociétés de chemins de fer françaises.

Le gouvernement de la République chargera un des administrateurs de la Banque d'Etat de l'établissement de ce rapport qui sera, avec les éléments qui en seront la base, communiqué aux censeurs, puis rendu public avec, s'il y a lieu, les observations que ces derniers croiront devoir y joindre d'après leurs propres renseignements.

ARTICLE 9.

Pour éviter autant que possible les réclamations diplomatiques, le gouvernement français s'emploiera auprès du gouvernement marocain afin que celui-ci défère à

618

un arbitre désigné ad hoc pour chaque affaire d'un commun accord par le consul de France et par celui de la puissance intéressée ou, à leur défaut, par les deux gouvernements de ces Consuls, les plaintes portées par des ressortissants étrangers contre les autorités marocaines, ou les agents agissant en tant qu'autorités marocaines, et qui n'auraient pu être réglées par l'intermédiaire du consul français et du consul du gouvernement intéressé.

Cette procédure restera en vigueur jusqu'au jour où aura été institué un régime judiciaire inspiré des règles judiciaires de législation des puissances intéressées et destiné à remplacer, après entente avec elles, les tribunaux consulaires.

ARTICLE 10.

Le gouvernement français veillera à ce que les ressortissants étrangers continuent à jouir du droit de pêche dans les eaux et ports marocains.

ARTICLE 11.

Le gouvernement français s'emploiera auprès du gouvernement marocain pour que celui-ci ouvre au commerce étranger de nouveaux ports au fur et à mesure des besoins de ce commerce.

ARTICLE 12.

Pour répondre à une demande du gouvernement marocain, les deux gouvernements s'engagent à provoquer la revision, d'accord avec les autres puissances et sur la base de la Convention de Madrid, des listes et de la situation des protégés étrangers et des associés agricoles au Maroc dont parlent les articles 8 et 16 de cette Convention.

Ils conviennent également de poursuivre auprès des puissances signataires toutes modifications de la Convention de Madrid que comporterait le moment venu, le changement du régime des protégés et des associés agricoles.

ARTICLE 13.

Toutes clauses d'accord, convention, traité ou règlement qui seraient contraires aux précédentes stipulations, sont et demeurent abrogées.

ARTICLE 14.

Le présent accord sera communiqué aux autres puissances signataires de l'acte d'Algésiras près desquelles les deux gouvernements s'engagent à se prêter mutuellement appui pour obtenir leur adhésion.

ARTICLE 15.

La présente convention sera ratifiée et les ratifications seront échangées à Paris aussitôt que faire se pourra.

Fait à Berlin le 4 novembre 1911 en double exemplaire.([6])

Signé (L.S.) JULES CAMBON.
Signé (L.S.) KIDERLEN.

([6]) [v. infra, pp. 831–4, App. IV.]

No. 627.

Sir F. Bertie to Sir Edward Grey.

F.O. 43774/13751/11/28.
(No. 499.)   Confidential.   *Paris,* D. *November* 5, 1911.
Sir :—   R. *November* 6, 1911.

I have the honour to inform you with reference to my despatch No. 495 of the
3rd instant([1]) that I had a further conversation with the President of the Council
yesterday morning but I did not succeed in moving him from his declared intention
to press on the Spanish Government the Regnault Projet.([2]) He maintains that in
view of the opinions in favour of obtaining large compensations from Spain in Morocco
which are held by prominent political persons of all parties and are urged on him by
them he must maintain his views which are those set forth in the Projet which
M. de Selves he says submitted to him and he approved. He argues that the 1904
Agreements have been broken by Spain and that France cannot be expected to make
them the basis for negotiations with the Spanish Government. I am however under
the impression that on further reflection and when he finds that unless he accepts
that basis His Majesty's Government will not give any assistance at Madrid to the
French negotiations there M. Caillaux will reconsider his position for his colleagues
in the French Cabinet are I understand not by any means all agreed that his present
attitude is good policy.

I have, &c.
FRANCIS BERTIE.

MINUTES.

The situation revealed by Sir F. Bertie's despatches([2]) is a grave one and deserves serious
consideration. M. Caillaux appears not unwilling to contemplate a situation in which the
Anglo-French Entente would no longer play any part.

Sir F. Bertie will no doubt carefully watch developments. It might perhaps be suggested
to H[is] E[xcellency] (? privately) that it would be advantageous to get into touch with
M. Delcassé, who must be presumed to carry some weight in the Ministry, although there is
always the danger—as Sir F. Bertie well knows—that in the face of M. Clémenceau's hostility,
M. Caillaux might be tempted to purchase a prolongation of his premiership by the sacrifice of
M. Delcassé.

Sir F. Bertie's proceedings should be approved.

E. A. C.
Nov. 6.

As M. de Selves and other members of the Cabinet are already doubtful as to the wisdom
of the policy M. Caillaux will probably abandon it if he gets no support from us.

W. L.

Sir F. Bertie's language recorded in his despatches([2]) should be entirely approved.

A. N.
F. D. A.
E. G.

([1]) [*v. supra,* pp. 603–4, No. 618.]
([2]) [*v. supra,* pp. 583–7, No. 598, and *encl.*; pp. 599–601, No. 614; and pp. 603–4, No. 618.]

No. 628.

Sir Edward Grey to Sir E. Goschen.

F.O. 44277/25883/11/28.
(No. 263.)
Sir,   *Foreign Office, November* 6, 1911.

Count Metternich communicated to me to-day the text of the Agreement between
Germany and France as to Morocco,([1]) and said that his Government asked for our
support of it.

([1]) [*v. supra,* pp. 615–8, No. 626, and *encl.*]

I replied that I would examine the Agreement, which I had not yet studied as a whole since it was signed, though the French had kept us informed as to it during the progress of the negotiations with regard to it. I would, however, at once express my great satisfaction at the conclusion of the negotiations. Count Metternich would remember that, when the Agreement of 1909 between Germany and France as to Morocco had been made,([2]) I had expressed great satisfaction, on the assumption that difficulties about Morocco were over, because difficulties about Morocco were sure to throw Germany and ourselves in opposite diplomatic camps. If, as I hoped, and as must apparently be the case, the present Agreement between Germany and France was a permanent settlement of the difficulties as to Morocco, it would be most satisfactory to us. It might be a little time before public opinion had calmed down sufficiently to realise the full consequences of it, but its effect must be to relax the tension and to remove a great obstacle from the path of European diplomacy.

Count Metternich said very cordially that he would certainly transmit what I had said to his Government.

[I am, &c.]
E. G[REY].

([2]) [v. supra, p. 136, No. 152. cp. Gooch & Temperley, Vol. VI, p. 230, Ed. note.]

No. 629.

Note Verbale communicated by Señor de Villa Urrutia.

Embajada de España en Londres,
F.O. 44251/13751/11/28.   *7 de Noviembre de 1911.*

Gobiernos Alemania y Francia han predido adhesion, tan pronto como sea posible, de Gabinete de Madrid á Acuerdo franco-aleman. El Gobierno de S[u] M[ajestad] ha contestado que habiendo sido reconocidos sus intereses politicos y particulares en Marruecos, no estará en condiciones de prestar la referida adhesion hasta haber obtenido las necesarias seguridades para los mismos. El Gobierno de S[u] M[ajestad] cree deber informar de ello á ese Gabinete como lo hace á los demás signatarios del Actá de Algeciras.

No. 630.

Sir M. de Bunsen to Sir Edward Grey.

Madrid, November 8, 1911.
F.O. 44288/13751/11/28.   D. 5·15 P.M.
Tel. (No. 86.) Confidential.   R. 9·30 P.M.

French Ambassador has received the Spanish answer to his Excellency's note communicating the Franco-German agreement concerning Morocco. He tells me that it is to the effect that the Spanish Government accept agreement, subject to the conclusion of satisfactory arrangements in accordance with the secret convention of 1904.

I understand that the reply received by the German Ambassador makes the consent of Spain conditional on new arrangements being concluded to replace, in a manner satisfactory to Spain, articles of General Act of Algeciras by which a special position was granted to Spain.

(Repeated to Paris.)

No. 631.

Sir Edward Grey to Sir F. Bertie.

Private.([1])

My dear Bertie,   *Foreign Office, November* 8, 1911.

Your conversations with de Selves, Caillaux, and the President([2]) have been most valuable, and I endorse and shall stick to every thing that has been said on our part about negotiations with Spain.

We can have nothing to do with a line that is mean and dishonourable. We have got to keep France straight in this matter, or to part company with her. I wish of all things to avoid the latter alternative, but we can only do so by carrying the former. This we shall carry.

The President put the matter exceedingly well : one could wish for nothing better than what he said.

Yours sincerely,

E. GREY.

([1]) [Grey MSS., Vol. 13.]

([2]) [*i.e.*, the President of the Republic, M. Fallières; M. Caillaux was President of the Council from June 27, 1911, to January 11, 1912; M. de Selves, Minister of Foreign Affairs, from June 27, 1911, to January 9, 1912.]

CHAPTER LIX.

NAVAL AND MILITARY NEGOTIATIONS.

I.—THE MOLDE INCIDENT, JULY 14–JULY 26, 1911.

[*ED. NOTE.*—As will be seen, during the period of gravest crisis, July 21–24, Herr von Kiderlen-Waechter and Sir Edward Grey were engaged in a negotiation of great delicacy and involving most confidential relations. This incident is complete in itself and is therefore given out of its strict chronological order.]

No. 632.

Sir E. Goschen to Sir A. Nicolson.

Private.([1])

My dear Nicolson,   *Berlin, July* 14, 1911.

Kiderlen sent for me today and said that his excuse for asking me to come out on such a hot day was that he wanted to speak to me on a very delicate matter. He said that I no doubt remembered that some time ago " Messieurs les Marins " had, very prematurely, talked about meetings of the German and British fleets as a method of improving the relations between the two countries. The Emperor, he knew, had been much taken with the idea, but he, Kiderlen, had thought at the time that the sailors had never realized what such meetings would mean nor the effect they might produce on other Powers, and he had been very glad when the idea had been squashed. Now there was a prospect of a British and a German squadron meeting at Molde, when The Emperor would be in the " Hohenzollern." " You know the Emperor pretty well " he said " and you can imagine how excited he will be at the sight of the two Squadrons. He will certainly want to make the most of the opportunity, and there is every chance that, as an Admiral in both Navies, he will amuse Himself by putting Himself at the head of the combined squadrons and going through a series of Naval Manœuvres—ending with a great Banquet, Toasts and God knows what." He added that this was a slack time with the newspapers (as they were being told nothing about Morocco and very little about Albania) and that I could imagine what a boon the meeting of a British and a German Squadron in the presence of the Emperor would be to them. Half of the Press would write that the meeting was a proof that a naval agreement between the two countries was a " fait accompli "; the other half would try to make out that one side or the other had arranged the meeting to over-awe the other side by a display of force. In fact there was no end to the nonsense which would be written with the result that the whole of Europe [would] be agog to know what the meeting really meant. Unwarrantable conclusions would be drawn, friends and allies might be scared, explanations would be asked and, in a word, the whole thing would be a great bore. This idea troubled him very much and he wanted to know if I could assist him in preventing anything of the sort happening. The following idea had occurred to him : the chief point was to prevent the Emperor from following his impulsive ideas and making a great fuss. The British Squadron was, he had heard, timed to be at Molde on the morning of the 29th while the Emperor was absolutely obliged by his engagements to leave that Port on the morning of the 30th. Would it be possible for the British Squadron to *move slowly* and appear in the Molde Fjord only on the *evening* of the 29th? A timely fog would, he said, be the best solution, but fogs he feared were not at the command even of the powerful British Navy. But if they could have some ammunition to shoot off, or delay their arrival by some other means known

([1]) [Carnock MSS., Vol. III of 1911.]

to sailors, it would be a great relief to his mind. If this was impossible the British Squadron might perhaps arrive by driblets—the Admiral preceding his Squadron and there would be no harm in a quiet little dinner on board the "Hohenzollern," but what he wanted to avoid, if possible, was that the Empires should have time to organize a big tra-la-la (as he put it) and furnish food for all the Quidnuncs of Europe. The moment for a combined naval demonstration, such as His Majesty would love, was, he added with a wink, not propitious and would not suit his present preoccupations at all! I said that I quite saw the point and personally was inclined to agree with him but that it seemed to me that if our Squadron arrived on the Saturday morning and the Emperor had to leave early on the following day, there would scarcely be time for anything more than the usual official visits. Kiderlen said "Ah! I see you don't know our Emperor as well as I thought you did! He will entirely lose his head when he sees the two Squadrons together, and even if the Chancellor and I were there and endeavoured to restrain His ardour we should be quite unable to prevent Him from getting to work at once!"

He added that I would understand that this was a very delicate matter for him to move in, but he was so convinced that he was right that he had no hesitation in asking me to help him. Of course if it ever came out that he had acted as he was now doing he would be dismissed from his Office at once, so he would beg that if anything could be done in the way which he had suggested every precaution might be taken to make any delay which might be arranged appear as natural as possible.

I said that as a rule the timing of the visits paid by our cruising Squadrons to the various ports was arranged long beforehand and was of a hard and fast nature, and that therefore there might be some difficulty, but that I would lay the matter confidentially before Sir Edward Grey and you who would decide whether anything could be done in the way which he had suggested.

Of course there is no doubt, if Kiderlen's diagnosis of the Emperor's probable proceedings is correct, that a meeting of the two Squadrons while the "Hohenzollern" is at Molde offers great disadvantages. If the Emperor gives free rein to his passion for naval display there will certainly be plenty of excitement and plenty of erroneous impressions and conclusions, therefore I rather think that Kiderlen is right and that it will be a good thing if the great "tra-la-la" which he anticipates can be conveniently avoided.

Yours very sincerely,
W. E. GOSCHEN.

No. 633.

Sir A. Nicolson to Sir E. Goschen.

Private.(¹)
My dear Goschen, *Foreign Office, July* 18, 1911.

Many thanks for your letter marked Secret. We had already been warned of the project of a meeting of the two Fleets and we were discussing steps whereby such an event could be prevented; but your letter gave us the first intimation that the Emperor himself contemplated being present. Grey intended to speak to McKenna yesterday evening, but I have not seen him since. I think the best plan would be that our Fleet should avoid Molde altogether, and we could always explain the change of programme in a manner which need not give offence. However, before the Bag goes I shall have an opportunity of talking the question over with Grey, and we will be able to tell you what has been decided. Even without the Emperor, a meeting of the two Fleets, especially at this moment, would have perplexed France very much and would have caused much comment and misunderstandings throughout Europe. Moreover I was under the impression that we were always against such

(¹) [Carnock MSS., Vol. III of 1911.]

meetings with whatever Power might be concerned. It is curious how persistent the Germans are to sow discord between us and France but I do not think there is the slightest chance of their succeeding. . . . .(²)

[A. NICOLSON.]

(²) [The rest of this letter is reproduced, pp. 374–5, No. 395.]

No. 634.

Admiral Bethell to Sir A. Nicolson.

Private.(¹)

My dear Sir Arthur, *Admiralty, July* 21, 1911.

We are rather anxious here about the German High Sea Fleet which is cruising in Norwegian Waters where the Atlantic Fleet is also to cruise.(²) It is desirable the two fleets should not meet. Indirectly I have heard that the Consul at Molde knows the dates the Germans will be there and possibly the Consul at Christiania or our Minister knows the German programme that is the dates they will be at Norwegian Ports. The First Sea Lord would be very grateful if you would enquire for us about this. It should be done by cable otherwise it will be too late.

Yours sincerely,
A. N. BETHELL.

The Molde dates are the most important to us to know but we should like to have as much information of the Germans movements as can be obtained.

A. N. B.

(¹) [Carnock MSS., Vol. III of 1911.]
(²) [The programme of the German Fleet was finally arranged on August 8. *v. G.P.,* XXIX, p. 314.]

No. 635.

Sir E. Goschen to Sir A. Nicolson.

Secret.(¹)

My dear Nicolson, *Berlin, July* 22, 1911.

You told me in your letter(²) that before closing it you would tell me what Sir E. Grey thought of the Molde meeting of the British and [German] Naval Squadrons: *but* as you didn't do so, I suppose you didn't have an opportunity of talking over the matter with him. Kiderlen asked me yesterday whether I had heard from you on the subject. I said that personally you agreed with him that a meeting of the two Squadrons under the eye of the Emperor might give rise to a good deal of comment and perhaps misconstruction, but that you hadn't had an opportunity yet of discussing the matter with Sir E. Grey. He said that the idea was still troubling him and that he hoped sincerely that something might be arranged in the way he had suggested. He said that there was no knowing what would happen when the two fleets met. At the end of three days they might either fraternise *too much* and exchange compliments to such an extent as to disturb the minds of other Powers: or they might on the contrary be shaking their fists in each others faces with an equally disturbing result. I said that speaking for myself it seemed to be that it would be better if they did not meet at all. "That of course," he said "would be the best solution, but I'm afraid that now that all arrangements are made that would be too marked!"

(¹) [Carnock MSS., Vol. III of 1911.]
(²) [*v. supra,* pp. 623–4, No. 633.]

Still there is no doubt that if that could be arranged without offence and if good reasons could be found for the change, it would be best.

Yours in great haste,
W. E. GOSCHEN.

K[iderlen] tells me that the Norwegians don't like the German fleet going to their waters to manœuvre—(and in fact there are articles in the Norwegian papers about it) "but," he said "where else can we go?"

[W. E. G.]

No. 636.

Sir A. Nicolson to Sir Edward Grey.

Private.(¹)
My dear Grey,   53, *Cadogan Gardens, S.W., July* 24, 1911.

Please do not think me demented—but Ottley has drawn my attention, once directly and once through Crowe, to the fact that the German High Sea Fleet, cruiser squadron and torpedo flotilla are all concentrated near and about the Norwegian coasts—and in a good position for a " bolt from the blue," a contingency which the Defence Committee, though considering it most highly improbable, did not deem that it should be quite ruled out. I have also thought it odd that Kiderlen was so anxious our Fleets should not meet—and it is just possible that he had in his mind that our vessels should not see what the others were doing. I daresay this is very far fetched—but I don't like to have Ottley's remarks quite disregarded—and so send them on to you. I am very glad the meeting of the Fleets is not to take place. I think there is absolutely no risk of a bolt from the blue.

Y[ou]rs sincerely,
A. NICOLSON.

(¹) [Grey MSS., Vol. 54.]

No. 637.

Sir Edward Grey to Mr. McKenna.

Private.(¹)
Dear McKenna,   *Foreign Office, July* 24, 1911.

Since I saw you, this letter(²) has reached me.

It is too much to say that relations are strained at the present moment, for we have asked nothing of Germany yet nor she of us, but they might at any moment become strained and we are dealing with people, who recognize no law except that of force between nations, and whose fleet is mobilized at the present moment—for I suppose mobilization for manœuvres at full strength could be used if desired for attack.

Yours sincerely,
E. GREY.

(¹) [Grey MSS., Vol. 48.]
(²) [The letter was from Colonel Repington, but has not itself been traced.]

[*ED. NOTE.*—According to *Churchill*, p. 48, Sir Edward Grey said to Mr. Churchill after the interview with Count Metternich on July 25: " I have just received a communication from the German Ambassador so stiff that the Fleet might be attacked at any moment. I have sent to Mr. McKenna to warn him." The warning orders were then sent to the Fleet.]

No. 638.

Sir A. Nicolson to Sir E. Goschen.

Foreign Office, July 26, 1911.
D. 12·15 P.M.

Tel. Private.(¹)

In consequence of what M[inister for] F[oreign] A[ffairs] has twice said to you asking us to avoid any meeting of British and German fleets we have cancelled cruise of Atlantic fleet, as only way of avoiding a meeting without risk of marked discourtesy. You should inform M[inister for] F[oreign] A[ffairs], saying that this change of plan has no other object. There have also been indications that visits of foreign fleets are not very welcome at present either to Norwegians or Swedes.

(¹) [Carnock MSS., Vol. III of 1911.]

II.—GENERAL.

[*ED. NOTE.*—Professor J. H. Morgan reports Lord Haldane as saying, in a conversation held on December 17, 1917, " Lord Roberts's idea of military preparation was a purely Home Defence force, proceeding on the assumption of the ' Blue Water ' school and that England would be invaded—he had no conception of an Expeditionary Force and thought nothing of the General Staff, he thought it altogether too continental. But I realised that our frontier was the East of France. The Navy's idea was, exclusively, a battle in the North Sea. At the time of Agadir they objected that they could not transport an Expeditionary Force. They wanted a " scrap " on the sea and to throw just two Divisions into German territory with no other artillery than ship's guns which in those days had no capacity for shrapnel. I pointed out to them that the Germans had a railway system which would envelop the two Divisions with a million men in a few hours." *v. Quarterly Review*, January 1929, Vol. 252, p. 185.]

No. 639.

Memorandum by Brigadier-General Sir G. N. Nicholson.(¹)

W.O. Liaison I/6.
Secret.

War Office, November 6, 1911.

Action taken by the General Staff since 1906 in preparing a plan for rendering military assistance to France in the event of an unprovoked attack on that Power by Germany.

In January 1906, when French and German relations were strained in connexion with Morocco, the General Staff with the approval of the Ministers of State concerned began to consider what steps could be taken to render military assistance to France in the event of an unprovoked attack on that Power by Germany, should His Majesty's Government in such an event decide to render such assistance.

The problem was treated as being of a secret and hypothetical nature, and all that was done at first was to estimate the force which could be made available and the period within which it could be mobilized at the stations where the several units

(¹) [The first seven paragraphs of this memorandum were published in *Gooch & Temperley*, Vol. III, pp. 186–7, No. 221 *b*. This part is here reproduced for the sake of convenience and the whole of the remainder is now published. It is printed at the beginning of the chapter, in spite of its date, since it summarizes earlier negotiations.]

composing the force were quartered. After due consideration, and having taken into account the requirements of home defence, the General Staff were of opinion that our military resources would admit of the formation of an expeditionary force for the purpose in view, consisting of four Divisions and a Cavalry Division. But if the scheme were to be of any value should the occasion arise for carrying it into effect, it was necessary to go further and to collect and formulate information regarding the ports of embarkation and railway transport thereto, transport by sea across the Channel, the ports of disembarkation, and railway transport therefrom to the assumed area of operations.

The consideration of some of these questions obviously involved secret and unofficial communication with one or more members of the French General Staff, and reference was made to the Foreign Office on the subject. In reply Lord Sanderson informed General Grierson, then Director of Military Operations, on the 15th January, 1906, that Sir Edward Grey in concurrence with the Secretary of State for War agreed to communications being entered into with Colonel Huguet, the French Military Attaché, for the purpose of obtaining such information as might be required, it being understood that the communications must be solely provisional and non-committal.

Colonel Huguet was accordingly consulted, and a preliminary scheme was drawn up with the assistance of the Admiralty in regard to the ports of embarkation and disembarkation and the arrangements for sea transport across the Channel. As secrecy was essential, no official letters passed on the subject between the War Office and the Admiralty.

Meanwhile the tension between France and Germany began to relax, and hopes were entertained, which were afterwards realized, that the dispute about Morocco might be capable of amicable settlement, at any rate for the time being.

In October, 1906, General Ewart succeeded General Grierson as Director of Military Operations, and found that the original scheme needed revision on account of changes in the organization of the Home Army. Intimation had also been received of certain changes in the French plans of mobilization and concentration, which affected the ports of disembarkation and the railway transport therefrom. A revised scheme was therefore prepared, but before communicating it to Colonel Huguet Sir Neville Lyttleton, then Chief of the General Staff, approached the Foreign Office and on July 26th, 1907, submitted a covering memorandum indicating the action which it was proposed to take. In this memorandum it was clearly laid down that the scheme was not binding on the British Government, but merely showed how the plans made in view of the situation in 1906 would be modified by the changes made in the organization of the Home Army in 1907. The memorandum with a few verbal amendments was approved by Sir Edward Grey, and Colonel Huguet was informed accordingly.

At the same time the Admiralty were unofficially acquainted with the changes in the scheme so far as that Department was concerned, and Lord Fisher, then First Sea Lord, authorized General Ewart to settle details with Sir Charles Ottley, then Director of Naval Intelligence, and the Director of Naval Transport.

The scheme was then further elaborated, and on December 3rd, 1908, it was laid before a Sub-Committee of the Committee of Imperial Defence appointed by the Prime Minister to consider the Military Needs of the Empire. This Sub-Committee was presided over by the Prime Minister and included among its members the Marquess of Crewe, Viscount Haldane, Mr. McKenna, Lord [Sir C.] Hardinge, and Lord [Sir J.] Fisher.[2] The question of rendering naval assistance to France in the event of an unprovoked attack on that Power by Germany was considered at a second meeting of the Sub-Committee on December 17th, 1908; and at a third

---

[2] [The Records of the Committee of Imperial Defence show that Lord Esher and the following technical advisers were present: Rear-Admiral Slade (succeeded by Rear-Admiral Bethell, March, 1909), Sir J. French, Sir W. Nicholson, Major-General Ewart, and Admiral Sir C. Ottley, Secretary.]

meeting on March 23rd, 1909, the question of rendering military assistance was further discussed, the following conclusion being unanimously arrived at—

" (a) In the event of an attack on France by Germany, the expediency of sending a military force abroad, or of relying on naval means only, is a matter of policy which can only be determined, when the occasion arises, by the Government of the day.

" (b) In view, however, of the possibility of a decision by the Cabinet to use military force, the Committee have examined the plans of the General Staff, and are of opinion that in the initial stages of a war between France and Germany, in which the British Government decided to assist France, the plan to which preference is given by the General Staff is a valuable one, and the General Staff should accordingly work out all the necessary details."

The Sub-Committee reported this conclusion to the Committee of Imperial Defence on July 24th, 1909. In their Report the Sub-Committee remarked that it would be possible in the course of a few months to strengthen the British Expeditionary Force of four Divisions and one Cavalry Division by the two remaining Divisions, thus bringing the force up to 160,000 men.

In accordance with the conclusion arrived at the General Staff continued to elaborate the scheme, certain alterations being made from time to time in the ports of embarkation and disembarkation in conformity with variations in the naval situation and in the French plans of military concentration.

In April last, when the recurrence of tension between France and Germany seemed not improbable, the possibility of at once despatching six instead of four Divisions besides the Cavalry Division came under consideration, and revised tables for the larger force with accelerated dates of mobilization were worked out. The tables for movements by rail, embarkation, sea transport, and disembarkation were similarly revised. This enlarged scheme was drawn up not in supersession of, but as an alternative to, the original scheme, from which it only differed in contemplating the immediate despatch of the two additional Divisions instead of in the course of a few months. As the greater includes the less, it is obvious that arrangements made for the despatch of a larger force would *a fortiori* provide for the despatch of a smaller force. It was recognized by the General Staff that the alternative scheme would have to be referred to the Committee of Imperial Defence for consideration, and it was submitted and explained in detail to the Committee on the 23rd August last,[3] the Prime Minister presiding and Sir Edward Grey, Mr. Lloyd George, Lord Haldane, Mr. McKenna, Mr. Winston Churchill, and the First Sea Lord[4] being present with other members. At the meeting doubt was expressed by some of those present as to the prudence of adopting the alternative scheme, more particularly in connection with the requirements of home defence, but no conclusion was arrived at.

It may be added that the greatest care has been taken throughout by the General Staff to treat the plans for rendering military assistance to France, should His Majesty's Government determine to render such assistance on occasion arising, as being secret, hypothetical, and non-committal. Personally I have never spoken on the subject to any French officer, not even to Colonel Huguet. It has been unavoidable for the Director of Military Operations to consult Colonel Huguet and a few experts of the French General Staff whom he has interviewed on technical matters at Colonel Huguet's request; but that the non-committal proviso has been rigidly adhered to is evident from a note which was made in French of a conversation which took place on July 20th, 1911.[5] This note is prefaced by a statement which may be translated as follows—" First and foremost, it is placed on record that these

[3] [Sir Henry Wilson's speech is described in his *Life and Diaries* (1927), *ed.* Gen. Sir C. E. Callwell, I, pp. 99–101, and in Churchill, *The World Crisis, 1911–4*, pp. 56–8.]

[4] [Admiral Sir Arthur Wilson.]

[5] [*v.* immediately succeeding document.]

communications are devoid of any official significance, and are in no way binding on the British and French Governments.''([6])

(Sd.)   W. G. N.,

War Office,

6-11-11.

([6]) [*cp.* Wilson, *Life and Diaries,* Vol. I, pp. 96–107.]

[*ED. NOTE.*—The difference between the military and naval points of view, and a summary of Admiral Sir Arthur Wilson's opinion as expressed at the meeting of the Committee of Imperial Defence of August 23, are in *Churchill,* pp. 58–9. The result of this disagreement was shown in Lord Haldane's demand for an Admiralty Board to work in full harmony with the War Office plans, *v.* Churchill, *The World Crisis, 1911–4,* p. 59; Asquith, *Genesis of the War* (1923), p. 96; and Haldane, *Autobiography* (1929), pp. 225–34.]

No. 640.

Memorandum of Meeting held on July 20, 1911, *between General Dubail and General Wilson.*

W.O.   *August* 21, 1911.

Le 20 juillet 1911, à 3 heures de l'après-midi, une conférence a eu lieu au Ministère de la Guerre à Paris, entre : M. le Général Dubail, Chef d'Etat-Major de l'Armée française, et M. le Général Wilson, Directeur des opérations militaires au War-Office, en vue de déterminer les conditions de la participation éventuelle d'une armée anglaise aux opérations des armées françaises du Nord-Est, dans une guerre contre l'Allemagne.

Assistaient à cette conférence :

M. le Général Regnault, sous-chef d'état-major de l'armée française.

M. le Colonel Huguet, attaché militaire à l'Ambassade de la République Française en Angleterre.

M. le Lieutenant-Colonel Hallouin, chef du bureau des opérations à l'Etat-Major de l'Armée française.

M. le Lieutenant-Colonel Crepey, chef du bureau des transports, à l'Etat-Major de l'Armée française.

Il a tout d'abord été déclaré :

Que les pourparlers engagés, dépourvus de tout caractère officiel, ne pouvaient lier en rien les Gouvernements anglais et français,

Que la conférence avait seulement pour but d'élucider certaines questions essentielles, et de prévoir les mesures préparatoires indispensables, de manière à assurer, le cas échéant, dans les meilleures conditions possible, la co-opération effective des Armées coalisées.

Dans cet ordre d'idées, la discussion a porté et l'accord s'est établi sur les points suivants :

    I. Composition de l'Armée anglaise de débarquement.

    II. Transports maritimes.

    III. Débarquements sur le territoire français et séjour dans des camps temporaires.

    IV. Transports en chemin de fer.

    V. Zone de concentration, date de l'achèvement des transports.

    VI. Alimentation.

I.—*Composition de l'Armée anglaise de débarquement.*

L'Angleterre consacrera aux opérations contre l'Allemagne la totalité des forces dont elle dispose pour les expéditions hors de son territoire, savoir :

> six divisions actives
> une division de cavalerie
> deux brigades montées
> des éléments d'Armée.

Les effectifs transportés en France s'éléveront à un total de 150,000 hommes, 67,000 chevaux, en chiffres ronds.

II.—*Transports maritimes.*

Ces troupes viendront atterrir sur le territoire français dans les ports de Rouen, le Havre et Boulogne.

Toutes les questions relatives aux transports maritimes, jusques et y compris celle de l'intensité des débarquements quotidiens seront étudiées et réglées par les soins de l'Amirauté anglaise.

Toutefois, l'Etat-Major français devra fixer l'Amirauté sur la longueur de quais réservée dans chaque port pour l'amarrage des bâtiments français.

III.—*Débarquements et séjour dans ces camps temporaires.*

Les dispositions relatives au débarquement à Boulogne, au Havre, à Rouen et à l'installation des troupes anglaises débarquées dans ces ports incomberont à l'état-major français.

Les débarquements s'effectueront :

> les 4e et 5e jours de la mobilisation anglaise pour l'infanterie.
> le 6e jour de la mobilisation anglaise pour les boulangeries et quelques organes de ravitaillement.
> du 7e au 12e jour de la mobilisation anglaise pour les troupes montées et les convois.

Autant que possible les troupes anglaises, au fur et à mesure de leur débarquement seront dirigées sur des camps temporaires où elles feront un séjour d'au moins 24 heures.

L'Etat-Major français procédera, dés à présent, à des reconnaissances en vue de déterminer les emplacements des camps et d'établir s'il y a lieu, les projets de travaux à effectuer, notamment en ce qui concerne l'adduction de l'eau.

Les tentes seront fournies par l'administration anglaise qui les transportera en temps utile.

Parallèlement aux reconnaissances faites, en vue de l'installation des camps temporaires, l'Etat-Major français tracera pour le cas d'une campagne d'hiver des zones de cantonnement à proximité des trois ports de débarquement.

IV.—*Transports par chemin de fer.*

Les transports par voie ferrée s'effectueront par deux lignes indépendantes :

> de Boulogne sur Douai.
> du Havre et de Rouen par Amiens sur Saint-Quentin.

Chacune de ces lignes a un débit de 42 trains par jour, soit 84 trains pour l'ensemble des deux courants.

En tenant compte du battement minimum de 24 heures entre le moment où une unité débarque en France et celui où elle est enlevée vers la base de concentration, les transports pourront commencer :

pour l'infanterie le 5ᵉ jour de la mobilisation anglaise.

pour les éléments montés et les convois le 8ᵉ jour de la mobilisation anglaise.

Les derniers éléments de convois partiront des camps temporaires le 13ᵉ jour dans la soirée ou le 14ᵉ jour au matin.

Les transports se diviseront en trois échelons :

		Débarquements dans la zone de concentration.
I. Infanterie, Etats-Majors, Boulangeries, quelques éléments de ravitaillement	100 trains environ ...	avant le 8ᵉ jour (moyenne 33 trains par jour).
II. Autres éléments combattants ...	250 trains environ ...	du 8ᵉ au 13ᵉ jour inclus.
III. Convois	100 trains (étude du 4ᵉ bureau)	(moyenne 60 trains par jour.)

Comme le montre ce tableau, l'utilisation de 2 lignes de transport permettra, tout en restant au-dessous du rendement maximum d'enlever les unités de toutes catégories à peu près au fur et à mesure de leur arrivée en France.*

V.—*Zone de Concentration.*

La zone des débarquements de concentration serait comprise entre Arras, Saint-Quentin et Cambrai.

Toutes les unités de l'Armée anglaise (y compris les convois) seront débarquées le 15ᵉ jour de la mobilisation.

Il est permis d'espérer que tous les éléments combattants pourront être à pied d'oeuvre le 13ᵉ jour.**

VI.—*Alimentation.*

L'alimentation des troupes anglaises sera assurée jusqu'au 7ᵉ jour inclus par l'administration anglaise : du 8ᵉ au 11ᵉ jour inclus, elle est à la charge de la France.

L'administration anglaise reprend les distributions à dater du 12ᵉ jour.

En résumé, l'armée anglaise forte de 6 divisions d'infanterie, 1 division de Cavalerie, 2 Brigades montées, débarquant à Rouen, au Havre et à Boulogne, sera transportée par deux lignes ferrées indépendantes sur St. Quentin et Douai. Elle pourra commencer les opérations actives au plus tard le 14ᵉ jour de la mobilisation anglaise, c'est à dire dans des conditions satisfaisantes pour coopérer utilement avec les Armées françaises, à la condition que le retard de la mobilisation anglaise ne soit pas trop considérable.

L'alimentation des effectifs débarqués ne sera à la charge de la France que du 8ᵉ jour inclus au 11ᵉ jour inclus. L'Etat-Major français se charge de l'installation des troupes anglaises, aussi bien dans les camps provisoires après leur arrivée sur le territoire français (tentes apportées par l'Armée anglaise) que sur la base de concentration.

A la fin de la conférence, M. le Général Wilson a demandé qu'il soit procédé à des études sur les points suivants :

Télégraphie.

Les agents anglais doubleront-ils purement et simplement les télégraphistes français, ou bien ces agents apporteront-ils leurs appareils pour exploiter eux-mêmes les lignes télégraphiques françaises?

* Dans le cas où l'infanterie serait débarquée dans les ports et prête à être enlevée longtemps avant l'artillerie, il vaudra mieux la maintenir dans les camps temporaires plutôt que de la transporter prématurément dans la zone de concentration, en laissant ensuite une lacune dans les transports.

** Il est entendu que les unités, au fur et à mesure de leur arrivée dans la zone de concentration, se placeront dans des conditions leur permettant de commencer le mouvement en avant aussitôt après l'arrivée des derniers éléments combattants.

Grand Parc à munitions.

Le Grand Parc à munitions doit-il être installé à Rouen, au Havre, ou à Boulogne?

Ravitaillement en pétrole.

L'administration française pourra-t-elle assurer le ravitaillement de l'armée anglaise en pétrole?

La conférence prend fin à cinq heures.

Fait à Paris le 20 Juillet 1911.

Le Chef d'Etat-Major de l'Armée Française :

(Sgd.)	DUBAIL.
(Sgd.)	HENRY WILSON,
	Director Military Operations.

21.8.11.

No. 641.

Sir F. Bertie to Sir Edward Grey.(1)

F.O. 34109/34109/11/17.
(No. 377.) Secret.   *Paris, D. August 25, 1911.*
Sir,   R. *August 29, 1911.*

I have the honour to transmit to you herewith a despatch as marked in the margin which I have received from Colonel Fairholme, Military Attaché to this Embassy reporting a conversation with General Joffre, Chief of the French General Staff, respecting strategical problems which would arise in a war between Germany and France and other matters.

I have, &c.
FRANCIS BERTIE.

Enclosure in No. 641.

Colonel Fairholme to Sir F. Bertie.

(No. 12.) Confidential.
Sir,   *Paris, August 24, 1911.*

I have the honour to report to Your Excellency that I was to-day received by General Joffre, the newly appointed Chief of the French General Staff, who, under the recent reorganisation of the High Command, occupies the position of supreme head of the main French Armies in Peace and War.

General Joffre, who took part in the defence of Paris as a Sub-Lieutenant in the Siege Artillery, and was transferred to the Engineers after the war, has seen service in several Colonial Expeditions, including Tonkin, in all of which he rendered eminent services. He commanded the IInd Army Corps (Amiens) up to last year, when he was appointed a Member of the Supreme Council of War.

I was favourably impressed by the personality of the new Chief, who is a big, square-built man, quiet in manner, but with an unmistakable air of confidence and resolution. He is 59 years of age.

(1) [Reprinted from *Gooch & Temperley,* Vol. VI, pp. 642–4, No. 475 and *encl.*]

1 found the General extremely well-disposed towards England, and anxious to maintain the cordial and intimate relations which have existed of late between the two Armies. He expressed his intention of affording all possible facilities for the interchange of information, and of visits by French and British officers, with a view to mutual improvement and understanding.

When the first reserve had worn off, he became more communicative than most French Generals in responsible positions, and it may interest Your Excellency to know what he said about the present political and military situation.

General Joffre considers that, though relations with Germany are undoubtedly very strained, ("très tendues"), the principal danger of the protracted negotiations lies in the possibility of incidents occurring which might inflame public opinion on either side.

The French Military Attaché in Berlin, who was formerly Chief Staff Officer to General Joffre, had, in letters to his late commander, for some time past predicted the present difficulties with regard to Morocco, but, in his opinion, Germany does not want war at the present moment. He thinks it probable that an unsatisfactory agreement, wanting in finality, will be patched up. He writes, however, that the German General Staff is very busy just now with war preparations.

On the French side, General Joffre said that he and his Staff have been, and are still, hard at work settling the details of their plans of campaign, which, he stated, will be ready in every particular in a few days' time.

The General then went on to discuss the strategical problem.

The one unknown factor is whether the Germans mean to come through Belgium or not. "I wish I knew that," he observed, "and I wish I knew that they intend doing so; it would be better for us. It would greatly hamper our dispositions if we did not know their intentions in this respect by about the fourth day of mobilisation, as it would be difficult to get back any considerable force in time for employment in the main theatre of operations which had been originally sent to oppose an advance through Belgium. Recent German preparations, construction of railways and detraining platforms, &c., point to an intention to move considerable bodies of troops in these regions."

The new Chief attaches the very greatest importance to the co-operation of a British expeditionary force, which concentrating somewhere between Douai and Cambrai, and falling on the right flank of the German advance, might produce great, and even decisive, results. But it would have to be sent early in the day; its intervention, for instance, on the 18th day of the French mobilisation, might not prove a bit too soon. As regards the provision by the French authorities of the requisite railway transport to convey the British contingent to the points of concentration which might ultimately be fixed on, he anticipates no difficulty, even should all the six British Infantry Divisions be dispatched.

He stated that arrangements have recently been made by which the carrying powers of the French railways in War have been considerably increased.

"In any case," he said, "Germany must pour a large force into Alsace and Lorraine, as if they allowed us to gain a footing there the populations of both provinces would rise. *This we know for certain.* And then every possible difficulty would be created for their railway transport, &c."

I gathered that, if the Germans should advance in force viâ Belgium, the French plan would be to hold them in check on that flank, and to attack vigorously on Alsace and Lorraine.

General Joffre remarked that if the Germans did not attack in force through Belgium, the front of contact between the two armies would become very restricted for such large forces.

I ventured to suggest that such a contingency might not prove disadvantageous to France in view of the notorious superiority of the German forces in numbers.

"That superiority," General Joffre replied, "does not trouble me very much. It would only amount to two or three Army Corps. Against the German Reserve

Corps we have our Reserve Divisions, and we can count on the active intervention of the Russian army, which would be on the move certainly before the 30th day of our mobilisation. But we should very much like to know what Austria would do."

On my mentioning Italy, the General said very positively, " Italy will make no move. Her interests lie on our side, not on that of Germany and Austria."

Speaking of the abandonment of the French Army Manœuvres, which has now been definitely decided on, General Joffre said that this is due to the prevalence of foot-and-mouth disease in the North of France; from his manner, and from the details he gave me, I am satisfied that this, and not the possibility of war, is the true reason for the change of plans.

He informed me that the manœuvres of the VIIth Army Corps, (Besançon), which, like the VIth, is a frontier corps of three Infantry Divisions, will be transformed into Army Manœuvres, but on a smaller scale than those originally contemplated. and that the Foreign Officers will be invited to witness these instead of those which have now been cancelled.

I have, &c.
W. E. FAIRHOLME, *Colonel,*
Military Attaché.

No. 642.

Mr. Lloyd George to Sir Edward Grey.

Private.([1])
My dear Grey, *Brynawelon, Criccieth, September* 1, 1911.

Winston has asked me to forward enclosed to you.([2])

The Kaiser is I believe sincerely anxious to keep the peace but Waechter has pushed him into a position whence he cannot retire with dignity. The agitation in Germany is making it increasingly difficult for him to give in and the Cartwright incident has added another complication.([3])

War is by no means inevitable but it is becoming an increasing probability. It is so much in the reckoning as to render it urgently necessary for us to take every step which would render the issue of war more favourable, always provided that such a step does not increase the chance of precipitating war.

I hope you have had a short respite from your anxieties.

Y[ou]rs sincerely,
D. LLOYD GEORGE.

([1]) [Grey MSS., Vol. 62.]
([2]) [This letter from Mr. Churchill cannot be traced.]
([3]) [The subject of the Cartwright interview is treated *infra* pp. 837–45, *App.* V.]

No. 643.

Sir F. Bertie to Sir Edward Grey.

F.O. 34910/34910/11/17.
(No. 391.) *Paris,* D. *September* 2, 1911.
Sir, R. *September* 5, 1911.

I have the honour to transmit to you herewith, a despatch which I have received from Colonel Fairholme, Military Attaché to this Embassy, relating to his interview with the Minister for War.

I have, &c.
FRANCIS BERTIE.

Enclosure in No. 643.

Colonel Fairholme to Sir F. Bertie.

Sir :—   *Paris, September 1, 1911.*

I have the honour to inform Your Excellency that I was to-day received for the first time by the new Minister for War.

I was much struck by the youthful and lively appearance of Monsieur Messimy, who might well be taken for a captain, or even for a senior lieutenant in the French Army.

He gave me the impression of a somewhat hot-headed personality, and one which might readily become pugnacious, so that I should hardly think that his presence at the War Office is a factor which would tend to throw oil on the troubled waters in the present political situation.

Speaking of the latter he said that France does not want war, but is not afraid of it. " If it is only a matter of ceding a few thousand square miles of Africa to Germany, that, he said, is not a matter for two great nations to fight over, but we are not, and I least of all, am not, going to stand any more nonsense from Germany, no ' manque de politesse,' and I expect you will have noticed that we have the nation at our back." This sentence he repeated almost in the same words no less than three times, and he seemed to me to attach almost more importance to the moral than to the material aspect of any injury which France might suffer.

Monsieur Messimy alluded with considerable warmth to what he called the rudeness and brutality of Herr von Kiderlin [*sic* : Kiderlen]-Waechter.

He said that Germany was always going behind agreements and wanting something more, but that France this time had made up her mind what she is ready to concede, and would go no further. She, France, must have a free hand in Morocco.

As regards the state of preparation for War, Monsieur Messimy said that when France got her warning, four years ago, she had begun to prepare, and had been preparing ever since, but that during the last two months the work of preparation had been most " intensive."

He was not prepared to say that he thought that there would be war, but if it came he thought that France would win.

I have, &c.
W. E. FAIRHOLME, *Colonel,*
Military Attaché.

No. 644.

Sir F. Bertie to Sir Edward Grey.

F.O. 35713/35713/11/28.
(No. 399.)   *Paris, D. September 8, 1911.*
Sir :—   *R. September 11, 1911.*

I have the honour to transmit to you, herewith, a despatch which I have received from Colonel Fairholme, Military Attaché to this Embassy, relating to the present condition of the French Army.

I have, &c.
FRANCIS BERTIE.

Enclosure in No. 644.

Colonel Fairholme to Sir F. Bertie.

Sir :—   *Paris, September 7, 1911.*

It has been generally noticed that the attitude of the French public, and of nearly the whole of the French Press, during the present period of strained relations with Germany, is being characterised by a spirit of calm confidence, such as they have not been known to exhibit in similar situations in the past.

In military circles, so far as I am able to judge, the same feelings prevail, there is no wish to pick a quarrel with Germany, but, should it come to a war, the French Army is not at all afraid regarding the result.

It may not be out of place at the present juncture, to consider how far, from the military point of view, the confidence of the French Nation is justified, and also to what extent the present moment should prove favourable, in the interests of France, for embarking on the struggle which all seem convinced must come within the next few years.

I have had no opportunity of seeing anything of the German Army for some years past, so that I do not feel qualified to hazard an opinion as to the relative values of the two armies at the present moment, nor to predict what would be the ultimate result, were war to break out now.

But I can affirm, without fear of contradiction, that the French Army has never, in modern times, been so well trained, or so ready for war as it is to-day.

The last two years have been marked by great general progress, and by the introduction of a number of highly important military reforms, such as no corresponding period in the past could show, while the annual expenditure on the army has increased, during the same period, by five and a half million pounds sterling.

During the past three months, abnormal activity has been displayed in preparing for war, organising the commands and staffs for the armies which would be formed, and in working out the plans of campaign, which, I understand, are now complete in every detail.

These measures have quite recently involved numerous changes affecting the holders of important posts, and I am in a position to state that the Generals to whom the conduct of affairs has now been entrusted, as well as their Chief Staff Officers, enjoy the fullest confidence of the Army.

Amongst the new appointments I would especially name General de Castelnau, First Assistant-Chief of the General Staff, who would assume the duties of Chief of the Staff of the principal Group of Armies on the outbreak of war. This officer is spoken of as " a French von Moltke."

As regards armament, the French have got, and know how to use, the best quick-firing field gun in existence, superior to the German gun in several respects.

The French Infantry rifle is, now that the Balle S. has been adopted, practically as good as the German rifle.

In efficiency of training, the French Infantry, judged by its work in peace time, and measured by British standards, leaves something to be desired; but its best qualities are only brought out by war, and it is probably the equal of the German infantry in most respects and its superior in dash and in intelligence.

The French Cavalry is admirably trained and horsed and it should prove to be at least as good as the German.

The French Field Artillery is somewhat weaker in guns than the German, 120 per Army Corps as against 144, but this disparity will be more than compensated by the marked superiority of the French gun itself, as well as by the better French artillery methods and training, and also by the four-gun battery organisation.

In Military Aviation the French have practically the monopoly of what may prove to be a very powerful auxiliary in war. Even should the actual usefulness of this new Arm turn out to be less than is expected, the confidence and the enthusiasm resulting from its possession form a moral asset of no small value, especially in view of the French national character.

Of dirigibles the French Army would have several available, though the Germans, in spite of very numerous casualties of late, would no doubt still hold the superiority in this respect; the value of these unwieldy and delicate structures, for war purposes, has however yet to be proved.

As regards numbers, France, with her stationary population, has for some time past been at a disadvantage, but it is by no means certain that, in a war on such a large scale, this difference would necessarily make itself felt to any very great extent, owing to the difficulties attendant on the application of these masses of men. I have the authority of the new Chief of the General Staff, General Joffre, for saying that the French Staff is not very much preoccupied by this consideration.

With regard to the plan of campaign, it is reassuring, from the French point of view, to note that the idea of taking the offensive, the military policy of the strong, and the only one which makes for decisive victory, now finds far more favour in French military circles than was the case even quite recently. It had often been noticed by foreign military observers, up to quite a short time ago, amongst others by my predecessor, Lieutenant-Colonel Lowther, that, in connection with Germany, defence, and defence only, was spoken and written about; "Sommes-nous défendus?" and the idea of carrying the war into the enemy's country did not seem to enter into the programme of the most optimistic. There has of late been a very marked change in this respect.

It does not come within my province to discuss Naval matters, but it is impossible not to be struck by the enthusiasm which has been caused by the recent Naval Review at Toulon, which seems to mark the dawn of a new era for the French navy, a service which, till quite recently had suffered from the continuous neglect of many successive administrations.

Turning now to a consideration of the opportuneness or otherwise, of the present moment for the war, the following would seem to be reasons in favour of it, from the French point of view:

1. The Government has just now got the whole nation at its back, which might not by any means be the case at some future time.
2. With her stationary population, France would meet Germany now on more favourable terms as regards numbers, than would be the case later on, when each succeeding year must increase the disparity.
3. A substantial increase in the French Field Artillery was completed last year, and any further increase, on a large scale, of that Arm, would be difficult. On the other hand, the German Artillery might improve as regards both armament and training.
4. France, at the expense of great sacrifices, in valuable lives and in money, has got a long lead in everything connected with aviation, whereas Germany has scarcely begun to occupy herself with that service.

On the other hand, the following may perhaps be considered as reasons against the war at the present moment:—

1. The Russian Army might perhaps be in a better position to afford active co-operation beyond the Russian frontiers after it has had more time to carry out the changes of organisation and distribution recently introduced.
   (But on the other hand, it might be more preoccupied by internal troubles at some future time than now.)
2. The effects of some of the important reforms recently introduced in the French Army will require some time to make themselves fully felt, and it may consequently be anticipated that, in this respect, that army would be still more efficient, a year, or even two years hence.

To sum up, it seems to me that the balance of evidence is in favour of a war at the present moment.

I have, &c.

W. E. FAIRHOLME, Colonel,
Military Attaché.

No. 645.

Mr. McKenna to Sir Edward Grey.

Private.([1])
Tel.

H.M.S. " Enchantress," Invergordon,
September 15, 1911.

Am with Home Fleet at Cromarty. If any danger of attack on ships at anchor here not safe at night. Do you think safer position necessary? No difficulty in moving if desirable though some comment may be made.

MINUTE.

Sir A. Nicolson and I thought it would be best to consult Sir Arthur Wilson as to this, and after doing so I have sent the annexed telegram in reply.([2])

H. M.
15.ix.1911.
E. G.

([1]) [Grey MSS., Vol. 48.]
([2]) [v. immediately succeeding document.]

No. 646.

Sir Edward Grey to Mr. McKenna.

Private.([1])
Tel.

Foreign Office, September 15, 1911.
D. 4·50 P.M.

Your tel[egram] today.

No special development to make danger of sudden attack greater since I saw you, but possible danger exists in present situation. We have consulted 1st Sea Lord who thinks that no further precautions are necessary beyond those ordinarily taken by the fleet.

([1]) [Grey MSS., Vol. 48.]

No. 647.

Sir Edward Grey to Sir A. Nicolson.

Private.([1])
My dear Nicolson,

Fallodon, September 17, 1911.

The negotiations with Germany may at any moment take an unfavourable turn and if they do so the Germans may act very quickly—-even suddenly.

The Admiralty should remain prepared for this: it is what I have always said to McKenna. Our fleets should therefore always be in such a condition and position that they would welcome a German attack, if the Germans decided to act suddenly.

We should of course give the Admiralty news immediately of any unfavourable turn in the Franco German negotiations, but German action might follow so soon after this that there would not be time to get our ships together, if they were not already in positions whence this could be done quickly.

I should like to be sure that the Admiralty are keeping this in mind.

([1]) [Carnock MSS., Vol. IV of 1911.]

I am puzzled by the German optimistic reports of the prospect of the Franco-German negotiations, they may be and probably are intended to prepare the way for a climb down : but they may be intended to mislead and lull suspicions before a rapid coup.

Y[our]s sincerely,
E. GREY.

[ED. NOTE.—An explanation of the British military and naval preparations during August and September was given by Lord Haldane to Captain Ostertag, the German military attaché in London, and reported by him on October 24, 1911, v. G.P., XXIX, pp. 247–9, and notes with further references; v. also Haldane, Autobiography (1929), p. 225.]

No. 648.

Lord Granville to Sir Edward Grey.

F.O. 42692/21735/11/28.

(No. 30.)   Confidential.   Berlin, D. October 20, 1911.

Sir,   R. October 30, 1911.

I have the honour to forward, herewith, a despatch, as marked in the margin, which I have received from Captain Watson, Naval Attaché to this Embassy, relating to The Campaign of the German Navy League for a larger Navy.

I have, &c.
GRANVILLE.

Enclosure in No. 648.(¹)

Captain Watson to Lord Granville.

(No. 30.)   Confidential.

Sir,   Berlin, October 17, 1911.

I have the honour to submit that in my previous letters I reported on the campaign of the German Navy League and its leader, Gross-Admiral von Koester, for an acceleration of replacement of old cruisers by large battleship-cruisers and an alteration of the present scheme of replacement to effect the same, which alteration the Navy League have up to the present contended will be within the limits of the present navy law.   The opponents of this proposal, namely, the press of the Liberals and Left, contend that such alteration constitutes a breach of the present navy law, and that a new fleet law will be required.

While these two parties present their different points of view in the press, the responsible authorities give no sign as to whether they intend to abide by the present navy law or yield to the pressure in favour of an earlier replacement of cruisers, which, if carried out, will surely lead in 1915 to a renewed demand for more work by the shipbuilding firms, and therefore to an ultimate permanent increase in the naval strength of Germany as at present laid down by her fleet law.

It has been stated that His Majesty the Emperor and Admiral von Tirpitz have been the mainstay of the German fleet increase in the past, and His Majesty has certainly given support to the proposals for further increase by his speech at Hamburg, before reported.   I would, however, report that now in one paper, the National Liberal "Blätter" (Liberal capitalists), Admiral von Tirpitz comes in for attack in that he is supposed to have informed the Finance Minister that the present navy law will be adhered to.   In connection with this report, an article in the "Täglische Rundschau" three weeks ago alluded to it with regret, and pointed out, with reference to recent events and a possible war against two Powers, and with the aid of comparative tables of naval forces of England, Germany, and France, what the building of only two armoured ships, instead of four, would mean for Germany.

(¹) [As the original text of this enclosure is not available in the Foreign Office archives, the above copy is taken from the Confidential Print.]

In the following paragraph of this letter, I report some of the influences that are being brought to bear on the Imperial Chancellor and Minister of Marine to obtain an increase of large cruisers as the minimum demand, while one writer goes considerably further in demands for increase than the Navy League does.

The activity of the Navy League and press appears to be considerable, and uses for its basis the action of England in the Moroccan affairs.

The Navy League publications and speeches, and some of the press have articles which give vent to a bias against England, from which the writers proceed to construct their case for a naval increase.

Whether the attack on Admiral von Tirpitz, before referred to, is justified or not, from the writer's point of view, events will show.

2. Of the recent principal support given to further increase of navy, I submit the following :—

Navy League.

October 10th.—Admiral v[on] Koester presided over a large meeting of Navy League at Kiel, and published his views as to increase in naval armaments. At the close of the meeting the following telegram was sent to the Imperial Chancellor :—

"The meeting here of 1,600 people of united groups of German Navy League at Kiel sends in great anxiety the urgent request to your Excellency to hurry on the building of the defensive power of the Empire by water, and to allow a suitable Bill to be laid before the legislative authorities for the estimate year 1912, and this in view of the threatened safety of the Empire through the present grouping of the Powers."

In addition to the above, meetings have been held in fifty other places in Germany, including several important cities, all of which have sent similar urgent requests to the above to the Imperial Chancellor urging on fleet building.

Press.

Articles in favour of naval increase have appeared in several papers including the following. As before stated, these articles commence by alluding to England, her action, and the thwarting of Germany in recent Moroccan affairs, and on that base the claim for a German naval increase.

One speaker at a Navy League meeting (Chaplain Hass) declared that faith in German diplomacy has sunk, that they must set their faith in the German sword and German ships. The meeting took place at Kiel, and is reported in the "Kieler Neueste Nachrichten" of the 5th October, last.

Papers quoted :—

"Deutsche Tageszeitung" of the 8th and 13th October.
"Täglische Rundschau" of the 27th September. As before mentioned.
"Kieler Neueste Nachrichten" of the 5th October. As before mentioned.
"National Liberal Blätter" of the 10th October.
"Vossische Zeitung" of the 11th October. Article by Admiral Stiege (retired).
"Hamburger Nachrichten" of the 10th October.
"Staatsburger Zeitung," Berlin, of the 13th October.
"Die Flotte" of October.
"Die Post" of the 8th October.

Demands a programme, instead of present navy law, of :—

1911–12	... ...	{ 4 battle-ship cruisers to replace " Hansa " class. { 1 battle-ship.
1912–13	... ...	{ 3 battle-ships to replace the old " Kaiser " class. { 2 battle-ship cruisers to replace " Victoria Luise " and " Kaiserin Augusta."
1913–14	... ...	{ 1 battle-ship. { 3 battle-ship cruisers to replace " Prince " class.
1914–15	... ...	{ 4 small cruisers. { 4 divisions of high sea torpedo boats.

As will be seen, this goes considerably further than the proposals of the Navy League, and would somewhat drastically alter the scope of the present navy law.

The writer concludes his arguments in favour of this programme with the following words :—

" Then, and only then, in 1917 shall we have a fleet ready to strike; a fleet which will know how to speak, and by means of which the German determination to be powerful will then be able to make itself heard amongst the Powers of Europe."

3. That the proposed increase meets with considerable opposition from Liberals and Left is shown from the press of those parties. Whether the present internal condition of Germany will allow the Chancellor to accede to the requests of the Navy League is a question of political conjecture, but the press of several parties seem to have found the action of the Government too weak for maintenance of Germany's prestige.

If therefore the proposals for naval increase are cleverly put, they may receive support from several of the parties in the present Reichstag, always excepting the Social Democrats and Left wing of the Liberal party, which together do not constitute a majority in present Reichstag.

An increase in naval estimates would, in case of pressure by powerful political circumstances, have passed the present Reichstag last winter without much difficulty. It may, I submit, be considered that, since the events of last two months, a naval increase has a better chance of doing so.

4. The following appear to be some of the courses open to the German authorities if they either contemplate an increase or are forced into it :—

(a.) Yield to the popular outcry against England and bring in a revision of the navy law before the present Reichstag dissolves before the elections.

(b.) Wait until March, and, if the elections give fair chance of success, then bring in an increase.

(c.) Bring out estimates, which shall adhere to present navy law, in the hope that England's estimates will give an excuse for either a supplementary or conditional estimates in 1912 or an increase in 1913, or in the hope that other countries' estimates may furnish an excuse.

I[t] would seem more likely that the German Admiralty would prefer to adopt one of the last two mentioned courses, as this would best serve German naval interests vis-à-vis England, should the respective political sides to the alternatives be equal.

I have before submitted by letter the report that the date of the production of German [estimates] may be altered to March, a date which coincides with the production of British naval estimates.

I have. &c.
HUGH WATSON,
Naval Attaché.

No. 649.

Lord Stamfordham to Mr. Churchill.

Private.(¹)
Secret.

Dear Churchill,   *Buckingham Palace, October 25, 1911.*

The King wishes me to let you know that yesterday he heard from a relation in Germany who had recently been in Berlin to the following effect :—

"Admiral Tirpitz said, at the time when the Morocco crisis had reached its acute stage, that Germany would have gone to war with England but her Fleet was not ready yet and would *not* be until 1915 when the Canal would be finished so that all the largest ships could pass through, and by that time they would have enough Dreadnoughts launched to deal with any Power. The mines from Heligoland to the mainland would not be ready until 1914. If war broke out now," the Admiral said, "the German Fleet would be smashed for no reason at all": (*i.e.* with no advantage to Germany).

The writer then went on to say:

"That is the reason why Germany gave in: so far as I can see we shall be fighting in 1915."

If he did not hear these views expressed by Admiral Tirpitz himself, he heard them second hand.

Yours very truly,
STAMFORDHAM.

(¹) [Grey MSS., Vol. 48.]

No. 650.

Admiralty to Foreign Office.

F.O. 42827/32046/11/28.
Confidential.

Sir,   *Whitehall, October 27, 1911.*

With reference to your letter No. 32046 of the 9th ultimo,(¹) enclosing copy of a despatch from the British Consul at Luderitzbucht, relative to a suggested lease of Penguin Island to the Government of German South West Africa, for use as a quarantine station, I am commanded by my Lords Commissioners of the Admiralty to acquaint you, for the information of the Secretary of State for Foreign Affairs, that although the actual intrinsic value of Penguin and Seal Islands, first annexed by Great Britain in 1867, would appear to be very small, now that the large guano deposits have been worked out, their real value lies in their position as forming a natural protection to the waters lying between them and the mainland, and as such, is very great.

2. The enormous utility of a fine first class harbour, situated on a stretch of coast barren of other harbours and without possibilities of them for very considerable distances on either side, is self evident, whether the matter be considered from a strategic or from a commercial point of view, and it is known that the German Government is most anxious to obtain a good harbour for German South West Africa and is now turning its attention to Luderitzbucht, after making a not very successful attempt to create a harbour at Swakopmund.

No objection would be seen to the lease of Penguin Island, if it were solely for the erection of a quarantine station, but as proposals were mooted in 1909 to build a mole between Shark Island and Penguin Island making the entrance to Robert

(¹) [Not reproduced.]

Harbour to the northward of the latter Island, it is considered unlikely that the German Government would be content with using the island for quarantine purposes only. It is almost certain that a footing once obtained, permission to build a break-water or carry out other harbour works would be asked for.

3. My Lords consider it undesirable to assist the German Government in forming a good harbour here, especially as the two islands, if retained intact, might have' a high value in any future bargaining in territory with that country, and they would suggest that the Secretary of State should communicate with the Colonial Office on the subject with a view to the desirability of not granting leases or other concessions being brought to the notice of the Government of the Union of South Africa.

I am, &c.
W. GRAHAM GREENE.

No. 651.

Lord Granville to Sir Edward Grey.

F.O. 42700/42700/11/28.
(No. 348.)   Confidential.   *Berlin,* D. *October* 28, 1911.
Sir,   R. *October* 30, 1911.

I have the honour to forward, herewith, a despatch, as marked in the margin, which I have received from Colonel Russell, Military Attaché to this embassy, relating to a certain feeling of nervousness in Germany regarding their military forces, which appears to me to be of considerable interest.

I have, &c.
GRANVILLE.

Enclosure in No. 651.

Lieutenant-Colonel Russell to Lord Granville.

Confidential.
My Lord,   *Berlin, October* 27, 1911.

From the tone and substance of recent notices in the press, and from other indications of various kinds, I am inclined to think that the confidence of the German people in the perfection and invincibility of their military forces, and particularly in the matter of the superiority of these forces over those of France, has been slightly shaken during the last few weeks. This feeling has not in my opinion communicated itself in any way to the army. I refer only to the general public.

The bold and confident attitude of France during the Morocco negotiations has produced an uneasy feeling that the French army must be very efficient and very strong.

I do not imply, my Lord, that there is anything approaching to a panic, and in the army the most unbounded confidence still reigns supreme. I refer more to a kind of nervous tremor which I believe to have passed through the civilian element of this country with regard to its military strength.

This feeling manifests itself by enquiries in the press as to whether the laws for universal service have been administered with sufficient stringency, whether the 90,000 young men who come of age each year and are fit, but are not called up to serve, might not perhaps with advantage have been given some military training, whether the provisions of the Quinquennial Law of 1911 were really adequate to the needs of the military situation in Europe, and similar questions of this nature. And further, why was not the great might of the German Empire exerted at once to decide by war, or threat of war, the differences which existed between them and France.

[19656]   2 T 2

The authors of articles on the manœuvres appear to me to go out of their way to reassure their readers that all is, indeed, well with the German army, whereas formerly such consoling communications would have been considered quite superfluous.

There exists, I think, also a feeling of indignant irritation at the possibility of France raising large bodies of coloured troops to be used against the German army on European battle-fields.

There would also appear to be a demand, as the supply is very plentiful, of articles on the armed strength of Great Britain. If these are couched in derogatory terms they are, I fancy, all the more palatable to the reading public.

I do not for a moment consider, my Lord, that the feeling I have referred to, which is in some respects akin to that which is now demanding an increase in the navy law, is sufficiently powerful to produce an agitation affecting in any way the systematic increase of the army which has already been fixed by law, particularly in view of the fact that more money may be required for the navy. I thought, however, that it was perhaps desirable that I should acquaint your Lordship with my opinion on the present state—even if only a transitory one—of the public mind on this subject.

The confidence of the army in itself is not, I am sure, as I have stated above, influenced in the least degree by the misgivings which appear to disturb the man in the street. The dominant feeling in the army at the present moment—and this feeling is not only confined to the army—is, I believe, one of intense hostility to ourselves. The chief origin of this sentiment is best illustrated by the remarks of some German officers, who recently assured my French military colleague that they could very easily and quickly have settled their differences with France over Morocco, if it had not been for the interference of the English.

A remark made to me by a German Officer is also illuminating: "What is the use of our having an army, as we do not use it?"

I am perfectly aware that I have failed in this despatch to substantiate my contentions by tangible evidence of any kind, but an opinion gained on the spot by numberless minor indications is perhaps not uninteresting.

I have, &c.
ALICK RUSSELL,
Military Attaché.

No. 652.

Mr Churchill to Sir Edward Grey

Private.([1])

My dear Grey,   *Admiralty, October* 28, 1911.

The foreign Naval Attachés called on me this morning by agreement, to pay their respects on my taking Office. The Russian had a communication to make which is not without its importance : and he told me that the Russian Government were very anxious to increase their Fleet in the Baltic. They had a Programme, which would shortly be passed through the Duma in the form of a Law, which would yield, by 1930, 16 Dreadnought Battleships in the Baltic, with 8 other Battleships in reserve. They were, however, very anxious to make more rapid progress, and they had reason to believe that, either now or in the near future, some first class units which were building in this country for South American States, or, as he hinted, more probably Turkey, would, owing to change of policy or failure of contracted conditions, be capable of being brought into the market. The Russian Government were prepared "in three days" to buy such a ship, or ships, and take it over from the Power for whom it was being constructed. But before in any way approaching the parties concerned, the Russians wished to know whether the British Admiralty favoured such a step. I promised I would give him a definite answer early next week. But I said the fact that I reserved my answer till I could consult you and my advisers ought not to leave him to suppose that we were not favourable to an immediate increase of Russian strength in the Baltic. On the contrary, the growth and revival of the Russian Fleet there would certainly be welcomed by us. Will you have the matter looked into, and let me know whether I am right in these assumptions, and whether there are any other objections to such a transfer? I do not see how either of the Powers concerned could complain if they defaulted or if their policy changed. After all, it would only be by agreement.

He then went on to say that the Russian Government hoped that we would favour their placing orders in this country for construction of ships. The Minister of Marine would be occupied during December with the Navy Bill in the Duma, and the discussions might be protracted into January, but as soon as the Navy Bill had been passed into law Admiral Gregorowski would propose to come over to England in order, as I gathered, to arrange for the placing of a number of orders here, and generally to inform himself about Naval progress. All this would be very satisfactory to us, and I told the Naval Attaché to assure the Minister of Marine of the gratification with which we should receive a visit from him, and begged him on no account to come to this country without giving me an opportunity of arranging that his visit shall be in every way pleasant and instructive.

As I have no doubt you will agree I only send this *ex abundante cautela* (!).

Yours very sincerely,
WINSTON S. CHURCHILL.

No. 653.

Sir E. Goschen to Sir Edward Grey.

F.O. 46072/26557/11/18.
(No. 386.) Confidential.   *Berlin, D. November* 17, 1911.
Sir,   R. *November* 20, 1911.

I have the honour to transmit, herewith, a despatch which I have received from Colonel Russell, Military Attaché to this Embassy, relating to the effect produced in Germany by the recent article in the "Times" on the subject of the German Army Manœuvres.

You will recollect that in my despatch No. 357 of the 3rd instant([1]) I had the honour to inform you that both the Imperial Chancellor and the Secretary of State for Foreign Affairs had expressed considerable irritation at the publication of these articles.

I have, &c.
W. E. GOSCHEN.

Enclosure in No. 653.

Lieutenant-Colonel Russell to Sir E. Goschen.

(No. 29.) Confidential.
Sir,   *Berlin, November* 16, 1911.

I have the honour to inform you that I recently received instructions from the War Office to report on the effect produced in Germany by the publication of a series of articles on the German Imperial manœuvres, which have lately appeared in the "Times" from the pen of the military correspondent of that journal, and to ascertain to what extent Lieutenant-Colonel Reppington [*sic* : Repington] was believed in this country to be associated with the British General Staff.

([1]) [Not reproduced.]

I replied at once that the Great General Staff was well informed with regard to this matter, and appreciated the fact that the military correspondent of the "Times," though editor of the new "Army Review," did not represent the views of our General Staff, but that the army in general did not realize to the same degree the personality of this brilliant military writer.

Since writing in this sense, I have had time to probe the matter further, and am now able to confirm the opinion I expressed in the first instance.

Some aspects of public opinion on the subject of these articles, as reflected in the press, are not, I think, without importance or interest.

Notices have appeared in the newspapers in this country stating that these articles in the "Times" had been inspired by the British military attaché in Berlin, and that he should in consequence not be invited to attend the Imperial manœuvres on future occasions.

I might perhaps quote in this connection a matter which came to my notice, and which appears to constitute a notable exception to the rule that the General Staff here is well informed with regard to the authorship of the articles in question. The Bavarian military plenipotentiary in Berlin, Lieutenant-General Freiherr von Gebsattel, informed me the other day that the War Minister had said to him, " I suppose Russell did not really write those articles in the ' Times'? " The indignant surprise contained in my comment on this remark caused General von Gebsattel to change his tone somewhat, and he hastened to assure me that it was of course only a bad joke on the part of the War Minister.

Writers in the newspapers here note with regret that the belief of foreign nations in the invincibility of the German army is no longer so firm as it used to be. The homage paid in the past to German military strength is now replaced by unfavourable criticism.

In most cases the authors of these articles hasten to assure their readers that there is no cause to apprehend that the German sword is not sharp and ready for immediate use. They assert, however, that a State which perpetually avoids war loses respect and prestige in the sight of its neighbours, and that a protracted attitude of defence engenders a disbelief in the offensive power of a nation. Germany has kept the peace so long they declare, that the saying now is: " So schnell schiessen die Preussen nicht."

The letters of the military correspondent of the "Times" are alleged to have been written with the special purpose of inspiring confidence in France, and all foreign criticism of German military and naval armaments is asserted to be part of the policy of encompassing Germany (" Einkreisungspolitik.")

The present occasion is not an opportune one for examining the contents of Lieutenant-Colonel Reppington's letters in detail, but my own opinion with regard to them from a general point of view—and this opinion is shared by all my military colleagues who have read the articles—is that, though brilliantly written and containing much that is quite incontrovertible, they are too severe in many instances in their judgment of the German soldiers.

If I may venture to express an opinion with regard to the desirability of publishing these articles, I am bound to admit that I can only deplore that they should have appeared in public print. My reasons for this opinion are as follows :—

1. I consider that these articles have contributed to increase ill-feeling against us.
2. I do not think that it is desirable to afford helpful criticism to a foreign country.
3. I believe that these articles will be misunderstood to a great extent by the British public.

With regard to 2, I am convinced that these most ably written letters will be studied with care by the German Great General Staff, and that this observant body will not fail to find much food for reflection and suggestions for improvement in this trenchant criticism of the Imperial manœuvres.

I should, perhaps, explain more fully the meaning I wish to convey by the third reason I gave above. I believe that the British public, too prone as it is to dismiss unpleasant truths, particularly when they have any reference to the armament and defence of their own country, will only too gladly accept this indictment of the German military forces and hasten to the conclusion that the German army is a bad one and may be taken as a negligible quantity.

That such an attitude is in the highest degree regrettable needs no demonstration.

I have, &c.

ALICK RUSSELL,
Military Attaché.

CHAPTER LX.

THE AFTERMATH, PRESS AND PUBLIC OPINION.

No. 654.

Sir E. Goschen to Sir Edward Grey.

F.O. 38211/38119/11/18.
(No. 292.)   *Berlin, D. September 28, 1911.*
Sir,   R. *September 30, 1911.*

The German papers last night quoted at some length the speech delivered by the First Lord of the Admiralty at Abersychan on the 26th instant and they commented in an unfavourable manner on certain passages.

The first part of the report of the speech as printed by them is substantially the same as that given in the "Times" and other London papers, but the latter portion, to which exception is taken in Germany, does not appear in the English papers which I have seen. The following is a translation of this portion as reproduced in the "Kreuz-Zeitung" :—

"There can be no enduring peace for the British Empire unless it be peace with honour. This phrase was coined by Lord Beaconsfield on his return from the Berlin Congress. Certainly something has changed in our country since Germany transferred to Morocco her methods of intimidation which have been so successfully employed against the Russians in Persia and even against Great Britain in the East. His Majesty's Government openly declared last July that they recognised the policy of the *entente cordiale*. They adopt a middle course. They admit that some of the German demands must unhesitatingly be conceded. England has always recommended to France that she should make some concessions to Germany. She has not abandoned her position since the change of front in the month of August in regard to compensations in Africa. This temperate attitude should not be looked upon as a sign of weakness. It is in accordance with the practice of English diplomacy which differs radically from that employed in the Wilhelmstrasse. In the Wilhelmstrasse much is asked in order to obtain a little. England chooses her ground at the first onset and fights thereon to the end. The words of a First Lord of the Admiralty must be animated by the same principles. England has made peaceful proposals and has suggested a reduction in the rate of naval construction, but at the same time she has made it clear that if her proposals are obstinately rejected and an attempt be made to shift the ground, she will steadfastly continue her policy of maintaining her fleet at the proper standard."

The "Kreuz-Zeitung" comments on this as follows :—

"This speech of Admiral McKenna's, who three years ago, by his allegations in regard to the German fleet which were known to be untrue, was the cause of violent Germanophobia, is a piece of impertinence ('eine Unverschämtheit')."

The "Berliner Tageblatt" considers the speech to be an indirect reply to that recently delivered by Admiral von Köster and it states that "in its whole tone, it will certainly not contribute to the improvement of Anglo-German relations."

The "Post" writes as follows :—"We should have had great pleasure in listening to a speech of this nature from the mouth of a responsible German Minister during the last months. It is very painful to have to allow an Englishman to say such things about German policy, all the more as unfortunately they constitute a legitimate criticism."

I have, &c.
W. E. GOSCHEN.

No. 655.

Sir E. Goschen to Sir Edward Grey.

F.O. 38378/38119/11/18.
(No. 296.)   *Berlin*, D. *September* 29, 1911.
Sir,   R. *October* 2, 1911.

With reference to my despatch No. 292 of yesterday respecting the reports of Mr. McKenna's speech which appeared in the German newspapers,(¹) I have the honour to inform you that the Wolf Telegraphic Bureau has issued the following communication :—

"Various German newspapers, all of which draw their information from the same source, published a report of the speech made on September 26th by the English Secretary of the Navy, according to which Mr. McKenna was made to talk of Germany's attempts at intimidation etc. In answer to an enquiry made by us in London we received a telegram from a competent source that McKenna said no single word, which in any way resembled the portion of the report to which we refer. The Secretary of the Navy made no reference at all in his speech either to Morocco or to Germany or to foreign politics of any kind. Nor did the London papers published on the morning of the 27th instant contain one word of the utterances ascribed to McKenna in the above-mentioned report. From this it would appear that the whole story was a pure invention."

The "Berliner Tageblatt" adds that the "Press Telegraph," the agency responsible for the original report had issued it in the form of a telegram purporting to come from London, but that the agency now offers the excuse that its report was taken from the Germanophobe "Echo de Paris" whose invidious comments were mistaken for part of the speech itself. The "Berliner Tageblatt" places two marks of exclamation after this explanation but makes no further comment.

I have, &c.
W. E. GOSCHEN.

(¹) [*v.* immediately preceding document.]

[*ED. NOTE.*—Sir V. Corbett's despatch No. 59 of September 29, 1911, R. October 2, reported that " Mr. McKenna's speech in North Monmouthshire on the 26th instant has excited an extraordinary amount of interest in the German press," and summarized several comments in the press of South Germany. *cp. supra*, p. 564, No. 579, and *infra*, pp. 653–5, No. 661, *note* (¹).]

No. 656.

Sir Edward Grey to Sir E. Goschen.

F.O. 38342/38119/11/18.   *Foreign Office, September* 30, 1911.
Tel. (No. 191.)   D. 7 P.M.

The passage about Morocco quoted in the Times of Friday from a German report of Mr. McKenna's speech is an absolute forgery. Mr. McKenna made no reference in his speech to Morocco or to foreign affairs. Mischief done by such misrepresentations in the German Press is so serious that I shall send you an official despatch for communication to German Government asking whether they cannot do something to discover their source or to counteract them.(¹)

(¹) [v. immediately succeeding document.]

No. 657.

Sir Edward Grey to Sir E. Goschen.

F.O. 39870/38119/11/28.
(No. 224.)
Sir,   *Foreign Office, October* 10, 1911.

H[is] M[ajesty's] G[overnment] have observed with great regret the extraordinary outburst of animosity against this country which has found almost daily expression in the columns of the German press for the last three months.

I do not wish to refer again to the attack recently made on His Majesty's Ambassador at Vienna in circumstances which have made on His Majesty's Government a most painful impression,(¹) and which have already been dealt with in my conversations with Count Metternich. Your Excellency's despatch No. 292 of the 28th ultimo(²) points to a further incident in what appears to be an organised campaign to mislead public opinion in Germany for the purpose of prejudicing it against England and of exciting animosity in one country against the other.

The utterance ascribed to the First Lord of the Admiralty, which has been made the subject of a series of grossly offensive articles against a British Cabinet Minister, was reported and reproduced in a large and influential portion of the German press before a statement issued by what is described as a semi-official press agency exposed the truth concerning it. The words imputed to Mr. McKenna are of course a pure invention, the passage which contained them having, with apparent deliberation, been fraudulently interpolated in the report of his speech.

With one or two honourable exceptions, the German papers have done nothing to repair the mischief which they have caused, the semi-official *démenti* being in many instances carefully relegated in small type to an obscure corner of the paper.

An incident of this kind, coming as it does so soon after the fabrication of a statement put into the mouth of Sir F. Cartwright, cannot leave His Majesty's Government indifferent. Indeed, the prevalence of the spirit of which these cases appear to be symptomatic is a matter which causes them serious concern. I shall no doubt find myself compelled before long to comment in the House of Commons upon the unprecedented perversion of Mr. McKenna's speech and the consequent attacks upon him, and I propose to take that or another suitable opportunity to give some public warning of the growing danger to which the good relations between the two countries must be exposed if embittered by the deliberate propagation of false news.

I should learn with satisfaction that the Imperial Chancellor, by giving some public warning such as I have suggested or by whatever method he thinks likely to be effective, would do what is possible on his part to counteract the mischief that has already been done and to prevent its recurrence.

(¹) [v. infra, pp. 837–45, *App.* V.]
(²) [v. supra, pp. 648–9, No. 654.]

I accordingly request your Excellency to make this suggestion to Herr von Bethmann-Hollweg, for I am confident that he is as desirous as His Majesty's Government to obviate the danger to which I have referred.

[I am, &c.
E. GREY.]

MINUTE.

This should be circulated to the Cabinet.

E. G.

MINUTE BY KING GEORGE.

App[rove]d.

G.R.I.

No. 658.

Sir Edward Grey to Lord Granville.

F.O. 40431/38119/11/28.
(No. 228.)
My Lord, *Foreign Office, October* 13, 1911.

I told Count Metternich to-day briefly the purport of the despatch which I was sending to you(¹) about the forgery interpolated in the report of Mr. McKenna's speech. I observed that this, in conjunction with numerous other things of the same kind, made me think that there must be some laboratory in which these things were manufactured.

Count Metternich did not dissent from this view, and observed that the source from which this falsehood had come was a French Agency, often employed by the German newspapers because it was cheap.

I said that I had seen the statement that the forgery in the report of Mr. McKenna's speech had been taken from the " Echo de Paris," but, in writing to you I had made no comment upon the source. My object was, whatever the source, to get people to be on their guard against the mischief done.

Count Metternich said that there was a current misstatement concerning himself, to the effect that he had misinformed his Government as to the attitude of England towards the question of Morocco.

I said that this statement ought never to have been made.

Count Metternich observed that anyone who had followed events for the last four or five years must have known that, whenever there was a difference about Morocco, England sided strongly with France.

I said that no doubt we had sided in that way at the Algeciras Conference and since; but I thought that the feeling of resentment in Germany had been unduly enhanced by statements that we had interfered in the negotiations beween France and Germany to prevent France from making concessions to Germany which, but for us, France would willingly have made. This was absolutely untrue.

Count Metternich did not dispute this, but he said that, if we had remained from the first entirely neutral in the question of Morocco, it might have been settled between France and Germany in a shorter time. The attitude of the British Press and of British public opinion, implying that we would go all lengths in support of France, had made a settlement less easy.

I replied that I did not wish to go over all the old ground again, and therefore I would only observe that this attitude might be attributed to the way in which Germany had opened the question by sending a ship to Agadir. I did not ignore that

(¹) [*v.* immediately preceding document.]

there had been differences of policy between the German and British Governments that had given rise to friction from time to time, but my point was that whatever resentment this might cause in Germany was bound to be increased many-fold, and quite unnecessarily, if false statements about us were made and believed.

Our conversation was quite friendly in tone, and though Count Metternich referred to complaints which might be made on his own or the German side, he gave me the impression of regretting the lengths to which the German Press had gone. On one or two other instances of misrepresentation which I gave him he made no comment except to minimize the importance of the German journal, the "Post," in which they had appeared.

[I am, &c.]
E. G[REY].

No. 659.

Sir E. Goschen to Sir Edward Grey.

Berlin, November 2, 1911.

F.O. 43364/38119/11/18.
Tel. (No. 95.) R.

D. 4·40 P.M.
R. 7 P.M.

I communicated to Chancellor to-day substance of your despatch No. 224.([1]) He said that cause of attitude of German press towards England was bad feeling which now unfortunately existed between the two countries, and for which Germany was certainly not responsible. I maintained that it was, on the contrary, to the press that this feeling was chiefly due, and that it was owing to misleading reports of the attitude of His Majesty's Government in the Moroccan and other questions published in German newspapers that public opinion in Germany had been so excited against England. It was, I added, the propagation of false and misleading news that was occupying your attention, and you hoped that his Excellency would help in fighting against this growing evil. His Excellency said that he would be obliged if I would communicate your despatch to Secretary of State for Foreign Affairs, with whom he would like to discuss the matter. I said that I would do so, but that you had wished me to speak on the subject to him, the Chancellor, in the hope that he might be disposed to make some statement in the Reichstag in the manner you had suggested. His Excellency said, after some further conversation, that he could tell me now that he was shortly going to speak in the Reichstag on the subject of Morocco, and that he would necessarily then have some remarks to make on the subject of the press. I asked his Excellency whether he would speak in the sense which you had suggested. He said that he would certainly call attention to the harm done by propagation of false reports, but he could say no more until he had discussed question with Secretary of State for Foreign Affairs. During our conversation he pointed out that German press had not monopoly of misrepresentations, and mentioned certain articles in "Daily Graphic" concerning movements of German troops which he had had to contradict, and more especially the recent articles in the "Times" respecting German army. I shall see Secretary of State for Foreign Affairs this evening.

([1]) [v. supra, pp. 650–1, No. 657.]

No. 660.

Sir E. Goschen to Sir Edward Grey.

Berlin, November 2, 1911.

F.O. 43365/38119/11/18.
Tel. (No. 96.) R.

D. 7·50 P.M.
R. 9·30 P.M.

Press: My immediately preceding telegram ( ).(¹)

Secretary of State for Foreign Affairs, who spoke bitterly on his side of the English press, states that before Chancellor can come to any decision with regard to acting on your suggestion he must know more or less what you propose to say in the House of Commons. He says that if you throw blame for present feeling in two countries entirely upon German press, it would of course be out of the question for Chancellor to endorse your views.

I said that it was evident from your despatch that you wished to give warning to press generally against danger of propagating false news, and that you hoped that Chancellor might take the same course. His Excellency said that he would like that to be made quite clear, and the best way would be that Chancellor should be informed of the language which you proposed to hold. He added that Chancellor was going to speak on Morocco on 8th November, so that matter was pressing.

(¹) [*v.* immediately preceding document.]

No. 661.

Sir E. Goschen to Sir Edward Grey.

F.O. 43699/38119/11/28.
(No. 357.)
Sir,

Berlin, D. November 3, 1911.
R. *November 6, 1911.*

I have the honour to report that in accordance with your instructions I communicated to the Imperial Chancellor yesterday the substance of your despatch No. 224 of the 10th ultimo(¹) respecting the general animosity of the German Press against Great Britain and, more particularly, the attacks on Mr. McKenna caused by the false reports of his speech published in the German newspapers.

In reply to my communication the Chancellor said at once that the animosity of the German Press was scarcely to be wondered at considering the ill feeling which had unfortunately arisen between the two countries during the Morocco negotiations between Germany and France. It was this ill-feeling, for which Germany was certainly not responsible, which had aroused the animosity of the German Press. The speech of the Chancellor of the Exchequer had, as I must have observed, created a most painful impression throughout Germany, and if anything could have added to that impression it was the tone and language used by the British press in reproducing the speech. I stated, in reply, that as he had mentioned Mr. Lloyd George's speech, I must also mention the despatch of the "Panther" to Agadir which had preceded it and which had created a most unfavourable impression throughout Great Britain. The Chancellor said that no objection had been raised to the French expedition to Fez: why should so much feeling have been aroused by the despatch of a German ship to Agadir? I said that the circumstances had been very different. The French expedition had been made to relieve a very dangerous and threatening situation at Fez, with the consent of the Sultan of Morocco, and after all the Powers had been duly informed of the intentions of the French Government. The German Government itself had not actually protested against it. The Chancellor said that they had done so.(²) I replied that then I must have been badly informed, for my

(¹) [*v. supra,* pp. 650–1, No. 657. Sir Edward Grey denied the authenticity of the German press reports of Mr. McKenna's speech in the House of Commons on November 7. *v. Parl. Deb.,* 5th Ser., Vol. 30, pp. 1450–1.]

(²) [Marginal comment by Mr. Villiers: "'The habit of mendacity' again."]

impression of the attitude of the Imperial Government at that time had been that they had raised no special objection but had merely pointed out to the French Government that if the expedition remained in Fez beyond a reasonable time a difficult situation would arise about which Germany would have something to say. The Chancellor admitted that this was correct but said that he considered that what the Imperial Government had said amounted to a protest against the French expedition.

As the conversation was rather straying from the subject which I had in hand, I said that I could not agree with His Excellency that Germany was in no way responsible for the clouding of the atmosphere between the two countries. Granting that the despatch of a ship to Agadir and Mr. Lloyd George's subsequent speech had created an unfavourable impression in Great Britain and Germany respectively, an improvement in the atmosphere since these two events had been rendered impossible through the systematic and deliberate manner in which the attitude of His Majesty's Government in the Morocco question had been misrepresented in the entire German Press. His Majesty's Government had all along, notwithstanding the clear and straightforward statements to the contrary made by the responsible British statesmen, been accused of endeavouring to throw difficulties in the way of an arrangement being come to between France and Germany, and indeed of making every effort to bring about a rupture of the negotiations. A prominent feature of this anti-British Press campaign had been the attacks on His Majesty's Ambassador at Vienna made on the strength of a bogus conversation reported in the " Neue Freie Presse "[3] and which had been continued in spite of Sir F. Cartwright's *démenti* and the categorical denial of His Majesty's Government. The Chancellor said that in this matter the Imperial Government had unreservedly accepted the statement of His Majesty's Government and had published a communiqué to that effect in the " Norddeutsche Allgemeine Zeitung." I said that I did not dispute for a moment the correct proceeding of the Imperial Government but that I was speaking of the German Press which had continued its attacks upon Sir F. Cartwright in spite of the formal statement of His Majesty's Government and of the acceptance thereof by the Imperial Government. Continuing, I said that the attitude of the greater portion of the Press with regard to Mr. McKenna's speech had been deplorable. An entirely false version of the speech had been published—a volley of abuse had been poured upon Mr. McKenna—and even when the semi-official Telegraph Agency had put the matter right and explained how the error had occurred, not a single one of the papers which had reproduced the false version of the speech and had abused Mr. McKenna had had the grace to express regret or retract one word which they had written. The Chancellor admitted that the incident had been regrettable but then again he had done all in his power to rectify matters by causing the semi-official Telegraph Agency to publish the correct version and explain the mistake which had been made. He added that, as regards general misrepresentation, he on his side had equal cause to complain of the British Press and he called my attention to certain false statements in the " Daily Graphic," which he had been obliged to contradict, and more especially to the articles written by the Military Correspondent of the " Times " upon the German army. I said that as regards the " Daily Graphic " it was a paper which I never read and therefore I did not know to what he was alluding, and that as regards the " Times " military articles they were criticisms of an institution, perhaps unjustified and incorrect, but still criticisms, and as such stood upon a totally different level to the abuse of an individual member of His Majesty's Government, abuse founded upon a falsification of his utterances, the falsity of which would, I should have thought, have been patent to any unprejudiced mind. The Chancellor then said that he would prefer that I should talk over the matter with the Secretary of State for Foreign Affairs, who was quite conversant with the attitude of the Press in both countries. I said that I would certainly do so, but that as a matter of fact

(3) [*v. infra*, pp. 837–45, *App.* V.]

your message was addressed to him, the Chancellor, as you hoped that he might join you in issuing some public warning to the Press respecting the danger caused to the maintenance of the good relations between the two countries by the propagation of false and misleading reports. His Excellency said that in a few days he was going to speak in the Reichstag on the subject of Morocco and that he would probably have something to say on the subject of the Press. I said that I hoped he would see his way to falling in with your suggestion, to which he replied that he would talk over the matter with Herr von Kiderlen after I had seen the latter.

In the course of conversation the Chancellor alluded somewhat bitterly to the fact that our previous negotiations, in which he had shown so much good will and anxiety for good relations with England had been twice interrupted by His Majesty's Government and that he was still waiting for an answer with regard to the exchange of naval information. I did not think it advisable to go deeply into this subject and only said that if there had been interruptions in our negotiations they had been owing to unavoidable circumstances which had been fully explained at the time.[4]

In the evening I saw Herr von Kiderlen who had just come from the Chancellor. I need not trouble you with his recriminations with regard to the attitude of the British Press, which were pungent, and in some cases, I must admit, not quite unjustifiable. As he mentioned the "Times" articles on the German army as being flagrant instances of the sort of language held in the British Press with regard to Germany, I pointed out to him, also, that criticism, however severe, was not the same as deliberate misrepresentation and personal abuse of a British statesman founded on a falsification of his public utterances. I added that the fact that none of the papers which had founded their attacks on Mr. McKenna on the false reports of his speech had, on being informed of their error, expressed the slightest regret for their baseless abuse, had made a very disagreeable impression both on His Majesty's Government and public opinion in Great Britain. Herr von Kiderlen said: "When, I should like to know, has any English newspaper expressed regret for its false statements with regard to Germany?" To which I replied: "When has any English newspaper published a false report of a speech by a German statesman, and then grossly abused him for what he did not say?"

I finally said that as it was not likely that I could get him to share my conviction that the balance of Press iniquities was heavily on the German side, we had better come to the point, which was whether the Chancellor was disposed to give some public warning of the growing danger to which the good relations between the two countries must be exposed if embittered by the propagation of false and misleading news.

Herr von Kiderlen said that it was not quite clear as to what form your proposed "public warning" would take and that therefore he would suggest that the Chancellor should be informed beforehand of the language you proposed to hold. He added that as the Chancellor was going to make a statement on the Morocco agreement on the 8th instant, he would be much obliged if I would lay his suggestion before you as soon as possible.

I have, &c.
W. E. GOSCHEN.

MINUTES.

Sir E. Goschen should be informed that his language to the Chancellor and M. Kiderlen is highly approved and that he dealt with a delicate question with much tact and firmness.
A. N.

I entirely approve.

E. G.

(4) [This paragraph is printed in *Gooch & Temperley*, Vol. VI, p. 647, No. 477.]

No. 662.

Sir E. Goschen to Sir Edward Grey.

F.O. 43702/43702/11/28.
(No. 360.)   *Berlin,* D. *November* 4. 1911.
Sir,   R. *November* 6, 1911.

With reference to my telegram No. 98 of yesterday's date([1]) I have the honour to report the announcement in the press this morning that the Emperor has accepted Herr von Lindequist's resignation and that Dr. Solf, Ex-Governor of Samoa has been appointed to take temporary charge of the Colonial Office.

The "Lokal-Anzeiger," which has often been used of late for semi-official utterances and may therefore be presumed in this case to be reproducing the views of the Foreign Office and the Imperial Chancery, blames Herr von Lindequist severely for his behaviour during the negotiations and for his resignation at the very moment of their conclusion; the paper describes him as a subordinate official and insinuates that it is monstrous for a person in that position to oppose the wishes of the Imperial Chancellor and to put difficulties in the way of negotiations conducted by him or under his auspices; it also hints pretty broadly that Herr von Lindequist is responsible for the indiscretions which have emanated from the Colonial Office both in regard to the course of the negotiations and to his own desire to resign, although it actually says that he is not personally responsible for them.

The "Tageblatt" on the other hand, the paper which published the indiscretions referred to, declares that it is in the best position to know that Herr von Lindequist is in no way responsible for them: it is indignant at the description of the Secretary of State for the Colonial Office as a subordinate official, and points out that, though by the Constitution the Chancellor is alone responsible for all the Imperial Offices and the various Secretaries of State are nominally subordinate to him, it is quite absurd that they should be so, and it greets with delight the attitude of one man who has at last been found with independent views and with sufficient strength of character to resign rather than give a false official approval to things of which he disapproves.

I have, &c.
W. E. GOSCHEN.

([1]) [Not reproduced.]

[*ED. NOTE.*—On November 6, 1911, M. Neratov congratulated Herr von Lucius, the German Ambassador at St. Petersburgh, on the successful conclusion of the negotiations. *v. G.P.* XXIX, pp. 430–1, and references in footnotes.]

No. 663.

Sir Edward Grey to Sir E. Goschen.

F.O. 43364/38119/11/18.
Tel. (No. 215.) R.   *Foreign Office, November* 6, 1911.
Your telegrams Nos. 95 and 96([1]).

The following question will be put in House of Commons to-morrow by a private member.

"Whether communications have passed between the Foreign Office and German Government relative to an alleged interview granted by a British Ambassador to an Austrian newspaper; and, if so, what was the purport or conclusion of those communications."

([1]) [*v. supra*, pp. 652–3, Nos. 659–60.]

The following is the answer I propose to give.

Two incidents have lately formed the subject of communications between His Majesty's Government and the German Government. One is the article published in an Austrian newspaper and referred to in the question, the other is the report in the German Press of a speech delivered by my right hon[ourable] Friend who is now Home Secretary. The communications between the Governments have been of a more or less informal character, and it is unnecessary and perhaps would not be suitable to publish them; but I may say that they were not of a nature to cause any difficulty between the two Governments.

I think, however, that it is desirable to state the facts. It was alleged, and in some quarters believed, that the British Ambassador at Vienna had been— through an interview or in some other way—a party to the publication of an article criticizing German policy([2]): it was reported that my right hon[ourable] Friend, then First Lord of the Admiralty, had in a public speech used language attacking German policy.([3]) Both these incidents were construed in Germany as a direct public and intentional affront to Germany on the part of a British Minister and a British Ambassador, and they have given rise to great resentment.

The facts are that the British Ambassador in Vienna was not in any way a party to the publication of the article complained of, nor had he any knowledge of it before its publication. My right hon[ourable] Friend did not use the language complained of in his speech: the passage in question was interpolated into the report of his speech from some entirely foreign source, and nothing of the kind was said by my right hon[ourable] Friend.

I would express the hope, after these incidents, that public opinion will be on its guard against being carried away by false statements. There are of course difficulties and friction from time to time between this country and others arising from a real divergence of policy at a particular moment. I believe that the Governments concerned will be able to overcome all such difficulties if facts are not exaggerated or distorted, but if false news is to be reported and believed, public excitement and resentment will some day get beyond what it is possible for Governments to control.

There has been a tendency in individual organs of the Press, sometimes in Great Britain, sometimes in Germany, to put a sinister construction upon action taken, or supposed to be taken, by the German or the British Government respectively in different parts of the world. I trust that, with the happy conclusion of negotiations between France and Germany on the subject of Morocco, the tension that has given rise to suspicion and misconstruction in the British and German Press will disappear.([4])

You should let Chancellor or M[inister for] F[oreign] A[ffairs] have a copy stating that I send it for information only but with the desire to suit the convenience of the Chancellor by letting him know it before he makes his own speech in Reichstag on Wednesday. You should add that I have drafted the reply and have specially inserted the last paragraph with a desire to avoid giving any embarrassment to the Chancellor.

([2]) [v. infra, pp. 837–45, App. V.]
([3]) [v. supra, pp. 648–51, Nos. 654–5–6–7.]
([4]) [For this question and the reply, v. Parl. Deb., 5th Ser., House of Commons, Vol. 30, pp. 1450–1.]

No. 664.

Sir E. Goschen to Sir Edward Grey.

F.O. 44306/25883/11/28.
(No. 368.)
Sir,

Berlin, D. *November* 6, 1911.
R. *November* 9, 1911.

With the Reichstag elections so near at hand and with their influence bearing heavily on all questions concerning both internal and foreign policy, it is difficult to come to any exact conclusion respecting the real feeling of German public opinion with regard to the arrangement just concluded between France and Germany.(¹) The portion of the press which is unfavourable to the Government, such as that representing Pan-German ideas, describes it as a national shame and a final nail in the coffin of German prestige. The language of the Radical papers is less violent but not much less hostile, and the Conservative Press is reserved. It is, in fact only the newspapers who are habitually used by the Government for semi-official communications which point out the advantages of this arrangement which, while removing a continual source of friction between France and Germany, gains for the latter Power a very valuable addition to her colonial possessions.

I should say that, as yet at all events, the balance of public opinion is unfavourable to the arrangement. But an effort is being made by some of the more independent papers to point out that it is undesirable from a German national point of view that, for electioneering purposes, such violent language should be used against the arrangement as it cannot fail to give the world outside the idea that Germany has suffered a diplomatic defeat. The "Kölnische Zeitung" takes this line. It certainly does not itself show any particular enthusiasm for the arrangement but it does point out that those who abuse it unreservedly, and refuse to acknowledge that it has its good points, are rendering a bad service to their country. The "Kölnische" says that for those who think that the position gained by France in Morocco is in no way counterbalanced by the concessions obtained in French Congo, and for those who had set their hearts on a slice of Morocco, it saves trouble to abuse the whole arrangement without going into the question of whether it contains any counterbalancing advantages. But that the quiet observer, whose mind is free from prejudice and sentiment, and who will take the trouble to go into the matter, will find no difficulty in coming to the conclusion that the Morocco question has been solved in a manner which sufficiently safeguards German dignity and which offers certain practical advantages. The paper adds that in any case the idea that Germany has given up something that she possessed in Morocco must be swept from people's minds. It puts the case thus: we never had a foot of ground in Morocco: what we had was what the Algeciras Act gave us, namely the open door for our commerce and industry, and a claim, in common with other Powers, to exercise a certain influence on the political development of Morocco. We have continually declared that we only claim economic rights in Morocco, any efforts, therefore, to obtain political rights would have been contradictory to our declarations, and moreover could only have been realized by a war, and a war for that object, even if successful, would have been too high a price to pay.

Finally the paper says that the protracted nature of the negotiations is the best proof of the firmness with which German interests were defended and shows "that what there was to be got out of the affair was got." "Whether," it adds, "anything more could have been obtained is a question which can only be decided by those acquainted with the details of the negotiations. The German Press is not in this position, so that those who consider that more might have been obtained will remain of that opinion, while those who shared the idea of the Government with regard to compensation outside of Morocco, lack material to disprove the contention of their opponents."

(¹) [*v. supra*, pp. 605–8, No. 619; and *infra*, pp. 831–6, App. IV.]

The " Kölnische Zeitung " tempers this very doubtful defence of the arrangement with a reservation to the effect that if, as the French Press maintains, Germany has to take over all the obligations of the French Government towards French concessionary companies in the territory now acquired, and that France is accordingly not bound to buy out the rights of those companies, then, even those who have hitherto been disposed to regard the compensation in the Congo as an acceptable addition to German colonial possessions, will have to admit that the compensations, if saddled with such a burden, are worthless.

Other papers which are not wholly against the arrangement, such as the " Hamburger Nachrichten," also say that perhaps the Government have obtained all that under the circumstances was obtainable, but point out that the worst part of the settlement is that while Germany's renunciation of all political interest in Morocco is definitive, the French assurances with regard to the open door, commercial equality, mines, etc., exist only on paper.

On this point the " Tägliche Rundschau " observes :—" If France holds to her assurances, well and good : but if she does not, what then? A new ground for disputes will have arisen, the result of which, in view of the paramount position of France in Morocco and the prejudices of other countries against us, can be easily foreseen."

There is almost as much controversy over the resignation of Herr von Lindequist, the late Secretary of State for the Colonies, as over the arrangement itself. Those who regard the latter with even half-hearted favour decry Herr von Lindequist's capabilities as a statesman and complain of the manner in which, though subordinate in authority to the Foreign Office, he all along hampered and delayed the negotiations, and particularly of the moment which he chose for deserting his colleagues. They moreover follow the example of an irritated Government in making both Herr von Lindequist and Herr von Danckelmann responsible for the indiscretions by which the public was informed of the divergence of opinion between the Colonial Office and the Foreign Office. On the other hand the out and out opponents of the arrangement maintain that Herr von Lindequist is head and shoulders above any other German statesman in knowledge of colonial affairs and they hold up both him and Herr von Danckelmann as martyrs to duty, who preferred rather to give up their posts than to have any part in an arrangement so damaging to German interests and so fatal to the reputation of German diplomacy.

Since I began to write this despatch the opinion on the Franco-German arrangement seems to be growing rather more favourable particularly in the more weighty and reputable organs of the German Press. The " Frankfurter Zeitung " and papers of that stamp, in their latest issues, state that now that the whole text is before them their first impression of the arrangement has changed for the better and that they do not consider that it deserves the violent abuse that has been lavished upon it from so many quarters; they moreover point out that it is to the fact that Germany and France have come to an agreement on a difficult question of such paramount importance that weight should be attached, rather than to the question as to whether a few points in the arrangement might not have been settled in a manner more favourable to Germany. All these papers are a little sceptical however as to whether the arrangement will lead to a permanent improvement of Franco-German relations and they all agree that the Imperial Chancellor and Herr von Kiderlen have a heavy task before them when they have to stand up to defend their Moroccan policy in the Reichstag and before the people.

The Imperial Chancellor himself told me that he anticipated hard times, but he maintains that the violent language which is directed against the arrangement in a certain portion of the Berlin and provincial press is due more to political hostility against himself than to any deep-rooted dissatisfaction with the result of the Morocco and Congo negotiations. He commented somewhat severely upon the action of Herr von Lindequist in resigning his office at such an inopportune moment, but said that it was due probably to loss of nerve through illness and overwork.

To sum up I consider that the nearness of the elections and internal political considerations are chiefly responsible for the abuse lavished on the Franco-German arrangement, and I have the impression, confirmed from many sources, that the German people at large are not really very dissatisfied with the result of the negotiations.

I have, &c.
W. E. GOSCHEN.

No. 665.

Sir E. Goschen to Sir Edward Grey.

F.O. 44120/38119/11/18.
Tel. (No. 99.) Urgent. R.

Berlin, November 7, 1911.
D. 11·55 A.M.
R. 1·45 P.M.

Your telegram No. 215.(¹)

Chancellor is very grateful for text of your answer and especially for last paragraph. Nothing you propose to say will cause him any embarrassment and he intends in his speech to call attention to your warning addressed to press of both countries and to say that he entirely associates himself with that warning. There is one point in ante-penultimate paragraph of your telegram which rather disturbs him, namely that you say "there *are* of course difficulties, etc." He fears this may give a handle to German press for again calling attention to divergence between two Governments on Morocco question and that it may weaken his proposed statement that His Majesty's Government have all along declared that they have no wish to hamper negotiations. He would like you to say "difficulties *may* of course arise." I said that I would inform you of his observations but that I thought subsequent words "from time to time" covered his objection. He said that he was perhaps over particular but that he was afraid of sense that your words might convey in German translation. His Excellency told me he would not be able to avoid allusion to Chancellor of the Exchequer's speech. He did not propose to criticize Chancellor's speech itself but to quote natural irritation caused in Germany by interpretation given to it by, and especially [by] the French, press.

(¹) [*v. supra*, pp. 656–7, No. 663.]

No. 666.

Sir Edward Grey to Sir E. Goschen.

F.O. 44120/38119/11/28.
Tel. (No. 218.) R.

Foreign Office, November 7, 1911.
D. 4 P.M.

Your telegram No. 99.(¹)

I have used words proposed by Chancellor.

(¹) [*v.* immediately preceding document.]

No. 667.

Sir Edward Grey to Sir E. Goschen.

F.O. 44120/38119/11/28.
Tel. (No. 219.)

Foreign Office, November 7, 1911.
D. 7·15 P.M.

Your telegram No. 99.(¹)

We cannot object to allusions to interpretation put by Press upon Chancellor of Exchequer's speech,(²) but I trust German Chancellor will not say anything that can be interpreted as criticism of the speech itself; that would of course make it necessary for us to reply by defending and justifying the speech. I leave it to your discretion whether it is necessary to say any word to this effect to the German Chancellor before he speaks.

(¹) [*v. supra*, p. 660, No. 665.]
(²) [*v. supra*, pp. 648–51, Nos. 654–7.]

No. 668.

Sir V. Corbett to Sir Edward Grey.

F.O. 44314/25883/11/28.
(No. 77.)
Sir,

Munich, D. November 7, 1911.
R. *November 9, 1911.*

The Morocco Convention, the full text of which is published here to-day, has been generally ill-received by the press. The "Frankfurter Zeitung" indeed welcomes the conclusion of the long-protracted negotiations without an appeal to the *ultima ratio regum* with satisfaction but without enthusiasm for the actual results attained. The "Schwaebischer Merkur," an independent National Liberal paper, remarks that it is perhaps a good sign that the agreement has been received without enthusiasm on either side and expresses approval of the acquisitions in the Congo.

With these two exceptions the newspapers universally lament a German diplomatic defeat and condemn the policy of the Government which led to it. The comments even of the clerical "Bayerischer Kurier" are unfavourable.

The line generally taken is to blame the policy of Prince Buelow rather than that of the present Chancellor or Herr von Kiderlen for what has occurred, but the action of the latter is not uncriticized : it is asked what was the object of sending a ship to Agadir if the only object of the German Government was to acquire a few thousand square miles of pestilential swamp in Central Africa.

It would be a waste of time to give you the press criticisms in detail. Suffice it to say that they are tinged throughout with party bias, and, if they at all accurately interpret the public sentiment, point to a grave dissatisfaction with the present system of Government and a general desire that the Imperial Ministry should be directly responsible to Parliament. This desire, if the Liberal and Socialist parties have their way, will largely influence the coming electoral struggle.

In many quarters, though in sufficiently guarded language, dissatisfaction is expressed with the influence of the Emperor, whose impulsive visit to Tangier is represented as the first of the series of events which have culminated in the definite exclusion of Germany from Morocco.

A sinister note is struck by some of the Nationalist papers which ask whether the milliards spent on the army have been spent in vain, and whether the military power of the Empire might not have been employed to prevent the present humiliation. The hope is expressed that it will be so employed in future.

The fiction of British intrigues during the course of the negotiations figures prominently in almost all the papers.

I have, &c.
VINCENT CORBETT.

No. 669.

Sir Edward Grey to Sir E. Goschen.

F.O. 44580/38119/11/18.
(No. 268.)
Sir,   *Foreign Office, November 8, 1911.*

Count Metternich read to me to-day a sentence that the German Chancellor intended to use in debate, giving in general terms the same sort of warning as I had given against false statements in the Press.

I said that I was very glad that he was going to reciprocate the warning which I had given. It would, I thought, be a good thing if he could give some illustration to point the moral, such as what had happened in connection with Mr. McKenna's speech. I supposed, however, that as the Chancellor would be making a long speech on the question of Morocco, and had German public opinion to consider, it might be a delicate matter for him to say anything about the German Press in particular.

[I am, &c.]
E. G[REY].

No. 670.

Sir F. Bertie to Sir Edward Grey.

F.O. 44453/44289/11/28.
(No. 507.)   *Paris, D. November 9, 1911.*
Sir,   *R. November 10, 1911.*

The publication by the "Matin" of the Secret Franco-Spanish Treaty of 1904 seems to have created a great stir in parliamentary circles.([1])

Various papers give accounts of the views expressed by prominent deputies in the lobbies on the subject.

I transmit to you herewith, as an instance of these accounts, an extract from the "Figaro" of to-day's date.([2]) As I have reported to you before, this paper nourished a particular animosity against M. Delcassé which is apt to colour its opinions.

It would seem, however, that the statement made by the "Figaro" that the current opinion in Parliamentary circles is that the value of the Franco-German Treaty is greatly diminished by the provisions of the secret Franco-Spanish Treaty represents the case.

The majority of the French papers publish maps to illustrate the latter Treaty with the Spanish zones clearly marked. The phrase currently used is that France is to receive, by the terms of the Treaty, a Morocco *sans façade* on the Mediterranean, and the view is generally expressed that the negotiations with Spain must alter the situation in France's favour.

The "Figaro" which has expressed itself against the policy of pressing Spain unduly, considers nevertheless that Spain can reasonably be expected to agree to a band of territory in her zone being neutralized for the purpose of serving for a French Railway from Tangier to Fez.

I have, &c.
FRANCIS BERTIE.

([1]) [For the text of the Convention, *v. infra*, pp. 826–9, *App.* IV.]
([2]) [Not reproduced.]

No. 671.

Sir F. Bertie to Sir Edward Grey.

F.O. 44637/16083/11/28.
(No. 511.)

Sir,

Paris, D. *November 9, 1911.*
R. *November 11, 1911.*

The " Temps " publishes this evening an article, obviously by its foreign editor, M. Tardieu, in which various arguments are put forward to prove that Spain is bound not to insist on the provisions of the secret Franco-Spanish Treaty of 1904 remaining intact, but must consider what compensation she is to give to France for the sacrifices which the latter has made in order to alter the international status of Morocco.

The article then asserts that England is in duty bound to bring home to the Spanish Government the necessities of the situation. England was the witness to the signature of the Franco-Spanish Treaty of 1904(1) and also advised the French Government to conclude the recent Franco-German Agreement. The article then reproduces reproaches which have been made against the sterility of the Anglo-French *entente* notably in the Near East in the past, and expresses the hope that this sterility will not show itself again during the next few weeks.

The article alludes to the fact that those who like M. Hanotaux and M. Judet who have never fully accepted the *Entente*, have not hesitated of late to call its value to France into question. The " Temps " which has shown its invariable fidelity to the friendship between France and England is therefore in a position to insist that it should now show its practical effects.

The article is evidently written with a view to exercising pressure on His Majesty's Government to support French claims as against those of Spain in the forthcoming negotiations concerning Morocco.

I have, &c.
FRANCIS BERTIE.

MINUTES.

There is no reason why H[is] M[ajesty's] G[overnment] should be influenced by articles in the " Temps."

E. A. C.
Nov. 11.

It would be easy to quote against the " Temps " as to the value of the *entente* many of its own articles during the last two months.

W. L.
F. D. A.
A. N.
E. G.

(1) [For text, *v. infra*, pp. 826–9, *App.* IV.]

No. 672.

Foreign Office to Board of Trade.

F.O. 43587/25883/11/28.

Sir,

Foreign Office, November 9, 1911.

I am directed by Sec[retar]y Sir E. Grey to inform you that he has received from the French Chargé d'Affaires a copy of the Convention as regards Morocco which has recently been concluded between the French and the German Gov[ernmen]ts.(1)

The Chargé d'Affaires stated at the same time that the French Gov[ernmen]t would be glad to receive at an early date a notification of the adherence of His Majesty's Gov[ernmen]t to the Convention.

Sir Edward Grey is anxious for political reasons that the assent of H[is] M[ajesty's] Gov[ernmen]t to the convention should not be unduly delayed, but before notifying to the French Gov[ernmen]t the adherence of H[is] M[ajesty's] Gov[ernmen]t he would be glad if Mr. Buxton would cause the articles of agreement

(1) [*v. infra*, pp. 831–4, *App.* IV.]

to be examined with a view to ascertain whether the commercial rights and economic equality in Morocco of British subjects are fully safeguarded under them.

I am to add that Sir Edward Grey proposes to call the attention of the French Gov[ernmen]t to the text of article 1 of the new convention in which the words "l'égalité économique entre les deux nations" occur, and to ask for an assurance that it is not intended by this article that any preferential economic rights should be conferred on the subjects of the two signatory Powers, and that British subjects in Morocco will not receive less favourable economic treatment than that accorded to the subjects of any other Power.

In view of the urgency of the matter, Sir Edward Grey would be grateful if he could be favoured with the views of Mr. Buxton on these points at the earliest possible moment. A copy of the convention is enclosed herewith.([2])

I am, &c.
F. A. CAMPBELL.

([2]) [v. infra, pp. 831–4, App. IV.]

No. 673.

Sir E. Goschen to Sir Edward Grey.

F.O. 44843/38119/11/18.
(No. 371.)   *Berlin,* D. *November* 10, 1911.
Sir,   R. *November* 13, 1911.

The answer you gave to the questions in the House of Commons([1]) with regard to the article in the "Neue Freie Presse," attributed by the German Press to Sir F. Cartwright's inspiration, has been reproduced in all the newspapers here, including the semi-official "Norddeutsche Allgemeine Zeitung," but so far without much comment. Still, from what I hear, it has had a good effect here and is regarded as denoting a desire on your part to improve the somewhat murky atmosphere which has recently hung over Anglo-German relations.

The "Frankfurter Zeitung," noticing that you introduced in your answer the incident of the falsification of Mr. McKenna's speech, said that that gross misrepresentation, due to the stupidity of an undisciplined Press Bureau and which you could easily disprove, stood on a rather different plane from the utterances of a British Ambassador, unless these utterances could also be proved to have been entirely fabricated. Such proof was, the "Frankfurter Zeitung" states, not to be found in your answer as you had only said very diplomatically that Sir F. Cartwright was not a party to the publication of the article and had no knowledge that it was going to be published. Sir F. Cartwright's innocence was therefore not proved as clearly as that of Mr. McKenna which you were able to make as clear as daylight. On the other hand, politically speaking, Sir F. Cartwright might now regard himself as sufficiently cleared by your declarations.([2])

By the terms of your warning to the Press, the paper says that you have clearly shown that it is the wish of the whole British Cabinet that the tension of the past summer should relax in favour of better relations with Germany, although it might be perhaps a little too early for any positive step in that direction.

The "Vossische Zeitung" intersperses a few remarks upon your answer in a homily addressed to England on the text that Germany will not suffer dictation of any sort, neither with regard to her dealings with other Powers, nor to the number of ships she wishes to build nor anything else. It refers to your answer concerning the "Neue Freie Presse" article in much the same terms as the "Frankfurter Zeitung." But it adds that the point is not whether Sir F. Cartwright was responsible for the publication of the article, but whether he had spoken as the article made him speak. "That he had done so there is no possible doubt. Not only had he done so, but the language he had used had been of a far more

([1]) [v. supra, pp. 656–7, No. 663.]
([2]) [v. infra, pp. 837–45, App. V.]

provocative and uncivil nature than the 'Neue Freie Presse' had allowed to appear. Nevertheless Sir F. Cartwright is still British Ambassador at Vienna.

Finally the "Vossische" does justice to the sincerity of your desire and that of His Majesty's Government to improve Anglo-German relations; and makes a sympathetic allusion to the recent speeches at the meeting of the Anglo-German Friendship Society at the Mansion House. But it says that there must be no more threats, no more lecturing and that Germany's friendship is only to be had on that condition.

"Therefore," it says, "if England so desires it, we can be friends, the best of friends, and be mutually of the greatest help to one another. If this is not England's wish, we can confine ourselves to 'correct relations' or perhaps become 'incorrect.' But if Sir E. Grey and England with him, sincerely desires to be friends with us, then we will draw a line through the past and say : 'Soyons Amis, Cinna!'"

The "Berliner Tageblatt," after reproducing your answer, says that it is not very clear why, though no question was asked on the subject, you felt called upon to refer to the falsification of Mr. McKenna's speech, a matter which had been at once satisfactorily cleared up and explained ;(³) and it supposes that you took this course in order to detract attention from the more important case of Sir F. Cartwright, which had only received an official but never a real explanation. The paper also says that your subsequent words give the impression that you wished to make the Press responsible for the failure of diplomacy to deal with a difficult situation. In conclusion the "Tageblatt" says that it heartily sympathises with your wish that the tension which has arisen between the two Countries during the Morocco crisis may disappear, but that it does not think that that happy result can be attained by the simple assertion that the British Ambassador in Vienna was no party to the publication of the anti-German "interview" in the "Neue Freie Presse."

The wounds caused to German self-esteem by the interpretation given to Mr. Lloyd George's speech(⁴) and by Dr. Münz's concoction(⁵) are, as you will have seen from these comments, and as you will see from some of the speeches just delivered in the Reichstag, still sensitive to the gentlest touch, and will still take some little time to heal. But I think it may be stated that the conciliatory words at the close of your answer have been well received and that they have set sensible people thinking whether the time has not nearly arrived when, as the "Kreuz Zeitung" puts it, a line should be drawn through the happenings of the last few months, and a fresh start made in the direction of more satisfactory relations between the two countries.

I have, &c.
W. E. GOSCHEN.

(³) [v. supra, pp. 648–55, Nos. 654–61, passim.]
(⁴) [v. supra, pp. 387–417, chap. LV, passim.]
(⁵) [v. infra, pp. 837–45, App. V.]

No. 674.

Sir E. Goschen to Sir Edward Grey.

F.O. 44845/25883/11/28.
(No. 373.)   Berlin, D. November 10, 1911.
Sir,   R. November 13, 1911.

Yesterday, before a very full house, the Imperial Chancellor made his anxiously looked for statement on the subject of the Franco-German Morocco Agreement.(¹) His Excellency's speech is criticised and commented on in the Press strictly on party lines. The Conservative organs consider that he made as good a speech as could be expected under the circumstances; Liberal papers say that he made a poor defence of a poor arrangement, and the small band of semi-official papers maintain exactly the contrary, namely that the speech left nothing to be desired and supported an

(¹) [This sentence is reproduced in A. & P. (1911), CIII (Cd. 5970), p. 447, but the word "very" is omitted before "full." The rest of the despatch is omitted, though the translation is published.]

excellent arrangement with admirably reasoned arguments. As a matter of fact the Chancellor's speech seems to have been worthy of the occasion, but it must be admitted that the cold, and to a certain extent, hostile atmosphere in which His Excellency spoke, had the effect of leaving upon his hearers a rather dismal impression.

A full translation of the speech is enclosed in this despatch.

In speaking of the despatch of the "Panther" to Agadir, the object of which, he said, was communicated to the Powers before the ship reached its destination, he stated that it had been represented in the foreign Press as a provocative and menacing act. This was a gross misrepresentation. "We threaten no one, but we protect our rights and we allow no one to prevent us from doing so."

As regards the resignation of Herr von Lindequist, on which his views were awaited with the greatest eagerness, he said, amidst almost continual interruption, that that Minister had from the first been opposed to the acquisition by Germany of a larger addition to her colonial possessions, and desired a smaller territory than that which had been obtained, one more advanced in cultivation, and easier and cheaper to administrate [sic].

He had more especially been against any cession of territory on the part of Germany. He had sent in his resignation in the summer, but it had not been accepted. On the 28th of October the newspapers had reported that he was about to resign, but with his consent this had been officially denied. He had however then announced his intention of retiring in the spring and using the interval for a tour through the Colonies. A few days afterwards he had renewed his request to be relieved from his office, accompanying it with a very sharp criticism against the text of the arrangement. He had at the same time stated that he was not ready to take any departmental responsibility for the arrangement in the Reichstag and had refused in fact to support the Government policy in any way. This had further been all communicated to the Press, His resignation had on this occasion been at once accepted, in order that the business of the Colonial Office might be carried on in such a manner as not to disturb the unanimity and solidarity necessary for the Government to carry on the affairs of the country.

The Chancellor then came to the accusations of timidity and subservience which had been made against the Government. He said that their programme had been all along to give to France an increase of political influence in Morocco, to obtain for Germany increased security for her economic interests, and to see that the negotiations were carried on without any outside interference. This programme had been carried out to the letter. All reproaches for weakness were totally undeserved. This programme had been settled in May and the Emperor had commanded that it should be strictly carried out, in full consciousness that every political action of a great Power contains within itself the fateful question: "Peace or War." After alluding to the Press rumours that Admiral Tirpitz had reported to the Emperor that the Navy was not ready for war, which he characterized as absolutely devoid of foundation, he came to Mr. Lloyd George's speech.

With regard to his remarks on this subject you have already noticed that in his efforts to defend the Imperial Government from the charge so freely brought against them of having yielded to intimidation and of having drawn back in the face of threats from a third Power, he gave a somewhat one-sided account of what had passed between the two Governments on the subject of the speech in question, and conveyed the impression, whether purposely or not, I do not know, that it was in consequence of a communication made to you by Count Metternich on the subject that "the British Government gave up their desire to interfere in the negotiations."

His exact words as given in the Official Report of his speech are as follows:—
"After that, the British Government expressed no further wish to interfere in the negotiations."

As regards the "Neue Freie Presse" article he repeated your observations and said that the Government regarded the matter as closed.

The rest of the speech was taken up with the defence of the arrangement. He claimed that the Government deserved all praise for not having pursued the "uptopia(²) of land-grabbing." Personally he regarded it as his duty so to conduct the affairs of the nation as to avoid any war that might be avoided and in which the honour of Germany was not at stake. Morocco had been a festering sore in German relations with England and France. That sore had now been cicatrized and the fact that Germany and France had been able to come to an understanding in such a delicate question was of far greater value than discussions of Arbitration Treaties and of arrangements for the limitation of armaments. That understanding might well become the corner-stone of their future relations with England and France. In conclusion he said that in the interest of the prestige of Germany, who could not possibly allow an international act like that of Algeciras to be set aside to her disadvantage, the Government had acted as they had done, and would, if necessary, have acted with the sword. "We expect no praise and we fear no blame."

After a speech from the leader of the party of the Centre of no great importance from an international point of view the Conservative leader, Herr von Heydebrand addressed the House. This gentleman has distinguished himself lately by sundry very anti-English speeches and particularly by his denunciation of the Chancellor of the Exchequer; it was therefore to be anticipated, even if he did not attack the Franco-German arrangement, that he would certainly take advantage of the opportunity to attack England. He was not long in getting to work; he said that the Chancellor had alluded to Mr. Lloyd George's speech as an after-dinner speech. Such after-dinner speeches were not to the taste of the German people. It might suit the English to forget what had been said after they had failed in their attempt to involve Germany and France in a war; but Germans had not forgotten it, and it was that after-dinner speech and Sir F. Cartwright's interview which had brought the flush of shame to every German cheek and shown Germany where her enemy lay. Germany now knew who it was that thwarted all her natural desires for expansion, and refused her a place in the sun. He did not know what answer the Imperial Government had given to these provocations, but he knew the sort of answer the German people would give. It was a matter which concerned Germany's very existence, and no country could stand such proceedings, least of all Germany. It was both the right and the duty of the Government to decide what was to be done, but we expect their decision to be compatible with the honour of the country. "I declare that we Germans are ready to make the necessary sacrifices ('Out of the pockets of the workmen,' from the Socialists). I repeat that in the name of my political friends I declare that when the hour, the country and our honour require it, we are ready to sacrifice both our lives and our property. It is not by yielding to threats, but by the German sword, that we can maintain our position in the world."

Herr von Heydebrand, considering that he is the leader of the party on whom the Chancellor has chiefly to rely, was not very amiable as regards the arrangement itself, but he tempered his somewhat severe criticisms by stating that the patience, self-sacrifice, and hard work which the Government had brought to bear on the arrangement was at all events worthy of praise. He added that the path chosen by the Government had not been the right one, but still they had not been entirely to blame as the right path had been practically closed to them by the policy of a former Government.

As Herr von Heydebrand had alluded to the article in the "Neue Freie Presse" in terms which implied disbelief of your statements on that subject, Herr von Kiderlen rose and spoke as follows:—"I must at once answer one point in the speech which we have just heard. An article appeared in the 'Neue Freie Presse' which was attributed to the British Ambassador in Vienna. We at once addressed a communication to the British Government on the subject and that Government stated to us officially, and authorised us to publish this statement, that the Ambassador had been in no respect a party to the publication of that article, and that the article had been in no way influenced by the Embassy." Here the speaker was interrupted by cries from the Right, "Who knows whether that is true?"

(²) [Thus in original.]

"It is surely," Herr von Kiderlen continued, "the least that can be expected from international courtesy, that when a Government gives an official explanation, we should attach credence to it, and no one has the right to demand that we should receive such an explanation with mistrust."

Herr von Kiderlen was followed by Herr Bebel, the Socialist leader, and later by Herr Bassermann, but owing to want of time I must reserve an analysis of their speeches and of those of any subsequent speakers of importance for a later despatch.

I have, &c.

W. E. GOSCHEN.

Enclosure in No. 674.

Translation of Speech delivered by Herr von Bethmann-Hollweg in the Reichstag, November 9, 1911.([3])

For the consideration of the agreements laid before you it will first of all be of value to inform you as to the latest phase of the Morocco question, and as to the important points of the agreements concluded. The Act of Algeciras was intended to maintain the independence of Morocco with a view to the economic development of the country for the benefit of the trade of all the Powers parties to it. It was soon evident that one of the essential conditions was lacking, namely, a Sultan who was actual ruler of the country, and was in a position to carry out the reforms provided for. Even Sultan Mulai Hafid could not do so in spite of his personal qualities. He fell more and more under foreign influence, and came into constantly increasing conflict with the tribes of his own country in consequence. This led to ever-growing influence on the part of France, for, of the four Powers which since the seventies possessed treaty rights to maintain military missions at the Sultan's Court, only the French mission had succeeded in establishing itself. In the same way France had for long supplied Morocco with money. The position of the Sultan, surrounded by hostile tribes and shut up in Fez, became eventually so precarious that France informed the Powers that grave apprehensions must be felt for the lives and property of her officers at the Sultan's Court and of the European colony.

France accordingly declared that she proposed to send troops to Fez, and to conduct the Europeans back to the coast. We had received no such threatening reports from Fez and, therefore, declared that our colony did not require foreign assistance. Since, however, we could naturally assume no responsibility for the lives of the French citizens who were alleged to be threatened, we raised no objection to the advance to Fez to bring back the threatened French citizens to the coast. We added the explicit reserve, however, which we also announced publicly that we retained our liberty of action, should the French expedition go beyond its alleged object, even should such action be merely the result of circumstances arising out of the expedition. This occurred, as was to be expected. France exerted practically unlimited sway over the Sultan in virtue of her influence, which had gradually become absolute. The independence of the Sultan assumed by the Act of Algeciras thus ceased to exist. It has, indeed, been urged that the Sultan himself summoned the French to his assistance, but a ruler who summons foreign troops to his assistance and who relies solely upon the support of foreign bayonets, is no longer the independent ruler on whose existence the Act of Algeciras was based. We let this be known and suggested to France an understanding leaving, of course, the initiative to her. We indicated the general outlines only of our programme to the effect that we would be ready to take into account the altered position of France necessitated

([3]) [The translation of this speech was originally made in the British Embassy at Berlin; it was however given a more literal rendering by Sir E. Crowe on its receipt at the Foreign Office. *cp.* his minute, *infra*, pp. 675–6. The above text is taken from the print of Sir E. Crowe's emended version, of which the original cannot be traced. A German report of the speech is given in the *Norddeutsche Allgemeine Zeitung* of November 10, 1911; *v.* also A. & P. (1911), CIII, (Cd. 5970), pp. 445–53.]

by the changed conditions, but that in return we must demand more precise guarantees for the equality assured to us in the domain of commerce and industry, especially in regard to public works, besides compensations for those rights assumed by France without previous understanding with us and contrary to the letter and spirit of the Algeciras Act. At first we received no positive proposals from Paris, whilst the French military power continued to spread in Morocco, and the fiction began gradually to become established not only in France but also in other countries that France was acting in pursuance of a European mandate. When, therefore, German interests appeared to be threatened in consequence of the events in Morocco, we sent a war-ship to Agadir. The despatch of this ship was primarily intended for the protection of the lives and property of our subjects. (Cries from the Social Democrats: "Subjects!") It represented at the same time a clear intimation of our right and our intention to defend our subjects (loud shouts from the Social Democrats: "There are no subjects") just as independently as France protected hers, so long as the latter came to no understanding with us. This object for the despatch of our war-ship and its limitation to this object was announced, immediately before the arrival of the ship, to the Powers through our Ambassadors and Ministers accredited to them. It is, accordingly, an untrue assertion if the despatch of a ship to Agadir was represented in the press—in the foreign press—as a provocation and a threat. We provoke and threaten no one; but we protect our rights and we shall not allow ourselves to be deterred or hindered by anyone.

The discussion with France then began. From a purely formal standpoint we might have demanded the restoration of the *status quo ante*, that is to say, the *status quo* before 1906; theoretically that would have been the correct thing to do, in practice it was impossible. It was hardly possible to clear Morocco again of foreign troops without incurring the danger of internal disturbances. The *restitutio in integrum* would further have been highly incomplete, since the lasting impression produced by the action of France would have continued to prevail even after the withdrawal of her troops. Finally we would have returned to a point, under unfavourable circumstances for us, which had resulted in constant friction to which both Governments desired equally to put an end. The assertion that the "Panther" was sent to Agadir with the object of acquiring territory in Morocco is incorrect. By the agreement of February 1909 the acquisition of territory in Morocco was already put out of the question. Our programme, which was drawn up long before the despatch of the "Panther," was conceived on the same lines. The incorrectness of the assertion is also established by the declarations which we made to the foreign Powers immediately before the arrival of the ship at Agadir. It is also made evident by the declarations which the Imperial Government issued through the organs of the press simultaneously with the arrival of the ship at Agadir. It is highly regrettable that this incorrect assertion should have been unpatriotically made use of even at home as a basis for the belief in a retreat of the Imperial Government and a humiliation of Germany.

In the negotiations with France the leading idea was that it had been shown to be impossible for the Moors to re-establish and maintain order in their country by their own efforts, and that the intervention of a foreign Power was required. As regards the greater part of Morocco, this Power could only be France. The greater the freedom which France obtained therefore, the easier it was for her to guarantee and assume responsibility for such order. In return we have obtained far-reaching and detailed guarantees for the equal treatment of non-French trade and for the rights of non-French nationals resident in Morocco. The details may be seen in the treaty laid before you.

After explaining the details in question the Chancellor went on to say :—

I come to the question of the compensations. In connection therewith I will speak first of all of the resignation of Herr von Lindequist. The Secretary of State for the colonies opposed from the very beginning the acquisition of a colonial possession of the extent of that which we have now obtained. He desired instead smaller but more cultivated territories, which would consequent'y be more easily and cheaply administered. Since it was found that this object was not attainable, he advocated mere roundings off of our colonial possessions and rectifications of frontier. I could not concur in this opinion, since I held the acquisition of a larger piece of colonial territory to be necessary for our activities. In regard to the Congo, which had years ago been mentioned in connection with previous informal discussions with France, there was also no longer any question of a *res integra*. These differences of opinion, and the belief that the Colonial Office was not permitted to exercise sufficient and decisive influence on the course of the negotiations, led Herr von Lindequist to decide as long ago as this summer to tender his resignation. His Majesty refused, however, at my request, to accept his resignation whilst the negotiations were still pending. The desires of the Colonial Office have been so far met in the course of the negotiations that the territory accruing includes all those portions on the frontier of the Cameroons which were indicated to me by the Colonial Office as being desirable. Herr von Lindequist was opposed in principle to the cession of German territory, though he told me that if no agreement could be reached without such cession, he considered the cession of the territory now made over to France to be acceptable. On the 28th October a rumour appeared in the press of the approaching resignation of Herr von Lindequist. This rumour was denied with the consent of Herr von Lindequist; the text of the *démenti* was submitted to him. In order, however, to refute any further press assertions, I would observe that Herr von Lindequist certainly spoke to me of the probability of his retirement next spring. But at the same time he definitely announced his desire to proceed to South-West Africa on a tour of inspection on the termination of the proceedings in the Reichstag. A few days later Herr von Lindequist again sent in his resignation. Shortly before, after the text of the projected agreement had been submitted to him, he had addressed to me an official minute in which great stress was laid on the disadvantages of our new acquisition, and which arrived at the conclusion that the 275,000 square kilom. of territory to be acquired would not even approximately counterbalance the loss which would be sustained by our colonial possessions through the cession to France of 12,000 square kilom. between the Logone and Shari rivers, and through the collateral agreements contained in the draft treaty. It was found possible to modify some of these collateral agreements, in accordance with the proposals of Herr von Lindequist, by negotiations with France. The position taken up by the Secretary of State in his minute compelled me, however, to ask him what attitude he proposed to adopt when the question came up for discussion in the Reichstag. It transpired that Herr von Lindequist was not prepared to undertake the defence of the agreements in the Reichstag as far as his department was concerned. This implied—with all personal respect—a misconception of the situation. Herr von Lindequist was not expected to assume personal responsibility for the Congo agreement. That agreement forms only a part of the whole political arrangement with France, and for that I am responsible. Herr von Lindequist was also not expected to defend the work before the Reichstag in all its bearings or even to praise it. I only asked of him an objective appreciation of the agreement from the colonial standpoint, in which the drawbacks of the agreement, especially the disadvantage of the cession of the Shari triangle, the concessionary companies, the sleeping sickness, and the partially unfavourable configuration of the land would be clearly set forth, and only the possibility, the hope of a favourable future development would not be disputed. Herr von Lindequist refused, however, to support my policy even·to this very limited extent, and therefore again tendered his resignation as I have already stated. Even more painful than the resignation of an official who had been tried by many years of colonial service, precisely at this moment, was the circumstance that the press learnt almost simultaneously with the Chancellor of the attitude adopted by Herr von Lindequist in the above-mentioned written minute in opposition to the Congo compensation. Though this certainly occurred without the concurrence and against the will of Herr von Lindequist, there was no other course open to me but to provide, by dealing rapidly with his resignation, for the conduct of the business of the Colonial Office in such a way as not to disturb the necessary continuity and uniformity of the Imperial Government.

This brings me back to the real point. I have just told you in detail why our claims for compensation were directed towards a compact enlargement of the Cameroons in Congo territory. I have further explained to you that the territory which has come to us includes those tracts of land, which those who know our colonies told us were worth striving after. Their acquisition is of value for the present, and at the same time it rounds off the Cameroons in the way we wished. But we also had to think of the value to us of gaining access to Africa's greatest river, the Congo, and to its tributary, the Ubangi. We also succeeded on that point. I do not contest the fact that in doing so we had also to take over countries of insignificant value, the administration of which will give us a good deal of trouble. I need not tell you it was just as hard for me as for the colonial administration to cede the territory on the Logone. (" Why did you do it then? " from the Left.) But we could never have achieved what we wanted without some sort of an exchange of territory. I admit that the new boundaries are to a certain extent inconvenient and difficult for the administration to deal with. Similar difficulties have also existed on the old southern boundary of the Cameroons and on the " Duck's Beak." In order to lessen these difficulties a wide scope of action has been afforded to the commission appointed for the delimitation of the frontiers. They are to pay particular attention to the natural boundaries and to the homogeneousness of the natives. For this purpose the commission is to have the right to deviate from the boundary laid down in general lines by treaty, sometimes in favour of one of the parties, sometimes in favour of the other. They have only to be careful to see that the net result of the deviations is the same for both parties. Far-reaching conditions have been laid down for the transit traffic of both countries. We have given one another mutual assurances respecting the extension and the linking up of the railways, and we are thereby now in a position to gain access by railway to the great rivers in case we should find it necessary. We guarantee the French a military road to the Benue for their North-East Congo territory similar to that granted to them by England in the Niger basin, which has led to no difficulties on either side.

The concluding article of the agreement has no present meaning, but it may acquire one in the event of territorial changes taking place in the Congo basin, to which we might then have something to say.

Gentlemen, a regular storm of indignation has now been raised against these acquisitions in the Congo by a large section of public opinion. No expression is strong enough to condemn the work done by the Government and to discredit it abroad. A correct opinion can only be found by not passing over the bad sides of the question, but also by not passing over the good side. There certainly exist among these new acquisitions tracts of little value, perhaps of no value at all, but this is also the case in our other colonies. The concessions are a heavy burden, but they are limited in point of time, and they will be under the sovereignty of German law and administration, which protects us against the misuse of the concessions. The sleeping-sickness which prevails in some districts is a doubtful blessing.

On the other hand, we receive valuable strips of country, country which is conveniently situated as regards the Cameroons. No one can deny that, not even the gentlemen who wish to disturb me with their interruptions. We gain access to the Congo and the Ubangi. The value of this access will only be realised in the future. But that it will be realised no one can deny. We get on the whole a most important new colonial territory. You should not reproach us with trying to get what we can, because Germany has only now, unfortunately much too late, joined the ranks of colonial nations.

I am firmly convinced that the favourable manner in which the Cameroons have developed, thanks to the activity of our merchants and the energy of our governors and Protectorate troops, will also find its echo in the newly acquired territory. Those who want to carry on a colonial policy with a definite aim in view should not forget the future possibilities in considering the present value. From a mere sand-box, to what has South-West Africa grown? Who saw furthest into the future: those who laughed at Rhodesia or the energy [*sic Tatkraft*] of the man who gave that country his name?

All the successes attained by the great colonial nations have only been won by the fact that these nations knew how to deal not with short but with very long periods of time, and by the courage with which they made light of the difficulties of the present for the sake of successes to be awaited in the often far-distant future.

Gentlemen, it is also not true that the French are glad to be rid of a part of the Congo territory. French statesmen have assessed at a high figure—and with reason—the advantages they have gained in Morocco, but with no light heart did they give up for it wide stretches of a territory for which for a generation so many experienced and distinguished French explorers and officers had sacrificed their strength and their lives.

Such is the sequence of events and such is the result.

From the outset our programme was as follows:—Recognition of increased political rights for France—in return only for an increased guarantee of our economic interests in Morocco—and in return for the acquisition of land in the Colonies. We never for a moment attempted to acquire land in Morocco. Negotiations between ourselves and France alone, not before an international congress and not in consultation with a third Power. We drew up this programme and we have adhered to it, nor have we allowed ourselves to be turned aside one single step from following it either by external or internal influences. All the reproaches of weakness which have been cast in our teeth during these last months, reproaches of weakness and and of yielding, the talk of a second Olmütz and what not, all fall to the ground before the facts as they are. The negotiations between ourselves and France have been carried on without interruption on both sides in the endeavour to come to a working agreement acceptable to both parties. From neither party and at no stage of the negotiations was any language used, any idea mooted, which would have been incompatible with the honour of one of the two parties. There was never any occasion for the "banging on the table with the fist," which was recommended to us. Moreover, I do not hold with this sort of threatening gesture. We no longer live in the Homeric days when threatening and bragging was part of a soldier's outfit. Germany is strong enough to do without that sort of armour. (Applause.) She will know how to draw her sword if need be. Foreign policy is only possible on such a basis. I must here make it quite clear, in order to contradict the misleading statements of the foreign and also of our own press that His Majesty the Emperor commanded that the programme, which was already drawn up in May last, should be adhered to in all phases of the negotiations, in the full knowledge that every political action of a great Power can evoke the fateful question of war or peace, and fully prepared at any time to draw the sword in defence of the nation's honour. Thus did the Emperor show himself to be at one with the nation, which during this whole time and in all its ranks has been imbued and inspired with the firm determination to defend its vital interests and its honour against all the world. There has also naturally never for a moment existed the slightest doubt as to the complete readiness for war of the army and navy. The reports, which are now being spread abroad to the effect that during a confidential discussion it was asserted that there were flaws in our readiness for war, especially in the navy, are pure inventions. They are in direct contradiction to the facts.

Now it has been asserted—and this assertion has eaten deep into the people— that we retreated before England. A speech made at a banquet by the British Minister, Lloyd George, has specially served in this connection. (Laughter and cheers on the Left.)—Gentlemen, I am speaking of a grave matter, and I beg you to allow me to finish my speech without interruption.—One of our Conservative papers, indeed, by substituting "Germany" for "England" right through the speech, brought out clearly that the speech, taken by itself, might equally have been made by a German statesman without giving occasion for criticism. What gave significance to the speech was the fact that the whole of the French press and a great portion of the English press, interpreted it in a chauvinistic sense and in a manner spiteful towards Germany, and that this interpretation was in no way repudiated from the English side. I found myself constrained to instruct the Imperial Ambassador in London to speak about the matter. My representation was to the effect that we were discussing the Morocco question with France; that England's interests were not so far affected thereby; and that if England should consider her interests to be affected by the result of the discussions, we expected the British Government to urge those interests upon the two contracting Governments only through the usual diplomatic channel. The British Government, after this, intimated no more desire of any kind to take part in our negotiations with France.

For all that, the ill-effects of that after-dinner speech remained. Owing to the interpretation given to it by the French and English press, it especially produced in wide German circles a very bitter feeling, which naturally found expression in a more or less forcible manner in our press. The effect of this speech was therefore not such as to further a good understanding with England. However sincerely I regret it, I must distinctly protest against the speech having been used as a handle for reproaching the Government with a weak and hesitating policy. Our programme of a reasonable settlement with France without interference on the part of a third Power and uninfluenced by irresponsible press intrigues has in fact been carried out.

The English Minister, Sir Edward Grey, in an appeal to the press of both countries, gave utterance to serious words in the House of Commons the day before yesterday, and especially warned the press against spreading false news.(⁴) I can only associate myself with this warning in order that ideas do not become established in the public opinion of both countries which would in the long run embitter the relations between the two great countries to their mutual disadvantage, and, I may add, to the disadvantage of the whole world.

I have pointed out to you that we have accomplished what we intended. In everyday life that is not usually called weakness, but reproaches were levelled at us from another point of view; that we ought to have tried for something else, but, above all things, for something more. What the honour and prestige of Germany demanded was either Southern Morocco or the restitution of the Act of Algeciras. In fact, one thing or another. Yes, gentlemen, he who considers the possession of Southern Morocco to be a vital interest for Germany, he who sees in the fact that this possession was not claimed a loss of prestige to Germany, for him there must be no alternative; he must demand that we go to war in order to conquer Southern Morocco. For him the restitution of the Act of Algeciras can be no real equivalent. There is nothing to be done with this formula, from the standpoint of Germany's honour and prestige or from the standpoint of practical politics.

Southern Morocco was not a desirable country for us as its protection and defence would have entailed constant sacrifices out of all proportion to the value of the land. That has been till the middle of last summer the general opinion. I will not speak of Bismarck, who expressed the desire that France might annex Morocco. You will reply that times have changed since then, but even since Bismarck the opinion has been steadfastly adhered to that we had no political interests to pursue in Morocco. This opinion was formally recognised by the treaty of February 1909, and all parties in the Reichstag agreed to this recognition on the discussion of the agreement. How has all this suddenly changed? Southern Morocco is doubtless a fine country (laughter); it is said to be very rich in ore, to have a fruitful soil on which German emigrants could settle. I will not argue this point, although there are many remarks which might be made with regard to a policy of colonisation in Morocco. I assume,

(⁴) [Following on his denial of the authenticity of the German reports of Mr. McKenna's speech, and of the Cartwright interview on November 7, v. Parl. Deb., 5th Ser., House of Commons, Vol. 30, pp. 1450–1.]

therefore, that it is in itself a very desirable piece of land. But I must say that for those who recognise it as Germany's task to conquer desirable countries by war, they would do just as well, in fact, perhaps, still better, if they were to attack some other countries than Morocco. Such things have, indeed, been done even in regard to European countries!

These are mere phantasies, and I am astonished that people can be found abroad who attach importance to them in connection with German policy. Germany can only pursue a strong policy, in the sense of a *Weltpolitik* if she keeps herself strong on the continent. It is only the weight which we exert as a continental Power which makes world commerce and colonial policy possible. Both must collapse if we do not maintain our power at home; if we acquire outlying possessions, the safeguarding of which can only be secured by frittering away and weakening our continental power, then we should be sawing at the branch on which we sit. Our policy in the last decades was therefore right in not pursuing political aims in Morocco, and therefore our present policy is also right in having excluded from the very beginning all thought of the acquisition of land in Morocco. I claim it as being particularly creditable to our policy that we did not pursue the utopia of the acquisition of land in Morocco. The complaints of a bad policy do not emanate only from those who wished to acquire a portion of Morocco. They have been raised from much wider circles. Should these complaints have any other aim than to put difficulties in the way of the Government's conduct of foreign affairs, then they must have a tangible aim. I am not speaking of those who were simply bent on war this summer. There were such people. And their number was not so big as the words they used. I will not waste words on the reprehensibility of their conduct. Others wanted a war of prevention, either against France, or against England, or against both. You all know what Bismarck thought of wars of prevention. He has said that his advice would never have been to go to war because a war was sooner or later inevitable. He regarded even a successful war as an evil which it should be the aim of the statecraft of nations to prevent. These are the principles on which we have acted. No one can tell whether Germany will not be fated to go to war with her neighbours. But on me who have now to bear the responsibility, it is incumbent so to conduct affairs that a war which is avoidable, and which is not demanded by the honour of the country, shall be avoided. Such have been the principles on which the last phase of Moroccan policy has been based.

Morocco was like a continually festering wound in our relations not only with France but also with England. The French advance to Fez led to an acute stage which rendered an operation necessary. We have performed this operation in order to heal the wound. We could never have reached the result achieved by the negotiations now before you, if both Governments had not had this same end in view. I consider it a great gain that it should have been possible for Germany and France to arrive at a peaceful understanding on such a delicate question as that of Morocco, involving as it did so many open and concealed dangers. This fact is worth more than all discussions on disarmament and arbitration treaties. It can become the foundation for the development and consolidation of relations in harmony with the true needs and progress of the two great nations. It is true that only the future can build on this foundation; but the present would have been guilty of a sin of omission had it cast aside the corner-stone instead of putting it in place.

I said just now that the Moroccan question also affected our relations with England. I would say one word more in regard thereto. In virtue of treaty stipulations, England stood ever on the side of France, at least diplomatically, in all Moroccan differences between us and France. Our understanding with France accordingly also cleans the slate in respect to our relations to England.

I return to the consideration from which I started. The depression and pessimism evinced by our people, which sought to urge the Government to other deeds, ought to indicate tangible aims, aims which could have been achieved simultaneously with the solution of the Morocco question. I have explained why we did not attempt to secure a piece of Morocco. It was especially strongly urged that we ought then at least to have broken off the negotiations with France, that we ought to have insisted on the restoration of the Act of Algeciras. It would have been easy enough to break off the negotiations, still easier perhaps not to begin them. But the restoration of the Act of Algeciras would have in no way benefited us. I see no advantage for Germany in the restoration of a situation which suffered from the no longer tenable fiction of the sovereignty of the Sultan of Morocco and the independence of the Shereefian Empire. We are sufficiently acquainted with this situation since 1906. It was materially and morally unsatisfactory for us. The desire for the Algeciras Act was also partially inspired by another motive. If we would not, or could not, have Southern Morocco, then, France must not have it. This was to be read often throughout this summer. In my opinion, the value of a policy does not consist in the injury done to others, but in the advantages gained for one's own country. A policy which aims at injuring another without considering whether it benefits the author is a shortsighted one. The animosity which it engenders must be paid for sooner or later. He, however, who sees in the increase of power accruing to France from her protectorate over Morocco a danger to Germany's existence, becomes an advocate of the war of prevention.

Hence, [sic] gentlemen, why this yearning for the Act of Algeciras? Did the prestige of Germany in any way demand it? No, gentlemen, our prestige as a Great Power demands that we should not suffer an international treaty, like the Act of Algeciras, which bears our signature, to be altered for the benefit of one party without our assent, to our disadvantage. For this we must fight, if necessary with the sword. For this we negotiated and the negotiation has been successful.

In conclusion, let me sum up. How did things stand before Fez and Agadir? Nominally Morocco was independent; de facto it has fallen under French influence. After Tangier and Algeciras this complicated and obscure situation was a standing menace to our relations with France. The "open door" existed indeed on paper, but it lacked the special guarantees which the obscurity of the internal situation rendered doubly urgent. We had renounced political aspirations in Morocco.

And now: we have given up nothing in Morocco which we had not already given up. In return we have obtained the economic guarante[e]s which were lacking. We have besides acquired a considerable colonial possession, which will bear fruit under our colonial administration. We have achieved this by means of a peaceful understanding with France. It has for the first time been found possible to solve by agreement with our western neighbour a great and difficult political question which contained the germ of great evil.

Such is the result. It is now for you, gentlemen, to weigh the pros and cons of a policy which has led to this agreement. We do not expect praise, but we also fear no reproach.

MINUTES.

Qu[ery]. Read in print, unless Sir E. Grey wishes to refer to the speech at once.

E. A. C.
Nov. 13.
W. L.
A. N.

Print as soon as possible—let me have a copy in print and circulate to the Cabinet.
As soon as the official text is received I should like to see it, especially to compare with this report the passage in the official report about the Ch[ancellor] of Exchequer's speech.

E. G.

The embassy have now sent us a copy of the official text, (annexed) without however anything indicating any divergencies from the unofficial version, and without any fresh translation. I have carefully gone over the original German of the two principal passages relating to the attitude of Great Britain, namely the passages marked on pp. 4 and 7 of our printed copy of the present despatch.(⁵) The first of these passages is quite accurately rendered, except for the few unimportant words which I have altered, or inserted.

As regards the second passage, I presume it would be desirable to render it as literally as possible, even at the expense of elegancy. I have accordingly re-translated the paragraph, and annex my version. Special importance attaches to the concluding sentence of the paragraph. It is almost impossible to render it verbatim, but I have endeavoured to do so. My version avoids the use of the expressed " *further* wish " and puts in its place an exact, but I admit not elegant, rendering of the actual German words used.

The question is whether my more literal, or Sir E. Goschen's prettier, translation of the paragraph should go to the Cabinet. I am holding back the copies for the Cabinet pending a decision on this point.

(I have not revised the remainder of the speech).

E. A. C.
Nov. 15.

For our purposes the more literal it is the better. Qu[ery] Substitute Sir E. Crowe's version.

W. L.

And then let me have a copy in print and with it the records of conversations with Count Metternich for which I asked on a separate paper for reference.

E. G.

(⁵) [These passages are the last two sentences of the 2nd paragraph, in which the changes are insignificant, and the fifteenth paragraph. The version given above is Sir E. Crowe's. The fifteenth paragraph in Sir E. Goschen's version ran as follows : " It has now been maintained and this assertion has made a very great impression on our people, that we retreated before England. A speech made at a banquet by the British Minister Mr. Lloyd George has been specially utilized for this purpose. Germany was not mentioned in this speech. (Laughter from the Left.) Gentlemen, I am now speaking seriously and I beg you to allow me to finish my speech without interruption. One of our Conservative papers at that time went so far as to assert that by changing the word " England " into the word " Germany " throughout, the speech taken by itself might quite easily have also been made by a German statesman. The speech gained importance by the fact that the whole of the French Press and a great portion of the English Press interpreted it in a chauvinistic and spiteful sense against Germany, and by the fact that no attempt whatever was made from the English side to counteract this interpretation, I found myself compelled to instruct the Imperial Ambassador in London to mention the matter. My representation was to the effect that we were discussing the Morocco question with France, that for the present England's interests were not affected thereby, and that if England should find her interests affected by the result of the negotiations we should expect the British Government to lay those interests before the two Governments interested only through the usual diplomatic channels. After that the British Government expressed no further wish to take part in our negotiations with France." *v. supra*, pp. 672–3.]

No. 675.

Sir F. Bertie to Sir Edward Grey.

F.O. 44930/16083/11/28.

(No. 515.)   *Paris,* D. *November* 11, 1911.

Sir,   R. *November* 13, 1911.

I had the honour to report to you the publication by the " Matin " on the 8th instant of the secret Franco-Spanish Treaty of 1904.(¹)

The " Figaro " of yesterday's date published the secret treaty negotiated but not signed between France and Spain in 1902 concerning Morocco.(²)

The " Temps " of to-day's date publishes the secret Franco-Spanish Treaty of September 1st 1905 respecting Morocco, and also makes public what it believes to be the contents of two secret clauses of the Anglo-French Convention of 1904.(³)

(¹) [For text, *v. infra*, pp. 826–9, *App.* IV.]

(²) [Reference to this subject is made in *Gooch & Temperley*, Vol. II, p. 279, No. 336; Vol. III, p. 30, No. 30, and *note* (¹).]

(³) [As a result of this indiscretion of the " Temps " and an impending parliamentary question. Sir Edward Grey asked the French Government to consent to the publication of these secret articles. *v. infra*, pp. 695–6, No. 693; p. 711, Nos. 706–7. This consent was given on November 19.]

I have the honour to transmit to you herewith extracts, as marked in the margin, from the papers mentioned in which these treaties are given, or alluded to.(⁴)

No explanation is forthcoming as to how these secret agreements have found their way into the hands of journalists.

I have, &c.
FRANCIS BERTIE.

Enclosure in No. 675.

Extract from " Le Temps " of November 11, 1911.

DEUX CLAUSES SECRÈTES DU TRAITÉ FRANCO-ANGLAIS DE 1904.

Divers journaux ont parlé des clauses secrètes du traité franco-anglais de 1904.

Nous croyons savoir que l'une de ces clauses enregistrait l'adhésion de la France à la suppression des capitulations en Égypte le jour où l'Angleterre négocierait en ce sens avec les puissances.

La seconde clause avait pour objet de déterminer dans le nord du Maroc, même sur sa côte Atlantique et jusqu'au sud de Larache, une zone dans laquelle l'action de la France devait être soumise à des restrictions du même ordre que celles exigées par l'Angleterre pour la rive méditerranéenne qui fait face à Gibraltar.(⁵)

MINUTES.

These revelations are getting intolerable. The reference to the secret articles of the Anglo-French Declaration of 1904 is likely to cause H[is] M[ajesty's] G[overnment] serious embarrassment. The " Daily News " [See No. 44998](⁶) is already protesting against parliament being kept in ignorance of the existence of any secret agreement, and there will in all probability be parliamentary questions which it will be difficult to deal with satisfactorily unless it is decided, in view of what has occurred, to publish the secret clauses textually forthwith. Since Germany has now recognized the position of France in Morocco, and since the Franco-Spanish secret convention has also become public, there would probably be no real objection to divulging the secret clauses of the Declaration of 1904 now.

But even if this were decided upon—after consultation with the French government,—I think we should address to them an earnest representation concerning the difficulties to which their failure to maintain the secret of such transactions exposes other governments. I think we should be entitled to request that a searching enquiry be made in order to trace the present grave indiscretion to the person responsible for it and that that person should be adequately punished.

E. A. C.
Nov. 13.

A very discreditable leakage of which the French owe us an explanation.

W. L.

We might ask Sir F. Bertie to draw the attention of M. de Selves to the leakage—and that we leave it to him to speak to M. de Selves in the sense which he may consider most appropriate and pertinent. We can well leave the matter in Sir F. Bertie's hands.

A. N.

Let me examine the secret clauses again with a view to their publication, I don't remember anything objectionable in them and if there is nothing I will instruct Sir F. Bertie to suggest in calling attention to this indiscretion that they should be published.

E. G.

Instruct Sir F. Bertie to point out to M. de Selves that the indiscretion in the Temps has given rise to questions here that make it difficult for me to refuse publication of the secret articles of the Anglo-French agreement of 1904 and to say that in view of the changed conditions in Morocco and the publication of the secret agreement between Russia and Spain there does not seem to be objection to the publication of our secret articles and to ask if M. de Selves agrees.

E. G.

(⁴) [These are contained in 3 enclosures of which the last only appears worth reproducing.]
(⁵) [*v. Gooch & Temperley*, Vol. II, pp. 373–98, No. 417.]
(⁶) [Not reproduced.]

No. 676.

Sir F. Bertie to Sir Edward Grey.

F.O. 44931/8755/11/28.
(No. 516.)   Paris, D. *November* 11, 1911.
Sir,   R. *November* 13, 1911.

The Paris Press comments very unfavourably on the explanations given yesterday by M. de Selves to the Commission for Foreign and Colonial Affairs of the Chamber of Deputies as to the statement made by His Excellency the previous day (see the enclosure in my despatch No. 514 of yesterday's date)(¹) to the effect that the French Government had neither protested nor made any reservations on learning of the Spanish occupation of Larache and Alcazar. M. Cruppi who was Minister for Foreign Affairs at that time and who is Minister of Justice in the present Cabinet addressed a letter—so the "Matin" declares—to M. de Selves expressing his surprise that the latter should have been kept in ignorance of an important *dossier* at the Ministry for Foreign Affairs containing the texts of the French protests against the occupation in question.

Yesterday M. de Selves, at the request of M. Caillaux made the following statement to the Commission :—

"En sortant hier soir du Palais Bourbon je fus assailli par un doute ; je me demandais si je ne m'étais pas trompé en affirmant à la commission que mon prédécesseur n'avait fait aucune objection au gouvernement espagnol au mois de juin dernier. Je consultai M. Bapst, directeur des affaires politiques, qui m'avait assisté devant la commission. Lui aussi n'était pas sans inquiétude. Rentré au Ministère je fis faire des recherches, et j'appris bientôt l'existence d'un dossier qui contenait les protestations du gouvernement français auprès du Cabinet de Madrid. Ce matin je demandai à votre President, M. Paul Deschanel, de bien vouloir convoquer la commission. Je tiens en effet à ne pas retarder plus longtemps une explication. Je viens ici dire très loyalement que j'étais insuffisamment informé quand j'ai répondu à un de vos collègues, M. Marcel Ribière. Voici en effet les protestations qui furent adressées au gouvernement espagnol. Il y a trois dépêches du ministre des affaires étrangères à notre ambassadeur à Madrid, M. Geoffray. Elles sont datées : la première du 8 juin ; la seconde, du 10 juin, et enfin la troisième du 13 juin 1911."

M. de Selves added that the protests of his predecessor, M. Cruppi, had been couched in very decided terms and that it was therein stipulated most strongly that France would not give her assent to any occupation other than that of the Ceuta zone.

This explanation is stated to have elicited numerous protests on the part of the Commission and M. Ribière declared that it was a proof of the disorder and anarchy reigning in one of the most important departments of the Ministry for Foreign Affairs. M. de Selves thereupon stated that M. de Bapst was at Biarritz on leave of absence when the French protests were made. This further explanation however failed to satisfy the Commission, two of whose members enquired how it was possible that M. Bapst on returning from leave did not make himself acquainted with what had occurred during his absence.

I have, &c.
FRANCIS BERTIE.

(¹) [Not reproduced.]

No. 677.

Sir E. Goschen to Sir Edward Grey.

F.O. 44846/25883/11/28.
(No. 374.)
Sir,

Berlin, D. November 11, 1911.
R. November 13, 1911.

I have the honour to transmit herewith a translation of a speech which the Chancellor made in the Reichstag yesterday in which he made an energetic protest against the violently chauvinistic language of Herr von Heydebrand, and the unjustifiable manner in which he had spoken of a country whose relations with Germany were of a normal character.(¹) Herr von Heydebrand's utterances might be made by an excited hustings orator, but they were utterly unworthy of an orderly deliberative assembly.

The Chancellor's speech, which the " Vossische Zeitung " describes as the Chancellor's first real political success, has created great excitement in all political circles. Never, the papers say, have such words been addressed to the Conservative Party by a Chancellor since the days of Bismarck, and it remains to be seen what the ultimate effect upon the present grouping of parties will be.

People are at a loss to understand the difference between the studied and somewhat monotonous tone of his first speech, and the fiery and energetic language of the second. I learn from a confidential source that the tone and language of the speech was arranged between the Emperor and the Chancellor on the evening of the first debate in the Reichstag, that is, immediately after Herr von Heydebrand had spoken. I do not know whether this is a fact, but if it is true it would certainly account for the energy of the speech.

I have, &c.
W. E. GOSCHEN.

Enclosure in No. 677.

Speech delivered by Herr von Bethmann Hollweg in the Reichstag, November 10, 1911.

(Translation.)

Gentlemen, I have heard it said the Government have suffered a severe defeat, Tripoli is the result of Agadir, we have inaugurated a mistaken policy of fraternisation, we ought not to have sent the " Panther " to Agadir, in short, that we have done everything wrong. Gentlemen, let me deal with two points.

Herr Bassermann has said that Tripoli was a result of Agadir. Gentlemen, if the Italian expedition to Tripoli had had any connection with the Moroccan events, it would have been connected not with Agadir but with the French advance to Fez. It was not we who raised the Moroccan question. It was the French who did so with their advance to Fez. This advance compelled us to open negotiations, and how can you then assert that the advance of the Italians to Tripoli was the result of Agadir?

Gentlemen, I have frequently seen the same view expressed in the foreign press, especially in that portion of the foreign press which is particularly ill-disposed towards Germany, which when trouble arises anywhere in the world says : " Of course Germany was the cause of it." Gentlemen, I must say quite openly that I was surprised that the leader of the National Liberal party should have associated himself with these views in contradiction to the facts.

Gentlemen, Herr Bassermann went on to make the following further criticism of our action. He said that when M. Rouvier was in office no offer was made to us in regard to Morocco; and that if such offer had been made, according to Herr

(¹) [This sentence of the despatch is reproduced, with the omission of " violently chauvinistic," in *A. & P.* (1911), CIII (*Cd.* 5970), pp. 453–56. The rest of the despatch is omitted in the published version, though not described as an extract. The text of the translation is the same as that given here.]

Bassermann, we ought not to have accepted it in view of our whole Eastern policy. Herr Bassermann indeed maintained that our present foreign policy, which is in his opinion extraordinarily bad in comparison with that formerly pursued, has destroyed the entire results of the Eastern policy which we have so carefully pursued during the last 20 years. Herr Bassermann however said not only that we ought not to have accepted an offer on the part of M. Rouvier, on account of our Eastern policy, but also because the England of King Edward VIIth's time would not have allowed it. Herr Bassermann therefore praises the policy of the past by having conformed in advance to the probable opposition of England, and he cannot sufficiently blame our present policy for weakness and cringing on account of an alleged yielding to England which has not occurred. I explained this to you yesterday.

Thirdly Herr Bassermann considers that we have undone the whole of our good Eastern policy. Our former policy was to avoid doing anything to offend Islam. But now Herr Bassermann has himself proposed that we might indeed have sacrificed the sovereignty of the Sultan of Morocco in the North and given over the protectorate to France, but that we ought to have maintained that sovereignty in the South. Gentlemen, how does that tally with an undoing of our Eastern policy?

Herr Bassermann has continued to speak—as did also other members—of the sovereignty of the Sultan, and said that we had made untold sacrifices in Morocco. Herr von Heydebrand made a like observation. Gentlemen, I ventured to explain to you yesterday—and everyone who has studied the facts must admit it—that the sovereignty of the Sultan of Morocco had long been a fiction—it existed no more. This was the case before we concluded our Morocco agreement. All these reproaches as to sacrifices are therefore baseless. Herr Schultz said just now that we had retired from Morocco. But, Gentlemen, we were never there. All these reproaches fall to the ground.

I began by saying that I would have been glad to hear positive proposals from you, as to how I ought to have acted. I have not heard very many, but some have indeed been made. Herr Bassermann said that we ought not to have sent a ship to Agadir, but that we ought to have taken measures on our western frontier. Yes, Gentlemen, but what sort of measures? Does he mean movements of troops? But, Gentlemen, movements of troops on our western frontier at a moment of tension are the beginning of mobilisation, and mobilisation at a critical time means war. I do not know whether such a measure would have been an appropriate intimation to France to sit down with us to negotiate a deal. I return once more to the proposal of Herr Bassermann to sacrifice the independence of the Sultan in Northern Morocco and to recognise the French protectorate, but to keep Southern Morocco free from it, in order that we could live there under better conditions. I cannot imagine how this idea could have been carried out. One and the same ruler is to be under the Protectorate of France in the North, but Sovereign in the South of Morocco, which is however ¡not so sharply divided from the North. That is not possible. Then again our economic interests and our trade can only flourish in a safe country, where order prevails—not police order, but internal order—where the Government is undivided. That is the necessary condition for the conduct of commercial and industrial undertakings. That you must admit. I see no possibility of it, however, if in Southern Morocco twenty different tribes under twenty different chiefs are held together by no undivided force. I see really no advantage in Herr Bassermann's proposal; and if we had achieved this result—Northern Morocco under a French protectorate and Southern Morocco under a so-called Sovereign Sultan— Gentlemen, Herr Bassermann would have had still worse things to say of me.

I come now to Herr von Heydebrand. He is, so far as I know, with the member already mentioned, the only one who has made positive suggestions. Herr von Heydebrand has admitted that it is easy to criticise but difficult to do better. But he added :—

"But we think that if we had retained an entirely free hand for our future demands and had possessed the will and determination to assert them at the proper time and in the proper circumstances, it would have been more sensible than that which is now laid before us." ("Quite right," from the National Liberals.) You cry "quite right," Gentlemen. I have carefully weighed this suggestion of Herr von Heydebrand, as I do all his words, but I must admit that I am still not clear what I ought to have done according to Herr von Heydebrand's idea. Wait for the proper time and circumstances! To do nothing then on the advance of the French to Fez, to sit still with folded arms? Gentlemen, that would have been a mistake. That would have been a policy of weakness which would have always been thrown in my teeth. There are times when one must act at once and even in certain circumstances take risks, and that we did. I can really make nothing of a proposal to wait and do something at the proper time.

I take more seriously what Herr von Heydebrand said about England. He, too, has again referred to the well-known article in the "Neue Freie Presse" which has been attributed to the British Ambassador at Vienna, and although the Secretary of State made a declaration yesterday with regard thereto, Herr Wiemer has also again returned to the subject.

Gentlemen, the matter is perfectly clear. I called the attention of the British Government to the justifiable indignation (Erregung) aroused in Germany by this article in the "Neue Freie Presse." I at the same time gave the British Government to understand that I would be glad to receive an explanation. To this the British Government replied that the British Ambassador at Vienna had neither inspired the well-known article in the "Neue Freie Presse" nor had he made the observations attributed to him by the author of the article. For me therefore the incident is thus closed. (Contradiction and cries of: "Diplomatically.") No, Gentlemen, also for the Reichstag. (Contradiction.) I beg, Gentlemen, that before you give such loud expression to your contradiction you will permit me to finish what I have to say. A great responsibility rests also with the Reichstag in this connection. And no doubt must be expressed in responsible quarters with regard to an official declaration on the part of a foreign Power.

Herr von Heydebrand prefaced his remarks on England with the observation that he had no intention of overthrowing the Government. He however stated almost in the same breath that he had heard language used in a speech resting on the responsibility of the whole British Cabinet, which must be described as a humiliation of, and a warlike challenge to, the German people, and which I had lightly passed over with the expression "After-dinner speech!" If Herr von Heydebrand meant by this that I had intended to dismiss a humiliating challenge to the German nation as it were with a paltry perversion of words, I must leave it to Herr von Heydebrand to say how he would reconcile this public aspersion on his own Government with his alleged intention not to overthow the Government and with his own conscience as a patriot.

Gentlemen, I must further deplore that language should have been used in this House in regard to our relations with a foreign country with which we are in normal relations which might be suitable to electoral meetings, but which is not customary in a Parliament conscious of its responsibility. When I, in the full consciousness of my responsibility, make use of carefully chosen words in regard to the speeches of foreign statesmen, this can and should lead to an improvement of our international relations. Passionate and extravagant language such as that used by Herr von Heydebrand may serve party purposes—but for the German Empire it is injurious. It would be to me a matter of regret if it should become the custom in this House to speak in this tone of our foreign relations. A strong man needs not to carry his sword in his mouth."

After expressing to the House his appreciation of the patriotism which after all inspired their criticism, he made a short reference to a statement by one of the previous speakers to the effect that the attitude adopted towards England by the Chancellor had given the first signal for the adverse criticisms.

"Gentlemen," he said, "I have explained to you and I hope I have convinced you that I have sacrificed nothing of the honour of my country, the honour of the nation to which I belong in our relations with England.

Gentlemen, there have been forces everywhere at work,—I must say it openly—which have more to do with the impending elections than with Morocco and the Congo. But if, Gentlemen, matters are so represented in the newspapers and in the Press as to make it appear that the Fatherland is in need, that we stand on the verge of collapse as a nation, this is not borne out by the facts. To inflame the national passions to fever heat for the sake of Utopian schemes of conquest and party aims, is to compromise patriotism and to squander a valuable asset.''

No. 678.

Sir F. Cartwright to Sir Edward Grey.

F.O. 45130/16083/11/28.
(No. 189.)   *Vienna, D. November* 11, 1911.
Sir,   R. *November* 14, 1911.

I have the honour to submit a résumé of the comments of the principal Viennese journals on the debate which took place in the German Reichstag the day before yesterday on the Moroccan question.

The '' Fremdenblatt '' says the new Agreement must be regarded from the point of view of an honourable and not disadvantageous settlement of the whole question. The German Chancellor set this aim before him, and if he has obtained, without disturbance of the peace, all that was obtainable, his success has been all the greater. It is, however, of greater importance to the World that an agreement should have been reached, by direct negotiation, between France and Germany in so difficult a matter—and they have rendered a great service to the cause of peace. Naturally a compromise never gives complete satisfaction, but the Chancellor may well be content in spite of all criticisms raised against his policy.

The '' Neue Freie Presse '' refers particularly to the extraordinary attitude of the German Crown Prince during the debate and the remarkable and undoubted evidence of His Imperial Highness's approval of the violent criticisms directed against the policy of the Kaiser's Minister and of the language used by Herr von Heydebrandt [*sic*] against England : such a thing has never before been experienced by Germany. Germany and France have now come to an understanding and the Morocco Affair is ended, but with the result that England has to reckon with a very bad feeling in Germany. The estrangement between these two appears unfortunately to be worse than it was before. Germany has suddenly recognised where the enemy is. '' The enemy is England.''

The '' Zeit '' believes the German Government's Morocco policy has suffered a severe defeat. When German diplomacy, after six years' struggle, gains no material advantage worth speaking of and arrives only at an evident relapse of relations with England, the dissatisfaction of the German people is not surprising. Austrians are sorry to see how German policy, once so masterly, has fallen into weak hands. But the outspoken and uncompromising criticism now shewn in Germany gives hope that her political prestige will soon recover what it has lost.

The '' Neue Wiener Tagblatt '' considers that the Chancellor, in his speech, destroyed the notion that the sending of the '' Panther '' was a surprise to the German Ambassadors in Paris and London and to the Governments to which they are accredited. The Chancellor took great trouble to point out that no territorial acquisition in Morocco was aimed at, and he was able to show how superfluous were the British warnings and threats in regard to German intentions which never really existed.

The '' Reichspost '' approves the boldness with which delicate matters of German policy were debated in the Reichstag, as a sign of national pride and conscious strength. The Chancellor's position must be considered as seriously weakened.

I have, &c.
FAIRFAX L. CARTWRIGHT.

No. 679.

Sir F. Cartwright to Sir Edward Grey.

F.O. 45131/16083/11/28.
(No. 190.)   *Vienna,* D. *November* 11, 1911.
Sir,   R. *November* 14, 1911.
With reference to my immediately preceding despatch on the attitude of the Austrian Press towards the Morocco debate in the German Reichstag I have the honour to append herewith translation of a telegram dated from Berlin which appeared in this morning's edition of the ' Zeit.'

" It is a pity that so little has so far been said in the Morocco debate with regard to diplomatic relations between England and Germany in the last few months. On the English side it is always maintained that Mr. Lloyd George was perfectly justified in making his sharp and sensational speech. Your correspondent learns from the circles of the British Embassy here that the German Government omitted to inform the British Government sufficiently with regard to the dispatch of the " Panther " to Agadir. As has been previously announced the explanations given by Count Metternich, the German Ambassador in London, were most inadequate. The London Cabinet asked therefore for an explanation through its Ambassador in Berlin. A second attempt was made a fortnight later. The London Cabinet declared that as Signatory to the Algeciras Act it was entitled to be acquainted with the intentions of Germany in Morocco. In the Berlin Foreign Office, however, silence was maintained and England was left without a reply. An extremely bad impression was created in London by this attitude. The situation became more and more critical and the possibility of an ultimatum to Germany was considered. The King of England and the Czar addressed letters to the Emperor William, in which it was stated that the situation was critical. Finally the idea of an ultimatum was rejected and Mr. Lloyd George was authorized to make his well known speech which perhaps sounded rather sharper than was intended. It was only then that Berlin decided on a reply which was sent 24 hours after the speech was delivered. It was announced that Germany did not aim at the acquisition of territory in Morocco but merely desired to negotiate with France. Thereupon the feeling in London became calmer, but in the subsequent speech of Mr. Asquith the fact was emphasized that Germany's action in sending a ship to Agadir had been undertaken with the intention of creating a new phase in her Morocco policy. The British Government was equally interested in this affair and did not desire only to be consulted when the ' Fait accompli ' was laid before her."

Though I do not for a moment believe that the above emanated from any British Embassy circles, it shows traces of coming from some authoritative source and I therefore venture to trouble you with it as being the first attempt that has been made in the Austrian Press to explain the situation existing beween England and Germany before the conclusion of the Morocco Agreement in a sense more or less exculpating the policy of His Majesty's Government. It will very likely lead to further correspondence.

I have, &c.
FAIRFAX L. CARTWRIGHT.

No. 680.

Sir F. Bertie to Sir Edward Grey.

F.O. 45121/16083/11/28.
(No. 519.)   *Paris,* D. *November* 12, 1911.
Sir,   R. *November* 14, 1911.

The "Matin" continues to represent the extreme claim of France to obtain compensation from Spain in the North West of Morocco.

I have the honour to transmit to you herewith an article on the subject in that paper in which the continued occupation of Alcazar and Larache by Spain is declared to be impossible. France, the article says, cannot consent, after all her sacrifices to leave "la tête du pays" in the hands of Spain.

The "Matin" points out the objections to two protectorates existing side by side in Morocco, and suggests that Spain should be allowed to annex outright the Riff region, including Tetuan and Ifni.

It declares that its view is that of the majority of people in France including parliamentary and diplomatic circles.

There is reason to believe that the "Matin" is directly inspired by the President of the Council.

I have, &c.
FRANCIS BERTIE.

MINUTE.

After the results of the municipal elections in Spain which went very badly for the Republican Party, the Spanish Gov[ernmen]t will stiffen still more in their resistance to French pretensions.
A. N.
E. G.

No. 681.

Sir E. Goschen to Sir Edward Grey.

F.O. 45540/25883/11/28.
(No. 377.)   *Berlin,* D. *November* 13, 1911.
Sir,   R. *November* 16, 1911.

In continuance of my despatch No. 373 of the 10th instant([1]) I have the honour to continue the analysis of the speeches made by leading politicians in the Reichstag debate on the Franco-German arrangement.

Herr von Heydebrand's violent speech was followed by a very long and rather depressing one from the Socialist leader, Herr Bebel. Like nearly all the other speeches delivered it was more an electioneering address and a manifesto against war, than a speech upon an important arrangement with a foreign country. A subsequent speaker said that the only person who had supported the arrangement was Herr Bebel, but I can find little trace of that support in his speech, except that he gave his opinion that any specific arrangement was preferable to war. He deprecated the prevailing idea that Socialists opposed everything, and reminded the House that they had saved the Russian Commercial Treaty for the Government and had done so because it was an instrument of public utility. But the arrangement by which Germany had practically handed over to France a country over which she had no rights and the integrity of which the Emperor had formerly promised to defend, was in a very different category and was on a par with Italy's piratical attack upon Tripoli. He then described the gradual change which had come over their Morocco policy since the Emperor's visit to Tangier, a change which had culminated in the announcement, made in the early part of this year, that the maintenance of the integrity of the Shereefian Empire was an impossibility, and that a portion of it must

([1]) [*v. supra,* pp. 665–8, No. 674.]

fall to Germany's share. Then came Agadir, general jubilation, and subsequently resentment at England's interference. He himself could not see how England could have acted differently, as both in her view and in the view of a considerable portion of the German public, an important change in the balance and distribution of naval strength was contemplated. In any case there was a feeling in the air at that time that the despatch of a ship to Agadir was a preliminary step to the acquisition of territory in Morocco. War was talked of freely and when the Emperor put his foot down at Swinemünde and said that he would not hear of a war on the Morocco question He was attacked by the Pan-German Press in a manner which would have cost Social Democratic Editors had they so written, years of imprisonment. He also alluded to the statements in the Press to the effect that the Secretary of State had called together a large meeting of political leaders and journalists and caused them to be informed that the despatch of a ship to Agadir had no other meaning than that a territorial footing in Morocco was to be secured. Herr Bebel gave a sort of negative defence of the arrangement by pointing out that it was of very little advantage to France and that it would be a drag on French policy rather than otherwise. It was nonsense to talk of the 60,000 African soldiers who were to reinforce the French army.

On the contrary France would have to send 60,000 French soldiers to keep the Morocco tribes in order. As regards the Congo arrangement he said that it was unnecessary for him to waste any words upon it. Its condemnation was to be found in the action and words of Herr von Lindequist, than whom no greater expert in Colonial affairs existed in Germany. In a tremendous peroration he fell on the Conservatives and Pan-Germans, predicted increase of armaments on all sides, resulting in war and national bankruptcy.

Herr Bebel was followed by Herr Bassermann, the National Liberal leader.

He complained of the lack of material supplied by the Government for the debate and said for that reason he would support the resolution that the arrangement should be referred to the Budget Committee. He defended Prince Bülow's policy and said that the reason it had not met with the success it merited was that the French had violated the Act of Algeciras. It was French action which had placed the Morocco question on a fresh basis, and which prepared the public mind for a radical change from Prince Bülow's peaceful policy. It was owing to that anticipated change which, under the circumstances, was welcomed by public opinion, that the despatch of the " Panther " to Agadir had caused such excitement and such hopes. Then came the speeches of British Ministers, and the jubilation of the public gave place to a feeling of intense resentment at England's interference and her cry of " hands off."

His following remarks seem to have been prompted by the suspicion that the original idea of the Government in sending a ship to Agadir had actually been to effect a footing in Southern Morocco. He is not clear on the subject, but this was what he said :—

" England's interference would seem to be utterly inexplicable except under the supposition that it was our intention to occupy Moorish territory. All the outbursts in the English Press were grounded on that idea. Now what are the real facts of the case? Were we certain that in sending a ship to Agadir we had the assent of the British Government as asserted by our Ambassador in London? Or were we completely taken by surprise by the ill-temper shown in England when the ' Panther ' arrived at her destination? The only thing which is certain is that our people expected great things from the despatch of the ' Panther,' and that when the news came out that she had only gone to Agadir temporarily to look after the lives and property of shadowy German subjects and that the German Government were seeking compensation not in Morocco but in the Congo, a storm of indignation and disgust swept through the whole country." He then also asked the Foreign Secretary whether it was true that at a meeting of politicians and journalists encouragement had been given by his Department to the idea of a German sphere of interest in Morocco.

As regards the arrangement itself he said that his party objected to it strongly. France got a Province and in that Province German interests were not sufficiently guarded. "*Without political influence commercial interests could not be maintained.*" And it was that influence which Germany had given up. In his opinion as regards the Congo compensations he, like Herr Bebel, referred the House to the action of Herr von Lindequist.

Returning to the subject of Agadir he said that the despatch of the "Panther" was from every point of view a huge mistake. If it had never been the idea of the Government either to occupy Moorish territory or to defend the integrity of the Shereefian Empire, then it was a useless proceeding and one, as it turned out, not at all favourable to German policy. If the ship was sent as a warning to France that Germany would not suffer her to turn a deaf ear to German remonstrances, that was also an error, as there were other and better ways of making a demonstration against France, ways which while more efficacious would not have brought England on to their backs.

He did not agree with the Chancellor that the arrangement would put a stop to all friction between the two Governments and considered that its effect would be equally disappointing with that of the Potsdam Agreement. Personally he thought that friction would be increased by the arrangement, and in any case it would require more than such an arrangement to wipe out the memory of Alsace and Lorraine.

He then said that the warlike feeling of the last few months had directed general attention to the German army and navy. He and his political friends felt sure that both services were in a condition to meet any serious situation; but they wished to take this opportunity of expressing the hope that if there should be any deficiencies in the army and the navy they would be promptly made good. He said this especially of the Navy, about which remarks had been made, and his Party hoped that those in authority would have both the will and the courage to do what was necessary, without any thought for the impression which an increase of German naval strength might make abroad.

His peroration reminds one of something one has heard before and was as follows :—

> The last months have caused us many sad reflections : but the fact remains that throughout Germany a strong national feeling, a readiness for war if necessary, has been brought to light, which shows that every German is prepared to give up his life for the sake of the Fatherland. Foreigners may be certain that if any attempt is made to trample our national honour under foot they will find a united Germany ready for its defence.

I should mention that the Chancellor was evidently excessively annoyed at the continued references to Sir F. Cartwright in connection with the "Neue Freie Presse" article, after he had said that the matter must be regarded as closed, and His Excellency instructed Herr von Kiderlen Waechter to say a few words to the House on the subject. Herr von Kiderlen rose and repeated the Chancellor's previous remarks, adding that international courtesy, if nothing else, demanded that credence should be attached to the statements of foreign Governments.

That did not, however, prevent the next speaker, Herr Wiemer, leader of the Progressive National Party, from again referring to the alleged "interview," and observing that neither that matter nor the communications with the British Government before and after the despatch of the "Panther" had been adequately cleared up by either the Chancellor or the Secretary of State. Herr Wiemer's speech was on the whole moderate. As regards England he said that as an advocate of friendly relations between the two countries, he had regretted Mr. Lloyd George's speech but still more the effect it had produced. He had no objection to the statement that England must maintain at all costs her position and her prestige among the nations, but England must also recognise that other nations had the right to do the same. He criticised Heydebrand severely for his chauvinistic and bellicose language and said that it had been most inopportune, coming, as it did, just after the friendly words which had been spoken in England by leading politicians and men of influence. It was equalled in irresponsible tactlessness by Mr. Bassermann's proposal to increase the German Navy just after the British First Lord had expressed the hope that the British Naval Estimates might next year be reduced, or at all events not increased. He reminded Herr Bassermann that to any increase in German naval construction, Great Britain could and would have only one answer.

As regards the Franco-German arrangement he said that he could not agree with the Chancellor's statement to the effect that the great thing was that Germany and France had been able to come to an agreement at all on such a delicate question, and observed that it would have been a greater thing if Germany had got what she wanted, and not given France the lion['s] share of the advantages exchanged. The arrangement might on the whole be considered fairly satisfactory, and he bore France no grudge for getting the best of it. Everything, however, would depend upon whether the latter Power kept her engagements.

Herr Wiemer also complained of the German Diplomatic Service, and of the class from which it was recruited; but his severest language was reserved for the manner in which the Crown Prince had chosen to display his chauvinistic tendencies in a serious assembly and during a debate on a peaceful arrangement.

Herr Schultz, the Vice President of the Reichstag then made a short and moderate speech upon the advantages and disadvantages of the Franco-German arrangement. Of those who took part in the debate he was one of the very few speakers who kept to the point under discussion and avoided reference either to Mr. Lloyd George or Sir F. Cartwright.

The Chancellor then rose and addressed the House for the second time in the speech of which I had the honour to transmit a translation in my despatch No. 374 of the 11th instant.([1])

After his Excellency had raised the House to a great state of excitement by the violence with which he had reproved Herr von Heydebrand, there were a few more speeches made, but they were of no special interest from an international point of view, and as a matter of fact, the Chancellor had given the House something else to think of than arguments for or against a Treaty which, as far as Germany was concerned, was an accomplished fact, and which had already been under discussion for three days.

I must mention however that before the close of the day's session Herr Bassermann explained that he had not advocated any increase in the German Naval Programme, he had only said that if, as some people averred, there were deficiencies they ought to be at once made good. That was a very different thing.

Herr von Kiderlen made no speech during the debate, but he gave one or two sharp answers which amused the House. In reply to the charge brought by Herr Bassermann and Herr Wiemer that German diplomats were ill-informed, His Excellency said:—" I must say a word in defence of our Representatives abroad. It has been stated in the Press and also just now in the Reichstag that they are ill-informed. This statement is devoid of all foundation, and those who make it have no knowledge of the subject and have been misinformed. It is a most remarkable thing that those who repeat this fiction that our diplomatists are worth nothing, get their information, and regard it as gospel, from young gentlemen who after a short period of service left our Diplomatic Service, well!—not exactly because they were well-informed! "

With regard to the question asked by Herr Bassermann and others as to whether it was true that at a meeting of politicians and journalists the Imperial Foreign Office had authorised or made a statement to the effect that the despatch of the " Panther " to Agadir meant that Germany intended to have a foothold in Morocco, and nothing else, Herr von Kiderlen replied that it was true that 50 or 60 people

([1]) [v. supra, pp. 679–82, No. 677, and encl.]

had met together and decided upon the annexation of Morocco. He had caused them to be informed that if they wished to annex Morocco they must do it themselves, as the Government would not stand behind them.

Herr von Kiderlen protested strongly against the language of Herr Bebel and others who had described the " Tripoli " campaign as an act of piracy. He said that they might all regret that the war had taken place but that it was not for Italy's allies to cast aspersions on Italian action. He must protest in the name of the Government against such language respecting an allied nation being used in the Reichstag.

On the conclusion of the debate it was unanimously resolved to refer the Conventions to the Budget Commission of the Reichstag.

I have, &c.
W. E. GOSCHEN.

No. 682.

Sir M. de Bunsen to Sir Edward Grey.(1)

F.O. 45365/45365/11/28.
Tel. (No. 91.) Confidential. P. *Madrid, November* 14, 1911.

The Spanish Government has received from the French chargé d'affaires an official note asking for the grant to the Government of Morocco of facilities for the coaling at a Spanish port of three small coastguard vessels, purchased by the Makhzen, on their way to Tangier. The usual custom of a communication addressed to the Spanish Minister at Tangier by the Sultan's representatives would in the opinion of the Spanish Minister for Foreign Affairs have been the correct course, and he considers that France is acting prematurely in exercising her protectorate before the Powers have recognised it, and his reply will probably be to that effect.

(1) [The original decypher of this telegram cannot be traced, and the above document is therefore taken from the printed copy of the paraphrase.]

No. 683.

Sir Edward Grey to Sir F. Bertie.

F.O. 43587/25883/11/28.
(No. 475.) Confidential.
Sir, *Foreign Office, November* 14, 1911.

On receipt of your Excellency's despatch No. 422 of the 28th September,(1) which I read with great interest, I immediately requested the Admiralty and the War Office to furnish me with their views as to the advisability of His Majesty's Government obtaining an assurance from the French Government that no part of the Moroccan coast should ever be fortified.

Both these departments have now informed me that they consider that it would be advantageous for His Majesty's Government to secure, if possible, such an assurance from the French Government.

I have meanwhile received from the French Minister at this Court a copy of the recently concluded Franco-German Convention.(2) In transmitting this document, Monsieur Daeschner stated that the French Government would be glad to receive at an early date a notification of the adherence to it of His Majesty's Government.

(1) [*v. supra*, pp. 552-4, No. 567.]
(2) [*v. supra*, pp. 615-18, No. 626.]

As Your Excellency is aware, His Majesty's Government are bound by their treaty engagements not to refuse their assent to the establishment of a French Protectorate in Morocco, and not to attach to such assent any conditions involving fresh engagements on the part of the French Government.

That a request for an assurance as regards the neutralization of the whole of the Moroccan coast-line would be so regarded by the French Government is shewn by the history of the 1904 negotiations between Great Britain and France.

After careful consideration of the opinions of the Lords Commissioners of the Admiralty and of the Army Council, I have come to the conclusion that in view of all the circumstances it would not be politic to attach such a condition to the adherence of His Majesty's Government to the convention.

In acquainting the Lords Commissioners of the Admiralty and the Army Council with this decision, I have informed them that I will endeavour to give effect to their wishes, should a suitable opportunity occur during the course of any future negotiations with the French Government.

I have thought it desirable in reply to Mr. Daeschner's communication to inform the French Government that the adherence of His Majesty's Government to the Declaration is given subject to the understanding that the provisions of Articles 4 and 7 of the Anglo-French Declaration of 1904 are in no way affected by the present convention, that British subjects in Morocco will receive no less favourable treatment than that accorded to the subjects of any other Power, and that definite arrangements will be made for the internationalization of the town of Tangier.

Your Excellency will note that His Majesty's Government are putting forward no new demands, but are merely putting on record what I believe to be the avowed policy of the French Government.

A copy of Monsieur Daeschner's note and my reply are enclosed herewith for Your Excellency's information.(³)

I am, &c.

E. GREY.

(³) [v. supra, pp. 604–8, No. 619, and encl., and infra, pp. 689–90, No. 685.]

No. 684.

Sir A. Nicolson to M. Daeschner.

F.O. 43587/25883/11/28.

My dear Minister :—   *Foreign Office, November 14, 1911.*

A note is being sent to you to-day announcing that, subject to certain observations His Majesty's Government have much pleasure in giving their adherence to the recently concluded Franco-German Convention with regard to Morocco.(¹)

We shall delay our reply to the German Government, who have also communicated to us the text of the Convention, till we receive the answer of your Government to our note and we should therefore be grateful if they were able to give it early consideration, and to let us have their views as soon as may be convenient.

I have, &c.

A. NICOLSON.

(¹) [v. immediately succeeding document.]

No. 685.

Sir Edward Grey to M. Daeschner.

F.O. 43587/25883/11/28.

Sir,   *Foreign Office, November 14, 1911.*

It was with much satisfaction that H[is] M[ajesty's] Gov[ernmen]t learnt of the definite conclusion of the negotiations which have been proceeding between the French and German Governments on the subject of Morocco.

H[is] M[ajesty's] Gov[ermen]t have, as you are aware, in no way endeavoured to influence the course of these negotiations, as they felt assured that the French Government would not set their hand to any agreement under which the legitimate and acknowledged interests of Great Britain in Morocco would be unfavourably affected.

You were good enough to transmit to me in your note of the 3rd inst[ant]([1]) a copy of the convention which has now been signed between the French and German Gov[ernmen]ts and at the same time you informed me that the French Government would be glad to receive at an early date a notification of the adherence to it of H[is] M[ajesty's] Gov[ernmen]t.

H[is] M[ajesty's] Gov[ernmen]t have given their careful consideration to the articles of the Convention, and in doing so, they have assumed that the engagements taken by the French Government towards H[is] M[ajesty's] Gov[ernmen]t as regards Morocco under articles IV and VII of the Anglo-French Declaration of 1904 will not in any way be affected by the present agreement.

H[is] M[ajesty's] Gov[ernmen]t note that in the articles of the present agreement renewed provision is made for the economic equality in Morocco of the subjects of all Powers. They observe however that under article 1 the German Government gives its assent to such measures of reorganization of control and of financial guarantees as the French Government may, in agreement with the Moorish Government, think fit to take, provided that the action of the French Gov[ernmen]t safeguards in Morocco economic equality between the *two* nations.

H[is] M[ajesty's] Gov[ernmen]t presume it is not intended by the use of these words to establish in favour of German nationals any superior claim to equality of treatment than is, under existing conditions, enjoyed by the subjects of all the Powers, as such a construction would conflict with the general spirit of the agreement itself, and they understand that British subjects will continue to receive in Morocco as favourable economic treatment as those of any other State.

In view of the freedom of action now conceded to France under the new Franco-German convention, H[is] M[ajesty's] Gov[ernmen]t take this opportunity to remind the French Government of the importance attached by both of them equally to the preservation of the exceptional character which the town of Tangier derives from the presence of the diplomatic body and from its municipal and sanitary institutions. H[is] M[ajesty's] Gov[ernmen]t feel confident that the French Gov[ernmen]t will accordingly concur in adequate arrangements being made for placing the town and municipal district of Tangier definitely under international control.

Subject to the above observations and in the belief that they are in harmony with the views and intentions of the French Government, H[is] M[ajesty's] Gov[ernmen]t have much pleasure in giving their adherence to the Franco-German Convention.([2])

[I have, &c.]
E. G[REY].

([1]) [v. *supra*, pp. 604–8, No. 619, and *encl.*]
([2]) [v. *infra*, p. 695, No. 692.]

No. 686.

Sir Edward Grey to M. Daeschner.

F.O. 43587/25883/11/28.
Sir :—
Foreign Office, November 14, 1911.
In the note which I had the honour to address to you to-day([1]) I informed you that, subject to certain observations, His Majesty's Government had much pleasure in giving their adherence to the recently concluded Franco-German Convention with regard to Morocco.

([1]) [v. immediately preceding document.]

His Majesty's Government have not yet received the text of the notes relevant to the Convention which they understood have been exchanged between the French and German Governments.

The notification of their adherence is, in these circumstances necessarily limited to the actual Convention the text of which you were good enough to enclose in your Note of the 3rd instant.([2])

[I have, &c.
E. GREY].

([2]) [v. supra, pp. 604–8, No. 619, and encl.]

No. 687.

Foreign Office to Admiralty and War Office.

F.O. 43587/25883/11/28.
Confidential.
Sir,   *Foreign Office, November* 14, 1911.

In your letter $\frac{\text{M.01410 Confidential}}{0159.428 \text{ (M.O.1.)}}$ of the 3rd instant,([1]) you informed me that the $\frac{\text{Lords Commissioners of the Admiralty}}{\text{Army Council}}$ considered it desirable that a formal undertaking should if possible be obtained from the French Government that no part of the Atlantic Coast of Morocco, South of the Sebou River, should ever be fortified.

Sir Edward Grey has now received from the French Minister at this Court a copy of the recently concluded Franco-German Convention and the French Government have intimated through him that they would be glad to receive at an early date a notification of adherence to it on the part of His Majesty's Government.

On receipt of this communication the question arose as to whether the assent of His Majesty's Government to the Convention should be made conditional on the obtaining of an assurance from the French Government as to the non-fortification of any part of the Moroccan Coast.

Careful and full consideration was given to the observations put forward on this subject by the $\frac{\text{Lords Commissioners and by the Army Council}}{\text{Army Council and by the Lords Commissioners of the Admiralty}}$ but in view of all the circumstances of the case, Sir Edward Grey decided that it would not be politic to attach such a condition to the adherence of His Majesty's Government to the Convention.

What has chiefly weighed with him in arriving at this conclusion is that His Majesty's Government are bound by their treaty engagements not to refuse their assent to the establishment of a French Protectorate in Morocco, and not to attach to such assent any conditions involving engagements on the part of the French Government additional to those embodied in the Anglo-French Declaration of 1904.

That a request for an assurance as regards the non-fortification of the whole of the Moroccan coast line would be so regarded by the French Government is shewn by the fact that, at the time of the negotiations which led to the conclusion of that Declaration, His Majesty's Government endeavoured to obtain from the French Government the assurance in question but were unable to secure their assent, and ultimately desisted from pressing the point.

His Majesty's Government obtained however from the French Government the engagement recorded in Article 7 of the Declaration of 1904, (see my letter of October 6th),([2]) and Sir E. Grey has now informed the French Government that he

([1]) [v. supra, p. 610, No. 620, and note ([2]).]
([2]) [v. supra, pp. 565–6, No. 581.]

[19656]   2 y 2

would be glad to receive an assurance that this Article is in no way affected by the present Franco-German Convention.

Although Sir E. Grey does not see his way to put forward the request for the non-fortification of the whole of the Moorish Coast in connexion with the present Agreement, he will not fail to bear in mind the wishes of the $\frac{\text{Lords Commissioners}}{\text{Army Council}}$ on this point, and he will endeavour to give effect to them should a suitable opportunity occur during the course of any future negotiations with the French Government.([3])

[I am, &c.
W. LANGLEY.]

([3]) [v. infra, p. 779, No. 757.]

No. 688.

Sir Edward Grey to Sir M. de Bunsen.

F.O. 45365/45365/11/28.
Tel. (No. 97.) R.   Foreign Office, November 15, 1911.

Your tel[egram] No. 91.([1]) The proper procedure would undoubtedly have been that the request should have been addressed through the Spanish Rep[resentati]ve at Tangier, but unless the Spanish M[inister for] F[oreign] A[ffairs] has already replied you might suggest to him that the Spanish Gov[ernmen]t might point out the irregularity of the procedure but agree on this occasion to request on condition that it should not be cited as a precedent and that any future requests from the Moorish Gov[ernmen]t should be communi[cate]d through the Spanish Rep[resentati]ve in Morocco till France and Spain have settled their negotiations.

([1]) [v. supra, p. 688, No. 682.]

No. 689.

Sir Edward Grey to Sir F. Bertie.

F.O. 44434/44289/11/28.
(No. 476.)
Sir,   Foreign Office, November 15, 1911.

The French Minister called at the Foreign Office on the 8th inst[ant] and stated that on several occasions the French Gov[ernmen]t had, as His Majesty's Gov[ernmen]t were aware, refused to agree to the Spanish proposal to publish the secret Franco-Spanish agreement respecting Morocco of 1904.([1]) The French Gov[ernmen]t had feared that publication of the agreement might compromise their negotiations with Germany but now that these negotiations were concluded, the objection held good no longer. Moreover the existence of the secret agreement seemed to be pretty generally known.

The French Gov[ernmen]t in these circumstances intended to give the document to the Commission of the Chamber which deals with foreign affairs, and M. Daeschner enquired whether His Majesty's Gov[ernmen]t had any remarks to make or objections to offer to this course, which implied publication of the agreement in the press.

M. Daeschner was informed that His Majesty's Government had no objection.

[I am, &c.
E. GREY.]

([1]) [v. infra, pp. 826-9, App. IV.]

No. 690.

Sir E. Goschen to Sir Edward Grey.

F.O. 46067/46067/11/28.
(No. 381.)
Sir,

Berlin, D. November 16, 1911.
R. November 20, 1911.

Yesterday's edition of the "Lokal-Anzeiger," a paper which has recently occasionally been inspired by the Government, publishes the text of that part of Mr. Lloyd George's speech of July 22nd(1) which deals with England's interests abroad. The paper states that the Chancellor tried in vain in the Reichstag to point out that there was nothing in the speech to justify the reproach which had been brought against him that he had silently swallowed a humiliation.

The paper goes on to say that people reading the speech without prejudice would not be able to close their eyes to the fact that the Chancellor's opinion respecting it was absolutely right. Lloyd George could not however be absolved from the reproach that he chose a very inauspicious moment for making this speech and that he did not rightly gauge what effects it might have. The German nation was quite rightly sensitive about and irritated at different events which had occurred in England and in particular about the utterances of the Jingo Press, and therefore Mr. Lloyd George, whose whole past showed that he belonged to the English "peace idealists," must have said to himself that his words, most carefully chosen though they were, must have awakened a most unfriendly echo in Germany just because they were spoken in a moment so critical to Germany.

The article concludes by saying that it is unjust to reproach the German Government with not having made this speech the motive for an "energetic" diplomatic intervention in England.

I have, &c.
W. E. GOSCHEN.

(1) [The speech was made on the 21st, *v. supra*, pp. 391–2, No. 412, *et sqq.*]

No. 691.

Sir E. Goschen to Sir Edward Grey.

F.O. 46069/25883/11/28.
(No. 383.) Confidential.
Sir,

Berlin, D. *November* 16, 1911.
R. *November* 20, 1911.

The debate in the Reichstag upon the Franco-German agreement was, owing to the circumstances that the Reichstag elections are near at hand, not of a nature to reveal the true sentiments of the political parties who took part in it. As a matter of fact there was scarcely a good word said for the arrangement from first to last. but I am assured by several of the political leaders themselves that if it had been put to the vote it would have been passed by a very large majority and that that verdict would have been ratified by the public at large.

But even if the debate was thus, as far as the Franco-German arrangement was concerned, a purely academic discussion, such as gave the leaders of parties an opportunity to lay their views and sentiments before the electorate, there are certain circumstances which render the debate interesting and in some respects memorable.

These circumstances were the violent chauvinistic language of Herr von

Heydebrand, the part played by the Crown Prince, and the vigorous onslaught upon Herr von Heydebrand by the Imperial Chancellor.([1])

The first idea of the Conservatives was that their chief speaker should be Count Kanitz, a man of moderate views and with a certain knowledge of foreign affairs. It was decided however that the occasion required someone with more "temperament," so Herr von Heydebrand was selected; and certainly in that respect he may be said to have fully justified the choice. It is a pity that Herr von Heydebrand's temperamental language was so obviously directed against England; for it has caused the Crown Prince to be represented in many quarters in England as having deliberately applauded anti-English sentiments. I do not think for a moment that His Imperial Highness had any such idea. I think that he regards the Franco-German arrangement, or rather the fact that an arrangement was come to at all, with considerable dislike, and like most young officers of his age, would have liked a war. Most of his friends would, so I hear, prefer a war with England, but I have every reason for believing that a war with France would be more to His Imperial Highness's taste. However that may be a lot of young officers seem to have got it into their heads that by the Franco-German arrangement Germany had knuckled down to France and England, and it was thought by these wiseacres a most excellent plan that the Crown Prince should go to the Reichstag and, by signifying pronounced assent every time the sabre was rattled, show what the Young Military Party thought of the Chancellor's (and the Emperor's) policy. The Crown Prince is plucky and impulsive but not much given to reflection and I do not believe that he dreamt for a moment that his little manifesto would be regarded as an anti-English demonstration. This is the generally accepted view in grown-up circles, even in those where his conduct was most blamed and against whom it was most directed.

The Chancellor's speech in answer to Herr von Heydebrand has created widespread interest, and everyone is asking what is meant and how it will affect the political situation. For His Excellency it was a personal triumph, in so far that everyone was surprised that the Chancellor, whom people persist in regarding as a calm and detached philosopher, could show so much energy and courage. There is no doubt about his courage in facing difficulties and he has shown it on more than one occasion; but what is really surprising is that, from his seat as Chancellor, and amidst the cheers of the Radicals and Socialists he should have administered such a sharp public reproof to the leader of a party on whose support he has, in ordinary times, chiefly to depend. For the parties of the left only cheered His Excellency because he rebuked the war-like language of Herr von Heydebrand and they will oppose his domestic policy as much as ever. If therefore on account of the speech the Conservatives fall away from him, it is difficult to see how he can get through any Government legislation at all. This will be so much the case if the Conservatives take the Chancellor's speech amiss and desert him, that many people say that Herr von Bethmann Hollweg, who, if no great statesman is at all events a capable politician, would never have allowed himself to fall into this position through inadvertence or impulse, and that therefore he must have spoken with his eyes open to the consequences: this could only mean that he had made up his mind to resign in the near future.

I do not see any particular reason why the Chancellor should resign at the present moment, at all events on the Morocco question. His arrangement with France was certainly not well received in the Reichstag, but it was not seriously attacked; day by day public opinion seems to be getting more favourable to it, particularly in the commercial and financial centres, and he has, I believe, the Emperor's esteem and support. The outlook for the elections is, from his point of view, bad, and he himself told me that he thought there would be at least 120 Socialists in the next Reichstag, but I do not think that he is the man to desert on the eve of a battle. However if the Government of the country is to be carried on upon the lines hitherto

([1]) [v. supra, pp. 665–75, No. 674; and pp. 679–82, No. 677, and encl.]

in use, either some new arrangement of parties must be made, which it is difficult to foresee, or the Chancellor will resign, or the Conservatives must tell Herr von Heydebrand that he has as a matter of fact gone a little far in his speech, and that it would be contrary to the interests of the party to separate from the Chancellor's "Bloc." From what I see in the Press the last seems to be the most likely solution.

I have, &c.
W. E. GOSCHEN.

MINUTE.

A further aggravation of the difficulty in which the German Government may find itself placed at the elections, will arise from the attitude of the Centre Party on the subject of an increase in naval armaments. The "Germania," which is the acknowledged mouthpiece of that party, has published an article violently opposing the plan of any such increase, on account of its necessary effect on Anglo-German relations.

E. A. C.
Nov. 30.
F. D. A.
W. L.
A. N.
E. G.

No. 692.

M. Daeschner to Sir Edward Grey.

F.O. 45859/25883/11/28.   *Ambassade de France, Londres,*
Monsieur le Secrétaire d'État,   *le 17 novembre,* 1911.

Mon Gouvernement a été heureux de prendre connaissance de la communication en date du 14 de ce mois(1) par laquelle Votre Excellence a bien voulu me faire savoir que le Gouvernement de Sa Majesté donne son adhésion à la Convention récemment conclue entre la France et l'Allemagne au sujet du Maroc. Il voit dans cet assentiment une nouvelle manifestation des sentiments d'amitié et de bonne entente qui unissent nos deux pays.

En me faisant part de cette décision du Gouvernement Britannique, Votre Excellence formulait diverses observations destinées à préciser en vue de leur interprétation éventuelle la portée possible de quelques clauses de cet accord. Je suis chargé par mon Gouvernement de donner à Votre Excellence l'assurance que le bénéfice des clauses économiques insérées dans la Convention précitée s'étend à toutes les Puissances et de lui confirmer également que l'accord dont il s'agit n'implique aucune dérogation aux articles 4 et 7 de la Déclaration franco-anglaise du 8 Avril 1904 relative à l'Egypte et au Maroc.

Veuillez, &c.
E. DAESCHNER.

(1) [*v. supra,* pp. 689–90, No. 685.]

No. 693.

Sir Edward Grey to Sir F. Bertie.

F.O. 44930/16083/11/28.
(No. 481.) Confidential.
Sir,   *Foreign Office, November* 17, 1911.

In your despatch No. 515 of the 11th instant(1) Y[our] E[xcellency] informed me that the "Temps" of that date had published what it believed to be the contents of two secret clauses of the Anglo-French Declaration of 1904.

From an examination of the extract from the paper which Y[our] E[xcellency] enclosed, it is clear that the secret Articles II and III of the declaration are those

(1) [*v. supra,* pp. 676–7, No. 675.]

alluded to, though the version published by the "Temps" corresponds but little either in text or in substance with the articles themselves.

The indiscretion in the "Temps" has however given rise to questions in this country, which will make it difficult for me to refuse publication of the Secret Articles of the Declaration of 1904.

I am not aware that any objection now exists to their publication, in view of the changed conditions prevailing with regard to Morocco, and of the publication of the secret agreement of 1904 between France and Spain.

I should therefore be glad if Y[our] E[xcellency] would enquire whether the French gov[ernmen]t agree to their publication.

[I am, &c.
E. GREY.]

No. 694.

Sir Edward Grey to Sir E. Goschen.

F.O. 46325/13911/11/28.
(No. 281.)
Sir,   *Foreign Office, November* 17, 1911.

I observed to Count Metternich to-day that, though I had not yet studied the official report, I had observed only one point in Herr von Bethmann-Hollweg's first speech,(¹) on the Agreement made with France, that would cause me any difficulty in my statement in the House of Commons.

The Imperial Chancellor had repelled in the Reichstag an attack which had been made upon him, to the effect that he had been menaced by the speech of the Chancellor of the Exchequer, and had recoiled before it. In repelling this attack, he had used words which had given the impression in some quarters that the German Government had made to us a menacing communication as to the speech of the Chancellor of the Exchequer, and that we had recoiled before their communication. I should have to defend us against this impression.

Count Metternich said that he did not remember a passage of this sort in the speech of the Imperial Chancellor.

I then told him what the passage was. But I explained to him that I was sure it had not been the intention of the Imperial Chancellor to give the impression to which I had referred; and, therefore, though I must deal with the point, I would do this in a way which would show that our feelings were not hurt by his speech.

I went on to tell Count Metternich that I found a most helpful passage in the speech of the Imperial Chancellor, to the effect that the settlement reached with regard to Morocco ought to improve the relations of Germany with both France and England. I intended to respond most cordially to this.

I admired very much the second speech of the Chancellor in the Reichstag,(²) and I would endeavour to reciprocate the tone and spirit of it.

I said that of course I was speaking quite unofficially, and I had not yet prepared a statement for the House of Commons; but I did not wish Count Metternich to think that the speeches of the Imperial Chancellor had not been appreciated.

There was another speech, made by some one else in the Reichstag, that contained a very violent attack upon England : but I had not yet read it carefully, or considered whether anything would have to be said about it.

Count Metternich thanked me for what I had told him as to the speeches of the Imperial Chancellor. He said that he thought Britain and Germany were now at the parting of the ways, and that relations between them might now get either much better or much worse. He did not suggest that anything very striking could be

(¹) [v. supra, pp. 665–75, No. 674, and encl.]
(²) [v. supra, pp. 679–82, No. 677, and encl.]

done very soon, but he thought it was very helpful to have speeches such as Herr von Bethmann-Hollweg had just made and as, he gathered, I intended to make.

He then, at some length, described to me what he thought was the feeling in England with regard to Germany; what German feeling now was towards England; and how it had seemed to public opinion in Germany that England had been anxious to get up a quarrel between Germany and France, in which she would join: while, on the other hand, English people had been convinced that Germany intended to make war upon England. Both these impressions were, of course, wrong.

I said that in France, during the early stages of the negotiations as to Morocco, the impression had been that Germany was making upon France demands which would force her to choose between humiliation and war. Of course, the fact the negotiations had now come to the settlement should remove this impression.

[I am, &c.]
E. G[REY].

No. 695.

Sir Edward Grey to Sir E. Goschen.

F.O. 46520/25883/11/28.
(No. 282.)
Sir,

Foreign Office, November 18, 1911.

Count Metternich gave me to-day the substance of a communication from the German Chancellor respecting his speeches.

Herr von Bethmann-Hollweg said that he had informed me, before he spoke, that he did not propose to criticise the speech of the Chancellor of the Exchequer, but only the Press comments upon it and the interpretation which had been given to it. I had replied that we could not object to criticism of Press comments on the speech, but that I hoped he would not criticise the speech itself, as that would impose on us the necessity of defending it. Herr von Bethmann-Hollweg hoped that I was satisfied with what he had said. He had endeavoured in his speech to remove the tension which had existed between the two countries in the summer, and he wished me to know that Herr von Kiderlen, in the Reichstag Committee, had also carefully refrained from saying anything that would reflect upon England.

The plenary sittings of the Reichstag had yet to come, and the interpellations to be made then would oblige Herr von Bethmann-Hollweg to refer again to the speech of the Chancellor of the Exchequer. He would therefore like to have, if possible, some clue that would guide him in his remarks, and it would be helpful if he could be informed of what I intended to say in Parliament about the speech.

Herr von Bethmann-Hollweg had seen a question, which had been put in Parliament by Mr. Goldman, attributing to him something which he had not said as to communications which had passed between the two Governments on the subject of the speech of the Chancellor of the Exchequer. What Herr von Bethmann-Hollweg really had said was that he had made a communication to us on the subject of the speech, and that after this the British Government expressed no desire to take part in the negotiations with France. He had said this in reply to attacks in ill-informed quarters of the German Press to show that we had not intruded unfairly into the negotiations.

I asked Count Metternich whether the German Chancellor had sent this communication after learning what I had said yesterday about his speeches.

Count Metternich replied in the negative.

I then observed that what I had said yesterday had to a great extent anticipated what the German Chancellor said in this communication. I could not say exactly how much might have to be said about the speech of the Chancellor of the Exchequer; but I would discuss the question with the Prime Minister and the Chancellor of the Exchequer, as we were all three cognisant of the speech. If the plenary sittings of the Reichstag were not to take place for some time, the German Chancellor would have a report of what was said here before they were held.

Count Metternich promised to let me know when the plenary sittings of the Reichstag were to take place. He himself had been unaware that there was to be a further debate in Berlin.

[I am, &c.

E. GREY.]

No. 696.

Sir F. Cartwright to Sir Edward Grey.

Vienna, November 19, 1911.

F.O. 46163/46163/11/28.　　　　　　　　　　　　　　　　　D. 2·57 P.M.
Tel. (No. 123.) Secret. Very Confidential.　　　　　　　R. 7·15 P.M.

Count Aehrenthal sent for the French Ambassador yesterday afternoon, and presented him with a curiously worded document, which the Ambassador read to me last night.([1]) The main drift of this document is that Austria-Hungary is ready in principle to recognise the Morocco Convention, and that delay in doing so is due to question of formality, how to secure [to] Austria-Hungary all the advantages, judicial and economic, granted to Germany in Morocco.

The document then goes on to speak of the excellent political relations existing between Austria and France, which should be extended to economic questions.

The document asserts that Franco-Austrian capital might well be employed together to benefit both countries in Near East, Morocco, and elsewhere. Finally a request is made that French Government should facilitate raising of a loan of a milliard francs by Austro-Hungarian Government in Paris.

Count Aehrenthal informed French Ambassador that he had not sent a copy of this document to Austrian Ambassador at Paris from a fear that he might explain it incorrectly to French Government, which might lead to misunderstandings. The document will not reach French Government by messenger for another week.

From Count Aehrenthal's language in discussing this document French Ambassador infers that we are nearing a turning in the roads, and that Count Aehrenthal is holding out a friendly hand to Triple *Entente* with a view to dissociating himself little by little from Germany, as he is beginning to realise that Germany may go to war with France at any moment.

French Ambassador believes that Count Aehrenthal would not have asked for so vast a sum of money from France if he were not prepared in his mind to give something substantial in return. What form those guarantees will take it is impossible to say at present, but the French Ambassador declares that France must insist on being thoroughly assured that, in the event of a war between Germany and France, even if Russia comes to the assistance of France, Austria (though perhaps mobilising) will remain neutral so long as Germany does not run any danger of being crushed.

([1]) [Apparently that printed in *Ö-U.A.*, III, No. 2942. *cp. infra*, pp. 713–5, No. 708.]

No. 697.

Sir E. Goschen to Sir Edward Grey.

F.O. 46402/46402/11/28.
(No. 387.)　　　　　　　　　　　　　　　　　　　Berlin, D. November 19, 1911.
Sir,　　　　　　　　　　　　　　　　　　　　　　　R. November 21, 1911.

I have the honour to report that the following telegram from Berlin, which appears to be of semi-official origin, was printed in the "Kölnische Zeitung" of the 17th instant :—

"The confidential "exposé" made by the Secretary of State for Foreign Affairs in the Morocco Commission of the Reichstag, so far as it dealt with the exchange of views with England, afforded proof that this portion of the criticism passed on German diplomatic action was not justified. Even the representatives of those sections which were strongly opposed to the Government were convinced that the language of the Foreign Office did not lack that emphasis which public opinion held to be required."

The truth of this latter assertion is denied by the Conservative "Kreuz-Zeitung" which states that it has made enquiries on the subject of all the sections concerned. The confidential communications made by the Secretary of State in regard to the attitude of Germany towards England contained nothing which was not already known and nothing which was calculated to alter the views entertained by the members of the Budget Commission.

The "Tageblatt" yesterday quoted articles from the Socialist "Vorwaerts" criticizing the alleged delay of the German Government in returning a reply to an enquiry from His Majesty's Government in regard to the despatch of the "Panther" to Agadir and stating that Mr. Lloyd George's speech was the result of this delay. To-day it quotes a further statement to the effect that Herr von Kiderlen did indeed assert before the Budget Commission that a reply had been made but that His Excellency was forced to admit that the answer was a verbal one. The instructions on the subject only reached the German Ambassador on the day on which Mr. Lloyd George delivered his speech, it was therefore probably not possible for him to deliver the message in time.

The "Tageblatt" states that Herr von Kiderlen is expected shortly to publish a statement on all points on which he does not desire to maintain secrecy and it adds that it understands that a unanimous wish has been expressed by the Commission that this statement will deal as fully as possible with the facts connected with Mr. Lloyd George's speech.

I have, &c.
W. E. GOSCHEN.

MINUTES.

The official report of Herr von Kiderlen's statement before the secret committee of the Reichstag has appeared in the press and is given in translation in to-day's Times (annexed hereto).(1)

The statement in the "Tageblatt" referred to in the last paragraph of the present despatch, indicates that the published account contains only so much as the German gov[ernmen]t do not think it necessary to keep secret, and that in fact he said much more—which is primâ facie probable.

Herr von Kiderlen's statement to the committee and its publication involves a breach of the well-established diplomatic rule that communications exchanged with foreign governments shall not be published without the latter's consent. The breach seems all the more flagrant as the recent communications from Count Metternich, embodied in the despatches to Sir E. Goschen, conveyed, if not a request, certainly a suggestion that in view of the very short and restrained reference made by the Chancellor in his recent speeches in the Reichstag to what passed between the British and German governments, Sir E. Grey should on his part say as little as possible on the subject. The fact that an elaborate, and in many respects misleading, statement had been made or was on the point of being made to the Reichstag in secret session by Herr von Kiderlen, was suppressed. This does not seem quite straightforward. If the publication in the German press had been made a day later, and if the Morocco debate in the House of Commons had, as previously intended, and announced, been held to-morrow, Sir E. Grey would have found himself placed in an embarrassing position.

As the German gov[ernmen]t have without consulting H[is] M[ajesty's] G[overnment] thought fit to publish their version of what passed between Count Metternich and Sir Edward Grey, Sir Edward is now free either to lay his record of the communications before parliament without further reference to Berlin, or to quote it in detail when speaking in the forthcoming debate.

E. A. C.
Nov. 22.

(1) [v. infra, pp. 700–3, Ed. note, and p. 715, No. 709.]

This performance on their part has certainly freed our hands.

W. L.
A. N.
F. D. A.

It has freed my hands or rather my mouth considerably.

E. G.

[ED. NOTE.—The following extract from the *Times* of Wednesday, November 22, 1911, gives a summary of Herr von Kiderlen-Waechter's statement of November 17. As shown in Sir E. Crowe's minute on the immediately preceding document (*v. supra*, p. 699) a copy was attached by him to that document. Although, therefore, the statement was made on the 17th, its substance was not published in Germany until the 21st, or in Britain until the 22nd.

STATEMENT BY THE GERMAN FOREIGN SECRETARY.

Berlin, Nov[ember] 21.

The extract officially published this evening of Herr von Kiderlen-Waechter's speech before the Budget Committee on Friday [the 17th], states that a telegram was sent on June 30 to all the German representatives accredited to the Powers signatory to the Algeciras Act announcing the despatch of the Panther to Agadir and explaining the reasons for the step. In addition, instructions were sent to the German Ambassador in London simultaneously directing him to make the following communication to the British Government :—

Although our information in regard to the situation of the Europeans at Fez did not accord with the French information, we raised no objection to the French advance to Fez. Meanwhile a situation has gradually arisen which has rendered the provisions of the Act of Algeciras illusory. In consequence of a situation created by the force of circumstances, we have found ourselves compelled to comply with the appeal of a number of well-known business houses, and undertake ourselves the protection of the lives and property of German subjects and *protégés* in Southern Morocco until orderly conditions are restored in the country, but we have had no intention whatever of expostulating with France on account of her action. In view of the position of affairs it might seem doubtful whether France will be able to return to the *status quo* of 1906. We are, therefore, eventually prepared, in common with France, to look for a way which may lead to a final understanding on the Morocco question and which will also be in accordance with the interests of the other signatory Powers. The method of direct negotiations could hardly encounter insuperable obstacles in view of the existing good relations between France and ourselves.

The British Government was therefore informed as to the German intentions before the arrival of the ship at Agadir, the above communication having been made on July 1.([2])

Interview with Sir Edward Grey.

During the course of the negotiations with France, Herr von Kiderlen-Waechter continued, it came to explanations with the British Government. No inquiry was made by England either of the German Ambassador in London or of the Government in Berlin with regard to the foregoing communication. The Foreign Secretary continued :—

It was not till July 21, the day of Mr. Lloyd George's speech, that an interview took place between Sir Edward Grey and the German Ambassador at the instance of the British Foreign Secretary. The opinion that Sir E. Grey had formed of our attitude, in spite of the explanations made by the Ambassador at the time of the despatch of the Panther, was again manifested at this interview. This opinion was the result of charges which the French and a section of the British Press and, indeed, some officials had consistently brought against our policy. Sir E. Grey expressed a wish to discuss the Morocco question unofficially with the Ambassador. He had from the first placed it beyond doubt that, in view of her great economic interests there, England must participate in any settlement of the Morocco question. He had been waiting, he said, in the hope of an agreement between France and Germany. Now, however, that the German demands, as he had learned, were of such a far-reaching character that it was obvious the French could not accept them, there was a danger that the negotiations would come to an end without a result and then the question would again come into the foreground, " What is Germany doing in the closed harbour of Agadir and its *Hinterland*? " He knew nothing of what was going on there. Agadir, Sir Edward pointed out, was suited for the construction of a war port. No one knew what Germany intended there. He must expect questions of this kind in Parliament and was not in a position to give an explanatory answer. If the Franco-German negotiations came to nothing, which, in view of the German demands might easily occur, the Agadir question, in which British interests were involved, would immediately arise. Sir E. Grey, therefore, believed the time had come when England should participate in the negotiations. He had held aloof so long as there was reason to hope for a Franco-German agreement outside Morocco as British policy was not affected if France and Germany sought to reach a colonial agreement by

([2]) [*v. supra*, pp. 322-3, No. 339.]

means of the regulation of the frontier of the Cameroons as had been suggested at first. As, however, France could not accept the German demands, it was probable that the actual Morocco question in which British interests were involved to a high degree would come into the forefront of politics and therefore the question of German intentions in regard to the closed harbour of Agadir and its *Hinterland* had again become acute. He wished again to emphasize that he was animated in bringing about the meeting solely by the desire not to find himself confronted by facts which would compel him to take up an attitude and as a consequence of which the political situation, already sufficiently complicated, would assume a decidedly more difficult and serious form.

The German Standpoint.

The German Ambassador said he had not been informed concerning the details of the German negotiations with France and could not admit that the German demands were obviously unacceptable as Sir E. Grey had said. In that case Germany would not have presented them. Sir E. Grey had asserted, even if unofficially, that the time had come to negotiate *à trois*. This contention was apparently based on the suggestion that Germany might build a naval station at Agadir and close the *Hinterland*. These were suppositions of which the Ambassador knew nothing. If, the Ambassador continued, any English interests were injured by Germany's action, let Sir E. Grey name them. As he (Sir E. Grey) could not do that, it would be more correct, the Ambassador said, to wait till he was able to prove that any British interest or right was affected. Germany had not the slightest intention of injuring British rights or interests. The course of events had brought about a moment when Germany found herself face to face with the necessity of coming to an understanding with France over the Morocco business. If, as Sir E. Grey assumed, the German proposals in another field were considered unacceptable, that only proved that France did not set as much value upon the free exercise of her claims in Morocco as might have been expected. She must, therefore, put up with the presence of a foreign war-ship in a Moroccan harbour as part of the bargain. A North African empire from the Tripoli frontier to Senegambia, with a predominant position in Morocco, was no small matter. England, the Ambassador pointed out, had been compensated in Egypt, which also was no trifling matter, but Germany had not been compensated with anything. If France wished that Germany, like England, while preserving her commercial interests, should retire into the background in Morocco, she must offer an equivalent approximately corresponding in value to the great aims she sought herself. The Ambassador could not hide from the Minister that he (Sir E. Grey) seemed to have one measure for France and another for Germany. If he laid such stress on the inviolability of Moroccan territory, he ought, before all, to request explanations from France.

Sir E. Grey replied that he would in no way oppose the extension of Germany's colonial possessions in the heart of Africa. He could not conceal from himself, however, that English interests might be most seriously affected by the Morocco question itself. He had, therefore, sincerely hoped for an agreement between France and Germany, and only in the undesired event of the failure to reach such an agreement had he been obliged to say plainly that the *démarche* at Agadir would lead to explanations (*eine Aussprache*) between England and Germany. He believed the situation would lose its acuteness if such a discussion took place between the two Governments before events occurred at Agadir in respect of which England would be obliged to take up a position.

Protection of German Interests.

Herr von Kiderlen-Waechter, continuing, pointed out that the foregoing conversation showed that Sir E. Grey openly assumed that Germany meant to establish herself in Morocco in spite of the communication made to him at the time of the despatch of the Panther. The Ambassador's despatch reporting the conversation with Sir E. Grey was received in Berlin on July 22. "An answer," the Foreign Secretary proceeded, "was immediately despatched from Berlin":—

The Ambassador was therein instructed to tell Sir E. Grey that we had from the first declared that our ship was merely to protect German interests at Agadir. A native attack on a German farm among other reasons gave special occasion for her presence there with that object. Up to the present nothing had occurred which justified the inference that there has been a change in our intentions. Not a man had yet been landed. We regretted that in England faith seemed to be placed in insinuations in regard to our intentions which obviously emanated from a source hostile to us. We had never thought of the establishment of a naval port on the Moroccan coast and would never think of such a thing. That was an hallucination. Also, we had no designs upon Moroccan territory, but we must demand that France should either adhere strictly to the Algeciras Treaty or, if she believed herself unable to do so, that she should enter into explanations with us. Negotiations had been begun on both sides and were guaranteed the strictest secrecy. We had taken the obligation seriously and had not even informed our allies. France had adopted another procedure and had supplied not only the Press, but, as appeared also, her friends with information which was incomplete and inexact and calculated to cast suspicion on our intentions. We, therefore, for the time ceased to negotiate until the secrecy of the negotiations was guaranteed. If the negotiations failed we had no designs upon Moroccan territory, but we must then demand from France with all emphasis a decision for the execution of the Algeciras Act in its letter and spirit and in its entirety. We counted on the support of the other Powers especially of England, if France did not wish for an understanding on the basis proposed by us and in that case we demanded the restoration of the *status quo ante* in Morocco.

Mr. Lloyd George's Speech.

Herr von Kiderlen-Waechter declared that the assertion that Germany had not answered an inquiry of the British Government for 14 days thus fell to the ground. He continued :—

As the answer to the questions raised by Sir E. Grey in his interview with the German Ambassador was despatched the text of the speech delivered by Mr. Lloyd George on the evening of July 21 became known in Berlin. It was sent on the very day, therefore, that the Ambassador and Sir E. Grey had their conversation. It was not necessary to comply with the suggestion of the British Minister which we afterwards received that he should be authorized to make use in Parliament of our declaration that we had no designs upon Moroccan territory. To have done so would have given rise to the impression that that declaration was a consequence of Mr. Lloyd George's speech.

On July 24 our Ambassador in London was instructed to point out that Mr. Lloyd George's speech had furnished a large part of the British and the entire French Press with an occasion for violent attacks upon Germany. The question how far this effect was intended by the English Minister need not be gone into. The British Government, however, could not fail to perceive that this effect of a speech made by one of its members must give rise to dissatisfaction in Germany to a high degree. Germany had made proposals to France which appeared entirely loyal and acceptable. They referred to regions in which British interests were neither directly nor indirectly concerned. If in spite of that, England believed she ought to declare her wishes, she could make these known through the ordinary diplomatic channel; if instead of doing this the British Government caused public declarations to be made by one of its members which could, at least, be interpreted as a warning intended for ourselves, and which actually were interpreted by the British and French newspapers as a warning bordering upon a threat, it was difficult to find grounds for that procedure. The British Government, the Ambassador was directed to point out, could not be in doubt that the friendly agreement between Germany and France which the British Government itself declared it desired would not be promoted thereby. In view of the tone adopted towards Germany by a part of the British and almost the entire French Press the British Government could not have been in any uncertainty as to the effect that was to be expected from Mr. Lloyd George's speech. If the British Government had had the intention of complicating and confusing the political situation, and bringing things to a violent outburst (*Entladung*), it could have chosen no better means of doing so than the Chancellor of the Exchequer's speech.

In reply the Ambassador reported that Sir E. Grey consented not to make Parliamentary use of the information concerning Germany's intention not to acquire territory in Morocco, but remarked that in that case he had no means of allaying public disquiet in regard to our alleged designs upon Agadir. Sir E. Grey defended Mr. Lloyd George's speech as moderate, and declared that it was quite right to deliver the speech.

British Interests.

The Ambassador then again drew the Minister's attention to the fact that the Anglo-French (*sic*) Press represented the speech as a threat against Germany. Sir E. Grey declared that Germany's eventual intention to undertake the restoration of the *status quo* in Morocco was alone calculated to lend the Morocco problem a still graver significance. He protested against the idea that the British Government did not desire a Franco-German agreement. He must, however, point out that in the event of British interests being touched in the course of the Morocco question the British Government must defend them.

The Ambassador thereupon said that nobody denied England that right. We never intended to dispose of English interests and rights. That intention existed only in the English imagination. The British Government had no ground for that suspicion, which had also been heard in Mr. Lloyd George's speech, in consequence of which the speech had a provocative effect. If occasion arose Germany would welcome the co-operation of the other signatory Powers for the purpose of restoring the *status quo* in Morocco. Only if that co-operation were wanting would she assert her right herself. Menacing warnings, the Ambassador added, would only encourage Germany to hold fast to her right.

Fresh instructions were sent to the Ambassador on July 26 in reply to Sir Edward Grey that he must have perceived from the official communications that British interests were not affected by the negotiations with France. We expected, therefore, from his tried loyalty that he would give expression to this fact in Parliament without entering upon the confidential portions of our communication. The Ambassador was further instructed gladly to take note of Sir E. Grey's assurance that a Franco-German understanding was desired by him to express the conviction that this would be in a high degree helpful to the progress of the negotiations.

That wish it was difficult to reconcile with the English assertion that our demands in the Colonial sphere could not be fulfilled, an assertion made without knowledge of the equivalent we were offering in the political sphere. It was Germany's earnest wish to diminish or entirely to remove causes of friction with France in the colonial sphere, especially in Africa. If Great Britain shared that wish then she could only promote its attainment by endeavouring to assuage the present highly-excited state of feeling in France which had been produced by false rumours and semi-indiscretions.

Herr von Kiderlen-Waechter then gave a summary of a statement issued by Reuter's Agency on July 22, which is described as obviously inspired, and added, " From this point on our negotiations with France made better progress."—*Reuter.*]

No. 698.

Sir F. Bertie to Sir Edward Grey.

(By Bag.)

F.O. 46373/46373/11/28.   *Paris,* D. *November* 20, 1911.
Tel. (No. 188.) *En clair.*   R. *November* 21, 1911.

Monsieur de Selves whom I saw by appointment this evening, wishes me to inform you that proposals have been drawn up by the President of the Council for an arrangement with Spain in regard to Morocco. He will communicate them to me in the next few days for your consideration.

No. 699.

Lord Acton to Sir Edward Grey.

F.O. 46706/38119/11/18.
(No. 44.)   *Darmstadt,* D. *November* 20, 1911.
Sir,   R. *November* 23, 1911.

The storm of abuse which has the British Government and people for its objective and which has been maintained by the German press with untiring energy during the past few months, is evidently not intended primarily for foreign consumption, as an undiplomatic weapon to harass the home Government by its recoil, but appears to have for its main purpose the education of the remoter portions of the population, to judge by the care which is expended on the concoction of printed matter which never meets other than German eyes. Intermittently, as will be seen below, views are put forward which testify to a genuine wish for a clarification of the atmosphere other than by powder and shot, and it would be as unfair to underrate the academic value of such utterances as to exaggerate the practical gravity of the more frequent type of comment. Indeed it is I think unwise to yield to the universal temptation and to attach excessive might to press opinion in Germany. It is perhaps an error to look upon the press as an invariably faithful reflector of public feeling. Leading articles are written to whet the appetite rather than to satisfy it. They are as often dictated by the personal rancour of the editor or the style exigencies of the hack, as by questions of circulation or of party loyalty. The most perfect compositions on topical themes are frequently unread by those who make war and peace, whether these stand at the apex or the base; and it can scarcely be questioned that the cataclysms of history are generally due to the interplay of cosmic forces against which the written or spoken word is of only superficial avail.

In spite of this attitude of detachment, it is however disappointing to find single-hearted demonstrations of friendship, such as a recent effusion of the " Daily Chronicle," received with contumely by local German organs that have no axe to grind in the international forge. The London paper had innocently hazarded the view that no insuperable obstacle stands in the way of an understanding. In giving prominence to this and similarly attuned passages in the same article, the " Darmstädter Tagblatt " of November 15 observes that it is curious that these

Germanophil utterances only make themselves heard now that the conclusion of the Morocco Agreement is an accomplished fact; and it suggests the inference that England's present good-humour and satisfaction at the issue of the Franco-German negotiations is a proof that Germany has got the worst of the bargain. The fact is that for the present at any rate nothing but what is evil can emanate from London. The "Frankfurter Zeitung," on the other hand, which a few days back admitted the injudiciousness of the Agadir escapade without adequate previous warning and its responsibility for our subsequent attitude; and which interpreted the Guildhall speech of the new First Lord as a wholesome hint to dreamers of the Flottenverein that the distance between the strength of the two navies can never be narrowed, returns to-night to the time-honoured theme and describes the recrudescence of bitterness as a comedy of errors. The writer regrets in vigorous terms that Germany should not be represented by a more statesmanlike diplomatist at the Court of St. James who would have given the Wilhelmstrasse timely warning of the probable effect of the meditated coup. (It may be noted in this connection that Baron Jenisch who is well known in London and who was at Wilhelmshöhe on behalf of the German Foreign Office on the occasion of King Edward's last visit, and whom, as I have reason to know, His Majesty would have wished to have seen installed in due course at Carlton House Terrace, is at present Prussian Minister at Darmstadt.) The "Frankfurter Zeitung," still unconvinced of the impregnability of the entente, thinks it not entirely outside the range of the possible that England may in the near future make a friendly démarche at Berlin if only to prevent the recent agreement between France and Germany leading to a political rapprochement between those two countries from which she would find herself excluded. The article generously concludes with the declaration that if, in the words of Nigra, England and Germany are nations who must be either bitter enemies or close allies, the writer would unhesitatingly opt for the latter.

Mr. Churchill's speech has not met with universally friendly comment in the German press. For example, the "Hannoversche Courier" remarks in respect of it that if any innocents still exist who are unable to explain the sharp antithesis between England's German policy and the siren whispers which are wafted across the Channel by friendly societies and by orators postprandially disposed, they will find a solution in the Guildhall speech, in which the declaration is made with telling force that so long as the naval competition continues the feeling of mistrust will endure. In other words, as soon as Germany abandons her policy of naval expansion the way will be paved for friendly conversation.

The recent criticisms by the "Times" Military Correspondent of the efficiency of the German army as revealed at the autumn manoeuvres forms the subject of a violent personal attack in the "Schlesische Zeitung" on Colonel a'Court-Repington whose family history is narrated with astonishing accuracy of detail in order to gauge the amount of credence which may be attached to his written statements. According to this journal the British critic who only spent four days with the opposing armies, had a threefold object in view. Firstly, he desired at that stage of the negotiations to incite the French to resistance à outrance by holding out a prospect of military success; secondly, by exploding the fable of her invincibility which has won her so many bloodless victories, the critic was endeavouring to diminish Germany's prestige abroad and to weaken the force of her diplomacy; thirdly, by attributing military imperfections to the lavish expenditure on the navy, the crafty penman with Printing House Square at his back, wished to warn the guileless electors to the new Reichstag that naval expansion is not in the true interests of a mainland empire and thus to arrest that competition which is so irksome to Great Britain.

This summary of random passages, chosen perhaps from too wide a field, will at any rate serve to show that at times there is honesty of purpose, and that where the purpose is less honest, the provocation is generally manufactured at home.

Apart from newspaper controversy, I understand that the flame of bitterness against England continues to burn very high in military circles here. A few weeks ago I came upon a striking illustration of this fact at a dinner given at the Castle of Philippsruhe by the Landgrave of Hesse. The General commanding the XVIII Army Corps who was among the guests, remarked with some vehemence to his neighbour at table, the wife of a well known English peer : " We now know who our real enemies are, and I hope that my sons and my sons' sons will never forget it." I need not add that the conversation arose on the staple theme of all political conversations here : the Chancellor of the Exchequer's July declaration. A more pleasing impression is derived from an account given me by Sir Hubert Jernyngham of a conversation during a recent visit to Friederichsof with Princess Frederick Charles of Hesse in which Her Royal Highness assured my informant that her Imperial brother holds that Providence has destined the Teutonic races to join hands in order to take the place of the moribund Latins in carrying forward the work of civilisation. Prince Henry of Prussia who is a frequent visitor to this capital is equally friendly in his references to public affairs, and if in conversation with me he sometimes deplores the retirement of Sir Frank Lascelles he perhaps pays thereby an unconscious tribute to the efficiency of his successor.

I have, &c.
ACTON.

No. 700.

Sir Edward Grey to Sir F. Bertie.

F.O. 45859/25883/11/28.
(No. 485.) Confidential.
Sir,

Foreign Office, November 20, 1911.

In my despatch No. 475 of November 14th,(¹) I transmitted to Your Excellency a copy of the note from the French Minister requesting the adherence of His Majesty's Government to the recently concluded Franco-German Convention. Your Excellency is aware from my despatch No. 479 of the 16th(²) instant that in reply I informed Monsieur Daeschner that His Majesty's Government had much pleasure in giving their adherence to the Convention subject to the following assumptions,—firstly, that Articles 4 and 7 of the Anglo-French Declaration of 1904, were not in any way affected by the recently concluded Convention; secondly, that British subjects would continue to receive in Morocco as favourable economic treatment as those of any other State—the attention of the French Government being specially directed in this connexion to the use of the words " the *two* nations " in the text of the Convention; and thirdly that adequate arrangements would be made for placing the town and municipal district of Tangier definitely under international control.

Monsieur Daeschner was at the same time informed semi-officially(³) that I should be grateful if the French Government could furnish me with their views on these points at an early date, as it was necessary for me to communicate with the German Government who had asked for the support of His Majesty's Government on behalf of the Convention.

I now transmit to Your Excellency a copy of a note from the French Minister, containing the reply of his Government to these observations.(⁴) The assurances of the French Government are satisfactory with regard to the first point, viz, : Articles 4 and 7 of the Anglo-French Declaration of 1904.

As regards the second point, while the French Government assure His Majesty's Government that the economic clauses of the Convention apply equally to the subjects of all Powers, no mention is made of the phrase " equality between the two nations " as to the meaning of which His Majesty's Government specifically enquired. In the version of the Convention communicated to me by the German Government and laid

(¹) [*v. supra*, pp. 688–9, No. 683; and pp. 604–8, No. 619, and *encl.*]
(²) [Not reproduced, but for the reply sent to M. Daeschner, *v. supra*, pp. 689–90, No. 685.]
(³) [*v. supra*, p. 689, No. 684.]
(⁴) [*v. supra*, p. 695, No. 692.]

[19656]

2 z

by them before the Reichstag, the word "two" does not occur and the first paragraph of article 1 of the Convention ends with the words "l'égalité économique entre les nations."

In these circumstances it is necessary for His Majesty's Government to ascertain which is the authoritative text. I shall be glad if Your Excellency will accordingly make the necessary enquiries of the French Government.

Finally the French Government in their reply omit all reference to the question of the internationalization of the town and municipal district of Tangier. His Majesty's Government are much embarrassed by this omission, and, assuming it to be intentional, they feel constrained to renew the statement that in adhering to the Franco-German Convention they expect the French Government to carry out their engagements towards Spain as to the internationalization of Tangier, engagements which were, in accordance with Article VIII of the Anglo-French Declaration of 1904, communicated by the French Government to His Majesty's Government and taken note of by them, and to which they are therefore practically parties. If the French Government actually contemplate a departure from the policy defined in that agreement His Majesty's Government would reluctantly be compelled to reconsider their position, and would in particular be obliged to take such steps at Madrid as would prevent the Spanish Government from agreeing to any modification of their agreement with France of 1904, which would not provide adequate safeguards for securing the international status of Tangier.

I should be glad if Your Excellency would take an opportunity of explaining the attitude of His Majesty's Government in regard to the above-mentioned matters to the French Government. I leave to your discretion the manner and form of such a communication, but Your Excellency will bear in mind that some formal record will be necessary either on the part of the French Government to the effect that the reservation of His Majesty's Government with regard to Tangier is understood and will be satisfactorily met by them, or on the part of His Majesty's Government to the effect that their adherence to the Franco-German Convention is subject to a satisfactory settlement of the international status of Tangier.([5])

In my opinion the substitution of an amplified note for that sent to me by Monsieur Daeschner would be the best solution of the difficulty, but Your Excellency may not consider it advisable to put forward such a suggestion in which case I do not in any way desire to press the proposal.

[I am, &c.]
E. G[REY].

([5]) [cp. infra, pp. 707–8, No. 703, and min.]

No. 701.

Sir F. Bertie to Sir Edward Grey.

Paris, November 21, 1911.

F.O. 46450/46450/11/28.   D. 8·35 P.M.
Tel. (No. 190.)   R. 11·30 P.M.

I have following confidential information from a reliable private source. There have been pour-parlers between the French and German governments in regard to withdrawal of the German man of war from Agadir.

German M[inister for] F[oreign] A[ffairs] demurred to withdrawing the ship before the ratification of the Franco-German convention. President of the Council said that he would guarantee approval by chamber. German M[inister for] F[oreign] A[ffairs] will not insist on preliminary formal ratification by President of the Republic. He will withdraw ship as soon as Chamber has approved convention.([1])

([1]) [v. G.P. XXIX, p. 435. Herr von Kiderlen-Waechter sent a definite assurance in secret to M. Caillaux through Baron von Schoen on November 25, 1911. For earlier discussions, v. G.P. XXIX, pp. 432–3.]

No. 702.

Sir F. Bertie to Sir Edward Grey.

F.O. 46431/46431/11/28.
Tel. (No. 189.)

Paris, November 21, 1911.
D. 9·40 P.M.
R. 11 P.M.

A Parisian financier and Doctor Schwabach lately British Consul-General at Berlin are jointly devising a project which the Parisian financier assures me has the approval of German M[inister for] F[oreign] A[ffairs] and M. Caillaux for forming syndicate of German French and British financiers for commercial undertakings in Morocco such as railways and other works. The Parisian financier enquires whether H[is] M[ajesty's] G[overnment] would view with satisfaction a British participation in such a syndicate. If so he would take steps to obtain it. It would he says have the support of the French Government.

MINUTES.

This looks like a revival of our old friend the Société de Travaux Publics. We killed the latter, because its object was a monopoly. There is no mention of a monopoly here, but we can hardly give an official assurance of support without further details.

We might instruct Sir F. Bertie to tell the " financier " that H[is] M[ajesty's] Gov[ernmen]t are in principle favourable [to] the association of British and foreign capital, but cannot give a formal assurance of support to any particular scheme until they are in receipt of detailed information notably as to the share to be allotted to this country, and Sir F. Bertie might endeavour to obtain such particulars.

Copy of correspondence to Board of Trade.

G. H. V.
21/11/11.

I feel some doubt about this report. The " Société de Travaux Publics " is not dead, but a properly constituted French Company. I suspect the present proposal is for a re-arrangement of the international basis of that Company. If so, all would depend on the proportionate share to be offered to British capital.

The course suggested in Mr. Villiers' above minute seems the right one.

Commercial Dep[artmen]t.

E. A. C.
Nov. 21.

We must certainly have further information. Dr. Schwabach, though an ex-British-Consul-General, does not represent either British finance or British commerce.

W. L.
A. N.
E. G.

No. 703.

M. Daeschner to Sir Edward Grey.

F.O. 46537/44289/11/28.
Monsieur le Secrétaire d'État,

Ambassade de France, Londres,
le 21 *novembre,* 1911.

Dans l'avant dernier paragraphe de la Note qu'elle a bien voulu m'adresser le 14 de ce mois,(¹) au sujet de l'adhésion du Gouvernement royal à l'accord franco-allemand du 4 Novembre, Votre Excellence m'avait signalé l'intérêt qu'elle attachait à la situation spéciale de Tanger.

Je suis autorisé à donner officiellement à Votre Excellence, pour faire suite à ma note du 17 courant,(²) l'assurance que le Gouvernement de la République ne se

(¹) [*v. supra,* pp. 689–90, No. 685.]
(²) [*v. supra,* p. 695, No. 692.]

prévaudra pas de ses accords avec l'Allemagne pour revenir sur la clause de la Convention franco-espagnole de 1904 relative à la situation spéciale de' la ville et de la région de Tanger.

> Veuillez, &c..
> E. DAESCHNER.

MINUTES.

This appears to be quite satisfactory. We expressed confidence in our note to M. Daeschner that the " French Gov[ernmen]t will concur in adequate arrangements being made for placing the town and municipal district of Tangier definitely under international control." The French now give a definite assurance that they will not go back on Art[icle] IX of the Franco-Spanish agreement which lays down that Tangier shall keep its " caractère spécial."(³) The French note could have been more satisfactorily worded but it seems to be sufficient.

Q[uer]y tel[egraph] to Sir F. Bertie.

" My despatch No. 485.

French Minister has just conveyed official assurances with regard to Tangier and you need say nothing to French M[inister for] F[oreign] A[ffairs] on this particular point."

> G. H. V.
> **21/11/11.**

It is a question whether we should not hold out for some more definite engagement than that embodied in the rather vague stipulation of article 9 of the Franco-Spanish convention.

In any case we must telegraph to Sir F. Bertie to suspend action on our previous instruction which no longer meets the situation.

After consulting Sir A. Nicolson I have accordingly sent the annexed tel[egram] to Paris.

> E. A. C.
> Nov. 21.

The present assurance is a considerable improvement on the total omission from the French note of any mention of Tangier, but it will be as well to get from the French Gov[ernmen]t some indication of their views as to the future administration of Tangier and its environs.

> W. L.
> E. G.

(³) [Added by Sir E. Crowe : " Art[icle] 9 :

' La ville de Tanger gardera le caractère spécial que lui donnent la présence du Corps Diplomatique et ses institutions municipale et sanitaire.' "]

No. 704.

Sir F. Bertie to Sir Edward Grey.

F.O. 46556/46556/11/28.

(No. 545.)   *Paris, D. November* 21, 1911.

Sir,   R. *November* 22, 1911.

I have the honour to transmit to you herewith an extract from the "Temps," in which an account is given of the questions put by Monsieur Millerand at a recent sitting of the Commission for Foreign Affairs of the Chamber of Deputies respecting certain points connected with the Franco German Treaty and the future position of Spain in Morocco.

Monsieur Millerand desired to receive information with respect to :—(1) the question of France's right of pre-emption of the Belgian Congo, (2) the retention by Germany of Post Offices in Morocco and (3) what extent responsibility of France would be engaged if Germany, after having recognised a French Protectorate over the *whole* of Morocco, had complaints to make as to occurrences in the Spanish zone.

Monsieur Millerand received explanations from Monsieur de Selves on the first two of the above mentioned points.

> I have, &c.
> FRANCIS BERTIE.

Extract from " Le Temps" of November 22, 1911.

A PROPOS DU TRAITÉ FRANCO-ALLEMAND.—CONVERSATION AVEC M. MILLERAND.

Nous avons eu l'occasion de nous entretenir avec M. Millerand de son intervention à la commission des affaires extérieures au sujet du traité franco-allemand, intervention très sommairement résumée par les communiqués officieux.

—Je me suis borné, nous a dit M. Millerand, à formuler non point des objections, mais de simples observations—des observations d'un caractère pratique, inspirées seulement du désir de faciliter et d'améliorer l'application du traité.

"Ce traité, il n'appartient pas, vous le savez, à la commission de le modifier. Elle ne peut que l'approuver ou le rejeter. Il m'apparaît d'ailleurs, ainsi que le *Temps* le montrait hier, comme la conséquence logique et nécessaire de la politique antérieure. Il était impossible de ne pas le négocier et il est impossible de ne pas le ratifier, même si l'on pense que certaines de ses clauses auraient gagné peut-être à être autrement rédigées.

"Cela dit pour préciser l'esprit dans lequel je suis intervenu, résolu à approuver le traité et soucieux seulement d'aider le gouvernement à l'appliquer dans les meilleures conditions possibles. D'où les trois questions que j'ai posées.

"J'ai demandé d'abord si l'article 16 de l'accord congolais portait atteinte au droit de préemption de la France au sujet du Congo belge. M. de Selves m'a répondu que non. La France s'engage, comme l'Allemagne, à conférer avec les signataires de l'acte de Berlin, si le statut territorial du bassin conventionnel du Congo venait à être modifié, par achat ou autrement. Mais s'il est question de conversation préalable, il n'est pas question, a ajouté le ministre, d'adhésion nécessaire. Le droit de la France subsiste donc.

"J'ai demandé ensuite des éclaircissements sur la déclaration de M. de Kiderlen, annonçant que les postes allemandes subsisteraient dans l'empire chérifien. J'estime en effet qu'elles doivent disparaître quand nous aurons créé une organisation nouvelle. L'Allemagne s'est engagée, selon moi, à cette suppression, en acceptant par avance, dans la première lettre explicative, le protectorat français. J'ai constaté que le gouvernement était de mon avis.

"Je me suis inquiété enfin—ici encore en vue de l'avenir et dans un esprit tout pratique—de la situation créée à la France par la coexistence de ses engagements vis-à-vis de l'Allemagne et de l'Europe d'une part, vis-à-vis de l'Espagne d'autre part. A ce sujet, voici ce que j'ai dit :

"Le document explicatif dont les journaux ont signalé l'existence qui n'a pas été publié, mais qui a été lu à la commission, définit les limites du Maroc, Algérie, Afrique occidentale, Rio-de-Oro. C'est pour tout cet empire que la France à traité avec l'Allemagne. Mais de cet empire, l'Espagne gardera une partie. Et enfin par le même document, l'Allemagne s'engage à ne pas intervenir dans nos négociations avec l'Espagne.

"Cela étant, j'ai envisagé l'hypothèse suivante. Supposons qu'ultérieurement une puissance, l'Allemagne par exemple, ait à se plaindre en matière économique, adjudication ou autre, de l'attitude de l'Espagne dans sa zone. Quels seraient en présence d'une plainte semblable les droits et les devoirs de la France, si l'Allemagne, en vertu de l'engagement pris par elle de ne pas se mêler des négociations franco-espagnoles, prétend ignorer cet accord et ne connaître au Maroc qu'une responsabilité : la nôtre ?

"J'ai indiqué qu'à mon sens, il y aurait lieu de conjurer ce risque en prenant soin d'informer exactement les puissances de la nature et de l'étendue de nos engagements avec l'Espagne, tels qu'ils sortiront de la négociation prochaine. C'est une précaution désirable et possible.

"Voilà à quoi s'est bornée mon intervention qui avait, vous le voyez, pour seul objet d'éclaircir certaines éventualités et ne s'inspirait à aucun degré d'un sentiment d'hostilité, soit à l'égard du traité négocié, soit à l'égard de ses négociateurs."

MINUTES.

The third question is a "poser." The case will very probably arise, but presumably the situation will be straightened out by the Franco-Spanish negotiations.

G. H. V.
22/11/11.

The French gov[ernmen]t hold that their rights of pre-emption over the Belgian Congo remain intact, although they have agreed not to act upon them without previous communication with the Powers signatories of the Berlin Act.

The German post-offices are understood to have to disappear on the proclamation of a French protectorate. (This will equally apply to the British and other foreign post-offices.)(¹)

I do not know whether there are foreign post-offices in Egypt,(²) but if so the question deserves consideration what steps we may eventually be free to take to suppress them.(³)

E. A. C.
Nov. 22.

African ⎫
Eastern ⎬ Dep[artmen]ts.
Commercial ⎭

W. L.
F. D. A
A. N.
E. G.

(¹) [Marginal comment by Mr. Langley : " But this must of course be by arrangement with the other Powers."]

(²) [Marginal comment by Mr. Vansittart : " There is a French post office in Egypt. R. G. V."]

(³) [Marginal comment by Mr. Norman : " If they suppress ours in Morocco, why should we not suppress their perfectly superfluous one in Egypt? H. N."]

No. 705.

Sir Edward Grey to Sir F. Bertie.

F.O. 46537/44289/11/28.
(No. 487.)

Sir,   *Foreign Office, November 22, 1911.*

In my telegram No. 306 of the 21st instant(¹) I requested Y[our] E[xcellency] to suspend action on my despatch No. 485 of the 20th instant,(²) as I had received a further note from the French Minister.

I now transmit to Y[our] E[xcellency] a copy of this communication,(³) from which you will see that the French Gov[ernmen]t assure H[is] M[ajesty's] Gov[ernmen]t that they will not avail themselves of the recent convention with Germany to depart from article IX of the Franco-Spanish agreement of 1904 relative to the special position of the town and district of Tangier.

H[is] M[ajesty's] Gov[ernmen]t have received this assurance with much satisfaction, and they are confident that the French Gov[ernmen]t intend to ensure that adequate arrangements will be made for placing the town and municipal district of Tangier definitely under international Control. They are confirmed in this belief by the wording of the draft French Declaration communicated to you by M. Regnault (see Y[our] E[xcellency's] despatch No. 455 C[on]f[idential], of Oct[ober] 21)(⁴) in connexion with the suggested text of a revised Franco-Spanish agreement. It is stated in the first article of this declaration that, in accordance with article IX of the Franco-Spanish agreement of 1904, the town of Tangier shall be administered under the sovereignty of the Sultan by a municipality of an international character.

(¹) [Not reproduced as its tenour is indicated. cp. p. 708, No. 703, min.]
(²) [v. supra, pp. 705–6, No. 700.]
(³) [v. supra, pp. 707–8, No. 703.]
(⁴) [v. supra, pp. 583–5, No. 598.]

Y[our] E[xcellency] informed me, in your telegram No. 188 of the 20th inst[ant]([5]) that proposals had been drawn up by the President of the Council for an arrangement with Spain in regard to Moroccco, and that they would shortly be communicated to H[is] M[ajesty's] Gov[ernmen]t for consideration. I trust therefore that these proposals will contain adequate safeguards for securing the internationalization of Tangier.

I should be glad if Y[our] E[xcellency] would take an opportunity of speaking in the sense of this despatch to the French M[inister for] F[oreign] A[ffairs] explaining the satisfaction of H[is] M[ajesty's] Gov[ernment] at the assurances already received and the importance they attach to a definite settlement of the matter. It is of course still necessary for H[is] M[ajesty's] Gov[ernment] to ascertain the authoritative text of the Anglo-French Convention, and I should be glad if Y[our] E[xcellency] will accordingly make the necessary enquiries of the French Gov[ernmen]t with regard to this point, as proposed in my despatch No. 485.

I am, &c.
E. GREY.

([5]) [v. supra, p. 703, No. 698.]

No. 706.

Lord Lansdowne to Sir Edward Grey.

Private.([1])

My dear Grey,   *Lansdowne House, November* 22, 1911.

Thanks for your note.

I do not think the publication of the secret articles will do much harm,([2]) or that it would have been possible to withhold them after all that has happened.

We shall at any rate hear no more of the confident statements, which are still being made, to the effect that we had bound ourselves by these articles to afford one another material assistance of a definite kind in certain eventualities.

Yours sincerely,
LANSDOWNE.

([1]) [Grey MSS., Vol. 69. cp. supra, pp. 676–7, No. 675; pp. 695–6, No. 693.]
([2]) [Publication took place simultaneously in London and Paris on, November 24, and Papers were presented to the House of Commons on that day, and to the House of Lords on November 27. The text is in A. and P. (1911), Vol. CIII, (Cd. 5969), pp. 358–60.]

No. 707.

Sir F. Cartwright to Sir Edward Grey.

F.O. 47100/46794/11/18.
(No. 198.)   *Vienna,* D. *November* 23, 1911.
Sir,   R. *November* 25, 1911.

I have the honour to report that the subject of Anglo-German relations during the past summer continues to occupy the Viennese Press. The 'Neue Freie Presse' increases in violence with each day, and in a leading article published this morning speculates on how Prince Bismarck would have treated the telegram reporting the conversation which you, Sir, had with Count Metternich.([1]) "Never since the founding of the German Empire," it declares, "has such a telegram been received in Berlin : never since the days of Benedetti and Ems has anyone attempted to

([1]) [cp. supra, pp. 390–1, No. 411, and reference in Sir E. Crowe's Memorandum, infra, p. 823, App. III. Count Metternich's report of this conversation is given in G.P. XXIX, pp. 199–203.]

intimidate Germany by sharp words : never since the Duke of Gramont has anyone except Sir Edward Grey threatened that mighty Empire with the outbreak of war.''

It maintains that you, Sir, at once adopted a bellicose tone in speaking to the German Ambassador, and that your words, spoken in private, were then underlined in public by Mr. Lloyd George's speech. What, it asks, would have been Bismarck's attitude? Would he have avenged the insult with the sword, or would his genius have found some better way?

The 'Neue Freie Presse' finds it incomprehensible that the British Government should wish to evoke the hostility of Germany on account of Morocco. ''Every word of Sir Edward Grey's burns,'' it says, ''like hot lead on the heart of the German nation.'' What possible advantage, it asks, can it be to England to arouse such feelings, in view of Germany's declaration that she was not seeking to acquire any Moroccan territory? Why, after Mr. Asquith's declaration that England had no objection to an increase in the German colonies in Central Africa, did Sir Edward Grey use language to the German Ambassador of a kind which as a rule is only employed immediately before the outbreak of war? England's duty as an ally of France is not, in the opinion of the 'Neue Freie Presse,' an adequate explanation : for that duty could never have compelled England to outdo France herself and to prepare her fleet for action while the French navy lay quiet. '' Sir Edward Grey spoke,'' says the 'Neue Freie Presse,' ''like a man whose temperament suddenly bursts out, and who is guided by personal dislikes and prejudices until he forgets what his aim is, and becomes the tool of alien purposes. Fidelity to a treaty cannot explain the fact that the British Secretary of State spoke with more heat than the French Minister for Foreign Affairs; and that only the prudence of some of the members of the British Cabinet prevented a war which would have been a historical crime.''

It now, continues this paper, lies with the English people to determine whether this policy is to continue in the future, now that it knows the facts as to the proximity of war during last summer. The article laments that your policy, Sir, should, as it alleges, have crushed the beginnings of reconciliation in regard to naval armaments, and should have rendered that question ten times more difficult by this pouring of oil on the flames. Threats can, it declares, never succeed in intimidating Germany, and England had better give up her mistaken policy before the German people become convinced that England is behind every attack on her : for it is impossible that the relations between the two countries should continue in their present condition. ''The necessary preliminary to a new naval policy in Germany is,'' it concludes, '' the adoption of quite a new foreign policy in England.''

Articles from the English newspapers are reproduced here *in extenso*, and the entire Viennese Press is much occupied by the approaching debate in the House of Commons. Your statement, Sir, is awaited with extreme interest.

I have, &c.

FAIRFAX L. CARTWRIGHT.

MINUTES.

The " Neue Freie Presse " is inspired by the German Ambassador at Vienna. This article is particularly disgraceful.

G. H. V.
25/11/11.

It betrays the cloven hoof. It is the Bismarckian tradition to concentrate the attack on the obnoxious person and bring about his fall. But Sir E. Grey is not in the position of M. Delcassé in 1905.

E. A. C.
Nov. 25.
F. D. A.
W. L.
A. N.
E. G.

No. 708.

Sir F. Cartwright to Sir A. Nicolson.

Private.([1])

My dear Nicolson,   *Vienna, November 23, 1911.*

Some time ago information reached me that General Conrad von Hötzendorf, chief of the Austrian Staff—as reported home in my telegram No. 91 of September 6th last([2])—was desirous of bringing the Austro-Hungarian Army up to a thorough state of efficiency, but that the cost of doing this, calculated at a sum of 600 million kronen, made it difficult for him to realize his plans. On Saturday last, the 18th instant, Aehrenthal sent for Crozier, the French Ambassador here, and taking a document out of his pocket, presented it to him to read. This document was marked "Notes confidentielles," and as Crozier read its contents to me that evening, I telegraphed its main drift home the next morning.([3]) Crozier could not take it upon himself to give me a copy of it without permission of his Government, so I am not able to furnish Sir Edward Grey with its exact wording. The document was evidently drawn up very carefully in the French language, and begins by laying stress on the good political relations which now exist between France and Austria-Hungary, which it declares it would be well to see extended to the economic field. It points out that French and Austro-Hungarian capital might with mutual advantage work together in Morocco, the Near East and elsewhere. With regard to the Morocco Agreement, it declares that in principle Austria-Hungary has no objections to raise to it, but that there are questions of formality which require to be attended to to assure to this country all the advantages which Germany secures for herself by this new agreement. Finally the document comes to the crux of the whole question, namely that Austria-Hungary is desirous of borrowing the sum of a milliard of franks [*sic*] in Paris, and asks the French Government to facilitate the raising of such a loan by instalments, and this when the political outlook allows of such a financial operation to take place.

Aehrenthal informed Crozier that he wished this matter to be treated directly between themselves here, and for that reason—and to avoid misunderstandings which might arise in Paris—he had not communicated the document to Szécsen, the Austro-Hungarian Ambassador there, but had merely instructed him to inform the French Government as to Austria-Hungary's delay—on the ground of formal reasons—in giving her immediate consent to the Morocco Agreement. It may be worth while pointing out to you that it occurs to me that this delay is due in part to the wish of Aehrenthal to see how the idea of a loan is received in Paris, but partly also to make it clear that because Germany has concluded an agreement with France, it does not follow as a matter of course that Austria-Hungary must give her immediate assent to it. On the contrary, Aehrenthal means to show that he will study the Agreement from a purely Austro-Hungarian point of view, and come to his conclusions with regard to it without consulting Germany.

I telegraphed home on November 4th, that Aehrenthal, in vague language, had given Crozier to understand that he had in his mind the possibility of asking for a loan from France, so Crozier was not actually unprepared when Aehrenthal made the formal request on Saturday last for French money, but he was somewhat overwhelmed at the demand of so vast a sum as a milliard of franks. He thought it best, under the circumstances not to enter into discussion with Aehrenthal about it, and after the exchange of some vague phrases, he put the document into his pocket and told Aehrenthal that he would communicate its contents to his Government.

Since then I have had various conversations with Crozier who looks upon this demand for a milliard as a matter of perhaps vital importance to France, for he cannot imagine that Aehrenthal would ask for a milliard under present circumstances without expecting to be asked to give something in return to France. The first point which will have to be cleared up is this, namely, whether Germany knows of

([1]) [Carnock MSS., Vol. VI of 1911.]
([2]) [Not reproduced.]
([3]) [*v. supra*, p. 698, No. 696, and *note*.]

Aehrenthal's demand and intends to profit, to a certain extent, by the influx of French gold into the Dual Monarchy; or is this a step taken by Aehrenthal independently and without the knowledge of Germany with a view to strengthen the Austrian army and the economic situation here, in order to place Austria-Hungary in a better position to offer resistance to pressure from Berlin, brought to bear here to force the Dual Monarchy to take part in an offensive war carried on by Germany against France? As far as I can judge at present I am somewhat inclined to accept the second view of this question. I will here mention that about a week ago Dr. Szeps called upon me, and on my asking him what attitude he thought Austria would assume in the event of war breaking out between Germany and France, he replied that he could not say what were the views of the Ballplatz, but his own personal impression was that if Russia mobilized, this country would have to do the same; Austria, however, would do all in her power through offers of mediation to bring the war to a close and to restore things in Central Europe to the "status quo ante," and so avoid the possibility of herself being dragged into a war in which she had no real interests to defend. Dr. Szeps told me that the declaration made a few days before by the new Minister of War here, that hostilities lasting a year would cost Austria-Hungary a sum of ten milliards of Kronen, had produced a profound impression on thinking people in the Dual Monarchy, whose one desire now seemed to be to keep out of any war. I may add that various articles have of late appeared in the newspapers here, written in that sense.

From the conversations I have had with Crozier I gather that he would advise his Government to act towards Aehrenthal's proposal in the following way :—he thinks the French Government should avoid returning a flat refusal to the Aehrenthal proposal, but should say that owing to the good relations which exist between France and Austria, and which the French Government desire to see still further improved, they had no objection in principle to the milliard loan; as Aehrenthal, however, himself declares in the "Notes confidentielles," that the loan seems to him 'only possible if the political atmosphere becomes serene, the French Government must observe that at the present moment the public mind on the Continent is in a nervous state with regard to the immediate future, and that this nervous state has certainly not been calmed by the speeches made in the Reichstag and by the Crown Prince's attitude on that occasion. Under these circumstances Count Aehrenthal must understand that no French Government could withstand the public indignation which would be aroused in France if it became known that they had given a helping hand to the Triple Alliance, and that French gold was perhaps being used to forge new arms which might at any moment be turned against France. The French Government might then declare that they would be glad to be in a position to supply Austria with the money she seemed to be in want of, but that they can only do so if Aehrenthal should be in a position to give such assurances to France as would completely reassure public opinion in that country as to the use the Austro-Hungarian Government would make of the money in question.

Crozier thinks that if his Government acted as mentioned above, Aehrenthal would be either forced to withdraw the demand altogether, without giving any reasons for doing so, or he would disclose his hand partially and perhaps hold out hopes of Austria remaining neutral in the event of a war breaking out between Germany and France.

Whether Aehrenthal has in his mind the possibility of going so far as to conclude some secret agreement with France, by which Austria would stand aside in the event of her declaring that Germany had begun an offensive war against France—against Austria's advice,—it is impossible to say as few people know the exact terms of the Dual Alliance between Germany and Austria.([4]) One thing I am pretty certain of, however, and that is that if convenient to him Aehrenthal will merely stick to the

([4]) [The terms were published in the press in 1887. The text etc. is in A. F. Pribram : *Secret Treaties of Austria-Hungary*, (Harvard University Press, 1920), Vol. I, pp. 18–35.]

very letter of the Treaty and to nothing more. Now it is commonly rumoured that when in 1879 Andrassy was on the point of signing the Alliance with Germany, it had the form of an offensive and defensive alliance against France. It is said that when the Emperor Franz Joseph saw the draft Treaty, he declared that nothing would induce him to enter into an offensive alliance against France, and the Treaty had consequently to be altered. This alteration forms the so-called "Gastein clause," and if it really exists one might conceive the possibility of Aehrenthal entering into an engagement with France that Austria will not take part in a war which, in his opinion, owed its origin to the offensive attitude assumed by Germany.

The French Government at the present moment are unfortunately weak, and as to the Quai d'Orsay it appears to be in a perfect state of disorganization, so that it is quite possible that the French Ministry may hesitate to commit themselves to any action with regard to Aehrenthal's proposal. It seems to me, however, that it would be a great pity if France lost this opportunity of probing how far the Austro-Hungarian Government are inclined to separate themselves from Germany in the event of the latter country bringing about a war between herself and France. . . . .(⁵)

Yours truly,
FAIRFAX L. CARTWRIGHT.

(⁵) [The rest of this letter refers to the Turco-Italian conflict over Tripoli, relations with Great Britain, and the internal affairs of Austria-Hungary.]

No. 709.

Sir Edward Grey to Sir E. Goschen.

F.O. 46863/46838/11/28. *Foreign Office. November 23, 1911.*
Tel. (No. 222.) D. 9 P.M.

It is most unusual, if not unprecedented, for German Minister for Foreign Affairs to have made public his version of conversations between German Ambassador and myself without previous communication with me.(¹) It would justify me in laying before Parliament my words of the conversations. I propose, however, in first instance, only to do in my speech on Monday what German Minister for Foreign Affairs has already done, and you should say nothing meanwhile to German Minister for Foreign Affairs on the subject of his speech or mine.

(¹) [v. supra, pp. 698–700, No. 697, and min.; also Ed. note, pp. 700–3.]

No. 710.

Sir Edward Grey to Sir F. Bertie.

F.O. 46431/46431/11/28.
(No. 488.)
Sir, *Foreign Office, November 23, 1911.*

I have received Y[our] E[xcellency]'s telegram No. 189 of the 21st inst[ant](¹) relative to the proposed formation of a syndicate of German, French and British financiers for commercial undertakings in Morocco.

I should be glad if you would tell the French financier who informed you of the proposal that H[is] M[ajesty's] Gov[ernmen]t are in principle favourable to the association of British and foreign capital, but cannot give a formal assurance of support to any particular scheme until they are in receipt of detailed information, notably as to the share to be allotted to this country.

Y[our] E[xcellency] might at the same time endeavour to obtain such detailed information.

[I am, &c.
E. GREY.]

(¹) [v. supra, p. 707, No. 702.]

No. 711.

Sir Edward Grey to Sir E. Goschen.

F.O. 47154/46794/11/18.
(No. 286.)
Sir,   Foreign Office, November 23, 1911.

The German Ambassador made to me this evening a communication from the German Chancellor to the following effect.

The disclosures made in the speech of Captain Faber, M.P.,([1]) as to which the German Government did not know how far they were true, but which had not been contradicted in England, had caused in Germany a commotion which was comprehensible. The German Government were being attacked, on the ground that they had not taken the public into their confidence, and had not replied sufficiently to the speech of the Chancellor of the Exchequer. The German Chancellor thought that the best way to allay this agitation would be to make a frank statement of what had taken place. Such a statement was more and more imperatively demanded by German public opinion. Herr von Kiderlen had, therefore, been instructed to make to the Budget Committee of the Reichstag the statement which had now been published. He had also made a statement about Captain Faber's disclosures that would be published shortly.

The comments in the British Press upon Captain Faber's speech and upon the British readiness to go to war with Germany on the side of France had greatly intensified the temper of public opinion in Germany. The German people thought themselves face to face with a coalition ready to pounce upon them at any moment; and, as they were unconscious of having any quarrel with England itself, they looked upon England as the principal Enemy: for while France took no warlike preparations last September, England was ready.

The speech which I was to make on Monday would have a great bearing on all these questions. If it was irritating to German feeling, there would for a long time be no prospect of allaying the ideas which had been roused in Germany.

The general trend of the German Chancellor's communication was that he hoped I would co-operate in the attempt which he had made in his speeches to soothe the feeling of antagonism.

I replied that the character of what I intended to say on Monday in dealing with the speeches of the German Chancellor would be the same as I had already, in previous conversations with Count Metternich, said that it would be. But it seemed to me very unusual, if not unprecedented, to disclose without consulting me, as Herr von Kiderlen had done, a version of what had been said in conversations between Count Metternich and myself.

Count Metternich observed that Herr von Kiderlen had not given the whole of what had passed, but only such things as he thought were necessary and useful for public opinion.

I replied that Herr von Kiderlen had made his own selection, without consulting me. I must now go through my records of the conversations, and make my selection. As Herr von Kiderlen had made public part of what had passed between Count Metternich and me as to the speech of the Chancellor of the Exchequer, it would be necessary for me to deal more fully with this speech than I would otherwise have dealt with it.

As to Captain Faber's speech: I had not expected to have to refer to it, and indeed I had so far read it only cursorily. It had apparently been founded upon such gossip as Captain Faber had been able to pick up, and my recollection was that

([1]) [The speech by Captain W. V. Faber, M.P. for West Hampshire, was made at the Mayoral Banquet at Andover on November 9, 1911. A report of it was printed in the *Daily Telegraph* for November 20, 1911, *cp.* *G.P.* XXIX, pp. 261–3, *note*. It is stated in the *Daily Telegraph* article, which contains a summary of the speech, that though delivered on the 9th the speech was not published until the 18th. The statement of the Berlin correspondent of the *Daily Telegraph*, written on the 19th, says that the speech had been reproduced there at considerable length. *cp. infra*, p. 731, No. 721; p. 740, No. 723; p. 746, No. 726.]

it referred solely to certain precautionary measures which we were alleged to have taken against attack.

Count Metternich said that he thought it included a statement that British cruisers had been sent to sea, with instructions to sink any German destroyers.

I said that any such statement was absolutely untru . We had not prepared for any aggressive action. The impression on the German public mind seemed to be that we were aggressive, while the apprehension in the British public mind was that Germany might be aggressive. If the two Governments were to embark upon a public controversy as to which had most reason to think the other aggressive,—a controversy which I hoped would never take place,—we should have to disclose the information which poured in upon us as to the study and exploration of a large part of our coast by German Officers, work that could be done only from the point of view of a German invasion of England.

Count Metternich deprecated the idea that there were German agents spying upon our fortified places; though two British officers had been taken when spying in Germany, the two Germans whom we had arrested were simply foolish or discredited persons and with regard to the rest of our coast, he said that British maps and charts were published which gave full information.

I replied that I was not thinking of spies, technically so called; but there was no doubt that a very careful exploration of our coast and open harbours had been made on behalf of Germany. However I had not mentioned this in order to be controversial, but only to point out that there was another side to the shield, and that if people in Germany took as evidence of aggressive intentions on our part such precautions of defence as those alleged in Captain Faber's speech, then some Captain Faber or other might pick up some gossip as to the German exploration of our coast, and might just as well excite people on this side about German aggressive intentions.

As to what had passed during the summer and autumn : there were times when we had been in the dark as to the objects at which Germany was aiming. Though I had never thought the idea probable, and though I had always refused to believe in it, there had been passages in some of Count Metternich's earlier communications, the tone of which gave the impression that Germany was going to force upon France the choice between demands so humiliating that France could not honourably accept them, and war. If German public opinion thought that it was we who had warlike intentions, it ought to be borne in mind that British public opinion had had the same apprehension with regard to Germany.

The conversation was on both sides very friendly in tone in spite of the subject matter of it.

[I am, &c.]
E. G[REY].

No. 712.

Minute by Sir E. Crowe.

Herr von Kiderlen's statement before the Budget Committee of the Reichstag.

F.O. 47153/46838/11/28.   *November* 23, 1911.

The attached extract from to-day's " Times "(¹) gives a second and final instalment of Herr von Kiderlen's statement. There are several points which merit attention.

(1.) We are now for the first time told on official authority that M. Rouvier in 1905 made overtures to Germany for a definite understanding concerning Morocco. We have known for some time that M. Rouvier was ready, and anxious, to sacrifice M. Delcassé in order to inaugurate a policy of a Franco-German understanding, and that he was subsequently exasperated on finding Germany as irreconcilable as before.

(¹) [*v.* immediately succeeding document. The British Government subsequently published a despatch from Sir E. Goschen, enclosing a corrected copy of this statement. *v. A. & P.* (1911), CIII. (*Cd.* 5992), pp. 465–76.]

(2.) Mr. Joseph Chamberlain is now officially declared to have proposed a partition of Morocco to Germany. There is no record of any such proposal in our archives, but unfortunately that is not a reason for questioning the accuracy of the statement. It is notorious that in the past the F[oreign] O[ffice] records have never been complete, but that on the contrary many of the most important questions of foreign affairs were treated as the private concern of the Secretary of State. It is also known that the German embassy here has frequently attempted to negotiate or discuss important questions with members of the British cabinet other than the Sec[retary] of State for Foreign Affairs. Mr. Chamberlain fell into the trap of conducting such pourparlers with Baron von Eckardstein and finally making at the—, I believe, written,—suggestion of the German Embassy his speech* in which he advocated an alliance with Germany and the United States, only to be promptly and mercilessly attacked by all the semi-official German press for daring to make such a proposal.

However we have no official knowledge of all this, and as there is no record of the alleged proposal of Mr. Chamberlain respecting a partition of Morocco, I presume H[is] M[ajesty's] G[overnment] will always, if necessary, be quite free to hold and declare that they had no knowledge of it, and that if Mr. Chamberlain made such a suggestion he must have done so in his private capacity, as, not being Sec[retary] of State for F[oreign] A[ffairs], he had no authority for negotiating with a foreign Power.

(3.) The evidently much compressed account of Germany's attitude in respect of the alleged violation of the Algeciras Act by France is full of inaccuracies, and in its general outline, altogether misleading. In the same sentence it was said that what France did (in the Shawia) did not constitute a violation of the Algeciras Act, and also that the best policy was to wait and take a certain course "in case of *persistence* in the violation of the Act." Moreover it is to be remembered that the Franco-German Agreement of 1909 which was subsequent to the Shawia events avowedly stands on the basis of the Algeciras Act, which cannot therefore have been considered by the parties at that time to have become inoperative through violation of its terms. The French have not, so far as I am aware, ever told us that Germany demanded a cession of territory as *compensation for the violation of the Act*. We have been under the impression that the German demand was justified as compensation for giving France a free hand in the future.—It is now stated that after M. Cambon was informed at Kissingen of what Germany was ready to concede in Morocco for compensation elsewhere no answer came from France. "Meanwhile France was establishing herself unceremoniously in Morocco and German traders asked for protection." "*From these considerations* followed the despatch of a war-ship to Agadir."

Nothing could be more misleading. No mention is made of the fact that M. Cambon, on returning to Paris from Kissingen, found the French gov[ernmen]t had resigned and that no Ministry was in existence. At that time the German ship was actually on its way to Agadir, and this was of course known to Herr von Kiderlen when he spoke to M. Cambon.

E. A. C.
Nov. 23.
W. L.

* Which he very lamely explained away in the H[ouse] of C[ommons]. [W. L.]

MINUTES.

Sir E. Grey might perhaps like to have copies of this minute by Sir E. Crowe sent to the Prime Minister, Lord Morley, Lord Haldane and Mr. Lloyd George with the extract from the Times.

A. N.

Yes.

E. G.
F. D. A.

No. 713.

Extract from the " Times " of November 23, 1911.([1])

ANGLO-GERMAN RELATIONS : THE OFFICIAL REVELATIONS IN BERLIN.

We publish below a continuation of the official extracts from Herr von Kiderlen-Waechter's speech before the Budget Committee of the Reichstag on Friday last. The extracts published yesterday dealt principally with the conversations which took place between Sir Edward Grey and Count Wolff-Metternich. The further extracts, published to-day, describe the subsequent course of the negotiations.

Berlin, Nov[ember] 21.

. . . . ([2]) Herr von Kiderlen-Waechter next gave an historic review of the Morocco question. He told how in 1880 at the time of the Madrid conference Prince Bismarck in a direct report to the Emperor took the view that Germany must welcome the firmest possible establishment of the French in Morocco. Mr. Chamberlain had a scheme for the partition of Morocco in 1899 by which England was to take Tangier and Germany to have a port on the Atlantic coast, but this never came to formal negotiations. In 1905, after the Emperor's visit to Tangier, M. Delcassé made an attempt at direct negotiation, which for want of positive proposals led to no result. Afterwards M. Rouvier again expressed, through semi-official and official channels, a desire to come to an understanding. The word " Congo " was then uttered for the first time. Positive proposals were demanded from the German side, but without leading to any result.

The Foreign Secretary continued :—

In the meantime, we had taken up the position that changes in Morocco could only be brought about with the assent of all the signatories to the Madrid Convention in order not to fall between two stools. Prince Bülow was accordingly unable further to discuss the French desires for an understanding which had never been accompanied by concrete proposals.

Coming to the occupation of Shawia he said :—

One day the Sultan, who naturally always sought to play off France and Germany against each other, protested in great excitement against the occupation of a certain village on the border of the Shawia country. The German Government considered for a long time what was to be done. An ultimatum might have been sent, but what sort of impression would it have made if the Chancellor had stated in the Reichstag that his Majesty the Emperor had declared war because the French occupied some village or other with an unpronounceable name on the edge of the Shawia? The situation for Germany was difficult because it developed gradually. One could never say the Algeciras Act was violated by such action at such a moment and we raised no objection. We therefore decided that the best policy was to wait and in case of persistence in the violation of the Algeciras Act to claim full freedom of action for ourselves. France, on the other hand, always represented herself as the mandatory of Europe for the restoration of order and insisted that the measures were merely temporary and that the Algeciras Act had not been violated.

VIOLATION OF THE ALGECIRAS ACT.

Other Powers, notably England, were disposed to concur in the French action. Germany stood alone in her opposition in connexion with which she never even hinted at a claim to part of Morocco. We only asked that France should come to terms with us in regard to the violation of the Act of Algeciras and that France, as the violation had been committed by her, must come forward with positive proposals. This view was finally expressed in a conversation between the Chancellor and the French Ambassador in Berlin, also in a conversation between Herr von Kiderlen-Waechter and M. Cambon at Kissingen in June.([2]) We constantly declared that Germany was willing to leave France a free hand politically, but must demand for herself better guarantees for the maintenance of the principle of the open door, and, furthermore, compensation in the colonial sphere as indemnity for the violation of the Algeciras Act committed by France in establishing herself in Morocco without a previous understanding. The French Ambassador took note of these views of the German Government, but no positive proposals were forthcoming from France. Her answer always was that later on they would be glad to come to an understanding.

Meanwhile France had established herself with ever diminishing ceremoniousness. Then as complaints from German subjects of oppression and appeals for protection were received, especially from Sus, the German Government said to itself, " France is not the mandatory of Europe; we must claim for ourselves the same right to protect our subjects." From these considerations followed the despatch of a war-ship to Agadir.

([1]) [This extract summarizes the remaining part of Herr von Kiderlen-Waechter's speech of November 17. The first part is given *supra*, pp. 700–3, *Ed. note.*]

([2]) [The paragraphs here omitted repeat the final paragraphs of the previous part, already printed, *supra*, pp. 702–3.]

([3]) [*v. supra*, p. 322, *Ed. note*; and pp. 353–4, No. 373.]

Herr von Kiderlen-Waechter concluded with an *exposé* of the reasons why Germany did not desire territory in Morocco. A colony in Morocco, he said, would have been a great burden. They would have had to contend with perpetual opposition from the French in Morocco and Algeria. Then there were economic and climatic difficulties in the way of German colonization. He then dealt with the " black peril," rehearsing already known arguments that it would be long before France could raise an army in Morocco and in case of war in all probability would have to keep a greater number of European troops in Morocco than the number of native soldiers she could take from her colonial army to Europe. They had guaranteed access to ore deposits in the Sus for German industry. German policy had attained in every respect the aim it set itself—namely, the recognition of French political influence in Morocco, better guarantees for the open door, and compensation for the violation of the Act of Algeciras through the cession of colonial territory. " As far as the Spaniards are concerned " he concluded " we must wait and see how the French come to terms with them. Germany can await the development of things with great tranquillity."

No. 714.

Sir Edward Grey to M. Daeschner.

F.O. 45870/25883/11/28.

Sir,   *Foreign Office, November 24, 1911.*

With ref[erence] to the Note which you were good enough to address to me on the 17th inst[ant],([1]) I have the honour to express to you the thanks of H[is] M[ajesty's] Gov[ernmen]t for the communication of the notes exchanged between the French Ambassador at Berlin and the German M[inister for] F[oreign] A[ffairs] in connection with the recent Morocco Convention.

His Majesty's Gov[ernmen]t have duly taken note of the documents in question.

[I have, &c.

E. GREY.]

([1]) [*v. supra*, p. 695, No. 692.]

No. 715.

Sir F. Bertie to Sir Edward Grey.

                                                            Paris, November 26, 1911.

F.O. 47136/41371/11/28.   D. 3·30 P.M.

Tel. (No. 193.) Confidential.   R. 5 P.M.

I have had this morning very satisfactory conversation with Minister for Foreign Affairs which renders it unnecessary that I should act on the instructions contained in your despatches Nos. 485 and 487 of 20th November and 22nd November([1]) respectively in regard to projected French negotiations with Spain on the subject of the Spanish zones in Morocco and the special position of Tangier.

MINUTES.

We shall no doubt receive a full report by despatch. If Sir F. Bertie is satisfied that the attitude of the French government is satisfactory on the question of the internationalization of Tangier, he was right in not acting on our instruction.

Qu[ery]. Await despatch.

E. A. C.
Nov. 27.
W. L.

([1]) [*v. supra*, pp. 705–6, No. 700; and pp. 710–11, No. 705.]

No. 716.

Sir F. Bertie to Sir Edward Grey.

F.O. 47479/41371/11/28.

(No. 561.) Very Confidential.   *Paris,* D. *November* 26, 1911.
Sir,   R. *November* 28, 1911.

The instructions contained in your Despatch No. 485 Confidential of the 20th instant, as modified by your Telegram No. 306 of the next day([1]) and your Despatch No. 487 of the 22nd instant,([2]) amounted in substance to directions to me to obtain in such manner as I might deem advisable more precise and definite assurances in regard to the internationalization of Tangier than have been given to you by the French Minister in London and the authoritative text of the Draft Franco-Spanish Convention. In regard to Tangier the French Minister informed you that he was authorized to give you officially the assurance that the Government of the Republic will not take advantage of its agreements with Germany to go back on the clause in the Franco-Spanish Convention of 1904 relative to the special situation of the town and region of Tangier.([3]) As a confirmation of your belief that the French Government intend to ensure that adequate arrangements will be made for placing the town and municipal district of Tangier definitely under international control, you refer me to the wording of the Draft French Declaration communicated to me by Monsieur Regnault on the 19th ultimo([4]) in connection with the suggested text of a revised Franco-Spanish Agreement, in the first Article of which Declaration it is stated that in accordance with Article IX of the Franco-Spanish Agreement of 1904 the town of Tangier shall be administered under the sovereignty of the Sultan by a Municipality of an international character. You further reminded me that in my Telegram No. 188 of the 20th instant,([5]) I informed you that proposals had been drawn up by the President of the Council for an arrangement with Spain in regard to Morocco and that they would shortly be communicated to His Majesty's Government for consideration. You therefore trusted that these proposals would contain adequate safeguards for securing the internationalization of Tangier. You desired me to speak in the sense of your Despatch No. 487 of the 22nd instant to M. de Selves, explaining the satisfaction of His Majesty's Government at the assurances already received and the importance they attach to a definite settlement of the matter.

With the object of acting on your directions so far as in conversation with Monsieur de Selves I might find necessary or advisable, I applied for an interview with him. He was not able to receive me yesterday, but he appointed 11 o'clock this morning for me to see him. I was anxious to avoid if possible any quotation of the papers left with me by Monsieur Regnault as I have treated the Projet of which that gentleman was the author under the inspiration of the President of the Council as dead so far as His Majesty's Government are concerned, as a consequence of a conversation which I had with Monsieur Caillaux on the 18th instant when, in reply to his observation that "il faut qu'un arrangement se fasse, il faut que nous en causions," I observed, "Oui, mais en tout cas pas le Projet Regnault" to which he answered "Proposez donc quelque chose d'autre."([6])

I began the interview with Monsieur de Selves by reminding him of a conversation which, as I had informed him I had had with Monsieur Cruppi on the 20th instant and the intention of that gentleman to invite me to meet Monsieur Caillaux at dinner. I remarked that the dinner was to be on the 1st December and inquired what MM. Caillaux and Cruppi, who evidently were acting together, were likely to say to me.

In the course of the above-mentioned conversation Monsieur Cruppi's standpoint was as follows :—In the superior interests of France and England the *entente* between

([1]) [*v. supra,* p. 701, No. 705, *note* ([1]).]
([2]) [*v. supra,* pp. 710–11, No. 705.]
([3]) [*v. supra,* pp. 707–8, No. 703.]
([4]) [*v. supra,* pp. 586–7, No. 598, *encl.* 2.]
([5]) [Not reproduced as its substance is here given.]
([6]) [*v. supra,* p. 318, No. 337.]

them must be maintained, and the British and French Governments should come to an understanding as to what is reasonable compensation for France to have for the sacrifices which she has made to Germany for the benefit of Spain or rather on account of which Spain will profit in Morocco. As France was more than justified in going to Fez, Spain acted contrary to Treaty in occupying Larache and Alcazar, and His Majesty's Government concurred in that view, and as the Spanish occupation was continued in spite of formal protests by the French Government they would have been within their rights if they had denounced the Secret Franco-Spanish Agreement of 1904. They had abstained from doing so out of regard for high political considerations, viz., the desire to be in unison with His Majesty's Government and to avoid giving plausible pleas to Spain for throwing herself into the arms of Germany. France has obligations to England under the Secret Anglo-French Agreement of 1904 in regard to the Atlantic Coast of Morocco, and England, as a so to say guarantor to Spain of the Franco-Spanish Secret Agreement, is in a delicate position. If His Majesty's Government, however, maintain that that Agreement is still in *full* force, the French Government would be justified in calling upon Spain to withdraw from Alcazar *and* Larache and all the territory occupied by Spanish troops in defiance of the terms of the Agreement, and notwithstanding the protests of the French Government; or if His Majesty's Government adhere to their view that Spain was not justified in such occupation, then they must admit that Spain is not entitled to the full benefit of all the advantages accruing to her under the Franco-Spanish Agreement if it had remained entirely respected and observed by the Spanish Government. Monsieur Cruppi understood and appreciated the reasons for which His Majesty's Government stipulated for and still maintain the necessity in their naval interest for the undertaking that Spain and not France shall hold the Atlantic Coast of Morocco as laid down in the Anglo-French Secret Agreement of 1904, and he considered that the engagement should be observed, but arrangements should be made for freeing from Spanish maladministration or ineptitude the territory between a certain circumference comprehending Tangier (to be neutralized or internationalized) and Alcazar for a Railway line giving secure passage for French communications and international trade between Tangier and Fez. This would, he considered, be impossible if the territory through which the railway would run were under Spanish authority, for there would be no kind of proper administration. There were, he said, two suggestions *en l'air*, one for a narrow band ("tuyau") of territory to be excised from Spanish occupation and administration for the purposes of the railway, and another that the Spanish occupation and administration of the Atlantic Zone allotted to Spain by Monsieur Delcassé's Secret Convention of 1904 shall be restricted to the Coast and a strip of territory behind it, the remainder (excepting Tangier and some territory in its immediate vicinity, which would be under international administration—though within the Spanish Zone) to fall to France. Monsieur Cruppi naturally preferred the second alternative.

Monsieur de Selves said that since that conversation and the one which, as I had informed him, I had had with the President of the Council on the 18th instant the situation had changed. He had made proposals to the Cabinet for the negotiations with Spain which, after hearing his arguments in their support his colleagues had accepted and the President of the Republic had approved. They were that inasmuch as France had in 1904 entered into engagements with England which still existed on the subject of Morocco, those engagements should be the basis for the negotiations with Spain in regard to such modifications as may be considered admissible by the British Government in the Franco-Spanish Agreement of 1904 with the view of giving compensation to France for the sacrifices which she has made in the French Congo to Germany for a settlement of the Moroccan question as between France and Germany, the result of which will be an improved position for Spain in Morocco. The terms which Monsieur de Selves would desire to arrange with Spain through the French Ambassador at Madrid with the aid of the British Ambassador, after a preliminary discussion and agreement between the French and British Governments, would be that no compensation should be asked of Spain in the North of Morocco. There should merely be a slight rectification of the Loukkos boundary line so as to obviate constant disputes in regard to it in the vicinity of Alcazar, that the compensation from Spain should be sought in the Spanish Southern Zone which should be claimed by France except Ifni, which out of consideration for Spanish susceptibilities and its position opposite to the Canaries should be left with some surrounding territory in Spanish possession. With regard to Tangier and its immediate vicinity, arrangements should be made for its internationalization, and the railway from Tangier viâ Alcazar to Fez should be constructed by the French Government in cooperation with the Spanish Government, viz., by a Syndicate or Board on which the Spanish Government would have representatives, the Railway Company to be empowered to take measures for the security of the line. With regard to the question of the relations between the Spanish and Moorish Governments on matters concerning the Spanish Zone, Monsieur de Selves suggests that the Sultan should appoint a sort of Commissioner with full powers to represent his Majesty and to treat all questions arising between the Spanish Authorities and the Makhzen.

Monsieur de Selves pointed out that the arrangement which he contemplated would leave Spain in the occupation of Larache and Alcazar, give to her all the zone on the North West of Morocco as well as the zone on the Mediterranean Coast allotted to her by the Convention of 1904. It would pay regard to Spanish interests on the subject of the Railway between Tangier and Fez. It would provide for the internationalization of Tangier and its vicinity, a matter to which you attached great importance, and would provide compensation in the South for French sacrifices as I had suggested, and it offered a solution of the difficult problem of how to deal with questions between the Spanish and Moorish Governments in the Spanish Zone. Monsieur de Selves said that in making these proposals he had been guided by the desire to act with His Majesty's Government and to preserve intact the *entente* with England which in the interests of both France and England was so necessary for the mutual protection of their general interests. He asked me whether I thought that his proposals would meet with your concurrence. I told him that I felt confident that you would consider the bases for the negotiations as satisfactory. He will furnish me with a projet for your consideration.

I have, &c.
FRANCIS BERTIE.

MINUTES.

The outline of the new French proposals as sketched by M. de Selves appear not only satisfactory from the British point of view, but ought to meet with a favourable reception at Madrid.

Sir F. Bertie has dealt with the matter with his usual tact, and his action and language should, I think be entirely approved.

We must clearly now wait, before we criticize the French proposals, until we have their text before us.

We cannot too closely scrutinize the arrangements which are to be made for the internationalization of Tangier. I think we must be prepared to find that France will make every endeavour, by using vague terms and dealing in general phrases only, to keep open a loophole by which French special interests can yet, in future, emerge in a privileged position in Tangier. They will no doubt lay stress on the control of the head of the railway which is to link Fez with the sea at Tangier. We must be on our guard not to encourage or allow any schemes by which large powers of police or armed assistance for the maintenance of order might be reserved to the Moorish gov[ernmen]t (*i.e.* France).

We have already some ominous indications of the way in which France is likely to try to secure such an object : There is the scheme reported in Sir R. Lister's telegram received today([1]) which would give a predominant position to Morocco (France) in one of the few municipal institutions already existing at Tangier. There are further the numerous articles in the inspired French press (see No. 47477 for instance from Sir F. Bertie also received to-day)([7]) which show what importance the French gov[ernment] attach to a French hold over Tangier.

We must keep our eyes open.

E. A. C.
Nov. 28.

([7]) [Not reproduced]

We must keep our eyes open but the present terms are an enormous improvement on those which M. Caillaux was prepared to offer and ought to be satisfactory to Spain.

W. L.

Sir F. Bertie should be entirely approved. M. Cambon will probably communicate to us the French text today (29th).

A. N.
F. D. A.
E. G.

No. 717.

Sir E. Goschen to Sir Edward Grey.

F.O. 47462/46450/11/28.
Tel. (No. 106.) R.
Morocco.

Berlin, November 27, 1911.
D. 7·56 P.M.
R. 10 P.M.

" North German Gazette " announced that German war-ship will leave Agadir to-morrow, as all is now quiet, and no further danger exists for German lives and property.

No. 718.

Sir Edward Grey to Count Metternich.

F.O. 47120/13911/11/28.
Y[our] E[xcellency],   *Foreign Office November* 27, 1911.
H[is] M[ajesty's] Gov[ermen]t have given their careful consideration to the Convention respecting Morocco concluded between Germany and France which Y[our] E[xcellency] was good enough to communicate to me on the 6th inst[ant]. I have much pleasure in informing Y[our] E[xcellency] that they have decided to adhere to it.

[I have, &c.]
E. G[REY].

No. 719.

Foreign Office to Board of Trade.

F.O. 45541/45363/11/28.
Sir,   *Foreign Office, November* 27, 1911.
With reference to the Foreign Office letter No. 20278 of June 9th 1910 and previous correspondence relative to the Union des Mines Marocaines I am directed by Sec[retar]y Sir E. Grey to transmit to you herewith a copy of a despatch from H[is] M[ajesty's] Ambassador at Berlin(¹) calling attention to the report—which has since been confirmed—that an agreement has been signed between the Union and the Mannesmann Morocco mining syndicate.

It will be remembered that when the Union was first formed a share of 50% was allotted to France, 25% to Germany and 25% to the other Powers together. 10% of this was promised to G[rea]t Britain but so far as Sir E. Grey is aware only 6% was taken up by British capitalists. Under the terms of the agreement now concluded 20% of the new combine is allotted to France, 40% to the Mannesmanns and 40% to the old Union. This amounts practically to an absolute control of the syndicate by France and Germany, and the reduction of the British share to a negligible quantity.

(¹) [Not reproduced.]

Sir E. Grey is considering the question whether it would or would not be advisable in the circ[umstance]s to intimate to the French Gov[ernmen]t his dissatisfaction with this particular arrangement and generally, as in the case of the Societé marocaine de Travaux publics, with the smallness of the share allotted to Great Britain in these international syndicates in Morocco. The difficulty is that Sir E. Grey understands there is no eagerness on the part of British capitalists to invest in these undertakings and it would obviously place H[is] M[ajesty's] Gov[ernmen]t in an awkward position if, after making representations to the French Gov[ernmen]t and obtaining a larger allotment, the necessary capital were not forthcoming.

Sir E. Grey would be grateful for an expression of the views of the Board of Trade as to the course they would advise should be adopted in the present case, and for any observations generally, on the subject, which they may desire to offer.

[I am, &c.

W. LANGLEY.]

No. 720.

Extract from Speech by Mr. Asquith in the House of Commons on November 27, 1911.

(*Parl. Deb.*, 5*th Ser.*, House of Commons, Vol. 32, pp. 106–7.)

. . . . The House has heard from my right hon[ourable] Friend the Foreign Secretary, and I believe has heard with universal satisfaction, that the world is now in possession of the whole of our Treaty obligations on this subject. There is no secret arrangement of any sort or kind which has not been disclosed, and fully disclosed, to the public, and we ask, from that point of view, that our conduct should be judged by the measure of our Treaty obligations which Members of the House are able to ascertain precisely for themselves. . . . .

No. 721.

Sir Edward Grey's Speech in the House of Commons, November 27, 1911.([1])

Great Britain and Germany.

The Secretary of State for Foreign Affairs (Sir Edward Grey): I beg to move, " That the foreign policy of His Majesty's Government be now considered."

I propose, in moving this Motion, that the House do enter upon the consideration of foreign affairs, to restrict myself in the speech in which I move it to one subject only, but I do that, not with the intention or desire of in any way restricting the limits of the Debate. I do it because the subject with which I wish to deal—which is, indeed, as I consider it, the primary cause of this day being set apart for foreign affairs—the subject of the recent Morocco negotiations and our relations with France and Germany—is so important, so serious, and at the present time still so delicate that for me in my speech to attempt to travel over other ground and mix up other matters would be for me personally exceedingly difficult, if not impossible, if I am to do justice to the one subject I want to deal with first; and I venture to say, as far as my opening speech is concerned, it might even be inconvenient for the House. So I propose to restrict myself to that subject in my speech in moving the Motion.

Let me say to the House that, had it been possible, I would gladly have waited before saying anything here on the Morocco question until the conclusion of the discussion in the French and German Parliaments as to the negotiations for a settlement between their two countries. France

([1]) [*Parl. Deb.*, 5*th Ser.*, House of Commons, Vol. 32, pp. 43–65.]

and Germany are the two principals in the matter. The Reichstag, as I understand, has not concluded its discussions, and the French Chamber has not yet begun its public discussions. But so much has been said in Germany already, especially by the recent disclosures of the German Foreign Secretary, that even at the risk of disturbing discussions which have still to take place in both France and Germany—a risk which I shall try to reduce to the smallest possible limit—I feel bound to make a somewhat full statement to the House. I wish to have every regard to the susceptibilities and difficulties of public opinion both in France and in Germany; but so much has been said about us in Germany in recent discussions that we must have some regard to our own public opinion, and I am sure it will be felt abroad that what has passed has made it impossible for us to postpone a full statement any longer. I am afraid I shall have to read to the House more than is usual in a speech, because I shall have to give an account of conversations which took place in the summer between myself and the German Ambassador, I want to make what I have to say about them as accurate as possible, and to do that it is necessary for me to read my own record of what actually took place.

The plan of what I propose to say to the House in my speech will be as follows : I propose to begin by a narrative, as clear as I can make it, of what passed between ourselves and Germany in the summer. I shall then proceed to examine what was the real ground of tension caused between Germany and ourselves by the Moroccan question. So much suspicion and gossip have collected in connection with this subject of tension in the summer that it is exciting men's minds and corroding their tempers, both here and in Germany, to a greater extent than ever before, though the crisis, whatever it was is past, I shall endeavour to alleviate that not by belittling what was really serious, but by trying to give a true estimate of the situation. The third part of what I wish to say shall be general remarks on foreign policy, and a response to certain passages in the speeches of the German Chancellor that seem to me of hopeful augury for the future.

If, in the earlier part of my statement, there seem to be some things which do not promise a hopeful or conciliatory development, I would ask the House not to jump at conclusions, but to remember, when I am recounting what has been the difficulty in the way, I am doing it not in order to emphasise or to perpetuate it, but to get it out of the way. I will now begin the narrative part. The German Foreign Secretary has already made not a complete but a large disclosure of what has passed in conversations between the German Ambassador in London and myself in the summer.([2]) In diplomatic procedure it is very unusual to make public an account of conversations without first consulting the other party to them. I had no knowledge of what the German Foreign Secretary was going to disclose or that he was going to make any disclosure of these conversations until I read the report of them in '' The Times.'' I understand that the exigencies of the situation in Germany made it impossible for me to be consulted beforehand, and I quite understand what the situation was. Had I been consulted as to the disclosures he made I should certainly have offered no objections, and I make no complaint now of their having been made. But, of course, they are not full disclosures. The German Foreign Secretary was presenting the case of his Government to the Budget Committee of the Reichstag. Here I have to give the complement of what he said by presenting our case, and I, of course, will do what he has done and disclose so much of these conversations as is necessary to put before the House the part which we took.

The German Chancellor and the German Foreign Secretary have already disposed of one misapprehension with regard to the Moroccan question. It was imagined in some quarters, I think I have seen it on the Paper of this House in a question put, that Germany had protested against the French action in going to Fez at all, and that France had persisted in going there in the face of the German protest. The German Government have now explained what the German view of the French going to Fez really was, and I have no comment or criticism to make upon what they said. I therefore begin my narrative not with the French expedition to Fez, but with the 1st July. On that day the German Ambassador came to the Foreign Office and made the following communication :—

'' Some German firms established in the south of Morocco, notably at Agadir and in the vicinity, have been alarmed by a certain ferment which has shown itself among the local tribes, due, it seems, to the recent occurrences in other parts of the country. These firms have applied to the Imperial Government for protection for the lives of their employés and their property. At their request the Imperial Government have decided to send a warship to the Port of Agadir to lend help and assistance in case of need to their subjects and employés, as well as to protect the important German interests in the territory in question. As soon as the state of affairs in Morocco has resumed its former quiet aspect, the ship charged with this protective mission shall leave the Port of Agadir.''

That was accompanied by an explanation given to us at the same time which seemed to me much more important than the actual communication of the sending of the ship. The explanation given to us made it clear that the Moroccan question was being opened—the whole Moroccan question—by the sending of the ship to Agadir. It made it clear that the German Government regarded a return to the *status quo* in Morocco as doubtful, if not impossible, and that what they contemplated was a definite solution of the Moroccan question between Germany, France, and Spain.(³) The whole question, or at least the kernel of the question, after that communication was received was what was the definite solution of the Moroccan question which Germany contemplated? If a return to the *status quo* was doubtful, if not impossible, then the only alternative was a definite solution of the Moroccan question. What was the nature of that? What was clearly the objective Germany contemplated? Was it to be the partition of Morocco, or what was it to be? That was what occupied our minds after receiving that communication. The communication was made to the Foreign Office on the Saturday. On the next Monday, the 3rd July, I asked the German Ambassador to come and see me. I informed him I had seen the Prime Minister, and that we considered the situation created by the dispatch of the " Panther " to Agadir as so important that it must be discussed in a meeting of the Cabinet. I would say no more pending the meeting of the Cabinet, but I wished the German Government to learn at once that, in our view, the situation was serious and important.(⁴) The next day, the 4th July, I asked the German Ambassador to come and see me again, and said that I must tell him—this was after the Cabinet meeting—that our attitude could not be a disinterested one with regard to Morocco. We must take into consideration our treaty obligations to France and our own interests in Morocco. We were of opinion that a new situation had been created by the dispatch of a German ship to Agadir. Future developments might affect British interests more directly than they had hitherto been affected, and, therefore, we could not recognise any new arrangements that might be come to without us. I made it quite clear to the Ambassador that this communication, and the exact words which I used, were those of His Majesty's Government sitting in Cabinet.(⁵)

After that there was a period of silence. The German Ambassador was not instructed to make any comment to me with regard to my communication, and we received no information from the German Government as to what their aims or desires were or as to what they had in mind when they spoke of a definite solution of the Moroccan problem. Some information reached us from other quarters, leading us to apprehend that the settlement contemplated by the German Government might be a partition of Morocco, arrived at by negotiations to which it was not intended we should be a party. I think, in the German mind, it has sometimes been assumed that our agreement made with France in 1904 entirely disinterested us with regard to Morocco, and if Germany wished to make a new settlement with regard to Morocco, it was going out of our way and intrusive for us, having given by our agreement of 1904 a free hand to France in Morocco, as far as we are concerned—it was going out of our way and intrusive to interfere with any other Power wishing to make her own arrangements. That does not take full account of the agreement of 1904 made by the right hon[ourable] Gentleman opposite. It is quite true we disinterested ourselves in Morocco politically, but we did it on conditions laid down—conditions both strategic and economic. What were the reasons of our being interested in Morocco? We have no jealousy of other Powers. It is obvious, if the Moroccan question was to be reopened and a new settlement made, unless we were consulted, unless we knew what was going on, unless we were in some way parties to the settlement, the strategic and economic conditions stipulated for between ourselves, France, and Spain in 1904 might be upset.

On the 12th July, the British Ambassador in Berlin had occasion to see the German Foreign Secretary on some minor matters, and took the opportunity to say that there had been at one time some mention of a conversation *à trois* between Germany, France and Spain, the inference being that we were to be excluded from it. The German Foreign Secretary told our Ambassador to inform us that there never had been any idea of such a communication and, except for this negative communication, we had no further information from the German Government of their views.(⁶) A little later it appeared in the Press that the German Government and indeed it was case—that the German Government had made demands with regard to the French Congo of an extent to which it was obvious to everybody who thought of it that neither the French Government nor the French Chamber could agree. That at once made me anxious as to the development of the situation. If Germany was going to negotiate with France an arrangement by which Germany received from France something in the French Congo and left France in Morocco as she is under our agreement of 1904, then of course we were prepared to stand aside and not to intrude, but if Germany, starting negotiations on that basis with France, made demands not for a portion, but for the greater part of the French Congo or anything of that kind, it was quite clear France must refuse those demands and negotiations would be thrown back on some other basis and the question of the possible partition would arise again. That is why I became anxious.

I therefore asked the German Ambassador to see me again on the 21st July.(⁷) I said to him I wished it to be understood that our silence, in the absence of any communication from the

(³) [*v. supra*, pp. 322–3, No. 339.]
(⁴) [*cp. supra*, p. 328, No. 347.]
(⁵) [*v. supra*, p. 334, No. 356.]
(⁶) [*v. supra*, pp. 356–7, No. 373.]
(⁷) [*v. supra*, pp. 390–1, No. 411.]

German Government—our silence since the Cabinet communication of the 4th July, and since the Prime Minister's statement of the 7th July in this House([8])—our silence since then must not be interpreted as meaning that we were not taking in the Moroccan question, the interest which had been indicated by our statement of the 4th of that month. We knew that a rectification of the frontier of the French Congo had been proposed as a basis for negotiations with France. We thought it possible that a settlement might be come to between Germany and France on this basis without affecting British interests. We would be very glad if this happened, and in the hope that it would happen at a later stage we had hitherto stood aside. But I had been made anxious by the news which appeared the day before as to the demands which the German Government had made on the French Government; demands which were in effect not a rectification of the frontier, but a cession of the French Congo, which it was obviously impossible for the French Government to concede. I heard that negotiations were still proceeding, and I still hoped that they might lead to a satisfactory result, but it must be understood that if they were unsuccessful, a very embarrassing situation would arise. I pointed out to the German Ambassador that the Germans were in the closed port of Agadir; that according to native rumours they were landing and negotiating with the tribes, so that, for all we knew, they might be acquiring concessions there and that it might even be that the German flag had been hoisted at Agadir, which was the most suitable port on that coast for a naval basis. We could not say to what extent the situation might be altered to our disadvantage, and if the negotiations with France came to nothing, we should be obliged to do something to watch over British interests and to become a party to the discussion of the matter. The longer the Germans remained at Agadir the greater the risk of their developing a state of affairs which would make it more difficult for them to withdraw and more necessary for us to take some steps to protect British interests. I wished to say all this now while we were still waiting, in the hope that the negotiations with France would succeed, for, if I did not say this now, it would cause resentment later on if the German Government had been led to suppose by our previous silence—our silence since the 4th July—that we did not take an interest in the matter.

The German Ambassador was not in a position to give me any information, but he deprecated the assumption that what I had sketched as the possible damage to British interests would be accomplished. He was sure that his Government had no intention of acquiring commercial monopolies, and unfairly prejudicing our interests. On this I observed that the fact that Germany remained in occupation of a closed port involved at least a monopoly of commercial opportunities. I had waited before saying anything further between the 4th July and the 21st July. I made that statement on the 21st July, because I was getting anxious because the situation seemed to me to be developing unfavourably.

The German Ambassador was still not in a position to make any communication to me from the German Government. In the course of that day, the 21st July, the Chancellor of the Exchequer told me that he had to make a speech on an occasion of importance at the Mansion House the same evening. He consulted the Prime Minister and me as to what should be said. It was fourteen days since the last public statement about Morocco had been made here, and that had been only the very short statement made by the Prime Minister in the House. We were anxious as to the way in which things were developing, and we all three felt that for a Cabinet Minister of first-rate importance to make a speech on a formal occasion and to say no word about foreign affairs after the interview would be misleading to public opinion here and everywhere. What I had said to the German Ambassador that day as to Agadir and the negotiations with France was obviously suitable only—I read it to the House now, because the German Foreign Minister has disclosed it, and there is no reason why it should not be said now—what I said to him that day as regards Agadir and the negotiations with France was obviously suitable only for diplomatic channels and not for public statement. The Chancellor of the Exchequer therefore made his speech in quite general terms. What he said is on record.([9]) He claimed no pre-eminence, no predominance for us in international affairs. It contained no menace, such as the saying of "Hands off!" to anyone anywhere. It did not say that there was any particular demand or claim on the part of Germany that was inconsistent with British interests. Its purport and its point was that where British interests were affected, we must not be treated as if we were of no account. If the time ever comes when this cannot be said by a Minister speaking in the position the Chancellor of the Exchequer was in then, we shall have ceased to exist as a great nation.

As a matter of fact, the first German comments on this speech that I saw in the Press were such as naturally might have been expected. One German Conservative newspaper said that if the word "Germany" were substituted for the word "England," the speech might have been made by a German Minister. The words of the speech were soon forgotten, and a sort of legend has grown up about them. For instance, a few weeks ago, I heard of one German who protested to an English friend of his and of mine against the speech, and was given a report of the

([8]) [v. supra, p. 342, No. 364. It will be seen that this statement was made on the 6th not on the 7th.

([9]) [v. supra, pp. 391–2, No. 412; for the results of this speech v. supra, pp. 387–417, chap. LV, passim.]

speech to read. Having read it, he said that what was objected to in Germany was, not the speech itself, but the fact that it had been made at a moment when France and Germany were coming to terms, and that it upset the negotiations. The exact contrary is the truth as to the particular circumstances of the negotiations existing at the time. I was afraid, and I spoke to the German Ambassador because I was afraid, that things were developing in a way that would bring up the Moroccan question, force the Moroccan negotiations back, not upon an arrangement between France and Germany about the Congo and Morocco respectively, but upon something in the nature of a partition of Morocco, or some sort of solution which might make the question of British interests to be directly affected, and which would certainly directly bring into operation our Treaty obligations with France.

On the 24th July, three days after the speech of the Chancellor of the Exchequer, the German Ambassador came to see me.([10]) He informed me that the German intention in sending a ship to Agadir had not changed. Not a man had been landed there. The German Government regretted the credence which was given to the insinuations as to the intentions of Germany that came from hostile quarters. Germany had never thought of creating a naval port on the coast of Morocco, and never would think of it. Such ideas were hallucinations. As to the negotiations with France, if the German demands were rather high his Government were ready to make concessions in Morocco as well as in Colonial matters, but the Chauvinistic tone of the French Press, and a part of the British Press, menacing Germany with the interference of the friends of France, did not tend towards a settlement. I said that I was likely to be asked in Parliament what was happening in Agadir, and I should like to know whether I might say that the German Government had informed me that not a man had been landed. The Ambassador asked me to make no public statement with regard to this communication until he had had time to communicate with his Government. The next day, 25th July, the German Ambassador came to see me again,([11]) and told me that the information that he had given me on the previous day was confidential, and that the German Government could not consent to its being used in Parliament in view of the speech of the Chancellor of the Exchequer. He then made to me in regard to that speech a communication which has now been published by the German Government, and which I need not read in full to the House, because it has been in the Press here already, except to say about it that that communication was a strong criticism upon the effect of the speech upon the Press rather than upon the substance of the speech itself.

The communication, however, was exceedingly stiff in tone, and I felt it necessary—for, of course, I had not expected any communication of this kind—to say at once that as the speech of the Chancellor of the Exchequer seemed to me to give no cause for complaint, the fact that it had created surprise in Germany was in itself a justification of the speech, for it could not have created surprise unless there had been some tendency to think that we might be disregarded. The speech had not claimed anything except that we were entitled to be considered as one of the great nations. It had claimed no pre-eminence, and that it had not even indicated that there was a crisis. It dealt in general terms with remote contingencies. The German Government had said that it was not consistent with their dignity, after the speech of the Chancellor of the Exchequer, to give explanations as to what was taking place at Agadir. I said to the Ambassador that the tone of their communication made it inconsistent with our dignity to give explanations as to the speech of the Chancellor of the Exchequer. Of course, by that I meant a public explanation. Explanations as to Agadir had already been given me by the German Ambassador, but it was the public explanation that the Government could not consent to. Then I thought it right to say further on the question generally, knowing that the interests of France were involved as well as our own, and that it was the desire of France that the negotiations should go smoothly —I said to the German Ambassador that it was not intended, by anyth[i]ng that had been said, or would be said here, to embroil the negotiations between Germany and France. On the contrary, we sincerely desired that they should succeed, but the tone of the German communication was unfavourable with regard to France as well as with regard to us, and made it more than ever evident that a very difficult situation would arise if the German negotiations with France should not succeed. There the matter was left by that conversation, and there it remained for two days, until the 27th July. Then the German Ambassador came to me again and made another communication from his Government, in conversation, so that I took down the words.([12]) The communication he made to me on the 27th July was this—I put it in the words I took down—

"We trust that Sir Edward Grey, by our very open and candid communication, has gathered the conviction that our pourparlers with France at the moment do not touch British interests. We trust to the Minister's great loyalty, that he has so often shown, that he will find it possible to state this fact in Parliament, without, however, giving any details of our confidential communication. We acknowledge with pleasure that the Minister has stated that he desires an agreement between Germany and France, and feel quite convinced that this will prove most helpful to the progress of the negotiations.

"But, having in view the wish expressed by Sir Edward, we cannot quite see how he can, in the present state of the pourparlers, describe our demands as obviously impossible, without

([10]) [v. supra, pp. 394–6, No. 417.]
([11]) [v. supra, pp. 397–9, No. 419.]
([12]) [v. supra, pp. 411–13, No. 430.]

knowing what we on our side have the intention to offer to France in the political and colonial territorial field. It is not possible in regard of the formal pledge of secrecy we have given——"

" We " means the German Government—

" to go into details; but as the territories to be eventually exchanged are exclusively German and French, we do not believe that special English interests could be touched, and that it seems advisable to leave it to the two parties immediately concerned to form an estimation of the value of the objects to be eventually exchanged.

" Adverse criticism from the English side must obviously render the negotiations more difficult. On the other hand, a public statement that England would be pleased to see a successful conclusion of the Franco-German pourparlers would have a most beneficial influence on an auspicious result; for which we most earnestly hope. We most seriously wish to diminish any points of friction we have with France in the colonial sphere, especially in Africa, and hope it may eventually be possible to make them disappear entirely. We could not look forward, even if this was done, to establishing intimate relations with France; but we believed that it would do away with a cause of frequently recurring tension. If the wishes of England are in the same direction, the best way to help to bring about this result would be by having a calming influence on public opinion in France, which just now, by half-truths and inaccurate statements, has been brought to considerable excitement."

The House will observe that the tone of that communication was exceedingly friendly, not only to ourselves, but to France. I at once expressed appreciation of the friendly tone in which the communication was couched. The German Ambassador and myself then had some further conversation of a general and informal kind, in the course of which he expressed some regret at the way in which our public opinion had been misled to adverse conclusions as to German action. I asked, on that, what else could have been expected, when the German Government suddenly sent a ship to Morocco, to a closed port, which was said to be the most suitable place on the west coast of Morocco for a naval base. Of course, this action has mobilised British public opinion. I also pointed out that, after I had made to him on 4th July a declaration on behalf of the British Government, we had had no communication from the German Government until 24th July, and even then their denial of any intention to establish a naval base had been in a form which I could not use to allay the suspicions which had been roused here. I suggested to the Ambassador, and he received the suggestion very cordially, that we should not pursue this point. I expressed the hope that this latest German communication might be taken as a new point of departure, and that we need not go back upon things which might lead to mutual recriminations. In the afternoon of the same day the Prime Minister made a statement in the House. That statement is on record, and anyone who reads that statement will, of course, see that the spirit in which we discussed the thing in public here corresponded to the spirit in which we had then been approached. From that date onwards there were no further difficulties between the German Government and ourselves about the Moroccan negotiations.

That is practically the end of my narrative part, and the comment I have to make upon it is this. In the disclosures made in the Reichstag by the German Foreign Secretary I find he has stated that the intention of taking a part of Morocco had never existed in Germany, as the Secretary of State—that is the German Foreign Secretary—distinctly stated at the time to a well-known Pan-German. Unfortunately, the gentleman in question did not believe it. If, after we had made the Cabinet statement to the German Ambassador on 4th July that intention had been confided to us as definitely as that, I think a good deal of misunderstanding might have been avoided. As regards the subsequent course of the negotiations, I need only say this : The French Government consulted us at every point where it seemed at all likely that British interests might be affected—most loyally at every point—and except perhaps once or twice on subsidiary points of purely economic detail in Morocco itself, we were able to say that British interests were not involved by the proposals or counter-proposals made in the course of the negotiations between France and Germany, and everything we said or did in our communications with the French Government was in the direction of helping and not impeding the negotiations.

Now I come to the more general part. I propose to examine, as people will continue to discuss it, the real nature of the tension which existed. An agreement has now been reached between the French and German Governments, in which both sides have made substantial concessions and substantial gains. That this has been accomplished and peace between the two countries preserved in the face of all the excitement which arose during the negotiations appears to us, who are onlookers, a fact very creditable to the diplomatists who negotiated the agreement and not discreditable to the part which we ourselves had taken, though that was a subsidiary part. In spite of that, this is the moment chosen by some people to excite themselves, and as many others as they can, in Germany or here, by discussion of how near we came to war. There are really some people who seem to take delight in suggesting or forming the opinion, from whatever gossip or information they can get in any quarter, that we were near to war, and the nearer we came to war the greater satisfaction they seemed to get out of it. I do not say we are peculiar in this respect at this moment. It is really as if in the atmosphere of the world there was some mischievous influence at work which troubles and excites every part of it. We are passing this year through a period of great excitement. It is so still. Some countries are in revolution, others are at war, and in several countries which are neither in revolution nor at war there are people who seem to delight in discussing how near they have been or are likely to be either to revolution or to war in the past, present, or the future. Really it is as if the world were indulging in a fit of political alcoholism, and the best that can be done by those of us who are in positions of responsibility is to keep cool and sober.

A speech has been made lately by the honourable and gallant member (Captain Faber).[13] I only refer to it because it really is the case that that speech has been forming the subject of discussion in the Budget Committee of the Reichstag· in Germany, and, I am told on quite good authority, has intensified the bitterness of the German feeling. Of course, I know it is quite possible for us to reply that there are one or two speeches made in the German Reichstag—not official speeches—and the honourable and gallant gentleman (Captain Faber) is not an official Member which, if correctly reported in the paper, gives us just as much reason for saying here that our public opinion has been offended and intensified by the speeches made there. Of course, one speech leads to another. I can only do the best I can to try to alleviate the suspicions and excited talk by examining what the tension and apprehension in the summer and on into September really were. Of course there was anxiety—diplomatic anxiety, not always, not constant, but intermittent—and at times considerable anxiety as to how the negotiations between France and Germany were to find a solution. They were very difficult for the two countries concerned in them, and had either of them broken off the negotiations—and there were times when it looked as if negotiations must reach a deadlock—had either abruptly broken off the negotiations it is very difficult to see what the next move would have been. We were in constant and intimate relations with France. We knew that France earnestly desired a settlement. We knew she would not break off negotiations abruptly. We did not believe that the German Government would do it either, though, of course, we were not in the same close touch with them, nor so cognisant of their view in the course of negotiations. Still, there was the possibility that negotiations might be broken off, though I never thought the probability. I never expected anything abrupt, but it did look once or twice late on in the summer as if the negotiations might reach a deadlock. If they reached a deadlock, what was the next step to do? Naturally the next step, the next diplomatic step, would have been for some Power which was a party to the Act of Algeciras to propose a conference. That was the step we had in mind, the step we should have been prepared to take if the negotiations had reached a deadlock. But in July, before the last German communication that I read to the House, what I called a friendly communication, I had sounded the German Government as to whether a proposal for a conference would be acceptable if negotiations reached a deadlock, and the reply I had received from the German Government, though not absolutely conclusive, pointed to the fact that a proposal for a conference might not be acceptable. That was what gave rise to anxiety in the diplomatic situation. The natural step would have been a conference if there was a deadlock; the doubt remained whether such a proposal would be welcome to the German Government, and if unwelcome to the German Government, then of course things might have been made not better, but worse, for making the proposal.

Then the House will say, supposing all that had happened, supposing negotiations reached a deadlock, supposing a conference was proposed and Germany would not agree to it, what would have been the situation then? Then you would have had this situation. You would have had France, Germany, and Spain in occupation of parts of Morocco, a German ship at Agadir—because, of course, the German ship could not leave Agadir with negotiations unsettled— you would have had at any rate the beginning of a partition of Morocco without agreement between the three parties—France, Germany, and Spain—who were in occupation of different parts of Morocco. You would have had us no party to the negotiations at that time, and you would have had on record the statement made publicly by the Prime Minister here, and the statement made by the German Government on the 4th July that we could not recognise any settlement come to unless we were consulted. You had, at any rate, the prospect, if negotiations broke down, of a very strained diplomatic situation; and undoubtedly the period was from time to time one of tension, not as to what was going to happen in the next twenty-four hours, but tension, because of the anxiety of what one saw might possibly take place. That I believe is as accurate and faithful an estimate as I can give—it is not a thing you can prove by documents—of the situation as it existed and of the amount of tension there was. I said I would not belittle what was serious, and I think I have not done so; but I would suggest that if that be accepted it is a statement of the truth of the actual facts of the situation which might be, and I think would be, disquieting and alarming if people had imagined that there had never been any great tension or serious difficulties, but which, considering the talk that now exists of the imminence of war, ought to be not alarming and disquieting but a sedative to the excited state of public opinion.

Now let me say something as to foreign policy generally. First of all let me try to put an end to some of the suspicions with regard to secrecy—suspicions with which it seems to me some people are torturing themselves, and certainly worrying others. We have laid before the House the secret Articles of the Agreement with France of 1904. There are no other secret

(13) [v. supra, p. 716, No. 711, and note; infra, p. 740, No. 723, encl.]

engagements. The late Government made that Agreement in 1904. They kept those Articles secret, and I think to everybody the reason will be obvious why they did so. It would have been invidious to make those Articles public. In my opinion they were entirely justified in keeping those Articles secret, because they were not articles which commit this House to serious obligations. I saw a comment made the other day when these articles were published that, if a Government would keep little things secret, *a fortiori*, they would keep big things secret. That is absolutely untrue. There may be reasons why a Government should make secret arrangements of that kind if they are not things of first-rate importance, if they are subsidiary to matters of great importance. But that is the very reason why the British Government should not make secret engagements which commit Parliament to obligations of war. It would be foolish to do it. No British Government could embark upon a war without public opinion behind it, and such engagements as there are which really commit Parliament to anything of that kind are contained in treaties or agreements which have been laid before the House. For ourselves we have not made a single secret article of any kind since we came into office.

Now let me say a word upon the general aspects of what I consider is the proper foreign policy of this country, and what the foreign policy of the Government has been. It is said to be, and in a sense that is quite true, a continuation of the policy of the Government in which Lord Lansdowne was Secretary for Foreign Affairs. Some years ago we had constant trouble and friction with France and Russia. Everybody remembers it. There were continual excursions and alarms, and more than once we were supposed to be on the brink of war with one or other of these two countries. I remember when I was Under-Secretary in the Foreign Office in 1893, there was much more abrupt talk of war about Siam, although I believe it would have been madness for the two countries to go to war about Siam in the light of what has happened since. It would have been madness and a crime. But for a short time there was great excitement on that point. An end has been put to all that as far as regards France and Russia. The late Government turned relations which had been those of friction and difficulty with France, not perpetual but intermittent, into relations of cordial friendship. The friendship which they made we have kept unimpaired. As far as there are records in the Foreign Office to give me any indication of Lord Lansdowne's intentions, I think he would have desired, had he remained in office to-day, something of the same kind with Russia. I do not say they had gone far, or that he had incurred any responsibilities or committed himself in the matter, but as far as I have any indication, that is the direction in which he would have gone. We have gone on in that direction, and what was accomplished with France has been accomplished with Russia. The relations have been changed from those of friction and difficulty into relations of friendship, and it is well that it has been so, because in different parts of the world British interests touch and rub against French and Russian interests, and where that is so, it is difficult to find a halfway house between constant liability to friction and cordial friendship. It is cordial friendship alone which provides sufficient mutual tolerance and good-will to prevent difficulties and friction which would otherwise arise.

In addition to that, our friendship with France and Russia is in itself a guarantee that neither of them will pursue a provocative or aggressive policy towards Germany, who is their neighbour and ours. Any support we would give France and Russia in times of trouble would depend entirely on the feeling of Parliament and public feeling here when the trouble came, and both France and Russia know perfectly well that British public opinion would not give support to provocative or aggressive action against Germany. And the same considerations *mutatis mutandis* apply to France and Russia. We know perfectly well that neither of them wishes to pursue an aggressive or provocative policy towards Germany, and if it were true, as is sometimes stated in a portion of the Continental Press, that we had tried to make difficulties between France and Germany, or Russia and Germany, if it had not been our policy, and if they had not known it was our policy to smooth the path of their diplomatic relations with Germany, the friendship with them would not have endured. One of the essential conditions of the friendship of ourselves with France and Russia in the last few years has been the certain knowledge that neither they nor we wish to pursue a provocative or aggressive policy.

Now let me say this : German strength is, by itself, a guarantee that no other country will desire or seek a quarrel with Germany. That is one side of the shield of which Germans may well be proud, but I think it ought to be remembered by German public opinion that there is another side to the shield, and that is if a nation has the biggest army in the world, and if it has a very big navy, and is going on building a still bigger navy, then it must do all in its power to prevent what would otherwise be the natural apprehensions in the minds of others, who have no aggressive intentions towards that Power, lest that Power with its army and navy should have aggressive intentions towards them. Germany is rightly proud of her strength. She is building a big fleet. Surely it is natural and obvious that the growth of that fleet must raise apprehensions, or at least make other nations very sensitive to apprehensions, lest the Power which is becoming strong should have aggressive designs towards themselves. I do not believe in these aggressive designs. I do not wish to have it interpreted in that sense, but I think it must be realised that other nations will be apprehensive and sensitive, and on the lookout for any indications of aggression. All we or the other neighbours of Germany desire is to live with her on equal terms.

There is one foreign policy different to the one which I have been endeavouring to sketch to the House, and it seems to me to be advocated in some quarters of the country. It seems to me to be simply disastrous. It is that we should give it to be understood that in no circumstances, however aggressively, provocatively, or wantonly, a friend of ours was attacked, we should give our friend any assistance whatever. That would be an attempt to revert to what was once called a policy of " splendid isolation." It would deprive us of the possibility of having a friend in Europe, and it would result in the other nations of Europe, either by choice or by necessity, being brought into the orbit of a single diplomacy from which we should be excluded. The idea of splendid isolation contemplated a balance of power in Europe to which we were not to be a party, and from which we were to be able to stand aside in the happy position of having no obligations and being able to take advantage of any difficulties which arose in Europe from friction between opposing Powers. That policy is not a possible one now. Any single Power that attempted to adopt that policy in Europe to-day would be felt as a public nuisance, and if we were that single Power, one result would be that in the course of a few years we should be building warships not against a two-Power standard, but probably against the united navies of Europe. As a matter of fact that policy, which would be disastrous, is not a policy. It is the negation of policy, and if it were accompanied, as I suppose it would be accompanied, with constant criticisms of individual Members of the House about the internal affairs and proceedings of other Governments, constant pressure upon the Secretary of State for Foreign Affairs of the day, to interfere and make representations about matters which do not directly concern us, then I say that the disastrous consequences of such an attitude of mingled interference and drift would soon become apparent in an expenditure on armaments, even greater than the present expenditure, and sooner or later the very peace that people desired to preserve would topple over. Such an attitude would not even gain us the friendship of Germany.

One does not make new friendships worth having by deserting old ones. New friendships by all means let us make, but not at the expense of the ones we have. I desire to do all I can to improve the relations with Germany, as I shall presently show. But the friendships which we have lasted now for some years, and it must be a cardinal point of improved relations with Germany that we do not sacrifice one of these, and what I desire—and what I hope it may be possible to have, though it may seem difficult at the present time—is that the improved relations may be such as will improve not only ourselves, but those who are our friends. We keep our friendships. We intend to retain them unimpaired, and the more we can do, so long as we can preserve that position, so much the better, and we shall endeavour to do it. That is an essential condition. Is the policy I have sketched out necessarily a bar to good relations with Germany? I do not believe it is. They say in Germany—I only take the opinions that are reported and as they appear in the Press in Germany—that it is part of our policy always to stand in Germany's way and object to Germany's expansion. It is unfortunate that the Morocco question has come up so often. But that is a special case by itself, where we have a special agreement and have special interests, to which we attach importance, which are set out in the agreement; but in my opinion—though I do not speak for more than myself personally when I say this—the wise policy for this country is to expand as little as possible, and certainly no further the African possessions.[14]

I do not say that there are not—of course there are—certain parts of Africa lying absolutely contiguous to British possessions, especially to those of the Government of the Union of South Africa, which, if there were territorial changes, we could not see pass into other hands; and if there are great territorial changes there are no doubt other things close to British territory in the nature of frontier rectification. If there are to be changes brought about by the good-will and negotiation with other Powers, then we are not an ambitious competing party, and, not being an ambitious competing party ourselves, if Germany has friendly arrangements to negotiate with other foreign countries, we are not anxious to stand in their way. I believe that is the wise policy for this country, and if it is the wise policy not to go in for great schemes of expansion ourselves, then I think it would be diplomatically and morally wrong to indulge in a dog-in-the-manger policy with regard to others. I think, indeed, the House may see something of that sort in the recent negotiations.

What was Germany's great objective, as I gather, in the later stages of the negotiations with France the other day? To obtain access to the Congo and Ubanghi. I have already said to the House we never for a moment demurred to that or put forward any plea of British interests. We have facilitated, so far as it lay with us to do anything, the negotiations. The German Chancellor recently made two speeches. He naturally presented the German view, and they were addressed mainly to German public opinion. I willingly recognise that in both those speeches of the German Chancellor, though he had a difficult situation to deal with, and those speeches put the German view of the case, he was studiously careful to avoid saying anything that might offend British public opinion; and if I may speak freely about those speeches of the German Chancellor, I would say that, while upholding the German view of the particular case, the tone and spirit of them were such as to inspire us with a belief in his desire to see his country strong, but not aggressive. If that is the spirit of German policy, then I am sure that in two

(14) [This is correct according to Hansard. The sense seems to be " certainly to expand no further the African possessions."]

or three years the talk about a great European war will have passed away, and there will have been a growth of good-will, not only between Germany and England, but between those two countries and the friends of both. There is a great responsibility upon the British Government and the German Government, and upon other Governments, to make the tone and spirit of these speeches, especially of the second speech, of the German Chancellor, prevail in the years which are immediately before us.

Do not let us imagine that we can force the pace at this moment in improving relations with Germany. We cannot compel suddenly, after the friction of the last few months, the favourable breeze of public opinion, either in Germany or here. At present the breeze is anything but favourable. Sometimes the breeze may be so adverse that the Governments, however well disposed, may not be able to pursue a favourable course without tacking. But what we want is not to cease to steer a favourable course, and to steer it straight ahead whenever we can. I say that on the assumption that that is the desire of the German Government too. It is certainly the natural inference from the tone and spirit of the speeches of the German Chancellor. If that is his assumption, then we shall respond to it, and in some ways, though public opinion may be adverse at the present moment excited as it recently has been, in some ways one can already see that the horizon is brightening. The German Chancellor said, in one of his two recent speeches, that Morocco is like a continually festering wound in German relations not only with France, but also with England, and that, in virtue of Treaty stipulations, England stood ever on the side of France—at least diplomatically—in all Moroccan difficulties between Germany and France. So that, as a matter of fact, the German understanding with France as to Morocco also cleaned the slate in respect of German relations with England. I welcome that statement, because the German Chancellor includes France and England in it, and I would now read for the House what I said to the German Ambassador in London on the 6th of this month, when he communicated to me the text of the agreement between Germany and France, and told me that his Government asked our support of it as both Governments had agreed to do. They had, of course, agreed to ask the other Powers, who are parties to the Act of Algeciras, to support the agreement.

I replied that I would examine the agreement which I had not yet studied as a whole since it was signed, although the French Government had kept us informed of it during the progress of negotiations. I would, however, at once express my great satisfaction at the conclusion of the negotiations. Count Wolff-Metternich would remember that when the agreement of 1909 between Germany and France as to Morocco had been made, I had expressed great satisfaction on the assumption that the difficulties about Morocco were over, because the difficulties about Morocco were sure to throw Germany and ourselves into opposite diplomatic camps. If, as I had hoped, and must apparently be the case, the present agreement between Germany and France was a permanent settlement of the difficulties as to Morocco, it would be most satisfactory to us. It might be a little time before public opinion had calmed down sufficiently to realise the full consequences of it; but its effect must be to relax the tension and remove a great obstacle from the path of European diplomacy.

The discussion upon the agreement has not yet concluded. I have had no difficulty in speaking to the House on this subject and discussing the matter fully with them. What I have dreaded has been the risk of introducing into the discussion in either Germany or France anything of a nature to disturb the discussion of their own settlement of their own relations with each other. Whether I have altogether been able to avoid that risk I cannot yet say. It was a risk that had to be taken because of what is due to the House of Commons here. The Anglo-French agreement of 1904 as to Morocco, with which certain arrangements with Spain are intimately connected, was a great element in the foundation of our friendship with France. It has since then continued unimpaired to the mutual satisfaction of each party, I believe not only of the Governments but also of the peoples of the two countries. During the last seven years, throughout all the strain of diplomatic discussion, closely connected as it has been with that agreement, the two Governments have held to it in letter and spirit, and during all this time our diplomatic relations have been intimate and cordial. If, as I hope is the case, the Franco-German Agreement as to Morocco has secured for France the great position in Morocco which recent events have made it quite clear must be held by some European country, and which France, in the interests of her Colonial Empire, could not allow to pass into hands other than her own; if it has also removed the great obstacle in the smooth path of the diplomacy of the greatest nations of Europe, then the Anglo-French Agreement as to Morocco will become, when the necessary adjustments have been made with Spain, not an active, but a passive factor in the relations between the two countries. But I trust that the fact that we have with France during the last seven years gone hand-in-hand through a great deal of rough diplomatic weather, without for a moment losing touch with each other, will have its influence in perpetuating in France and here confidence in our mutual good faith and goodwill, our intention to keep in touch.

It would be presumptuous and invidious for me to appraise, or to attempt to appraise, the merits to Germany and France respectively of the bargain they have made about Morocco and the French Congo, and the comparative value of their gains and losses, or I would call it the gains and concessions to each that they are now engaged in discussing. Each Government, the French Government and the German Government, is defending the agreement before its own public opinion; each Government, the French Government and the German Government, finds critics in France and in Germany. It is difficult perhaps for us at the time, and it is still more difficult for France and Germany, to see the wood for the trees at the moment. But a few years hence I believe that to-day's estimate, whatever it be in France or in Germany, of the balance of losses and gains of each country respectively in the recent negotiations will seem a comparatively small matter. The great matter will be that Morocco will no longer trouble the peace of Europe. For years that question of Morocco has been the discomfort of diplomatists. There was a risk in leaving it unsolved. We all knew that. It was left unsolved because there appeared to be even a greater risk in attempting to find the solution. I trust that now a solution has been found. The part we have played has been a subsidiary one. The credit belongs to France and to Germany, the two principals. But for us to have taken less interest than we have done would have been to fall short of due care of British interests, and to fail in being honourably consistent in the fulfilment of Treaty obligations with France. If this settlement between France and Germany receives the approval of both nations it ought to secure that the Moroccan question has been honourably and permanently settled without breaking the peace of Europe. If that is so, then I do claim with confidence, as against critics, whether at home or abroad, that the part His Majesty's Government has taken has contributed, and contributed materially, to the realisation of that expectation, and I trust that that will be the general sense of the House.

No. 722.

Sir Edward Grey to Sir M. de Bunsen.

F.O. 47912/13751/11/28.
(No. 123.)
Sir, *Foreign Office, November 28, 1911.*

The Spanish Ambassador came to see me to-day, and asked whether, as reported in the Press, the French Government had opened negotiations with us as to an arrangement with the Spanish Government as regards Morocco.

I said that I heard from Sir Francis Bertie that the French Government were intending to consult us,([1]) but I had not yet seen their proposals. He would remember that I had some time ago expressed the opinion that the Agreements of 1904 should be the basis of the negotiations, but that if Spain was getting a free hand in her sphere in Morocco in consequence of the Franco-German Agreement, and was not asked for anything by Germany, she ought to make some concession to France.

The Ambassador agreed that, in such a case, some concession should be made by Spain, but it should not be in parts of Morocco that were vital to her. The railway from Tangier to Fez could go through the Spanish zone and be secured to France without a concession of territory there. He was afraid that the French wished to become *de facto* the supreme authority in Tangier, and that they hoped to obtain this by means of the railway terminus which they would establish there. Germany was to share in the railway: this participation was a sort of *pot-de-vin* to her, and was not consistent with the equal economic advantages which were so much talked of.

I observed that equal economical advantages could hardly be construed to mean that every railway was to be completely international. On the general question of a Franco-Spanish Agreement, I said that he would no doubt recognise that the prospect was much more favourable than a short time ago, when he had spoken to me on the subject, and had expressed great apprehension.

The Ambassador entirely admitted this improvement, and said that it was due to the representations which we had made in Paris, and the publication of the secret Franco-Spanish Agreement.

([1]) [Probably refers to *supra*, pp. 721–3, No. 716.]

I urged that Spain should now remain as quiet as possible, and avoid any incidents in Morocco of an untoward nature.

The Ambassador assured me that his Government were doing this, and would continue to keep things as quiet as possible.

[I am, &c.]
E. G[REY]

No. 723.

Sir E. Goschen to Sir Edward Grey.

F.O. 47977/47677/11/28.
(No. 400.)   *Berlin, D. November* 29, 1911.
Sir,   R. *December* 1, 1911.

Your speech upon Foreign Affairs([1]) was awaited in Berlin with the deepest interest. Late in the evening of the 27th the "Lokal-Anzeiger" sent out a flying sheet containing the text of the first part of the speech, and an announcement that a further sheet would be at once issued containing the rest of the speech. The second sheet however contained nothing further than a revised edition of the first part of the speech together with a few words of the remainder. It is necessary to mention this as the morning papers of the following day based their comments on the first part of your speech which was all that they had before them. These comments were not very enthusiastic and in some cases far from friendly.

The "Berliner Tageblatt" said that the speech would cause neither profound disappointment nor great enthusiasm. It agreed that the publication by Herr von Kiderlen-Waechter of the conversations between you and the German Ambassador, without previous agreement, was a breach of diplomatic procedure and usage. It also pointed out that although in your conversations with Count Metternich on the 3rd and 4th July([2]) you had made no actual request for information, such a request had been implied, and it was extraordinary that the Secretary of State for Foreign Affairs had made no mention of these conversations, as thereby he had given it to be understood that it was only on the 21st July that you had made known your views on the situation to the Imperial Government. After criticizing Herr von Kiderlen's procedure in this matter the "Tageblatt" referred to your statement that if the British Government had not been left so long without information, so much mistrust would not have arisen, mistrust which had been increased by the "inacceptable" German demands for compensation. This statement, the "Tageblatt" said, was scarcely logical, because even on the 3rd July your language to Count Metternich had been full of mistrust of German designs; still the fact remained that it was quite incomprehensible why between the 4th and the 21st of July the German Government had neither said nor done anything which might have tended to avoid a very serious crisis.

Up to this point, therefore, the "Tageblatt" had summed up, as regards the July conversations, rather in your favour and against Herr von Kiderlen-Waechter; it then proceeded to deliver one or two criticisms of your attitude. They consisted mainly of two points. Firstly that while pleading anxiety with regard to German designs on Morocco, which was obviously feigned, as you knew perfectly well that no such designs were entertained, your real preoccupation and your real reasons for interference, were your fears lest Germany should acquire the Coast of French Congo. Secondly that your utterances indicated that Great Britain claimed the right to a deciding voice in the disposal of territory in every corner of the world.

([1]) [*v. supra*, pp. 725–35, No. 721.]
([2]) [*v. supra*, p. 328, No. 347; and p. 334, No. 356.]

The " Frankfurter Zeitung " treated your speech with great reserve and confined itself to stating the opinion that it would not much contribute to the improvement of the relations between the two countries.

The " Börsen-Courier " had an article on your speech in which not a single pleasant word is to be found. It complained that your speech was not what Germany had had a right to expect. You had confined your remarks to the episodes of July alone and had thrown no light whatever on the broad question of Anglo-German relations. Therefore your speech was not calculated to induce people in Germany to change their opinion with regard to you and your colleagues. You had attached no weight to the feeling aroused in Germany by the French proceedings in Fez, nor had you given any explanation as to why these proceedings had been regarded so benevolently by the British Government and British public opinion, while the action of Germany in sending a ship to Agadir had been regarded with so much distrust and suspicion. Further you had said nothing to remove the impression that you had intended to oppose the alleged far-reaching demands of Germany with regard to French Congo. The article also found fault with your defence of Mr. Lloyd George's speech and said that what was chiefly to be condemned in your speech was that you had not uttered one word of reproof for the provocative and insulting interpretation which had been given to Mr. Lloyd George's remarks by the British and French Press. Finally the article repeated that your speech was not calculated to improve Anglo-German relations, and said that for the moment it supposed Germany must rest content with the knowledge that the Franco-German arrangement meets with your approval and that you desired that the present tension between Great Britain and Germany should be relaxed.

The " Vossische Zeitung " is not so unfriendly as might have been anticipated from its previous utterances. Its first criticism is directed against your statement in regard to the action of the German Government in publishing conversations with you without having previously obtained your concurrence. In this connection it quotes from a speech made by Prince Bismarck in 1885 in which the British Government was reproached with publishing confidential conversations, and it says that England has no right to complain now if other nations make use of the right which she herself had exercised.

It goes on to admit that, so far as could be judged from the telegraphic reports, your tone in speaking of the differences of opinion between England and Germany was polite, " or that you at least rejected any policy which implied a challenge to Germany."

It then points out the discrepancies between the accounts given by you and by Herr von Kiderlen, in that the latter made no mention of the conversations which took place on July 3rd, 4th and 12th. Presumably, it says, the importance of these conversations was differently estimated in Berlin and in London. The German Secretary of State laid stress on the absence of an enquiry, the British Minister on the failure to furnish information. It still remained an enigma what gave rise to the British pronouncement at the close of the " period of silence." As regards Mr. Lloyd George's speech it was only natural that the British Government should have denied that it was of a threatening character. They had already attempted to defend it as being reasonable and had avoided everything which might have the appearance of undue yielding. Germany on the other hand refused to authorize the use in Parliament of the information that she had no designs on Moroccan territory since it would otherwise have appeared as if this declaration had been the result of Mr. Lloyd George's speech. Whilst then both sides were attempting to avoid the appearance of weakness war became even more imminent, and in spite of your tribute to the skill of the diplomatists who brought about the agreement between France and Germany, the credulity with which British statesmen accepted the accusations levelled against German policy could hardly have contributed to facilitate the maintenance of peace. It was difficult, it said, to make advances when they may be represented, even though falsely, as the result of outside pressure.

After mentioning your hope that the relations between the two countries might improve and your statement that England, whilst holding to all her old friendships, would gladly have intercourse with Germany on a footing of equality, the article says that it was nothing but equality that the German people had claimed. Germany made no more bids for friendship, she did not expect a declaration of affection to ensue after ten days. So far as was to be seen from the telegraphic report at present to hand your speech would not affect the political situation and political feeling.

For some reason or other the concluding part of your speech, that is to say the part dealing with the Imperial Chancellor's speeches was not given out by the Wolff Bureau last night with the rest of the speech, so that the morning papers had not seen it when they made their comments this morning. The "Tageblatt" in its evening issue calls attention to this and, though it says that the addition of the missing part makes no material change in the impression produced by the first part, still it must be admitted that the concluding part of your speech "does not make too unfavourable an impression." To this somewhat faint praise, however, it adds that the effect of the speech was not altogether "unsympathetic" as it was always "sympathetic" to find a Statesman who knew exactly what he wanted. "We do not exactly want," it continues, "the same as Sir E. Grey does, his point of view is in fact widely different from ours, but we recognise that he stated his views logically and with both clearness and dignity. Certainly the tone of his speech was somewhat reserved and cool, but we prefer that to a lot of fine phrases which say nothing and convince no one."

The "Tägliche Rundschau" said that the formal and polite tone of your speech gave emphasis to the studied reserve of your observations with regard to Germany, and added that as you were unable to hold out any immediate hope of improvement in Anglo-German relations, it was just as well that you made no attempt to draw a veil over that fact by means of resounding phrases. At any rate Germany now knew how they stood with regard to Great Britain. It added that the most important sentence of your speech was that concerning the stability of the Triple *Entente*, in which you stated that those who wished to be on friendly terms with Great Britain must also be friends of her friends.

The "Hamburger Nachrichten" said that the reasons you gave for desiring to intervene in the Franco-German negotiations were not convincing, but that on the whole the tone of your speech was not unsatisfactory, as it showed at all events that His Majesty's Government had no desire to accentuate the differences between the two countries.

The "Post" found much to criticize in the policy of His Majesty's Government and harped on the well-worn theme of Great Britain's desire to prevent Germany from obtaining a place in the sun. It also pointed out that your utterances confirmed the idea that in the Morocco negotiations Great Britain was all along the real opponent. "It was England," it said, "that put the drag on those negotiations and hindered us from obtaining a favourable settlement with France. England had threatened us, humiliated us and beaten us. That neither can nor will be forgotten by a free and independent country like Germany." Nevertheless the "Post" pays a high tribute to your speech and to that of the Prime Minister and to the general high level of the debate in the House of Commons.

This is what it says :—

"When we compare the course of the debate on Moroccan affairs in the Reichstag with that of the House of Commons we have reason to regard the latter with feelings of profound envy. In England a skilful statesman discussed an extremely difficult question on broad and stately lines. Both Sir E. Grey's speech and that of the Prime Minister were clear, elegant in form and breathing the very spirit of independence; every word was well weighed and dictated by statesmanlike wisdom. Their speeches were listened to by the House with the earnestness which the occasion required and were received with expressions of the highest approval. How different was the scene in the German Reichstag. The best friend of the Chancellor cannot say that his speeches on the Morocco question were either skilful, statesmanlike, or successful. Twice during his speech his utterances were received with derisive laughter by the Reichstag and at its conclusion there was an icy silence." After a short and scornful reference to Herr von Kiderlen's failures as an orator, the article continues:—"The regrettable difference between the two debates is easily explained. In England two really gifted statesmen defended their successful policy with skill and tact; whereas in Germany men of the best intentions, but lacking the necessary ability, had endeavoured to justify a faulty policy by faulty means."

A Berlin telegram, published by the "Kölnische Zeitung" last night says that anyone who expected that your speech would reveal that British policy had taken a new direction must have been disappointed. The English Minister was satisfied with the policy hitherto pursued and even the Opposition expressed its approval of it. It had been repeated over and over again that England was animated by no unfriendly intentions towards Germany and that she had never thought of hampering the Franco-German negotiations but the fact remained that Germany met with opposition almost every time that she attempted to take action in any part of the world. The telegram goes on to observe that you had failed to make it clear from what source you had derived the information as to the alleged intentions of Germany in regard to a partition of Morocco, and it expresses astonishment that credence should have been attached to coast rumours as to the landing of German crews and the hoisting of the German flag. It could only be explained by a pronounced irritation which appeared to have often assumed a personal form. It seemed as though people in England had from the first been very sensitive because they had not been admitted to the Franco-German negotiations and that this sensitiveness had considerably increased during the further progress of events.

As regards the future it says that the desire expressed by you to live on terms of equality with Germany was in entire accordance with German wishes, but in spite of this theoretical agreement Germans had not always had the feeling that they were treated by England on an equal and friendly footing. This fact could not be got over and it explained the embittered feeling prevailing in Germany.

Germany, it continues, also did not believe in the possibility of a violent hastening of improved relations with England, but at the same time it was convinced that an improvement could only be slowly effected even if England showed herself a little better disposed towards Germany and did not always place difficulties in the way of German aims even when no British interests were involved. The "mischievous influence" of which you spoke was not to be sought in Germany, for all her interest pointed to the pursuit of a peaceful development and the avoidance of collisions so long as this was compatible with her dignity and position as a Great Power.

In a later edition, the "Kölnische Zeitung" says that after your utterances, which promised a peaceful solution of the tension, the armament competition must begin again with increased vigour. England evidently regarded with suspicion the German declarations as to the dispatch of the "Panther." This suspicion, for which no reasonable ground was to be perceived, was not mentioned in so many words in your speech, but it took the form of an expression of anxiety in regard to England's position as a Great Power. From your utterances it was evident that England continued to stand shoulder to shoulder with France, not only in the sense of a justifiable friendship, but also in the sense of a diplomatic demonstration directed against the German Empire.

As you will have seen from the above extracts your speech has met with a very mixed reception. Even such praise as has been accorded to it has been tempered in nearly every case by a certain amount of cavilling. I hope however that after a little time for reflection the cavilling will cease and that your straightforward and frank utterances will meet with the appreciation which most of those who are now attacking them are probably fully aware that they deserve.

I have not yet heard any official opinion of your speech, but I trust that it is not represented by the Article in the "Lokal-Anzeiger" of which I have the honour to enclose a translation.

I have, &c.

W. E. GOSCHEN.

Enclosure in No. 723.

Translation of Leading Article in the "Lokal-Anzeiger" of November 29, 1911.

What is bound to strike everyone most in Sir Edward Grey's speech is his confirmation of the two facts—(1) that on July 1st he was informed by the German Ambassador of the reasons why Germany was sending a warship to Agadir, and (2) that he was kept *au courant* with the progress of the negotiations in the most loyal and conscientious manner by the French Government. Sir Edward Grey must therefore also on July 21 have been fully informed by the French Government as to what compensation Germany had actually demanded and whether precise demands had really already been made; he preferred, however, to appear to the German Ambassador to be quite uninformed, and in the most unusual manner, to say the least of it, to have supported the mistrust felt by his Government with regard to the official declaration of the German Government by exercising his influence on the views of the Press. It is equally new in diplomatic usage to expect that a formal and official statement should be characterised by a later statement as "final." According to our usage an official statement can only be final. The situation in July was actually as follows :—

In the period between the 1st and 21st July Germany first attempted to convince her French neighbour, who was holding obstinately to the treaty of 1909, of the need for fresh negotiations, and a feeler was put out for a suitable basis for an understanding. This basis had not yet been definitely discovered by July 21; the negotiations hung fire; neither France nor Germany were able to make any positive communication to England respecting the basis of the understanding which they were striving to bring about, and that aroused the suspicion in England that France and Germany might be able to come to a rapprochement, leaving England out of it and pushing her on one side. Lloyd George was therefore put forward, to whose speech only the most meagre reference was made by the British Secretary of State in the House of Commons.

That which is bound to calm that portion of Germany [*sic*] public opinion, which would not believe in the firmness of the German Government, is the English confirmation of the fact that the action of Germany against Lloyd George's speech was by no means tame but, according to Sir Edward Grey's words, extremely sharp. And it could not be otherwise, for the lasting impression of the events of the last months must, even after the recent debate in the House of Commons, be that England's attitude with respect to us during the whole crisis was unnecessarily and aggravatingly unfriendly, not to say arrogant. The fiction that England was the last and only Court of Appeal in all questions appertaining to the political possession of harbours and coasts, was also on this occasion fully maintained by the British Government. That Government did not attempt by a single word to refute the general belief in an immediate outbreak of hostilities against Germany in the event of her not arriving at a settlement with France, although it would have been easy for her to do so already in July by simply pointing out that a Conference in such case would become necessary. Instead of censuring Captain Faber's speech for having excited public opinion, it would have been better if Sir E. Grey had refuted the allegations brought forward by Captain Faber,([3]) for although during the whole crisis no English and also no German warship had been placed on a war footing and no other preparations for war worth mentioning had been made, his own country was allowed to believe the whole time, and the belief is still allowed to remain

([3]) [v. supra, p. 731, No. 721.]

to-day that England was equipped for war and that she could 'have been compelled at any moment to draw the sword (for foreign interests). The British Government wilfully allowed the world to believe that there was a danger of war and is therefore responsible for that wave of frantic war fever which swept over the whole world in the last months.

The reference to the Bosnian crisis, so popular in England, is not quite apt. Absolutely no negotiations on the Bosnian question took place, after the annexation had been declared, which could be disturbed by foreign intervention and during the whole Bosnian crisis German statesmen abstained from mystic speeches and unfriendly demonstrations against other nations.

In the circumstances in which it was made and in view of the present mistrust which has been once again aroused against German policy, Sir E. Grey's speech could not have had any other effect than it has. Nothing else was expected in our Government circles. Anglo-German relations will for a long time to come not be particularly friendly, but they have become normal again—till the next crisis, which we hope is a long way off.

No. 724.

Sir E. Goschen to Sir Edward Grey.

F.O. 47978/46838/11/28.
(No. 401.)   *Berlin,* D. *November* 29, 1911.
Sir,   R. *December* 1, 1911.

With reference to my despatch No. 391 of the 23rd instant.([1]) enclosing translation of a semi-official communiqué in regard to the statement made by the Imperial Secretary of State for Foreign Affairs on the subject of Morocco at a secret sitting of the Budget Commission held on November 17th, I have the honour to report that the following notice appears in the "Berliner Tageblatt" this morning:—

"Wolff's Telegraph Bureau requests us to state that Herr von Kiderlen-Waechter had nothing to do with the communications published by the Bureau in regard to his statement in the secret sitting of the Budget Commission."

The fact remains that the semi-official "Norddeutsche Allgemeine Zeitung" published the complete text of the protocol of the sitting on the evening of November 23rd and that the same text is contained in a Parliamentary Paper of which I enclose a copy herein.([1])

I have, &c.
W. E. GOSCHEN.

([1]) [Not reproduced.]

No. 725.

Sir F. Bertie to Sir Edward Grey.

F.O. 47973/13751/11/28.
(No. 569.)   *Paris,* D. *November* 30, 1911.
Sir,   R. *December* 1, 1911.

I have the honour to transmit to you herewith a copy of the draft Convention between France and Spain respecting Morocco which, as I informed you in my despatch No. 561 Confidential of the 25th instant,([1]) M. de Selves promised to send

([1]) [*v. supra*, pp. 721–3, No. 716. The despatch was of the 26th inst.]

to me for your consideration. It was brought to me to-day by M. Geoffray, French Ambassador at Madrid who said that it was communicated to me " à titre officieux." He explained in reply to my enquiry as to the internationalization of Tangier that it would be the subject of an annex to the Convention. It was not quite complete as it required some amendments. He would communicate it to me to-morrow.

M. Geoffray informed me by direction of M. de Selves that he (M. de Selves) would be glad to have your observations on the Projet de Convention at as early a date as possible so that M. Geoffray might without undue delay return to Madrid to resume negotiations with the Spanish Government.

I have, &c.
FRANCIS BERTIE.

Enclosure in No. 725.

Avant-Projet de Convention Franco-Espagnole.

Préambule.

Le Gouvernement de la République française et le Gouvernement de Sa Majesté le Roi d'Espagne déclarent qu'ils demeurent fermement attachés au principe de l'intégrité de l'empire marocain.

Article 1er.

Le gouvernement français reconnaît qu'il appartient à l'Espagne de prêter dans la zone d'influence espagnole, son assistance au gouvernement marocain pour l'introduction de toutes les réformes administratives, judiciaires, économiques, financières et militaires dont il a besoin.

De même que dans la zone française, les règlements d'application concernant ces réformes seront arrêtés par le Makhzen; ils auront un caractère général et ne comporteront aucune clause spéciale relative à l'une ou à l'autre zone sans l'assentiment préalable de la puissance qui y exerce son influence.

Ils seront appliqués par les autorités marocaines et contrôlés par des agents de nationalité espagnole dans la zone espagnole.

Article 2.

La zone d'influence espagnole est déterminée de la manière suivante :

Au nord, par le littoral et les présides espagnols.

Au sud, partant de l'embouchure de la Moulouya, la limite remonte le thalweg de ce fleuve jusqu'à 2 km. en aval du gué de Mechra-klita, au nord de Moul-el-Bacha.

De là elle gagne par un parallèle les hauteurs de Djebel Fizen; elle suit l'alignement de la crête des hauteurs séparant les bassins de l'oued Kert et de l'oued Inaouen, laissant ainsi au sud de la vallée de l'oued Meknassa, pour gagner par la crête la plus septentrionale le Djebel Moulay Bouchta.

Cette limite est tracée sur la carte qui est annexée en deux exemplaires au présent accord.(²) Elle pourra, s'il devient nécessaire d'adopter de nouvelles précisions géographiques faire l'objet de rectifications opérées d'un commun accord entre les deux gouvernements, mais en se rapprochant le plus possible des données ci-dessus.

Tout le territoire marocain situé au sud et à l'est de cette limite constitue la zone d'influence française.

Article 3.

Les régions comprises dans la zone d'influence espagnole spécifiées à l'article 2 restent placées sous la souveraineté du sultan. Elles seront administrées par un haut-commissaire espagnol et par un khalifa nommé par Sa Majesté chérifienne et agréé par le Gouvernement espagnol.

(²) [Not reproduced.]

Le khalifa résidera à Tétouan; il sera muni d'une délégation générale et permanente du sultan en vertu de laquelle il exercera tous les droits appartenant au sultan tels que : nomination de fonctionnaires et agents chérifiens dans ladite zone espagnole, application des règlements, &c.

Le gouvernement espagnol déclare assumer la responsabilité de l'ordre et de la sécurité dans la région soumise à son influence. Il assurera l'application des traités, conventions et engagements antérieurement signés par le Makhzen, ainsi que l'accord du 4 novembre 1911 entre la France et l'Allemagne approuvé par Sa Majesté chérifienne tant au regard de l'Allemagne qu'en celui des autres puissances signataires de l'Acte d'Algésiras qui ont accédé au dit accord.

Article 4.

L'Espagne s'engage à n'aliéner ni à céder sous aucune forme, même à titre temporarire [*sic*], ses droits dans tout ou partie du territoire composant sa zone d'influence.

Article 5.

Afin d'assurer le libre passage du détroit de Gibraltar, les deux gouvernements conviennient de ne pas laisser élever de fortifications ou des ouvrages stratégiques d'aucune sorte autres que ceux déjà existants sur la partie de la côte marocaine comprise entre la Moulouya et le Loukos.

Article 6.

Ne se trouve comprise dans aucune des deux zones la ville de Tanger qui, conformément aux principes posés dans les accords de 1904 et de 1905, sera administrée par une municipalité conformément aux dispositions arrêtées dans le règlement annexé à la présente convention.(²)

Article 7.

Les écoles, les consulats et agences consulaires et tous les établissements espagnols et français actuellement existants au Maroc seront respectés dans l'une et l'autre zone d'influence.

Les deux gouvernements s'engagent à faire respecter dans leur zone la liberté et la pratique extérieure de tout culte existant au Maroc. Le gouvernement espagnol fera en sorte que les privilèges religieux conférés au clergé régulier et séculier espagnol soient désormais localisés à la zone d'influence espagnole.

Article 8.

Il ne sera apporté aucune entrave au passage des convois de ravitaillement destinés au Makhzen, aux voyages des fonctionnaires étrangers ou chérifiens qui se rendront de Tanger à Fez et inversement, non plus qu'aux passages de leur escorte, de leurs domestiques, de leurs armes et bagages. En ce qui touche le port d'armes on se conformera au règlement chérifien sur la matière.

Article 9.

Les crédits ouverts par l'article 6 de l'acte d'Algésiras pour la police des ports devant être épuisés au 1ᵉʳ janvier 1912, la police dans les villes de Larache et de Tétouan et dans la zone d'influence espagnole sera assurée par des troupes indigènes recrutées dans ces régions et organisées, comme il a été stipulé dans le traité hispano-marocain de 1910. Les effectifs de ces troupes seront fixés par le haut-commissaire espagnol et par le khalifa du Sultan.

(²) [Not reproduced.]

Article 10.

Les ressources constituées par les impôts et taxes prévus au traité hispano-marocain de 1910 seront affectées aux dépenses d'entretien de troupes visées à l'article précédent ainsi qu'au traitement des fonctionnaires chérifiens, aux dépenses de travaux publics et d'administration de la zone.

Article 11.

Il est stipulé que le gouvernement chérifien ne pourra être appelé à participer à aucun titre aux dépenses de la zone espagnole. Le gouvernement royal assumant les responsabilités visées à l'article 3 paragraphe 3 de la présente convention, le gouvernement chérifien ne pourrait être mis en cause ni supporter une responsabilité quelconque du chef de réclamations motivée[s] par des faits qui se seraient produits dans la dite zone.

Article 12.

Le gouvernement français et le gouvernement espagnol constatent que la création dans l'empire chérifien de zones d'influence ne peut porter atteinte aux droits, prérogatives et privilèges antérieurement concédés à des tiers pour tout le territoire de l'empire, par le gouvernement marocain.

En conséquence, (le Trésor français créancier d'une annuité de 2,740,000 francs), l'Administration du contrôle de la dette qui représente les porteurs des emprunts 1904 et 1910, la Banque d'Etat du Maroc, la Régie cointéressée des tabacs continueront de jouir dans la zone d'influence espagnole de tous les droits qu'ils tiennent des contrats qui les régissent, sans diminution ni réserves et sans que les délimitations de zone puissent faire obstacle à leur action, notamment en ce qui concerne la surveillance et la répression de la contrebande, les excédents de douane réalisés dans les ports.

Le gouvernement espagnol, responsable de sa zone d'influence, reconnaît expressément ces situations antérieures et s'engage à faciliter aux institutions ci-dessus le libre et complet exercice de leur droit.

Ces institutions pourront, d'accord avec le gouvernement chérifien et les deux puissances signataires modifier les conditions de leur fonctionnement en vue de les mettre en harmonie avec l'organisation territoriale de chaque zone.

En ce qui concerne les droits de douane à l'entrée et à la sortie, ils ne pourront être modifiés dans chaque zone que d'accord avec les deux puissances signataires, sous réserve des droits ci-dessus rappelés et les stipulations des traités et conventions en vigueur.

Article 13.

Le gouvernement espagnol s'engage à établir dans le délai de trois mois à dater de la signature de la présente convention le bureau de douane de Mellila dans les conditions prévues par la convention hispano-marocaine de 1910.

Article 14.

Les chemins de fer seront placés pour tout l'Empire sous l'autorité du ministre des travaux publics chérifien. Il en sera de même du service des postes et des télégraphes chérifien. Les tarifs et le régime administratifs seront unifiés sur toute l'étendue du territoire marocain. Le personnel local et les agents d'exécution étrangers seront recrutés suivant les zones parmi les ressortissants des deux puissances signataires.

Article 15.

Par dispositions spéciales et en dérogation des stipulations de l'article précédent résultant des engagements intervenus entre la France et l'Allemagne relativement à la construction d'une ligne directe de chemin de fer de Tanger à Fez, le gouvernement espagnol donne son adhésion à la construction immédiate de la dite ligne.

Les études de cette ligne et la surveillance des travaux seront assuré[e]s par le gouvernement chérifien qui choisira tels organes d'exécution qui lui paraîtront convenables.

Les travaux seront mis en adjudication conformément à l'article 6 de la convention franco-allemande du 4 novembre 1911.

En ce qui touche l'exploitation de la dite ligne, le gouvernement chérifien en déterminera librement les conditions, conformément au paragraphe 3 du même article 6.

Le gouvernement chérifien ou la Compagnie à laquelle il aura concédé l'exploitation de la ligne auront la faculté de prendre toute mesure de police et de garde que comportera l'exploitation et la surveillance de la ligne.

Article 16.

Les puissances signataires s'engagent à prêter dès maintenant, dans leurs possessions d'Afrique leur entier concours au Makhzen pour la surveillance et la répression de la contrebande des armes et munitions de guerre.

Lorsqu'il s'agira du droit de visite dans les eaux territoriales marocaines, les deux gouvernements établiront d'un commun accord les règles à observer pour l'efficacité de la répression en se conformant aux règlements douaniers chérifiens.

Article 17.

Les différends qui viendraient à s'élever entre les parties contractantes au sujet de l'interprétation et de l'application des dispositions de la présente convention et qui n'auraient pas été réglés par la voie diplomatique seront soumis à un tribunal arbitral constitué dans les termes de la convention du 18 octobre 1907 ; un compromis devra être dressé et il sera procédé suivant les règles de la même convention en temps qu'il n'y serait pas dérogé par un accord exprès au moment du litige.

Article 18.

Toute clause des traités, conventions et accords antérieurs qui seraient contraires aux stipulations qui précèdent sont abrogés.

MINUTES.

Under this draft convention the Spanish zone would be restricted to the northern portion only of Morocco; the part allotted to Spain under the 1904 convention in the south-west of Morocco, including Iffni, would be absorbed by France.

The maps in our possession do not show the Djebel Mulai Bouchta which is to be the point where the southern boundary of the Spanish sphere is to reach the Atlantic. But the general description of the line (in article 2) does not seem to differ widely from that adopted in the 1904 convention.

The proposal that Spain should now give up the southern sphere originally assigned to her, does not seem unreasonable provided that Spain after parting with it is not called upon by Germany for further concessions to that Power. The attitude of Germany is for the present an unknown quantity.

The Sultan's authority is not only in theory maintained, but is to be exercised by Moorish officials. That is probably a prudent arrangement, though a clearer situation would have been created if the precedent of Cyprus had been followed, and France and Spain had undertaken with the Sultan's authority, the absolute " occupation and administration " of their respective spheres. This however would have deprived the Sultan in the eyes of the natives of every right of sovereignty, and may well be considered to be too drastic and difficult a change.

It is a satisfactory arrangement that in the Spanish zone the Moorish Khalifa is to reside not at Tangier but at Tetuan.

All previous and existing Moorish treaties remain operative. This secures the rights of the treaty Powers (art. 3).

Spain renews the engagement not to alienate any portion of her sphere (art. 4).

Article 5, forbidding the erection of any new fortification or works, is somewhat categorically worded. The principle is correct. The wording might be held to prevent Spain from strengthening her existing batteries at Melilla! But this clearly is not intended.

Art[icle] 6, provides for the internationalization of Tangier. But all details are relegated to a separate agreement, of which the text is promised for tomorrow.

The financial arrangements appear, so far as is possible to judge on a rapid perusal of the articles (9–11) to be reasonable.

Art[icle] 12 provides for the maintenance on their present basis of the State Bank, the Control of the Debt, and the Tobacco Régie, as well as the Customs Tariff, subject in all cases, to fresh agreements between all the treaty Powers. This is as it should be.

Art[icle] 14 may possibly cause some difficulties. It stipulates for unified railway, post and telegraph services under the authority of the Moorish gov[ernmen]t. Presumably such authority can only be exercised through the two Khalifas' residing respectively in the French and Spanish zones.

Art[icle] 15 reserves the Tangier to Fez railway for special treatment. This will no doubt give rise to much discussion at Madrid. I see no objection to the general principles laid down, except that whilst the Moorish gov[ernmen]t and the Railway Co[mpany] are authorized to police the line (presumably by the aid of French and Spanish police forces in the respective zones) there is no indication as to who is to exercise that right in Tangier where the principal terminus will be. It seems to me important that when arrangements are made for the police at Tangier it should be placed so far as possible under the international municipality, and that neither France nor Spain should have the policing of the terminus.

On the whole, and on a rapid survey of the articles, which must be rather perfunctory, I should say that they offer a satisfactory *basis of discussion* with Spain, but that H[is] M[ajesty's] G[overnmen]t cannot well definitely commit themselves to a final approval without further opportunity of study and examination and without some indication of such objections, if any, as may be raised by Spain.

Seen by Sir E. Grey.

See tel[egram] to Sir F. Bertie, No. 329 of today.([3])

E. A. C.
Dec. 1.

([3]) [*v. infra*, p. 748, No. 727.]

No. 726.

Sir E. Goschen to Sir Edward Grey.

F.O. 48297/47677/11/28.
(No. 405.) Confidential.   *Berlin,* D. *November* 30, 1911.
Sir,   R. *December* 4, 1911.

Since writing my despatch No. 400 of the 29th instant([1]) I have not noticed any improvement in the tone of the German press with regard to the policy of His Majesty's Government as set forth in your speech. The chief complaint now seems to be that as Great Britain had no secret agreement with France providing for mutual support nor any military convention with that Power, her action in endeavouring to intervene in the Franco-German negotiations and her readiness to give France military and naval support, as shown by Captain Faber's speech,([2]) and by the mobilization of the Fleet, had been clearly dictated by hostility to Germany. This conclusion does not seem to be logically sound or to be justified by the premisses, but it is the opinion most generally in vogue here, at all events in German journalistic circles.

The "Germania" is especially strong on this point of the policy of His Majesty's Government being dictated by hostility to Germany, and not by any Treaty obligations to support France, and couples with this complaint the indictment, made so freely in the German Press, that in your speech you made it more clear than ever that Great Britain had no intention of abandoning her pretensions to have the final word in the disposal of territories all over the world. The "Germania" says that this attitude does not in the least harmonise with the language in which you were good enough to state that Great Britain claimed no predominance in international affairs and that Germany had equal rights to make her voice heard. "The fact is" the

([1]) [*v. supra*, pp. 736–41, No. 723.]
([2]) [*v. supra*, p. 716, No. 711, and *note*.]

" Germania " says, " that last summer Great Britain assumed the position of the leader of the world, and, what is far worse, Sir E. Grey's speech clearly shows that the British Government consider that attitude a perfectly natural one to adopt. We must draw our own conclusions as to the consequences of this attitude, and we must admit that the conflict between the two nations is not only not set aside, but has the appearance now for the first time of becoming inevitable. Or should we wait to see whether the proud Englishmen will perhaps become a little more modest in their pretensions? Previous experience shows that that would be a foolish proceeding. Or are we to suppose that the German Michael intends humbly to submit to being placed under the guardianship of England? That of course is utterly out of the question. Therefore it must come sooner or later to a thorough clearing up of accounts (Abrechnung) between the two nations. As for Sir E. Grey's fine phrases about new friendships and understandings we attach to them, in the face of the logic of events, very little importance or—none whatever. How is it possible for Great Britain to come to an understanding with Germany when Downing Street founds its policy towards us upon mere uncontrollable rumours. Sir E. Grey must himself admit that that was what happened in the summer."

I have ventured to bring this article to your notice as in my despatch under reference, I omitted to make mention of the opinions held by the Party of the Centre, of which the " Germania " is the representative organ.

The belief that in your conversations with Count Metternich you founded your reference to the unacceptable German demands for compensation in the Congo upon newspaper reports only, is common to the whole German Press. This belief has always existed, but in any case it was confirmed by the omission in the German translation of your speech of the words: " And, indeed, it was the case." As the Berlin correspondent of the " Times " rightly pointed out, this omission has tended to delude public opinion on the point.

I have unfortunately not had an opportunity of seeing either the Chancellor or the Secretary of State for Foreign Affairs since you made your speech, but from conversation with others I have gathered that while admitting that your speech was unimpeachable in form and friendly in tone, the feeling in official quarters is that it will not have the desired effect of calming public opinion here. From a person, who is in constant communication with the Chancellor, I hear that the latter fully appreciated the references which you made to him and his speeches in the Reichstag, but rather wished that you had thought of all his genuine efforts to come to a better understanding with England before assenting to Mr. Lloyd George's speech. It is possible of course that the Chancellor said this, but I rather think that the view expressed was that of my informant, for he went on to say that the speech in question had placed the Imperial Chancellor in a most difficult position and that it was entirely owing to Mr. Lloyd George's utterances that His Excellency had had to sit down after a long and important speech in the Reichstag without one single encouraging cheer from any side of the House. This deadly silence, my informant said, was the reply of the representatives of the Nation to Mr. Lloyd George's speech. He added that it was owing to this speech that your own speech had been so much criticised in the German Press and that the rather unfriendly reception accorded to it had surprised no one.

My informant desired that his remarks should be treated as confidential.

The forthcoming debate on Foreign Affairs in the Reichstag will probably enlighten us more with regard to official opinion; in the meantime it is obvious that some time must elapse, probably until the Reichstag elections are over, before any real improvement can take place in the relations between the two countries.

I have, &c.

W. E. GOSCHEN.

No. 727.

Sir Edward Grey to Sir F. Bertie.

F.O. 47973/13751/11/28.   *Foreign Office, December* 1, 1911.
Tel. (No. 329.) R.   D. 5 P.M.

I regard it as very satisfactory that French Gov[ernmen]t intend to make proposals to Spain upon basis of 1904 agreements. I have not had time to study carefully the French draft,(¹) which was only received here this afternoon, and it would not be fair to regard us as pledged to all details till Spain has had an opportunity of expressing her view. But the draft is one to which I will give general support as affording a fair basis for discussion after it has been presented to Spanish Gov[ernmen]t. I notice that there is no mention of Ifni, which I thought France was willing to leave to Spain. I presume that point is not decided adversely. We shall be ready to give our good offices if required when discussion takes place at Madrid. Spain will of course expect to be assured that Germany will not also claim compensation from her as well. You should inform M[inister for] F[oreign] A[ffairs] of my views.

(¹) [*v. supra*, pp. 742–5, No. 725, *encl.*]

No. 728.

Sir F. Bertie to Sir Edward Grey.

F.O. 48398/47849/11/28.
(No. 573.)   *Paris*, D. *December* 2, 1911.
Sir,   R. *December* 4, 1911.

Monsieur Millerand, who has been taking an active part in the discussion of the recent Franco-German Treaty in the Commission for Foreign Affairs, yesterday gave an address to the Socialist-Radical group of the Chamber on foreign affairs. He recommended the approval by Parliament of the Treaty, in spite of the drawbacks to it, which had been pointed out. Germany had received by it no privileges which other Powers did not share. France had secured a Protectorate over Morocco. It was inevitable that her action would at the beginning be embarrassed by the obstacles ("entraves") which were inherited by the present situation from the past. It would be for the French Government to realize fully this Protectorate by taking their time about it, as had been done in the case of Tunis. He called attention to the possibility that might arise, if care were not taken, of France as a result of the future agreement with Spain, being held responsible by other Powers for the latter country's proceedings.

England would have to be closely associated with the settlement to be reached with Spain for she was the "témoin" of French agreements with Spain in 1904. It was right that England should be so associated for a higher reason, namely for the sake of the "Entente Cordiale." It was the bounden duty of France to maintain and strengthen it and to go hand in hand with England in this as in all other questions of foreign policy.

I have, &c.
FRANCIS BERTIE.

No. 729.

Sir F. Bertie to Sir Edward Grey.

F.O. 48399/47805/11/28.
(No. 574.)   *Paris, D. December 2, 1911.*
Sir,   R. *December 4, 1911.*

I have the honour to transmit to you herewith a letter published in the "Temps" and addressed to the President of the Council by Baron d'Estournelles de Constant on the subject of the desire alleged to have been expressed at one time by Mr. Chamberlain to bring about the partition of Morocco between England and Germany.

The letter has reference to an article written by Monsieur Stéphane Lauzanne in the "Matin" which I forwarded to you in my Despatch No. 553 of the 25th ultimo.([1])

Monsieur d'Estournelles de Constant declares that no such desire existed on the part of Mr. Chamberlain in 1903 and 1904 and gives his reasons for making this statement.

Monsieur Stéphane Lauzanne writes a reply to Monsieur d'Estournelles de Constant in the "Matin" of to-day's date.([2]) He points out that the matter was brought up by Monsieur de Kiderlen-Waechter before the German Commission for Foreign Affairs, and that the views attributed to Mr. Chamberlain were held by him in 1899, if not in 1903. Monsieur Lauzanne quotes a speech made by Mr. Chamberlain on November 30, 1899, advocating an alliance between England, Germany and the United States.

I have, &c.
FRANCIS BERTIE.

Enclosure in No. 729.

Extract from "Le Temps" of December 2, 1911.

———

M. J. Chamberlain et la Question du Maroc.

M. d'Estournelles de Constant vient d'adresser au président du conseil la lettre suivante où il proteste contre une allégation récente à propos de la politique de M. Chamberlain, l'ex-premier ministre anglais [*sic*].

Monsieur le président du conseil,   *Paris, le 1er décembre.*

Pour justifier un nombre inconnu de traités secrets auprès desquels le "secret du Roi" n'est plus qu'un enfantillage, on crée des légendes. C'est dans l'ordre. On nous dit : le traité franco-anglais de 1904 avait pour objet, en réalité, de couper court à une manœuvre de l'Angleterre ou du moins du parti unioniste anglais lequel rêvait, en la personne de M. Chamberlain, de soustraire le Maroc à l'action française pour le partager entre l'Espagne et l'Allemagne. C'est cette conception machiavélique que le traité secret de 1904 a fait avorter.

Je dois protester, dans le double intérêt de la vérité et des bonnes relations franco-anglaises, contre cette invention démentie par les faits que vous connaissez comme moi-même. Je le dois d'autant plus que M. Chamberlain, malade, ne peut se défendre.

La vérité est qu'en 1904 M. Chamberlain n'a pas rêvé et ne pouvait rêver un partage du Maroc entre l'Espagne et l'Allemagne, pour plusieurs motifs, notamment :

1°. Tout le monde sait que le gouvernement dont il faisait partie considérait comme inadmissible la cession non pas de la moitié du Maroc, mais même d'un seul port du Maroc à l'Allemagne ; inutile d'insister sur ce point.

([1]) [Not reproduced.]
([2]) [Not reproduced, as sufficiently indicated above.]

2°. M. Chamberlain pouvait si peu songer, en 1904, à prendre parti contre la France qu'il s'était prononcé publiquement pour la politique de l'entente cordiale, l'année précédente, devant vous, devant moi, devant tous ceux de nos collègues français qui ont pris part à la réception grandiose du Parlement britannique, le 22 juillet 1903. Personne encore n'avait cru pouvoir prononcer ces mots : "Entente cordiale"; ce fut lui qui en prit l'initiative; le texte de son discours figure dans les bulletins de notre groupe, et ce discours fit sensation.

Ce n'est pas tout. En politique pratique, M. Chamberlain ne s'est pas contenté de cette manifestation et c'est lui qui le premier a demandé qu'elle fût suivie d'une sanction diplomatique : il ne l'a pas fait sans y être encouragé par ses collègues du cabinet, sans parler de l'entourage du roi; c'est lui qui a suggéré, réclamé verbalement et par écrit la réalisation d'un accord diplomatique franco-anglais. J'ai rendu compte de ces conversations et de sa correspondance personnelle avec moi au ministre des affaires étrangères par une communication publique du 3 août 1903 que tous les journaux ont reproduite. J'ai lieu de croire que cette lettre n'a pas été sans influence sur l'orientation des négociations engagées depuis lors.

Il est donc pour le moins étrange aujourd'hui, qu'on cherche à égarer l'opinion au point de lui persuader que l'entente cordiale ne serait l'œuvre que d'un parti alors que, réalisée par les uns, préparée par tous, elle est l'œuvre de l'Angleterre et de la France.

Veuillez, &c.
D'ESTOURNELLES DE CONSTANT.

MINUTES.

The question at issue is only of academic interest. We have no official record of this alleged plan of Mr. Chamberlain.

G. H. V.
4.12.11.

But historically of much interest, as showing why the French were particularly anxious to conclude an agreement with this country.

E. D.
4.12.11.
E. A. C.
A. N.
W. L.

No. 730.

Sir E. Goschen to Sir Edward Grey.

F.O. 48299/21735/11/28.
(No. 407.)   *Berlin,* D. *December 2, 1911.*
Sir,   R. *December 4, 1911.*
I have the honour to forward, herewith, a despatch, as marked in the margin, which I have received from Captain Hugh Watson, Naval Attaché to this Embassy, relating to a conversation between His Majesty the Emperor and the Chilean Minister in Berlin on Naval ship-building.

I have, &c.
W. E. GOSCHEN.

Enclosure in No. 730.

Captain Watson to Sir E. Goschen.

(No. 32.) Confidential.
Sir,   *Berlin, November 27, 1911.*
I have the honour to report that I am informed on excellent authority that the Chilean Minister in Berlin had, about two months ago, an interview with His Majesty

the Emperor, which lasted about three-quarters of an hour, Herr Zimmermann of Foreign Office being present. The subject of the interview was naval. His Majesty spoke strongly of the excellence of German ship-building and said Captain Mischke, of the German-built "Von der Tann," whom His Majesty described as one of his best officers, had said that his ship could beat the "Minas Geraes" (a Brazil ship built in England) in an hour. His Majesty further remarked that they had many great secrets in German ship-building which people did not know of. His Majesty further alluded to there being thousands of English spies about. (The exact connection of this remark with the others I do not know, but it was made in connection with the foregoing remarks.)

On the Chilean Minister remarking that their naval attaché was given very few facilities for seeing the best German work, His Majesty said he would give orders on the subject. (I understand that the effect of such orders, if given, is not yet perceptible; probably because Chilean orders for ships have been placed in England. I have before reported on the attitude of German authorities towards their failure to get Chilean orders in my letter, Secret, of the 24th May last.([1]))

2. The interview shows not only His Majesty's great interest in the naval ship-building yards, but also is evidence that the supply of an adequate amount of work to these yards is a matter of considerable concern to His Majesty, and presumably to his responsible officials.

The incident bears out what I have before reported, that either Germany must from 1912 to 1917 keep her own annual naval ship-building programme up to previous years instead of reducing as at present proposed by fleet law, or get foreign orders if she is to avoid dislocation of the naval ship-building trade in the years that elapse before she can, under her "fleet law life" for an armoured ship of twenty years, commence her annual rate of replacement-building of her fifty-eight armoured ships of three armoured ships per annum after 1917.

The foreign orders do not appear, up to the present, to have come to Germany in sufficient amount to supply the six private ship-building yards in Germany, which, together with the two biggest Government yards, have been dividing the four armoured ships per annum between them for [the] last few years, and will now have only two to divide each year until 1918 if present navy law is adhered to.

That this result is causing great anxiety, both in view of the dislocation of the armoured ship-building trade that is bound to result from a reduction of present keen competition and in view of labour questions connected with the coming elections, is undoubted. The position of affairs naturally gives great point to the advocates of a further navy increase in Germany.

Even if, for political reasons, external or internal, the Government do not add armoured ships to the present number proposed for 1912 under the navy law (viz., 2), it is improbable that, after the elections and when political matters at home and abroad are calmer, the same policy will be pursued in 1913 and subsequent years; which policy, unless foreign orders are received, would emasculate the large naval ship-building trade of Germany, built up rapidly with expensive plant under the fleet law, and would render it totally unfitted by a loss of continuity of work to efficiently carry out the replacement-building of three armoured ships per annum that Germany will require after 1917.

3. The number of ships Germany must build after 1917 for replacement purposes under present fleet law, viz., 3, will bring a heavy burden on her possible naval opponents, especially if they have to make up leeway at the same time, or if Germany increases in any way or at any time on her fleet law, a contingency and possibility her present ship-building resources render her easily able to carry out by herself, without taking into account possible help from allies.

I have, &c.
HUGH WATSON,
Naval Attaché.

([1]) [Not reproduced.]

No. 731.

Sir F. Bertie to Sir Edward Grey.

F.O. 48609/13751/11/28.
(No. 576.)   Confidential.   *Paris,* D. *December* 3, 1911.
Sir,   R. *December* 5, 1911.

As I had the honour to inform you in my despatch No. 561 very confidential of the 26th([1]) ultimo M. Cruppi invited me to meet the President of the Council at dinner on the 1st instant. M. Cruppi's object in wishing me to meet M. Caillaux and the latter's intention in accepting M. Cruppi's invitation were I have no doubt to remove from your mind the bad impression which they realized must have been produced by M. Caillaux's imprudent language to me which I reported to you in my despatches Nos. 495 Confidential and 499 Confidential of the 3rd and 5th ultimo respectively([2]) and their desire to bring me round to some of M. Caillaux's modified views in regard to the negotiations with the Spanish Government on the subject of Morocco so that I might urge them on you as the reconsidered and essential and reasonable claims of the French Government.

No reference whatever was made during dinner to the question of Morocco. It was only after about an hour and a-half that M. Caillaux, seeing that I was not likely to start the subject, began it by observing that the reconsidered proposals of the French Government in regard to the Spanish zones in Morocco, which the Minister for Foreign Affairs must have communicated to me, had been drawn up with every desire to meet as far as possible the views of His Majesty's Government, which I had expressed to him so plainly (*si nettement*) and he hoped that they would be considered as satisfactory and be urged by them on the Spanish Government. I said that I had a general knowledge of the proposals but I had not gone into the questions raised by them. M. Caillaux stated that out of deference to the views of His Majesty's Government the French Government would abstain from claiming Larache and Alcazar. Ifni would out of regard to Spanish susceptibilities as being opposite to the Canaries be omitted from the compensation in the South which France would require, but such compensation would not suffice. It would be absolutely essential that the line of the Spanish zone described in the 1904 Agreement should be altered in the Lukkos district; guarantees must also be given for the security of the Tangier Alcazar railway, and for French commercial enterprise of all kinds in the Spanish zone. These requirements must be regarded as very moderate and the least that France had the right to expect for the sacrifices which she had made to Germany and which would benefit Spain. If after the construction of the Tangier–Alcazar–Fez railway the Spanish authorities threw difficulties in the way of its efficient working as the carrier of trade the result would be that that trade would find its inlet and outlet through Algeria or the Atlantic Coast under French authority which would be circuitous routes and not to the advantage to trade in general and to British interests in particular. It would therefore be necessary to have very real guarantees for a railway passing through the Spanish zone.

As during the conversation in which I took but little part and M. Cruppi acted and spoke as a moderator in the zeal and arguments of the President of the Council, and frequently insisted on the necessity of maintaining the *entente* intact, M. Caillaux frequently spoke of the concessions which he was offering to Spain, I reminded him that any compensations for France would be concessions from Spain as they would be derogations from the engagements of France towards Spain under the Agreements of 1904 to which England had been a party; and as he expressed the opinion that His Majesty's Government had unduly supported the Spanish case, on the principle —a mistaken one he thought—of taking the part of the weak against the strong, I told him that for reasons which I had on previous occasions explained to him the

([1]) [*v. supra,* pp. 721–3, No. 716.]
([2]) [*v. supra,* pp. 603–4, No. 618; p. 619, No. 627.]

general policy of England was no doubt to keep Spain in unison with her but that in the particular case of Morocco His Majesty's Government asked for no more than an observance by the French Government of their Treaty engagements of 1904 towards Spain and England with such variations as might be necessary for reasonable compensation to France for the advantages accruing to Spain through the change in the *status quo* resulting from the Franco-German Convention. Compensations must however be found where they would not be inconsistent with the important interests of Spain and England.

I have, &c.
FRANCIS BERTIE.

No. 732.

Sir F. Bertie to Sir Edward Grey.

F.O. 48610/48610/11/28.
(No. 577.) Confidential.   *Paris,* D. *December* 4, 1911.
Sir,   R. *December* 5, 1911.
Opinion in Paris appears to be divided on the question whether the Ministry will survive the interpellations on foreign policy which are expected to begin on the 10th instant.

There is a movement on foot in Parliament which receives considerable support to approve the Franco-German Treaty first, and then to continue the debate on foreign policy.

This would not suit the Ministry for its best safeguard for the present is to induce the Chamber to approve by one vote both the Treaty and the policy of the Ministry with regard to foreign affairs generally.

The Editor of the "Figaro" in the course of an article published to-day advocating the division of the debate into two parts, says :—"Mais que M. Caillaux n'oublie pas que l'Angleterre est l'associée de l'Espagne au Maroc, et qu'il se garde comme d'un crime contre la patrie, des pressions qu'il a un instant, hélas, exercées déjà, et qui abattraient, s'il les continuait, des humiliations ou des catastrophes incommensurables sur la France privée dès lors de tout appui."

I have, &c.
FRANCIS BERTIE.

No. 733.

Sir Edward Grey to Sir F. Bertie.

F.O. 47973/13751/11/28.
Tel. (No. 334.) R.   *Foreign Office, December* 4, 1911.
French Ambassador has now given me the draft proposals for Tangier and the police. I have said that I must have some days to study them. I have explained that you suspended action on my telegram No. 329,(¹) as you were sending further information about Tangier.

I think you can now safely give support to first document as a basis for discussion as in my telegram No. 329 saying that we must not be regarded as committed to details as we do not yet know what is the modification that the French desire of the 1904 line and the question of Ifni remains to be discussed. Reservation with regard to Spanish views is already made in my telegram No. 329.

(¹) [v. supra, p. 748, No. 727.]

It must also be understood that I can express no opinion yet about Tangier proposals.   (End of R.)

(Very Confidential.)

French Ambassador tells me that it is intention to leave Ifni as well as Alcazar and Larache to Spain, but that French Gov[ernmen]t do not wish to say so immediately.

No. 734.

Sir Edward Grey to Sir M. de Bunsen.

F.O. 48748/48748/11/28.
(No. 125.)
Sir,   *Foreign Office, December 4,* 1911.

· The Spanish Ambassador asked me to-day whether you would take part in the negotiations between France and Spain in Madrid, and said that if the French Government desired that you should do so the Spanish Government would be very glad that the negotiations should be *à trois.*

I replied that I was not yet sure as to this point; but I had contemplated that you should in any case be ready to use your good offices if they were required.

In reply to further enquiries from the Ambassador, I said that I had not yet read the actual proposals of the French Government as to Tangier; but the general lines of the Agreement as to Morocco were based on the Agreement of 1904, and were therefore satisfactory in principle.   Certain details of great importance had been reserved, and I was not so far aware of what the French proposals would be with regard to them.

[I am, &c.]
E. G[REY].

No. 735.

Sir Edward Grey to Sir M. de Bunsen.

F.O. 48919/48748/11/28.   *Foreign Office, December 6,* 1911.
Tel. (No. 102.)   D. 6·15 P.M.

As French Government are very willing and Spanish Gov[ernmen]t desire that you should associate yourself with their negotiations you may do so.

Confidential.

, Examination of French draft about Tangier shows that municipality proposed is not really international.   Draft is therefore inacceptable on this very important point. A despatch to Sir F. Bertie is being drawn up stating our objections: when this is ready they will be explained to you.

No. 736.

Sir F. Bertie to Sir Edward Grey.

F.O. 48927/13751/11/28.
(No. 583.)   *Paris,* D. *December 6,* 1911.
Sir,   R. *December 7,* 1911.

I had the honour to inform you by my telegram No. 198 of to-day's date([1]) that I had received this morning from M. Geoffray, in a letter dated the 4th instant a fresh edition of the Franco-Spanish Draft Convention respecting Morocco which

([1]) [Not reproduced.]

differed from the version forwarded to you in my despatch No. 569 Confidential([2]) of the 30th ultimo in respect to Articles 2 and 12, and I embodied in my telegram above mentioned a translation of the new version.

I enclose herein the text in French of the two articles in question.

I have, &c.
FRANCIS BERTIE.

Enclosure in No. 736.

Avant-Projet de Convention Franco-Espagnole.

Article 2.

La zone d'influence espagnole est déterminée de la manière suivante :

Au Nord, par le littoral et les présides espagnols.

Au Sud partant de l'embouchure de la Moulouia, la limite remonte le thalweg de ce fleuve jusqu'à l'alignement de la crête des hauteurs les plus rapprochées de la rive gauche de l'oued Defla. De ce point et sans pouvoir, en aucun cas, couper le cours de la Moulouia, la ligne de démarcation gagne aussi directement que possible, la ligne de faîte séparant les bassins de la Moulouia de l'oued Inaouen de celui de l'oued Kert, puis elle continue vers l'ouest par la ligne de faîte séparant les bassins de l'oued Inaouen et de l'oued Sebou de ceux de l'oued Kert et de l'oued Ouergha pour gagner par la crête la plus septentrionale le djebel Moulai-Bou-Chta. Elle remonte ensuite vers le Nord en se tenant à une distance d'au moins 25 kilomètres à l'est de la route de Fez à Ksar-el-Kébir par Ouezzan jusqu'au point le plus rapproché de la source de l'oued Loukkos. Elle est ensuite constituée par le thalweg de l'oued Loukkos dont elle descend le cours jusqu'à la rencontre d'un point situé à 10 kilomètres au sud de la ville de Larache. Elle suit ensuite ce parallèle jusqu'à la mer. La ligne générale de cette délimitation est tracée sur la carte annexée en deux exemplaires au présent accord.

Toutefois l'absence de connaissances géographiques précises sur la région montagneuse du Riff, ne permettant pas de définir cette limite exactement, elle sera déterminée, s'il y a lieu, sur le terrain par une commission de délimitation qui s'inspirera des modifications exposées ci-dessus.

Tout le territoire marocain situé au Sud et à l'Est de cette limite constitue la zone d'influence française.

Article 12.

Le Gouvernement français et le gouvernement espagnol constatent que la création dans l'empire chérifien de zones d'influence ne peut porter atteinte aux droits, prérogatives et privilèges antérieurement concédés à des tiers pour tout le territoire de l'empire, par le gouvernement marocain.

En conséquence, le trésor français créancier d'une annuité de 2,740,000 francs, l'administration du contrôle de la Dette qui représente les porteurs des emprunts 1904 et 1910, la Banque d'Etat du Maroc, la Régie co-intéressée des tabacs continueront de jouir dans la zone d'influence espagnole de tous les droits qu'ils tiennent des contrats qui les régissent, sans diminution ni réserve et sans que les délimitations de zone puissent faire obstacle à leur action, notamment en ce qui concerne la surveillance et la répression de la contrebande, les excédents de douane réalisés dans les ports.

Le Gouvernement espagnol, responsable de sa zone d'influence, reconnaît expressément ces situations antérieures et s'engage à faciliter aux institutions ci-dessus le libre et complet exercice de leur droit.

Ces institutions pourront, d'accord avec le Gouvernement chérifien et les deux puissances signataires modifier les conditions de leur fonctionnement en vue de les mettre en harmonie avec l'organisation territoriale de chaque zone.

([2]) [*v. supra*, pp. 741–5, No. 725, and *encl.*]

En ce qui concerne les droits de douane à l'entrée et à la sortie, ils ne pourront être modifiés dans chaque zone que d'accord avec les deux puissances signataires, sous réserve des droits ci-dessus rappelés et des stipulations des traités et conventions en vigueur.

A l'époque où le Gouvernement marocain pourra envisager l'éventualité de la conversion des emprunts de 1904 et de 1910, l'Espagne, en échange des perceptions douanières dont la zone espagnole bénéficierait, devra assumer une partie des charges de l'emprunt de conversion.

No. 737.

Sir F. Bertie to Sir Edward Grey.

F.O. 48928/1375/11/28.
(No. 584.)   *Paris,* D. *December* 6, 1911.
Sir,   R. *December* 7, 1911.

When I saw M. de Selves this afternoon the Spanish Ambassador had just been with him and had, so the Minister informed me, asked by direction of the Spanish Government whether the French Government would have any objection to Sir Maurice de Bunsen taking part in the negotiations about to recommence at Madrid between the French and Spanish Governments on the subject of Morocco. M. de Selves had assured him that the French Government, far from objecting to the British Ambassador joining in the negotiations, would welcome his doing so. I then informed M. de Selves that you had been glad to receive confirmation from me of the intention of the French Government to negotiate with Spain on the basis of the 1904 Agreements. You had not yet examined thoroughly the "Avant Projet de Convention"(¹) communicated to me by M. Geoffray on November 30 which reached the Foreign Office on December 1. You were not able therefore to give a definite opinion on the details of the Projet without knowing the views held in regard to it by the Spanish Government. You were, however, ready to give a general support to it as the basis of discussion with the Spanish Government, which would of course expect an assurance from the French Government that Germany will not demand compensations from Spain in the matter of Morocco.

You had noticed that no mention is made in the "Projet de Convention" of Ifni, which, together with Larache and Alcazar, are, in conformity with the assurances given by M. de Selves and the President of the Council, to be reserved to Spain.

I further stated to M. de Selves that the communication which I was making to him did not take into account the new text of Articles 2 and 12 which I received this morning from M. Geoffray in a letter dated the 4th instant, and which I had forwarded to you to-day.

I also informed M. de Selves that you did not consider that the proposals with regard to Tangier, as set forth in the Annex to the "Projet de Convention," were acceptable, and that several modifications would be required in them.

M. de Selves reminded me that he had communicated the Draft Convention and annexes to me for your observations. Larache and El Kazar would in conformity with the assurances which he had given to me, be within the Spanish zone of which the boundary would, as he had informed me, require modification in order by an easily established line to obviate frontier difficulties. He had no doubt that in this and other matters, including the question of Tangier, the French and British Governments would be able to come to terms.

(¹) [*v. supra,* pp. 742–5, No. 725.]

In order that M. de Selves might fully appreciate the purport and extent of the communication which I was authorized to make to him I gave him a Memorandum of it in French, of which after reading it he had a copy made as an *aide-mémoire,* returning to me the original.

I have, &c.
FRANCIS BERTIE.

<hr>

No. 738.

Sir E. Goschen to Sir Edward Grey.

F.O. 49074/49074/11/28.
(No. 415.)   *Berlin,* D. *December* 6, 1911.
Sir,   R. *December* 8, 1911.

I have the honour to report that yesterday the Imperial Chancellor addressed the Reichstag for the third time on the events preceding the Franco-German Morocco–Congo Agreement. A translation of His Excellency's speech is enclosed, herewith,([1]) and you will observe that it differs considerably both in tone and in the manner in which it was received in the Reichstag, from his first two speeches.([2]) In fact the best comment on his speech of yesterday is that it was greeted throughout with cheers from those quarters in the House where his first two speeches were received with such strong disapproval. This may be attributed to the fact that His Excellency dwelt with emphasis on the points which had formed the basis of the Conservative and Nationalist attacks on England, namely the prejudiced and provocative attitude of Great Britain towards Germany throughout the Morocco negotiations, the mistrust with which His Majesty's Government had received the German explanations and the general claim of Great Britain to have a deciding voice in the direction of the world's affairs.

In the short debate that followed, the Conservative speaker stated that he regarded the Chancellor's speech as a complete justification for the speech delivered by Herr von Heydebrand, and that appears to be also the view of a large portion of the Press.

The Chancellor's speech seems to have made a very favourable impression upon public opinion here, and, as far as I am at present able to judge, is hailed with satisfaction by the greater part of the Press.

I must reserve my own comments upon it for a later despatch.

At the conclusion of the Debate the Reichstag passed in all its readings a Bill proposed by the Budget Commission providing that the following sentence should be added to § 1 of the Protectorates Law :—

> "An Imperial Law is required for the acquisition and cession of a Protectorate or portions thereof. This provision does not apply to rectification of frontiers."

An Imperial message was then read by the Chancellor closing the present sitting. The Reichstag has however not yet been formally dissolved.

I have, &c.
W. E. GOSCHEN.

([1]) [*v.* immediately succeeding document. The first sentence of this despatch, with some alterations, was reproduced in *A. & P.* (1911), CIII, (*Cd.* 5994), p. 460. The rest of the despatch was omitted, but the translation was given in full.]

([2]) [*v. supra*, pp. 668–75, No. 674, *encl.*; and pp. 679–82, No. 677, *encl.*]

<hr>

No. 739.

Speech of the Imperial Chancellor, Herr von Bethmann Hollweg, December 5, 1911.([1])

(Translation.)

Gentlemen,

I rise to speak immediately after your reporter, in order to state first of all that the Federal Governments are prepared to agree to the proposal for the modification of the Protectorates Law. We consider with you that it is not only proper, but also desirable, that alterations in the extent of our protectorates should in future be dependent on an Imperial law.

I desire, further, at the outset to deal with the reproach contained in the oft-heard question : Why did the Government not do more for the information of public opinion? Why did they not attempt sooner to dissipate the depression and displeasure felt in large circles by correcting misapprehensions and throwing light on what was obscure? Gentlemen, the reason was not bureaucratic love of secrecy, which would have been particularly foolish in this instance. It did not come from any remissness on the part of the persons who deal officially with press matters. The true reason for the slight action taken by the Government to meet that dissatisfaction lay elsewhere, and was based on careful reflection.

The difficult nature of our negotiations, the secrecy which we demanded from France, the passionate excitement aroused by the attitude of England, imposed great restraint on us. The nation was certainly exposed thereby to a severe trial of patience. But, gentlemen, what must be our first consideration in critical times? Surely to arrive at the desired understanding with France and alone. To this supreme object we had to subordinate everything else, and especially consideration for the impatient and certainly comprehensible desire for more light on the diplomatic proceedings.

Gentlemen, had we, as has at various times been demanded in the commission, replied publicly to public utterances in England, and had we announced to the world the protest which we had lodged with the London Cabinet, we should not have rendered freer or more easy the course towards our goal; on the contrary, we should have barricaded it. We had especially to reckon with the reaction on public opinion in France. I do not believe that in such an event it would have been possible for the French Government to overcome the opposition to an agreement on the basis desired by us, and, gentlemen, do not forget that we had by our action begun a very difficult task, and had assumed a very great responsibility.

Certainly—and we foresaw it from the first—the feeling in our own country was bound to become through our reserve ever more and more excited and impatient, ever more critical of its own Government. That has been a great evil, and one difficult to bear. But we took it on ourselves and bore it in the hope that, after the conclusion of the business with France, we should succeed in reducing the patriotic excitement and critical zeal to proper proportions.

Perhaps, gentlemen, you will object that on the presentation of the agreement to the Reichstag the time had at least come to say everything which has subsequently been made known in the commission by the Secretary of State. Gentlemen, I will not argue with you whether the disclosures and indications made by me in the full sitting of the House were not sufficient, or whether they have been everywhere judged correctly and without prejudice. If I had foreseen what was said in England during the course of the proceedings of the commission in regard to certain preparations in September, and which was bound to increase considerably the excitement here, I would certainly then have not withheld any longer the publication which has now been made. It is not our fault if we have been now compelled, in order to allay unrest, to proceed to a publication which we had long delayed on well-considered grounds, and I note with satisfaction that this has also been understood in England.

([1]) [The translation referred to in the immediately preceding document has not been traced, and the text is here reproduced from the *Confidential Print*.]

As the course of the deliberations of your commission shows, our relations with England have hitherto played a large part in all negotiations in regard to our arrangements with France. The declarations of the English Minister are now also before us, and I gladly recognise that they are couched in a conciliatory tone. I, for my part, will not go further into the past than is necessary for a consideration of the future.

The English Minister for Foreign Affairs spoke quite openly of the apprehensions aroused in him by the dispatch of the "Panther" to Agadir, and by the plans of our Morocco policy generally. The advance of the French to Fez and the action of Spain had, apparently, aroused no apprehensions on the part of England as to their prejudicial effect on her Moroccan interests. I do not know on what the English assumption was based that we desired to create for ourselves a naval base on the Atlantic Ocean. What we really wanted with Agadir, England knew from the instructions sent to our Ambassador in London on the 30th June last, which have been made known to the commission. We had, therefore, on our side given no cause for doubt. France too, who was, indeed, most directly interested, and Russia, her ally, never distrusted our plans. But France was—Sir E. Grey has said so—during the whole course of the negotiations, in close communication with England and asked for England's advice in all questions which could affect English interests. In these circumstances it is difficult to understand how England could consider her interests threatened. These interests could indeed, since we were negotiating with France, not be endangered without the knowledge of France. If, however, in spite of all, doubts were entertained by England, either on account of rumours among the natives at Agadir, to which the English Minister alluded, or on account of press utterances, I would at all times have been ready to dispel these doubts if questioned by the English Government.

Gentlemen, the English Foreign Minister spoke of the period of silence from the 4th to the 21st July. Now this silence was a mutual one. Once only, on the 12th July, did the English Ambassador here speak to the Secretary of State of the possibility of a negotiation à trois in regard to Morocco, between Germany, France, and Spain, and added the remark that this would make an unfavourable impression in England. It was replied to the Ambassador on the same day as an official statement of the German Government that such an intention had never existed. In spite of its negative form, this reply had the very positive meaning that any apprehension on the part of England that we aimed at a partition of Morocco with Spain and France was baseless.

Our Ambassador in London had just as little opportunity of imparting information in reply to an enquiry on the part of the British Government. Sir Edward Grey stated in his speech that in his conversation with Count Metternich, on the 4th July, he had characterised the dispatch of the "Panther" to Agadir as creating a new situation, and that the British Government were disturbed on account of possible future developments directly affecting British interests. We could not see in this utterance any enquiry requiring an answer. The answer that would have been made, was made by Count Metternich himself on his own initiative. In his report of the 4th July he said :—

"I replied to the Minister that, according to my idea, the Imperial Government had absolutely no wish to exclude England from a new arrangement of things, or to prevent any possible safeguarding of British interests in Morocco."

But, even if this reply had not appeared to be sufficient, a further explanation could easily have been obtained by reference to us before the 21st July, the day of the next conversation between Sir E. Grey and Count Metternich and the speech of the British Chancellor of the Exchequer. Far be it from me to complain of the fact that this course was not adopted. For the choice of means, the interest of one's own country—in this case therefore England's interest—is the only deciding factor. I cannot, however, pass over the effects as they appear to me. And I must certainly say that, in my opinion, the tension and the fact that the situation had become more acute could have been avoided if greater confidence had been placed in our declarations of the 1st July, and if the period of silence had not been broken on the part of England by a prominent member of the English Cabinet.

Following the good example set by the English Minister, I will not enter into recriminations, for they will not help the future. I will, therefore, also not reopen the question of the effect of the above-mentioned statement on public opinion in Germany. I spoke about the feeling it caused three weeks ago, and it found still more passionate expression in speeches made in this House, speeches which—in this I cannot follow Sir E. Grey—cannot be placed on a parallel with the actual assertions of an English Member of Parliament respecting preparations for war in England. The English Minister will not be able to recognise, as we do, the justice of this feeling, which dominated a large section of our people, but he will at least find it intelligible, in view of the public demonstration made by the British Government on the 21st July. I would like to add a further observation, one which appears to me to be not without importance for the establishment of future relations. Sir Edward Grey said that the Chancellor of the Exchequer, Mr. Lloyd George, by his speech wished to make it clear, without provocation, that, where English interests were affected, England could not be treated as if she did not count. If the day ever came when that could no longer be clearly stated, then England would have ceased to exist as a Great Power.

Gentlemen, I claim the same right for Germany. When, however, I look back into the past, I find that the Moroccan complications arose because this right had not always been accorded to Germany. The year 1904, in which England and France disposed of Morocco without consideration for the interest which Germany had for the settlement of the Moroccan problem, was the *proton pseudos*. Out of this rose the necessity for us to go to Algeciras and then to Agadir, *i.e.*, the necessity for us to safeguard our economic interests ourselves, and to show the world that we are firmly resolved not to allow ourselves to be pushed on one side.

If, as the ultimate result of this, alleged or actual readiness for war ensued in England—which of these is true I cannot decide—and further an acute state of excitement arose, which the English Minister has called " political alcoholism," we can only note it with regret. But we must also refuse to take the responsibility for this just as we had to refuse to allow ourselves to be diverted from the path which the maintenance of our interests and the dignity of the Empire had marked out for us. That state of excitement led to playing with the idea of war. To a sober observer the facts, from a German point of view, are as follows :—

What did we negotiate about with France? About the cession of considerable political rights to France; that was not in opposition to the Anglo-French agreements of 1904. About the increased guarantees of our economic interests in Morocco, not only of our interests, no! of all Powers, including English interests, in accordance with the principle of the open door, which has been the fundamental principle of the English view of Government and law. About colonial compensations in Africa. And Sir Edward Grey expressly declared that England did not think of standing in our way if we wished to conclude peaceful agreements with other Powers in respect to Africa.

Our negotiations with France were also carried out by both sides in the most difficult moments, as has been proved, with the invariable good-will to arrive at a peaceful understanding. This was also not unknown in England, for Sir Edward Grey stated that it never seemed probable to him that the negotiations would be broken off.

And finally, as I proved in detail on the 9th November, we have attained the object that we had in view from the outset. This object did not directly affect any English interests, and therefore contains in itself the refutation of the English apprehensions. The best proof lies in the fact that England had officially expressed her satisfaction at the conclusion of the negotiations.

And in spite of all this, a situation has developed which, in English eyes, brought near a war against us, *i.e.*, a world war. If all the bearings run so hot, gentlemen, then the machine must have a serious defect.

The English Ministers have unanimously expressed a desire for better relations with us, and I associate myself entirely with this desire, which was also shared by the other speakers in the English Parliament. But I notice that although this desire has already been frequently expressed in recent years on both sides, and also in this House, yet we have had to go through what we have gone through.

My remark has been taken up in England that by the settlement of the Morocco question a " clear table " has been made in this respect between England and Germany also. The Englishmen speak of a " clean slate," of a slate that has been wiped clean. Gentlemen, this slate has been written on quite recently with a hard pencil, and the slate has become scratched in consequence. It must not be mistrust which guides the pencil, if the slate is to be covered with clear writing.

The English Minister for Foreign Affairs is right in seeing no aggressive designs behind Germany's growing strength, and I welcome the fact that in agreement with him the English Prime Minister rejects every thought of envy or ill-will towards the aspirations of our growing nation. We also, gentlemen, sincerely desire peace and friendship with England. But the actual development of good relations between the two countries will only keep pace with the desire in so far as the English Government is prepared to give by her policy practical expression to her desire for such relations.

Other nations, too, must reckon with the forward development of Germany. This development cannot be checked. In what spirit it is carried out is shown by the history of Germany for the last forty years. We shall be able to continue working in the same spirit if we keep ourselves strong. For in this, too, I agree with Sir Edward Grey: the strength of Germany is in itself a guarantee that no other country will seek a quarrel with us.

Permit me, gentlemen, to recall, in conclusion, something which I said recently. I said: " The dominant chord of the passionate feeling which prevails in wide circles is the will of Germany to enforce her position in the world with all her strength and capacity "; and I continued: " That was the good and great revelation which we have experienced, and which has supported me, though as far as words were concerned it was directed against me."

It is now a question of encouraging this feeling, and holding firmly to its dominant chord. We have passed through a difficult, serious, and threatening time. This the nation has rightly felt. May it now clearly perceive what it owes to itself. That is to say, neither depression nor provocative arrogance, but a free outlook, cool blood, calm strength, and steadfast unity in great national questions.

MINUTES.

Sir E. Goschen confirms the impression which the telegraphic summary of the speech has made here.

It has been decided to lay the Chancellor's and Herr von Kiderlen's previous speeches before parliament. The question arises whether the present speech should also be laid. If so, there will just barely be time to get out the bluebook before the debate in the House of Commons next Thursday.

E. A. C.
Dec. 8.

It would make the B[lue] B[ook] complete.

W. L.
A. N.

Herr von Kiderlen's published statement should be laid by itself as soon as possible without waiting for this last speech of the German Chancellor.

E. G.

No. 740.

Sir E. Goschen to Sir Edward Grey.

F.O. 49398/48824/11/28.
(No. 416.)
Sir,

Berlin, D. *December* 6, 1911.
R. *December* 11, 1911.

   In his speech of yesterday(¹) the Imperial Chancellor can hardly be said to have poured oil on the troubled waters. But it is only fair to His Excellency to say that had he done so, he would not have improved his position in Germany—a matter of the utmost importance to him at the present moment in view of the impending elections. As it is, the entire Press, with the exception of that representing the Socialist party, are loud in their praise of the Chancellor and state that he has quite atoned for the past and regained the position he had lost. His Morocco policy continues to be criticized to a certain extent, but as regards the language he held respecting England there is practically unanimity. It was the same in the Reichstag, when, as is pointed out cheerfully by a Conservative paper, the only member who said a word in defence of Great Britain, was the Socialist Herr Bebel. I fear that this is only too clear an indication of the present feeling of the country towards England. It is also a sign of the times that even among the Socialists, notwithstanding what is said in their papers, there is a feeling that pro-English and anti-war sentiments must not, in view of the coming elections, be too freely put forward in the addresses of the candidates, and that considerable care must be exercised in that respect.

   Altogether, considering the Chancellor has regained the confidence of the Conservatives by more or less confirming the opinions which had led to their attacks on England, and by his adroit use of Captain Faber's alleged revelations, his speech must be regarded as a great personal success from the point of view of German internal politics.

   If it were not for the fact that internal political exigencies required a certain amount of vigorous language on the part of the Chancellor, it might cause surprise that he took so much pains to temper his reciprocation of your and the Prime Minister's friendly words and wishes with certain qualifying observations of a not particularly cordial character. But again here he had to please the public, and as the phrase : '' We want deeds and not words,'' has been the stock phrase in almost every article which has been produced by the German Press during the last 2 months, he felt, I presume, that it would be well to bring it in and to amplify it in language suitable to the occasion. Still in the Chancellor's mouth it gained greater significance and what particular '' deeds '' His Excellency had in his mind has been a very fruitful source of discussion in Berlin diplomatic circles. My French colleague, who saw the Chancellor yesterday, asked His Excellency straight out what he had meant when he had spoken of the necessity for His Majesty's Government to give some practical evidence of their good-will. Had he had any special case in his mind? The Chancellor replied in the negative, adding that for the moment there was no particular question of importance being discussed between the two Governments. What he had meant to indicate was that in every part of the world where Germany had, or wished to create, interests she almost invariably met with opposition from England in one form or another. His words had been intended as a warning that unless that attitude of opposition was changed, it would be impossible for Germany and England to be friends. M. Cambon told the Chancellor that he still considered that his speech had been rather unnecessarily strong after the friendly words which had been spoken in the House of Commons and that as the Chancellor had such a high reputation for sincerity, his words carried so much weight that they could not fail to create a rather uneasy feeling abroad as to the present state of Anglo-German relations. His Excellency replied that no one was more anxious than he to have

(¹) [*v.* immediately preceding document.]

good relations with England, and no one had tried harder to establish them, but that for the moment those relations certainly left much to be desired in the way of cordiality and he would have lost any reputation for sincerity which he might possess if he had endeavoured to convey a different impression or if he had spoken otherwise than he had done.

As I said in my previous despatch on this subject, the best comment on the Chancellor's speech is to be found in the extravagant praise accorded to it by a Press which for the moment is manifestly ill disposed towards England. I do not propose to trouble you with a series of extracts from the newspapers, because they are all pitched in the same key, but I enclose a translation of a Berlin telegram published in the " Kölnische Zeitung " which, owing to its manifestly official source, may be of some interest.(²)

I cannot however resist from quoting the following gem from an article published in the Centre organ, the " Germania." It is a fair sample of the more exaggerated outpourings of the Conservative Press.

" For a gourmet capable of understanding and appreciating delicate satire, it was a real joy to notice the deliciously clever fashion in which the Chancellor copied the tone and form of Sir E. Grey's speech, and so drove the British Minister off the field with his own weapons. We hope that in Downing Street this irony will be appreciated at its full value. ' Fortiter in re suaviter in modo ' is the motto to be applied to the Chancellor's speech. While not using one single strong word against England, he told her any number of the bitterest truths, and launched arrows against her which will no doubt wound our dear cousins to the quick."

I have, &c.
W. E. GOSCHEN.

MINUTE.

The Chancellor unhappily takes up the traditional Berlin attitude that when Great Britain has interests to defend which somehow or other stand in the way of Germany's ambitions, then Great Britain must either abandon her interests or stand convicted of hostility to Germany.

E. A. C.
Dec. 11.
W. L.
A. N.
E. G.

(²) [Not reproduced.]

No. 741.

Sir M. de Bunsen to Sir Edward Grey.

Madrid, December 7, 1911.
D. 11·35 A.M.
R. 1·30 P.M.

F.O. 49043/13751/11/28.
Tel. (No. 94.)

French Ambassador having returned to Madrid first meeting between him and M[inister for] F[oreign] A[ffairs] was held yesterday afternoon at the Ministry of State. At the request of both parties I was present at the interview. French Ambassador handed to the M[inister for] F[oreign] A[ffairs] the draft Convention relating to the Spanish sphere of influence in Morocco. The M[inister for] F[oreign] A[ffairs] promised to examine it carefully but said that he could not enter upon the negotiations without receiving assurance that after ceding a portion of Spanish Southern zone to France Spain would not be called on to make a further cession to Germany in exchange for German recognition of new arrangements. French Ambassador pointed out that it would be useless to sound Germany with regard to her ultimate intentions at present stage and he suggested that negotiations should proceed and that before signature Spain and France might agree that the engagement involving cession of Spanish territory should be made conditional on Germany not exacting further compensation. M[inister for] F[oreign] A[ffairs] concurred. French Ambassador said he expected to receive within a few days regulations concerning Tangier mentioned in Article 6.

(Repeated to Paris.)

No. 742.

Sir Edward Grey to Sir F. Bertie.

F.O. 49037/48749/11/28.
Tel. (No. 338.) R.   *Foreign Office, December 7, 1911.*

Police in Morocco. Mandates to France and Spain for policing ports expire Dec[ember] 31. We understand that State Bank wishes to be informed before Dec[ember] 20 what arrang[emen]ts will be made after end of year, in regard to payment of officers and men at several ports. Please ascertain if French Gov[ern-men]t would be disposed to suggest to the Powers that mandates should be prolonged for six or three months. Such a prolongation would seem desirable.

No. 743.

Sir Edward Grey to Sir F. Bertie.

F.O. 48918/46431/11/28.   *Foreign Office, December 7, 1911.*
Tel. (No. 342.) R.   D. 10·15.

Your telegram No. 200.(¹)

You should inform financier that provided British capital participates on equal terms with foreign capital H[is] M[ajesty's] G[overnment] will, if the syndicate is supported by the French and German Gov[ernment]s, equally support it as far as they properly can.

(¹) [Not reproduced. It enquires whether His Majesty's Government have made any decision as to participation in the proposed syndicate for commercial undertakings in Morocco. *v. supra*, p. 707, No. 702; and p. 715, No. 710. *infra*, p. 768, No. 749.]

No. 744.

Board of Trade to Foreign Office.

F.O. 49100/46431/11/28.   *Board of Trade, D. December 7, 1911.*
Sir,   R. *December 8, 1911.*

I am directed by the Board of Trade to acknowledge the receipt of your letter of the 2nd December (No. 47480),(¹) with its enclosures, relative to a proposed Moroccan International Syndicate; and in reply, I am to inform you that the Board see no objection to the reply which Sir E. Grey proposes to make.

I am, &c.
H. LLEWELLYN SMITH.

(¹) [Not reproduced. *cp.* immediately preceding document, and *note*.]

No. 745.

Sir Edward Grey to Sir M. de Bunsen.

F.O. 49274/49274/11/28.   *Foreign Office, December 8, 1911.*
Tel. (No. 104.)   D. 6·45 P.M.

Spanish Ambassador says that impression made upon Spanish Gov[ernmen]t by French draft is exceedingly bad. Spain does not get, especially in control of customs the free hand in her sphere that would have been given her by the draft of September and that France will have in French sphere.

I replied that I had expressed opinion to the French that draft is a fair basis for discussion, but had not committed myself as to details pending expression of Spanish view and had observed that the question of Ifni remained for discussion. I expressed disappointment that Spanish Gov[ernmen]t showed no satisfaction that Larache and Alcazar about which they had felt such apprehension were left to them. I said I quite understood Spanish desire for as free a hand in their zone as French had in theirs, but the objections seemed to be points of detail. It would never do for Spain to reject the draft as not affording basis for discussion. I said you would be present at the next meeting at Madrid when I supposed Spanish objections would be stated and you would report to me what French Ambassador said in reply to them.

No. 746.

Sir F. Bertie to Sir Edward Grey.

F.O. 49674/13751/11/28.
(No. 588.)   *Paris,* D. *December 8, 1911.*
Sir,   R. *December 11, 1911.*

The President of the Council, whom I met last night at the dinner given by the Minister for Foreign Affairs in honour of the Russian Minister for Foreign Affairs, and who was most effusive in his manner, asked me whether His Majesty's Government had expressed their complete concurrence in the Franco-Spanish Draft Convention. He hoped that they were satisfied for the proposals were most moderate. I replied that you accepted the draft Convention in principle as a basis for discussion with the Spanish Government but the proposals concerning Tangier in the annex were not acceptable. His Excellency asked me in what respect. The French Government would be quite ready to modify them. I said that I had not yet received your views on the subject.

I have, &c.
FRANCIS BERTIE.

No. 747.

Sir F. Bertie to Sir Edward Grey.

F.O. 49675/13751/11/28.
(No. 589.)   *Paris,* D. *December 8, 1911.*
Sir :—   R. *December 11, 1911.*

The Spanish Ambassador having told me yesterday evening that he desired to have some conversation with me came to the Embassy this morning. He is an orator and speaks well but at unnecessary length. His discourse occupied over an hour, with few interjections from me. He began by thanking me on the part of the Spanish Government for what I had been able to do by your instruction to mitigate the cupidity of the French Government in Morocco. He said that the Avant Projet of Convention which the French Ambassador at Madrid had communicated to the Spanish Minister for Foreign Affairs(¹) had been a great disappointment to the Spanish Minister for Foreign Affairs. It might be treated as a base for discussions but it was unacceptable as it stood and would require much modification and Señor Garcia Prieto would prepare a Contre Avant Projet. The French Draft would put on Spain great responsibilities and give her but little authority to deal with them. The representative of the Sultan in the Spanish zone would be in reality supreme and he would depend on the Maghzen alias the French Government. What Spain required was an entirely free hand in her zone, just as free as that of France in the rest of Morocco. He understood that Larache and El Kazar would remain in Spanish hands and that compensation to France for her sacrifices in her Congo colony was to be found in the South. No mention was however made of any reservation of Spanish rights in the South and it seemed to be intended that Ifni should pass to France which would be quite inacceptable to Spain. M. Perez Caballero then proceeded to dilate on the grievances of Spain and the misdeeds of the French Government. He contended that no compensation was really due to France, for Spain had gained nothing from the Franco-German agreement. She would lose much of what she was really entitled to under her agreements with France. The French Government should have negotiated with the Spanish Government and have come to an agreement as to the respective positions of France and Spain in Morocco before settling with the German Government how Spanish rights were to be disposed of. He had urged this on M. Cruppi, but that Minister had turned a deaf ear to his representations. The Spanish Government had offered to take part in the expedition to Fez. Their offer had been rejected. He had warned M. Cruppi that if the French Government sent the expedition to Fez Spanish troops must of necessity occupy Larache and El Kazar in order to maintain the rights of Spain contingent on a change in the *status quo* in Morocco which would be entailed by the expedition to Fez. His warnings had been treated as bluff and the French Government feigned surprise when the Spanish Government acted as he had intimated they would do. Unfortunately Spain had neither a fleet nor an army to ensure respect for her rights by France. The allegations of Spanish negotiations with the German Government were false. Why had the French Government assumed to dispose of a right which was inalienable. France could not legally dispose of the right of pre-emption in regard to Spanish Guinea and the Spanish Government would be ready to refer the question and other matters at issue to a Court of Arbitration even to the French Court of Cassation as he had stated to the French Minister for Foreign Affairs and honourably abide by the decision. Moreover, Spanish Guinea and the island of Fernando Po were included in the agreement of 1907 by which France, Spain and England had bound themselves not to dispose of any of their maritime possessions in the Mediterranean and on the coast washed by the Atlantic. This agreement included the French, Spanish and British Possessions in the Gulf of Guinea. The German Government might perhaps not require from Spain the cession of Spanish Guinea on the present occasion, but it was evident that they contemplated doing so in the future on some pretext or another. M. Caballero then returned to the question of the position assigned to Spain in Morocco by the Draft Franco-Spanish Agreement. He said that it would be an impossible one and he trusted that the British Ambassador at Madrid would support the Spanish Government in their negotiations with the French Ambassador at Madrid with the object of rendering the position of Spain in Morocco tolerable and that I should be instructed to renew the representations in favour of Spain which he was thankful to say had already had some effect.

I said but little during the Spanish Ambassador's speech, except that I had not understood that the Spanish, French and British maritime possessions in the Gulf of Guinea had been considered by the Spanish, French and British Governments as

(¹) [*v. supra*, pp. 742–5, No. 705, and *encl.*]

included in the agreements of 1907, and that I hoped that the negotiations at Madrid would result in arrangements more favourable to Spain than M. Caballero at present seemed to consider probable.

I have, &c.

FRANCIS BERTIE.

MINUTES.

The most important point is that of the eventual position of Spain in the Spanish zone of Morocco. I still think that the legitimate desires of the Spanish Government would best be met by letting them enter into a treaty with the Sultan by which the Spanish zone is given over to be "occupied and administered" by Spain, just as Cyprus is by England.

E. A. C.

Dec. 11.

The Spanish Gov[ernmen]t have complained, generally, that the French proposal is unsatisfactory. What is wanted is a counter proposal setting out in detail the points which they consider objectionable. The only one mentioned, Ifni, will we know give rise to no difficulty.

W. L.

A. N.

Let me see the 1907 agreement. France has actually ceded to Germany a small piece of coast on the Atlantic. We knew of this during the negotiations but Spain did not. This however is not the point that Spanish Ambassador takes.

E. G.

12.12.11.

Spain might it seems to me fairly contend that the cession of territory made by France to Germany on the coast of Africa is a change of the territorial status quo about which under the agreement of 1907 Rennie should have made communication to Spain, but we need not raise this point.

E. G.

13.12.11.

F. D. A.

No. 748.

Sir E. Goschen to Sir A. Nicolson.

Private.([1])

My dear Nicolson,
Berlin, December 8, 1911.

I was so sorry to learn from your letter that you too have been suffering from influenza, and I think it is very nice of you to have found time to write to me under those depressing circumstances. There are enough subjects for depression just now without having influenza on the top of it. The only fault I could find in your letter was that you forgot to tell me whether you were amused by the cartoon in "Simplicissimus" which I sent you. That reminds me that Granville has just come back from shooting with the Crown Prince. The latter talked a great deal of his demonstration in the Reichstag, but expressed no repentance for the demonstration itself, which he admitted was directed against Bethmann Hollweg. *But* he was horrified at the idea that it should have been taken as a demonstration against England. Nothing was further from his thoughts; he was, he confessed, not at all averse from a war with France, rather the contrary, for he loathed the French, but the idea that he should have been thought to have demonstrated against his English friends made him quite unhappy. He begged Granville to tell me this and to write it to his friends. He expressed the greatest wish that Germany should be friends with England and said that it was a perpetual worry to him that the two countries did not seem to hit it off together.

([1]) [Carnock MSS., Vol. VI of 1911.]

It has surprised me greatly that the English Press has given such a good reception to Bethmann's speech. It is much better so, but I don't think that the British public would be quite pleased if they had been obliged, as I have, to read all that the German papers have to say about it. All the diplomats here thought it awfully strong and were agog to know what would be thought of it in England. Cambon thought it so strong that he rather attacked the Chancellor about it; but you will read about that in one of my despatches. I did not report, however, that Cambon attacked Kiderlen about it too. The latter said "Well! if you want people in England to understand, you must put things very plainly, and this time the language was plain enough!" Then Cambon said to him, "Voulez vous que je vous dise ce que je pense du discours du Chanceller? Eh bien! c'est cet animal de Kiderlen qui l'a écrit!" Kiderlen roared; he only denied the accusation *very* faintly. I have thought all along that the voice was Jacob's but that the hands were those of Esau! There were so many things in the speech that had the Kiderlen touch. . . . .([2])

Yours very sincerely,
W. E. GOSCHEN.

([2]) [The rest of this letter refers in general terms to European relations and Eastern affairs.]

No. 749.

Sir Edward Grey to Sir F. Bertie.

F.O. 48918/46431/11/28.   *Foreign Office, December 9, 1911.*
Tel. (No. 347.) R.   D. 12 P.M.

My tel[egram] No. 342 (Dec[ember] 7—Morocco Syndicate).([1])
Financier will of course understand that our conditional promise of support does not involve obligation on H[is] M[ajesty's] G[overnment] to give *exclusive* support to the syndicate.

([1]) [*v. supra*, p. 764, No. 743.]

No. 750.

Sir M. de Bunsen to Sir Edward Grey.

F.O. 49900/13751/11/28.
(No. 198.)   *Madrid, D. December 10, 1911.*
Sir,   R. *December 13, 1911.*

In my telegram No. 94 of the 7th instant([1]) I had the honour to report the meeting which took place on the previous afternoon between the Spanish Minister for Foreign Affairs and the French Ambassador, immediately after the return of the latter from his consultation with the French Government at Paris. I felt myself authorized by your telegram No. 95 of October 26,([2]) informing me of the extent to which I am at liberty to support the proposals submitted by the French Government, to accede to the courteous suggestion which was made to me on the same day by both parties that I should be present at the discussion which was to be opened between them in respect of the relations between the French and Spanish zones in Morocco. I have since had the honour to receive, by your telegram No. 102 of the 6 instant,([3]) your full permission to attend the meetings in question.

([1]) [*v. supra*, p. 763, No. 741.]
([2]) [*v. supra*, p. 594, No. 607.]
([3]) [*v. supra*, p. 754, No. 735.]

The French invitation to attend the meeting at the Ministry of State was conveyed to me by telephone from the French Embassy at midday. Soon after I received a letter from Señor Garcia Prieto in which he was good enough to say that he had just heard "that the French Government would welcome with the same pleasure as the Spanish Government my presence at the ensuing conversations," adding that he was arranging for a meeting to take place at 5 o'clock.

I have ventured to trouble you with the above particulars in view of the comments that I notice my participation in the opening conversation has provoked in a portion of the French and Spanish press. The evening *Epoca* of the 9th instant explains clearly the intimate relation which exists between England, France, and Spain in regard to the new Morocco settlement and the treaties out of which it has grown. It expresses surprise at the ignorance which appears to prevail on the subject in the public mind, and it points out how natural it is that the representatives of the above three countries should jointly confer with regard to a question affecting the interpretation of a set of engagements accepted by them all.

As to what passed at the opening meeting, I have little to add to my above mentioned telegram. The Spanish Foreign Minister remarked, on receiving the draft Convention from the hands of the French Ambassador, that he must make a preliminary point of the absolute necessity which existed for the Spanish Government that they should be assured, before entering upon the negotiation, that they would not have to pay twice over for the recognition of their rights in Morocco. There was still in his mind the fear which he had expressed during the brief conversations held at San Sebastian in the summer that after ceding territory to France the Spanish Government would be called upon to cede more to Germany. Monsieur Geoffray having expressed the opinion that it would be useless at this early stage to approach the German Government in order to ascertain what they would do on the completion of the arrangement between France and Spain, I suggested that Señor Garcia Prieto might see his way to leaving the point he had raised in abeyance till near the conclusion of the negotiations, when it might be agreed that any Spanish engagement involving a cession of territory should be conditional on no further territorial demands being made on Spain from other quarters. M. Geoffray adopted the suggestion and Señor Garcia Prieto appeared to concur, promising to study carefully the draft Convention, and to let us know when he was ready for a further interview. The conversation was entirely friendly. It was agreed that the negotiation should be kept as secret as possible, and I may say that, apart from your telegram No. 104 of the 8 instant([4]) I have since received no indication whatever of the impression produced by the French proposals. The Spanish press has received no hint of what passed at the first meeting.

I have, &c.
MAURICE DE BUNSEN.

([4]) [v. supra, p. 765, No. 745.]

No. 751.

Sir R. Lister to Sir Edward Grey.

F.O. 50332/47410/11/28.

(No. 351.) Confidential.
Sir,

Tangier, D. December 10, 1911.
R. December 16, 1911.

As I had the honour to report in my telegram No. 159,([1]) the proposal of the Commission d'Hygiène to add to its numbers 12 Moorish Notables, to be nominated by the Maghzen may be considered as completely defeated.

([1]) [Not reproduced as its tenour is indicated.]

After receiving my annotation and that of the French Chargé d'Affaires the substance of which was reported in my despatch No. 344 of the 1st Instant,([2]) the Circular of the President of the Conseil Sanitaire went on to the Russian Minister. M. Botkine wrote that he shared the view expressed by the President and me, and I understand that all the other representatives have declared themselves of the same opinion.

M. de Billy's attempt has proved a sad failure, and I hear that he now more than ever throws all the blame on Ali Zaky Bey.

I regret to state that the feeling amongst the French Colony in Tangier is very bitter against England, with regard to the arrangement to be made between France and Spain. The key of the situation, they say, was in the hands of England, as Spain would have done whatever she told her. Presuming that Alcazar and Laraiche, as well as the Northern shore, are to remain in the hands of Spain, they consider that they have been defrauded of the fruits they had a right to expect. (1) by the vast concessions they have been obliged to make to Germany. (2) by the danger of war to which they were exposed during 4 months, and (3) by the fact that Spain had broken her obligations under the Treaty of 1904, and that consequently a new situation had been created. They do not appear to realise that the question is one which affects our own vital interests, and that it was with a view of safeguarding these that Article 3 of our Secret Treaty was drawn up, which formed the basis of the Franco-Spanish Secret Treaty of 1904. I am glad to say that M. de Billy has shown more wisdom on this occasion, and the Legation are doing their best to calm the agitation.

I have, &c.
REGINALD LISTER.

([2]) [Not reproduced.]

No. 752.

Sir E. Goschen to Sir Edward Grey.

F.O. 50508/50508/11/28.
(No. 427.)
Sir,

Berlin, D. December 11, 1911.
R. *December* 18, 1911.

I have the honour to report that yesterday the Pan-German League held a general meeting at Lübeck under the Presidency of Dr. Class, the author of the pamphlet against Herr von Kiderlen-Waechter's Morocco policy which was published on the 24th September last and to which frequent allusion was made during the sittings of the Budget Commission of the Reichstag.

At a meeting of the Working Committee of the League, held on the preceding day, a unanimous vote of approval of this pamphlet was passed and a report issued stating that the charges it had brought against the Secretary of State for Foreign Affairs had neither been contradicted nor disproved, and that the attitude of the President of the League in the Morocco question was in thorough harmony with the wishes of the League and of the majority of the nation.

The following resolution was put to the general meeting and was passed unanimously :

"That the German Empire has handed over to France political and therefore commercial supremacy in Morocco; that the territory acquired by Germany in the Congo in return for German territory in the Cameroons must, in view of the unanimous opinion of experts and above all that of the former Secretary of State for the Colonies, Herr von Lindequist, be regarded as distinctly disadvantageous to the German Empire; that the confidence of the entire world of Islam in the German Empire has been severely shaken and that the depreciation by the Chancellor of the well-founded national excitement during the recent crisis had placed serviceable weapons in the hands of the opponents of a national policy which would be most certainly used in the forthcoming elections. The Presidency of the League therefore held it to be their duty, both as patriots and citizens to point out that nothing but a change in the directors of German policy would offer any guarantee that henceforward the policy of the Empire would be conducted in a manner corresponding to the greatness of its past and to its hopes for the future."

At the close of the meeting a telegram was sent to Herr von Lindequist, thanking him for his courageous attitude towards the Congo arrangement.

The pamphlet written by Dr. Class accused the Secretary of State for Foreign Affairs of breach of faith and untruth on the ground that in the Budget Commission Herr von Kiderlen-Waechter had used words to the following effect :—'' The notion that it was the original plan of the Government to obtain a territorial footing in Morocco itself was disseminated chiefly through the pamphlet of Dr. Class.'' The latter has maintained all along and, as it appears from the report of the general meeting, still maintains that the Secretary of State had distinctly informed him that the above had been his original plan.

The '' Post '' in commenting upon the discrepancy between these statements says that Dr. Class's allegation is supported by other politicians who declare that a similar communication was made to them by Herr von Kiderlen-Waechter.

The '' Post '' adds that public opinion is profoundly surprised that the Secretary of State for Foreign Affairs has not thought it necessary to make any answer to the charge which was publicly brought against him of breach of faith and untruth. This charge had now been repeated at the meeting of the Pan-German League, and it seemed out of the question that the Imperial Government should continue to pass over the matter in silence. It was in any case a very regrettable state of things that such charges should be brought against the leading directors of German foreign policy and the '' Post '' hoped that an official explanation with regard to the affair would soon be forthcoming.

I have, &c.
W. E. GOSCHEN.

No. 753.

Sir Edward Grey to Sir F. Bertie.

F.O. 48176/48102/11/28.
(No. 522.)
Sir,   *Foreign Office, December* 11, 1911.

H[is] M[ajesty's] G[overnment] have been much gratified by the assurances of the French Gov[ernmen]t that provision would be made, in the proposed Franco-Spanish agreement respecting Morocco, for the internationalization of the town and district of Tangier, and they have given most careful consideration to the draft regulations on the subject enclosed in Y[our] E[xcellency]'s despatch No. 571 of the 1st instant.(¹) I transmit to Y[our] E[xcellency] herewith a memorandum prepared in this Department,(²) in which the principles embodied in the French proposals, and the more important points of detail are critically examined.

The memorandum, in the conclusions of which I concur, shows that there are weighty objections to the general lines on which the French scheme has been drawn up, the cardinal defect being that it does not in fact provide for real internationalization.

(¹) [Not reproduced.]
(²) [Not reproduced as its conclusions are sufficiently indicated.]

The scheme is based on the abortive proposals laid before the Diplomatic body at Tangier last spring, nominally by the Moorish Gov[ernmen]t, but in reality, as was not at the time concealed, under the advice of the French Legation. The proposals did not meet with the approval of the Committee, consisting of the representatives of Great Britain, Germany and Spain, as well as of France, to which it was referred for consideration, for the very reason that it practically left supreme power to the Moorish Gov[ernmen]t in the affairs of the proposed municipality.

The objections then entertained now derive additional force from the important political changes which are foreshadowed in the recent Franco-German Convention, and which are to be consolidated by the agreement now being negotiated between France and Spain. The practical outcome of these changes will be that the Sultan's authority over his dominions is henceforth to be exercised only under the advice, and with the assistance, of a European Gov[ernmen]t. His administration will be under French control as regards the French sphere, and under Spanish control as regards the Spanish sphere. Tangier, it is agreed, is to be outside either sphere; and it is obviously impossible that Tangier and its district should continue free from European control, and be governed by the very Sultan or Maghzen whose incapacity to carry on an efficient Government in the rest of Morocco forms the basis of, and justification for, the definite introduction of a system of European tutelage. Once it is admitted that there must be effective European control in the municipality of Tangier, and that such control is not to be exercised by either France or Spain or any one single Power, there can be no alternative to the controlling authority being placed in the hands of all the Treaty Powers jointly. This implies subordinating the Sultan's authority in Tangier definitely and unequivocally to that of the foreign community, whose voice must be made to prevail in all questions of municipal government. Among others, matters so important as the management of the police, including the regulation of numbers and pay, as also the water supply and the control of the port of Tangier, seem essentially such as ought to be entrusted to the municipal government.

How far it may be possible, by amending the scheme proposed by the French Gov[ernmen]t, to provide adequately for the requirements which have in the opinion of H[is] M[ajesty's] G[overnment] to be met in order to give effect to the general principles above outlined, it is difficult to decide without consulting the foreign Representatives at Tangier, whose local knowledge could alone offer a safe guide in estimating the practical effect of any detailed arrangements contemplated, and on whose co-operation if not direct participation the success of any scheme must to a large extent ultimately depend.

For this reason it appears to H[is] M[ajesty's] G[overnment] that if and when there is agreement as to the general principles which should be followed in setting up the proposed Municipality, it would be well to entrust the elaboration of details to the Diplomatic body at Tangier. This procedure would have the further advantage of bringing into the discussion the other Treaty Powers, whose consent and willing support will be necessary before an international municipality can be satisfactorily worked. It is suggested in the memorandum that the international settlement at Shanghai offers a sufficiently close analogy to justify its organisation being accepted as serving, in regard to many points of importance, as a useful model. A copy of the "Land Regulations and Bye-Laws for the foreign settlement of Shanghai" will be found at pp. 664 et sequitur (Vol: 2) of Hertslet's China Treaties (1908), a copy of which is in Y[our] E[xcellency]'s possession.

To enable Y[our] E[xcellency] more fully to understand the character and scope of the abortive "projet de règlement municipal" of January, 1911, to which reference has been made above, I transmit herewith a copy of that document(³) with the request that it may eventually be returned to me, as it is the only copy in the archives of the F[oreign] O[ffice], and it has been impossible to obtain a duplicate from Tangier.

(³) [Not reproduced.]

I beg Y[our] E[xcellency] to take an early opportunity of explaining the views of H[is] M[ajesty's] G[overnment] to the French M[inister for] F[oreign] A[ffairs] in such manner and form as may appear to you most suitable and judicious. I leave it to Y[our] E[xcellency]'s discretion, more particularly, to make use of so much of the considerations and arguments set forth in the enclosed memorandum as you may think desirable.

Y[our] E[xcellency] might also consider in this connection whether M. de Selves's attention should not be drawn to the recent attempt on the part of the French Legation at Tangier to swamp the European representation in the "Commission d'hygiène" by adding twelve Moorish members to that body. The incident was reported in Sir R. Lister's despatches Nos. 342, 343, and telegram No. 159 of which I enclose copies,(4) and, although the proposal was subsequently defeated when brought before the Conseil Sanitaire, it affords a good illustration of the impracticable nature of any scheme founded on the idea of placing the Moorish Gov[ernmen]t in a position of real authority as regards the duties of municipal administration at Tangier.

[I am, &c.]
E. G[REY].

(4) [Not reproduced. cp. supra, p. 769, No. 751, note (1).]

No. 754.

Sir Edward Grey to Sir M. de Bunsen.

F.O. 50222/13751/11/28.
(No. 133.)

Sir,   *Foreign Office, December* 12, 1911.

The Spanish Ambassador informed me to-day that his Government desired to thank us for what we had done with regard to the Franco-Spanish negotiations. They considered it due to us that the question of Alcazar was settled favourably. They were very glad that I had mentioned the question of Ifni to the French Government, because Spain had held Ifni prior to the Agreement of 1904, and the Spanish Government could never propose its cession to the Spanish Parliament. The Spanish Government would be willing to cede the "hinterland" in the south; but with regard to the coast they felt that it would be very difficult to allow it to pass into the hands of a strong foreign Power, as that would make the possession of the Canary Islands insecure.

I said that I had not yet considered the question of the whole coast, but only of Ifni itself, as the Ambassador had spoken of it with very great emphasis.

He replied that he had mentioned the coast before, but admitted that it was of Ifni that he had spoken most urgently. He then told me that his Government had replied to the French proposal, saying that they could not discuss the question of compensation until they knew what they were going to gain, and what their position would be in their own sphere. They observed that the 1904 Agreement was not referred to in the French proposal, except in connection with Tangier. They also noticed that the wording as to fortifications varied from that contained in the Anglo-French Agreement and the Franco-Spanish Agreement, and was open to the interpretation that the fortifications of Ceuta were to be demolished, and Ceuta turned into a commercial port. This was a matter which could interest only Great Britain, but the Ambassador did not suppose that we had suggested this alteration of wording.

I replied that we had not suggested it. I asked him whether he had yet received the French proposal as to Tangier.

He answered that his Government had not yet received it, and he enquired whether I had said any thing to the French on the subject.

I told him that we had represented to the French that the internationalisation of Tangier must be a real one.

The Ambassador said that this was exactly what his Government also desired : they did not wish to have the internationalisation rendered illusory by a control over Tangier that would be nominally Moorish, and really French.

[I am, &c.]

E. G[REY].

No. 755.

Sir Edward Grey to Sir F. Bertie.

F.O. 49873/48749/12/28.

Tel. (No. 367.) R. *Foreign Office, December 13, 1911.*

Your tel[egram] No. 206 (Morocco Police).([1])

French gov[ernmen]t will presumably inform Spanish gov[ernmen]t. Arrangement is unlikely to meet with objection from the other Treaty Powers and has our concurrence.

([1]) [Not reproduced. It announced the intention of the Moorish Government to ask the State Bank for funds for a prolongation of the mandates for policing the Moroccan Coast. The French Government did not consider it necessary to consult the Powers. *cp. supra*, p. 764, No. 742.]

No. 756.

Sir M. de Bunsen to Sir Edward Grey.

F.O. 50657/13751/11/28.

(No. 199.) *Madrid, D. December 14, 1911.*

Sir, R. *December 18, 1911.*

With reference to my telegram No. 96 of the 12th instant,([1]) reporting that I had attended on the previous day a second meeting between Señor Garcia Prieto and Monsieur Geoffray, I have now the honour to forward an abstract of the written comments handed in on that occasion by the Spanish Minister for Foreign Affairs with regard to the draft Convention concerning Morocco which the French Ambassador had communicated to His Excellency at their first meeting.

It will be seen that the principal Spanish objections to the French proposals bear on the extent of the territorial compensation demanded by France and on the character of the proposed arrangements for the administration of the Spanish zone.

On the first point, the sacrifice demanded of Spain includes three pieces of territory, two in Morocco and the third, in the Spanish view, outside Morocco, namely :—

(1) A triangle based on 36 kilometres of the coast southwards from the mouth of the River Lucus.

Spain objects on the ground that this cession would deprive her of several fords across the Lucus which are essential to the maintenance of the communications between Laraiche and Elksar. She holds to the definition of her sphere of influence given in the Franco-Spanish Convention of October 1904.

([1]) [Not reproduced. It reports the same conversation between Señor Garcia Prieto M. Geoffray, and Sir M. de Bunsen, in shorter form.]

(2). Some 500 kilometres of coast from the mouth of Wady Mesa southwards to North Latitude 27″ 40. See Articles IV, V and VI of the 1904 Convention. This portion includes Ifni.

Spain urges that public opinion at home and especially in the Canary Islands would resent the surrender of this important piece of coast.

(3). Some 200 kilometres of coast line between Latitudes 26″ and 27″ 40.

This region, which adjoins the Spanish possession of Rio de Oro, was declared by Article 6 of the 1904 Convention to lie outside Morocco and to be open immediately to the free action of Spain.

Senor Garcia Prieto declared that nothing would induce the Spanish Government to surrender it. When, in September last, His Excellency called attention to the new definition of the southern boundary of Morocco which the negotiators of the Franco-German Convention at Berlin were understood to have agreed upon, namely a definition, since confirmed, by which that boundary was shifted from North Latitude 27″ 40 to the Northern boundary of the Rio de Oro territory, Monsieur Geoffray had given the express assurance that this Franco-German agreement did not and could not affect the engagements existing between France and Spain on the point in question. The explanations then given are recorded in the last two paragraphs of my confidential despatch No. 155 of the 19th September 1911.([2]) The Spanish Government persists in regarding the definition of the boundary made in 1904 as the only correct one as between itself and the French Government.

Monsieur Geoffray said that he was authorised to meet as far as possible the wishes of Spain by offering to leave within her zone a stretch of 50 kilometres of coastline including Ifni and extending from 20 to 30 kilometres into the interior. He placed a sketch map defining this region in Senor Garcia Prieto's hands.

Senor Garcia Prieto did not think that Spain could make any territorial contribution (to make good the losses incurred by France) other than a portion of the hinterland of her South Morocco zone, excluding the region lying (in her view) outside Morocco.

The French Ambassador warned His Excellency that the French Government were not likely to give way on the territorial question. It was only, he declared, by pointing to a considerable territorial gain at the expense of Spain that they would have any chance of passing the new arrangement with Spain through the Chamber of Deputies. It was agreed however that Senor Garcia Prieto should embody in the counter draft, which he undertook to prepare, a statement of the utmost territorial compensation which Spain would be able to offer.

On the question of the administration of the Spanish zone, the Foreign Minister began by remarking generally that under the proposed arrangements France would practically exercise her protectorate, to some extent at least, over the Spanish as well as over the French zone. The "règlements d'application concernant les réformes" having to be drawn up by the Makhzen, France, standing behind the Makhzen, would become the lawgiver for the whole of Morocco. The powers of the "Khalifa" for the Spanish zone would be limited to the mere application and enforcement in that zone of a set of regulations drawn up at the dictation of France. This, he said, was a very different thing from the entirely Spanish administration of the zone which was contemplated in the preliminary propositions submitted in September.

His Excellency said he could not understand why the powers to be exercised by Spain in her zone should be less extensive than those vested in France by the German Convention. As France ceded to Spain by paragraph 2 of Article II of the Convention of October 1904 the whole of the powers vested in her by virtue of Article II of the Anglo-French Declaration of April 1904, so Spain thinks it reasonable that France should now cede to her, in the same way, with reference to the Spanish zone, the whole of the powers specified in Articles 1 and 2 of the Franco-German Convention of November 1911 as appertaining to France in Morocco.

([2]) [v. supra, p. 541, No. 559.]

In other words, in addition to the right to lend her assistance to the Government of Morocco for the introduction of all necessary reforms, whether "administrative, economic, financial or military," Spain demands that she shall be invested with the more ample powers conferred upon France by the German Convention, such as the power to lend her assistance also to the Makhzen in respect of all new regulations or alteration of existing ones; to take, in agreement with the Makhzen, all necessary measures of financial reorganisation and control; to extend, if need be, her faculty of control and protection; to exercise a full liberty of action; to dispose, as she sees fit, of the troops and police of her zone, in the interest of public order and security for trade.

Spain contends further that the continued control of the Customs within her sphere by the officers of the Public Debt, who represent the holders of the 1904 and 1910 loans, would involve an intolerable degree of French interference. She much prefers the suggestion contained in the September proposals (which were generally approved by the British Government) to the effect that the sums due in respect of existing loans should constitute a charge on the revenues of her zone for which Spain should be responsible. The same observation applies to the annuity due to the French Treasury in respect of the indemnity on account of French military operations in Morocco. Spain seeks, in short, to exclude from her zone, as far as possible, all French taxcollectors and controllers of taxes.

Monsieur Geoffray said it was materially impossible to alter the arrangements made with the issuing banks respecting the 1904 and 1910 loans. This could only be done with the consent of every individual holder of the loan stock, which it would be impossible to obtain. The control over the Morocco Customs must therefore be maintained in the hands of the "Administration du Contrôle de la Dette."

Criticizing the French proposals concerning the projected Tangier–Fez Railway, the Spanish Government object to the powers proposed to be left to the Shereefian Government, that is to the French protecting Government, in respect of (1) choice of the "organes d'exécution," (2) the working conditions of the line, and (3) its police and protection.

After listening patiently to Senor Garcia Prieto's explanations on these points and the others mentioned in the accompanying abstract, the French Ambassador set forth briefly the French view of the different questions raised and impressed upon the Spanish Foreign Minister the importance of an early settlement, in view of the extreme sensitiveness of French opinion at the present moment, and the likelihood that, if a change of Government took place at Paris, the new Administration would seek to curry favour with the Chamber by imposing much more arduous conditions on Spain than those which after protracted and laborious discussions he had at length succeeded in inducing the Government of Monsieur Caillaux to allow him to submit.

He begged Senor Garcia Prieto to put his comments into the concrete form of a counterproposal, omitting any merely captious objections, and keeping, as far as possible, the phraseology of the French original.

Although the Foreign Minister manifested great dissatisfaction with the proposed settlement in some of its aspects, the general tone in which he conducted the conversation was not unconciliatory and Monsieur Geoffray and myself were left under the impression that the Spanish Government really desired to come to terms.

I have, &c.
MAURICE DE BUNSEN.

Enclosure in No. 756.

Abstract of Written Comments by Spanish Minister for Foreign Affairs.

The marginal observations of the Spanish Government are to the following effect:—

Commenting on the Preamble, it is remarked that the present moment is not the most opportune for declaring anew the attachment of the two Powers to the principle of the integrity of Morocco. That principle is closely connected with the sovereignty of the Sultan, which is about to be profoundly modified at the demand of France.

Article 1. Why should not the attributes of Spain in her sphere of influence be defined in the same words and to the same extent as the attributes of France throughout Morocco are defined in Articles 1 and 2 of the Franco-German Convention of November 4 1911?

If the regulations for carrying out the necessary reforms are to be drawn up by the Makhzen, this will imply the intervention of France (who stands behind the Makhzen) in the affairs of the Spanish zones, and will place the Spanish Government in a position of dependency on that of France. This paragraph is in contradiction with the preceding one, which professes to invest Spain with the right to advise the Moorish Government in all important respects.

Article 2. The proposed rectification of the southern boundary of the northern Spanish zone, by shifting 25 kilometres further to the north the point at which it touches the Atlantic Ocean under the Convention of 1904, is inadmissible. Its effect would be to exclude from the Spanish zone the fords of the River Lucus most needed for keeping up communications between Elksar and Laraiche. The proposal is further inacceptable on strategic grounds.

The French claim that the whole of Morocco lying to the South and East of the above boundary is to be considered as falling within the French sphere of influence is open to the following objections. In the first place, Spain cannot admit that France has any right to claim the region between North Latitudes 26 and 27.40, which is expressly declared in Article 6 of the Secret Convention of 1904 to lie beyond the limits of Morocco. The region referred to is that which lies immediately to the north of the Spanish possession of Rio de Oro.

Further, Spanish public opinion would not acquiesce in the cession of the coast-line embracing Ifni. Admitting the principle that some territorial compensation is due by Spain to France, this compensation could only comprise a portion of the hinterland.

Article 3. Nomination of the *Khalifa* (to reside in the Spanish sphere) by the Sultan is equivalent to his nomination by France. The Khalifa should be invested with all the powers appertaining to the Sultan, and it is therefore inexpedient to specify the power of appointing officials and applying the regulations. Nor is there any reason why the place of residence of the Khalifa should be fixed.

Why is Spain called upon to declare that she will keep order and apply existing Treaties, including the new Convention between France and Germany, in her own sphere, when no such stipulation has been required of France?

Article 4. Spain having bound herself by Article 7 of the Convention of October 1904([3]) not to alienate or cede in any form any portion of her sphere of influence, there is no need to repeat this engagement.

Article 5. Similarly there is no need to repeat Article 14 of the Convention of October 1904, which defines the zone within which no fortifications may be erected.

Article 6. Pending receipt of the draft regulations concerning the position of Tangier, it is remarked that the Convention of 1904 did not expressly exclude Tangier from the Spanish sphere. It merely stipulated that Tangier should preserve its special character.

Article 7. Regard for existing schools is already provided for in Article II of the Convention of 1904. Why add Consulates?

Article 8. The proposed stipulation respecting the free passage of convoys, officers, etc., goes beyond what was proposed in the draft submitted last September. The Arms Regulations referred to could only mean, in the Spanish sphere, regulations drawn up by the Sultan's Khalifa residing in that zone.

([3]) [*cp. infra*, p. 828, *App.* IV, Art. vii: " L'Espagne s'engage à n'aliéner ni à céder sous aucune forme, même à titre temporaire, tout ou partie des territoires désignés aux articles II, IV et V de la présente convention."]

Article 9. Organisation of troops is a question of administration, appertaining to the Khalifa.

Article 10. Prefers text proposed by Monsieur Geoffray in September providing that " les revenus de toute nature des régions administrées par l'Espagne seront affectées aux besoins de ces régions, à leur administration et aux améliorations jugées nécessaires."

Article 11. Agrees that the Makhzen will not be responsible for expenses or claims arising in the Spanish zone. This is a reason the more for investing the Sultan's Khalifa for that region with full administrative powers.

Article 12. France demands that the rights secured by Treaty to

The French Treasury (annuity of 2,740,000);
Board of Control, representing holders of the 1904 and 1910 loans;
State Bank;
Tobacco Régie;

shall remain intact.

On this the Spanish Government remarks that the zones of influence date from October 3 1904; only the rights secured to the holders of the 1904 loan are anterior to that date, and even these are subject to modification on the expiration of the first period of application of the Convention of October 1904; if these rights have since been extended, this was done without consultation with Spain and in disregard of her objections; Spain did not cease to object to the arrangements affecting her zone, as well as that of France, which were made in 1910 between France and Morocco in respect of a new loan and a French Treasury annuity. Last September Monsieur Geoffray put forward the equitable principle that the annual sum due from the Spanish zone in respect of the service of existing loans should constitute a charge on the revenues of the Spanish zone. Spain prefers a settlement on the above lines, by which alone French intervention in her zone, through the Board of Control, can be prevented.

Article 13. Three months is too short a period for the establishment of the Melilla Custom House. It will be set up as soon as possible.

Article 14. Railways, posts and telegraphs. Repetition of observations on Article 1. Spain claims the entire administration in her sphere.

Article 15. As regards the Tangier–Fez railway Spain would object to the Makhzen (that is France) reserving to itself the power to " choisir les organes d'exécution qui lui paraîtront convenables; déterminer librement les conditions d'exploitation de la ligne; prendre toute mesure de police et de garde que comporteront l'exploitation et la surveillance."

Article 16. The required undertaking respecting contraband is made in Article 13 of the 1904 Convention and need not be renewed.

Paragraph 2 requires explanations.

The remarks of the Spanish Government conclude with an enquiry as to how the following questions will be dealt with, namely :—

Protection of natives;
Consular Jurisdiction;
Who will be the intermediary between the Khalifa for the Spanish zones and the foreign representatives as regards questions arising in those zones?
Arbitration of claims;
Annuity by Morocco to the Spanish Treasury;
Action of State Bank and Tobacco Monopoly.

MINUTES.

The two parties will probably be able to come to terms about the cession of territory and many of the Spanish objections seem purely captious. But the question of the Contrôle de la Dette is very ticklish. The Spaniards, not without reason, object exceedingly strongly to French agents of the Dette in their sphere. The French will almost certainly insist on their retention, not only because of the bondholders, but to ensure the proper administration of the Customs-houses.

There certainly are some difficult points to settle but there is as yet no reason to be pessimistic with regard to the outcome of the negotiations.

G. H. V.
14.12.11.

The Spaniards seem to me to be prepared to offer very little to France, and many of their objections to the French proposals are quite unreasonable. As regards Articles 4 and 5, it is certainly necessary that these should be embodied in the new convention, and it might be well to tell Sir M. de Bunsen that we expect this, unless it is expressly provided that the corresponding portions of the 1904 convention will remain in force (which seems unlikely). As regards Article 6, it would be quite as, if not more, objectionable that Tangier should be under Spanish control as under French, and we might remind the Ambassador that we expect proper arrangements to be made as regards the internationalization of Tangier and that the town and district must not be in either the French or Spanish sphere.

E. D.
18.12.11.
E. A. C.
Dec. 18.
W. L.

For us the question of Tangier is the predominating one. We might write to Sir M. de Bunsen in the sense suggested by Mr. Drummond.

A. N.

I do not think the Spaniards are altogether unreasonable in contending that what was agreed in their favour to be outside Morocco in 1904 should not be brought into it and claimed by the French now. And the contention of the Spanish Ambassador is that Spain is being asked to concede to France an area actually larger than France has given Germany in the Congo. Write to Sir M. de Bunsen as regards Article 4 and 5 etc. as proposed.

E. G.

No. 757.

Admiralty to Foreign Office.

F.O 50391/38006/11/28.
Confidential.
Sir, *Admiralty, December* 14. 1911.

I am commanded by my Lords Commissioners of the Admiralty to acknowledge the receipt of your letter No. 43587 of the 14th ultimo,(¹) respecting the adherence of His Majesty's Government to the recently concluded Franco-German Convention, and to request you to inform the Secretary of State for Foreign Affairs that while accepting his decision, they are glad to learn that he does not intend to lose sight of the wishes of the Admiralty in the matter of the fortification of the Atlantic Coast-line of Morocco, should a suitable opportunity occur for pressing these views on the French Government.

I am, &c.
W. GRAHAM GREENE.

(¹) [*v. supra*, pp. 691–2, No. 687.]

No. 758.

Sir F. Bertie to Sir Edward Grey.

F.O. 50338/50338/11/28.
(No. 602.) *Paris,* D. *December* 15, 1911.
Sir :— R. *December* 16, 1911.

I have the honour to inform you that before the debate which was fixed to take place in the Chamber of Deputies yesterday respecting the Franco-German Convention of the 4th of November last, the following motion proposed by the deputies of the Right, MM. de Mun, Delafosse, Denys Cochin, and Chambrun, was discussed and put to the vote : " Les soussignés ont l'honneur de demander l'ajournement du débat sur l'accord franco-allemand et sur les interpellations jusqu'au moment où le Gouvernement sera en mesure de donner à la Chambre des indications précises sur l'état des négociations avec l'Espagne, et sur l'adhésion des Puissances signataires de l'Acte d'Algésiras.''

Count Albert de Mun, who for eleven years past had not taken part in the debates of the Chamber, proposed this motion in a speech of great eloquence and was repeatedly cheered by various sections of the Chamber. He began by expressing the opinion that the debate on the Convention should be adjourned until more light could be thrown on the obscurity surrounding it. By that Convention a vast tract of French territory was ceded to a rival nation without any battle being lost, and this was the first time so great a sacrifice had been asked of France. Nor was this all, for from certain observations as to future territorial aggrandizements of Germany in Central Africa let us fall by M. de Kiderlen Waechter and by M. de Bethmann-Hollweg, and from a passage in your speech in the House of Commons to the effect that England would not adopt a dog-in-the-manger policy towards such aggrandizements, it might be inferred that some obscure design was already in process of evolution. What was that design? It was necessary for the Chamber to know before entering on a discussion of the Convention. What reasons had induced the Government to conclude a Treaty so painful for France and so perilous for others? When and how did the idea originate of the surrender of territory which is called the price of a Protectorate over Morocco? Why had Germany gone to Agadir? It had been stated that she had gone thither to induce the French Government to resume an interrupted conversation. There had been a conversation then? Since when and about what? Since when and why had that conversation been broken off? Even before Agadir the Congo had been mentioned, but why? A French Protectorate over Morocco might have been obtained more rapidly, with far fewer sacrifices and above all with far fewer complications if the French Government had considered the Moroccan question as an Algerian question and not as an European one. But what was the Protectorate which France now acquired? and why was it necessary for France to purchase it?

M. de Mun then proceeded to enquire into the events leading up to the Franco-German Agreement of 1909(¹) and into the manner in which that Agreement had been kept. If it were true that Germany had, in an explanatory annex to the Agreement, signified clearly her political disinterestedness in Morocco and had admitted the superiority of French commercial interests over German commercial interests in that country, why had the French Government negotiated with Germany again and to obtain what? and why had a French Colony been given up owing to the presence of a German ship at Agadir? In reality the Agreements of 1909 and of 1911 were the same in their two most essential points. The Morocco of 1909 and the Morocco of 1911 were one and the same Morocco, an international Morocco and a Morocco burdened with the Spanish mortgage. The Chamber and the country at large could no longer endure a system whereby France could be tied in regard to England and tied in regard to Spain for seven years without the public knowing it. M. de Mun concluded by enquiring what direction M. Caillaux had given to French external policy three months ago and what direction he would give to it in the future. He alluded to the passage in your speech dealing with the old friendships of England and declared, amidst considerable applause, that France had no more reason than England to forget her old friendships, and that neither country had in the present state of Europe any other friendships to exchange them for.

M. de Selves evidently intended to cut short the discussion of M. de Mun's motion and to reserve his explanations of the policy followed by the French Government until the debate on the Treaty itself had more fully developed. His Excellency therefore confined himself to a few words in answer to M. de Mun. He asked him

(¹) [v. infra, p. 830, App. IV.]

to withdraw his motion. When that was done, the Government would then be able to explain their policy. "Nous venons demander à M. de Mun," he said, "de nous relever du silence auquel il nous condamne par sa proposition préjudicielle." After this statement M. de Selves returned to his place, but the Chamber showed such manifest signs of dissatisfaction at the matter being thus summarily treated that, after a hurried consultation with the President of the Council, M. de Selves went again into the Tribune and said that as the Chamber seemed to insist on immediate explanations on his part, he would give them.

His Excellency then proceeded to give an account of the situation which he found in existence when he took office at the end of June. A conversation with Germany was already in progress. The Fez expedition had taken place and it appeared to Germany that the state of things resulting from the Act of Algeciras and from the the Franco-German Agreement of 1909 had been totally modified. The German Ambassador at Paris informed him a few days after he had taken office, that Germany had sent a warship to Agadir. The reasons given were that there were German interests there and that these interests were threatened. The warship would, however, be withdrawn as soon as order was re-established in Morocco. Shortly afterwards, M. de Selves declared that Germany was desirous of having a conversation with France; that she hoped it would be carried on rapidly, and that no unfriendly idea had inspired the despatch of the ship to Agadir. He (M. de Selves) had answered that he regretted the decision of the German Government to send a ship; that the French Government did not and had not refused a conversation with the German Government, but that he feared that the despatch of the ship to Agadir would "underline it in an unfortunate manner." This was on the eve of his departure with the President of the Republic for Holland. On his return the French Ambassador left Paris for Berlin with instructions to resume the interrupted conversation.

M. de Selves then alluded to the criticisms addressed to the French Government for not having sent a warship to Agadir. They had considered the question. They had been constantly in touch on all matters with the friends and allies of France. But it appeared to them, according to the information which they had received, that if Germany had sent a ship to Agadir, she had no intention of effecting a landing there, and the French Government considered that the question of sending a ship could be adjourned. He had been asked why France had not demanded the meeting of a new conference, as Morocco was under the régime of the Algeciras Act. But he knew that Germany had clearly stated that she would not have anything to do with a Conference except on condition that the actual state of affairs was re-established as it was left by the Algeciras Act; that is to say, that France should evacuate the positions which she had occupied in Morocco. If the French Government had insisted upon a meeting of a Conference, who could have said that Germany might not have effected a landing at Agadir in order to come to the Conference in a new "de facto" situation? All the ideas about a Conference were built up on a false conception, namely that the Sultan was in a position himself to ensure order and tranquillity in Morocco. France only was in a position to undertake this responsibility and therefore it was better, as the question had been raised by Germany, to face it frankly and to negotiate as that Power had invited France to do.

M. de Selves then gave the Chamber a sketch of the conditions on which the French Government had entered upon the negotiations. Any German territorial pretension in Morocco was excluded. The German Government had been told that the French Government would keep their friends and allies informed of the negotiations although they were "à deux," and finally the adhesion of the Signatory Powers of the Algeciras Act was laid down as necessary. Germany had replied that she agreed. "Take Morocco," she said, "establish your Protectorate there, but as you have negotiated already about Morocco with England, Italy and Spain, on what basis are you going to negotiate with us? Our public opinion will not allow us to abandon anything without compensation elsewhere."

At this point M. de Selves remarked that it was easy to say that France should establish a Protectorate over Morocco without making any sacrifices elsewhere, but it was easier said than done.

This remark appeared to cause great indignation in the Chamber, and M. de Selves' speech was for a time interrupted. He resumed it to give an account of how the question of cession of territory in the Congo was first mooted. Various members continued to interrupt and press His Excellency on this point. It has frequently been asserted of late that the French Government offered to give up territory in the Congo before the German Government asked for it, and in certain quarters great indignation has been expressed in regard to this offer. M. de Selves was at pains to prove that this indignation was unfounded as the German Government themselves first mentioned the Congo. He recounted to the Chamber how the French Government had refused to continue the conversation if M. de Kiderlen-Waechter should maintain his demand for the whole of the French Colony from the Sangha to the sea. There was a period of tension at this point, and various reports had been circulated, so His Excellency said, about this matter. It had been said that the friends of France had instigated her to a conflict. This was an absolute error. It was true that they had stood by the side of France ready to give her their aid— all the aid which the circumstances might demand—But they had never let fall an irritating word; on the contrary they used peaceful and conciliatory language, which they were able to do all the more as the vital interests and dignity of France were not at stake.

M. de Selves then continued his account of the progress of negotiations at Berlin. He would not, he said, enter into all the details of the portion relative to the Congo for the Minister of the Colonies would explain them to the House, but he would mention the matter of the French right of pre-emption over the Belgian Congo. He did not think that there was much chance of this right being exercised, for Belgium was jealously desirous of preserving her colonial domain. The French Government had never thought of abandoning their right in favour of Germany. Besides they were not in a position to do so, as such a right was a personal and not a transferable one. What had been done was to insert a clause in the agreement to the effect that if modifications in the territorial status of the conventional basin of the Congo were effected, France would not refuse to " causer " with Germany as with all other signatory Powers of the Berlin Act of 1885.

M. de Selves summed up the result of the negotiations with Germany by stating that, on one side, France was now able to take all administrative, military and financial measures which she judged necessary in Morocco. Her hands were free. She would represent Moorish interests *vis-à-vis* to foreign Powers. Such Powers as have interests in Morocco would approach the Moorish Government through an intermediary of the French Representative. The political liberty of action of France was complete and absolute, more than was the case when the protectorate over Tunis was established. On the other side, the agreement, in the region of economical matters, gave equality to all and privilege to none.

Negotiations with Spain had already been begun; it was impossible to give the House details of these negotiations, but two ideas inspired them : firstly, that it was just to ask Spain for some compensation in view of the sacrifices made by France to obtain advantages in which Spain would share; and secondly to have regard for Spanish feelings and dignity, for a great country like France should never take undue advantage of its strength (" abuser de sa force ").

The latter words of M. de Selves caused a commotion in the Chamber and he was again prevented from continuing his speech for some minutes.

He concluded his speech by emphasising the advantage resulting from the fact that Morocco would henceforth be banished from the chess-board of France's foreign policy. In that direction, France's hands were freed—an advantage which should not be underestimated when the situation abroad was carefully considered. France should be attentive to and take part, in a pacific sense, in all that was happening, for a country which isolated itself from external events was a country which was failing and growing less. The French Government would strive to strengthen the friendships and alliances of France. In so doing, they would only be responding to the sentiments expressed before the British Parliament "by a great Foreign Minister," and by the eminent Russian Minister for Foreign Affairs who had just visited Paris.

M. Lebrun, Minister of the Colonies, then rose to defend the cession of territory made by France to Germany under the Convention. He gave a fairly lengthy description of the territory ceded, of the part of the Bec du Canard which France had obtained and of the vast territories which still remained to her. The conclusion which he drew was that no vital part of French territory had been surrendered, that the Government had been able to prevent the French Congo from being cut in two and that by the Protectorate established in Morocco the desire of all French explorers had been fulfilled, viz., that French civilisation should be spread over the largest extent possible of African territory.

M. Jaurès, the Socialist leader, having expressed the hope that France would not endeavour to break her treaty engagements with Spain, the President of the Council declared that France in the negotiations with Spain which were based on the 1904 agreement, intended to respect the dignity of Spain but to safeguard at the same time her own interests.

M. Deschanel, President of the Commission for Foreign Affairs, then spoke briefly but strongly against M. de Mun's motion of adjournment which was finally thrown out by 448 votes to 98.

The texts of the speeches made by the Minister for Foreign Affairs and the Minister for the Colonies are enclosed herein.([2])

I have, &c.
FRANCIS BERTIE.

MINUTES.

It will probably be thought more convenient to read the speech in our print.

M. de Selves made some important contributions to public knowledge of the negotiations :—

1. He stated that the French gov[ernmen]t from the outset claimed liberty to communicate information resp[ecting] the negotiations to H[is] M[ajesty's] G[overnment].

2. He made it clear that it was France who independently of any advice from England declared the German original demands (on which Germany insisted until some time after Mr. Lloyd George's speech) to be such as France could in no circumstances accept, and that the French gov[ernmen]t so informed H[is] M[ajesty's] G[overnment].

3. He added that, throughout the discussion, H[is] M[ajesty's] G[overnment] urged the French gov[ernmen]t to be conciliatory in all matters not vitally affecting French interests.

4. He revealed the German demand (in September) for a privileged position for German commerce in a particular zone in Morocco.

It is for consideration whether the speech should be translated and laid before parliament.

If there were any desire in Germany to appreciate the real course of the negotiations, with sole regard to the truth, these statements ought finally to dispose of all the allegations of England's unjustifiable interference. But this is of course a vain hypothesis.

E. A. C.
Dec. 18.
W. L.
A. N.

I fear it would be impossible to translate and to lay the speech apart from the interruptions and with the interruptions it would make rather a ragged paper.

E. G.
23.12.11.

([2]) [v. infra, pp. 806–20, App. II.]

No. 759.

Sir E. Goschen to Sir Edward Grey.

F.O. 50518/50518/11/28.
(No. 437.)
Sir,

Berlin, D. *December* 15, 1911.
R. *December* 18, 1911.

The semi-official " North German Gazette " publishes the following communiqué to-day :—

The " Humanité " has published some articles containing disclosures respecting German intrigues against the Portuguese Republic, which, in spite of their fantastic character, have been faithfully reproduced by the " Vorwärts " and other newspapers. They contain for example the nonsensical assertion that the Secretary of State for the Foreign Office demanded from the French Ambassador a free hand in Angola instead of the compensations in the Congo. Two points however require to be properly explained.

Firstly the allegation that with the knowledge of the German Government two ships have lain at Hamburg with arms and ammunition for the Portuguese Royalists, the departure of which was only prevented by representations on the part of two Great Powers. The facts are as follows :—

On October 18th the Imperial Minister at Lisbon reported that the Portuguese Government believed that they had obtained information to the effect that two Portuguese, alleged to be the leaders of the monarchical movement, were staying in Hamburg for the purpose of buying war-ships or war material there. The German Government immediately caused enquiries to be made on the spot, the result of which was that the two gentlemen, whose presence had been notified from Lisbon, had actually been in Hamburg in the middle of October, but that in the meantime they had left for Paris without having purchased weapons or anything else of that description. No representations whatever with regard to this question had been made by a third party. The Portuguese Government shortly afterwards stated that in Hamburg at the end of November several ships had been loaded with artillery materials and ammunition for the Royalist conspirators. As a result of this communication further researches were instituted in Hamburg. So far they have led to no result.

Further, the allegations of the " Humanité " respecting the occupation by Germany of Portuguese forts and territories in the Kubango District must be rectified. Libebe actually lies in German territory. In the neighbourhood of this place the Portuguese have erected a fort, also in German territory. Germany's act of violence against this fort is limited to the fact that representations were made in Lisbon a short time ago by Germany, with a view to obtaining the withdrawal of the fort into Portuguese territory.

I have, &c.
W. E. GOSCHEN.

No. 760.

Sir F. Bertie to Sir Edward Grey.

F.O. 50642/50338/11/28.
(No. 607.)
Sir,

Paris, D. *December* 16, 1911.
R. *December* 16, 1911.

I had the honour to report to you by my despatch No. 602 of yesterday([1]) the proceedings during the first day of the debate in the Chamber of Deputies on the recent Franco-German Treaty.

([1]) [*v. supra*, pp. 779–83, No. 758.]

The debate was continued yesterday when four long speeches were made on the subject.

M. Vaillant gave the Socialist view of the matter. His party disliked the Moroccan part of the Agreement even more than that relating to the Congo, for France was thereby pushed still further along the path of colonial adventure. At the same time, the signature of the Agreement was satisfactory in that it removed the nightmare of a war. The Socialist Party hoped that it would prove to be the beginning of an "accord généralisé" with Germany. They did not wish to see France entangled in the strife between two rival Imperialistic ambitions, that of England and that of Germany, but rather to see her as the "trait d'union" between those two great peoples.

M. Abel Ferry made an instructive speech to the House based on personal knowledge of Morocco. He was followed in the tribune by M. Jules Delahaye, a Deputy of the Right, who, in an interminable speech, developed all the accusations on special and general points which his party habitually bring against the present and indeed all Republican Governments. He accused them among other things of being ruled and "run" by International Financiers. "Un groupe," he said, "qui sous les noms de Banque de Paris et des Pays-Bas, d'Union Parisienne et d'autres encore, règne et domine . . . .([2]) groupe qui fait la loi en France—occultement et à un degré que la plupart de vous ne soupçonnent guère—à tout :—Banque de France, Crédit Foncier, établissements de crédit, grandes entreprises métallurgiques et industrielles, transports, chemins de fer, presse, Chambre et Gouvernement."

The important speech of the sitting was made by M. Millerand as the spokesman of the "Republican Socialist" group. It was a serious and eloquent argument in favour of the adoption of the Treaty. After examining its meaning and the advantages accruing therefrom to France, he alluded to the future policy to be pursued in Morocco, and advocated a slow policy of assimilation and pacific penetration rather than one of conquest with all the expense and risks which it entailed. It was highly desirable to avoid losses of men and money which would alarm French public opinion and were not indispensable. Wisdom and patience were needed in establishing France's protectorate over Morocco. The negotiations with Spain should be carried on in a friendly and cordial spirit. The Agreements of 1904 must be duly considered and no one he believed would propose to repudiate the signature which French Ministers had in the past set at the foot of engagements made in the name of France. England as the witness of these Agreements should be associated in the present pourparlers between France and Spain. It was fitting that she should be so associated for higher and more general reasons than her participation in the 1904 Agreements. Certain eminent people, he continued, had conceived another system of equilibrium than that actually existing, but the first duty of French foreign policy was to take account of realities, and this entailed the obligation of proceeding in company with those who had stood at France's side in difficult hours and of holding firmly to existing friendship and ties. "Nos amitiés et notre alliance n'ont . . . .([2]) de pointe dirigée contre personne." The stipulation that recourse should be had to the Hague Tribunal in the event of difficulties between France and Germany was of great practical and even greater moral value. France was attached to peace, but it must be a peace with honour. She meant to defend her own rights, while respecting those of others. Her desire was to interpret the Agreement with Germany with scrupulous loyalty;- to avoid a policy of adventure and conflicts but to draw from that Agreement all the advantages which legitimately could be derived from it.

M. Millerand's statesmanlike speech evidently made a considerable impression on the Chamber and is greatly praised by the Press this morning. On leaving the tribune he was warmly congratulated by M. Caillaux. Several papers express the opinion that he has shown himself to be eminently qualified for the post of Minister for Foreign Affairs in the future.

([2]) [Thus in original.]

I have the honour to transmit to you herewith the text of his speech extracted from the " Journal Officiel."(³)

I have, &c.
FRANCIS BERTIE.

(³) [Not reproduced.]

No. 761.

Sir E. Goschen to Sir Edward Grey.

F.O. 50521/50338/11/28.
(No. 440.)
Sir,

Berlin, D. *December* 16, 1911.
R. *December* 18, 1911.

M. de Selves' speech in the French Chamber(¹) has, considering the revelations made to the German public as to the methods of German diplomacy, met with comparatively little comment.

The " Berliner Tageblatt " says that unfortunately nobody in the Reichstag had asked either Herr von Kiderlen or the Chancellor point blank " What did you demand from France at the beginning of the negotiations?" Both had maintained complete silence on this point, and now the French Minister stated that Herr von Kiderlen had told M. Cambon that Germany would be prepared to agree to an exchange in Togoland and in the Cameroons, but she demanded Gabon and the Congo from the sea to the Sangho. This statement was a confirmation of the " Times " and " Matin " reports of July 19th and 20th respectively, and it was now announced officially that Germany had demanded nearly the whole of the Congo Colony together with the coast, and that France had refused this demand.

The " Berliner Tageblatt " continues as follows :—

" We have already said that we did not, like the Pan-Germans, see in the subsequent yielding of the German Government, which began after Sir E. Grey's intervention of July 21st, any sign of a retreat; for in such commercial deals one always begins by asking for the whole though one eventually accepts a third. But it is rare to receive, instead of a third, a comparatively valueless remnant. According to M. de Selves the German Government also attempted to obtain the creation of two zones in Morocco, and they wanted in one of these two zones special privileges for Germany—a desire also frustrated by French opposition. Did not the whole of our official Press deny the announcements which appeared in the French papers at the end of August respecting this demand for special privileges, a demand which contrasted so very strongly with the " Equal Rights " thesis always held by Germany and which could not be granted without the consent of the other Algeciras Powers? "

The article concludes as follows :—" Yes! If Bethmann-Hollweg and Kiderlen had, in the negotiations as to that unfortunate Congo, avoided the appearance of compulsion and not sent their cruiser to Agadir, then distrust of Germany would not to-day be the sole, the ruling and determining feeling in France. Then the last word in this Franco-Spanish conflict would not yet have been spoken, and every Frenchman would give clearer expression to his displeasure against England, who is trying to secure for Spain such a large piece of the Moroccan coast, and who is detracting so much from the value of the French conquest. Yesterday's session of the French

(¹) [v. infra, pp. 806–14, App. II; and cp. supra, pp. 781–3, No. 758.]

Chamber shows how German diplomacy, by wrong methods, falls short of the very sensible aims which it sets itself to attain, and how it actually does attain exactly contrary aims. We are told that the "highest circles" are uncommonly satisfied with the work done. This satisfaction can only be explained by optimistic self-deception or by a highly developed sense of contentedness."

The Liberal "Voss" says "Yesterday's debate disclosed a few facts hitherto unknown; that they were unknown is regrettable, for the German people had the right to learn them not from a French Minister but either from the Imperial Chancellor or from the Secretary of State for Foreign Affairs. The impression made by the fact that Herr von Kiderlen kept all the diplomatic conversations of the third, fourth and twelfth of July, first disclosed by Sir Edward Grey, both from the Budget Committee and from the public was bad enough; and it is no less unfortunate that it is from the lips of French Ministers that we first learn that Germany did not, from the very beginning—as was first supposed—, demand mere economic equality in Morocco, but had asked special rights in a certain zone; that, moreover, Germany had given France permission to keep the Entente Governments 'au courant' with all phases of the negotiations, and that consequently the oft made reproach of indiscretion is unjust; finally that the French Government, when Herr von Kiderlen demanded the Gabon and the Congo between the sea and the Sangho, stated their inability to continue negotiations on this basis. Since this statement was undoubtedly communicated to the British Cabinet, their view that the negotiations might fail was based, not, as might be thought from the German account, on irresponsible Press rumours or inaccurate reports from the British Ambassador in Paris, but obviously on official French disclosures."

The "Voss" article concludes with the usual "deeds and not words" paragraph, and with an expression of the "desire that, now the Morocco question is over a rapprochement of all the States concerned may be brought about."

The Conservative papers are almost unanimous in maintaining complete silence on the subject. A careful search through the chief Conservative organs only reveals two paragraphs bearing on the subject. The first of these is a short comment in the "Hamburg Nachrichten" which takes the view that Monsieur de Selves' utterances provide a proof that "the Imperial Government have not failed for one instant of the negotiations to uphold German interests," and says that the purpose which instigated the despatch of the "Panther" has been fully carried out. France had entered upon negotiations only upon condition that Germany should demand no territory in Morocco, but as the latter had never even thought of such a thing, she could cede to the French demands in this respect without accusing her of cowardly surrender.

The fact that France had, according to Monsieur de Selves, come strengthened out of the deal contained no reproach to Germany, and the only important question was whether the latter had gained or lost by the negotiations with France. That question had been practically answered by Count de Mun who had stated that the agreement had opened to Germany the door to the interior of Africa, and that far-reaching changes, not detrimental to this Empire, would probably now be made.

The only other Conservative comment is contained in a—presumably inspired —Berlin telegram to the "Kölnische Zeitung." It is to the following effect:— Attention will naturally be given to the debate in the French Chamber and especially to Monsieur de Selves' speech. In it less weight was laid on details than on the certainty resulting from the whole course of the debate that there existed an undoubted majority for the acceptance of the treaty. That many of the deductions of Monsieur de Selves rested upon a one-sided French standpoint was explained by the circumstance that Monsieur de Selves exerted himself to make the events which happened during the negotiations appear as far as possible in a light most advantageous to France. The telegram proceeds to point out that if certain portions of the speech were to be looked at from a German point of view the picture could be somewhat altered, but that this would serve no practical purpose. All the essential points were, however, clear, so that it was now a question no longer of retrospective observation but rather of the practical results which, as the "Kölnische Zeitung" hopes, the treaty will have for the benefit of both nations.

I have, &c.

W. E. GOSCHEN.

No. 762.

Sir F. Bertie to Sir Edward Grey.

F.O. 50645/50338/11/28.

(No. 610.)   *Paris,* D. *December* 17, 1911.

Sir,   R. *December* 18, 1911.

In continuation of my despatch No. 607 of yesterday's date([1]) I have the honour to report that the debate on the Franco-German Treaty was continued yesterday in the Chamber by Messrs Sembat, Deschanel, and Denys Cochin.

Monsieur Sembat, who is a Socialist of a moderate type, concluded, after a wide survey of the state of foreign affairs, that not only French Socialists, but intelligent and far-sighted men of all parties were beginning to comprehend that the interests of France called not only for a policy of peace but one of "entente" and conciliation with Germany.

Monsieur Deschanel spoke as President of the Commission for Foreign Affairs which was charged with the preliminary examination of the Treaty, and advocated its acceptance by the House.

Monsieur Denys Cochin, the well-known Conservative Deputy, criticised the Treaty from various points of view and declared his intention of not voting for it.

It is thought that the debate will be over by the 19th instant at any rate. The Treaty, if passed, will then go before the Senate. There are signs that the Chamber is becoming surfeited with long speeches on the subject in which nothing new is said. The President of the Council's speech is awaited however with curiosity.

I enclose the text of Monsieur Deschanel's speech extracted from the "Journal Officiel."([2]) Some interesting remarks on the working of the agreement respecting the powers of the Moorish Customs Commission, the Adjudication Commission, the State Bank, and the management of public works will be found on p. 4046 of the "Journal Officiel."

I have, &c.

FRANCIS BERTIE.

([1]) [*v. supra,* pp. 784–6, No. 760.]

([2]) [Not reproduced.]

No. 763.

Sir E. Goschen to Sir Edward Grey.

Private.([1])

My dear Grey,   *Berlin, December* 17, 1911.

I dined with the Chancellor last night and we had a little friendly conversation together upon recent events. We have one great thing in common which is love of music. I asked him whether he had had time lately to play his usual Beethoven Sonata before going to bed. He said "My dear Friend you and I like classical music with its plain and straightforward harmonies; how can I play my beloved old music with the air full of modern discords?" I said that even the old composers used discords to lead to harmonies, and that the latter sounded all the sweeter for the discords which preceded them. He agreed, but said that in modern music as in the

([1]) [Grey MSS., Vol. 23.]

present political atmosphere the discords predominated. He then said that, speaking as a friend and not as a Chancellor, he felt bound to state that he had found your speech *very* cold. I told him that I was very disappointed to hear him say that, as I thought he would have been pleased at your references to him and your general tone towards Germany. He said "No! I thought Sir Edward Grey's tone cold, and though he did say some friendly words there were too many 'ifs' tacked on to them." I said that I had not found his last speech particularly remarkable for warmth. He said "I admit that it wasn't, but in the irritated stated of public opinion here I *had* to speak as I did." I added that if he would forgive me for making 'Tu quoque' I must say that his speech, particularly the end of it, was not devoid of 'ifs.' "But only one," he said. "Yes, but a very big one!" I replied. This he admitted, but said that our continual policy of opposing Germany had made it necessary for him to put in that big 'if.' I pointed out to him that you had said that it was *not* the policy of His Majesty's Government—far from it—to oppose German expansion and German interests. He replied that that was so and that he had been delighted to hear it, *but* why had you not said it earlier in the day? I replied that you had probably thought it unnecessary to emphasize such a well-known fact before, and that it was only now, since the debates in the Reichstag and countless articles in the German Press had shown that the idea that England was opposed to Germany's expansion was so deeply rooted in the German mind, that you had thought it necessary to show that that idea was incorrect. I then said that, as we were talking about these matters, I wished he would tell me exactly what he meant by "Deeds and not words." Had he anything, any particular question in his mind? He said that he had 'everything' in his mind. Everything almost that had happened since he had been Chancellor. I would do him the justice to admit that he was a sincere and truthful man. Well! the first time he had seen me after he had taken office he had told me that the chief object of his foreign policy would be to bring about good relations with England. In his efforts to attain this object he had not met with whole-hearted support from England. I denied this and said that, though on certain broad points you had not seen things quite in the same light as he had, you had always shown every desire to meet him half way. He said that he didn't want to recriminate in any way, but the fact remained that his efforts had been unavailing, and that Anglo-German relations were worse now than when he had taken office. This was a great disappointment to him. The fact was, he added, that the British Government did not talk enough with the Imperial Government. "Why on earth, for instance, after the conversation with Metternich on the 6th of July, did not Sir Edward Grey tell you to come and have a confidential talk with me and ask me for information?" I said "Simply because Sir Edward Grey's language to Metternich showed clearly that more information was desired and would be welcomed. Metternich's answer that he had no information to give proved that information had been sought." He implied that Metternich's answer had nothing to do with the matter and that it would not have been consistent with the dignity of the German Government to give unasked information in addition to that which had already been given and which ought to have removed all distrust. The conversation gradually drifted to pleasanter subjects, and we parted with the mutual hope that 1912 would prove a better year all round than 1911. . . . .(²)

I remain,
Yours very sincerely,
W. E. GOSCHEN.

(²) [The closing paragraphs make passing reference to the Anglo-German Friendship Society, and Sir E. Goschen's leave.]

No. 764.

Sir Edward Grey to Sir M. de Bunsen.

F.O. 51176/13751/11/28.
(No. 135.)
Sir,   *Foreign Office, December 18, 1911.*

The Spanish Ambassador, after expressing to me to-day the relief which his Government felt now that the possession of Alcazar and Larache had been settled in their favour, and telling me how grateful they were for the influence which we had exerted on their behalf, said that there were two points on which he wished me to know the views of his Government.

It had been a great shock to them to find that the territory to the south of Morocco, which by the Franco-Spanish Agreement of 1904([1]) had been recognised as outside Morocco, was now brought into the negotiations and claimed for France. It was true that, in the negotiations with Germany, Morocco had been defined as including this territory. But the Spanish Government were given to understand that this was done only in order to prevent Germany from raising questions about it, which would have been inconvenient to France and Spain. As however, the district had been recognised by the Agreement of 1904 to be outside Moorish territory, the Spanish Government could not agree to allow the question of its ownership to form part of the negotiations. The cession of this territory would mean giving to France more in area than she had given to Germany in the Congo; and the Canary Islands would be dominated from the coast by France.

I observed that, when the Spanish Government had laid great stress upon the possession of Ifni, I had assumed that they regarded Ifni as an "enclave," and did not attach the same importance to the rest of the coast.

The Ambassador said it was true that special mention had been made of Ifni; but he had also mentioned the coast. He had now ascertained that there were at least two places on the part of the coast demanded by France that might become good ports.

The other point on which he wished me to know the views of his Government was with regard to the administration of the customs in the northern zone of Morocco.

The French Government claimed the administration, because the Customs receipts were pledged to French creditors. But the Spanish Government would be willing to guarantee the payment of the sum realised by the Customs, if they had the administration.

By this, I understood him to mean that, even if the Customs did not realise for the creditors under Spanish administration the amount that was expected, the Spanish Government would make good the amount.

I said that I assumed these two points were raised in the counter-project submitted by the Spanish Government to the French Government. The latter had no doubt been much occupied by the debate in the French Chamber, and I did not yet know their views. I was now in possession of the Spanish view on these points, but I must wait to hear what the French Government had to say about them before I could commit myself definitely to an opinion.

[I am, &c.]
E. G[REY].

([1]) [*v. infra*, pp. 826–9, *App.* IV.]

No. 765.

Sir F. Bertie to Sir Edward Grey.

F.O. 50928/50338/11/28.
(No. 613.)   *Paris,* D. *December* 19, 1911.
Sir,   R. *December* 20, 1911.

The interest of yesterday's debate in the Chamber of Deputies on the Franco-German Treaty(¹) centred in the very able defence of French policy on the part of the President of the Council, which seemed to make a strong impression on the Chamber.

Monsieur Caillaux began by showing how the continuity of French policy and aspirations from 1830 onwards had gradually led up to the present Agreement which, it might be said, crowned all the efforts made hitherto to constitute a great French Empire in North Africa by opening Morocco to French action. He referred to the attacks brought against M. Jules Ferry some thirty years ago for his Tunisian policy and inferred that the present Ministry were being attacked in the same unjust manner for a policy which would in the future be hailed as one of the greatest value to France.

This reference to the attacks on M. Jules Ferry was understood by the Chamber as a side-hit at M. Clemenceau, who was the principal opponent of M. Ferry's Tunisian policy, and who is stated to be strongly opposed to the Franco-German Treaty and to intend to vote against it in the Senate.

M. Caillaux proceeded to review the former Agreements dealing with Morocco, in the course of which he made perhaps the best answer which has yet been given by any French statesman to the charges brought against France of violating the Act of Algesiras. The intervention of Germany in 1905 had temporarily hindered France from pursuing her own independent line of action in the Moroccan question and induced her to consent to an attempt to introduce reforms into Morocco on international lines. He, (M. Caillaux), believed that the régime set up by the Act of Algesiras was an impracticable one. It contained an inherent contradiction which vitiated it, for while recognizing the special interest of France in the maintenance of order there, it refused to give her means to protect and ensure it. "En deux mots, il lui imposait à la fois le devoir d'agir et l'impossibilité d'agir." France was consequently obliged to take action which, if not in contradiction with the Act of Algesiras, was outside it. . . . .(²) the naval demonstration at Tangier, the occupation of Oudja, of Casablanca, of the ·Shawia district, and finally the Fez Expedition, undertaken at the request of the Sultan, and rendered necessary by the fact affirmed by the French Consul at Fez that the triumph of the revolt would have entailed a massacre. It was evident, ever since 1907, that the rights obtained by France under the International Arrangement (Act of Algesiras) were inadequate if she was to carry out the duties which the necessities of the situation laid upon her. She was inevitably thrown back on the policy of individual as against collective action. Everything indicated the necessity for her to return to the former policy, which was the only practical one and the only one befitting the dignity of a great country like France when it had such interests at stake. A first attempt was made in 1909 by the Agreement of that year with Germany. It was a happy initiative in that it inaugurated a period of direct negotiation between France and the only Power which barred her way in Morocco. In 1909 Agreement was, however, altogether too incomplete and vague. Difficulties were sure to arise therefrom. In the first place, it was almost impossible to establish a distinction between political and economic issues, for they were intimately connected. When it was a question of deciding about such matters as the organization of the ports, the lighthouses and, above all, the railways, it became apparent that the interpretations placed on the Agreement were widely divergent. On one side a claim was made to a large share in furnishing

(¹) [*v. supra,* pp. 604–8, No. 619, and *encl.;* also *infra,* pp. 806–20, *App.* II.]
(²) [Thus in original.]

the materials, but the stipulations for the equality of other Powers in the Act of Algesiras interfered, and among these Powers were France's friends and allies. The question of the exploitation of a great network of railways was also a difficulty for it had to be settled whether it was one of politics or economics.

M. Caillaux then explained to the Chamber the situation with which his Ministry was confronted when it took office. France was holding, in addition to the Shawia region, Rabat, Mequinez and Fez. An engagement had been given to evacuate these towns, but how was that possible without running the risk of being forced to send another expedition a few weeks later and without compromising French prestige in the eyes of the Moors and of France's own subjects in Algeria? Moreover, the resources of the Makhzen were exhausted. The meeting of a Conference was open to objections and perils from the French point of view. Only one alternative remained; a direct negotiation with Germany, to free France from the mortgage laid on Morocco by the Act of Algesiras.

M. Caillaux at this point turned to the objections and attacks made in various quarters on his Ministry for having given up French territory in exchange for the " shadow of a Protectorate in a mutilated Morocco." He said that other countries had sacrificed territory in negotiation. England, for instance, had ceded Heligoland to Germany, and in 1904, had given up to France a band of territory in the North of Nigeria, as well as the Loos Islands. Moreover, France in 1894—at this time M. Hanotaux was Foreign Minister—had ceded a territory of 250,000 square kilometres in extent to Belgium in order to have liberty of action in the Bahr-el-Ghazal. As regards the advantages gained in Morocco, France had obtained a position there which the Treaty of Bardo had not given her in Tunisia. France had had to wait for 15 years before she had been able to obtain in Tunisia as free a hand as the Franco-German Agreement gave her in Morocco.

Turning to the economic point of view M. Caillaux enumerated the various restrictions on the action of France imposed by the Treaty. These restrictions—the only real ones—were firstly the State Bank, secondly the principle of economic equality or in other words the principle of adjudication in regard to public works, and thirdly the principle of the open door. The State Bank could not be done away with, contracts entered into with third parties and which only expired in 1936 rendered it obligatory to maintain that institution. Moreover, where was the danger arising from its existence? The State Bank would merely, like the Bank of France in France, gather in receipts and make the necessary payments without having any right to interfere in any way in administrative matters. Out of 14 votes on the Board of Administration 9 could be counted as French, and this majority could in the future be increased. In fact a Bank placed under French law, whose President and Vice-President were Frenchmen, which had a certain number of French Directors and which had at Tangier a French Director and a Spanish sub-Director and the greater part of whose personnel was French, could not hamper French action in Morocco.

As to the obligation to have recourse to adjudication for public works, such adjudication existed in fact in all French Colonies. In Tunis an attempt had been made to abolish the adjudication system but that attempt had not been successful.

There remained the third restriction—the principle of the open door. That principle, however, existed in a greater degree in the conventional basin of the Congo, where it was stipulated by the Treaty of Berlin that no Customs duty of more than 10 per cent. must be imposed whereas those duties in Morocco were at present $12\frac{1}{2}$ per cent. On the Ivory Coast and Dahomey the policy of the open door also existed and those Colonies were among the most prosperous of the French possessions in Africa. France had at present 45 per cent. of the total commerce in Morocco and she had 45 per cent. of the total commerce in all her Colonies taken together. When her political preponderance was established in Morocco that proportion would become still greater. M. Caillaux declared that for all new countries which were opened out to commerce the policy of the open door was the only policy possible. He pointed out that in future if Morocco were called upon to conclude international agreements it was France who would negotiate those agreements, that if public works were undertaken there it was the Sultan, protected by the French, who would be master of them. In conclusion M. Caillaux declared that the most lasting guarantee of peace was the existence of a powerful military force backed up by solid credit, and that France had, by the noble and reassuring example which she had set, given to French foreign policy the firmest support and the surest guidance.

I have the honour to transmit to you herewith the text of M. Caillaux's speech from the "Journal Officiel,"(³) and a summary of Press opinions on that speech which is published by the "Matin."(³)

I have, &c.
FRANCIS BERTIE.

MINUTE.

I think that the Algeciras Act only gave France the right of maintaining order in the districts adjoining the Algeciras frontier—in the same way as Spain was accorded the right of maintaining order in the districts adjoining her Presidios. I do not think that the Act gave France the mandate to maintain order throughout Morocco.

A. N.
E. G.

(³) [Not reproduced.]

No. 766.

Sir F. Bertie to Sir Edward Grey.

F.O. 51213/50338/11/28.
(No. 615.)   Paris, D. December 21, 1911.
Sir,   R. December 22, 1911.

I have the honour to inform you that the Chamber of Deputies yesterday evening passed the Franco-German Treaty respecting Morocco and the Congo by 393 against 36 votes. There were 141 abstentions.(¹)

The latter part of the debate was chiefly occupied by M. Jaurès speech which began the day before yesterday and was continued yesterday. It was one of those great oratorical efforts which the Chamber is accustomed to hear from M. Jaurès at important moments, and which, while they irritate it, at the same time compel its interest and occasionally its admiration.

The first part of M. Jaurès speech caused violent interruptions, especially at one point, where he alluded to the low standard of international morality at present prevailing, and declared that he regretted that France had also her responsibility for "les violations universelles de la foi jurée, dans cet abaissement de la signature et de la loyauté internationale."

He devoted a considerable part of his speech to an examination of the manner in which French policy was influenced by great financial Syndicates, and appealed to the Government to be careful not to yield to the temptation of straining the sense of the Treaty too much in favour of these interests which would create further conflicts. The value of the Agreement lay in the fact that, if wisely applied, it would bring more "serenity" into European relations. He also made an eloquent appeal to the Government to treat the native population of Morocco with justice. "Une politique," he said, "est nécessaire qui protège non seulement la liberté de leurs coutumes et de leurs traditions, mais qui protège, en fait, contre les avidités, contre les roueries des hommes d'affaires leur propriété traditionnelle. Vous pouvez transformer et améliorer leurs habitudes de culture sans leur dérober le sol sur lequel ils vivent indépendants depuis des siècles; et prenons garde d'étendre au Maroc tout entier les procédés d'expropriation pseudo-légale qui déjà à Oudjda ont volé aux Marocains toute la riche et féconde terre" (see my despatch No. 468 of October 26).(²)

(¹) [v. report of Herr von Schoen on this day, *G.P.* XXIX, pp. 438–43.]
(²) [Not reproduced. It summarises reports in the French press respecting local conditions at Oudjda.]

The end of M. Jaurès' speech was an impassioned argument against war and against the light-hearted and irresponsible manner in which a possible outbreak of war was often discussed. He pictured the calamities which must ensue from a war between great European Powers and the wholesale disasters which must follow, and insinuated that the upper classes would do well to work for peace, for in the social upheavals which accompanied or followed wars, no one could tell what might happen.

I inclose herein a portion of M. Jaurès' speech,([3]) in which he refers to the Peace Movement in the United States and Mr. Taft's efforts in favour of an Arbitration Treaty with England, and to the rivalry between England and Germany.

After M. Jaurès, various speakers explained why they would vote against the Treaty. One of these, M. Lefébure, read out a declaration on behalf of himself and twelve other Deputies of the Eastern frontier Departments to the effect that they could not vote for the Agreement with Germany as their action might be interpreted as "un oubli du passé."

This declaration occasioned a curious scene in which M. Lebrun, Minister of the Colonies, played the chief rôle, and which is described as follows by the "Matin":—

"Assis entre M. Caillaux et M. de Selves, M. Albert Lebrun a écouté cette lecture dans une tension de tout son être. M. Lebrun est Député de Briey; il est Lorrain. Son cœur éclate, et dans un sanglot qu'il ne peut arriver à dominer, il se cache la tête dans les mains. La Chambre a vu la scène; plus profondément encore, si possible, elle est remuée par la douleur patriotique du Ministre des Colonies. Pour bien montrer qu'ils lui gardent toute leur confiance et toute leur sympathie, de nombreux députés se précipitent au banc des Ministres et prodiguent à M. Lebrun des paroles d'amitié et de réconfort. La minute après, le Ministre des Colonies quittait la Chambre. Tous sès collègues du Cabinet, M. Caillaux en tête, tinrent à lui apporter, dans un bureau voisin, le témoinage de leur solidarité et de leur affection."

As I had the honour to report to you, M. Lebrun made, on the 14th instant, an able and effective speech in defence of the Treaty, which was cheered by the Chamber and was regarded as considerably increasing M. Lebrun's prestige.

Speaking generally, the debate which ended yesterday was conducted in an unusually calm tone. The Chamber listened with patience to long discourses on the negotiations and the Treaty itself which contained little that was novel. M. de Selves' speech was considered disappointing, but MM. Lebrun and Caillaux both made an effective defence of French policy. Various speakers advocated a "rapprochement" with Germany, but their words on this subject were received with marked coldness by the Chamber. Numerous references to the friendship and support of England were made and invariably evoked manifestations of cordial appreciation in the Chamber. Several speakers alluded in a highly eulogistic manner to your speech in the House of Commons on the 27th ultimo respecting the Morocco question.([4])

The Treaty will now go before the Senate. It will be first considered by a Special Committee appointed by the Senate to examine its clauses, and it is not expected that the public discussion in that House will take place before the middle of next month.

I have, &c.
FRANCIS BERTIE.

([3]) [Not reproduced.]
([4]) [v. supra, pp. 725–35, No. 721.]

No. 767.

Sir Edward Grey to Sir E. Goschen.

Private.(¹)

My dear Goschen,   *Fallodon, December 29, 1911.*

I wish I could have shared in your conversation with the Chancellor at dinner on the 16th : you send me a very pleasant account of it. (²) It would be very tempting to explain to the Chancellor the extraordinary disingenuousness of Kiderlen's statement to the Reichstag Committee and the criticisms that occurred to me on reading the Chancellor's second speech, but I have no type-writer here to whom to dictate a letter, so I won't even blow off steam to you.

Indeed I put aside criticisms on the Chancellor's last speech by considering that in his position, with the German elections in prospect and public feeling in Germany being what it is, he was bound whatever I had said to make finally the sort of speech that he did make. If I am right in this view, then an effusive speech from me on November 27 would not have altered the sort of speech he made subsequently; though it would have enhanced the effect of it, for I should have appeared as having made an overture and been snubbed, and the German Government would have had a great opportunity of scoring with their own public at my expense : an opportunity that in their present position they could not have afforded to neglect. I should also have made the French uneasy and this among other untoward consequences would have made the passage of the Morocco Agreement through the French Chamber more difficult. So much for my speech having been cold. . . . .(³)

Yours sincerely,

E. GREY.

(¹) [Grey MSS., Vol. 23.]
(²) [*v. supra*, pp. 788–9, No. 7.63.]
(³) [The rest of this letter refers to the question of the Portuguese Colonies, which will be treated in a later volume.]

[*ED. NOTE.*—The following memorandum written in July 1912 is reproduced here as it relates to conversations of this period.]

Memorandum on Conversations with Herr von Kiderlen-Waechter during three days in November, 1911.(¹)

July 25, 1912.

The German Foreign Minister in the course of three days, talked quite freely and frankly to a great personal friend, my informant, on all matters of international politics, especially those affecting Germany.

In discussing the Agadir business, he said that the plans were discussed and put before the Emperor as early as May, and after considerable delay the German Emperor gave permission for them to be carried out with the strongly expressed condition that on no account was it to lead to war. The object of the Agadir move, according to Herr von Kiderlen-Waechter, was not war at all, so that the Emperor's stipulation was by no mean displeasing. The main idea underlying this vigorous act of policy was to test the sincerity of the Anglo-French Entente. The speeches, newspaper articles and private utterances of more or less prominent people in England, and the known attitude of some politicians in France, had led Kiderlen-Waechter to presume that the strength of the Entente was much less than was supposed, and he confessed his surprise at finding that England stood so firmly to it. In this matter he admitted that he was surprised, and disappointed, for he had led the Emperor to believe that as a result of German action in Morocco a wedge had been driven between France and England which it would be possible in the future to drive further home. As a result of his miscalculations he had to endure the anger of the Emperor, which very nearly resulted in his resignation : but Herr Bethmann-Hollweg told the Emperor quite bluntly that if the Foreign Minister went, he would go to[o], and it was entirely owing to this that the Foreign Minister did not send in his resignation, for, as he put it to my friend, the Emperor " was unwilling to lose another Chancellor so quickly, as he was afraid of the sharp criticism that would follow." . . . .

H. A. G[WYNNE].

(¹) [Grey MSS., Vol. 68. A covering letter from Mr. Gwynne, then Editor of the *Morning Post*, states that the conversations recorded here took place between Herr von Kiderlen-Waechter and M. Také Jonescu. *cp. Gooch & Temperley*, Vol. VI, pp. 760–1, No. 594, where the rest of this memorandum is reproduced. *cp.* also *supra*, p. 357, No. 373, *min.*, and *infra*, pp. 821–26, App. III.]

APPENDIX I.

THE GERMAN FINANCIAL CRISIS.

Consul-General Sir F. Oppenheimer to Sir Edward Grey.

F.O. 42175/36569/11/28.

(No. 10.) Consular. *Frankfort-on-Main*, D. *October* 21, 1911.

Sir, R. *October* 26, 1911.

I beg to acknowledge receipt of the despatch dated September 23rd to the effect that it would be of interest to H[is] M[ajesty]'s Government to have reliable information on the present financial position in Germany as affected by the recent course of the Morocco negotiations and asking for a report on the subject.

The report asked for is herewith enclosed; the delay in its transmission is due to the fact that the request was received a few days after my departure on leave of absence.

I have, &c.

FRANCIS OPPENHEIMER.

Enclosure.

Report replying to Question how far the Negotiations concerning Morocco have affected the Financial Position in Germany.

To gauge the extent to which the financial position of Germany may have been affected by the recent course of the negotiations concerning Morocco and to summarise the financial position in Germany as it to-day presents itself, it will be necessary first to picture the financial situation in Germany as the negotiations concerning Morocco found it.

A. *Constellation before Agadir.*

Industrial recovery and discount rates.

In 1907 a financial check had brought the brilliant boom of the preceding four years to an end (Bankrate—November 1907 $7\frac{1}{2}$%). A slow but steady industrial recovery has since taken place. Even if it had not yet during the first half-year of 1911 reached the uniform activity characteristic of a boom, the usual barometers registered a high industrial pressure. The continued needs of money for industrial purposes had again begun to stiffen the discount rates, viz. :

Bankrate Berlin—1909	1910	1911
annual average		January
3·93	4·35	4·5

The average for the two first quarters of 1911 was again a few points higher than that of 1910.

Government Stock.

Government stocks had steadily declined and were still dropping because available cash was invested in "industrials" which during a boom form a more lucrative investment. The German Government stock had been quoted at :

			4%	$3\frac{1}{2}$%	3%
July 1st 1909	...	...	101·	95·	86·60
July 1st 1910	...	...	101·10	93·	84·70
July 1st 1911	...	...	100·83	92·70	83·90

Period of speculation at home.

This last commercial recovery can boast a feature of its own : a wave of speculation, different in character from similar epidemics, has swept over the country. Hardly ever before have such vast numbers throughout Germany been involved in speculation, never before has the fever so entirely seized the "Mittelstand"—the smaller capitalists who as a class are nothing more than dilettanti in financial as in political matters. The increased cost of living in Germany has most directly affected that class; for that class the hope of an increased income has become an irresistible temptation. When the last industrial slump had been overcome (1908) without the dreaded concussions, partly owing to the iron grip which the syndicates have over the leading branches of manufacture, partly owing to a carefully studied management of the money market, an optimistic belief in the future penetrated the banking and the industrial world. The "outsider" was quick to catch this optimism : he was on the alert for a lucrative chance. A mass of new industrial issues which were put upon the market to ease the still outstanding credits (which during the preceding boom had been granted by the banks), found ready buyers among masses of the population. The banks, seeing a chance of remunerative business, played up to the public: they established a closer contact with these would-be "investors" by means of their Depositen-Kassen—branch establishments opened in all quarters of the towns and worked by enterprising managers. Possible clients were personally interviewed; the neighbouring areas were freely circularised. As the branch offices of different banks worked in competition their zeal became that of bucket-shops. Speculation increased with the force of an avalanche.

For the masses time bargains in industrial shares have been practically abolished by the more recent Stock Exchange legislation; where the last modification of the law has again facilitated them, they are still hampered by bureaucratic paternal precautions. The wave of speculation then was practically throughout a speculation by cash. The order to purchase was accompanied by a deposit as a margin against unlikely losses. To obtain the funds for these deposits permanent investments (stocks) were readily sold or mortgaged; private banking credits were pledged to the utmost extent. By the end of July 1911 (note)* the credits in the leading Berlin banks exceeded those of the preceding year by 401 million marks; deposits had risen by 326 million marks; stocks and shares in the hands of the banks had increased by $72\frac{1}{2}$ million marks. Already in 1909 (October) the Imperial Bank had issued a manifesto warning against the excrescences of this speculation; by the middle of 1911 its proportions had become so vast that even the banks which had at first encouraged it became alarmed, more especially as the first clouds were gathering on the economic horizon.

In consequence of the speculative fever which had lasted for quite three years, German industrial shares had reached quotations which were out of proportion to the working yield and which no confidence in the future, however sanguine, could justify (German Colonials; coal shares; "Phœnix," etc.). *[margin: Quotations in excess of working returns.]*

It was, moreover, notorious that the speculating public had spread its field of operations abroad. Owing to the practical impossibility of concluding time bargains at home, Germans had indulged in heavy speculative engagements in London, Paris and the States (viâ London); there were not unfounded misgivings that clients who had pledged their home credits to their fullest extent had, notwithstanding, entered also into unwarrantable obligations towards foreign banks. The German public was notoriously heavily engaged in gold mining shares, rubber shares, American rails, and even in such gambling shares as kinematographs, skating rinks, etc. *[margin: Speculation abroad.]*

The American market became the first subject for practical concern. The campaign there carried on against the trusts harassed the industrial world and prevented the expected recovery. Large orders for the iron and other works contemplated by the railroads were held back; industrial quotations receded. Yet the German bourses showed an unexpected resistance to the fluctuations of the American market, though, as a rule, any industrial adversities in the States are readily echoed in the financial centres of Germany. This unaccustomed resistance to the American set-back was still accepted as a welcome proof of the strength of the home markets. The banks, though already on the alert, were still inclined to profit from the German speculative fever as long as there was no cause for precaution nearer home. *[margin: American alarm.]*

Before long there were forced upon them the first doubts in the continuance of the native industrial recovery from purely domestic causes. If in 1907 the first diffidence in the future was awakened by the abnormal bankrate, it was in 1911 due to the abnormal rise in the price of all victuals. In the home market the increased cost of living must reduce the capitals available for the lesser necessaries of life and so curtail the demand for other commodities. It was also argued that the increased cost of living must lead to labour troubles which would be disastrous, whatever their *[margin: Industrial prospects at home. Cost of living.]*

* NOTE.—Figures *end* of *July* are given as picturing more accurately the true state of affairs than the figures of half-yearly balance sheets *end* of *June* when, for purposes of publication, the status of the banks is made to appear as "liquid" as possible.

result. If they led to increased wages, they must in the end handicap the competitive capacity of Germany's international trade.

Syndication.   At the same time the consequences of syndication in the leading German industries were clearly becoming a menace to the prosperity of the future. The leading syndicates are approaching the period of their possible renunciation, others have run out, some have collapsed prematurely. In each case the members of these syndicates, past and present, aim at an increased production which will insure a larger figure of participation, should a new syndication of their manufacture be effected. For this purpose works are increased to unremunerative dimensions—for, as a rule, it is the size of the works which determines the calculation of the figure of participation. Vast sums are invested, not because the works are insufficient to meet the present demand, but because the present figure of participation is deemed insufficient if it is to be fixed for a new and prolonged period of years. Thus the law syndicating the alcali mines directly involved an additional capital exceeding 400 million marks in the construction of new shafts and mines. The position is similar in the coal mining and iron industries. The coke syndicate had decreed a production amounting to only 40% of the actual figure of participation, so that the works were foregoing 60% of their possibility of production upon which, however, they are liable for interest. At the same time the heavy contributions towards the management of syndicates (coal syndicate 12% of the takings) further increase the cost of production.

B. *Agadir Incident to early September.*

These considerations admonished the banks to caution, quite regardless of the Agadir incident which so unexpectedly supervened on July 1st.

Speculating public confidence for various reasons.   The earlier diplomatic consequences of the Agadir incident did not perceptibly affect the German speculating public; its knowledge of international affairs is insignificant. The German Stock Exchange survey for the week following upon the Agadir incident registered in no case drops of more than 2%. The money market was and continued remarkably easy. The industrial boom of the three preceding years had increased capitals; the industrial issues had brought considerable profits to the banks; the transfer of shares had let profits into the hands of the sellers; owing to the reform of the Imperial finances (1909) the Empire had been able to refrain from an issue of stock for more than 18 months (since February 1910).

Banks diffident.   But while the speculating public was prepared to hang on, the banks brought pressure to bear upon their clients to reduce or redeem their credits. The misgivings concerning the industrial prospects which had prevailed during the preceding period still continued; new ones were added. The American market was becoming more unsettled with a tendency to go from bad to worse. In different parts of Europe the labour market was becoming restless; it was feared that the serious labour troubles in England might prove contagious in Germany. The procrastination in the international pourparlers naturally underlined the bankers' diffidence in the future.

Bankers bring pressure to bear upon public.   There is no doubt that the banks in view of the industrial situation used the Morocco entanglement at first only as a welcome and timely justification for a more energetic handling of their clients—for ridding themselves of precarious accounts, the result of a speculation which they had encouraged at an earlier period, but over which they had since lost all control. Under pressure from head-quarters the managers of the "Depositen Kassen" who are paid a percentage on the profits of their individual establishments, became alarmed and pressed their clients for the redemption of exaggerated risks.

Result: first check in upward tendency.   Thus, after three years, occurred the first definite set-back in the upward movement of the share market. By the middle of August the weakest elements among the speculating public had probably been removed. Those professionally engaged upon the Bourse had effected profit-taking sales on a more extended scale because the margin was still greatly in their favour. But that part of the speculating public which was financially strong enough still preferred to sell sound stocks to increase their deposits or to buy the shares outright. The public has learned that industrial quotations, if the scrip can be held sufficiently long, have eventually a way of righting themselves.

It was natural that the banks should have become more insistent as time advanced, even if there had been no Morocco question to obscure the future, because the second half of the third quarter is notoriously the one in which, even in ordinary times, the heaviest demands of the year are made upon the money market. In 1911, moreover, these demands were likely to present themselves earlier than usual because the harvests had been gathered in advance of the usual date. At the same time the amount of bills was likely to be exceptionally large at the settlement at the end of September because the new regulations of the Reichsbank concerning advances against securities (Lombard) had increased the cost of that class of loans. *Bankers' view justified.*

To these economic reasons was finally added one of a political kind. When the prolonged diplomatic negotiations were beginning to show a more serious aspect, not only were French holdings of German consols put on the German market, but French capital was being withdrawn; at the usual critical financial moment this hostile measure would lead to an unusual and unexpected shortage of cash. The "Times" (September 25th) had estimated that the amount of French money in the course of the negotiations actually withdrawn from Germany amounted to probably £10,000,000; I am informed on good authority that the actual amount was probably more than double that sum. These withdrawals began long before the fateful days early in September; they were prompted by political, not by financial, reasons. There exist very intimate connections between the German and the French "Haute Finance" and the position of the German money market is as well known in Paris as in Berlin. For many a year French capital has been attracted to Germany on account of the more lucrative rates at which it can there be invested, temporarily or for longer periods. With this prolonged experience the French have learned to read the meaning of German balance sheets; they appreciate the great publicity given to German banking affairs, more especially since the leading German banks have undertaken to publish their status bimensally—a publicity (and hence also a security) far in excess of what they are accustomed to at home. There is a very strong suspicion in Germany that this withdrawal of French capital was effected as the result of broad hints thrown out by the French Government. French finance is always to a certain extent dependent upon the Government of the day because the French Bourse is at the latter's mercy: no issue could there be effected against the wishes of the Cabinet. The Haute Finance no doubt deemed it advisable to follow official suggestions which were intended to embarrass Germany financially at a time of some political difficulty. *Withdrawal of French money.*

C. September and after.

Towards the end of August the German public was prepared to take a gloomy view of the political situation. Nothing had so entirely robbed it of what was left of confidence as the German press comment upon the speech delivered by the Chancellor of the Exchequer (August 24th 1911). The bona fide holders of shares became reconciled to the prospect of an impending period of stagnation, possibly of reaction. Yet they hoped at least for financial benefits from their American holdings which they had of late increased very considerably to cover expected losses in the German market. *Lloyd George's speech. Diffidence of public.*

These American purchases led towards the end of the month to enormous losses because nearly unprecedented differences had to be settled in the very shares which are popular among Germans. This was the real beginning of the déroute on the German market. The American losses made the public nervous concerning its German holdings. During the week ending September 2nd the Berlin Bourse did all in its power to save the situation. *Losses in Americans start the déroute.*

On the following Monday, September 4th, the provincial orders to sell poured in and, as is usual in times of anxiety, these provincial orders unhinged the market; it was swamped by material far in excess of what it could have consumed. The thunder clouds in the political sky, the wild rumours of war which frightened one into selling, frightened all alike; all were anxious to be first out of the market; there *September 4th "Black Monday."*

was a senseless stampede. As orders to sell were given without reserve prices, industrial shares dropped within a few hours 5, 8, and 10% ; some recorded losses in one day of 20, even 30%. Government stock (sold to pay for shares) receded by $\frac{1}{2}$ per cent. These drops of the "Black Monday" spelled heavy losses indeed and in a number of cases prepared ruin. The bankruptcies registered during the third quarter of 1911 number 2015 as against 1907 in 1910 and 1808 in 1909, in spite of the continuance of a wave of industrial prosperity.

Débâcle explained. no "countermine." How is such a débâcle to be explained?

The vast crowd of "amateur" speculators in Germany had for years speculated for a rise. Among that class the counter speculation "à la baisse," which could have stepped in as buyers as soon as certain drops had been reached, was non-existent. For though the dilettanti in the share market will risk to buy what they cannot afford, they dare not sell what they do not possess. As a result, an order to sell even a small parcel of shares may, even during ordinary times, have a very adverse effect upon quotations.

insufficient day speculators. At moments of more extended sales a further disadvantage of the Stock Exchange legislation in Germany is felt. The steady increase in the stamp duty on Stock Exchange transactions has greatly reduced that considerable group of day speculators who in former years had been regular attendants upon the Stock Exchange and who, carefully watching the fluctuations of the market, would become sellers or buyers whenever the constellation of the moment seemed favourable. The members of this useful professional group had been content with small daily profits; to-day such a calling offers little temptation because the profits on a day's bargains are too easily swallowed up by the Government tax payable on the day's business.

Haute Finance abstains from intervention. The leading bankers were conscious of the damage which the déroute of September 4th was inflicting upon the prestige of German finance ; they would have been prepared to intervene, if the Government had given them the least indication concerning the course of the diplomatic negotiations. There can be little doubt that the giant banks are strong enough to intervene successfully on the Stock Exchange at any given moment and that they command an effective machinery for such intervention through their many branch offices, affiliated houses, dependent private banks, Depositen Kassen. But the Secretary of State for Foreign Affairs declined to throw out any hints. Perhaps this refusal made the political situation appear more critical at a critical moment, but it is more likely that the bankers' inactivity was intended as a demonstration against the bureaucratic methods adopted by the German Foreign Office. They were determined to leave the Bourse to its own devices in order to impress official quarters with their power and to demonstrate ad oculos the advisability of in future letting the Haute Finance at least to some extent into the secrets of the Wilhelmstrasse.

Run on Savings banks. The fact that none of the large banks had intervened to save the situation supplied for the general public a semblance of justification for its grave fears concerning the political situation. This fear on the part of the small speculators spread to the small and smallest capitalists. There resulted a run on the savings banks. Depositors withdrew their accounts and demanded payment in gold—nothing but gold would satisfy them and gold was given. It is said that these withdrawals amounted to only 4 million marks out of deposits totalling sixteen thousand million marks. But I have reason to believe that the published sum remains far below the actual figures, more especially in the frontier districts. At the branch office of the Reichsbank in Metz, e.g., the telephonic calls for gold, not only by the savings banks, but by local banks to satisfy larger depositors never ceased for days. If it had been the small capitalists only calling for gold, the rush might have been explained as the outcome of a fear of war on the part of the uneducated who, having lived for four decades in undisturbed peace, regarded war still as a time of mediæval pillage and of forced contribution. But the fact that the call for gold came also from bankers and industrialists, from a stratum above that which uses the savings banks, tends to prove that there were in some quarters misgivings as to the soundness of the financial situation, at least in certain neighbourhoods.

As a direct result of the crisis two banks have failed—both at Göttingen. I am collapse of two
local banks. told that the Reichsbank was prepared for the collapse of two further banks in the same locality.

D. *Situation reviewed.*

In view of the political situation during which these events occurred it is natural that the financial situation of Germany thus revealed should have been very differently judged by the Press at home and abroad.

The foreign press summed up German finance by describing it as a house of abroad. cards for the collapse of which wild rumours had sufficed. It was asked what must be the effect of a genuine war scare if the contingent risk of war, more or less well founded, already had such a disastrous effect upon German finance. The run on the savings banks was adduced to prove German diffidence in her own financial strength; it was argued that after such a rude lesson Germany must be the first to realise how little she was financially entitled to enter upon a policy of " sabre rattling."

The German press was as ready to deduct a proof of financial strength from at home. these same events. It was pointed out that a rise in the discount rate of only 1% 19th Sept[ember] during a prolonged period of international complications with vast sums of foreign gold withdrawn, with the most exacting annual settlement at the door, with a premature call for money owing to an exceptionally early harvest is an irrefutable argument in favour of the soundness of German finance. The fact is underlined that the savings banks paid the clamouring crowd in gold upon demand without insisting upon the notice to which they are by law entitled in case of the withdrawal of deposits of more than 300 marks. It was argued that the collapse of two small banks in one town is an insignificant local calamity and proves, not a general weakness, but a general strength. It is boastingly proclaimed that the wealth of the German financial resources, as manifested by the crisis, has surprised the Germans themselves. It is even said that, as far as the German money market is concerned there never was any real cause for alarm; that the panic was a coup cleverly engineered by French antagonists to frighten the German chauvinists into a more conciliatory attitude.

It probably is a fair criticism upon these criticisms that the situation was under- independent
view. rated abroad and overrated at home. In justice it must be stated that the German financial situation was no better and no worse than that of the other leading money markets at that period. Its picture was reflected at greater disadvantage than it deserved because the news published, concerning the German Exchanges dealt most conspicuously with German industrial shares. In France very few similar industrial share companies exist nor are the few used for speculative purposes by the native crowd. Speculation there gambles in rubber shares, African mines, American rails, etc., which, at the same time provide the subject for popular gambling in Great Britain, in the States and also in Germany. When the market for these shares collapses no conclusions can in consequence be drawn to discredit the finance or money market of any particular country.

Even if it be admitted that the drops that occurred on the German Exchanges on September 4th have been more sudden (for reasons previously set out) than those registered elsewhere, they were certainly not more considerable than the drops of the international shares mentioned above spread over a number of days in that very period. But even the low water mark reached in Germany for German shares on September 4th was in most cases still considerably higher than the quotations of these shares at the beginning of the same year. Shares in concerns of those industries which had a particularly good year were only temporarily affected *e.g.* electrical industry, chemical industry, etc.; for other shares the retrogression was only partly made good because the quotations had been previously run up beyond anything justifiable by the working returns. The following is a table of German share quotations selected at random on January 2nd, August 15th and September 4th, and compared with the quotations of October 16th :—

(NOTE.—" ex " means quotation without dividends due.)

	2nd January.	15th August.	4th September.	16th October.
Badische Anilin	485	508	490	500
Elberfeld Farben	484	508	494	502
Höchster	515	541	523	539
Chem. Riedel	214	292	271	290
Arenberg Mining Co.	393	384	370	366
Charlotten Foundry Co.	177	215 ex	202	204
Concordia Mining Co.	311	308	276	275
Donnersmark Foundry Co.	301	303	291	300
Hasper ,, ,, ...	164	174 ex	160	167
Hösch ,, ,, ...	289	328 ex	308	310
Oberkoks ,, ,, ...	168	186	173	177
Rhein-Nassau ,, ,, ...	305	350	330	338
Westf. Wire Works, Langendreer ...	226	200 ex	173	187
Kleyer Motor Co.	434	462	446	466
Dürkopp ,, ,, ...	417	515	481	465
Egestorff Machine Co.	307	295 ex	272	...
Halle ,, ,, ...	401	430	415	415
Hofmanna Railway Carriage Co. ...	560	681	646	729
Vogtländer Machine Co.	369	460 ex	425	439
Plauener Lace Co.	121	131 ex	118	128
Etc.	Etc.	Etc.		

Nor ought German finance to be too harshly stigmatised for the drop in German consols ; British consols reached a particularly low level at the same period. Again about the same time in which the German official discount rate was raised, the rate was raised also by the same amount (1%) by the other central note-issuing banks in Europe. The discount rate itself in Germany was no higher than is customary towards the end of the third quarter, viz. : 5%. Again, if there were two bankruptcies of German local banks, the amounts involved in both were below those involved in the collapse of the Bank of Egypt.

There was on the German Exchanges a panic—the fact cannot be explained away—but it could have been prevented had the amour propre of the leading banks been officially studied. It is a fact that a similar occurrence was afterwards actually prevented by an official statement issued to the banks. Official quarters stood reproved and accepted the lesson. The banks had achieved their purpose. As the political situation lost its tension the market quickly recovered ; the confidence of the public was rapidly restored. The gold which had been demanded from the savings banks and others was promptly returned—in many cases the actual rolls of sovereigns with the seal of the Reichsbank untouched. Accounts had been closed and money thus flowed back into the banks. Subsequently even such incidents as the publication of the Cartwright interview (September 13th) remained without effect upon the market, though it aroused German feeling no less than the Chancellor of the Exchequer's speech. The banks, relieved of a mass of doubtful accounts, nursed the Stock Exchange and the general situation became one of renewed optimism. The harvest results proved better than was expected ; the railway returns were excellent ; the half-yearly balance sheets of the banks showed considerable profits ; on September 22nd the vast labour movement in the German metal industry was finally arrested ; many branches of industry were fully occupied in connection with orders for the coming winter.

French money returns to Germany.

If French money (and British too) had been withdrawn during the political negotiations, other foreign money remained in the country ; its amount was even increased by the early raising of the German discount rate, probably advanced in date for the very purpose of tempting foreign lenders. French money was again freely offered—no doubt with the tacit sanction of the French Government—but preference could be given to offers from New York—this snub being an answer to the earlier withdrawals of French money from the German market.

By the end of September no traces were left of the short, sharp panic—which never went below the surface of the financial situation. On October 1st 100 million 4% Imperial Bonds and 145 million Prussian Treasury Bonds were due. The Imperial Government had more than a week before announced that it was its intention to redeem 40 millions in cash and to exchange 60 millions against stock redeemable in 1915. The Prussian Government proposed to renew its 145 millions and to increase the amount by 40 millions. The whole transaction was effected without a hitch and of the re-issue more was even applied for from abroad than had been sent in for the purposes of the conversion. *cash redemption of Treasury bonds.*

The events of September 4th did not test the quality of the German money market; assisted by a continued industrial boom, they left the financial situation if anything improved because it was relieved of undesirable elements; their removal was a salutary and painless operation benefiting the body as a whole. *Conclusion: the events of Sept[ember] 4th no test of German finance.*

E. *The Lesson.*

The foregoing pages contain a considered description of the German financial situation before the negotiations concerning Morocco were begun and of the German financial situation during the progress of these negotiations. They show that the negotiations concerning Morocco have (as yet) had no great or general effect upon the financial situation in Germany, but there have been two minor adverse effects: one, transitory, if general—the panic on the Stock Exchange; and one, more lasting, if locally restricted, the collapse of two banks. Can any conclusions be drawn from these two events? Can they be taken as proofs that there are certain risks below the surface which were not really touched in September last and which, during a less favourable economic constellation than that of 1911, (*e.g.* during an industrial slump or during a period of high rate of discount), could have matured into serious trouble? Is it from these two events that the real lesson of 1911 is to be drawn? *German banking: its dangers.*

In the German banking world three different groups of banking establishments must be distinguished: the Imperial Bank (Reichsbank), standing by itself; the limited group of the leading banks (Grossbanken) and the host of smaller banks.

1. The Reichsbank. No words need be wasted upon the merits of the Imperial Bank in times of peace. It is an institution above suspicion, managed by an experienced body of officials and erring, if at all, on the side of caution. Its dealings are circumscribed and safeguarded by law; its status is permanently the subject of public knowledge. It is at all times watched by the keenest financial brains of the country and supported by the business world at large. Its business and power have steadily increased; it enjoys the well earned confidence of the country. It is, physically and morally, the backbone of German banking. *Reichsbank: in peace.*

In case of war the " Reichsbank " becomes the " Kriegsbank," and it is generally believed that it is equally well prepared for this emergency. It will take supreme and active control of the financial situation according to a scheme said to be ever held in readiness and which, with the declaration of war or the beginning of hostilities, would automatically come into operation. Part of this secret scheme no doubt decrees a " moratorium ": all withdrawals of deposits from the Reichsbank, from other banks and savings banks will be stopped; an embargo will be laid upon all gold. The Reichsbank will be freed from those guarantees as to its issue of notes to which it is bound in times of peace; it will be empowered to issue notes to any necessary amount, regardless of the cover in gold and cash prescribed for ordinary times. Its gold reserves will be exclusively used for the needs of the country. *Reichsbank: in war.*

2. The Grossbanken, the second group, led by seven banks (one with its head office in Cologne), with a total capital of 1,039 million marks and possessing 322 million marks of reserves, are the outcome of the process of concentration which during the last decade or two has become characteristic of German industry generally and German banking in particular. This concentration has given German *Grossbanken.*

banking unprecedented financial strength and has helped to make the existence of the giant concerns of German industry possible. The control of the German money market, the Stock Exchange and of German banking generally lies practically in the hands of this restricted group. Their head offices are in Berlin, but they are in intimate touch with the industrial centres throughout Germany and with the public at large by means of their branch offices, dependent banks, Depositen Kassen, distributed all over the country. They are keenly, yet cautiously, managed and have for a number of years paid high if steady dividends. To earn these dividends their vast resources are turned to lucrative account—the cautious think without the necessary regard to the possession of sufficient liquid securities which in the hour of need could be converted into cash. This charge has long been raised against these giant banks—and in this respect their position is not above suspicion; their finance is too thoroughly based upon the experiences of a prolonged peace. Of late greater pressure has been brought to bear upon them to hold larger amounts invested in Government Stocks. But the conversion of the investments at present held must necessarily be a slow one because the high dividends which have been therewith declared have proved the banks' best advertisement and the public would interpret a sudden reduction of dividends, even if due to an exchange for safer investments, as a sign of weakness and not of consolidation. The collapse of any one of these banks is inconceivable; so tremendous are the interests involved, that the Reichsbank would be forced to step in to ease the situation were there even a contingent risk of such an unlikely national calamity.

Smaller banks.

3. The third group is the group of smaller banks, many of which combined could not approach the financial importance of only one in the previous group. The majority of these smaller banks are of more recent birth also, for the best known private banks of olden times have been swallowed up by the aforementioned Ogre banks, determined thus to obtain a ready-made footing in valuable industrial markets. But it would be unfair not to differentiate between these smaller banks. There remain some of the old-fashioned establishments to which the modern rise of German industries is primarily due. These survivals of olden times have been joined by others of equally high standing. Their independent business is to-day pre-eminently one of an administrative kind: they manage private funds, private accounts; for any participation in the more important banking business they stand poor chances in competition with the giant banks unless they work for that purpose in harmony with, often in dependence upon them. As long as their methods are sound, they are patronised and secretly supported by the large banking concerns which have in fact helped to swell their number, for they regard them as valuable supporters in local markets.

Speculative banks.

Apart from these, there is a host of smaller private banks which, for purposes of their own, aim at independence. They are, as a rule, financially weak and would resent even a confidential revelation of their methods and resources. They are known to embark upon risky business propositions, to ply for more speculative clients, they are prepared to take greater risks. During any difficult constellation at home, or even abroad, their position becomes precarious. It is among these smaller speculative banks (the true character of which may only be known to those with inside knowledge) that any financial difficulty will invariably originate. In the hour of need no serious bank will be prepared to come to their aid because it is better for the banking world that these speculative concerns should vanish. Their interests are generally locally circumscribed; they become partners in local risks; the collapse of one such institute tends to implicate others of the same kind; this is the hotbed of any possible financial " Krach." If at the beginning of such a calamity the general constellation of the country, industrial and political, were one of serene confidence, if there be no risk of an industrial slump or of war, assistance might perhaps be tendered by a combination of serious banks (with the co-operation of the Reichsbank) to arrest a serious local catastrophy [sic]. But if the constellation be one of real difficulty, more especially of political difficulty, no assistance could be forthcoming because the local public, alarmed by the first collapses, would lose its confidence in the other local banks, however sound

Those banks which are dependent upon the giant banks would be supported, no doubt; but how often and for how long could even the large banks under adverse circumstances intervene? A run begun upon the small banks would eventually spread to their own establishments. They are not at present prepared for such an emergency, for if war is in the air, the majority of their securities cannot be readily realised and their liquid resources would not suffice to meet such a prolonged run upon their cash reserves. At such a moment no doubt the "Haute Finance" would bring pressure to bear upon the Government in self-defence: the political tension would have to be brought to an end either by an action unmistakably making for peace or by the commencement of hostilities. In the former case the public will be appeased; in the latter case, according to the scheme prepared, there is an automatic embargo laid upon all deposits—in either case the run is arrested.

In the light of this argument the two incidents which occurred during the progress of the negotiations concerning Morocco—the short panic due to the refusal of the "Haute Finance" to intervene and the collapse of the two banks at Göttingen —must stand out in quite a new relief. The "Haute Finance," officially slighted, gave a double proof, a negative and a positive one so to speak, of its power: first by standing aloof, and then by arresting the déroute. The collapse of the banks at Göttingen after so short a set-back and the temporary run on the savings banks prove how little is needed to upset the class of banks of which these establishments were representative members. During the progress of the diplomatic negotiations concerning Morocco any further risk was averted by the reassuring statement communicated to the "Haute Finance" by the German Government and the banks were ready thereupon to intervene also, because the general industrial outlook filled them with confidence. What must have happened if the Government had expressed a view less confident or if the economic situation had been one of real difficulty? Thus during the recent negotiations already the "Haute Finance" has chosen to some extent to force the hands of the Government from reasons of wounded pride; it may some day be driven to do so from reasons of self-defence. ^{The lesson of 1911.}

This then is the lesson of the recent events: delicate diplomatic negotiations too long drawn out may become under the present system of banking in Germany the cause of great difficulty to the "Haute Finance"—and the latter may then under an unbearable strain successfully insist upon a rapid progress of the negotiations—either towards peace or war.

MINUTES.

This extremely interesting report is worthy of Sir Francis Oppenheimer's high reputation. It shows that though the events of Sept[ember] 4th were no real test, yet the weakness of the German financial position was greatly exaggerated. In any time of stress the riskily managed small bank and the private gambler are almost bound to go; in the present instance it seems that even this could have been prevented by la haute finance. It was currently stated that it was the financial situation which had deterred Germany from going to war. In the light of Sir F. Oppenheimer's report this opinion will have to be revised and we may take it that it was the state of the navy and not of finance that proved the deterrent.

Thank Sir F. Oppenheimer for his most valuable report which has been read with the greatest interest and which forms a noteworthy contribution to the information on which a correct judgment of the international situation can be based. G. H. V.

26/10/11.

The most important points brought out by this report are the really sound position of the German banks; the existence of a definite scheme for financing a big war, which will come into force automatically when war is declared; and the pressure which the banks will inevitably exercise, at a time of prolonged crisis, to bring about—not so much a peaceful—but *any* solution, peaceful or warlike; since it is the period of expectancy and indecision which is fatal to the banks, whilst they are prepared to meet the situation once war is actually decided upon.

Copies of this despatch might be sent (secret) to the Treasury, Admiralty, War Office, Committee of Imperial Defence, Berlin. E. A. C.

Oct[ober] 26.

The intervention of the Banks had this good effect that as the German Gov[ernmen]t were not prepared for war they had to declare for peace and were unable to prolong the period of uncertainty whether it suited them to do so or not. W. L.

Very interesting and a valuable help in forming sound conclusions. E. G.

APPENDIX II.

Extract from the "Journal officiel" of December 15, 1911 (enclosed in Sir F. Bertie's despatch, No. 602, of December 15, 1911, *v. supra*, pp. 779–83, No. 758.)

DEBATE IN THE FRENCH CHAMBER RESPECTING MOROCCO.

December 14, 1911.

M. de Selves, Ministre des Affaires étrangères. Avec toute la Chambre nous avons applaudi l'apparition à cette tribune de l'éloquent orateur que vous venez d'entendre (*Très bien! très bien!*); et sur nombre de points qu'il a traités, vous verrez que nous sommes plus en communauté de vues avec lui que nous ne le paraissons dès l'abord.

Mais si je comprends le souci de l'honorable M. de Mun et de la Chambre d'obtenir du Gouvernement des explications complètes sur l'accord franco-allemand et sur les questions que l'honorable M. de Mun a soulevées, je comprends moins la proposition d'ajournement qu'il vient de formuler.

Je ne conçois pas que je puisse, si on l'accueille, fournir les explications qu'il désire et sur l'accord congolais et sur les négociations qui ont été suivies.

Les raisons qu'il nous donne sont que, pour que la Chambre puisse connaître complètement l'accord franco-allemand, il faut que la question espagnole soit réglée, d'une part, et il faut, d'autre part, que les nations qui doivent donner leur adhésion se soient prononcées.

En ce qui concerne l'accord franco-espagnol, je ne vois pas bien en quoi la solution de la question sera favorisée par le fait que la Chambre ne se sera pas prononcée sur l'accord franco-allemand. Il m'apparaît que c'est l'inverse qui en sera le résultat.

D'autre part, en ce qui concerne l'adhésion des puissances, qu'il conviendrait d'attendre pour que nous discutions la question, qu'il me permette de lui dire qu'un certain nombre d'entre elles ont déjà donné leur adhésion, parmi celles qui pouvaient le donner sans consulter leur parlement.

M. Jules Delahaye. Et l'Autriche?

Au Centre. Et les Etats-Unis?

M. le ministre des affaires étrangères. L'Autriche-Hongrie, les Etats-Unis, la Belgique, nous ont fait connaître qu'elles n'avaient aucune objection à soulever, mais qu'elles étaient obligées de consulter leurs Parlements et tout naturellement, au cours de la réponse qu'elles nous fournissaient à cet égard, elles indiquaient que notre Parlement lui-même ne s'était pas encore prononcé, qu'il y avait quelque chose d'un peu gênant pour elles à insister devant leurs propres Parlements, tant que le Parlement français n'avait pas encore pris sa responsabilité.

M. Armand Jousselin. Ce n'est pas de notre faute.

M. le ministre des affaires étrangères. En telle sorte, messieurs, que, désireux au plus tôt d'aborder la question, de répondre aux observations qui ont été faites, aux questions qui ont été posées, de donner à la Chambre . . . . .([1])

M. Joseph Caillaux, président du conseil. . . . . . toutes les explications.

M. le ministre des affaires étrangères . . . . . toutes les explications et tous les éclaircissements auxquels elle a droit et qu'elle désire, nous venons demander à l'honorable M. de Mun et demander à la Chambre elle-même de nous relever du silence auquel il nous condamne par sa proposition préjudicielle. (*Mouvements divers.*)

Je lui demande d'y renoncer; je demande à la Chambre d'écarter la motion d'ajournement de M. de Mun et aussitôt je reviendrai à cette tribune, abordant la question franco-allemande et répondant à l'honorable M. de Mun dans toute la mesure qu'il demande.

M. le ministre des affaires étrangères descend de la tribune et retourne à son banc.— Exclamations et bruit prolongé.)

M. Jules Delahaye. Et c'est tout?

M. Tournade. C'est tout ce que vouz avez à dire?

M. Georges Berry. C'est la politique du silence que nous faisons ici maintenant.

Plusieurs membres. Expliquez-vous dès maintenant!

(*M. le ministre des affaires étrangères remonte à la tribune.*)

M. le ministre des affaires étrangères. Puisque la Chambre me marque le désir d'explications immédiates, je les donne sur-le-champ.

M. de Mun rappelait tout à l'heure que, lorsque nous nous étions présentés devant vous au mois de juillet dernier, nous vous avions dit que des conversations étaient engagées à ce moment entre la France et l'Allemagne. Nous vous demandions de nous permettre de les continuer en vous donnant l'assurance qu'elles seraient conduites avec le souci le plus entier des intérêts de ce pays et la préoccupation constante de ce que sa dignité comporte. L'heure est en effet venue, messieurs, de vous fournir les explications que vous souhaitez. (*Très bien! très bien!*)

M. Jules Delahaye. Ce n'est pas trop tôt!

M. le ministre des affaires étrangères. Messieurs, au moment où je suis arrivé au Quai d'Orsay—M. de Mun vous le disait très justement tout à l'heure—des conversations étaient commencées entre la France et l'Allemagne.

([1]) [The omission marks here and throughout this document are in the original.]

C'était après l'expédition de Fez. Il était apparu à l'Allemagne que l'état de choses résultant de l'Acte d'Algésiras et de l'accord de 1909 avait été profondément modifié.

L'Acte d'Algésiras, d'après la thèse allemande, reposait sur ce principe, non plus seulement de la souveraineté du sultan au Maroc, mais de la possibilité effective, pour le sultan, de faire respecter cette souveraineté et d'assurer l'ordre. Le traité de 1909, qui constituait un progrès pour la France, puisque l'Allemagne y reconnaissait l'influence politique que la France avait au Maroc, après cette affirmation, en contenait une autre, qui consistait à déclarer que la France et l'Allemagne associeraient, dans la plus large mesure, au Maroc, les intérêts de leurs nationaux.

M. Jules Delafosse. Les intérêts économiques.

M. le ministre des affaires étrangères. Mais l'acte de 1909, prolongement de l'acte d'Algésiras, ne donnait, dans la pensée de l'Allemagne, à la France aucune action politique au Maroc, (*Mouvements divers*), il apparaissait à l'Allemagne que la situation s'était, je le répète, profondément modifiée par le fait que la France, sur nombre de points, occupait le Maroc, et le fait de l'expédition de Fez lui semblait avoir compliqué la situation que j'indique. (*Mouvements divers.*)

Des conversations étaient donc engagées. Elles portaient sur les intérêts respectifs des deux pays, sur des points divers, mais en particulier avaient pour objet de traiter certains aspects de la question marocaine. (*Mouvements divers.*)

Ces conversations s'étaient engagées à Berlin entre notre ambassadeur et le chancelier. Elles s'étaient poursuivies à Kissingen entre M. Cambon et le ministre des affaires étrangères.([2])

M. Jacques Piou. Etait-il alors question du Congo? (*Mouvements divers.*)

M. le président du conseil. Attendez! on va vous le dire.

M. le ministre des affaires étrangères. Les choses en étaient là, messieurs, lorsque le cabinet auquel j'appartiens se constitua. Notre ambassadeur était venu à Paris pour nous mettre au courant et nous demander s'il devait reprendre et continuer ces conversations.

J'étais depuis quelques jours au quai d'Orsay, lorsque l'ambassadeur d'Allemagne demanda à me voir. Il me déclara, au nom de son gouvernement, que l'Allemagne venait d'envoyer un bateau à Agadir.([3]) Il m'en donnait pour raisons qu'il y avait à Agadir des intérêts allemands, que ces intérêts étaient menacés. Il ajouta que le bateau se retirerait d'ailleurs, dès que l'ordre serait rétabli au Maroc.

Peu après, messieurs, M. de Schoen me déclarait que l'Allemagne était désireuse de causer avec la France, qu'elle souhaitait que ces conversations fussent menées rapidement et qu'aucune pensée inamicale n'avait inspiré l'idée de l'envoi du bateau à Agadir.

Je reçus avec calme, mais avec froideur, la communication qui m'était faite. (*Mouvements divers.*) Je marquai tout de suite à l'ambassadeur d'Allemagne tout le regret que j'éprouvais de la détermination du gouvernement allemand. Je lui dis que nous ne nous refusions pas et que nous ne nous étions pas refusés à une conversation, mais que je craignais que l'acte de l'Allemagne, par l'envoi d'un, bateau à Agadir, ne la soulignât d'une façon fâcheuse. J'ajoutai que quelque urgence qu'il y eût à engager la conversation, cette urgence n'était pas telle, que je dusse engager tout de suite l'entretien, que j'avais à accompagner M. le Président de la République en Hollande et que la conversation se continuerait dès mon retour.

Voilà les premiers faits. Dès mon retour, notre ambassadeur repartait pour Berlin avec les instuctions qu'il avait reçues et allait poursuivre la conversation antérieurement commencée.

Je sais que, sur ce que nous avons fait et sur ce que nous devions faire à ce moment, des questions diverses ont été posées. On m'a dit notamment: "Lorsque vous avez appris que l'Allemagne envoyait un bateau à Agadir, pourquoi n'en avez-vous pas fait autant?"

Messieurs, cette question de l'envoi d'un bateau français à Agadir, nous l'avons examinée. Nous avons dès le commencement, comme en toutes circonstances, été en contact permanent avec nos amis et nos alliés avec lesquels nous avons eu des échanges de vues ininterrompus. Mais il nous est apparu, d'après nos renseignements, que si l'Allemagne envoyait un bateau à Agadir, elle n'avait pas l'intention d'y opérer un débarquement. (*Mouvements divers.*) Et nous avons estimé qu'il y avait lieu d'ajourner la question.

Une autre question qui, à ce moment-là, nous a été posée, est celle-ci: Puisque vous étiez sous le régime de la conférence d'Algésiras, pourquoi n'avez-vous pas demandé la réunion d'une nouvelle conférence? Et une critique a été formulée à ce propos.

J'avoue qu'en ce qui me concerne je n'ai pas cru un instant qu'il y eût lieu, à cette heure, de provoquer la réunion d'une conférence.

Une première raison, à mon sens, décisive, se présentait: une conférence n'a d'effet utile que si les puissances intéressées consentent à y prendre part.

Or, l'Allemagne déclarait très nettement, je le savais, qu'elle n'accepterait pas la réunion d'une nouvelle conférence . . . . (*Mouvements divers.*)

M. Jules Delafosse. Ce n'est pas une raison.

M. le ministre des affaires étrangères. . . . . qu'elle n'irait pas, qu'elle n'en tiendrait pas compte et que, si quelqu'un parlait de réunion de la conférence, il y a une première condition qu'elle y mettrait: c'est que la situation de fait fût rétablie telle qu'elle était de par l'Acte d'Algésiras, c'est-à-dire que la France évacuât les positions qu'elle occupait au Maroc.

([2]) [*v. supra*, pp. 353–4, No. 373.]
([3]) [*v. supra*, pp. 323–4, No. 340.]

M. Denys Cochin. Voulez-vous me permettre de vous poser une question? (*Mouvements divers.*)

A gauche. Non! non!

Au centre et à droite. Parlez! parlez!

M. Marcel Sembat. Puisque vous êtes inscrit, monsieur Denys Cochin, vous parlerez à votre tour; laissez parler, monsieur le ministre.

M. Jules Delahaye. Alors, nous ne pouvons plus poser des questions? (*Non! non! à gauche.*)

M. le président. L'orateur désire continuer.

M. le ministre des affaires étrangères. Messieurs, je vous en prie, ne voyez, dans mon attitude à votre égard, rien de désobligeant. Mais, comme je parle de questions graves, je demande à la Chambre de m'entendre avec le même sentiment dans lequel je lui parle. (*Parlez! parlez!*)

Messieurs, je vous citais des faits. Des complications étaient possibles si on avait insisté pour la réunion de la conférence. Qui vous dit que l'Allemagne n'eût pas débarqué à Agadir, afin de se présenter à la conférence avec une nouvelle situation de fait?

Dans ces conditions y avait-il lieu de songer à réunir une conférence, et au surplus les faits qui s'étaient produits au Maroc depuis l'acte d'Algésiras n'avaient-ils pas démontré que les solutions qui pouvaient découler d'une conférence internationale n'étaient point de nature à répondre aux besoins de la situation telle qu'elle s'était révélée au Maroc. (*Très bien! très bien! à gauche.*)

Toutes ces solutions venaient d'une idée qui avait été démontrée fausse. Cette idée consistait à croire l'autorité du sultan suffisante pour assurer au Maroc l'ordre et la tranquillité.

Il n'était plus possible de pourvoir au maintien de l'ordre sans créer du même coup une situation nouvelle qui n'eût plus été le résultat d'un accord international; une puissance devait être chargée d'exercer une action directe et aussi large que possible afin d'assurer au Maroc l'ordre et le calme nécessaires à la prospérité de ce pays et à ses besoins généraux.

Or, messieurs, ai-je besoin de dire que la puissance par excellence indiquée pour l'œuvre à laquelle je fais allusion, cette puissance, c'était la France? (*Très bien! très bien! sur divers bancs à gauche.*)

Et dès lors il m'a paru que puisque la question était soulevée, que puisque l'acte de l'Allemagne l'avait posée, c'était une occasion de la résoudre. Alors, la prenant corps à corps. nous n'avons pas hésité à engager la conversation à laquelle l'Allemagne nous conviait.

M. Georges Berry. C'est là où vous avez eu tort.

M. Joseph Caillaux, président du conseil, ministre de l'intérieur. Nous verrons cela.

M. le ministre des affaires étrangères. Certains, lorsque cette conversation avec l'Allemagne s'est engagée, m'ont demandé:

"Pourquoi n'avez-vous pas admis l'Espagne à y participer, et pourquoi, du même coup, n'avez vous pas tranché la question espagnole?"

Eh bien, messieurs, à ceux qui pourraient être tentés de poser une semblable question, je demande de réfléchir.

Avec l'Espagne, nous avons toujours traité seul à seul; et quand une tierce puissance a pu être avisée de nos conversations, quand une tierce puissance a pu avoir à se préoccuper de ce qui passait entre l'Espagne et nous, cette puissance a été l'Angleterre.

Pouvais-je admettre qu'une modification aussi important fût créée et que la question espagnole, au lieu de se résoudre entre nous et l'Espagne, au lieu de se résoudre, s'il fallait un témoin, avec l'Angleterre, fût résolue avec une autre puissance?

Songez à toutes les conséquences qui pouvaient être le résultat de ce changement et vous saisirez bien vite la raison pour laquelle l'Espagne n'a pas pris part à la conversation franco-allemande.

Dès lors, messieurs, la conversation s'est engagée. Et avant d'entrer dans le détail de cette conversation, nous avons dit à l'Allemagne:

"Il est bien entendu, que si, comme vous l'indiquez, vous avez l'intention de réclamer une compensation, ce n'est point au Maroc qu'elle pourra être trouvée. Il est bien entendu que vous n'élèverez pas de revendication territoriale au Maroc."

Ensuite nous avons dit:

"Nous devons vous prévenir, bien que nous causions à deux, que nos amis et nos alliés seront tenus au courant de tout."

Et enfin nous avons ajouté:

"Il est non moins entendu que nous demanderons aux puissances signataires de l'acte d'Algésiras d'adhérer à l'accord que nous aurons pu conclure au sujet du Maroc."

Voilà, messieurs, la triple condition que nous avons mise à nos conversations.

Pourquoi, dès le début, avons-nous précisé? C'est parce que—et vous le sentez avec moi—le Maroc a pour la France un intérêt spécial. Le Maroc, c'est la continuation de nos possessions algériennes et à l'heure où nous sommes, l'Algérie et la France, il me semble que c'est la même chose. (*Vifs applaudissements*.)

Admettre qu'une tierce puissance vienne s'installer au Maroc, c'est une occasion de conflits, mais cela peut être en outre un danger permanent pour la France, et il n'est pas besoin de réfléchir beaucoup pour s'en apercevoir.

Oh! je n'examine pas en ce moment la question du Maroc au point de vue de ses richesses, des avantages divers qu'il peut procurer pour la France.

Je regarde plus et plus loin et j'entrevois, messieurs, dans l'histoire—et pour l'histoire, il faut tout entrevoir—des conflits possibles, de grands conflits possibles, que, malgré tous leurs efforts et toute leur volonté de paix, les hommes d'Etat ne sont pas toujours en mesure d'éviter. A cette heure, supposez donc une agitation se produisant dans ces pays, un effort qui vous y retienne, la France attaquée ailleurs et prise à revers au Maroc! C'est à ce point de vue particulier, spécial, que j'ai constamment examiné la question marocaine; c'est avec cette préoccupation constante que j'en ai recherché la solution. (*Applaudissements*.)

Alors, messieurs, que nous avions ainsi posé la question, l'Allemagne nous a dit : Soit! nous acceptons. Prenez le Maroc, installez-y votre protectorat. Mais, alors que vous avez traité avec l'Angleterre à cette occasion, que vous avez traité avec l'Italie, que vous traitez avec l'Espagne. . . .

M. Tournade. Nous ne le savions pas!

M. le ministre des affaires étrangères. . . . . sur quelles bases traiterez-vous avec nous?

Notre opinion publique ne permet pas que nous n'obtenions pas par ailleurs quelque compensation à l'abandon que nous allons vous consentir. . . . .

A droite. De quoi?

M. le ministre des affaires étrangères. . . . . et à la promesse que nous allons vous donner que notre diplomatie s'emploiera à faire ratifier par les puissances l'accord que nous aurons conclu.

M. de Lanjuinais. Alors, c'est une commission?

M. le ministre des affaires étrangères. Il est aisé de dire que l'on pouvait résoudre autrement la question marocaine et que la France pouvait établir sur le Maroc son protectorat sans songer à supporter par ailleurs quelques sacrifices; mais cela est plus facile à dire qu'à réaliser (*Exclamations à droite*) et je voudrais recevoir de la bouche de ceux qui critiquent la solution proposée. (*Applaudissements à gauche*.)

Nous nous sommes alors retournés vers l'Allemagne et notre ambassadeur, dans les conversations qu'il engageait, a dit : "Précisez. Qu'entendez-vous? Quelle est la base de discussion que vous proposez? Quel est l'objet de la demande que vous formulez?" L'ambassadeur d'Allemagne, dans une conversation qu'il avait eue avec moi, m'avait dit—et c'est ainsi que, pour la première fois, le mot a été prononcé devant moi—: "C'est du côté du Congo que vous pouvez trouver la solution de la question."

Et M. de Kiderlen-Waechter, lorsque, dès son retour, M. Cambon le pressait, lui tenait le même langage, et il lui disait, quelques jours après la conversation que j'avais eue moi-même à Paris : "C'est du côté du Congo que nous trouverons la compensation."

M. le Comte Albert de Mun. On n'en avait jamais parlé avant? (*Mouvement*.)

M. le président du conseil. Jamais dans mon cabinet.

M. Jules Delahaye. Toute la question est là. Vous nous devez la vérité.

M. Georges Berry. Quand en avait-on parlé?

M. le vicomte de Villebois-Mareuil. On en avait parlé à Bruxelles.

M. Georges Berry. Je répète ma question: quand en a-t-on parlé?

M. le ministre des affaires étrangères. Le 10 juillet.

Messieurs, les conversations vont se pou[r]suivre. Je désirerais—j'aurais désiré qu'elles fussent plus rapides. J'aurais désiré que les négociations fussent moins longues. A diverses reprises, j'ai marqué le regret que j'éprouvais de ces lenteurs, de même que j'avais exprimé le regret de l'envoi d'un bateau à Agadir. (*Exclamations à droite*.)

La raison, je l'ai dite : je craignais, et je l'ai manifesté, que ces lenteurs elles-mêmes ne diminuassent la valeur du résultat qui serait obtenu. Il n'a pas dépendu de nous qu'elles fussent moindres. Et lorsque je m'en vais vous tracer, à grands traits, les phases par lesquelles ont passé les négociations, vous verrez que, de ces lenteurs, il n'y a pas, messieurs, à nous savoir mauvais gré, puisqu'elles sont le résultat de la résistance même que nous avons constamment apportée aux prétentions formulées. (*Applaudissements à gauche*.)

M. Tournade. C'était prévu.

M. le ministre des affaires étrangères. Au moment où l'Allemagne a eu prononcé le mot de "Congo". . . .

M. Jaurès. La première?

M. le ministre des affaires étrangères. La première.

M. Jaurès. Ah!. . . .

M. le ministre des affaires étrangères. . . . . et où M. Cambon, regardant une carte avec M. de Kiderlen-Waechter le secrétaire d'Etat, lui dit : "Eh bien! nous pouvons arriver à des échanges. Nous vous abandonnerons le Togoland, nous vous ferons des cessions territoriales dans le haut Cameroun. Mais voici ce que nous demandons," et M. de Kiderlen-Waechter indiqua sur la carte tout le Gabon, tout le Congo qui se trouve entre l'Océan et la Sang'ha (*Mouvement*),—

messieurs, je raconte les faits—à ce moment-là, nous déclarâmes tous sans hésitation qu'ainsi engagée, dans des conditions pareilles, la conversation ne pourrait pas se continuer.

M. *Maurice Barrès.* Voilà qui est mieux.

M. *le ministre des affaires étrangères.* Il y eut à ce moment une période de tension dont vous avez gardé le souvenir et que, en ce qui me concerne je ne saurais oublier. A ce moment, des bruits divers ont circulé et on a dit que nos amis nous poussaient à un conflit. (*Interruptions.*) C'est une erreur absolue, messieurs.

M. *Jaurès.* Très bien!

M. *le ministre des affaires étrangères.* . . . . et je dois à la vérité de déclarer qu'il n'en a jamais été ainsi. (*Très bien! très bien! à gauche et sur divers bancs.*)

Certes, ils furent à nos côtés, prêts à nous accorder le concours, tout le concours que les circonstances pourraient commander. (*Vifs applaudissements sur un grand nombre de bancs.*) Mais à aucun moment ils ne nous firent entendre une parole irritante. Ce furent, au contraire, tout le temps des paroles d'apaisement et de conciliation qu'ils formulèrent, tout autant que les intérêts vitaux de la France et sa dignité n'étaient point en jeu. (*Vifs applaudissements.*)

Messieurs, à côté des bruits qui ont couru à ce moment, vous me permettrez de dire qu'il y eut aussi des calomnies; certains en vinrent jusqu'à insinuer que le ministre des affaires étrangères et le Gouvernement qui résistaient n'étaient pas éloignés de désirer un conflit. (*Mouvements divers*).

Sur divers bancs. Personne ne l'a dit.

M. *le ministre des affaires étrangères.* Messieurs, jamais un pareil sentiment ne fut le nôtre, j'ai à peine besoin de le dire.

Mais si nous ne l'avons pas éprouvé, j'ose déclarer très simplement que nous ne nous sommes jamais départis un instant du souci des intérêts de ce pays et de sa dignité, et que notre résistance à ce moment comme dans tous les autres, a été uniquement dictée par notre devoir.

Nous avons donc, messieurs, répondu en indiquant que la conversation ne pouvait se continuer si des demandes pareilles étaient maintenues.

Et alors, on nous a dit : " Eh bien! cherchons; mais en tout cas, nous devons vous le déclarer, il nous faut obtenir un accès au fleuve Congo."

On s'est demandé pourquoi il avait été ainsi parlé de ces cessions territoriales. Pourquoi ces questions-là avaient été examinées? je vous l'ai dit déjà, c'est parce que la première parole qu'avait prononcée le ministre des affaires étrangères en Allemagne avait consisté à dire : " Le Maroc, vous l'aurez "—il avait même ajouté : " Installez-y votre protectorat, libellez vous-même l'accord qui doit en déterminer les précisions."

Cependant comme les négociations traînent, nous donnons des instructions à notre ambassadeur et nous lui prescrivons d'ajourner la conversation sur les questions territoriales.

On nous a dit : Rédigez l'accord sur le Maroc. Or il ne faut pas qu'il y ait d'ambiguïté et de malentendu. Nous allons parler Maroc et nous ne causerons cessions territoriales que lorsque la question marocaine aura été réglée elle-même, lorsque nous serons tombés d'accord sur les clauses diverses du contrat que nous préparons.

M. *Tournade.* Mais vous en aviez accepté le principe.

M. *le ministre des affaires étrangères.* Messieurs, à ce moment, les difficultés s'accusent encore, et, il vous en souvient, une interruption se produit dans la conversation. M. de Kiderlen-Waechter part en voyage et M. Cambon, notre ambassadeur, vient à Paris. Et ceci nous amène au 30 août.

A ce moment, notre Ambassadeur repart pour Berlin, nanti d'un projet d'accord sur le Maroc et avec instruction de ne parler de rien autre tant que l'accord sur ce projet ne sera pas intervenu.

Sur ce projet, les conversations reprennent et l'Allemagne nous répond par un contre-projet à la date du 7 septembre. Ce contre-projet non seulement apportait certains modifications aux précisions que nous avions formulées pour tout ce qui nous paraissait se rattacher à la liberté politique, à l'action politique au Maroc, mais il formulait, au point de vue économique, des demandes que nous avons jugées absolument inadmissibles. Ce projet consistait à diviser le Maroc, au point de vue économique, en deux zones : une zone qui comprenait le Sud et dans laquelle il devait se produire, comme dans l'accord de 1909, des associations d'intérêts entre les Allemands et les Français, associations d'intérêts dans lesquelles les Allemands figureraient à concurrence de 70 p. 100 et les Français de 30 p. 100, l'autre zone comprenant la partie au Nord et dans laquelle c'était le contraire, les Allemands figurant à concurrence de 30 p. 100 dans les associations d'intérêts qui se formeraient, et les Français à concurrence de 70 p. 100.(⁴)

J'ai à peine besoin de dire que ce projet fut immédiatement écarté par nous. On invoquait les principes qui avaient marqué l'accord de 1909, il nous parut inadmissible d'accepter, au Maroc, autre chose que le principe de la liberté commerciale et économique pour tous, sans privilège pour quiconque.

Les choses n'allèrent pas sans difficulté. Le temps s'écoula. Et le 28 septembre encore, l'Allemagne reprit un certain nombre des propositions qu'elle nous semblait avoir abandonnées. Elle formula quelques demandes nouvelles et ce n'est que dans les premiers jours d'octobre que, sur les diverses parties de l'accord marocain, nous pûmes penser que les conversations étaient suffisamment avancées.

(⁴) [*v. supra*, pp. 509–10, No. 538; pp. 515–6, No. 539; pp. 532–3, No. 556; p. 534, No. 537, *encl.*]

Mais il y eut, à ce moment, un point que nous soulevâmes et que certainement vous serez tout disposés à apprécier. Nous voulûmes que la convention qui était intervenue fût une convention ne prêtant pas, ou prêtant le moins possible à des difficultés ultérieures.

Toute convention, quelque soin que l'on ait pris à la rédiger, peut, dans son interprétation, prêter à un moment donné, à des difficultés. Pour prévenir ces difficultés, messieurs, nous demandâmes, et nous avons obtenu que l'Allemagne consentît, au cas où des divergences d'interprétation se produiraient par la suite, qu'il fût précisé et stipulé que la cour de la Haye serait appelée à les trancher dans les conditions où elle fonctionne ordinairement.

Certains peuvent n'attacher aucune importance à cette précision. En ce qui nous concerne, nous avons considéré comme un point important, comme un point de premier ordre, cette affirmation que, si des difficultés survenaient, il fût précisé qu'elles seraient résolues par ce moyen pacifique et d'avenir, je me plais à le penser malgré tout, qu'est la cour de la Haye. (*Applaudissements*.)

La convention relative au Maroc, les lettres interprétatives de cette convention furent signées et paraphées le 11 et le 14 octobre,([5]) et c'est à ce moment seulement que furent reprises avec des précisions les conversations relatives aux cessions territoriales.

Etant admis que nous ne pouvions pas obtenir ce que nous avions obtenu au Maroc sans un certain sacrifice, quelque douloureux qu'il fût, nous examinâmes ce qu'il était possible de faire.

Nous l'examinâmes en nous inspirant de ces préoccupations qui consistèrent à veiller à ce qu'aucune atteinte ne fût portée à la vitalité de nos colonies dans l'Afrique équatoriale; à ce que—pour répondre au sentiment que l'opinion publique, avec une persistance grande, avait manifesté—les communications ne fussent pas interrompues entre les diverses parties de nos colonies.

Nous arrivâmes à nous mettre d'accord; et si je n'entre point dans le détail, c'est que M. le ministre des colonies vous dira tout à l'heure, avec une précision que je n'y saurais mettre, tout ce qui se réfère à cette partie de notre domaine colonial; il vous dira tout ce qu'il pense, tout ce qui est, toutes les conséquences qui découlent de l'accord que nous avons conclu.

Je ne veux toucher en ce moment qu'un seul point. M. de Mun, tout à l'heure, parlant du Congo, des stipulations que nous y avons insérées, a abordé la question du droit de préférence que nous possédions sur le Congo belge.

Messieurs, à l'heure actuelle, je ne présume pas que ce droit de préférence ait grande chance de s'exercer.

M. Pierre Leroy-Beaulieu. On n'en sait jamais rien.

M. le ministre des affaires étrangères. Le gouvernement belge et la Belgique sont très jalousement soucieux de conserver leur domaine colonial . . . .

M. Denys Cochin. Plus soucieux que vous.

M. le ministre des affaires étrangères. . . . et j'avoue que je n'entrevois pas l'heure où une succession s'ouvrira de ce côté. Mais jamais nous n'avons eu la pensée nous ne pouvions pas avoir la pensée, d'abandonner au profit de l'Allemagne ce droit de préférence qui nous **avait** été reconnu.

Au surplus, nous ne le pouvions pas. Chacun sait qu'un droit de préférence est un droit personnel et incessible, et, par conséquent, il ne pouvait pas entrer dans notre pensée de céder quoi que ce fût de ce côté.

Et si vous vous rappelez, messieurs, les débats qui se sont produits au sein du Reichstag, vous y verrez que le secrétaire d'Etat des affaires étrangères l'a reconnu comme nous et a donné à notre droit de préférence le même caractère que je lui donne en ce moment.

Qu'avons-nous fait dès lors? Nous avons inséré un article disposant que, si des modifications dans le statut territorial du bassin conventionnel du Congo venaient à se produire, alors la France ne refuserait pas de causer avec l'Allemagne . . . .

M. le comte de Lanjuinais. Ces conversations nous coûtent cher.

M. le ministre des affaires étrangères. . . . . comme aussi avec toutes les puissances signataires de l'acte de Berlin de 1885.

M. Pierre Leroy-Beaulieu. C'est la renonciation au droit de préemption.

M. le ministre des affaires étrangères. De sorte, messieurs, que, si vous voulez bien y réfléchir, non seulement vous ne trouvez pas le moindre danger dans cette clause, mais vous y trouvez une garantie, lorsque des changements profonds viendront à se produire—s'ils viennent à se produire—dans le bassin conventionnel du Congo.

MM. Jaurès et Marcel Sembat. Viendraient à se produire!

M. le ministre des affaires étrangères. Oui, sans aucun doute, viendraient. Est-ce que vous vous imaginez que nous pouvons empêcher que des conversations se produisent entre les grands pays qui se trouveront là?

Et alors, qu'avons-nous fait? Nous avons par avance régularisé ces conversations inévitables, et au lieu de se produire entre tel et tel, elles devront nécessairement se produire, si elles se produisent, dans cette grande conférence de tous les pays signataires de l'acte de Berlin de 1885. (*Mouvements divers*.)

Et, messieurs, les puissances qui ont examiné cette clause ne s'y sont pas méprises; et, loin de voir un danger dans les stipulations que nous avons insérées au contrat, c'est une garantie que l'on doit y trouver.

M. Paul Escudier. Une garantie pour elles.

([5]) [*v. supra*, p. 569, No. 587; pp. 571–4, No. 589, *encl.*]

M. le ministre des affaires étrangères. Voilà donc conclu dans ses deux éléments essentiels l'accord marocain.

Quelle est sa signification? Quelle est sa portée?

Il se devise en deux parties. D'un côté il consacre la liberté d'action politique absolue de la France. La France désormais . . . .

M. Georges Bonnefous. Pas seule.

M. le ministre des affaires étrangères. . . . . doit pouvoir prendre au Maroc toutes les mesures administratives, militaires, financières, qu'elle jugera nécessaires.

M. Paul Escudier. Et la banque? Et la poste?

M. le ministre des affaires étrangères. Elle est libre de ses mouvements. Elle pourra réglementer toutes les portions du Maroc que les besoins comporteront.

Elle aura la représentation à l'étranger des intérêts marocains. Les puissances étrangères qui auront des intérêts su Maroc interviendront auprès du gouvernement marocain par l'intermédiaire du représentant de la France.

Par conséquent, c'est dire que, d'une façon précise, complète, absolue, la liberté de la France, au point de vue de son action politique dans le Maroc, est entière, aussi complètement précisée que possible, comme elle ne l'a pas été lorsque le protectorat tunisien a été organisé. (*Interruptions à droite.—Très bien! très bien! à gauche.*)

M. le président du conseil. Parfaitement!

M. Charles Benoist. C'est vrai, historiquement.

M. Pierre Leroy-Beaulieu. Et l'Espagne, vous l'oubliez, monsieur le ministre.

M. le ministre des affaires étrangères. Si vous voulez vous reporter à l'époque du protectorat tunisien, si vous voulez bien rapprocher les droits qui, à ce moment, furent les droits de la France, des droits que consacre l'accord marocain, vous verrez qu'il nous a fallu une série d'années pour arriver, en Tunisie, à posséder les droits que l'accord marocain accorde à la France.

Au point de vue économique—c'est la deuxième partie—qu'établit l'accord?

De privilège pour personne. . . . .

M. Paul Pugliesi-Conti. Pas même pour nous.

M. Pierre Leroy-Beaulieu. Surtout pas pour nous!

M. le ministre des affaires étrangères. J'entends qu'on dit : pas pour nous, non, pas pour nous. Est-il possible de restreindre, au Maroc, la situation que les puissances possédaient pas l'Acte d'Algésiras?

M. Jules Delahaye. Alors, à quoi bon le protectorat?

M. le ministre des affaires étrangères. Croyez-vous que vous eussiez obtenu leur accession à l'accord que vous allez leur soumettre si, en le leur soumettant, vous n'aviez eu que ce langage à leur tenir : Je restreins sur le terrain de la liberté commerciale et économique, les droits dont vous bénéficiez jusqu'à ce jour.

M. Jules Delahaye. Et le Congo, alors? (*Exclamations à gauche.*) Ah! vous trouvez cela tout simple. (*Nouvelles exclamations.*) Oh! vous ne m'empêcherez pas de dire ce que j'ai à dire.

M. le président. Monsieur Delahaye veuillez garder le silence et permettre à M. le ministre de s'expliquer.

M. le ministre des affaires étrangères. Donc, messieurs, aucun privilège pour qui que ce soit, entendez-le bien; l'égalité commerciale et économique pour tout le monde. Et laissez-moi vous dire que je considère que cette précision est utile au Maroc, puisqu'elle va permettre d'y développer des éléments de richesse et de prospérité qui auraient pu être, eux, écartés et entravés, sans le principe même de cette liberté commerciale et économique que je vous indique. (*Mouvements divers.*)

Messieurs, c'est ainsi que se trouve terminée cette question et, permettez-moi de dire, terminée par une solution pacifique. (*Applaudissements.*) Car, je ne saurai trop le dire, ceux qui la critiquent pourraient bien, à côté des critiques, marquer la solution à laquelle ils auraient eu recours. (*Très bien! très bien! sur divers bancs à gauche.*)

Nous vous apportons donc une solution pacifique de la question; nous vous apportons une solution qui nous paraît, je vous l'ai marqué tout à l'heure, assurer la sécurité de nos possessions algériennes, et développe la force de la France elle-même. Nous vous apportons une solution pacifique, je le répète, et que, malgré toutes les critiques formulées contre le résultat de ces négociations, j'ose croire satisfaisante de par le jugement que l'on porte au sujet de l'accord, partout et notamment à l'étranger. Oui, messieurs, à l'étranger, qui nous juge quelquefois avec plus d'équité que nous ne jugeons nous-mêmes (*Très bien! très bien! à gauche*), si bien que quelquefois, c'est là qu'il faut regarder si l'on veut savoir comment les choses doivent être appréciées.

M. le président du conseil. Oui! croyons-en nos amis et nos alliés.

M. le ministre des affaires étrangères. . . . . j'ose croire que vous estimerez avec nous que nous sortons de ces négociations, que la France sort de ces négociations, avec une situation qui est loin d'être amoindrie . . . . (*Vifs applaudissements à gauche et sur divers bancs au centre.*)

M. Lefas. Grâce à elle-même.

M. le ministre des affaires étrangères. . . . qui est loin d'être amoindrie, je le dis avec joie, dans l'opinion du monde.

Certes, nous ne prétendons pas que les négociations que nous avons conduites, avec quelque dignité, quoi qu'on en dise, nous ne prétendons pas que ces négociations soient la seule cause de cet état d'esprit. Cet état d'esprit général dans le monde, nous y sommes peut-être pour une faible part, mais je reconnais, je suis heureux .de constater, que le pays y est pour la plus large part. (Vifs applaudissements.)

On avait raison de dire tout à l'heure, comme le disait M. de Mun, que nous avons été soutenus par le pays.

M. Tournade. Vous ne l'avez pas suivi.

M. le ministre des affaires étrangères. Nous nous sommes sentis soutenus par lui. La fermeté. . . .

M. Pourquery de Boisserin. Le sentiment de notre force.

M. le ministre des affaires étrangères. . . . . la fermeté dont il a fait preuve, fermeté sans jactance, calme et digne, a révélé au monde et nous a révélé . . . . (Exclamations et mouvements divers.)

M. Maginot. A vous-même, peut-être?

M. Dalbiez. Il y a longtemps que nous nous connaissons.

M. Auguste Bouge. La France s'est reconnue, elle ne s'est pas révélée à elle-même.

M. le ministre des affaires étrangères. . . . . a révélé une France ayant plus que jamais le sentiment de sa force et de sa dignité.

Ce que je voudrais—vous me permettrez bien cette réflexion, je le dis pour moi comme je le dis pour les autres—ce que je voudrais c'est que nous ne diminuions pas nous-mêmes les effets heureux qui ont été produits.

M. le président du conseil. Très bien !

M. le ministre des affaires étrangères. On vous disait que nous avions commencé nos négociations avec l'Espagne. Nous les poursuivons.

Je ne puis, messieurs, vous donner à l'heure où je vous parle et vous le comprenez, les détails des négociations; mais ce que je puis dire pour répondre à des sentiments qui ont été exprimés à cette tribune, c'est que nous les poursuivons avec une double orientation, l'une qui consiste à dire à l'Espagne : Ce que nous avons acquis au Maroc, nous l'avons acquis au prix d'un sacrifice; vous allez participer à ce que nous avons acquis nous vous demanderons, dans une mesure juste et équitable, de reconnaître le sacrifice que nous avons consenti.

Cela, messieurs, nous le lui dirons, et nous le lui disons dans l'esprit le plus amical, ayant le souci de ménager la dignité et la fierté de ce grand pays. (Vifs applaudissements.)

Nous ne voulons rien faire qui puisse lui porter atteinte, nous estimons qu'un grand pays comme la France. . . .

A l'extrême gauche. Et comme l'Espagne !

M. le ministre des affaires étrangères. . . . . ne doit jamais, messieurs, abuser de sa force. (Vives exclamations au centre, à droite et sur divers bancs à gauche et à l'extrême gauche.— Bruit.)

M. Plichon. Pour qui dites-vous cela?

M. César Trouin. Ce langage est intolérable !

M. Paul Pugliesi-Conti. La France est vraiment digne d'un langage plus fier ! Retirez cette parole.

M. Jaurès. Je demande la parole.

M. le ministre des affaires étrangères. Je ne comprends pas cette émotion qui ne peut que dénaturer le sens de mes paroles, au moment même où je vous disais que c'était dans l'esprit le plus amical que ces négociations étaient conduites et que la solution en serait recherchée. (Applaudissements.)

Nous considérons que ce serait une faute, une faute politique, en même temps que ce serait un acte blâmable que de comprendre nos négociations et nos rapports avec l'Espagne autrement que dans l'esprit amical que je vous indiquais tout à l'heure. (Applaudissements.)

Un mot encore. Je vous ai dit tout à l'heure les avantages divers que me paraissaient résulter, pour la France, de la solution de la question marocaine.

Il y en a un sur lequel je vous demande la permission d'insister en terminant. Il consiste à avoir débarrassé l'échiquier de notre politique extérieure de la question marocaine (Exclamations sur divers bancs), qui était et qui pouvait être une source de conflits permanents.

M. d'Elissagaray. Puissiez-vous dire vrai.

M. le ministre des affaires étrangères. La France, de ce côté, a désormais les mains libres, et ce n'est point un mince avantage au moment où la situation extérieure comporte une attention toute particulière.

Messieurs, la France doit être attentive à tout ce qui se passe, participer, par son action pacifique à tout ce qui a lieu, considérant qu'un pays qui s'isole des événements extérieurs, est un pays qui diminue et qui déchoit.

Comment participerons-nous à tous ces événements? Dans l'esprit pacifique qui nous anime, avec ce souci de ne' contribuer qu'au progrès général.

Quels seront pour participer à cette œuvre et pour la réaliser nos points d'appui?

Messieurs, ce n'est pas au moment où nous venons d'une façon particulière d'apprécier les bienfaits de nos amitiés et de nos alliances que nous pourrions être tentés d'y porter une atteinte, si petite soit-elle. (Vifs applaudissements.)

C'est en les resserrant, s'il est possible, que nous avons le désir et le devoir d'accomplir la tâche qui nous incombe. Nous ne ferons, au surplus, que répondre aux sentiments que manifestait il y a quelques jours devant le Parlement d'Angleterre un grand ministre des affaires étrangères (*Applaudissements*), comme aussi aux sentiments que manifestait récemment, au cours d'une visite dont nous garderons le souvenir et dont nous sentons tout le prix, l'éminent ministre des affaires étrangères de la puissance alliée. (*Applaudissements à gauche et au centre.*)

M. Albert Lebrun, ministre des colonies. Je demande la parole.

M. le président. La parole est à M. le ministre des colonies.

Sur divers bancs. Nous demandons une suspension de la séance.

Voix nombreuses. Non! non! Parlez!

M. Massabuau. Et la motion d'ajournement? (*Interruptions à gauche.*)

M. le Président. Tout le monde sait que les membres du Gouvernement ont la parole quand ils la demandent.

M. le vicomte de Villebois-Mareuil. Alors c'est un ministre qui répond à un autre ministre?

M. Tournade. Ainsi donc, il n'est plus question de la motion préjudicielle?

M. le président. On me parle de la motion préjudicielle. Ainsi que tout le monde a pu le voir, j'allais la mettre aux voix lorsque M. le ministre des affaires étrangères a demandé à nouveau la parole, or les membres du Gouvernement ont toujours la parole quand ils la demandent.

C'est maintenant le tour de M. le ministre des colonies. Je lui donne la parole. (*Très bien! très bien!*)

M. Albert Lebrun, ministre des colonies. La Chambre comprend sans doute combien est délicate à cette heure la tâche qui est imposée au ministre des colonies. (*Très bien! très bien!*)

Il est pris, en effet, entre un double écueil : ou bien, dans son souci légitime de défendre au mieux devant la Chambre la partie congolaise de l'accord, il risque de se laisser aller à un optimisme excessif et, par là même, de paraître s'accommoder trop aisément d'une cession de territoire qui, en tout état de cause, lui demeure comme à tous ses collègues, infiniment douloureuse; (*Applaudissements vifs et prolongés sur un grand nombre de bancs*) ou bien, détournant sa pensée de la partie du traité ou la France reçoit pour ne la fixer que sur celle où elle donne, la seule à vrai dire sur laquelle il ait à s'expliquer à la Chambre à cette heure, le ministre, encore dominé par l'angoisse qu'il a connue cet été, risque de ne pas paraître convaincu des bienfaits du traité du 4 novembre et de ne pas mettre en une suffisante lumière les arguments qui, à son sens, doivent déterminer la Chambre à le voter. (*Vifs applaudissements sur les mêmes bancs.*)

Messieurs, je m'efforcerai d'éviter ce double écueil. J'apporterai ici en toute simplicité, en toute sincérité, réponse aux questions très nombreuses qui ont été posées de toute part depuis quelques semaines; j'aurai le souci—je le dis tout de suite au début de mes explications—de ne déprécier en rien les territoires abandonnés en Afrique équatoriale, mais aussi de les montrer tels qu'ils se comportent, avec leurs imperfections, leurs difficultés d'exploitation.

Il faut expliquer au pays, avec une entière netteté, les clauses et les conséquences de cet accord; il ne nous pardonnerait pas, d'avoir abandonné la moindre parcelle de son empire sans qu'il ait été mis à même de mesurer la valeur et l'importance des territoires cédés. (*Très bien! très bien!*)

Que donnons-nous en Afrique équatoriale, que nous reste-t-il après cette cession; qu'en pouvons-nous, qu'en devons-nous faire demain?

Telles sont les questions que successivement je voudrais envisager ici.

Messieurs, au cours des négociations difficiles qui se sont poursuivies cet été, le Gouvernement, en tant qu'il s'agissait de la partie congolaise de l'accord, a obéi à une triple pensée. Le principe de la compensation en Afrique équatoriale admis—et sur ce point mon collègue des affaires étrangères s'est expliqué tout à l'heure—il s'agit d'abord à ce que les cessions portent le moins possible sur cette partie de la colonie, qu'il considère comme la plus intéressante par sa proximité de la côte et par ses possibilités d'avenir, j'entends dire le Gabon et le Moyen-Congo jusqu'à la Sangha.

Il s'est efforcé, en second lieu, de sauvegarder au mieux la grande voie de pénétration vers le centre africain constituée par les fleuves Congo, Oubangui, Gribingui, Chari, qui forme en quelque sorte comme l'épine dorsale de notre possession.

Enfin il a fait effort pour que les cessions n'intéressent que les parties de notre possession qui avaient été le moins colonisées par la France où elle avait le moins dépensé de son or et de son sang, qu'en un mot elle avait le moins marquée de son empreinte, de telle sorte que l'abandon en fût moins sensible à son amour-propre et à ses intérêts matériels. (*Vifs applaudissements.*)

Dans quelle mesure avons-nous réussi à ce triple point de vue? J'ai le devoir de l'expliquer à la Chambre.

Messieurs, quand on envisage d'ensemble l'histoire de l'Afrique équatoriale, on est frappé dès l'abord par des constatations qui paraissent particulières à l'évolution de cette colonie.

Voici près de trois quarts de siècle que nous sommes à Libreville, voici plus de trente ans que notre pavillon flotte à Brazzaville et cependant nous n'avons rien fait ou presque rien dans cette fraction de la colonie d'un accès relativement aisé.

Cela s'explique, messieurs, parce que tout l'effort de la métropole s'est porté vers l'hinterland, vers le Congo moyen, vers l'Oubangui, le Chari et leurs affluents, en vue de gagner nos rivaux de vitesse et d'atteindre au plus tôt le centre africain; les événements qui se déroulent à cette heure au Ouadaï et qui auront, je l'espère, une prochaine et heureuse solution, ne sont que le couronnement de ce long et héroïque effort.

Pendant que nous poursuivions cette œuvre, nous avons négligé la fraction de la colonie voisine de la côte, et cela contrairement à ce qui s'était passé dans toutes nos colonies, notamment en Cochinchine pour l'Indo-Chine, et au Sénégal pour l'Afrique occidentale.

Quel est le tableau que nous avons sous les yeux? A l'heure actuelle, on peut à peine accéder à Libreville de nuit tant les passes sont mal éclairées. Le port rudimentaire, construit par la marine voici quarante ans, ne comporte des installations que pour les chalands et les embarcations légères.

Il n'y a pas de matériel pour charger et décharger les colis, pas de moyens de transport. A Cap-Lopez, la situation est la même dans les rades plus méridionales, celles de Setté-Cama et de Loango elle est pire encore.

Les fleuves, voies de pénétration naturelle vers l'intérieur, mais qui ne sont navigables qu'à une petite distance de la côte à raison de l'orographie de cette partie de l'Afrique et spécialement des monts de Cristal qu'ils descendent en rapides, ces fleuves n'ont pas été aménagés. Les sociétés concessionnaires auxquelles on avait à tort pensé pouvoir confier la création de l'outillage économique de la colonie, n'ont rien ou presque rien fait; de ce côté, tout espoir doit être abandonné.

J'ai donc le droit de dire—les chiffres sont là pour en témoigner—que ce que nous avons fait jusqu'en ces toutes dernières années dans cette fraction de la colonie est négligeable. Le Gabon avait en 1898-99 un mouvement commerciale de 9 millions de francs. Dix ans après le chiffre des transactions était sensiblement le même.

Pourtant—et j'arrive à un point essentiel—il faut considérer que cette fraction de la colonie en est la partie la plus précieuse, à raison de sa proximité de la mer et des facilités d'accès qu'elle présente; pourvu qu'on veuille bien les aménager, les deux ports de Libreville et de Cap-Lopez sont les plus sûrs de la côte occidentale d'Afrique, depuis Dakar jusqu'à Saint-Paul de Loanda. A l'intérieur, les populations sont commerçantes, belliqueuses il est vrai, mais elles donnent, par là même, la mesure de ce qu'elle pourront faire. C'est là une règle générale en Afrique, et il y a quelques jours je recevais un télégramme du colonel Largeau, dans lequel il me disait qu'il avait rencontré des peuplades belliqueuses et qu'il s'en félicitait, car il y voyait pour l'avenir des concours actifs pour le commerce et l'agriculture.

De plus, ce pays du Gabon est infiniment riche par ses possibilités actuelles et d'avenir. Je ne parle pas du caoutchouc, sur lequel tout le monde est très suffisamment informé, mais des cultures de cacao, café, vanille, qui doivent réussir parfaitement, ainsi que le démontrent des exemples malheureusement trop restreints encore, mais que nous pouvons multiplier.

Les bois présentent des essences nombreuses. Enfin, on a découvert dans la région de Mboko-Sangho, du Mindouli et du Djoué, une zone cuprifère qui ouvre à l'exploitation des mines un bel avenir.

Ces renseignements vous montrent combien nous étions fondés dans cette première préoccupation, qui a consisté à retenir la plus possible de cette fraction de la colonie qui, j'ai le droit de le dire, même détachée de tout l'hinterland, représente un ensemble homogène, puisqu'il ne comprend pas moins de 500,000 kilomètres carrés de superficie, et que, je le rappelle en passant, les deux diagonales, Libreville—Ouesso et Libreville—Brazzaville, mesurent près de 800 et de 900 kilomètres. Ces espaces sont suffisants pour former une colonie prospère. On a pu redouter à un moment donné—et M. le ministre des affaires étrangères y faisait allusion—que l'emprise ne fût plus considérable. Elle se réduit heureusement à une superficie de 30,000 à 35,000 kilomètres carrés.

Certes, ce sacrifice n'est pas négligeable, quand on veut bien se rappeler qu'il comporte, notamment, la rive gauche du rio Muni et une partie des affluents Nord de l'Ivindo. Mais ce qu'on peut dire, messieurs, c'est que, ni par son étendue territoriale, ni par sa disposition même, cet abandon ne constitue un danger pour la partie de la colonie qui nous demeure. Il dépend exclusivement de nous, comme je l'indiquerai, tout à l'heure, il dépend de notre courage, de notre énergie, de notre foi dans l'avenir de ce pays, de faire que le nouveau voisinage qui lui est imposé n'entraîne point de conséquence mortelle pour le reste de la colonie. (Applaudissements.)

Il s'agissait, en second lieu, comme je l'indiquais tout à l'heure, de sauvegarder la grande voie maîtresse qui conduit vers le centre africain et de garder intacts les liens entre les diverses fractions de la colonie.

Messieurs, avec son clair génie le pays a compris que dans l'immense superficie de notre empire africain, certaines fractions pouvaient être abandonnées pour acquérir par ailleurs des avantages équivalents ou supérieurs. Il en a admis le principe, mais à une condition, c'est que ce qui nous resterait ne fût pas touché indirectement et que nous ne fussions pas contraints de solliciter l'intervention de tierces puissances pour atteindre les domaines qui nous restaient. En un mot, au mois de septembre dernier, le pays s'est opposé à la coupure. Nous croyons avoir suffisamment résolu la question sur ce point et donné au sentiment national les garanties qu'il exigeait.

Voici, en effet, quelle est la situation à l'heure actuelle. Avant le traité—et je m'excuse de donner ici quelques précisions, je les crois nécessaires (Parlez! parlez!)—avant le traité, trois voies d'accès conduisaient à nos possessions d'Afrique équatoriale. La voie septentrionale, celle de l'Afrique occidentale, c'est la voie Niger–Tchad, la voie Niamey–Zinder–Nguigmi. C'est la plus courte kilométriquement et c'est, à l'heure actuelle, celle que suit le fil télégraphique; c'est peut-être, pour une fraction des transports au moins, celle qui sera suivie demain.

J'indique, en passant, messieurs, que c'est par cette voie que les renforts envoyés au Ouadaï au lendemain des événements douloureux de l'Ouadi-Kadja et de Doroté sont passés. Donc, même si la coupure par le Sud avait été réalisée, nos troupes du Ouadaï n'eussent pas été isolées comme on l'a écrit à tort plusieurs fois cet été.

Cette première voie demeure intacte. Je n'insiste pas.

La deuxième voie de pénétration est celle qui emprunte la Nigeria anglaise et le Cameroun allemand : c'est la voie dite de la Bénoué. Les marchandises venues par mer débarquent à Burutu, port anglais à l'embouchure du Niger, elles sont transportées ensuite par vapeurs fluviaux sur le Niger et la Bénoué jusqu'à Garoua, en territoire allemand et, de là, acheminées, par chalands, pirogues, charrettes ou porteurs jusqu'au Logone.

Il vous apparaît tout de suite, messieurs, que cette voie était viciée et précaire par son caractère international. Elle ne pouvait donner satisfaction que si nous étions en bons rapports avec les nations dont elle traverse les territoires. Mais c'était là une situation antérieure à l'accord du 4 novembre.

Ce que pouvait l'accord du 4 novembre, c'était ne pas modifier en mal cette situation. Eh bien, nous en avons eu la préoccupation, et puisque les territoires de Léré au Logone étaient compris dans la cession, nous avons prévu une série d'enclaves permettant d'utiliser, dans les mêmes conditions qu'hier, peut-être même—des techniciens me l'ont confié depuis—dans des conditions meilleures la voie ancienne.

Au centre. Oh non!

M. le ministre des colonies. Je tiens ces renseignements d'officiers qui ont commandé dans ces régions.

La troisième voie de pénétration est celle du Congo et de l'Oubangui, qui est à proprement parler notre voie nationale. Nous nous sommes efforcés de lui garder ce caractère. (*Très bien! très bien!*)

Oh! je sais—M. de Mun y a fait allusion—il y a les deux pointes de la Sangha et de la Lobaye, et on n'a pas manqué de critiquer ces deux enclaves. On a voulu y voir comme deux agrafes d'une tunique de Nessus destinée à brûler un jour les flancs de notre colonie. Messieurs, la réalité est heureusement moins tragique.

Oui, l'Allemagne possédera de 12 à 20 kilomètres de rives sur un ensemble fluvial qui a près de 1,500 kilomètres; mais—vous ne l'avez pas oublié—l'accord stipule en même temps que les rives ne pourront pas être fortifiées.

Il dit aussi qu'il y aura liberté de transit sur ces rives. Et si ces garanties, messieurs, pouvaient vous paraître insuffisantes parce qu'elles ne sont qu'écrites, il suffirait de se rappeler qu'au droit de Bonga, à l'embouchure de la Sangha, le Congo a plus de 10 kilomètres de largeur, et qu'en face de la Lobaye, vis-à-vis de Mongoumba, l'Oubangui a plus de 1 kilomètre aux basses eaux.

Ces chiffres démontrent que la navigation française sur le Congo et l'Oubangui n'est nullement menacée. (*Très bien! très bien!*)

Enfin—et on paraît l'oublier toujours quand on parle Congo et Oubangui—nous sommes dans le bassin conventionnel du Congo, qui a reçu un statut spécial par l'acte de Berlin de 1885.

Aux termes de cet accord diplomatique et par suite, dès avant le traité du 4 novembre, les navires allemands pouvaient en toute liberté et avec les garanties assurées par l'acte de 1885, circuler et sur le Congo, et sur l'Oubangui et sur la Sangha.

M. Pierre Leroy-Beaulieu. Alors pourquoi les Allemands ont-ils demandé accès à ces deux fleuves?

M. le ministre des colonies. Il est vrai,—et on a beaucoup parlé au cours de cet été—que la navigation se pratique dans ces régions dans des conditions un peu spéciales, parce que les chaudières sont chauffées au bois. Un jour viendra où elles le seront au pétrole, mais, en attendant, la puissance qui ne détient pas une des rives n'est pas certaine de pouvoir assurer sa navigation sur le fleuve.

Je pense que l'étendue de rives que nous avons conservées prouve une fois de plus que nous sommes absolument maîtres de la navigation dans cette partie du Congo, depuis Brazzaville jusqu'à Bangui. (*Très bien! très bien!*)

Quant à la dernière fraction de cette grande voie de pénétration dont je parlais tout à l'heure jusqu'au Chari et au delà de Bangui, elle n'est pas touchée; je me trompe, elle est améliorée d'une manière sensible par l'abandon qui nous a été fait par l'Allemagne des territoires compris entre le bas Logone et le bas Chari.

M. le comte de Lanjuinais. On nous cède la moitié d'un bec de canard et on nous prend deux trompes d'éléphant. (*Exclamations.*)

M. le ministre des colonies. J'entends bien, messieurs : ces douze ou quinze mille kilomètres carrés ne constituent pas un accroissement de richesse très appréciable pour notre Afrique équatoriale, mais ces territoires ne sont pas négligeables et les documents distribués au Reichstag allemand à l'occasion de la discussion du traité indiquent qu'au delà du Rhin on considère cette partie comme ayant une valeur égale à celle que nous cédons entre le Logone et la frontière orientale du Cameroun, et que nous nous plaisons à considérer comme de très grande valeur.

Mais cet abandon a eu pour résultat de rendre le fleuve Chari français jusqu'à Fort-Lamy. Quand on sait l'importance de Fort-Lamy, chef-lieu du territoire militaire du Tchad, ou reconnaît que ce n'est pas là un petit avantage; la sécurité de nos voies de communication a été accrue dans une très large mesure. *(Très bien! très bien!)*

Il ne suffisait pas d'avoir sauvegardé les voies d'accès; il était encore désirable de cantonner, en quelque sorte, les territoires cédés dans la partie de la possession où nous avions fait jusqu'ici les moindres efforts. Ce but a été atteint. J'ai fait dresser, aussi approximativement que possible, l'état des dépenses effectuées par la colonie jusqu'à ce jour, d'une part dans les parties cédées, d'autre part dans les parties conservées. Je scinde cette période en deux fractions, l'une qui va jusqu'en 1909—c'est la date à laquelle ont commencé les travaux de l'emprunt de 21 millions—la seconde qui comprend les deux dernières années.

Avant 1909, on avait effectué dans les territoires cédés environ 100,000 fr. de travaux pour une série de postes; au contraire, pour les territoires demeurés français, on arrive à un total d'environ 5 millions pour les installations de postes, à Libreville, à Loango, à Brazzaville, à Ouesso, à Bangui, etc.; et à 1 million pour les lignes télégraphiques.

Ainsi, en résumé avant 1909, sur une dépense d'environ 6,100,000 fr., 100,000 fr. ont été dépensés dans les territoires cédés.

Depuis 1909, c'est-à-dire depuis la mise en exécution de l'emprunt de 21 millions, dans les territoires cédés, il a été fait une dépense de 400,000 fr. Dans les territoires conservés, au contraire, il a été fait une dépense d'environ 8 millions, pour les lignes télégraphiques, la route de Fort-Sibut à Fort-Crampel, les études des deux voies ferrées, des études hydrographiques, etc.

Ainsi, en résumé, pour cette seconde période, il a été fait 8,400,000 fr. de dépenses, dont 400,000 fr. dans les territoires cédés.

J'avais le devoir de faire passer ces chiffres sous les yeux de la Chambre. *(Très bien! très bien!)*

Sans doute, pour être complet, faudrait-il ajouter à ces chiffres les dépenses effectuées par les missions religieuses et par les sociétés concessionnaires. Mais, d'abord, les premières demeurent presque toutes entières en territoire français. Quant aux secondes, les éléments d'appréciation m'ont fait défaut.

Toutefois, je puis affirmer que, sauf dans la région de la Haute-Sangha, pour laquelle un effort sérieux a été tenté, les sociétés n'ont pas fait preuve d'une très grande activité. Je m'excuse devant la Chambre de ces détails. Mais je crois que mon devoir est de les lui fournir. Je n'aurais pas pleinement rempli ma tâche si je ne l'avais pas fait. *(Très bien!—Parlez!)*

En les envisageant d'ensemble, voici en résumé l'importance des territoires cédés. Ils mesurent une superficie qu'on peut évaluer à 225,000 kilomètres carrés, chiffre faible, qui m'est venu du gouvernement [*sic.* gouverneur] général de l'Afrique équatoriale, mieux placé que personne pour l'établir à 275,000 kilomètres carrés, chiffre fort.

Ces territoires ont une population d'environ 1 million d'habitants. Les effectifs militaires que nous y entretenons sont de quatre ou cinq compagnies. Les agents civils de l'administration sont au nombre d'une cinquantaine environ. Le nombre des agents de factoreries, des commerçants et colons est à peu près double. Le montant des importations et des exportations, autant que j'ai pu l'établir, s'élève à 8 millions de francs en chiffres ronds.

Enfin pour ce qui est des impôts, je me permets de rectifier des chiffres qui ont paru. Voici ceux que j'ai reçus du gouverneur général de l'Afrique équatoriale et je l'ai prié de les vérifier à nouveau, parce qu'ils me paraissaient inférieurs à la réalité.

Les recettes effectuées dans les territoires cédés s'élèvent à environ 1 million de francs pour les douanes et les domaines, et à 750,000 fr. pour les impôts de capitation.

Envisageant d'un autre point de vue ce même ensemble, voici comment il se présente : à peu près 50,000 kilomètres carrés de parcelles inondées ou marécageuses, où l'eau, la terre, la végétation s'entremêlent au point que l'homme n'y peut pas vivre et qu'il n'y pénètre que pour la chasse.

Ensuite de 60,000 à 80,000 kilomètres carrés de forêts vierges très serrées, où, à la vérité, se trouvent des peuplements caoutchoutifères de première importance, mais où se trouvent aussi les germes qui provoquent le mal redoutable que vous savez, auquel je ne ferai ici qu'allusion, mais sur lequel je devrais m'étendre plus longuement, si je lui donnais la place qu'il doit tenir dans cet exposé.

Enfin de 100,000 à 140,000 kilomètres carrés de terres légères, aptes à la culture et à l'élevage, découvertes dans la plus grande partie de cette étendue habitées par des populations intelligentes, déjà habituées aux travaux de l'agriculture et de l'élevage, et préparées par l'islamisme à une discipline sociale. C'est la région qui s'étend à l'est de la frontière orientale actuelle du Cameroun.

J'indique, pour finir, qu'à peu près les trois quarts ou les quatre cinquièmes des territoires cédés sont entre les mains de sociétés concessionnaires dont le privilège d'exploitation prend fin, pour les unes, en 1920, et, pour les autres, en 1930.

Tel est, messieurs, défini aussi exactement que possible, le bilan de ce que nous cédons en Afrique équatoriale.

Si douloureusement que nous soyons affectés par ce sacrifice, nous ne devons pas nous laisser aller à certaines exagérations que cet été j'ai entendu exprimer par des esprits d'ordinaire plus mesurés. N'est-on point allé jusqu'à dire que le traité du 4 novembre compromettait irrémédiablement l'avenir de notre empire african?

Quand on songe, messieurs, que cet empire comporte près de 6 millions de kilomètres carrés exploitables, et je ne parle pas, bien entendu, du Sahara; qu'il est habité par à peu près 33 millions d'habitants; qu'il comporte un commerce de près de 2 milliards, j'ai le droit de dire qu'en mettant en balance ces chiffres et ceux que j'indiquais à l'instant, on ne peut pas déclarer que nous ayons affaibli sensiblement notre position en Afrique. J'ai le droit de dire—et je le fais sans aucune passion politique—que la troisième République, qui a reconstitué le domaine colonial de la France, mutilé par les régimes antérieurs, ne peut être accusée d'avoir inscrit dans les fastes de notre histoire des pages qui rappellent en quelque façon que ce soit notre abandon des Indes, de la Louisiane et du Canada. (Applaudissements à gauche et au centre.)

Messieurs, que reste-t-il en Afrique équatoriale et que devons-nous faire de ce qui nous reste? C'est là l'œuvre de demain, c'est celle qui nous presse.

J'ai dit tout à l'heure ce qu'est la partie côtière, celle qui s'étend de l'Atlantique à la Sangha, je n'y reviens pas. On a parlé ensuite avec quelque dédain de l'enclave qui nous demeure entre le Likvuala aux Herbes et l'Oubangui. Messieurs, quand on songe que ce territoire mesure 400 kilomètres le long de l'Oubangui et 150 kilomètres de largeur à la hauteur de Bera Njoko, que dans le passé et dans un avenir très long encore la seule voie de pénétration dans cette région sera le fleuve Oubangui, quand on fait cette constatation, on se demande pourquoi cette fraction de notre colonie, telle qu'elle se comporte à l'heure actuelle, n'aurait pas le développement qu'elle aurait en avant l'accord. J'ai d'ailleurs rappelé déjà les raisons d'ordre politique et économique qui nous avaient empêchés de l'abandonner.

Pour les régions situées plus au Nord, dans l'Oubangui–Chari–Tchad notamment, elles sont, il est vrai, légèrement écornées à leur extrémité occidentale.

Messieurs, on a représenté tour à tour ces régions comme des réserves de richesses mystérieuses et comme des terres maudites. Il est certain qu'on ne peut pas fonder de très vastes espoirs sur des terres isolées en quelque sorte à l'intérieur d'un grand continent. Les difficultés d'accès et de transport les empêchent de prétendre sur le marché mondial à une place prépondérante; mais ces régions, ne l'oublions pas, sont les réservoirs de races denses et vigoureuses dont nous avons un si grand besoin dans notre Afrique, où la densité moyenne de la population est faible. Ne nous y trompons pas, quand nous aurons apporté à ces populations la sécurité et la paix, quand nous aurons débarrassé ces régions des tyranneaux locaux, qu'ils appellent comme hier Rabah ou comme aujourd'hui Doudmourrah, quand nous y aurons porté les premiers éléments de la civilisation, sous forme de routes, d'écoles, de dispensaires, de marchés, elles prendront le même développement qu'ont pris, à l'étonnement de beaucoup de coloniaux mêmes, les régions du Soudan, si décriées autrefois.

Messieurs, nous avions, en outre, pour conserver cette région, des considérations politiques impérieuses.

Nous ne pouvions pas admettre qu'une autre nation que la France donnât le mot d'ordre sur les confins du Sahara, où le moindre bruit, la moindre agitation ont des répercussions si étrangement lointaines.

Si enfin ces considérations d'ordre économique ou politique n'avaient point suffi pour nous faire apprécier à leur juste valeur ces territoires, je dirai après M. de Mun qu'il y avait une raison majeure, bien qu'une raison de sentiment, pour les garder.

Quand au cours de cet été je lisais les objurgations adressées au Gouvernement, quand de toutes parts on vous conjurait de ne point céder le sol qui avait bu tant de sang de nos soldats et de nos explorateurs, j'avais la satisfaction de penser, et j'en apporte l'expression très loyale devant la Chambre, que, sauf deux ou trois tombes qui se trouvent dans la partie cédée, presque toutes demeurent dans le territoire conservé, et, demain comme hier, les cendres de Crampel et de Bretonnet, de Lamy et de Behagle, de Fiegenschuh, de Moll et de tant d'autres reposeront à l'ombre du drapeau national. (Applaudissements.)

Dans cette Afrique équatoriale qu'allons-nous faire? Faut-il nous laisser aller au découragement où certains pessimistes voudraient nous conduire?

Ne faut-il pas au contraire répondre au coup qui a frappé la colonie par un redoublement d'efforts?

J'ai indiqué que peu de choses avaient été faites dans cette colonie. Je dois maintenant préciser.

Il est exact que, jusqu'il y a deux ans, presque rien n'avait été fait au Congo, mais, depuis deux ans, un effort sensible a été effectué et les résultats de cet effort ont été tels qu'ils ont mis en évidence pour cette colonie une possibilité d'exploitation, et des espoirs qui ne seront pas tous démentis. Il n'y a pas à hésiter, la France doit immédiatement s'employer à réparer un passé qu'on peut regretter aujourd'hui.

Voici d'un mot quelle est en cette fin d'année 1911 la situation de la colonie.

Neuf bataillons l'occupent, trois au Tchad, six répartis dans les trois colonies du groupe. Trois cents administrateurs ou agents civils sont répartis dans une centaine de postes. On peut affirmer qu'à la fin de l'année 1912 nous aurons pris possession de toute la colonie.

Quand on pense qu'au début de 1908 un cinquième à peine était occupé, on peut mesurer le chemin parcouru depuis trois ans.

L'armature de la colonie est dès maintenant constituée. Elle peut, elle doit se développer suivant les mêmes méthodes que celles employées dans toutes nos grandes colonies. Et voici que déjà les résultats financiers indiquent que ces espoirs ne sont pas vains. Les budgets du Moyen-Congo et de l'Oubangui-Chari sont en excédent, leurs caisses de réserves sont au maximum. Le budget général, il est vrai, n'en est pas au même point. Mais je dois indiquer que, l'année dernière, il est arrivé à éteindre la dette de 1 million qui, depuis plusieurs années, grevait son passif. Dans le projet de budget que j'ai reçu ces jours derniers pour l'année 1912, le gouverneur général avait pu inscrire l'annuité nécessaire à l'amortissement de la seconde tranche de l'emprunt de 21 millions. Lorsque la Chambre a voté cet emprunt, elle avait pensé cependant en conserver toujours la charge au budget colonial.

Enfin, messieurs, le mouvement commercial, également depuis deux ans—je souligne ces mots, car je ne voudrais point paraître, en ce moment, plaider une cause contraire à celle que je défendais tout à l'heure—ce mouvement qui ne s'est dessiné que depuis deux ans, indique un chiffre de 40 millions double de celui d'il y a dix ans. Ce mouvement ne peut que s'accroître, parce que nous rendons au commerce libre des espaces de plus en plus vastes, et qu'en même temps, une administration plus attentive surveille mieux les sociétés concessionnaires et saura les diriger dans une voie plus conforme au sain développement économique de la colonie. (*Applaudissements à gauche et au centre.*)

Telle est la situation. Pourquoi ne ferions-nous pas pour cette Afrique équatoriale ce que nous avons fait pour les autres colonies, pour l'Indochine, pour l'Afrique occidentale, pour Madagascar, quand nous avons prêté 300 millions à la première, 200 millions à la seconde et 100 millions à la troisième?

Messieurs, il s'agit de savoir si la France voudra consentir ces sacrifices. Je puis vous dire que le Gouvernement, en possession des études entreprises sur l'emprunt de 21 millions, sera en état au cours de l'année 1912, de vous présenter un programme qui permettra à la colonie de prendre le développement auquel je faisais allusion. Ces études sont complètes et détaillées. Je ne saurais trop rendre hommage aux officiers qui les ont entreprises là-bas dans les conditions difficiles que vous savez.

Le projet de voie ferrée de Pointe-Noire à Brazzaville, avec une installation de port à Pointe-Noire est prêt. La France se doit de faire cette voie ferrée pour se constituer à elle-même une voie de pénétration exclusivement française et ne plus être obligée d'emprunter la voie belge de Matadi à Kinchassa qui semble d'ailleurs avoir atteint son maximum de rendement.

Cette voie française sera assurée d'un trafic certain, non seulement par le transit qui dépasse déjà 3 millions, mais par l'exploitation des produits de la forêt de Mayumbe et des mines de cuivre de M'Boko Songho et de Mindouli.

En second lieu, ce programme comprendra l'amélioration des communications de Brazzaville au Tchad, d'abord en mettant à profit les résultats de la mission Roussilhe, de façon à aménager le fleuve Congo et le fleuve Oubangui, puis en terminant la route de Bangui à Fort-Archambault, dont la section médiane est en voie de construction.

Enfin, messieurs, et je tiens à le dire ici, nous devrons faire également le chemin de fer de la partie Nord du Gabon. . . . .

M. *Tournade.* C'est très intéressant, mais ce n'est pas la question. (*Exclamations à gauche.*)

M. *le président du conseil.* Mais si, c'est tout à fait la question.

M. *le ministre des colonies.* L'honorable M. Tournade me dit : C'est très intéressant, mais ce n'est pas la question.

M. *Fernand David.* Vous tenez un très beau langage, à tous égards. (*Applaudissements.*)

M. *Tournade.* Je ne dis pas non, mais ce n'est pas la question.

M. *le ministre des colonies.* J'ai indiqué tout à l'heure, afin que la Chambre en fût juge, l'étendue des territoires cédés. Puis, pour répondre à certain pessimisme, que je ne crois pas voulu, j'ai eu le devoir de dire ce qu'il nous restait de notre Afrique équatoriale et ce que surtout elle pourrait être demain si nous voulions bien faire pour elle ce que nous avions fait pour les autres colonies. (*Applaudissements à gauche et sur divers bancs.*) Par conséquent, messieurs, j'ai le droit de dire que je suis au cœur de la question. (*Très bien! très bien!*)

On vous a dit : "Vous avez blessé mortellement la colonie." J'ai démontré qu'il n'en est rien et qu'il suffit de la volonté et de la méthode de notre part pour la remettre dans l'état où elle aurait dû être si elle n'avait pas été délaissée. (*Applaudissements à gauche et sur divers bancs.*)

Et je termine, messieurs, ce que je disais lorsque j'ai été interrompu; il faudra faire aussi le chemin de fer du Nord du Gabon. Peut-être le tracé qui paraissait devoir être adopté subira-t-il quelques modifications, mais je considère comme nécessaire d'entreprendre au plus tôt la ligne de N'Djolé à Kandjama, qui, en prolongeant par le rail la voie navigable de l'Ogooué, viendra drainer toutes ces régions de l'Ogooué et de l'Ivindo et au besoin permettra la pénétration jusqu'à Ouesso et au delà si les événements le font juger nécessaire.

J'ai dit que la France se devait à elle-même de faire cet effort et qu'elle le devait aussi à ceux de nos compatriotes, fonctionnaires, officiers ou colons qui sont en Afrique équatoriale et qui ont accueilli l'accord avec les sentiments que je viens de vous faire connaître. Ils n'ont pas protesté; ils ont dit leur tristesse; mais quand ils nous en ont envoyé l'écho, voici quelques semaines, ils ont ajouté qu'ils se sentiraient consolés si la mère patrie, au lieu d'abandonner ce qui reste de la colonie, voulait bien, par un nouvel et vigoureux effort, faire ce qu'elle n'avait pas fait dans le passé. Ils ont pensé unanimement qu'ainsi notre œuvre en Afrique équatoriale était pleinement sauvegardée. (*Applaudissements.*)

Messieurs, au cours des négociations, au fur et à mesure que se dessinaient les linéaments de la nouvelle frontière qui devait être assignée à notre Afrique équatoriale, l'opinion française, c'est son honneur, connut des heures d'émoi. Même ceux qui, bien informés, comprenaient que la France devait sortir de ce traité grandie en force et en puissance, ne se résolvaient pas aisément à l'idée de l'abandon d'une partie de nos possessions. Il leur apparaissait difficile que ces territoires qui avaient connu, à un moment donnée, la paix française, qui avaient reçu une première empreinte de notre civilisation, pussent passer en d'autres mains. (*Applaudissements.*) Et des voix émouvantes se faisaient entendre qui rendaient plus aiguë encore la crise où se débattait le sentiment national.

Je n'ai pas besoin de dire que nulle part plus qu'au Gouvernement, on ne ressentit ces doutes et ces angoisses, que nulle part on n'était mieux placé pour revivre l'histoire de ces régions, pour évoquer les noms des de Brazza, des Mizon, des Ballay pour ne parler que des morts. En poussant à travers l'Afrique mystérieuse leurs pointes hardies, ces valeureux pionniers avaient comme première idée de rendre la France plus grande.

Ah! certes, ils n'étaient point partis au hasard et, comme le disait tout à l'heure très justement l'honorable M. de Mun, ils suivaient un programme bien tracé.

Quand Fourneau et Gaillard remontaient pour la première fois la Sangha, quand ensuite de Brazza et Mizon, venus l'un du Sud, l'autre du Nord, se rencontraient également dans l'arrière Cameroun, ils comprenaient parfaitement qu'à ce moment ils ouvraient la voie française le long du Congo, qu'ils mettaient en relation directe nos possessions gabonaises avec nos possessions sahariennes; de telle sorte qu'on pût aller, comme le disait M. de Mun, en terre française depuis Alger jusqu'à Libreville. Mais ce qu'ils voulaient par-dessus tout, c'est que notre civilisation qu'ils savaient généreuse et accueillante aux faibles—et nul, je crois, plus que de Brazza ne l'a montrée sous ce jour au cœur de l'Afrique (*Vifs applaudissements*)—c'est que notre civilisation s'étendît sur la plus vaste partie possible du continent africain. (*Applaudissements.*)

Eh bien! leurs désirs sont réalisés; leur mémoire peut être satisfaite. (*Applaudissements.*)

Oui, il est vrai, demain le doux nom de France ne se répercutera plus sous les voûtes pleines de silence et de mystère d'une partie de la forêt équatoriale, mais par ailleurs il sonnera bien haut dans la plaine marocaine et sur les sommets du grand Atlas. Et quand on écrira l'histoire de ces événements, il faudra dire que ce Maroc nous a été donné en partie par ceux-là mêmes que leur vocation avait d'abord conduits vers l'Équateur. (*Vifs applaudissements.*) Je suis certain, messieurs, qu'à cette heure la France ne pourra que leur ouvrir plus larges encore les portes du temple de la Reconnaissance qu'elle élève à ceux de ses fils qui l'ont bien servie. (*Applaudissements vifs et répétés à gauche, à l'extrême gauche et au centre.—M. le ministre, de retour au banc du Gouvernement, reçoit les félicitations de ses collègues.*)

APPENDIX III.

Memorandum by Sir E. Crowe respecting Franco-German Negotiations.

F.O. 1950/1950/12/18.   *January* 14, 1912.

In the light of recent revelations, it may be useful to reconstitute, in brief outline, the history of events of which we have hitherto, it appears, had only a fragmentary knowledge. The revelations explain a good deal that was up to now somewhat mysterious in the attitude of the German Government.

The Franco-German agreement of 1909 was, as we suspected at the time, only a portion of a wider plan which comprised, at least so far as German intentions were concerned, a far-reaching scheme of co-operation between the two Governments in other parts of the world besides Morocco, and which would have formed, perhaps, to begin with, a counterpoise to, but eventually the end of, the *entente*. For the kind of co-operation aimed at in Turkey, and more particularly with respect to the Bagdad Railway, could obviously not co-exist with the Anglo-French understanding for action on parallel lines and reciprocal consideration for one another's interests in the East. That this view of the situation was present to the mind of M. Caillaux, the instigator and promoter of the policy of general co-operation with Germany, is proved by the secrecy of his negotiations and the absolute silence preserved upon them at Berlin at a moment when conversations were going on between England and Germany as to the possibility of some Anglo-German understanding to which France could become a party. If Germany was sincere in her suggestion that such an arrangement was practicable and easy, how is it to be explained that not a word was ever said about the fact that discussions, having that very object in view, were actually at the time proceeding with France? It must be concluded that, at least in the opinion of the German Government, the understanding with France was an alternative to the understanding with England, and not a step towards it.

This view is confirmed by the way M. Caillaux expressed himself, rather incautiously, to Sir F. Bertie. It will be remembered that his remarks culminated in the practical avowal that he did not see any advantage in the Anglo-French *Entente*, a view which, given the position at present occupied by France on the international chess-board, could only be explained and justified on the assumption that France was prepared to enter the orbit of the Triple Alliance.

These then were the larger, the governing, considerations which brought the German and French secret negotiators together. We do not know the whole plan even in outline. But it seems beyond doubt that, apart from France getting a free hand in Morocco, including the Spanish sphere, where France, no longer relying on English friendship, but able to count on German support, was ready to fall upon Spain, and apart from the compensation to be paid to Germany for this in the shape of the cession of the whole French Congo, there were in contemplation large and important schemes for a Franco-German control of Turkish finance, and for pushing the Bagdad Railway on in its advance to the Gulf with the assistance of French money and the French money-market. There seem also to have been discussions of a very large loan to Austria-Hungary to be negotiated in Paris, which was to be employed mainly for the purpose of considerably increasing the armaments of the Triple Alliance, with the necessary corollary of large orders for Krupps.

These secret negotiations were dragging on slowly, much too slowly for the German Government, who were becoming somewhat impatient to conclude something definite, but who believed that the French Government, in spite of M. Caillaux's unofficial commitments, were rather elusive, and had, more particularly, shown themselves reluctant to carry through certain preliminary arrangements (Morocco railways, Congo–Cameroon railways, &c.) which formed part of the wider scheme.

In the French march on Fez, the German Government saw their opportunity of squeezing the French. The terms of the 1909 agreement made it impossible to protest against a measure for " maintaining peace and internal order," in Morocco, which Germany had thereunder expressly recognised to be the duty of France. No objection was accordingly raised to the French advance, but unpleasant hints were let drop as to Germany "recovering her liberty of action" if France proceeded to occupy Fez permanently or made a "prolonged stay" there. These hints apparently did not lead to a hastening of the secret negotiations, which still hung fire. There followed the Kissingen interview,(1) at which Herr von Kiderlen, speaking to M. Cambon, whom he knew not to be in the secret of M. Caillaux's overtures, proposed in a most friendly tone, an amicable general settlement with France, by which she would be given a free hand in Morocco in return for something vaguely hinted at as a rectification of frontiers, on the Congo. This wrapping-up of the concession to be paid to Germany in a phrase so vague as to be necessarily misleading to anyone not in the secret, at a time when M. Caillaux appears already to have assented to the cession of the whole Congo, is explained by the fact that M. Caillaux was not as yet in a position to impose his unavowed policy on a Cabinet of which he was the Minister of Finance only.

At this moment (end of June) the German gunboat was actually on its way to Agadir. What exactly was in the mind of the German Government in taking that step, has been a matter of a good deal of speculation. No doubt there was the intention to give an unmistakable hint to France that Germany meant business and must be satisfied. But on the assumption that German demands had for the first time been foreshadowed at the Kissingen interview, the moment chosen for this "dig in the ribs" has hitherto seemed singularly inopportune. I remember Admiral Von Holzendorff telling me, when we talked about this in September last, that if I only knew what had preceded the Kissingen interview, the impatience of the German Government with France, of which the dispatch of the ship (disapproved by him) was the outcome, would become quite intelligible. I did not understand this at the time, and was unsuccessful in getting any further explanation. It is clear now that Herr von Kiderlen, having M. Caillaux's concessions as it were in his pocket, and seeing that the French Government were not active or prompt in redeeming their Finance Minister's pledges, thought the dispatch of the ship would make an impression in Paris sufficient to strengthen M. Caillaux's hands in getting his Cabinet to accept the policy of a general understanding with Germany.

Some time after the event, it will be remembered, Herr Zimmermann, the Under-Secretary of State in the German Foreign Office, let out confidentially to Sir Edward Goschen that the real object of sending the "Panther" was to facilitate the position of the French Government in yielding to the German demand.(2) This appeared almost in the light of a joke at the time, so incomprehensible did it seem that the German Government should have believed they could, by ostentatious pressure of this kind, make it easier for a French Government to give in to a German demand. In any case the miscalculation seems gross—and we know that it was not left uncriticised in German naval and Government circles—but we must now admit that Herr Zimmermann's statement, which seemed so extraordinarily far-fetched an explanation, was literally true.

Meanwhile, and before the "Panther" actually reached Agadir, the French Government resigned owing to the sudden accident to M. Monis, and M. Caillaux became Prime Minister.(3) Whatever effect his arrival at supreme power in the French Cabinet might have had on the negotiations in other circumstances, it soon became clear that the coup of Agadir, far from helping him, made it exceedingly difficult for him, in the face of the excitement of public opinion, to broach to his Cabinet the secret of his commitments to Herr von Kiderlen. But whilst the French Cabinet, including the Minister for Foreign Affairs and also the French Ambassador at Berlin, were kept in the dark, the secret communications with Herr von Kiderlen through unofficial channels appear to have been resumed. M. Caillaux's position must have

(1) [v. supra, p. 322, Ed. note; and pp. 353-7, No. 373.]
(2) [v. supra, pp. 487-8, No. 518.]
(3) [June 27, 1911.]

been a difficult one in these circumstances. On the one hand he could not but authorise the communications which M. de Selves entered into very naturally with the British Government with a view to common or at least parallel action of France and England in Morocco. No doubt he felt the less embarrassed in doing this, as he knew—what neither his Cabinet nor His Majesty's Government knew—that it was no part of the German plan to establish German authority in Southern Morocco.

It also now becomes intelligible what seemed so extraordinary at the time that Germany, having sent her ship to Agadir, absolutely declined to formulate any demands. She declared that it was for France to make an offer in return for Germany's evacuation of Agadir. We can now see that Herr von Kiderlen expected and wished M. Caillaux to come forward with the proposal to give up the French Congo to Germany. Why M. Caillaux did not come forward, but insisted on the proposal coming from Germany, can only be conjectured. Presumably he did not consider himself strong enough in his own Cabinet to venture so far.

When Herr von Kiderlen thereupon made his demand, he must still have been confident that it would be accepted. Had he not M. Caillaux's bond? But the opposition in France among the public was so loud and threatening that M. Caillaux was unable, not merely to avow his past negotiation, but even openly to advocate the course to which he was committed. What was he to do?

Here, again, is a point on which the recent revelations do not explicitly touch. But, judging from what we know took place then and after, it may safely be guessed that he thought it judicious to shelter himself behind Great Britain. He allowed M. de Selves and M. Paul Cambon to keep the closest touch with His Majesty's Government and discuss all eventualities on the basis of Anglo-French co-operation. To Herr von Kiderlen he most probably explained that his hand was being forced by England, which did not favour a Franco-German settlement on the terms offered.

On this hypothesis the attitude of the German Government towards England becomes much more intelligible and less ambiguous than it seemed hitherto. They genuinely believed that they had the French Congo and a good deal more in their pocket. Their secret friend and ally was the Prime Minister of France. He tells them that he cannot move because England objects. It had not so far occurred to them that any real difficulty could come from England, since their bargain, which involved German withdrawal from Morocco, but did not directly touch any specific British interests, was practically settled with France.

All of a sudden Count Metternich reports that Sir Edward Grey, after a silence of nearly three weeks, speaks strongly on the subject of Agadir and of the danger involved in Germany's insistence on demands which no French Government could accept. Mr. Lloyd George makes his speech. M. Caillaux, at the same time, points to the attitude of His Majesty's Government as making it impossible for him, at the moment, to redeem his former pledges. It was not unnatural that the German Government should turn upon England and should complain, and never cease complaining, that it was English intervention which prevented them from getting the terms from France which they had every reason to expect they would obtain.([4])

The immediate result was that Germany expressed readiness to take a good deal less. But, curiously enough, a pause took place in the official negotiations, and these dragged on irregularly with long and frequent pauses right into October. This is now explained by the fact that M. Caillaux again took up his private negotiations. M. Clemenceau has declared that he had positive proof that in the month of September M. Caillaux went so far as to express his readiness to enter into a secret arrangement with Germany for active co-operation against England. The patent fact is that throughout the long negotiations, and since, the official and semi-official German press never deviated from the line that the French attitude throughout gave no real reason for complaint, and that there must be a friendly understanding between France and Germany, but that England was the enemy, and must be wiped out eventually.

([4]) [cp. p. 795, Ed. note.]

All English assurances that there never had been any attempt or any desire to place obstacles in the way of a Franco-German understanding, were disbelieved and openly flouted. This was a not unnatural consequence of the belief, confirmed, as I think probable, by M. Caillaux, that the attitude of His Majesty's Government had been the exact contrary throughout.

Meanwhile, M. Caillaux's real intentions began to reveal themselves. M. de Selves formed his suspicions, found them confirmed in several ways, saw them react on the attitude of France towards Spain, and finally obtained proof of their correctness. The whole secret gradually came out. The shock to public opinion in France was such as to cause the downfall of M. Caillaux's Government and the unanimous condemnation not only of his tortuous methods, but of the policy which he thereby pursued.

If the foregoing is a fairly correct account—as I think it is—of what occurred, it is necessary to revise somewhat the view which our less complete knowledge of the events made us form of the methods of Herr von Kiderlen's diplomacy. It remains clear that his sending the " Panther " to Agadir was a blunder. It is open to some doubt whether, if the ship had not been sent, he might not have made it possible for M. Caillaux to get the French Cabinet to accept the African settlement which had been prearranged with the German foreign secretary. Had this been successfully done, perhaps further steps would have become easier for a closer rapprochement, ending in the severance of the *entente*. It is impossible to exculpate the German Government from having very deliberately set their plans for attaining this object. There is no necessity to blame them for adopting such a policy. It is quite natural and intelligible from their point of view. The important thing for us is to see and note that this was the kernel of Herr von Kiderlen's policy. We always suspected it; now we have very convincing proof. Whilst, therefore, the methods of German diplomacy now appear less Machiavellian than was generally thought at first, the direction of German policy stands the more clearly revealed as one of the search for understandings with France not with a view to promote the general peace of the world, but designed to separate the two western Powers which in combination offer the only obstacle to German plans for predominance in Europe. It was the transparency of this policy which in the end frustrated M. Caillaux's schemes. . . . .[5]

The question may be raised, how England on her part is affected by these revelations. So far as our relations with France are concerned, M. Caillaux's disappearance from the sphere of foreign policy can only be regarded as a blessing. He might or might not have acquired the power to direct French policy into a channel hostile to England. He was clearly not reluctant to make the attempt. The public opinion of France, on the other hand, rose to the occasion, and the sound sense and instinctive judgment shown in every quarter is a most encouraging feature in the situation. We might have been led into a quarrel with M. Caillaux's Government. Now he has been dismissed by a popular outcry, we have no quarrel with France.

As for our relations with Germany, it might at first sight appear that here was good opportunity for making a move for their improvement. We could, so it might be urged, go to Berlin and say : " These revelations show that your late acute ill-feeling against us arises from a complete misunderstanding. We on our part now see that your demands could not appear to you to be humiliating to France, since the French Prime Minister had already spontaneously agreed to them as reasonable. On the other hand, you must now admit that it was not we who stood in the way of your obtaining a settlement that a French Government could have accepted as satisfactory. You were under a misapprehension, but an intelligible misapprehension as to what France, as distinguished from M. Caillaux, could be expected to agree to. On this point, in fact, M. Caillaux unwittingly deceived you. But that is not England's fault, and England, unaware of M. Caillaux's commitments, was in honour bound to stand by France if the effect of her refusal to make what the French

[5] [A sentence referring to M. Caillaux is here omitted.]

Government regarded as a humiliating surrender to German dictation, was that she found herself involved in a war with you over Morocco."

Such an appeal might conceivably lead to the re-establishment of a better feeling between England and Germany. This must be a powerful temptation in the present circumstances. But it is essential to remember that such a course can only be followed at the risk of a breach between us and France. For it would amount to Germany and England agreeing that the blame for the grave misunderstanding between them rests on French Ministers, and it cannot unfortunately be doubted for a moment what use the German Government would make of any British advances in the sense suggested.

The distinction between methods of diplomacy and political ends remains all-important. In the last resort our quarrel with Germany arises, not from the peculiar methods of German diplomacy—although these have done much at all times to cause trouble and difficulties—but from a conflict of policies. German policy seeks the fulfilment of many ambitions, territorial, idealistic, and other, through the acquisition of a general ascendency in Europe—or, rather, the world—such as will make it impossible for any other State to oppose whatever wishes or designs she may consider herself justified in entertaining. There is nothing reprehensible in the abstract in such a policy, provided it does not refuse to pay due regard to the rights and liberties of other independent States. In practice the pursuit of the German policy leads to aggressive designs upon the territories and the fiscal, economical, and political independence of other States, who resist if they can, but whose chance of resisting would be gone the moment Germany's ascendency were secured.

England stands for the maintenance of existing rights and liberties so far as they are not incompatible with the orderly progress of the world. She is a strong supporter of the existing balance of power as most conducive to the continuance of independent States, on whose interaction and peaceful rivalry the progressive evolution of highest social ideals seems to depend.

If Germany will take her place among other nations in working out such a policy of free international co-operation, the symptoms of a conflict with England should rapidly disappear. They cannot be made to disappear by any arrangement, even if favoured by England herself, by which Germany is encouraged to work out her self-centred policy of a universal German ascendency. If we are wrong in ascribing such designs to the German Government, that is if Germany favours the same general policy as England, then the much-dreaded collision between the two countries will not be brought about by the mere fact that we do not rush to throw our arms round Germany's neck immediately after it has become apparent that she has failed in an attempt to break up the friendship between England and France.

If, on the other hand, Germany is still pursuing the policy of *divide et impera*, it is important that we should not play into her hands. Until, therefore, some unmistakable proof is forthcoming that Germany has given up the plan of sowing distrust between her neighbours in order to triumph over them separately, it is England's paramount duty to hold fast to the *entente* with France and Russia in order to maintain the balance of power. This would not be facilitated by any effort we might make to overcome our own difficulties with Germany by uniting with her to throw blame on France for the immediate results of M. Caillaux's adventure. For although France has unmistakably repudiated the policy of M. Caillaux, it is impossible entirely to dissociate the political action of a Prime Minister from his Government and his country. If we go too far in explaining away all cause of misunderstanding with Germany by dwelling on M. Caillaux's misleading diplomacy, and if a reconciliation with Germany and ourselves were brought about in virtue of our adopting such a course, then German opinion must necessarily fasten upon France as the source of all the trouble; there will be an outburst of anti-French feeling, which will, with some truth, be directly or indirectly traced to our action; and the consequence would unquestionably be mistrust between us and France. We cannot afford to run this danger, the less so as we are fully aware that, after all, the fatal policy of M. Caillaux, although he has been made the scapegoat by consent of all the parties, was in reality the policy of the German Government, and, in so far as we should excuse or condone German action, we should inevitably, in the eyes of France, appear in a sense to endorse the very principles underlying M. Caillaux's policy which we, in fact, agree with France in absolutely condemning.

In these circumstances, it seems to me that any advances on our part to Germany, based on the ground, or pretext, that the recent French revelations have removed an important cause of disagreement between us, are so likely to be misunderstood, and would lend themselves so readily to misrepresentation, that it will be wiser for the present to maintain an attitude of dignified reserve.

E. A. C.

Foreign Office, January 14, 1912.

APPENDIX IV.

Franco-Spanish Declaration and Convention respecting Morocco.([1])

(*Signed at Paris, October* 3, 1904.)

Déclaration.

F.O. France 3686. *Paris, October* 3, 1904.

Le Gouvernement de la République Française et le Gouvernement de Sa Majesté le Roi d'Espagne, s'étant mis d'accord pour fixer l'étendue des droits et la garantie des intérêts qui résultent pour la France de ses possessions algériennes, et pour l'Espagne de ses possessions sur la Côte du Maroc, et, le Gouvernement de Sa Majesté le Roi d'Espagne ayant en conséquence donné son adhésion à la Déclaration Franco-Anglaise du 8 Avril, 1904, relative au Maroc et à l'Égypte dont communication lui avait été faite par le Gouvernement de la République Française. DÉCLARENT qu'ils demeurent fermement attachés à l'intégrité de l'Empire Marocain sous la souveraineté du Sultan.

En foi de quoi, les soussignés, Son Excellence le Ministre des Affaires Étrangères et Son Excellence l'Ambassadeur Extraordinaire et Plénipotentiaire de Sa Majesté le Roi d'Espagne près le Président de la République Française, dûment autorisés à cet effet, ont dressé la présente Déclaration, qu'ils ont revêtue de leurs cachets.

Fait, en double exemplaire, à Paris, le 3 Octobre, 1904.

(Signé) DELCASSÉ.

F. de LÉON y CASTILLO.

Convention.

Le Président de la République Française et Sa Majesté le Roi d'Espagne, voulant fixer l'étendue des droits et la garantie des intérêts qui résultent, pour la France, de ses possessions algériennes, et, pour l'Espagne, de ses possessions sur la Côte du Maroc, ont décidé de conclure une Convention et ont nommé, à cet effet, pour leurs Plénipotentiaires, savoir :

Le Président de la République Française, S[on] Exc[ellence] M. Th. Delcassé, Député, Ministre des Affaires Étrangères de la République Française, etc.; et

Sa Majesté le Roi d'Espagne, S[on] Exc[ellence] M. de Léon y Castillo, Marquis del Muni, son Ambassadeur Extraordinaire et Plénipotentiaire près le Président de la République Française, etc.;

([1]) [Also printed in *Gooch & Temperley*, Vol. III, pp. 48–52, Nos. 58–9. It was published as a Parliamentary Paper in December 1911, *v. A. and P.* (1912–3), CXXII, (*Cd.* 6010), pp. 29–37.]

Lesquels, après s'être communiqués leurs pleins pouvoirs, trouvés en bonne et due forme, sont convenus des articles suivants :—

ARTICLE I.

L'Espagne adhère, aux termes de la présente Convention, à la Déclaration Franco-Anglaise du 8 Avril 1904 relative au Maroc et à l'Égypte.

ARTICLE II.

La région située à l'Ouest et au Nord de la ligne ci-après déterminée constitue la sphère d'influence, qui résulte pour l'Espagne de ses possessions sur la Côte Marocaine de la Méditerranée.

Dans cette zone, est réservée à l'Espagne la même action qui est reconnue à la France par le 2ème paragraphe de l'article II de la Déclaration du 8 Avril 1904,([2]) relative au Maroc et à l'Égypte.

Toutefois, tenant compte des difficultés actuelles et de l'intérêt réciproque qu'il y a à les aplanir, l'Espagne déclare qu'elle n'exercera cette action qu'après accord avec la France pendant la première période d'application de la présente Convention, période qui ne pourra pas excéder quinze ans à partir de la signature de la Convention.

De son côté, pendant la même période, la France, désirant que les droits et les intérêts reconnus à l'Espagne par la présente Convention soient toujours respectés, fera part préalablement au Gouvernement du Roi de son action près du Sultan du Maroc en ce qui concerne la sphère d'influence espagnole.

Cette première période expirée, et tant que durera le statu quo, l'action de la France près du Gouvernement Marocain, en ce qui concerne la sphère d'influence réservée à l'Espagne, ne s'exercera qu'après accord avec le Gouvernement Espagnol.

Pendant la première période, le Gouvernement de la République Française fera son possible pour que, dans deux des ports à douane de la région ci-après déterminée, le délégué du Représentant Général des porteurs de l'emprunt marocain du 12 Juillet 1904 soit de nationalité espagnole.

Partant de l'embouchure de la Moulouia dans la Mer Méditerranée, la ligne visée ci-dessus remontera le thalweg de ce fleuve jusqu'à l'alignement de la crête des hauteurs les plus rapprochées de la rive gauche de l'Oued Defla. De ce point, et sans pouvoir, en aucun cas, couper le cours de la Moulouia, la ligne de démarcation gagnera, aussi directement que possible, la ligne de faîte séparant les bassins de la Moulouia et de l'Oued Inaouen de celui de l'Oued Kert, puis elle continuera vers l'Ouest par la ligne de faîte séparant les bassins de l'Oued Inaouen de l'Oued Sebou de ceux de l'Oued Kert et de l'Oued Ouergha pour gagner par la crête la plus septentrionale le Djebel Moulai Bou Chta. Elle remontera ensuite vers le Nord, en se tenant à une distance d'au moins vingt-cinq kilomètres à l'Est de la route de Fez à Kçar-el-Kébir par Ouezzan jusqu'à la rencontre de l'Oued Loukkos ou Oued el Kous, dont elle descendra le thalweg jusqu'à une distance de cinq kilomètres en aval du croisement de cette rivière avec la route précitée de Kçar-el-Kébir par Ouezzan. De ce point, elle gagnera, aussi directement que possible, le rivage de l'Océan Atlantique au dessus de la lagune de Ez Zerga.

Cette délimitation est conforme à la délimitation tracée sur la carte annexée à la présente Convention sous le No. 1.([3])

ARTICLE III.

Dans le cas où l'état politique du Maroc et le Gouvernement Chérifien ne pourraient plus subsister ou si, par la faiblesse de ce gouvernement et par son

([2]) [Printed in *Gooch & Temperley*, Vol. II, p. 404, *App.*, and *A. and P.* (1904), CX, (*Cd.* 1952), p. 323.]

([3]) [Printed *B.F.S.P.*, Vol. 51, p. 930.]

impuissance persistante à assurer la sécurité et l'ordre publics ou pour toute autre cause à constater d'un commun accord, le maintien du statu quo devenait impossible, l'Espagne pourrait exercer librement son action dans la région délimitée à l'article précédent et qui constitue dès à présent sa sphére d'influence.

ARTICLE IV.

Le Gouvernement Marocain ayant, par l'article VII du traité du 26 Avril 1860, concédé à l'Espagne un établissement à Santa Cruz de mar Pequeña (Ifni), il est entendu que le territoire de cet établissement ne dépassera pas le cours de l'Oued Tazeroualt depuis sa source jusqu'à son confluent avec l'Oued Mesa, et le cours de l'Oued Mesa depuis ce confluent jusqu'à la mer, selon la carte No. 2 annexée à la présente Convention.(4)

ARTICLE V.

Pour compléter la délimitation indiquée par l'article I de la Convention du 27 Juin 1900,(5) il est entendu que la démarcation entre les sphères d'influence française et espagnole partira de l'intersection du méridien 14° 20' Ouest de Paris avec le 26° de latitude Nord qu'elle suivra vers l'Est jusqu'à sa rencontre avec le méridien 11° Ouest de Paris. Elle remontera ce méridien jusqu'à sa rencontre avec l'Oued Draa, puis le thalweg de l'Oued Draa jusqu'à sa rencontre avec le méridien 10° Ouest de Paris, enfin le méridien 10° Ouest de Paris jusqu'à la ligne de faîte entre les bassins de l'Oued Draa et de l'Oued Sous, et suivra, dans la direction de l'Ouest, la ligne de faîte entre les bassins de l'Oued Draa et de l'Oued Sous, puis entre les bassins côtiers de l'Oued Messa et de l'Oued Noun jusqu'au point le plus rapproché de la source de l'Oued Tazeroualt.

Cette délimitation est conforme à la délimitation tracée sur la carte No. 2 déjà citée et annexée à la présente Convention.(4)

ARTICLE VI.

Les articles IV et V seront applicables en même temps que l'article II de la présente Convention.

Toutefois, le Gouvernement de la République Française admet que l'Espagne s'établisse à tout moment dans la partie définie par l'Article IV, à la condition de s'être préalablement entendue avec le Sultan.

De même, le Gouvernement de la République Française reconnait dès maintenant au Gouvernement espagnol pleine liberté d'action sur la région comprise entre les 26° et 27° 40' de latitude Nord et le méridien 11° Ouest de Paris qui sont en dehors du territoire marocain.

ARTICLE VII.

L'Espagne s'engage à n'aliéner ni à céder sous aucune forme, même à titre temporaire, tout ou partie des territoires désignés aux articles II, IV, et V de la présente Convention.

ARTICLE VIII.

Si, dans l'application des articles II, IV, et V de la présente Convention, une action militaire s'imposait à l'une des deux parties contractantes, elle en avertirait aussitôt l'autre partie. En aucun cas il ne sera fait appel au concours d'une Puissance étrangère.

ARTICLE IX.

La ville de Tanger gardera le caractère spécial qui lui donnent la présence du corps diplomatique et ses institutions municipale et sanitaire.

(4) [Not reproduced.]
(5) [Printed B.F.S.P., Vol. 92, pp. 1014–5.]

ARTICLE X.

Tant que durera l'état politique actuel, les entreprises de travaux publics, chemins de fer, routes, canaux partant d'un point du Maroc pour aboutir dans la région visée à l'article II et *vice versâ*, seront exécutées par des Sociétés que pourront constituer des français et des espagnols.

De même, il sera loisible aux français et aux espagnols au Maroc de s'associer pour l'exploitation des Mines, carrières, et généralement d'entreprises d'ordre économique.

ARTICLE XI.

Les écoles et établissements espagnols actuellement existants au Maroc seront respectés. La circulation de la monnaie espagnole ne sera ni empêchée ni entravée. Les espagnols continueront de jouir au Maroc des droits que leur assurent les Traités, Conventions, et usages en vigueur, y compris le droit de navigation et de pêche, dans les eaux et ports marocains.

ARTICLE XII.

Les Français jouiront, dans les régions désignées aux articles II, IV, et V de la présente Convention, des mêmes droits qui sont, par l'article précédent, reconnus aux Espagnols dans le reste du Maroc.

ARTICLE XIII.

Dans le cas où le Gouvernement Marocain en interdirait la vente sur son territoire, les deux Puissances Contractantes s'engagent à prendre, dans leurs possessions d'Afrique, les mesures nécessaires pour empêcher que les armes et les munitions soient introduites en contrebande au Maroc.

ARTICLE XIV.

Il est entendu que la zone visée au paragraphe I de l'article VII de la Déclaration Franco-Anglaise du 8 Avril 1904,([6]) relative au Maroc et à l'Égypte, commence sur la côte à trente kilom[ètres] au Sud-Est de Melilla.

ARTICLE XV.

Dans le cas où la dénonciation prévue par le paragraphe III de l'article IV de la Déclaration Franco-Anglaise, relative au Maroc et à l'Égypte, aurait eu lieu, les Gouvernements français et espagnol se concerteront pour l'établissement d'un régime économique qui réponde particulièrement à leurs intérêts réciproques.

ARTICLE XVI.

La présente Convention sera publiée lorsque les deux Gouvernements jugeront, d'un commun accord, qu'elle peut l'être sans inconvénients.

En tous cas, elle pourra être publiée par l'un des deux Gouvernements à l'expiration de la première période de son application, période qui est définie au paragraphe III de l'article II.

En foi de quoi, les Plénipotentiaires respectifs ont signé la présente Convention et l'ont revêtue de leurs cachets.

Fait, en double exemplaire, à Paris, le 3 octobre, 1904.

(L.S.)   (Signé)   DELCASSÉ.
(L.S.)   (Signé)   F. DE LÉON Y CASTILLO.

([6]) [Printed in *Gooch & Temperley*, Vol. II, p. 405, *App.*, also in *A. and P.*, (1904), CX, (*Cd.* 1952), p. 324.]

EXCHANGE OF NOTES BETWEEN GREAT BRITAIN AND FRANCE, OCTOBER 6, 1904.

M. Cambon to the Marquess of Lansdowne.

F.O. France 3686.   *Ambassade de France, Londres,*
Cher Lord Lansdowne,   *le 6 octobre,* 1904.

Je suis chargé de vous communiquer les arrangements qui viennent d'être conclus
entre la France et l'Espagne au sujet du Maroc—Ils ont été signés le 3 c[ouran]t
par notre ministre des affaires Étrangères et l'Ambassadeur d'Espagne à Paris; ils
se composent d'une déclaration générale destinée à être publiée et d'une convention
qui doit rester secrète.

En me prescrivant de vous remettre le texte de cet accord, conformément aux
dispositions de l'article VIII de notre déclaration du 8 avril 1904, M. Delcassé a insisté
sur le caractère confidentiel de cette communication et m'a chargé de vous prier de
vouloir bien tenir la convention absolument secrète.

Veuillez, &c.
PAUL CAMBON.

The Marquess of Lansdowne to M. Cambon.

F.O. France 3686.
Dear M. Cambon,   *Foreign Office, October* 6, 1904.

I have had the pleasure of receiving your letter of to-day's date covering the two
documents which you had been instructed to communicate to me in accordance with
Article VIII of the " Declaration respecting Egypt and Morocco " of the 8th of April
last.

I need not say that the confidential character of the " Convention " entered into
by the President of the French Republic and the King of Spain in regard to French
and Spanish interests in Morocco, is fully recognised by us and will be duly respected.
The shorter paper, or " Declaration " made by the two Governments is I understand
public property.

With best thanks, I am, &c.

LANSDOWNE.

FRANCO-GERMAN DECLARATION RESPECTING MOROCCO.

(*Signed at Berlin, February* 9, 1909.)

F.O. 371/695.
5888/1780/09/28.

Le Gouvernement de la République Française et le Gouvernement Impérial
Allemand, animés d'un égal désir de faciliter l'exécution de l'Acte d'Algésiras, sont
convenus de préciser la portée qu'ils attachent à ses clauses en vue d'éviter toute
cause de malentendus entre eux dans l'avenir.

En conséquence,

Le Gouvernement de la République Française, entièrement attaché au maintien
de l'intégrité et de l'indépendance de l'Empire Chérifien, résolu à y sauvegarder
l'égalité économique et, par suite, à ne pas y entraver les intérêts commerciaux et
industriels Allemands—,

et le Gouvernement Impérial Allemand, ne poursuivant que des intérêts
économiques au Maroc, reconnaissant d'autre part, que les intérêts politiques
particuliers de la France y sont étroitement liés à la consolidation de l'ordre et de la
paix intérieure et décidé à ne pas entraver ces intérêts—,

déclarent qu'ils ne poursuivent et n'encouragent aucune mesure de nature à
créer en leur faveur ou en faveur d'une Puissance quelconque un privilège économique,
et qu'il chercheront à associer leurs nationaux dans les affaires dont ceux-ci pourront
obtenir l'entreprise.

[JULES CAMBON.]
[KIDERLEN-WAECHTER.]

FRANCO-GERMAN CONVENTION AND EXCHANGE OF NOTES RESPECTING MOROCCO.([7])

(Signed at Berlin, November 4, 1911.)

F.O. 46809/25883/11/28.

Convention entre la France et l'Allemagne relative au Maroc.

Le Gouvernement de la République Française et le gouvernement de Sa Majesté l'Empereur d'Allemagne, à la suite des troubles qui se sont produits au Maroc et qui ont démontré la nécessité d'y poursuivre, dans l'intérêt général l'œuvre de pacification et de progrès prévue par l'Acte d'Algésiras, ayant jugé nécessaire de préciser et de compléter l'accord franco-allemand du 9 février 1909, ont résolu de conclure une convention à cet effet. En conséquence, M. Jules Cambon, ambassadeur extraordinaire de la République française auprès de Sa Majesté l'Empereur d'Allemagne et M. de Kiderlen-Waechter, secrétaire d'État des Affaires étrangères de l'empire d'Allemagne, après s'être communiqués leurs pleins pouvoirs, trouvés en bonne et due forme, sont convenus des dispositions ci-après :

ARTICLE 1er.

Le gouvernement impérial allemand déclare que, ne poursuivant au Maroc que des intérêts économiques, il n'entravera pas l'action de la France en vue de prêter son assistance au gouvernement marocain pour l'introduction de toutes les réformes administratives, judiciaires, économiques, financières et militaires dont il a besoin pour le bon gouvernement de l'Empire, comme aussi pour tous les règlements nouveaux et les modifications aux règlements existants que ces réformes comportent. En conséquence, il donne son adhésion aux mesures de réorganisation, de contrôle et de garantie financière que, après accord avec le gouvernement marocain, le gouvernement français croira devoir prendre à cet effet, sous la réserve que l'action de la France sauvegardera au Maroc l'égalité économique entre les nations.

Au cas où la France serait amenée à préciser et à étendre son contrôle et sa protection, le gouvernement impérial allemand, reconnaissant pleine liberté d'action à la France, et sous la réserve que la liberté commerciale, prévue par les traités antérieurs, sera maintenue, n'y apportera aucun obstacle.

Il est entendu qu'il ne sera porté aucune entrave aux droits et actions de la Banque d'Etat du Maroc, tels qu'ils sont définis par l'Acte d'Algésiras.

ARTICLE 2.

Dans cet ordre d'idées, il est entendu que le gouvernement impérial ne fera pas obstacle à ce que la France, après accord avec le gouvernement marocain, procède aux occupations militaires du territoire marocain qu'elle jugerait nécessaires au maintien de l'ordre et de la sécurité des transactions commerciales, et à ce qu'elle exerce toute action de police sur terre et dans les eaux marocaines.

ARTICLE 3.

Dès à présent, si Sa Majesté le Sultan du Maroc venait à confier aux agents diplomatiques et consulaires de la France la représentation et la protection des sujets et des intérêts marocains à l'étranger, le gouvernement impérial déclare qu'il n'y fera pas d'objection.

Si, d'autre part, Sa Majesté le Sultan du Maroc confiait au représentant de la France près du gouvernement marocain le soin d'être son intermédiaire auprès des représentants étrangers, le gouvernement allemand n'y ferait pas d'objection.

ARTICLE 4.

Le gouvernement français déclare que, fermement attaché au principe de la liberté commerciale au Maroc, il ne se prêtera à aucune inégalité pas plus dans

([7]) [*v. supra*, pp. 615–8, No. 626.]

l'établissement des droits de douane impôts et autres taxes que dans l'établissement des tarifs de transport par voie ferrée, voie de navigation fluviale ou toute autre voie et notamment dans toutes les questions de transit.

Le gouvernement français s'emploiera également auprès du gouvernement marocain afin d'empêcher tout traitement différentiel entre les ressortissants des différentes puissances ; il s'opposera notamment à toute mesure, par exemple à la promulgation d'ordonnances administratives sur les poids et mesures, le jaugeage le poinçonnage etc.... qui pourraient mettre en état d'infériorité les marchandises d'une puissance.

Le gouvernement français s'engage à user de son influence sur la Banque d'Etat pour que celle-ci confère à tour de rôle aux membres de sa direction à Tanger les postes de délégué dont elle dispose à la Commission des valeurs douanières et au Comité permanent des douanes.

ARTICLE 5.

Le gouvernement français veillera à ce qu'il ne soit perçu au Maroc aucun droit d'exportation sur le minerai de fer exporté des ports marocains. Les exploitations de minerai de fer ne subiront sur leur production ou sur leurs moyens de travail aucun impôt spécial. Elles ne supporteront, en dehors des impôts généraux, qu'une redevance fixe, calculée par hectare et par an, et une redevance proportionnée au produit brut de l'extraction. Ces redevances, qui seront assises conformément aux articles 35 et 49 du projet de règlement minier annexé au Protocole de la Conférence de Paris du 7 juin 1910 seront également supportées par toutes les entreprises minières.

Le gouvernement français veillera à ce que les taxes minières soient régulièrement perçues sans que des remises individuelles du total ou d'une partie de ces taxes puissent être consenties sous quelque prétexte que ce soit.

ARTICLE 6.

Le gouvernement de la République française s'engage à veiller à ce que les travaux et fournitures nécessités par les constructions éventuelles de routes, chemins de fer, ports, télégraphes, etc.... soient octroyés par le gouvernement marocain suivant les règles de l'adjudication.

Il s'engage également à veiller à ce que les conditions des adjudications, particulièrement en ce qui concerne les fournitures de matériel et les délais impartis pour soumissionner, ne placent les ressortissants d'aucune puissance dans une situation d'infériorité.

L'exploitation des grandes entreprises mentionnées ci-dessus sera réservée à l'Etat marocain ou librement concédée par lui à des tiers qui pourront être chargés de fournir les fonds nécessaires à cet effet. Le gouvernement français veillera à ce que, dans l'exploitation des chemins de fer et autres moyens de transport comme dans l'application des règlements destinés à assurer celle-ci aucune différence de traitement ne soit faite entre les ressortissants des diverses puissances, qui useraient de ces moyens de transport.

Le gouvernement de la République usera de son influence sur la Banque d'Etat afin que celle-ci confère à tour de rôle aux membres de sa direction à Tanger le poste dont elle dispose de délégué à la Commission générale des adjudications et marchés.

De même, le gouvernement français s'emploiera auprès du gouvernement marocain pour que, durant la période où restera en vigueur l'article 66 de l'Acte d'Algésiras, il confie à un ressortissant d'une des puissances représentées au Maroc un des trois postes de délégué chérifien au Comité spécial des travaux publics.

ARTICLE 7.

Le gouvernement français s'emploiera auprès du gouvernement marocain pour que les propriétaires de mines et d'autres exploitations industrielles ou agricoles, sans distinction de nationalité, et en conformité des règlements qui seront édictés en s'inspirant de la législation française sur la matière, puissent être autorisés à créer des chemins de fer d'exploitation destinés à relier leurs centres de production aux lignes d'intérêt général ou aux ports.

ARTICLE 8.

Il sera présenté tous les ans un rapport sur l'exploitation des chemins de fer au Maroc qui sera établi dans les mêmes formes et conditions que les rapports présentés aux assemblées d'actionnaires des sociétés de chemins de fer françaises.

Le gouvernement de la République chargera un des administrateurs de la Banque d'Etat de l'établissement de ce rapport qui sera, avec les éléments qui en seront la base, communiqué aux censeurs, puis rendu public avec, s'il y a lieu, les observations que ces derniers croiront devoir y joindre d'après leurs propres renseignements.

ARTICLE 9.

Pour éviter autant que possible les réclamations diplomatiques, le gouvernement français s'emploiera auprès du gouvernement marocain afin que celui-ci défère à un arbitre désigné ad hoc pour chaque affaire d'un commun accord par le consul de France et par celui de la puissance intéressée ou, à leur défaut, par les deux gouvernements de ces Consuls, les plaintes portées par des ressortissants étrangers contre les autorités marocaines, ou les agents agissant en tant qu'autorités marocaines, et qui n'auraient pu être réglées par l'intermédiaire du consul français et du consul du gouvernement intéressé.

Cette procédure restera en vigueur jusqu'au jour où aura été institué un régime judiciaire inspiré des règles judiciaires de législation des puissances intéressées et destiné à remplacer, après entente avec elles, les tribunaux consulaires.

ARTICLE 10.

Le gouvernement français veillera à ce que les ressortissants étrangers continuent à jouir du droit de pêche dans les eaux et ports marocains.

ARTICLE 11.

Le gouvernement français s'emploiera auprès du gouvernement marocain pour que celui-ci ouvre au commerce étranger de nouveaux ports au fur et à mesure des besoins de ce commerce.

ARTICLE 12.

Pour répondre à une demande du gouvernement marocain, les deux gouvernements s'engagent à provoquer la révision, d'accord avec les autres puissances et sur la base de la Convention de Madrid, des listes et de la situation des protégés étrangers et des associés agricoles au Maroc dont parlent les articles 8 et 16 de cette Convention.

Ils conviennent également de poursuivre auprès des puissances signataires toutes les modifications de la Convention de Madrid que comporterait le moment venu, le changement du régime des protégés et des associés agricoles.

ARTICLE 13.

Toutes clauses d'accord, convention, traité ou règlement qui seraient contraires aux précédentes stipulations, sont et demeurent abrogées.

ARTICLE 14.

Le présent accord sera communiqué aux autres puissances signataires de l'acte d'Algésiras près desquelles les deux gouvernements s'engagent à se prêter mutuellement appui pour obtenir leur adhésion.

ARTICLE 15.

La présente convention sera ratifiée et les ratifications seront échangées à Paris aussitôt que faire se pourra.

Fait à Berlin le 4 novembre 1911 en double exemplaire.

Signé   (L.S.)   JULES CAMBON.

Signé   (L.S.)   KIDERLEN.

M. de Kiderlen-Waechter, Secrétaire d'Etat pour les Affaires Etrangères, à M. Jules Cambon, Ambassadeur de la République française à Berlin.

F.O. 45870/25883/11/28.

Mon cher Ambassadeur,   *Berlin, le 4 novembre,* 1911.

Pour bien préciser l'accord du 4 novembre 1911 relatif au Maroc et en définir la portée, j'ai l'honneur de faire connaître à Votre Excellence que dans l'hypothèse où le Gouvernement français croirait devoir assumer le protectorat du Maroc, le Gouvernement impérial n'y apporterait aucun obstacle.

L'adhésion du Gouvernement allemand, accordée d'une manière générale au Gouvernement français par l'article 1 de ladite convention, s'applique naturellement à toutes les questions donnant matière à réglementation et visées dans l'Acte d'Algésiras.

Vous avez bien voulu me faire connaître d'autre part que, dans le cas où l'Allemagne désirerait acquérir de l'Espagne la Guinée espagnole, l'île Corisco et les îles Elobey, la France serait disposée à renoncer en sa faveur à exercer les droits de préférence qu'elle tient du traité du 27 Juin 1900(⁸) entre la France et l'Espagne. Je suis heureux de prendre acte de cette assurance, et d'ajouter que l'Allemagne restera étrangère aux accords particuliers que la France et l'Espagne croiront devoir faire entre elles au sujet du Maroc, étant convenu que le Maroc comprend toute la partie de l'Afrique du Nord s'étendant entre l'Algérie, l'Afrique Occidentale française et la Colonie espagnole du Rio de Oro.

Le Gouvernement allemand, en renonçant à demander la détermination préalable de parts à faire à l'industrie allemande dans la construction des Chemins de fer, compte que le Gouvernement français sera toujours heureux de voir des associations d'intérêt se produire entre les ressortissants des deux pays pour les affaires dont ils pourront respectivement obtenir l'entreprise.

Il compte également que la mise en adjudication du Chemin de fer de Tanger à Fez, qui intéresse toutes les nations, ne sera primée par la mise en adjudication des travaux d'un autre chemin de fer marocain et que le Gouvernement français proposera au Gouvernement marocain l'ouverture du port d'Agadir au commerce international.

Enfin, lorsque le réseau des voies ferrées d'intérêt général sera mis à l'étude, le Gouvernement allemand demande au Gouvernement français de veiller à ce que l'administration marocaine ait le plus réel souci des intérêts économiques du Maroc, et à ce que, notamment la détermination du tracé des lignes d'intérêt général facilite dans la mesure du possible la jonction des régions minières avec les lignes d'intérêt général ou avec les ports appelés à les desservir.

Votre Excellence a bien voulu m'assurer que, le jour où aura été institué le régime judiciaire prévu par l'article 9 de la Convention précitée et où les tribunaux consulaires auront été remplacés, le Gouvernement français aura soin que les ressortissants allemands soient placés sous la juridiction nouvelle exactement dans les mêmes conditions que les ressortissants français. Je suis heureux d'en prendre acte et de faire connaître en même temps à Votre Excellence que, au jour de l'entrée en vigueur de ce régime judiciaire, après entente avec les Puissances, le Gouvernement allemand consentira à la suppression, en même temps que pour les autres Puissances, de ses tribunaux consulaires. J'ajoute que, dans ma pensée, l'expression

'' les changements du régime des protégés '' portée à l'article 12 de la Convention du 4 Novembre 1911 relative au Maroc, implique l'abrogation, si elle est jugée nécessaire, de la partie de la Convention de Madrid qui concerne les protégés et les associés agricoles.

Enfin, désireux de donner à ladite Convention le caractère d'un acte destiné non seulement à écarter toute cause de conflit entre nos deux pays, mais encore à aider à leurs bons rapports, nous sommes d'accord pour déclarer que les différents qui viendraient à s'élever entre les parties contractantes au sujet de l'interprétation et de l'application des dispositions de la convention du 4 Novembre et qui n'auraient pas été réglés par la voie diplomatique, seront soumis à un tribunal arbitral constitué dans les termes de la Convention de La Haye du 18 Octobre 1907.(⁹) Un compromis devra être dressé, et il sera procédé suivant les règles de la même convention, en tant qu'il n'y serait pas dérogé par un accord exprès au moment du litige.

Veuillez, &c.

[von KIDERLEN-WAECHTER.]

M. Jules Cambon, Ambassadeur de la République française à Berlin, à M. de Kiderlen-Waechter, Secrétaire d'Etat pour les Affaires Etrangères.

F.O. 45870/25883/11/28.

Mon cher Secrétaire d'Etat, *Berlin, le 4 novembre,* 1911.

J'ai l'honneur de prendre acte de la déclaration que Votre Excellence a bien voulu me faire que, dans l'hypothèse où le Gouvernement français croirait devoir assumer le protectorat du Maroc, le Gouvernement Impérial n'y apporterait aucun obstacle, et que l'adhésion du Gouvernement allemand, accordée d'une manière générale au Gouvernement français par l'article 1ᵉʳ de l'accord du 4 novembre 1911 relatif au Maroc s'applique naturellement à toutes les questions donnant matière à réglementation visées dans l'Acte d'Algésiras.

D'autre part, j'ai l'honneur de vous confirmer que dans le cas où l'Allemagne désirerait acquérir de l'Espagne, la Guinée espagnole, l'île Corisco et les îles Elobey, la France est disposée à renoncer en sa faveur à exercer les droits de préférence qu'elle tient du traité du 27 juin 1900(¹⁰) entre la France et l'Espagne. Je suis heureux par ailleurs de recevoir l'assurance que l'Allemagne restera étrangère aux accords particuliers que la France et l'Espagne croiront devoir faire entre elles au sujet du Maroc, étant convenu que le Maroc comprend toute la partie de l'Afrique du Nord s'étendant entre l'Algérie, l'Afrique Occidentale française et la colonie espagnole du Rio de Oro.

Je me plais aussi à vous informer que le Gouvernement allemand renonçant à demander la détermination préalable de parts à faire dans l'industrie allemande dans la construction des chemins de fer, le Gouvernement français sera toujours heureux de voir des associations d'intérêt se produire entre les ressortissants des deux pays, pour les affaires dont ils pourront respectivement obtenir l'entreprise.

Vous pouvez également tenir pour certain que la mise en adjudication du chemin de fer de Tanger à Fez qui intéresse toutes les nations, ne sera primée par la mise en adjudication des travaux d'aucun autre chemin de fer marocain et que le Gouvernement français proposera au Gouvernement marocain l'ouverture du port d'Agadir au commerce international.

Enfin, lorsque le réseau des voies ferrées d'intérêt général sera mis à l'étude, le Gouvernement français veillera à ce que l'administration marocaine ait le plus réel souci des intérêts économiques du Maroc et à ce que notamment la détermination du tracé des lignes d'intérêt général facilite dans la mesure du possible la jonction des régions minières avec les lignes d'intérêt général ou avec les ports appelés à les

(⁹) [This subject will be treated in a later volume.]
(¹⁰) [Printed *B.F.S.P.*, Vol. 92, pp. 1014–5.]

desservir. Votre Excellence peut également compter que le jour où aura été institué le régime judiciaire prévu par l'art[icle] 9 de la convention du 4 novembre 1911 relative au Maroc, et où les tribunaux consulaires auront été remplacés, le Gouvernement français aura soin que les ressortissants allemands soient placés sous la juridiction nouvelle exactement dans les mêmes conditions que les ressortissants français.

Je suis heureux d'autre part de prendre acte, qu'au jour de l'entrée en vigueur du nouveau régime judiciaire après entente avec les Puissances, le Gouvernement allemand consentira à la suppression, en même temps que pour les autres Puissances, de ses tribunaux consulaires. Je prends acte également que dans la pensée de votre Excellence, l'expression " le changement du régime des protégés " portée à l'article 12 de la convention précitée implique l'abrogation, si elle est jugée nécessaire, de la partie de la convention de Madrid qui concerne les protégés et associés agricoles.

Enfin désireux de donner à la convention du 4 novembre 1911 relative au Maroc le caractère d'un acte destiné non seulement à écarter toute cause de conflit entre nos deux pays, mais encore à aider à leurs bons rapports, nous sommes d'accord pour déclarer que les différends qui viendraient à s'élever entre les parties contractantes au sujet de l'interprétation et de l'application des dispositions de ladite convention et qui n'auraient pu être réglés par la voie diplomatique, seront soumis à un tribunal arbitral constitué dans les termes de la convention de La Haye du 18 octobre 1907.([11]) Un compromis devra être dressé et il sera procédé suivant les règles de la même convention en tant qu'il n'y serait pas dérogé par un accord exprès au moment du litige.

Veuillez, &c.
[JULES CAMBON.]

([11]) [This subject will be treated in a later volume.]

APPENDIX V.

The Cartwright Interview.

[*ED. NOTE.*—The documents relating to the so-called Cartwright Interview are placed in an Appendix in order not to interrupt the story of the Franco-German negotiations. The Editors do not think this incident quite worthy of the importance attached to it at the time, but they think it well to publish the relevant material. For Dr. Münz's version of the incident *v.* his article "The Cartwright Interview of August 1911," *Contemporary Review*, March 1930, which contains a translation of the interview published in the *Neue Freie Presse* and of Dr. Münz's letter of August 30, to Sir F. Cartwright, *cp.* G.P. XXIX, pp. 237–243; Ö.-U.A. III, Nos. 2603–4–5, 2737. The main references in the text of this volume are *supra*, p. 493, No. 524, *encl.*; p. 634, No. 642, and *note;* pp. 656–7, No. 663; pp. 664–5, No. 673; *v.* also Subject Index, *sub* Press, Austro-Hungarian, *infra*, p. 910.]

Sir F. Cartwright to Sir Edward Grey.

F.O. 33698/33698/11/28.   *Vienna,* D. *August* 26, 1911, 6·30 P.M.
Tel. (No. 85.) Confidential.   R. *August* 26, 1911, 7·00 P.M.

The "Neue Freie Presse" of yesterday morning published an article purporting to give views of a highly-placed English diplomatist on the Morocco question. The article is unsigned, but I am told was written by Dr. Münz, a well-known literary man who accosted me on the last day of my stay at Marienbad, and with whom I had a few moments' conversation. The article contains nothing that is not well known, and no views which have not appeared in leading English or French newspapers. German Embassy here want to hold me responsible for it, and intend, I am informed, to start a campaign in the German press against the French Ambassador here and myself. German Embassy yesterday summoned all the correspondents of the German newspapers and told them to attack me. The chief fury of the Germans seems to be directed against the "Neue Freie Presse" for its independence in publishing an article giving Anglo-French views of the situation.

I must decline all responsibility for this publication, and, although some of the views expressed may be mine, I did not express them to Dr. Münz (who is deaf), and the greater part of the article is mere guess-work on his part.

Article by post to-day.

Sir E. Goschen to Sir Edward Grey.

                                           Berlin, August 26, 1911.
Private.(¹)   D. 8·23 P.M.
Tel.   R. 9 P.M.

Interview with a "British diplomatist" published by "New Free Press" is here openly attributed to Sir F. Cartwright. If this is not correct would it be advisable for me to contradict? I hear that Imperial Foreign Office feels rather strongly about it.

(¹) [Grey MSS., Vol. 23.]

Count Metternich to Sir Edward Grey.

                              Kaiserlich Deutsche Botschaft,
Private.(¹)   9, *Carlton House Terrace, S.W.,*
Dear Sir Edward,   *London, August* 29, 1911.

On the 25th inst. the Vienna "Neue Freie Presse" has published an article "by an English diplomatist in an important position." This article contains striking outbursts against German policy, the entourage of His Majesty the Emperor, and diplomatic Representatives of the German Empire.

A great part of the German as well as the Austrian press declares Sir F. Cartwright, the British Ambassador at Vienna, to be the author of this article.

The German Government are unwilling to believe that this assumption corresponds to facts, as a journalistic activity of such a kind by a British diplomatic Representative would be most unusual and very trying to Anglo-German relations.

(¹) [Grey MSS., Vol. 23.]

With a view to the great and justified excitement caused in Germany by this incident, the Imperial Chancellor deems that an official utterance, made by you, would be of great value.

I should be much obliged if you would let me know your view on the matter.

Believe me,
Yours sincerely,
P. METTERNICH.

Sir Edward Grey to Sir E. Goschen

F.O. 33939/33698/11/28.   *Foreign Office, August 30, 1911.*
Tel. (No. 171.)   D. 12·40 P.M.

Your private tel[egram] of Aug[ust] 26.(¹)

You can contradict report of an interview in whatever way you think most desirable.

(¹) [*v. supra*, p. 837.]

Sir Edward Grey to Count Metternich.

Private.(¹)
Dear Count Metternich,   *Fallodon, August 30, 1911.*

Neither Sir F. Cartwright nor I nor any British diplomatist that I know of had any cognizance of the Article in the Neue Freie Presse before it appeared.

The statement to the contrary has caused me considerable resentment; some time ago a statement of a very mischievous kind about British diplomacy came into the German Press from an unofficial Austrian source; I had a contradiction of it given, and, if my recollection is correct, the contradiction did no good and the statement was repeated. I am doubtful whether any more good would be done by an official denial now, but I shall be in London on Monday and Tuesday next and shall be glad if you will come to see me about it at the Foreign Office on either day.

Y[ou]rs etc.
E. GREY.

(¹) [Grey MSS., Vol. 23. The letter is printed in *G.P.* XXIX, pp. 238–9. A German translation was telegraphed by Count Metternich to Berlin on September 1.]

Sir Edward Grey to Sir F. Cartwright.

F.O. 34351/33698/11/28.
Tel. (No. 95.)   *Foreign Office, August 31, 1911.*

Statement in Neue Freie Presse that article reached it from an English diplomatist invites a more categorical denial than your telegram to Berlin news agency.(¹) I propose therefore to communicate to press a statement that the article was not communicated nor inspired by you nor had the British Gov[ernmen]t any cognizance of it. Would you prefer that this communication was made by you at Vienna or by F[oreign] O[ffice] in London?

(¹) [Sir F. Cartwright's telegram was reproduced in a communication from the *Times* correspondent at Berlin dated August 28. It was printed in the *Times* on August 29. The text was as follows : " Je ne me tiens pas responsable des articles anonymes paraissant dans les journaux et desquels des gens mal renseignés m'attribuent l'origine."]

Sir F. Cartwright to Sir Edward Grey.

F.O. 34362/33698/11/28.   *Vienna,* D. *August* 31, 1911, 8·30 P.M.
Tel. (No. 86.) Confidential.   R. *August* 31, 1911, 10·15 P.M.

Your telegram No. 95 (   ).(¹)

I think denial had better come from the Foreign Office, as being more authoritative.

Dr. Muenz asked me for an interview while at Marienbad, which I refused. He then pursued me for ten minutes on promenade. On that he founded an article. He has confessed

(¹) [*v.* immediately preceding document.]

to French Ambassador that he talked to a number of people, and out of what they said manufactured an article, which, he thought, represented the opinion of the British Government on the Morocco question. Dr. Muenz has written me a letter of apology and has asked to see me, but I have refused to do so. Dr. Muenz saw " Times " correspondent at Marienbad, and as latter is very outspoken in his language, Muenz may have got opinions from him which he then put into my mouth. The " Arbeiter Zeitung " points to this as probable source of article, as it is known I frequently see " Times " correspondent, and it is assumed, therefore, that the latter's views must be mine.

French Ambassador and myself have strong reasons to believe that German Embassy had a hand in the preparation of the article. It was retarded two days, during which time it was telegraphed to Berlin for improvements.

I am sending an account of all the information which I can obtain in a private letter to Sir A. Nicolson by messenger, and French Ambassador is sending home a full report to his Government to-night, which he has read to me and which I have suggested should be communicated to you.

Sir F. Cartwright to Sir A. Nicolson.

Private.(¹)

My dear Nicolson,   *Vienna, August 31, 1911.*

A great deal of stir has been made by the Germans over an anonymous article published by the " Neue Freie Presse ", and purporting to give the views of a British diplomatist. The moment this article appeared the German Embassy summoned the correspondents of German newspapers here and told them to blaze away at me and to make as much noise as possible over the article in question. A large number of usually inspired newspapers in Germany have taken up the cry and published most absurd stories against both myself and Crozier, the French Ambassador, some being even too absurd to be quoted. The whole thing looks like a prepared coup by the German Embassy here to try and get rid of Crozier and myself, as Tschirschky hates us both because since we have been in Vienna we have steadily laboured to bring about and to maintain good relations between Austria-Hungary and our respective countries, and our personal relations with Aehrenthal are well known to be remarkably good, whereas Tschirschky's are notoriously bad.

Some ten days ago Dr. Muenz, the reputed author of this article, tried to see Crozier with a view of obtaining from him an interview. Crozier happened to be with Lahovary, the Roumanian Minister in Paris, at the time Dr. Muenz called, so that the latter was not able to give reins to his imagination in reporting the conversation, as a witness was present. Nevertheless he manufactured an interview, full of false statements, which ended with a violent attack by Crozier upon Schoen, the German Ambassador in Paris. Now if there is one German diplomatist for whom Crozier entertains a personal affection, it is Schoen, with whom he was a long time at Copenhagen, so to represent him as his enemy was an absurdity. The German press attempted to raise a stir over this article but it fell somewhat flat, and they therefore tried the same manœuvre with myself in the hope of better success. Dr. Muenz was sent to Marienbad to see me. He knew that I went out every morning at 8 o'clock; he waylaid me one day and came up to me near the Colonnade, and asked me to fix an hour to have an interview with him. I told him I gave no interviews to journalists and walked on. He followed me, saying that the Moroccan question was in such a critical state that he wished to know what the English views were on the situation. I referred him to Mr. Asquith's speech and the views expressed by the English leading newspapers. He continued to follow me across the Promenade, explaining the German view of the situation. I shrugged my shoulders, and the only observation I can remember I made to him was that if the situation was very critical, it was in great part due to the attitude assumed by the Pan-Germans who, by their press organs, had led the German public to expect unreasonable concessions from France which, in my opinion, it would be difficult to realize, therefore deception and disappointment would follow. As soon as I reached the hairdresser at the Hotel Klinger, I went in to be shaved and so got rid of Dr. Muenz; he followed me in all a distance of about a hundred yards.

Dr. Muenz has now come back to Vienna and has gone to see Crozier, as I decline to see him, and he has expressed to the French Ambassador his regret that he had had anything to do with the publication of the interview. He declares that he merely wrote a private letter to Benedickt, the proprietor of the " Neue Freie Presse ", in which he told him that he had seen me and that I considered the situation to be grave, and that I laid the blame for the present state of things at the door of the Pan-Germans. Out of this the " Neue Freie Presse " manufactured an interview in which they gave what they presumed to be my views on political matters in general. The " Arbeiter Zeitung ", which ridicules the " Neue Freie Presse " and their bogus interviews, declares that Steed, the Times correspondent, comes frequently to see me, and that therefore Steed's opinions—which are well known—reflect my own, and that they have been used in the manufacturing of the sham interview. There may be some truth in this.

(¹) [Carnock MSS., Vol. IV of 1911.]

Since the appearance of this interview, I have been exposed to the most ridiculous accusations by the German press, some so silly that they are not worth repeating, but anything serves just now in Germany to excite the indignation of the public against England's policy of standing firm by France. The most virulent newspaper seems to be the Munich "Neueste Nachrichten", which is inspired from Berlin, and it declares solemnly that while in Munich I kept a host of newspaper men in my pay to write against Germany, and that I represented the worst features of King Edward's nefarious policy—relentless hatred of Germany. Some German newspapers state that I intrigued with Isvolsky against Germany, and I may remind you that last year, when I met Isvolsky in Munich, I was assailed by the German press, and the Vienna "Zeit", the mouthpiece of Tschirschky, called upon Aehrenthal to send me my passports because I had gone to see a well known enemy of Austria. As a matter of fact, I informed Aehrenthal at Marienbad that I would probably meet Isvolsky in Munich, and the day of my return to Vienna I saw Aehrenthal and told him of my interview with the Russian Foreign Minister. Aehrenthal told me that he was very pleased to have at first hand information as to Isvolsky's views with regard to Austria. Another German newspaper declares that I aroused Turkish animosity against Germany at the time of the Potsdam interviews, and that I am always at work in the Austrian press with a view to turn it against Germany. Maximilian Harden in the "Zukunft" of the 19th instant explains the real grievance of Germany against me in the following sentences :— "Der unsteten, doch immer schwachgemuten Torheit deutscher Politik hat Frankreich andere wichtige Buendnisse zu danken. Russland, England, Italien, Spanien, die Vereinigten Staaten und Japan sind ihm durch Vertraege assoziirt. Belgien, Holland und die Schweiz sind bereit ihm—Frankreich—wenn es sich ohne Lebensgefahr machen laesst, gegen Deutschland gefaellig zu sein; Oesterreich–Ungarn ist durch das Duett Crozier–Cartwright in den Wunsch geschmeichelt worden, voe dem Daemmern der Schicksalstunde leise der Pflicht zu unbequemer Wahl zwischen Deutschland und Frankreich zu entschluepfen." It suits the Germans to attribute to Crozier and to myself Aehrenthal's attempts at independence from the control of Berlin, and for this we shall never be forgiven. People in Germany will not see the reality of things, but Austria, as she gains in self-respect and strength, must inevitably some day get tired of feeling the weight of Germany's pressure on her flank.

I need hardly mention that Dr. Friedjung attacks me violently in the Berlin "Vossische Zeitung", accusing me of being at the bottom of all the anti-German intrigues in Vienna, and of inspiring personal attacks which have appeared in German newspapers against Tschirschky. As the most virulent of these attacks have appeared in the "Zukunft", I suppose Dr. Friedjung will soon be stating that I keep Maximilian Harden in my pay. Friedjung's hatred against England is well known, and he will never forget Steed's castigation of him in the "Times" for his connection with the forged documents in the Serbo-Croatian conspiracy case. . . . .[2]

Yours truly,

FAIRFAX L. CARTWRIGHT.

P.S.—I have received a letter of apology from Dr. Muenz of which I enclose a copy.[3] I have refused his request that I should receive him. To Crozier, who has seen Dr. Muenz since the "Neue Freie Presse" article appeared, the latter has been more explicit than he is in his letter to me. According to what Crozier tells me, Dr. Muenz declared to him that he intended to write an article representing what he thought were the views of the British Government with regard to the Moroccan question. For this purpose he gathered all the information he could from a number of persons he saw—scraps from here, scraps from there—and out of all this he manufactured an article which he sent to Benedickt, the owner of the "Neue Freie Presse", with the intimation that it should be published as coming from their correspondent in London. In the letter to Benedickt Muenz mentioned that he had seen me, and the former at once, without Muenz' knowledge, and apparently with the connivance of the German Embassy, saw that a sensation could be produced by publishing the article with such indications that the German public might be led to believe that I was the originator of it.

[2] [The last paragraph of this letter is omitted. It reports a conversation with M. Paul Doumer which has no bearing on the Cartwright Interview.]

[3] [Not reproduced. An English translation has appeared in an article by Dr. Münz "The Cartwright Interview of August 1911", *Contemporary Review*, March 1930.]

Sir Edward Grey to Sir F. Cartwright.

F.O. 34486/33698/11/28.
Tel. Private.   *Foreign Office,* September 1, 1911, 12·30 P.M.

German Ambassador informs me that German Chancellor considers that in view of excitement caused by statement in German and Austrian Press that you are author of article in Neue Freie Presse an official utterance by me would be of great value. I have replied that neither you nor any British diplomatist that I know of had cognizance of the article in the Neue Freie Presse before it appeared, that I am doubtful whether an official denial will do much good but will see German Ambassador about it in London on Monday or Tuesday.

Have you sufficient ground to justify me in saying to German Ambassador that I have reason to suppose that this attack upon you has been inspired by German Embassy at Vienna?

Sir F. Cartwright to Sir Edward Grey.

                                                        Vienna, September 1, 1911.
F.O. 34577/33698/11/28.   D. 6·10 P.M.
Tel. (No. 87.)   R. 7 P.M.

Your telegram unnumbered of today.

Reuter's agent here was in the office of the "Neue Freie Presse" on the night of Wednesday, 23rd August, and was told that a sensational article would appear in the morning. On the following day he was told that it would appear later, and it did so on Friday morning. During that time I have been told that the article was telegraphed to Berlin for comment. On Friday morning, quite early, the German chargé d'affaires, who is living at some distance from Vienna, came into the town, which was unusual, and summoned at once the correspondents of German newspapers here to the embassy, and, I am told, gave instructions that they should make as great a stir as possible about the article and point to me as the author of it. Anyhow it is certain that the German newspapers, which usually get their inspiration from official sources in Berlin, began to attack me without waiting for any verification of the authorship of anonymous article. The German chargé d'affaires has studiously avoided coming to see me, and has made no attempt to enquire of myself, before launching the accusation, whether I had anything to say about the article in question. No member of the German Embassy has had any contact with members of mine, even indirectly, since the beginning of the campaign.

Sir Edward Grey to Sir E. Goschen.

F.O. 35516/33698/11/28.
(No. 208.)
Sir,   *Foreign Office,* September 5, 1911.

I asked Count Metternich to come to see me to-day and said that I was now in a position to reply more fully to the message which the German Chancellor had sent me through him on the subject of the article in the "Neue Freie Presse."(¹) I was entirely convinced, not only of the German Chancellor's good faith, but also of his good-will in this matter, and of his desire to stop the mischief which had been done by the article. I therefore wished Count Metternich to tell the Chancellor himself the facts which I had ascertained.

The article was written by Dr. Münz. Dr. Münz had asked for an interview with Sir Fairfax Cartwright, but the latter had refused it. Dr. Münz had subsequently pursued him on the promenade, and had obtained a few minutes of conversation, which Sir Fairfax Cartwright could not refuse without rudeness, but I gathered that the conversation was of a perfunctory nature.

My first impression was that Dr. Münz had forced these few minutes of conversation in order that he might have a pretext for attributing his article to Sir Fairfax Cartwright's inspiration. But this impression has been dispelled by the fact that Dr. Münz had written a letter of apology to Sir Fairfax, and he therefore could not have intended the attacks which were made upon him.

Reuter's Agent in Vienna had been informed on the Wednesday evening that an important article was to appear next day. The article had been kept back till Friday, and had in the interval been communicated to Berlin, I supposed to some Press connection there.

So much for the facts as regards the writing of the article.

On the day when the article appeared, the German Chargé d'Affaires had gone to the Embassy in Vienna, and had sent for the correspondents of the German newspapers. This, of course, left a strong presumption that what passed had to do with the article, and was not of a calming nature, seeing that the German Press became very violent. But, as I could not know for certain what passed in the German Embassy in Vienna, I gave this only as a natural inference. The

(¹) [For Count Metternich's account of this interview, *v. G.P.* XXIX, pp. 240–2.]

comment I wished to make upon this was that, as the German Chargé d'Affaires was on perfectly good personal terms with Sir Fairfax Cartwright, the natural thing would have been for him to go to Sir Fairfax, tell him about the article, and ask for a denial, which he would at once have received. He would then have been in a position to calm the German Press. Even if Sir Fairfax Cartwright had not been able to deny the authorship of the article, I thought that in so serious a matter the German Chargé d'Affaires, before communicating with the Press, should have communicated with his Government, who would no doubt have referred the matter to me.

I had read some of the articles in the German Press. Their violence was such that clearly no denial from us would by itself have the least effect. Therefore all I could suggest to the German Chancellor was that some communication should be made to the Press, avowing that communications had passed between the two Governments, and that the German Government, being in possession of the facts, were satisfied that Sir Fairfax Cartwright was not cognizant of the article and had not inspired it.

Count Metternich said that he would tell me frankly that, in the view of his Government, the important point was not whether Sir Fairfax Cartwright was responsible for the appearance of the article, but whether he might not have expressed to some prominent journalist the opinions contained in it, and thus have been indirectly responsible for the writing of the article.

I replied that some person might no doubt be found who would object to everything in the article : one to one thing, and one to another. But there were things in it which, as isolated opinions, might have been expressed by almost anyone in conversation. There was even in it one thing at least which Count Metternich himself might have said. I could not, therefore, say that Sir Fairfax Cartwright had never expressed in conversation any of the opinions in the article. But I could say, for Sir Fairfax had explicitly told me this, that he had not expressed them to Dr. Münz, who was the writer of the article, and who had admitted that he had manufactured it after talking to a number of people.

Count Metternich then said that he thought the communication to the Press that might be satisfactory would be to the effect that his Government were satisfied that Sir Fairfax Cartwright was in no way responsible for the article, and did not express to the writer of it the opinions contained in it to which exception had been taken. He told me that he would suggest to the Chancellor that this should be said by the German Government; and he asked whether, if they agreed to this, it should be said at once, or whether he should see me again first.

I replied that I intended to return to London next Thursday evening or Friday morning, and I should be glad if he would see me before the announcement was made, in order that I might see the exact terms.

[I am, &c.]
E. G[REY].

Sir Edward Grey to Sir E. Goschen.

F.O. 35517/33698/11/28.
(No. 209.)
Sir,   *Foreign Office, September 8, 1911.*

Count Metternich showed me to-day([1]) the text of the communication which the German Government would be willing to make. It was as follows : " The Imperial Government have received from the British Government, on enquiry, information to the effect that the British Ambassador at Vienna has neither inspired the article published in the " Neue Freie Presse ", nor has the Ambassador made the statements ascribed to him to the author of the article."

I said that this communication omitted all mention of the fact that the German Government were satisfied, of which I had made a point in my previous conversation with Count Metternich. I feared that this communication would be received as a mere perfunctory official denial on the part of the British Government, and that it would not put an end to the attacks in the German Press. I suggested that the words " to the effect " should be left out after the word " information ", and that the words " which has satisfied the German Government " should be inserted there.

Count Metternich proposed that, if this was done, there should be inserted after the word " that " the words " in the opinion of the British Government."

I said that this would not serve to protect Sir Fairfax Cartwright from the attacks made upon him. I very much resented these attacks, and I might have taken an even stronger line, had it not been that the negotiations with France about Morocco were being resumed this week, and I did not wish to disturb the atmosphere. If a denial was published now, and the attacks were repeated, the situation would be made worse than ever.

([1]) [For Count Metternich's report, *v. G.P.* XXIX, p. 243.]

Count Metternich said that the object of the German Government was, not to protect the British Ambassador at Vienna, but to remove the foundation for the attacks.

I agreed the objects were separate, but they would both be achieved by putting a stop to the attacks in the Press, and unless this was done, neither object would be accomplished.

He told me that he would refer the point to his Government, and I observed that I would like to have an opportunity of submitting this point to the Prime Minister.

Sir E. Goschen to Sir Edward Grey

Berlin, September 14, 1911.

F.O. 36153/33698/11/28.
D. 8·10 P.M.

Tel. (No. 70.)
R. 10·15 P.M.

Following communiqué is published in " Norddeutsche " (" North German Gazette ") to-night—

" The Imperial Government have been informed by British Government, in reply to an enquiry, that the British Ambassador at Vienna neither inspired well-known article in the ' Neue Freie Presse ' nor did he make statements attributed to him by author of the article. The incident is thus satisfactorily closed as far as the Imperial Government are concerned."

Sir F. Cartwright to Sir A. Nicolson.

Private.(¹)

My dear Nicolson,
Vienna, September 14, 1911.

Your telegram of two days ago in which you send me the text of the communiqué which the German Government propose to issue with regard to the article in the " Neue Freie Presse ", seems to me to be satisfactory, and the communiqué ought finally to dispose of the false accusation that I am responsible for the composition or for the appearance of the above article. Dr. Muenz, the writer of the article, is, I am told, in despair over the trouble he has caused, and he bitterly blames the editor of the Neue Freie Presse for his unpardonable offence in attributing the article to me, merely in order to create a sensation, or was it perhaps done at the instigation of the German Embassy here? Dr. Muenz has declared to many persons in Vienna that his intention was to write an article which would give what he imagined to be the English view of the Moroccan question. He got his information by talking to all manner of diplomatists at Marienbad, and he drew much of it from English newspapers. Out of all this he made an article which he thought would be interesting; he sent it to the Neue Freie Presse with instructions to date it from London, and as coming from a correspondent there. I suspect he mentioned to the Neue Freie Presse that he had seen me for a few moments, and the editor then saw his opportunity of creating a sensation by attributing the whole of the article to me. It is strange, as I have already pointed out in my telegrams, that the publication of the article was delayed for two days. This was evidently done for some purpose and I have considerable grounds for believing that during that time the text of the article was telegraphed to Berlin. I may tell you that Dr. Friedjung frequently writes in the Neue Freie Presse, and has also the " entrée " to the German Embassy. As he also writes in the Berlin " Vossische Zeitung ", and as that newspaper began the violent attack against myself on the same day as the article appeared in the Neue Freie Presse, I cannot help thinking that Dr. Friedjung and the German Embassy between them had a hand in deliberately misleading for purposes of their own German public opinion as to the real origin of the anonymous article. As to the attitude of the German Government in this matter, I can only say that it seems to me that t has been inspired either by imbecility if they genuinely jumped at the conclusion that the article was really written by me without having given themselves any tro[u]ble to enquire into the matter, or by knavery if they wanted to seize an opportunity of letting the German public explode against Great Britain, and creating thereby a stream of Anglophobia in Germany which it will take a long time to stem. As for the German Chargé d'Affaires, he still keeps carefully out of my way; he is an amiable, weak man who, I think, has been the tool of Tschirschky and of the authorities in Berlin who probably instructed him not to go in search of a " démenti " from me before the German press had time to start the campaign against me. It is strange that in Germany, where the press gets information and direction to such an extent from official sources, nothing should have been done to prevent a violent explosion against Great Britain by the issuing of a note of warning to the newspapers to be careful and wait until it was ascertained who was really responsible for the production of the article in the Neue Freie Presse. The German Government cannot escape

(¹) [Carnock MSS., Vol. IV of 1911.]

from the responsibility of having remained aloof with folded arms, and in so doing, of having led everyone to believe that if they did not actually encourage the campaign against Great Britain, they certainly had no intention to stop it.

In Austria, comparatively speaking, little interest has been taken in the controversy; the Neue Freie Presse has been very silent on the matter; the "Tageblatt", the Vienna newspaper with the largest circulation, has hardly touched the matter, and the official "Fremdenblatt", Aehrenthal's organ, has refrained from mentioning the subject altogether. The only newspapers which have handled the question, are the two clerical organs, the "Reichspost" and the "Vaterland", who could not miss the opportunity of violently attacking the Jewish free-thinking Neue Freie Presse, on the grounds of the mischief it has caused by the unscrupulous publication of forged documents. The fact is that the Press Bureau at the Ballplatz have steadily declined to accede to German wishes that they should direct the Austrian press to take up the cry raised against me in Germany. . . . .([2]).

> Yours truly,
> FAIRFAX L. CARTWRIGHT.

([2]) [A part of this letter which treats of the Moroccan question is printed *supra*, pp. 526–7, No. 548. The remaining paragraphs are of a merely general character and are omitted.]

Sir Edward Grey to Sir F. Cartwright.

Private.([1])

My dear Cartwright, *Foreign Office, November* 9, 1911.

You will see that the German papers persist in saying that you made the statements attributed to you in the Neue Freie Presse and one paper asserts that Dr. Münz gave in the article "only the British Ambassador's own words."

We shall have a debate here, probably on the 22nd, and I may have to deal with the subject again.

Of course we may all of us say in informal conversation from time to time things that we never intend for publication and that never ought to be published, but from what you told me in telegrams or letters I should be justified in giving a denial to the statements that continue to be made, and I shall be glad if you will let me have the most explicit form of denial that is accurate, in case I want to use it.

> Yours sincerely,
> E. GREY.

([1]) [Grey MSS., Vol. 2.]

Sir Edward Grey to Sir F. Cartwright.

Private.([1]) *Foreign Office, November* 17, 1911.

Tel. D. 1·30 P.M

Private. My private letter of Nov[ember] 9.([2])

As there may be a discussion on foreign affairs next week in the House of Commons and the Vienna Messenger is not due till the week after, I shall be glad if you will telegraph to me at length in reply to my letter.

([1]) [Grey MSS., Vol. 2.]
([2]) [*v.* immediately preceding document.]

Sir F. Cartwright to Sir Edward Grey.

Vienna, *November* 18, 1911.

Private.([1]) D. 3·44 P.M.

Tel. R. 6·45 P.M.

Your private letter and your telegram of yesterday.

In the conversation I had with Dr. Müntz, at Marienbad, I referred him to Mr. Asquith's speech for an exposition of British policy, and blamed Pan-German press for raising expectations in Germany which I did not think would be satisfied. I made no criticism of the German Emperor (see my private letter of 31st August to Sir A. Nicolson).([2]) I would also specially refer

([1]) [Grey MSS., Vol. 2.]
([2]) [*v. supra*, pp. 839–40.]

you to Dr. Müntz's letter of apology to me and the draft letter which he proposed to send to the " Vossische Zeitung " (which formed the enclosure in my private letter of the 5th September([3]) to Sir A. Nicolson).

1. In this document Dr. Müntz declares that he never heard me make any objectionable criticism of the German Emperor.

2. Dr. Müntz declares that this year he had only a very short and insignificant meeting on the Marienbad parade with me.

3. Dr. Müntz declares that it is an absolute falsehood if German press state that the British and French Ambassadors at Vienna have been conspiring to bring about an agitation against the conclusion of an agreement between France and Germany over Morocco.

4. Dr. Müntz declares that neither the French nor British Ambassador has had anything to do with the publication of the interviews attributed to them. If the question of the " Neue Freie Press " article is again raised in detail it will, I am afraid, lead to fresh polemics in the German press, which it might be as well to avoid, as nothing we may say will find credence in Germany in the present state of feeling existing there against England. Dr. Müntz, who was very penitent six weeks ago, is now talking big about the accuracy of the article in order to try and re-establish his damaged reputation. Nearly all the embassies here have closed their doors against him as being an untrustworthy and inaccurate person. If he sees a chance he will be glad to seize it to pit his version of what occurred against mine. Under these circumstances, I venture to suggest that you, might make a declaration, if necessary, somewhat to the following effect :—

(R). " The British Ambassador had no hand in the composing of the anonymous article in an Austrian newspaper, neither did he know of it before its publication, neither did he directly or indirectly inspire or authorise any person to give publicity to his supposed views on the political events of the day." (End of R.)

It might perhaps be well to express satisfaction at the language held by the German Minister for Foreign Affairs and Chancellor in the Reichstag on this subject.

I am sending a private letter by Lord Rosebery,([4]) who leaves to-morrow.

([3]) [Not reproduced. *cp. supra*, pp. 839–40, and *note* ([3]).]

([4]) [This letter (F.O. 47601/8457/11/28) gives in detail the statements made in Sir F. Cartwright's telegram above, and encloses translations of Dr. Münz's denials, already mentioned in Sir F. Cartwright's private letter to Sir A. Nicolson, of August 31, 1911. *v. supra*, pp. 839–40, and *note* ([3]).]

APPENDIX VI.

Movements of German Warships S.M.S. " Berlin," " Eber " and " Panther," July 1911.

[*ED. NOTE.*—The Editors think it desirable to print below all the information which they have been able to collect as to the movements of the German vessels, the " Panther," the " Berlin " and the " Eber," which were concerned in the Agadir crisis. The most important point on which difficulty has arisen is as to the date of the arrival of the " Panther." No definite information is given on the subject in the *Grosse Politik*, and the British Foreign Office archives, though not equally silent, gave inconclusive evidence. A telegram from Vice-Consul Johnstone (at Mogador) to Mr. White (enclosed in Mr. White's despatch No. 210 of July 8, F.O. 27869/25641/11/28) referred to July 2 as the date, while Sir M. de Bunsen in his Annual Report for 1911 gave July 1 (*v. supra*, p. 309, No. 336). Information from the British Admiralty also gave July 1, and the Editors have been able to obtain information from the Naval Archives at Berlin, which confirms this. There is conflict also as to the date on which the " Berlin " arrived. The date given in the British naval records is the 7th, but the *Grosse Politik* gives the 4th (*v. G.P.*, XXIX, p. 153, *note*), and there is some confirmation of this in the British Foreign Office archives, in the same despatch from Mr. White to which reference has been made above. The departure of the " Panther " is not given in the British Admiralty records, but she is there said to have reached Mogador on the 6th. This, however, is almost certainly inaccurate, as Vice-Consul Johnstone gives the date of arrival of the " Panther " at Mogador as " an early hour " of the 8th. It may be assumed therefore that the " Panther " left Agadir on the 7th or 8th (*cp.* also Reuter's Agency, *Times*, July 10, 1911, p. 5). The " Berlin " did not finally leave Agadir until the end of November, but there is some confirmatory evidence for the fact, suggested by the record of her movements supplied by the British Admiralty, that her stay was not continuous. Possibly the " Panther " (*v.* Vice-Consul Johnstone's report printed *supra*, p. 418, No. 435) and certainly the " Eber," acting as an auxiliary, relieved her from time to time. During this long period therefore there was always one warship at Agadir and sometimes two.]

(a)

Movements Recorded by the British Admiralty.([1])

	Arrived.	Departed.
Cruiser *Berlin*—		
Kiel	...	1. 7.11
Arrived in Moroccan waters	? 5. 7.11	...
Agadir	7. 7.11	...
Tenerife	16. 7.11	18. 7.11
Tenerife	1. 8.11	2. 8.11
Las Palmas	2. 8.11	3. 8.11
Las Palmas	22. 8.11	28. 8.11
Agadir	29. 8.11	...
Las Palmas	17. 9.11	24. 9.11
Agadir	25. 9.11	...
Las Palmas	11.10.11	14.10.11
Agadir	15.10.11	...
Las Palmas	29.10.11	7.11.11
Agadir	...	21.11.11
Las Palmas	21.11.11	28.11.11
Casablanca	30.11.11	...
Gunboat *Eber*—		
Duala	...	30. 6.11
Las Palmas	14. 7.11	17. 7.11
Tenerife	17. 7.11	22. 7.11
Agadir	23. 7.11	23. 7.11
Tenerife	25. 7.11	29. 7.11
Agadir	31. 7.11	4. 8.11
Tenerife	6. 8.11	19. 8.11
Agadir	21. 8.11	30 8.11
Tenerife	31. 8.11	2. 9.11
Las Palmas	3. 9.11	7. 9.11
Agadir	9. 9.11	11. 9.11
Las Palmas	11. 9.11	15. 9.11
Agadir	17. 9.11	25. 9.11

([1]) [These movements were recorded at the time from reports received from various sources. The Editors have been informed that the actual reports are not now available.]

					Arrived.	Departed.
Las Palmas	...	...	...	...	27. 9.11	3.10.11
Agadir ...	...	...	...	...	4.10.11	...
Las Palmas	...	...	...	...	6.10.11	9.10.11
Las Palmas	...	...	...	...	17.10.11	27.10.11
Agadir ...	...	...	...	...	28.10.11	...
Las Palmas	...	...	...	...	10.11.11	19.11.11
Agadir ...	...	...	...	...	20.11.11	...
Casablanca	...	...	...	...	30.11.11	...

Gunboat *Panther*—

					Arrived.	Departed.
Agadir (from Tenerife)	...	...	...	1. 7.11	...
Mogador	...	...	...	...	6. 7.11	6. 7.11
Tenerife	...	...	...	...	8. 7.11	9. 7.11

The following note appears in the records, but the authority for this note is not quoted : (" Has gone 120 miles N. of Tenerife to transmit orders by W/T to ' Berlin ' at Agadir ").

					Arrived.	Departed.
Tenerife	...	...	...	...	10. 7.11	13. 7.11
Tenerife	...	...	...	...	21. 7.11	22. 7.11
Tenerife	...	...	...	...	22. 7.11	27. 7.11
Cadiz	...	...	...	...	29. 7.11	3. 8.11
Vigo	...	...	...	...	4. 8.11	5. 8.11
Flushing	...	...	...	...	9. 8.11	11. 8.11
Wilhelmshaven	...	...	...	...	12. 8.11	...

(*b*)

The following information from the Naval Archives at Berlin, communicated by the German Government, was received in October 1931.

(Translation.)

His Majesty's Ship " Panther " anchored in the harbour of Agadir on the evening of July 1st at 8 o'clock. On July 2nd the " Panther " merely altered her place of anchorage slightly.

INDEX OF PERSONS.

SHOWING WRITERS OF DESPATCHES, &C., AND OFFICIAL POSITIONS DURING
THIS PERIOD OF THE PRINCIPAL PERSONS MENTIONED IN THE TEXT.

AMADE, D', French General.
81–2 (No. 94), 109 (No. 119), 110 (No. 120), 111 (No. 122), 112 (No. 123), 132 (No. 147).

ANFLUS, KAID.
70 (No. 83, *encl.*), 94 (No. 105), 418 (No. 435).

ARCHER-SHEE, MAJOR M., M.P. for Central Finsbury, 1910–18, Finsbury, 1918–23.
Question asked in House of Commons, April 25, 1911, 201 (No. 219).

ARCOS, DUC D', Spanish Ambassador at Rome, 1905–7.
Conversation with Sir E. Egerton, 39 (No. 53).

ASQUITH, RT. HON. H. H., British Prime Minister and First Lord of Treasury, 1908–16.
Reply to question in House of Commons, 342 (No. 364), 356 (No. 373).
Speeches by, in House of Commons, 406 (No. 426), 412 (No. 430), 413–4 (No. 431); November
27, 1911, 725 (No. 720).

AZCARATE, SEÑOR, Spanish Deputy.
301 (No. 315).

AZZOUS, MOHAMMED BEN, Moorish Envoy to Berlin, 1908, 1910.
Mission to Berlin, February 1910, 147 (No. 163).

BALDING, SERGEANT.
150 (No. 166), 200 (No. 217).

BALFOUR, MR. A. J. (since 1922, 1ST EARL OF), British First Lord of the Treasury, 1895–1905;
Prime Minister, 1902–5.
Question by, in House of Commons, 342 (No. 364).

BAPST, M. EDMOND, *Directeur Politique* at the French Ministry for Foreign Affairs, 1909–13.
318 (No. 337).
Conversation with M. Isvolski, 531 (No. 554).

BARRÈRE, M. CAMILLE, French Ambassador at Rome, 1897–1924.
Conversation with Sir E. Egerton, 39 (No. 53).

BARRINGTON, SIR ERIC, Private Secretary to the Marquess of Lansdowne, 1900–5; Assistant
Under-Secretary of State for Foreign Affairs, 1906–7.
Minute by, 9 (No. 9), 20 (No. 22), 27 (No. 30), 30 (No. 35), 43 (No. 56).

BASSERMANN, HERR E., Member of the Reichstag.
Speech by, in the Reichstag, Herr von Bethmann Hollweg's comments on, 679–80 (No. 677,
encl.); Sir E. Goschen on, 685–6 (No. 681).

BEAUMARCHAIS, M. D. C. DE, 2nd Secretary at French Legation at Tangier, 1911.
183 (No. 199).
Conversation with Mr. R. Lister, 183–4 (No. 199).

BEBEL, HERR AUGUST, Member of the Reichstag.
Speech by, in the Reichstag, 684–5 (No. 681), 762 (No. 740).

BELL, MR. C. F. MOBERLY, Manager of the *Times*.
463 (No. 490).

BENCKENDORFF, ALEXANDER, COUNT, Russian Ambassador at London, 1903–17.
Communication from, 329–30 (No. 349).
Conversation with Sir E. Grey, 335 (No. 357), 407 (No. 427), 466 (No. 494), 479 (No. 507),
502 (No. 529).

BEN GHAZI.
70 (No. 83, *encl.*).

BERCKHEIM, COUNT, Councillor of French Embassy at Berlin, 1908–12.
Conversation with Sir F. Lascelles, 91–2 (No. 103).
Conversation with Herr von Schoen, 79 (No. 92).

3 I

BETHMAÑN HOLLWEG, HERR T. VON—(*continued*).
  Conversation with Sir E. Goschen, 276–7 (No. 306), 652 (No. 659), 653–5 (No. 661), 659
    (No. 664), 660 (No. 665), 788–9 (No. 763).
  Conversation with Don Polo de Bernabé, 331–2 (No. 352).
  Policy of, Herr Harden's criticism of, 443–5 (No. 467).
  Speech by, in the Reichstag, November 9, 1911, 665–8 (No. 674); *Text*, translation of, 668–75
    (No. 674, *encl.*).
    November 10, 1911, 679–82 (No. 677, *encl.*); Sir E. Goschen on, 694–5 (No. 691).
    December 5, 1911, 757 (No. 738); *Text*, translation of, 758–61 (No. 739); Sir E.
      Goschen on, 762–3 (No. 740).

BILLY, M. R. DE, 1st Secretary at French Legation at Tangier, 1909–12 (sometimes *Chargé
  d'Affaires*).
  Conversation with Mr. R. Lister, 175–6 (No. 189), 177 (No. 191), 184–5 (No. 199),
    262 (No. 289).
  Conversation with Mr. Rattigan, 217–8 (No. 239).
  Conversation with Mr. H. White, 297 (No. 334), 366 (No. 385), 393–4 (No. 416).

BISMARCK, OTTO PRINCE VON, German Imperial Chancellor, 1871–90.
  Policy of, 364 (No. 383, *min.*).

BOISSET, M., French Vice-Consul at Alcazar, 1911.
  291 (No. 325), 310 (No. 336), 320 (No. 337), 377 (No. 398).

BOLESTA-KOZIEBRODZI, LEOPOLD COUNT, Austro-Hungarian Minister at Tangier, 1904–9.
  115 (No. 127).

BOWLES, MR. GIBSON, M.P. for King's Lynn, 1892–1906, 1910.
  And Defence of Gibraltar, 1 (No. 1, *ed. note*).

BRANDT, HERR F., Austro-Hungarian Consul at Casablanca, 1907–14.
  113 (No. 124), 132 (No. 147).

BRÉMOND, CAPTAIN (later COLONEL), French Military Mission in Morocco, 1909–11.
  194 (No. 210), 202 (No. 220), 204 (No. 223), 208 (No. 230), 216 (No. 236), 225–6 (No. 248),
    232 (No. 258), 301 (No. 335).

BROOME, MR. G.
  418 (No. 435).

BRULARD, COLONEL, Commander of French forces in Morocco, 1911.
  248 (No. 270, *encl.*).

BUCHANAN, SIR GEORGE W., British Ambassador at St. Petersburgh, 1910–9.
  To Sir E. Grey, 357–8 (No. 374), 465 (No. 492), 469 (No. 496), 473–6 (Nos. 501–2), 477–8
    (Nos. 504–5), 527–8 (No. 550).
  Conversation with M. Louis, 357 (No. 374), 465 (No. 492), 469 (No. 496), 473–6 (Nos. 501–2),
    478 (No. 505).
  Conversation with M. Neratov, 357–8 (No. 374), 465 (No. 492), 475–6 (No. 502), 477 (No. 504),
    527–8 (No. 550).
  Conversation with M. Stolypin, 473–4 (Nos. 501–2).
  Private Letter—
    To Sir A. Nicolson, 478–9 (No. 506).

BÜLOW, BERNARD COUNT VON (since 1905, PRINCE), German Imperial Chancellor, 1900–9.
  Conversation with M. Jules Cambon, 66 (No. 81), 107 (No. 116), 124 (No. 137).
  Conversation with Sir C. Hardinge, 59 (No. 73).
  Policy of, 685 (No. 681).
  Speech by, in Reichstag, 79–80 (No. 92).
  Speech by, to the Agricultural Association, 1909, 143 (No. 160).

BUNSEN, MR. (later, SIR) M. DE, Secretary of British Embassy at Paris, 1902–5; British Minister
  at Lisbon, 1905–6; Ambassador at Madrid, 1906–13.
  To Sir E. Grey, 1 (*ed. note*, No. 1), 9 (No. 9), 14–15 (Nos. 15–16), 60 (No. 74), 87–9
    (No. 101), 100 (No. 111), 108 (No. 118), 135 (No. 150), 138 (No. 154), 139–40 (No. 156),
    144 (No. 161), 147 (No. 164), 158–60 (Nos. 170–1), 161–2 (No. 173), 162–3 (No. 175),
    168–9 (No. 182), 170–2 (No. 184), 200 (No. 218), 206 (No. 228), 212–4 (No. 235), 219–20
    (No. 241), 223–5 (No. 246), 231–2 (Nos. 257–8), 233–4 (No. 261), 238–43 (No. 266), 255–6
    (No. 277), 257 (No. 280), 258 (No. 283), 260 (No. 286), 263 (No. 290), 264–70 (Nos. 292–3),
    275 (No. 303), 321 (No. 337, *ed. note*), 442 (No. 465), 446 (No. 469), 489–91 (Nos. 521–2),
    500–1 (No. 527), 521–2 (No. 541), 528 (No. 551), 539–41 (No. 559), 543–4 (No. 563),
    577–81 (Nos. 594–5), 592 (Nos. 603–4), 593 (No. 606), 595–6 (No. 609), 611 (No. 621),
    620 (No. 630), 688 (No. 682), 763–4 (No. 741), 768–9 (No. 750), 774–8 (No. 756).

MENEBHI, MEHEDI EL. Moorish Minister for War, 1901, 1904, 1905, 1908.
77 (No. 91), 94 (No. 105), 98 (No. 108), 108 (No. 118), 184 (No. 199).
Conversation with Mr. R. Lister, 184 (No. 199).
Conversation with Mr. H. White, 97–8 (No. 108).

MENSDORFF-POUILLY-DIETRICHSTEIN, ALBERT COUNT, 1st Secretary at the Austro-Hungarian Embassy at London, 1904; Ambassador at London, 1904–14.
Conversation with Sir E. Grey, 46 (No. 58), 233 (No. 260), 381 (No. 404).

MERRY DEL VAL, SEÑOR ALFONSO, Spanish Minister at Tangier, 1908–11.
158 (No. 169).
Conversation with Mr. Harris, 324 (No. 341).
Conversation with Mr. R. Lister, 149 (No. 166), 284 (No. 315).

MESSIMY, M. ADOLPHE, French Minister for War, 1911, 1911–12, 1914–5.
Conversation with Colonel Fairholme, 635 (No. 643, *encl.*).

METTERNICH, COUNT PAUL VON WOLFF-, German Ambassador at London, 1901–12.
Conversation with Sir E. Grey, 47–8 (No. 60), 256 (No. 278), 328 (No. 347), 334 (No. 356), 390–1 (No. 411), 394–6 (No. 417), 397–9 (No. 419), 411–3 (No. 430), 598 (No. 613), 619–20 (No. 628), 651–2 (No. 658), 662 (No. 669), 696–7 (No. 694), 697–8 (No. 695), 716–7 (No. 711), 726–30 (No. 721).
Conversation with Sir A. Nicolson, 322–3 (No. 339), 336–7 (No. 359), 367–8 (No. 388), 374–5 (No. 395), 456 (No. 482).
Aide-mémoire by, 322 (No. 338).
Private Letter—
To Sir E. Grey, 837–8 (*App.* V).

MIKWAR, Moorish Minister for Foreign Affairs, 1911.
Appointed Minister for Foreign Affairs, 230 (No. 255).

MILLERAND, M., French Deputy, Minister for War, 1912–3, later President of the French Republic.
On, Franco-German Treaty, November 1911, 708–9 (No. 704, and *encl.*).
Speech by, addressed to Socialist-Radical group of French Chamber, December 1, 1911, 748 (No. 728).
Speech by, in Chamber of Deputies, 785 (No. 760).

MOINIER, General in French Army, Commander of forces in Morocco, 1910, 1911.
248 (No. 270, *encl.*), 262 (No. 289).

MOKRI, HADJI MOHAMMED EL, Moorish Minister for Finance, 1909–11; Ambassador at Madrid, 1910; Grand Vizier, 1910–12.
94 (No. 105), 147 (No. 163), 343 (No. 365).
Hispano-Moroccan Convention signed by, 155–7 (No. 169), 170–7 (No. 184), 298 (No. 335).

MONTEIRO, SENHOR L., Portuguese Minister for Foreign Affairs, 1907.
Conversation with Sir F. Villiers, 42 (No. 55).

MONTGOMERY, MR. (since 1927, SIR) C. H., Clerk in British Foreign Office, 1900–19; Assistant Secretary, 1919; Assistant Under-Secretary of State for Foreign Affairs, 1922–30; Deputy Under-Secretary, 1930– .
Minute by, 27 (No. 30), 638 (No. 645).

MOREAUX, CAPTAIN, of French Military Mission in Morocco, 1909–11.
185 (No. 199), 291 (No. 325), 294 (No. 330), 297 (No. 334), 310 (No. 336).

MORET, Spanish Prime Minister and Minister for the Interior, 1909–10.
Conversation with Sir M. de Bunsen, 579 (No. 594).
Conversation with Sir A. Nicolson, 3–4 (No. 2), 14 (No. 15).
And Anglo-Spanish proposed treaty, 1898, 1 (No. 1, *ed. note*).
And Anglo-Spanish relations, 1907, 14 (No. 15).

MORGAN, PROFESSOR J. H.
Article by, in the *Quarterly*, 626 (No. 639, *ed. note*).

MORLEY, MR. JOHN (since 1908, VISCOUNT MORLEY OF BLACKBURN), British Secretary of State for India, 1905–10.
In temporary charge of the Foreign Office, April 1911, 208–10 (Nos. 230–1).

M'TOUGI, KAID.
365 (No. 385), 394 (No. 416), 418 (No. 435).

MUAZA, EL, Moorish Ambassador at Madrid, 1909–10.
And negotiations for Spanish-Moorish Convention, 1910, 154–5 (No. 169), 170 (No. 184).

MÜHLBERG, DR. VON, German Under-Secretary of State for Foreign Affairs, 1900–7; Minister to the Vatican, 1908–18.
  Conversation with M. Jules Cambon, 42 (No. 56).
  Conversation with Sir F. Lascelles, 42–3 (No. 56).
  Conversation with Don Polo de Bernabé, 42 (No. 56).

MÜNZ, DR. SIEGMUND, Austro-Hungarian Journalist, Correspondent of the *Neue Freie Presse*.
  Article by, in *Neue Freie Presse* (*v. sub* PRESS, Austro-Hungarian (*Subject Index*)).

MULAI, ABDUL HAFID, Sultan of Morocco, 1908–12.
  70 (No. 83, *encl.*), 73 (No. 87), 366 (No. 385).
  Conversation with Dr. Vassel, 97–8 (No. 108).
  Interview with M. Gaillard, 152 (No. 168).
  Proclamation of, as Sultan, 73 (No. 87, *note*), 93 (No. 105); *Recognition* of, 74–108 (Nos. 88–118); unpopularity of, 231 (No. 256); misrule of, 231 (No. 256).
  And Franco-Moorish convention, 1910, 146–7 (No. 163).

MULAI, SLIMAN.
  Reported proclamation of as Sultan of Morocco, 182 (No. 198).

MULAI, ZIN, Pretender to the throne of Morocco, 1911.
  Announcement of proclamation as Sultan of Morocco, 230 (No. 255); treatment of after occupation of Fez, 272 (No. 295), 272 (No. 296), 273 (No. 299).

MUN, COUNT ALBERT DE, French Deputy, 1911.
  Speech by, 780 (No. 758), 787 (No. 761).

MUNI, MARQUIS DEL.
  (*v. sub* LEON Y CASTILLO, MARQUIS DEL MUNI.)

MURRAY, MR. O. A. R., Principal Assistant Secretary, British Admiralty, 1911–7; Permanent Secretary, 1917–
  To Foreign Office, 610 (No. 620).

NATTER & NAVARRETTE, MESSRS.
  314 (No. 336).

NERATOV, M. A. A., Russian Acting Minister for Foreign Affairs, 1911.
  To Count Benckendorff, 329–30 (No. 349).
  Conversation with Sir G. W. Buchanan, 357–8 (No. 374), 465 (No. 492), 475–6 (No. 502), 477 (No. 504), 527–8 (No. 550).
  Conversation with M. Louis, 329–30 (No. 349), 464 (No. 491 (*b*)).

H.I.M. NICHOLAS, Emperor of Russia, 1894–1917.
  Conversation with M. Louis, 476 (No. 502).

NICHOLAS NICHOLAÏÉVIC, Grand Duke of Russia.
  473 (No. 501), 475 (No. 502).

NICHOLSON, SIR G. N. (since 1912, 1ST BARON), BRIGADIER-GENERAL (later FIELD-MARSHAL), Chief of General Staff, British War Office, 1908–12.
  Memorandum by, 626–9 (No. 639).

NICOLSON, SIR ARTHUR (since 1916, 1ST BARON CARNOCK), British Ambassador at Madrid, 1905–6; at St. Petersburgh, 1906–10; British Representative at Conference at Algeciras, 1906; Permanent Under-Secretary of State for Foreign Affairs, 1910–6.
  To M. Daeschner, 689 (No. 684).
  To Sir E. Grey, 40–1 (No. 54), 118 (No. 130), 120 (No. 133), 121–3 (No. 135), 124–5 (No. 138), 434–5 (No. 458).
  To Lord Lansdowne, 3 (No. 2, *ed. note*), 3–4 (No. 2).
  Conversation with M. Paul Cambon, 166–7 (No. 178, *min.*), 181–2 (No. 196), 186 (No. 202), 208–9 (No. 230), 258 (No. 282, *min.*), 292–3 (No. 327, *min.*), 295–6 (No. 331, *min.*), 333 (No. 354), 360–1 (Nos. 379–80), 375 (No. 395), 574–5 (No. 590), 596–7 (No. 610), 602 (No. 617).
  Conversation with M. Daeschner, 196–7 (No. 213).
  Conversation with M. Isvolski, 40–1 (No. 54), 120 (No. 133), 121–3 (No. 135).
  Conversation with Count von Metternich, 322–3 (No. 339), 336–7 (No. 359), 367–8 (No. 388), 374–5 (No. 395), 456 (No. 482).

3 K 2

SAN GIULIANO, MARQUIS DI, Italian Minister for Foreign Affairs, 1905–6; Ambassador at London, 1906–10; at Paris, 1910; Minister for Foreign Affairs, 1910–4.
   Conversation with Sir Rennell Rodd, 252 (No. 273), 425 (No. 445).

SATOW, SIR E. M., British Minister at Tangier, 1893–4; at Tôkiô, 1895–1900; at Peking, 1900–6; 2nd Delegate at Hague Conference, 1907.

SAUNDERS, MR. G., Correspondent of the *Times* at Berlin, 1897–1908; Paris, 1908–14.
   Conversation with Mr. L. D. Carnegie, 133–4 (No. 148, *encl.*).
   Conversation with M. Clemenceau, 133 (No. 148, *encl.*).

SCHEBEKO, M. R. VON, Councillor of Russian Embassy at Berlin, 1909–12 (sometimes *Chargé d'Affaires*); Minister at Bucharest, 1912–3.
   Conversation with M. Jules Cambon, 212 (No. 234).
   Conversation with Sir E. Goschen, 225 (No. 247), 464 (No. 491 (*a*)).

SCHIEMANN, THEODOR, Professor of History at the University of Berlin, Contributor to the *Kreuz-Zeitung*.
   19 (No. 22), 434 (No. 457).
   Article by, in the *Kreuz-Zeitung*, 388 (No. 410).

SCHOEN, HERR WILHELM (since 1909, BARON) VON, German Ambassador at St. Petersburgh, 1905–7; Minister for Foreign Affairs, 1907–10; Ambassador at Paris, 1910–4.
   Conversation with Count Berckheim, 79 (No. 92).
   Conversation with M. Jules Cambon, 80–1 (No. 93), 106 (No. 115), 124 (No. 137), 143 (No. 160).
   Conversation with Sir E. Goschen, 142–3 (No. 159).
   Conversation with Sir E. Grey, 71–2 (Nos. 85–6).
   Conversation with Sir F. Lascelles, 89 (No. 101, *min.*).
   Conversation with Señor Perez Caballero, 220 (No. 242).
   Conversation with M. de Selves, 323 (No. 340), 343–4 (No. 366), 458 (No. 484), 485–6 (No. 514).
   Speech by, in Reichstag, 79–80 (No. 92).

SCHWABACH, DR. PAUL VON, British Vice-Consul at Berlin, 1897; Consul-General, 1898–1909.
   707 (No. 702).
   Conversation with Sir Eyre Crowe, 114 (No. 126).

SECKENDORFF, BARON VON, German Minister at Tangier, 1910–4.
   177 (No. 191), 481 (No. 509).
   Conversation with Mr. Lister, 225–6 (No. 248).
   Conversation with Mr. H. White, 393 (No. 416).

SELVES, M. DE, French Minister for Foreign Affairs, 1911–2.
   To Sir F. Bertie, 429 (No. 452, *encl.*), 571 (No. 558, *encl.*).
   To M. Jules Cambon, 529–30 (No. 553), 546–9 (No. 565).
   Conversation with Sir F. Bertie, 315–8 (No. 337), 343–4 (No. 366), 347–8 (No. 369), 352–3 (No. 372), 362–3 (Nos. 381–2), 371–2 (No. 392), 377 (No. 398), 378 (No. 400), 383 (No. 406), 383–4 (No. 407), 393 (No. 415), 421–2 (No. 440), 423 (No. 441), 424 (No. 442), 431 (No. 454), 435–6 (No. 460), 458 (No. 484), 467–9 (No. 495), 469–70 (No. 497), 471–2 (No. 499), 472 (No. 500), 482–3 (No. 510), 484–7 (Nos. 513–7), 494 (No. 525), 505 (No. 533), 505–6 (No. 534), 507–8 (No. 537), 524 (No. 545), 526 (No. 547), 531 (No. 554), 532–3 (No. 556), 535 (No. 558), 543 (No. 562), 549 (No. 566), 559 (No. 572), 560 (No. 575), 562 (No. 577), 569–70 (No. 588), 575 (No. 591), 576 (No. 593), 582 (No. 597), 584–5 (No. 598), 599–601 (No. 614), 703 (No. 698), 720 (No. 715), 721–3 (No. 716), 756–7 (No. 737).
   Conversation with Señor Perez Caballero, 377 (No. 398).
   Conversation with M. Isvolski, 469–70 (No. 497), 471–2 (No. 499).
   Conversation with Sir R. Lister, 534–5 (No. 557, *encl.*).
   Conversation with Baron von Schoen, 323 (No. 340), 343–4 (No. 366), 458 (No. 484), 485–6 (No. 514).
   Memorandum by, communicated to Sir F. Bertie, 381 (No. 403, *encl.* 2).
   Note, communicated to Sir F. Bertie, 568 (No. 584, *encl.*).
   Speech by, in Chamber of Deputies, 780–2 (No. 758), 806–14 (*App.* II).
   Statement by, to the Commission for Foreign and Colonial Affairs, 678 (No. 676).

SEMBAT, M. MARCEL, French Deputy.
   Article by, in *Humanité*, 560 (No. 574).
   Speech by, in Chamber of Deputies, 788 (No. 762).

SMITH, SIR H. LLEWELLYN, Permanent Secretary of the British Board of Trade, 1911–9.
   To Foreign Office, 764 (No. 744).

SUBJECT INDEX.

AFRICA.

Congo, Belgian.

Pre-emption rights of : Germany and, 379 (No. 402), 395 (No. 417); Great Britain and, 379 (No. 402), 384 (No. 407); Belgian attitude towards sale of, 419 (No. 436); French right of pre-emption, 427 (No. 449); Great Britain and, 427 (No. 449), 441 (No. 464); Germany and, 436 (No. 460); anxiety over possible German designs on, 595 (No. 608); Herr von Kiderlen-Waechter's request to France asking for consultation with Germany in eventuality of question arising of taking over Belgian Congo, 596–7 (No. 610); M. de Selves' suggested formula, 597 (No. 612); Sir E. Grey on undesirable effect of a present discussion, 598 (No. 612); Franco-German Treaty, 1911, and, 708–10 (No. 704 *and encl.*).

Congo, French.

Question of handing over to Germany, June 1911, 279 (No. 308); compensation to Germany over Morocco question and, 309 (No. 336), 344 (No. 366), 345 (No. 367), 354 (No. 373); desires conversations upon, 346 (No. 368), 348 (No. 369); Sir Eyre Crowe on German policy, 349 (No. 369, *min.*); British attitude, 349 (No. 369, *min.*); 359 (No. 377); Herr von Kiderlen-Waechter's suggestion of compensations in rectification of Cameroon and French Congo frontier, 362 (No. 381), 364 (No. 384); Sir F. Bertie on excessive German requirements, 370 (No. 391); Sir A. Nicolson on, 375 (No. 395); Franco-German discussions, 371–2 (No. 392), 373 (No. 393), 388 (No. 410); Sir E. Grey on German demands, 382 (No. 405), 390 (No. 411); Sir F. Bertie on, 384 (No. 407); M. de Selves prepared to offer rectification of frontier, 393 (No. 414), 393 (No. 415); Herr von Kiderlen-Waechter suggests cession of whole colony to Germany, 403 (No. 424), 404–5 (No. 425); opinion of French Government on, 405 (No. 425); nothing prejudicial to British interests in French proposed concessions, 405 (No. 425); France could not give up whole of French Congo, 416 (No. 433), 422 (No. 440); revised proposals, 428 (No. 451), 430 (No. 453), 431 (No. 454), 434–5 (Nos. 458–60), 442–3 (No. 466); German renewed demands, 447–8 (Nos. 471–2), 449 (No. 474); M. Caillaux on limits of French concessions, 461 (No. 488); decision on offers to be made, Aug. 22, 482 (No.

AFRICA—(*continued*).

Congo, French—(*continued*).

Question of, &c.—(*continued*).

510), 484 (No. 512); details of cessions offered, 484–6 (Nos. 513–4); discussed, 485–6 (No. 514); German view that they are insufficient, 502 (No. 528), 506 (No. 534); M. de Selves on French offer and German attitude, 506 (No. 534); Congo question chief difficulty, Sept., 532 (No. 555); opposition of French Colonial party, 545 (No. 564); and growing hostility of public opinion, 559–60 (No. 573); M. Herbette on, 564 (No. 579); M. Paul Cambon on, 565 (No. 580).

Germany and cession of the Congo : statements subsequent to the Franco-German treaty of 4 Nov., 1911, Sir E. Grey on, 727–8 (No. 721); Herr von Bethmann-Hollweg on, 760 (No. 739); Count A. de Mun on, 780 (No. 758); M. de Selves on, 782 (No. 758); German press comments on, 786–7 (No. 761); debate in French Chamber, 806–20 (*App.* II); Sir Eyre Crowe on Franco-German negotiations and M. Caillaux's offers, 822–4 (*App.* III).

(*v.* also *sub* Morocco, Franco-German negotiations, 1911.)

Gold Coast Colony.

Cession of part of to France, proposed, 535 (No. 558).

Portuguese Colonies.

Question of sale of, 427 (No. 449); Angola : Anglo-German Secret Convention, 382 (No. 405); Sir F. Bertie on British policy, 441 (No. 464); Germany and, 784 (No. 759).

South Africa.

South African War :

Portugal and, 441 (No. 464); Germany and, 441 (No. 464).

Africa, Tropical.

Sir E. Grey on British interests in, 382 (No. 405).

Cape to Cairo Railway.

Great Britain and Germany, 384 (No. 407).

AGADIR.

Opening of port of, and effect on Mogador (*v. sub* Mogador).

Sending of the " Panther " to (*v. sub* Morocco).

AGREEMENTS (*v. sub* Treaties).

ALCAZAR.

Reservation of to Spain (*v. sub* Morocco, Franco-Spanish negotiations).

Spanish occupation of (*v. sub* Morocco).

MOROCCO—(*continued*).
Negotiations—(*continued*).
  1. *Bombardment, &c.*—(continued).
    and France : Man of war leaves for Dar-al-Baida, July 1907, 52 (No. 63); and to Mazagan, 54 (No. 66); action to be confined to re-establishing order, punishing offenders and protection of Europeans, 54 (No. 66), 61 (No. 75); organisation of police to be hastened, 54 (No. 66); French action notified to Great Britain, 55 (No. 67), 55–6 (No. 68), 56 (No. 69), and signatory Powers, 57 (No. 70); Franco-Spanish police force advocated, 56 (No. 69); Spanish uneasiness at this proposal, 58–9 (No. 72); French proposal for preservation of order within individual spheres of influence, 60 (No. 74); M. Pichon regards Spanish attitude as unsatisfactory : his justification of extent of French military precautions, 61–2 (No. 76); no intention of an expedition into the interior, 62 (No. 76); M. Pichon disagrees with Spanish suggestion for superior command at Tangier, September, 65 (No. 80); M. Regnault's negotiations with Sultan of Morocco; French satisfaction, November, 70–1 (No. 83); Franco-Spanish proposal for international commission upon Casablanca claims, 71 (No. 84); Yellow Book on : Sir G. Lowther's comments on timidity of French policy, December 1907 : general state of anarchy, 72–4 (No. 87).

    and Germany : German unfriendly press comments and desire for establishment of proper police, 53–4 (No. 65 *and min.*); German friendly policy towards France in Morocco, 57 (No. 70 *and min.*); Prince Bülow anxious for improved relations : no German intention of creating difficulties, 59 (No. 73), 61 (No. 75), 64 (No. 78), 65 (No. 79), 72 (No. 86); Herr von Tschirschky regrets Spanish action in Morocco, 64 (No. 78); Sir F. Lascelles suggests Franco-Spanish joint action was distasteful, 64 (No. 78); Herr von Tschirschky on German wish that Morocco events should not arouse complications with the Powers, 65 (No. 79); Prince Bülow admits right of searching of German vessels for contraband, October, 66 (No. 81); but considers Spanish action far from satisfactory, 66 (No. 81); German reply to Franco-Spanish proposal for international commission on Casablanca claims, November, 71 (No. 84); claims to have a privileged position, 71 (No. 84);

MOROCCO—(*continued*).
Negotiations—(*continued*).
  1. *Bombardment, &c.*—(continued).
    and Germany—(*continued*).
      German commission instituted, 71 (No. 84), 71–2 (No. 85).
    and Great Britain : Relies on force sent by France, July 1907, 52–3 (No. 63, *ed. note*); no British ships to be sent, 53 (No. 64), 55 (No. 67, *min.*), 57–8 (No. 71), (No. 76); Franco-Spanish co-operation advised, 56 (No. 69), 57 (No. 71), 60 (No. 74, *min.*), 63 (No. 76, *min.*); British assurance to Spain of confidence in French measures and hope for continued Franco-Spanish co-operation, September, 63 (No. 77); acceptance of Franco-Spanish proposal for international commission on Casablanca claims, November, 71–2 (No. 85); but cannot accept German claims for a privileged position, 72 (No. 85).
    and Spain : Franco-Spanish proposals for maintenance of order communicated to Great Britain, 57–8 (No. 71); and the Powers, *Text*, 58 (No. 71, *encl.*); Franco-Spanish co-operation complete within limits of Algeciras Act : Spanish fear of a French forward policy, 58–9 (No. 72); will carry out engagements of Algeciras Act, but beyond this requires concurrence of Powers, 60 (No. 74), 61 (No. 76); Spanish police force of 400 men sent to Casablanca, 60 (No. 74), 61 (No. 76); Spanish uneasiness at extent of French military precautions, 62 (No. 76); M. Pichon regards Spanish attitude as unsatisfactory, 61–2, (No. 76); Spanish desire for superior command at Tangier : M. Pichon does not agree, 65 (No. 80); Spanish anxiety about Franco-Spanish secret agreement about Morocco, 65–6 (No. 80); *Text* of agreement of 23 February, 1907, 67–9 (No. 82, *encl.* 2); Franco-Spanish proposal for international commission upon Casablanca claims, November, 71 (No. 84).
  2. *Recognition of Mulai Hafid.*
    General outline of events :
      Sultan Abdul Aziz invites German intervention to restrain France, January 1908, 75 (No. 89); Mulai Hafid asks Germany to prevent France from supporting Sultan Abdul Aziz, 76 (No. 89); French secret agreement with Sultan Abdul Aziz, February, 78 (No. 91, *encl.*); German question of reception of envoys of Mulai Hafid, May, 80–1 (No. 93); General d'Amade to abstain from further military operations, 81–2 (No. 94); German

MOROCCO—*(continued)*.
  Negotiations—*(continued)*.
    3. *Casablanca deserters*—(continued).
      and Germany—*(continued)*.

satisfaction of German press at solution, 128–9 (No. 143); Herr von Kiderlen-Waechter considers incident closed: German policy not aggressive, 129 (No. 144); Arbitration Agreement signed, 129 (No. 144, *note*); *Text* of arbitration award, 130–1 (No. 145, *and ed. note*).

      and Great Britain : British view that the matter is one to be referred to arbitration, 118 (No. 129, *min.*); King Edward VII on, 118 (No. 129, *min.*); Sir E. Grey on, 119 (No. 131), 123 (No. 136); not advisable to make preparations or movements of ships, but Admiralty should keep in readiness, 119–20 (No. 132); Sir A. Nicolson on British support to France in event of unprovoked war, 120 (No. 133), 122 (No. 135); Sir E. Grey thinks that the question will be arranged, 121 (No. 134); that France is in the right, 121 (No. 134); British comments on final arbitration award, May 1909, 130 (No. 145, *min.*).

      and Russia : M. Isvolski's anxiety over German attitude, November, 118 (No. 130), 119 (No. 131), 120 (No. 133); Sir E. Grey suggests Russia and Italy might join in strong appeal to Germany and France to arbitrate, 121 (No. 134); M. Isvolski views the situation as being exceedingly serious, 121–2 (No. 135).

    4. *Franco-German Agreement, February* 1909.

German desire for *détente* in her relations with France in Morocco : reported by Mr. Lister from Tangier, January 1909, 131–3 (Nos. 146–7); Prince of Monaco's visit to Paris, February, 134 (No. 148, *encl. and min.*); Mr. Spicer and Mr. Langley on the suggested *rapprochement*, 134 (No. 148, *min.*); agreement negotiated whereby Germany disinterests herself in Moroccan affairs, 134 (No. 149); question of *quid pro quo*, 134–5 (No. 149 *and min.*), 142 (No. 158); agreement communicated to Great Britain, 134 (No. 149), 136–7 (No. 153); to Spain, 135 (No. 150), 137 (No. 153); to Morocco, 135–6 (No. 151); M. Paul Cambon on origin of the agreement, 137 (No. 153), 140–1 (No. 157); *Text* communicated to Great Britain, 138–9 (No. 155, *and encl.*), 141 (No. 157); letter to Baron von Schoen on interpreta-

MOROCCO—*(continued)*.
  Negotiations—*(continued)*.
    4. *Franco-German, &c.*—(continued).
      German desire, &c.—*(continued)*.

tion of, 141 (No. 157); Sir C. Hardinge and Sir E. Grey on the agreement, 140 (No. 157, *min.*), commercial relations in Morocco, 142 (No. 158); Baron von Schoen satisfied at success of the agreement, 142 (No. 159); German Emperor's congratulatory telegram to Prince Radolin and effects of, 143 (No. 160); Prince Bülow and, 143 (No. 160); German interests in Morocco economic, 269 (No. 293, *encl.*), 421 (No. 440), 521 (No. 540); German complaint at French neglect of agreement, July 1911, 354 (No. 373); Germany now regards agreement as non-existent, 29 July, 1911, 420 (No. 438), 421 (No. 440); French distrust of Germany over repudiation of, September, 542 (No. 560).

      and Austria-Hungary : Opinion that France had made a mistake in concluding the agreement, 350 (No. 371).

      and Great Britain : Sir E. Grey's satisfaction at : British interest in Morocco to preserve equal opportunities for commerce, 136 (No. 152); on " open door " in Morocco, 137 (No. 153); agreement removes a stumbling-block between Germany and England, 142 (No. 158).

      and Spain : Communication of to Spain, 135 (No. 150), 137 (No. 153); Spanish attitude to the agreement, 138 (No. 154), 140 (No. 156); irritation at being omitted from, 142 (No. 159) (*v.* also *infra* Spanish-German Agreement).

    5. *Spanish-German Agreement*, 1909.

Proposal for, February 1909, 135 (No. 150); Germany raises no objection to Spanish proposal, 138 (No. 154); France would prefer Spanish adherence to Franco-German declaration, 138 (No. 154), 140 (No. 156); Spanish-German negotiations opened, 140 (No. 156); German opinion that an agreement was unnecessary, 142–3 (No. 159); German recognition of Spanish special political position in Morocco, June 1909, 144 (No. 161); *Text* of communications from German Government to German Minister at Madrid *and* Spanish Ambassador at Berlin to German Secretary of State, 145–6 (No. 162, *encl.*).

3 M

MOROCCO—(*continued*).

Negotiations—(*continued*).

14. *Approach to the crisis*—(continued).

and Great Britain—(*continued*).

suggestion of exchange of territories in Northern Nigeria, 458 (No. 485), 460 (No. 487), 461 (No. 488), 462 (No. 489).

and Italy.

Marquis di San Giuliano states Italian position, 425 (No. 445).

and Spain.

Spanish Guinea, question of cession to Germany, August 1911, 429 (No. 451), 431 (No. 454), 436 (No. 460), 441 (No. 464), 467 (No. 495), 540 (No. 559), 615 (No. 625, *min.*), 766 (No. 747).

Spanish suggestion for resumption of conversations with France interrupted in June, August 1911, 442 (No. 465), 447 (No. 470); France does not desire resumption at present, 445 (No. 468); M. Geoffray on effect of proposed Franco-German agreement upon Spanish position, 446 (No. 469); Sir E. Grey discourages resumption of conversations, 447 (No. 470).

15. *Russian démarche.*

Definition of Russian attitude : Germany informed that Russia has no objection to measures which France found it necessary to take in Morocco, and is in complete agreement with them : Russia would stand by France, especially in any dispute which might arise with Germany, 464 (No. 491); M. Neratov does not believe that Germany would push matters to extremes, July 1911, 465 (No. 492); effect on Germany of Russian support, 466 (No. 494); origin of the " *démarche*," 466–7 (No. 494, *ed. note*); M. Isvolski deplores idea of a war on account of Morocco : his view on French and British interests, 467–8 (No. 495); a Franco-German war would lead to a general European war, 468 (No. 495); M. de Selves on satisfactory promise of Russian support to France, 468 (No. 495); formal assurance given of diplomatic and military support, 469 (No. 496).

M. Isvolski asks M. de Selves whether France would accept arbitration and whether the Emperor of Austria would be a suitable arbitrator, 470 (No. 497), 471 (No. 499); similarly to M. Jules Cambon, 480 (No. 508); Sir F. Bertie on M. Isvolski's suggestions, 470 (No. 498), 476 (No. 503); M. Isvolski's representations upon avoidance of war and suggestion of arbitration, 471 (No. 499); M. Isvolski's suggestions and communications to M. de Selves, of his

MOROCCO—(*continued*).

Negotiations—(*continued*).

15. *Russian démarche*—(continued).

own inspiration, 472 (No. 500), 473 (No. 501), 480 (No. 508).

Russian support as an ally, 472 (Nos. 500–1); Russian army not yet in a position to render great help to France, September 1911, 473 (No. 501, *min.*); M. Stolypin's disbelief in any serious danger of war, 474 (No. 502); M. Neratov denies that Russia had been asked to give counsels of moderation, 475 (No. 502), 477 (No. 504); M. Isvolski's instructions prompted by desire to impress grave consequences of approaching final negotiations in an unconciliatory spirit, 475 (No. 502), 476 (No. 503); reassurances of Russian support, 474 (No. 502), 477 (No. 504), 478 (No. 505); Emperor Nicholas on the situation, 476 (No. 502); his avoidance of a political conversation with Sir G. Buchanan, 478–9 (No. 506); Count Benckendorf on desire to avoid war, 479 (No. 507).

and Austria-Hungary.

Triple Alliance and question of Austro-Hungarian support to Germany, 468 (No. 495).

and France.

Satisfaction with diplomatic support given by Russia, July 1911, 465 (No. 492); Sir F. Bertie on grave effect of a French occupation of Mogador or landing at Agadir, August, 467 (No. 495); M. de Selves informs M. Isvolski that the Emperor of Austria would not be a suitable arbitrator in the question, 470 (No. 497); no question of considering arbitration at the moment, 471 (No. 499); M. de Selves resists Russian suggestions and re-affirms French position, 471–2 (No. 499).

and Germany.

Effect of Russian support to France, August 1911, 466 (No. 494); Baron von Schoen on necessity for a formula over Morocco, 467 (No. 495); possibility of conversations between Baron von Schoen and M. de Selves, 468 (No. 495); German request to Great Britain and Russia to use influence to prevail upon France to be conciliatory, 471–2 (No. 499).

and Great Britain.

British firm determination to stand by France, 1 August, 1911, 465–6 (No. 493); not inciting France to resistance : anxious for a speedy and satisfactory termination of the negotiations, 474 (No. 502); Sir E. Grey informs Count Benckendorff

MOROCCO—*(continued)*.
Negotiations—*(continued)*.
16. *Crisis and its settlement*—(continued).
and France—*(continued)*.
minerals, 562 (No. 577); publication of new proposals in French press before being officially communicated, 563 (No. 578); M. Herbette anticipates difficulties upon Congo discussion, 564 (No. 579); M. Paul Cambon on French feeling against large concessions in Congo, 565 (No. 580); M. de Selves on equality of Powers as regards industrial enterprises in Morocco, 569–71 (No. 588).
5th draft agreement with Germany prepared, 565 (No. 580); conclusion of Morocco agreement and signing of final draft convention, 568–9 (Nos. 585–7).
6th *Text* of portion of the convention, 571–4 (No. 589).
Opposition very considerable, October 1911, 574–5 (No. 590); M. Jules Cambon's personal suggestion giving Germany a point of contact on the Ubanghi and Congo, 575 (No. 592); accepted by Herr von Kiderlen-Waechter, 582 (No. 596); M. de Selves on, 582–3 (No. 597); negotiations practically settled, 588 (No. 599); Herr von Kiderlen-Waechter's request for assurance *re* Belgian Congo, 596–7 (No. 610); M. de Selves' suggested formula, 597 (No. 612); M. Paul Cambon's expectation of conclusion of negotiations, 589 (No. 601).
Text of Franco-German convention respecting Morocco, 604–8 (No. 619).
Agreement signed at Berlin, 4 November, 611 (No. 622); communicated to Great Britain and adhesion to asked for, 3 November, 604–5 (No. 619); communicated to Spain, 611 (No. 621), 611–2 (No. 623); letters exchanged between Herr von Kiderlen-Waechter and M. Jules Cambon, *Text*, 612–4 (Nos. 624–5); summary of, 614 (No. 625, *min.*); Franco-German convention and exchange of notes respecting Morocco, *Text*, 831–6 (*App.* IV).
17. *Negotiations with Spain.*
Franco-Spanish draft convention prepared, 489–91 (No. 521), 491 (No. 522); provisions of, 490 (No. 521); question of cession of Ifni to France, 490 (No. 521), 491 (No. 522); anxiety for British support for convention, 489 (No. 521), 491 (No. 522); *Text* of draft convention, 494–7 (No. 525, *encl.*); Sir F. Bertie on: omission of Spanish sphere at Ifni and Tangier stipula-

MOROCCO—*(continued)*.
Negotiations—*(continued)*.
17. *Negotiations with Spain*—(continued).
tion not definite, 494 (No. 525); M. de Selves hopes that Spanish rights at Ifni would be made over to France, 494 (No. 525); views of British statesmen on the draft convention, 497–8 (No. 525, *min.*); draft convention communicated to Spain: cession of Ifni region expected, 500 (No. 527); Sir M. de Bunsen on the convention, 501 (No. 527); Franco-Spanish conversations resumed, September, 539–41 (No. 559).
M. Paul Cambon on suggestion that Spain should annex her sphere, 574–5 (No. 590); Sir A. Nicolson on, 575 (No. 590); M. de Selves' views on, 576 (No. 593); British comments on, 576–7 (No. 593, *min.*); resumption of negotiations postponed, 577 (No. 594); divided opinion as extent of Spanish influence in Morocco, 577 (No. 594); new draft convention received by M. Geoffray: summary of, 577–8 (No. 594); Sir M. de Bunsen on, 578–9 (No. 594); *Text* of articles relating to Tangier, 581 (No. 595, *encl.*); M. Regnault's *Projet d'Accord Hispano-Marocain* and *Déclaration Française* for settling respective positions of France and Spain in event of a French Protectorate: Sir F. Bertie on, 583–5 (No. 598), *Text*, 585–7 (No. 598, *encl.* 1, 2); British comments on, 587–8 (No. 598, *min.*); M. Regnault's *Projet* discussed by M. de Selves and Sir F. Bertie: M. Caillaux reported as intending to press the proposals upon Spain: Great Britain could not support such a policy: negotiations should be on basis of 1904 agreements: M. de Selves advised to abandon the *Projet*, 599–601 (No. 614); French protest to Spain *re* Colonel Silvestre's demands to Raisuli, 592 (No. 603); Spanish reply, 593–4 (No. 606); M. Caillaux's attitude reported to be very hard, 598 (No. 613); Sir F. Bertie and M. Caillaux discuss the *Projet*: M. Caillaux's unconciliatory attitude: French grievances against Spain: effect of British support to Spain upon Anglo-French goodwill: 603–4 (No. 618): M. Caillaux on essential French interests, 604 (No. 618): Franco-German convention *re* Morocco communicated to Spain and adherence invited, 611 (No. 621), 611–2 (No. 623); M. Caillaux's intention of pressing the Regnault *Projet*: Sir F. Bertie

PRESS—(*continued*).

  German—(continued).

    Individual papers—(*continued*).

Hamburger Nachrichten, on improbability of war, July 1911, 409 (No. 428); on suggested cession of Togoland, 433 (No. 457); on Franco-German agreement, November, 659 (No. 664); on Sir E. Grey's speech, 738 (No. 723); on M. de Selves' speech on Franco-German agreement, December, 787 (No. 761).

Hannoversche Courier, Anglo-German relations, November 1911, 699 (No. 703).

Kölnische Zeitung, on disturbances at Casablanca, July 1907, 53 (No. 65); anti-French attitude, September 1908, 97 (No. 107); Casablanca deserters, October, 114 (No. 125); Agadir harbour and visit of French vessel, December 1910, 173 (No. 186, *note*); denial of a Franco-German *détente* on Morocco question, 244 (No. 267, *encl.*); Franco-German conversations, July 1911, 388 (No. 410), 399 (No. 420); on Mr. Lloyd George's speech and Agadir question, 407 (No. 428); Franco-German conversations, 433 (No. 457); denies impending resignation of Herr von Kiderlen-Waechter, August 1911, 440 (No. 463); Germany and Belgian Congo, October, 595 (No. 608); on Franco-German agreement, November, 658–9 (No. 664); Herr von Kiderlen-Waechter's speech to Reichstag Morocco Commission, 698–9 (No. 697); on Sir E. Grey's speech, 739 (No. 723); on M. de Selves' speech, December, 787–8 (No. 761).

Kreuz-Zeitung, Franco-German suggested understanding on Morocco, July 1911, 388 (No. 410); publication of Mr. McKenna's speech, 26 September, with an interpolated passage, September, 648–9 (No. 654); Herr von Kiderlen-Waechter's speech before Reichstag Morocco Commission, November, 699 (No. 697).

Münchener Neueste Nachrichten, German policy in Morocco, September 1908, 102 (No. 112); Germany and Agadir question, July 1911, 388–9 (No. 410); Mr. Lloyd George's speech, 408 (No. 428); anti-British attitude, October 1911, 564 (No. 579), 567 (No. 583).

Münchener Zeitung, German attitude on the "*Panther*" incident, July 1911, 340 (No. 362).

National-Zeitung, compensation to Germany over Morocco, July 1911, 388 (No. 410).

PRESS—(*continued*).

  German—(continued).

    Individual papers—(*continued*).

Norddeutsche Allgemeine Zeitung, recognition of Mulai Hafid as Sultan of Morocco, 1908, 83 (No. 96); on unfriendly attitude of English press, September, 100–1 (No. 112); denies Russian mediation to bring about a Franco-German *détente*, May 1911, 244 (No. 267); announcement of sending of the "Panther" to Agadir, July 1911, 324–5 (No. 342); protest against article in *Post* suggesting humiliation of Germany in Franco-German conversations, August, 438–9 (No. 463); no further publicity to be given to the deliberations, 440 (No. 463); departure of "Panther" from Agadir announced, November 1911, 724 (No. 717); denial of disclosures respecting intrigues against Portugal, December 1911, 784 (No. 759).

Post, on French expedition to Fez, 278–9 (No. 308); Franco-German conversations, July 1911, 408 (No. 428); announcement of a *rapprochement* viewed as a national humiliation, and suggests resignation of Herr von Kiderlen-Waechter, August, 438–40 (No. 463), 443–4 (No. 467); on Franco-German Moroccan negotiations, October 1911, 582 (No. 596); on Sir E. Grey's speech, November, 738–9 (No. 723); Dr. Class's criticism of Herr von Kiderlen-Waechter, December, 771 (No. 752).

Schlesische Zeitung, on Colonel Repington's articles in the *Times*, 704 (No. 699).

Schwäbischer Merkur, British press attacks on Germany, September, 101 (No. 112).

Süddeutsche Reichskorrespondenz, Germany and Morocco, September, 1908, 91–2 (No. 103).

Tägliche Rundschau, on Franco-German agreement, November 1911, 659 (No. 664); on Sir E. Grey's speech, 738 (No. 723).

Vossische Zeitung, on Casablanca disturbances, August 1907, 54 (No. 65); comments on Sir E. Grey's statement on false report of Mr. McKenna's speech, November 1911, 664–5 (No. 673); on Sir E. Grey's speech, 737 (No. 723); on debate in French Chamber on Franco-German agreement, December 1911, 787 (No. 761).

Zukunft, Herr Harden on Franco-German conversations, and policy, August 1911, 443–5 (No. 467).